ART BOOKS

FROM CRESCENT MOON PUBLISHING

Leonardo da Vinci
by James Pearson

Early Netherlandish Painting
by Rosalind Mutter

Piero della Francesca
by Naomi Haskell

Giovanni Bellini
by Julia Davis

Eric Gill: Nuptials of God
by Anthony Hoyland

Minimal Art and Artists In the 1960s and After
by Laura Garrard

Postwar Art
by George Knighton

Vincent van Gogh: Visionary Landscapes
by Stuart Morris

Max Beckmann
by Stuart Morris

Egon Schiele: Sex and Death in Purple Stockings
by D. Simon Eade

Mark Rothko: The Art of Transcendence
by Julia Davis

Jasper Johns
by L.M. Poole

Brice Marden
by Laura Garrard

Frank Stella: American Abstract Artist
by James Pearson

EROTIC ART

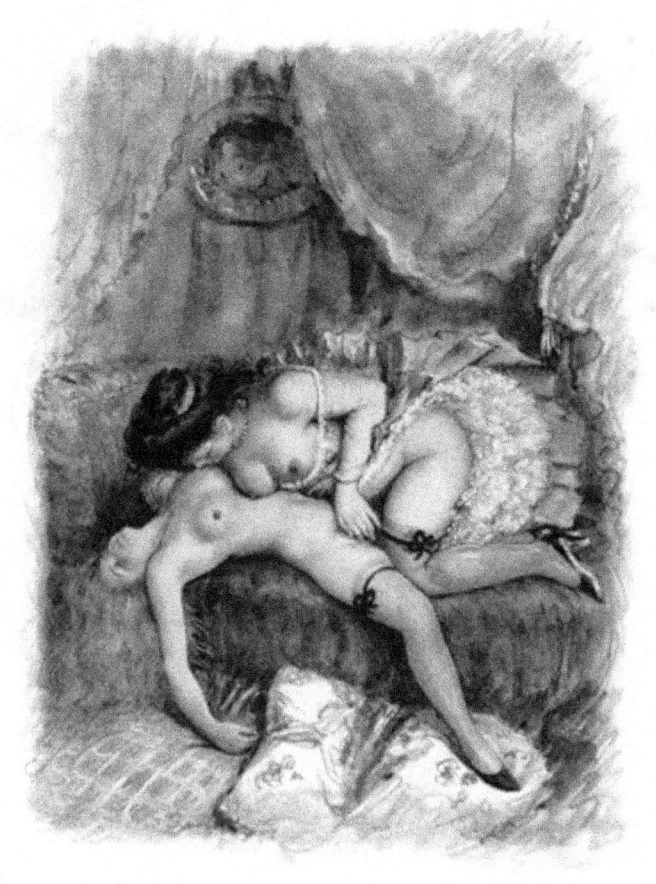

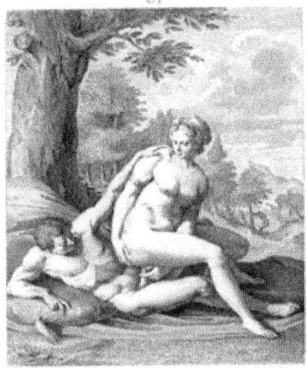

ANGELIQUE ET MEDOR.

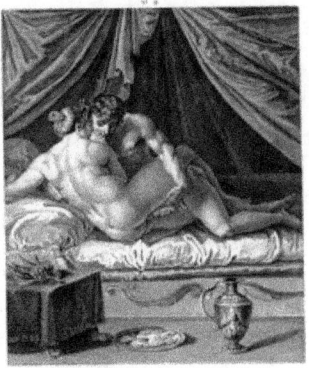

ANTOINE ET CLEOPATRE

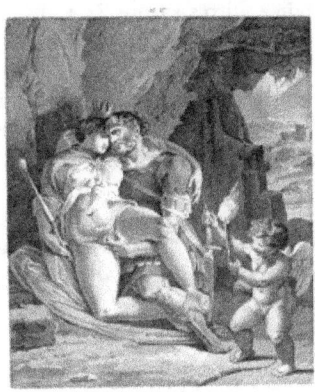

ENÉE ET DIDON

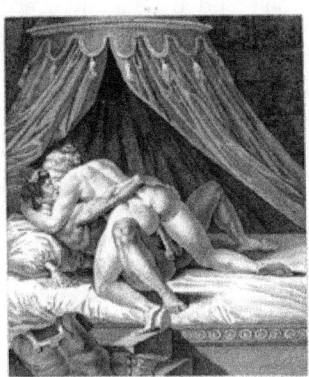

MARS ET VENUS

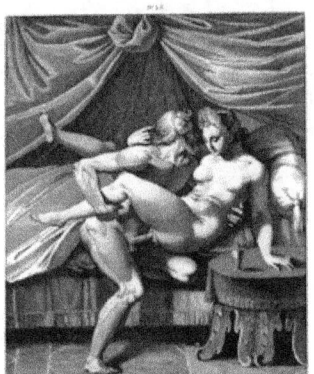

JUPITER ET JUNON

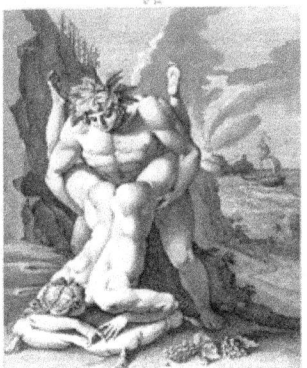

BACHUS ET ARIANE.

EROTIC ART

Cassidy Hughes

Crescent Moon

First published 2015.
© Cassidy Hughes 2015.

Printed and bound in the U.S.A.
Set in Book Antiqua 10 on 14pt.
Designed by Radiance Graphics.

The right of Cassidy Hughes to be identified as the author of *Erotic Art*
has been asserted generally in accordance with sections 77 and 78 of the
Copyright, Designs and Patents Act 1988.

British Library Cataloguing in Publication data

Hughes, Cassidy
Erotic Art
I. Title
704.9

ISBN-13 9781861715005(Hbk)
ISBN-13 9781861715142(Pbk)

CRESCENT MOON PUBLISHING
P.O. Box 1312, Maidstone, Kent, ME14 5XU
Great Britain, www.crmoon.com

CONTENTS

Then Beatrice looked at me, her eyes
sparkling with love and burning so divine,
my strength of sight surrendered to her power –

with eyes cast down, I was about to faint.

Dante Alighieri, *The Divine Comedy: Paradiso*

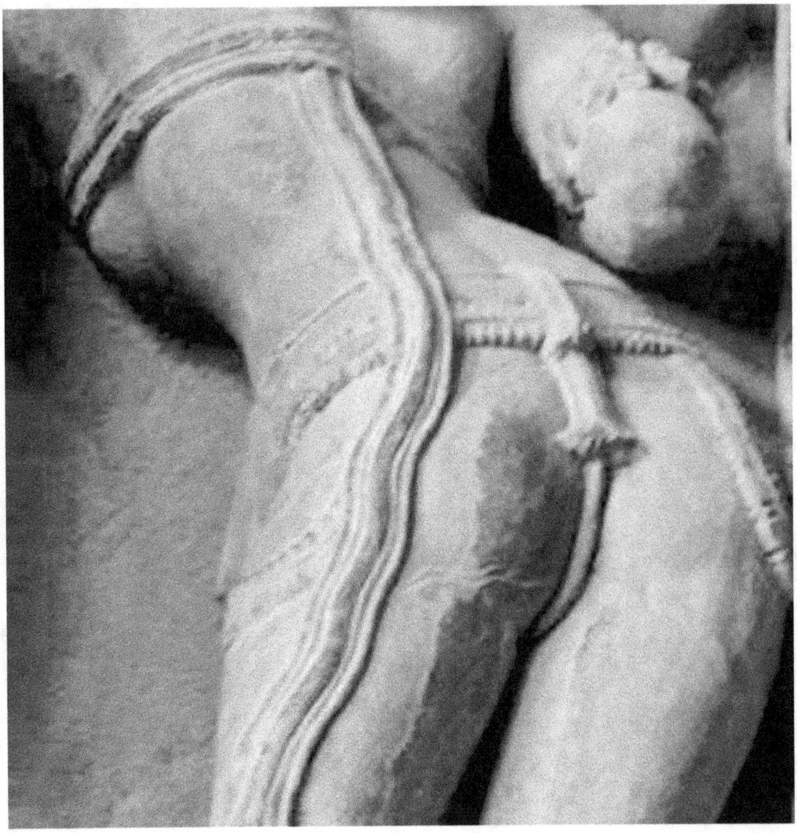

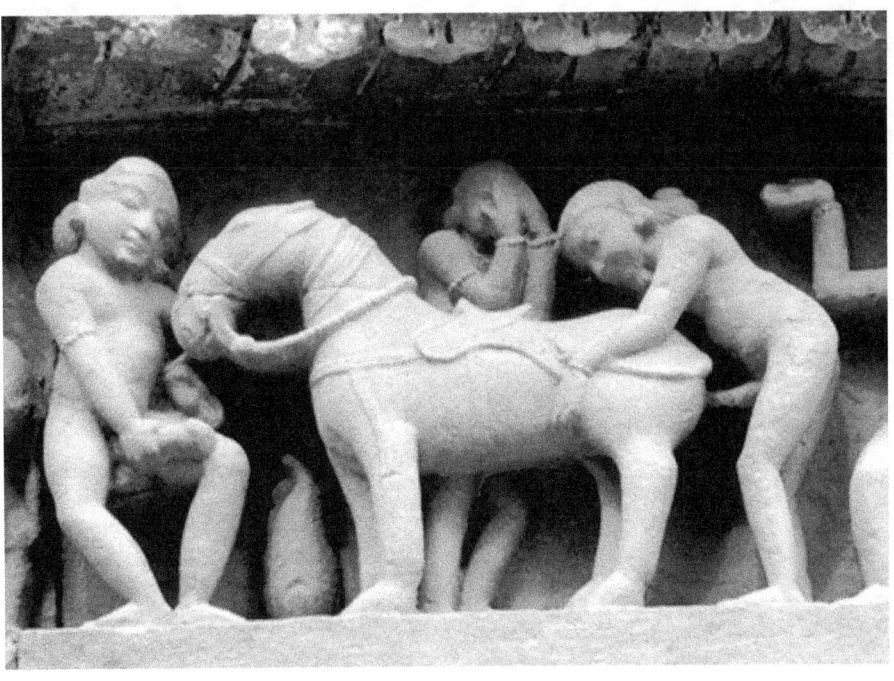

Khajuharo Temple, India

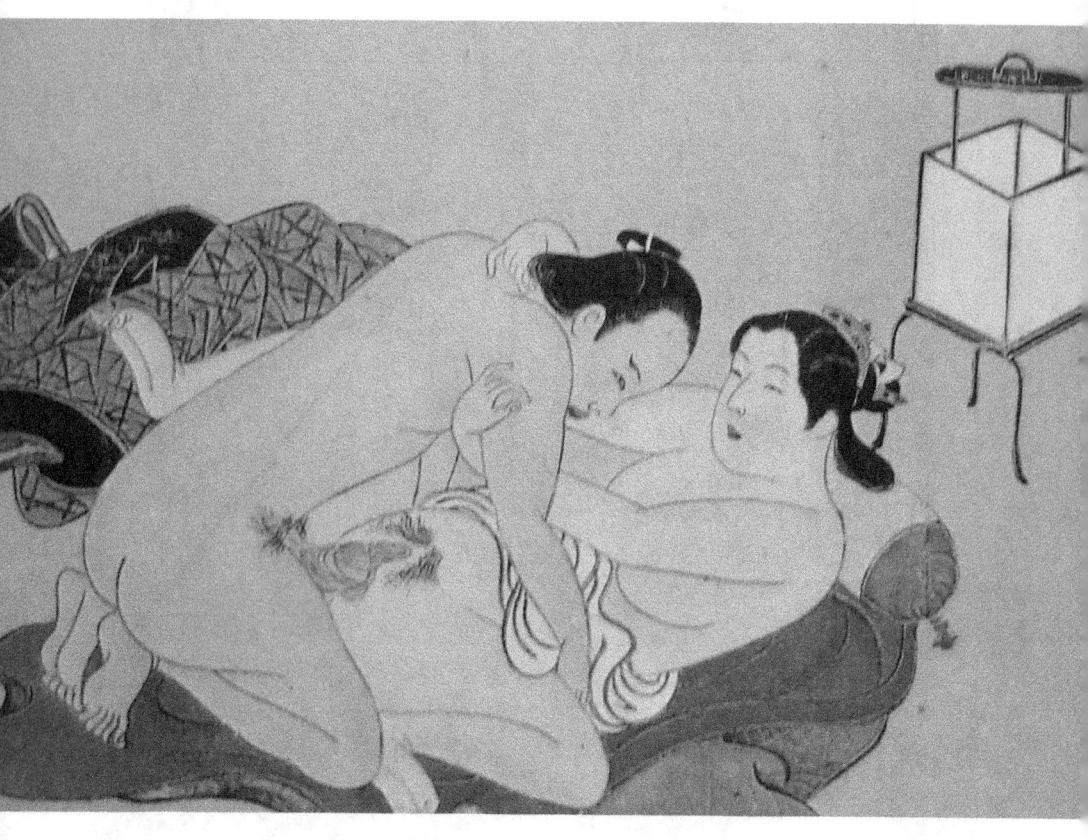

Sukenobu, shunga scroll, early 18th century

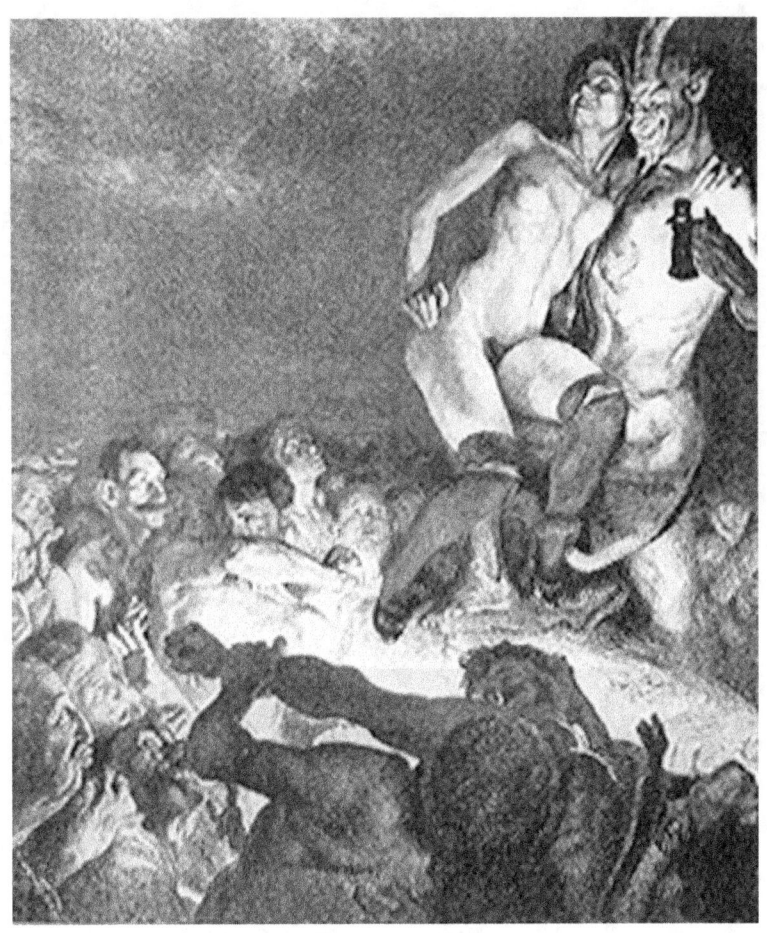

Otto Grenier, The Devil Showing Woman To the People, 1897

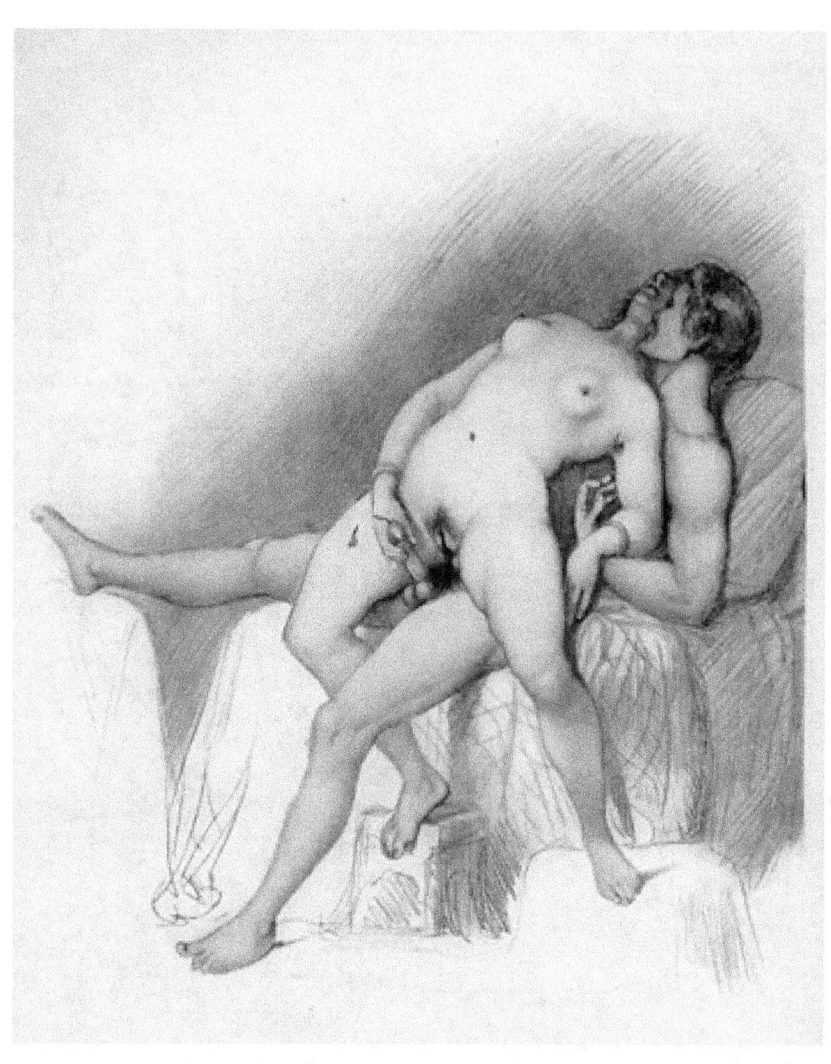

Johann Nepomuk Geiger (1805-80)

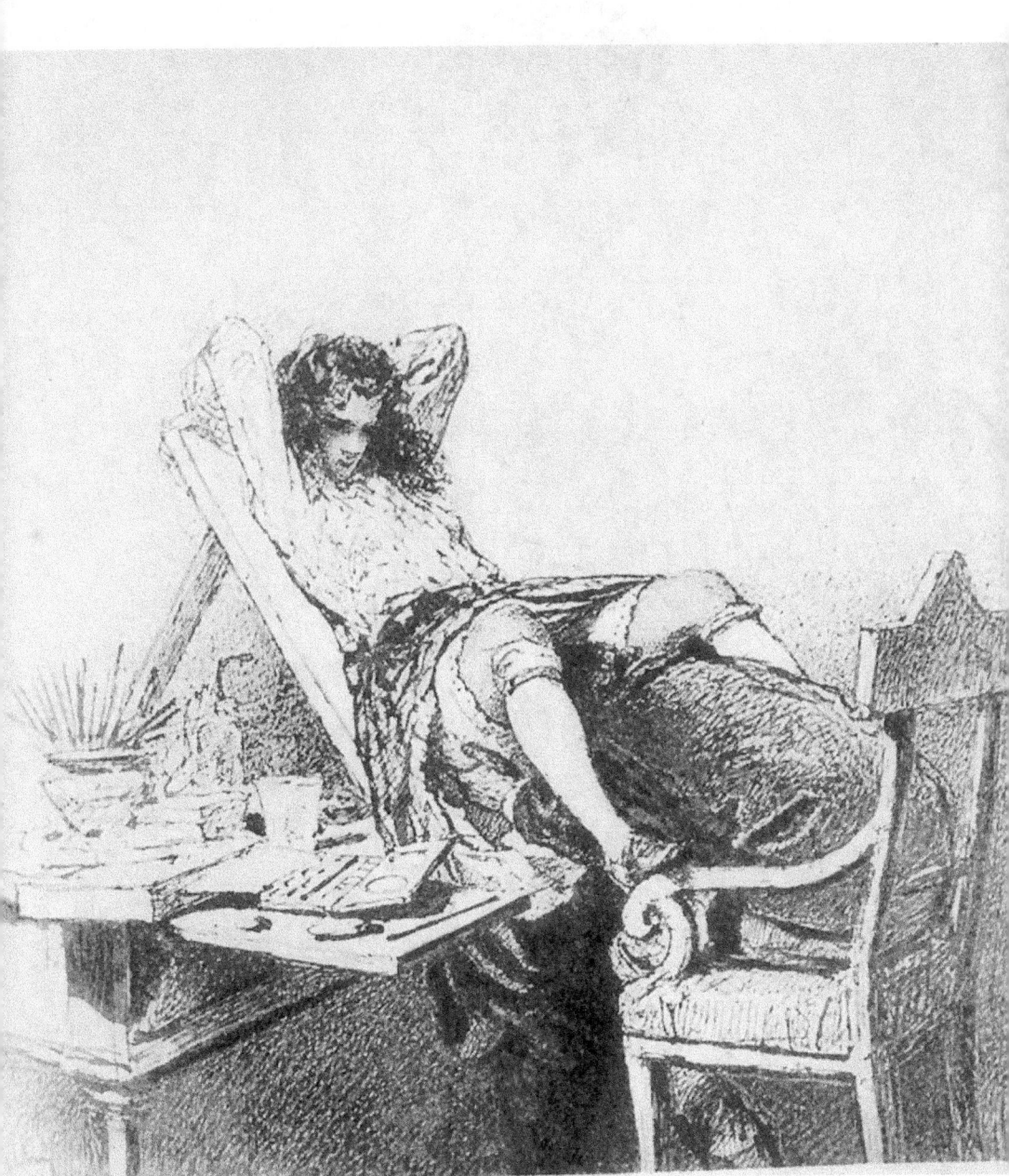

Mihály Zichy

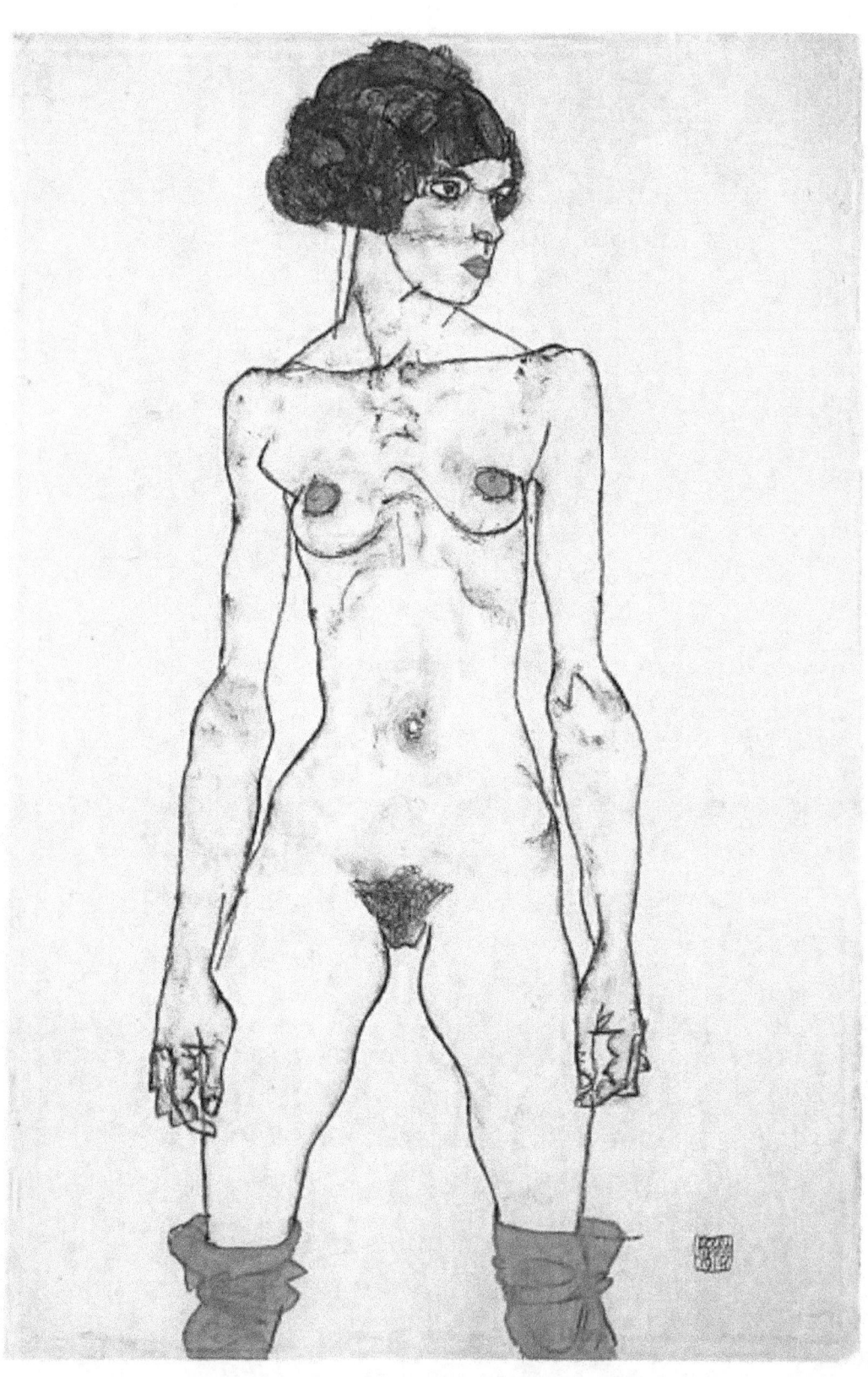

Egon Schiele, Nude, 1914

In this book on the history of erotic art, short entries on aspects of erotic art comprise the first section. The bulk of the second part of the book focusses on the history of erotic art, from prehistory to the modern era. There are also sections on the celebrated erotic artists. Many anonymous works are included. The appendices contain some more classics of erotic art.

EROTIC ART AND PORNOGRAPHY

The establishment art historical view of erotic art and pornography is that true erotic or high art engenders quiet contemplation, a detached ravishing of the senses, a meditation on Platonic, Aristotlean and Kantian ideas of 'beauty' and æsthetics. 'High art', which is legitimate art, art which justifies itself by its 'genius' or obvious 'greatness', is about distance and disinterested pleasure. The high art nude, in painting or sculpture, in the patriarchal view, justifies its existence by the brilliance of its production, the sumptuousness of its colour and form, the marvel of its human touches, the grandeur of its design, the loftiness of its ambition, the dynamism of its structures, and so on. As that producer of exquisite bodies, French Neo-Classical artist J.A.D. Ingres, wrote:

> There are not two arts, there is only one: it is the one which has as its foundation the beautiful, which is eternal and natural.[1]

---

1 J.A.D. Ingres, quoted in R. Goldwater, 216

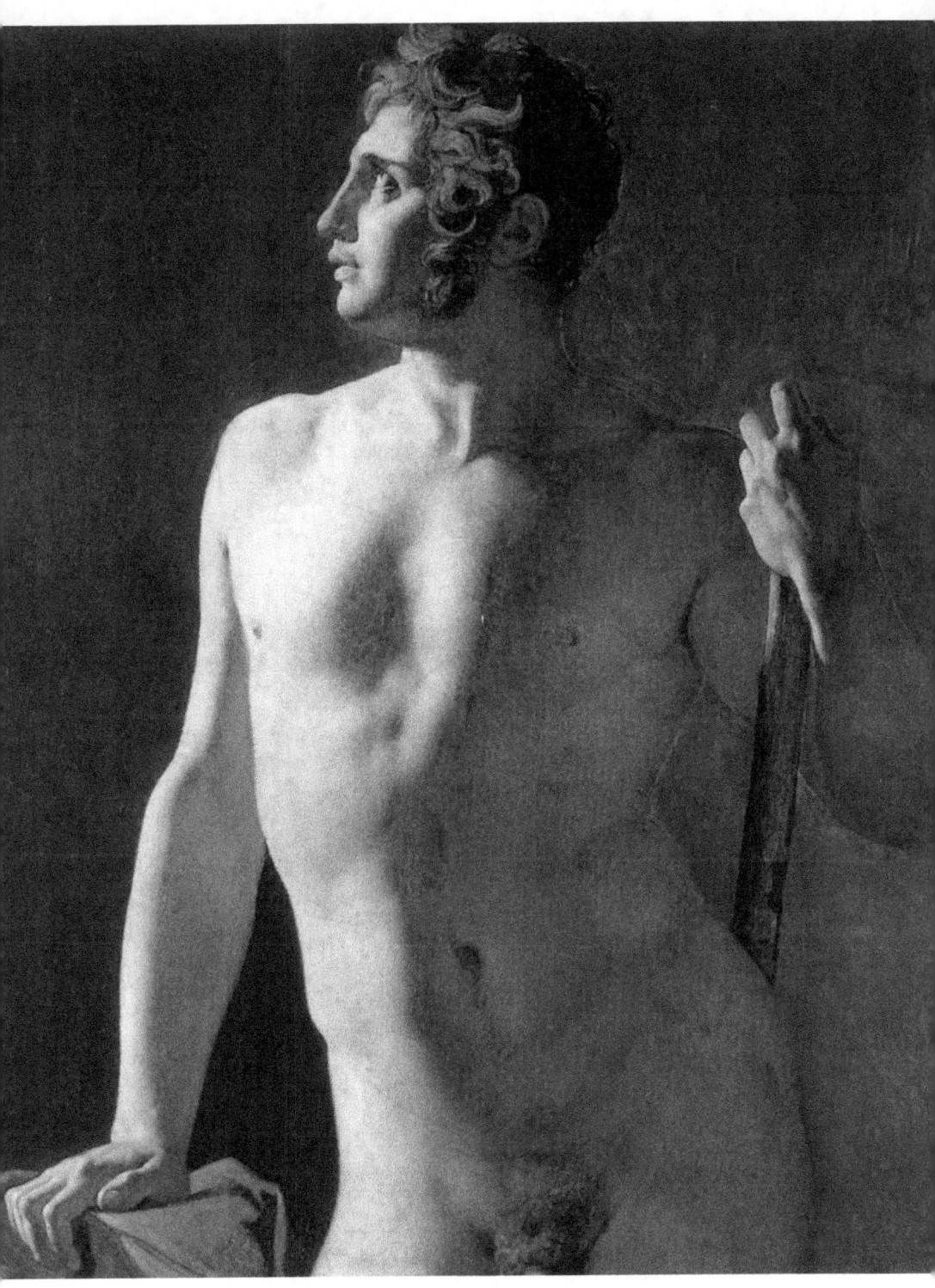

J.A.D. Ingres, Study of a Male Nude, 1801

EROTIC ART VERSUS PORNOGRAPHY

We know the male/ patriarchal view of the art versus pornography debate. Eroticism is justified and good because it is 'high art', it is superbly crafted, it is a 'work of art'. Thus the Kronhausens, the organizers of a major exhibition of 'erotic art' (of 1968),[1] write:

> one can perhaps distinguish between pornography and art. The criterion would be that the more a picture contains evidence of interpretative, creative elaboration, the closer it is to art.[2]

For the Kronhausens, as for so many artists and philosophers and intellectuals, erotic art is art because it is done well. Pornography is simply bad art.

Many guardians of æsthetics, many professors of art history and dons of 'the beautiful' go along with this view. Kenneth Clark is a typical establishment critic who puts forward the patriarchal view: nudes are OK provided they are æsthetically pleasing, provided they remain 'in the realm of contemplation' as he put it.[3]

---

1 The 'first international exhibition of erotic art' was at the Museum of Art, Lund, Sweden, and Aarhus, Denmark, in 1968
2 Phyllis & Eberhard Kronhausen: *Erotic Art: A survey of erotic fact and fancy in the fine arts*, W.H. Allen, 1971, 3
3 Quoted in Lord Longford: *Pornography: The Longford Report*, Coronet, 1972, 99f

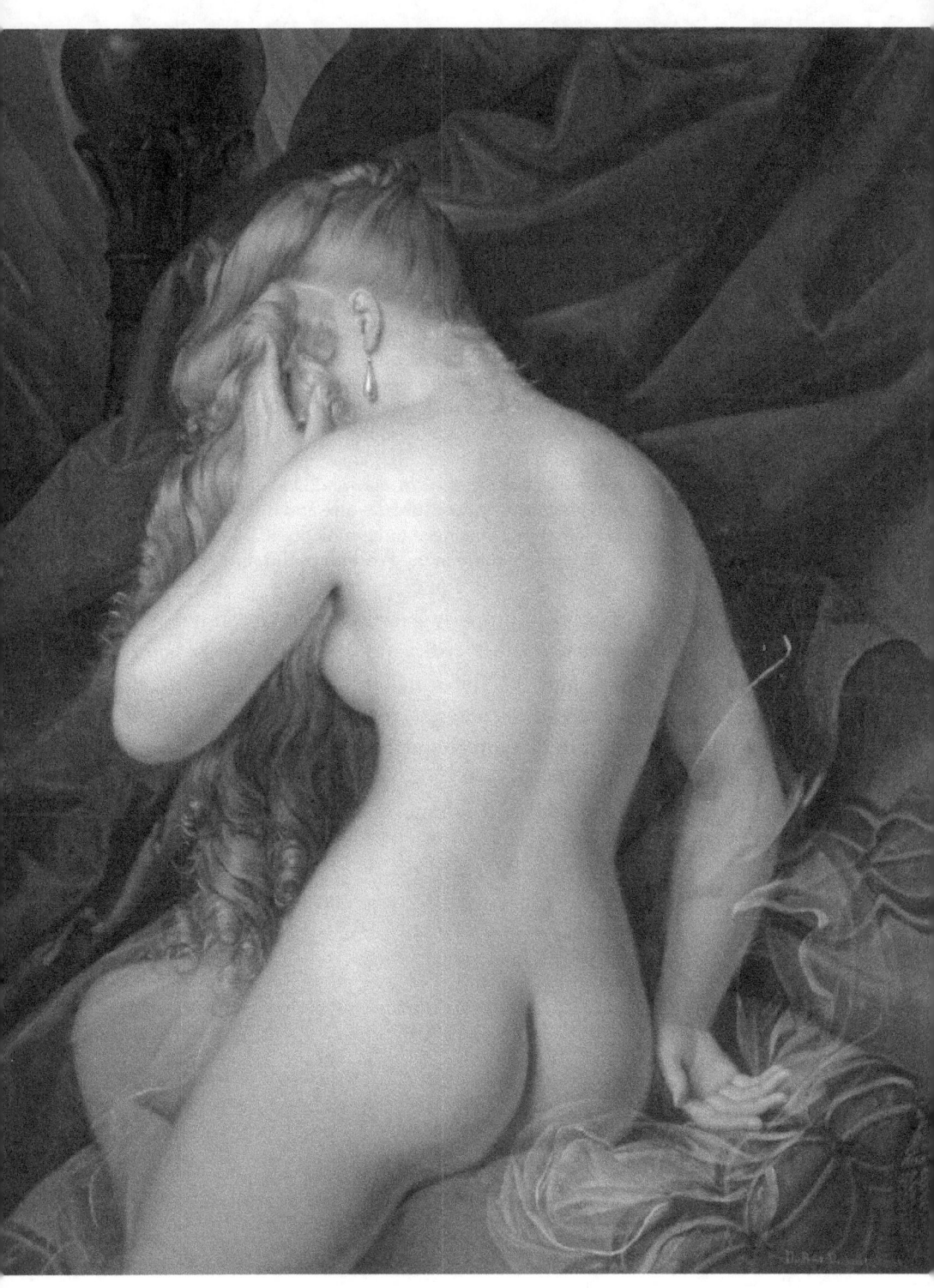

Alexandre-Jean Dubois-Drahonet,
Female Nude, 19th century

THE FEMALE NUDE

The 'sublime' qualities of high art, to use one popular adjective of art criticism, are crucial to its success, as Carol M. Armstrong notes in her essay on Edgar Degas:

> One of the things any painted object does is to resist signification at some level because of its very objecthood. And the female nude – because of *its* objecthood may be seen as almost emblematic of that level of resistance. In fact, the female nude has been linked to that stratum of painting most in tension with the work of signification – the stratum we connect to what we call, inadequately, "abstraction"; facture, the handling of paint per se, foregrounded as an obvious fact of the painting. Femaleness and facture, facture and the female nude, they go together somehow. One need only think of Titian, the first great painter of the female nude in the Western tradition.[1]

Much as worshippers properly gaze at an icon or an image of a deity with wonder, the art critic and historian kneels before 'great art' and worships it.[2] The female nude is the highest form of non-religious art, and it confers a religious awe in its æsthete consumers. The emphasis is on Neoplatonic terms such as 'purity', 'beauty', 'form' and 'symmetry'. As Aristotle puts it: '[t]he chief forms of beauty are order and symmetry and definiteness.'[3]

1 Carol M. Armstrong; "Edgar Degas and the Representation of the Female Body", in S. Suleiman, 223
2 See Pierre Bourdieu: *Distinction: A Social Critique of the Judgment of Taste*, tr Richard Nice, Routledge & Kegan Paul, New York 1984
3 Aristotle: *Metaphysics*, book XIII, in Albert Hofstadter & Richard Kuhns, eds: *Philosophies of Art and Beauty: Selected Readings in Aesthetics From Plato to Heidegger*, Random House, New York 1964, 96

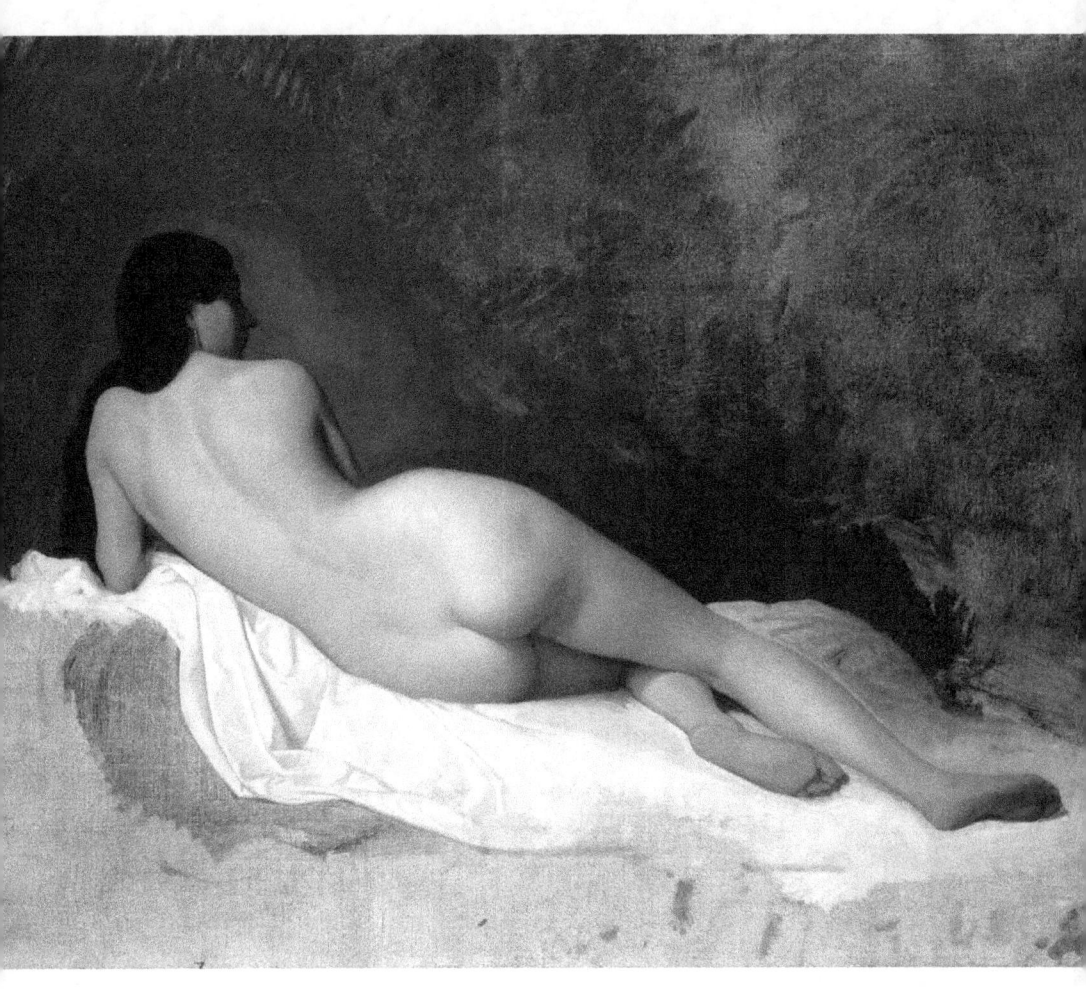

Isidore Pils, Nude Woman, c. 1841

THE FEMALE NUDE

Depictions of the female nude and of erotic gestures or acts can be problematic. The female body, for instance, is already 'objectified' even before it is painted or represented. Once painted, it becomes a cultural artifact, a mass of codes, meanings, signs and values, none of them fixed, all of them dependent on the context of consumption, dependent on the socio-political make-up of the viewer, and so on. None of this, however, has prevented erotic nudes and female nudes from being produced.

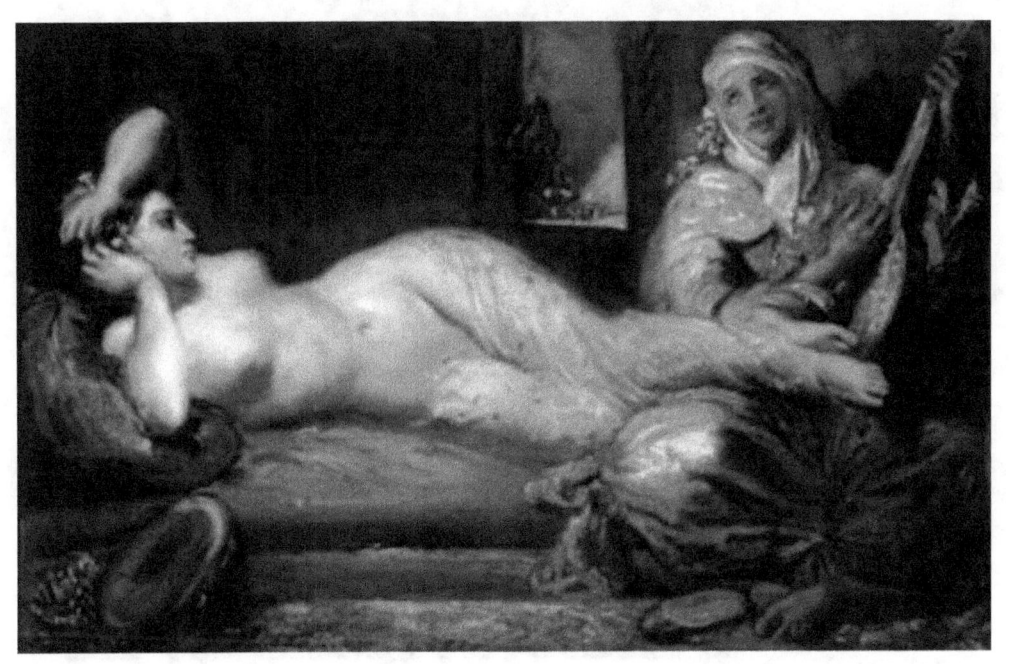

Théodore Chasséreau (1819-56)

William Bouguereau,
The Birth of Venus,
above

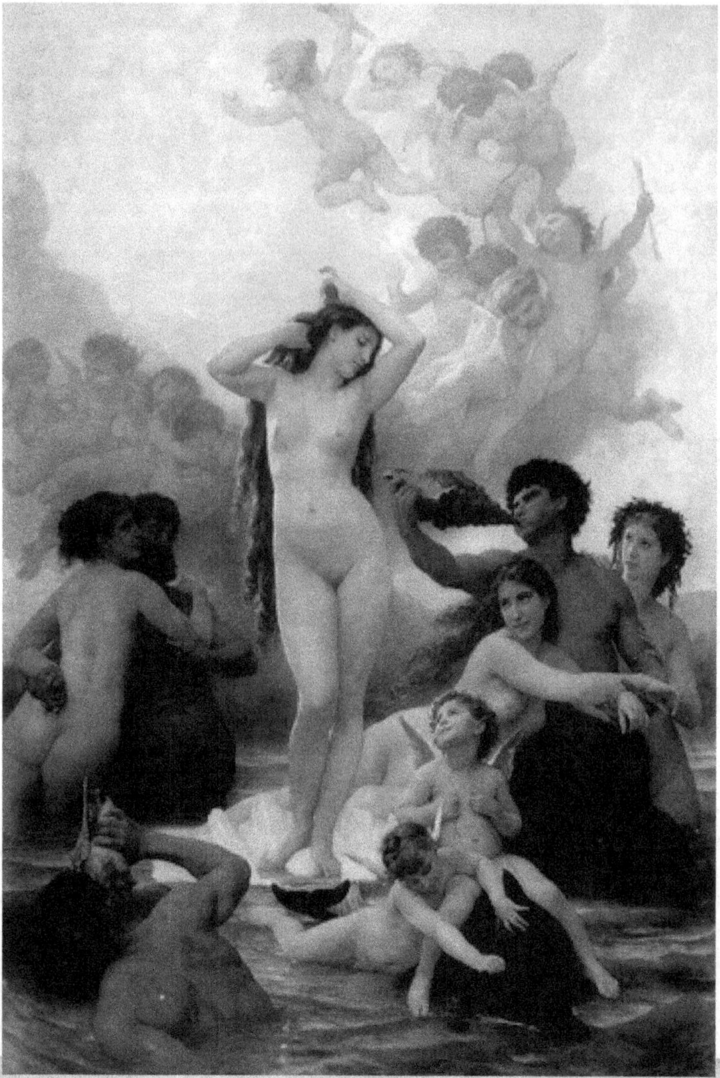

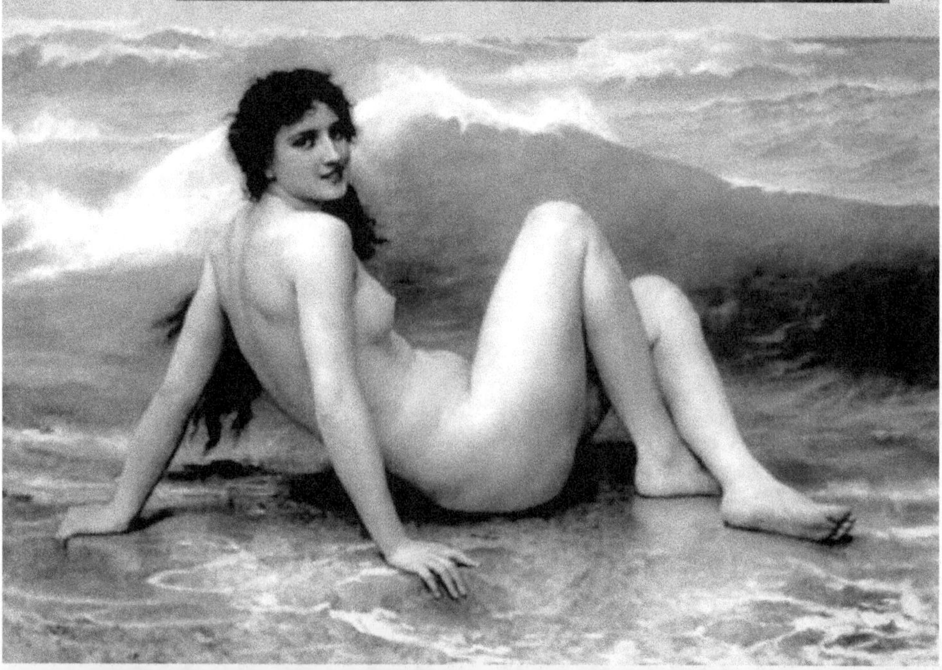

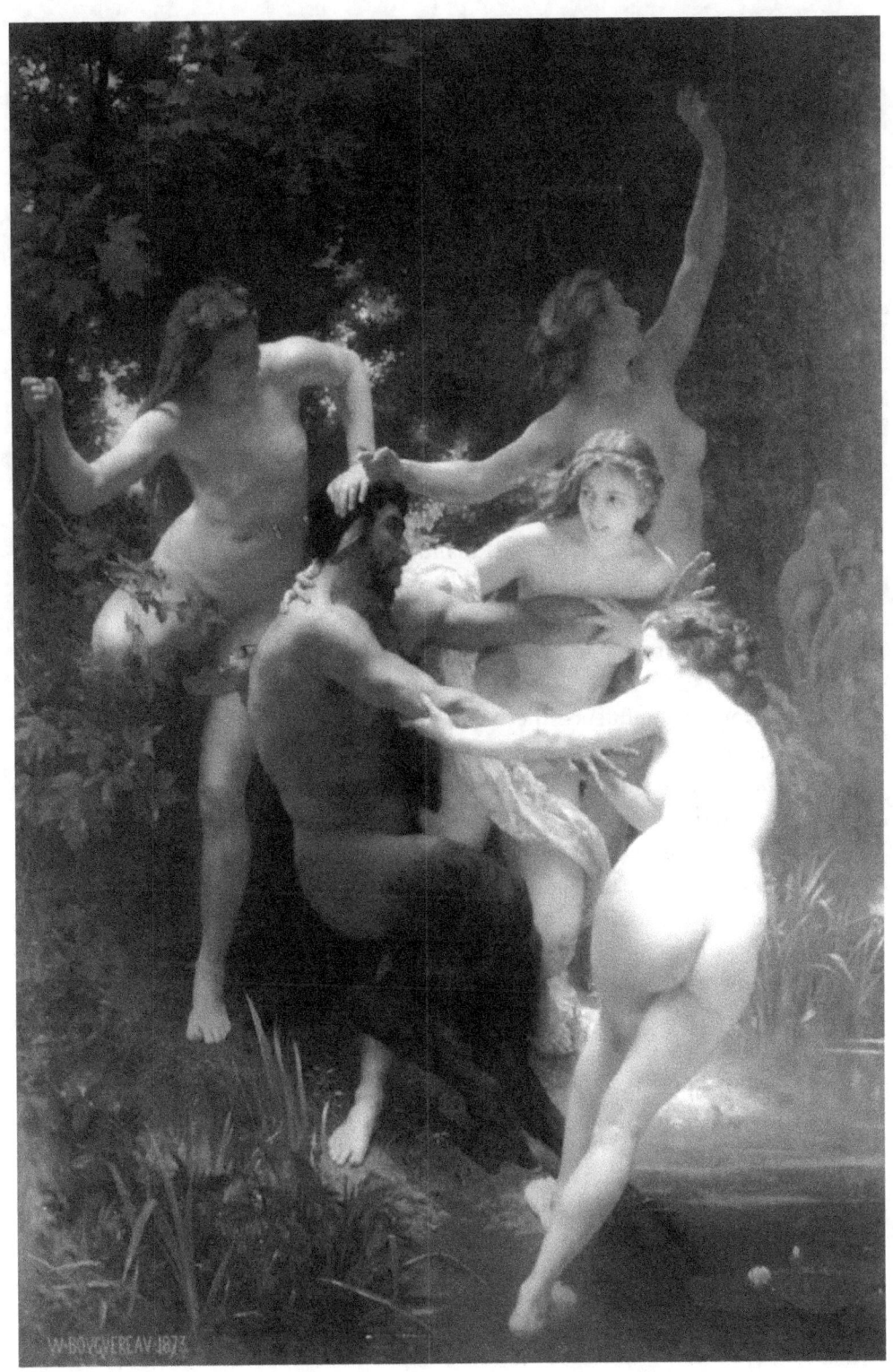

William Bouguereau, Nymphs and Satyr

THE FEMALE NUDE

Context is crucial in matters of eroticism. An image that is seen as 'erotic' in one context can easily be seen as 'pornographic' in another context. Take an image out of context, and soon a new, often ironic set of meanings are set in motion. Jacques Derrida has shown that a text may have many contexts, and is not fixed in one context forever.[1] Feminist artists have explored meanings and contexts, by placing traditional images in new contexts. Meanings are constantly in a state of flux. Nothing is fixed anymore. As Catherine Belsey writes: 'meanings circulate between text, ideology and reader' (144). Roland Barthes wrote that '[a]ll images are polysemous...they imply, underlying their signifiers, a floating chain of signifieds'. The consumer has the ability to 'choose some and ignore others'.[2] The cultural environment, socialization, economy, power relations, education, any number of factors can influence the meanings drawn from an image. With the female nude, in painting or erotica, the meanings are context-ualized as erotic. As Anne Hollander notes, the nude always has a sexual dimension to it.

For instance, men can 'possess' and yet never 'possess' a female nude painting. It remains an image. The 'possession' or consumption is of a cerebral order, which is why critics and professors such as Kenneth Clark, Bernard Berenson, Jacob Burckhardt, Walter Pater, John Ruskin, Aby Warburg, Roger Fry, Ernst Gombrich and other art critics emphasize the *intellectual* nature of enjoying art. Art for the head, not the body, art for the eyes, not the full five senses.

1 Jacques Derrida: *Eperons. Les styles de Nietzsche*, Flammarion, Paris 1978, 103f
2 Roland Barthes: *Image-Music-Text*, Hill & Wang, New York 1977, 39

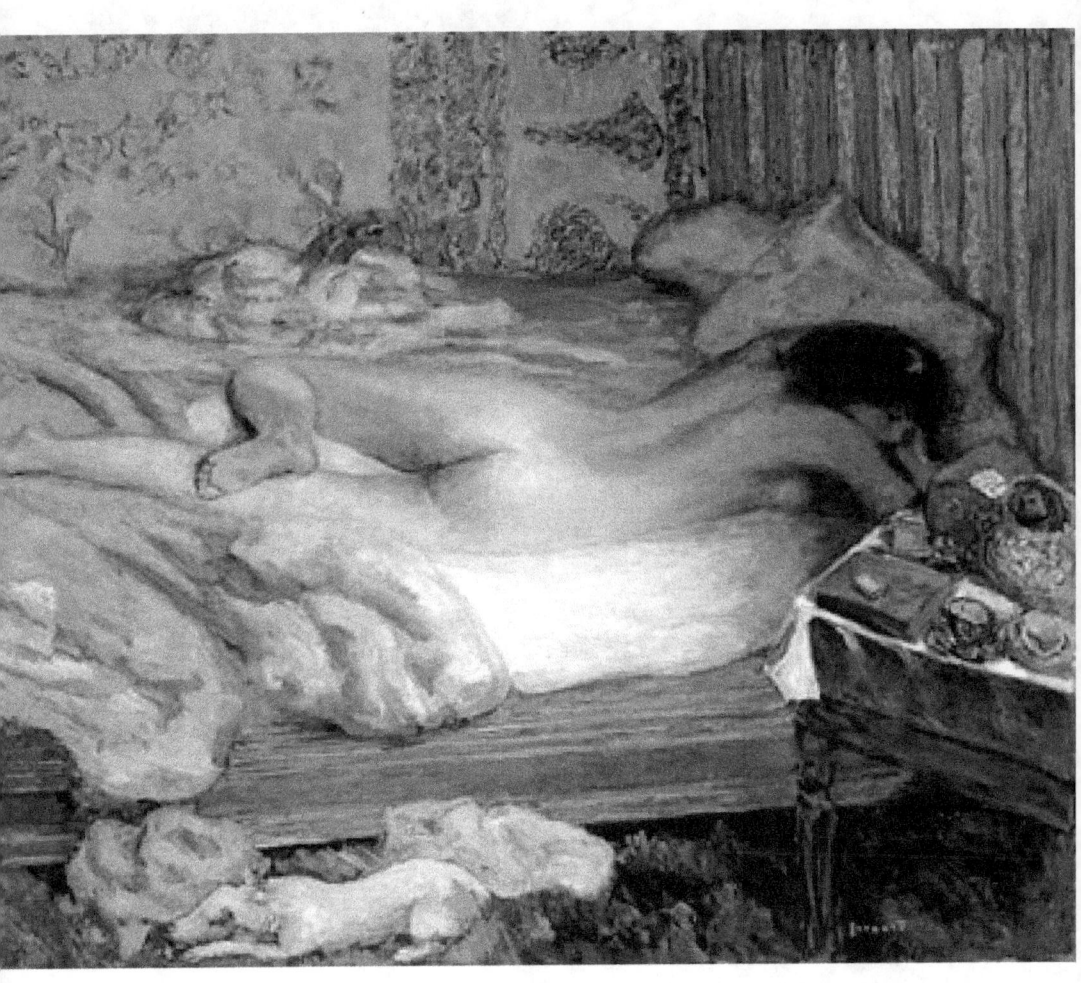

Pierre Bonnard

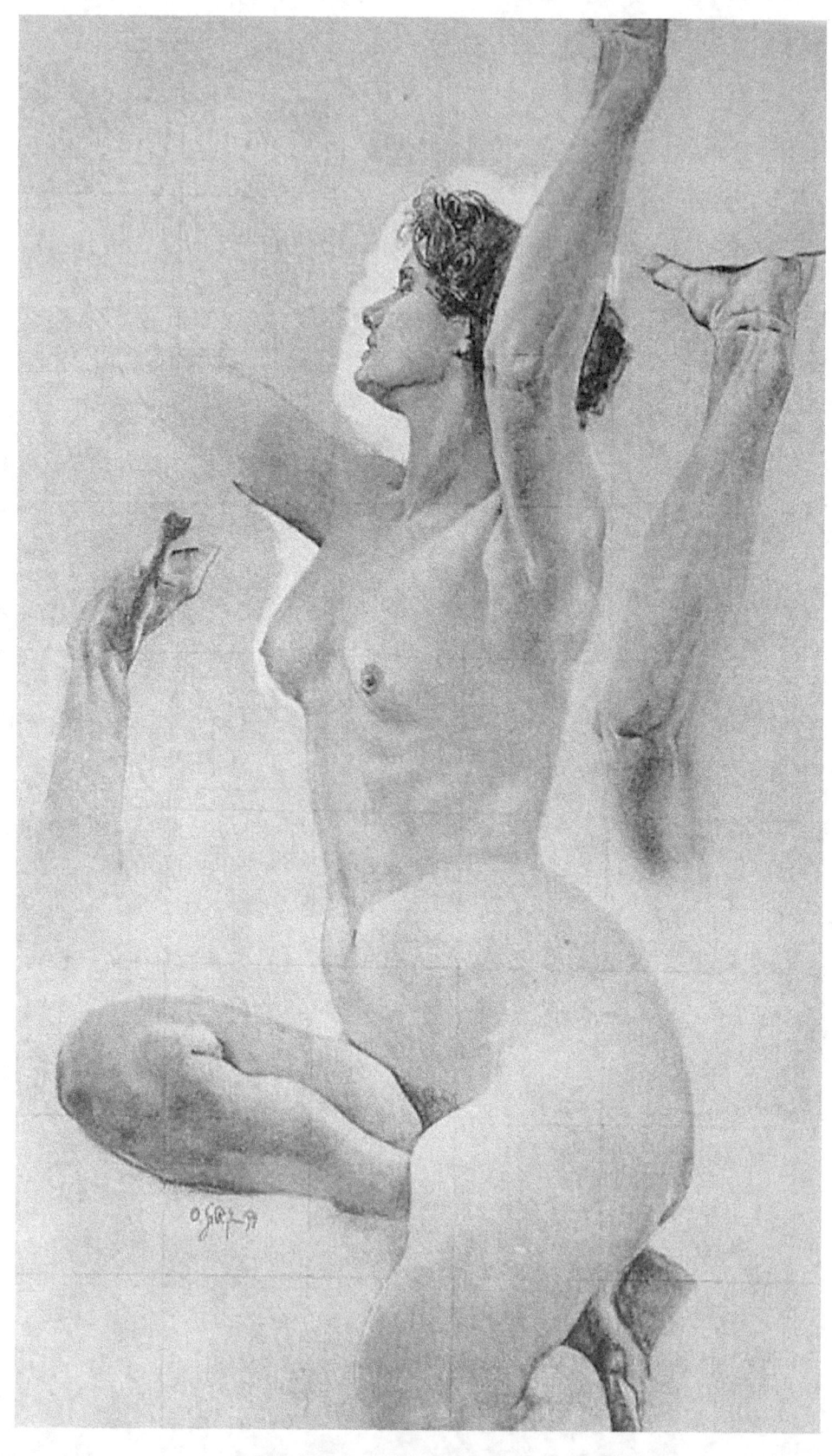

Otto Grenier, Study For Odysseus, 1912-33

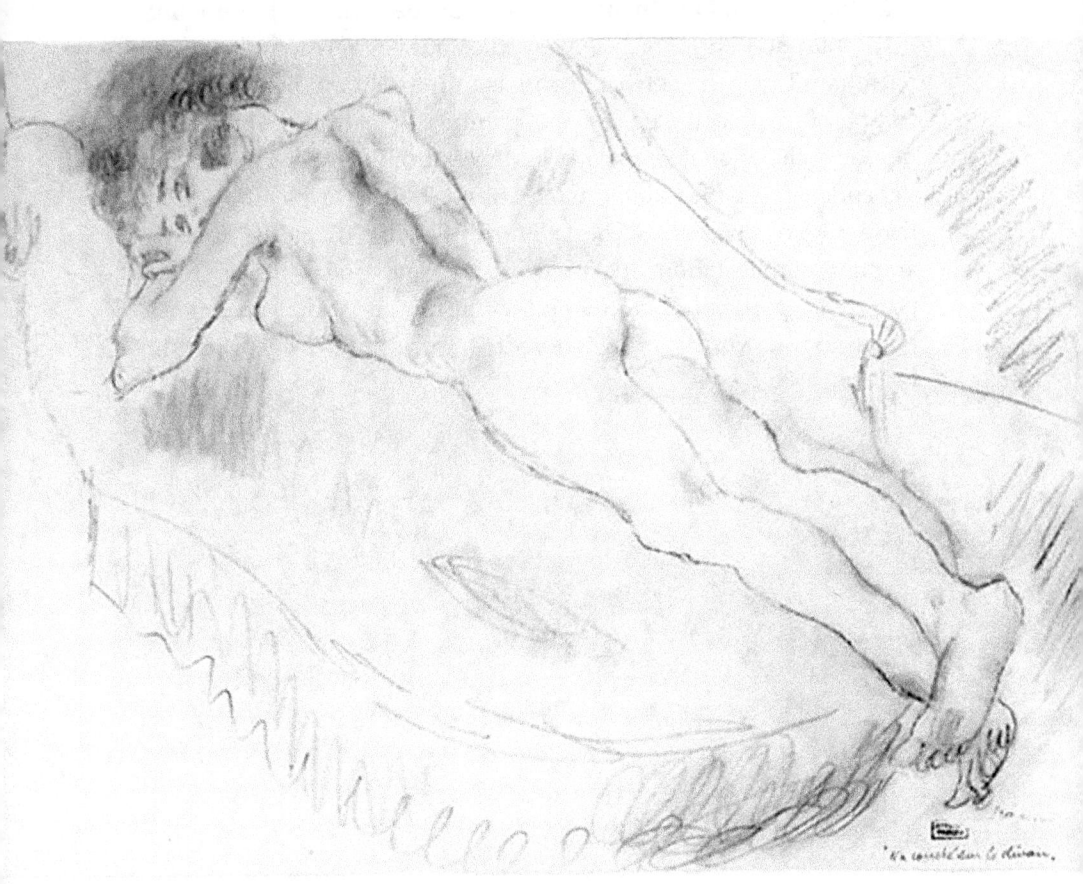

Jules Pascin

THE FEMALE NUDE

The high art nude, then, is a site of political and economic manipulation, an expression of the power relations between patron and painter, between connoisseur, artist and model. In the trinity of people linked by the painting – patron, painter and model – the model is clearly at the bottom of the pile. She is dependent on both painter and patron. She has to please both of them to be successful. The relation of artist to model thus is another manifestation, like that of husband and wife, of male power, of patriarchal culture in action, of the sexual economics which are at work everywhere in the world, and everywhere in history.

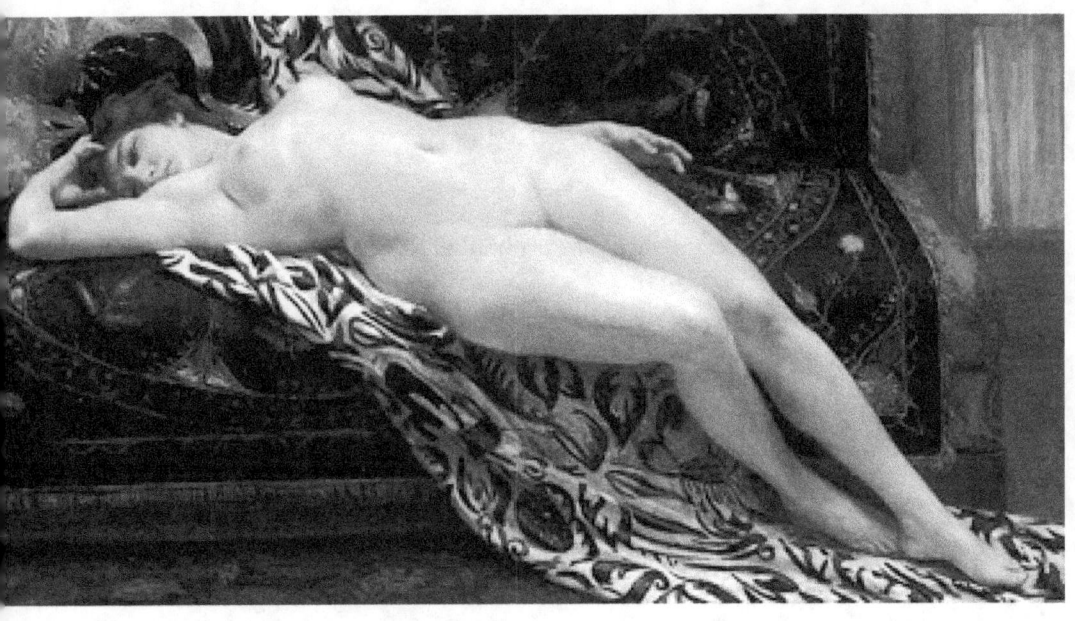

Guillaume Seignac, L'Abandon (above).
The Wave (below).

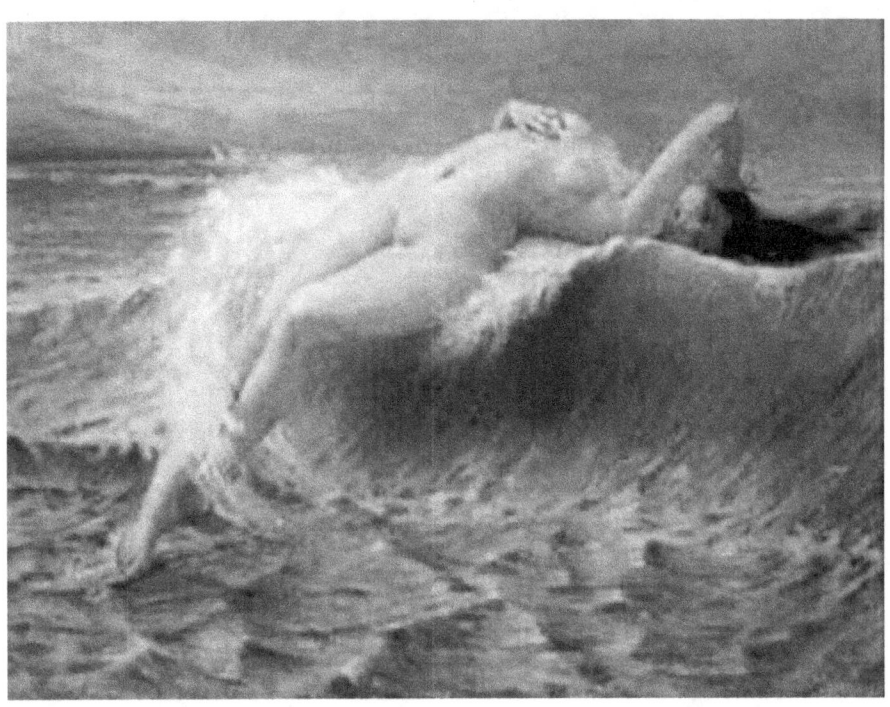

MALE NUDES

The male nude can be seen as a phallus, as Gill Saunders pointed out:

> The male body, while not constructed as the site of sexual pleasure, is often symbolic of phallic power. The whole body, muscular, potent, active, may come to represent the phallus.[1]

The penis isn't a phallus, so, to make up for the disappointing insufficiency of the penis, macho masculinity is demonstrated by bulging muscles, clenched fists, sturdy poses. The male nude poses with a body of 'rippling muscles', bizarrely exaggerated, or gripping a gun, or standing next to a motorcycle, a car, a machine, something that can connote phallic power.

---

1 G. Saunders: *The Nude*, 26.

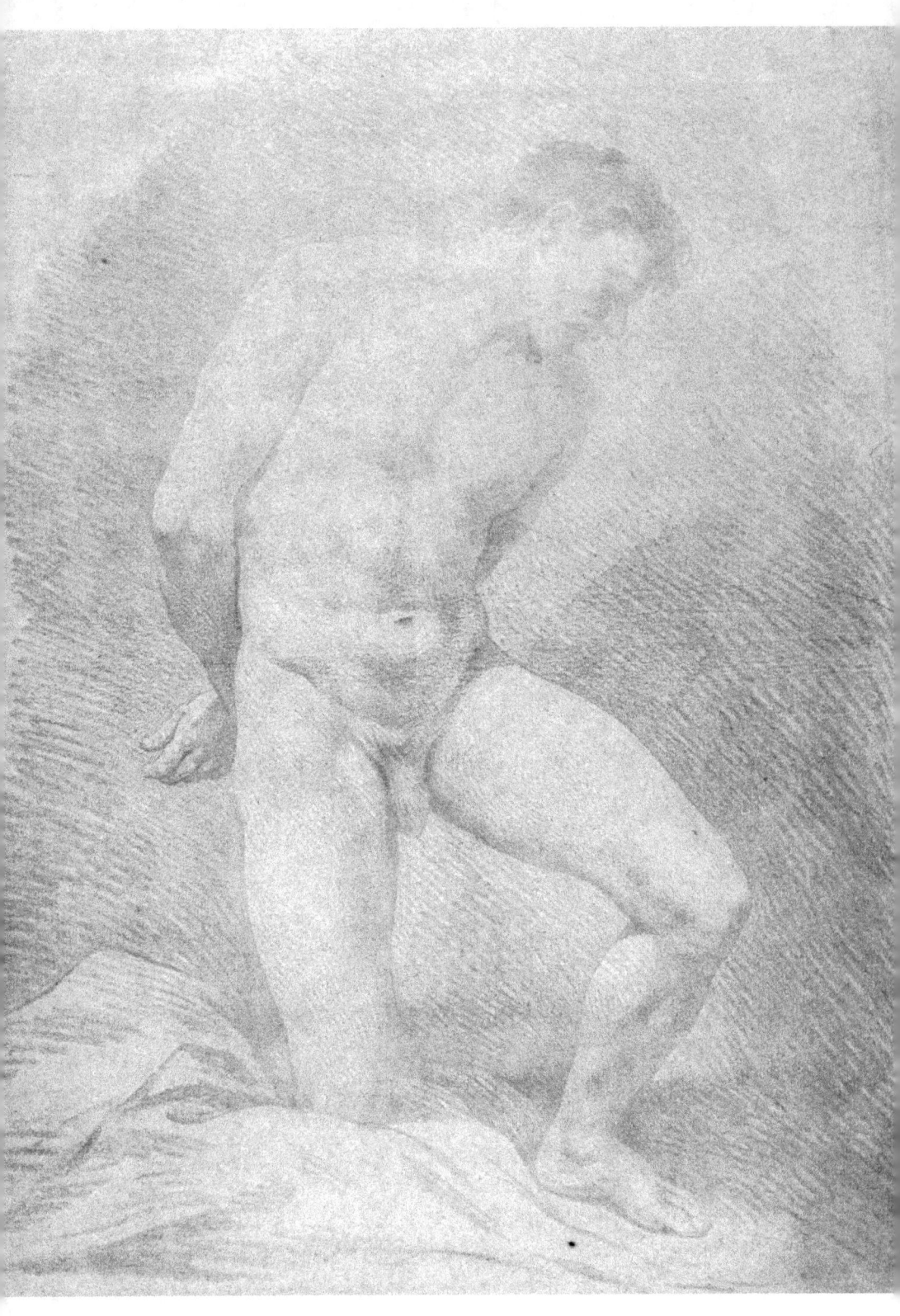

Male Nude, 19th century

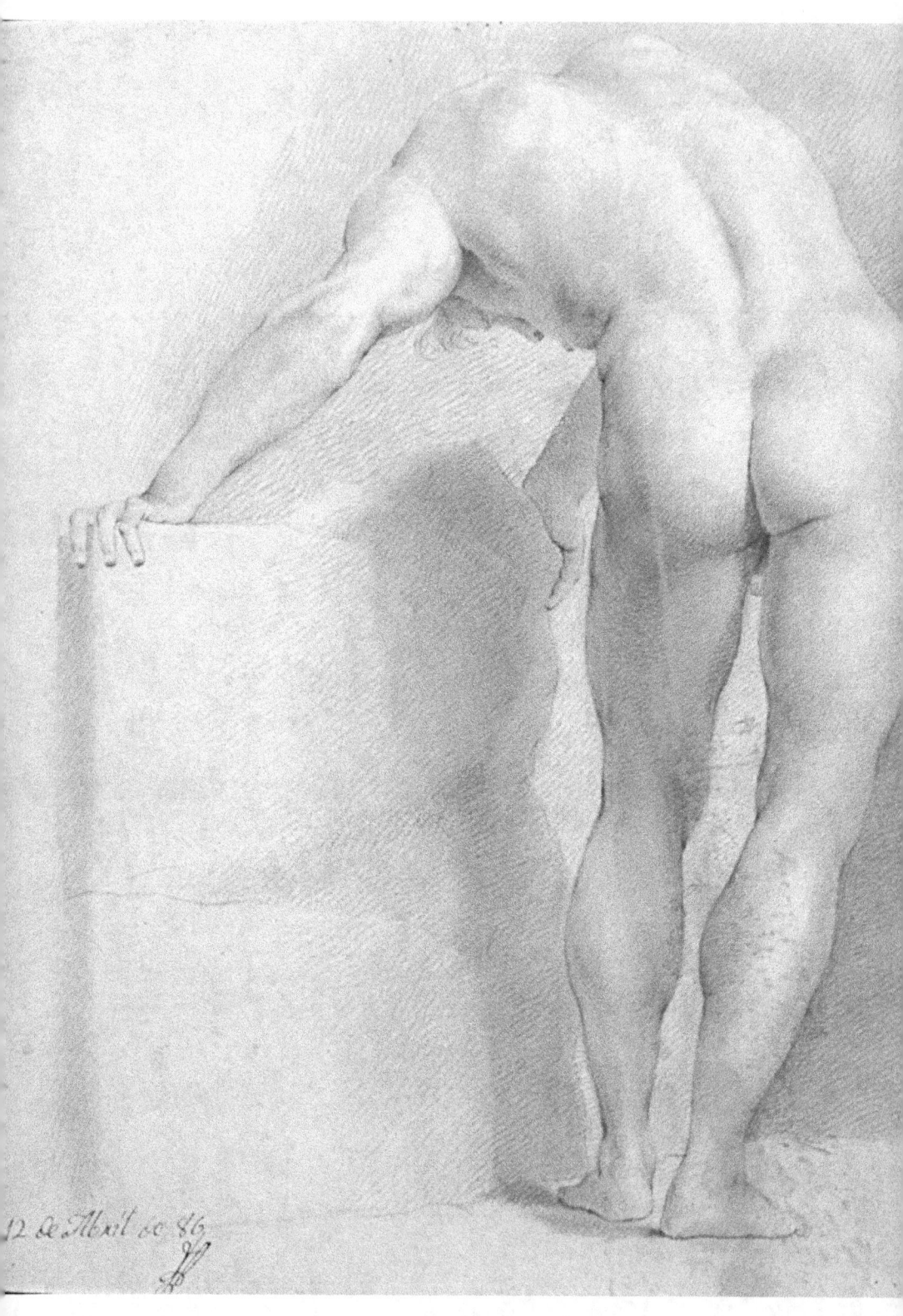

12 de Abril de 86

Mariano Amare, Male Nude, 1786.

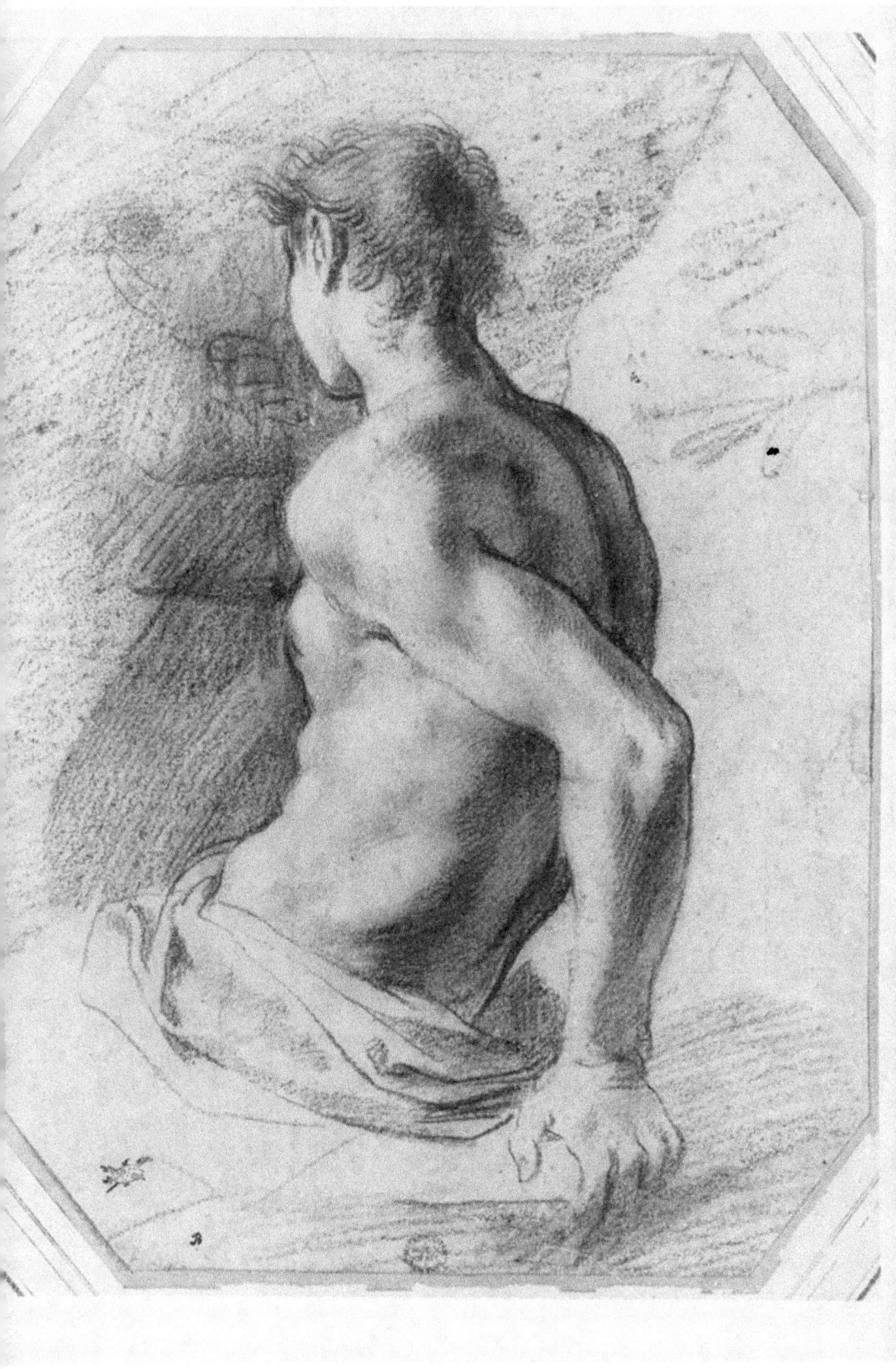

Annibale Carracci, Male Nude, Half-Figure, 16th century

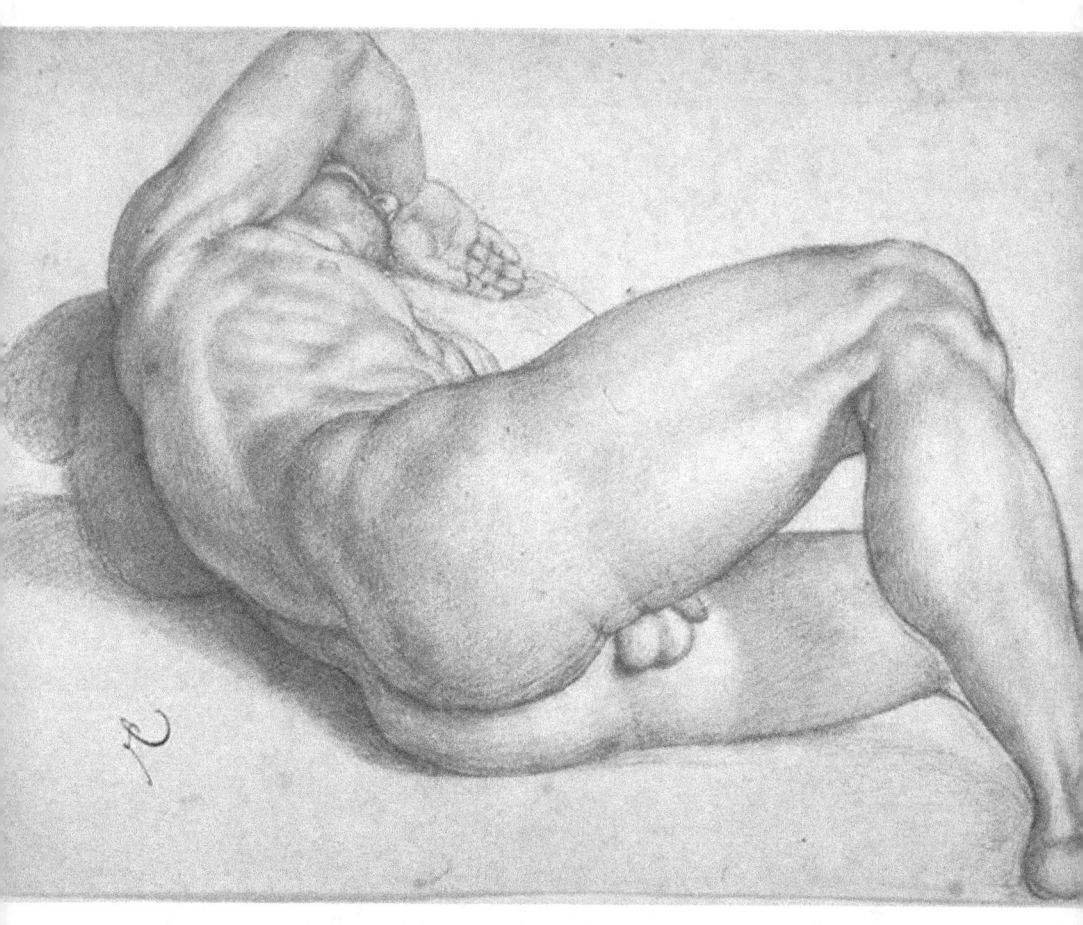

Agnolo di Cosimo (Il Bronzino),
Naked Man Lying On His Back, 16th century

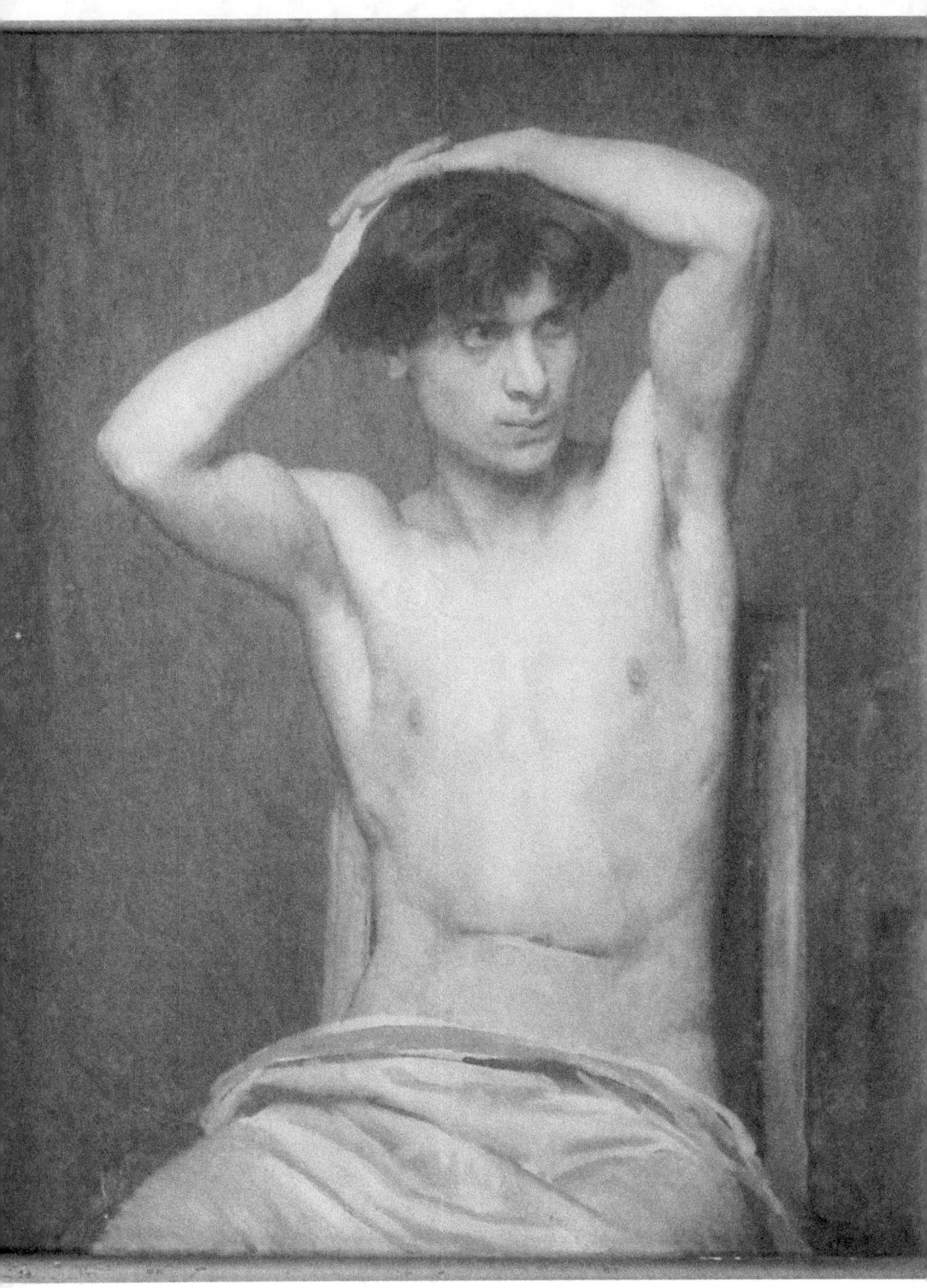

Henri-Lucien Doucet, Half-Nude Figure, 1879

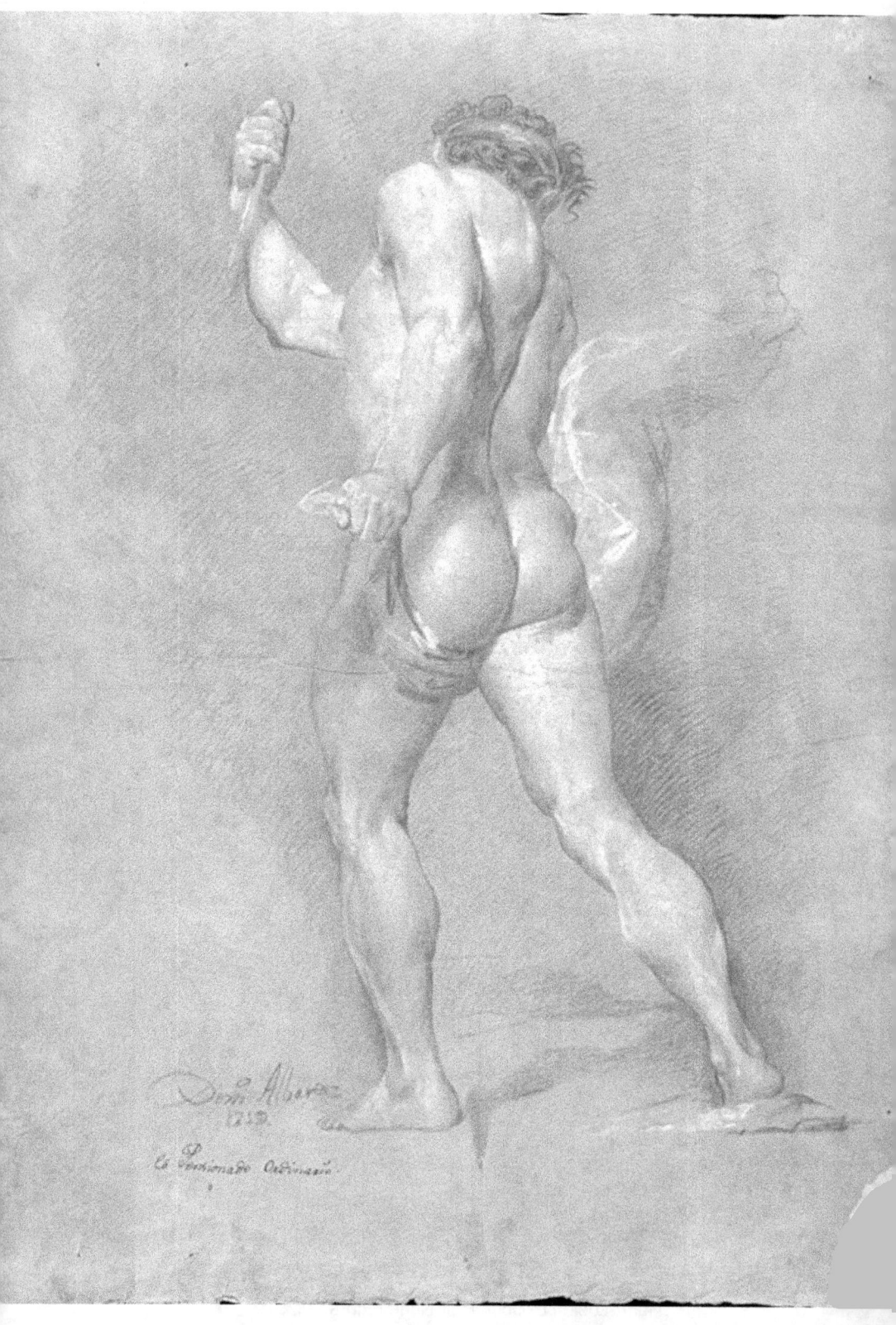

Domingo Alvarez Enciso, Male Nude, 1759

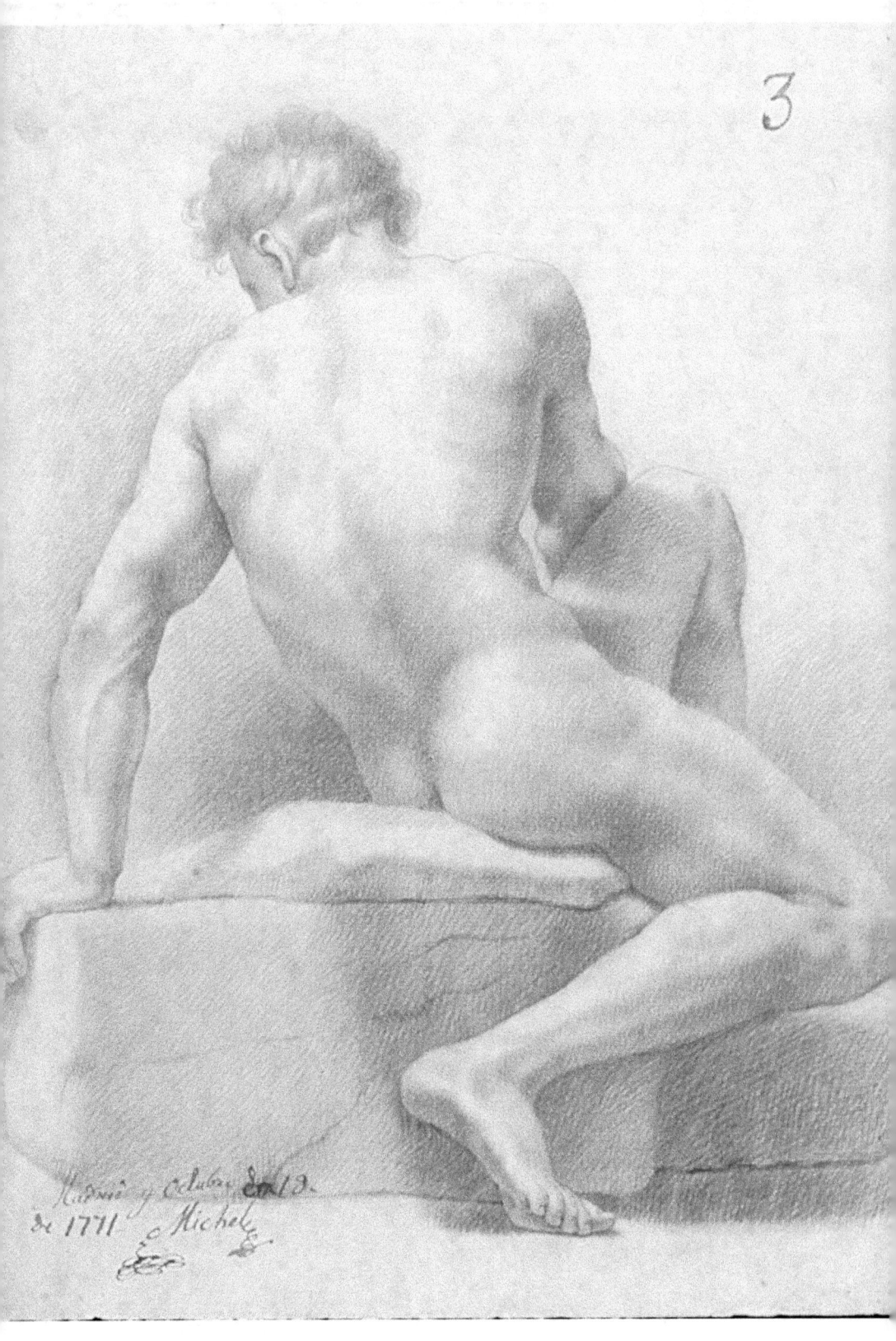

Pedro Pascual Munoz, Seated Male Nude, 1771

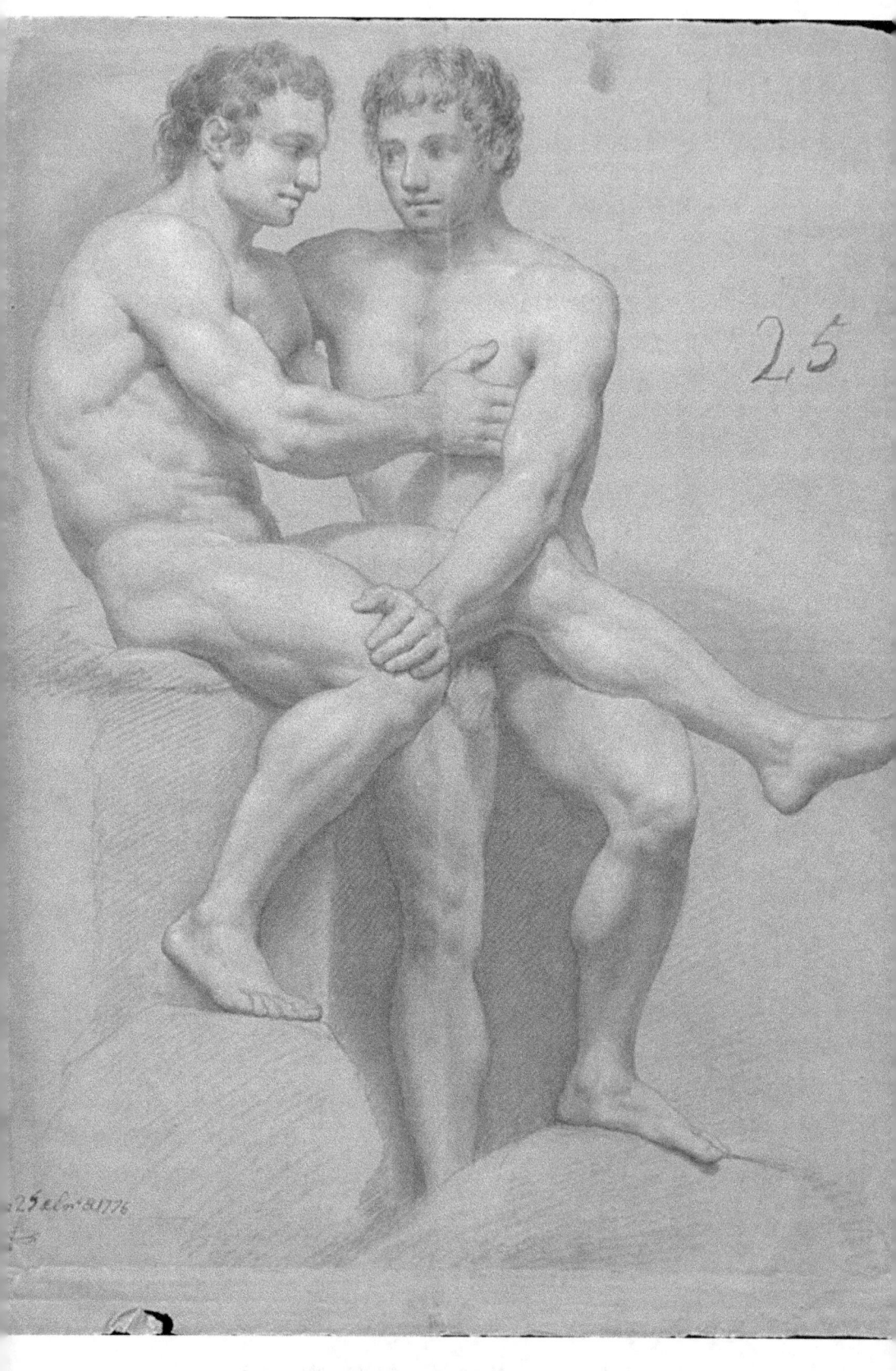

Gustin Esteve Marques, Two Male Nudes, 1776

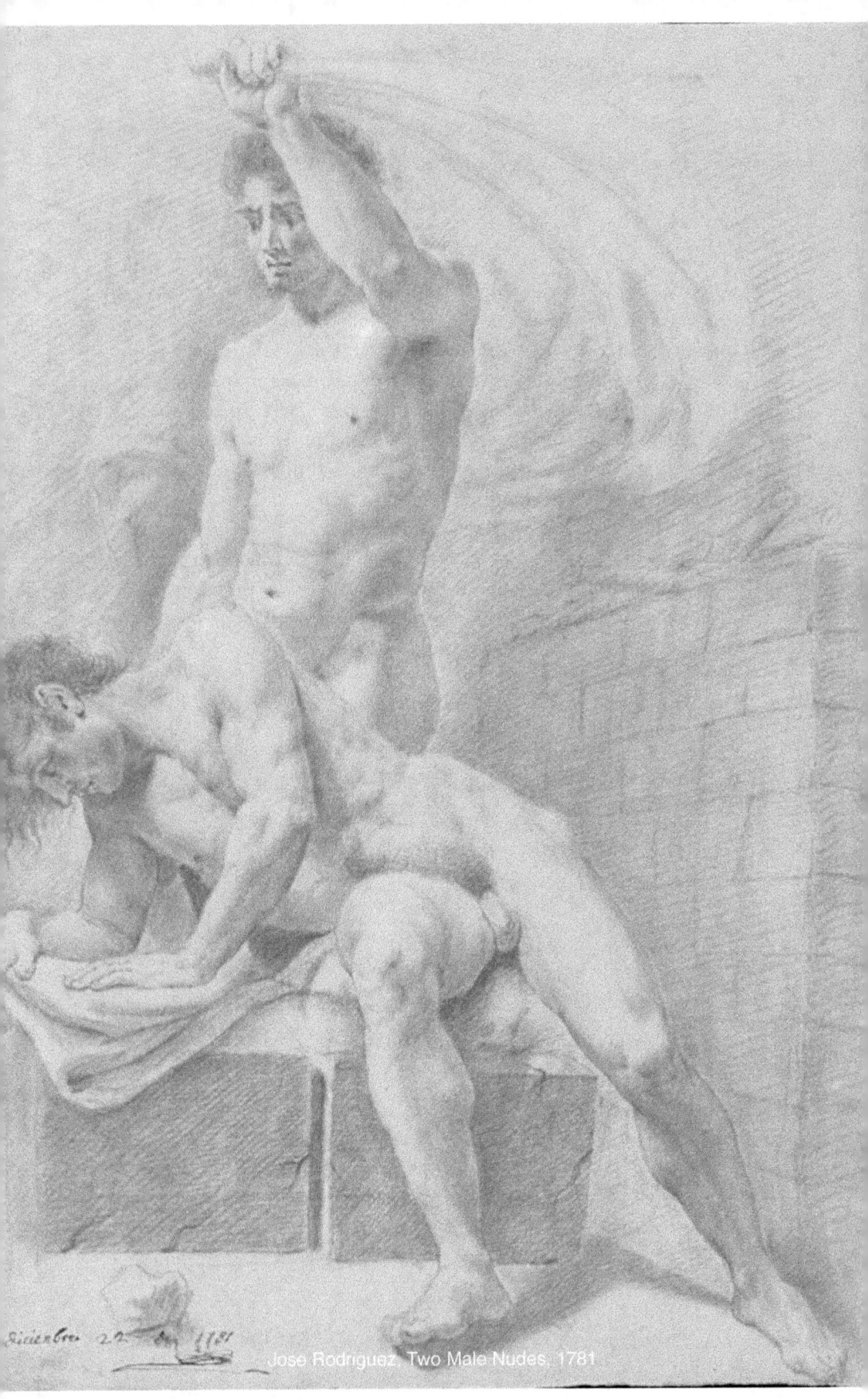

Jose Rodriguez, Two Male Nudes, 1781

MALE NUDES

The male nude can be appear uncomfortable. He doesn't like his photograph or painting or sculpture to be looked at like female nudes. He is used to being the one doing the looking. When the roles are reversed, ambiguity and confusion seeps in. The male nude is set up as spectacle, and as a passive object. To counter the awkwardness of this passivity, the male nude is shown *doing* something. Running, throwing a spear, fighting, etc. It tries to engage a position of activity, because to be the 'looked-at' one, the passive sex object, is very disquieting. Further, the activity of the male nude, which's seen everywhere – in photographs by Eadweard Muybridge,[1] in sculptures by Michelangelo Buonarroti, in movies, in gay porn – aims at portraying phallic power. 'Even in an apparently relaxed, supine pose,' Richard Dyer in 1983,

> the model tightens and tautens his body so that the muscles are emphasized, hence drawing attention to the body's potential for action. More often, the male pin-up is not supine anyhow, but standing taut ready for action.[2]

1 See L. Williams: "Film Body, an implantation of perversions", *Cinétracts*, vol. 3, no.4, Winter 1981, 19-25.
2 Richard Dyer: 'Don't Look Now", *Screen*, vol. 23, 3/ 4, 1983, 20, and in Angela McRobbie, 206

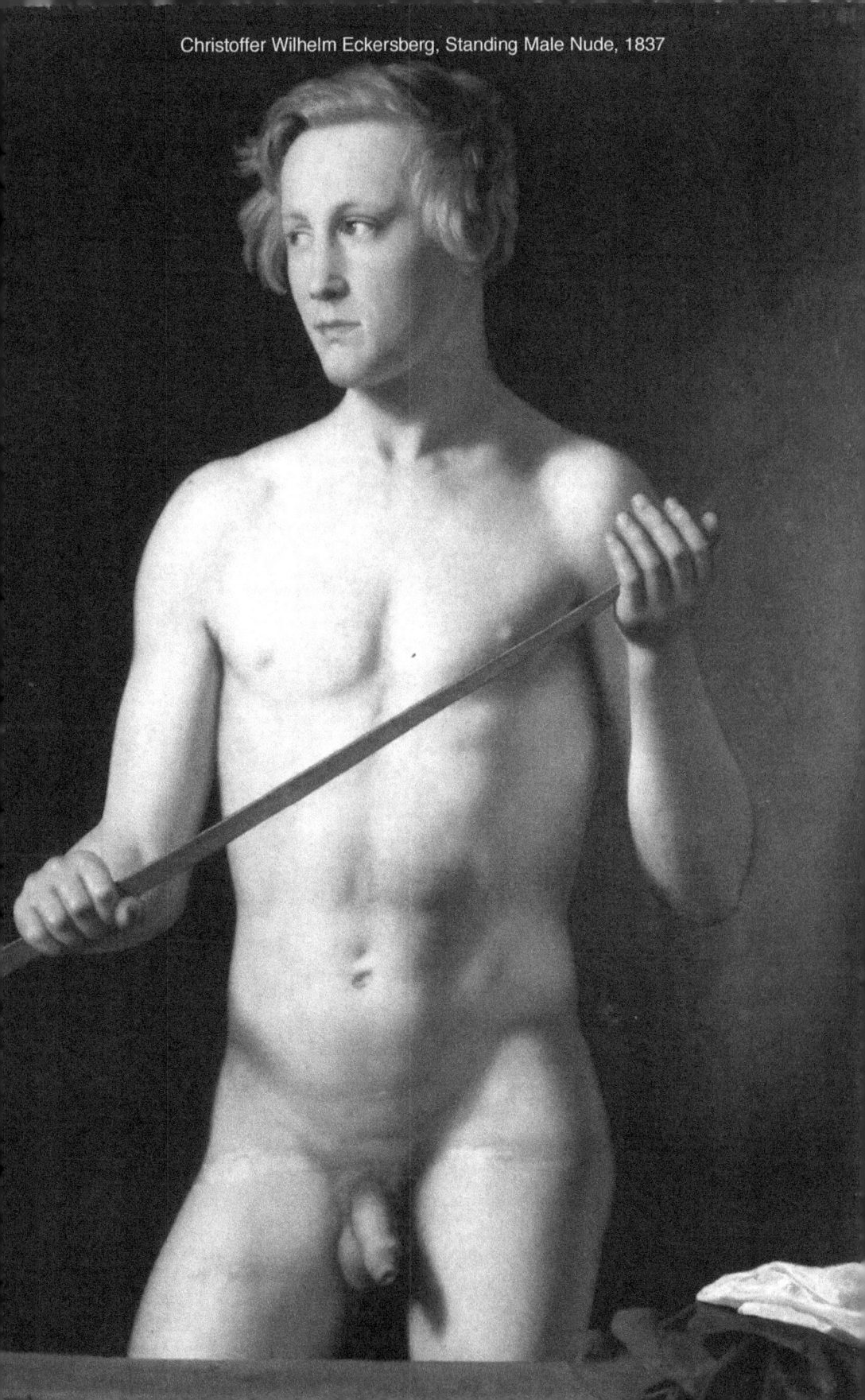

Christoffer Wilhelm Eckersberg, Standing Male Nude, 1837

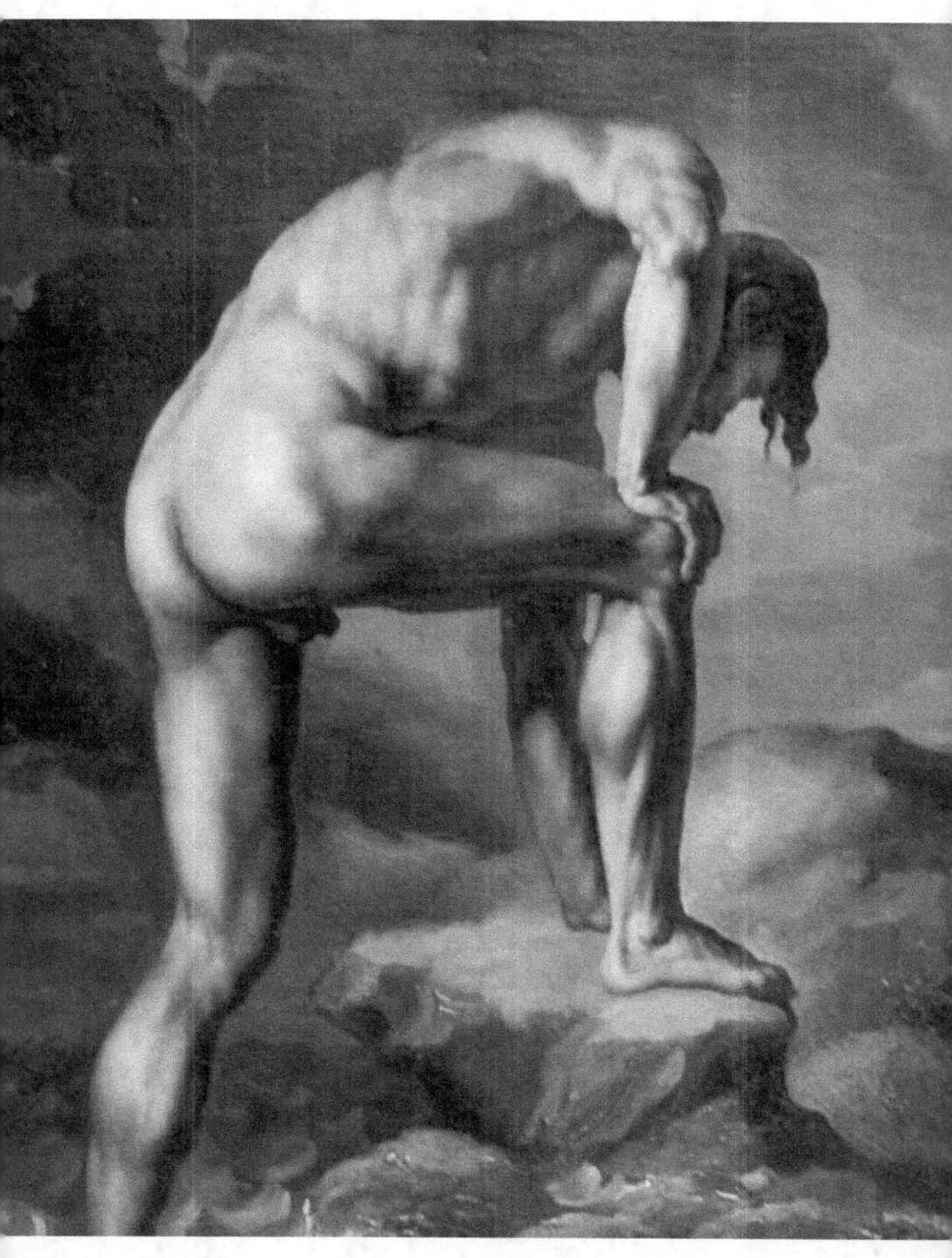

Jean-Louis Andre Theodore Géricault, A Shipwreck, c. 1819

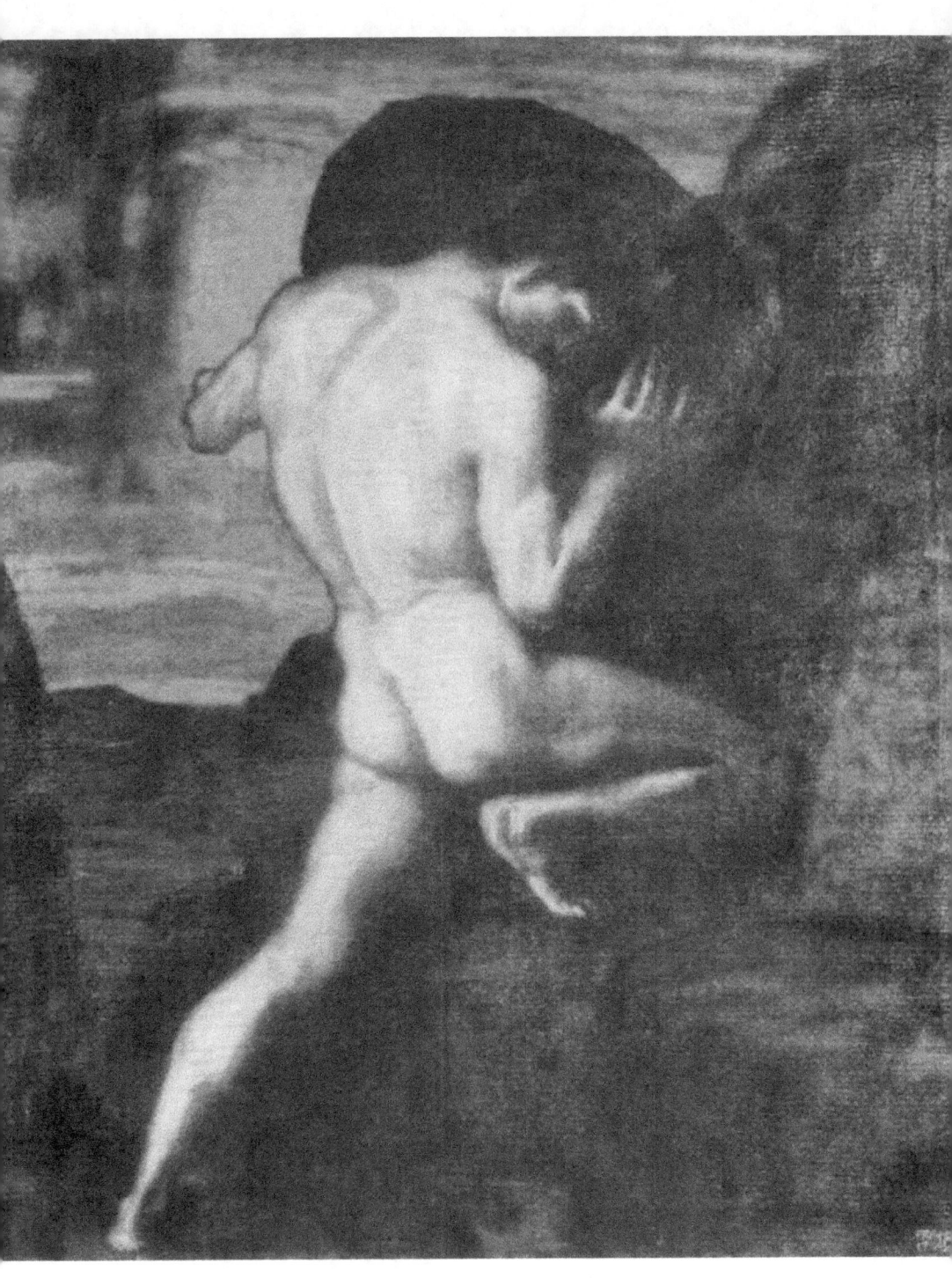

Franz von Stuck, Sisyphus

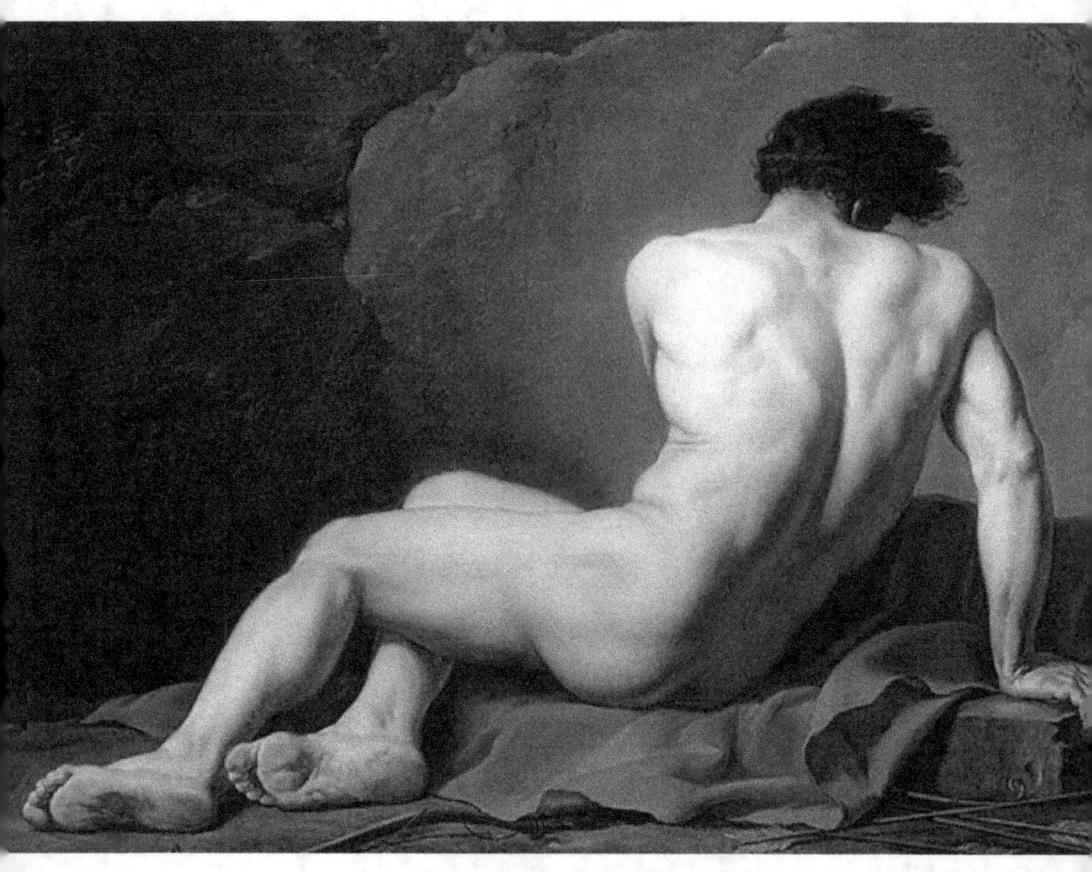

A classical French male nude painting
by Jacques-Louis David (known as Patrocles)

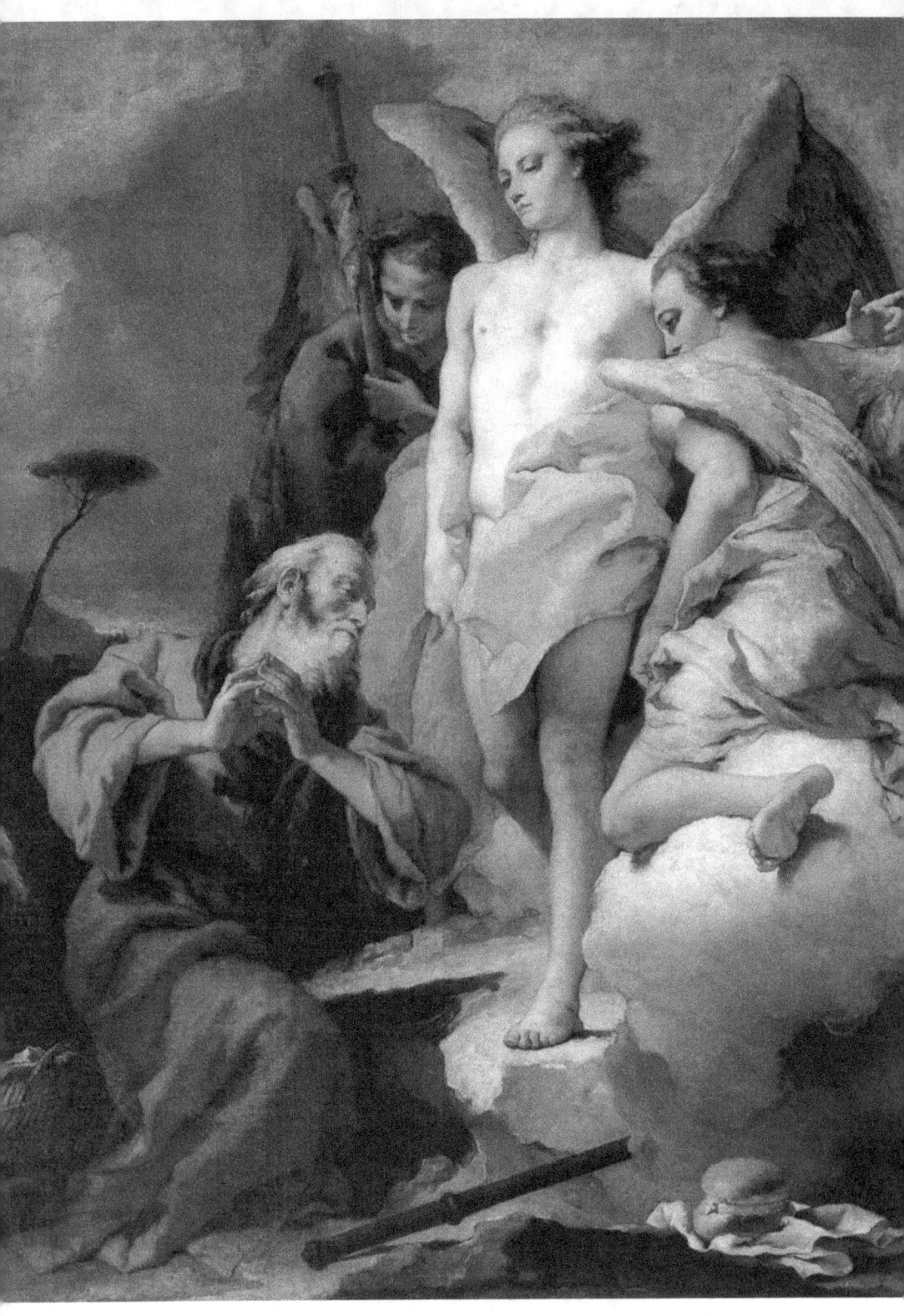

Giovanni Battista Tiepolo, Abraham and Three Angels, c. 1770

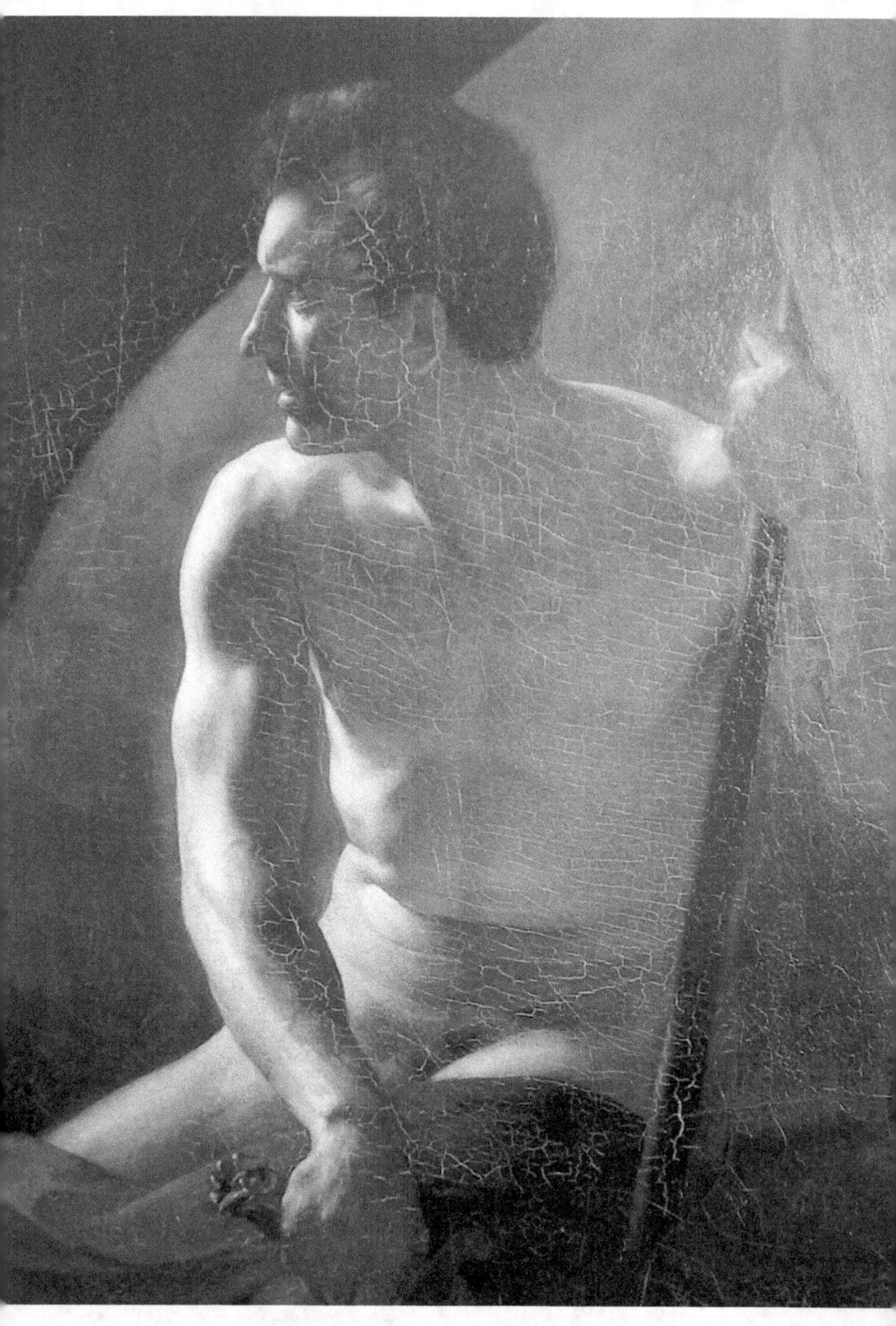

Hippolyte Dominique Holfeld, Half-Nude Figure, 1831

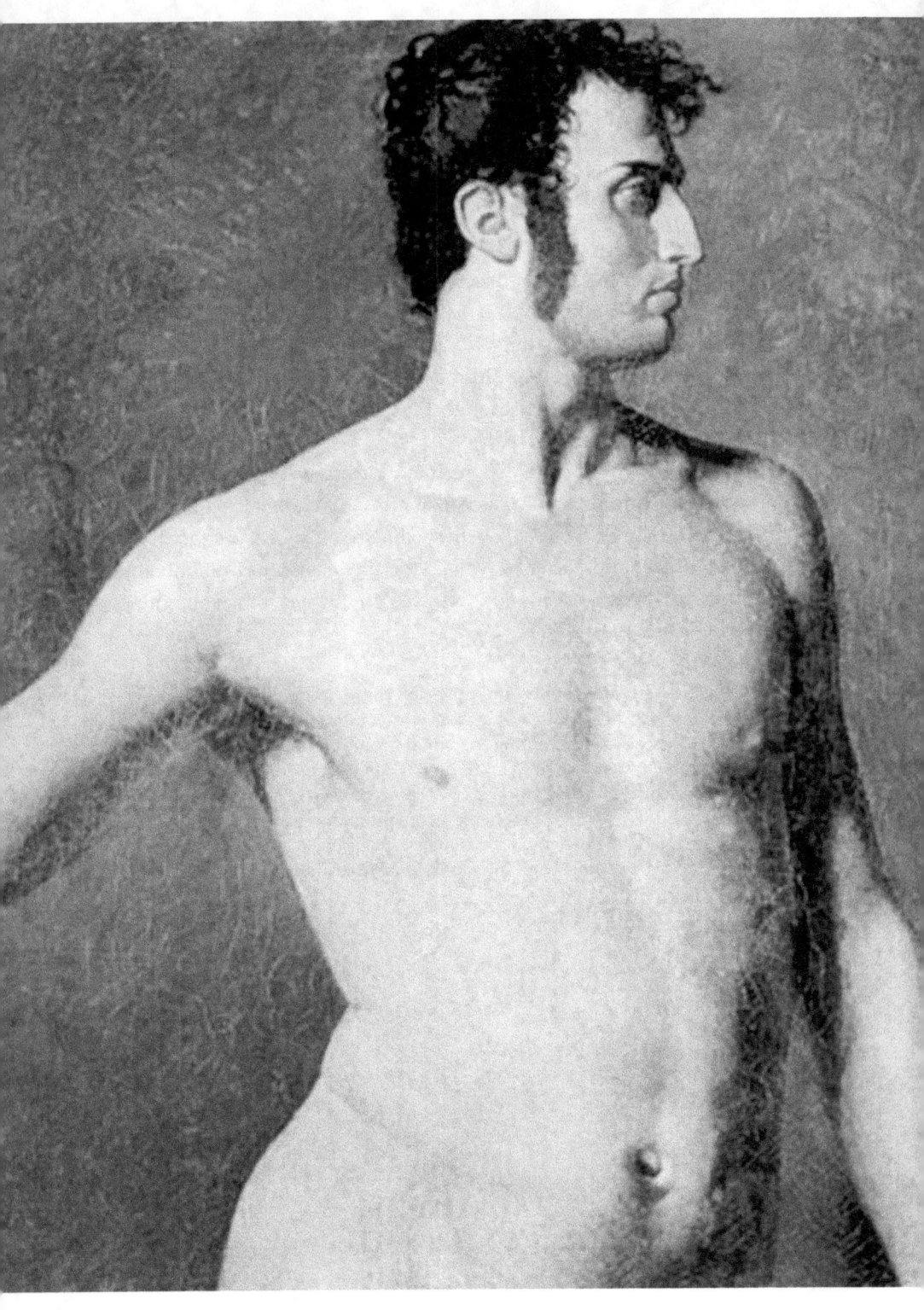

J.A.D. Ingres, Male Torso, 1801, Musée Ingres

MALE NUDES

The male nude image is subject to the same changes in culture as anything else: if you look at the nudes included here, you'll see the changes in fashion and style, at the superficial level, as well as the developments in the politics and society of the time, reflected in the nude images. Even though the body is nude, there are still numerous marks of culture upon it.

In the advanced capitalist, technological world, the body is not a 'natural' form any more, as Elizabeth Grosz explains in *Volatile Bodies*: clothing, exercise, jewellery, lifestyle, habits, negotiations of the cultural and social as well as the physical environment, and all sorts of activities alter it, inscribe it, turn it into something definitely not 'natural':

> Makeup, stilettos, bras, hair sprays, clothing, underclothing mark women's bodies, whether black or white, in ways in which hair styles, professional training, personal grooming, gait, posture, body building, and sports may mark men's. There is nothing natural or ahistorical about these modes of corporeal inscriptions. Through then, bodies are made amenable to the prevailing exigencies of power. They make the flesh into a particular type of body – pagan, primitive, medieval, capitalist, Italian, American, Australian. (142)

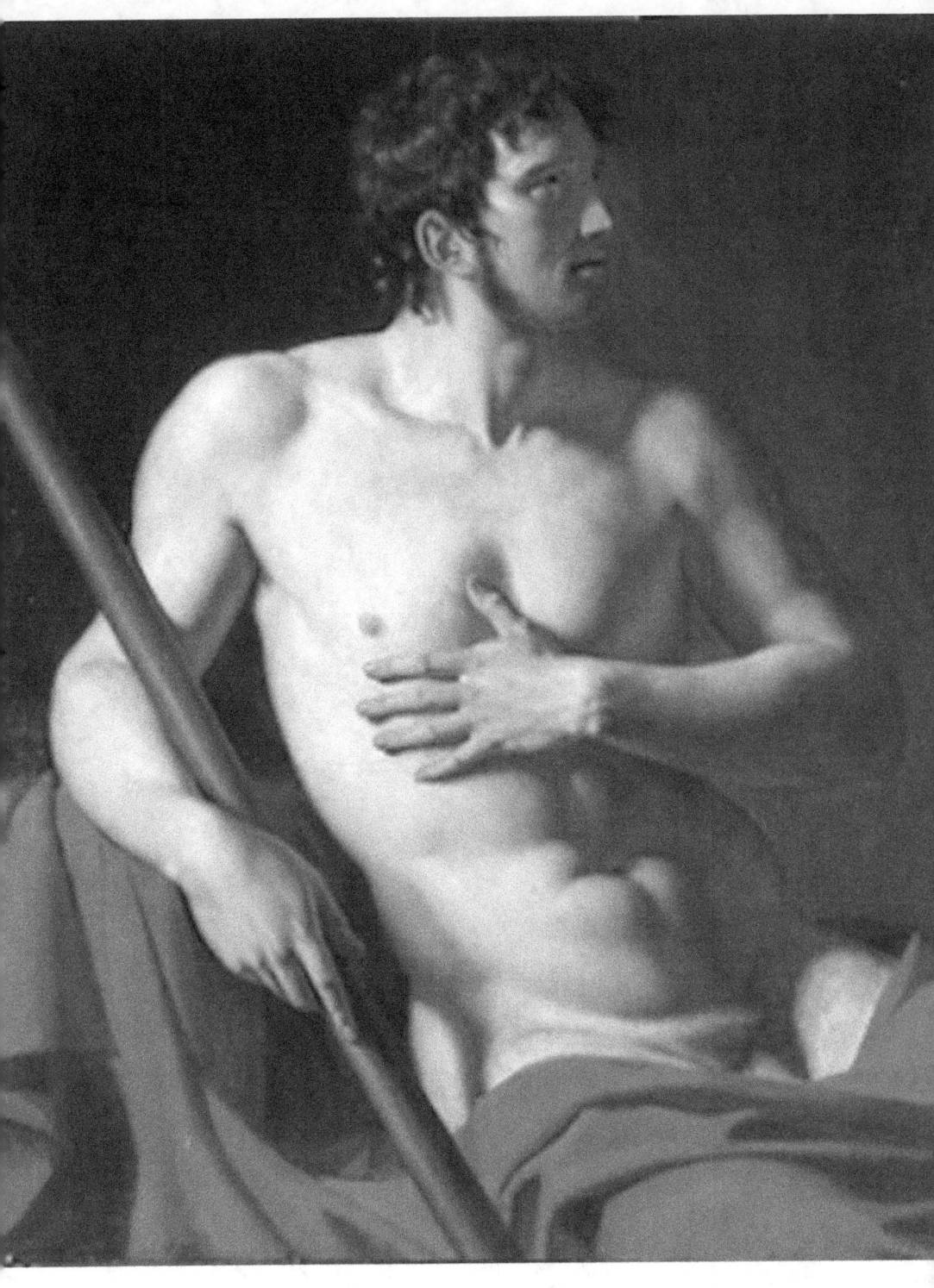

Auguste-Alphonse Gaudar de la Verdine, Male Nude, 1799

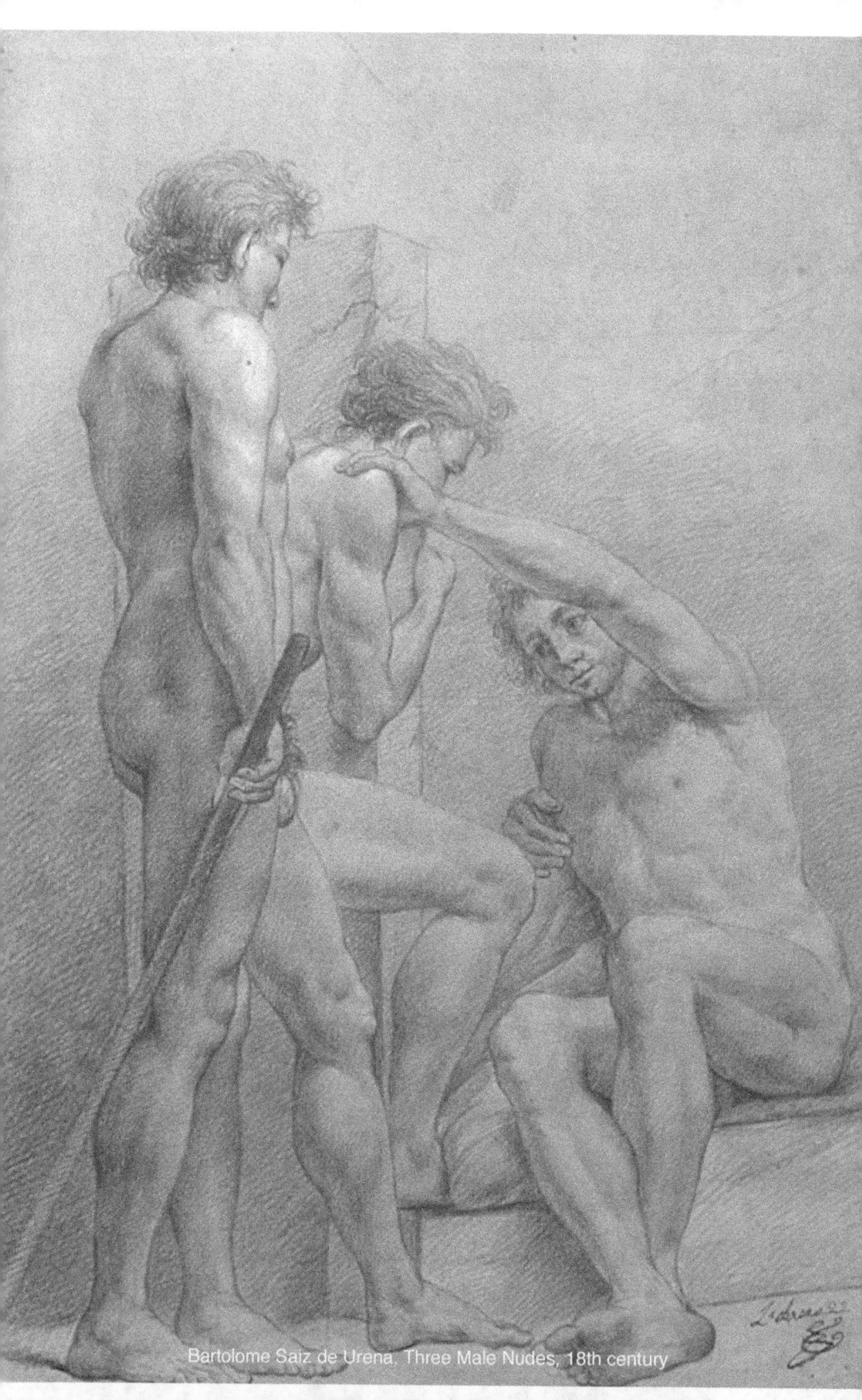

Bartolome Saiz de Urena, Three Male Nudes, 18th century

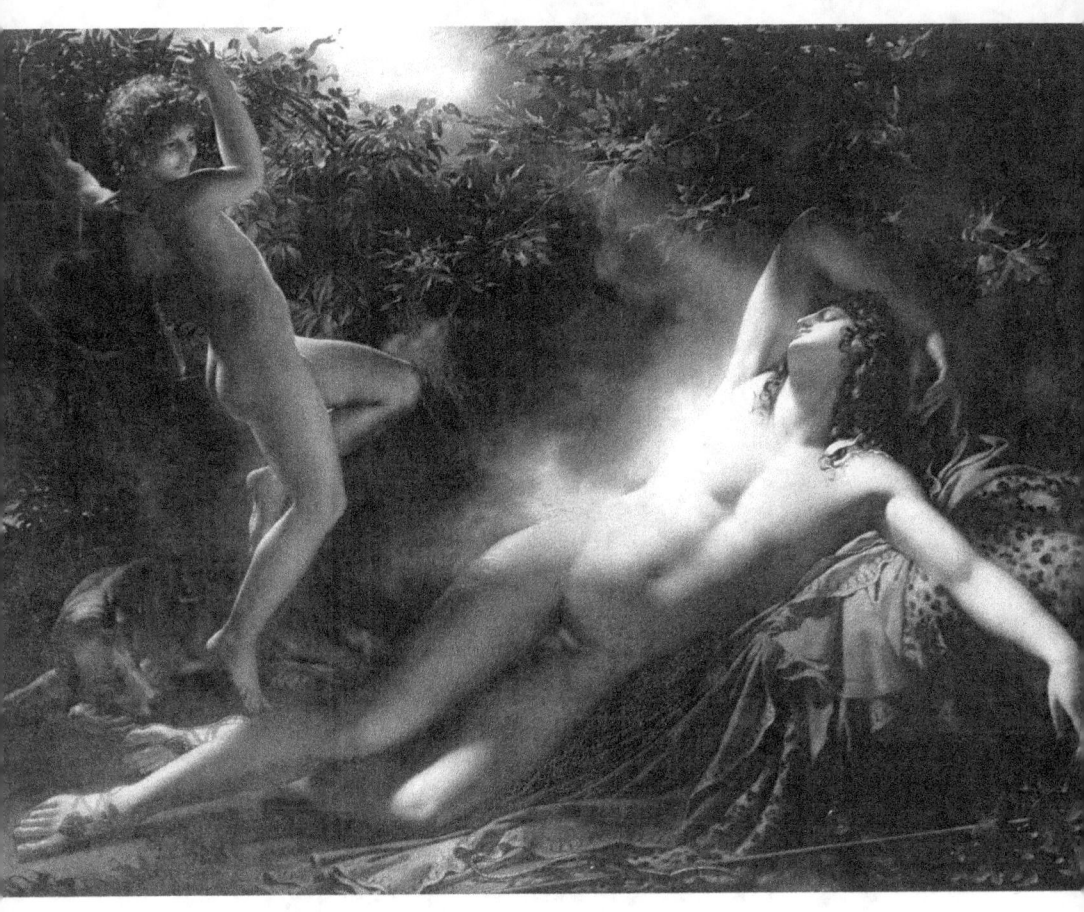

Anne-Louis Girodet-Trioson, Endymion, 1793

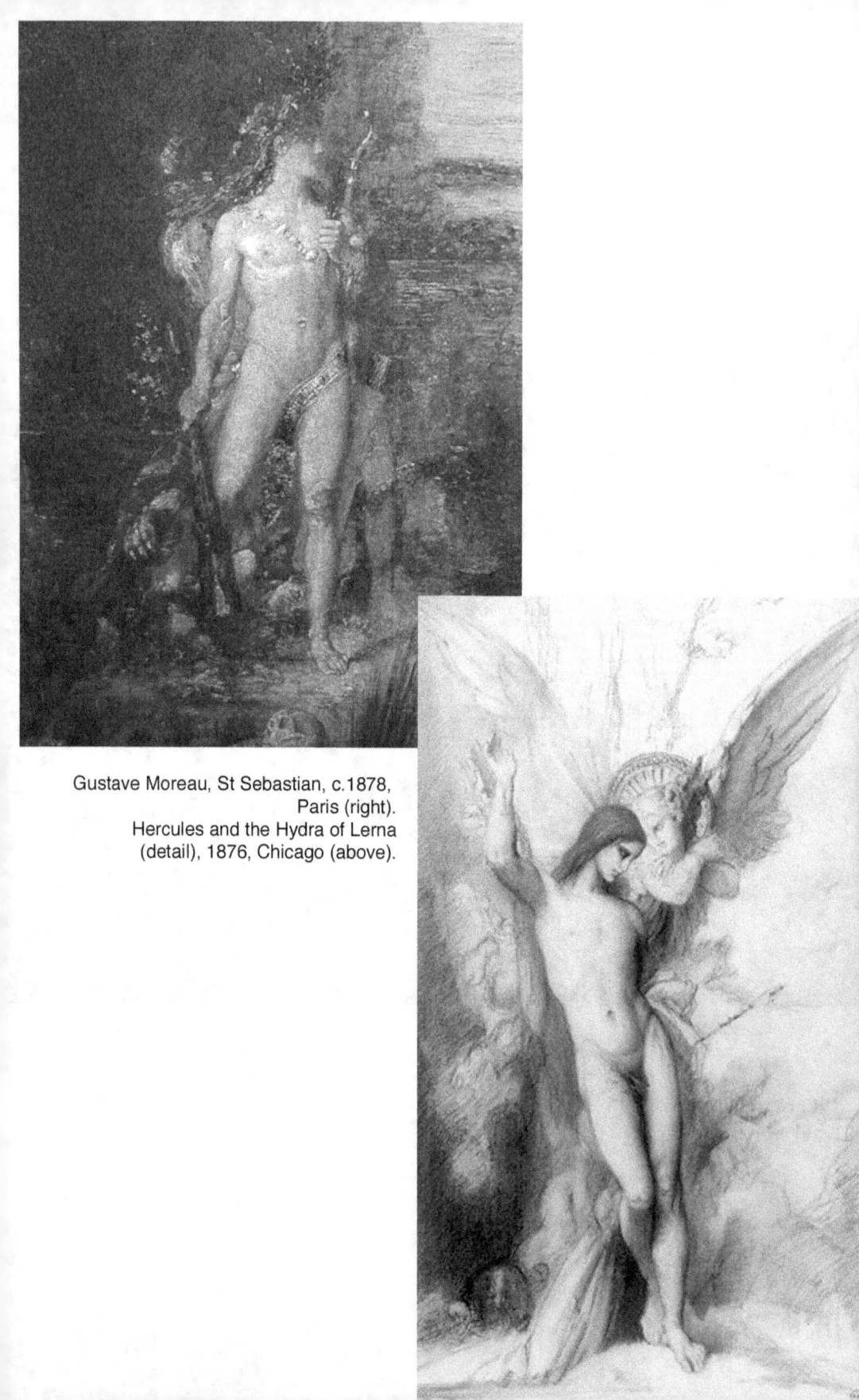

Gustave Moreau, St Sebastian, c.1878,
Paris (right).
Hercules and the Hydra of Lerna
(detail), 1876, Chicago (above).

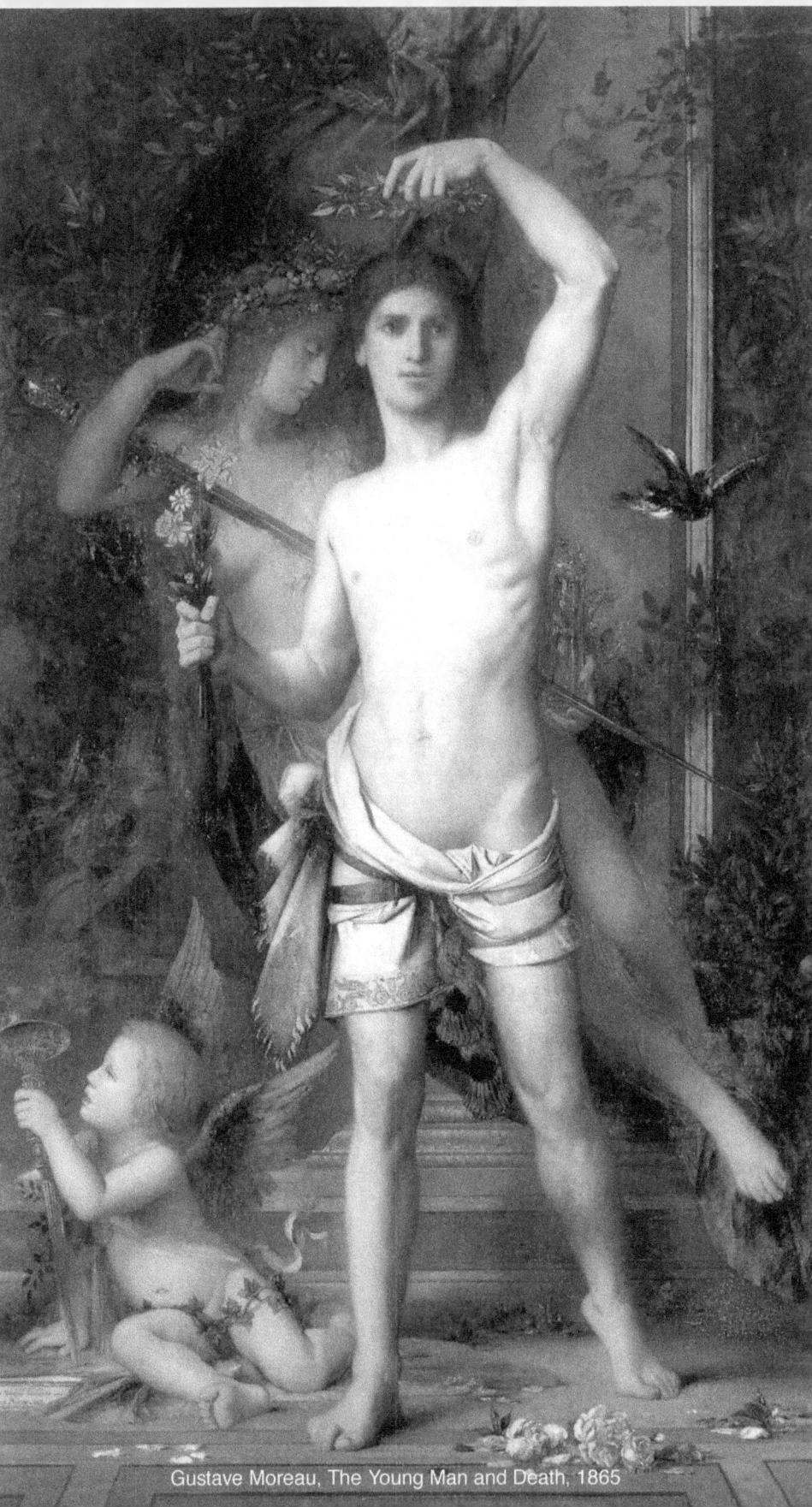

Gustave Moreau, The Young Man and Death, 1865

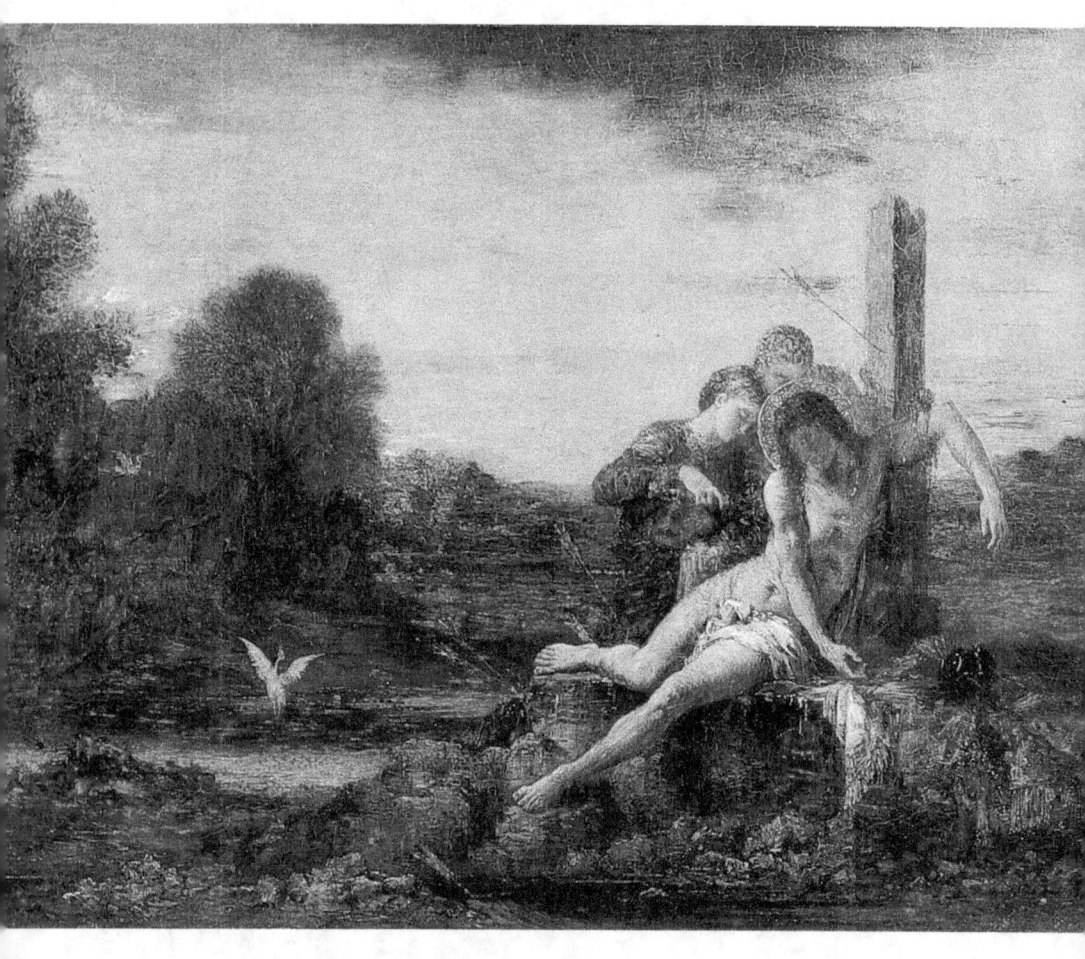

Gustave Moreau, St Sebastian, 1869

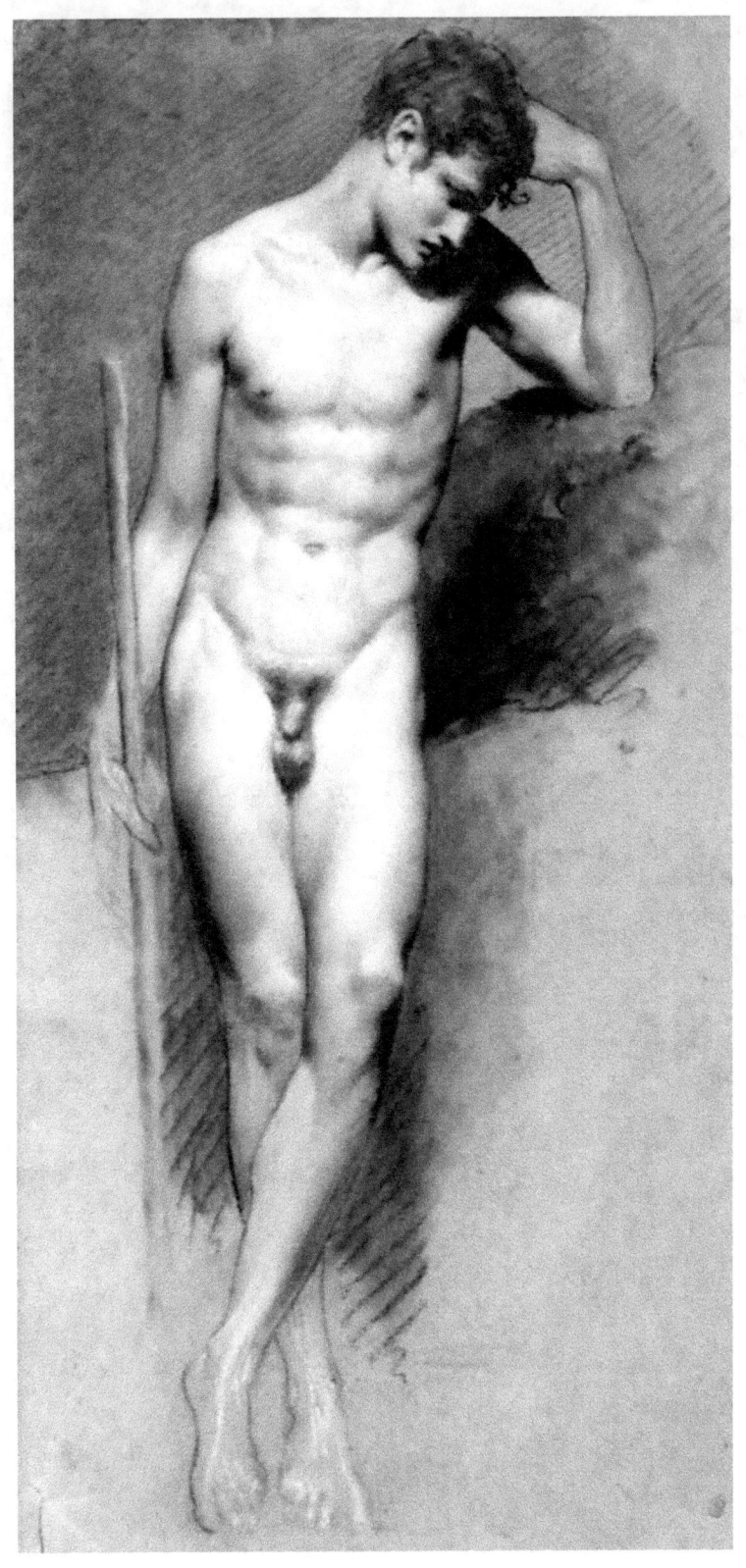

Pierre-Paul Prud'hon (1758-1823), Male Nude Standing

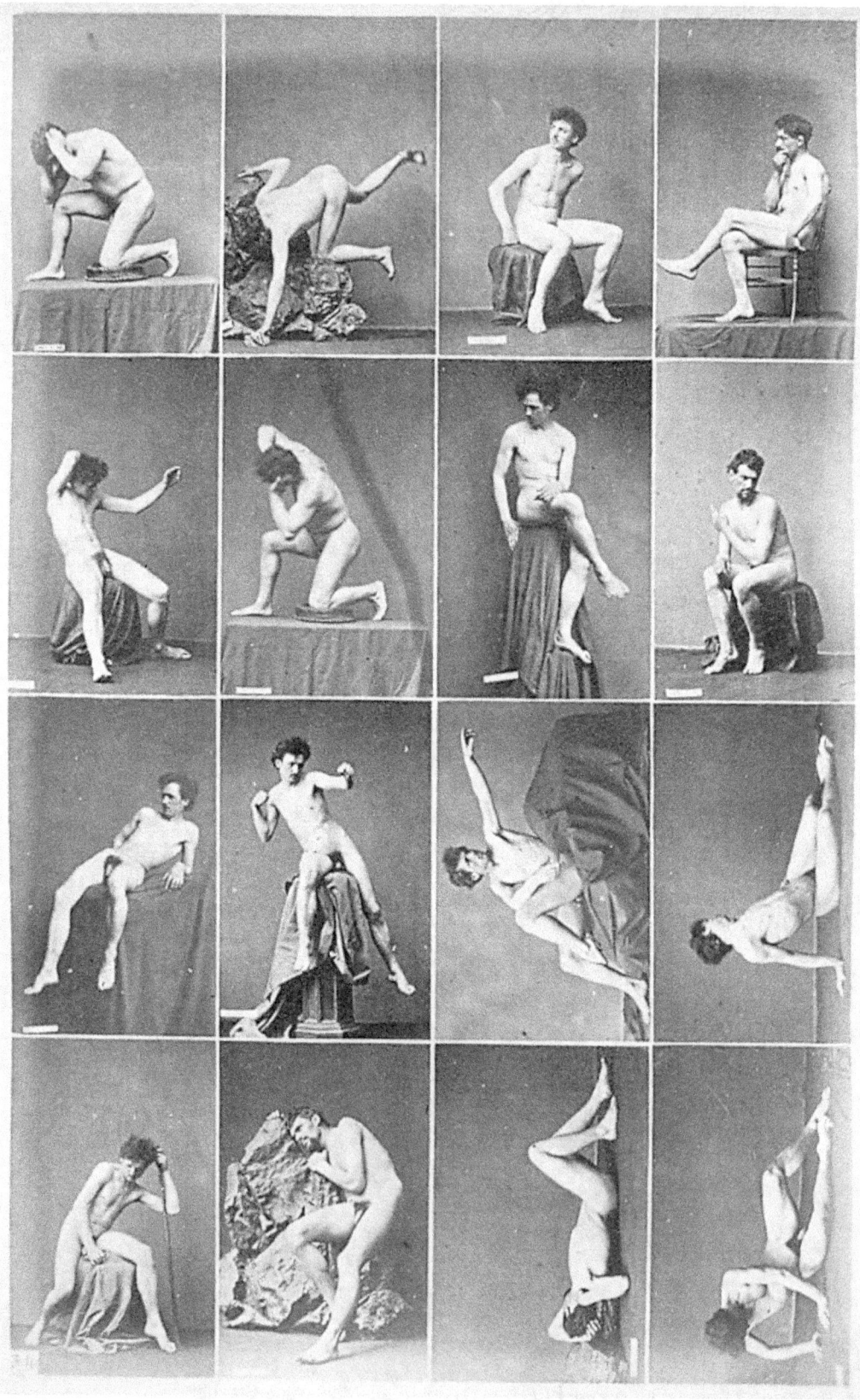

Ignout, Male Nude Studies, 1875

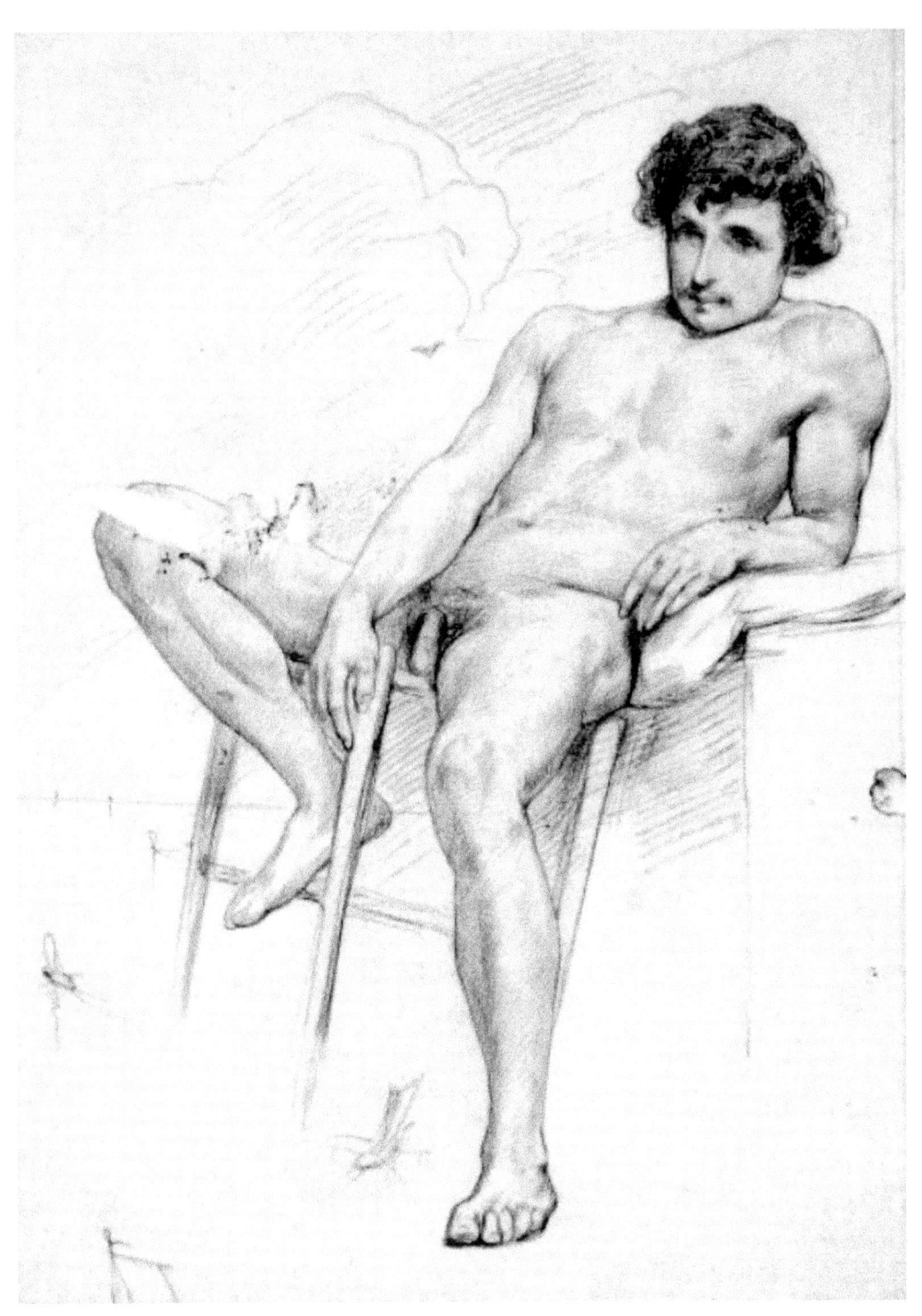

Lord Leighton, life drawing

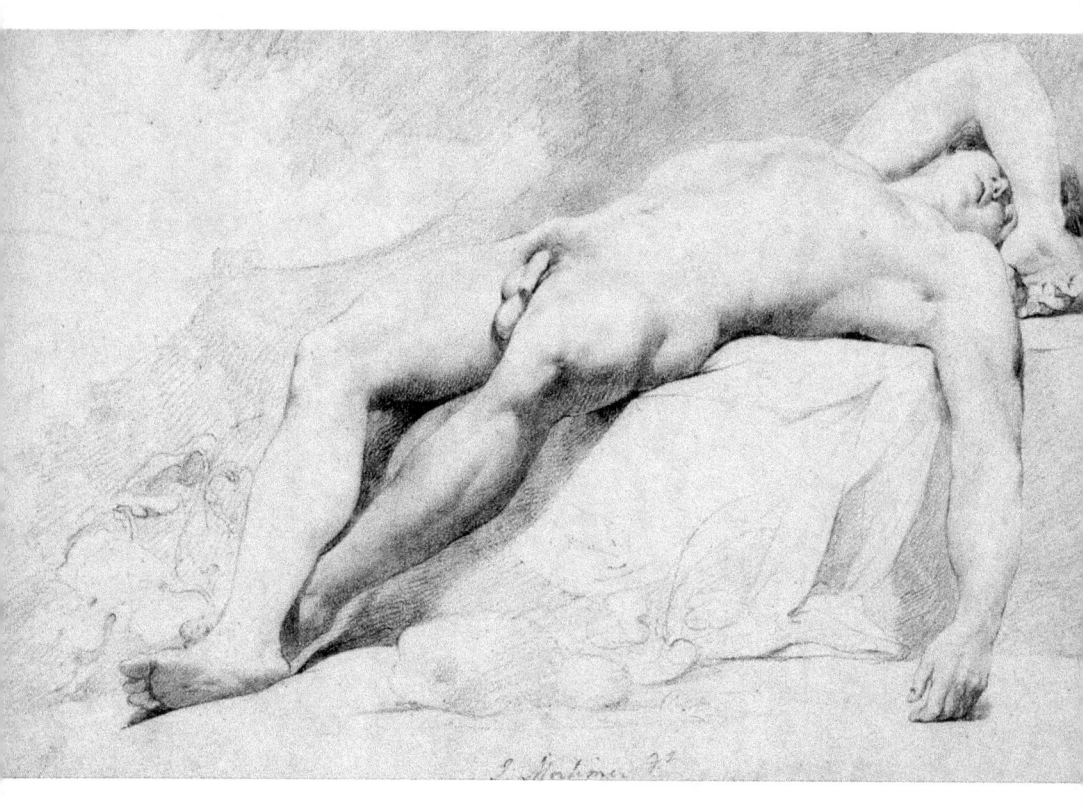

John Hamilton Mortimer, Recumbent Male Nude, c. 1773

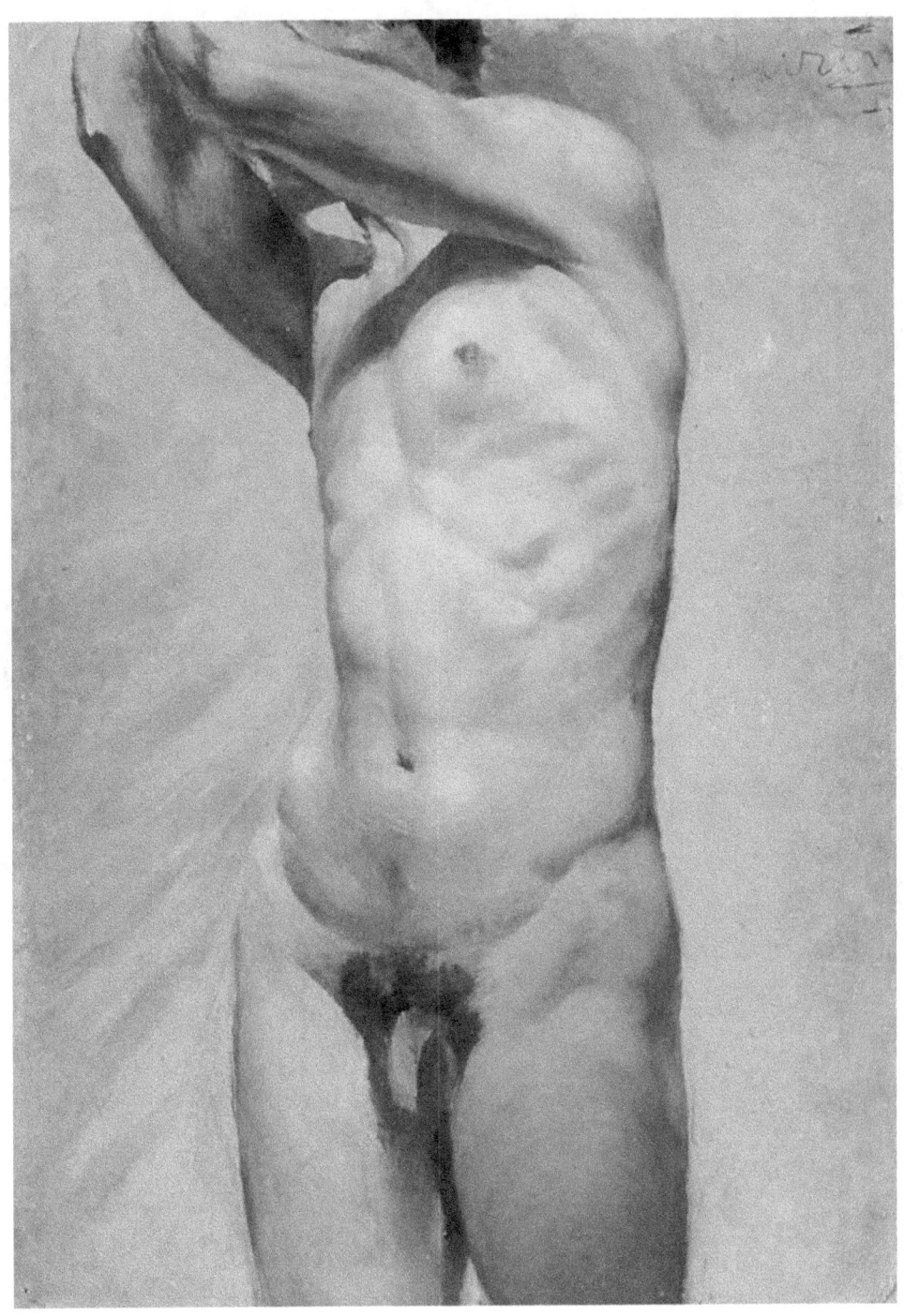

French school, c. 1890

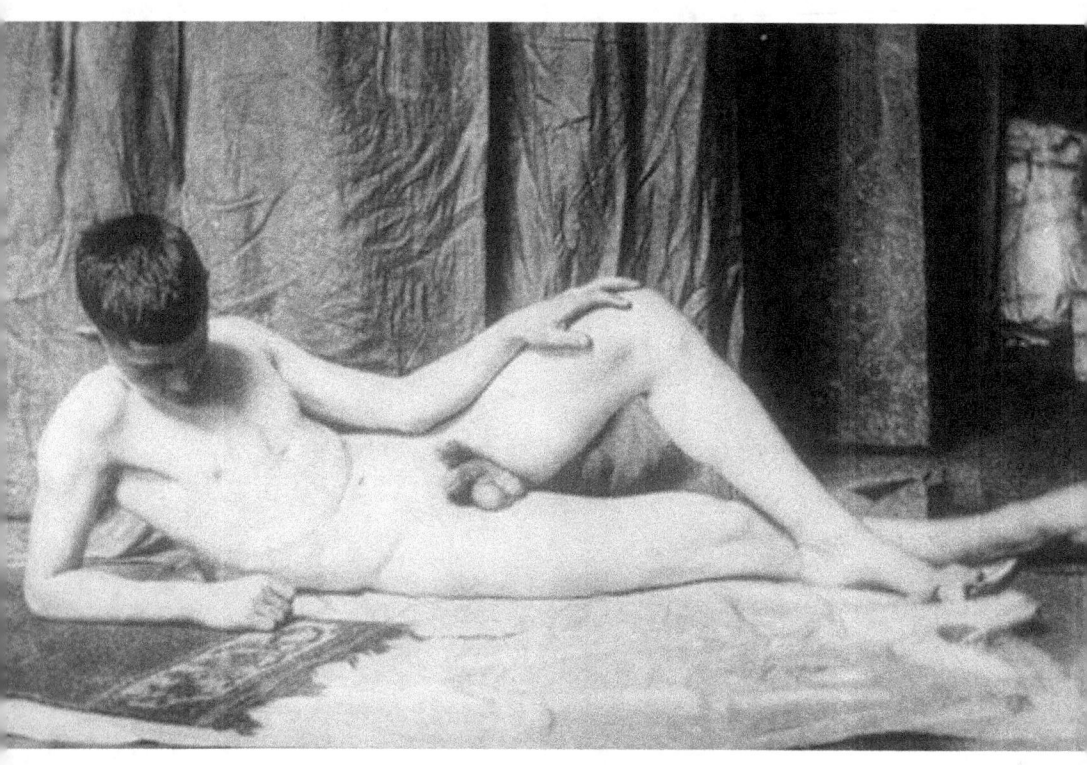

Reclining Male Nude, 1887–92,
Thomas Eakins, platinum print

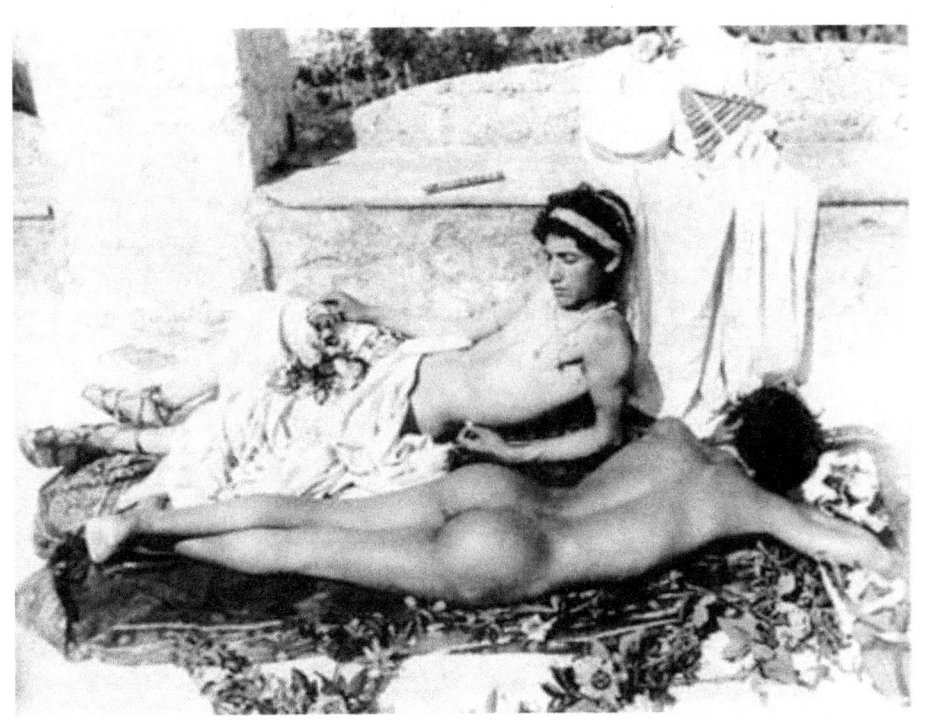

Wilhelm von Gloeden, c. 1900

PORNOGRAPHY

There are many different kinds of pornography, as there are many different kinds of art or feminism. Seen through cultural or postmodern or deconstructionist or semiological theory, pornography can be viewed as a realm of codes, meanings, contexts, signifiers, values, experiences and attitudes, which are politically controlled, manufactured by social, economic and political needs and demands. Pornography is thus the *representation* of... something; maybe certain kinds of sexuality, maybe somebody's thoughts on certain kinds of sexuality. Pornography is not *sexuality in itself*, it is mediation, representation, communication, a relic, a trace.

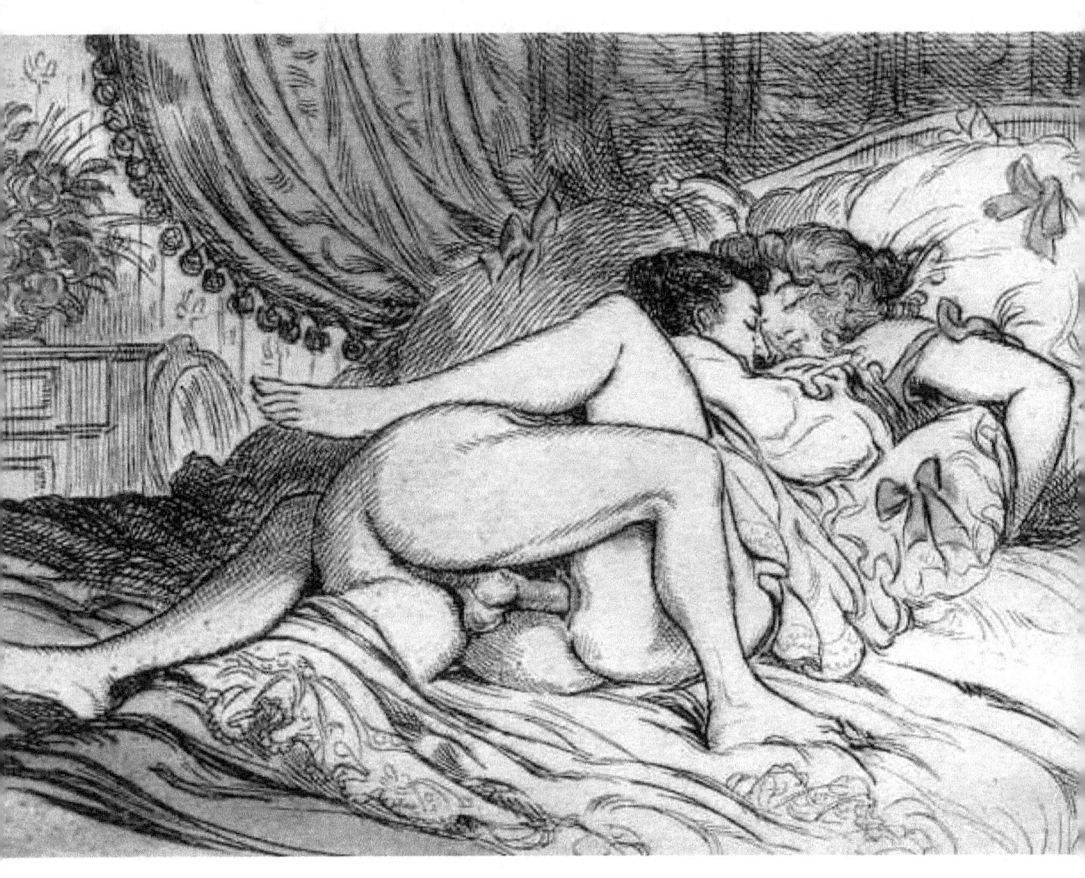

Anonymous, 19th century

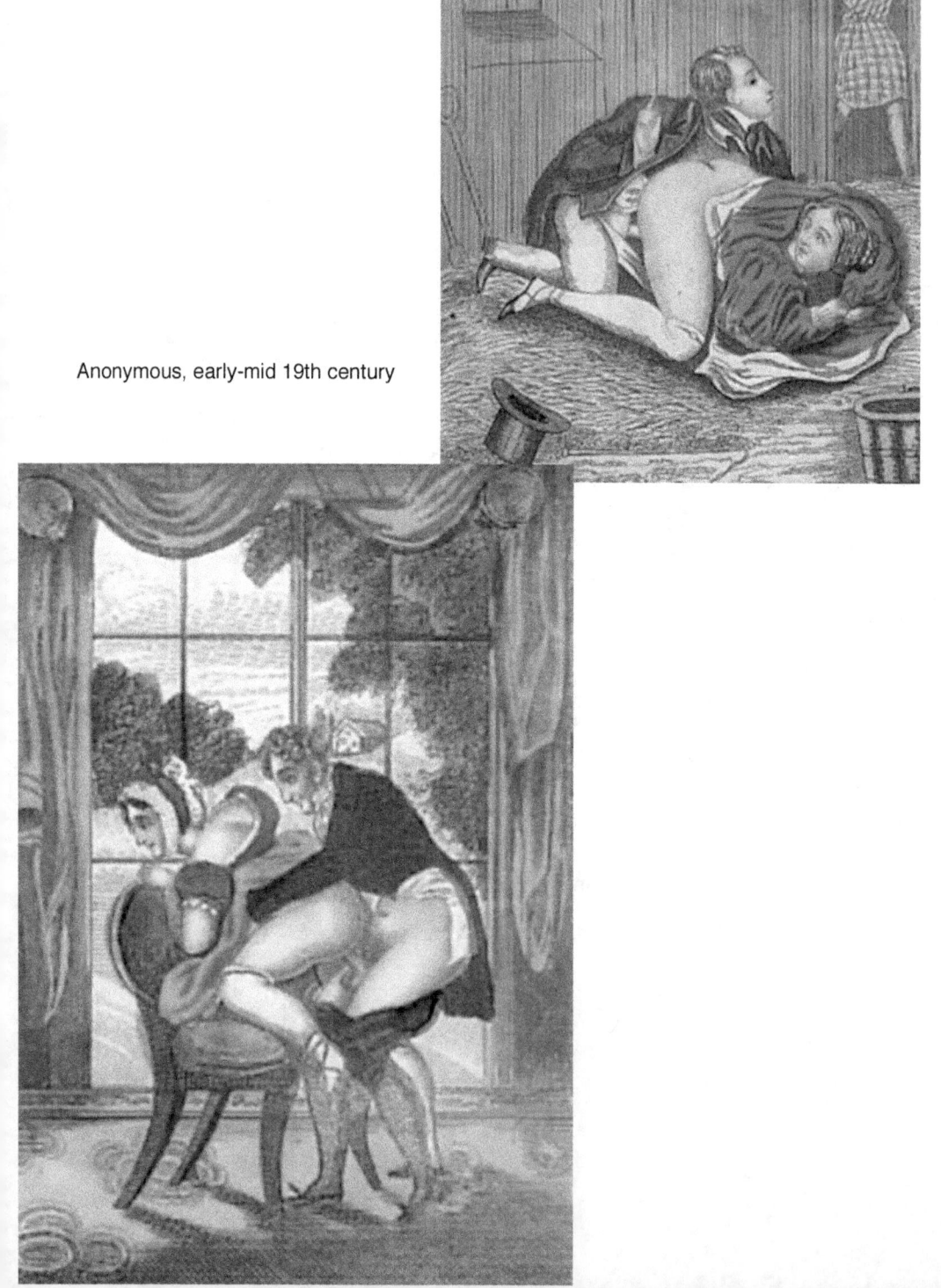

Anonymous, early-mid 19th century

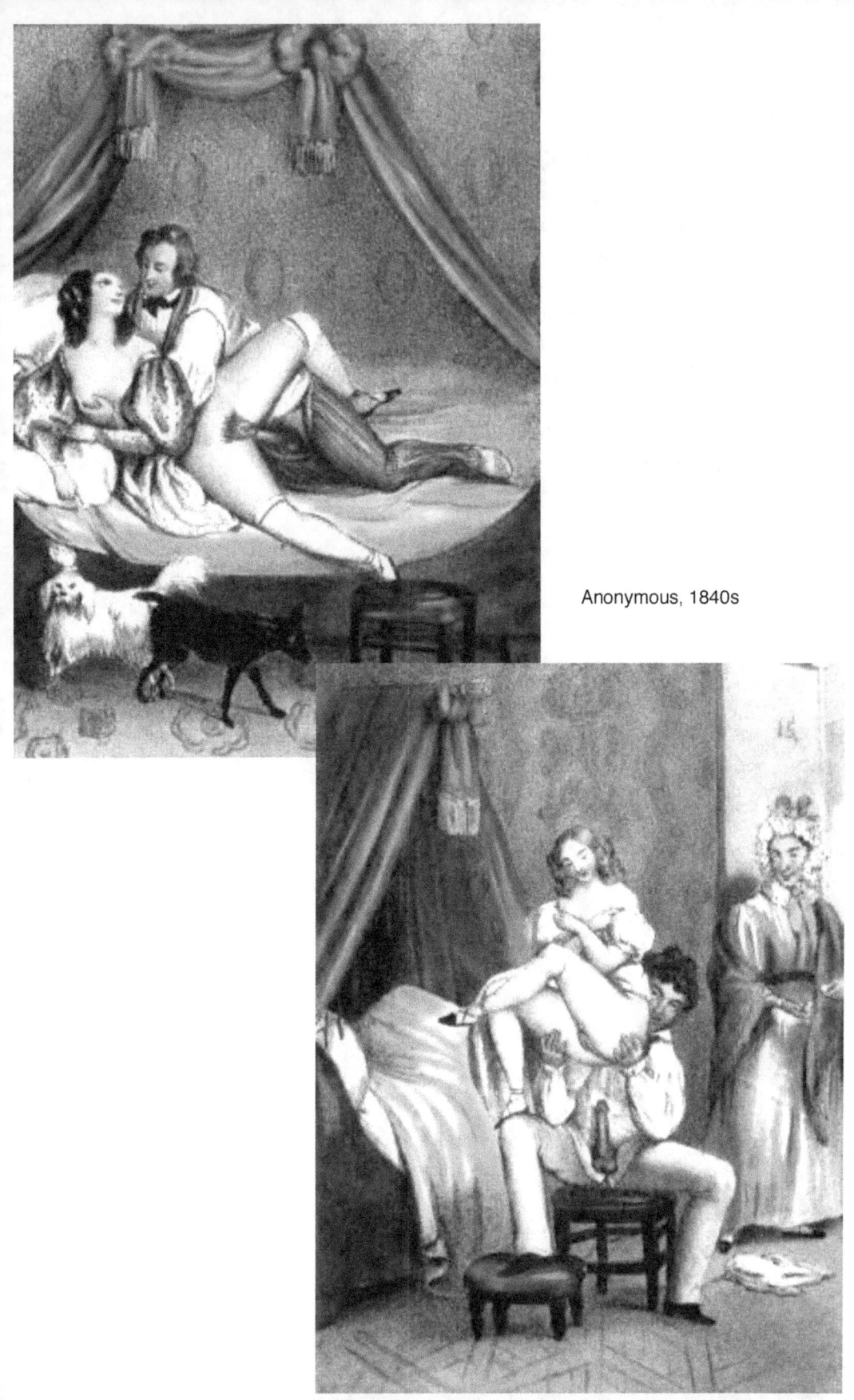

Anonymous, 1840s

Pornography has its own 'genres' of sub-categories: there is S/M, hardcore, lesbian, gay porn, soft core, and pornography geared to any number of fetishes; rubber, leather, boots, large breasts, bondage, etc.[1] What's your fetish? Porn will have something for you!

The history of art too has its categories and forms of erotic art, with the reclining (female) nude as perhaps the most well-known, and the most celebrated in art criticism. Other forms include humans and deities, humans and animals (often gods in beast-form), sexual positions, religious subjects, mythological subjects, Venus and Cupid, etc.

---

1 These sub-genres are institutions in themselves, with their own codes and structures, but their institutionalized sexual images do not express the real eroticism that people experience (they suggest it, perhaps, or reflect parts of it).

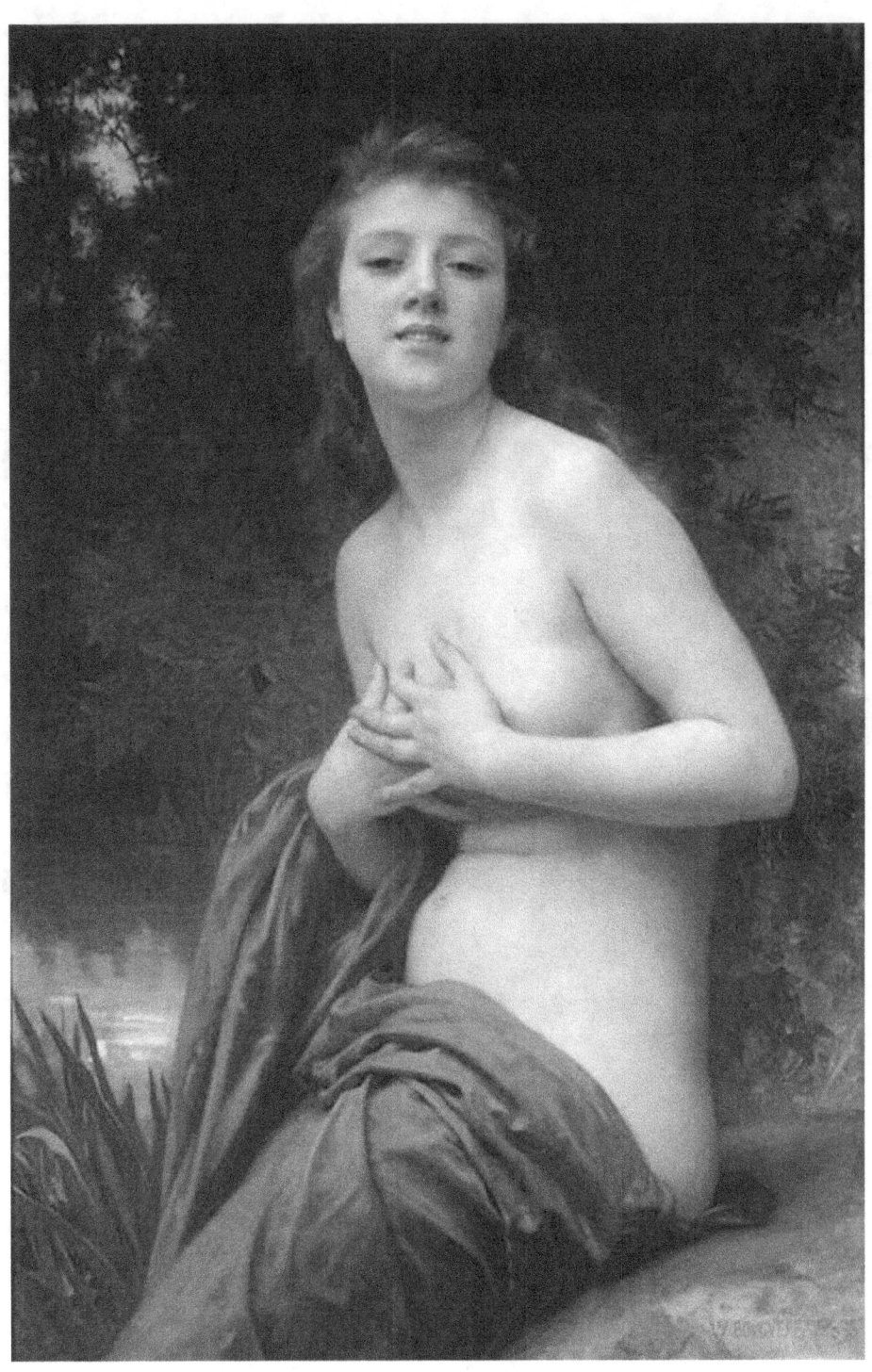

William Bouguereau, Spring Breeze, 1895

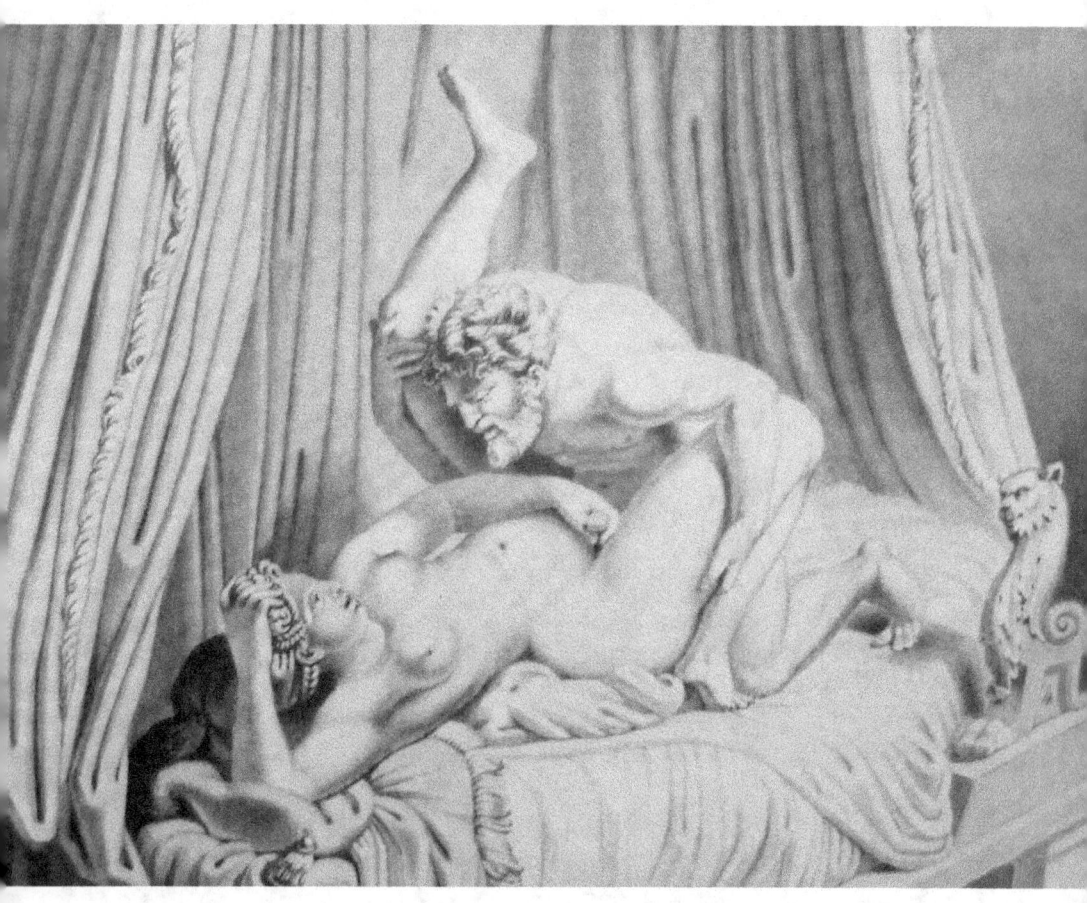

Friedrich von Waldeck, from Postures, c. 1858
(This page and following pages)

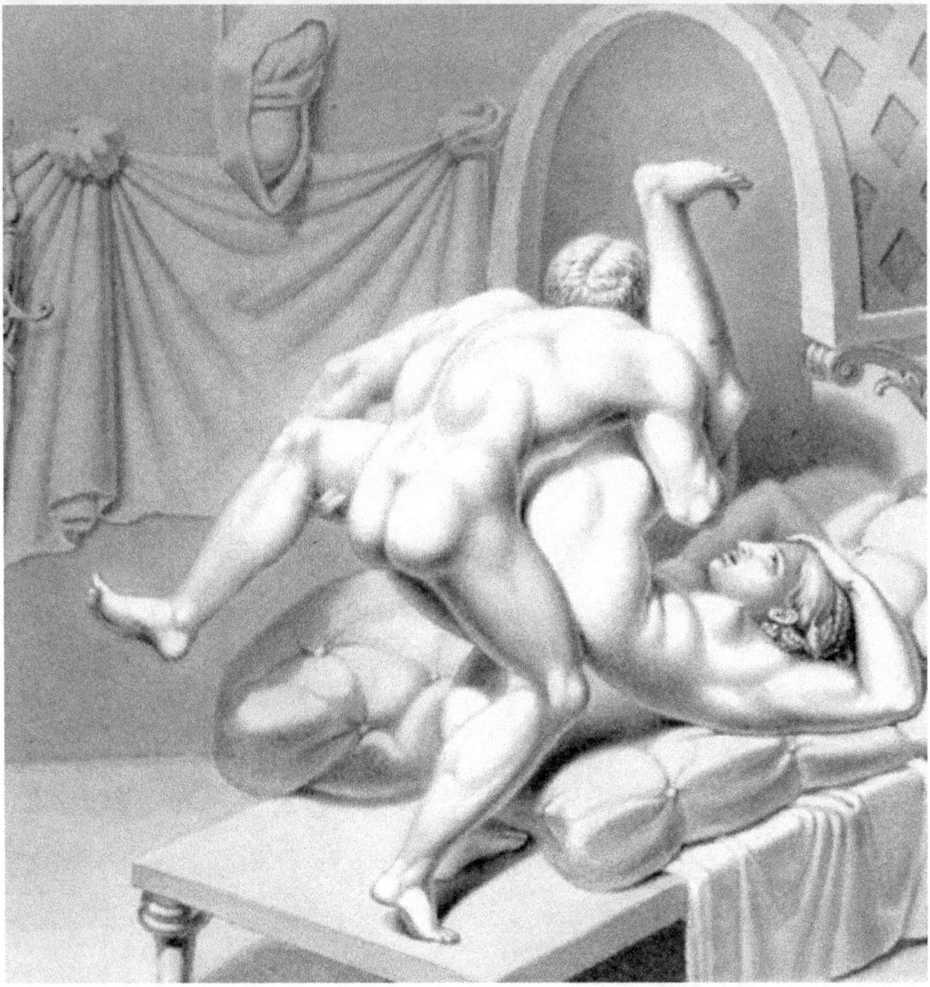

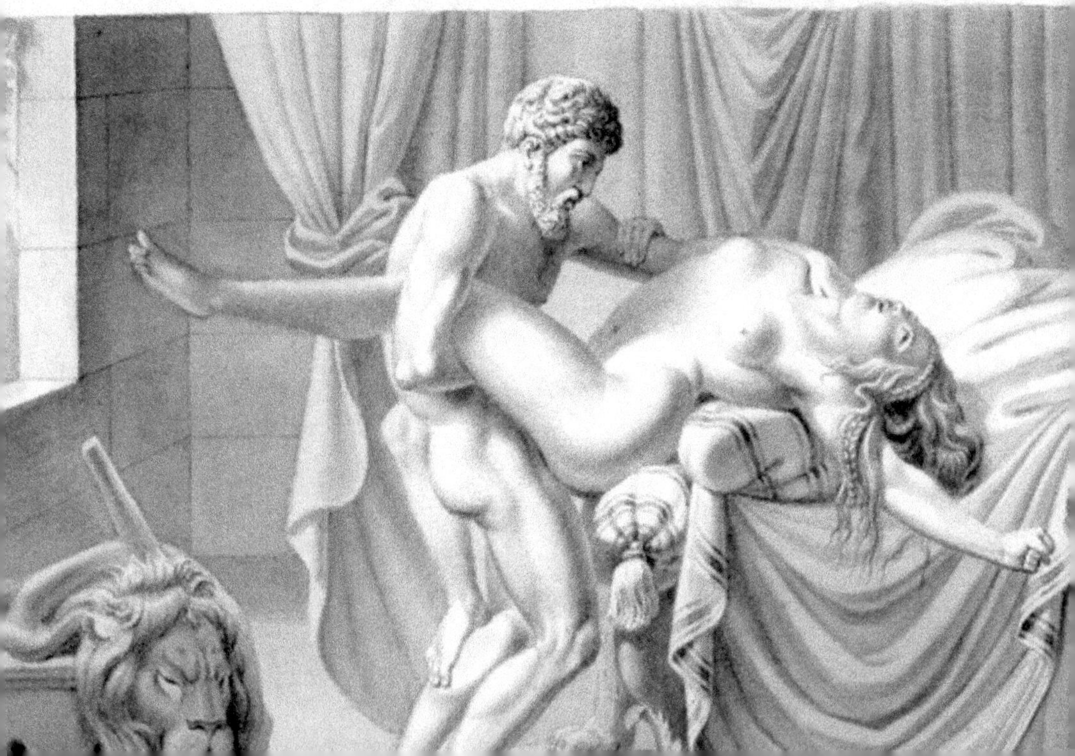

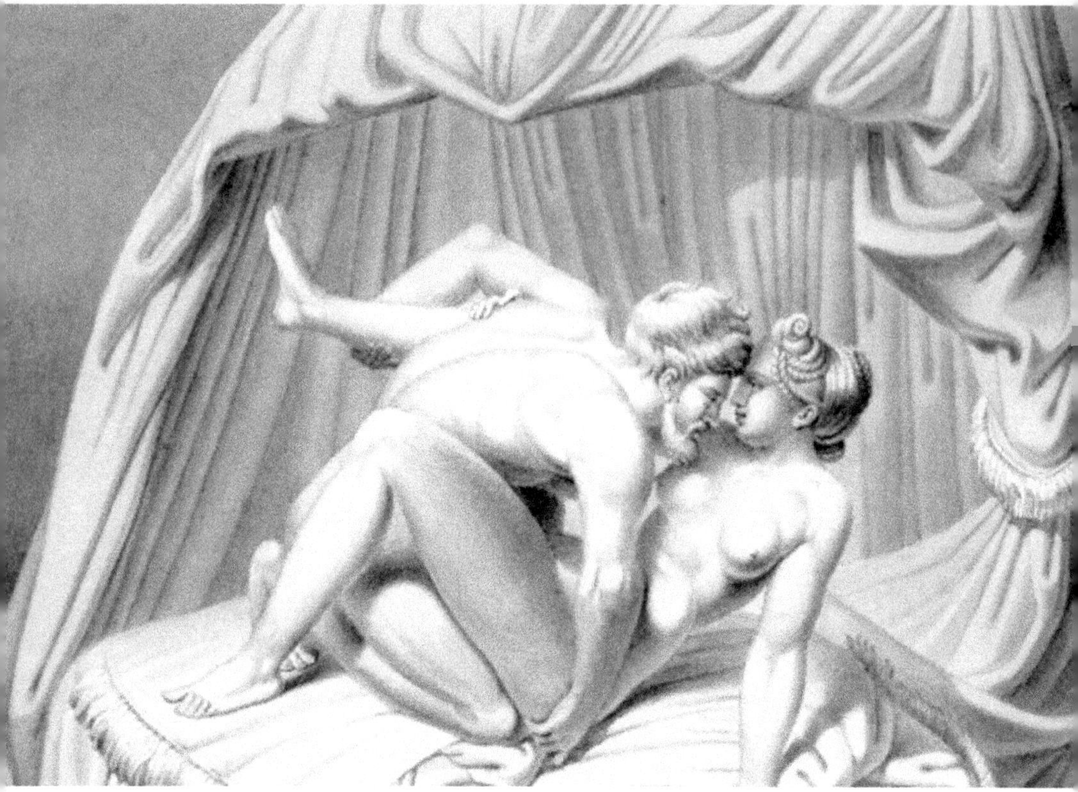

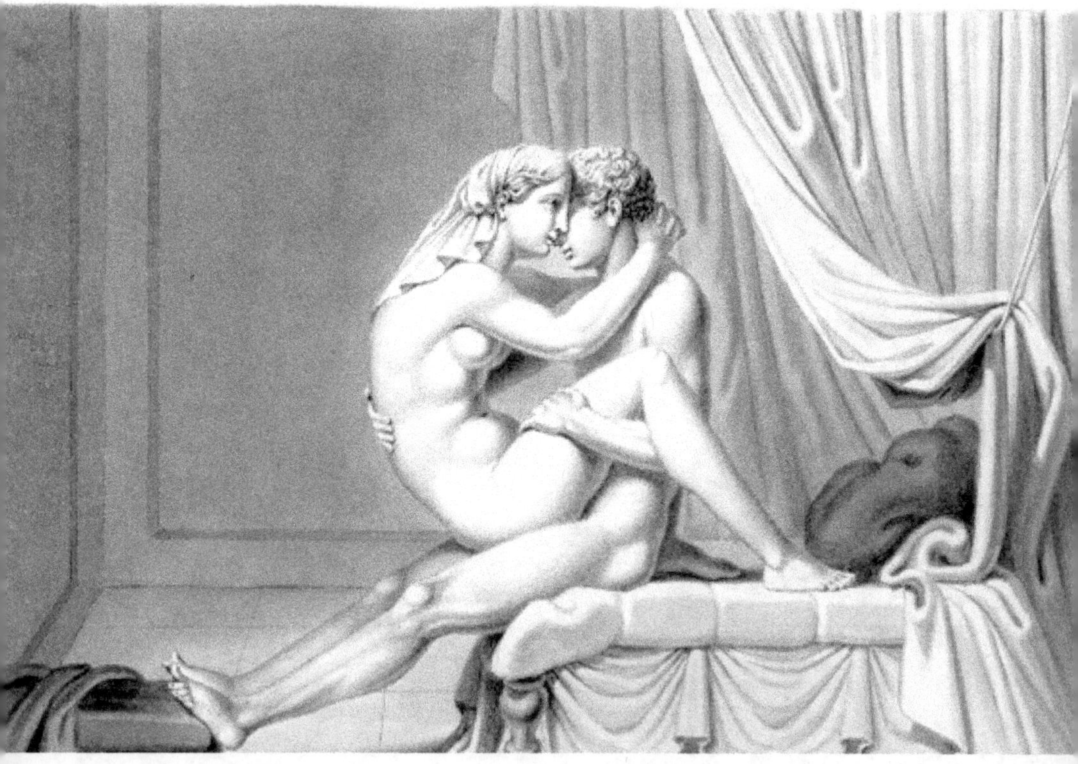

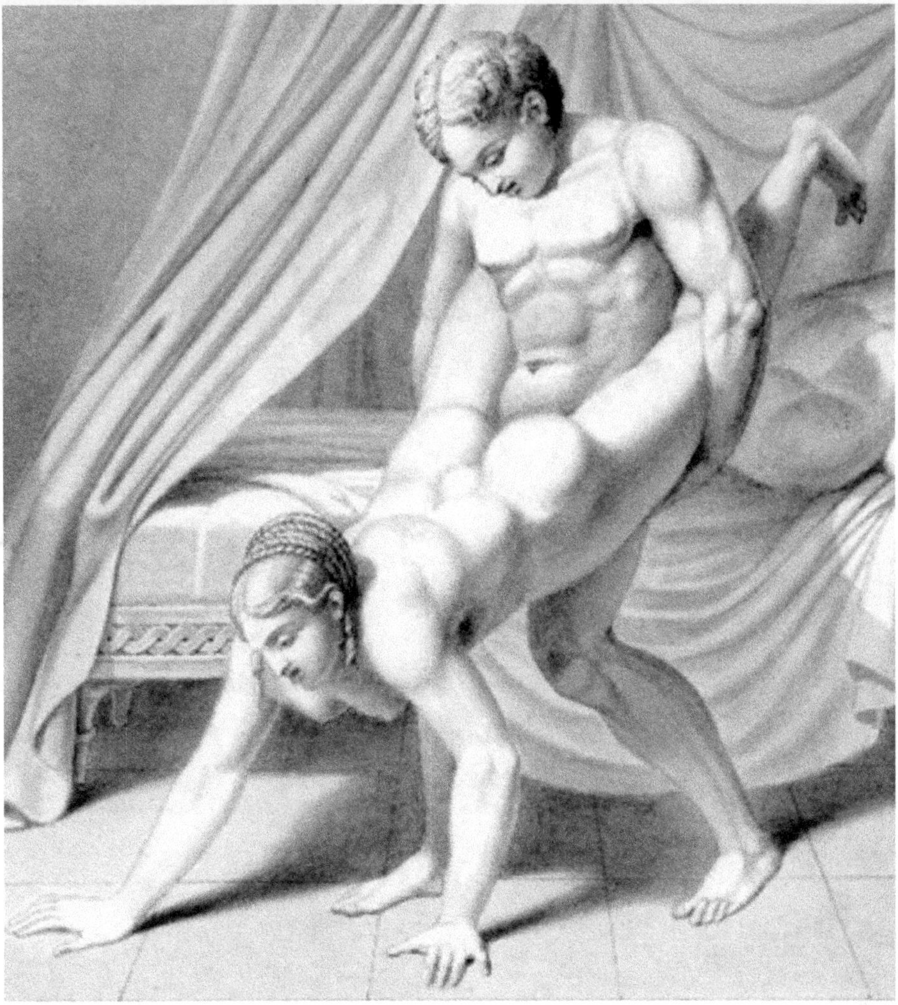

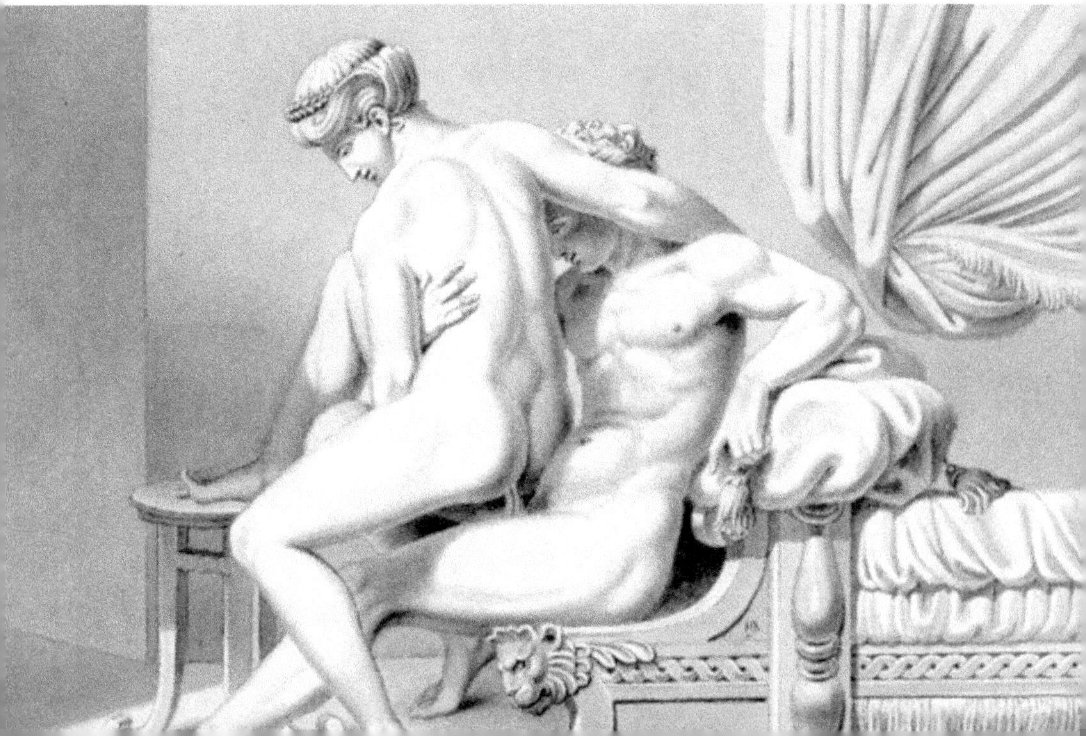

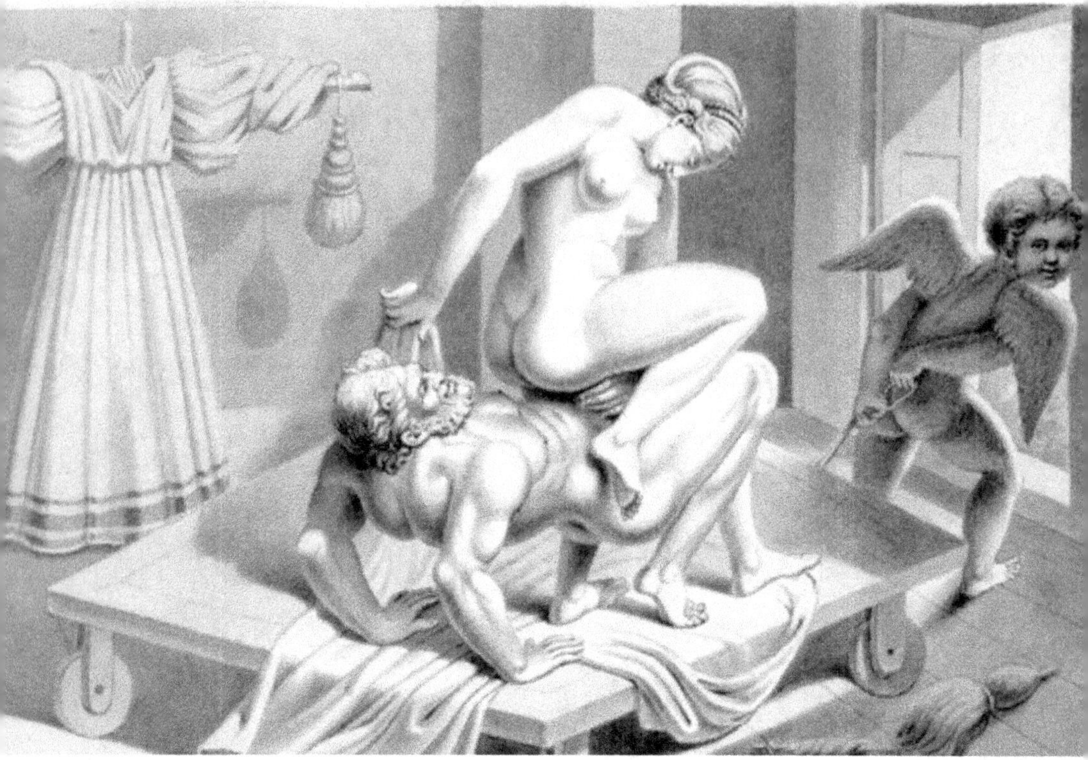

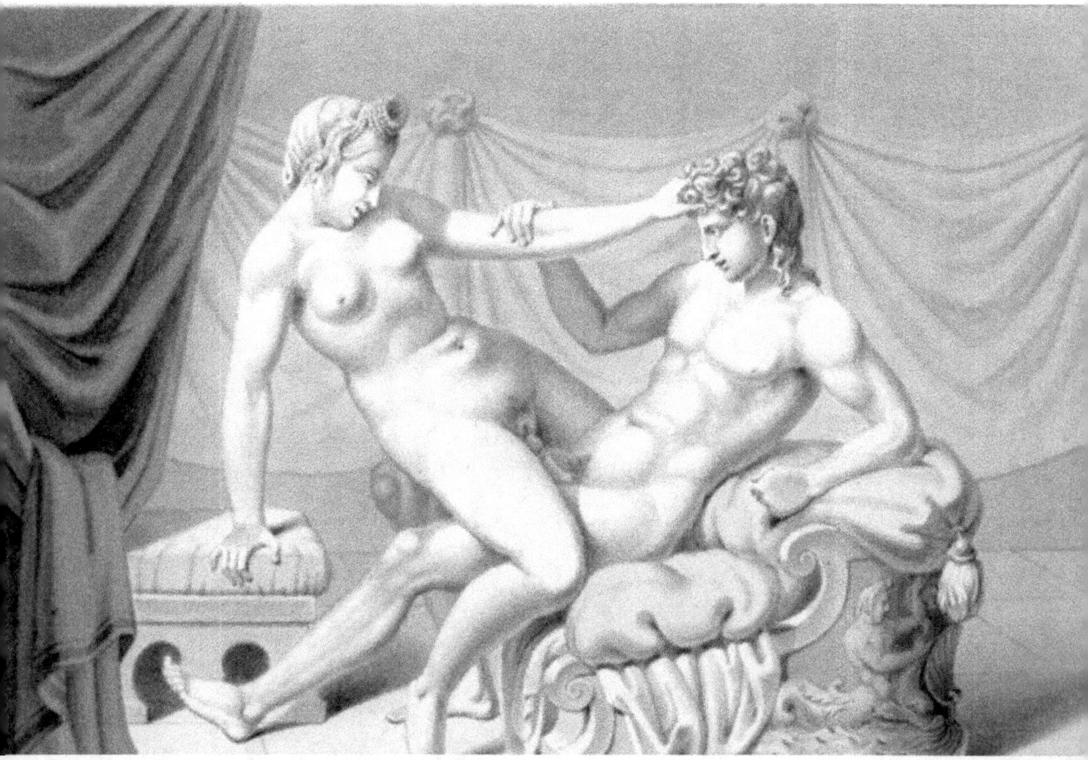

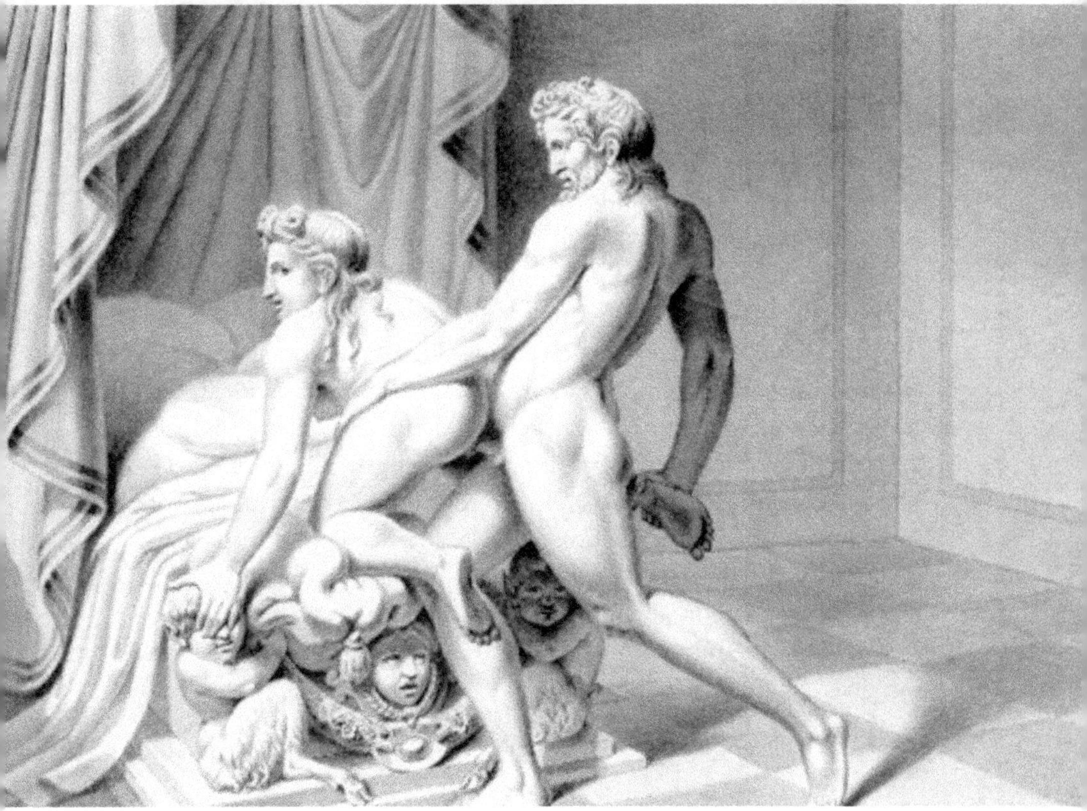

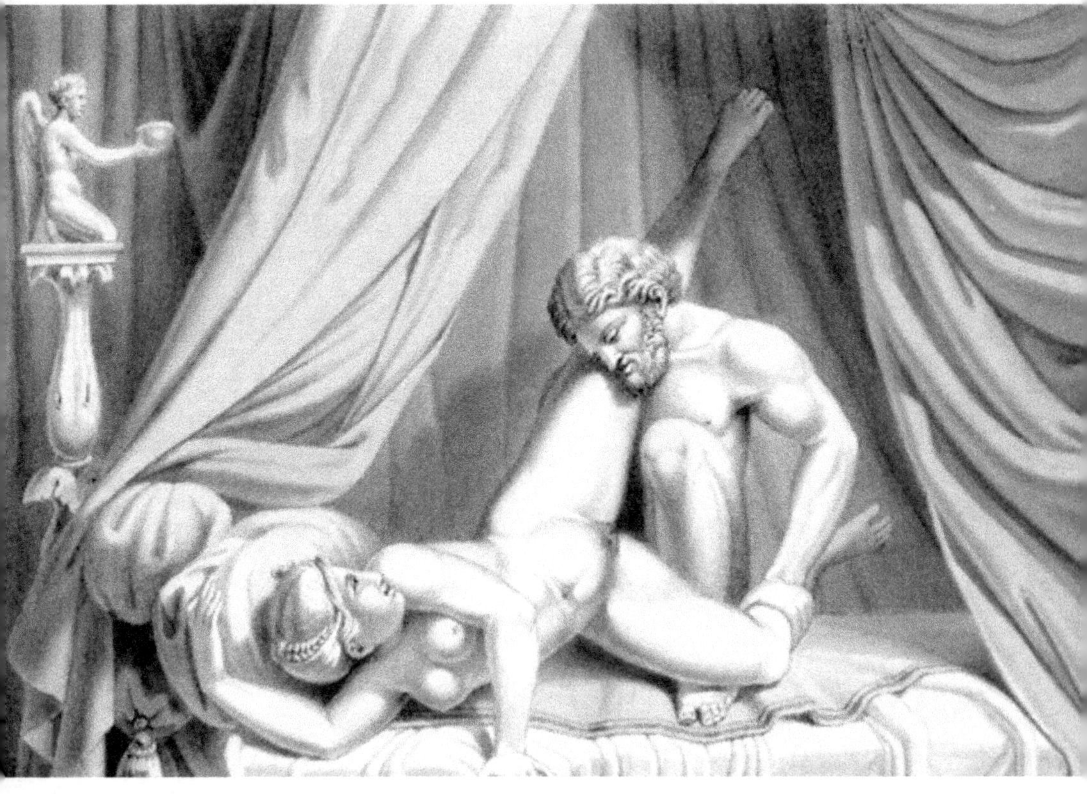

What occurs in most Western art, from Greek and Roman sculpture through the glories of the Renaissance to the latest pornography are male representations of female eroticism. Feminists say that there are no real depictions of female *jouissance* in art or literature. 'In my opinion,' wrote Marguerite Duras, 'women have never expressed themselves.'[1] What she means, perhaps, is that women have expressed themselves thus far in the terms and means and social structures defined by men. There is no 'feminine' or 'women's' writing, according to some feminists. Hélène Cixous reckons she's found only three 'inscriptions of femininity' this century: Colette, Marguerite Duras and Jean Genet.[2] In art, there are many women artists who have tackled erotic issues, but in the history of art, going back to, say, the Renaissance, the number of women artists who have survived are far fewer.

---

1 Duras, interview in *Signs*, Winter 1975, in E. Marks, 175.
2 H. Cixous: "The Laugh of the Medusa", *Signs*, summer 1976, in E. E. Marks, 249.

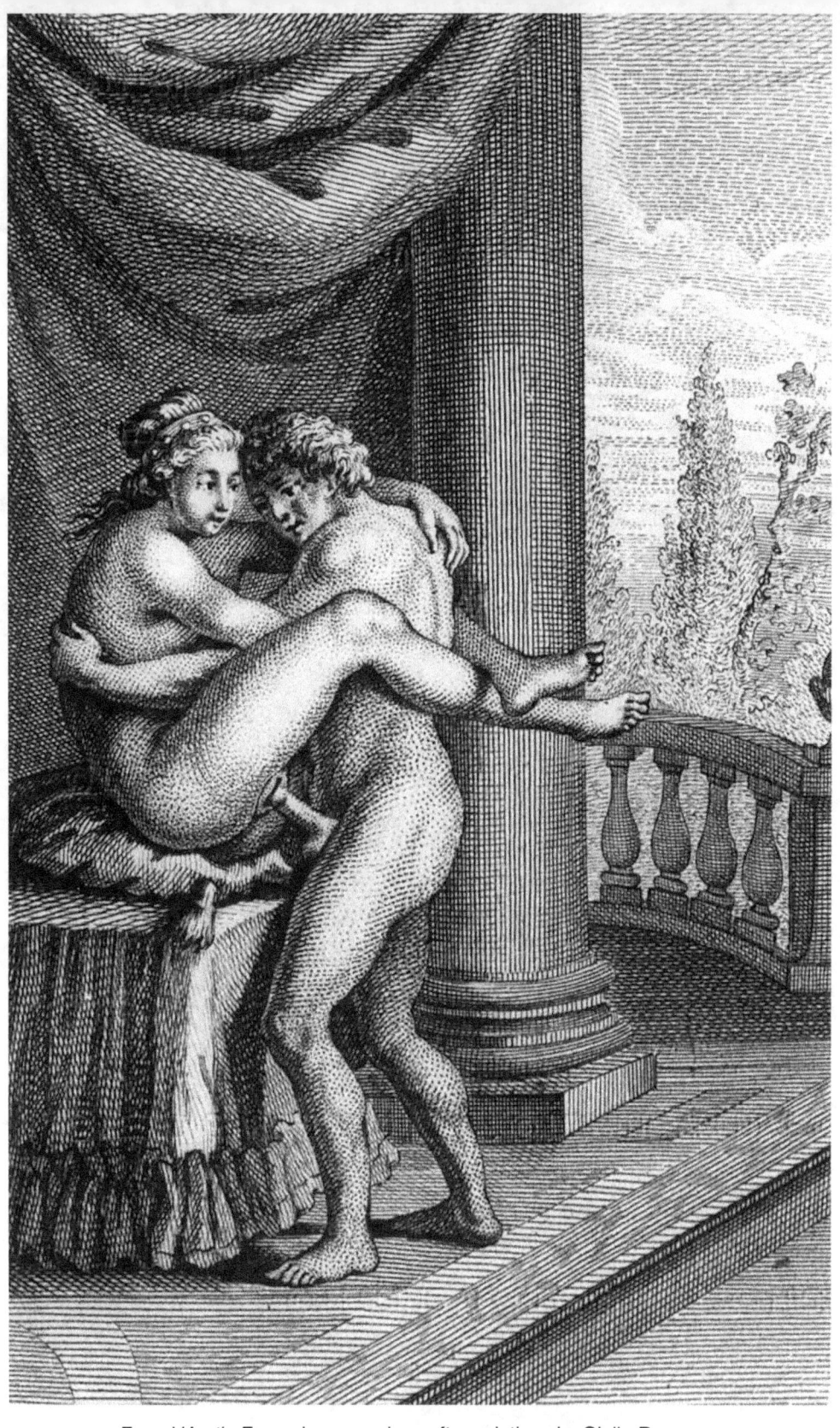

From L'Aretin Francais, engravings after paintings by Giulio Romano,
illustrating the Sonnets of Pietro Aretino
(this page and following pages)

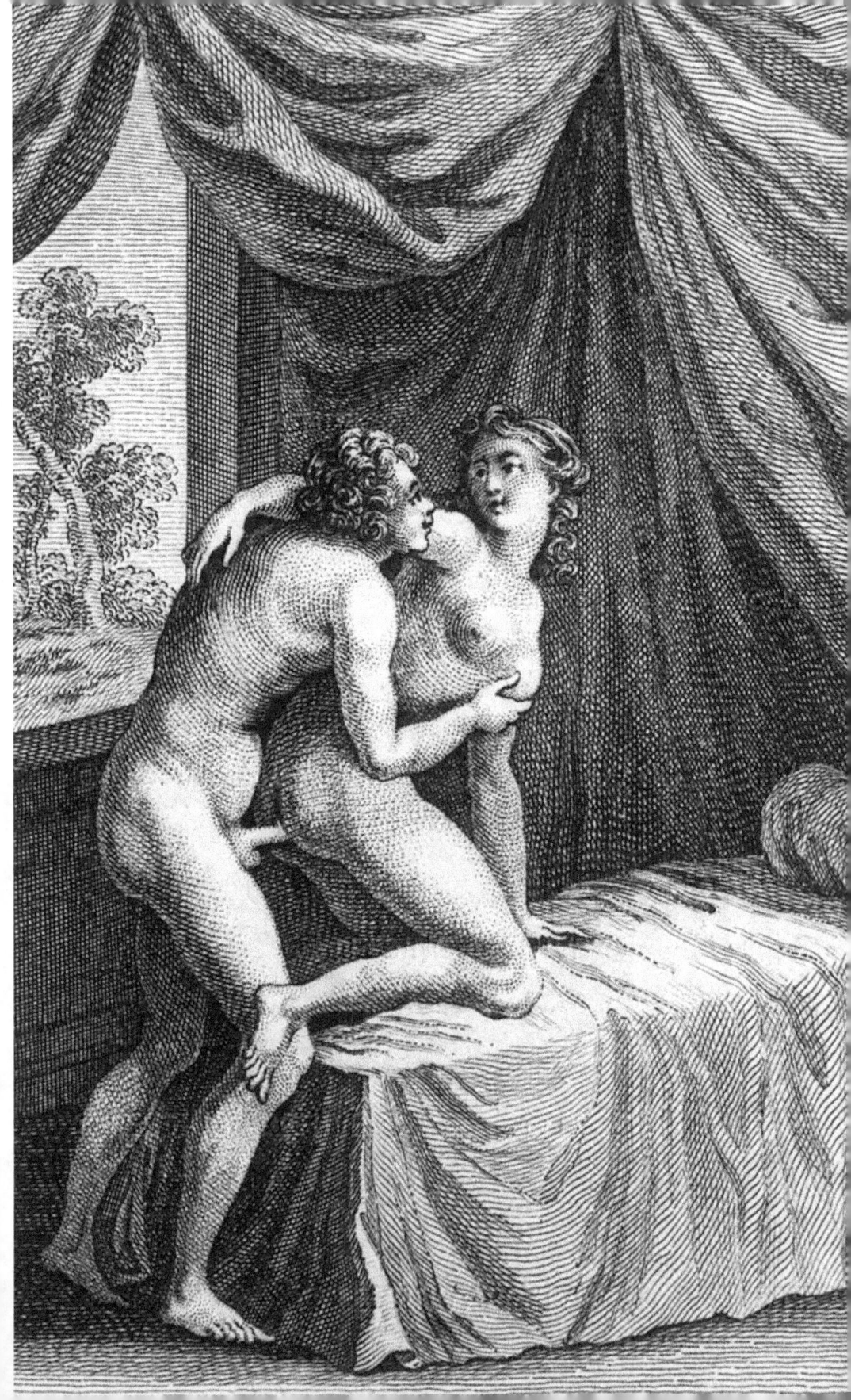

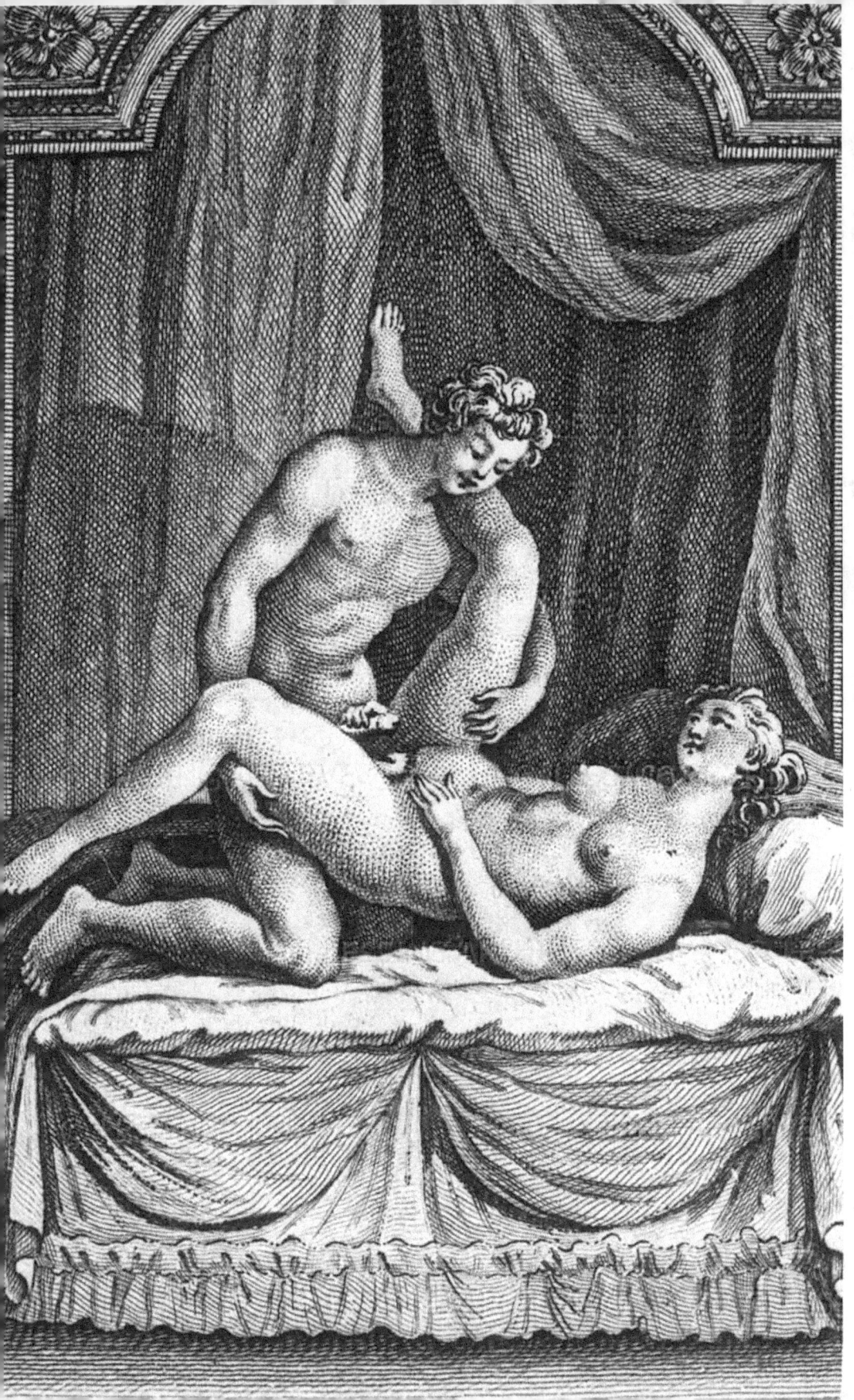

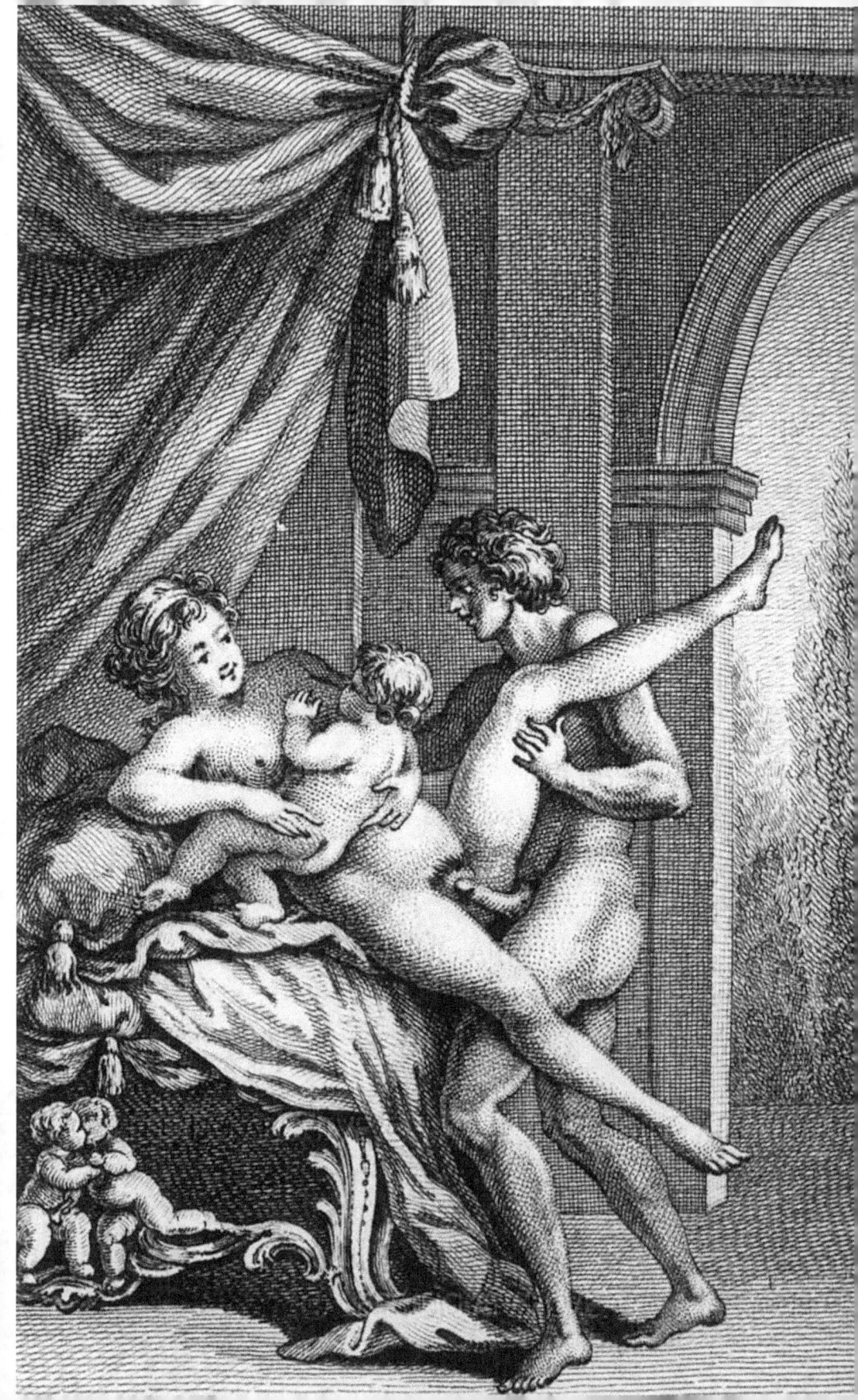

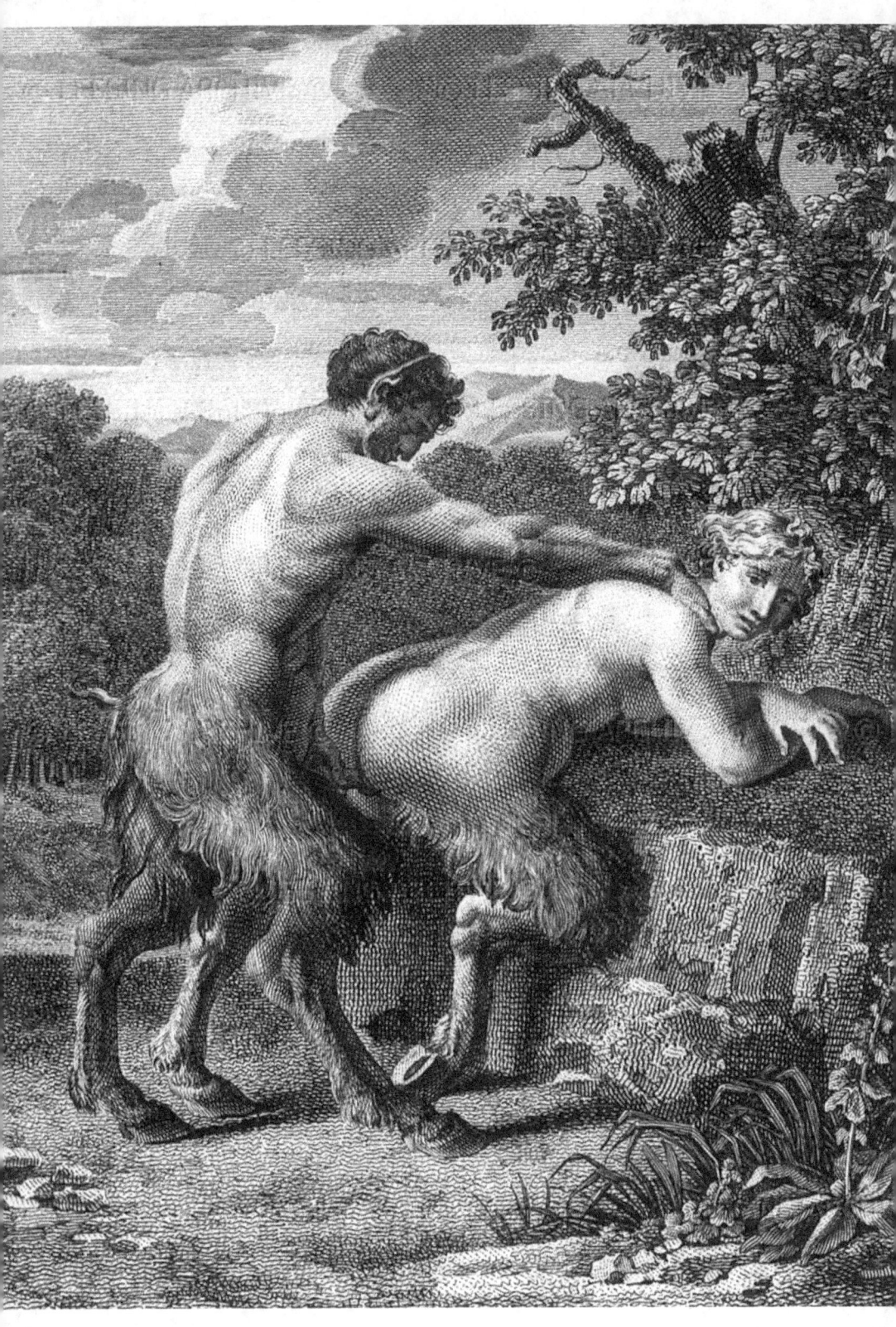

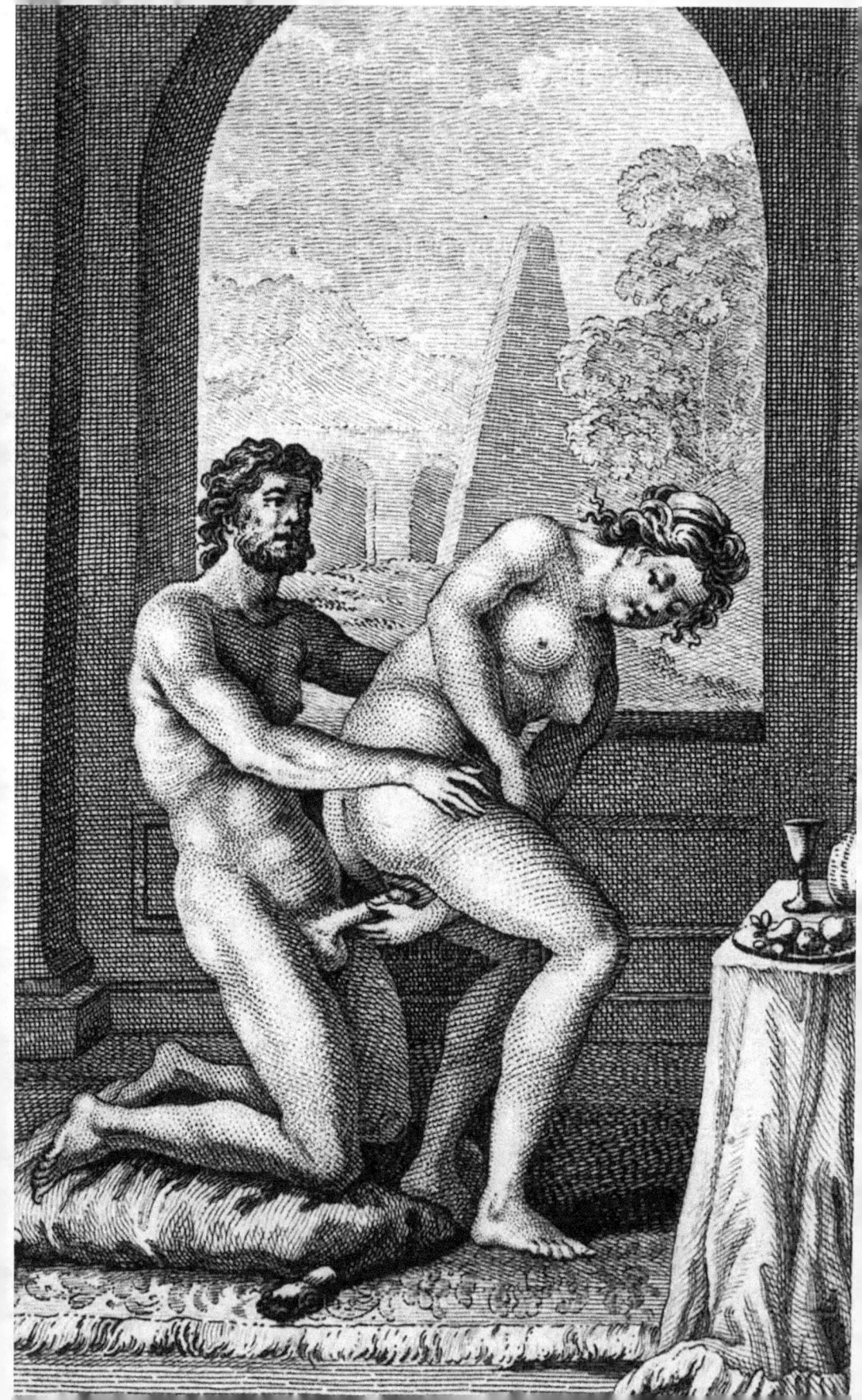

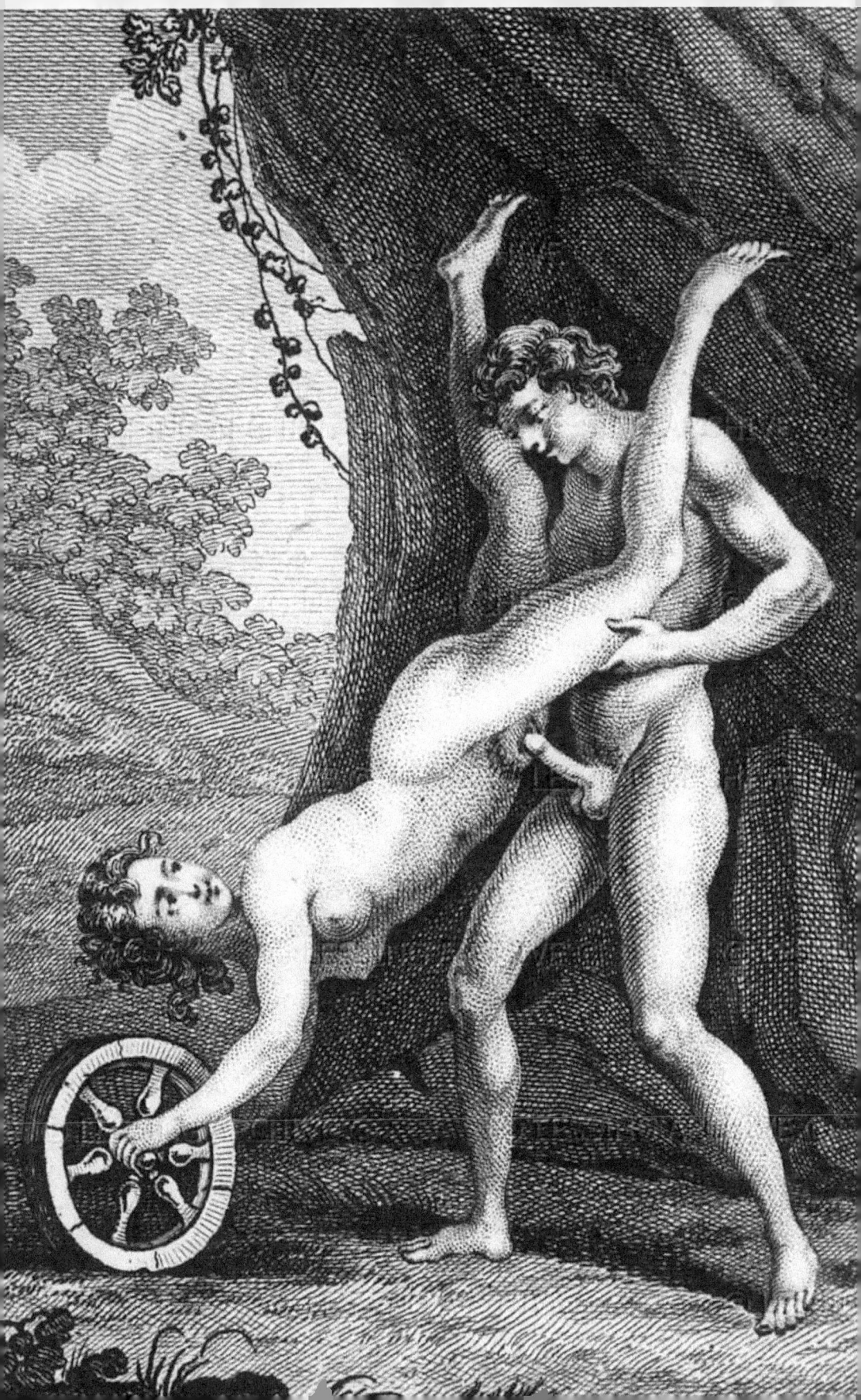

For law-abiding citizens, it seems, the 'line' has to be drawn somewhere. Somewhere between public and private, between sex and love, between visible and invisible, between freedom and control, between secrecy and publicity, between availability and censorship. Indeed, Walter Kendrick said the only definition of pornography is in terms of its forbidden or secret nature.[1]

Pornography brings the secret life of people out into the open. What the Western world holds most dear – the primacy and holiness of the individual, and the primacy and holiness of (heterosexual) love, of marriage, of the family – is cast into doubt by pornography.

Hardcore pornography, in particular, tries to make everything as clear and as visible as possible, and is thus disruptive and unsettling for the establishment. There are, thus, many close-ups of genitals in hardcore pornography. Sex is ecstatic, so hardcore pornography has to show this ecstasy. It does this by focussing on the genitals.

---

1 W. Kendrick: *The Secret Museum: Pornography in Modern Culture*, Viking, New York, NY, 1987.

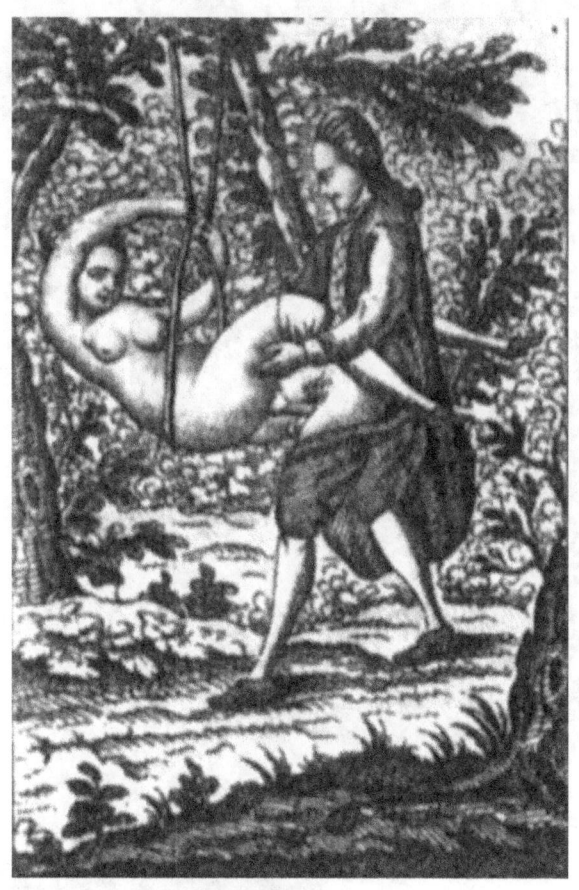

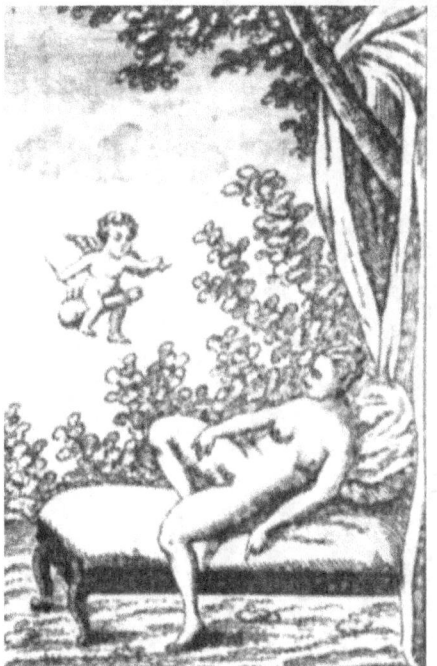

Anonymous,
Memoires du Suzon

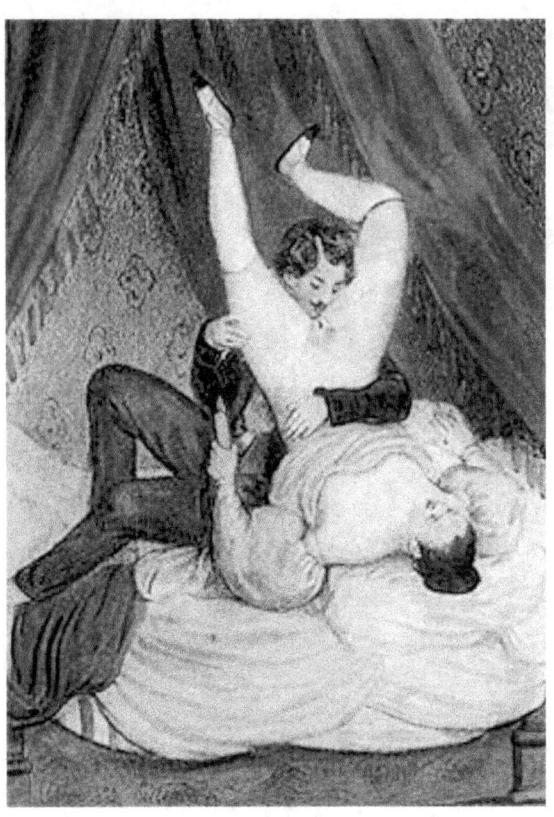

Anonymous, 19th century

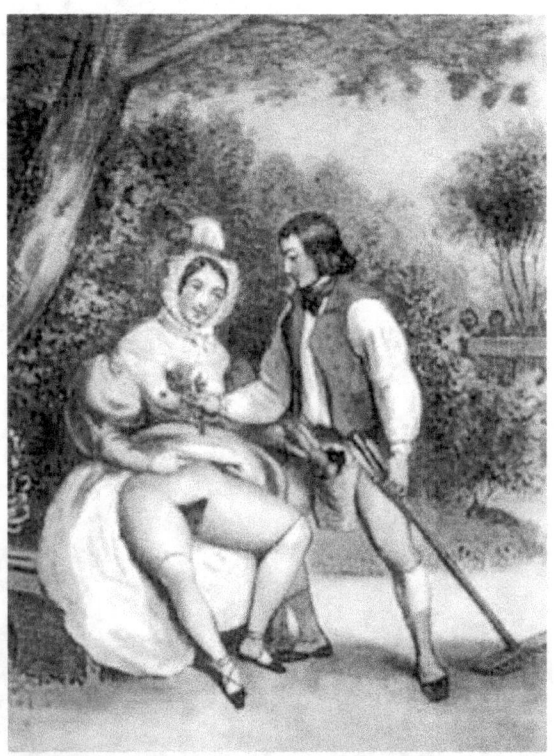

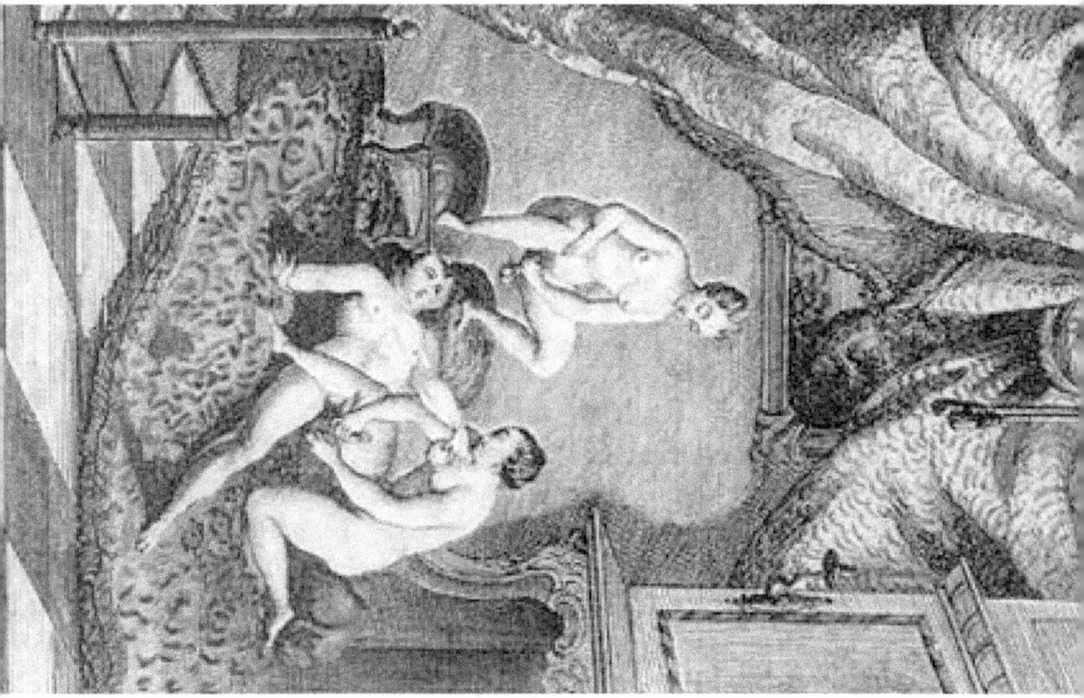

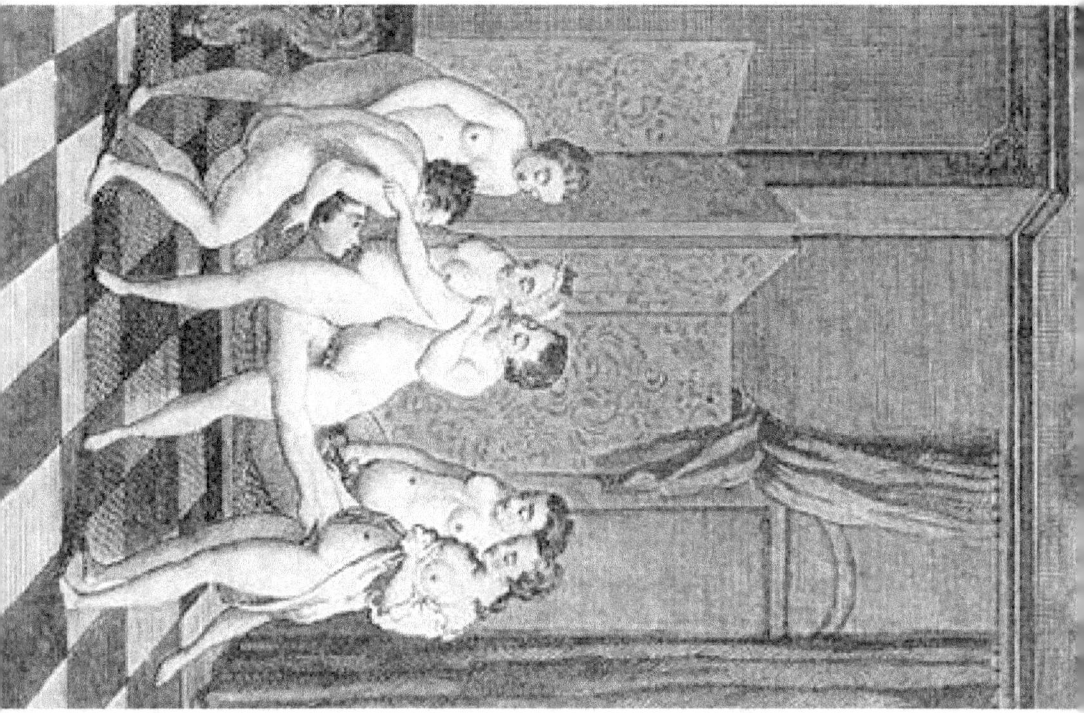

Anonymous, early 19th century

What occurs in most Western art, from Greek and Roman sculpture through the glories of the Renaissance to the latest pornography are male representations of female eroticism. Feminists say that there are no real depictions of female *jouissance* in art or literature. 'In my opinion,' wrote Marguerite Duras, 'women have never expressed themselves.'[1] What she means, perhaps, is that women have expressed themselves thus far in the terms and means and social structures defined by men. There is no 'feminine' or 'women's' writing, according to some feminists. Hélène Cixous reckons she's found only three 'inscriptions of femininity' this century: Colette, Marguerite Duras and Jean Genet.[2] In art, there are many women artists who have tackled erotic issues, but in the history of art, going back to, say, the Renaissance, the number of women artists who have survived are far fewer.

1 Duras, interview in *Signs*, Winter 1975, in E. Marks, 175.
2 H. Cixous: "The Laugh of the Medusa", *Signs*, summer 1976, in E. E. Marks, 249.

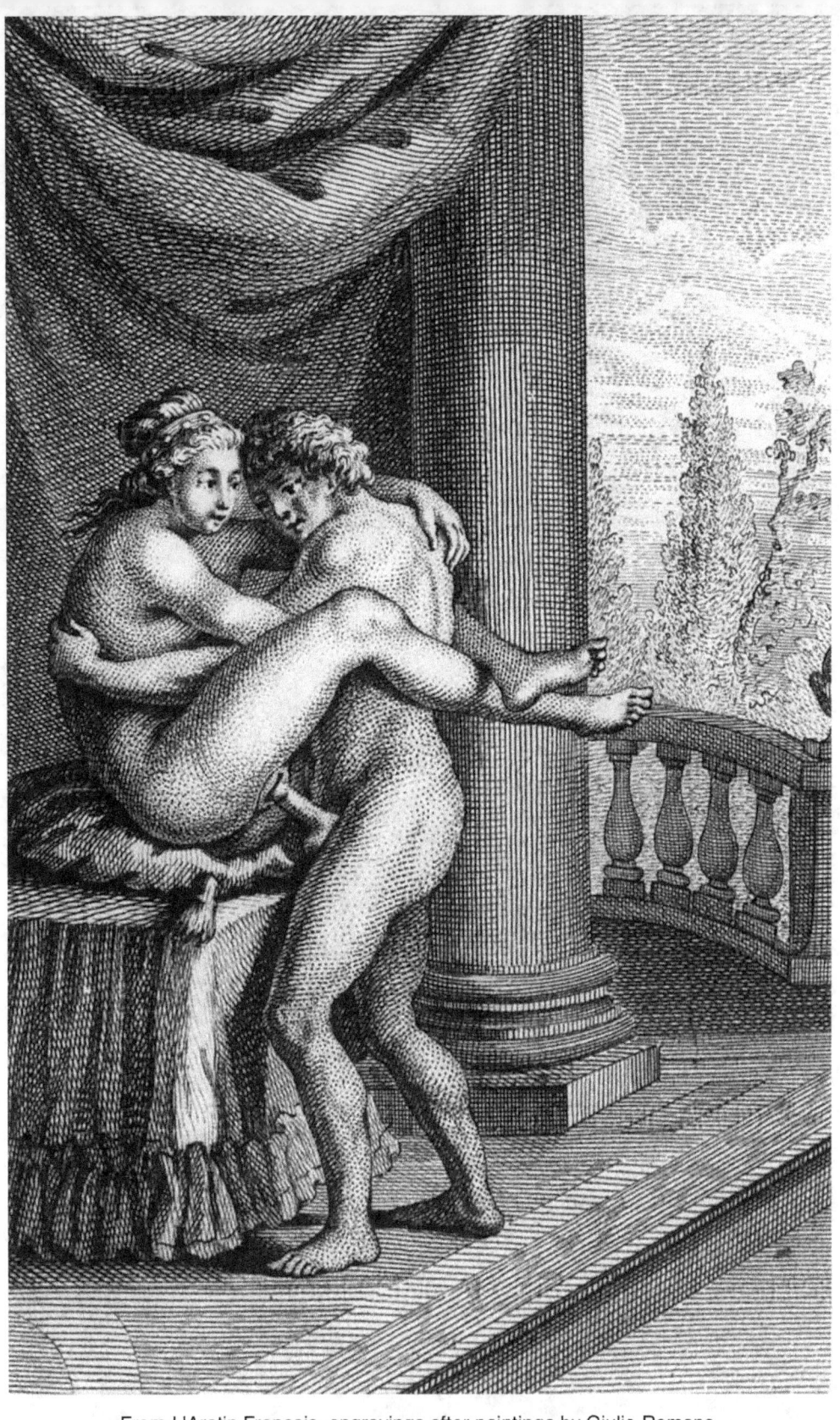

From L'Aretin Francais, engravings after paintings by Giulio Romano,
illustrating the Sonnets of Pietro Aretino
(this page and following pages)

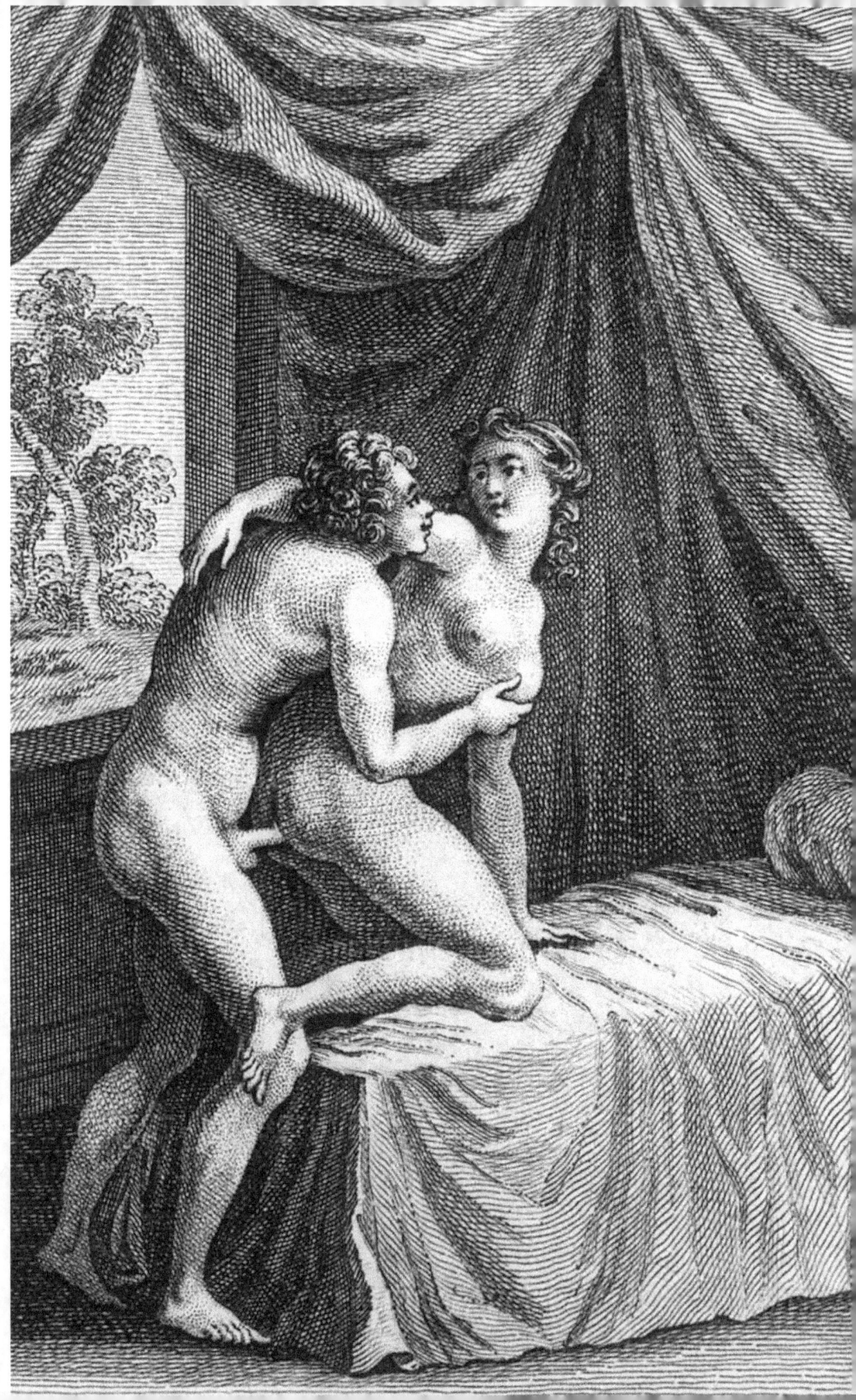

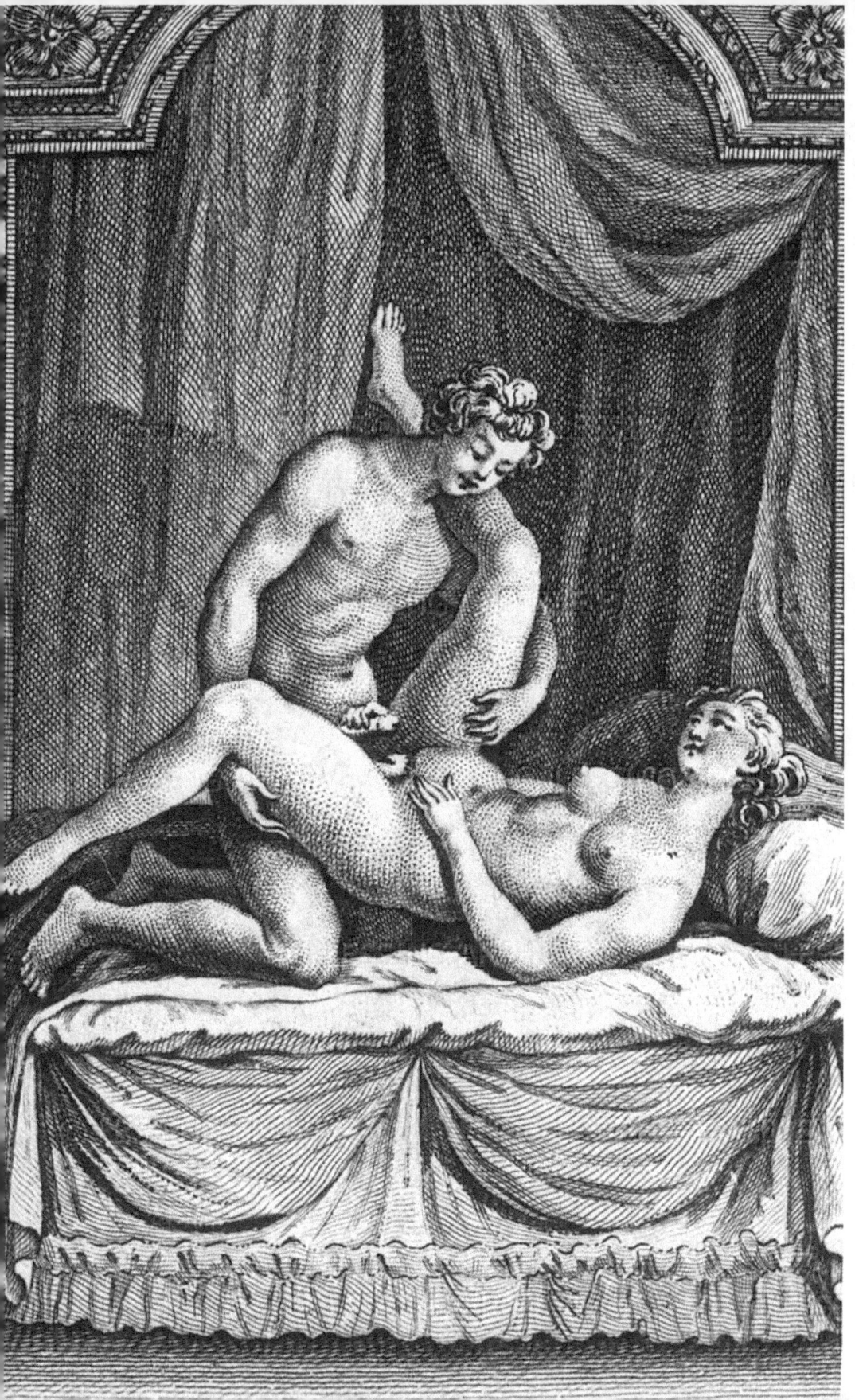

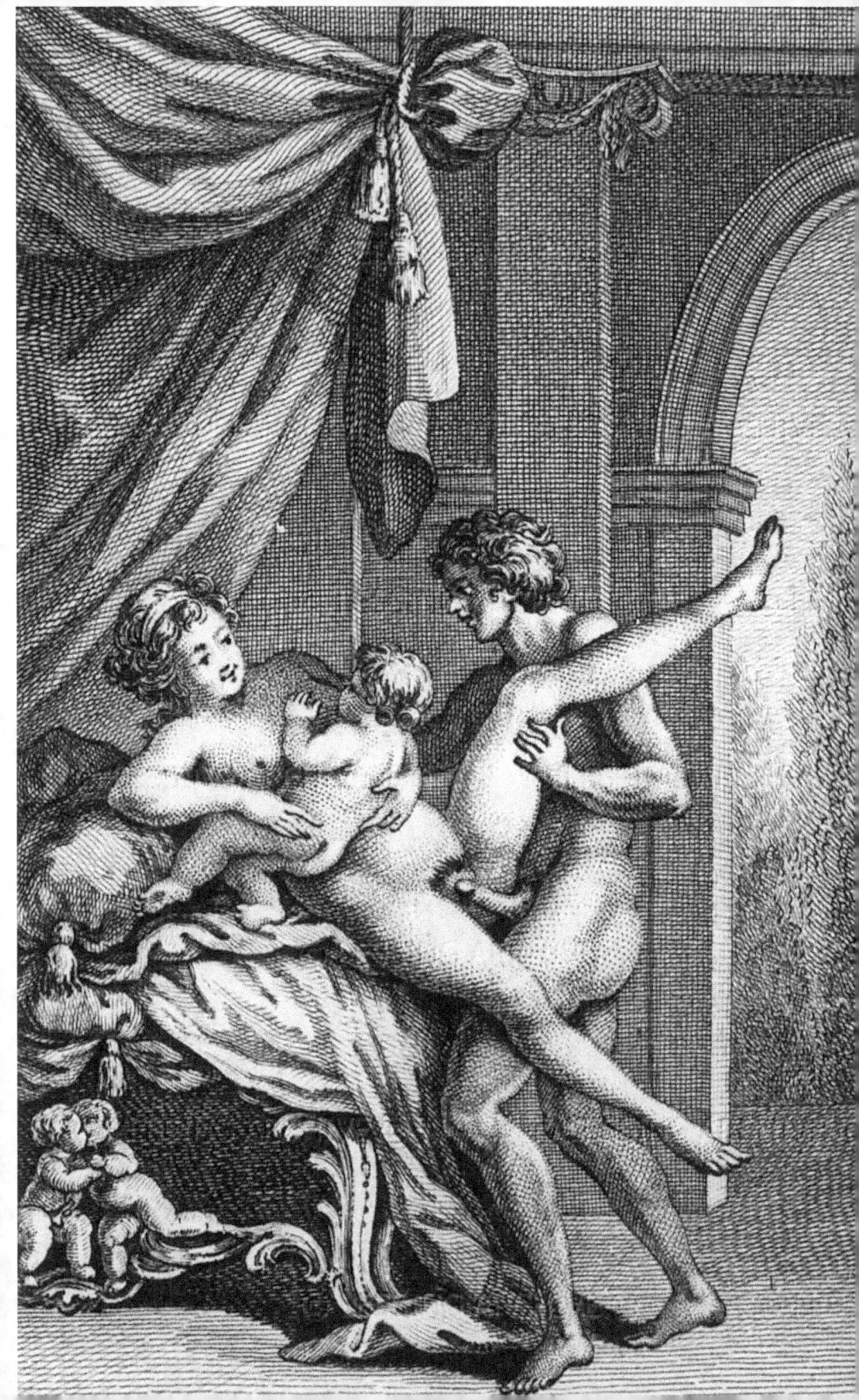

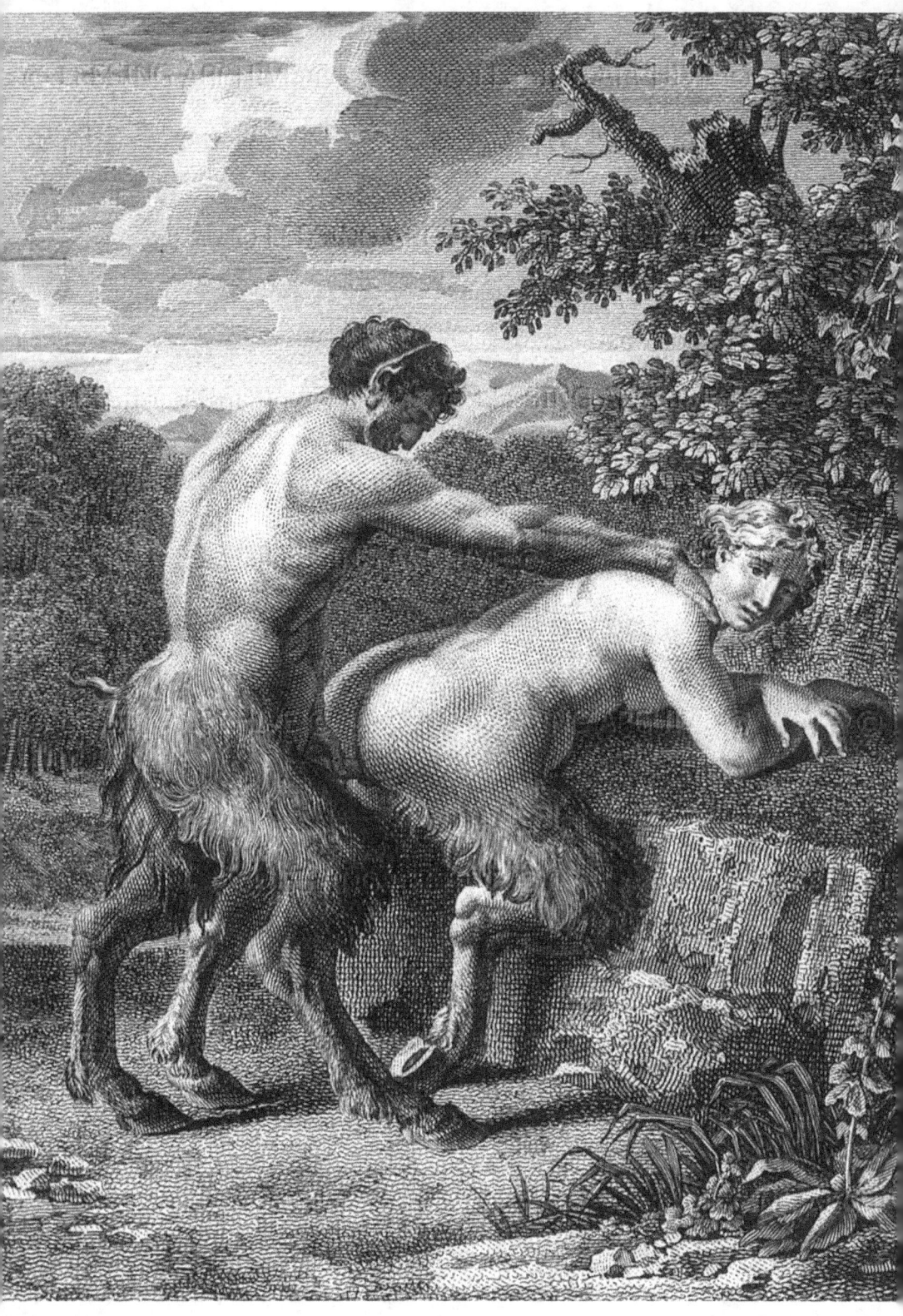

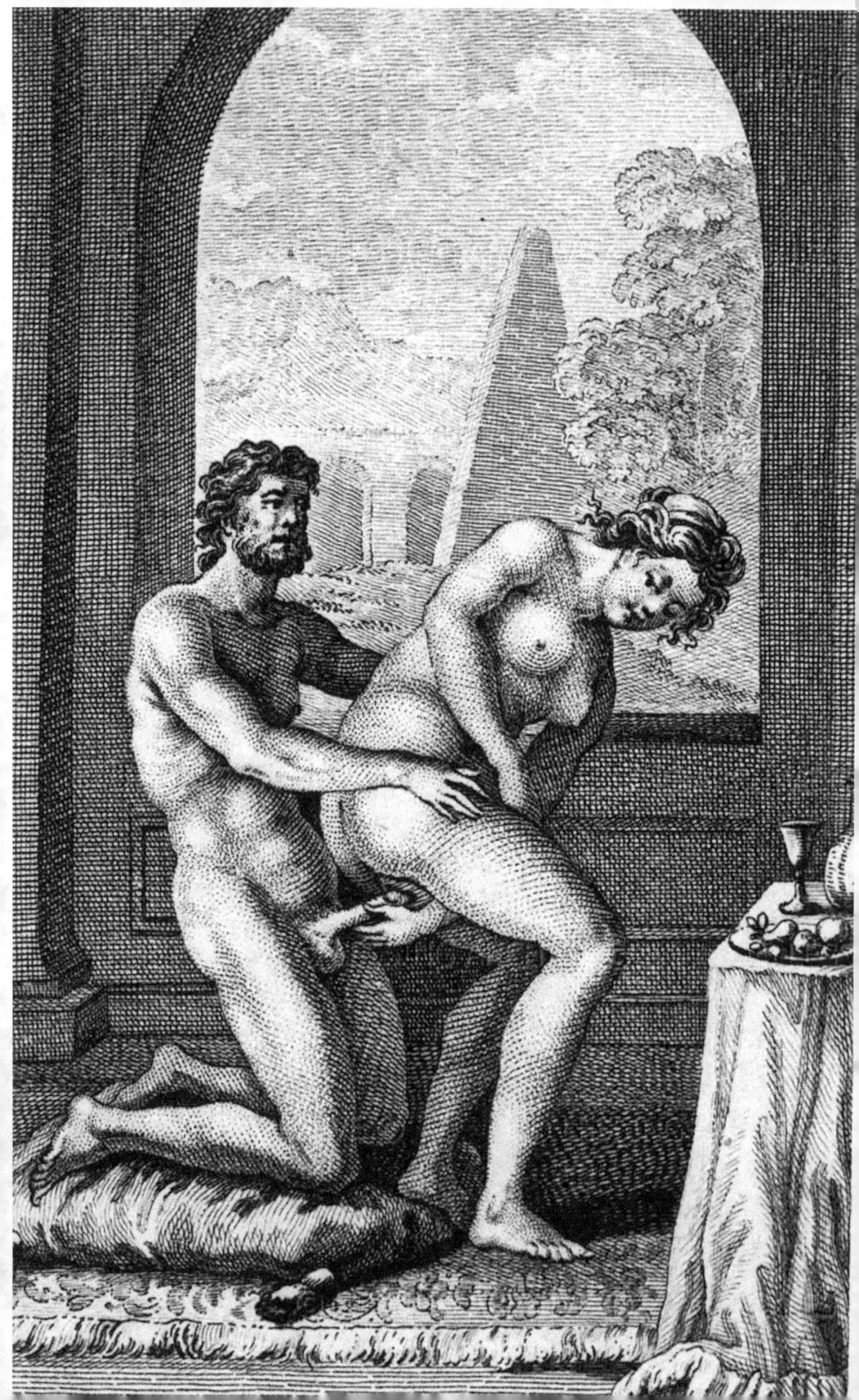

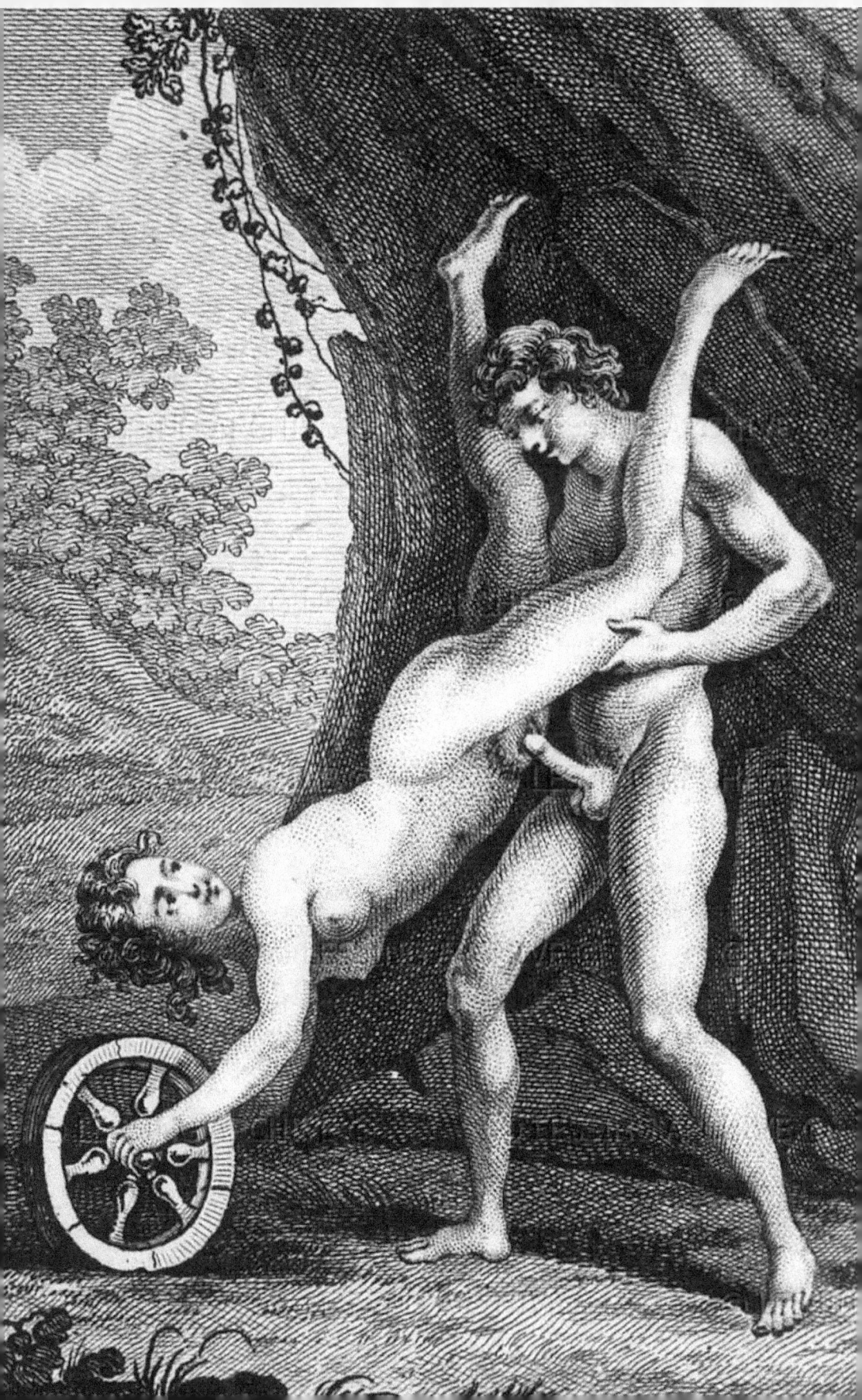

For law-abiding citizens, it seems, the 'line' has to be drawn somewhere. Somewhere between public and private, between sex and love, between visible and invisible, between freedom and control, between secrecy and publicity, between availability and censorship. Indeed, Walter Kendrick said the only definition of pornography is in terms of its forbidden or secret nature.[1]

Pornography brings the secret life of people out into the open. What the Western world holds most dear – the primacy and holiness of the individual, and the primacy and holiness of (heterosexual) love, of marriage, of the family – is cast into doubt by pornography.

Hardcore pornography, in particular, tries to make everything as clear and as visible as possible, and is thus disruptive and unsettling for the establishment. There are, thus, many close-ups of genitals in hardcore pornography. Sex is ecstatic, so hardcore pornography has to show this ecstasy. It does this by focussing on the genitals.

1 W. Kendrick: *The Secret Museum: Pornography in Modern Culture*, Viking, New York, NY, 1987.

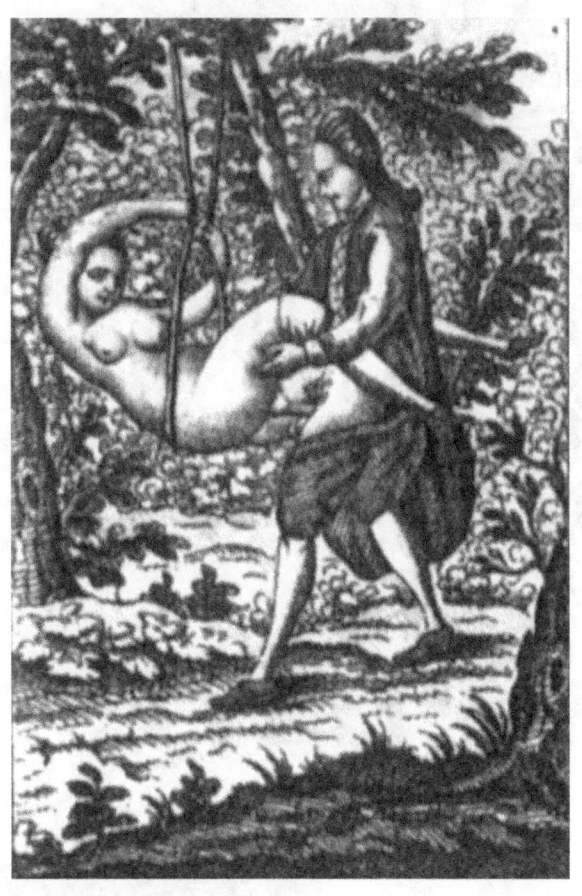

Anonymous,
Memoires du Suzon

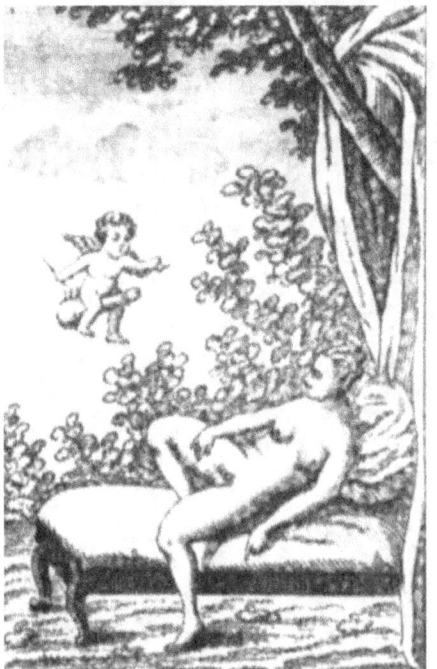

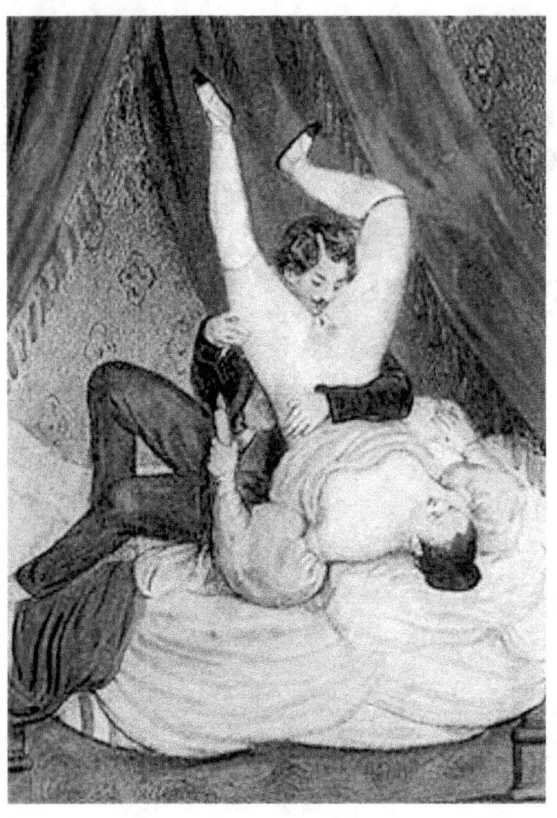

Anonymous, 19th century

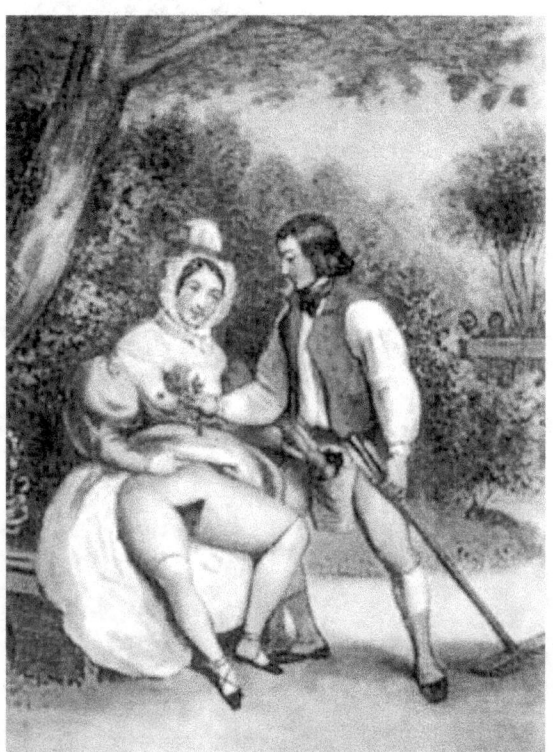

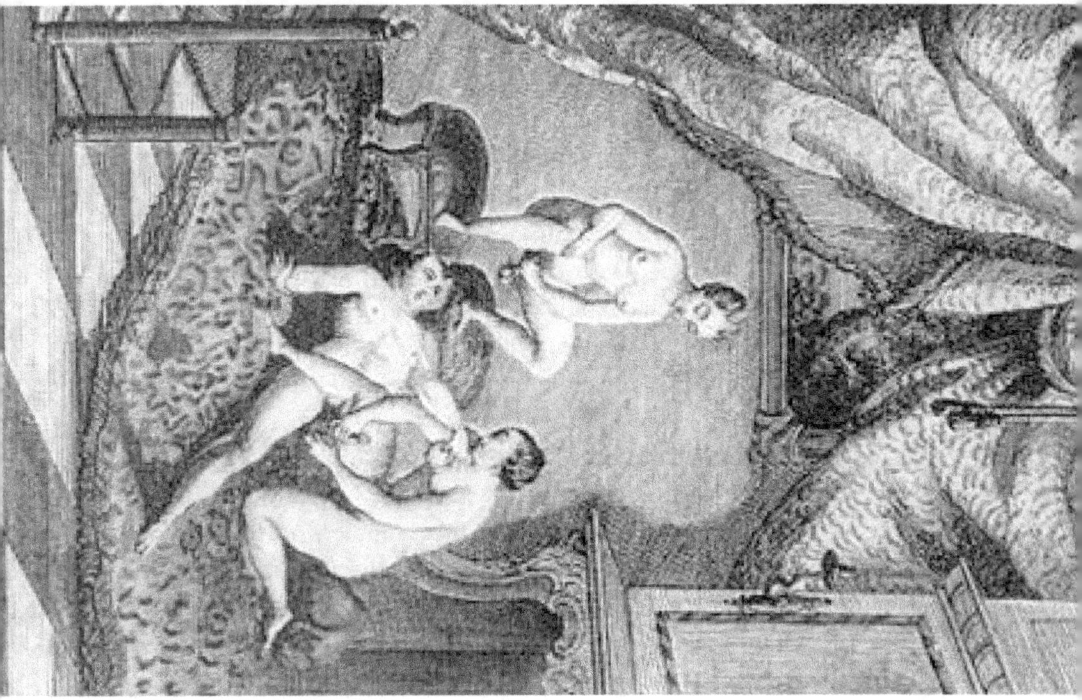

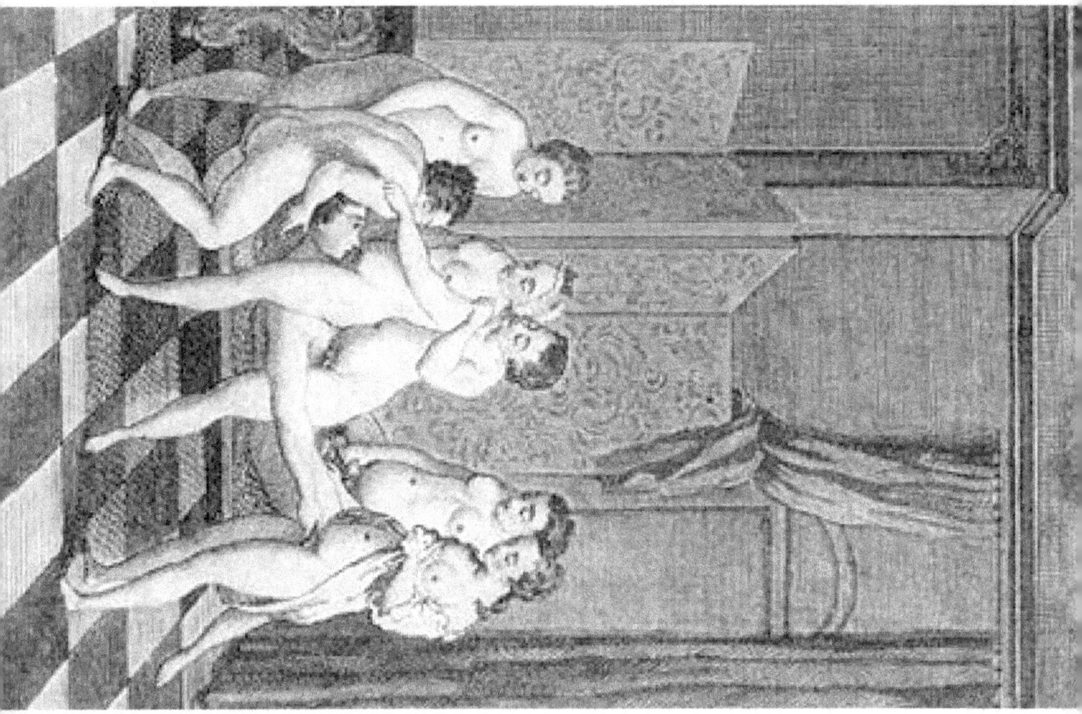

Anonymous, early 19th century

Pornography is the culture of eroticism in the West. There is sex on TV, in fiction, in blockbuster movies, in theatre, in pop music, but it is in pornography that erotic feelings are most frequently communicated. Yet pornography is commodified sex, materialist sex, sex manufactured into particular types, genres, roles and modes. There are standard pornographic encounters, standard pornographic camera angles, standard pornographic orgasms. Eroticism, as Sigmund Freud knew, is powerful, whether emotionally, psychologically, culturally or politically. Pornography, then, deals with really wild eroticism by categorizing it, putting into particular genres or narratives. The visual aspect of pornography helps to deal with the wildness and passion of erotic feeling. Pornography produces images and representations, which are easier to tackle than the real thing. Jane Gallop wrote that the 'visual mode produces representations as a way of mastering what is otherwise too intense'.[1] Experiences such as orgasm and erotic desire can be too overwhelming to be communicated in words. Putting these experiences into visual representations enables them to be controlled, packaged, commodified.

1 J. Gallop: *The Daughter's Seduction: Feminism and Psychoanalysis*, Cornell University Press, New York, NY, 1982, 35.

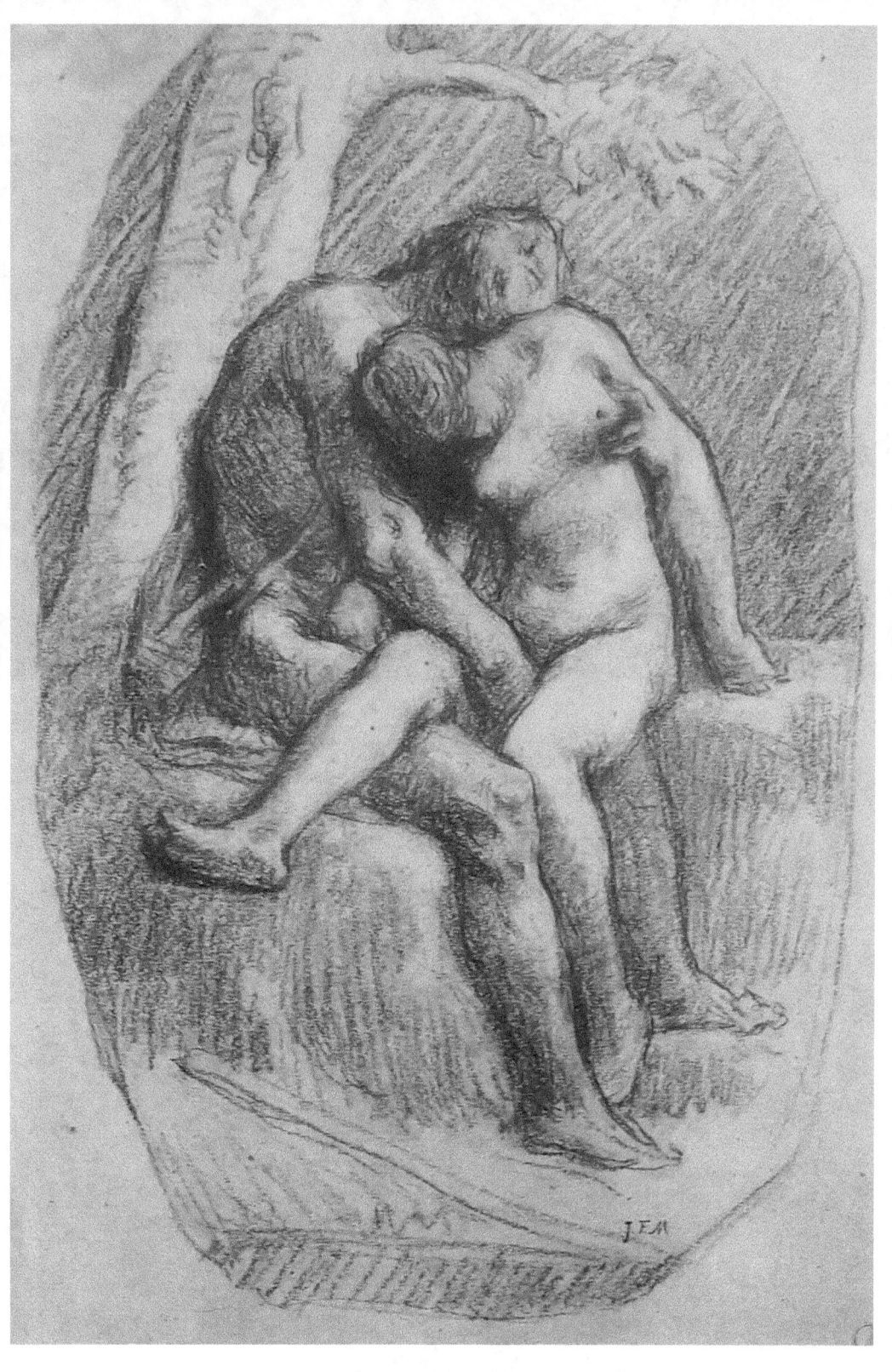

Jean-François Millet, The Lovers,
1848-50, Art Institute, Chicago

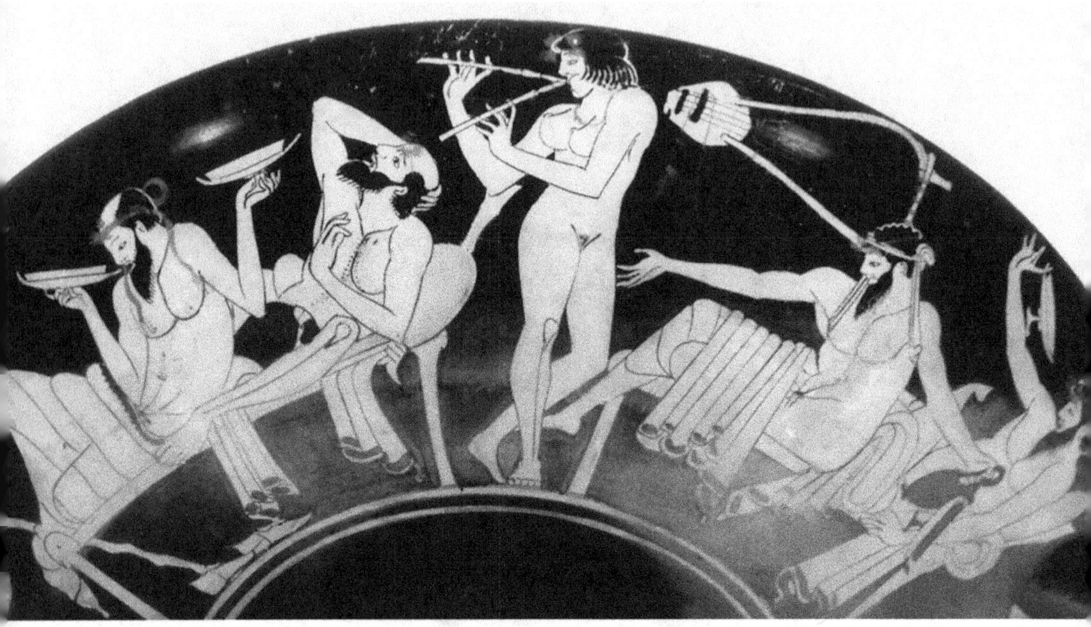

Ancient Greek vase art

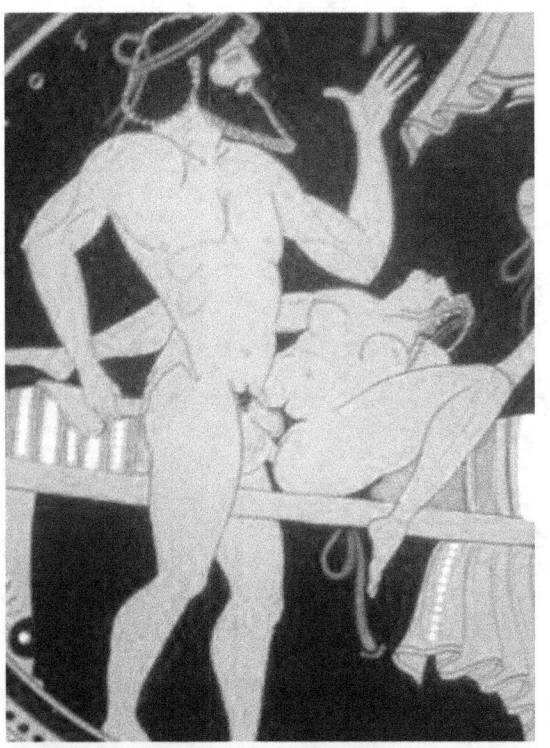

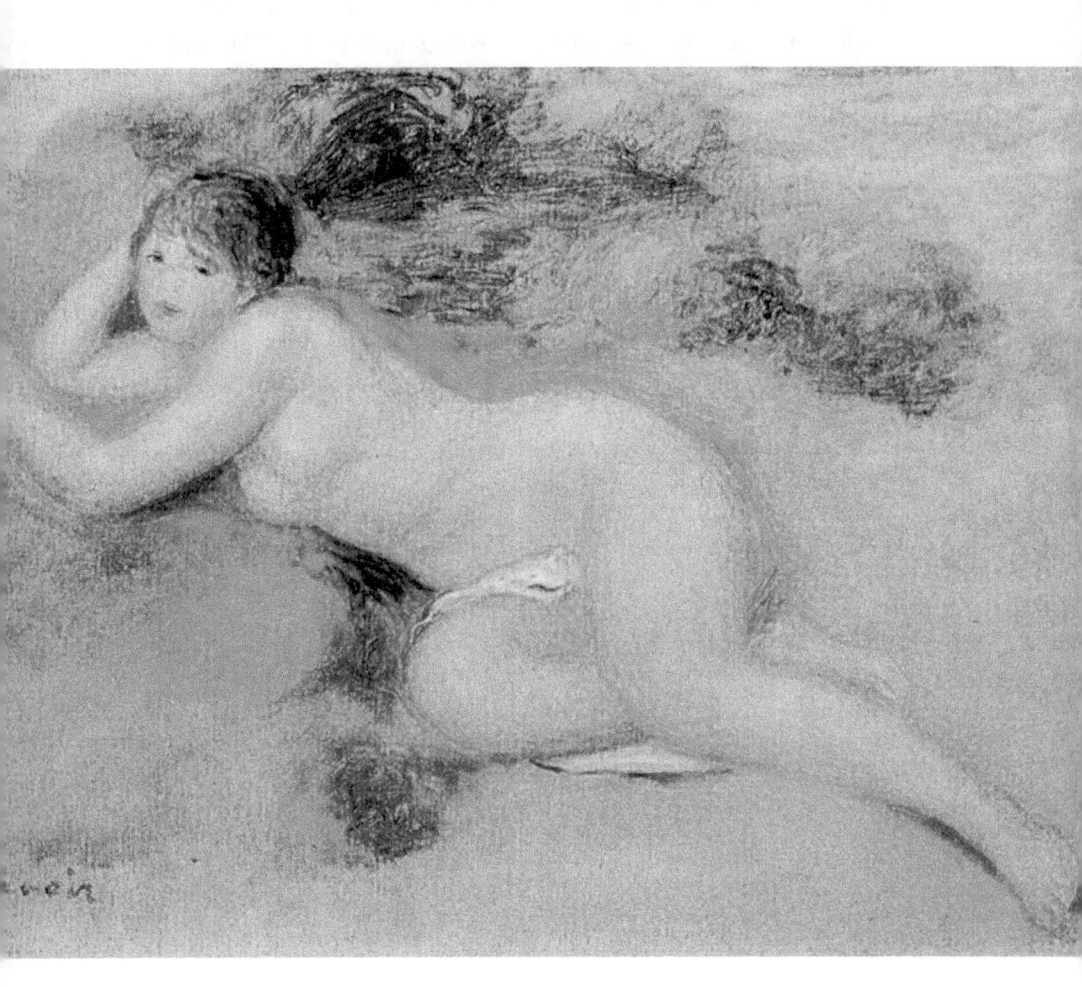

Pierre Renoir

Pornography is *fantasy*, as well as genre, product, system, and materialism. Pornography does not offer the consumer real people, but images, narratives, ideas, suggestions. The visual dimension of pornography helps to create certain kinds of representations of erotic feelings which the consumer can deal with, because they are communicated in recognizable forms. So now we're in an S/M narrative – masters, mistresses and slaves Or, over here we're in the narrative where a sexually frustrated male picks up a female hitchhiker. Or, here we are in the 'bored housewife' scenario: sex-starved, she humps the plumber over the washing machine. The consumer always knows where she or he is with pornography.

Pornography delivers the goods.

It delivers the goods: which's why it's bigger than the movie or pop music industries.

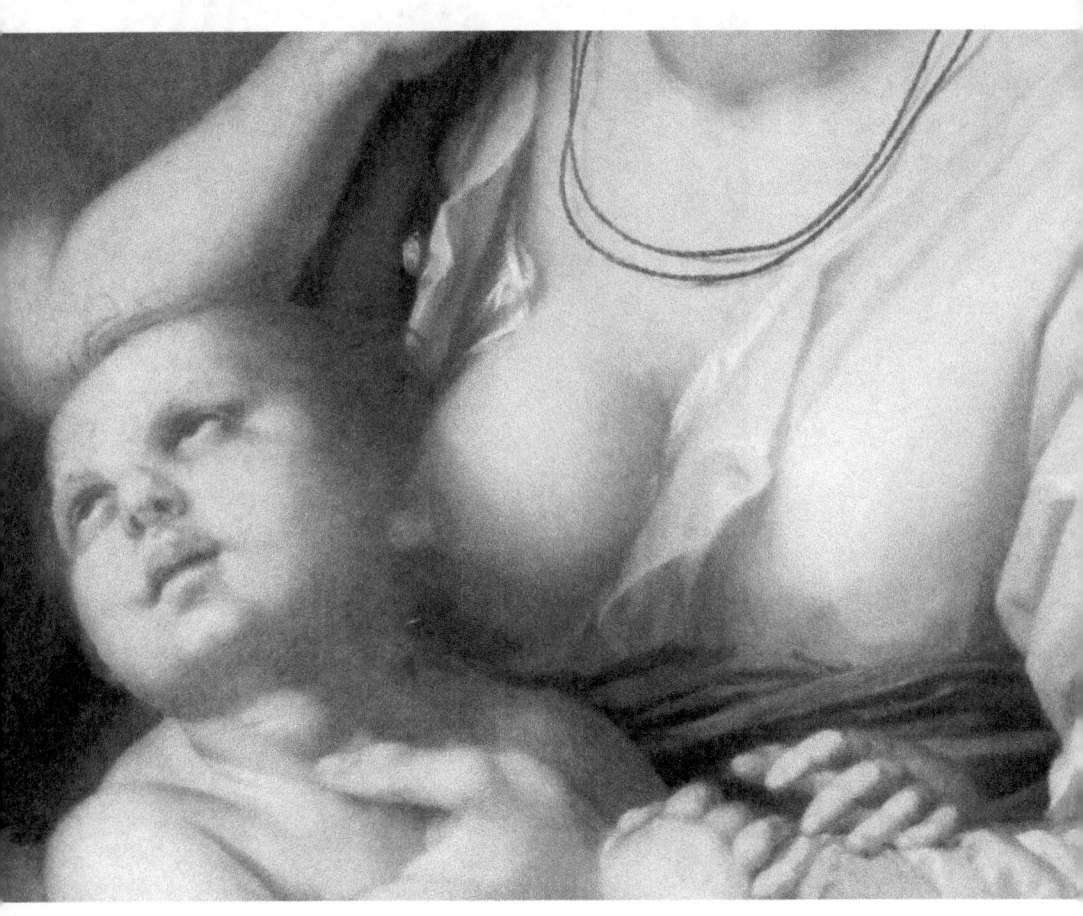

Andrea del Sarto, Madonna and Child, detail

Ferdnand Knopff,
Ishtar

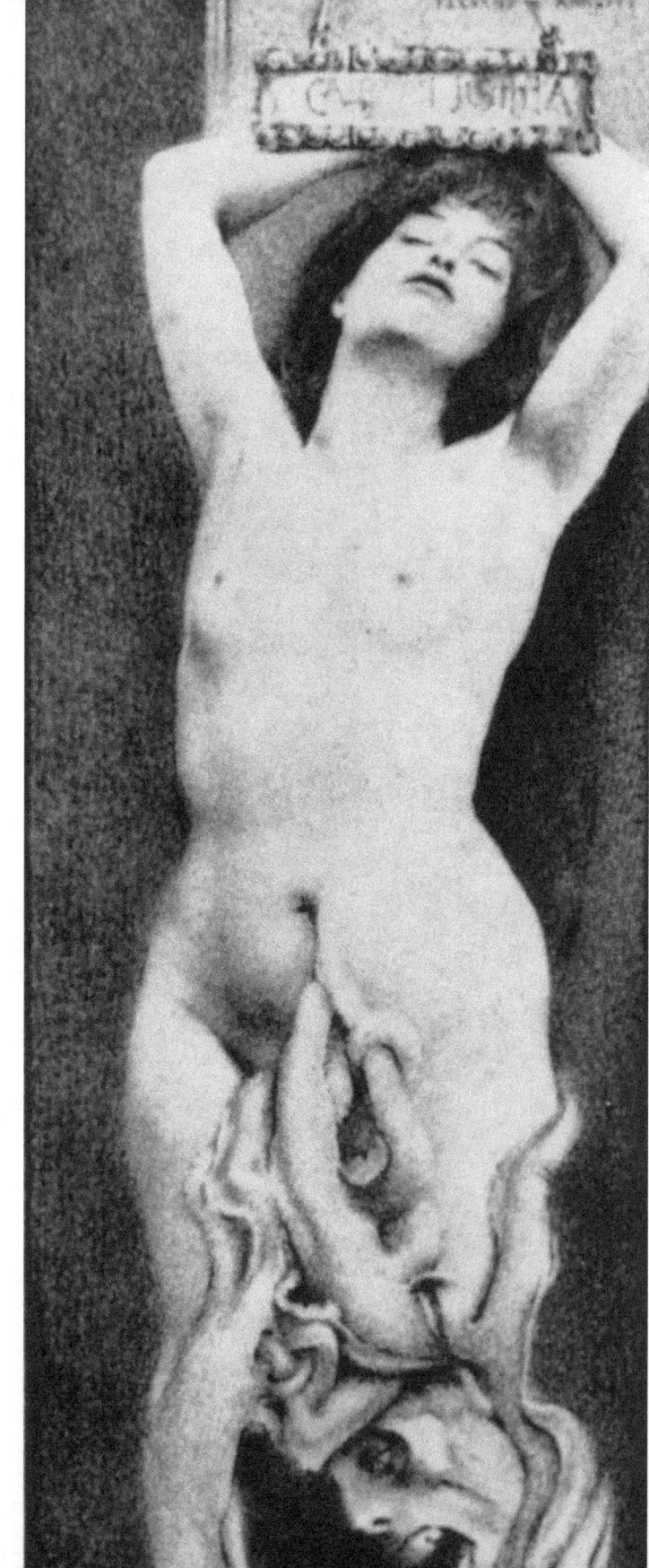

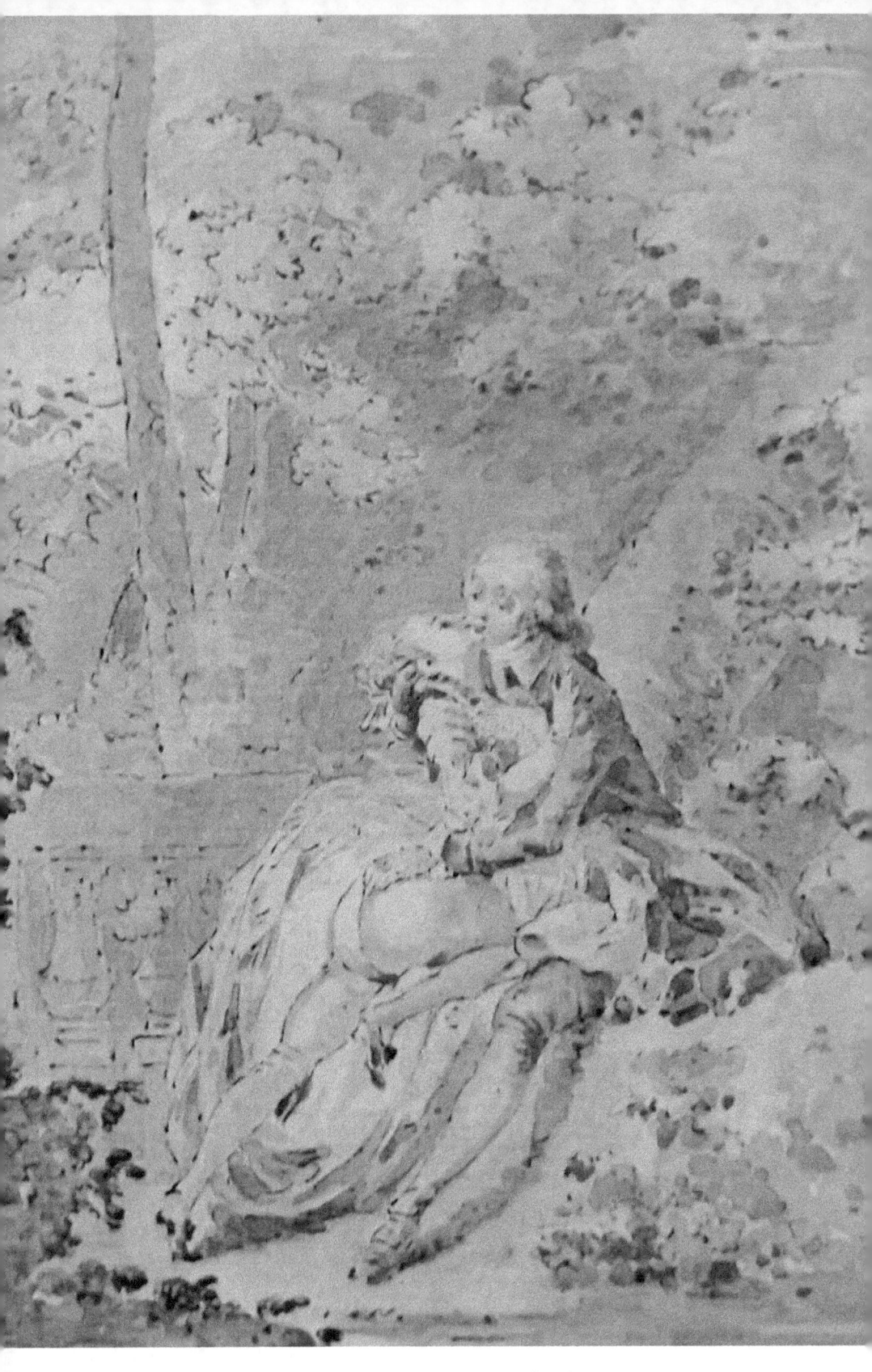

Niclas Lafrensen, 18th century, Sweden

If some work is erotic – a scene on TV, a photo, a sculpture, a dance – it's because, in the opinion of some people, you don't 'see' everything. Something is hidden. The 'erotic' in art is about anticipation, waiting, yearning. It's about potential and possibility, hidden but not hidden, partially clothed. As the photographer Grace Lau, who has made many pictures of fetishism, wrote: 'I prefer images that conceal, rather than those that reveal all.'[1]

Pornography, meanwhile, has people doing it now. They undress, and start attacking each other immediately. There's nothing to get in the way, not contraception, not fear, not aversions, not menstruation, not impotence, not interruptions, not anything. In short: it's *fantasy*.

Pornography turns 'what if?' into a reality. What if somebody took their clothes off in this train carriage and started having sex? is a typical question that erotic art suggests but pornography answers. What if this woman at home turns out to be a nymphomaniac and this repair guy turns out to be a superstud? What if the wedding guest who just smiled at you turns out to be the Fuck of a Lifetime? In pornography, people *do* rip their clothes and start mashing each other up.

Pornography presents as a normal, everyday occurrence what is hidden away, what is desired but unspoken. Pornography is the ultimate in fantasy, for in the fairy tale world of pornography, every dream comes true. And it is not only 'true', it is 'real'.

---

1 Grace Lau: "Confessions of a Complete Scopophiliac", in P. Gibson, 195

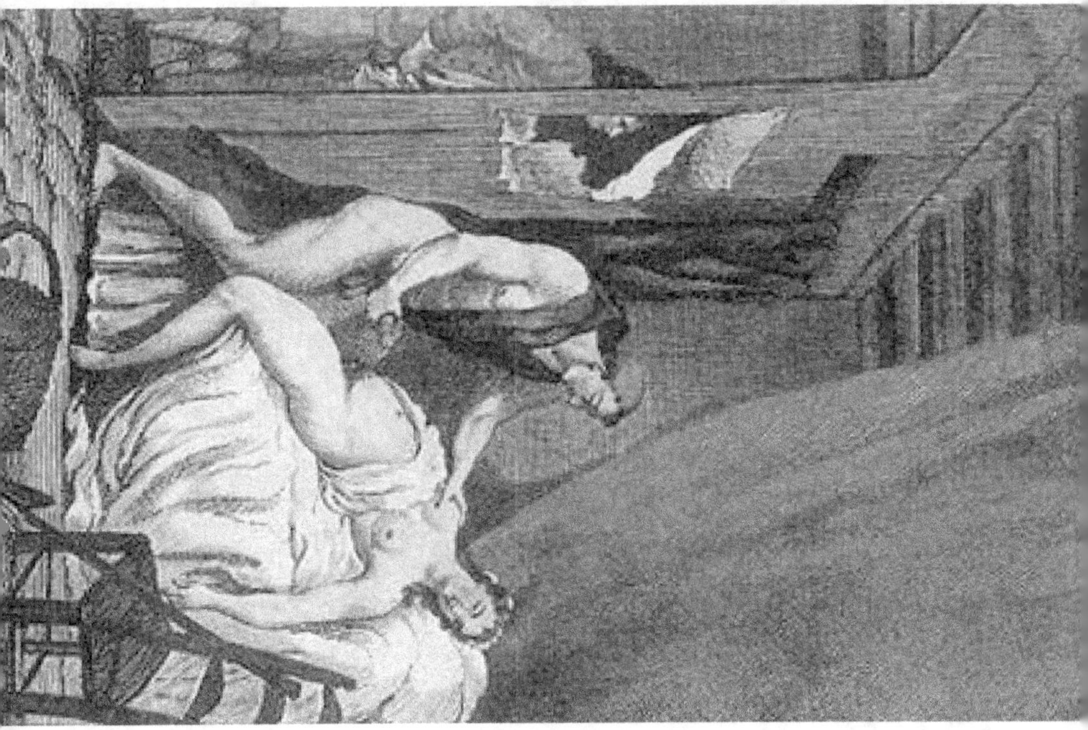

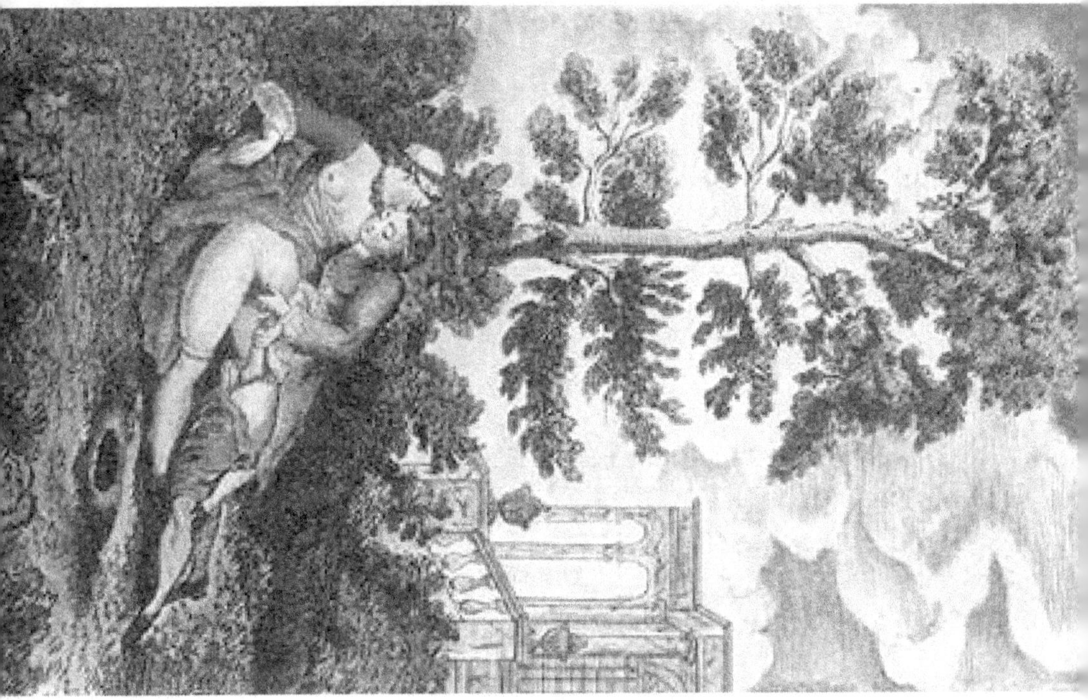

Anonymous, 19th century

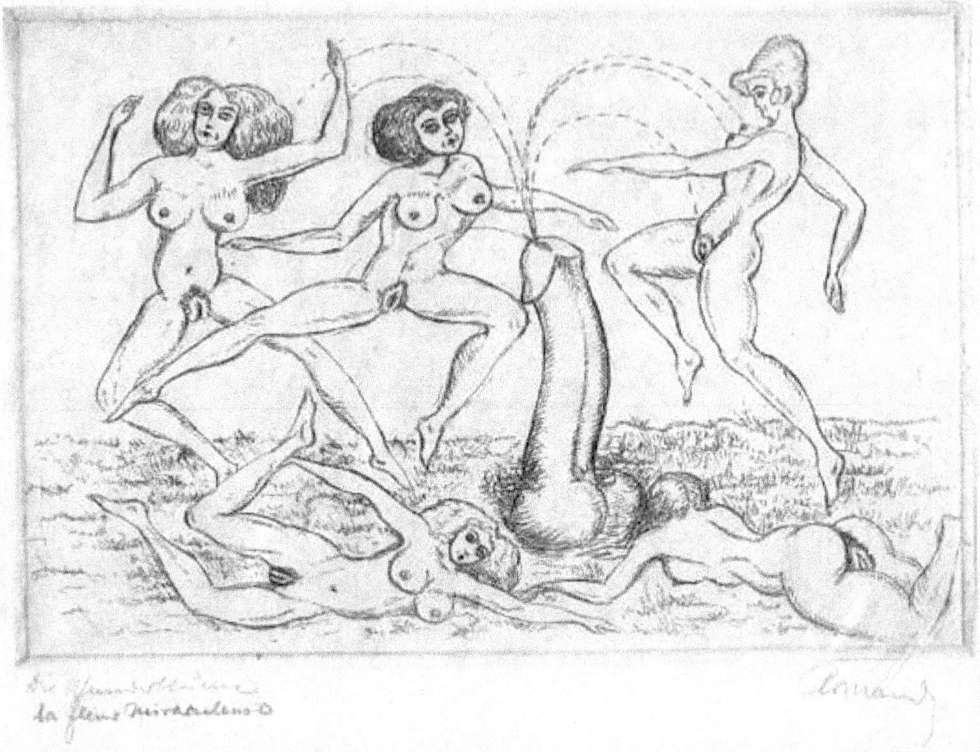

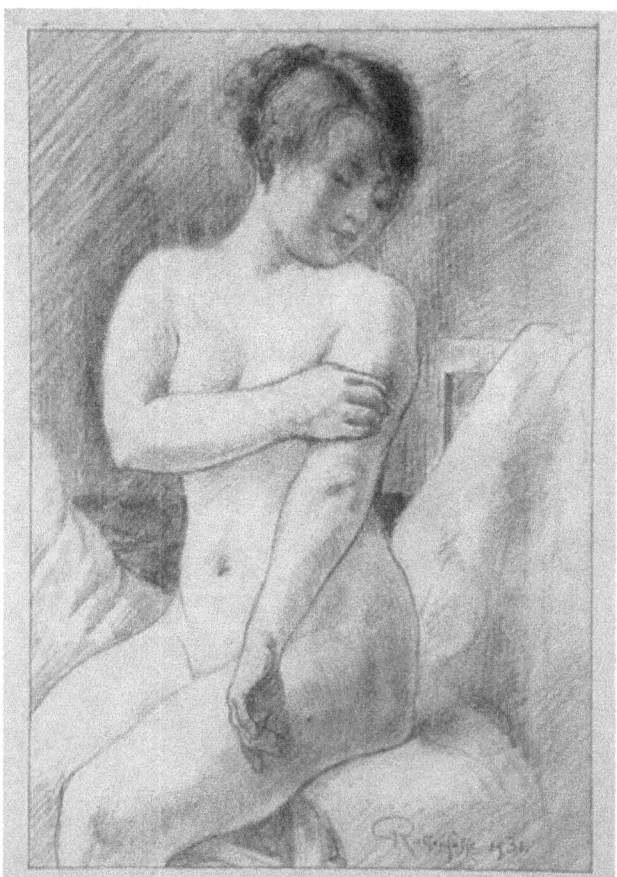

Armand Rassenfosse
(1862-1934)

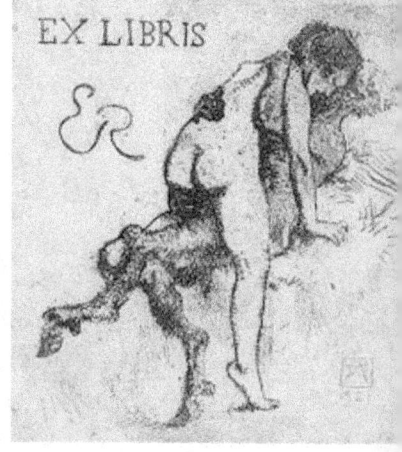

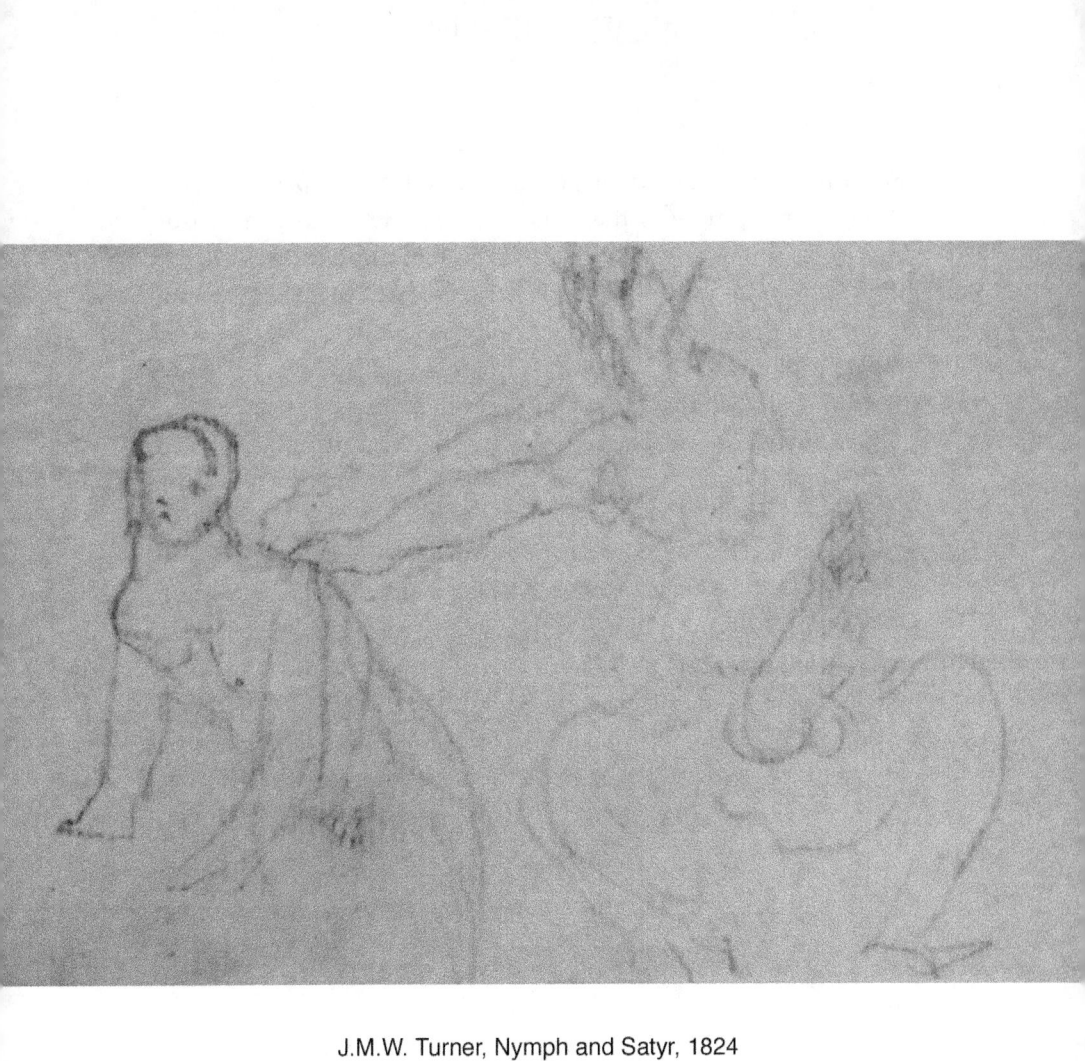

J.M.W. Turner, Nymph and Satyr, 1824

CENSORSHIP

One of the most contentious and fiercely debated aspects of erotic art and pornography is the issue of obscenity, taste and censorship. Throughout the history of art and pornography, different individuals or groups of people have sought to defend certain territories, whether moral, psychological, emotional, spiritual, religious, philosophical, political or ideological. There is always some line between the 'acceptable' and the 'obscene'.

The history of censorship is long and complex. In the 20th century there were many confrontations between artists and the establishment: with D.H. Lawrence's *Lady Chatterley's Lover*, with *Ulysses*, with films such as *Last Tango in Paris, Kids, Natural Born Killers, The Killing of Sister George, Performance, Trash, A Clockwork Orange* and countless others, with the *Oz* trials, with Senator Jesse Helms trying to stop NEA tax payers' money funding 'obscene' work, with reference to the photographer Robert Mapplethorpe (whose photos have created much 'controversy'),[1] with internet porn, with punk rock and gangsta rap, and so on.[2]

---

1 See M. Schoofs: "Robert Mapplethorpe: Exquisite Subversions", *Windy City Times*, 16 Mch, 1989; H. Kramer: "Mapplethorpe Show at the Whitney: A Big, Glossy, Offensive Exhibit", *The New York Observer*, 22 Aug, 1988; A.C. Danto: *Encounters & Reflections*, Farrar Straus Giroux, New York 1990; E. Kastor & Carla Hall: "Mapplethorpe Aftermath", *Washington Post*, 23 June 1989; T.A. Yasui: "The Mapplethorpe Bonanza", *Washington Post*, 21 Aug, 1989; P. Schjeldhal: "The Mainstreaming of Mapplethorpe: Taste and Hunger", *7 Days*, 10 Aug, 1988; R. Rooney: "The unambiguous stare of Mapplethorpe's lens", *Australian*, 25 Feb, 1986.
2 More Mapplethorpe articles: D. Dominick: "Robert Mapplethorpe's Proud Finale", *Vanity Fair*, Feb, 1989; "Robert Mapplethorpe: Aestheticizing the Perverse", *Artscribe International*, Nov/Dec 1988; J. Ribalta: "Decorative Heroism, The death of Mapplethorpe", *Lapiz*, Apl, 1989.

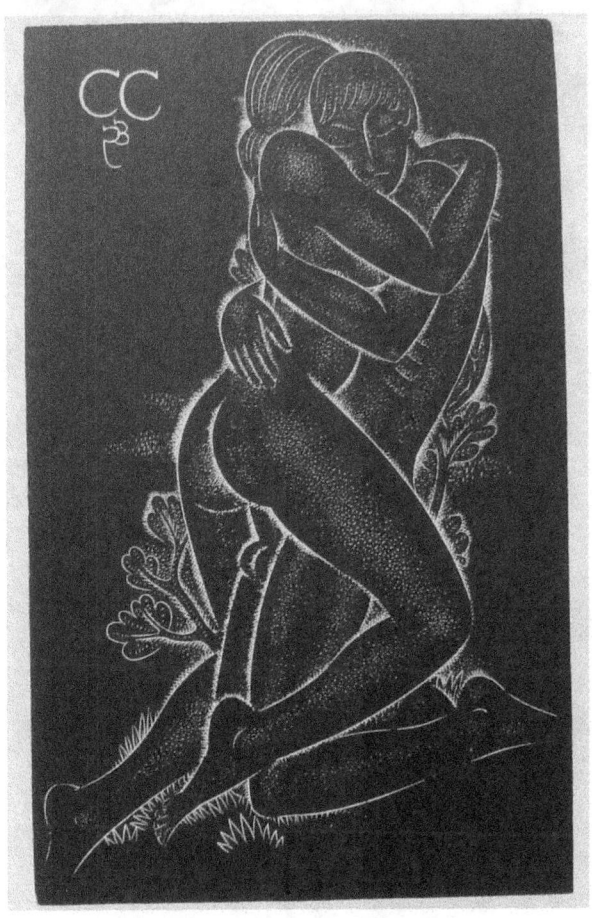

Fucking a flame into being: one of
Eric Gill's illustrations for D.H. Lawrence's book

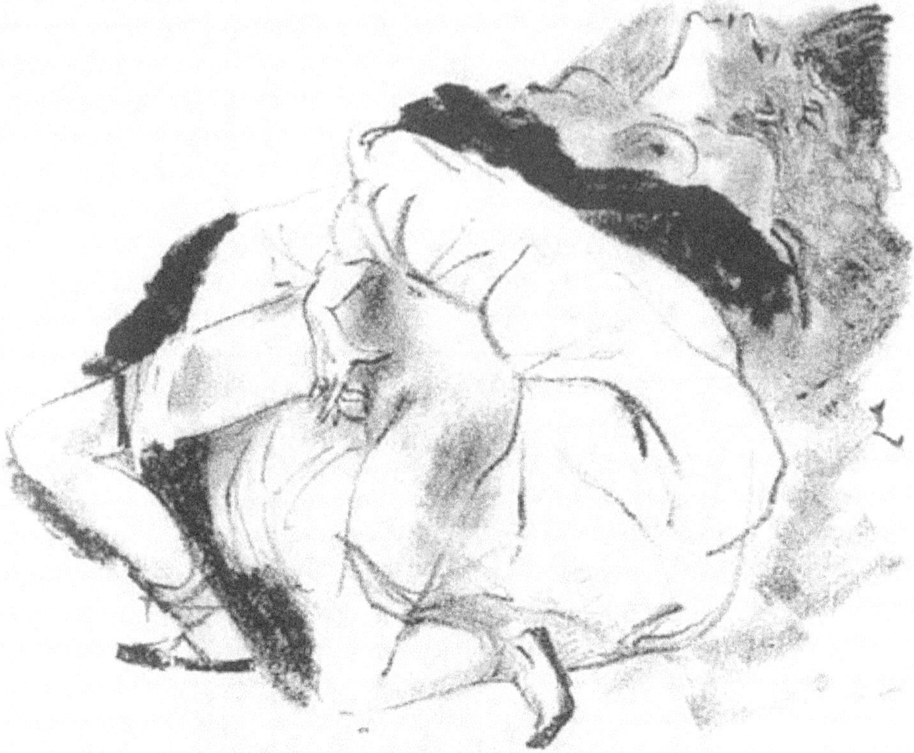

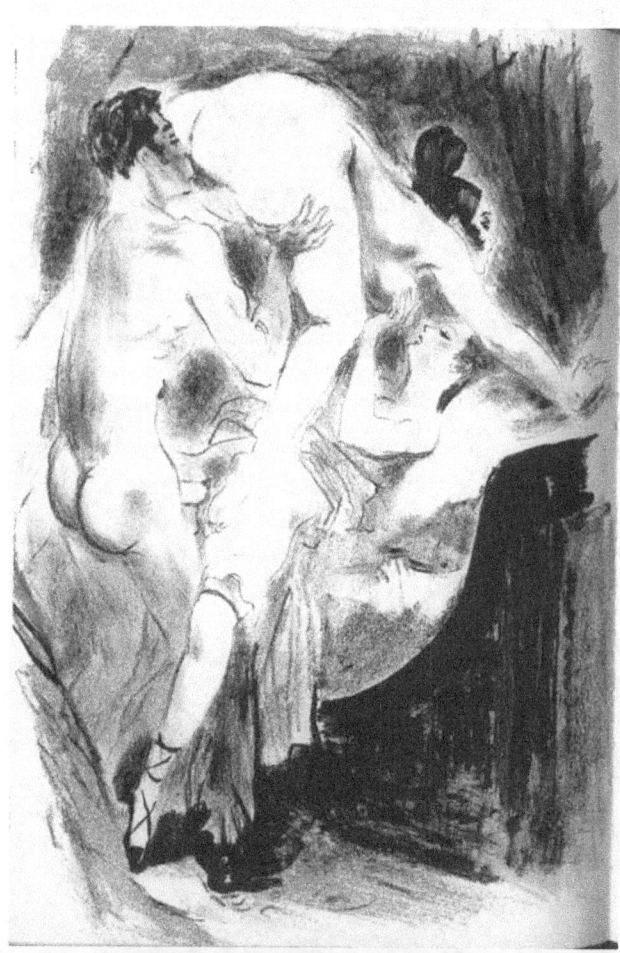

Louis-André Berthomme
Saint-André, Gamiani ou Deux Nuits
d'Excés, by Alfred de Musset

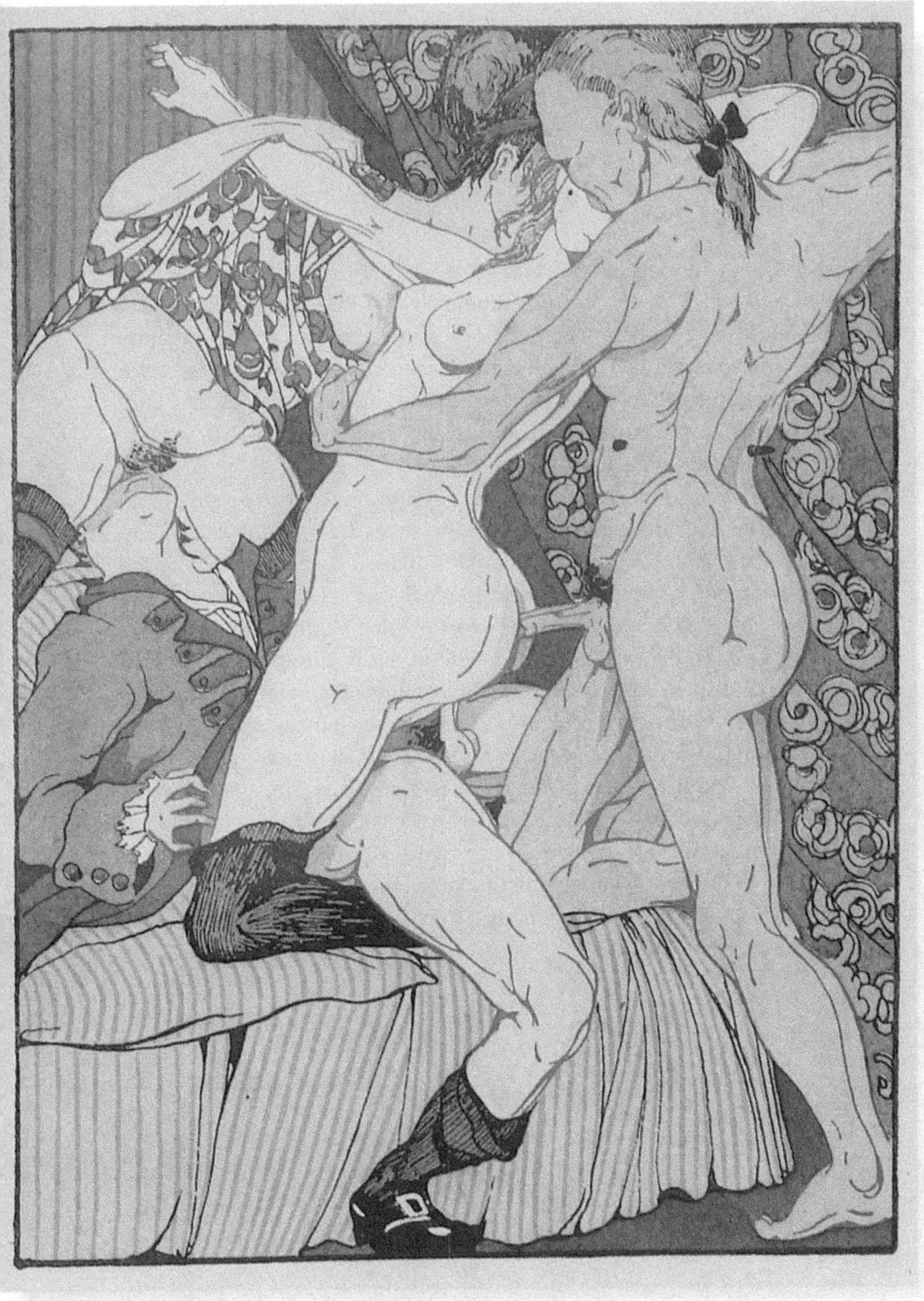

Illustration for the Marquis de Sade,
Le Bordel de Venise, 1921,
by Couperyn (a.k.a. George A. Drains), Paris

CENSORSHIP

The many debates concerning several Obscene Publications Acts and bills, the First Amendment of the American constitution, different regulatory groups, pressure groups, media organizations, publishers, and all manner of intellectuals and artists, have been intense, complex, protracted, and often a shambles. The confusions and ambiguities are at the centre of Western society. Pornography debates produce, very quickly, all manner of confusions and hypocrisies, of a moral, religious, psychological, social and ideological nature.[1] For some, though, the censorship debate is 'in fact, a little internal quibble between sections of the bourgeois community' (according to Suzanne Kappeler).

Pornography goes to the heart of what people hold dear: their identities, their feelings, their philosophical, spiritual and political views, their view of the 'quality of life'. Pornography unsettles these notions and structures. The fervour and uncertainty of the many attempts at legislation and policing show how problematic pornography is. In a case of recent years, five 'homosexual sadomasochists' were convicted in 1990 of inflicting 'injuries on each another's genitals during ritual sex' which involved 'cutting each other's genitals with surgical scalpels, sandpapering scrotums and pushing hooks into penises'. Their appeal was rejected by the courts.[2]

1 See *Art in America*, May 1990; C.H. Rolph: *The Trial of Lady Chatterley*, Penguin, London, 1961; G. Robertson: *Obscenity: an Account of Censorship Laws and Their Enforcements in England and Wales*, Weidenfeld & Nicolson, London, 1979; *The Attorney General's Commission on Pornography – the Meese Commission – Final Report*, US Government Printing Office, Washington DC, 1986; L. Lederer, ed, op. cit.
2 I. MacKinnon: "Lords reject appeals by sado-masochists", *The Independent*, 12 Mch, 1993.

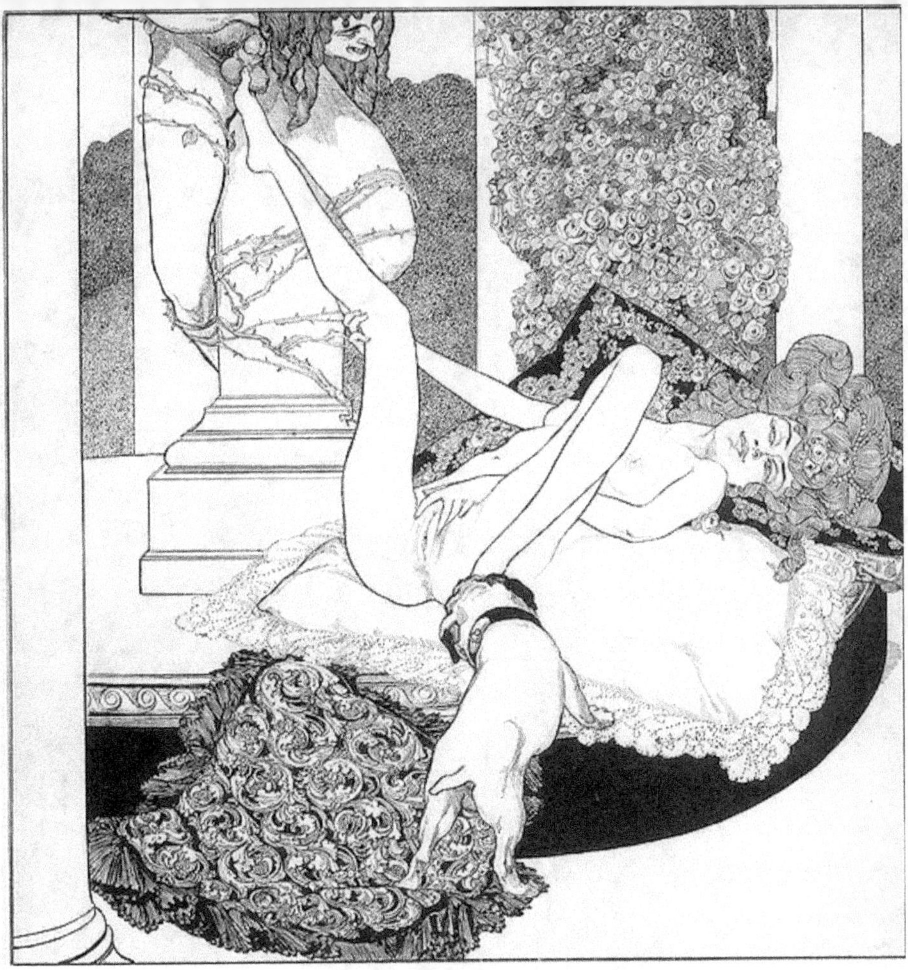

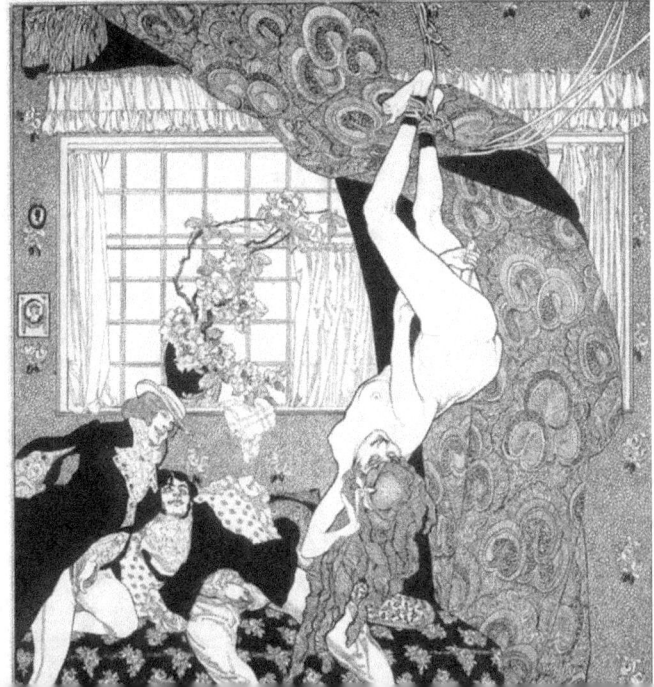

Franz von Bayros (1866-1924),
Der Toilettentisch, Tantalus, 1908

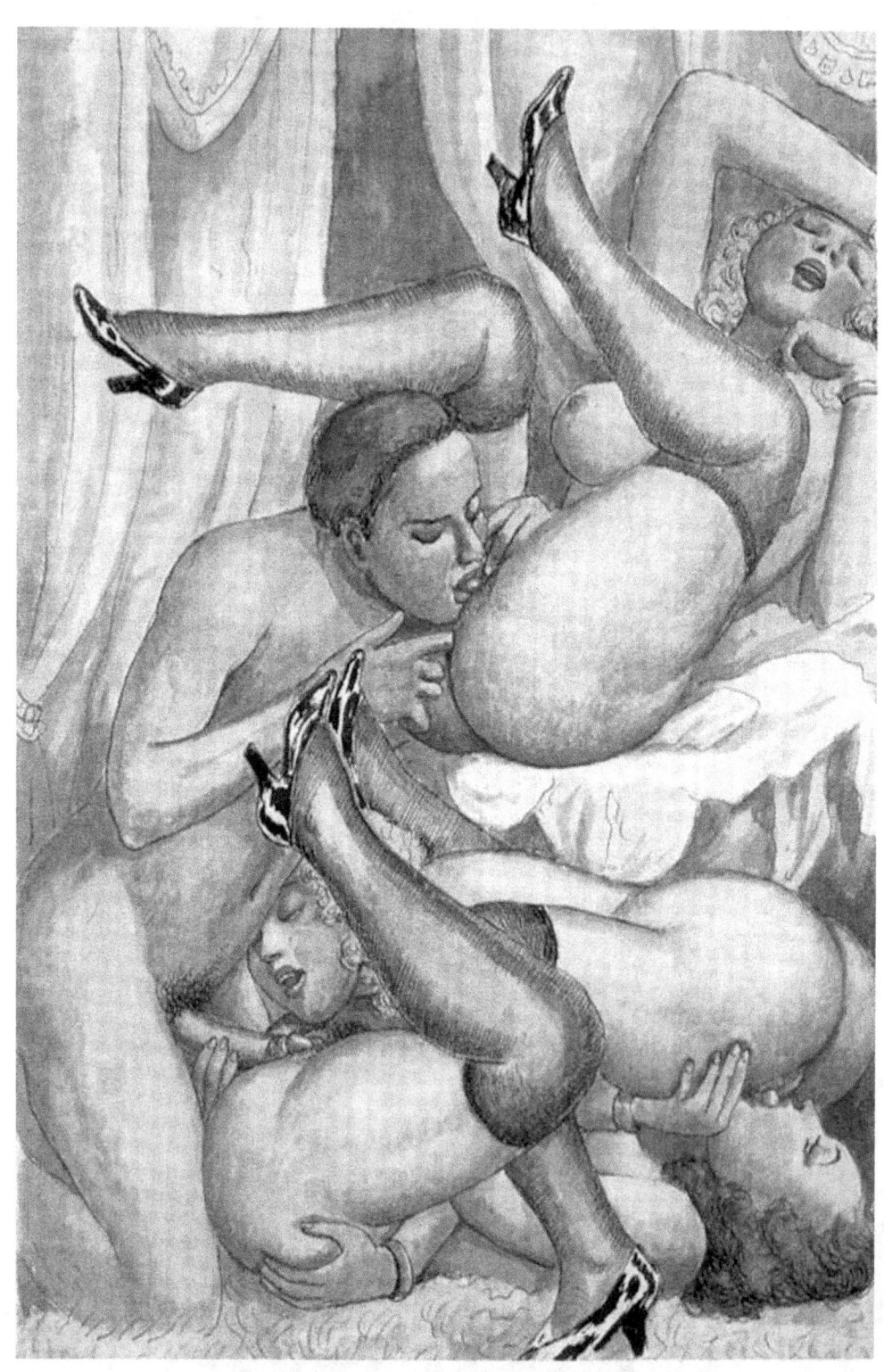

Anonymous, early 20th century

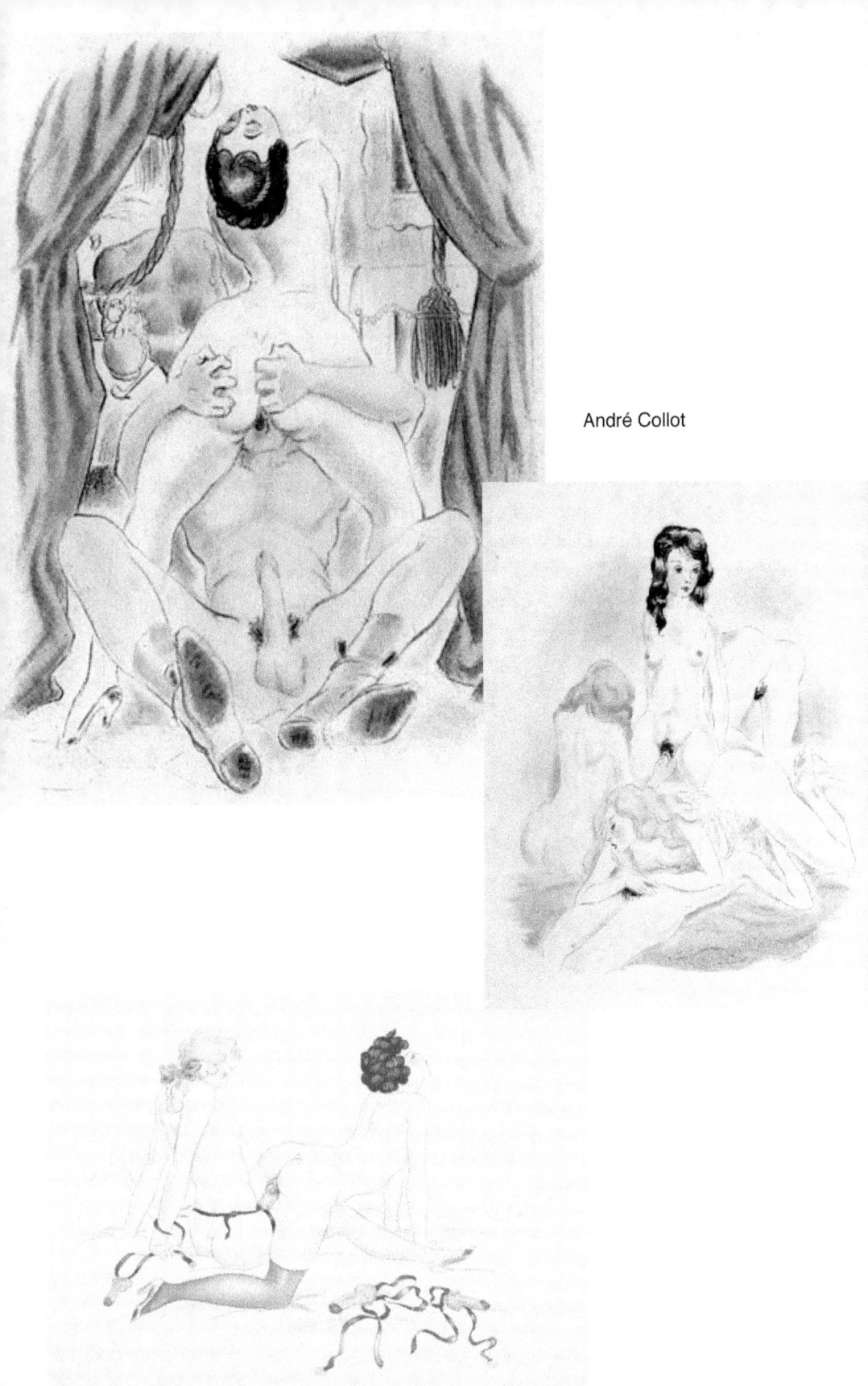

André Collot

FEMALE ORGASM

The female orgasm is 'anatomically invisible', as far as erotica is concerned. So the history of erotica and porn, for some commentators, 'is the history of visual strategies to overcome the anatomical invisibility of the female orgasm'.[1] In erotica, female orgasm is regarded with confusion and ambivalence. What actually is it? eroticists ask, what does it feel like? (Note that most eroticists throughout history have been men, forever excluded from directly experiencing the female orgasm). Thus the controversy over clitoral and vaginal orgasm, over female 'ejaculation', over 'multiple' orgasms. Female 'ejaculation' is 'visible evidence' of orgasm, yet it is censored by pornographers themselves at times.[2]

---

1 L. Nead, 98; see also L. Williams, 1990.
2 See S. Bell: "Feminist Ejaculations", in Arthur and Marilouise Kroker, eds: *The Hysterical Male: New Feminist Theory*, St Martin's Press, New York, 155-169; also C. Straayer: "The Seduction of Boundaries: Feminist Fluidity in Annie Sprinkle's Art/Education/Sex", in P. Gibson, ed, 168f

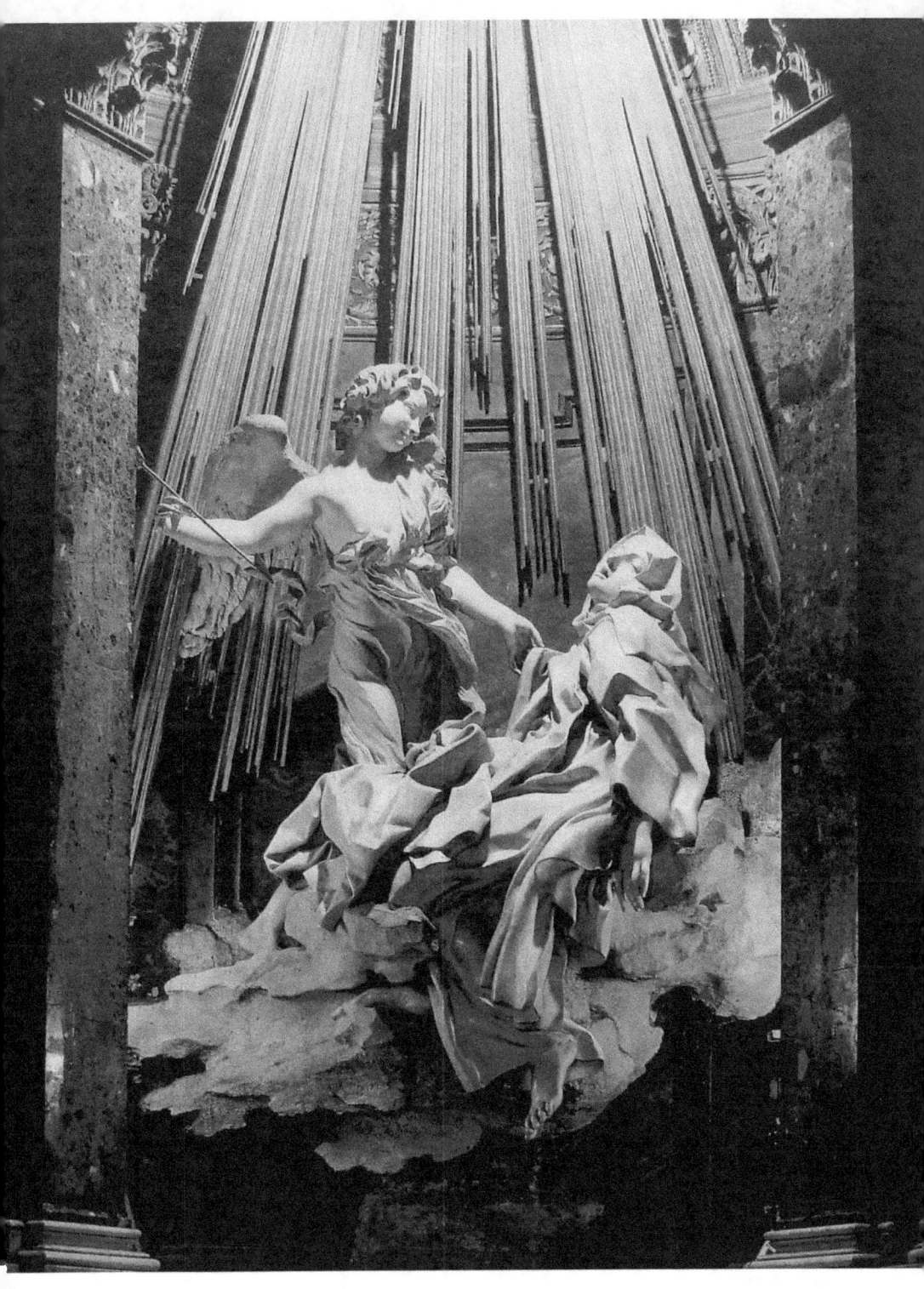

Gianlorenzo Bernini, The Ecstasy of St Theresa, 1652, Rome

ORGASM

Sexuality is not what you *are,* but what you *do.* It is not *who* is fucking *whom,* but *how.*[1] The question is *how is this fucking being done?* Never *why,* always *how.*

For patriarchal people, of either or any sex, it seems it is essential to know *who* is speaking about sex. Is the author male or female (or some other gender)? What is her/ his sexual identity? Patriarchal people are disturbed when their expectations of gender are disrupted. When, say, a male author writes of lesbian sexuality as if from the 'inside', as if in the 'character' of a lesbian. For example, who is the speaker and who is the subject of this poem:

> First, I want to make
> > kiss you...
> I want to make you come
> in my mouth like a storm.[2]

It seems the speaker (Marilyn Hacker) is female and she is describing lesbian sex. But the words could just as apply hetero-sexual or homosexual eroticism. Only when parts of the body are mentioned – clitoris, nipples, penis, breasts – is it possible to decipher the gender of speaker, text or subject, and sometimes not even then.

---

1 see Valerie Traub, in V. Wayne, 83
2 Marilyn Hacker: 'Noces', from *Love, Death and the Changing of the Seasons,* Arbor House 1986

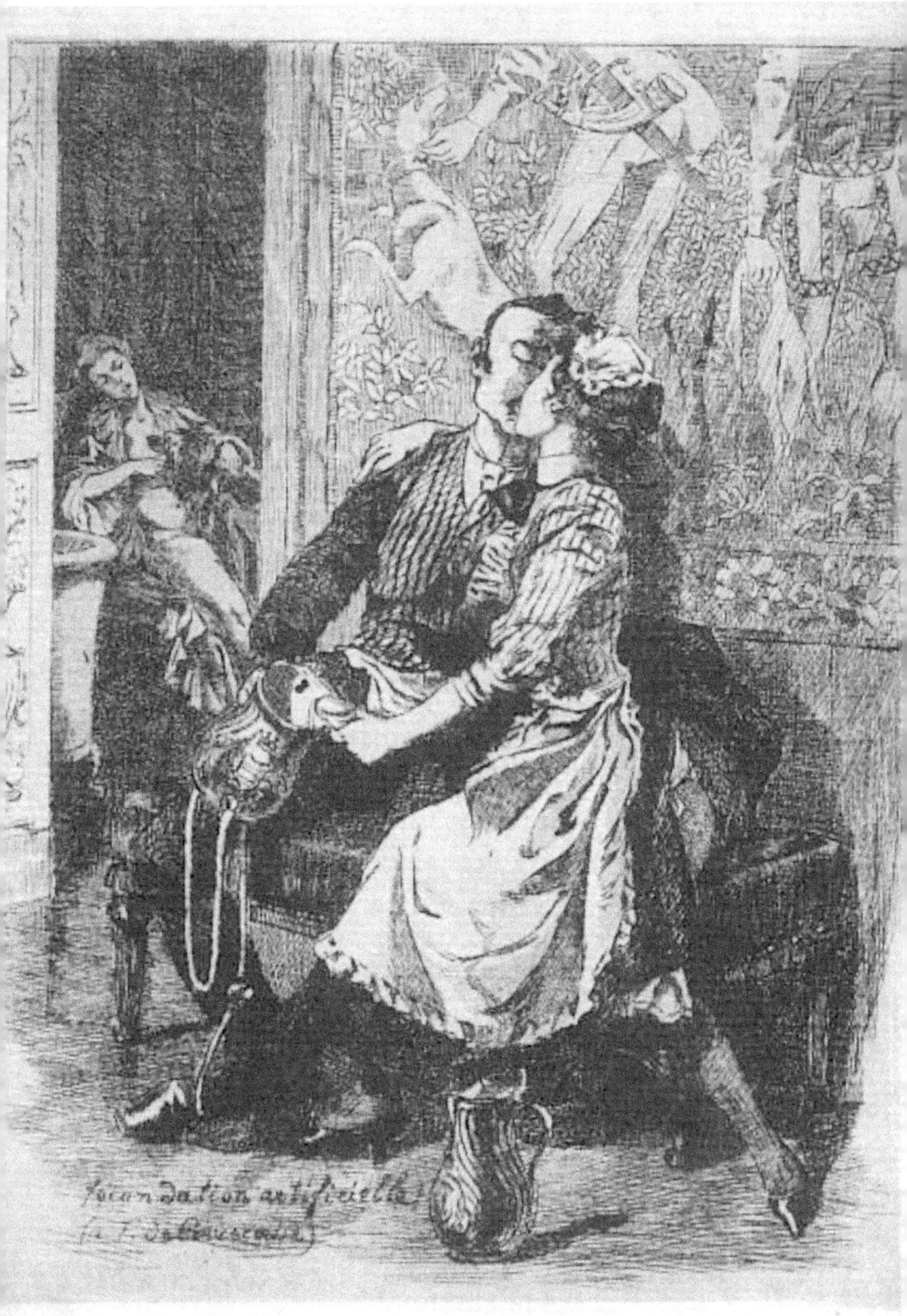

Martin van Maele

THE PHALLUS

In pornography, the great signifier is the phallus, while the site of pleasure is the woman's body. Reclining on a million couches in artists' studios, the female nude offers itself up as a country to be colonized. It is both a pleasure machine and a fantasy. The orchestrator of pleasure in this pornographic scenario is that little slip of flesh, the penis. The phallus is good, whole, true, unifying, as opposed to the bad, fragmented, impure, chaotic vagina.[1] The phallus is the emblem of male power, as many commentators, not only feminists, note: '[t]he supreme power is the power that prevails over mortality', and this power is 'reasonably equated with the phallus'.[2] For feminists, the West is a phallic/ phallocentric/ phallogocentric society, where the phallus, the sublime signifier, the most censored image in the West, is the beginning and the end of sexual pleasure. For Madeleine Gagnon, the phallus is an emblem of male narcissism:

> The phallus... represents repressive capitalist ownership, the exploiting bourgeois... The phallus means everything sets itself up as a mirror. Everything that erects itself as perfection.[3]

---

1 See T. Moi: *Sexual/ Textual Politics*, 66f; S.M. Gilbert & S. Gubar: *The Madwoman in the Attic: The Woman Writer and the Nineteenth Century Literary Imagination*, Yale University Press, New Haven, CT, 1979.
2 L. Steinberg: *The Sexuality of Christ in Renaissance Art and in Modern Oblivion*, Pantheon, New York, 1984, 90.
3 M. Gagnon: "Corps I", *La venue à l'écriture*, UGE, 10/18, Paris 1977; in E. Marks, 180.

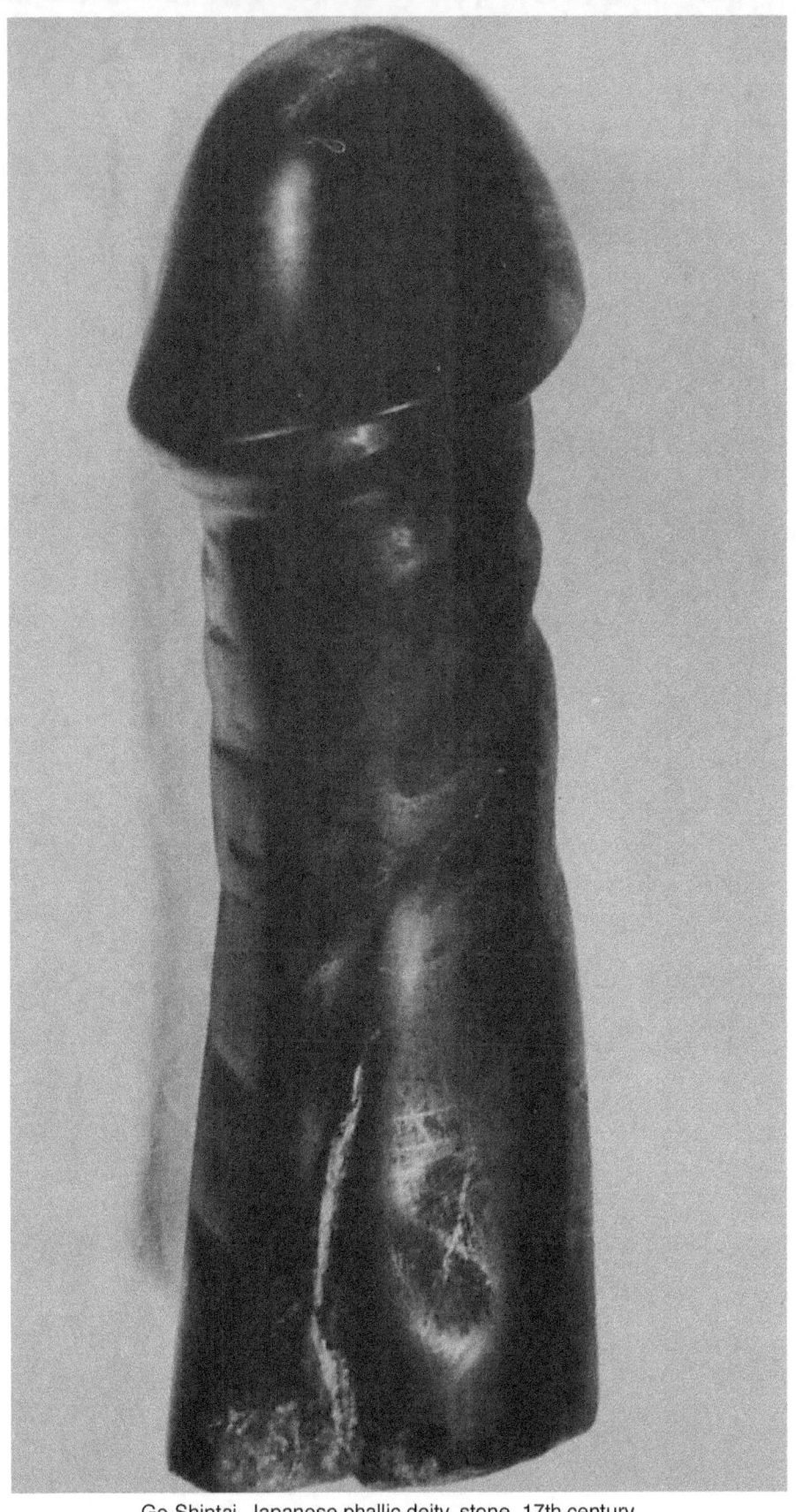

Go-Shintai, Japanese phallic deity, stone, 17th century

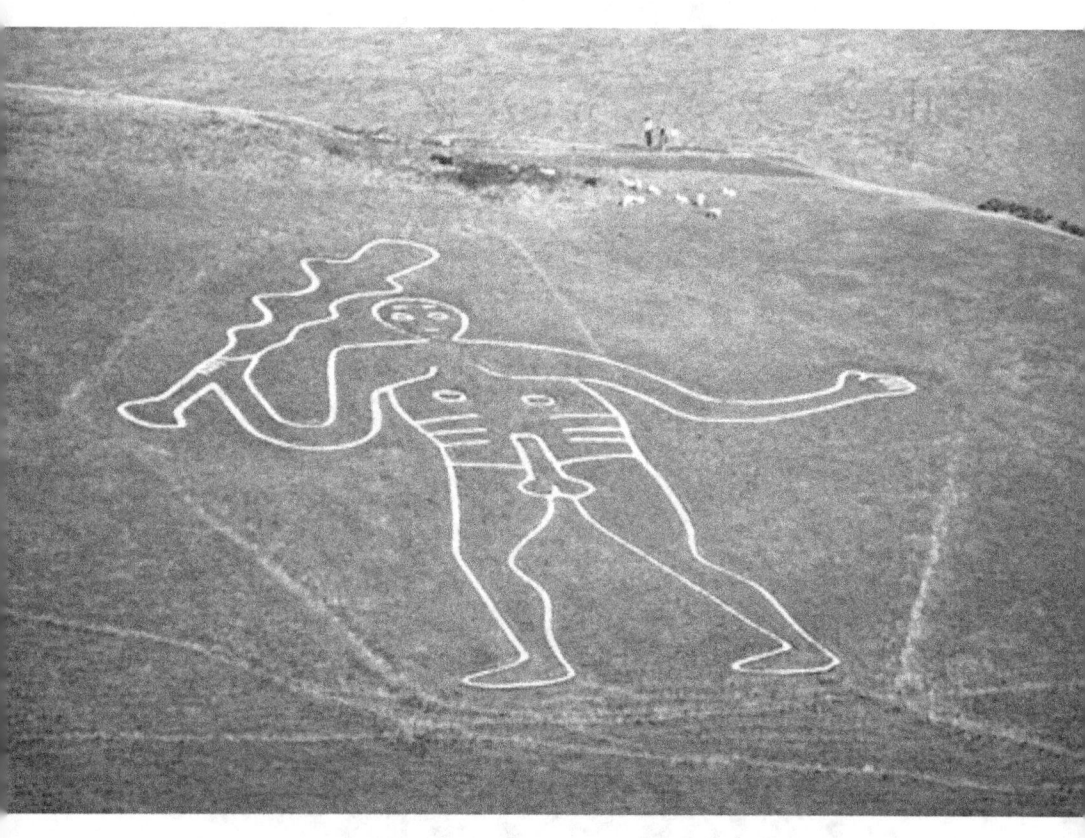

Cerne Giant, Dorset, England

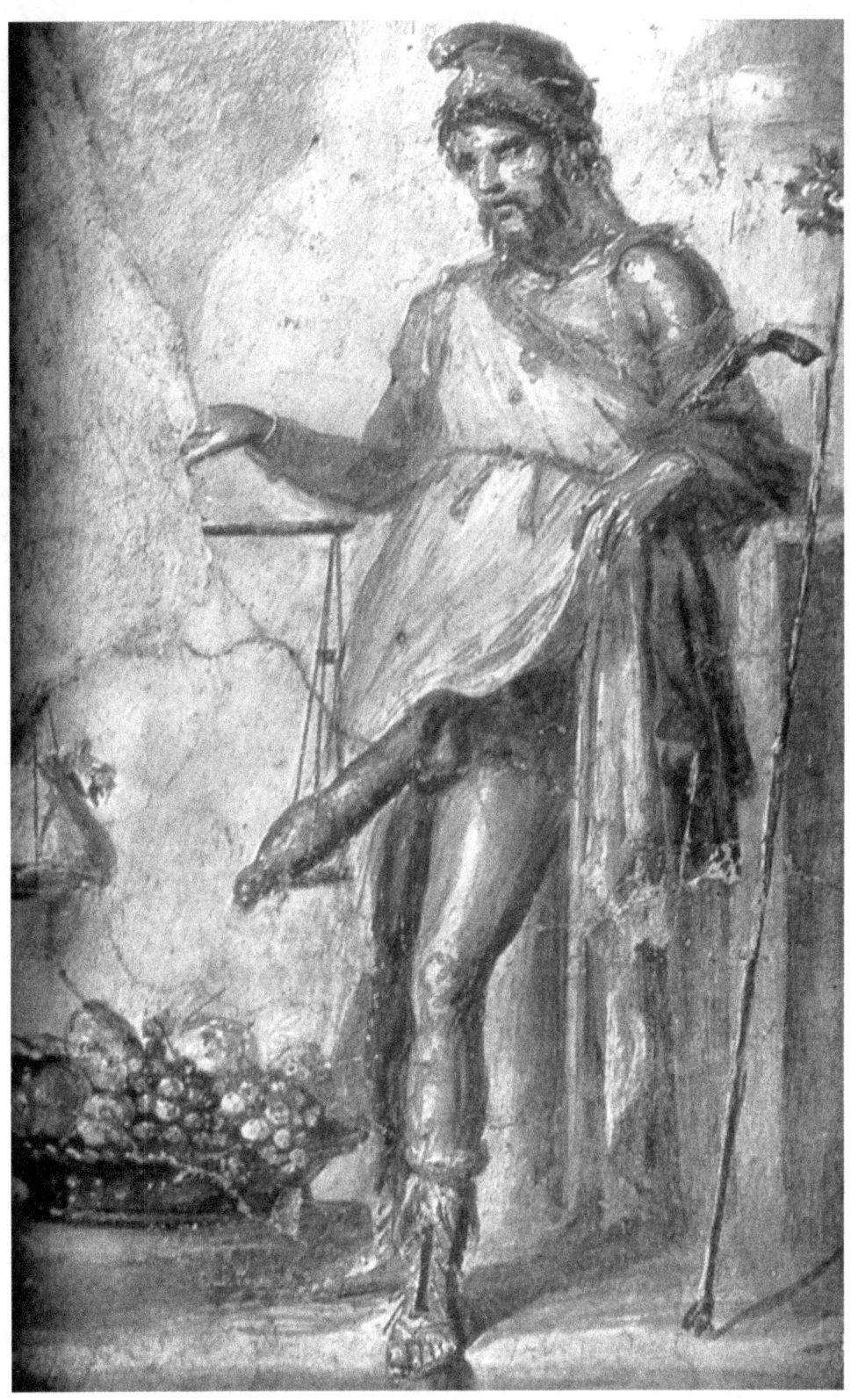

Fresco, Ancient Roman

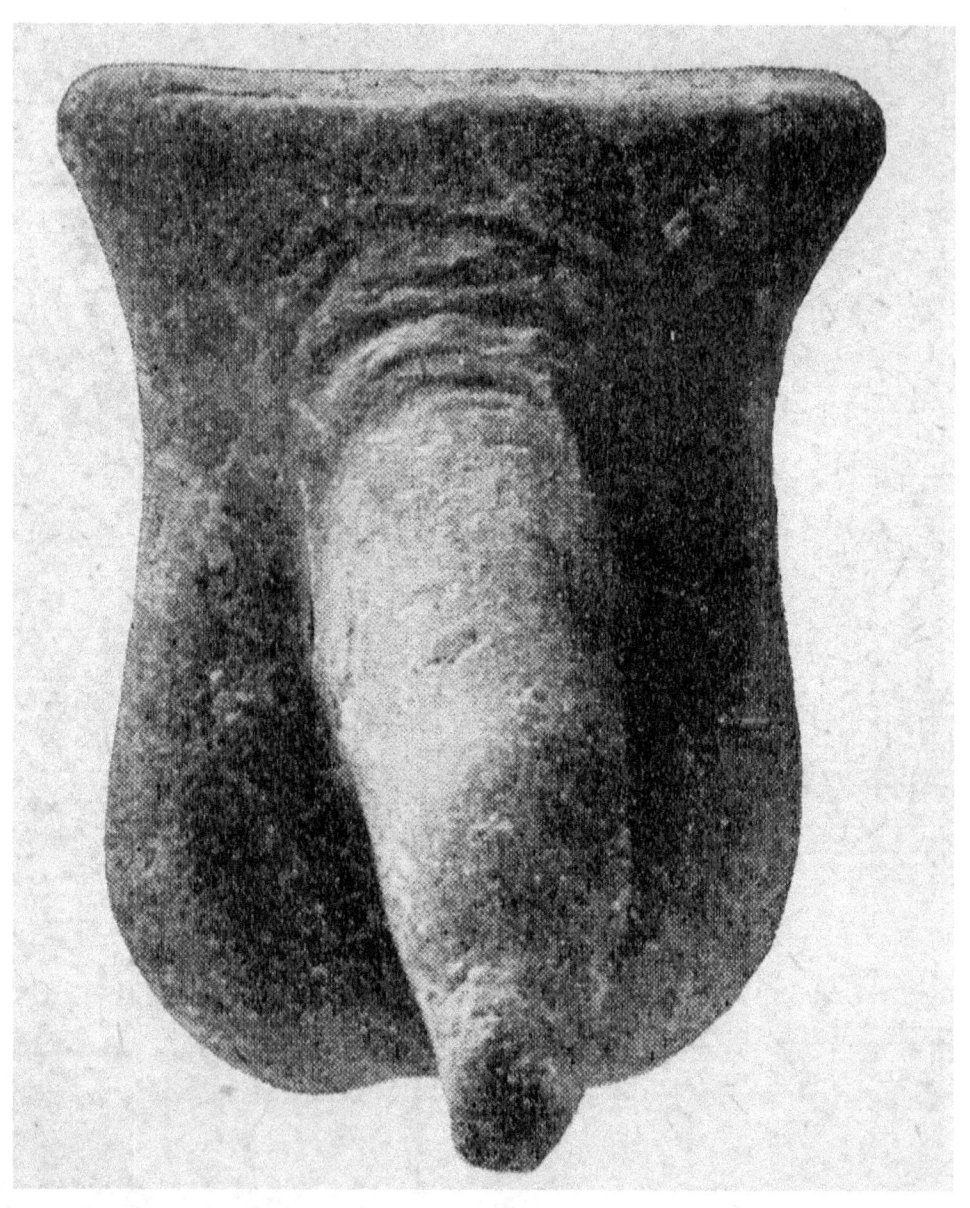

Ancient Votive Phallus, from Albert Moll, Handbuch der
Sexualwissenschaften, Verlag Von F.C. Vogel, Leipzig, 1921

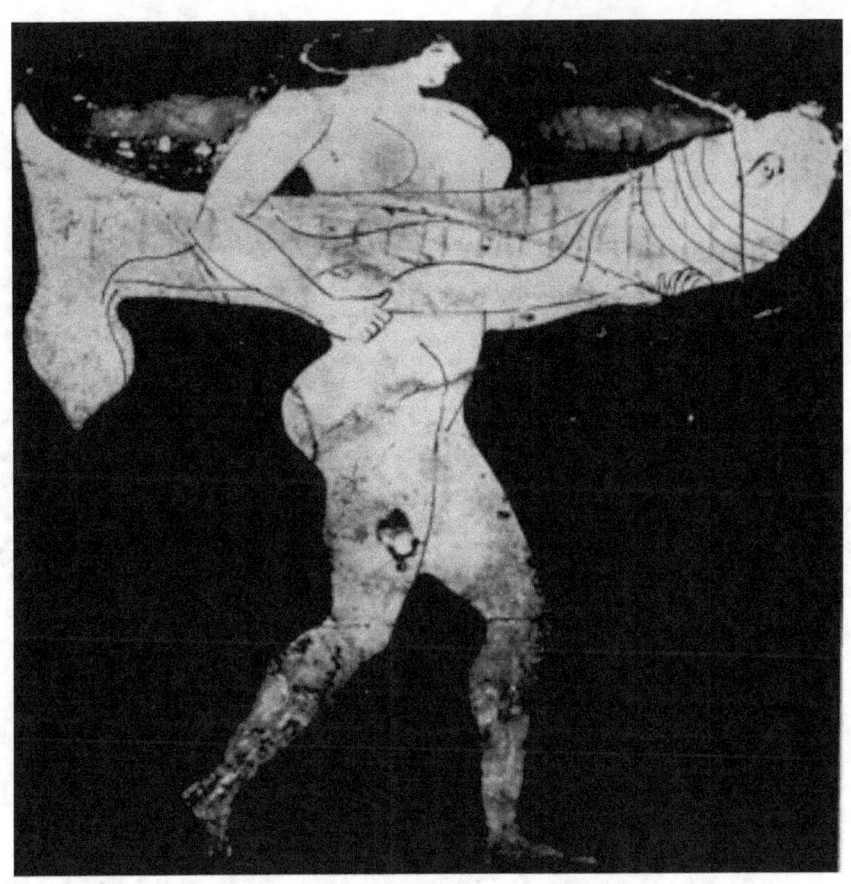

Vase, Ancient Greek

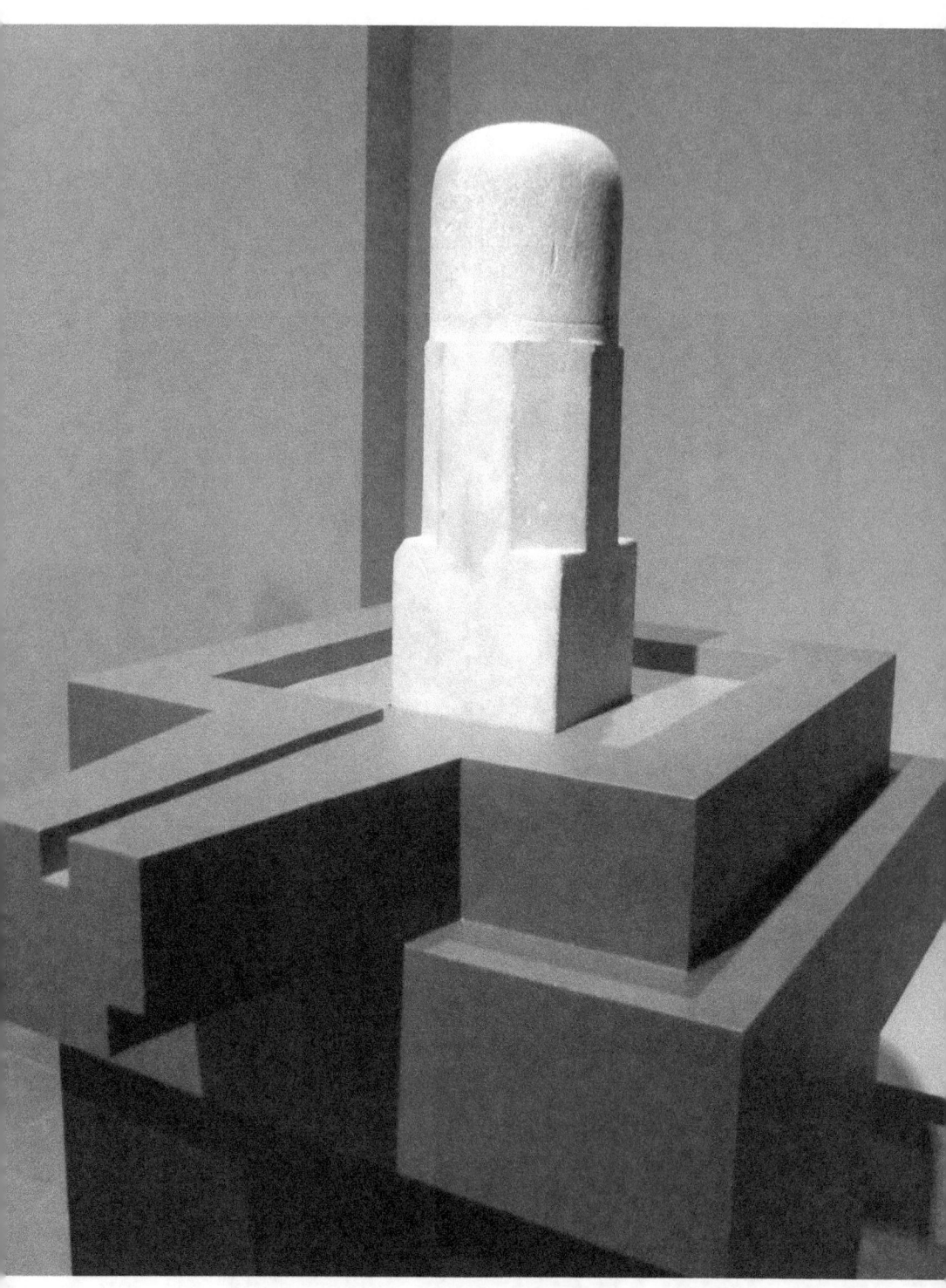

Lingam and Yoni, Cambodian, Norton Simon Museum, Pasadena, CA

Wood figure, Ivory
Coast

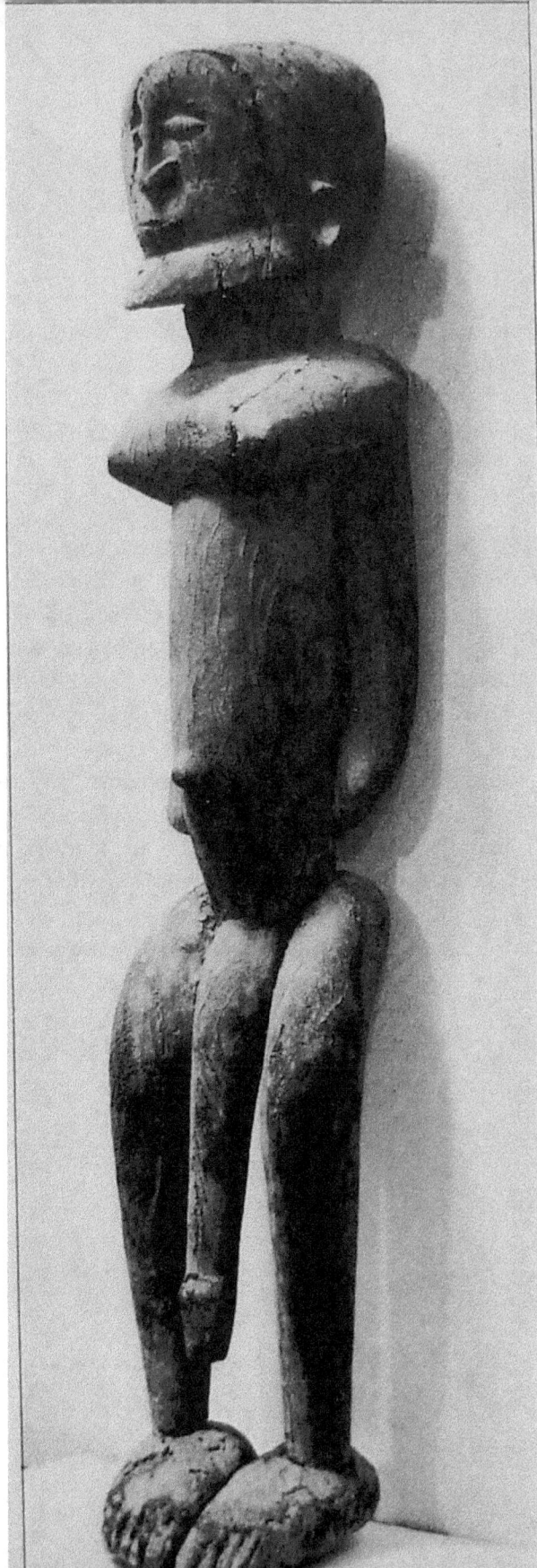

THE PHALLUS

Whole philosophic systems are based on the phallus, yet, as Juliet Mitchell remarked in "Feminine Sexuality':

> It's extraordinary what happens when you get rid of the centrality of the concept of the phallus. I mean, you get rid of the unconscious, get rid of sexuality, get rid of the original psychoanalytic point.[1]

If men reduce people to their sexual identities, as some feminists claim, then at the heart of this is the penis. Women are reduced to 'cunt', as Kate Millet put it, while men are all phallus. There are certainly no shortage of phallic symbols and artifacts about. The real thing, the real penis, is censored, carefully guarded – it's not much to look at anyway – so men displace their phallic sexuality onto thrusting cars, lorries, missiles, bombs, towers, cameras, computers, guitars, cigarettes, telephones, swords, guns, eyes, etc. These things abound in (patriarchal) art, and throughout the history of art (and pornography adds a million further fetishes). The trouble is that the penis ain't much of a thing, after all. As Richard Dyer commented: 'the fact is that the penis isn't a patch on the phallus. The penis can never live up to the mystique implied by the phallus'.[2]

1 J. Mitchell: "Feminine Sexuality: Interview with Juliet Mitchell and Jacqueline Rose", *m/f*, 8 (1983), 15.
2 R. Dyer: 'Don't Look Now", *Screen*, vol. 23, 3/4, 1983, and in A. McRobbie, 206.

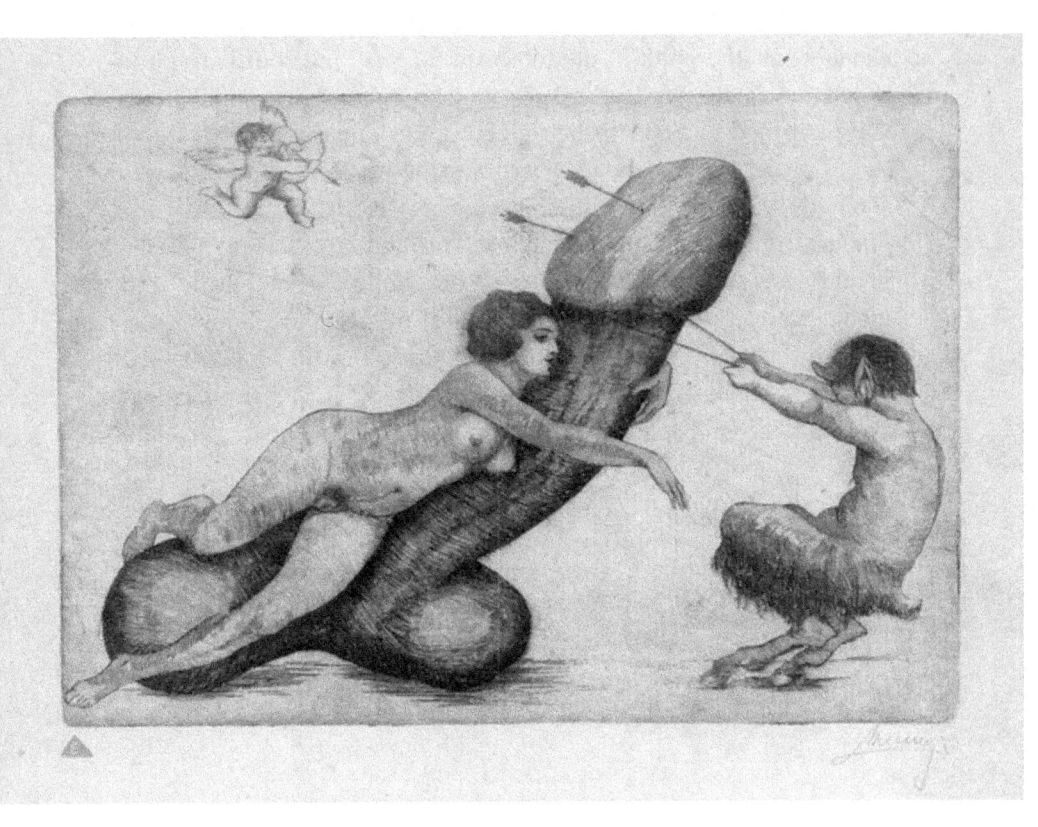

After Max Klinger (1857-1920)

In the (second wave) feminist view, the pornographer creates with his penis – the paintbrush, camera, computer or pen – these things are called 'tools', a common euphemism for the penis (there are thousands of other phallic control devices, such as game consoles, TVs, digital cameras, hi-fis, factory machinery, aeroplanes, etc). The quill, stylus or 'sharp projective' is a crucial element in the male's manufacture of art and pornography.[1] When Pierre Renoir was asked how he painted when he hands were crippled by arthritis he replied, '[w]ith my prick'.[2]

In pornography, the eye becomes the phallus, and looking is equated with caressing the obscure object of desire with the phallus (in the Lacanian system). Throughout Western art the phallus has been that visually absent but psychologically and ideologically present object. It is central in erotic art. Look at the Western art nudes – by Titian, Picasso, Ingres, Boucher: the phallus is there even though one doesn't see it. It's the same in any number of books, poems, sculptures, plays, operas, installations.

1 See J. Derrida: *Spurs: Nietzsche's Styles*, tr. B. Harlow, University of Chicago Press, Chicago 1979, 37-9; on the penis as a paintbrush, see Carol Duncan: "The Esthetics of Power in Modern Erotic Art", *Heresies*, 1, 1977, 46-50.
2 In J. Hobhouse, 135.

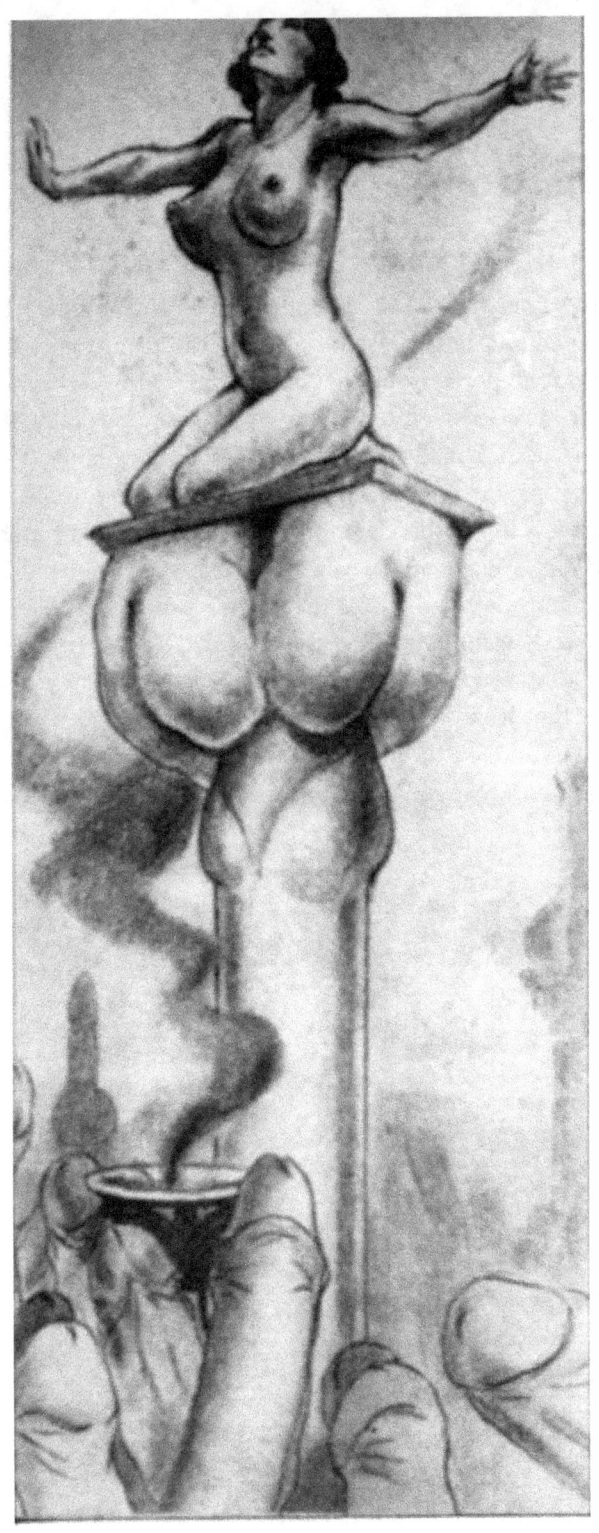

Anonymous, 19th century

LESBIAN EROTICISM

Lesbian sex is marked in contemporary cultural theory by the *lack* of the phallus. Hence, lesbian eroticism must always be 'deviant', because it departs from the patriarchal norms which exalt the phallus. Lesbianism must always be 'other', sexually, and many feminists note that the otherness of lesbian sexuality is one of the reasons that men and their patriarchal institutions are very threatened by lesbianism.[1] Lesbian attacks patriarchy at its powerbase. Men cannot control lesbians: '[l]esbians, by loving women and not men, pose a direct threat to the very basis of male supremacy', write Alice, Gordon, Debbie and Mary.[2] The lesbian is crucial, argued Monique Wittig, because she 'is the only concept that I know of which is beyond the categories of sex (man and woman)'.[3] Wittig moved towards a view of culture that goes beyond gender, beyond 'biological dimorphism', and biology.

---

1 T. Atkinson: *Amazon Odyssey*, Links Books, New York 1974; Alice, Gordon, Debbie and Mary: "Separatism", in S.L. Hoagland & J. Penelope, eds: *For Lesbians Only: A separatist anthology*, Onlywomen Press 1988, 31-40; A. Rich: "Towards a woman-centred university", in *On Lies, Secrets and Silence*, Novotny, New York 1979; J. Johnston: *Lesbian Nation: The Feminist Solution*, Simon & Shuster, New York 1974; S. Rowbotham: *Beyond the Fragments: Feminism and the making of Socialism*, Merlin 1979.
2 Alice, Gordon, Debbie and Mary, op. cit., 31-40.
3 M. Wittig: "One is not born a woman", in S. Hoagland, op. cit., 446-7.

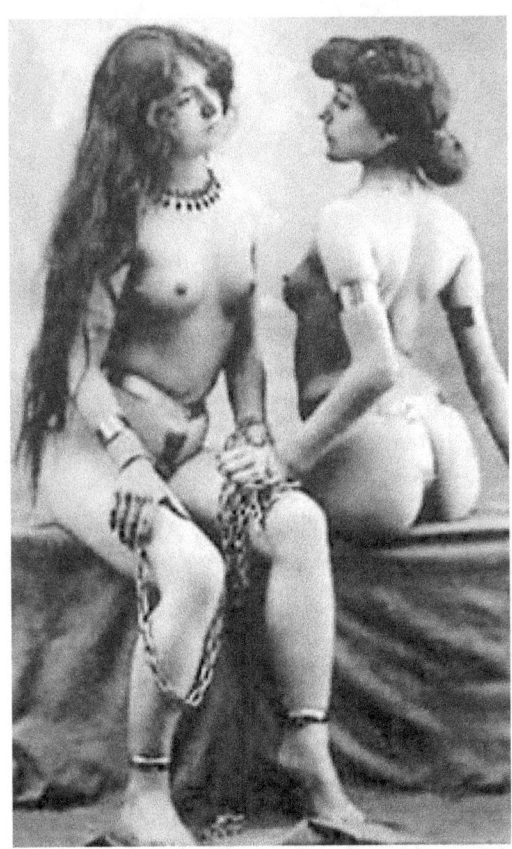

Anonymous, lesbian photograhs,
19th century

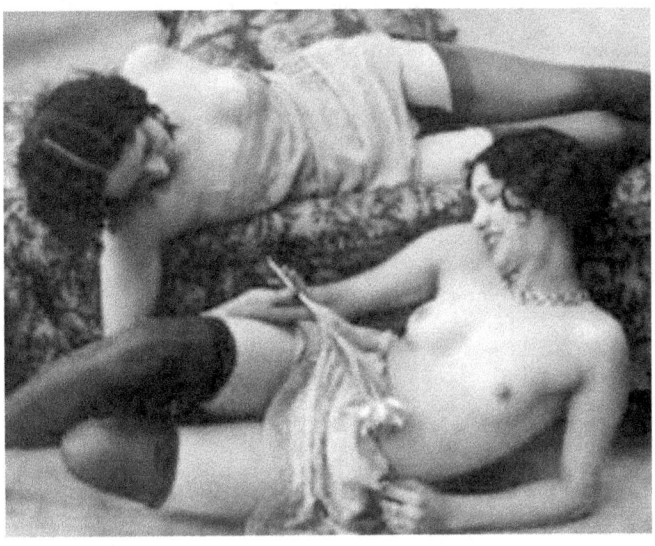

LESBIAN EROTICA

In heterosexual pornography, lesbian eroticism is often intro-
duced, but always controlled by a patriarchal force. Typically, in a
soft porn scenario, two bisexual women cavort on a bed overseen
by a male ('I've always wanted to see ya with another woman',
drools the man to his wife/ girlfriend; or, frequently, 'I got back
from work an' saw my wife an' her best friend writhin' on the
bed'). Towards the end of the scene, the man makes love to both
women. Why? Because they needed the phallus, they needed a
man to be fulfilled. Variations on this scenario occur endlessly in
pornography. The male presence (the phallus) is seen as
necessary for the true satisfaction for women (for valorization, for
authenticity: i.e., it's not *true* sex without the phallus).

Lesbian or women's pornography, made by women for
women, disappoints some feminists. Elizabeth Carola, who called
herself as a 'radical feminist lesbian', described magazines such as
*On Our Backs, Bad Attitude, OW! – Outrageous Women: A Journal of
Woman-to-Woman SM, Yellow Silk* and *The Power Exchange* in
"Women, Erotica, Pornography":

> Like all porn, this new 'woman's' porn is neither about nor for
> women. Like all porn it is, in a most basic sense, *against* women and
> *about* male fantasy – the basic male fantasy of Woman as Wholly
> Sexual Object whose Purpose is To Be Fucked – which feeds men's
> egos, fuels their violence…[1]

---

1 Elizabeth Carola: "Women, Erotica, Pornography: – Learning to Play the Game", in G.
Chester, 172.

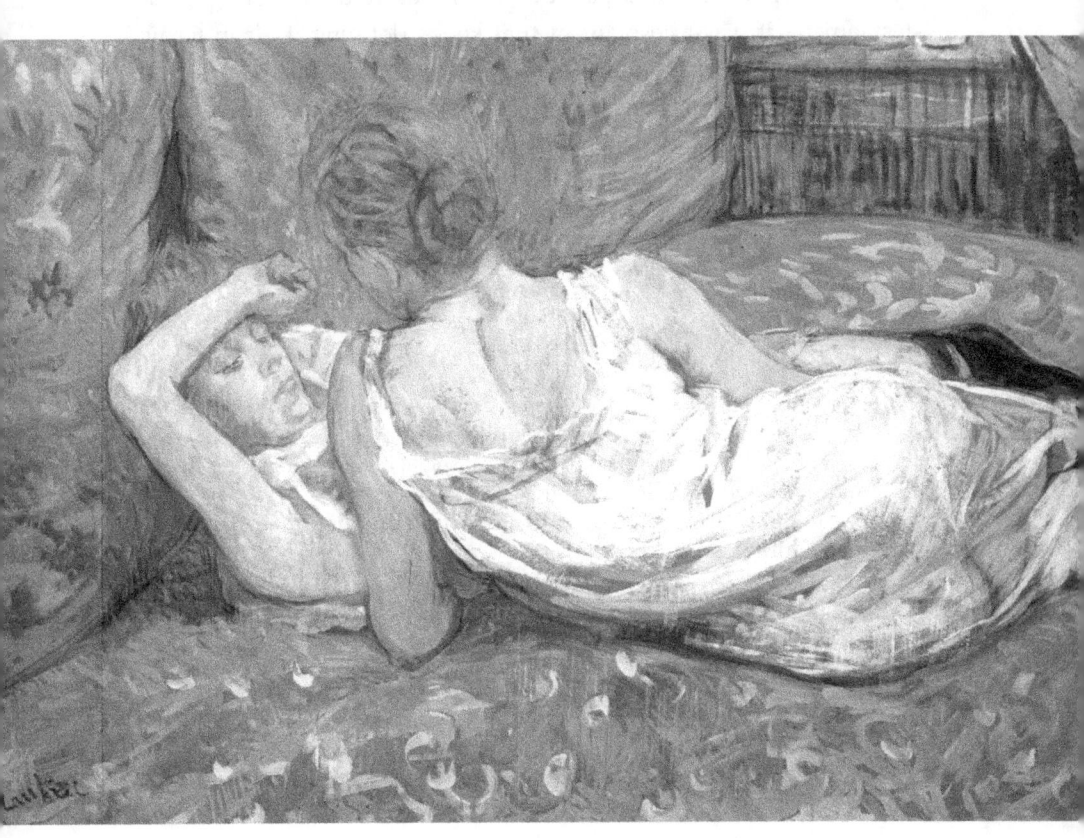

Henri de Toulouse-Lautrec (1864-1901), Two Friends

LESBIAN EROTICISM

Not all feminists agree about the revolutionary potential of lesbianism, if it is a lesbianism that keeps defining itself in terms of patriarchy. Elizabeth Mees reckoned that 'lesbianism, as an attack on hetero-relations, takes (its) place within the structure of the institution of heterosexuality. The lesbian is born of/ in it.'[1] There is no escape, it seems, from patriarchal and heterosexuality: the world is permeated with these ancient structures. As Sheila Jeffreys wrote: '[e]very woman grows up in a heteropatriarchal world',[2] while Ann Barr Snitow remarked in "Mass Market Romance':

> One of our culture's most intense myths, the ideal of an individual who is brave and complete in isolation, is for men only. Women are grounded, enmeshed in civilization, in social connection, in family and in love (a condition a feminist culture might well define as desirable) while all our culture's rich myths of individualism are essentially closed to them.[3]

1 E. Mees, in K. Jay & J. Glasgow: *Lesbian Text and Contexts: Radical Revisions*, New York University Press, New York, NY, 1990, 82.
2 S. Jeffreys: "The Censoring of Revolutionary Feminism", in G. Chester, 139.
3 A. Snitow: "Mass Market Romance: Pornography for Women Is Different", *Radical History Review*, no. 20, Spring/Summer, 1979.

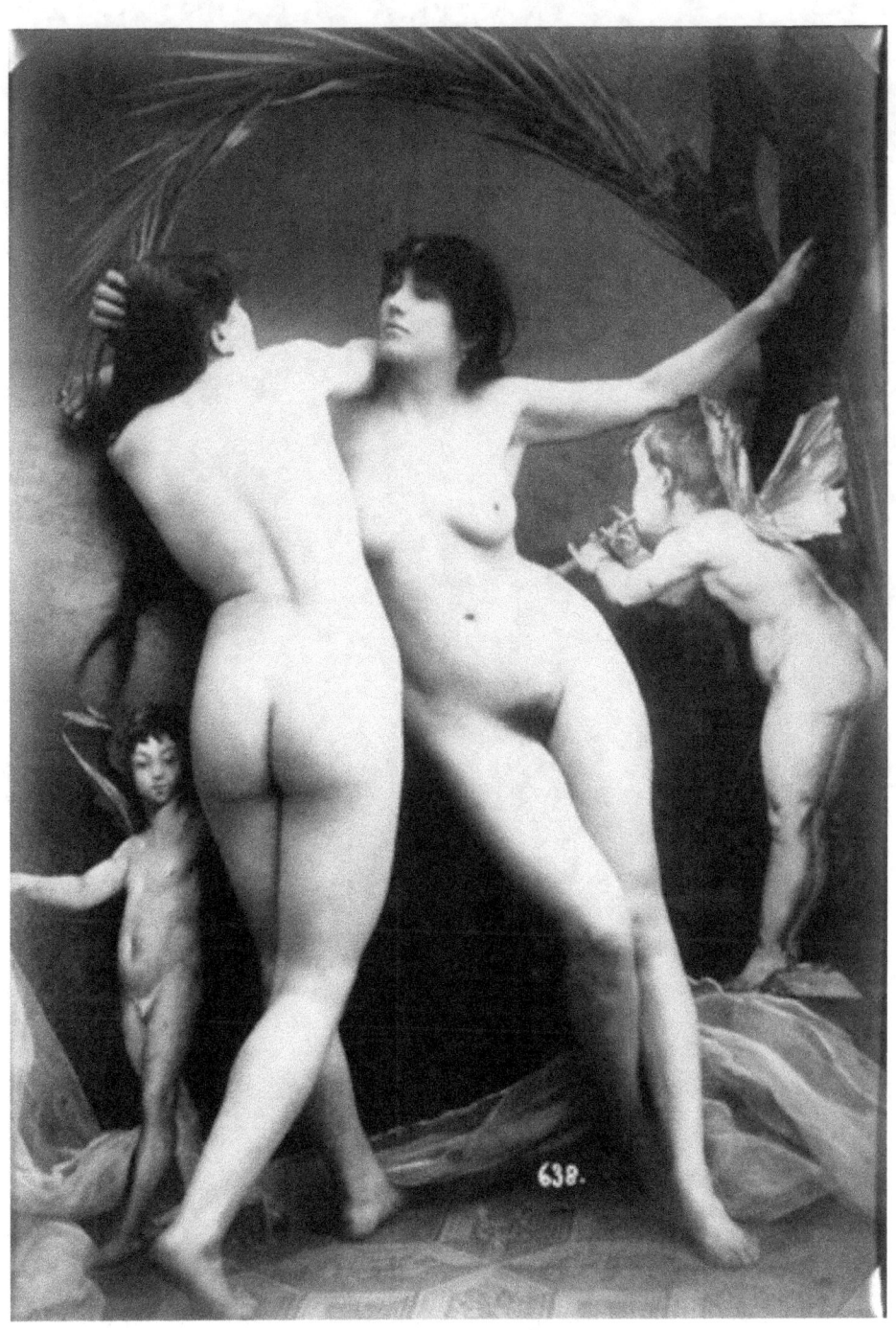

Gaudenzio Marconi (1841-85), Nudes and Angels, 1880s

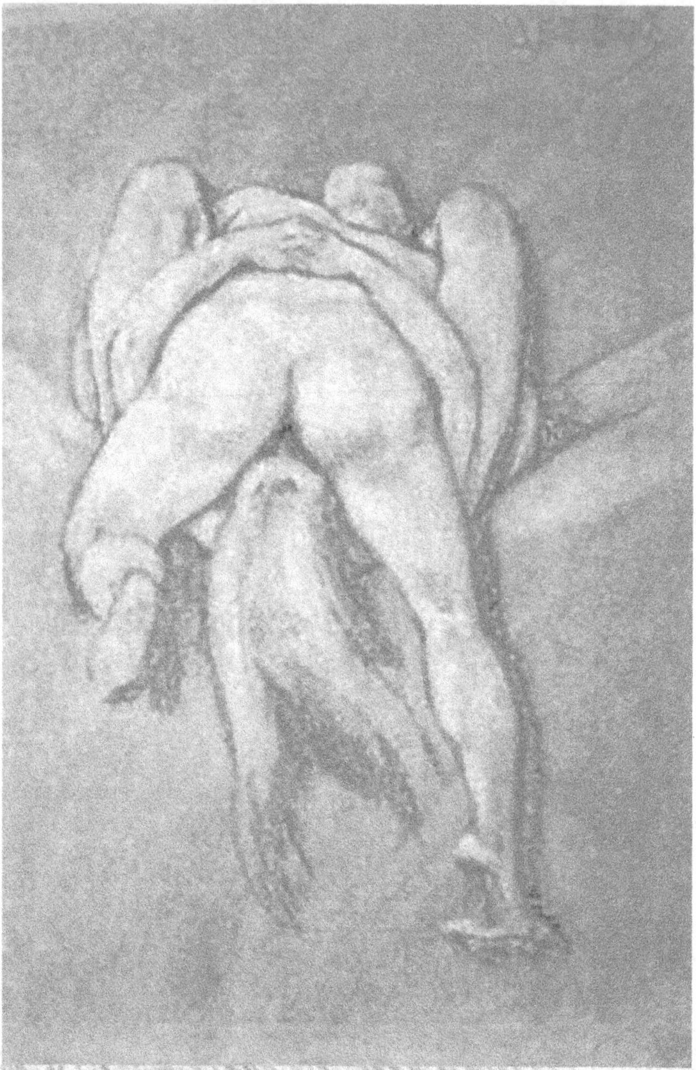

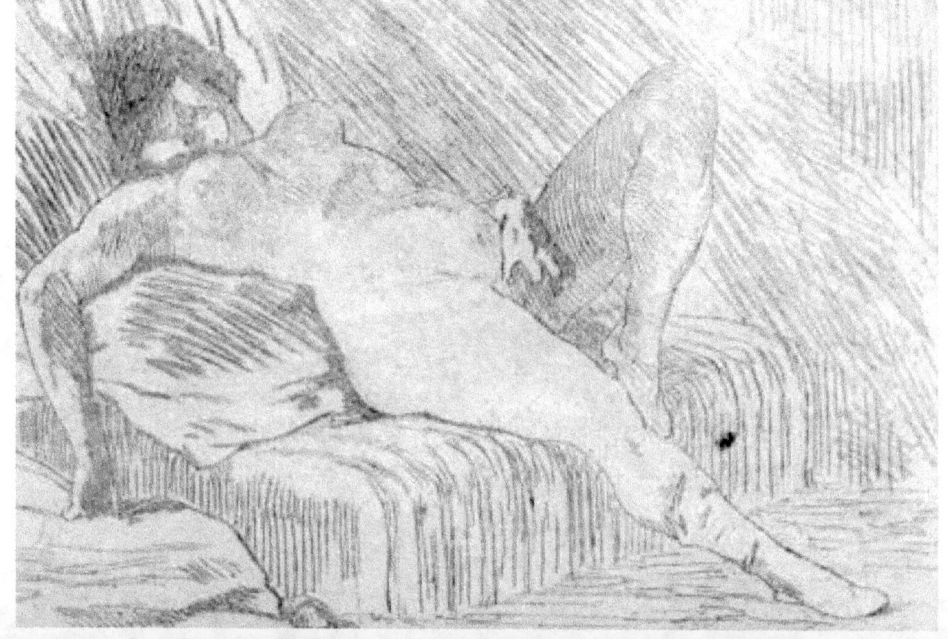

Félicien Rops,
Lesbians (left).

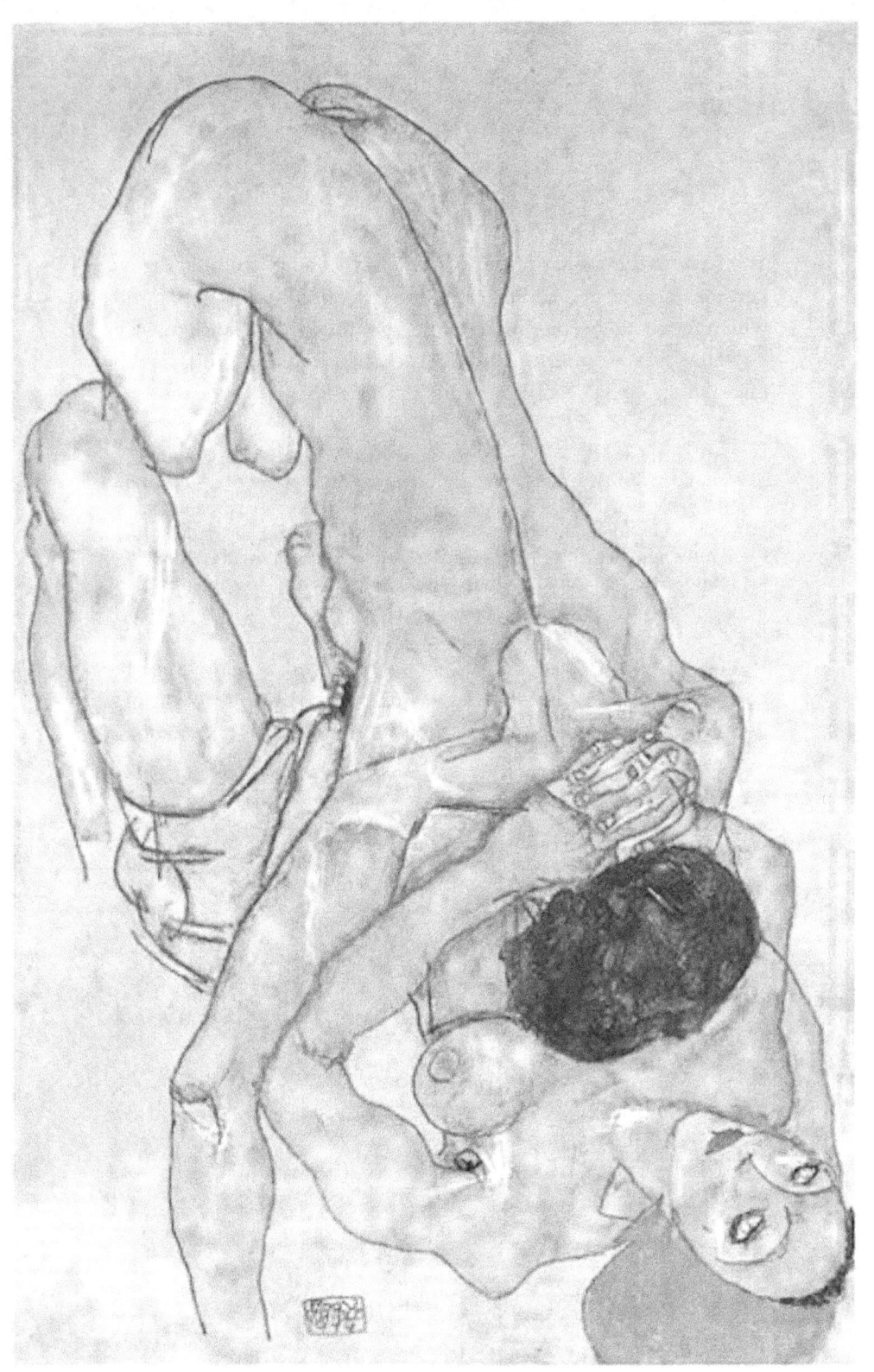

Egon Schiele, Two Women Lovers, 1914

VOYEURISM

The Lacanian Look emphasizes eroticism. Seeing is erotic, the eye becomes a kind of phallus, caressing the obscure object of desire, which it can never 'possess'. As the poet Rainer Maria Rilke wrote '[g]azing is a wonderful thing.'[1] The act of looking eroticizes the object. Jack Zipes describes it thus in *Don't Bet On the Prince*:

> For him [Lacan], seeing is desire, and the eye functions as a kind of phallus. However, the eye cannot clearly see its object of desire, and in the case of male desire, the female object of desire is an illusion created by the male unconscious. Or, in other words, the male desire for woman expressed in the gaze is auto-erotic and involves the male's desire to have his own identity reconfirmed in a mirror image.[2]

The look is an assertion of male power and sexuality. For the gaze is male, and feminists have grappled with the notion of a 'female' gaze, whether there can be such a thing as a 'female' or 'feminine' gaze.[3]

1 R. Rilke, letter to Clara Rilke, 8 March 1907, in *Gesammalte Briefe 1892-1926*, Insel Verlag, Leipzig 1940, II, 279f
2 Jack Zipes: *Don't Bet on the Prince: Contemporary Feminist Fairy Tales in North America and England*, Gower, Aldershot 1986, 258
3 Maggie Humm: "Is the gaze feminist? Pornography, film and feminism", *Perspectives on Pornography*, eds G.Day & C. Bloom, Macmillan 1988; Lorraine Gamran & Margaret Marshment, eds: *The Female Gaze*, Women's Press 1988; E.D. Pribram, ed: *Female Spectators: looking at film and television*, Verso, 1988

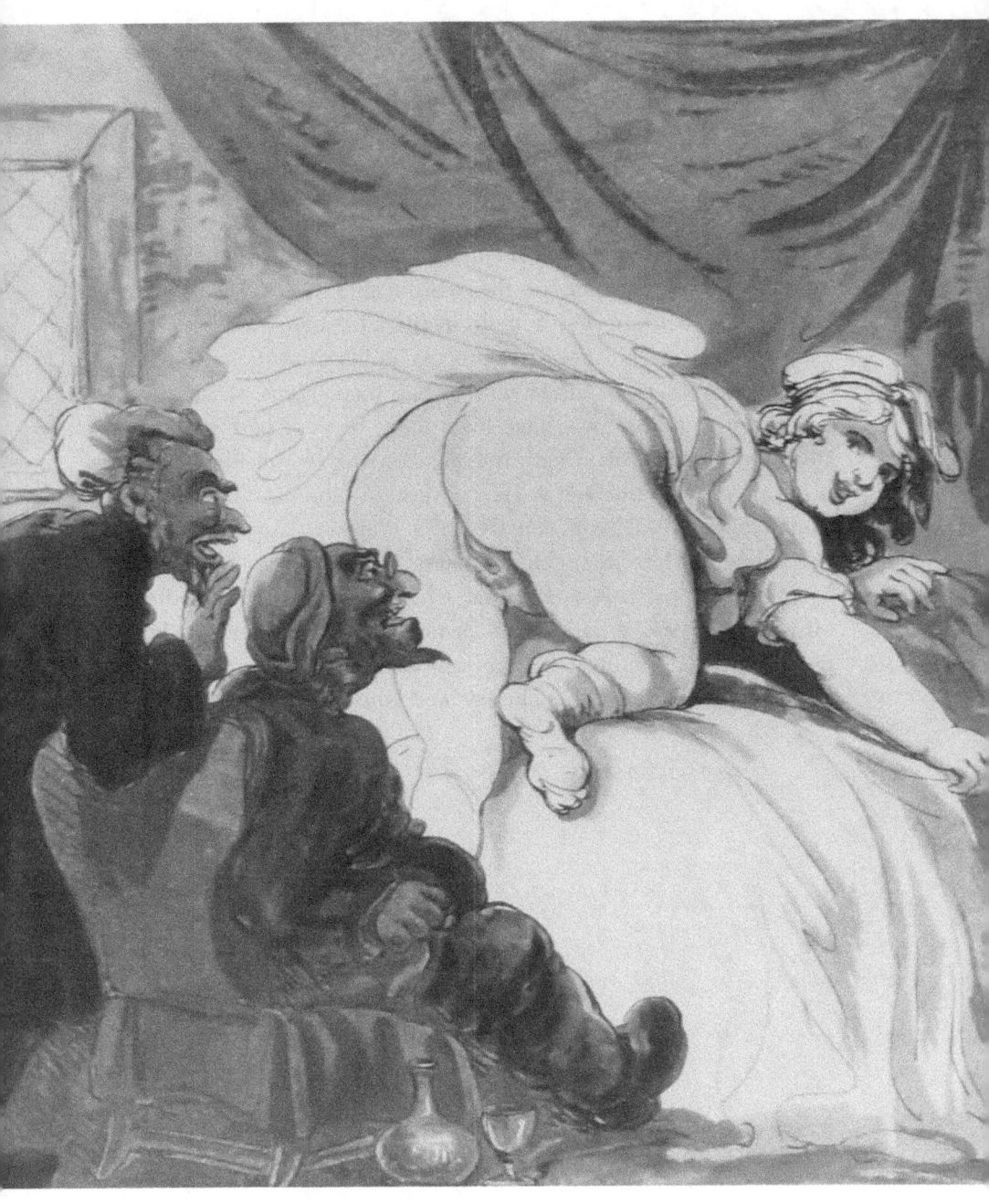

Thomas Rowlandson, Susannah and the Elders, 1820, London

SEX AND DEATH

Pain is good, because it means you are fully alive. This is the Existential view of patriarchal culture. 'Sensual pleasure is agony in the strictest meaning of the word', says C. Mauclair in a Freudian tone.[1] Suffering is holy, in the Christian tradition. The journey from martyrdom to sainthood and beatification is swift. The West exalts pain. Christ *suffered*, say theologians, so he must have been right, he must have lived hard, because he died hard. Death becomes heroic. Death transfigures people. Suicide is even better, if you can manage it. Hence Marilyn Monroe, Vincent van Gogh, Johann Wolfgang von Goethe's Werther, Virginia Woolf. Die young, and become famous (many artists have followed this equation: Egon Schiele, Frédéric Chopin, Wolfgang Amadeus Mozart, Georges Seurat, James Dean, Paula Modersohn-Becker, D.H. Lawrence, Jimmy Hendrix, Jim Morrison, Arthur Rimbaud, Raphael, John Keats, Percy Shelley, and Novalis.

---

1 C. Mauclair: *Magie de l'amour*, 145, quoted in Julius Evola, 84

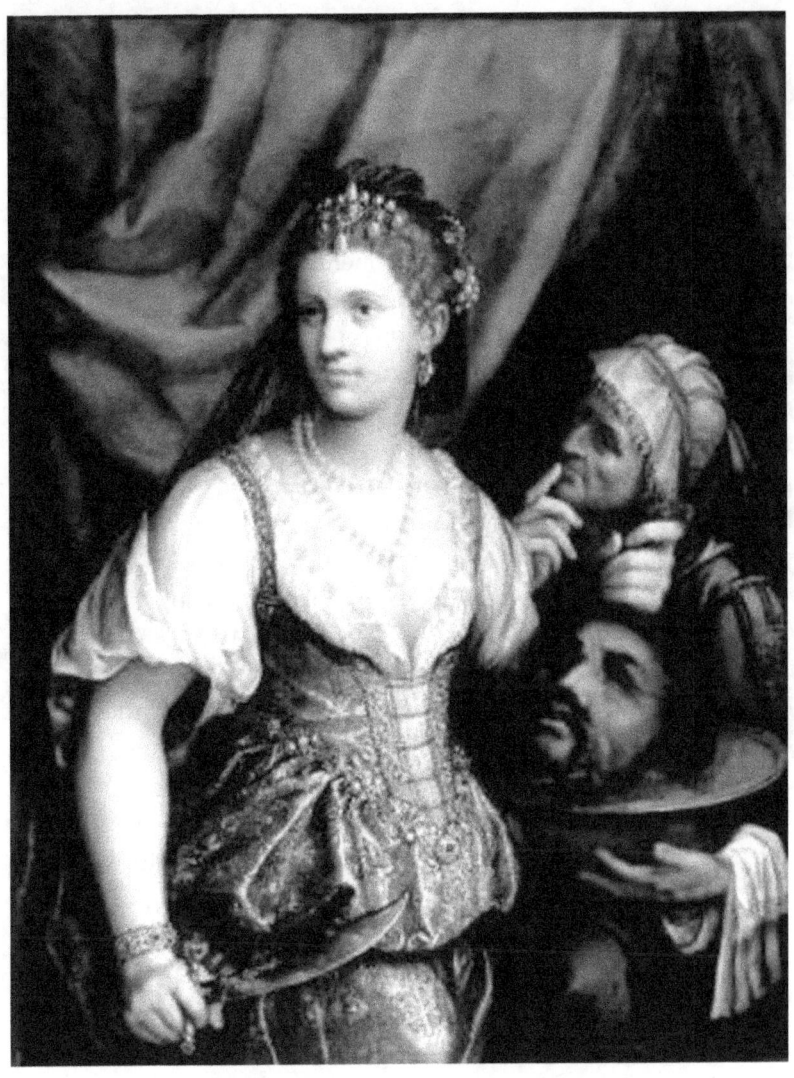

Fede Galizia, Judith with the Head of Holofernes,
Museum of Art, Sarasota, Florida

PREHISTORIC ART

It would be possible to argue that prehistoric art is patriarchal and masculine in nature, with its images of hunting and killing animals, its emphasis on death and survival (masculine, Existential concerns, from Charles Darwin to Jean-Paul Sartre), and the harshness of its environment. A discourse of heroic survival against the odds, against a hostile and unforgiving natural world. In fact, there is a mass of 'feminine' mystery and imagery in prehistoric art: for instance, in the many statues or figurines of nameless Goddesses, known as "Stone Venuses", which have been found.[1] (The modern artist Louise Bourgeois has produced sculptures that are very much like the "Stone Venuses": her *Stake Woman* is a rounded, headless, armless form, with two prominent 'breasts' and the overall shape of a vessel).[2] There is a widespread acceptance of Goddess worship as being older than God worship. The Goddess, wrote Robert Graves, is 'immortal, changeless, and omnipotent'.[3] In the beginning, it seems, was the Mother, not the Father. As Robert Briffault remarkedin*The Mothers*: '[t]he All-Mother is older than the All-Father'.[4] Some commentators extend Goddess religion back beyond the cults of Classical and ancient Goddesses – before the era of ancient world deities such as Isis, Ishtar, Aphrodite, Diana – to prehistoric times.

1 *Venus of Willendorf*, Austria, limestone, palæolithic (end of Gravettian); *Venus of Kostenki*, Moravia, mammoth ivory, palæolithic (Gravittian)
2 Louise Bourgeois: *Stake Woman*, c. 1970, pink marble, 11.4cm high, private collection
3 Robert Graves: *The Greek Myths*, I, Penguin 1948, 13
4 Robrt Briffault: *The Mothers: A Study of the Origins of Sentiments and Institutions*, Allen & Unwin 1927, III, 180

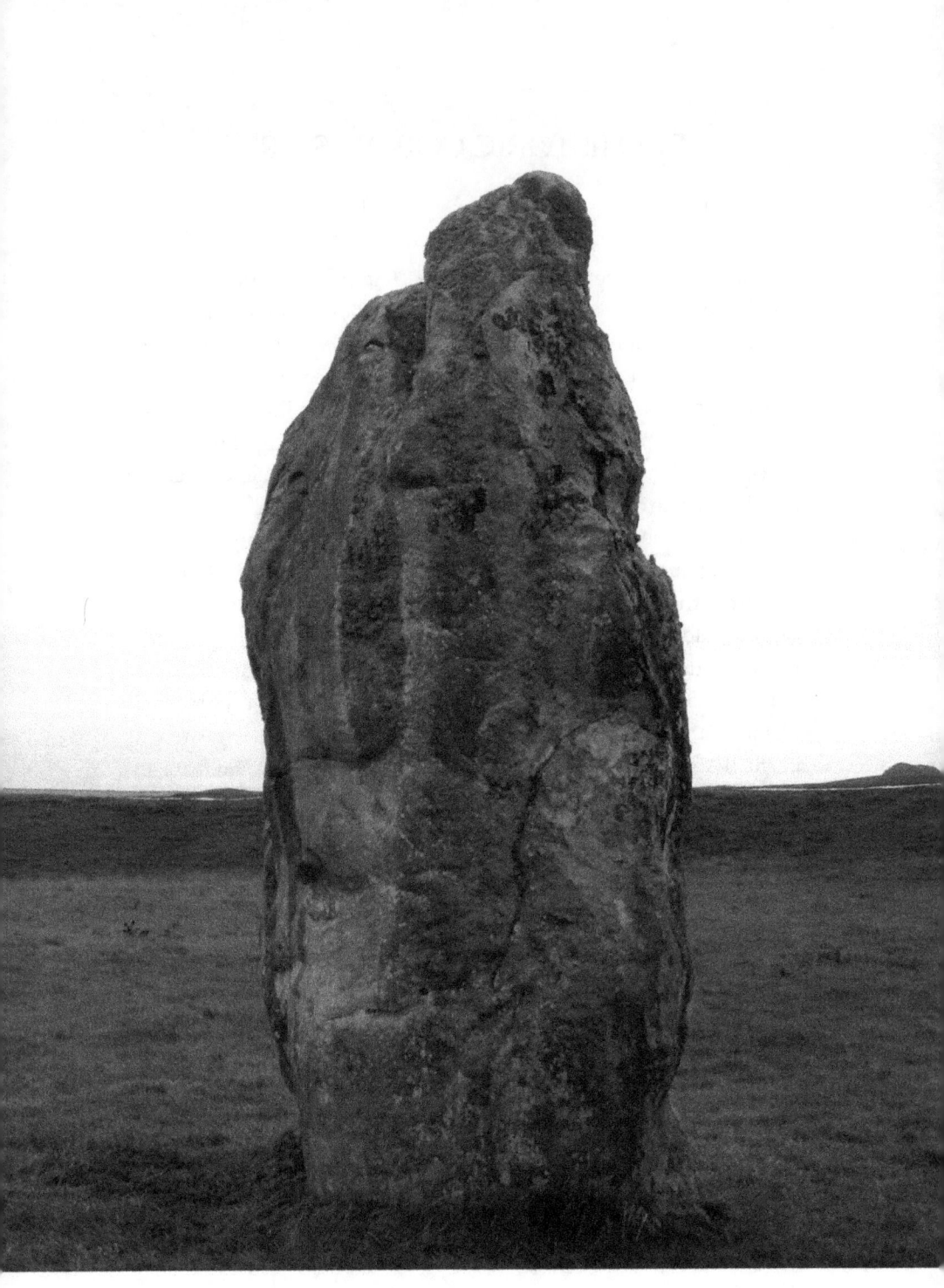

Avebury, Wiltshire, England

PREHISTORIC GODDESS ART

If you want to see evidence of the 'feminine' or the Goddess everywhere, you can. It's easy. Take the circular shapes of Avebury or Stonehenge, Britain's two great stone circles: these have to do with the ancient symbolism of the circle, with time, seasons, cycles, infinity, the 'great round' of life: this is the Goddess. The circle becomes a womb, if you like, the circular space in which the mysteries of life are experienced, and later are ritualized. The circle is 'female', if you want.

One can see the Goddess or the 'eternal feminine' in those "Stone Venus" figurines, and, later, in the Neolithic stones or menhirs, the standing stones, some of which had Goddesses carved onto them.[1] One can see the 'feminine' in the long uterine passages and entrances to tombs, so that the 'poetic' connection of womb = tomb has an ancient dimension, as well as occurring in Elizabethan poetry, for instance (William Shakespeare in particular was fond of the womb/ tomb trope, later taken up by Samuel Beckett). Thus, the bones covered in red ochre are put back into the 'womb' of the Earth, and bodies in burial lie in the foetal position.

Female eroticism plays a large part in prehistoric art. Women, in the carved figurines are mothers, and birth and motherhood are exalted. Hence some people think women were at the centre of prehistoric life in some places. Women, some thinkers reckon, held positions of power: they controlled 'trade' in sexual pleasure, for instance; they could withhold pleasure, and thus, with their knowledge of the menstrual cycle, they could exert power over men.[2]

1 Menhir statue of a woman, sandstone, St-Sernin, France. Neolithic, c. 2000 BC, Musée des Antiquités
2 See Chris Knight: *Blood Relations*, Yale University Press 1991; Peter Redgrove: *The Black Goddess*; Penelope Shuttle & Peter Redgrove: *The Wise Wound*

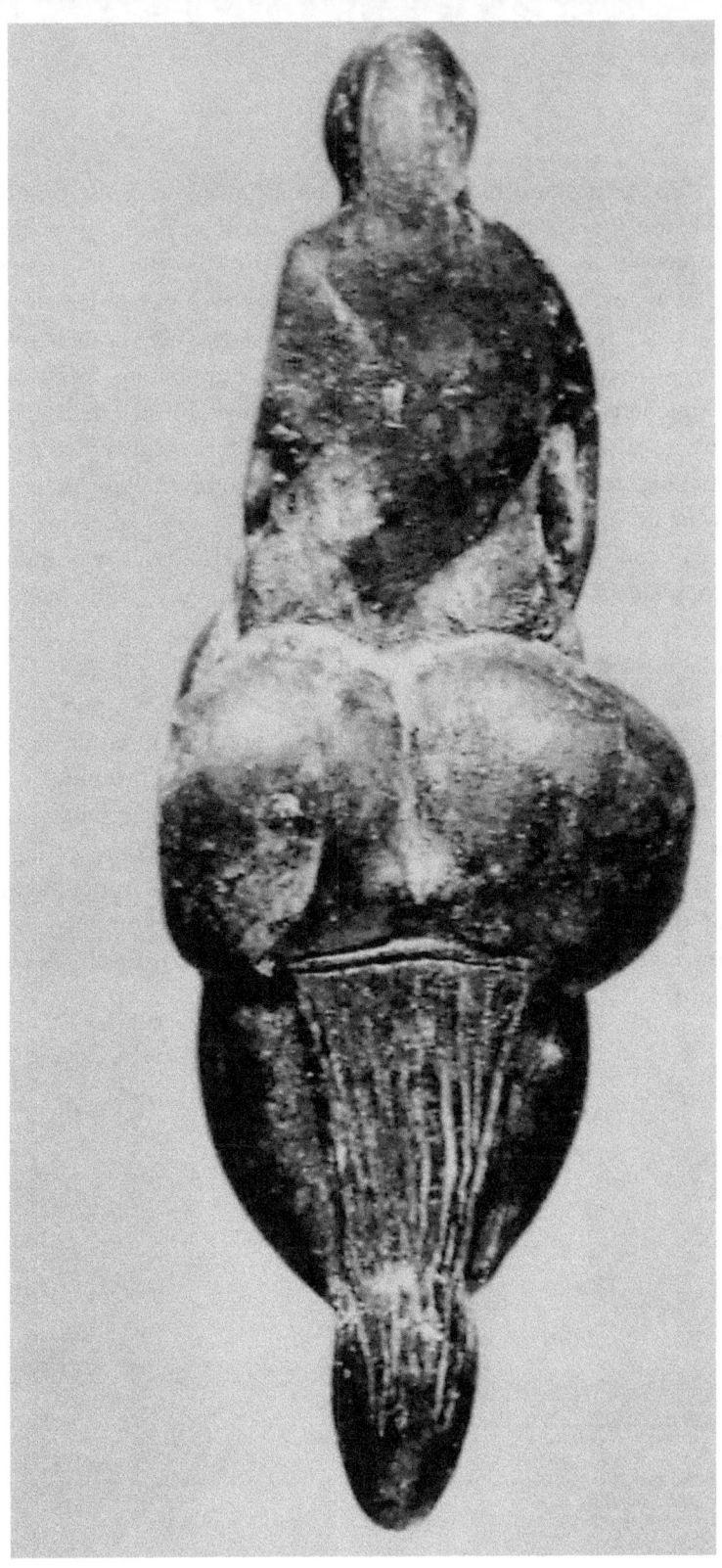

Venus of Willendorf, prehistoric, Vienna

Art critics and historians look back fondly on erotic primitive art, for there was a time, it is felt, when sexuality was freely expressed in art, without the 'hang-ups' of the modern era. Clearly, art critics, sociologists, historians and psychologists look back at prehistoric and primitive art nostalgically, in their search for a 'sexually liberated' space, to use that telling 1960s term. Depictions of sex abound, or seem to, in prehistoric and ancient art. A 2000 B.C. terracotta relief from Babylonia shows two people making love from behind; a Libyan demon makes love to a woman, in a 5000 B.C. engraving; someone sucks someone else's penis on a ceramic vessel from 500 A.D. Peru; two animals copulate in a 300 B.C. Peruvian carving.[1] Figures with over-size erections are commonplace – they are fertillity figures, aids in magical rites, talismans and fetishes.

In prehistoric art, sexuality is associated with religion; sexuality is religious, and the religious dimension has an erotic element in it. Notions of fertility, magic, sexuality, agriculture and so on are entwined. The obviousness of such statements needs to be remembered constantly, especially since our era is so unmagical. J.G. Frazer prudishly writes in *the Golden Bough*: 'ruder races in other parts of the world have consciously employed the intercourse of the sexes as a means to ensure the fruitfulness of the earth.[2]

1 *Terracotta relief depicting copulation from behind*, Mesopotamia, Babylonian period, c. 2000 BC; *Semi-human sexual demon*, rock engraving, Ti-n-Lalan, Libyan Fezzan, c.5000 BC, Fabrizio Mori, Rome; *Ceramic Vessel*, Mochica Culture, Peru, c. 500 AD, Institute for Sex Research, Indiana University
2 J.G> Frazer: *The Golden Bough*, abridged edition, Macmillan 1959, 136

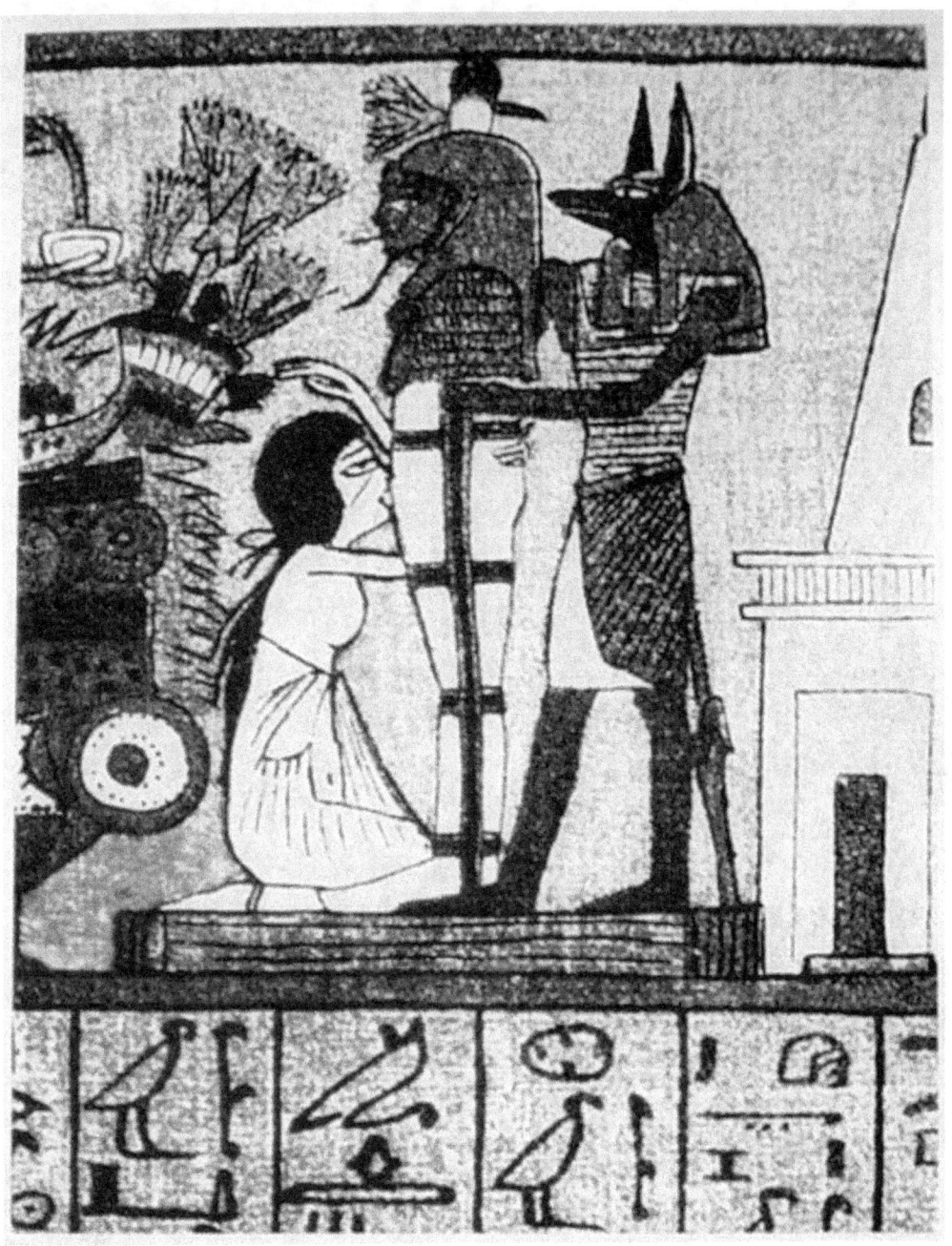

Ancient Egyptian, Isis and Osiris

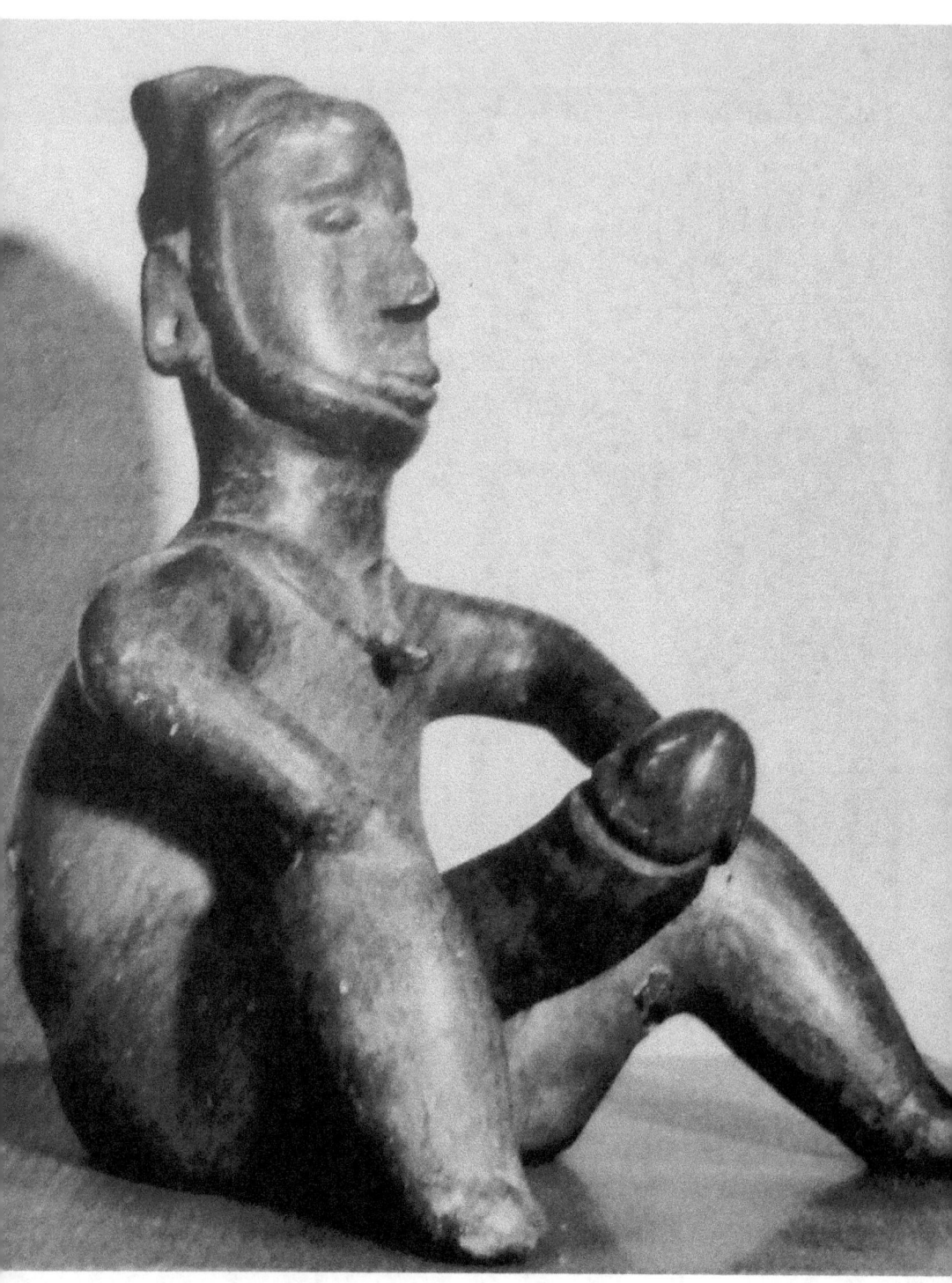

Terra cotta figure, 3rd century BC. Mexico

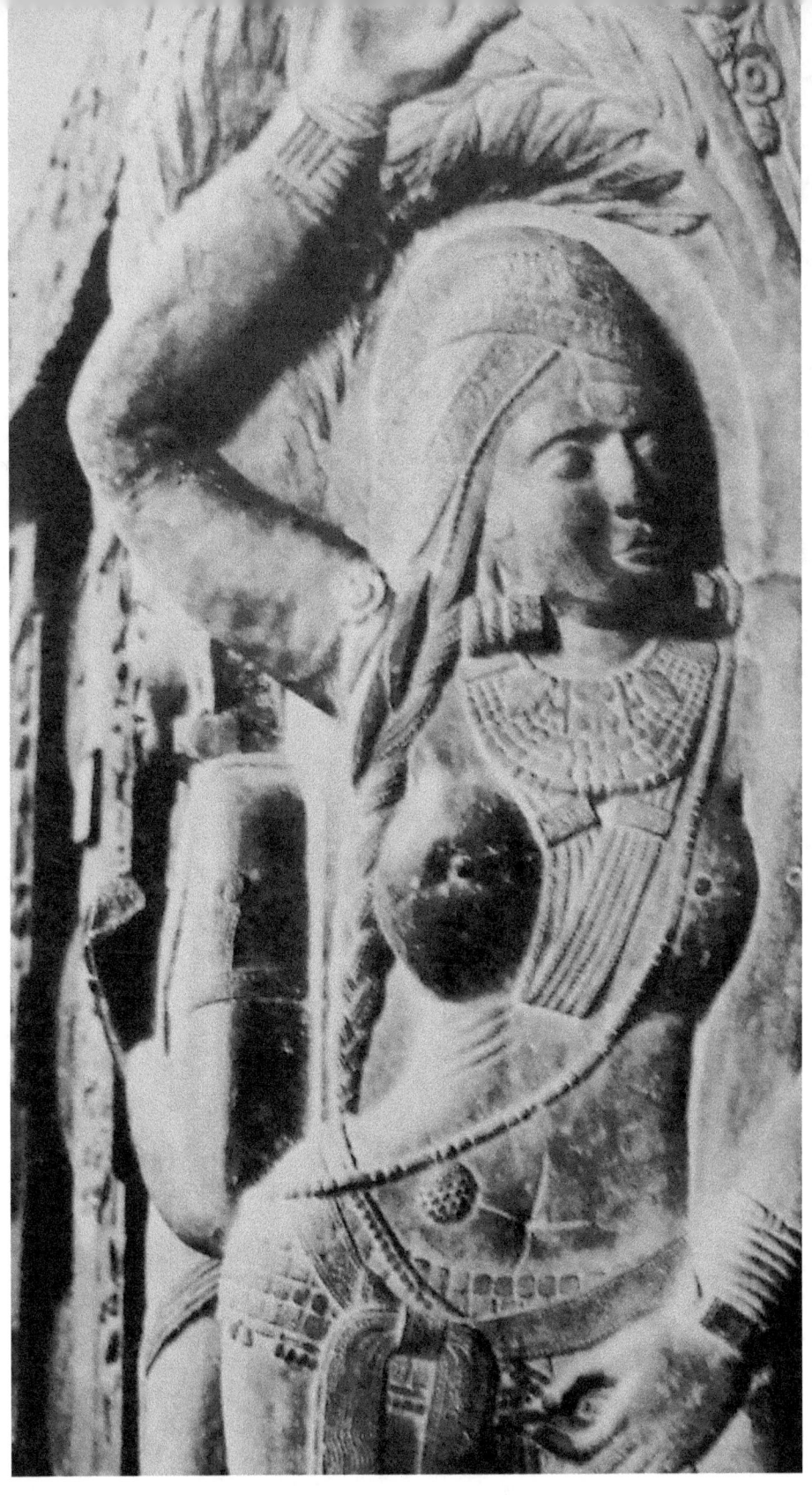

Yakshi figure, Indian Museum, Caluctta

POMPEII

Some of the most celebrated and widely-known examples of erotic art in the ancient world are the wall frescoes at Pompeii. One of the reasons is surely the clarity of the imagery – it's easy to see what's going on here. Also, the visual approach, in flattened two dimensions, which looks forward to the development of Renaissance space. And of course the sweetness and tenderness of the sex acts depicted.

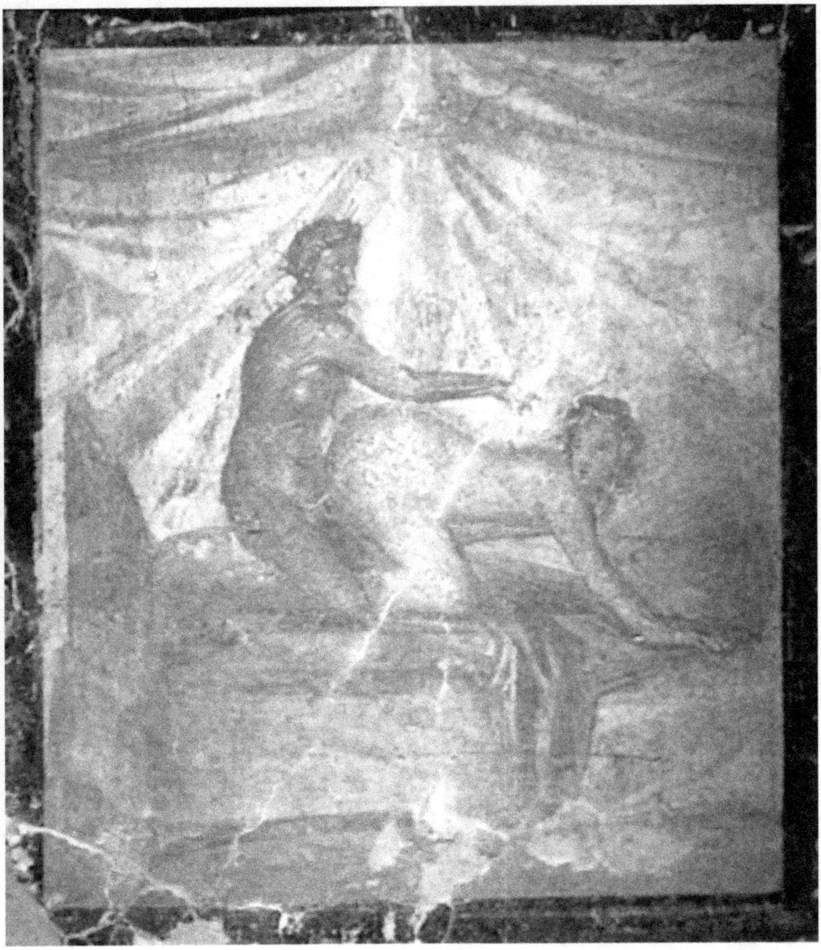

Ancient Roman art, Pompeii

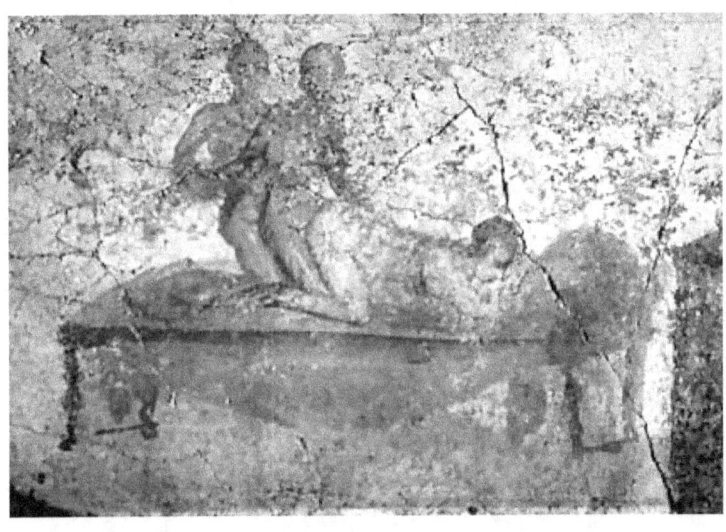

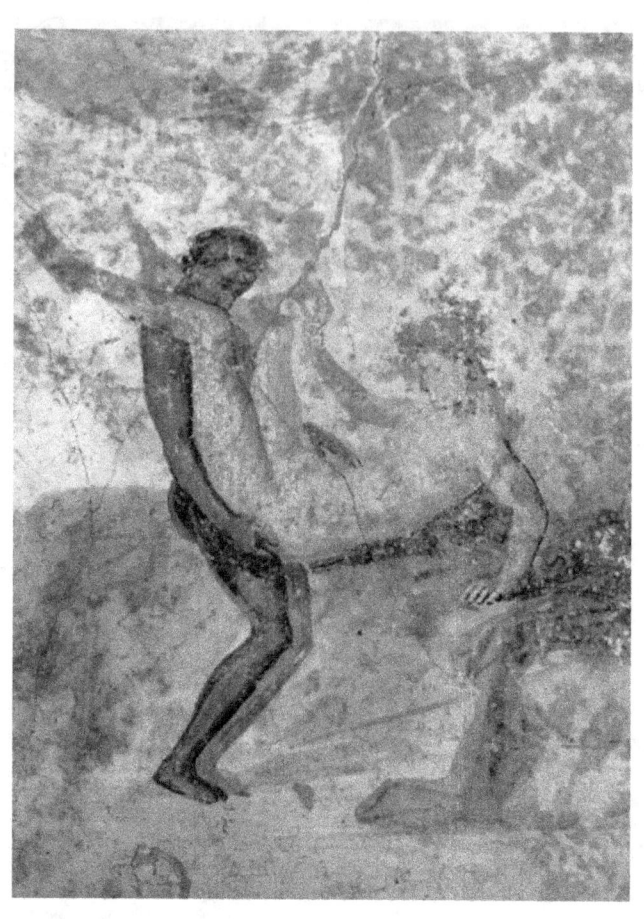

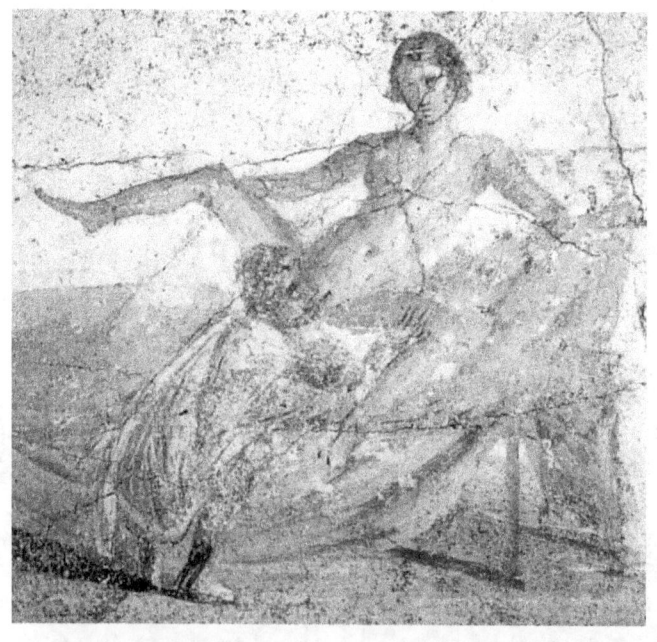

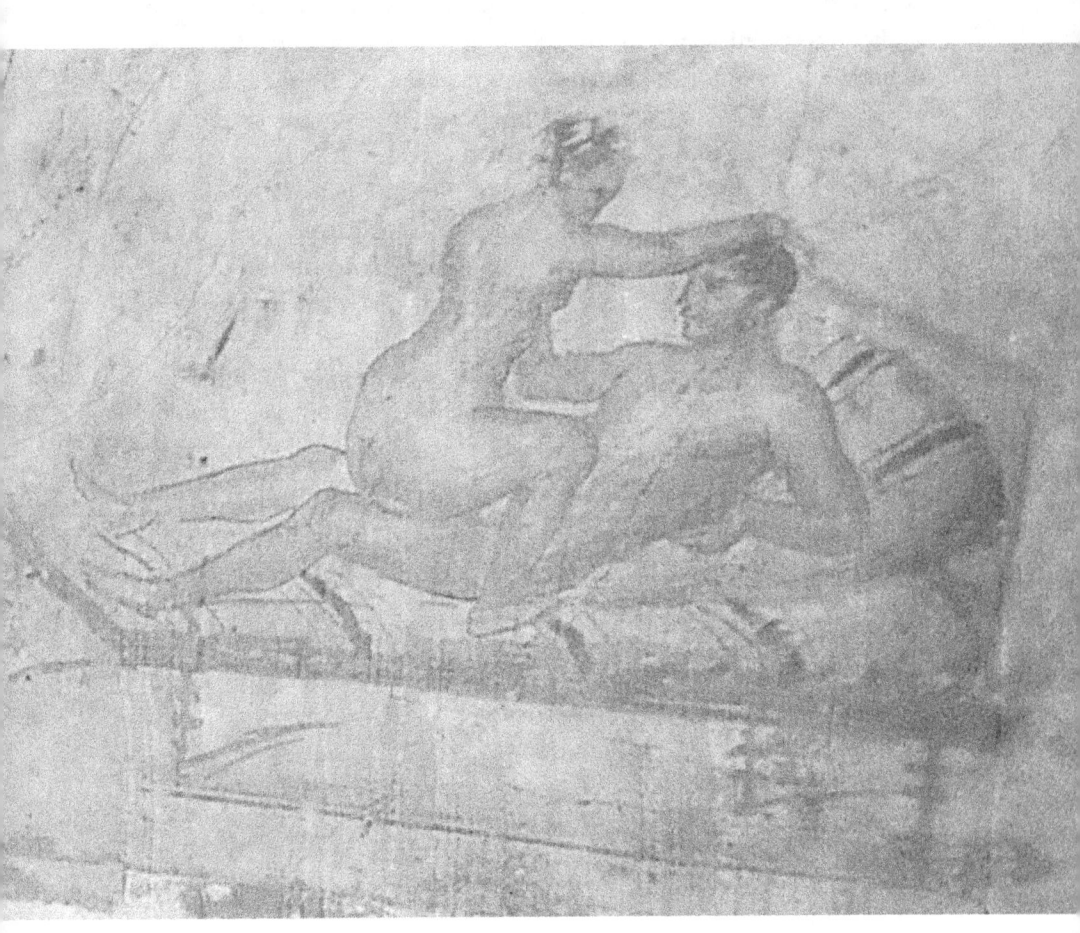

Pompeii wall painting

GREEK ART

Ancient Greek culture is everywhere celebrated as the one of the foundations of Western culture. So much of ancient Greek culture – the arts, politics, philosophy, writing, structures and ideas – is found throughout Western culture. Ancient Greek art remains the highpoint of Western art. You name it, the ancient Greeks did it – and much better than just about all the artists that followed them. Poetry, sculpture, architecture, philosophy, mathematics, science, political systems, erotic art – the ancient Greeks were brilliant at everything, it seems. The great leap in art made by the ancient Greeks from what had gone on before seems much larger than the 'improvement' of the Renaissance compared to mediæval art, or the emergence of abstract art at the beginning of the 20th century. What the ancient Greeks did overshadows the Renaissance, and modern art. Art may have had its true highpoint 2,000 years ago. Ancient Greek art is truly 'beautiful', to use the most apposite of all Neoplatonic terms. Look at Greek sculpture, from the female figures of Auxerre to the wonderful *Victory of Samothrace*.[1]

Here, in ancient Greek art, one finds the birth of modern æsthetics, modern notions of 'beauty', of ideal form and of the stature of 'high art'. In ancient Greek art, one finds the amalgamation of art and philosophy – that 'great' art must be produced from a 'great' philosophy – which has remained with 'high art' ever since.

---

1 *Female Figure*, from Auxerre, c. 625BC, limestone, daedalic style, Louvre, Paris; *Victory of Samothrace*, c. 200BC, marble, Louvre, Paris

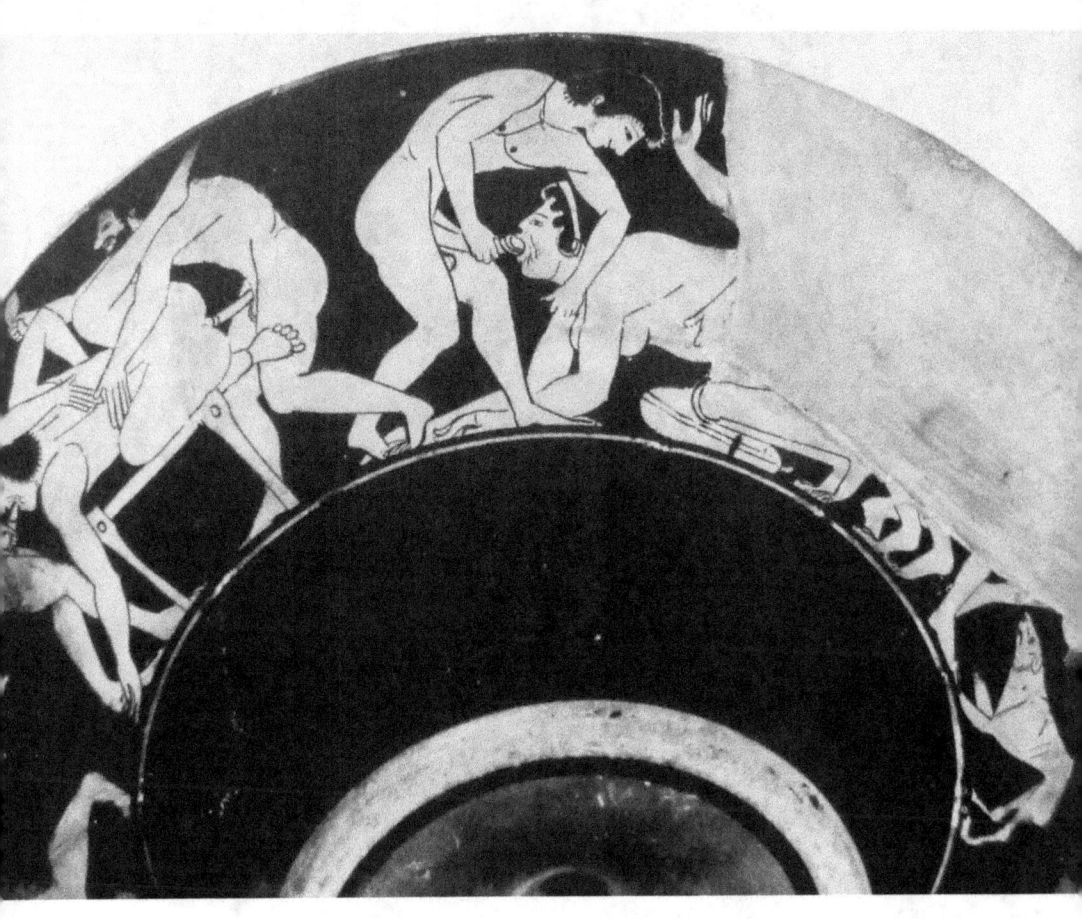

Greek Cup, Attic, attributed to Skythes

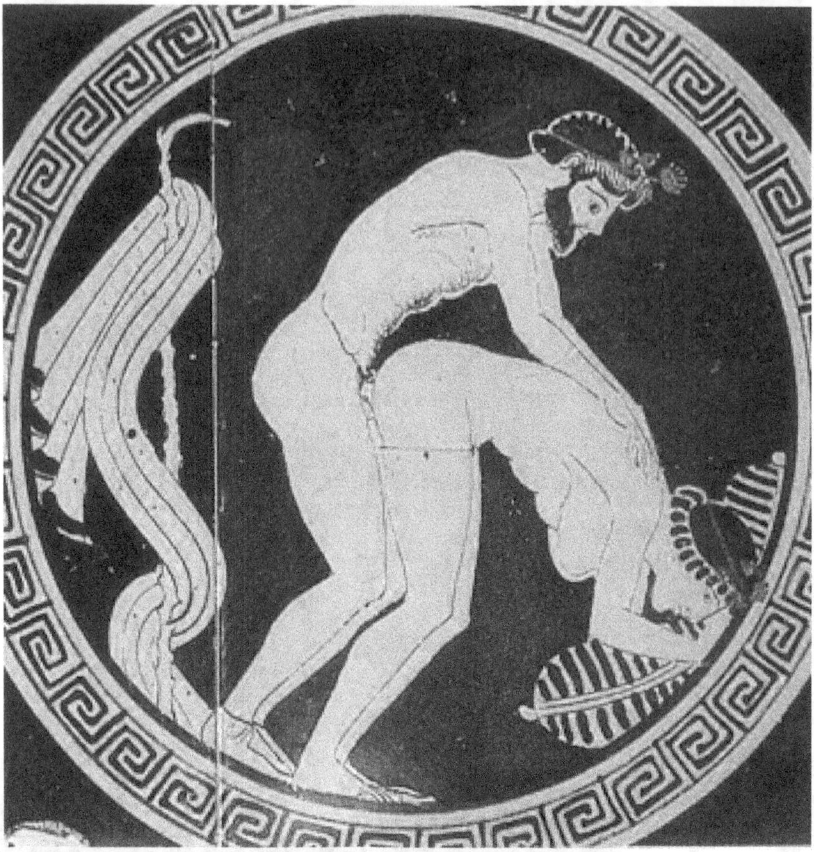

Ancient Greek
vase art

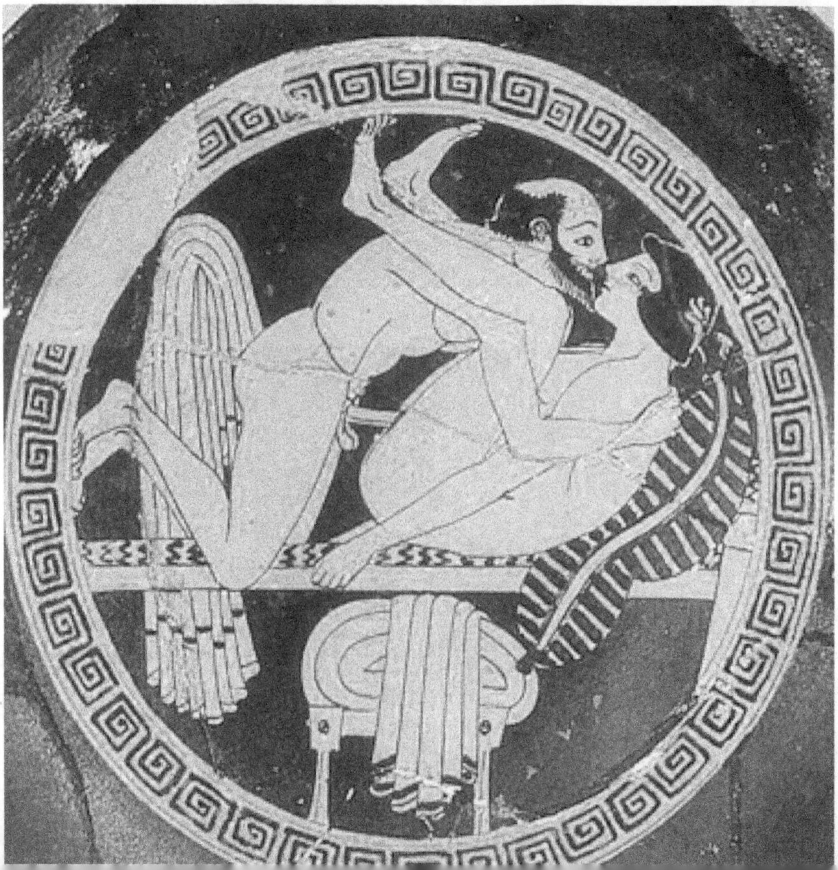

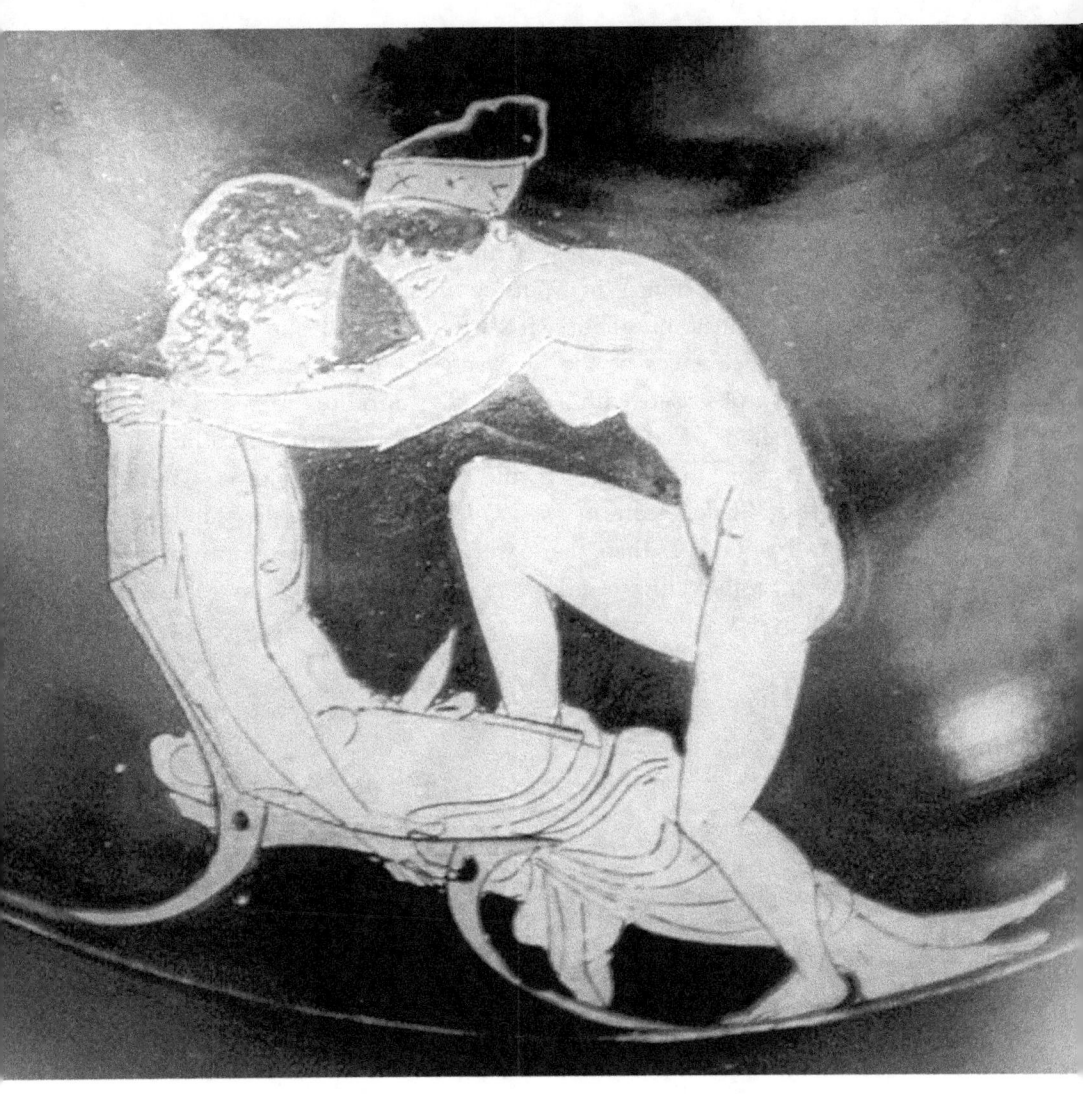

Shuvalov Painter, Ancient Greek, Berlin

GREEK ART

The art-pornography debate centres around power, politics, acceptability, philosophy and pleasure. The proper response to high culture is a detached enjoyment; pornography is disruptive, disturbing, debasing. Looking at a piece of high art, the pornographic response is lust while the high art response is rarefied contemplation. When pornographic responses to high art occur, the result is indignation from the art establishment. There are famous incidences of the 'debasing' of high art, as when a youth was so obsessed with a statue of Aphrodite of Cnidos that he masturbated on it, leaving a stain, as recorded in Pliny's *Natural History*; then there is the myth of Pygmalion, later reworked by Shakespeare in *The Winter's Tale*, where the statue is sensually responsive; then there was Henry George Quinn who sneaked into the Uffizi Gallery to 'fervently kiss' the Medici Venus all over.[1]

1 Nicholas Penny: "Goddesses and Girls", in *London Review of Books*, 2-29, December 1982, 20; Simon Wilson: "Short History of Western Erotic Art", in Robert Melville: *Erotic Art of the West*, Weidenfeld & Nicolson 1973, 16

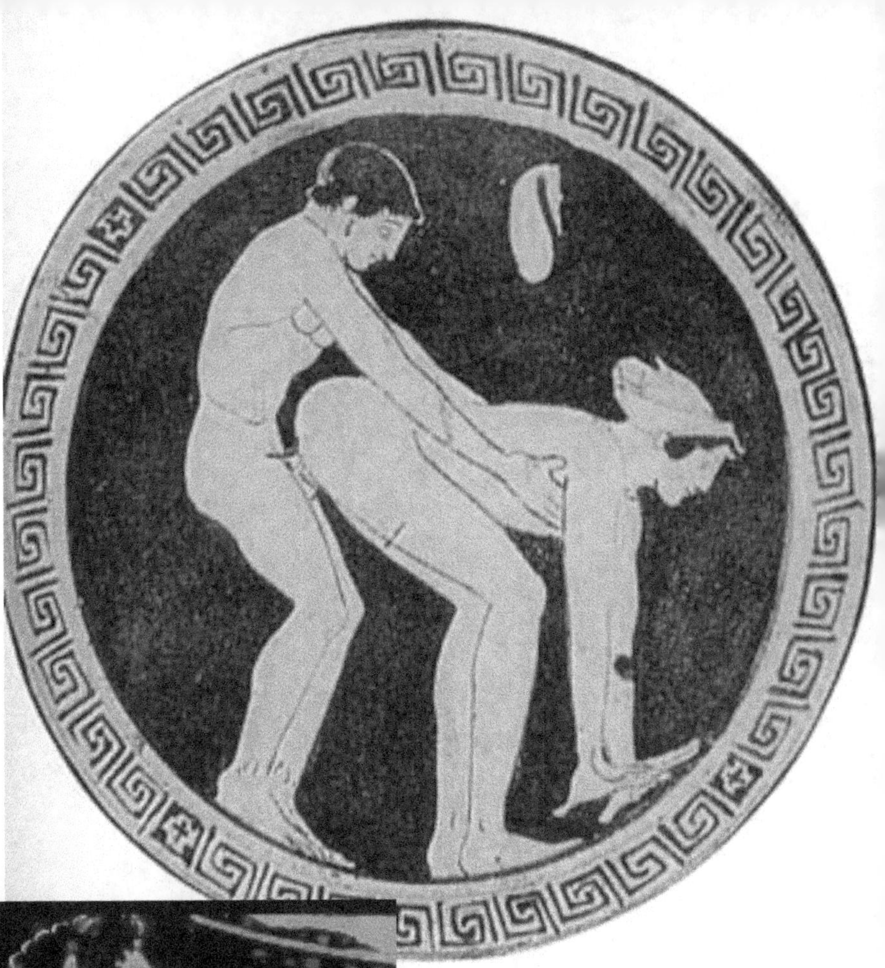

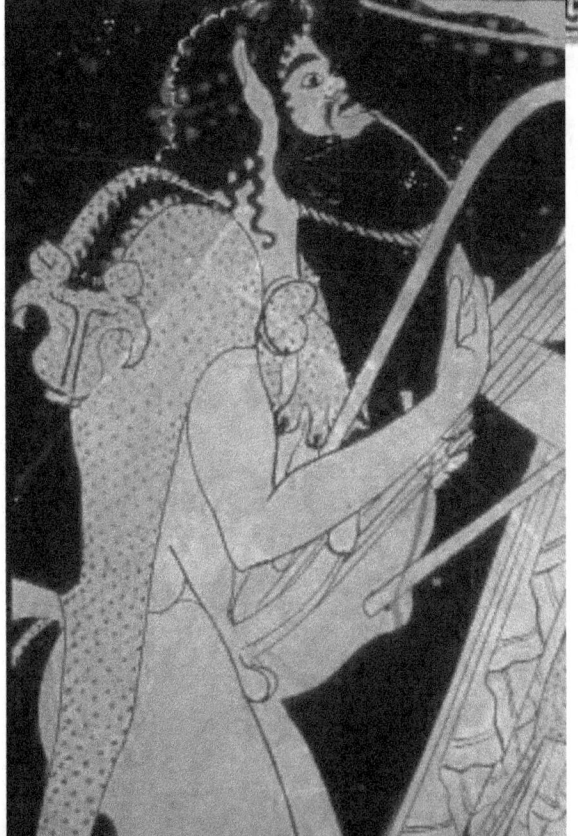

Art on ancient Greek vases

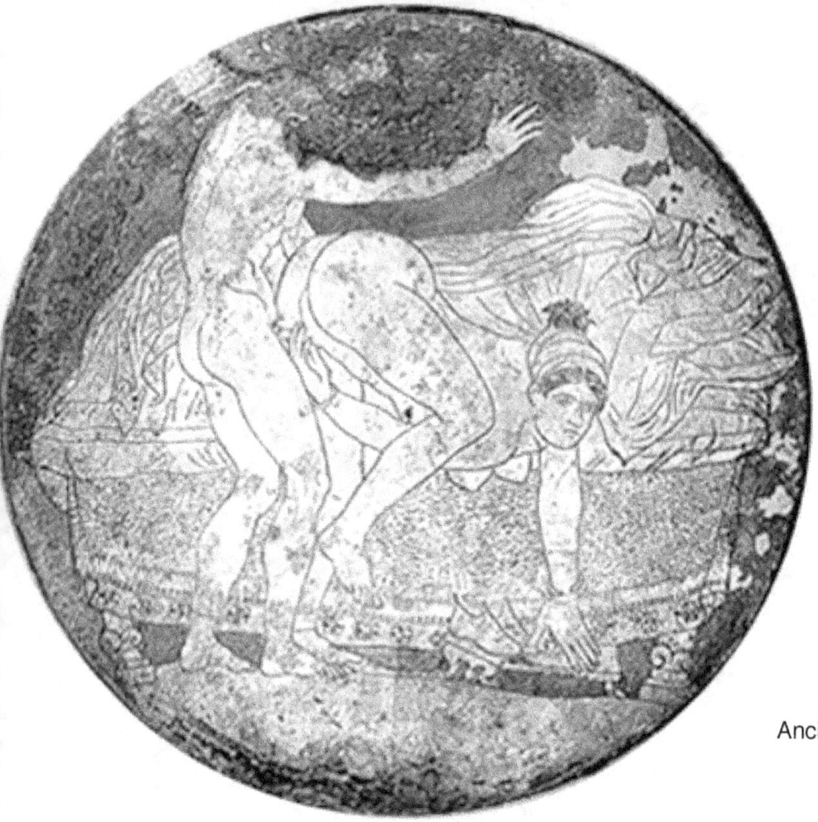

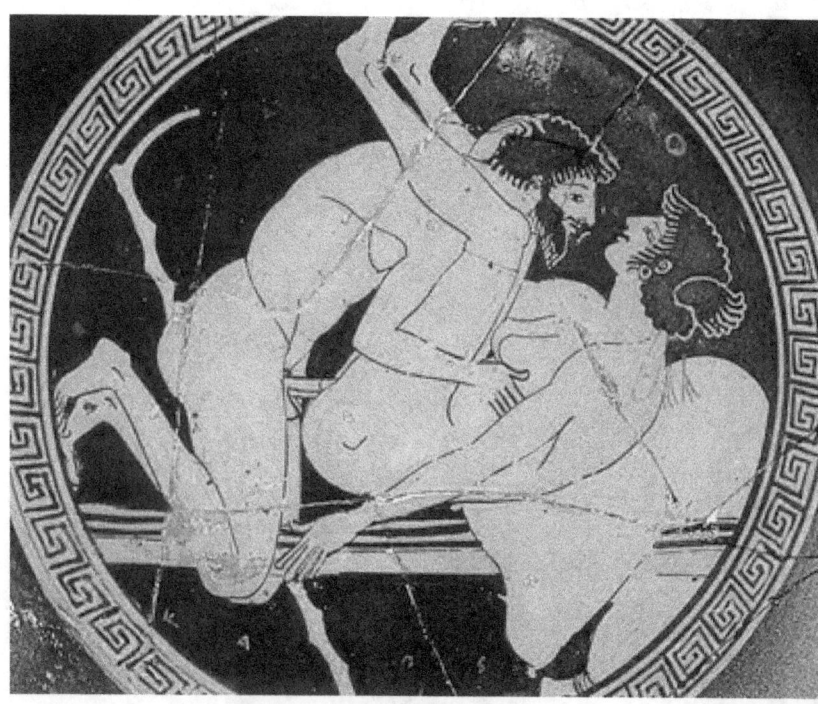

Ancient Greek art

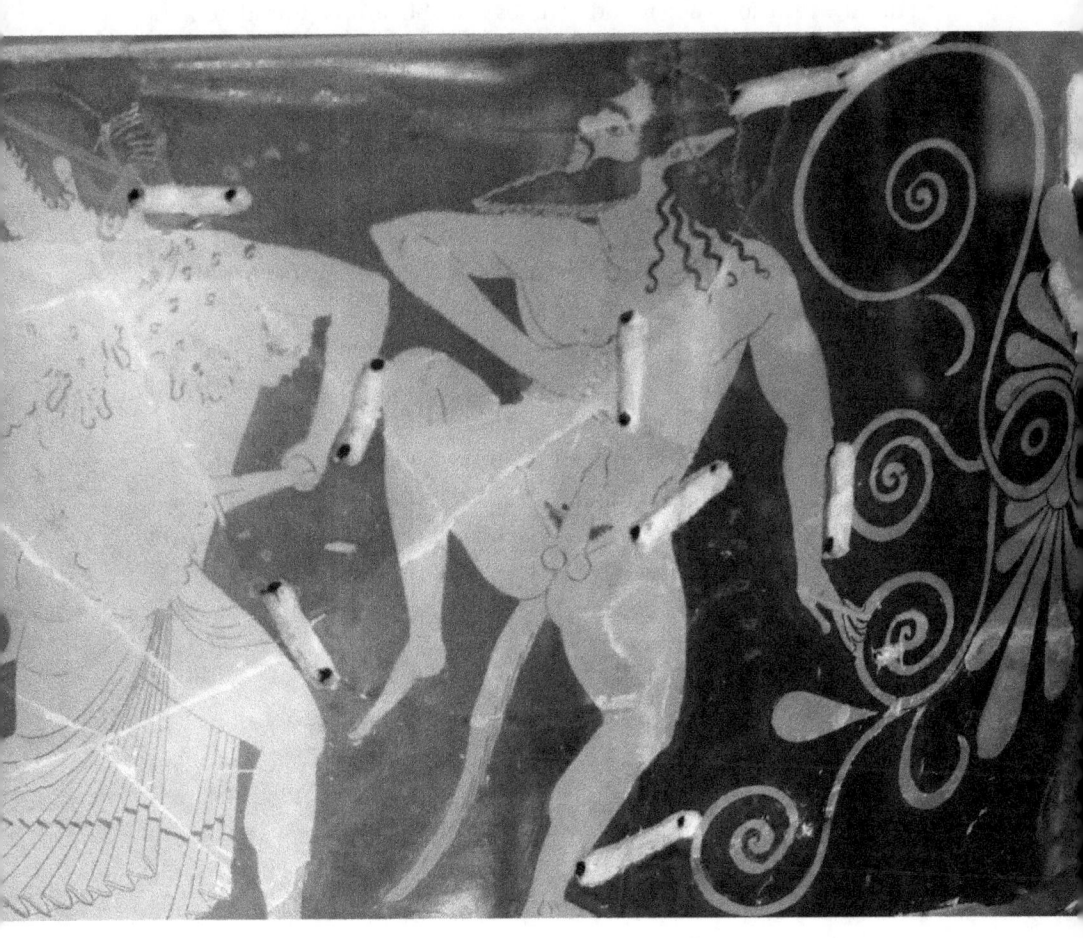

Greek Vase, 5th century, Louvre Museum, Paris

ERORTIC ART IN THE EAST

Hindu, Tantric, Taoist and Chinese erotic art is founded in a religion quite different in some key areas from Western religion. There seems to be less guilt, sin, body-hating and repression in Indian, Japanese and Chinese erotic art (this discussion will focus primarily on erotic art in India, Japan and China). The cosmic energy of life has a sexual dimension which is gloriously celebrated. Indian, Japanese and Chinese erotic art may be just as sexist and misogynist and patriarchal as Western erotic art, but it is also freer, more exuberant, more joyous.

In Oriental erotic art, sexuality is a cosmic energy, an essential part of an authentic religious worldview. Indian, Chinese and Japanese erotica is thoroughly sexist, though. As with witches' covens and Western magic, erotic energy manifests itself in men and women in erotic pairings, in heterosexual components, and the symbols of the *lingam* and *yoni* are, yet again, the penis and vagina.

Maithuna, the figures of lovemaking couples, are found on Indian temples, though, again, it is nearly always men and women that are depicted writhing together. Lesbian and gay and other forms of sexual identity and practices are rarely depicted. There are renditions of lesbian and gay 'sex acts', in the Moghul Indian erotic manuals, for instance, and in the Turkish Khamas poems.[1]

In Indian religion there are *shiva and shakti* as the cosmic forces; in China it is the *yin* and *yang*. Always there is an emphasis on the masculine and the feminine, and the union of the two. As the *I Ching* puts it: '[s]exual union of man and woman gives life to all things.'[2]

---

1 *Lesbian scene*, 17th century, Koka Shastra, Bibliotheque Nationale, Paris; *Homosexual scene*, Khamsa poems, Ata'î, Turkey, 19th century, Museum of Turkish and Islamic Art, Istanbul
2 *I Ching*, tr James Legge, Dover, New York 1963, 1

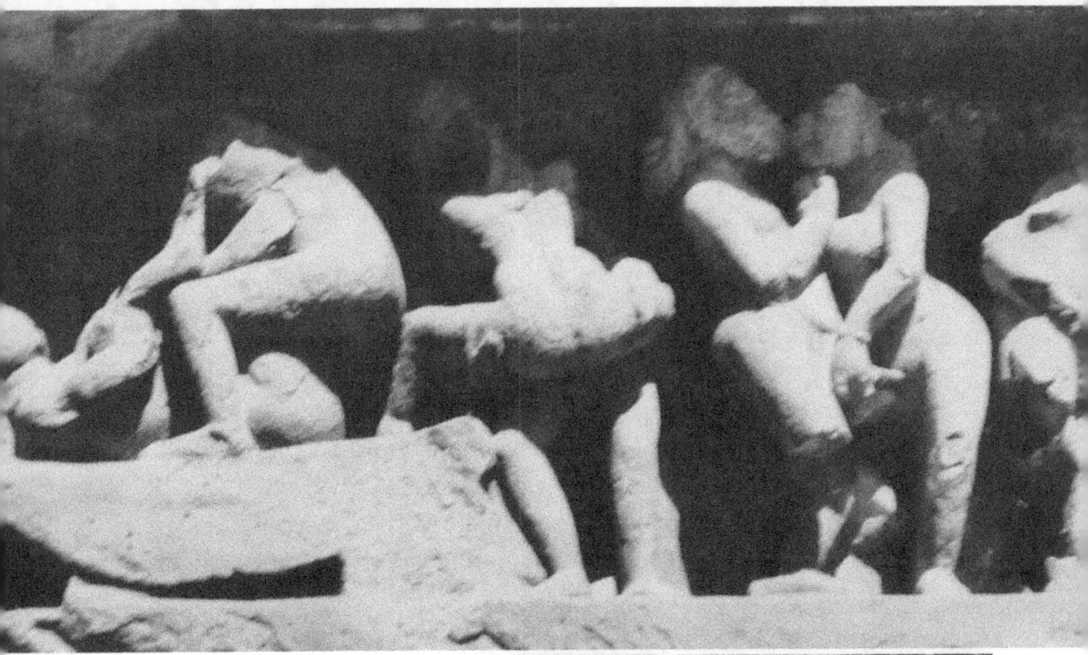

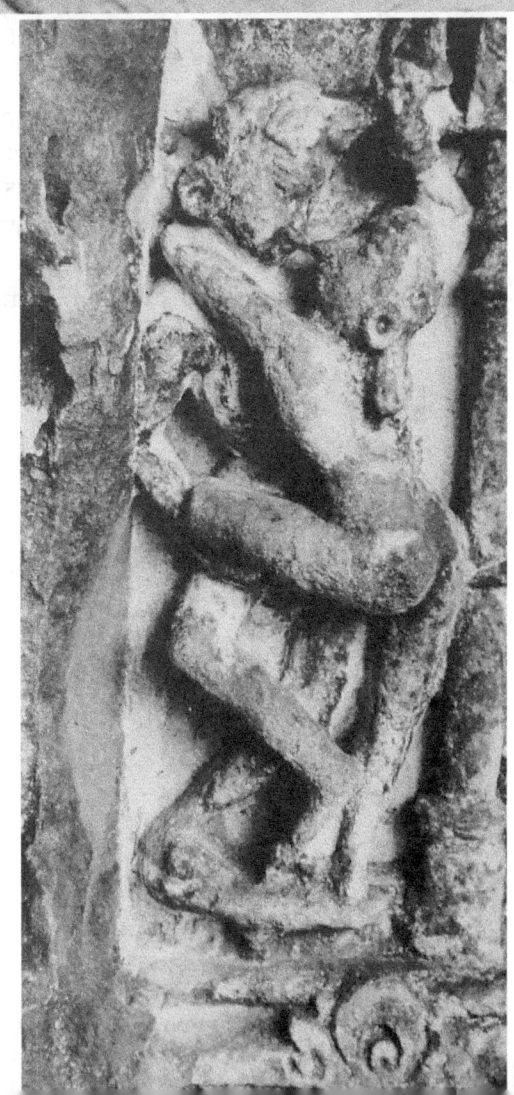

Khajuraho temple, 9-11 century,
Northern India, right.

Temple, 11th century, Mount Abu
area, Northern India

KHAJAHURO TEMPLE

The figures on the temples of Khajuraho or in Rajasthan, they're having a great time. They make love and they *smile*. Hey! sex is fun – and those carvings on the Indian temples show lovemaking as intimate, sensual pleasure, unblemished by death-consciousness or sin or guilt.[1] (A view regularly trotted out by modern writers is that sex is actually difficult, smelly, rough, dirty, nerve-wracking, etc. Oriental erotic art shows that there are other forms of sexual behaviour).

The carvings on the temples of India, such as Khajuraho temple, are among the most celebrated examples of erotic art from the history of art, and rightly so. The images of a woman climbing up a man's body, thighs spread, with him deep inside her, and the two of them kissing, are rapturous and totally unforgettable. These stone couplings are among art's most ecstatic images – and the effect is greatly enhanced by the frieze format, by collecting so many figures into the same space. And all of them are making love, or standing there exuding infinite desire.

---

1 Couple from the 'heaven bands of a temple, Rajasthan, 13th century, sandstone, 11in high; naked ascetic coupling with a Yogini, from Laksmana temple at Khajuraho

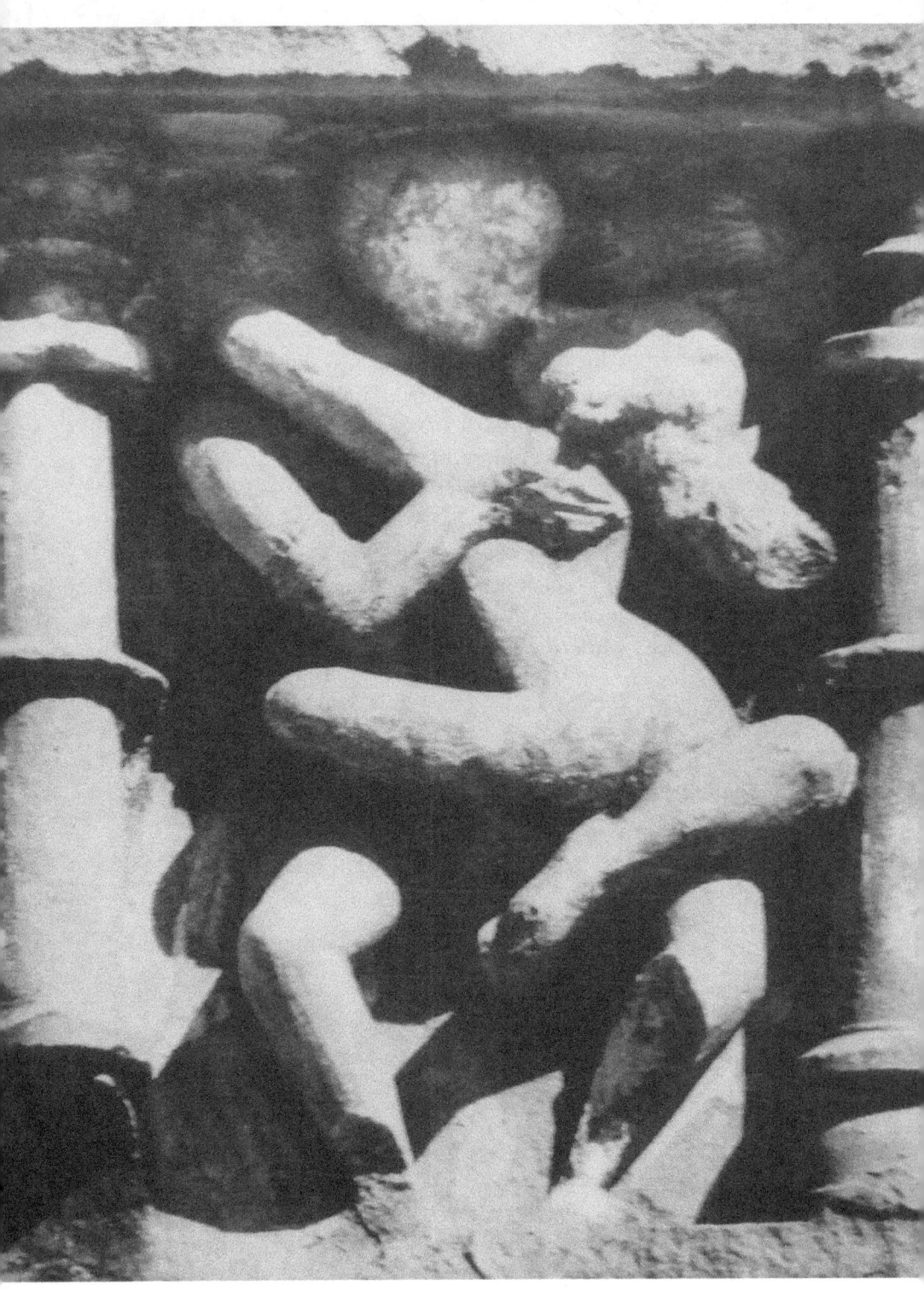

Khajuraho temple, 9th-11th century, North India

Hindu Tantric sex magic is very sensual, with its rites using meat, wine, butter, etc. There is an 'extreme' version of Tantric sex magic, the so-called 'left hand' ritual, where sex is practised when the woman menstruates. The aim, again, is to harness and channel wild sexual energies. The 'left hand' paths of Eastern sex magic were fascinating for groups of Western artists and writers, who were interested in gaining power over the world.

Tantrism is a life-affirming cult, with pleasure as a goal. But sexual practise is always contextualized within a cosmic, religious, and philosophical framework. It is never pleasure for pleasure's sake, never simply a series of multiple orgasms, so the text books say, although sex magic, East or West, is about cultivating the energies of the orgasm. As John Mumford commented: '[s]ex magic operates upon the premise that whatever is held in the imagination at the moment of orgasm will come to pass.'[1] Orgasm is that prime mystical state, the *jouissance* at the heart of mysticism. As Mumford wrote: '[o]rgasm is the only spontaneous, natural experience of a deathless, breathless, timeless, sorrowless dimension.'[2]

1 John Mumford: *Ecstasy Through Tantra*, Llewellyn Publications, St Paul, Minnesota 1988, 93
2 J. Mumford, op.cit., 33

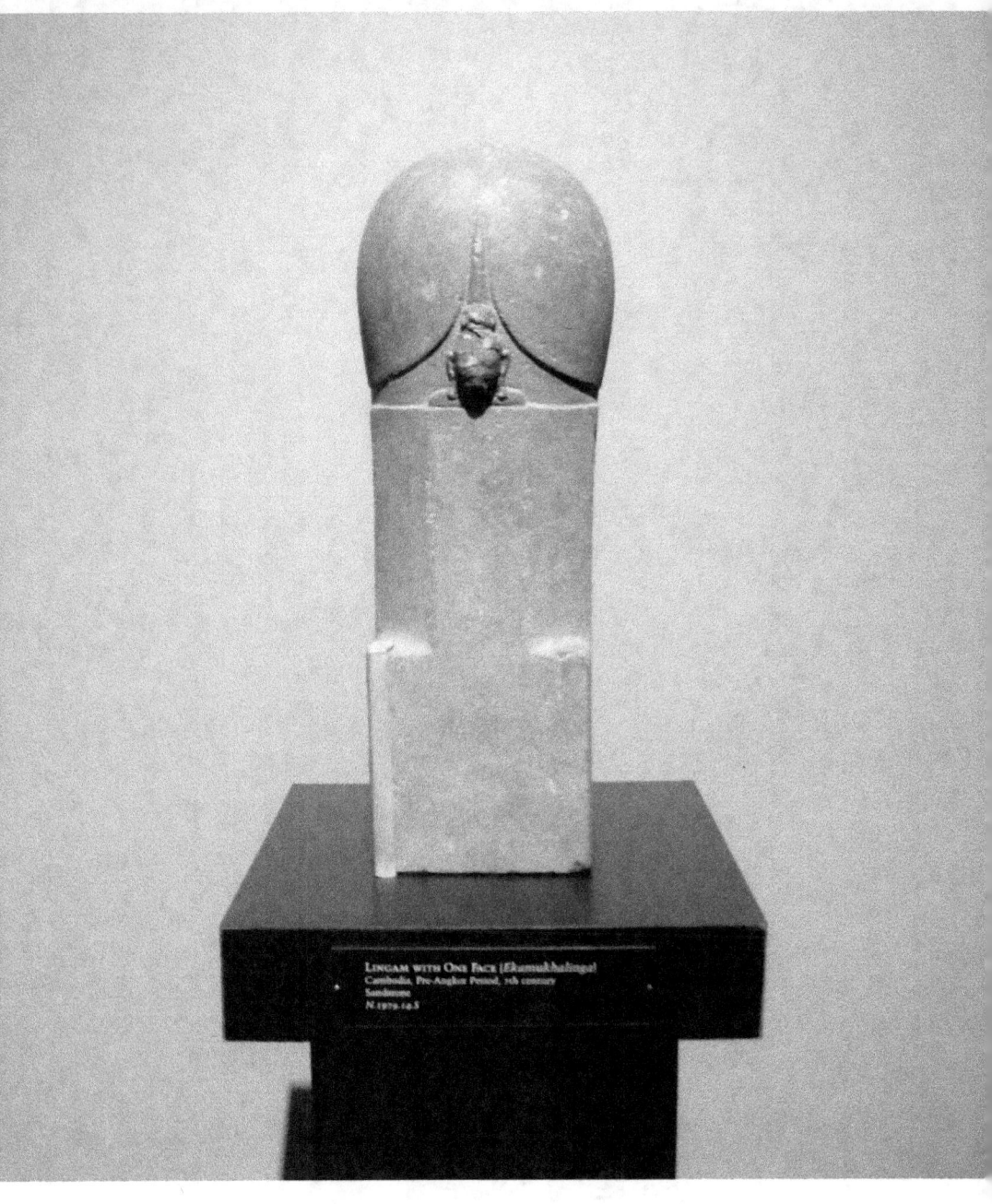

Lingam, Cambodia, 7th Century,
Norton Simon Museum, Pasadena, CA

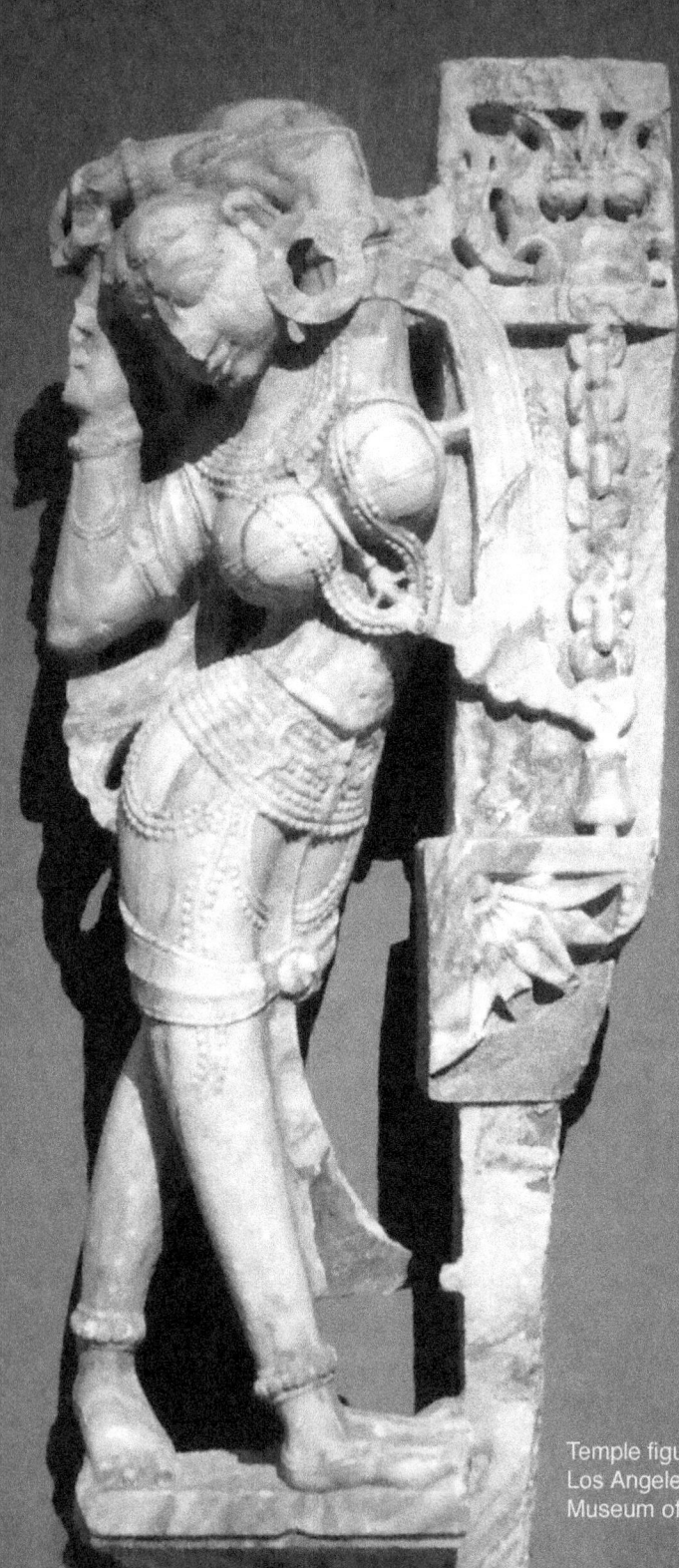

Temple figure, Indian,
Los Angeles County
Museum of Art

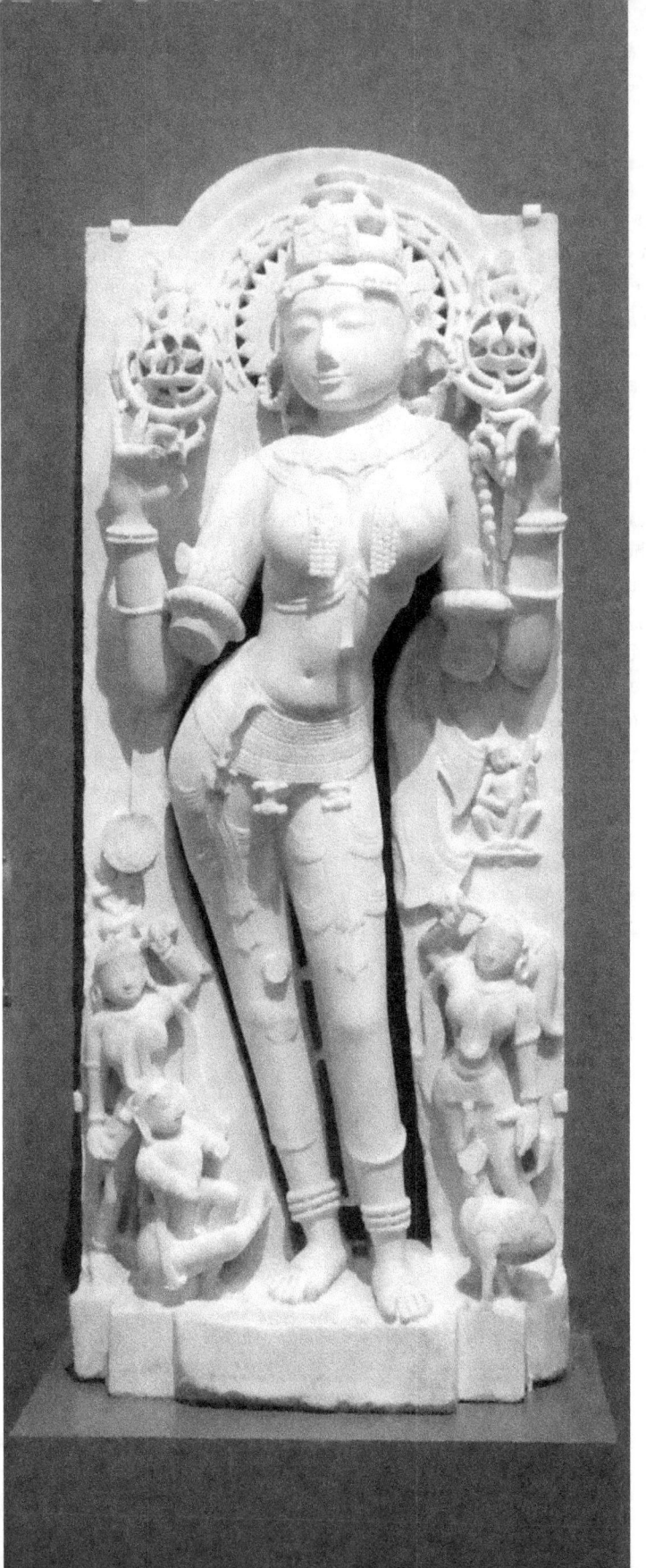

Indian temple figure,
Norton Simon Museum,
Pasadena, CA

Oriental erotic art is famous for its 'athletic' sexual positions – i.e., sex that goes beyond the missionary position or woman on top position of so much of Western erotic art. The variety of sexual positions are propounded in Oriental texts such as *The Perfumed Garden*, *Anangaranga*, or the *Kama Sutra*, which demonstrates 64 ways of fucking. The positions themselves have a religious aspect, being associated with yoga, with meditation and sex magic. The positions of the body echo or are manifestations of cosmic, religious energy. (Focussing on other sexual positions is partly a graphic function, too: it's easier to depict sexual positions outside of the missionary position if you want to concentrate on genitals touching. The missionary position hides everything. Which's why it's used as the main position in commercial cinema, for instance).

Chinese/ Taoist eroticism features quaint titles for sexual positions: *Two Fishes Side-by-Side*, *Turning Dragon*, *Leaping Wild Horses*; there are types of 'thrusting' (nine shallow, one deep); cute names for orgasms ('the bursting of the clouds'); the penis is the 'Jade Stem', the vagina is the Palace, or Gateway of Jade, or the Peach.

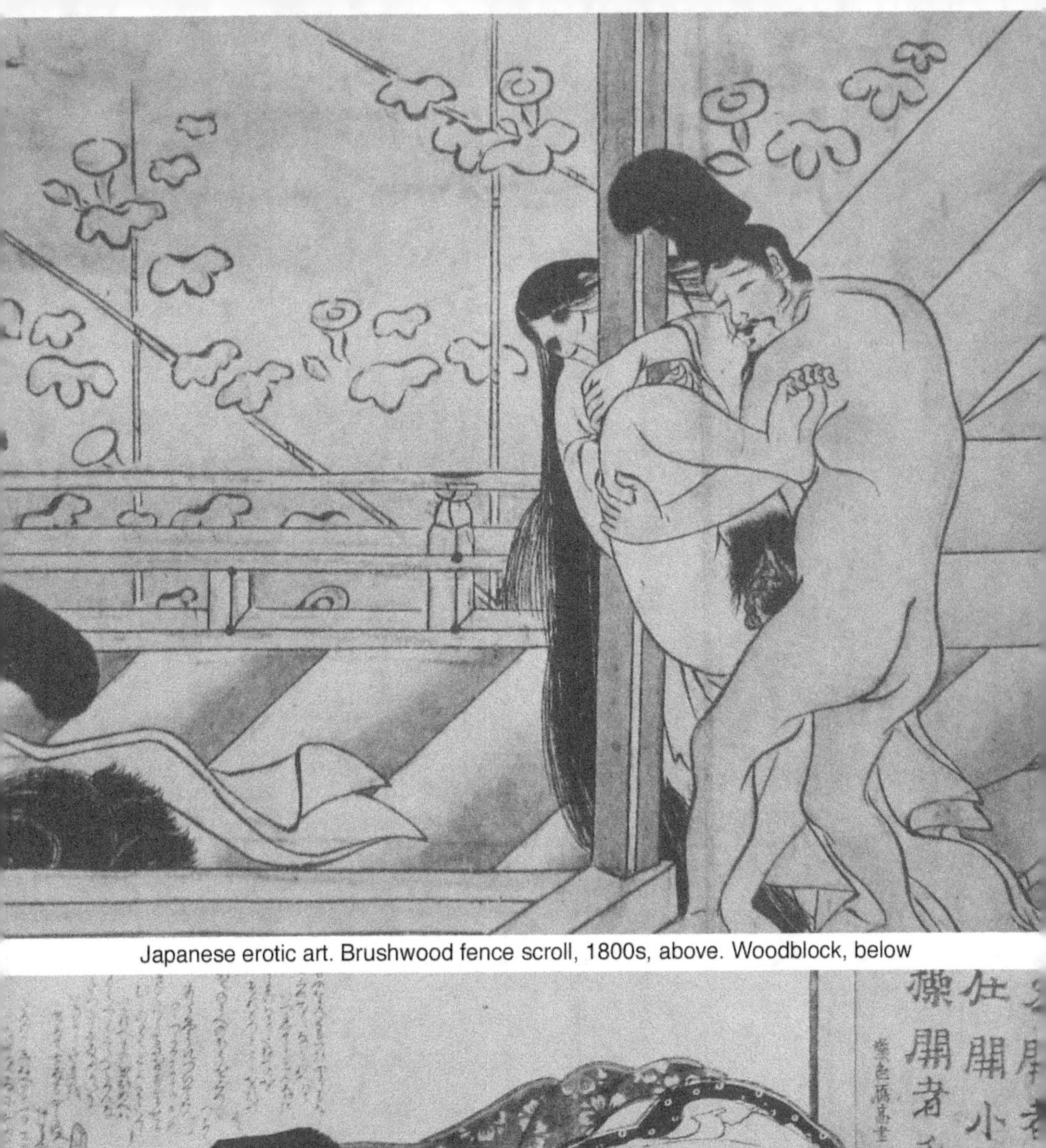

Japanese erotic art. Brushwood fence scroll, 1800s, above. Woodblock, below

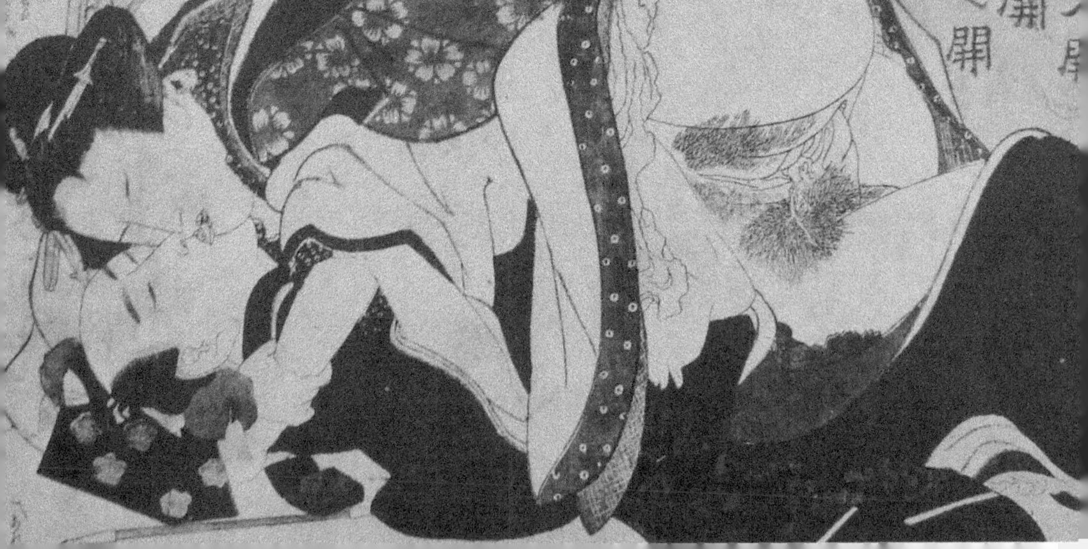

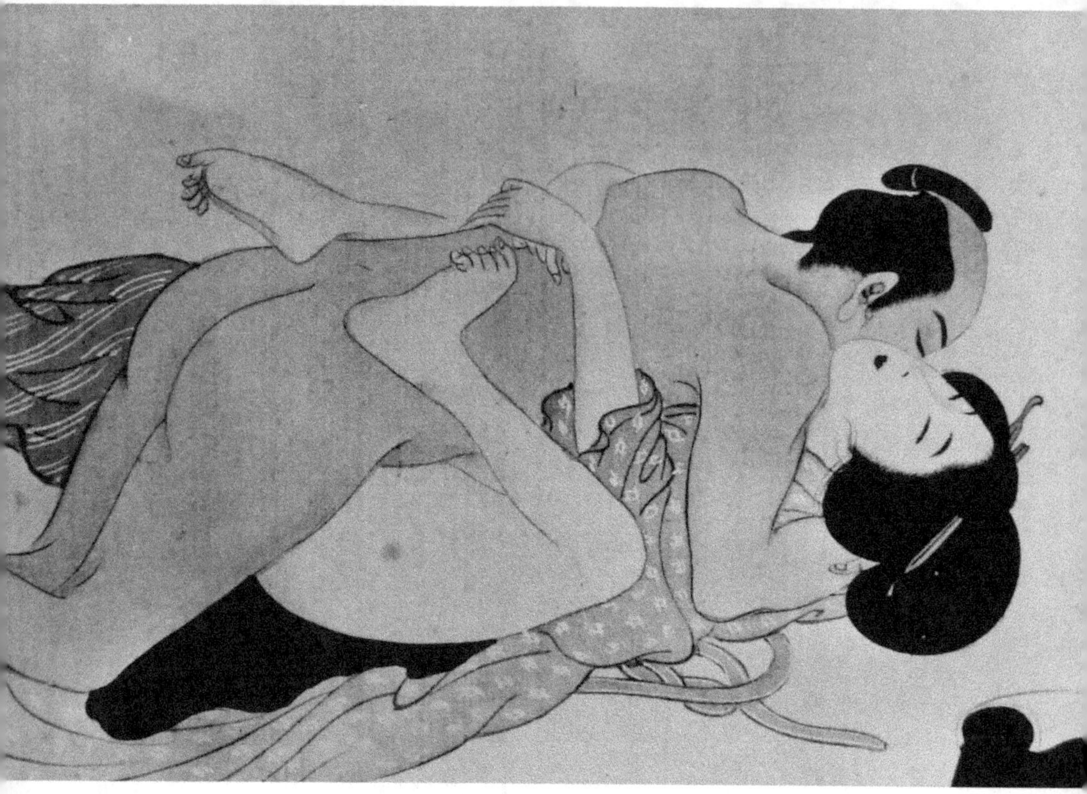

Two Hokusai school pictures: woodblock, 19th century, below.
Hokusai school, c. 1830, above.

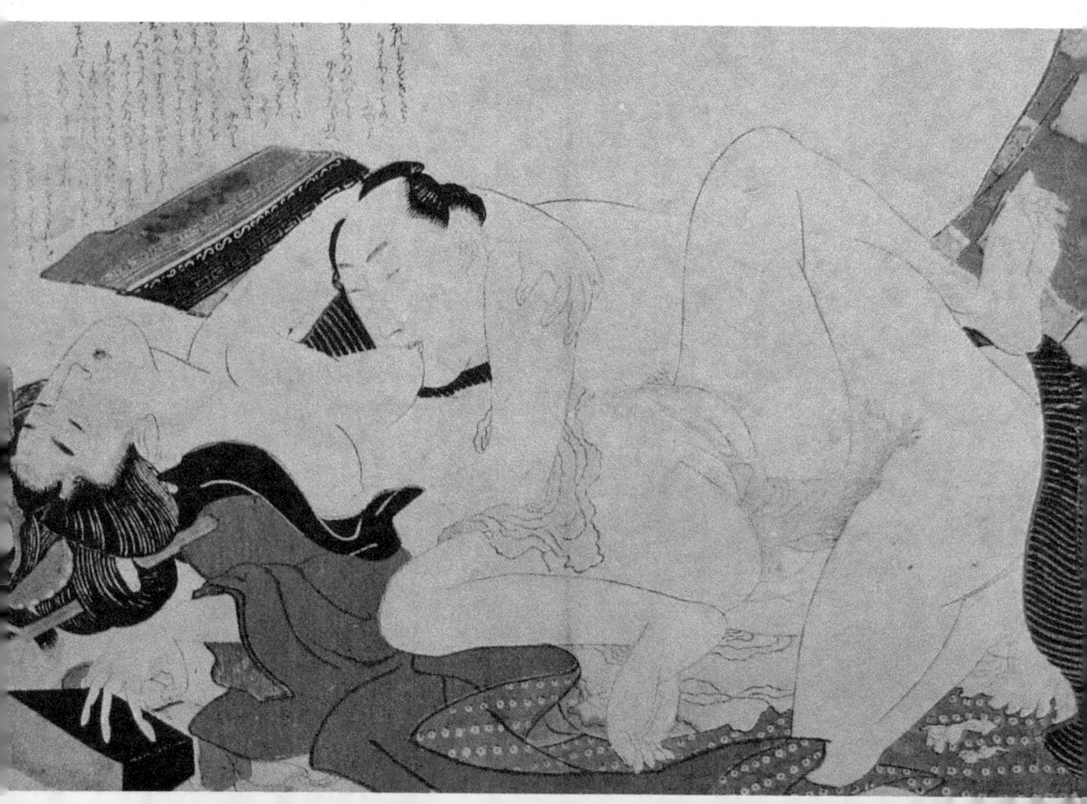

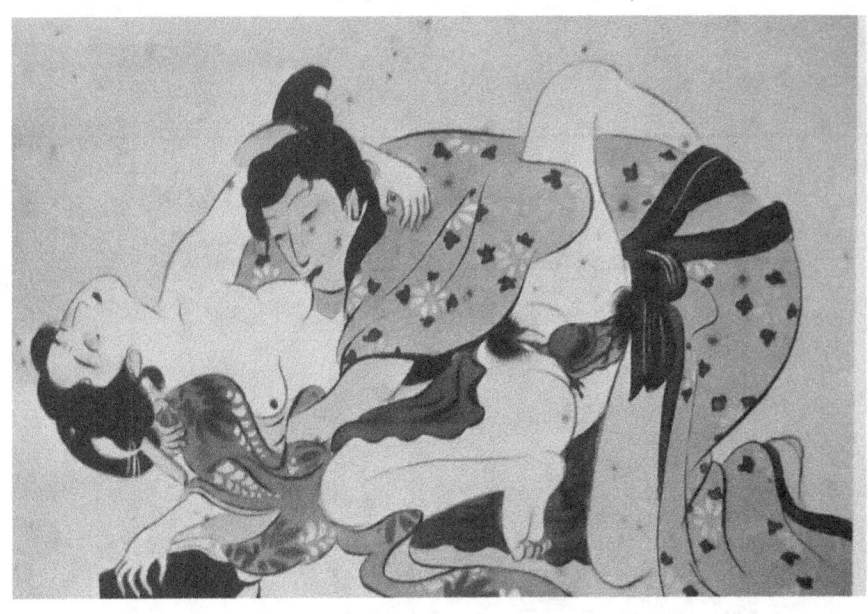

Anonymous, Painted Scroll, c. 1910, ukiyo-e school (above).
Shunchosai, woodblock print, 1770s (below)

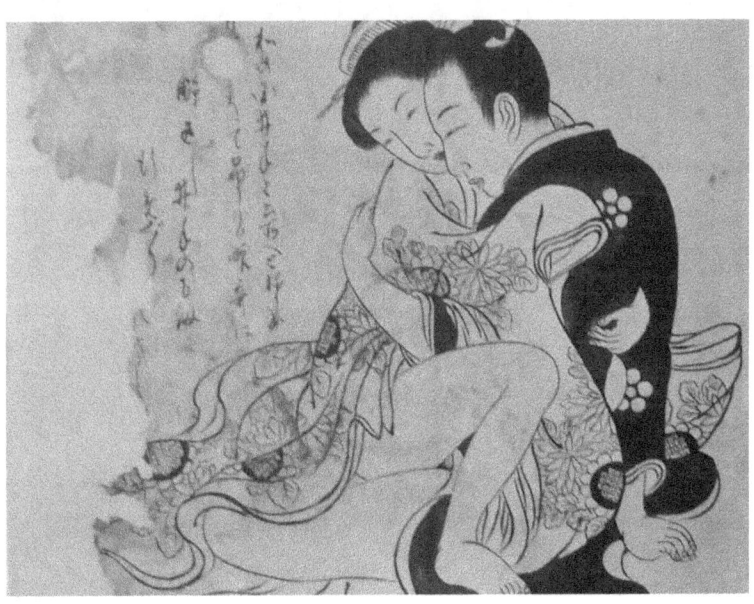

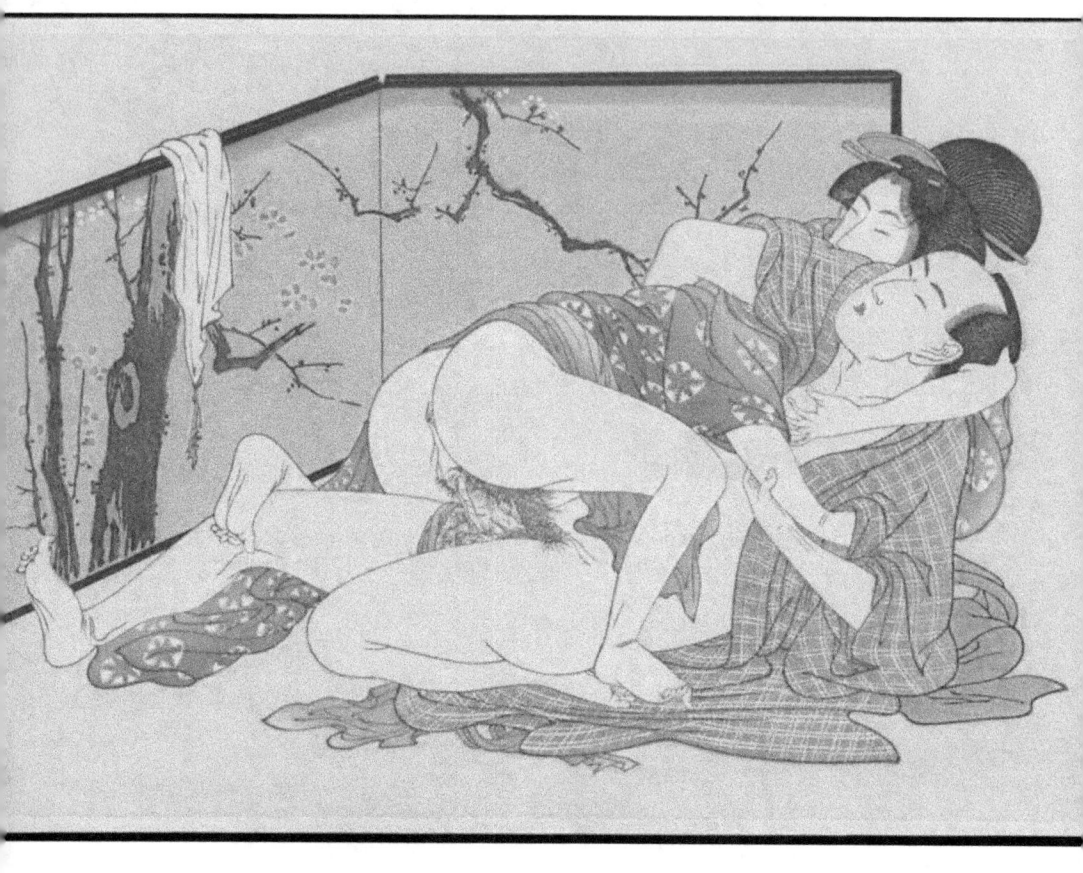

Kitagawa Utamaro (1753-1806), this page and over.
Some images are from Prelude To Desire, 1799

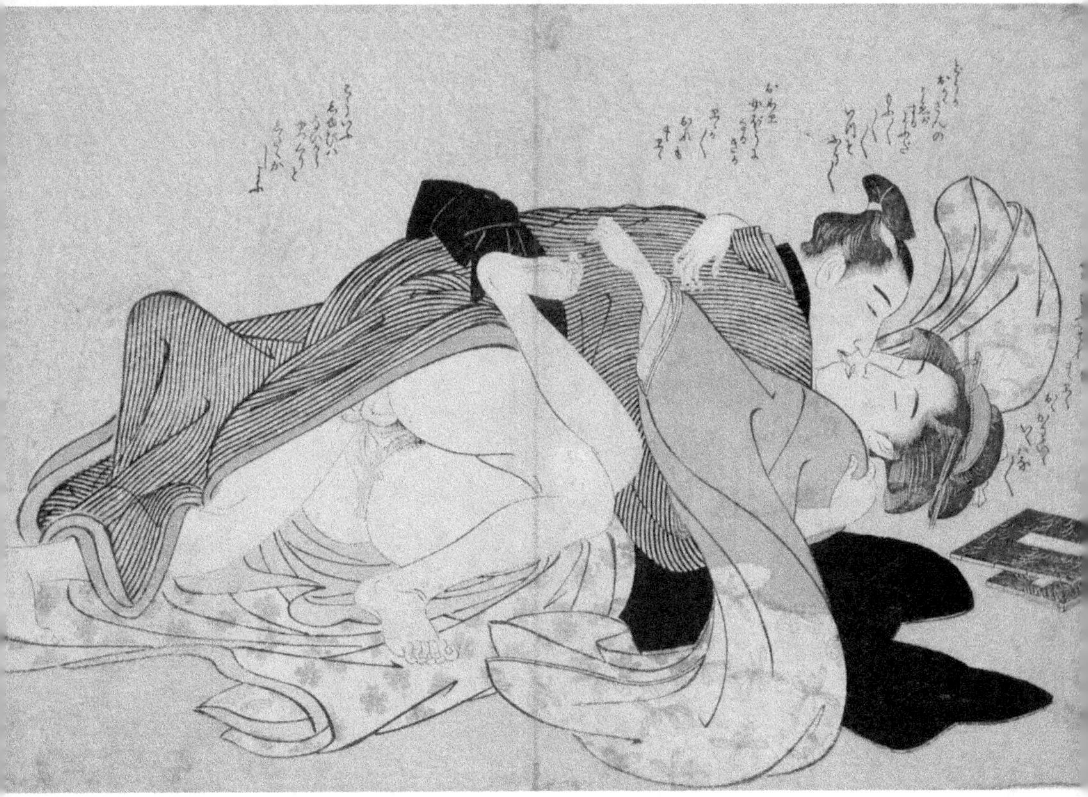

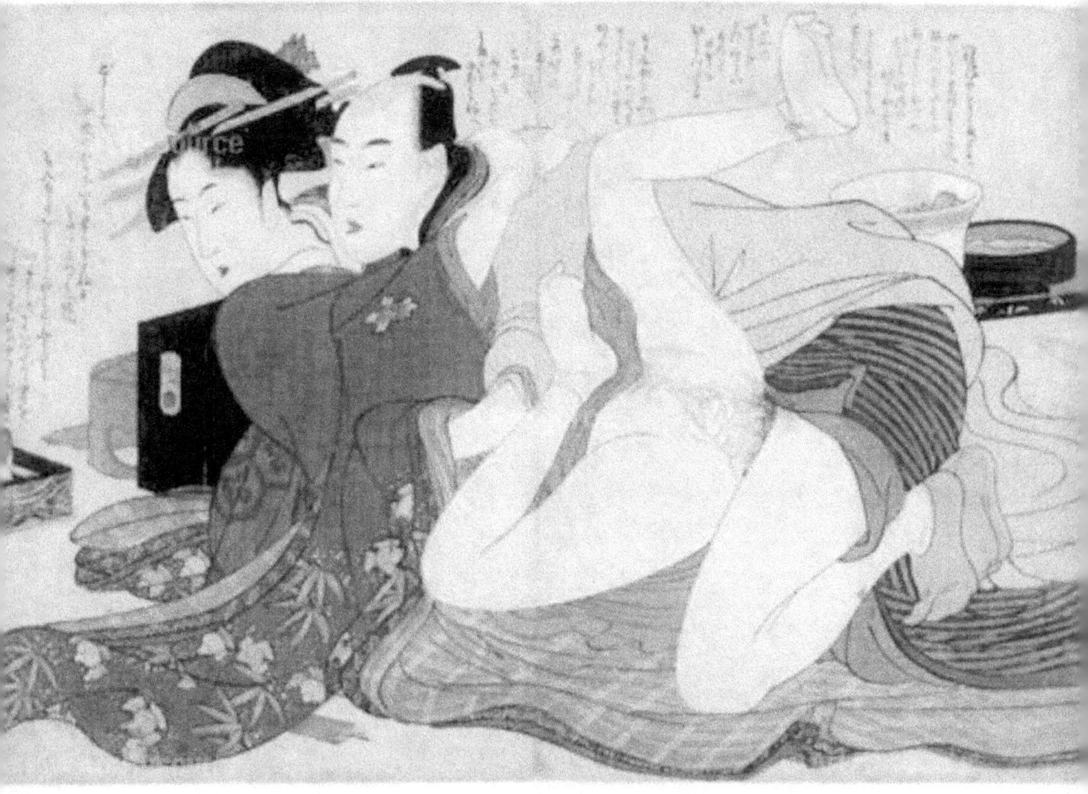

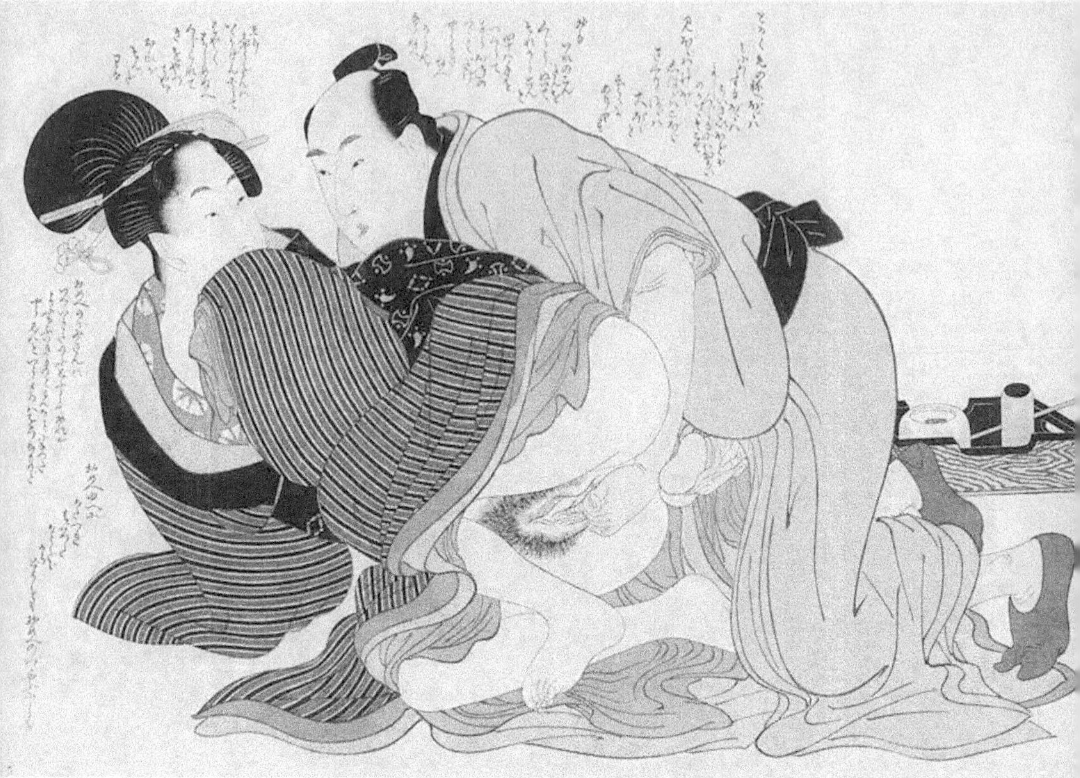

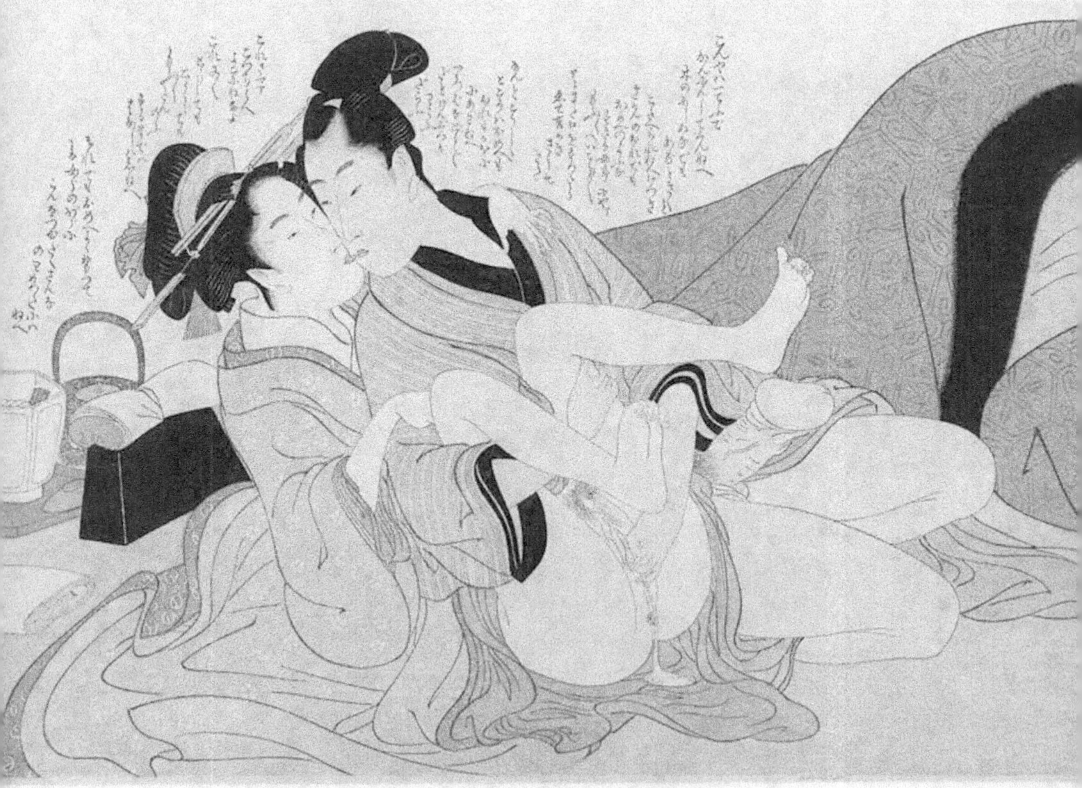

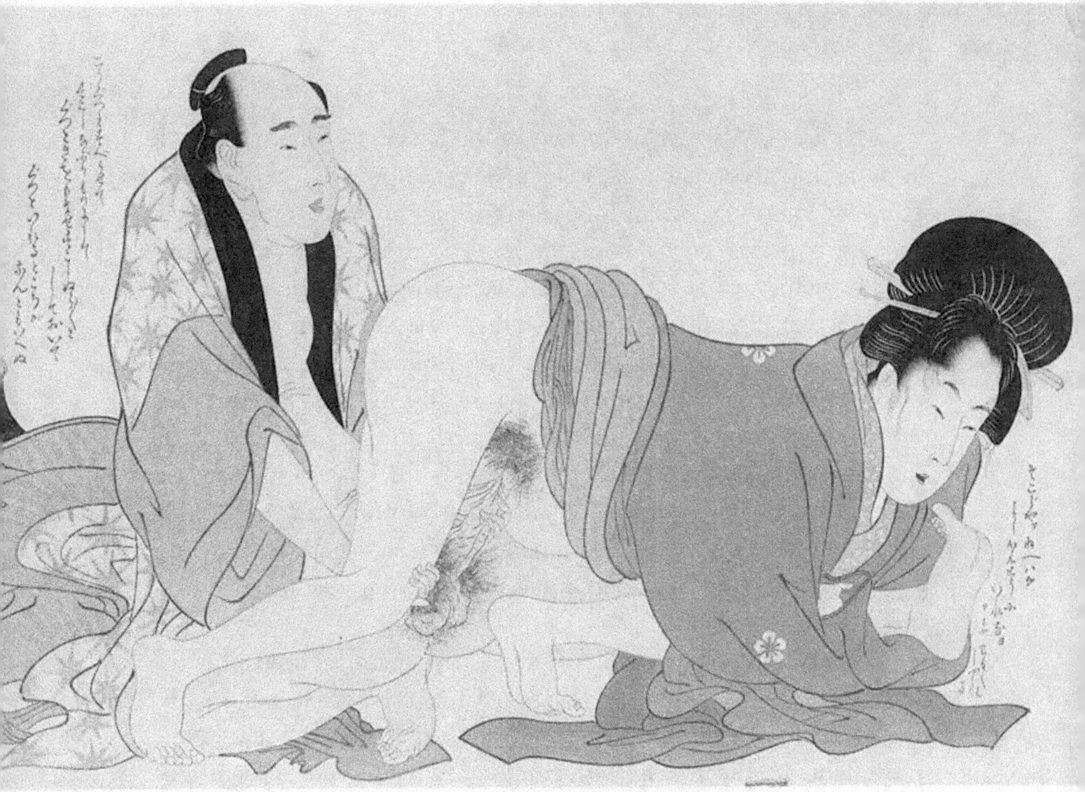

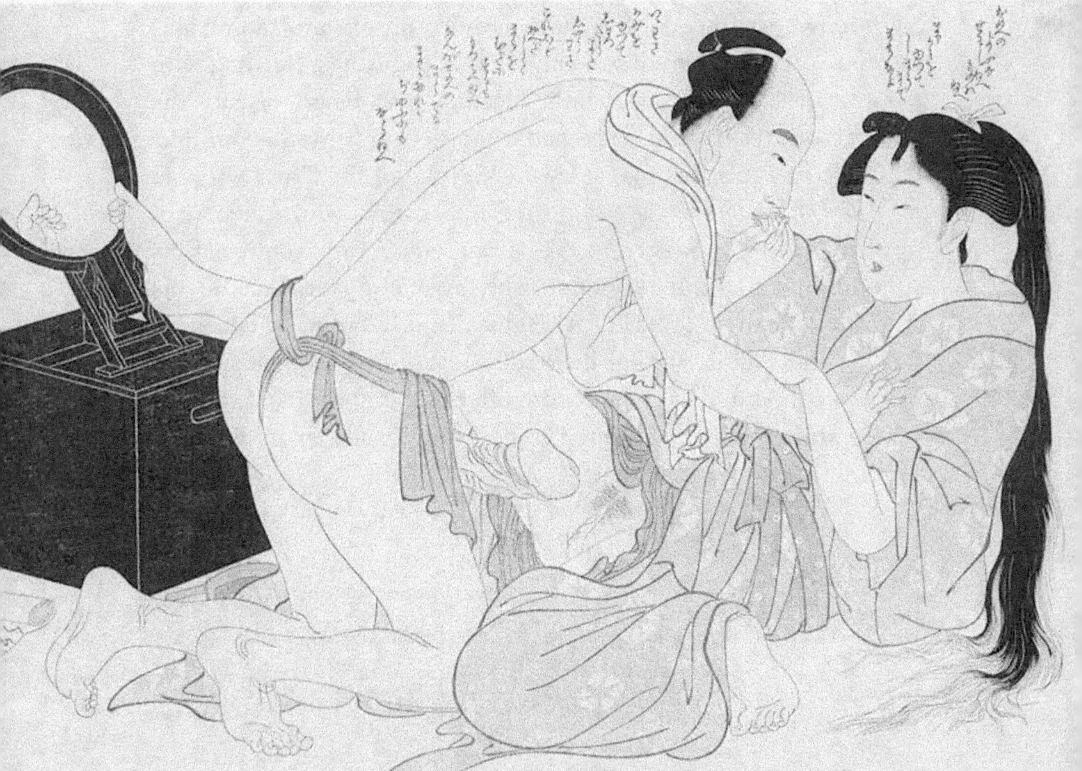

Mystical orgasm is the ecstasy at the heart of Western as much as Oriental mysticism. Catholic mystics, especially, experienced blinding, burning, tumultuous, orgasmic mystical ecstasies. St Theresa experienced some of the most intense religious orgasms in the history of mysticism, and her swooning was caught in Gianlorenzo Bernini's famous statue. The eroticism of female mysticism is apparent in so much of women mystics' writings. Marie of the Incarnation (d. 1671) wrote: '[i]t owes its origin to the mutual embraces of the soul and this most adorable Word who by the kisses of His divine mouth fills her with His spirit and with His life.' Later, she noted: '[h]er being is entirely penetrated and possessed by Him. It is consumed by caresses and acts of love which cause it to expire in Him by suffering deaths the most sweet'.[1]

For mystics of the mediæval and early modern era, God is the ultimate, Divine Lover, much as Christ is regarded as the bridegroom who 'marries' the bride, the church. The New Jerusalem, in the *Revelations*, comes down arrayed 'as a bride'. Nuptial imagery – that is, thoroughly erotic imagery – occurs throughout Judæo-Christianity, from the multi-sensual *Song of Songs* onwards. Indeed, the more ascetic and austere the mystic, the more erotic and joyous the mystical outpourings. Burning with the fire of love, pierced hearts bleeding the blood of life, the imagery of mysticism is drenched in eroticism. It is all about, like Tantrism or Taoist sex magic, desire. St John of the Cross wrote in his *The Dark Night of the Soul*: 'love is like fire, which ever rises upward with the desire to be absorbed in the centre of its sphere.'[2] Even seemingly unbudgably ascetic mystics such as the Arabic, Persian and Sufis, Al-Hallaj, Rumi, Jami, Al-Ghazzali, Rab'ia and Hafiz wrote incredibly erotically of being God-intoxicated, and Allah was seen often as the Divine Lover in whose arms the mystic desired to be extinguished in an excess of rapture that is clearly sexual.

1 *The Autobiography of Venerable Marie of the Incarnation, O.S.U., Mystic and Missionary*, tr J.J. Sullivan, Loyale University Press, Chicago, 1964, 56f
2 St John of the Cross, *Dark Night of the Soul*, tr E.A. Peers, Doubleday, New York 1959, 175

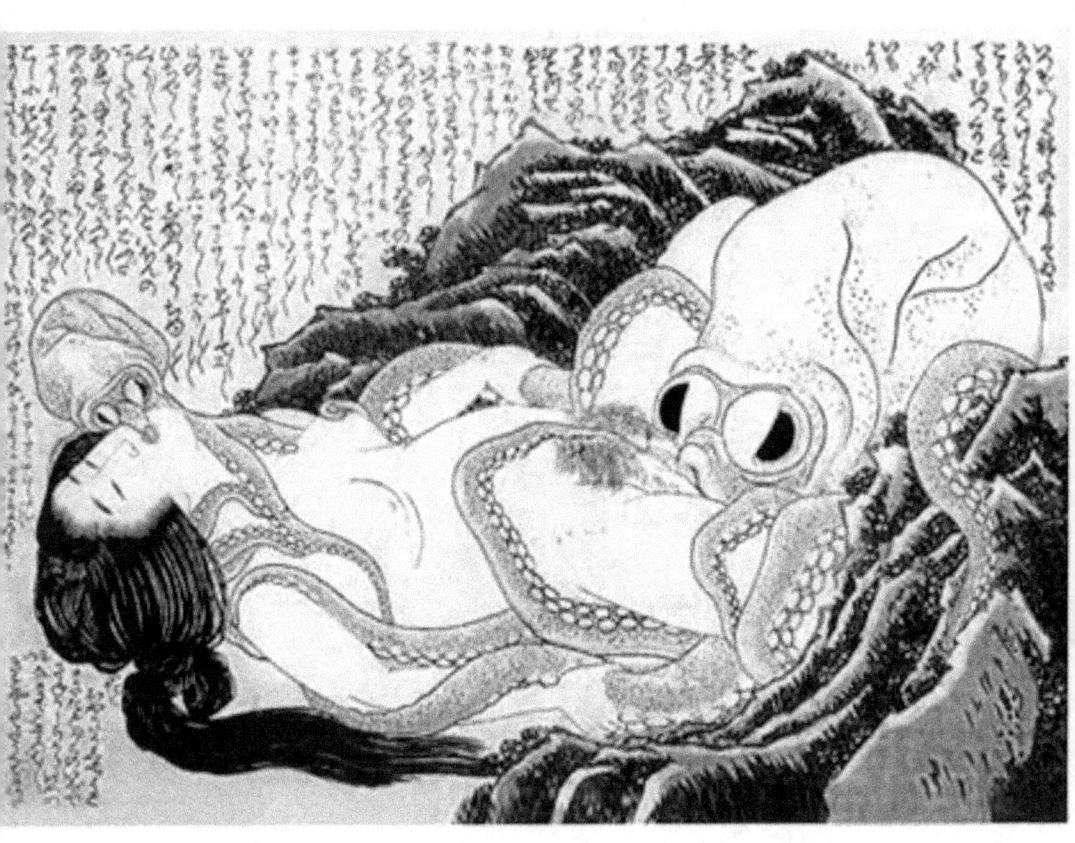

Katsuhika Hokusai, The Dream of the Fisherman's Wife, 1814

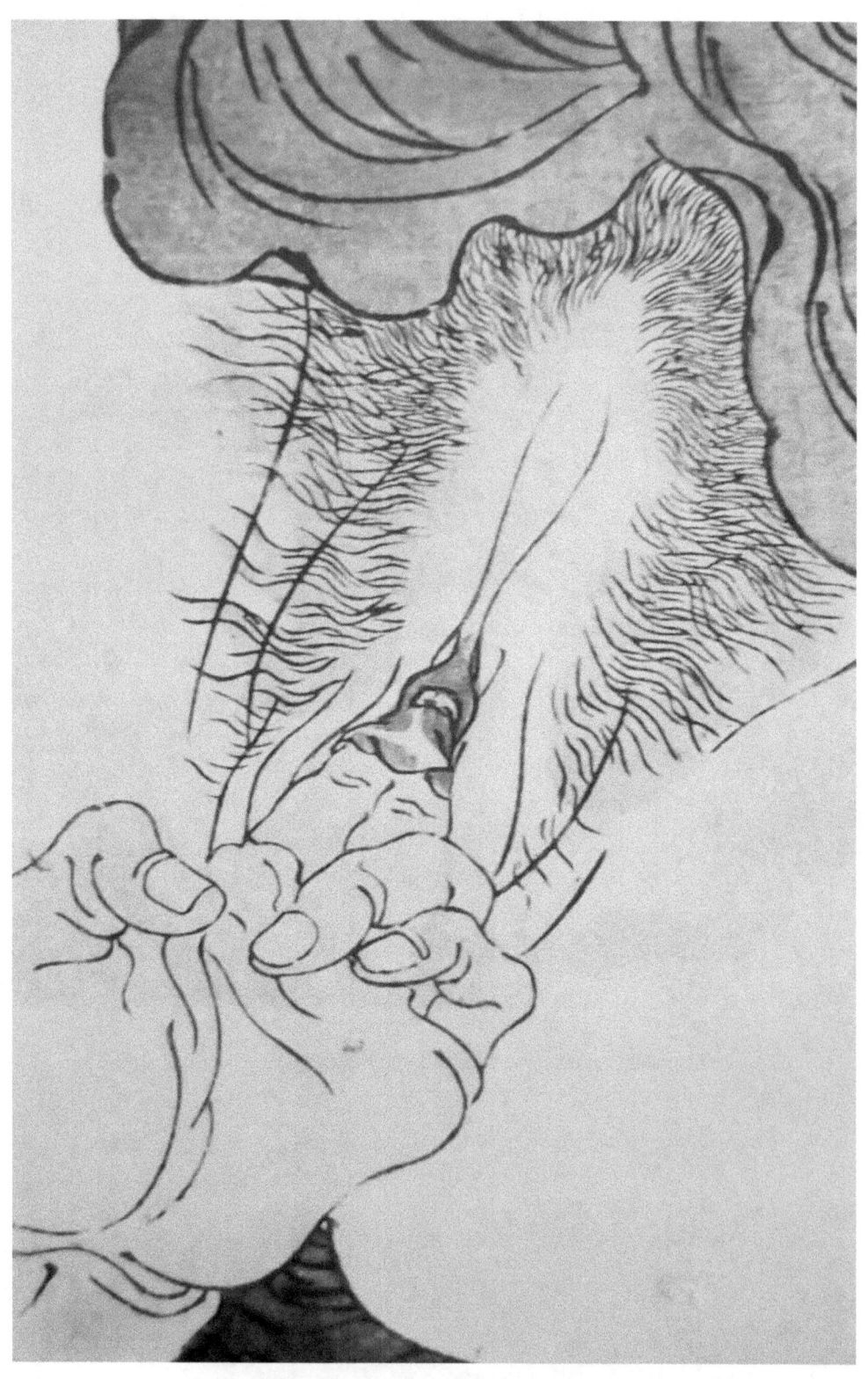

Utagawa Kunisada, from Shunshoku Bidan, 1840

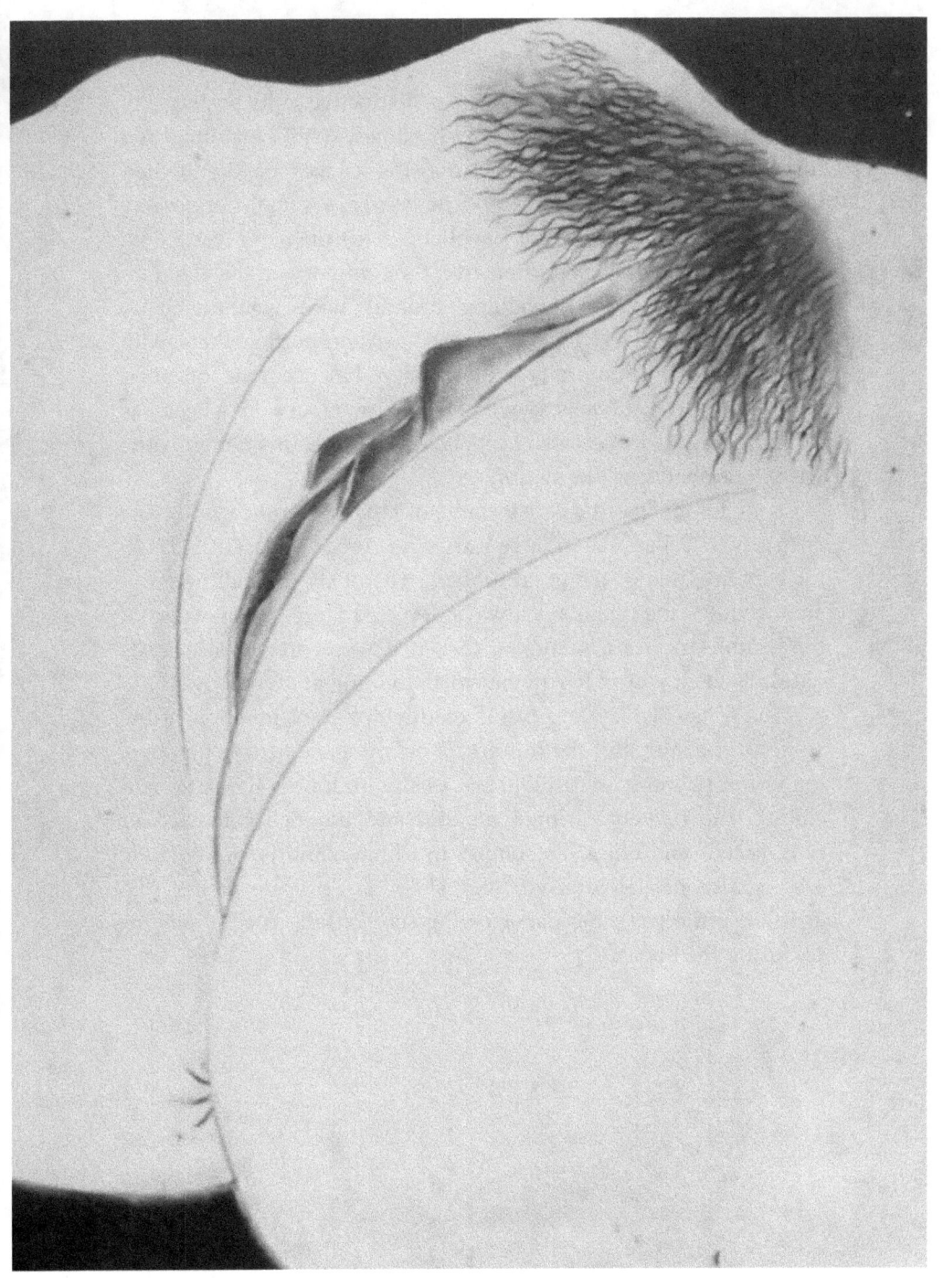

From Vaginal Album, Japanese,
ukiyo-e painting on paper, mid-19th century

Chinese and Japanese erotic art is distinctive in its portrayal of the human figure, the elegant flowing lines, with the clothes and furnishings and bedding mirroring the curves of the bodies. Genitals are greatly enlarged – penises are hugely engorged, poised at the entrance of swollen, wide-open vulvas, with clitorises aroused and prominent. It's common in this kind of erotic art to see guys walking around with gigantic cocks, sometimes a few feet long, with the men supporting them with their hands. In humorous erotica, men balance fans on their schlongs, or carry buckets, or ride their members on wheels, as cannons. In satirical scrolls, by Jichosai (18th century), men battle with their phalluses like swords.

Exaggerated genitals are a staple of Japanese erotica, and have been since at least the 12th century: the Abbot Toda (1053-1140), for instance, one of the great erotic artists of the period, noted in an anecdote: 'the phallus is always depicted large, far in excess of the actual size. As a matter of fact, if it were drawn only in its natural size, it would hardly be worth looking at'.[1]

The sense of play and fun is readily apparent in amongst the scenes of fucking. But the tupping is only one element in amongst the visual richness on display: just as significant are the patterned clothes, the flowery, printed textiles, and the rich colouring of reds, greens and blues. The bodies in Chinese and Japanese erotic are usually partially naked, and show up as pale cream (the artists use the base, the paper or the scroll itself, as the basis for colouring the bodies).

---

1 Quoted in P. Kronhausen, 260.

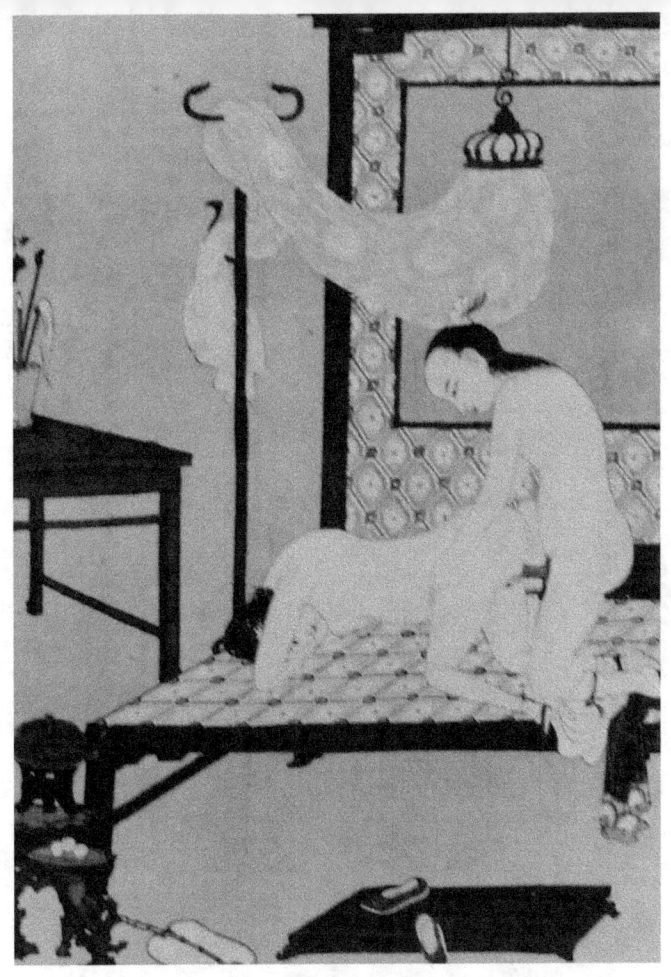

Chinese erotic art: erotic album, above.
Painted scroll, ukiyo-e school, c. 1640, below

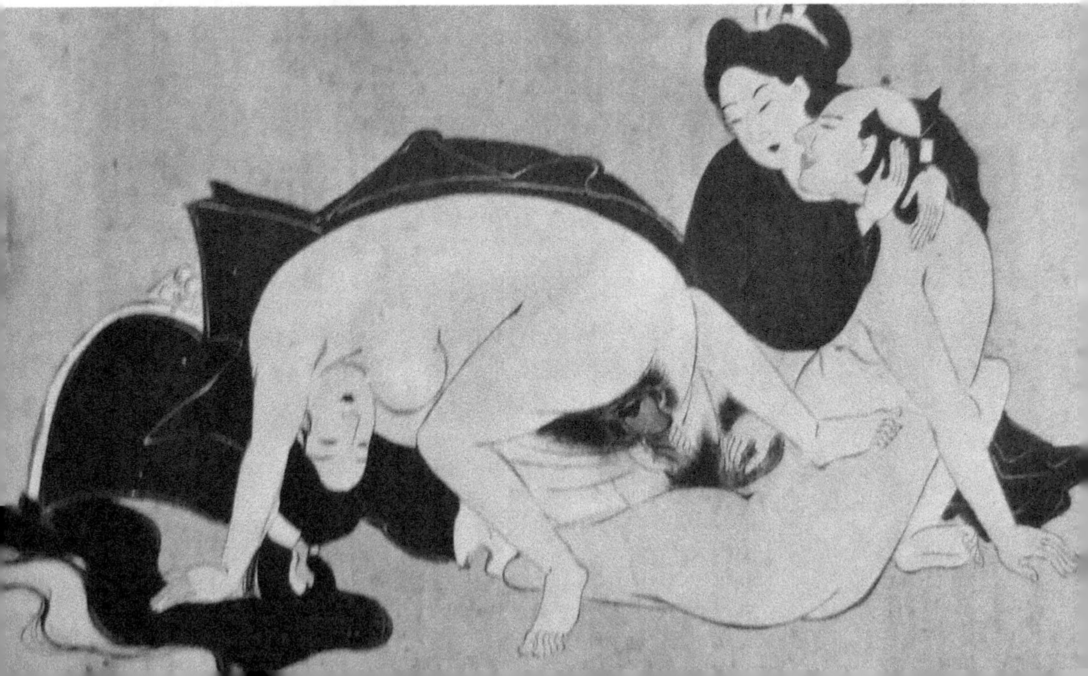

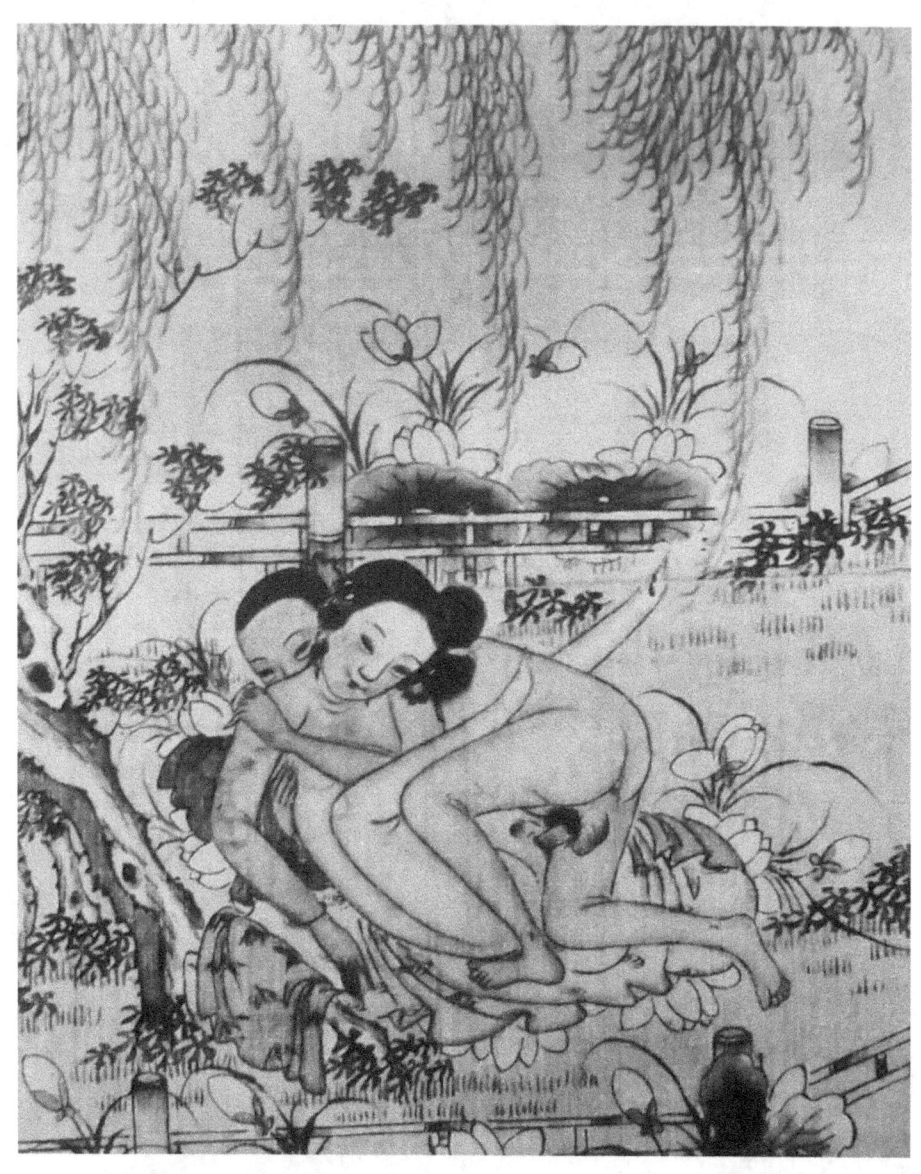

Erotic album, painted on silk, Chinese

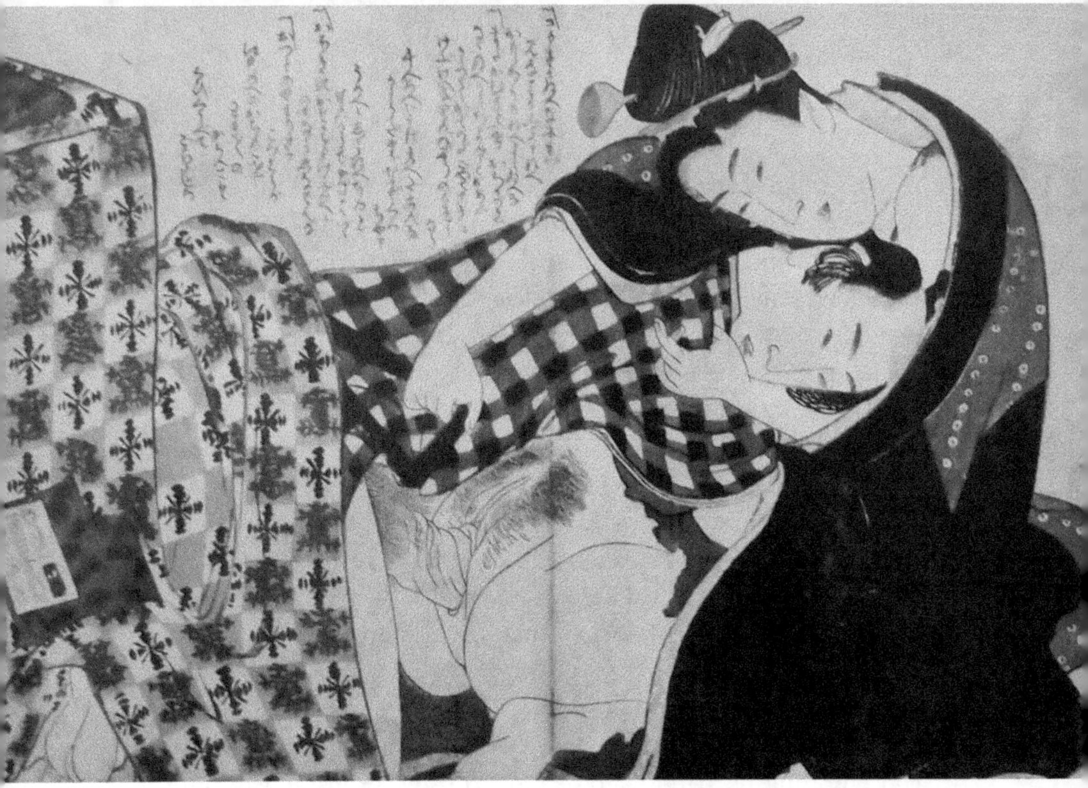

Katsushika Hokusai: Geisha and Lover (above),
and Yoshiwara Courtesan and Lover (below).

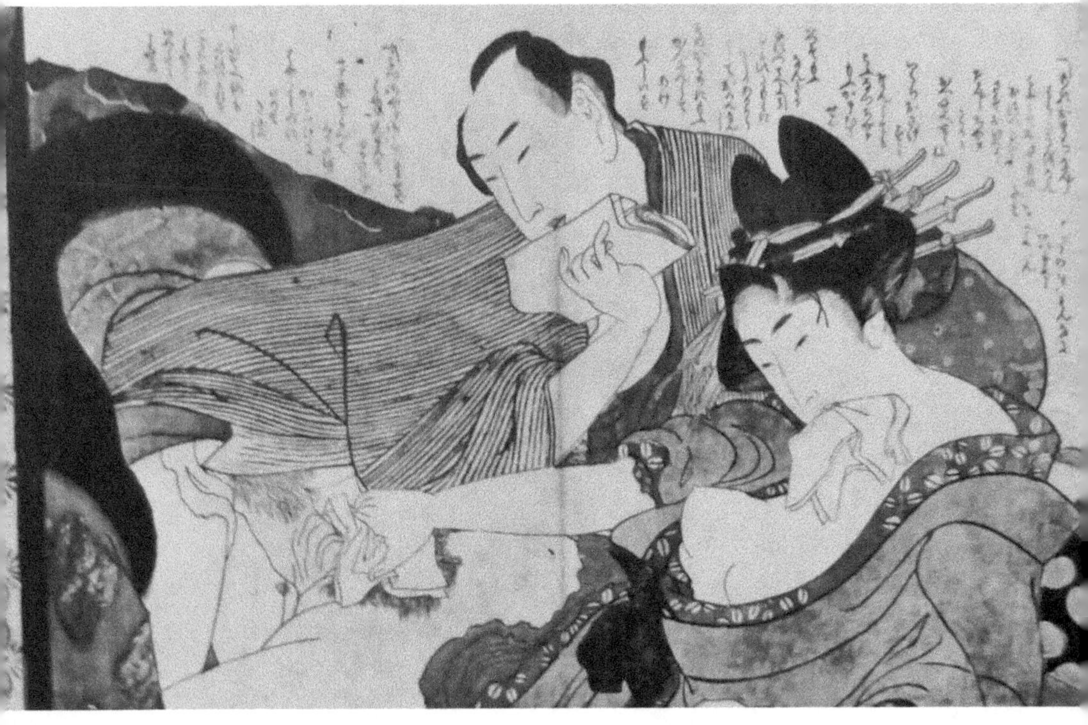

In Indian erotic art, the participants have a wonderfully serene temperament: in sets of miniatures and paintings, the couples go through every variety of sexual position, while calmly smiling to themselves or to each other. It's explicitly erotic art, with the genitals on display: the thighs of men and women are bent right back, to reveal the penis entering the vagina.

The people are *types*, as they are in contemporary pornography. They are not individualized: they are simply *a* man and *a* woman. It doesn't really matter *who* they are. They are, though, definitely the leisure class, aristocrats and the bourgeoisie. Indian erotic art includes depictions of tupping on the back of an elephant, lovemaking during a tiger hunt, a woman using a bow to fire a phallic arrow into a woman, and an antelope mounting a woman.

The other striking thing about Indian, Chinese and Japanese erotic art is how *decorative* it is, how much the artists are concentrating on patterns, on shapes, on the props and furniture in the pictures. The world of Oriental erotic art is certainly visually stunning, and luxurious, with its couches and hangings, its large windows opening onto pleasure gardens, its rich carpets and furnishings, and the lavish costumes (the patterned kimonos, for instance). There is little modelling: rather, the pictures, prints and scrolls are flattened visually, with line and colour doing all of the work (shadows, textures, and modelling are dispensed with).

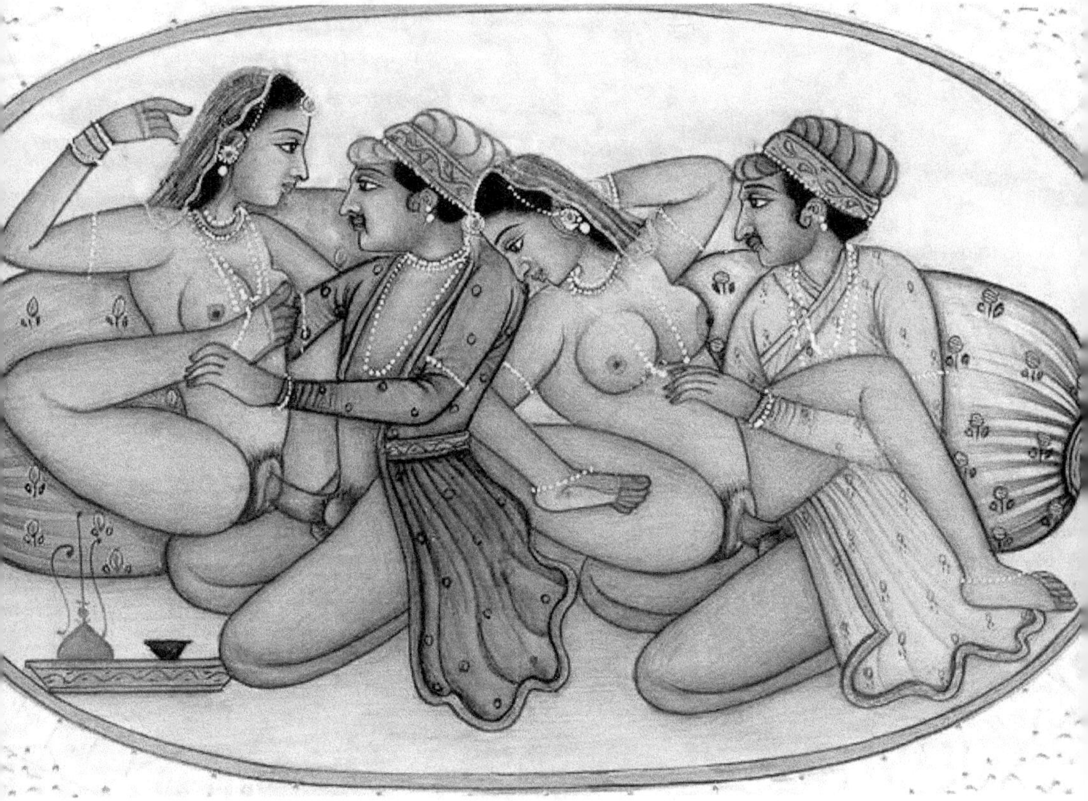

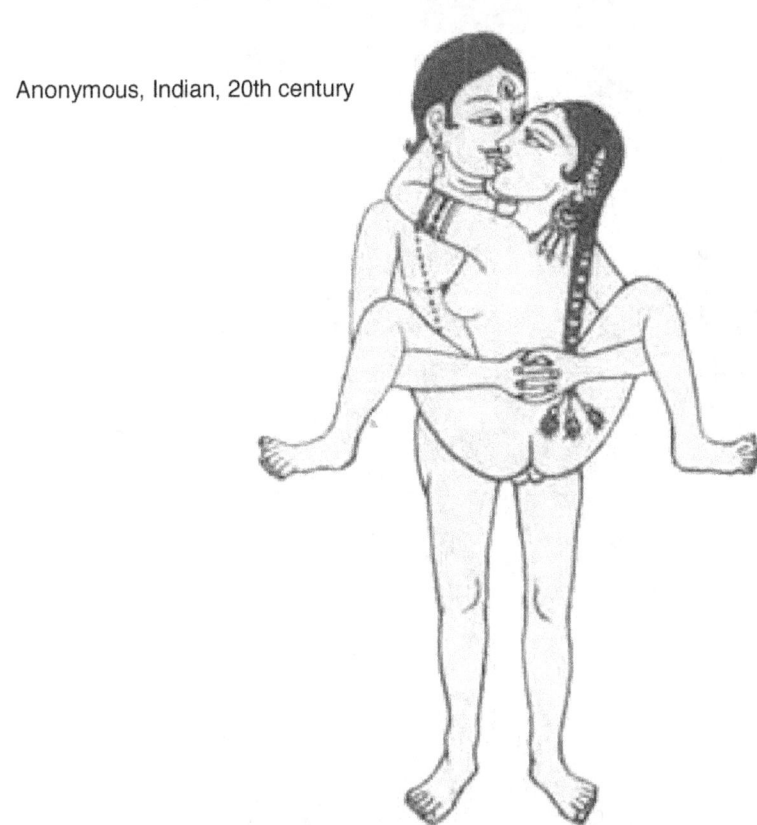

Anonymous, Indian, 20th century

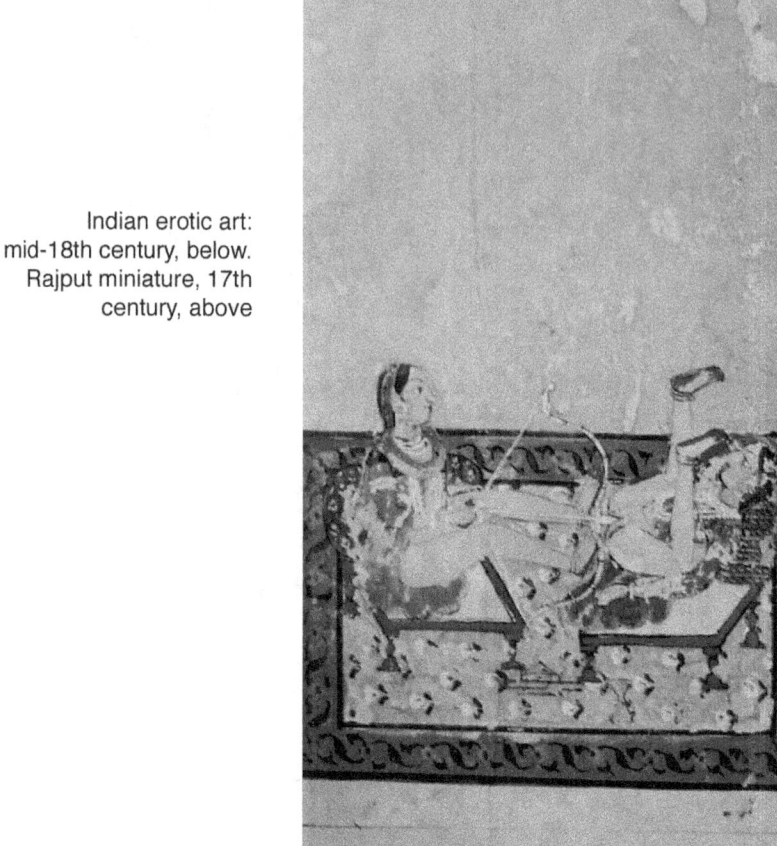

Indian erotic art:
mid-18th century, below.
Rajput miniature, 17th
century, above

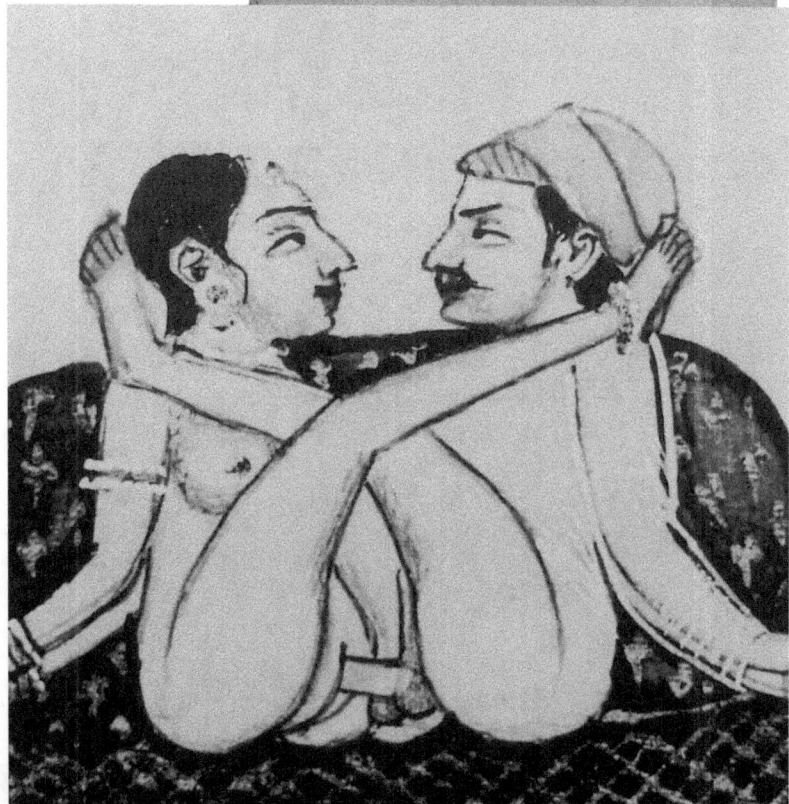

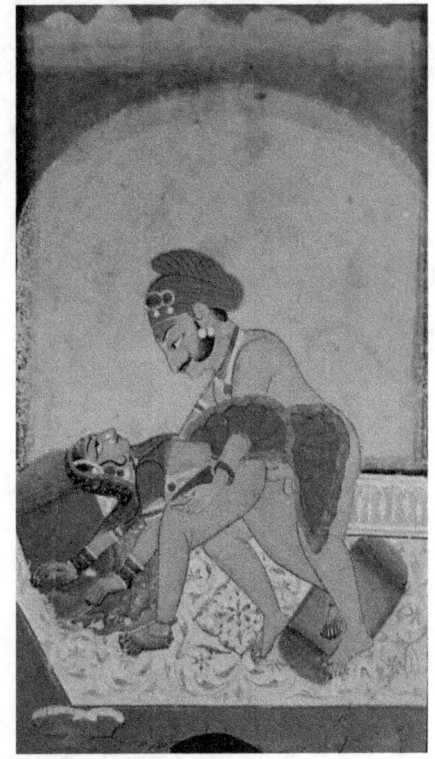

Indian erotic art:
Rajput, late 18th century, above.
Mogul style, 18th century, below.

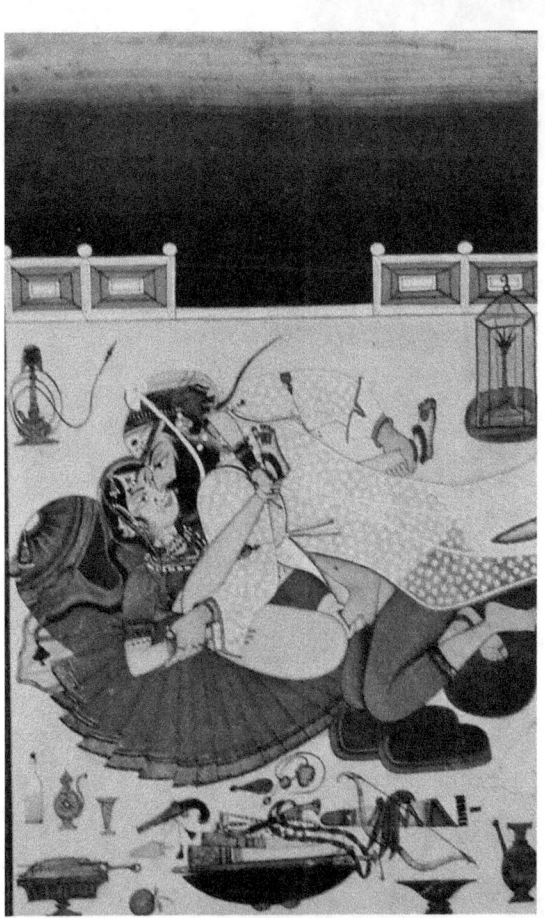

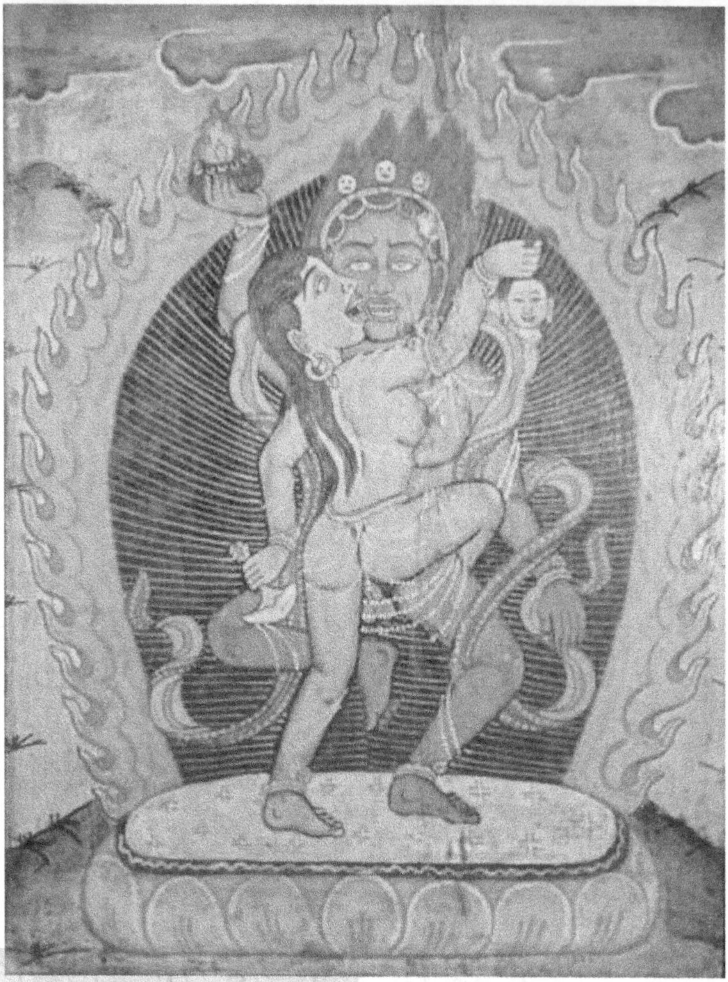

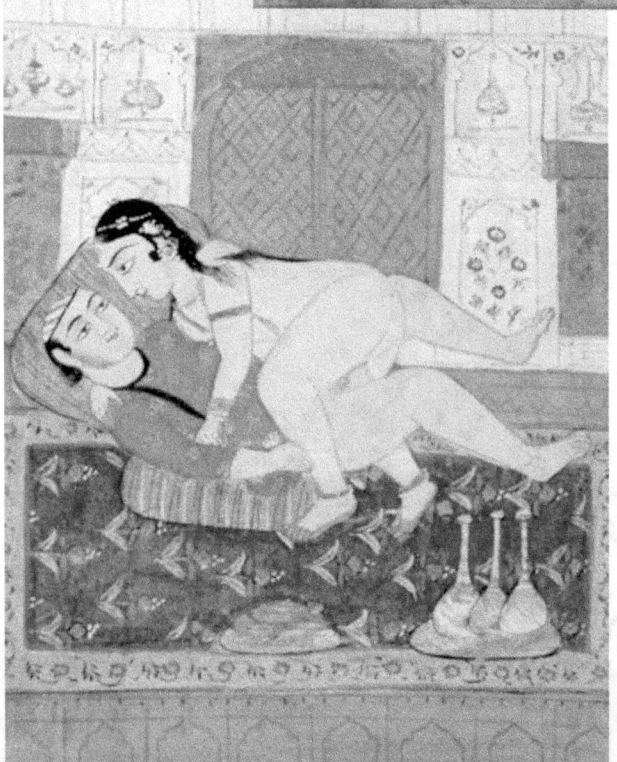

Indian Painting, 19th century,
Erotic Museum (above).
Indian school print (left).

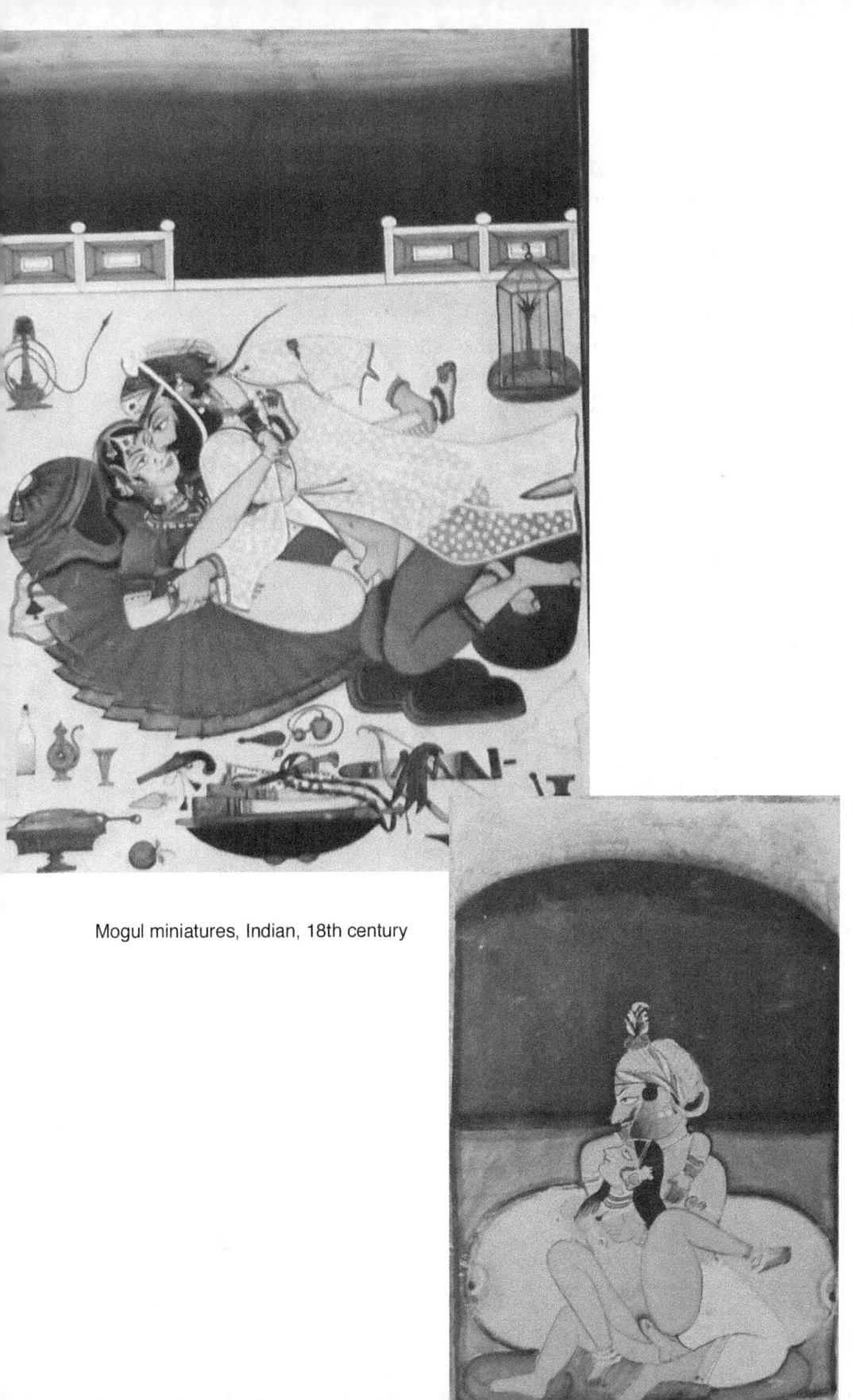

Mogul miniatures, Indian, 18th century

Erotic art in Japan goes back way before *hentai manga* and *animé,* to the woodblock print tradition (of the Edo period), and beyond – back to *shunga* ('posture'/ 'reclining postures') of the 7th and 8th centuries.

Japan has a history of erotic art, going back to woodblock prints in the Edo period, the *ukiyo-e* ('floating world pictures'), developed in the 17th century, and pillow books or *makura-e.*

Also it's not only the phallus that gets the royal treatment in Japanese erotic art: albums were also produced of women's genitals – whole erotic albums and sets of woodblock prints of vaginas. Katsushika Hokusai, for instance, created the *Elontsubi no hinagata* (*Models of the Vulva*), a set of twelve colour prints.

In Indian, Japanese and Chinese erotic art, people are shown gleefully and gymnastically contorting and entwining around one another. On hammocks, swinging from trees, on balconies, beds, cushions, tables, beside lakes, they copulate anywhere and everywhere. The depictions, by many anonymous artists, and also by celebrated artists such as Katsushika Hokusai, Utagawa Kunisada, Kitagawa Utamaro, Nishikawa Sukenobu and Torii Kiyonobu, show all manner of sexual activities, including a woman being licked by an octopus (Hokusai's famous image), rape by demons, and a blowjob while waiting in line at Burger King (just kidding).

Japanese *shunga* prints, especially, depict lovemaking as an innocent, pleasurable activity. The couples tup amidst serene Eastern landscapes, with vases filled with flowers, little fences, beautiful gardens, bo trees, lakes and streams. It all seems so pastoral and sublimely tranquil.[1]

1 Harunobu: *A Fantasy*, late 1760s, anonymous: *Trio in a Garden*, 18th century, China; *The Attack from the Rear, or 'The Leaping White Tiger'*, painting on silk from an album of the K'ang-hsi period, 1662-1722, C.T. Loo Collection, Paris; *In the Garden on a Rocky Seat*, painting on silk, K'ang-his period, C.T. Loo Collection, Paris

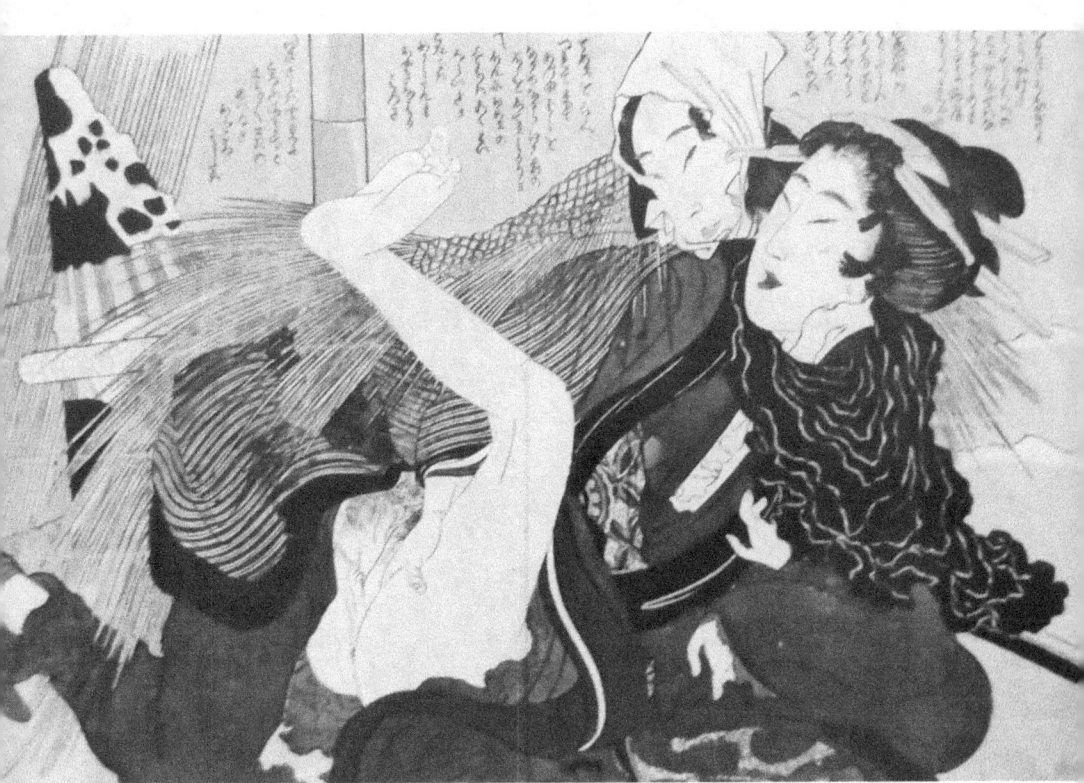

Katsushkia Hokusai, Lover and Geisha

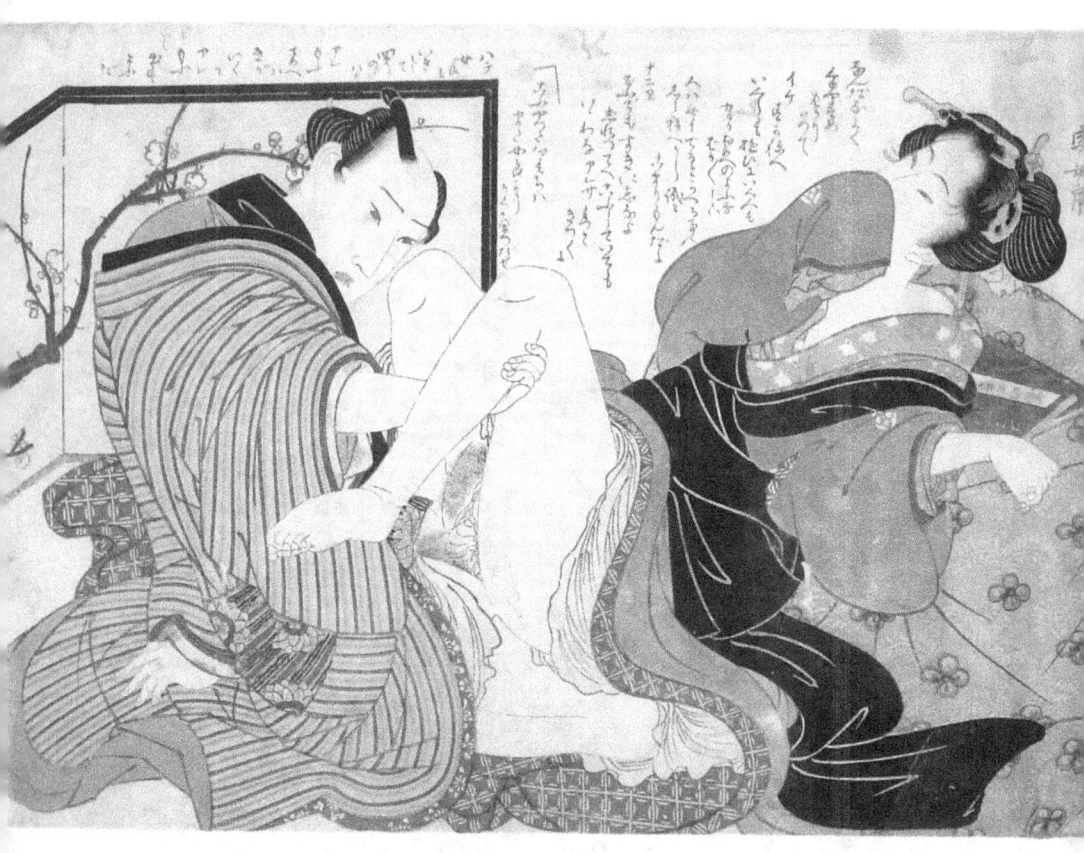

Japanese print, by Eizan

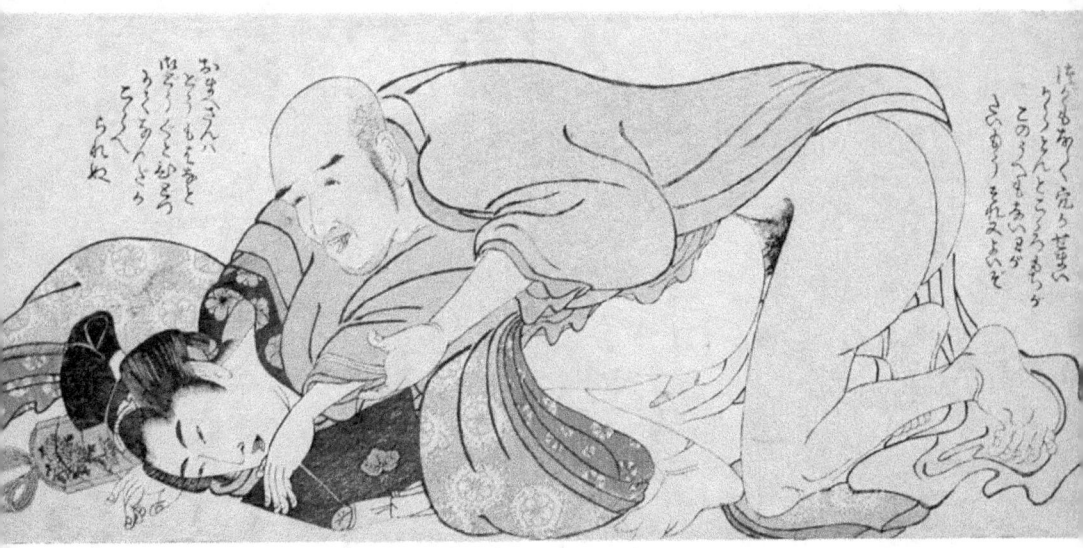

Two homoerotic images by Kitagawa Utamaro

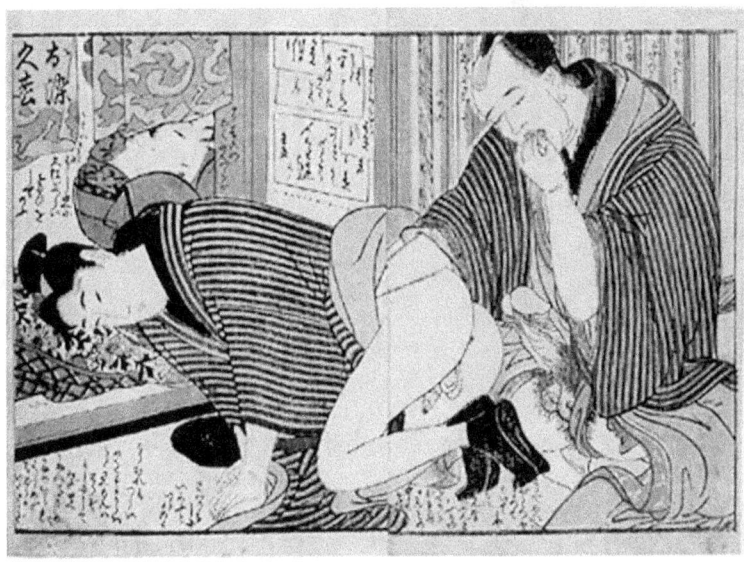

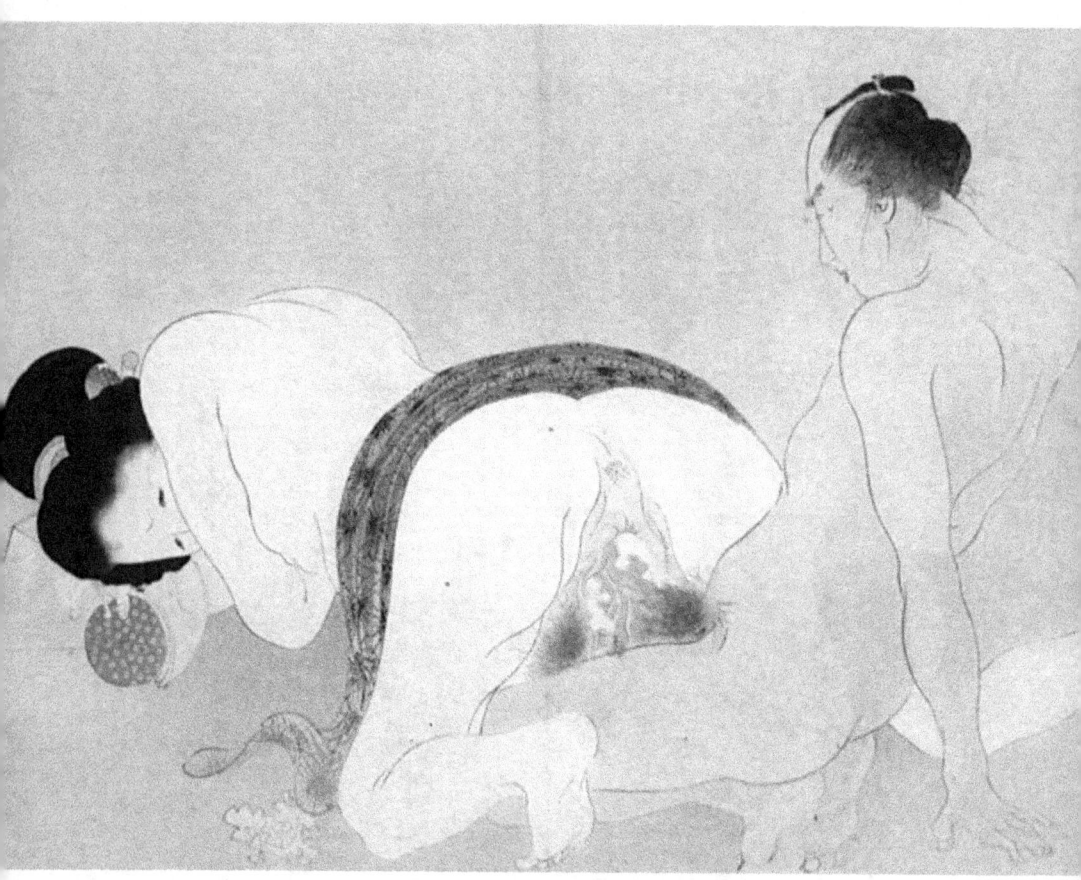

Shunga erotica, attributed to Tomioka Eisen (1864-1905)

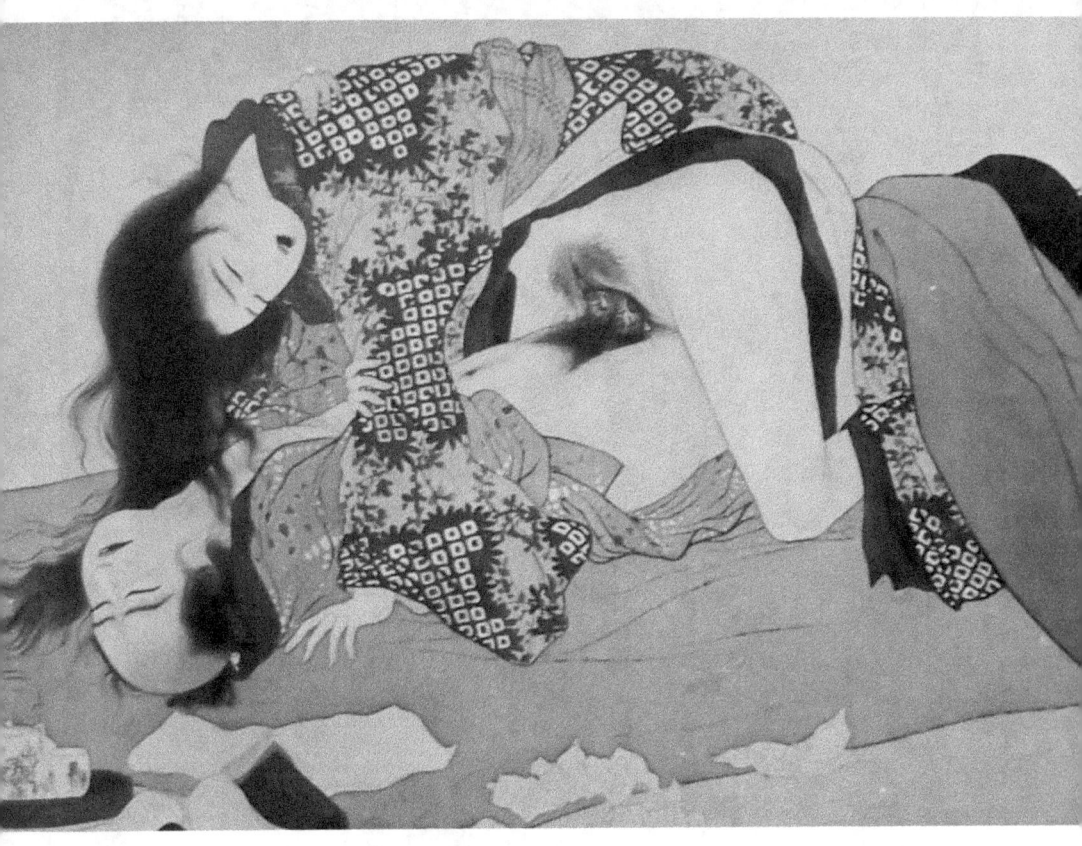

Uemara Shoen (1875-1949),
painted album, Japanese

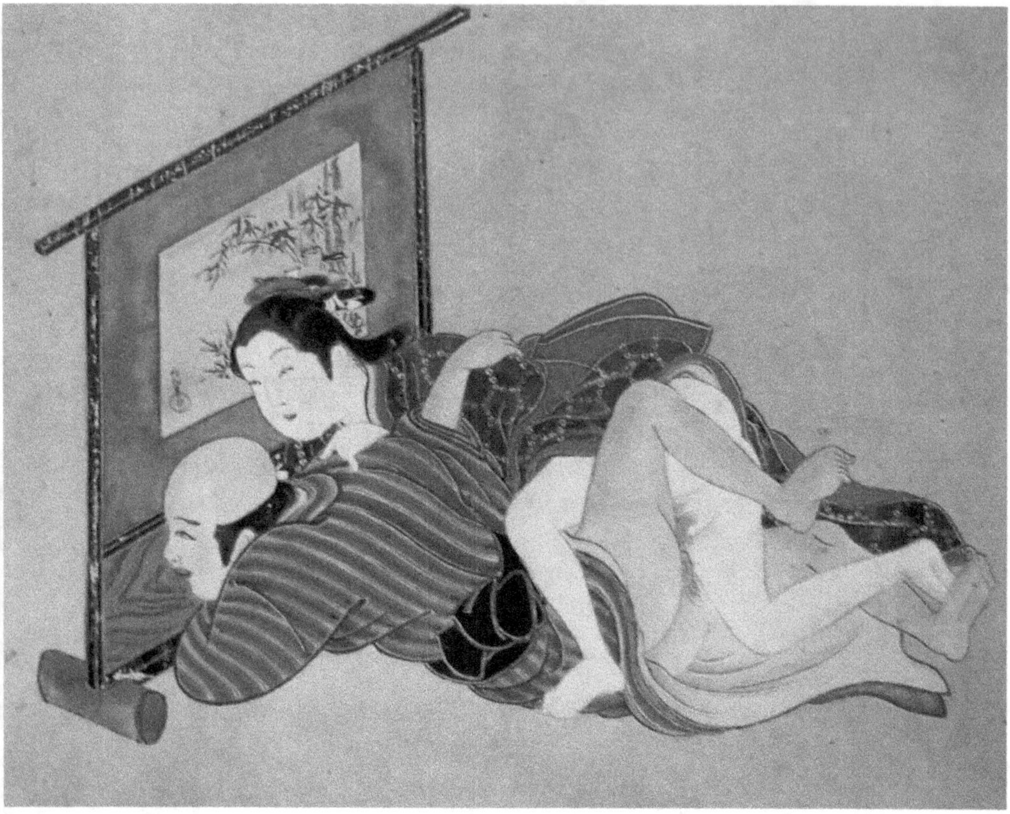

Nikikawa Sukenobu, early 18th century, Japanese

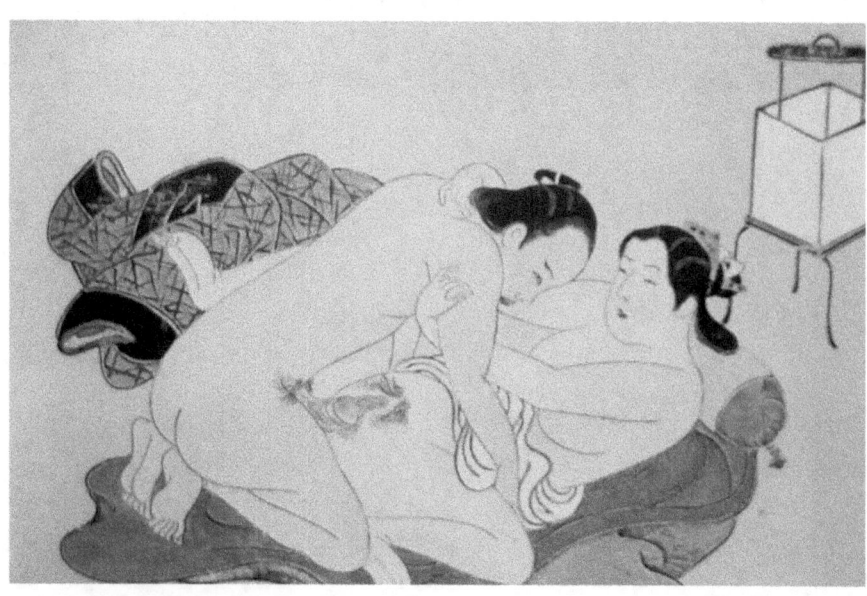

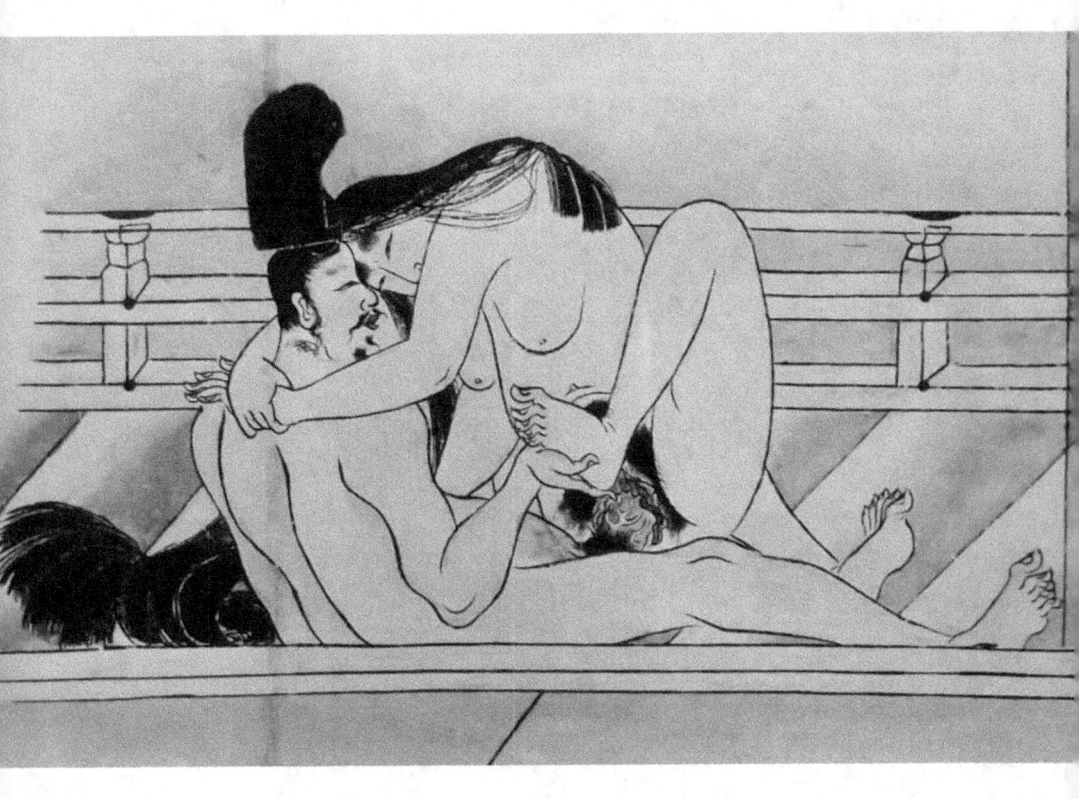

Keitoku, after Brushwood-Fence Scroll
(Koshibargaki-Zoshi), 12th century, Japan

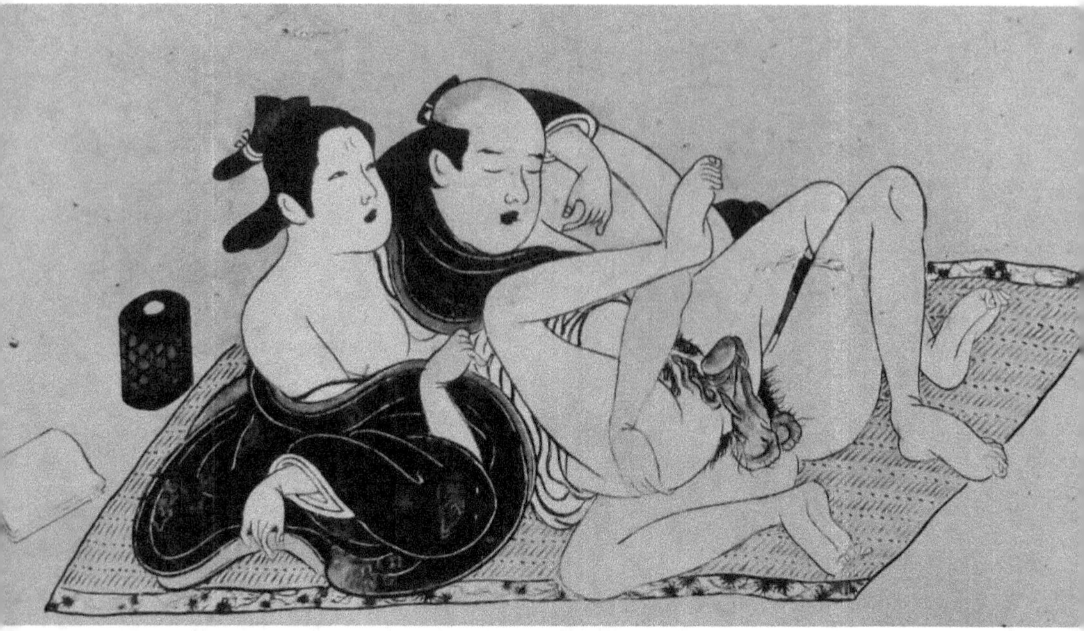

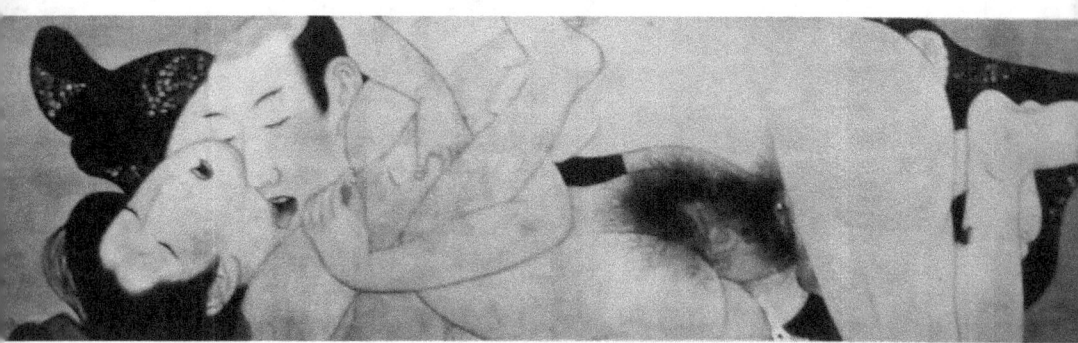

Nishikawa Sukenobu (1671-1751), ukiyo-e scroll, Kyoto, Japan (above).
Settei, Okyo school, 1780s, Japan (below)

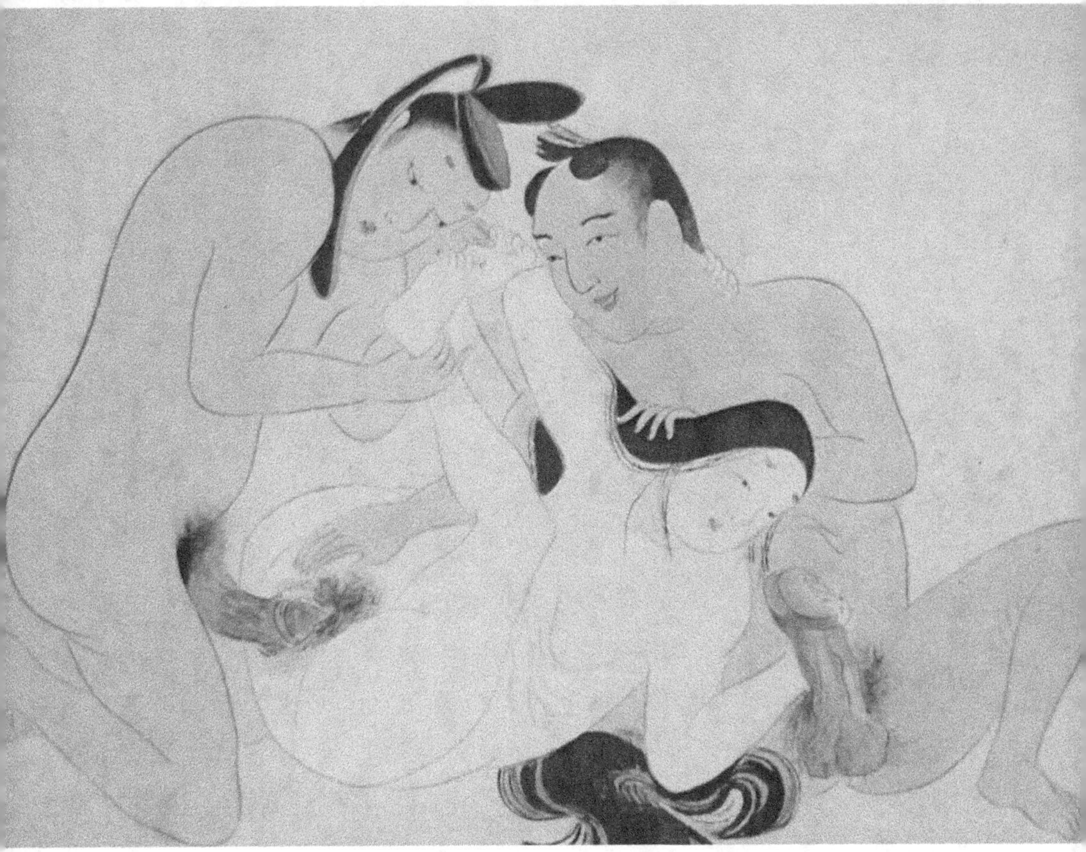

Late 18th century, Japanese (above).
Kangyo, late 19th century, Japanese (below)

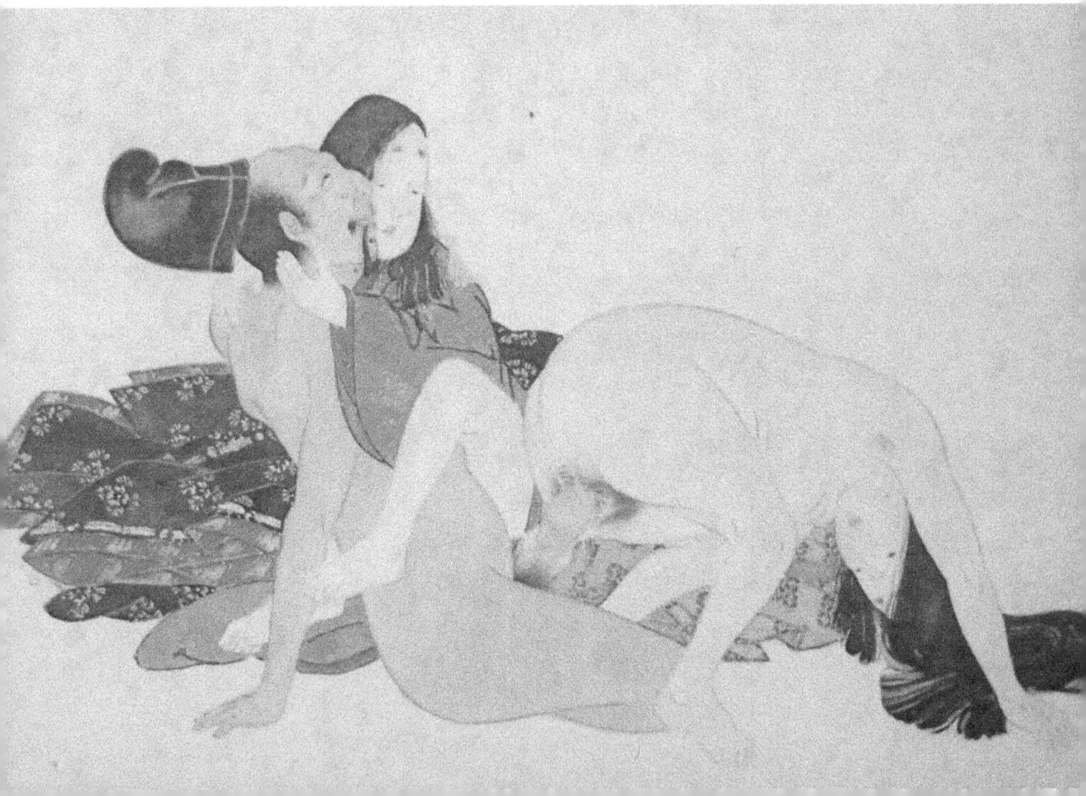

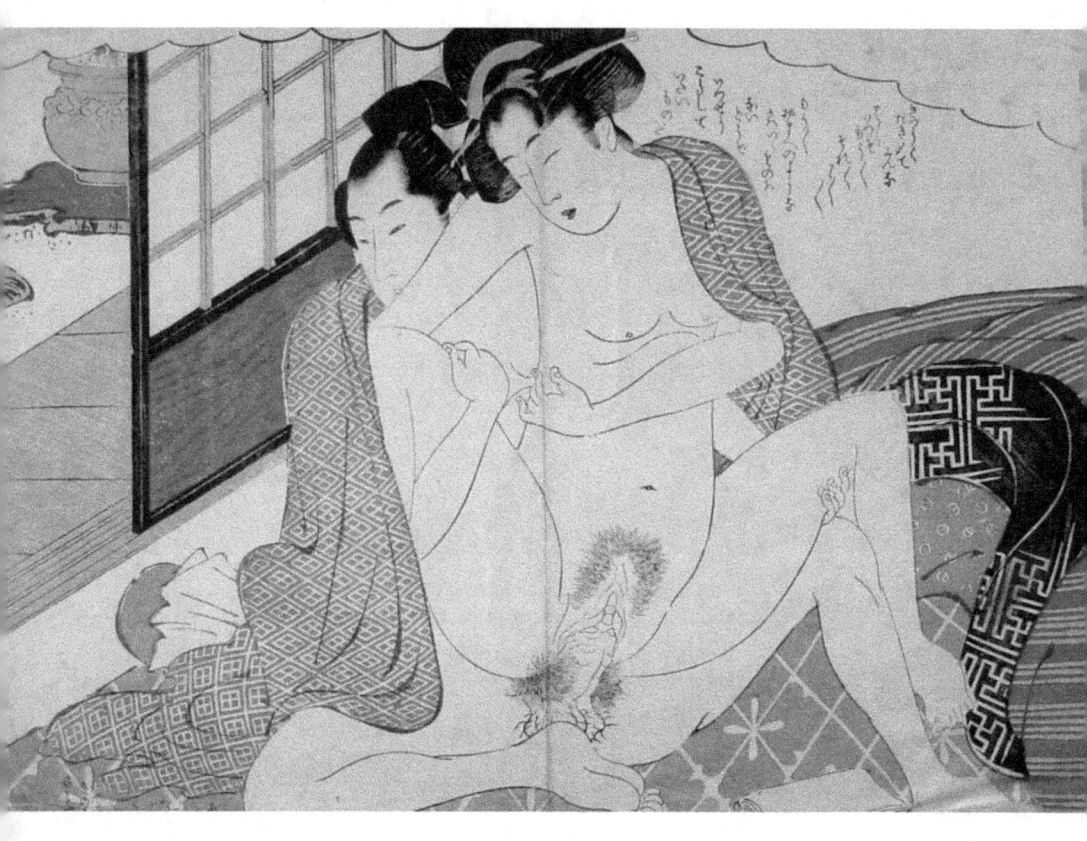

Japanese shunga print, 19th century
(this page and over)

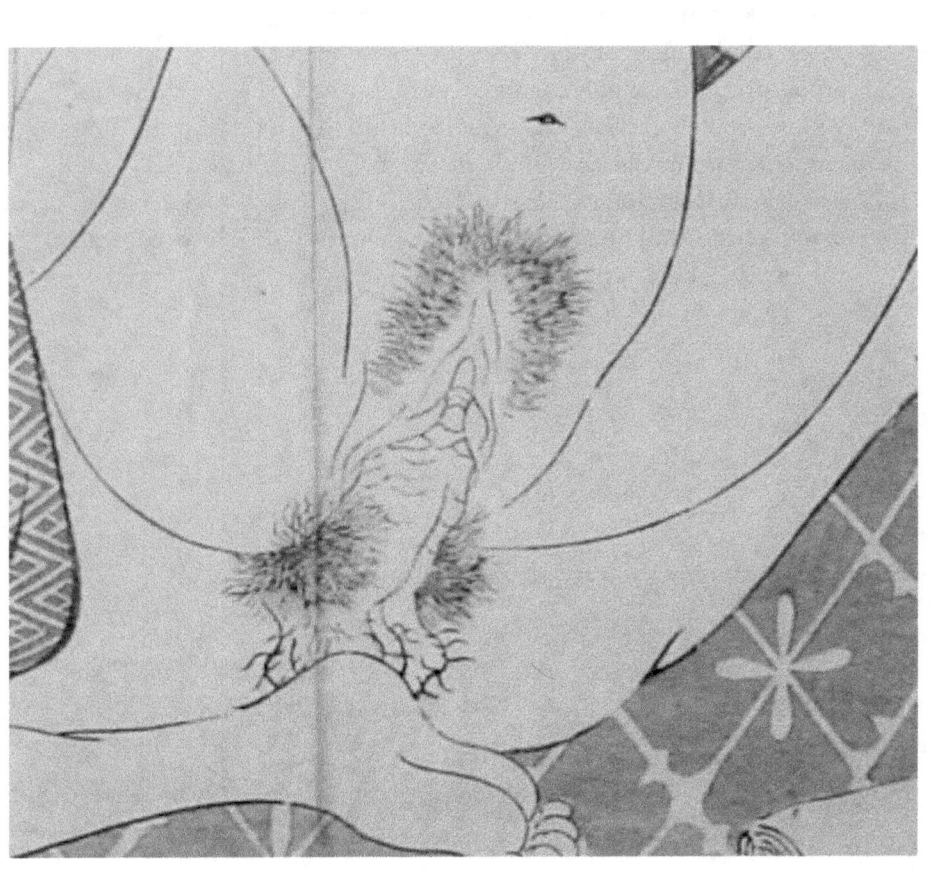

The inheritance of Japanese erotic art is the *manga* and *animé* tradition of contemporary Japan, in comics, comic books and animated movies and OAVs. Among the most famous of these is the *Legend of the Overfiend* series of animated movies, which draws inspiration from many sources, but also from Japanese erotic art, particularly in its more eccentric (and violent) aspects. *Manga* and *animé* comics and cartoons also use the human types of Japanese erotic art, and exaggerate them even further. The emphasis on young women (*shojo*), for instance, with their huge eyes, tiny mouths, large breasts and voluptuous bodies, are notorious – not only because of their sexual objectification, and the violence in many of the situations (with rape a favourite), but also because they are (or more correctly, *appear to be*) very young.

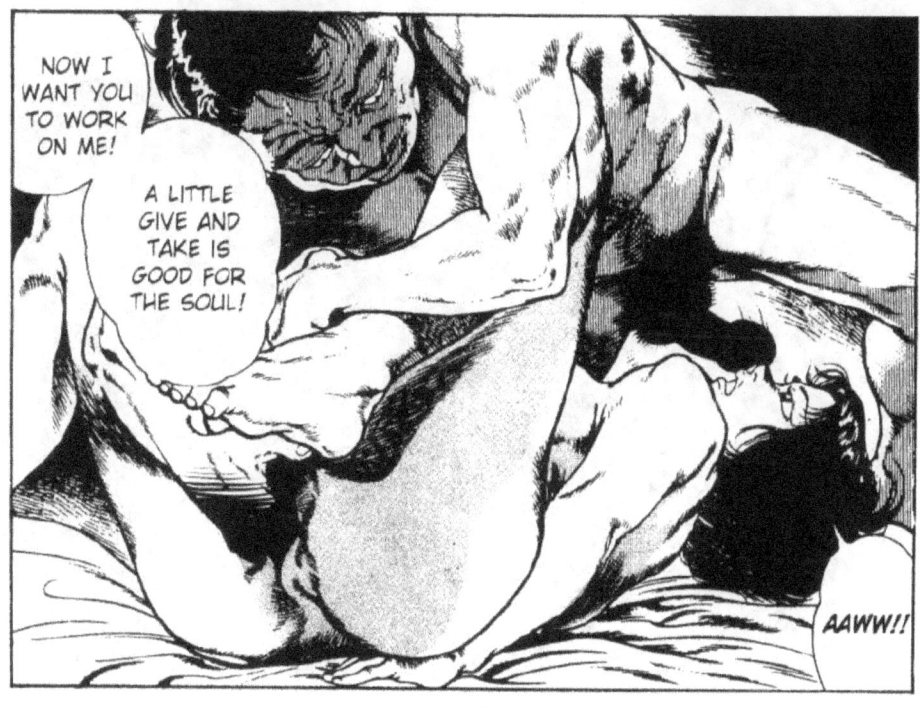

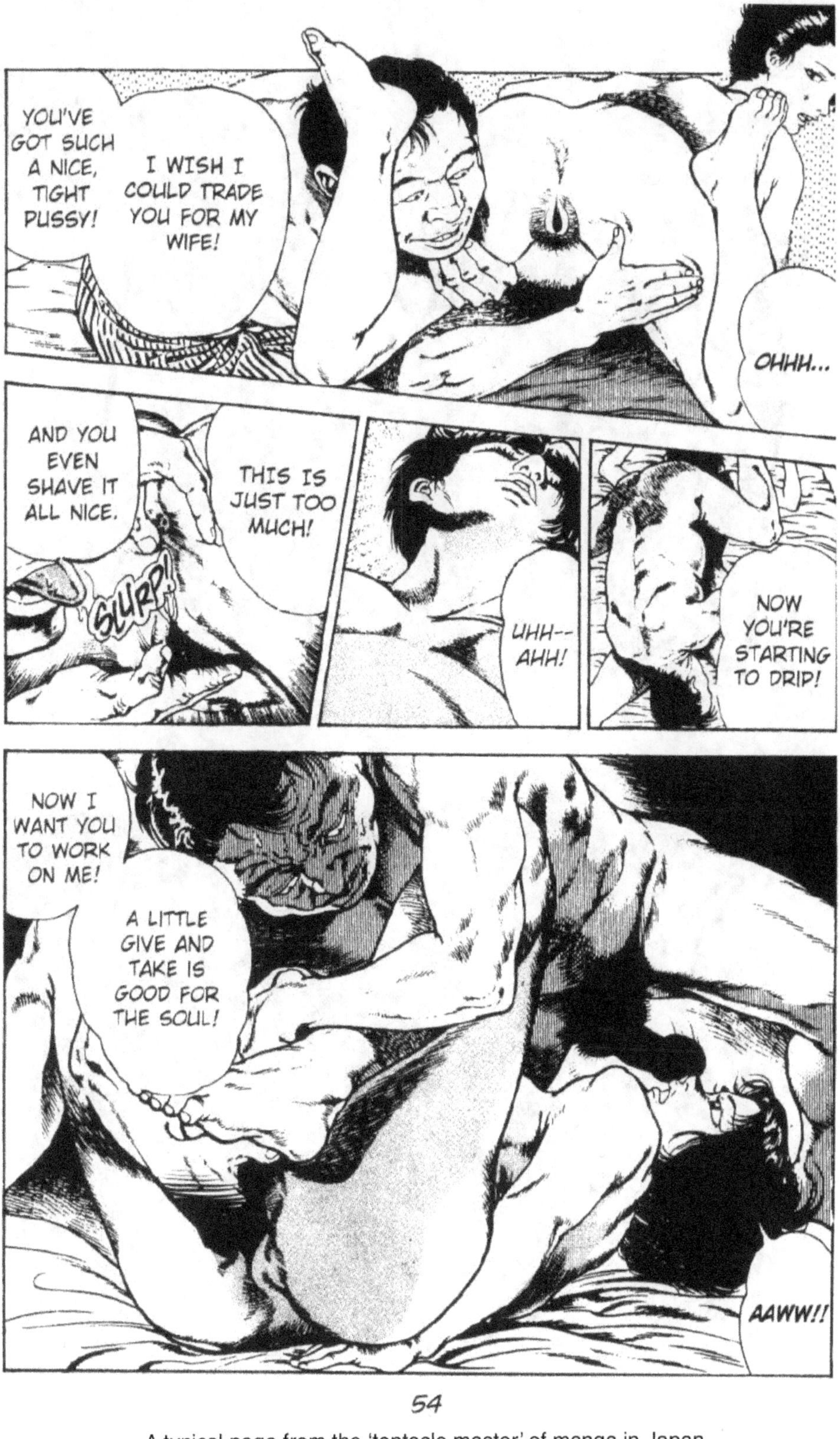

54

A typical page from the 'tentacle master' of manga in Japan,
Toshio Maeda (from his signature work, Urotsukidoji –
Legend of the Overfiend)

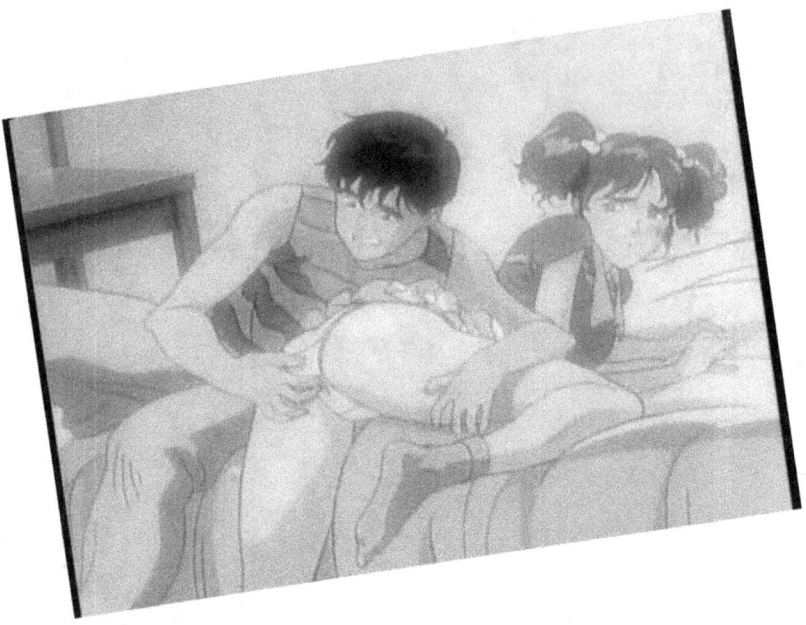

Legend of the Overfiend (1989)

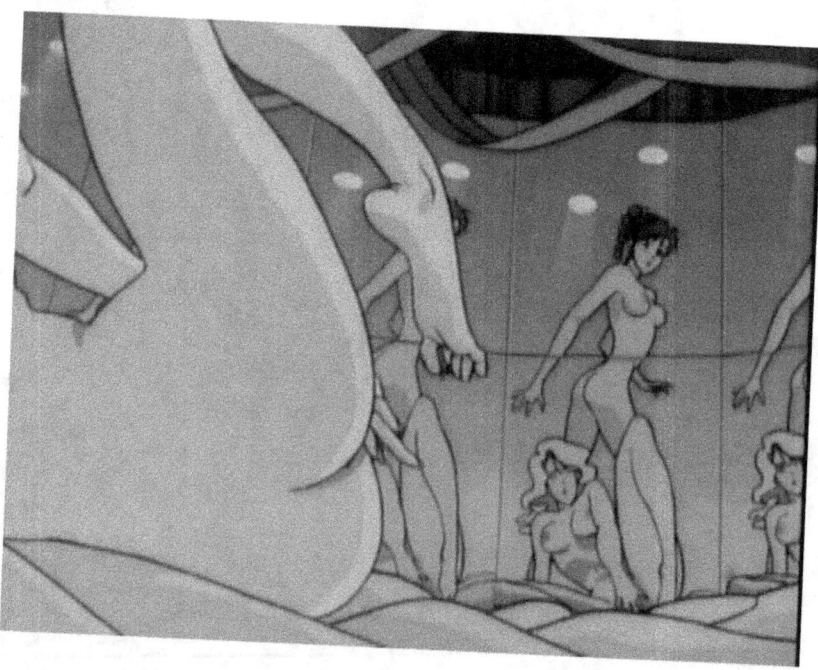

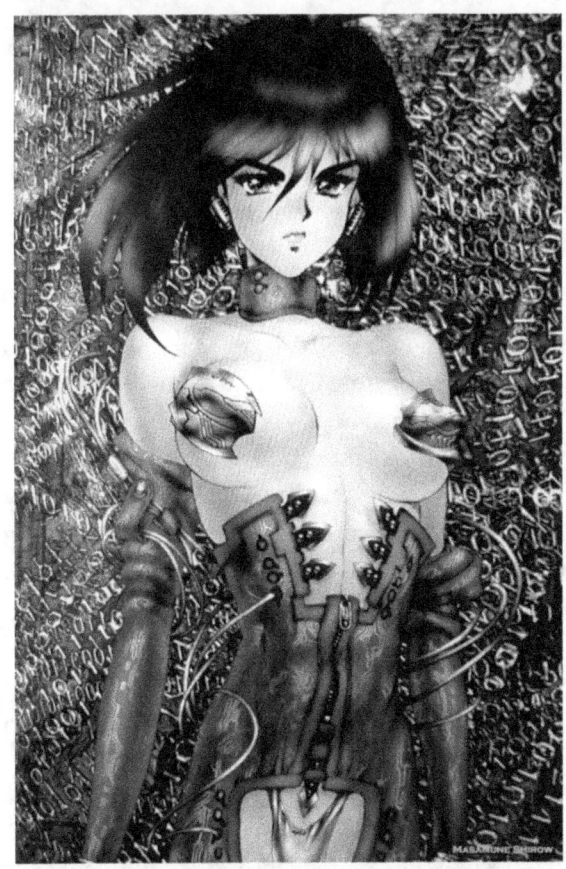

The extraordinary
cyberpunk art of
Masamune Shirow
(best known for
Ghost In the Shell)

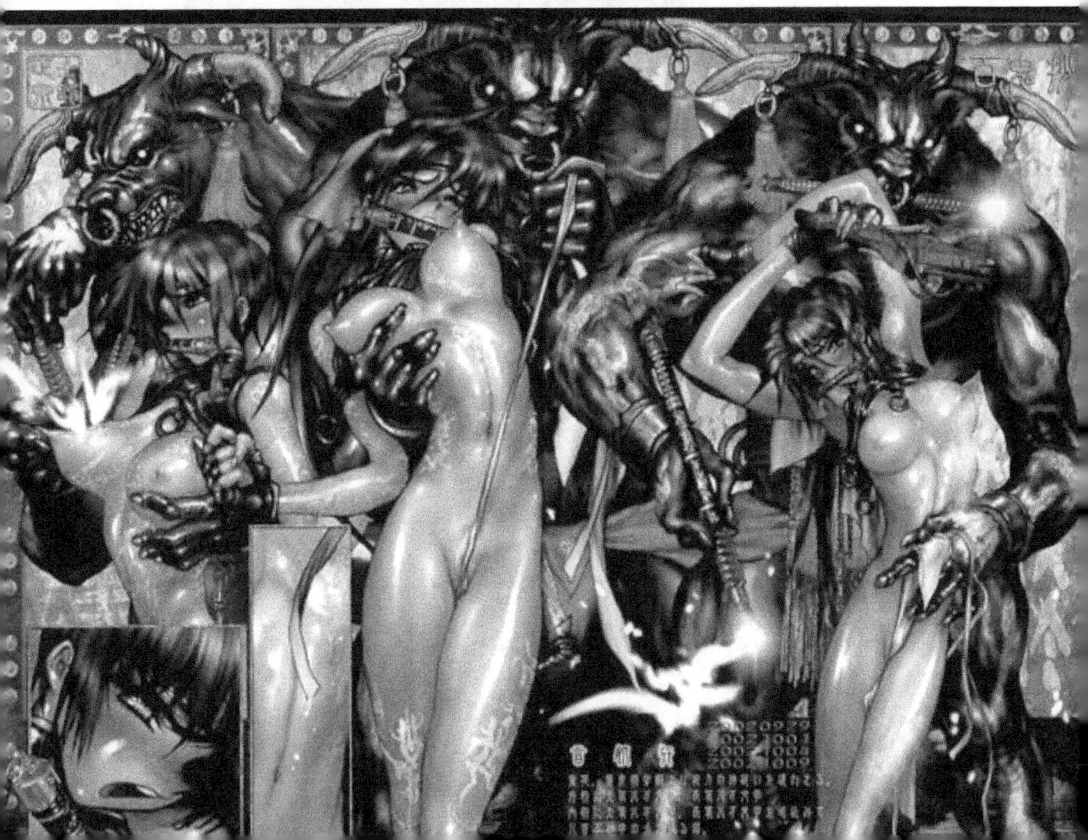

EROTIC ART IN THE RENAISSANCE

Imagine a nude painting of the Blessed Virgin Mary. The idea, to patrons, critics and consumers of Renaissance and mediæval art is shocking, as well as blasphemous. A naked Mother of God, it is unthinkable in terms of Renaissance and mediæval painting. There is a cult of the Virgin baring one breast, to suckle the baby Jesus. Here painters could depict breasts and nipples being sucked and it was all sanctified by the Catholic establishment. Anthony Van Dyck, Titian, Jan Gossaert (Mabuse), Hans Baldung, Joos van Cleeve, Rembrandt van Rijn and Peter Paul Rubens, among many others, painted the breasts of the Madonna.[1] The scene is usually a Holy Family, in Christ's childhood, with Jesus one or two years old, in some house, a room somewhere. Or the scene is a landscape in those paintings entitled *The Rest on the Flight Into Egypt*. Here, Joseph, always depicted as an old man, looks on longingly as Jesus is breast-fed. Joseph is an onlooker, a way into the picture, for the (male) viewer looks at the mother and child through Joseph's eyes. (The viewer is assumed to be masculine in most Renaissance paintings). In one painting of the Virgin breastfeeding Christ, by Orazio Gentileschi, Joseph has fallen asleep.[2] We do not see the mother and child through his vision. Instead, Jesus looks directly out at the viewer while he sucks his mother's nipple. The viewer is thus embroiled in this erotic mother-child relationship.

1 Titian: *The Virgin and Child*, c. 1570s, 75.6 x 63.2cm, National Gallery, London; Jan Gossaert: *The Virgin and Child*, c. 1530s, 47.7 x 38.2cm, Gemäldegalerie Staatliche Museen Preussicher Kulturbesitz, Berlin; Hans Baldung: *The Virgin and Child with an Angel*, 91 x 64cm, Gemäldegalerie Staatliche Museen Preussicher Kulturbesitz, Berlin; Anthony Van Dyck: *The Rest on the Flight into Egypt*, c. 1627, 134.5 x 114.5cm, Alte Pinakothek, Munich; Joos van Cleeve: *The Rest in the Flight into Egypt*, 54 x 67.5cm, Musées Royaux des Beaux-Arts, Brussels; Rembrandt van Rijn: *The Holy Family*, c. 1640, 41 x 34cm, Louvre, Paris; Peter Paul Rubens: *The Holy Family with the Apple Tree*, 1620-2, 353 x 233cm, Kunsthistorisches Museum, Vienna
2 Orazio Gentileschi: *the Rest on the Flight into Egypt*, 175.3 x 218.4cm, Birmingham Museum

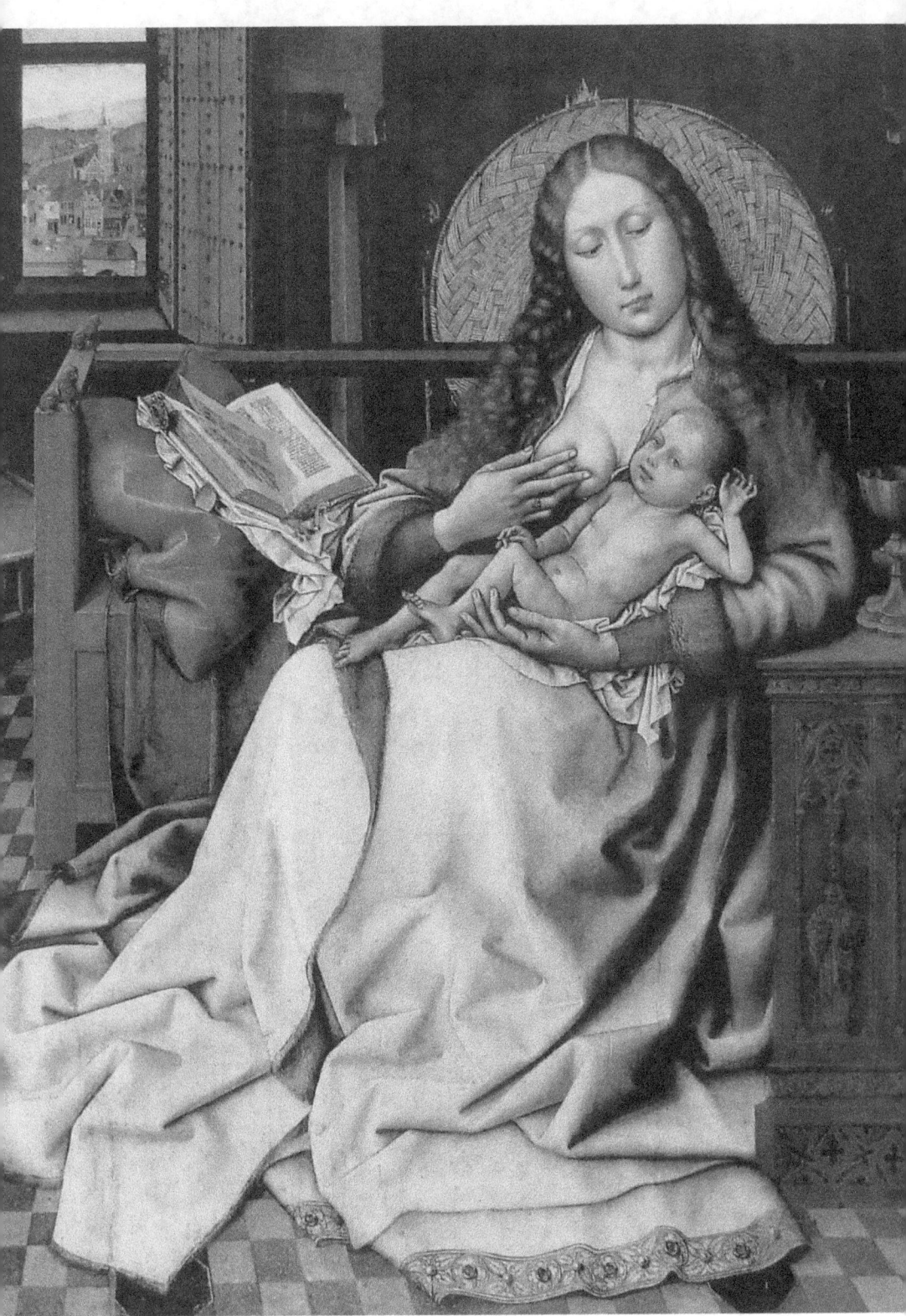

Robert Campin, Madonna With the Firescreen, National Gallery, London

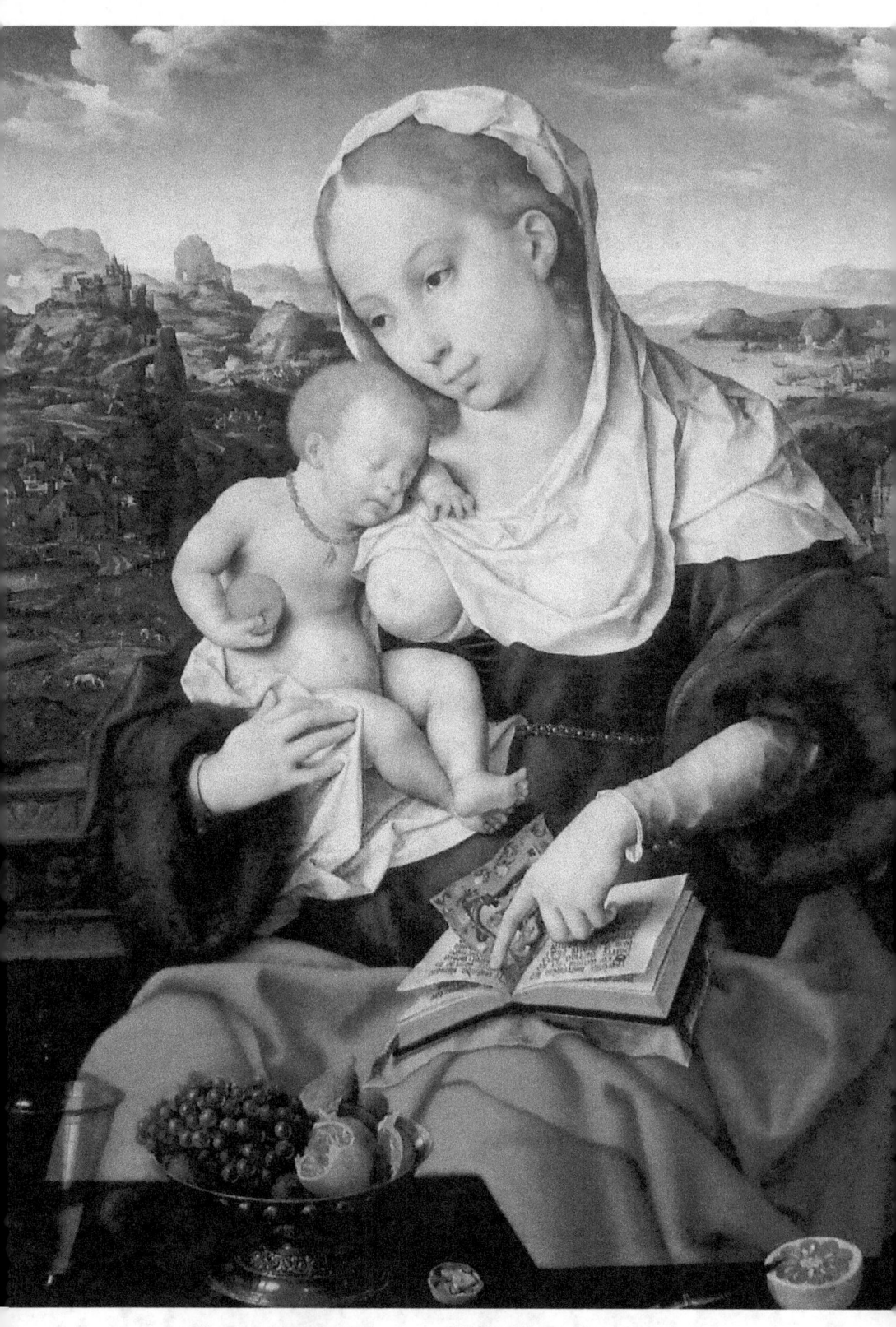

Joos van Cleve, Madonna and Child, Metropolitan Museum,
New York City

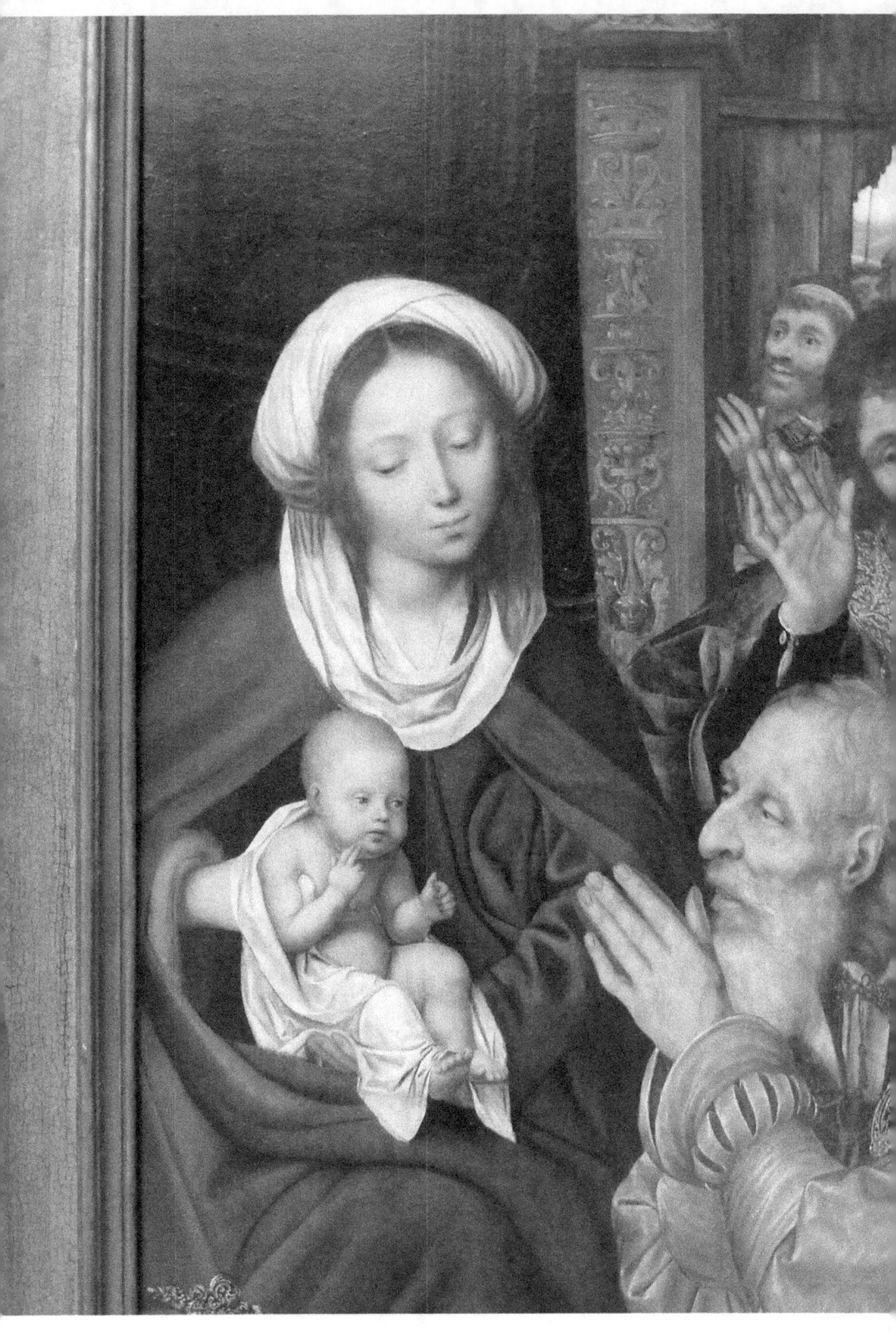

Gerard David, Adoration of the Magi, detail, Metropolitan Museum of Art

Greek mythology enabled Renaissance artists to use images and themes of a wilder, stranger and more erotic nature than the images, themes and codes of Christianity. While Catholicism suppressed sex at every opportunity, only allowing it to express itself in figures such as Mary Magdalene, who had to be portrayed as an eternal penitent, Greek mythology was fully human. The Greek gods and goddesses are playful, stupid, silly, deceitful, jealous, angry, wily, poetic, ignorant and erotic, quite unlike Jehovah or Jesus. Greek myths were subjects in which painters and sculptures could let themselves address erotic issues. The myths, drawn from Ovid, Plato, Apuleius and others, are contain many erotic moments, such as Zeus/ Jupiter making love to Leda in the form of a swan, or Apollo pursuing Daphne – to escape him, she changed into a laurel tree (this was a favourite myth of Francesco Petrarch's), or Actaeon seeing Diana naked, or Pygmalion falling in love with his statue of Venus which comes alive, or the god Zephyr chasing Chloris: when he embraces her, flowers spill from her mouth, as depicted in Sandro Botticelli's famous *Primavera*. Jean-Léon Gérôme painted an indubitably erotic depiction of Pygmalion: the statue comes alive and the sculptor embraces her passionately: the woman's legs are still white marble, but her upper body is already flesh. Typically, Gérôme makes sure that the groin and hips of the statue-becoming-woman are fleshly, for the woman is clearly destined to be the artist's whore, a statue made for sex.

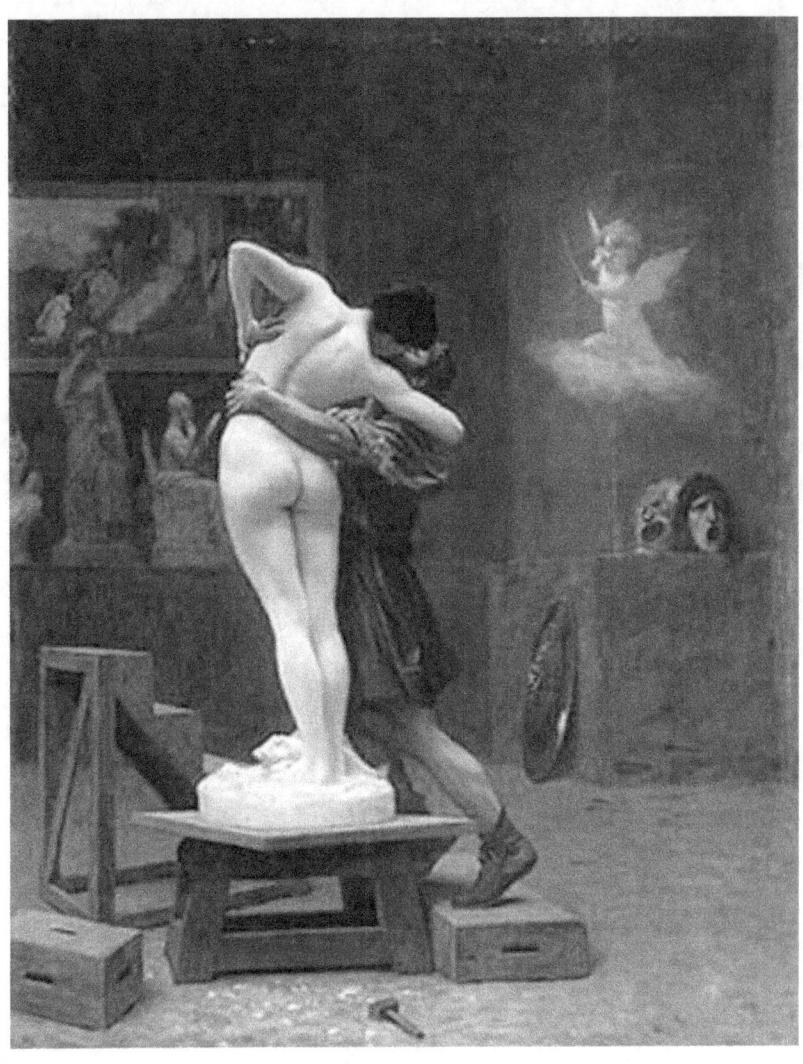

Jean-Léon Gérome, Pygmalion and Galatea,
Metropolitan Museum, New York

The common subject of the Renaissance nude was Venus. As the Goddess of Love in mediæval and courtly love poetry, Venus, with her phallic assistant, Cupid, as the cherub armed with bow and arrow, presided over erotic experiences. The poetry of the troubadours was distinctly erotic and physical, despite its insistence on manners, etiquette and morals. The aim of courtly love poetry was to get into the bed of the beloved woman, basically. Venus was called upon to aid the lover in this pursuit of the Holy Grail, the mystic cauldron of Woman, her womb. Venus is both Holy Whore and chaste Mistress of 'Love'. She is Love personified. The Louvre birth plate, *c.* 1400, shows the Goddess Venus hovering over a Tuscan Garden of Love attended by two angels. Below are six 'famous warriors'. All of them are staring intently at the genitals of the floating Goddess.[1] The lines of sight are marked on the painted salver. The Goddess is depicted in a mandorla, just like the Virgin Mary in *Assumption* images. The centre of the picture is Venus's vulva.[2]

Countless female nudes depict Venus in different poses of shyness and abandonment. Giorgione's *Sleeping Venus* makes the looking at the body easier, because she is asleep.[3] Yet this depiction is created very definitely for the pleasures of eroticism, made for the *jouissance* of looking. Other Renaissance Venuses, from Sandro Botticelli's *Birth of Venus* to Titian's *Venus of Urbino*, to the Master of Flora's *Birth of Cupid*, are offered as gorgeous depictions of women, of mythical women painted sublimely, of women who expose their 'looked-at-ness' for all to see.[4] Even 'unusual' visions of the female nude, such as the paintings of Lucas Cranach, come across, finally, as erotica.[5]

---

1 See Paul Watson: *The Garden of Love in Tuscan Art of the Early Renaissance*, Associated University Press 1979, 17, 23
2 *The Triumph of Venus*, anonymous, birth plate, School of Verona (?), c. 1400, Louvre, Paris
3 Giorgione: *Sleeping Venus*, c. 1508, oil on canvas, 108 x 175cm, Staatliche Kunstsammlungen, Gemäldegalerie, Dresden
4 Titian: *Venus of Urbino*, 1538, oil on canvas, 119.5 x 165cm, Uffizi, Florence; Sandro Botticelli: *The Birth of Venus*, c. 1482, tempera on canvas, 173 x 279cm, Uffizi, Florence; Master of Flora: *Birth of Cupid*, c. 1540/60, oil on wood, 108 x 130.5cm, Metropolitan Museum of Art, New York
5 Lucas Cranach: *the Nymph of Spring*, Palitz Collection, New York; *The Judgement of Paris*, panel, 40.2 x 27.8in, Metropolitan Museum of Art, New York

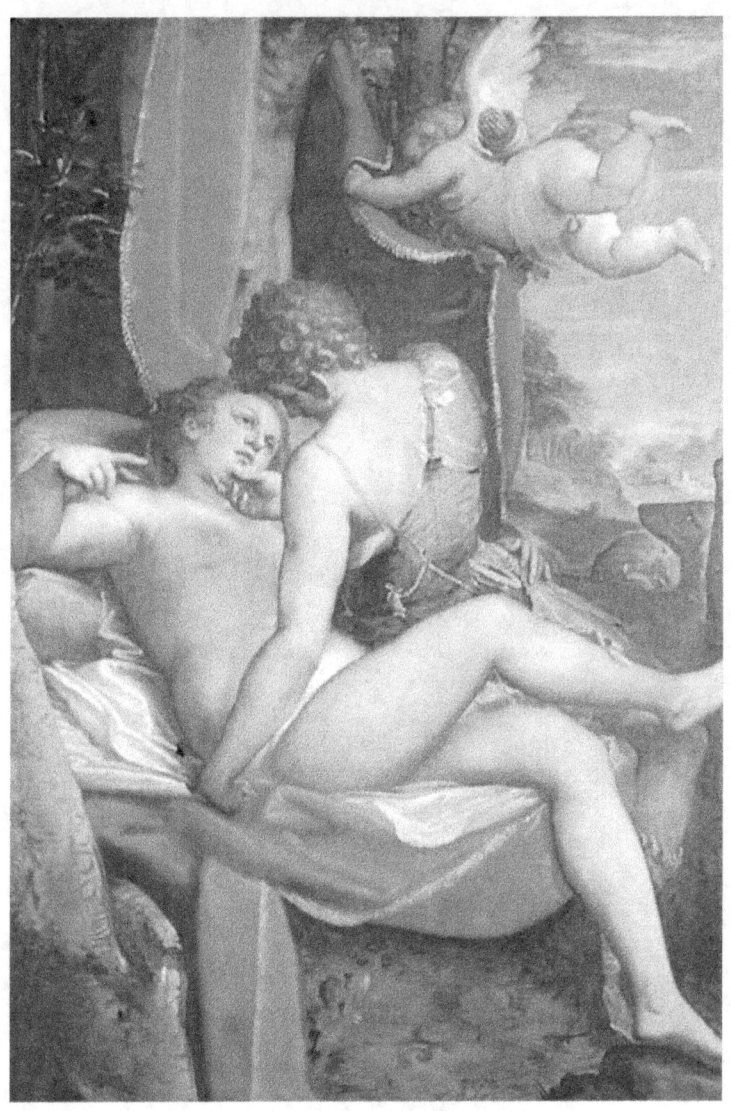

Luca Cambiaso, Venus and Adonis, 16th century

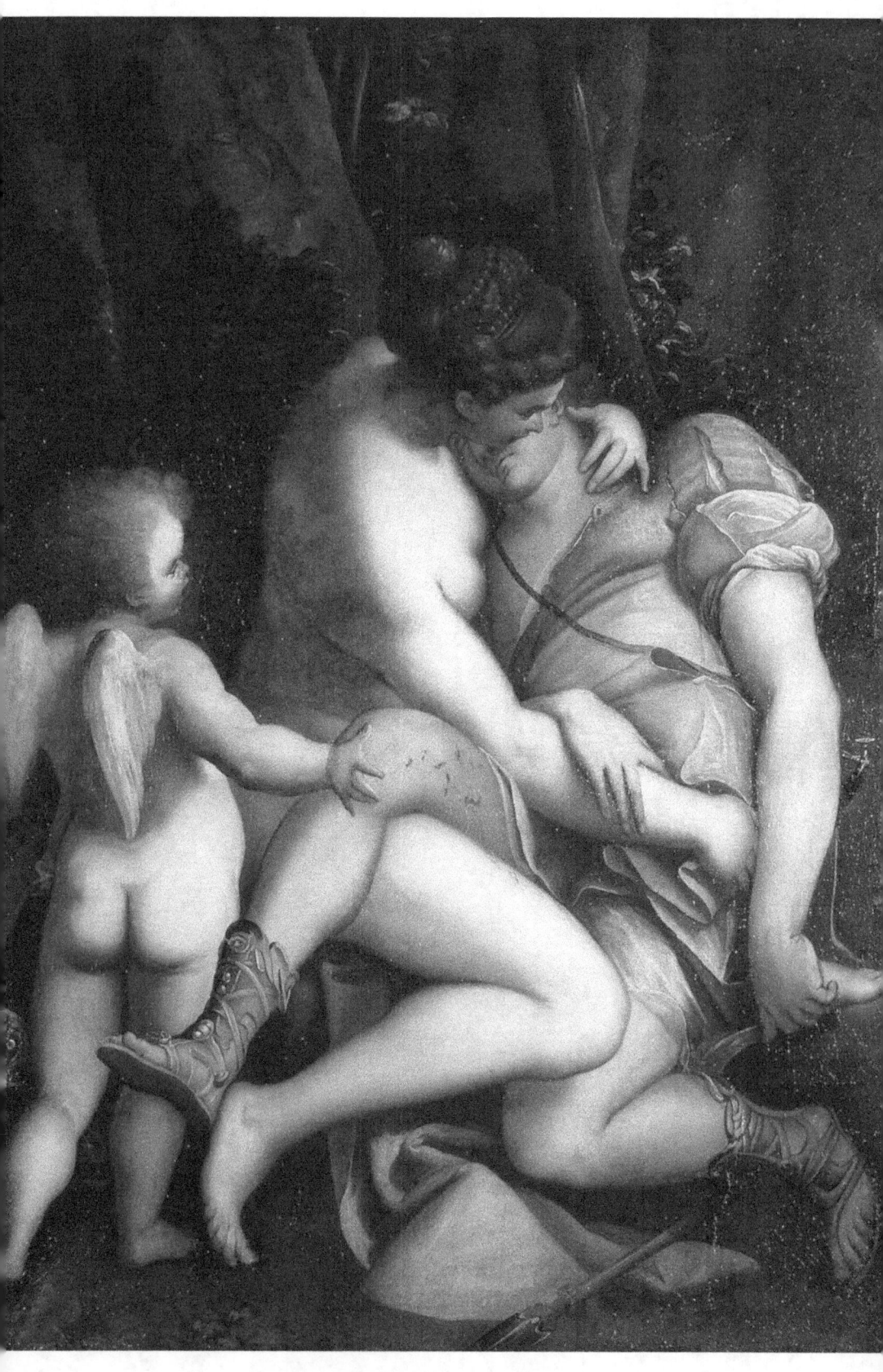

Luca Cambiaso, Venus and Adonis, c. 1565

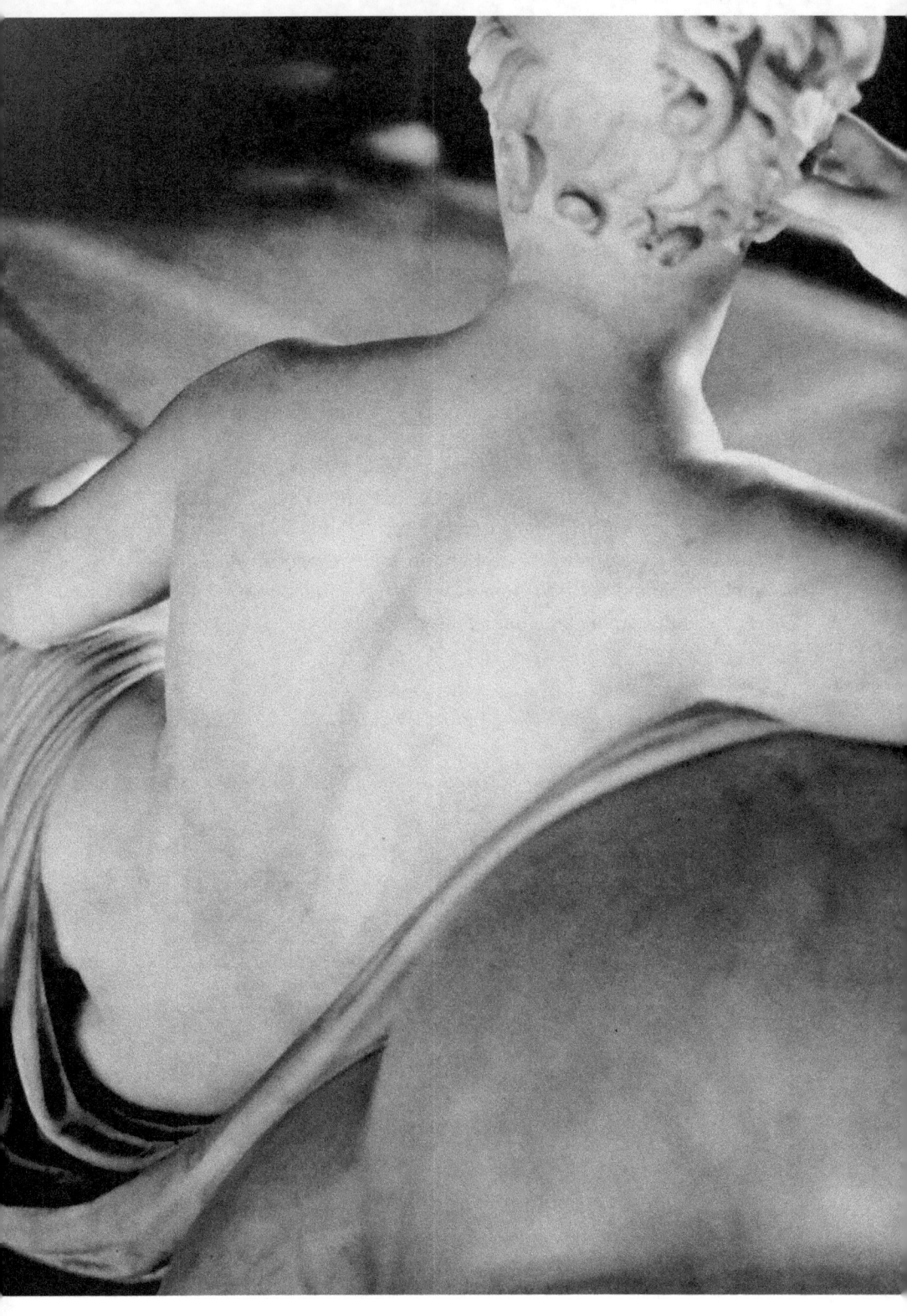

Antonio Canova, Venus Victorious, 1808

Even in unexpected places, such as in Early Italian Renaissance art, such as Pietro Lorenzetti, one finds erotic objectifications of women that look towards the 'high art' nude. And otherwise chaste and sober painters, such as Giovanni Bellini, produced female nudes made to be looked at erotically.[1] Piero di Cosimo's Neoplatonic, mythological paintings are called 'mysterious' by critics, but they also contain female nudes that are pornographic.[2] Antonio Pisanello's drawing of the personification of 'Luxury' undoubtedly depicts a prostitute: his drawing is a form of Renaissance pornography, given 'high art' status because Pisanello was a 'major' artist.[3] Some images of the Renaissance and later nudes contain men in the picture, who modulate the viewer's gaze.[4] The man in the picture stands in for the viewer, and the gaze is distinctly erotic (and male, except in certain cases, such as Simon Vouet's image of Psyche and Amor, where the female contemplates the male body).[5]

1 Ambrogio Lorenzetti: *Peace*, in *Good Government*, c. 1338-40, Palazzo Publico, Sienna; Giovanni Bellini: *A Young Woman at Her Toilet*, 1515, Kunsthistorisches Museum, Vienna
2 Piero di Cosimo: *Simonetta Vespucci*, c. 1477, tempera on panel, 22.4 x 16.5in, Condé Museum, Chantilly; *Venus, Mars and Cupid*, c. 1490, panel, 72 x 182cm, Staatliche Museen, Berlin
3 Pisanello: *Allegory of luxury*, drawing, Albertina, Vienna
4 Antonio Allegri de Correggio: *The Sleep of Antiope*, c. 1525, oil on canvas, 189.8 x 124.1cm, Louvre, Paris; Peter Paul Rubens: *Angelica and the Hermit*, c. 1625-8, oil on wood, 43 x 66cm, Kunsthistoriches Museum, Vienna
5 Simon Vouet: *Psyche Looking at the Sleeping Amor*, 1626, oil on canvas, 112 x 165cm, Musée des Beaux Arts, Lyons

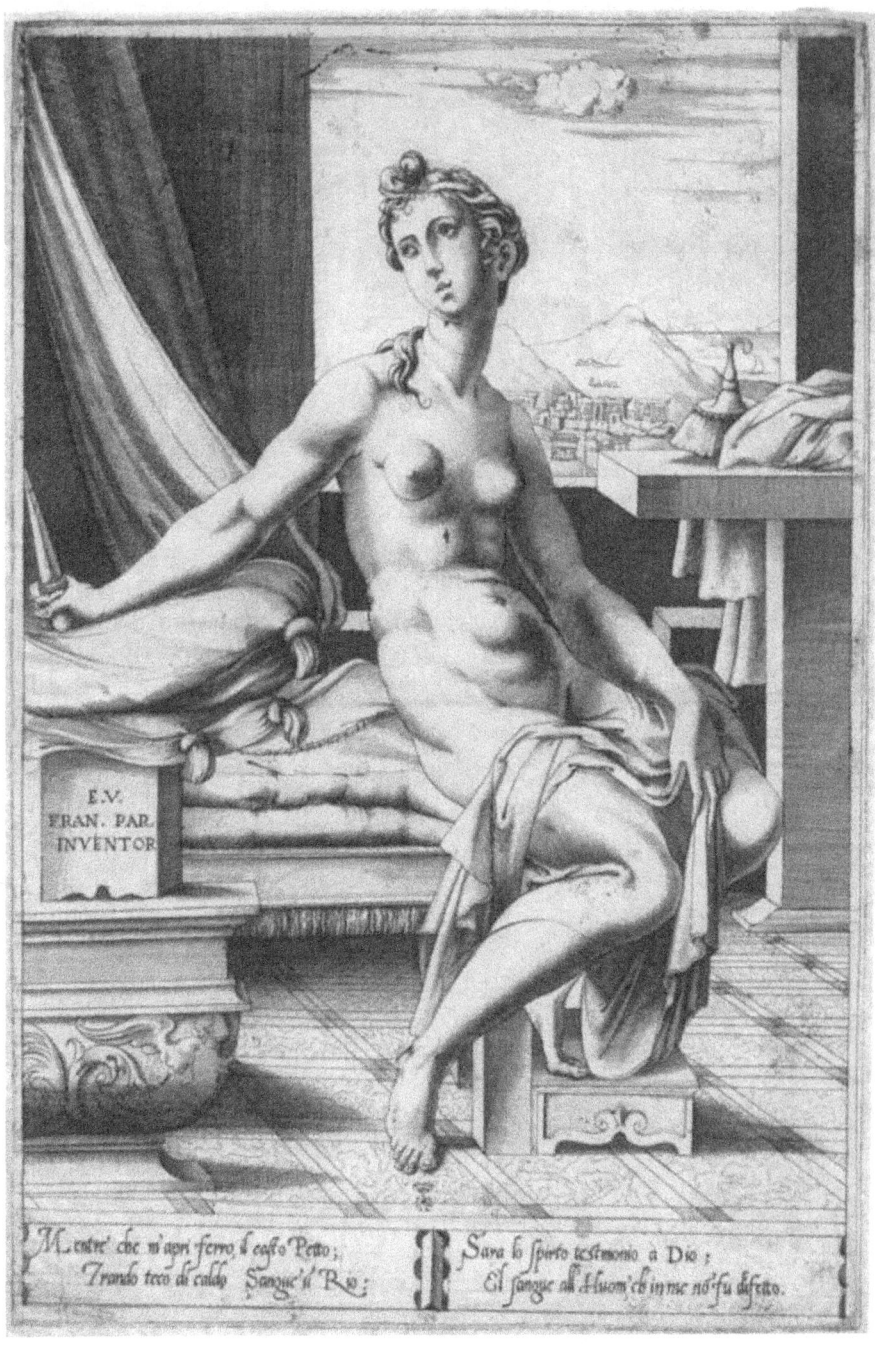

Enea Vico

VENUS AND VIRGIN

In the Neoplatonic, Aristotlean, Renaissance view of the fine art establishment, there is good art and bad art, there is art of 'taste', 'decency', 'refinement', 'purity' and 'civilization', and there is the vulgar, the uncouth, the disrespectful, the unornamental, the unlearned. Pornography falls into the latter category. In mediæval culture, there is Sacred and Profane love, drawn from Plato's *Symposium*, and the Venus Vulgaris (Earthly Venus) and Venus Coelestis. The Heavenly Venus is the one to aspire to, even though the Earthly Venus may be much more exciting.

These dichotomies are found throughout art. There is the chaste, passive, motherly Virgin Mary and the sexual, active, lascivious Mary Magdalene.[1] There is good and evil. There is Heaven and Hell. There is male and female. Throughout the history of Western culture we come across the same dualities, in one form or another. The female is clearly on the 'left' side, on the wrong side of the 'right' way. Women are the 'second sex', 'second class citizens': Sherry Ortner writes there is an opposition between culture and nature, and women are lower down in the male-made hierarchy:

> my thesis is that woman is being identified with – or, if you will, seems to be a symbol of – something that every culture devalues, something that every culture defines as being of a lower order of existence than itself.[2]

1 See Marina Warner: *Monuments and Maidens*; Kenneth Clark: *The Nude*; Lynda Nead, 19;
2 Sherry B. Ortner: "Is Female to Male as Nature is to Culture", in M. Evans, ed: *The Woman Question*, Fontana 1982

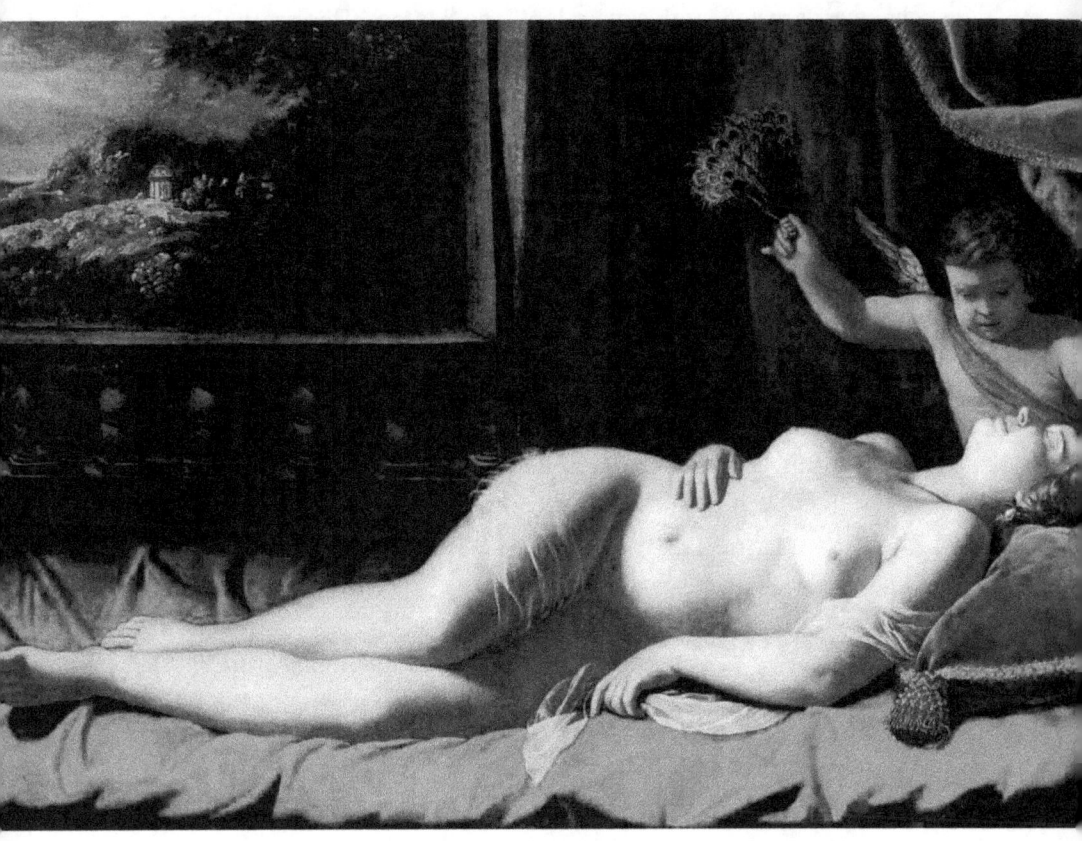

Artemisia Gentileschi, Sleeping Venus, 1625-30,
Barbara Piasecka Johnson Foundation, Princeton, New Jersey

The myth of Venus is based on that of the Greek Goddess Aphrodite. According to Homer, Aphrodite, the 'foam-born', was birthed from the severed, castrated genitals of the god Uranus, which were cast into the sea, creating white foam. The Goddess was blown ashore by the West wind, Zephyrus, to Cyprus, where she was greeted and covered by the Horae. This is the scene Sandro Botticelli depicts, and the sexual origin of Venus lies behind all those female nudes of the Renaissance.

Venus and the Virgin thus represent the twin poles of patriarchal culture: the sexual and asexual, the naked and the clothed, the lover and the mother, etc. The two merge, confusedly and ambiguously, in many Renaissance artworks. The Virgin is both Mother and Lover of Christ, just as, according to psycho-analysis, the mother is the child's first lover. The cults of the milk and breasts of the Madonna emphasize the erotic nature of the child-mother relation. The structure of the Madonna and Child image, with the child seated on the other's lap, echoes that of Osiris sitting on the 'throne' of his mother Isis, who is also his lover, in ancient Egyptian art.

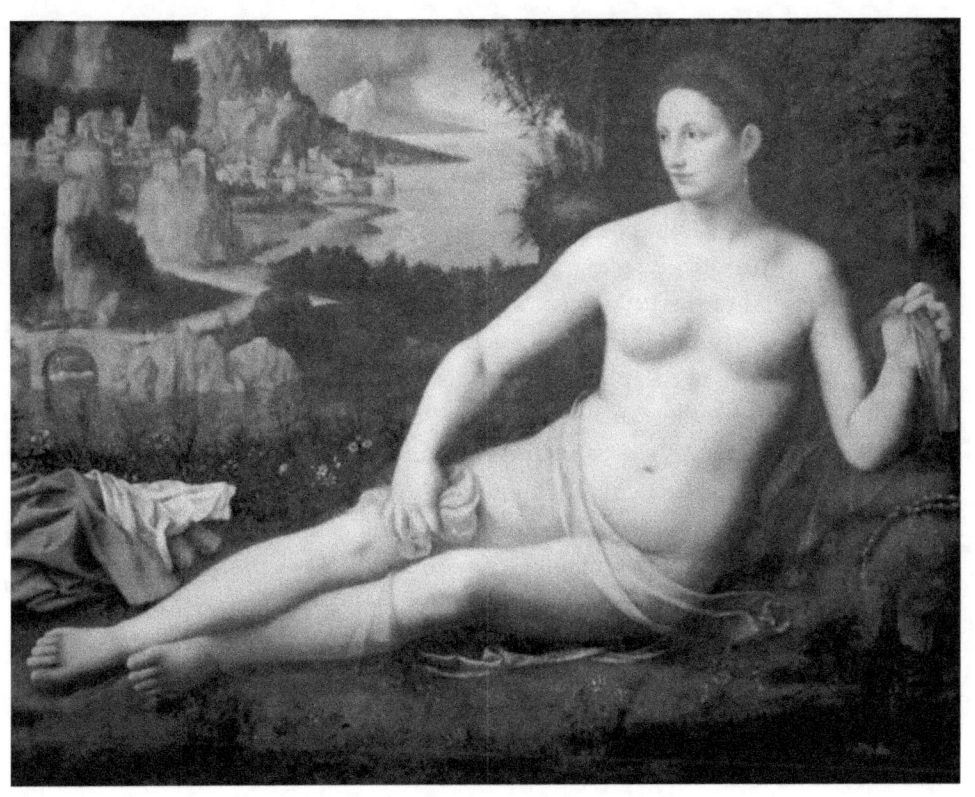

Bernardino Luini, Venus, 1530

FRAGONARD, DAVID, INGRES

After the astonishing output of Leonardo and Michelangelo, Renaissance art lost some of its passion, although it became increasingly openly erotic. Images such as Peter Lely's *Nymphs by a Fountain*, anything by Peter Paul Rubens, Jean Honoré Fragonard's *Bathers*, Jacques-Louis David's *Cupid and Psyche*, and Jean Auguste Dominique Ingres' study for *Ruggiero and Angelica* are openly erotic, displaying the body as a sensual object.[1] Myths such as that of the Judgement of Paris and the Three Graces allow ample opportunity for painting acres of quivering female flesh, as in paintings by Raphael, with his Neoplatonically idealized figures, or in the work of Rubens, Lucas Cranach and Hans Baldung Grien.[2] Artists such as Tintoretto, Veronese, Boucher, Tiepolo, Watteau, Reni, Rembrandt, Guercino, Correggio, Gros, Girodet, Géricault, and Delacroix do not hide their depictions of erotic bodies behind mythological narratives. Their images often put eroticism in the foreground: the pretence at mythological or historical painting is not longer upheld, and the nude form becomes primary.

---

1 Peter Lely: *Nymphs by a Fountain*, c. 1650-5, canvas, 129 x 144.8cm, Dulwich Picture Gallery, London; David: *Cupid and Psyche*, 1817, canvas, 184.1 x 241.6cm, Cleveland Museum of Art; Jean-Honoré Fragonard: *Bathers*, canvas, 64 x 80, Louvre, Paris; Jean-Auguste-Dominique Ingres: *Study for Ruggiero and Angelica*, c. 1819, canvas, 84.5 x 42.5cm, Musée Ingres, Montauban
2 Rubens: *The Judgement of Paris*, c. 1638-9, Prado, Madrid; Lucas Cranach: *The Judgement of Paris*, 1530, Staatliche Kunsthalle, Karlsruhe; Hans Baldung Grien: *The Three Graces*, c. 1540, Prado, Madrid; Raphael: *The Three Graces*, c. 150, panel, 6.6 x 6.6in, Condé Museum, Chantilly

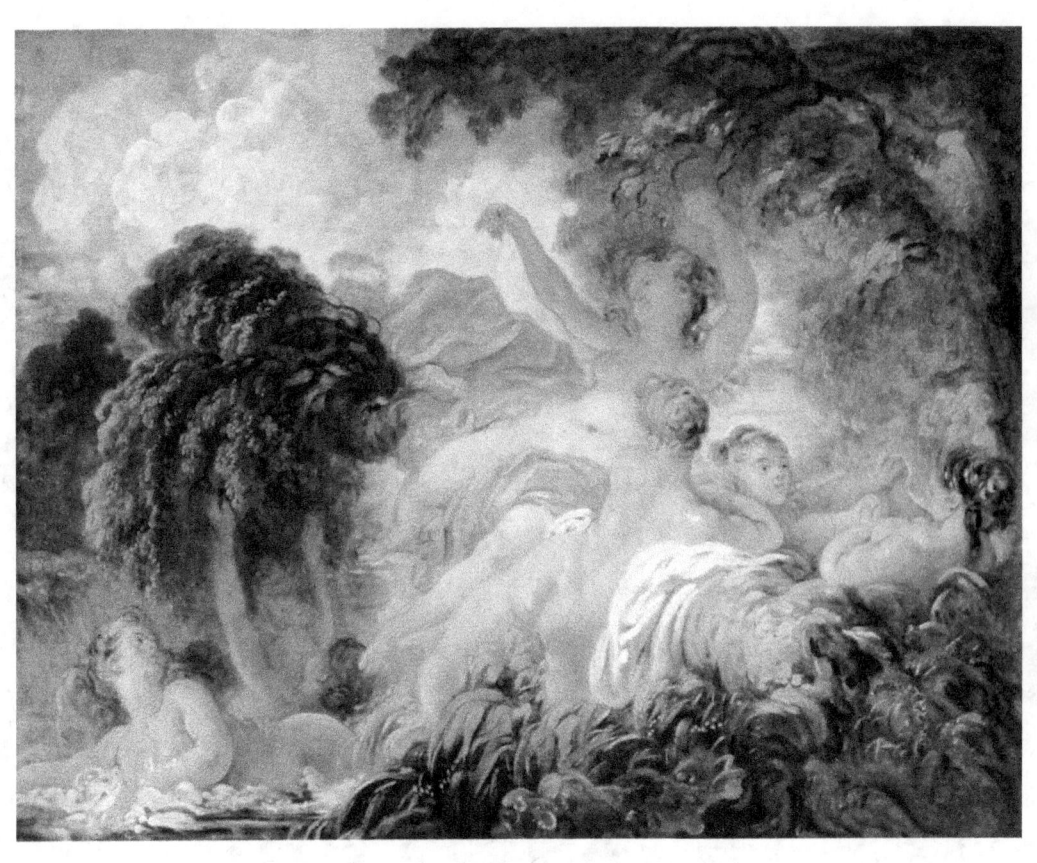

Jean-Honoré Fragonard, Bathers, 1756

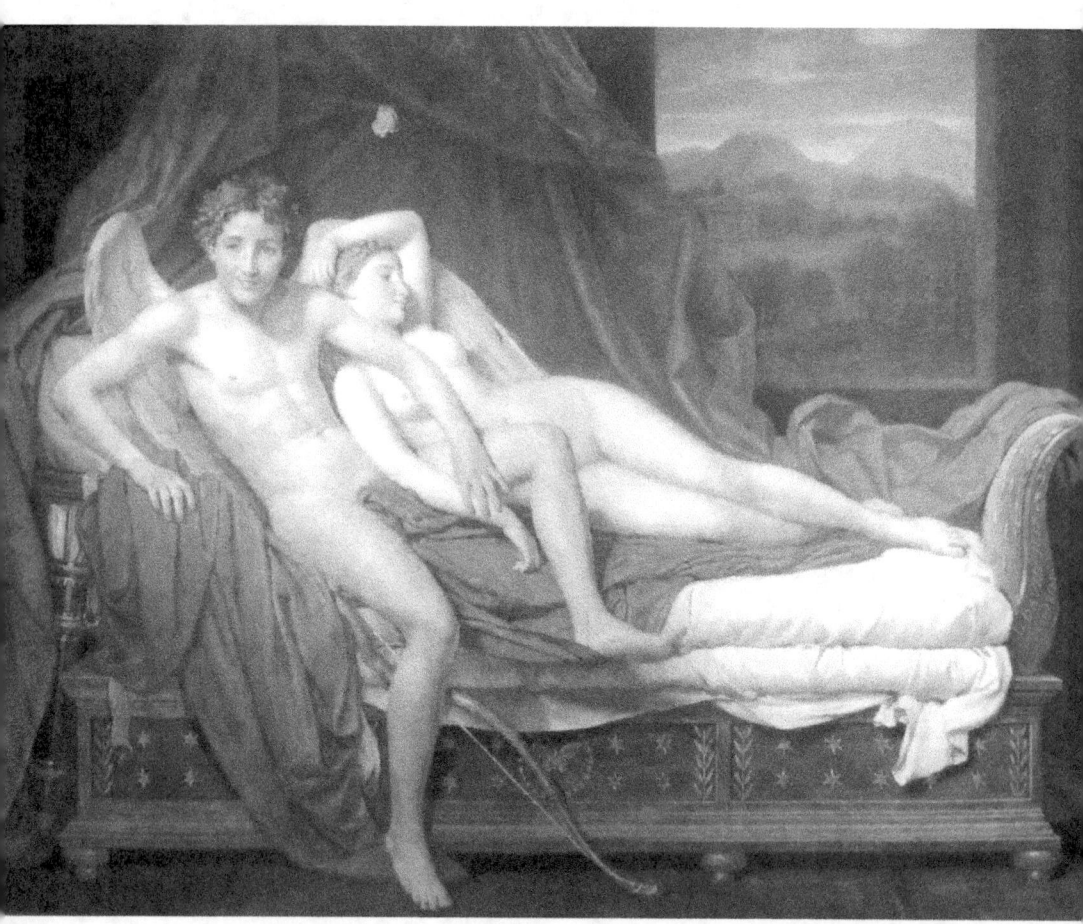

Jacques-Louis David, Cupid and Psyche, 1817,
Cleveland Museum of Art

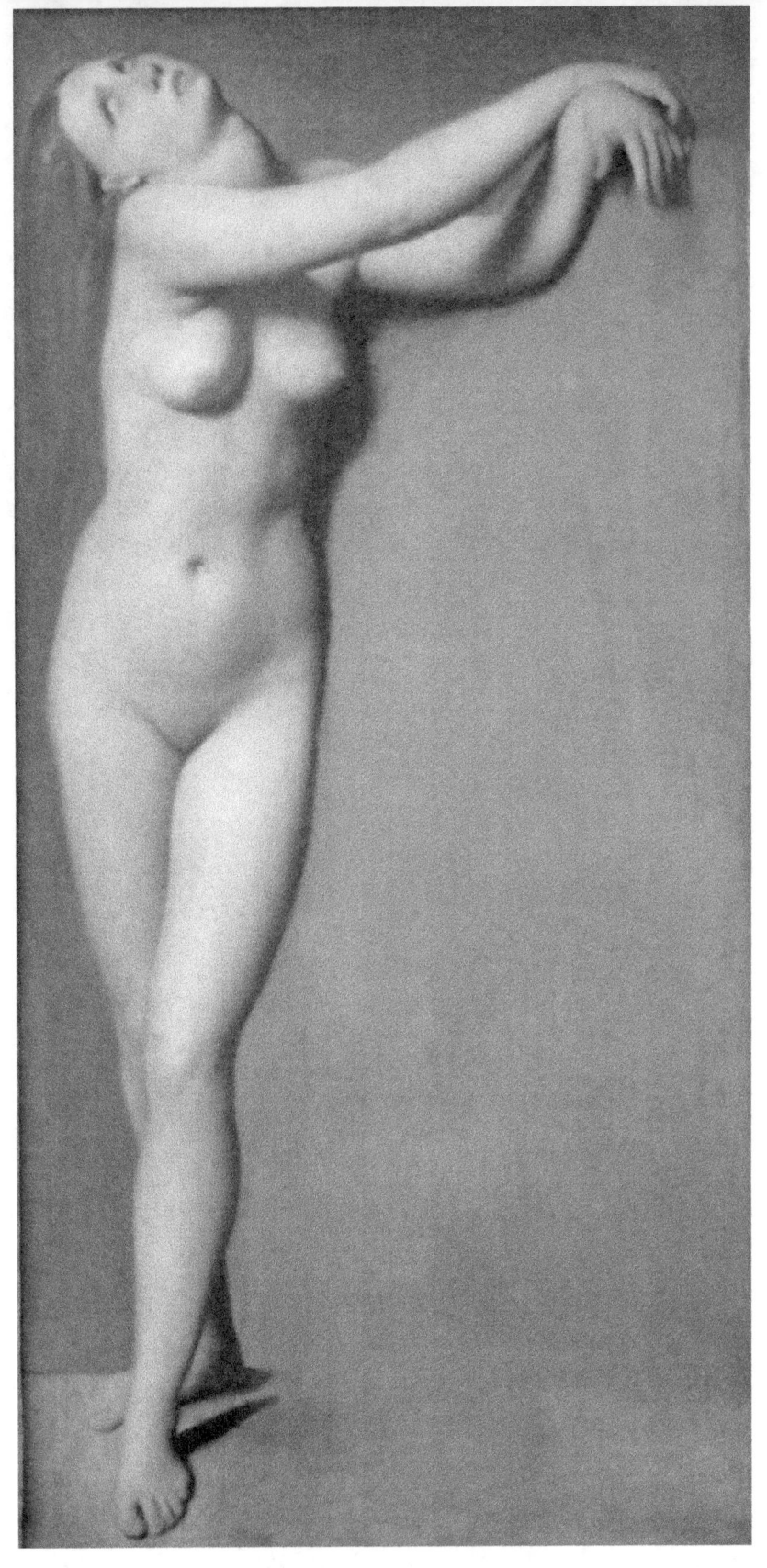

J.A.D. Ingres, study for Ruggiero

TINTORETTO, CORREGGIO, BALDUNG

See, for instance, the voluptuous nude in Correggio's *Jupiter and Antiope,* the acres of female flesh in *The Three Graces* by Tintoretto, or in his *Susannah and the Elders,* where the image of a woman admiring herself in a mirror occurs, to shift the focus from masculine vanity, or the ample back view of a woman, nude of course, stared at by two men, clothed of course, or the luminous skin of the women, nude of course, in Hans Baldung's *Adam and Eve.*[1]

---

1 Tintoretto: *Susannah and the Elders,* c. 1560, oil on canvas, 76 x 95.6in, Kunsthistorisches Museum, Vienna, *The Three Graces,* 1578, oil on canvas, 57.5 x 61in, Ducal Palace, Venice; Correggio: *Jupiter and Antiope,* c. 1525, oil on canvas, 74.8 x 48.8in, Louvre, Paris

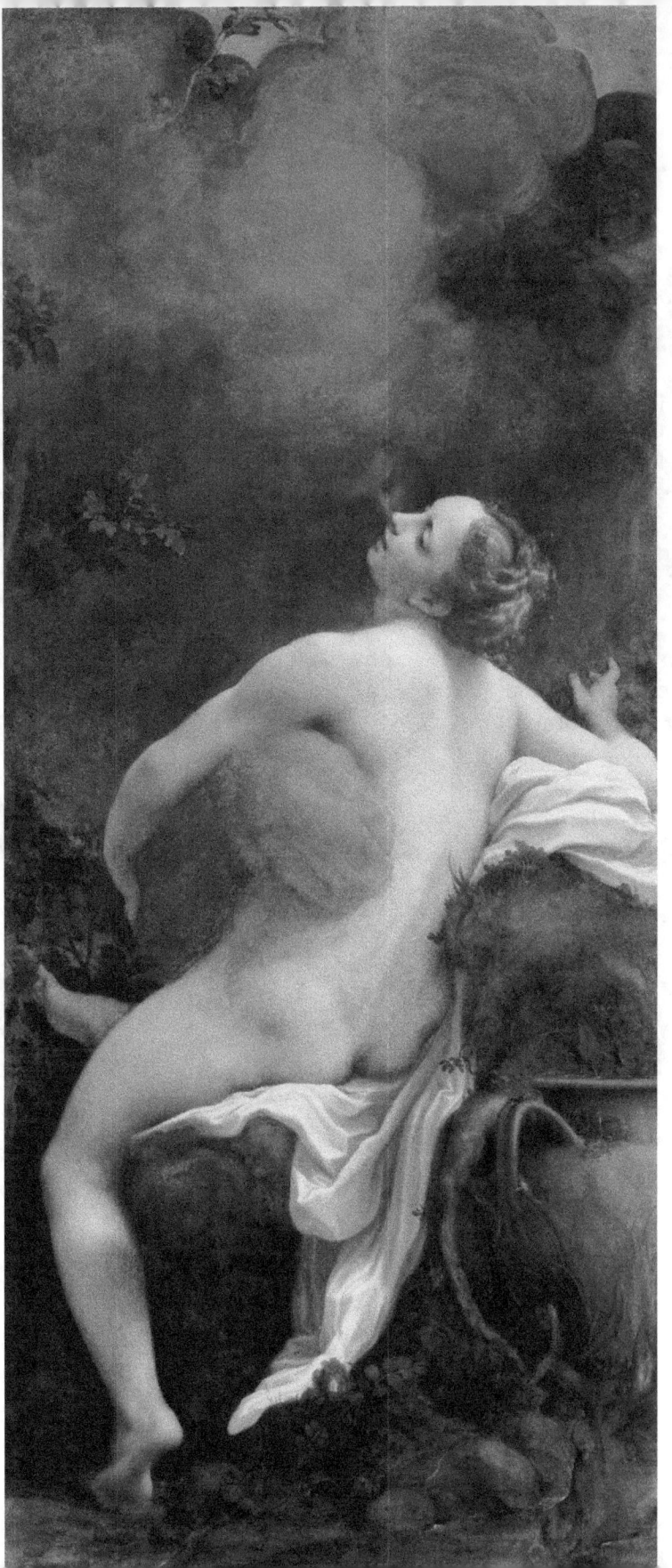

Correggio,
Jupiter and Antiope

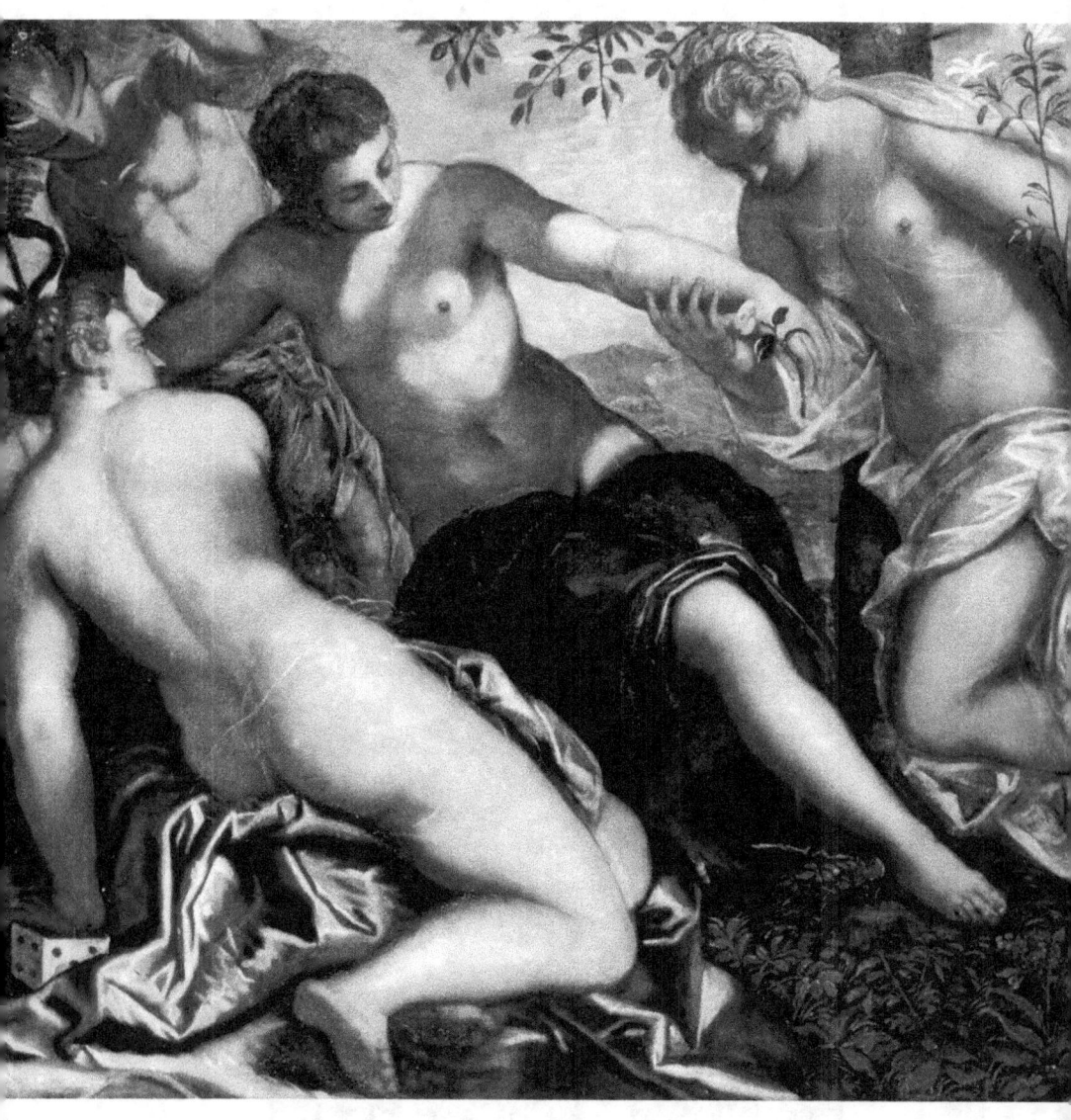

Jacopo Tintoretto, Mercury and the Graces, 1577

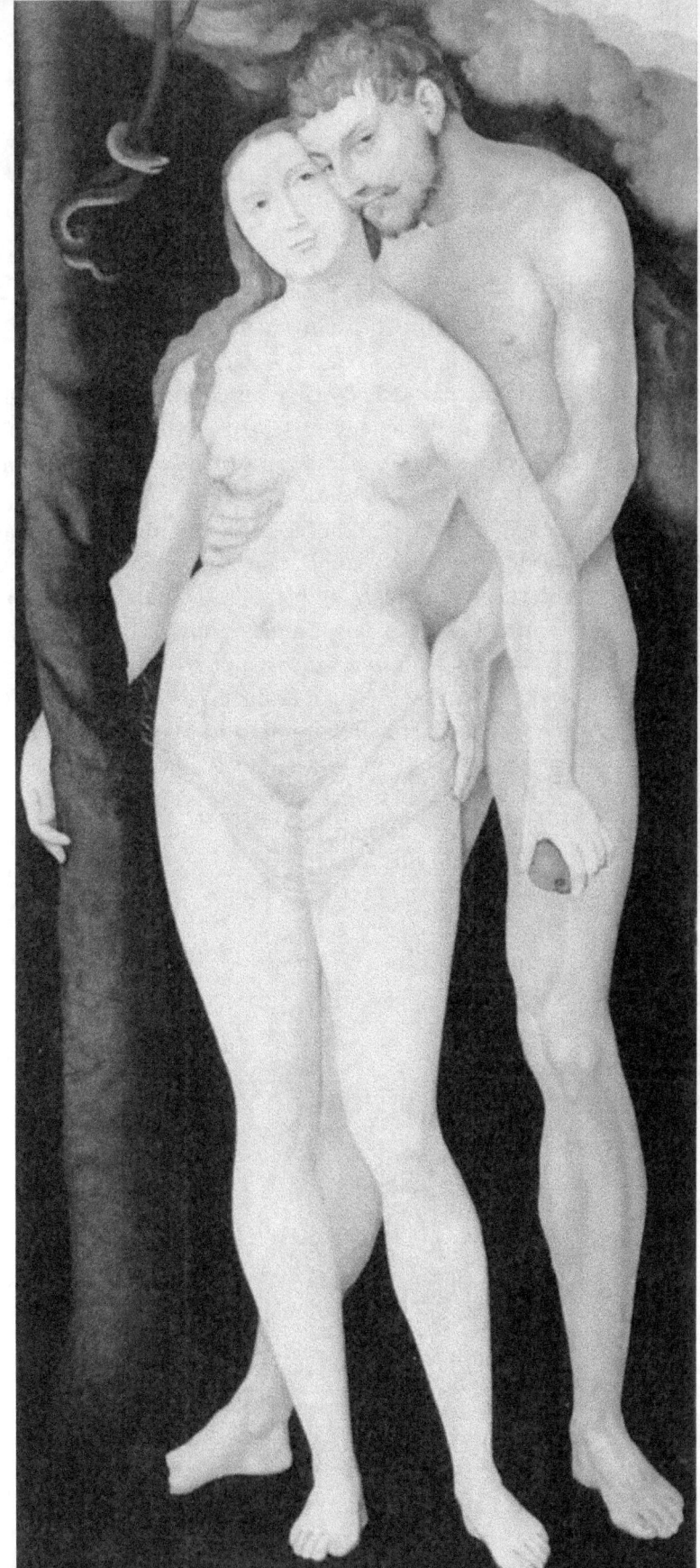

Hans Baldung,
Adam and Eve,
1531-35

CHRIST

One aspect of Christian imagery and Renaissance art that most Christian thinkers would not acknowledge is the eroticism of the Saviour's naked body. It is certainly a significant element in the celebrated depictions of Christ on the Cross: by Peter Rubens, Diego Velásquez and Andrea Mantegna, among many others.[1] Christ's nakedness sends conflicting signals. Clearly, nudity has a religious or mythic aspect, connoting nature/ naturalness, purity, birth, creation, renunciation, unveiled reality, truth.[2] In art, however, nudity is ambiguous: in religious contexts it is both spiritual and sexual.[3] Christ's body is often sexless, or androgynous, or feminized.[4] Christianity is an ambivalent cult; it has a clothed, virginal woman as the object of worship on the one hand, and a naked, equally virginal and chaste man on the other. In the most holy of churches, nudity is sanctified by the statues, icons and paintings of Christ on the Cross.

1 Andeas Mantegna: *Calvary*, 1459, 67 x 93cm, Paris, Louvre; Rubens: *Christ Between the Two Thieves (Coup de Lance)*, 1620, 429 x 311cm, Musée des Beaux Arts, Antwerp; Velásquez: *Christ Crucified*, 1630, 248 x 169cm, Prado, Madrid
2 See J.C. Cooper: *An Illustrated Encyclopaedia of Symbols*, 112-3
3 See Marina Warner: *Monuments and Maidens*, 304
4 See William Thompson: *The Time Falling Bodies Take to Light*, 109

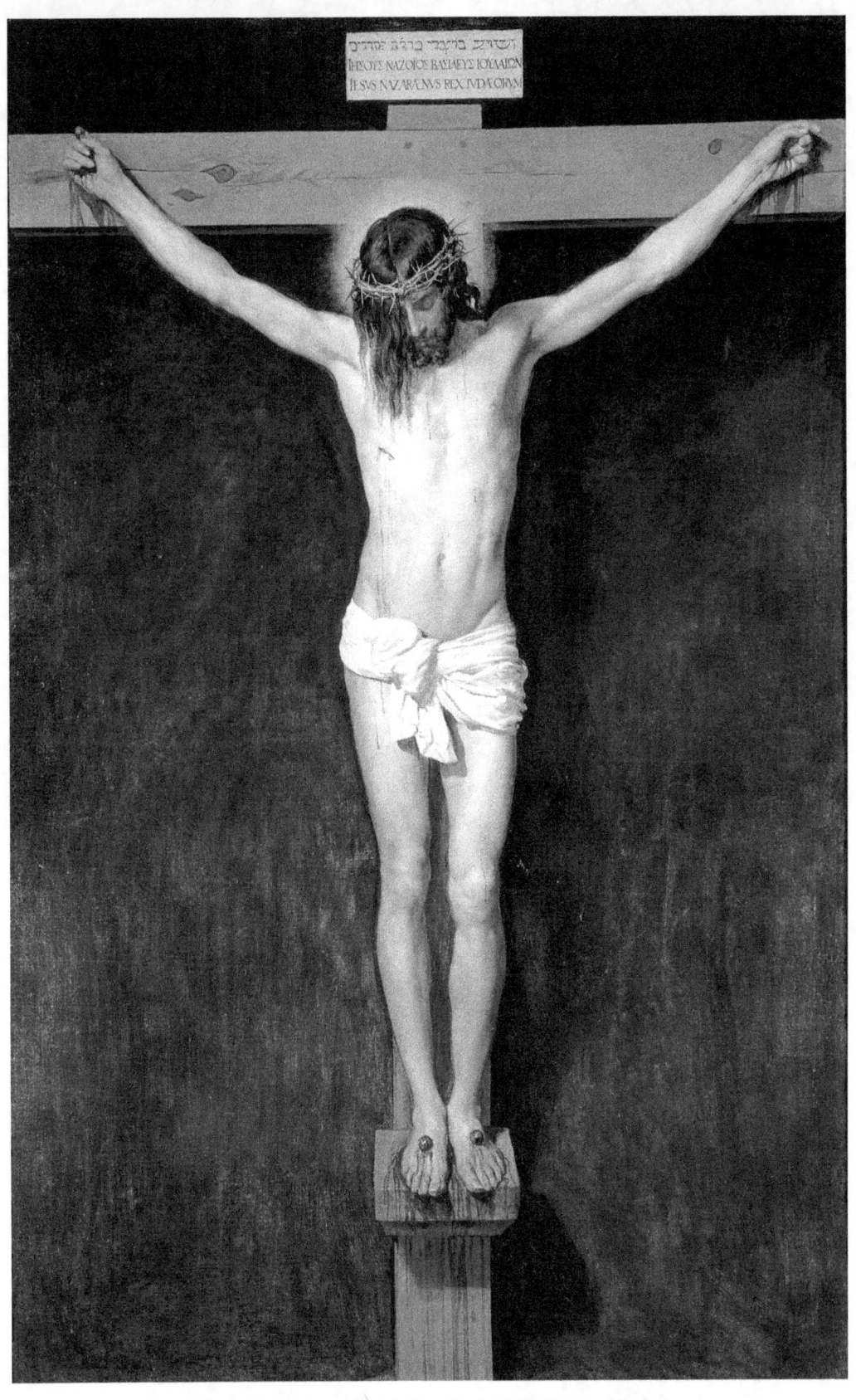

Diego Velásquez, Christ Crucified, 1632, Prado, Madrid

CHRIST

Christianity cannot deal with expressions of sexuality; or it prefers not to. It has a long history of suppressing sexuality, of body-hating, of repressing eroticism and erotic art. What Christianity does is to ignore erotic feelings, or to marginalize them in the outpourings of mystics. Other religions, such as Hinduism, acknowledge eroticism. There is room for the expression of sexual feelings in Hinduism; there are many gods, for a start. Such polytheism allows, as in the Greek pantheon of deities, for all manner of feelings. Renaissance painters understandably looked to the *Old Testament*, to historical figures and the Greek and Roman mythologies.

The dying or dead Christ, naked but for a slip of cloth and sometimes depicted entirely naked but with his legs bent to one side, hiding the 'transcendent signifier', the phallus, is an image of homoeroticism. Theologians and art historians down the ages did not or would not admit that Christ was or could have been an object of lust. Yet this is clearly the case in some depictions of the naked Saviour, such as paintings by Giovanni Battista Rosso, Michelangelo Merisi da Caravaggio, or Antonello da Messina.[1] These nude figures send a mass of signals, from the pathetic to the narcissistic, from the erotic to the spiritual.

---

1 Antonello da Messina: *Crucifixion*, 1475, 52.5 x 42.5cm, Musée des Beaux Arts, Antwerp; Caravaggio: *Entombment*, 1604, 300 x 203cm, Vatican, Rome; Rosso: *Dead Christ Supported by Angels*, c. 1524-7, oil on wood, 133.6 x 104.4cm, Museum of Fine Arts, Boston

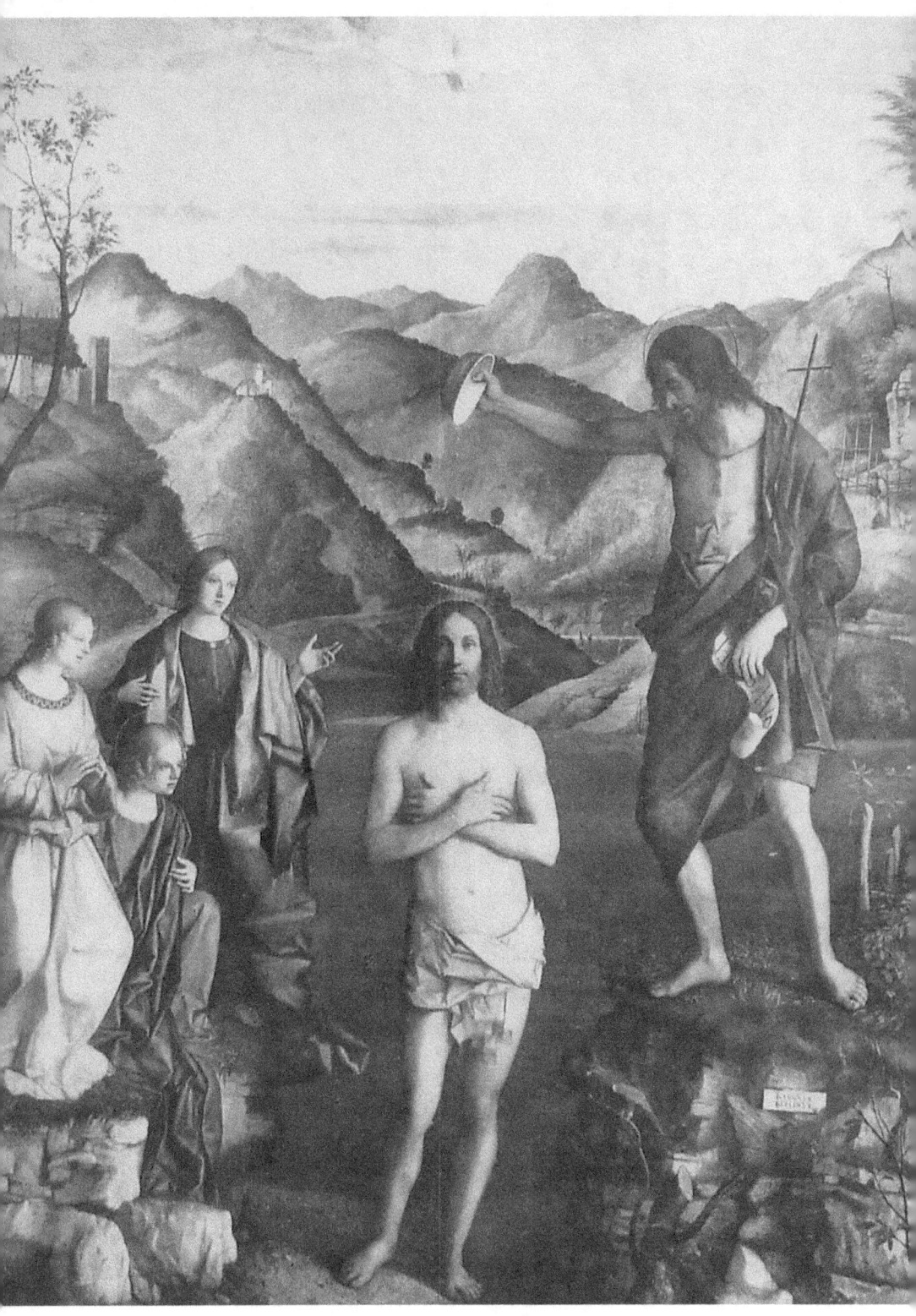

Giovanni Bellini, Baptism, early 16th century

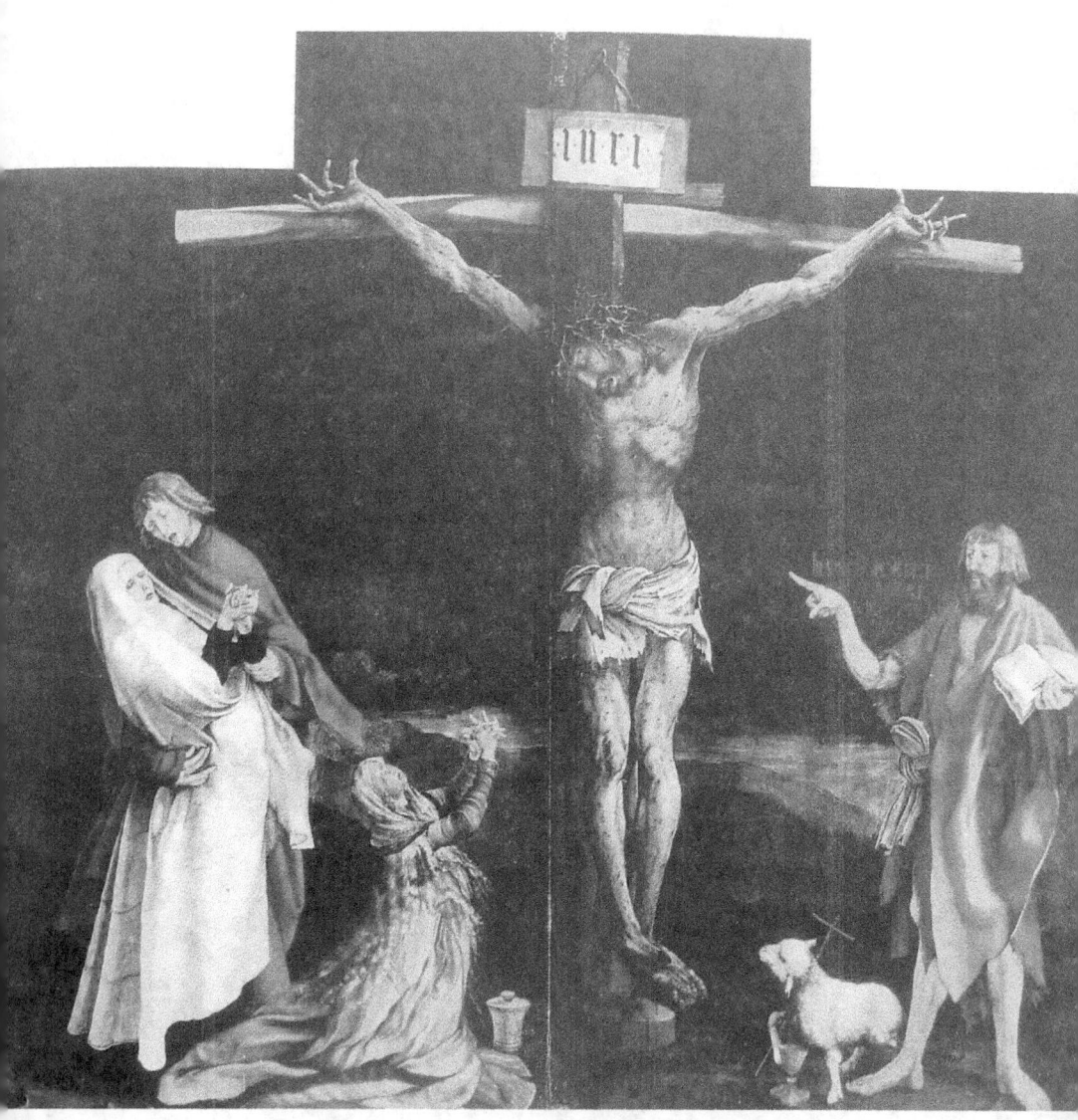

Matthias Grünewald, Crucifixion, Isenheim Altarpiece

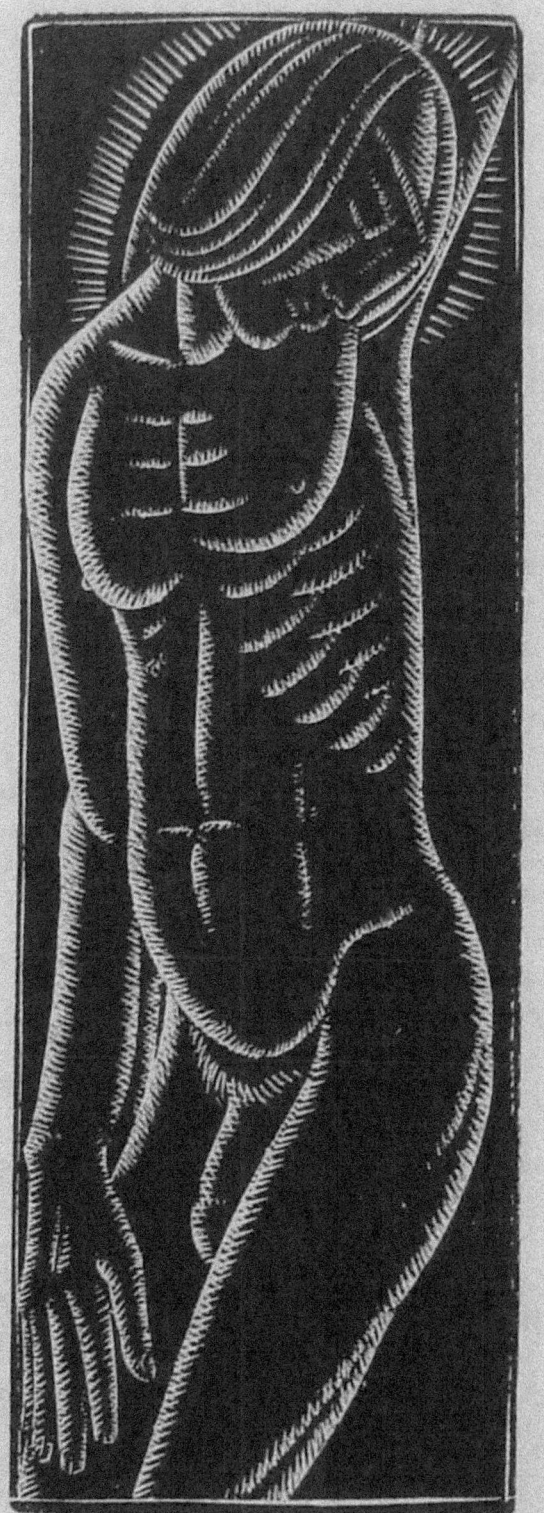

Eric Gill, Deposition, 1924

CHRISTIANITY AND PORNOGRAPHY

A good bout of flagellation goes down well with Christians too, and many Renaissance painters painted Christ being whipped or tortured by the guards, and being crowned with thorns. Examples include Titian's two *Christ Crowned with Thorns* paintings, which make suffering a sublime, heroic experience,[1] or the ritualized whipping in Piero della Francesca's *The Flagellation of Christ*, a much-discussed Renaissance painting, or Luca Signorelli's more staid approach to the torture.[2]

Not to be out-done, Vittore Carpaccio painted a bizarre picture: the crucified Jesus sitting on a throne, dead, with his eyes closed, with two semi-naked old men sitting on either side of him. The title is *Meditation On the Passion of Christ*.[3] There's the Saviour, looking very dead, on a throne, in a ruined landscape, while two old men sit right next to him and muse upon his death. Bizarre.

Sebastiano del Piombo goes even further: his *The Martyrdom of St Agatha* depicts the saint, nude of course, being tortured by a bunch of men, fully clothed of course.[4] They are applying gigantic metal pliers to her nipples. This is a depiction of sadism (in Christianity the euphemism is 'martyrdom'). Naturally, it seems, this is *sexual* torture, painted in such a straightforward fashion, the woman centre frame, the men surrounding her intent on brutalizing her. The rape, which must follow this torture, is not shown, and it is never shown in Renaissance art, and rarely in Western art. When rape occurs, as it must have done millions of times through the Christian era, men dragging away women are depicted, or Jupiter as a swan screwing Leda, but not the rape itself.

---

1 Titian: *Christ Crowned with Thorns*, mid-1450s, panel, 303 x 180cm, Louvre, Paris; *Christ Crowned with Thorns*, c. 1570-6, canvas, 280 x 181cm, Alte Pinakothek, Munich
2 Piero della Francesca: *The Flagellation of Christ*, c. 1450, panel, 59 x 81.5cm, Ducal, Urbino; Signoreli: *Flagellation*, c. 1480, canvas, 80 x 60cm, Brera, Milan
3 Carpaccio: *Meditation on the Passion of Christ*, c. 1505, panel, 70 x 86cm, Metropolitan Museum of Art, New York
4 Sebastiano del Piombo: *The Martyrdom of St Agatha*, 1520, 31 x 175cm, Pitti Palace, Florence

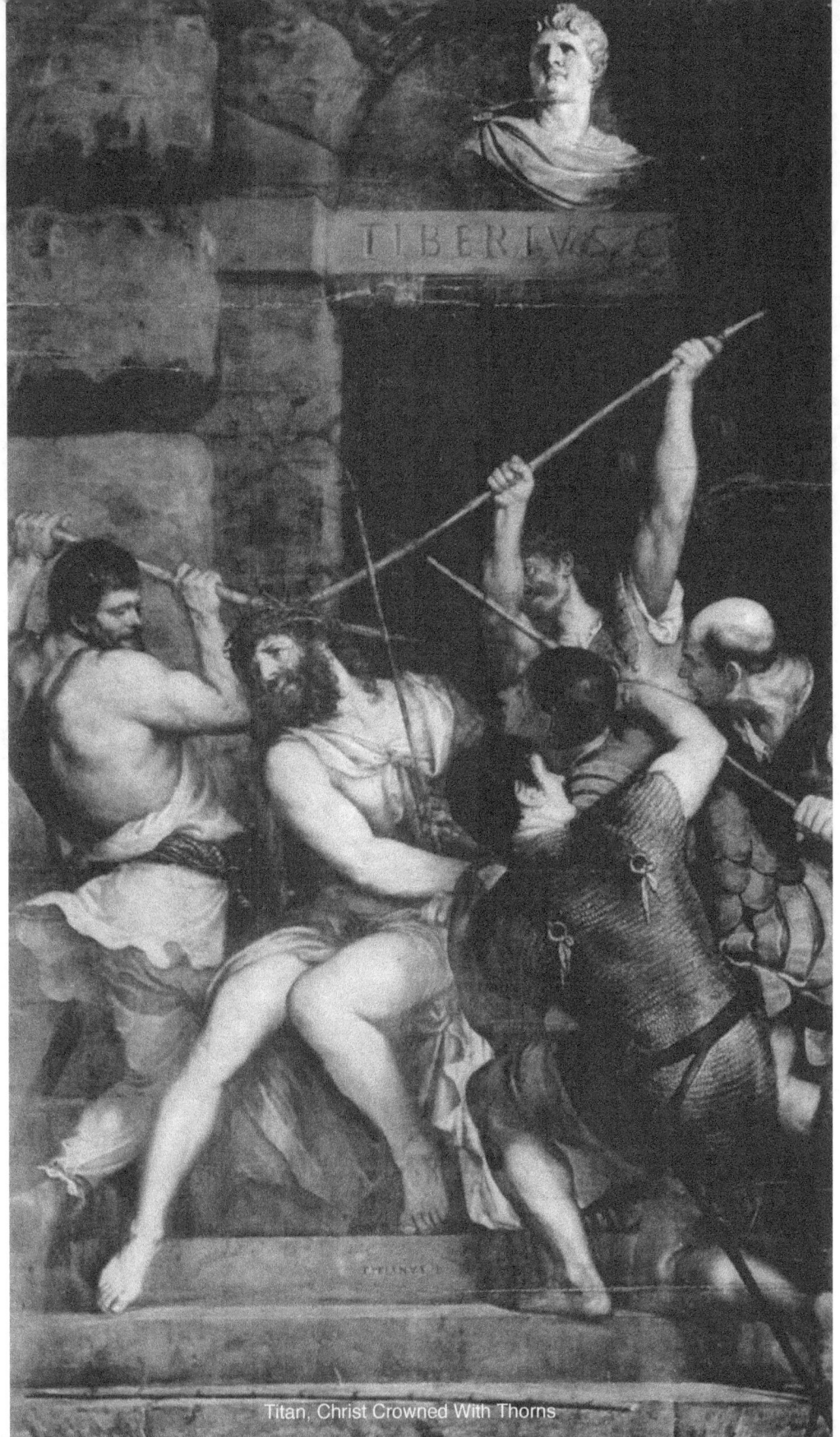

Titan, Christ Crowned With Thorns

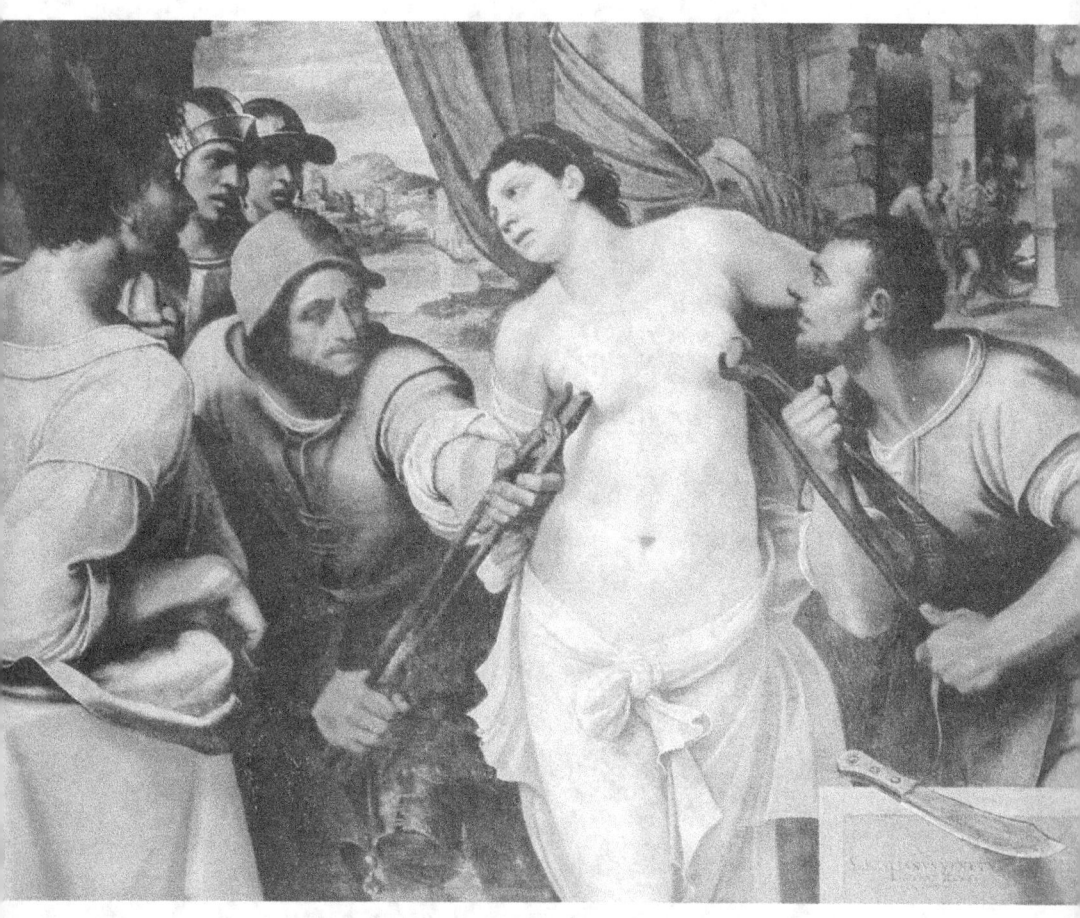

Sebastian del Piombo, The Martyrdom of St Agatha, 1520, Pitti
Palace, Florence

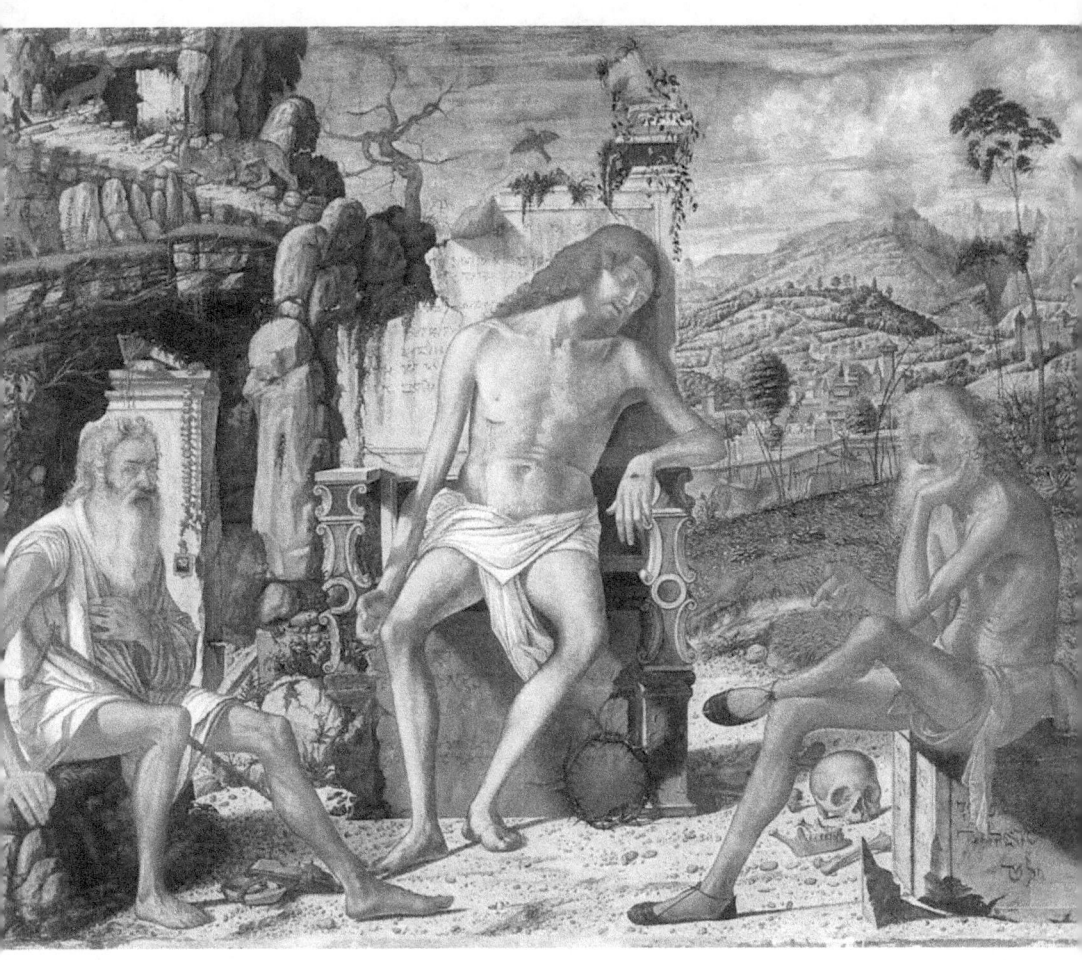

Vittorio Carpaccio, Meditation On the Passion

CRUCIFIED WOMEN

Artistic transgressions of Christian religion upset some people. Witness, for instance, the complaints of the clergy and the church about women priests. In 1984 an artwork of a crucified woman, *Christa*, was taken out of a church in New York because it was 'theologically and historically indefensible'.[1] A crucified *woman*, now there's a blasphemous image to conjure with. It's the not the first time a woman's been seen in a satire on the crucifixion. Félicien Rops often used the motif.

---

1 K.A. Briggs: "Cathedral Removing Statue of Crucified Woman", *New York Times*, 28 Apl, 1984.

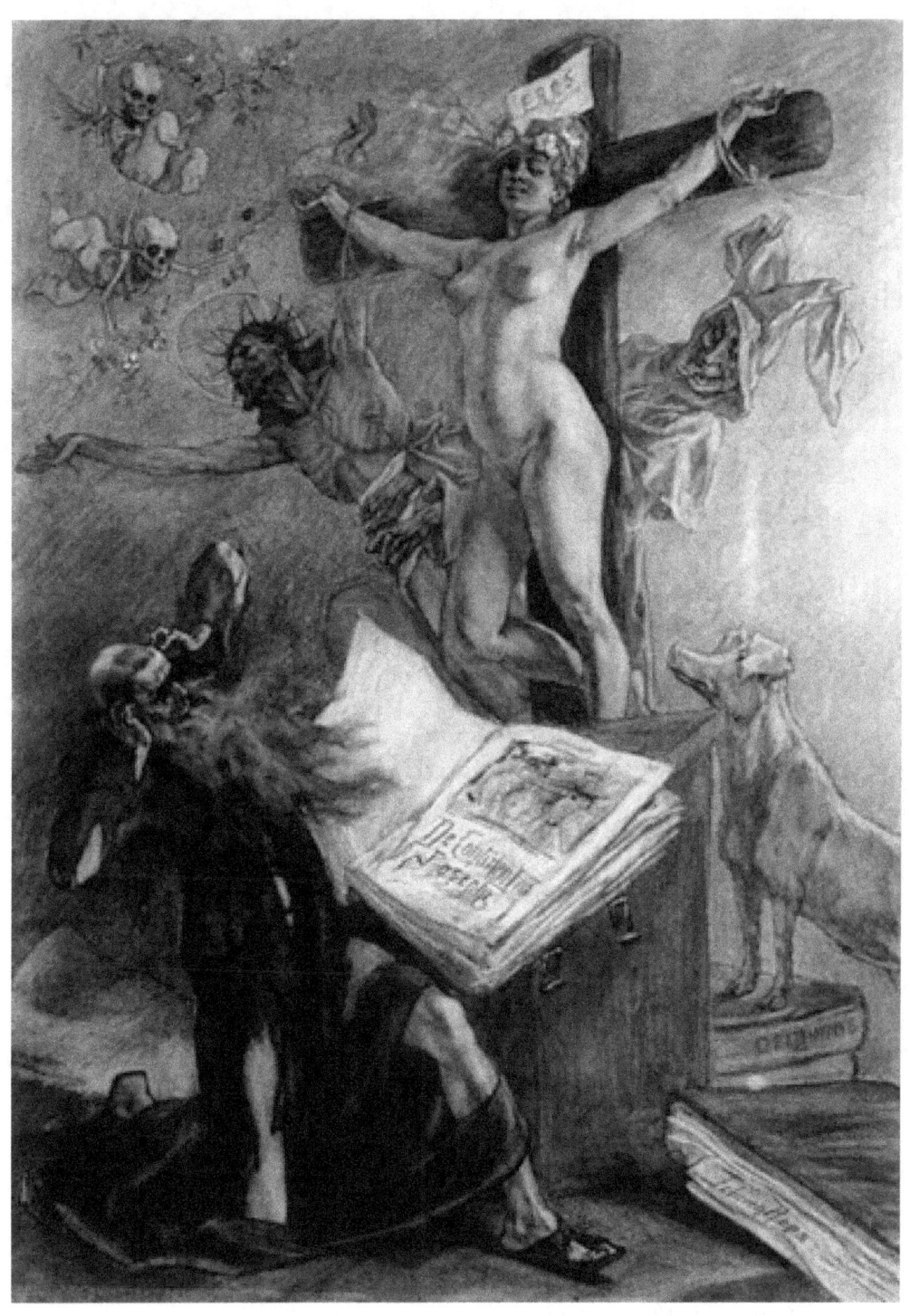

The Temptation of St Anthony, a popular subject of the era, by Félicien Rops

THE ANNUNCIATION

Even such seemingly gentle occasions such as the Annunciation are not free of sexist, patriarchal and erotic/ porn connotations. For a start, Mary is simply living her life when the Archangel Gabriel rushes in and tells her she is to bear the Son of God. Mary replies: 'how can this be, seeing I know not a man' (*Gospel of Luke*). As soon as she accepts, in the very moment she assents, she conceives Christ in her womb. It is literally the Word become Flesh.

Renaissance painters, such as Fra Angelico, depict the Annunciation as a delicate, silent moment, the two figures, Gabriel and Mary, kneeling together in spiritual communion. Angelico's Virgins are shy, passive, sad creatures.[1] For Mary in the *Gospels* is a 'good wife'; she accepts the Word of God.

Yet the Annunciation is clearly also a spiritual coercion. The woman is passive and humble. Her opinion or sanctity or dignity is not taken into account: she is forced to accept God's seed inside her. She cannot refuse the Word of the Lord. So it is sex by force for some feminists, because it is sex without consent (but is it sex? Or is it conception? These are theological paradoxes which much concerned theologians in the mediæval era).

---

1 Angelico: *The Annunciation*, c. 1440, fresco, San Marco Museum, Florence; *The Annunciation*, late 1440s, 194 x 194cm, Prado, Madrid; *The Annunciation*, c. 1443, fresco, 187 x 157cm, cell three, San Marco Museum, Florence

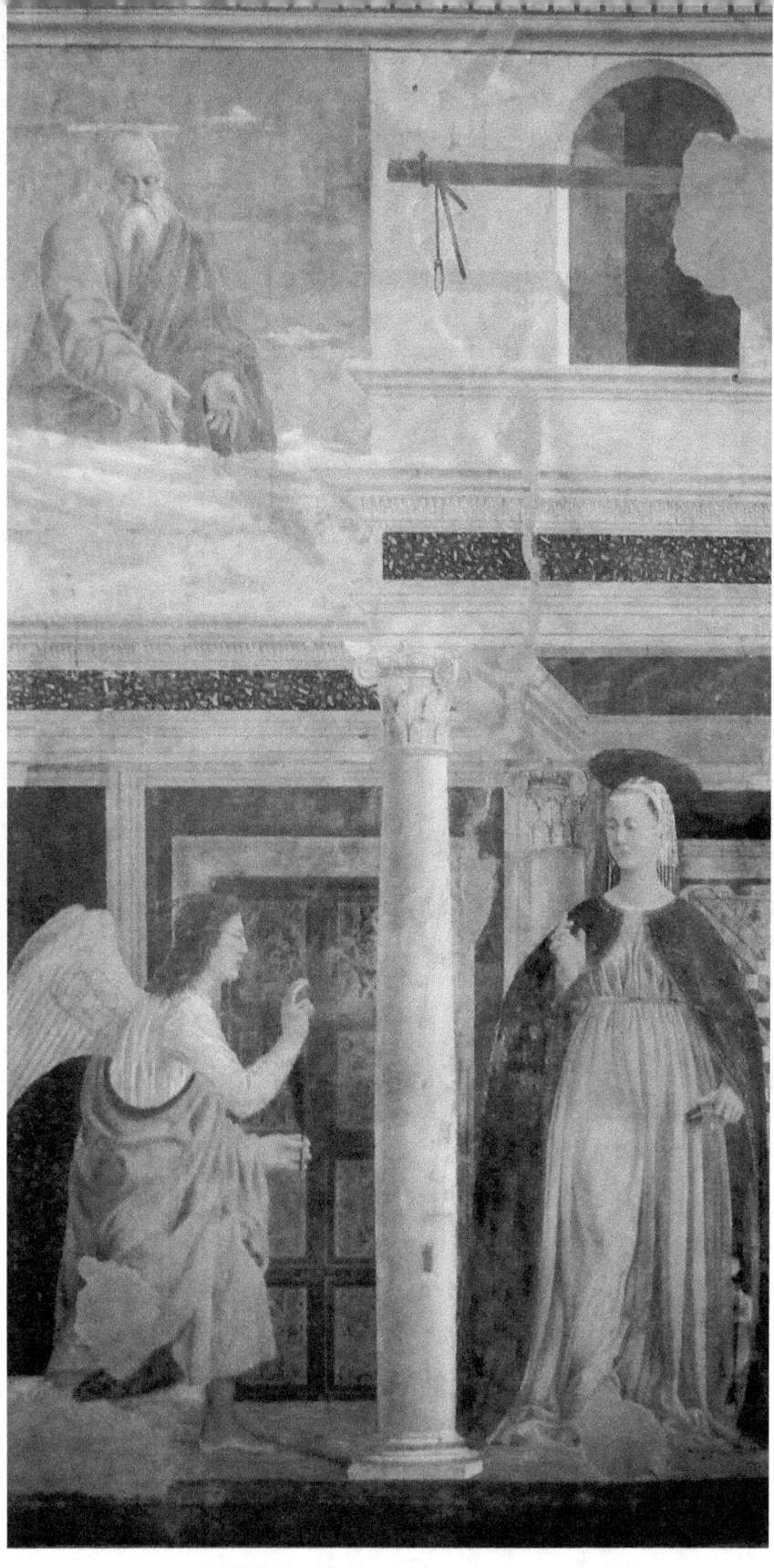

Piero, The Annunciation, Arezzo

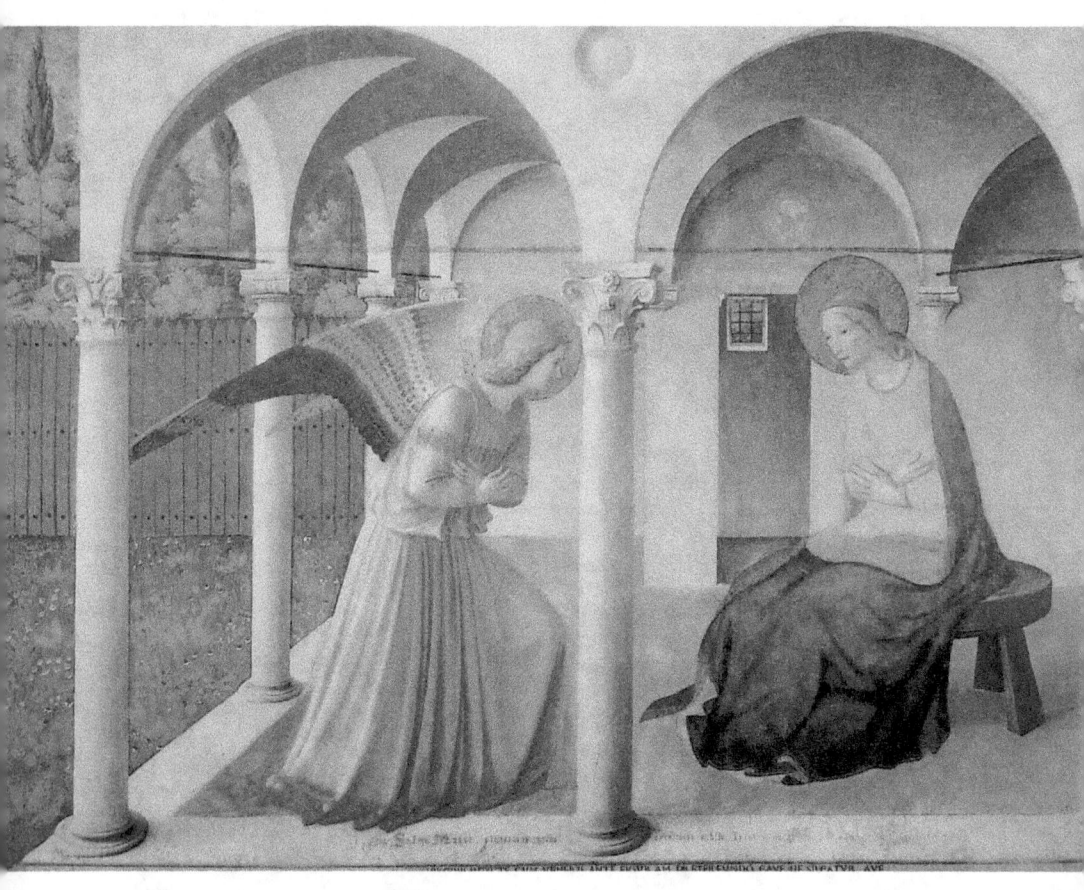

Fra Angelico, The Annunciation, San Marco, Florence

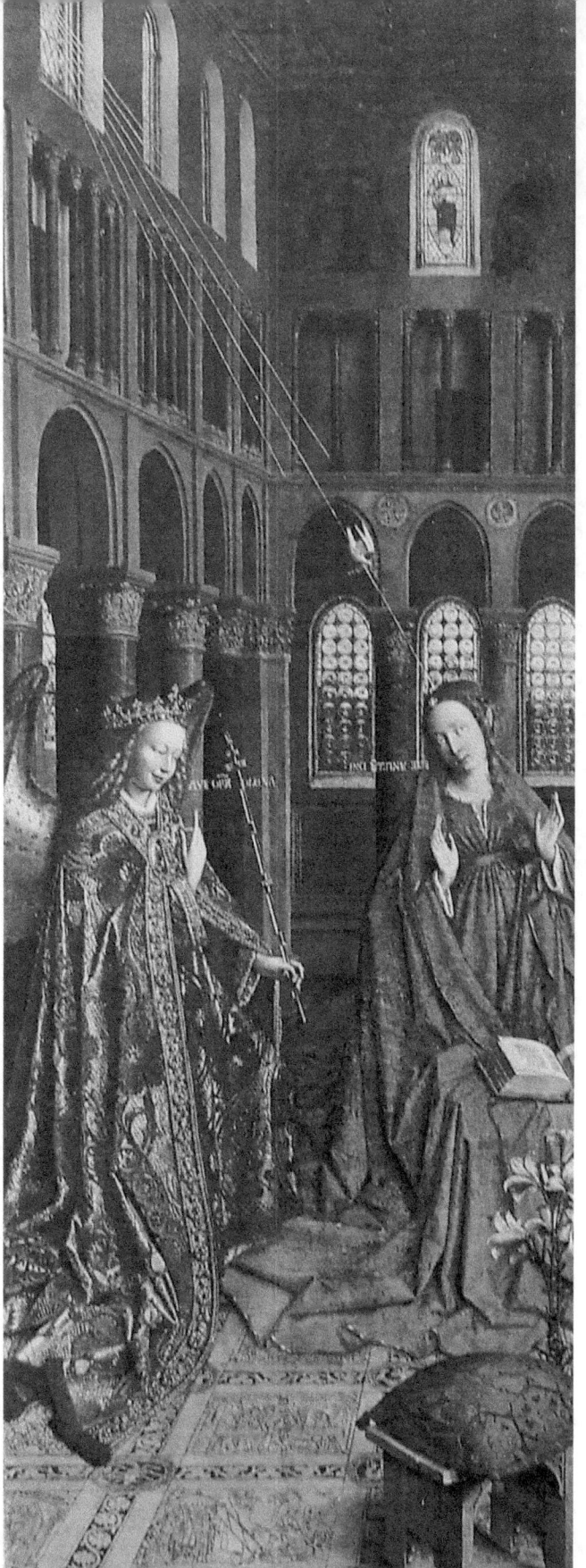

Jan van Eyck, The Annunciation, National Gallery of Art, Washington, DC

DEMONS AND NUNS:
RELIGION AND EROTICA

A good deal of erotica in the West of the early modern period revolves around religion (and Catholicism in particular). Demons, nuns, monks, crosses and churches are the familiar background. All of the reasons for employing religious imagery and settings are obvious. One is that creatures such as devils or monsters are obviously unreal or supernatural, and thus can be used to depict far more extreme sexual acts than 'realistic' portrayals of humans.

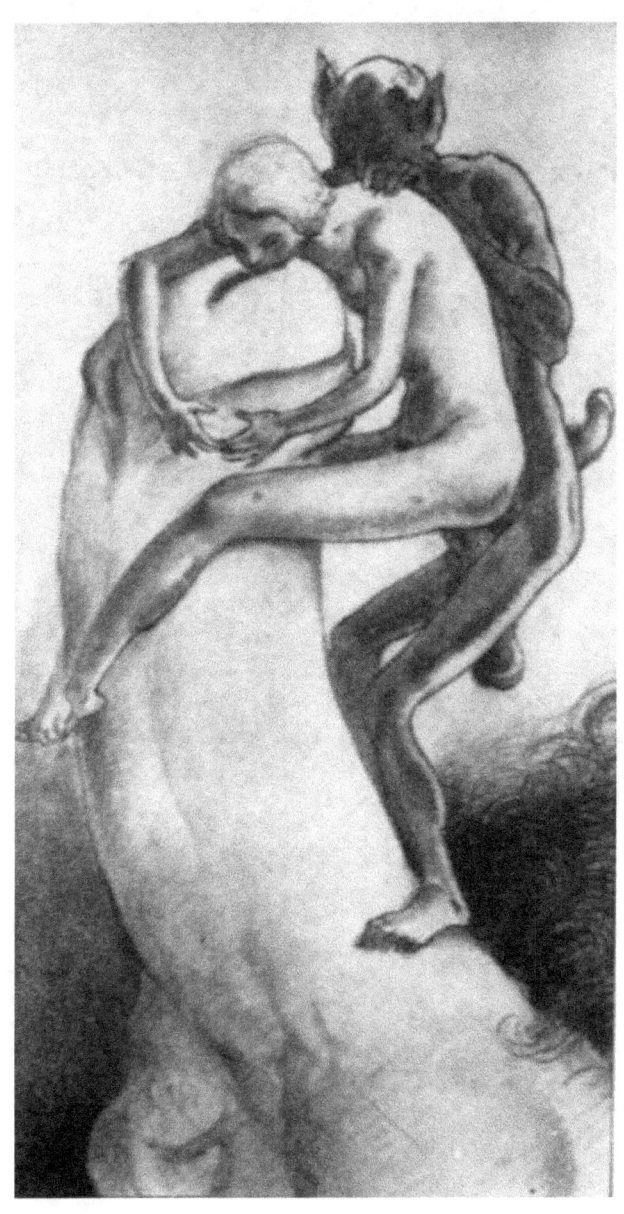

Anonymous, 19th century

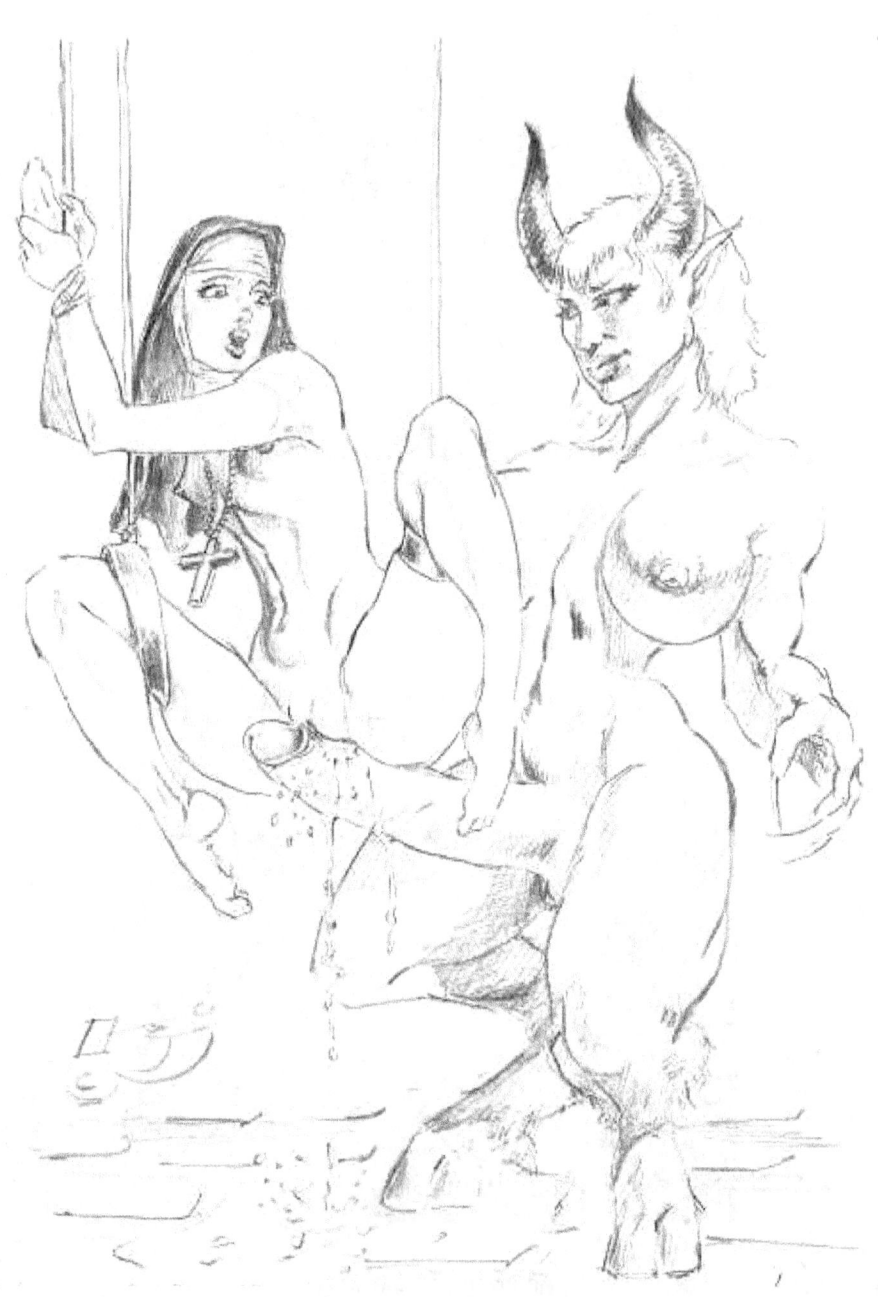

Anonymous, early 20th century

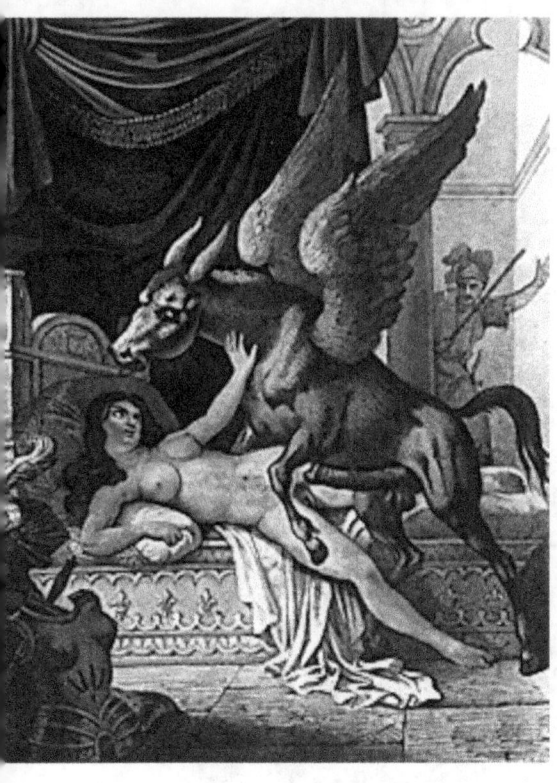

Puccelle d'Orleans

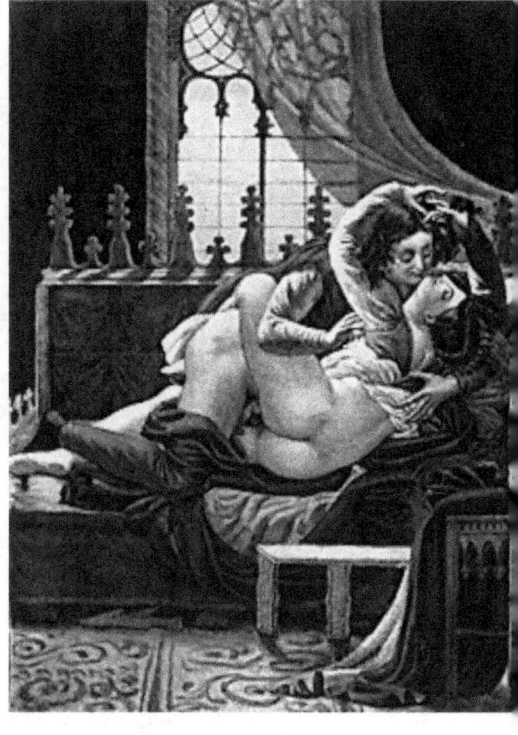

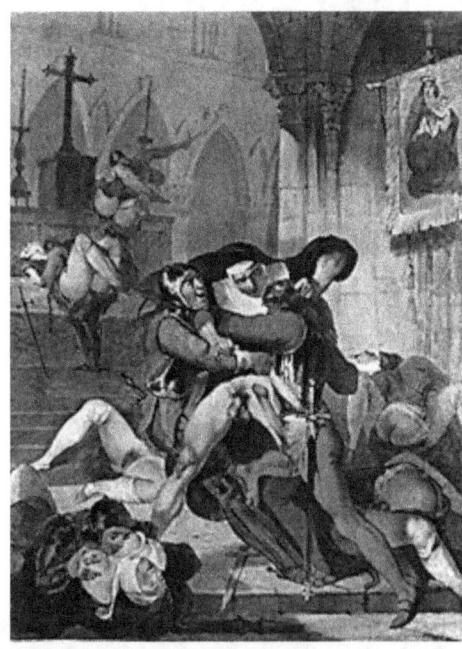

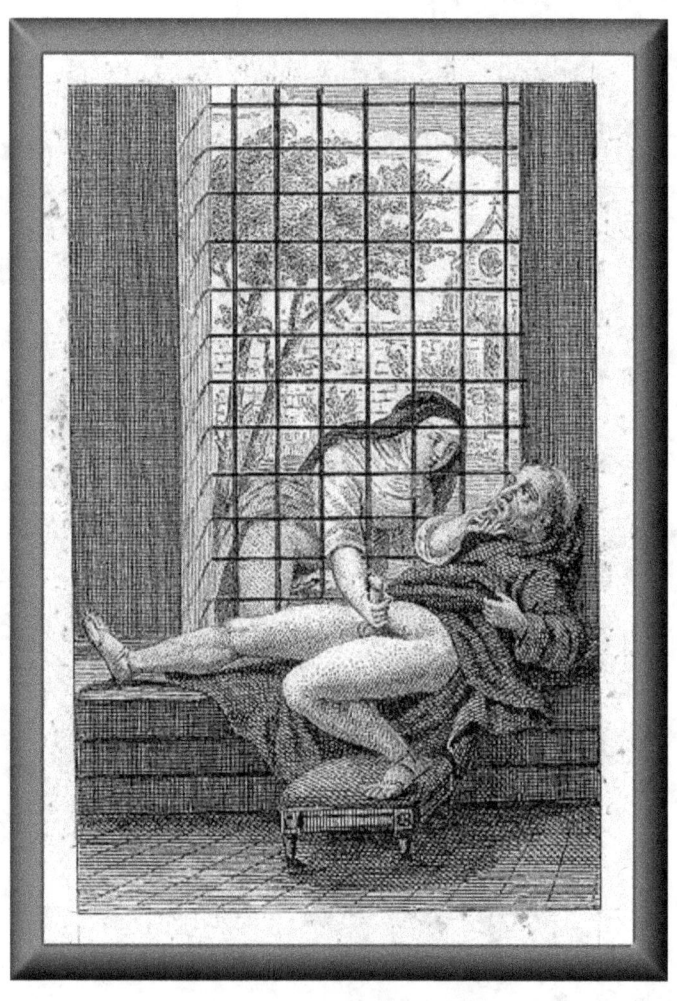

Anonymous, early 19th century

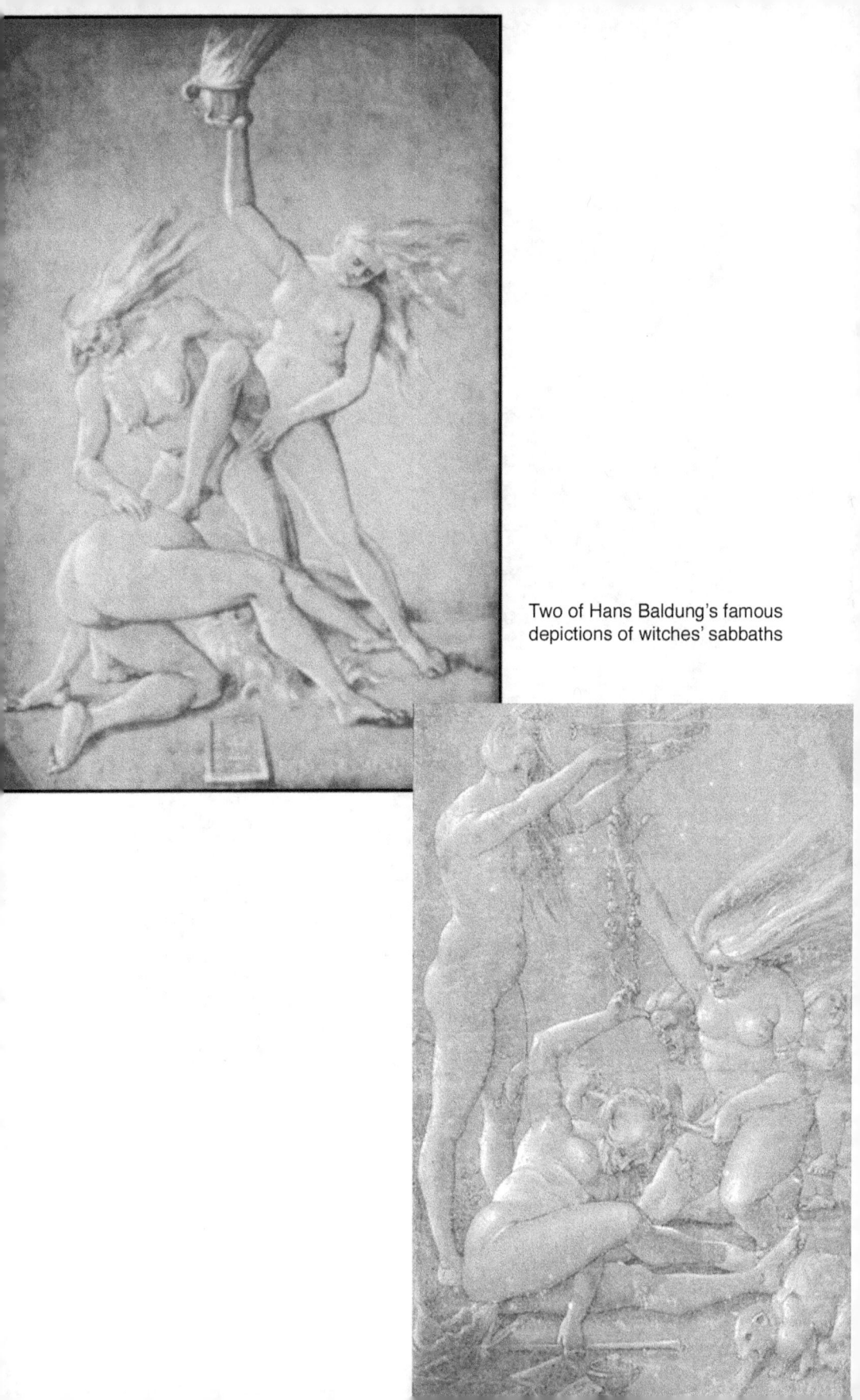

Two of Hans Baldung's famous
depictions of witches' sabbaths

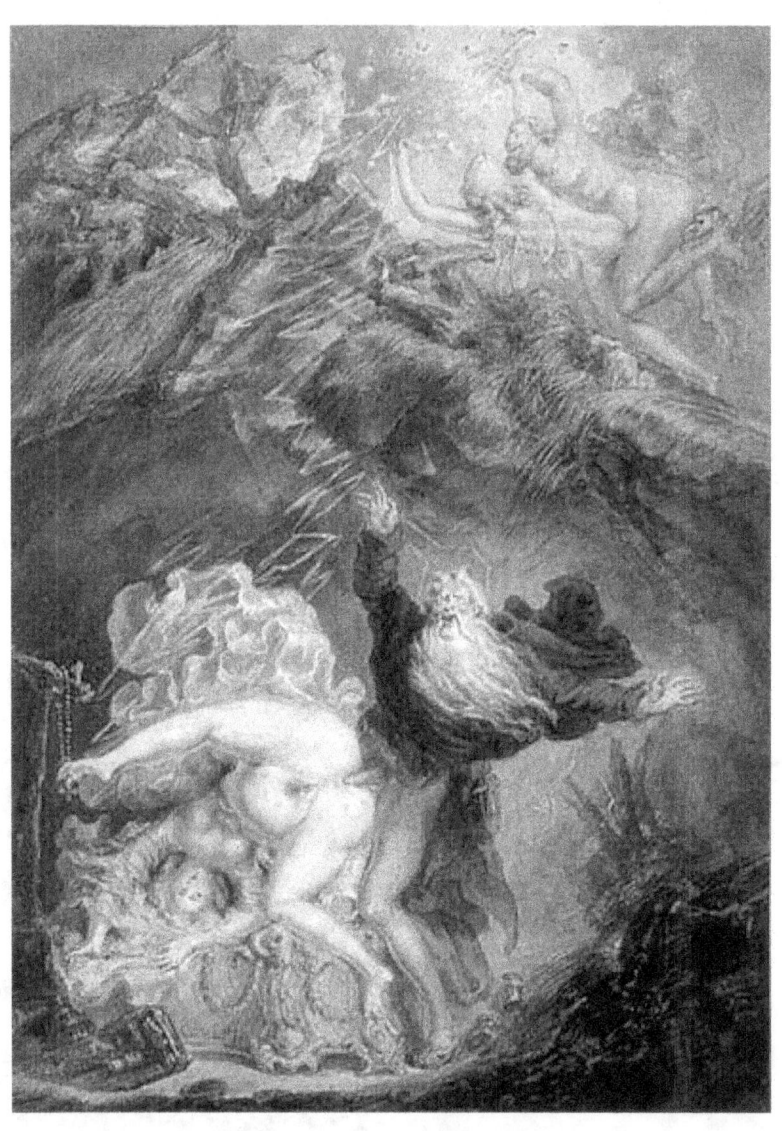

Giove Pluvio, Histoire Sainte

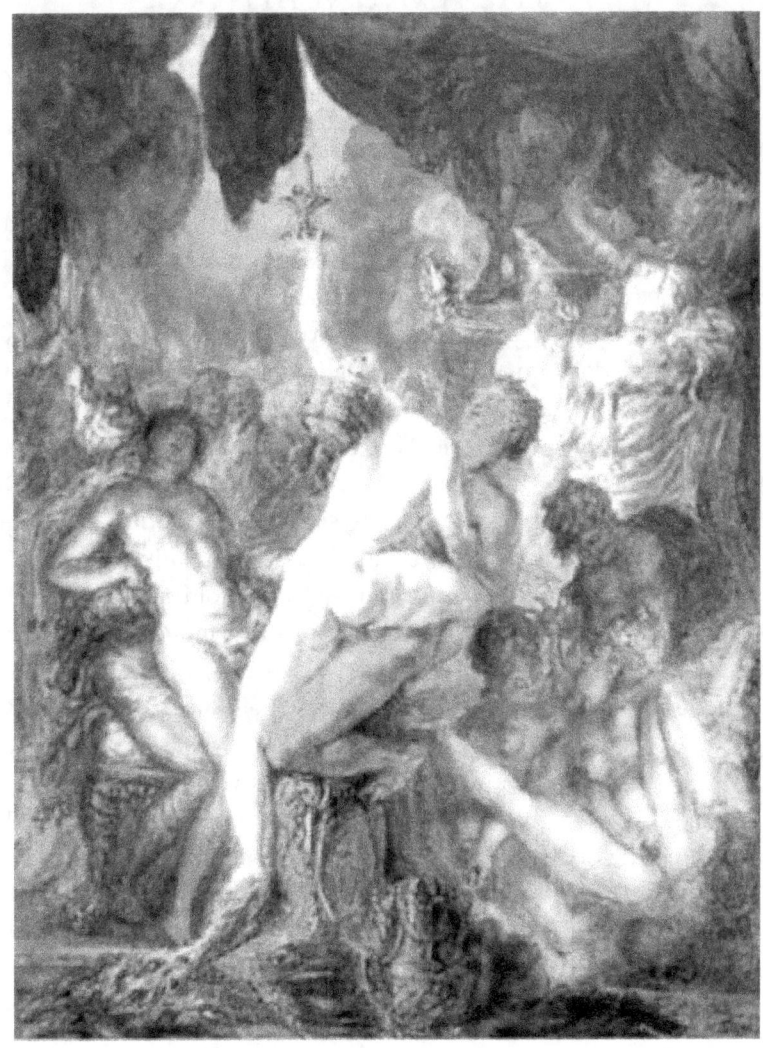

From Histoire Sainte, Adorazione del vitello d'oro

SANDRO BOTTICELLI:
THE ANNUNCIATION

Sandro Botticelli's *Annunciation* is violent. It depicts an aggressive sexual approach of a woman, though the pressure here is psychological and spiritual: the Archangel, as in all other depictions of the Annunciation, does not touch the Virgin. That would be too lascivious, if the Archangel's hand were placed on the breast or belly of the Virgin Mary. That would be too direct. So Gabriel does not touch the Madonna, but makes love to her from a distance, as God makes love to the Virgin from a distance, from the privileged position of Heaven. God sits on his heavenly throne, spiritually penetrating and impregnating the Virgin, who remains a Virgin, despite the physicality and pain of pregnancy and labour. The Virgin is too passive, fatally passive, for feminists. *Ecce Ancilla Domina* she says: 'behold the handmaid of the lord' (J. Metford, 28). The Virgin Mary moves from being a virgin, from 'knowing not a man', to becoming pregnant, in one anguished moment. Like Tess Durbeyfield in Thomas Hardy's 1892 novel *Tess of the d'Urbervilles*, she knows little of men. Then, the first time she knows 'love' (i.e. sex) she gets pregnant. This, then, is for some feminists a vicious kind of possession, which has the blessing of the top guy in the West, God.

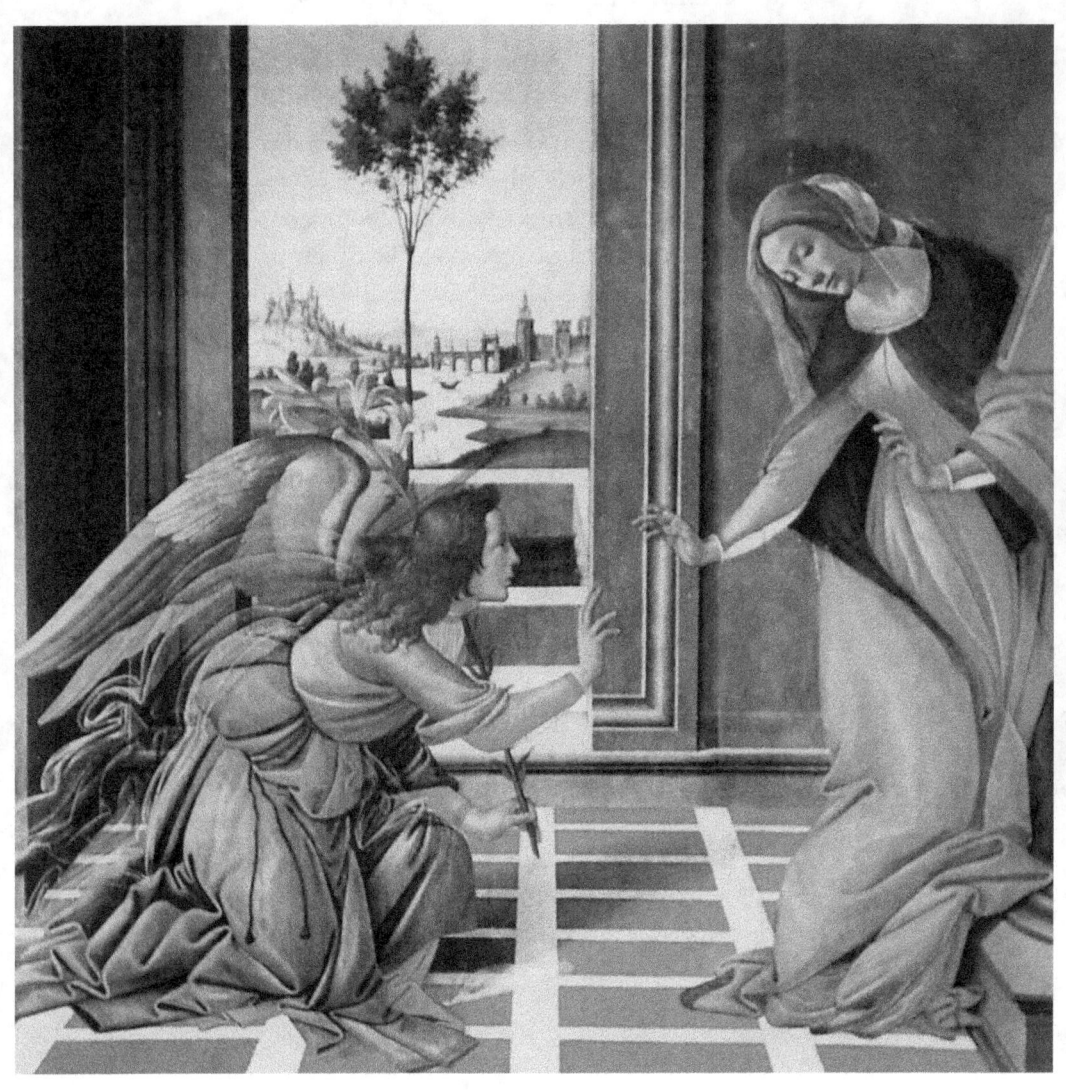

Sandro Botticelli, The Annunciation, Uffizi Gallery, Florence

LEDA AND THE SWAN

Like Michelangelo Buonarroti, Leonardo da Vinci produced an erotic version of *Leda and the Swan*. Both Michelangelo's and Leonardo's images are lost. We know both, though, because they were copied.[1] Michelangelo's picture is explicitly erotic: the huge swan lies between the deity's legs, the feathers of his wing over her vulva, a touch that expresses male 'possession' of the woman's sexuality.

Leonardo da Vinci made his *Leda and the Swan* as erotica is made; at the request of a (male) client: 'I executed the painting... for a lover. He wished to see the features of his goddess mirrored so that he might kiss them without arousing suspicion', Leonardo wrote.[2] In Antoine Coypel's (?) picture of *Leda and the Swan*, Jupiter's genitals are again the focus of the image, as the woman sits astride his legs.[3]

1 After Michelangelo: *Leda and the Swan*, 16th century, Royal Academy, London
2 quoted in Peter Webb, 112
3 Antoine Coypel (?): *Jupiter with Leda and the Swan*, from *Histoire Universelle*, c. 1750, British Museum

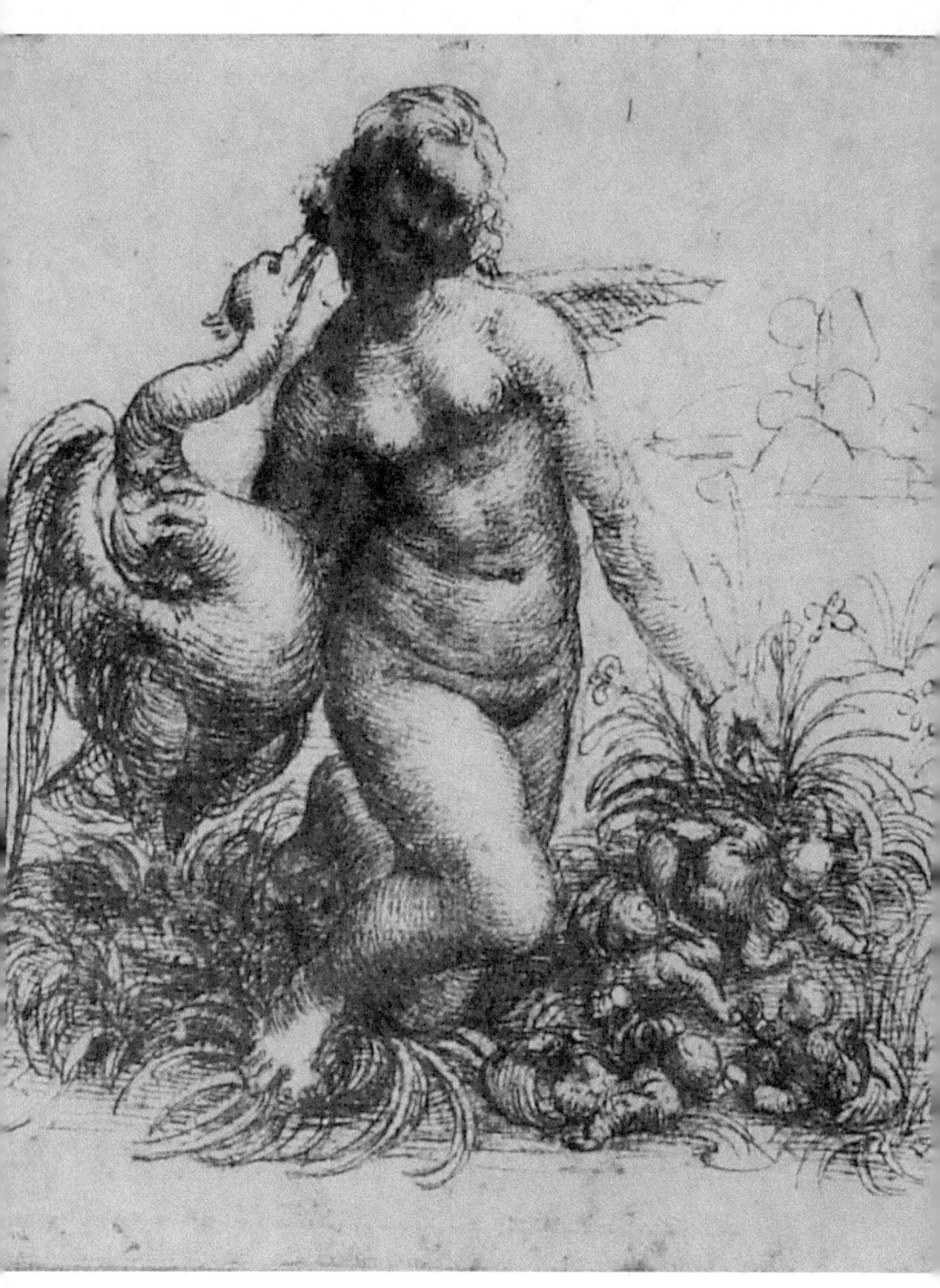

Leonardo da Vinci, Study for Leda and the Swan

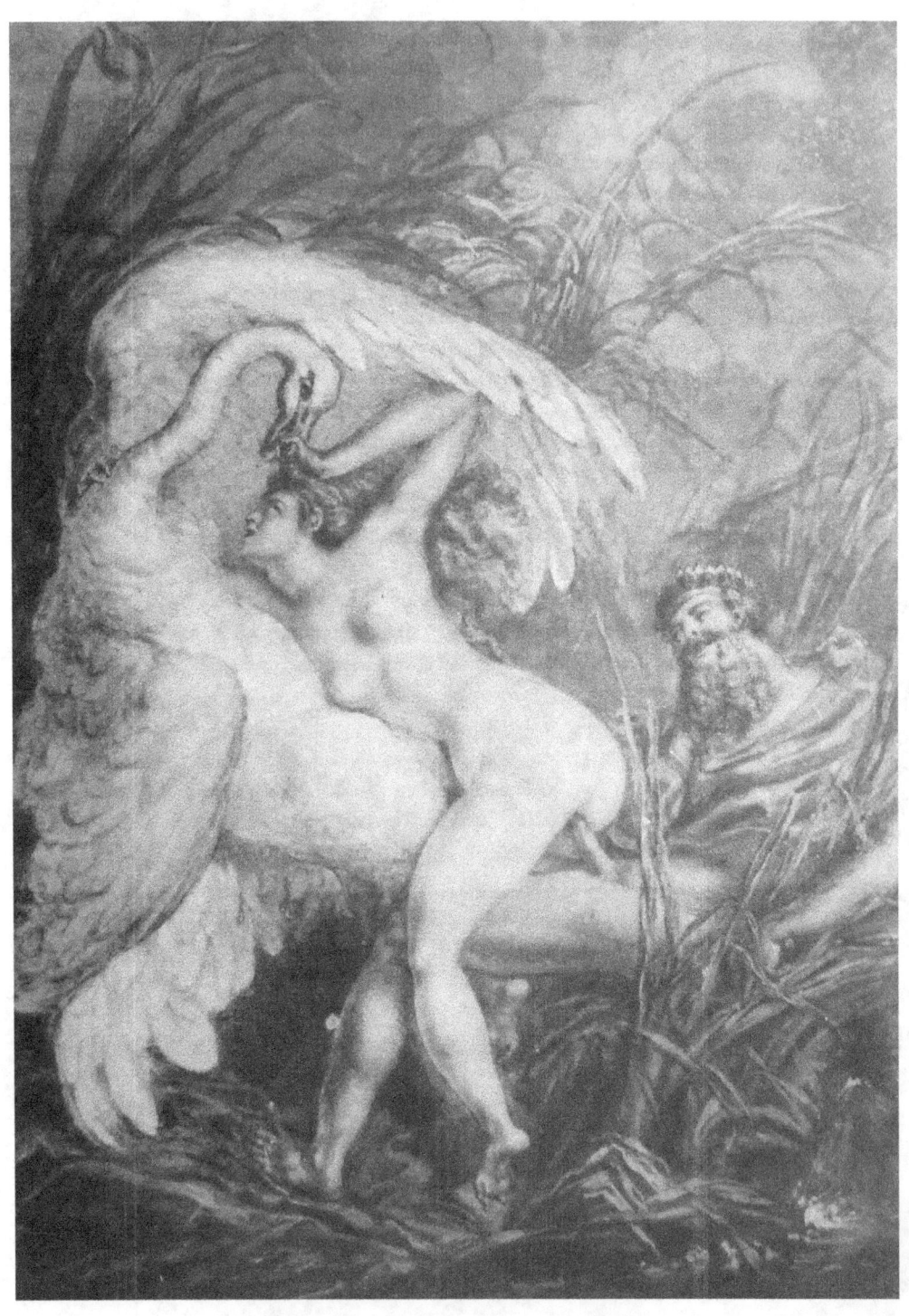

Antyoine Coypel, Jupiter With Leda and the Swan, c. 1750

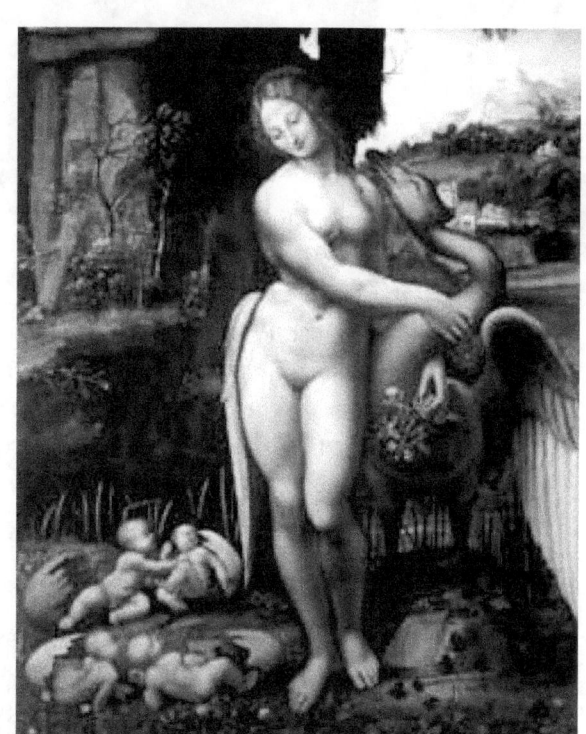

Leda and the Swan.
After Leonardo da Vinci (right).
After Paolo Veronese (below).

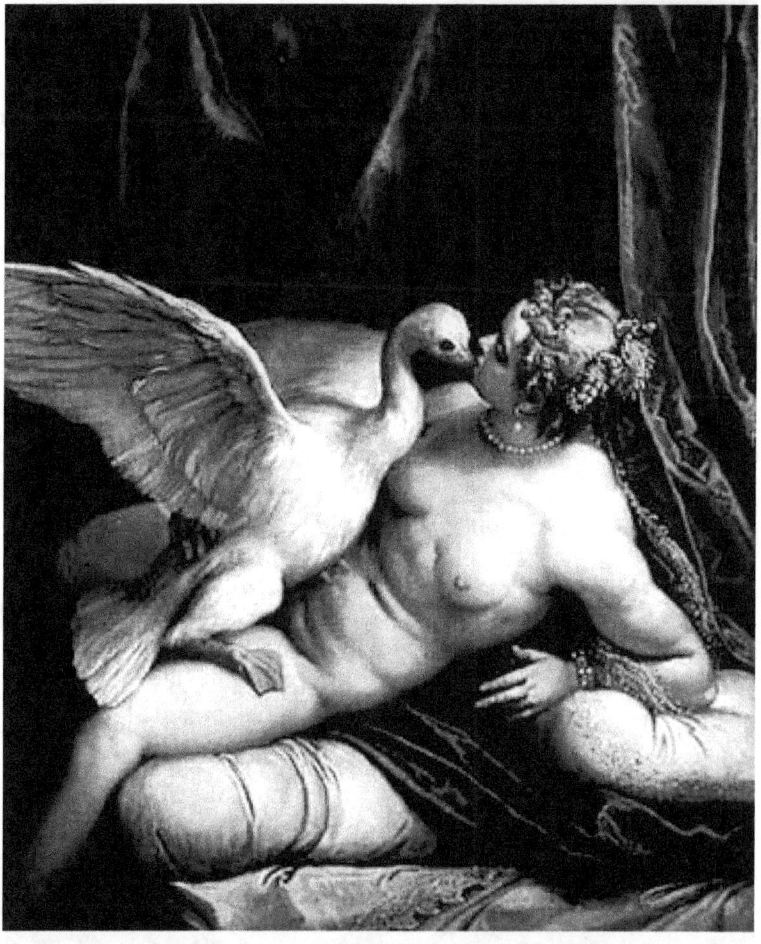

TITIAN: *NUDES*

Throughout history, female nudes of the high art type have been made for clients and connoisseurs – Titian made many nudes for such private, privileged consumption. Pornography too has been manufactured for the same clients and connoisseurs. When does a refined, rarefied enjoyment of erotic art become the vulgar, debased gratification of pornography? When does the connoisseur become the pornographic consumer?

In the art of Titian, as in Leonardo da Vinci, the sensuality of the paint surface is primary in the 'genius' of the art, in the critical acclaim the art generates. Whatever the subject, Titian manages to produce marvellous paintings.[1] Titian's soft colouring, his blurring of forms, his use of luminous lighting and his open use of paint look towards Impressionism and modern painting. Paintings such as *Venus Anadyomene* can stand happily beside Pierre Renoir as a modern depiction of a woman, a typical representation of 'woman' as erotic object, of 'woman' as Goddess and earthbound, flesh-and-blood being.[2]

Titian's nudes are the highpoint of the 'high art' nude; his nudes are as voluptuous as possible, for instance the woman reclining in bliss in the foreground right-hand corner of Titian's *Bacchanal of the Andrians*.[3]

---

1 Titian: *The Pesaro Altarpiece*, 1519-20, canvas, 478 x 268cm, Santa Maria Gloriosa dei Frari, Venice; *Christ Crowned with Thorns*, mid-1540s, 303 x 180cm, Louvre, Paris; *Pietà*, up to 1576, 353 x 348cm, Galeria dell' Academia, Venice
2 Titian: *Venus Anadyomene*, c. 1520, canvas, 76 x 57.3cm, Duke of Sutherland Collection, on loan to the National Gallery of Scotland, Edinburgh
3 Titian: *Bacchanal of the Andrians*, 1523-4, canvas, 175 x 193cm, Prado, Madrid

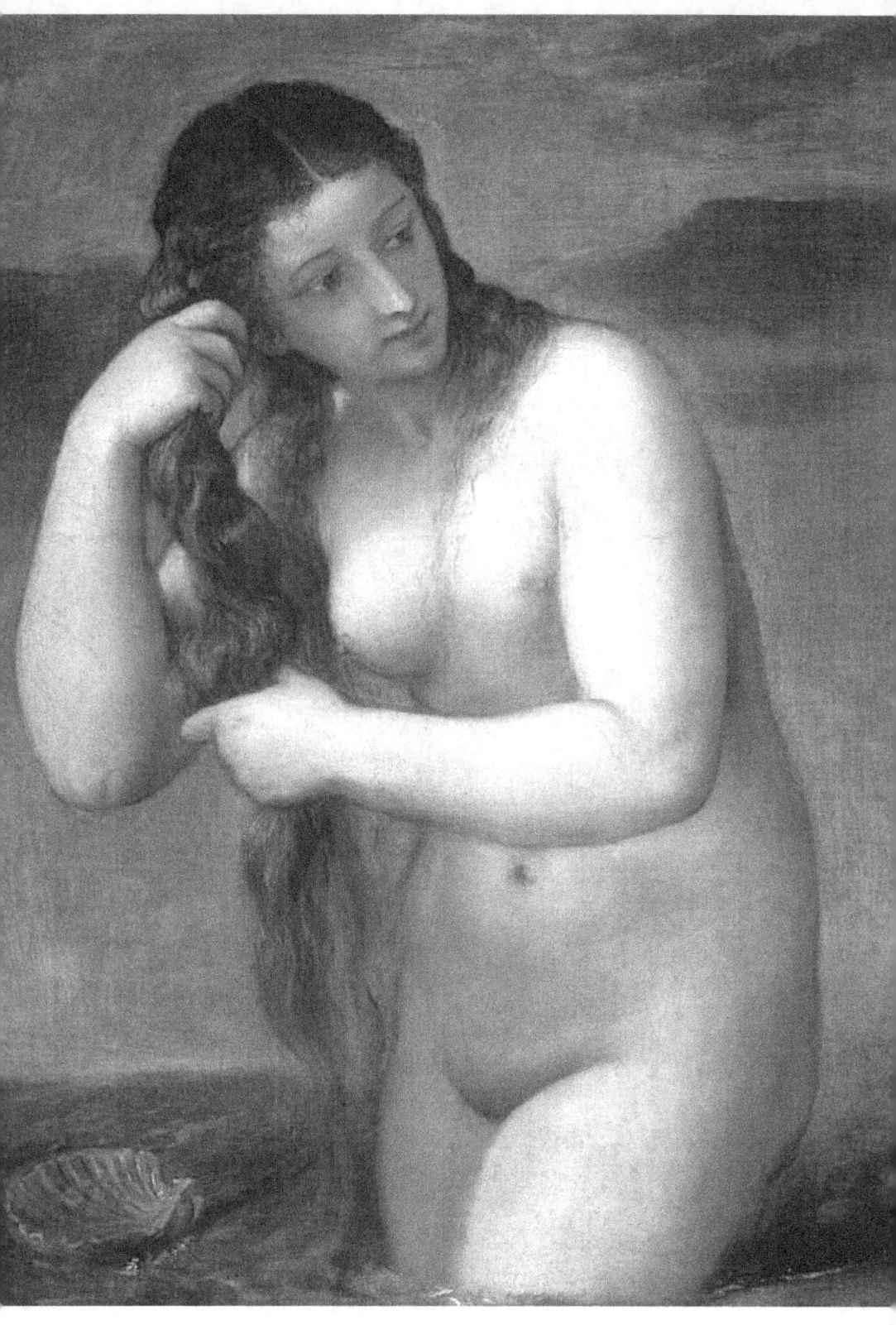

Titian, Venus Rising From the Sea, 1520, Scotland

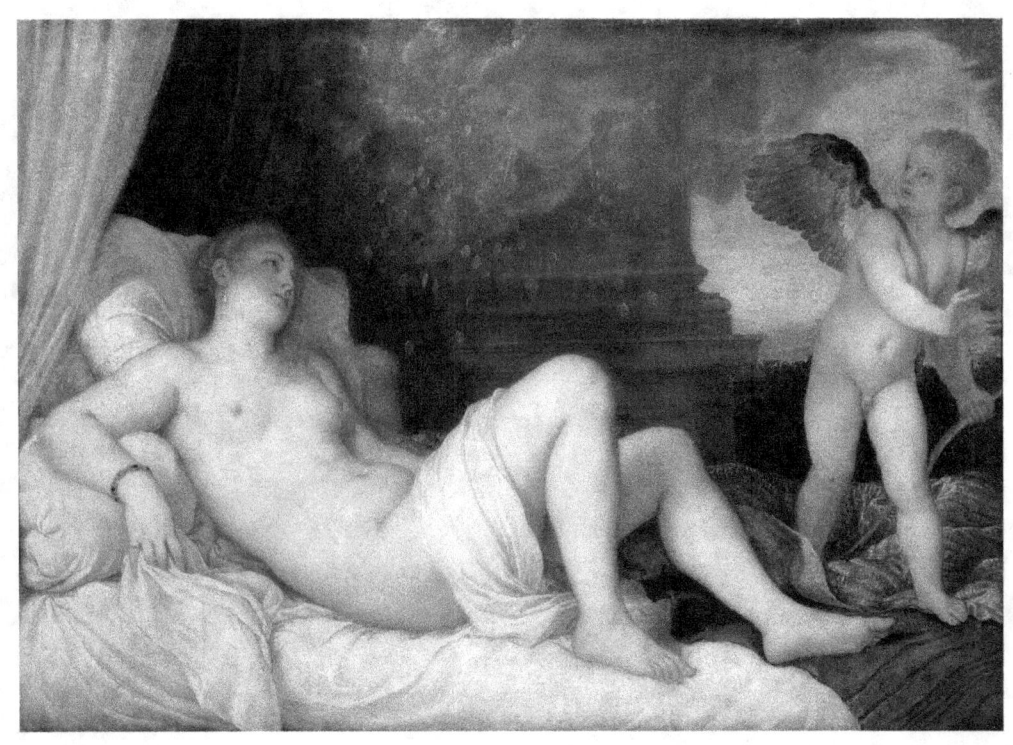

Titian, Danaë, 1544, Naples

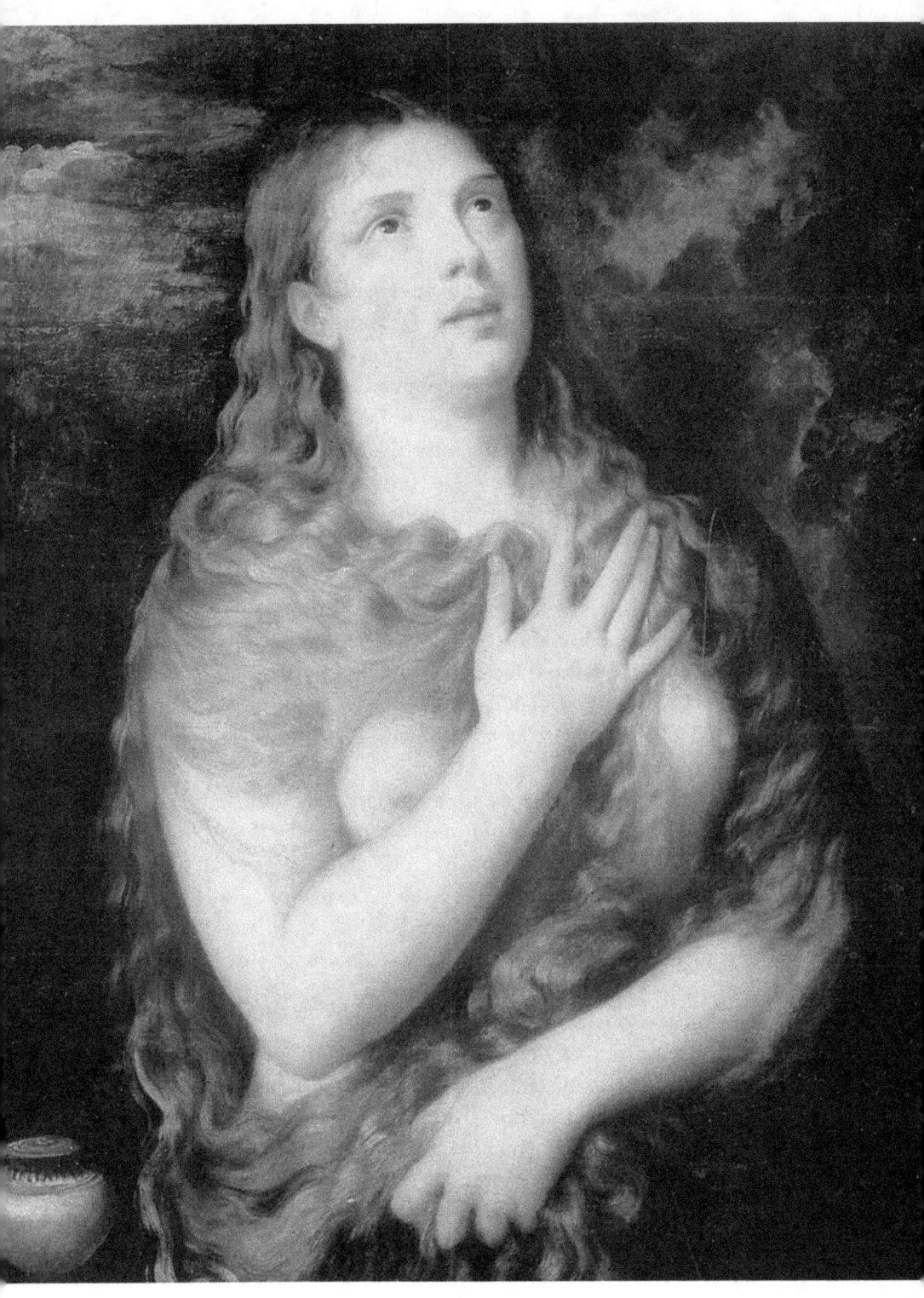

Titian, Mary Magdalene, 1533, Pittit Palace, Florence

MICHELANGELO MERISI
DE CARAVAGGIO

When you enter one of the biggest galleries in the Louvre Museum in Paris, you can halt on your way following the crowds to the *Mona Lisa* to have a look at numerous masterpieces on either side. You should definitely spend some time in front of Michelangelo Merisi de Caravaggio's *The Death of the Virgin*, of course, but be sure you don't miss the remarkable picture *The Fortune-teller* (1594, a.k.a. *The Good Fortune*). Luckily, *The Fortune-teller* is hung (at the moment) not too high up, so you can get a good view (why do so many museums and galleries hang major, major works of art way too high? Are we giants all of a sudden?).

Without a doubt, *The Fortune-teller* is a fabulous image of romance and sexuality and erotic love. It might not appear so at first, but have a closer look. On the top level, the painting portrays a woman and man, both young. The woman is a fortune teller and the man is a client, a punter, someone who's going to have their fortune told.

So the youth offers his hand, and the young woman takes it. In the act of telling his fortune from his palm, she is stealing his ring. So already this is fabulously erotic stuff, because all of the time it is written in neon signs by the exchange of *looks* between the two protagonists. In other words, the guy *knows* that the young woman is stealing his ring, and the young woman *knows* that the man *knows* she's trying to take his jewellery. And that's one of the reasons this painting is so erotic – it's the tease, the unspoken gestures, the eye contact, it's the guy saying, 'I know what you trying to do and you shouldn't be doing it, but I'm going to let you do it', and it's the woman saying, 'I'm going to take your ring, though you might not want me to, but really, *really* you do.'

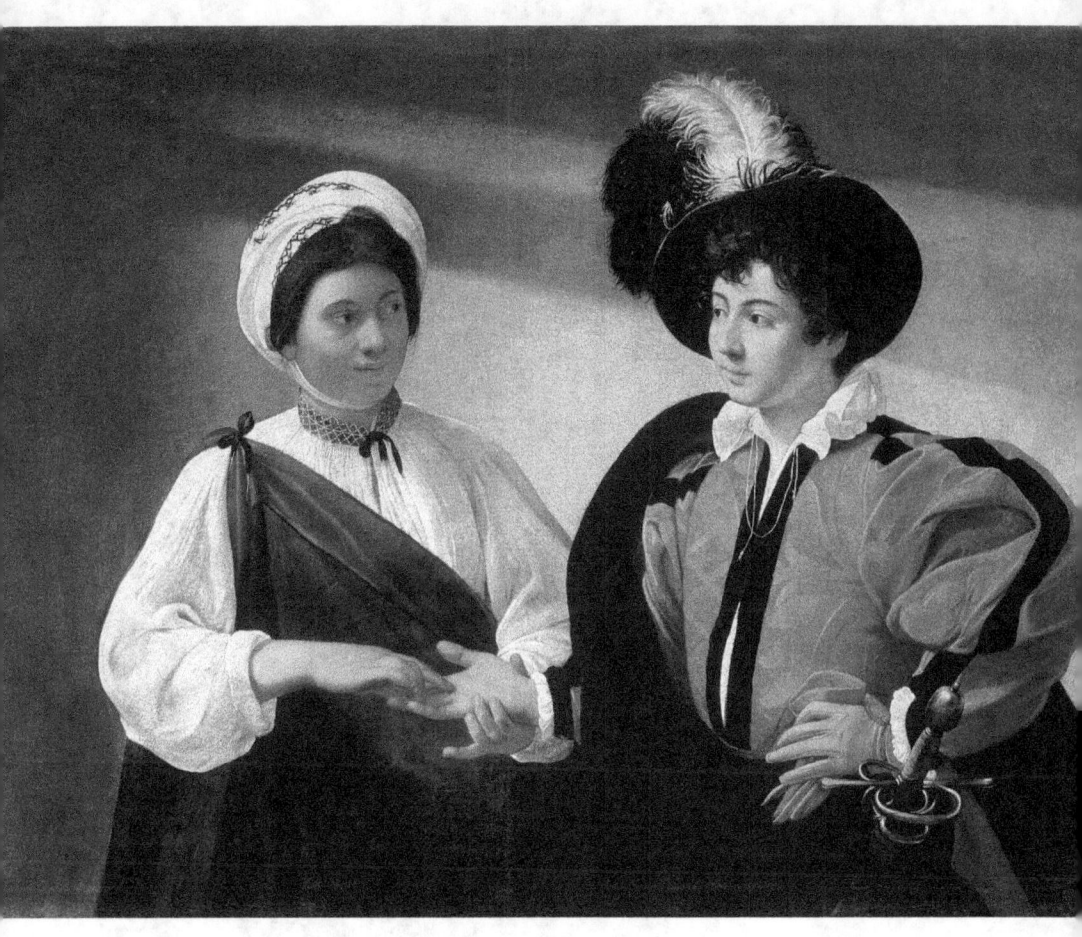

Michelangelo Merisi da Caravaggio,
The Fortune-Teller, Louvre, Paris

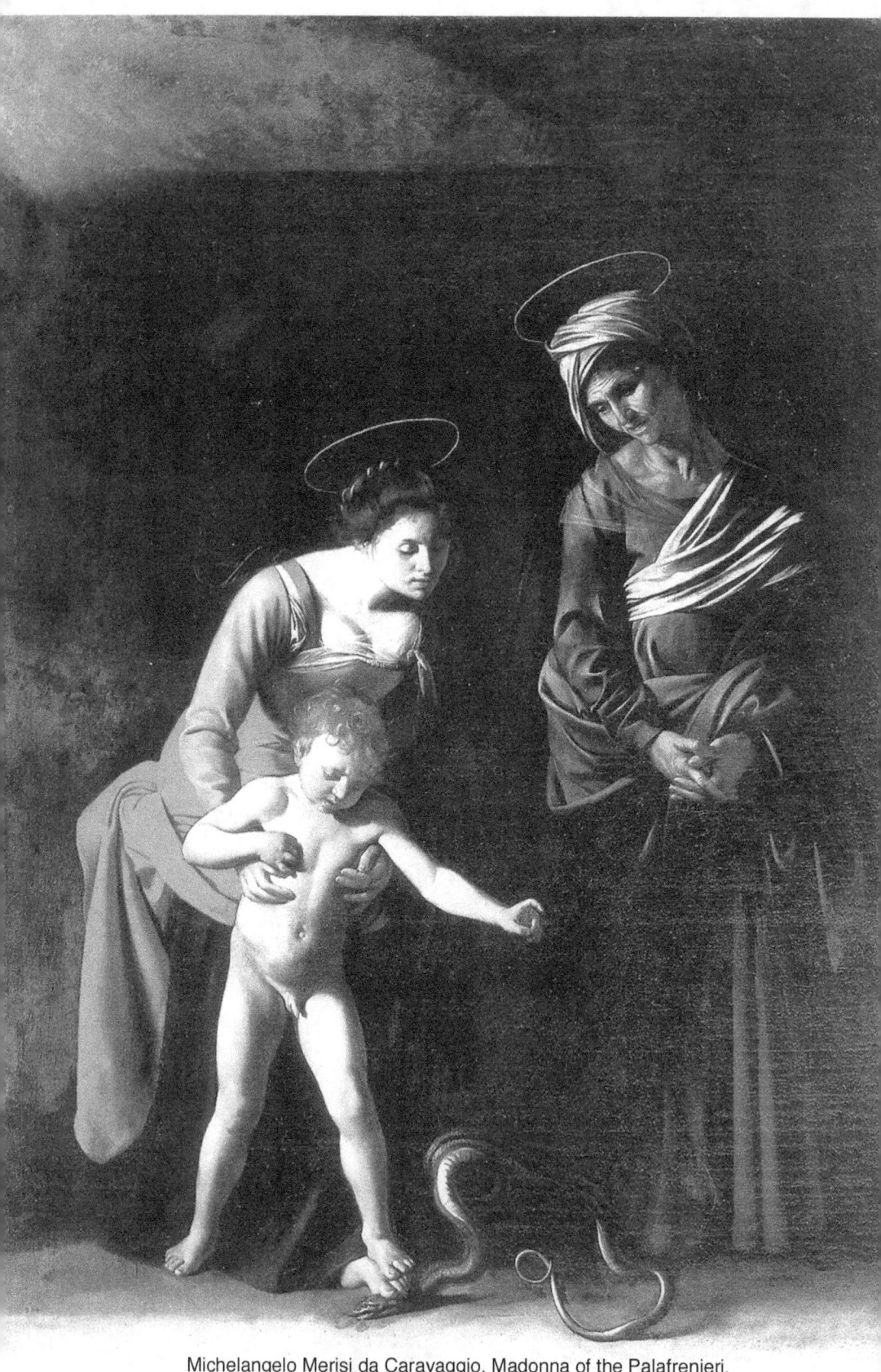

Michelangelo Merisi da Caravaggio, Madonna of the Palafrenieri,
1605-06, Galleria Borghese, Rome

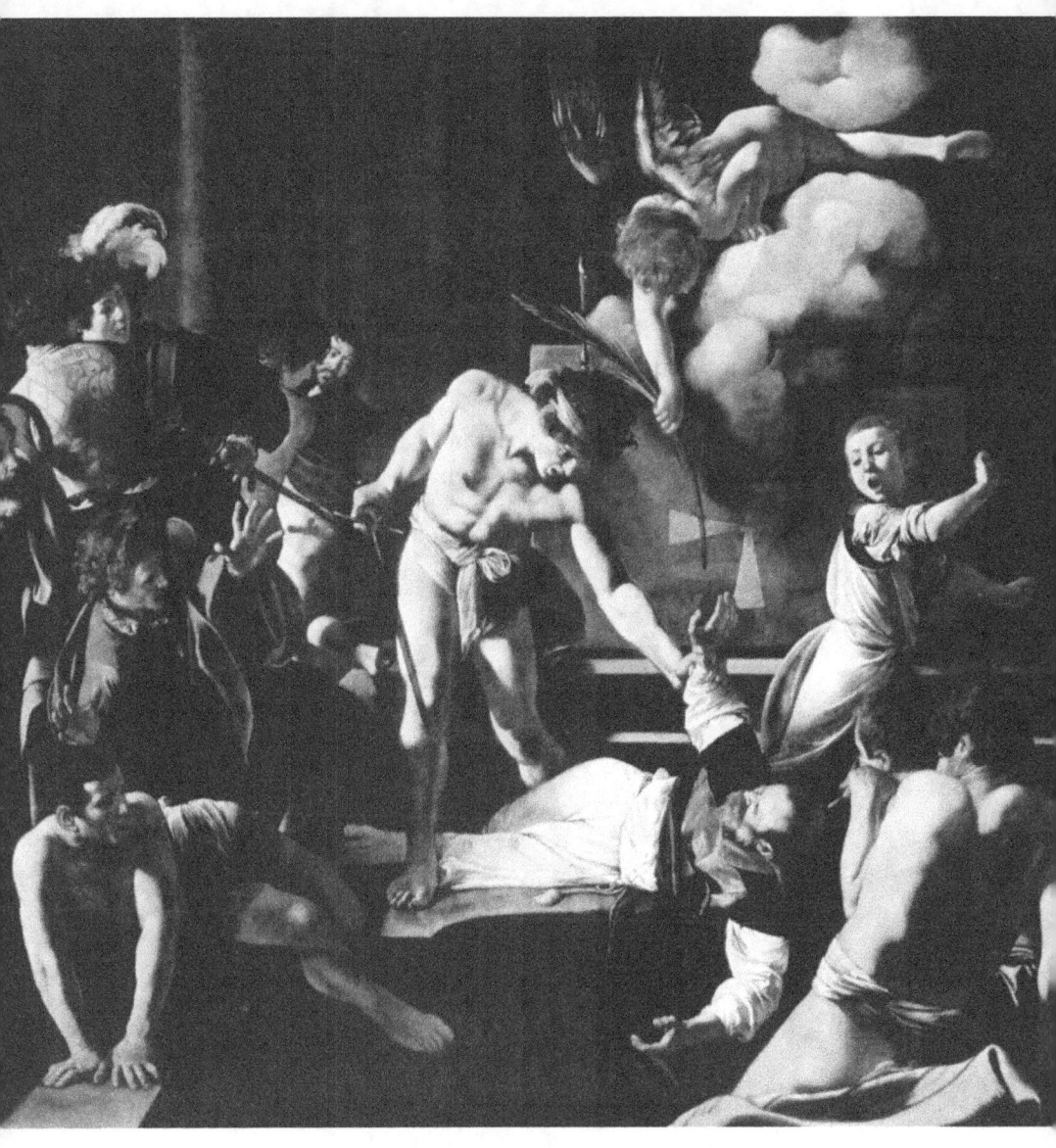

Caravaggio, The Martyrdom of St Matthew, 1600-01,
San Luigi dei Francesci, Rome

LUCAS CRANACH

The *Adam and Eves* and Venuses of Lucas Cranach (1472-1553, born in Vienna) are utterly distinctive: nobody in the history of painting has portrayed the human form quite like this. The nudes of Cranach (and other Northern Renaissance painters) are nudes that are not aware of their bodies being portrayed as spectacle. Yet Cranach's nudes must be conscious of their nudity too. Indeed, surely any Renaissance nude must be aware of its nakedness, otherwise it could not be a 'Renaissance' artwork. A mediaeval nude might be able to display itself without erotic self-awareness, but not a Renaissance nude, for Renaissance art is always aware of itself *as art*. It knows what it is doing.

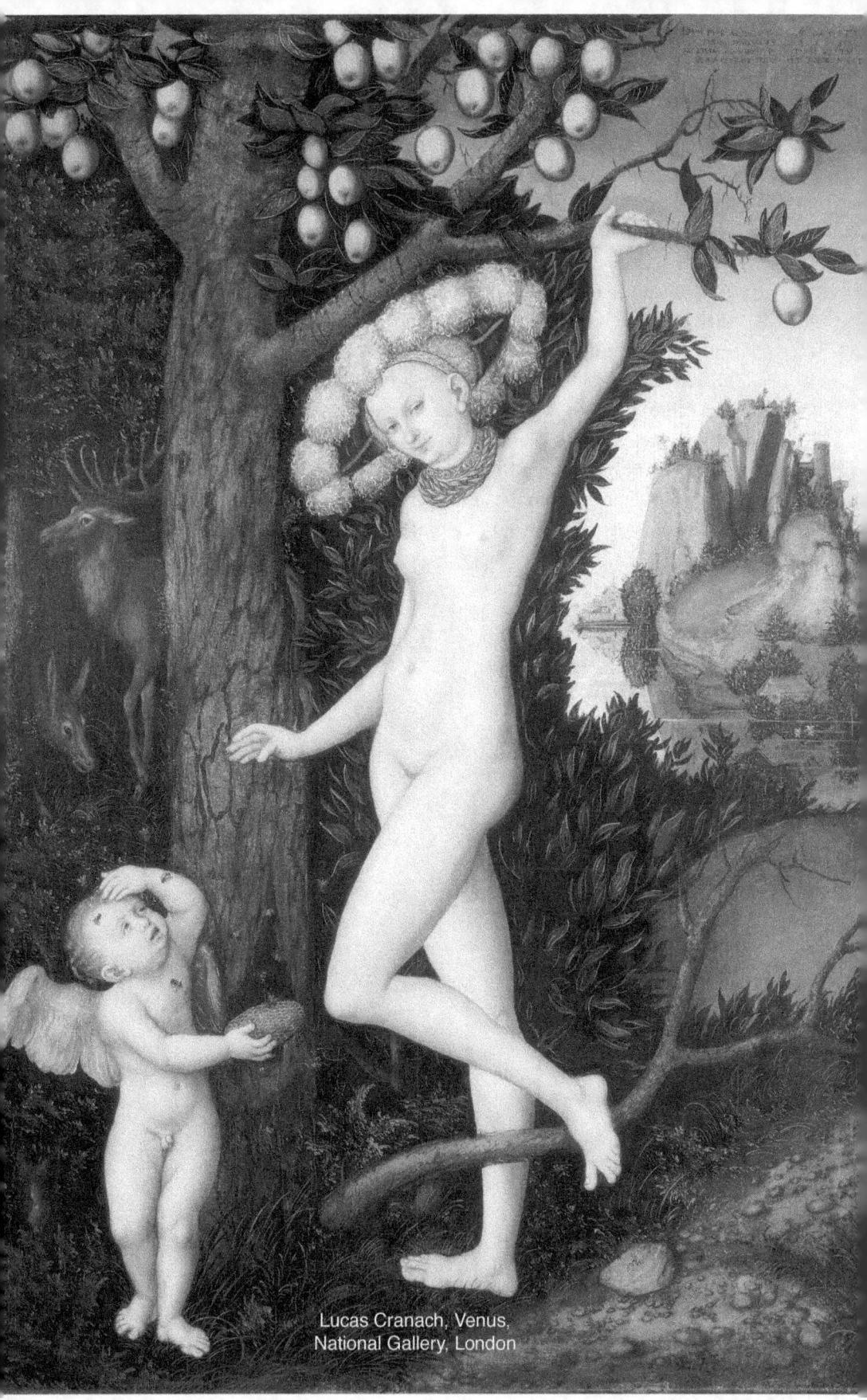

Lucas Cranach, Venus,
National Gallery, London

ARTEMISIA GENTILESCHI

Artemisia Gentileschi (1593-1653) is one of the celebrated women artists of the late Renaissance period, well-known for her marvell-ous *Judiths*, and her luminous *Self-Portrait*. Daughter of the painter Orazio Gentileschi, Artemisia was involved in a famous rape trial: Agostino Tassi was accused by her father of raping Gentileschi when she was 19 (Tassi was subsequently imprisoned). Inevit-ably, critics have linked the rape trial to the depictions of the *Old Testament* heroines that Gentileschi painted, including of course Judith cutting off the head of Holofernes.

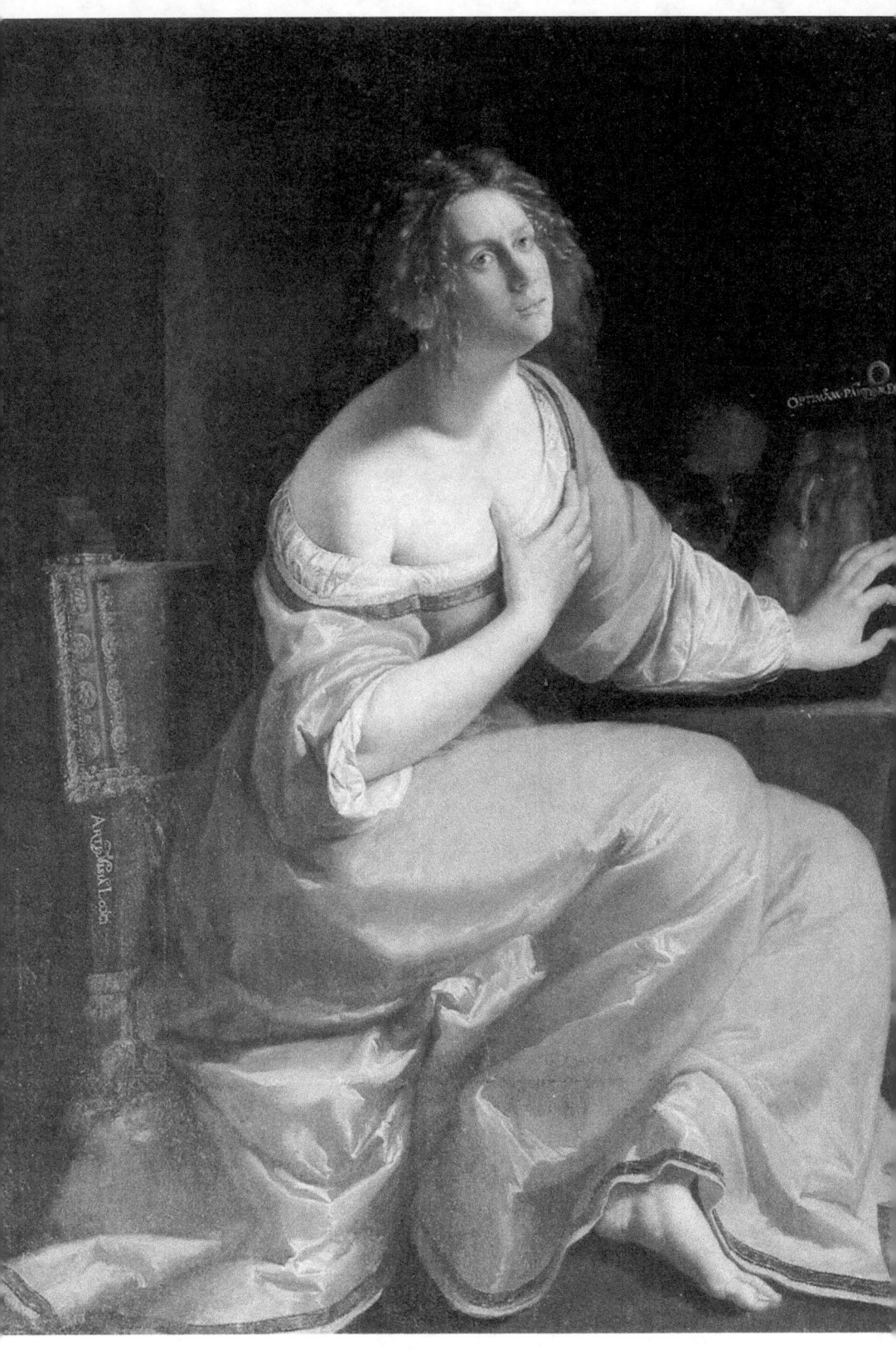

Artemsia Gentileschi, Mary Magdalene

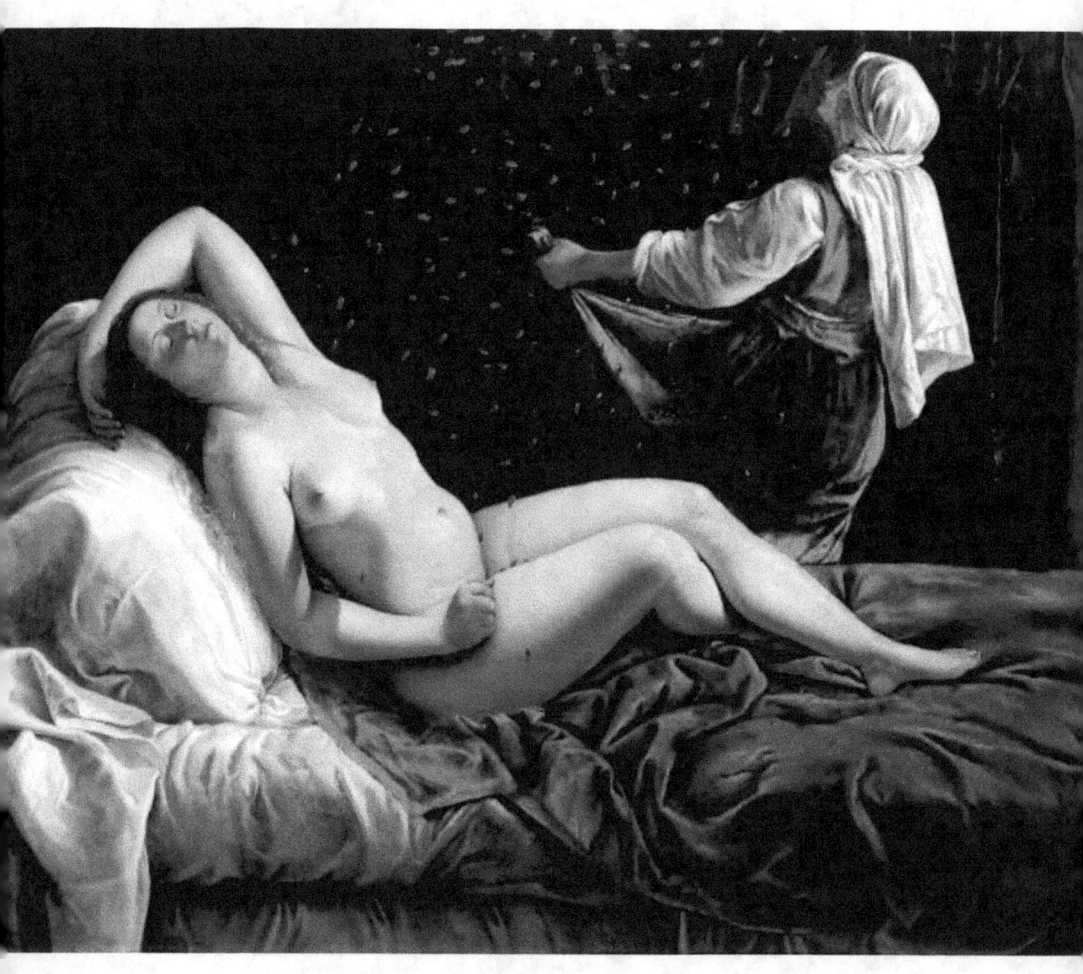

Artemisia Gentileschi, Danaë, c.1612, St Louis Art Museum.

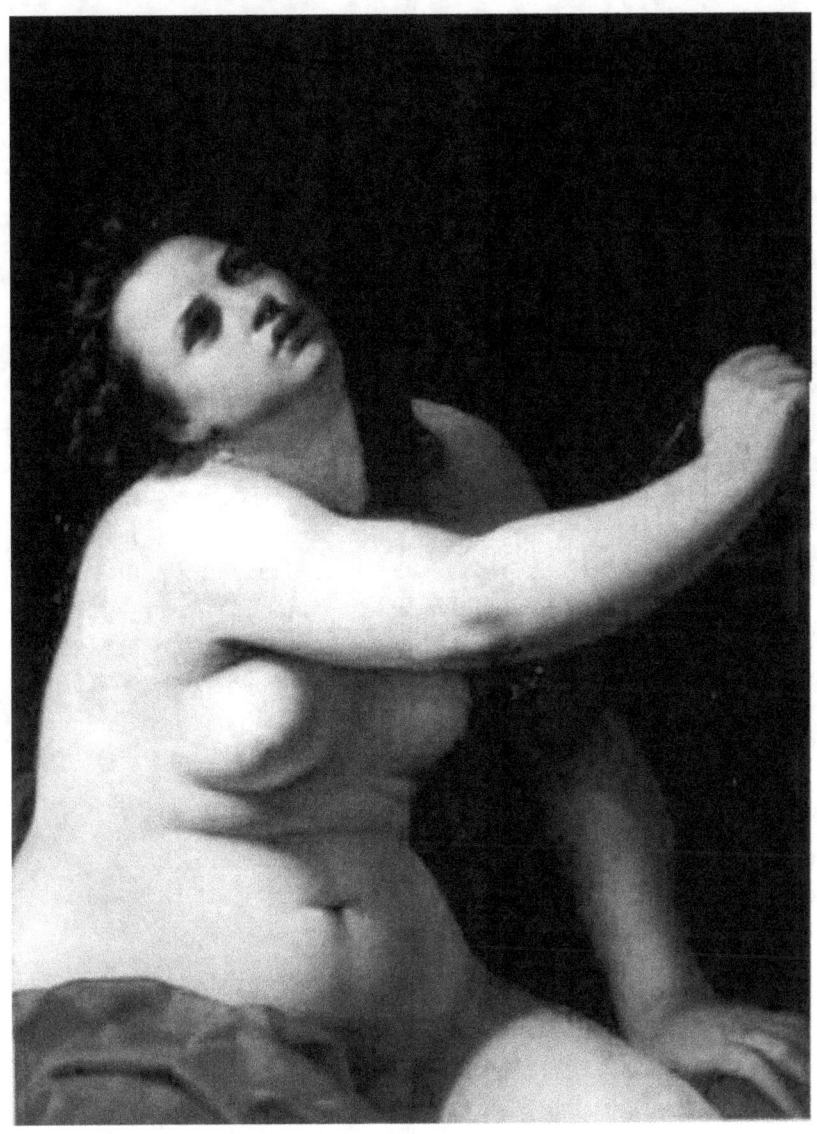

Artemisia Gentileschi, Cleopatra,
Cavallini-Sgarbi Foundation, Ferrara

MICHELANGELO BUONARROTI

Beside Michelangelo Buonarroti (1475-1564), the precocious, religious, obsessive hero of the era, other Renaissance sculptors often seem lightweight, insubstantial or hackneyed. Michelangelo's sculptures are full of the spirit of life which is expressed with an assurance of touch and modelling that is in itself erotic. His sculptures assert their eroticism, whatever the subject, from the superb *Dawn* and *Dusk* of the Medici tomb, to the late *Pietà*.[1]

There is undeniably a vivacious enjoyment of the male form in Michelangelo Buonarroti's *Ignudi* in the Sistine Chapel,[2] while his *Dying Slaves* are among the most sensual images of eroticism combined with death in Western art.[3] Michelangelo's slave dies utterly voluptuously, his arms pulled up to expose his body. Michelangelo's figures are confident in their nudity and their sexuality. They exude confidence – too much, it seems, for the owners of the Sistine Chapel: figures in Michelangelo's *Last Judgement* had to have drapes painted over their genitals during the Counter-Reformation.[4] And in 1970 the use of Michelangelo's *David* on a poster was banned.[5]

1 Michelangelo: *Tomb of Lorenzo de' Medici*, h. 173, Medici Chapel, Florence; *Pietà*, late 1550s, marble, 226cm high, Florence cathedral
2 Michelangelo: *Ignudi*, 1508-10, fresco, Sistine Chapel, Vatican, Rome
3 Michelangelo: *Dying Slave*, 1513, marble, 229cm high, Louvre, Paris
4 Michelangelo: *The Last Judgement*, 136-41, fresco, 1375 x 120cm, Sistine Chapel, Vatican, Rome
5 'In 1970, a bookseller in Sydney, Australia, was arrested for displaying a poster of the nude *David*, and the same happened in South Africa in 1973.' Peter Webb, *The Erotic Arts*, 4-5

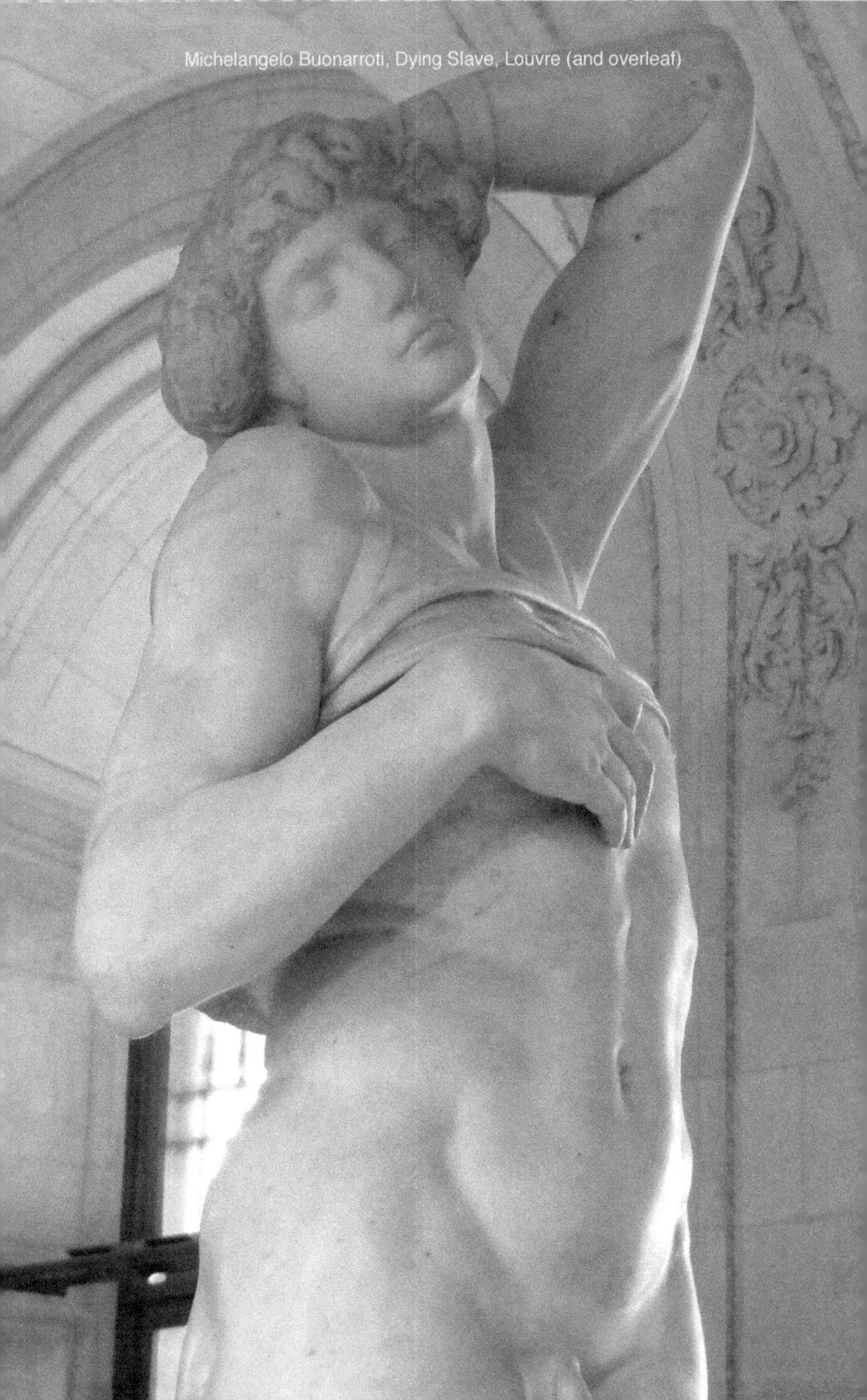

Michelangelo Buonarroti, Dying Slave, Louvre (and overleaf)

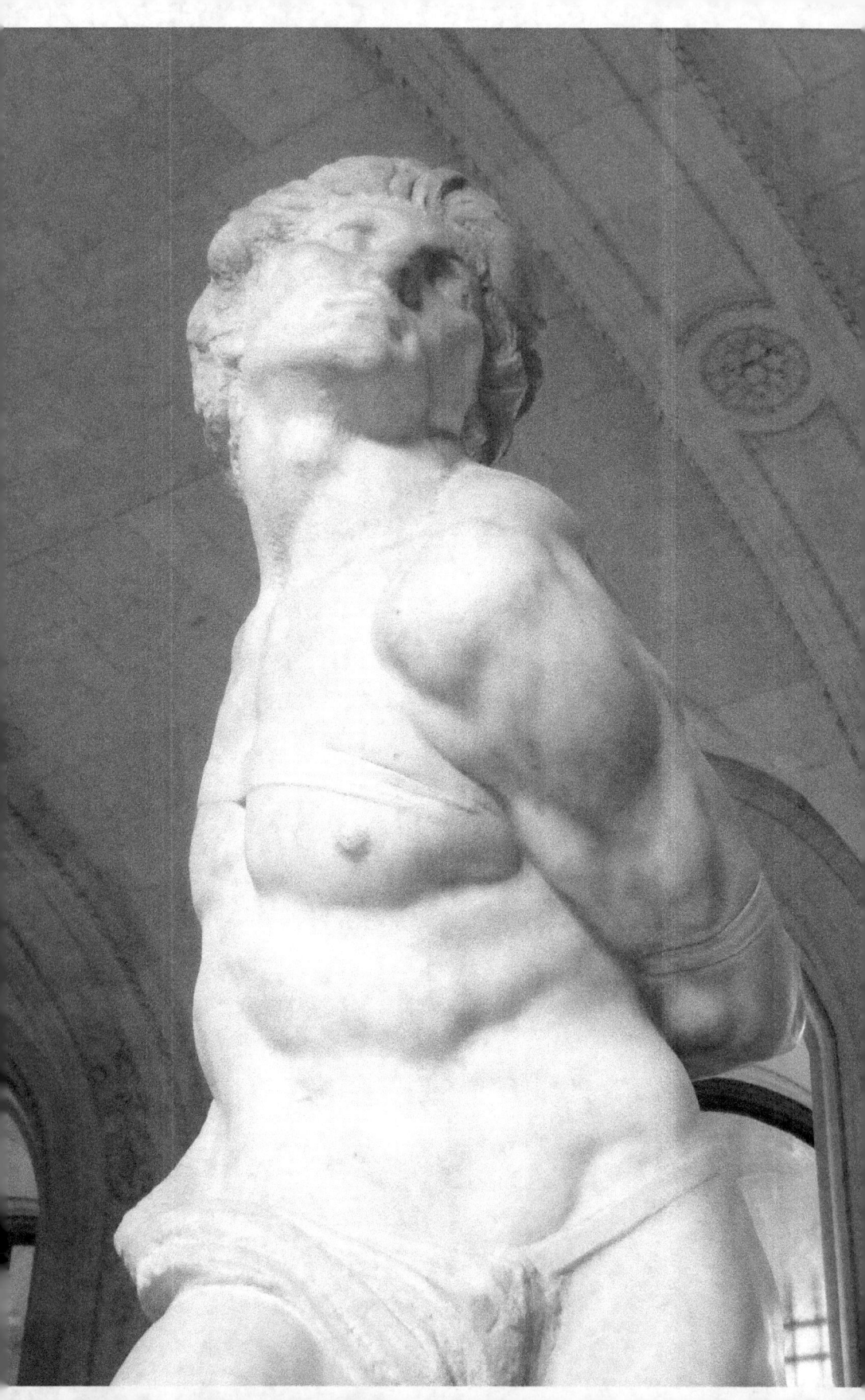

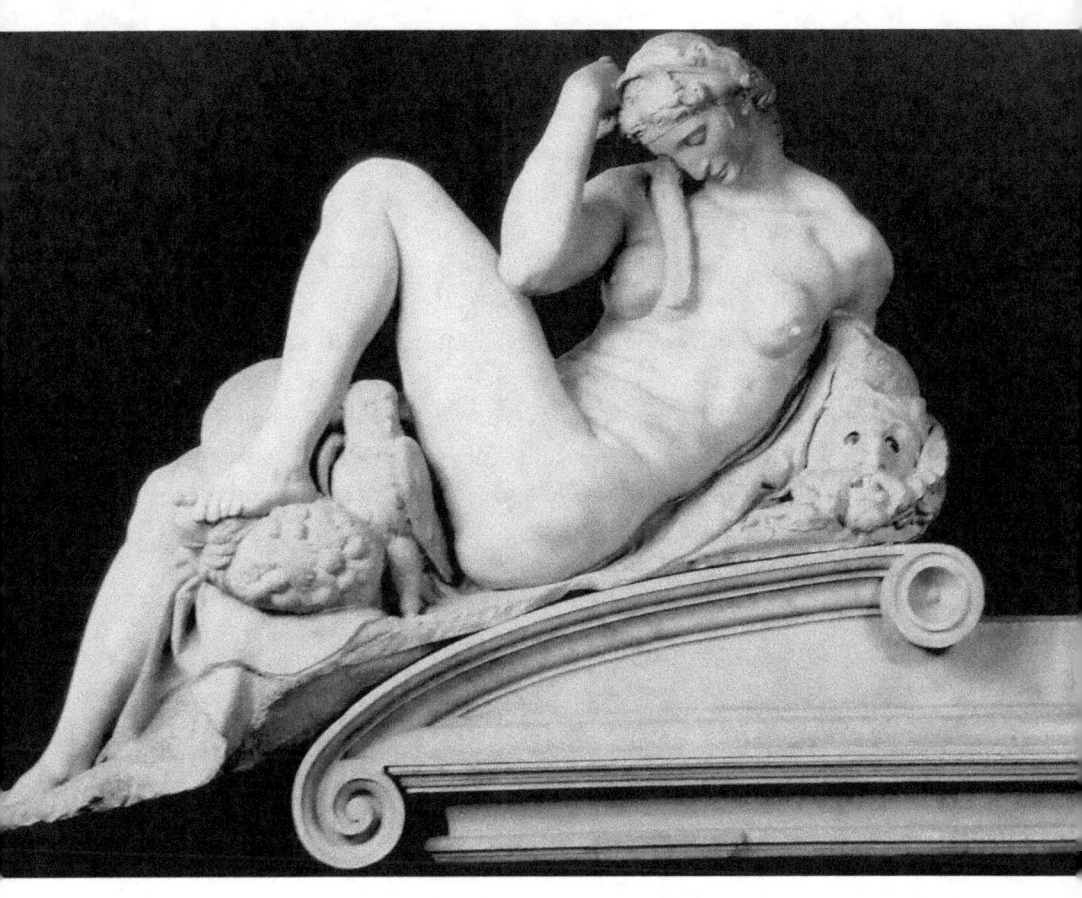

Michelangelo, Night, Medici Chapel, Florence

MICHELANGELO BUONARROTI

Michelangelo Buonarroti's figures add angst-ridden and 'modern' tensions – of self, identity, passion and Existential awareness – to the basically life-affirming gestures of ancient Greek sculpture. Michelangelo takes the anonymous, often indifferent eroticism of Greek statues and turns it into something modern or Renaissance, something decidedly individual and subjective. The anguish of (some of) Michelangelo's figures is that of a 'great' artist striving to achieve the Holy Grail or Philosopher's Stone of sculpture, the perfect form, that Neoplatonic impossibility. Beautiful as they are ('beauty' is precisely the right term for Renaissance's notions of perfection), Michelangelo's statues are not final, finished forms. They are fluid, aching for the touch of completion which nobody can give them. In Michelangelo's art, eroticism is passionately – sometimes desperately – asserted.

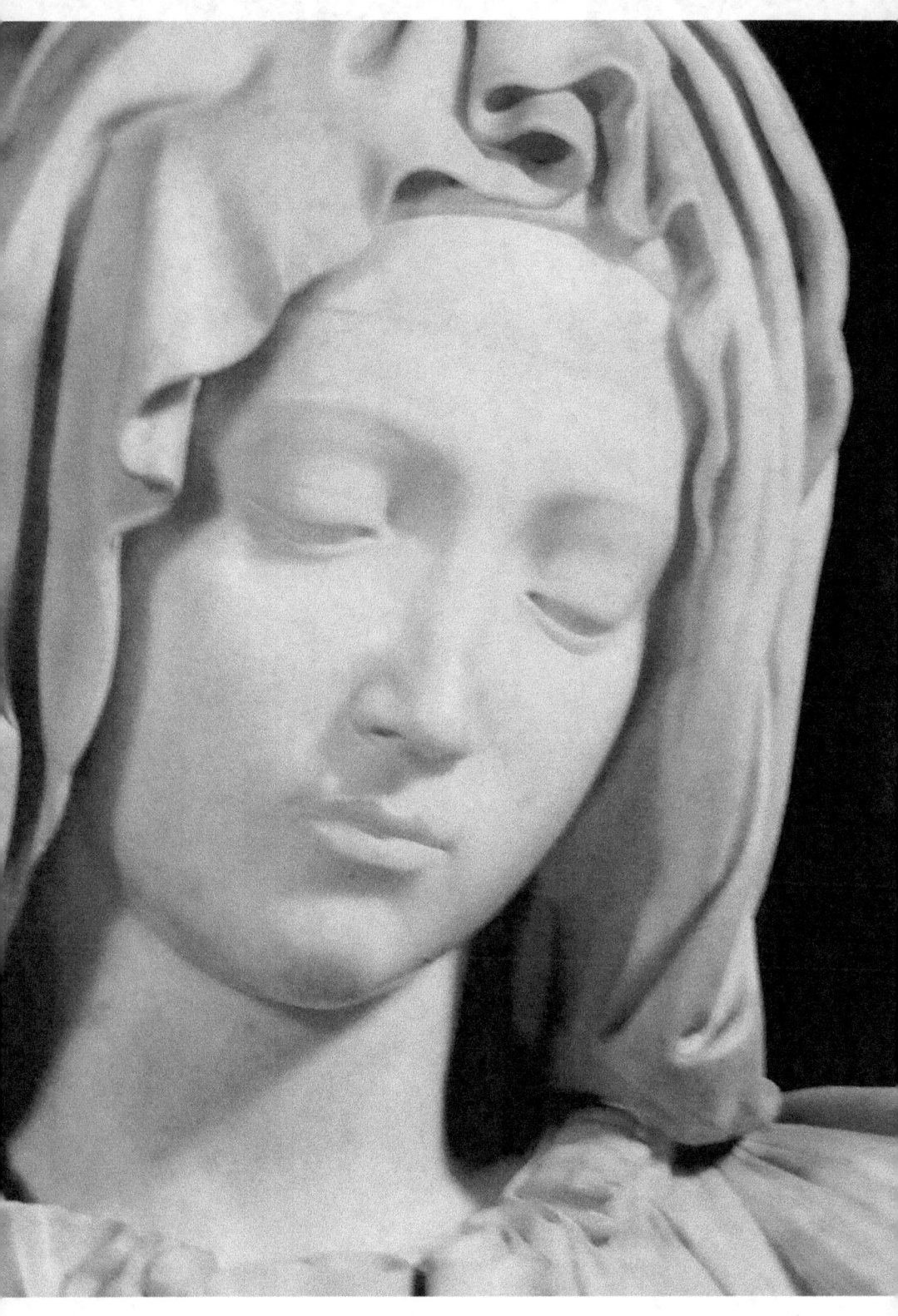

Michelangelo, Pietà, detail, Vatican, Rome

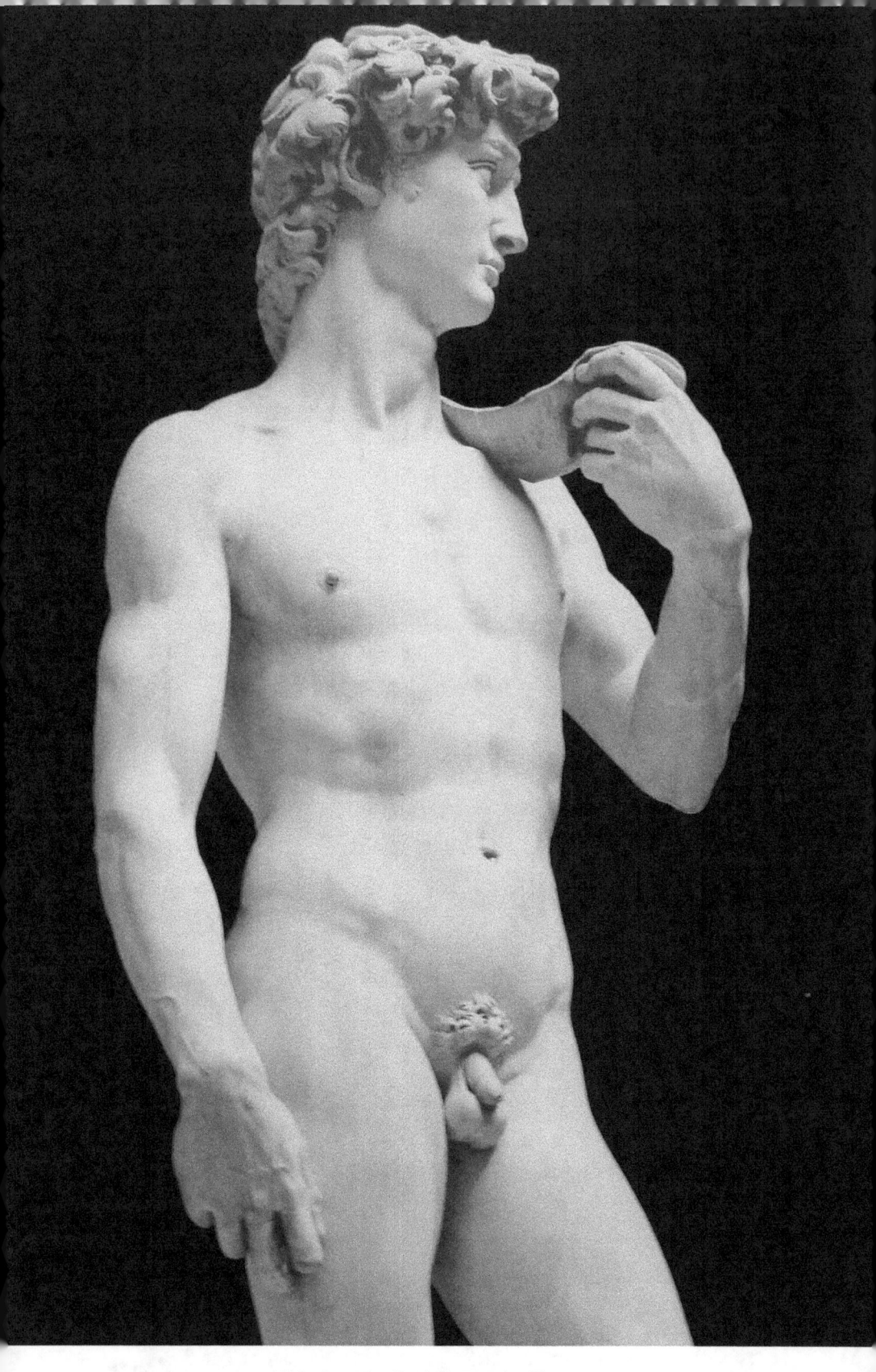

Michelangelo, David, 1501-04, Florence

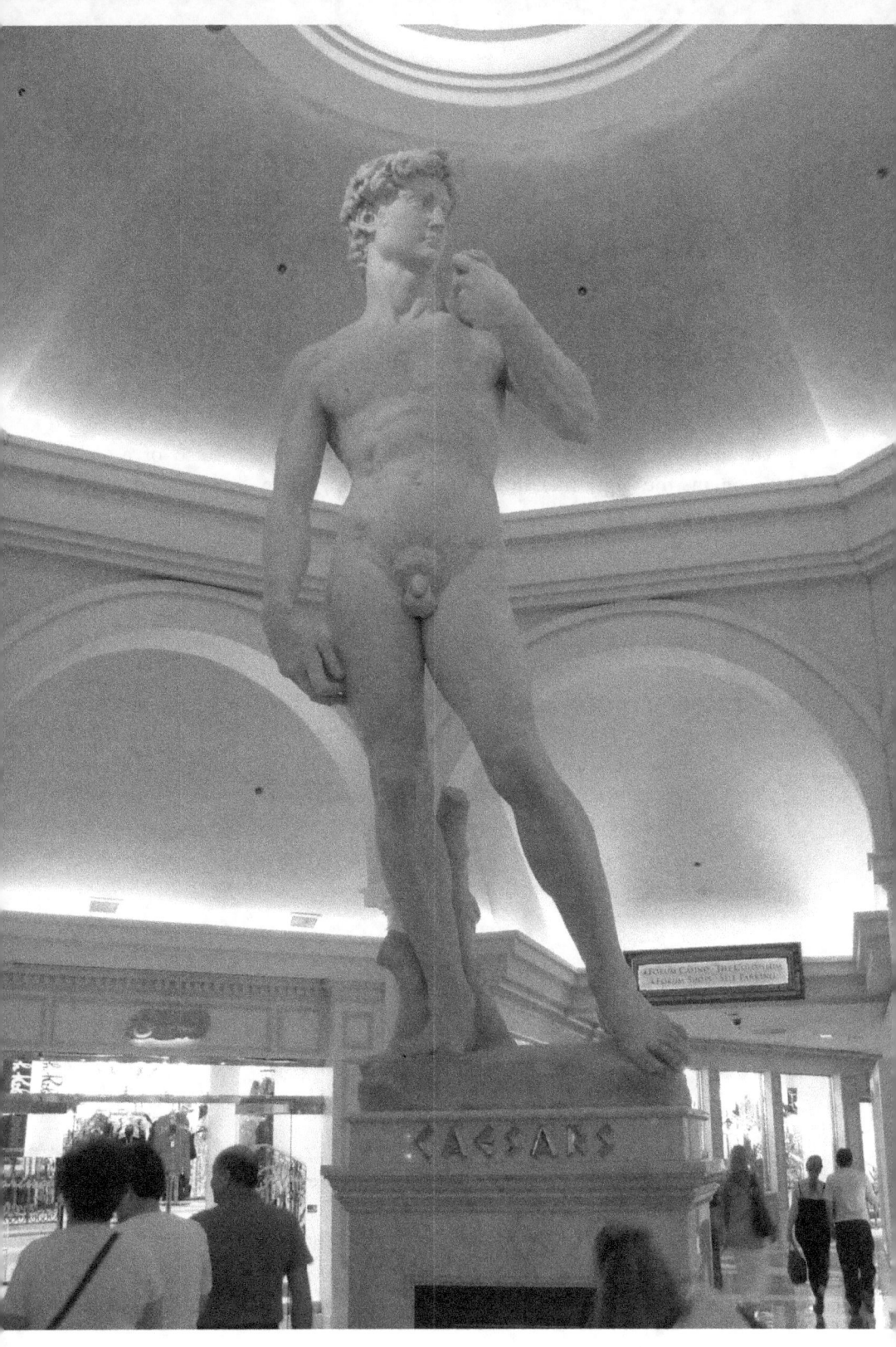

Michelangelo's David in Caesar's Palace, Las Vegas (photo: author)

MICHELANGELO BUONARROTI:
ADAM AND EVE

There is deep sexism in the Judæo-Christian Fall, for it is the woman who picks the apple and offers it to Adam. From the beginning, in the Judæo-Christian tradition, it is the woman who makes men 'fall'. In some depictions, the sexism is doubled, by having the serpent shown as a snake-woman – the torso of a woman, the legs, like those of a mermaid, as in Michelangelo Buonarroti's *Temptation and Expulsion* (1508-12).[1]

The symbol of the half-woman half-fish, still in use today,[2] is another manifestation of patriarchal people's projection of their sexual fears onto women, so that what lies 'below the waist' is feared and objectified as something slimy and fishlike, something dark, from the depths of the unconscious, which is the sea. The mermaid appears sculpted on mediæval churches, some of the mermaids expose their genitals, like the *sheila-na-gig* figure, which again fuses sacred and profane, spiritual and sexual, desire and fear.[3] The mermaid appears in much of Victorian art, as an image of men's ambivalent views of female sexuality – in E.M. Hale's *Mermaid's Rock* (1894), for instance, or John William Waterhouse's Pre-Raphaelite *A Mermaid* (1901).[4]

---

1 Michelangelo: *Temptation and Expulsion*, 1508-12, fresco, Sistine Chapel, Vatican, Rome
2 See the depiction of the Mary Magdalene in the wilderness sequence of Universal's film *The Last Temptation of Christ* (1988, USA)
3 See Anthony Weir & James Jerman: *Images of Lust: Sexual Carvings on Mediæval Churches*, B. T. Batsford, 1986, 48ff
4 John William Waterhouse: *A Mermaid*, 1901, 38.5 x 36.3in, Royal Academy of Arts, London; Edward Matthew Hale: *Mermaid's Rock*, 1894, 48 x 78in, City Art Gallery, Leeds

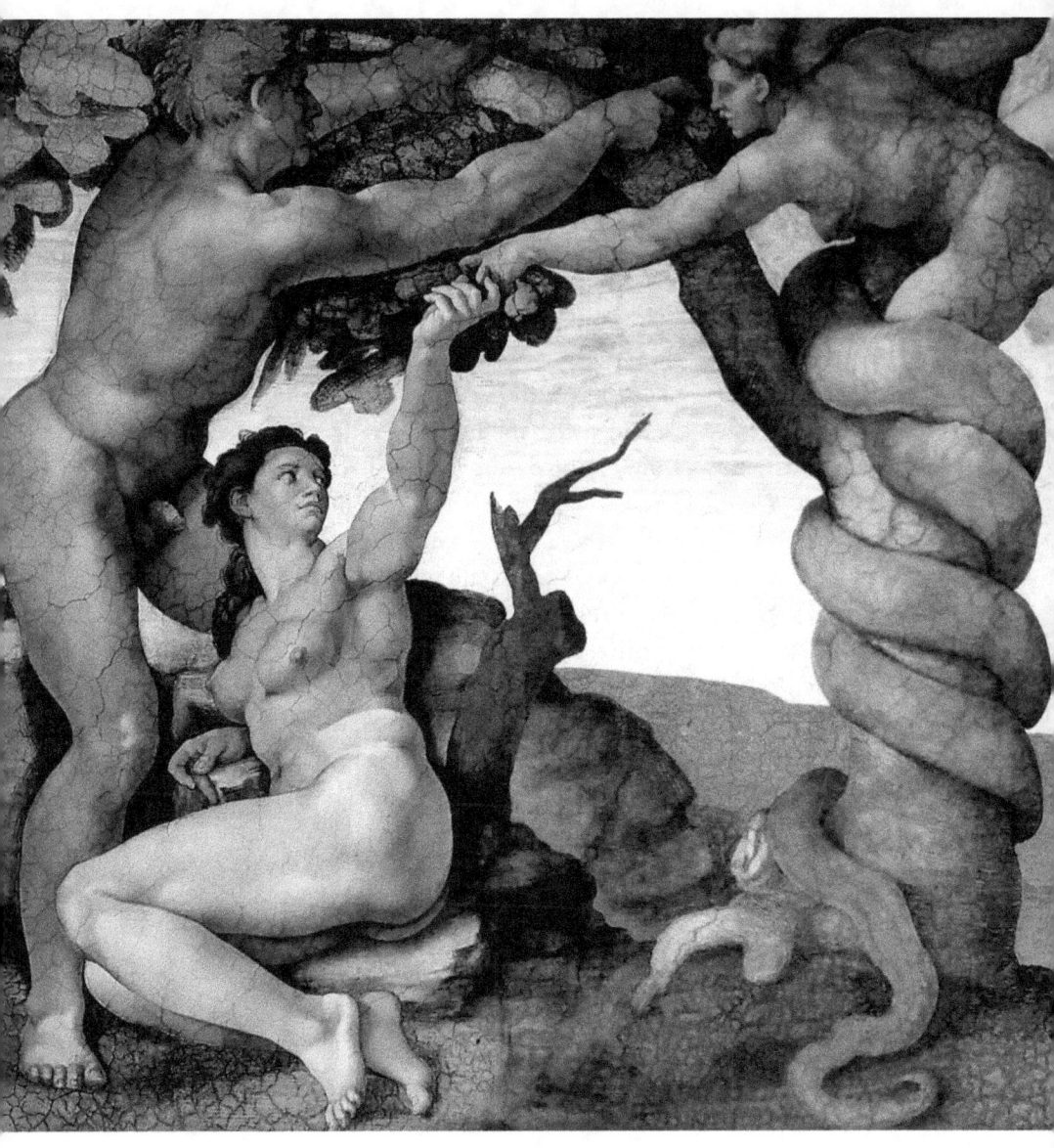

Michelangelo Buonarroti, from The Last Judgement, Rome

LEONARDO DA VINCI

The most erotic artist of the Renaissance, the one who created the darkest and the strangest images, who created the most hypnotic smile in art, who took Western painting to the highest point it has reached, was not Michelangelo Buonarroti, Andrea del Sarto, Fra Angelico, Sandro Botticelli, Pieró della Francesca, Andreas Mantegna, Giovanni Bellini, Raphael Sanzio, Titian, Caravaggio, Simone Martini, Fra Bartolommeo, Lucas Cranach or Masaccio, but Leonardo da Vinci.

Leonardo da Vinci is one of the most celebrated of artists, he's perhaps the most exalted artist in the West. He is the artist-as-hero, the artist-as-genius, undisputed genius (like William Shakespeare or Sophocles). Leonardo is enshrined for his amazing mind, his scientific curiosity, his ideas on botany, anatomy, architecture, weaponry, engineering, etc. But it is Leonardo's *sfumato* painterly technique, his brilliant manipulation of oil colours, that makes him so profoundly erotic. Stendhal wrote of Leonardo's 'soft, melancholy tones, full of shadows'.[1] The most common adjective applied to Leonardo's art is 'mysterious'. Walter Pater wrote famously of the *Mona Lisa*, in a way which says more about Pater and late Victorian and Decadent art than it does about Leonardo:

> She is older than the rocks among which she sits... [she embodies] the animalism of Greece, the lust of Rome, the mysticism of the Middle Ages with its spiritual ambition and imaginative loves, the return of the pagan world, the sins of the Borgias.[2]

1 Stendhal: *Histoire de la peinture en Italie*, 1877
2 Walter Pater: *The Renaissance*, Fontana 1964, 123

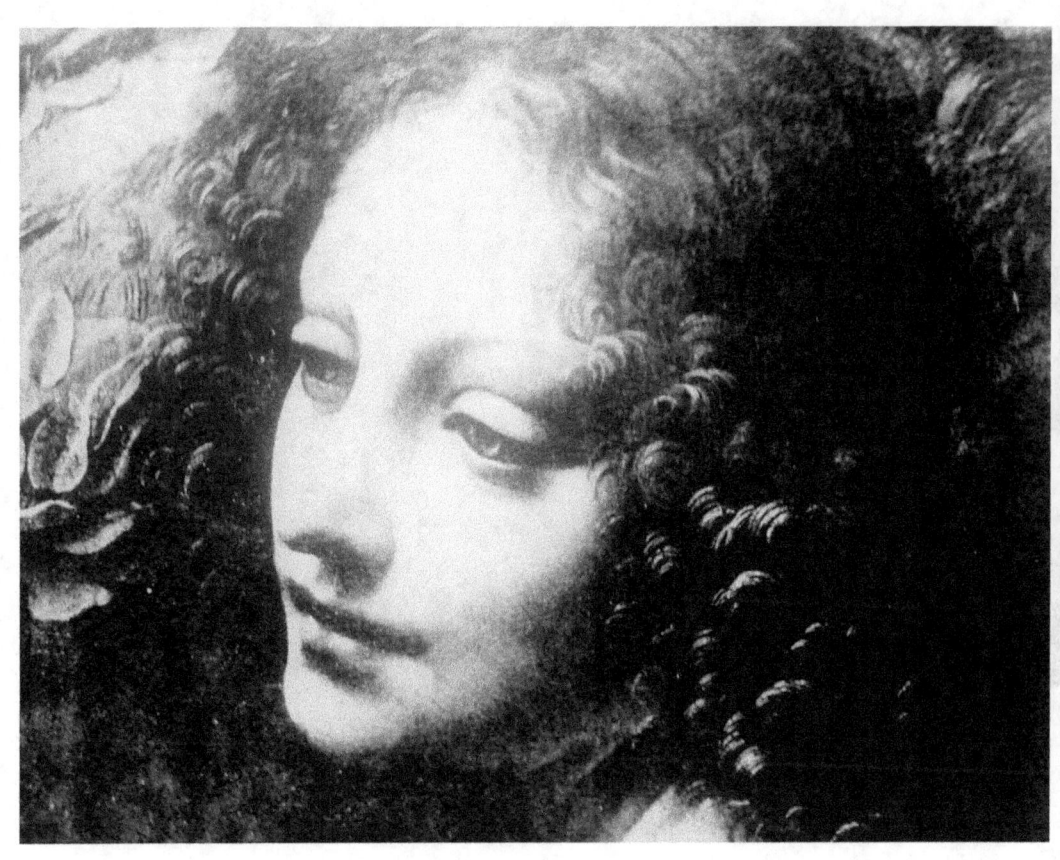

Leonardo's immortal faces: from *The Virgin of the Rocks*.

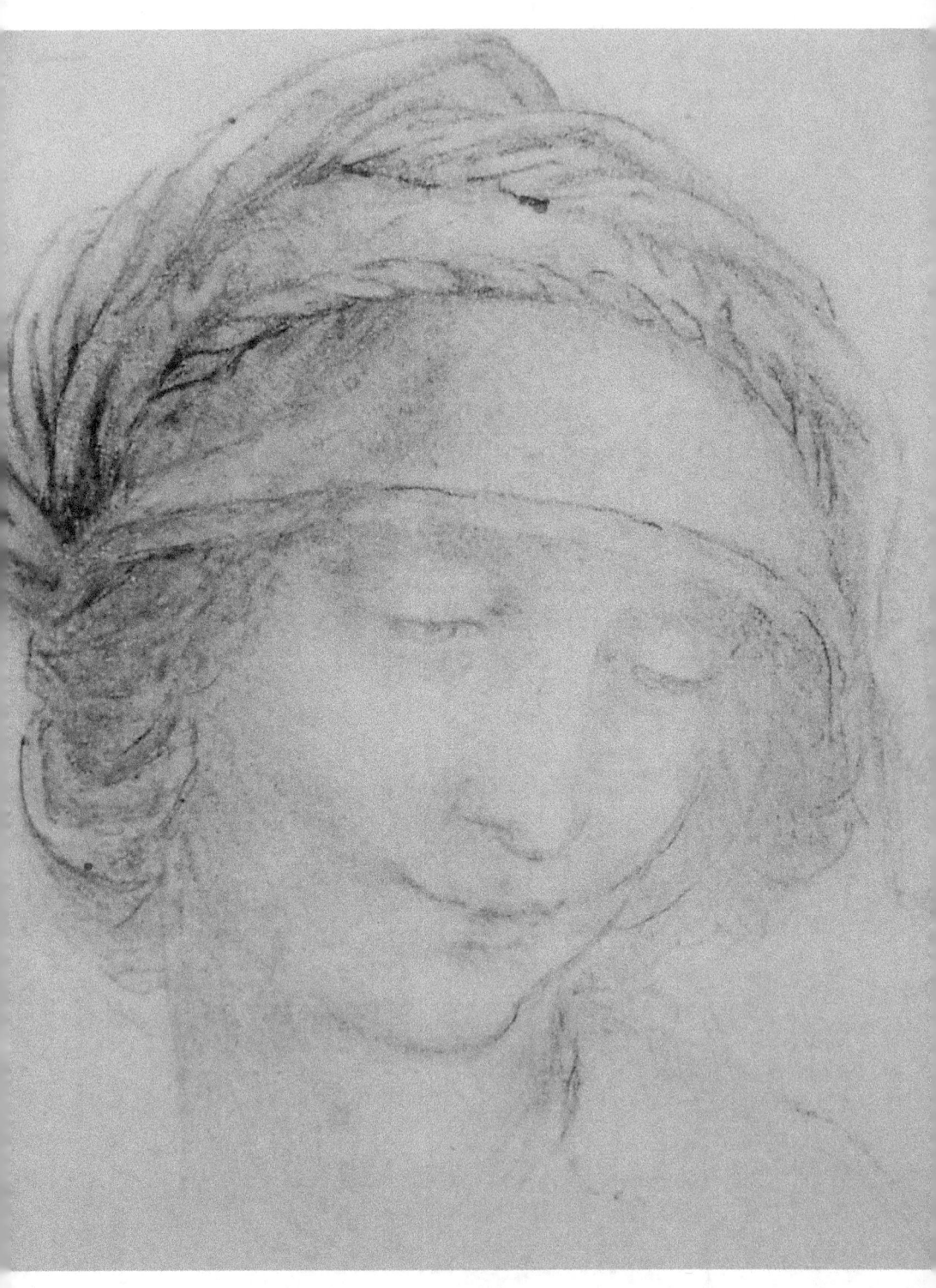

Leonardo, Study for The Virgin and Child With St Anne

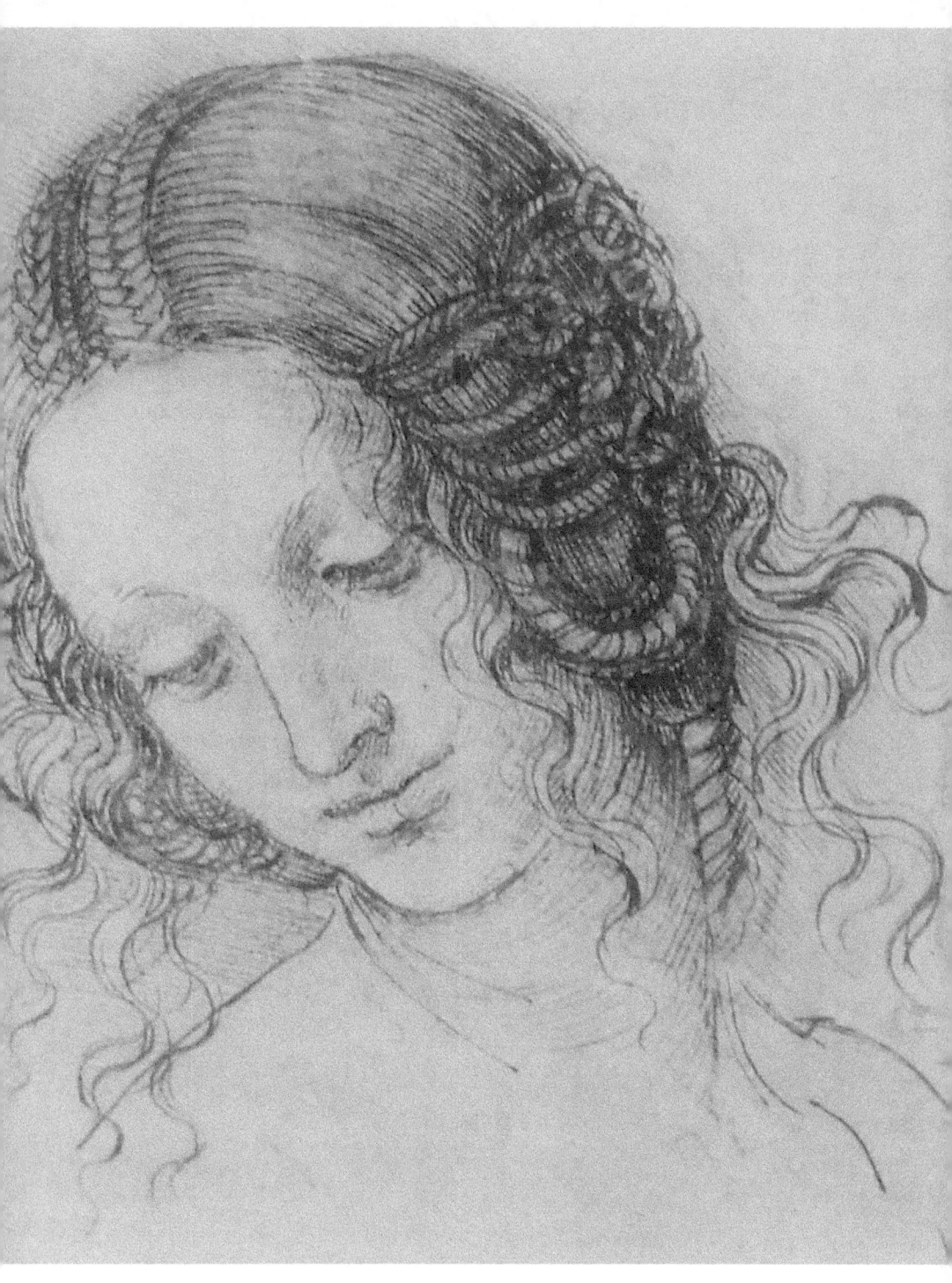

Leonardo, Study For the Leda and the Swan

FRANCISCO DE ZURBARÁN

Francisco de Zurbarán (1598-1664) was one of the central group of Spanish painters who formed the 'Golden Age' of Spanish painting (the others were El Greco, Diego Velásquez and Giuseppe de Ribera). Zurbarán's motifs included (aside from the usual Christian iconography of *Pietàs* and the like), monks in shadowy hoods and habits, and saints in meditation. Zurbarán's art is full of depictions of a devout Catholicism.

Francisco de Zurbarán's art is marked by the high contrast kind of lighting one finds in the art of Michelangelo Merisi de Caravaggio. Zurbarán, who lived in Seville, had never seen a Caravaggio painting in the flesh, but knew of Caravaggio's paintings from copies. As with Caravaggio's painting, Zurbarán's art aimed for a heightened realism, in which every detail of a person's clothing, for example, would be rendered sharply. The drive towards increased realism derived from the Church's demands: in the Counter-Reformation, 'extreme "spirituality" lay in extreme realism' (R. Hughes, 1990, 66).

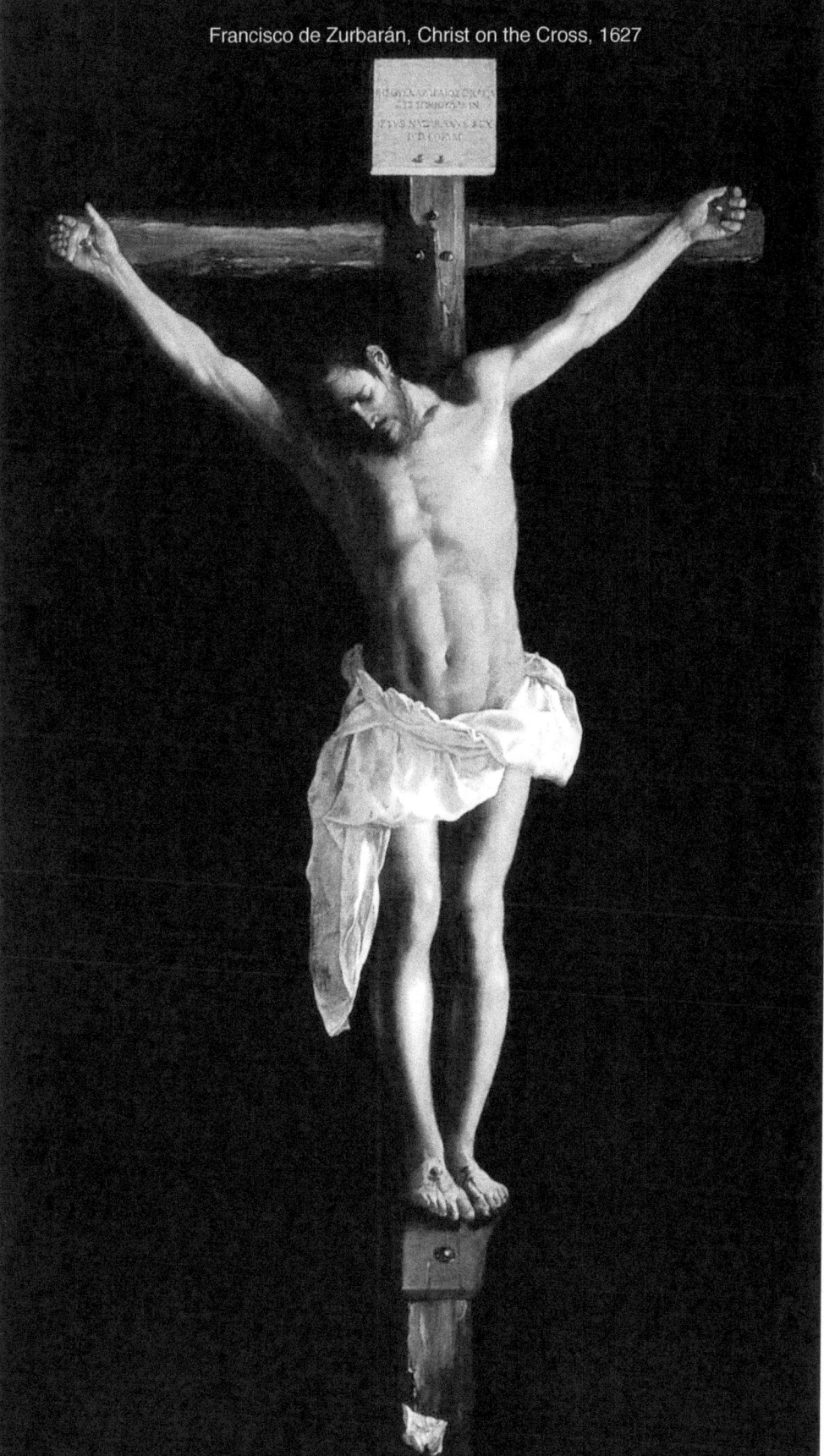

Francisco de Zurbarán, Christ on the Cross, 1627

GUILIO ROMANO

The sexploits of phallic deities such as Zeus/ Jupiter, whether he's chasing Leda as a swan or impregnating Danae as a golden shower, provide many opportunities for artists to make erotic art which is justifiably 'noble' because it comes from Classic mythology. It also means that sex with beasts can be depicted legitimately. Thus, one finds Guilio Romano depicting Jupiter with an erect penis about to tup Olympia.[1]

1 Guilio Romano: *Jupiter and Olympia*, 1525-35, Mansell Collection, London

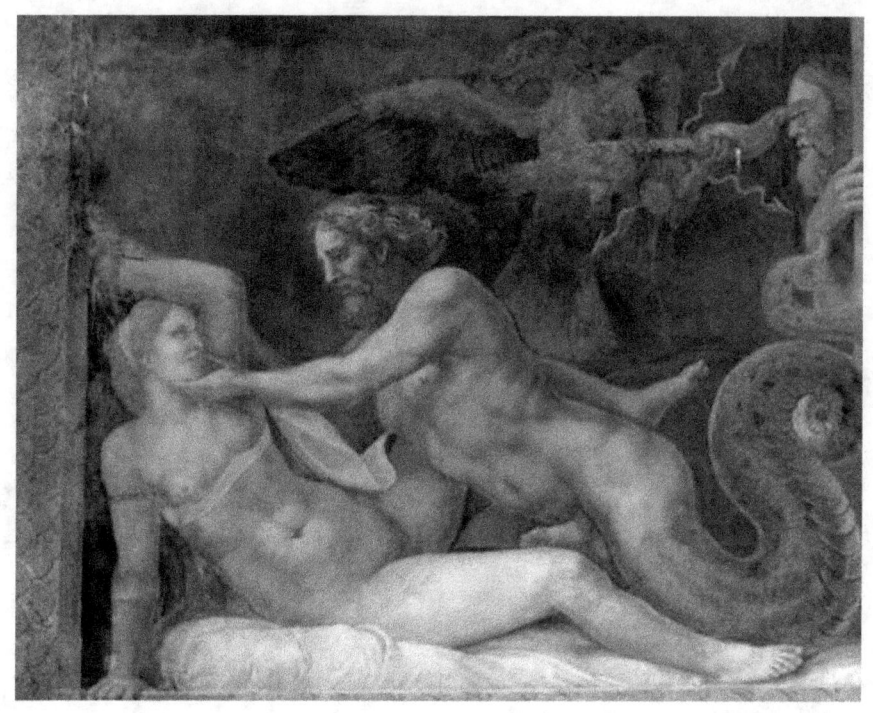

Giulio Pippi, a.k.a Giulio Romano

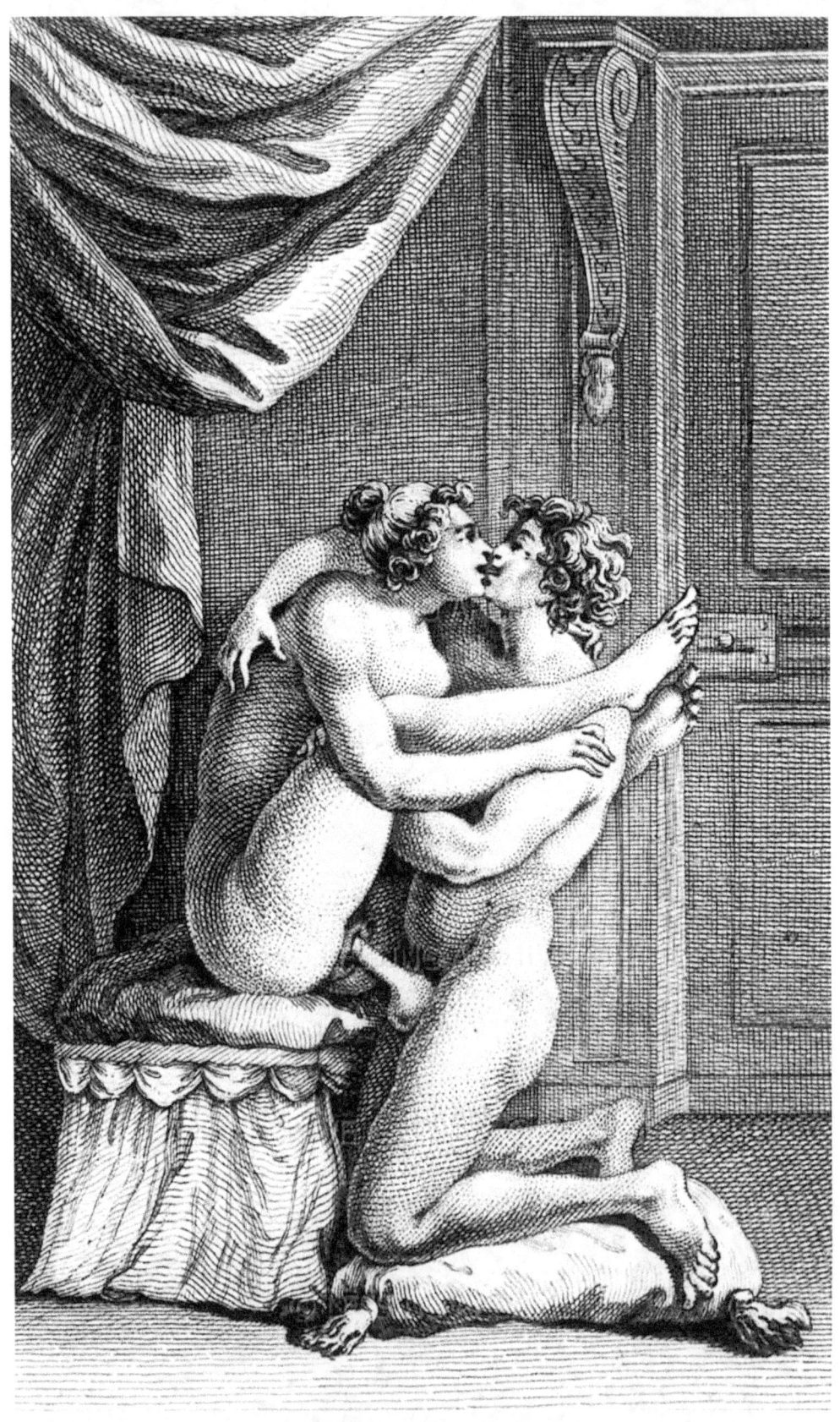

After Guilio Roman, 18th century

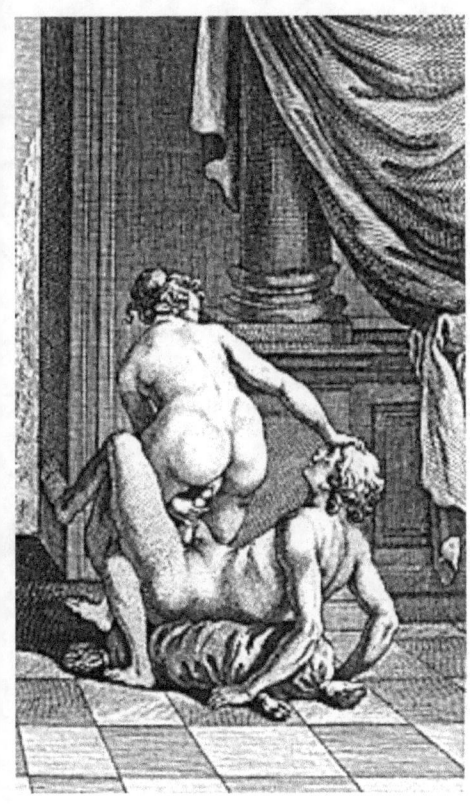

After Giulio Romano and Marcantonio Raimondi,
I Modi, 1524/ 27

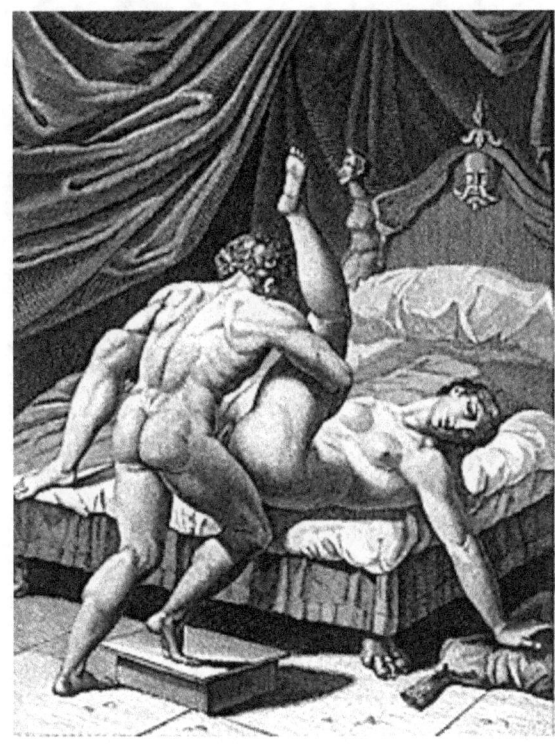

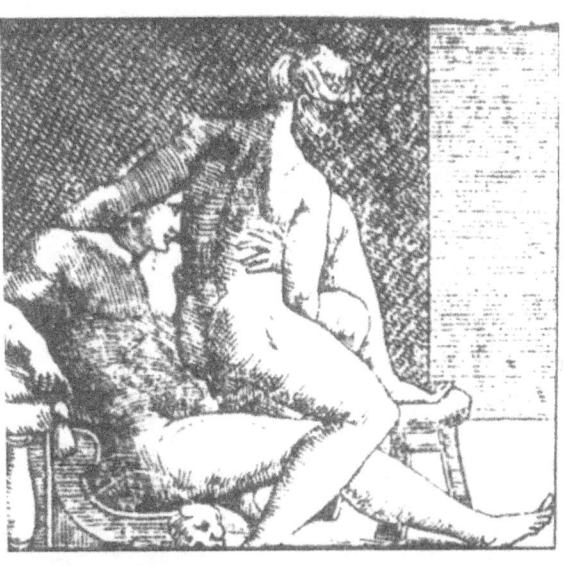

AGOSTINO CARRACCI: *THE WAYS*

The *I Modi* (*The Ways*) by Agostino Carracci is a celebrated 16th century collection of Italian Renaissance erotica. It has been much copied and pirated. It's a kind of Western, Renaissance version of the *Kama Sutra*. There's no denying the imagination and skill of the drawing on display here.

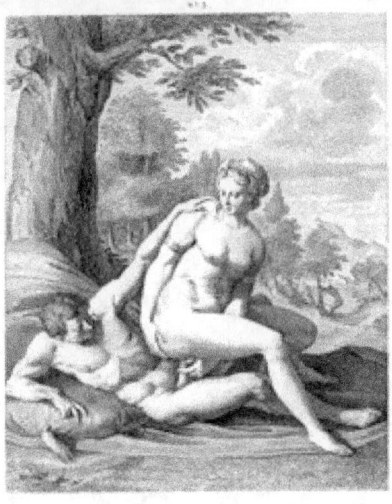

ANGÉLIQUE ET MEDOR.

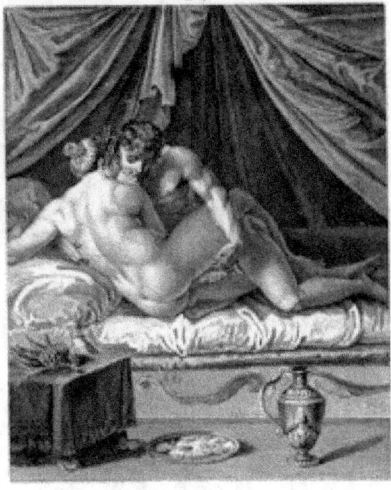

ANTOINE ET CLÉOPATRE

Jacques Joseph Coiny, after Agostino Caracci,
I Modi, 1524, and Pietro Aretino

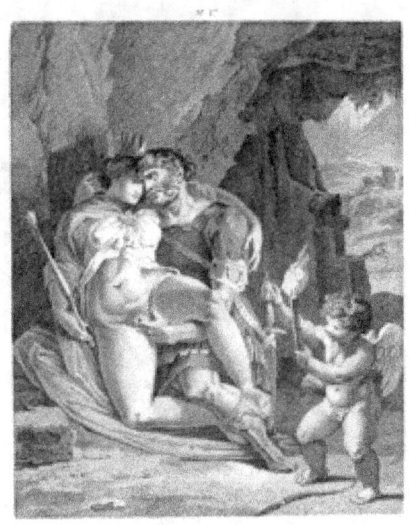

ENÉE ET DIDON

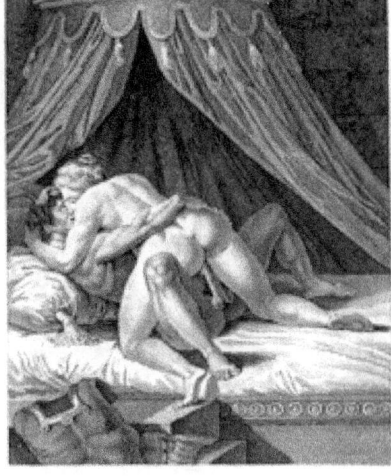

MARS ET VENUS

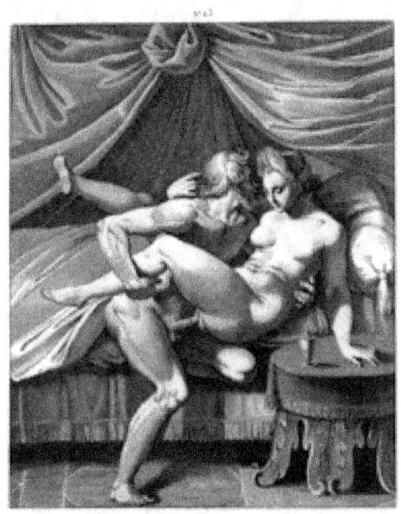

JUPITER ET JUNON

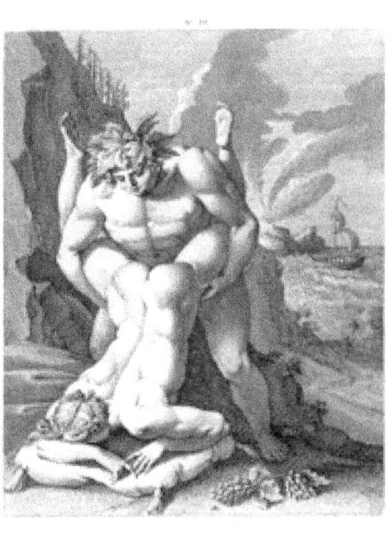

BACHUS ET ARIANE

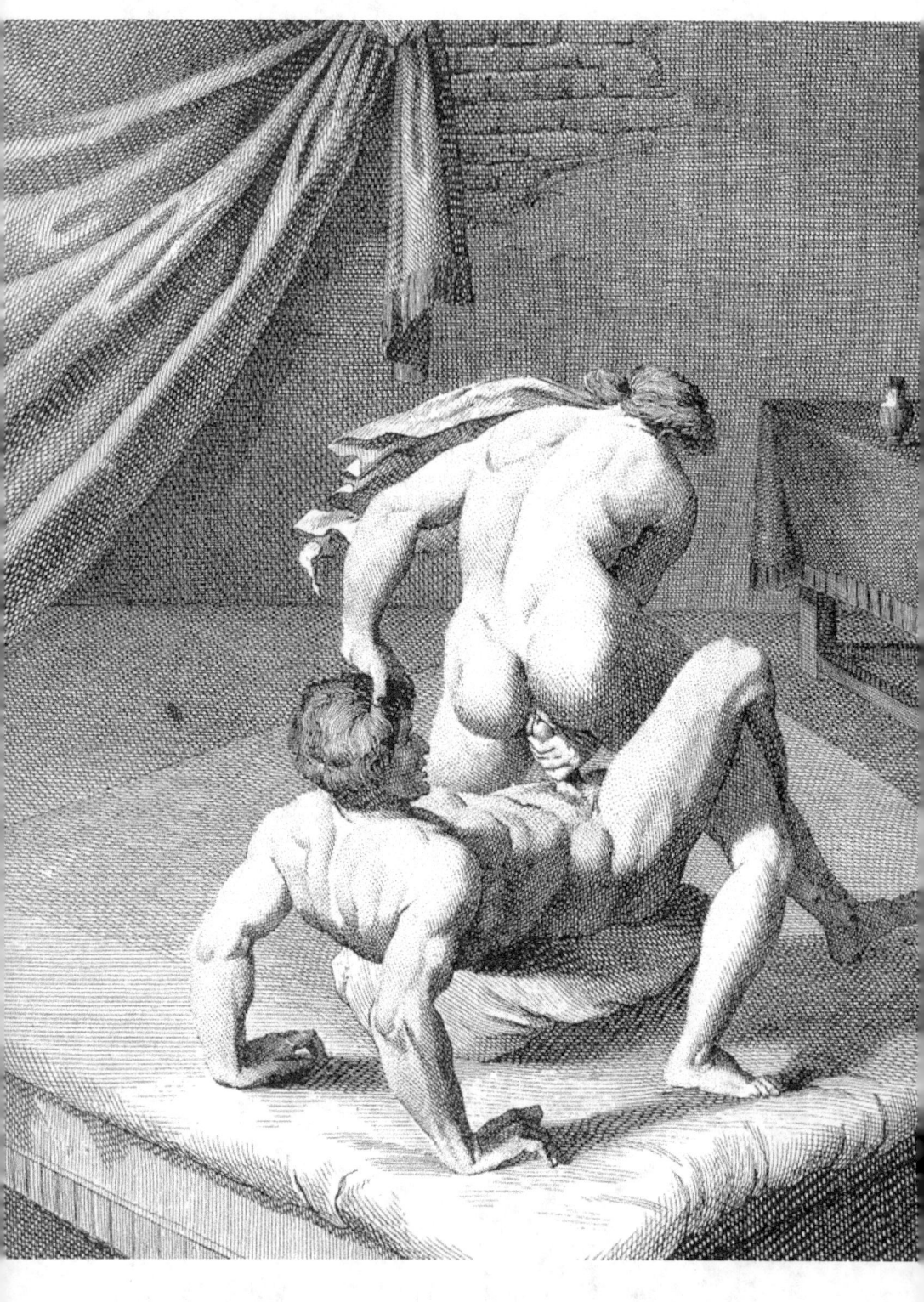

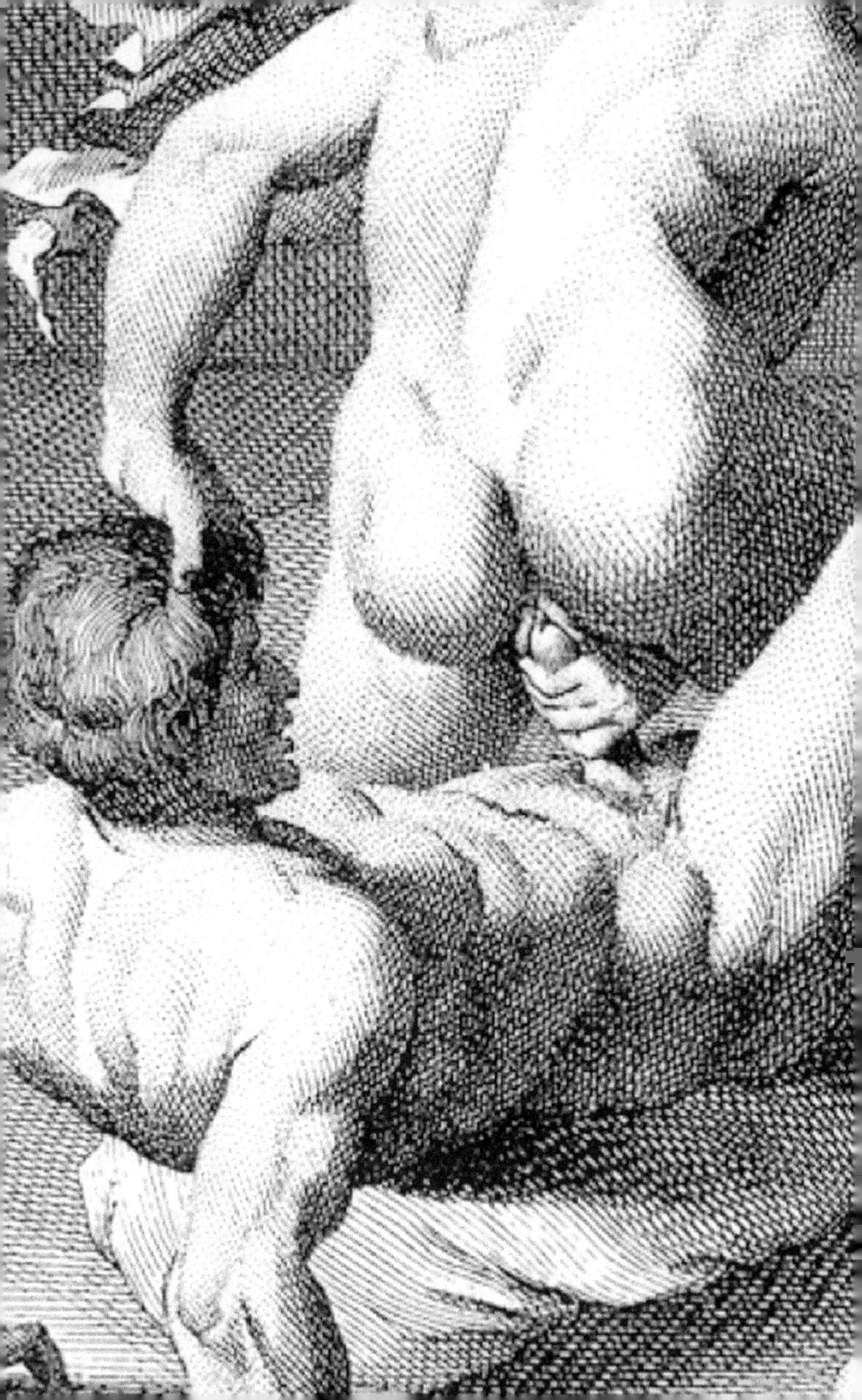

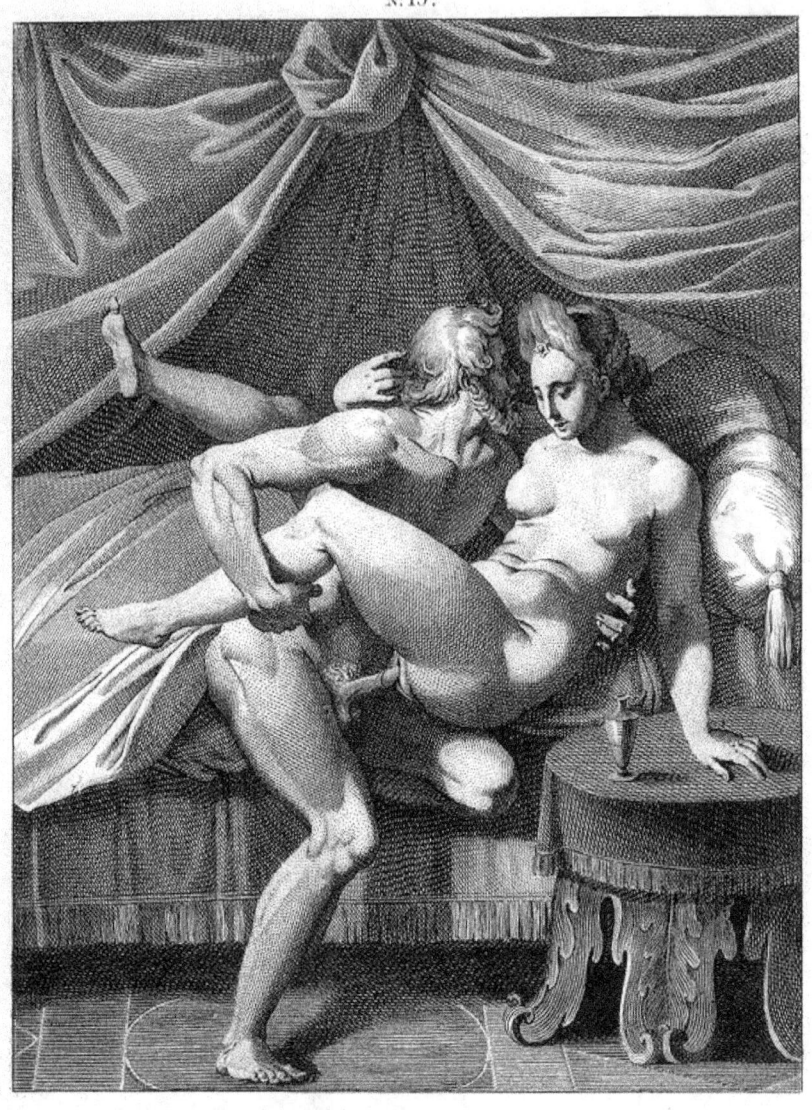

JUPITER ET JUNON

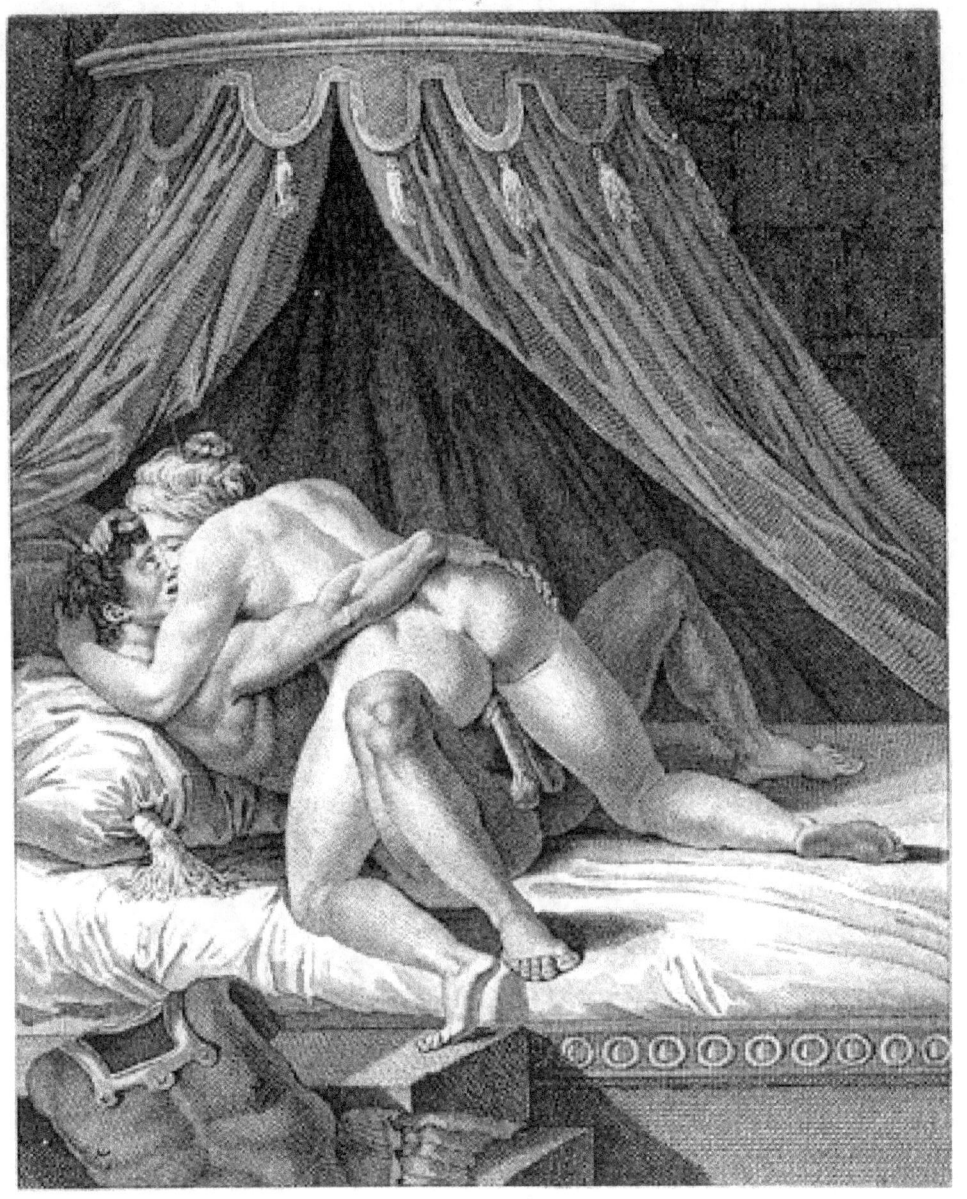

MARS ET VENUS

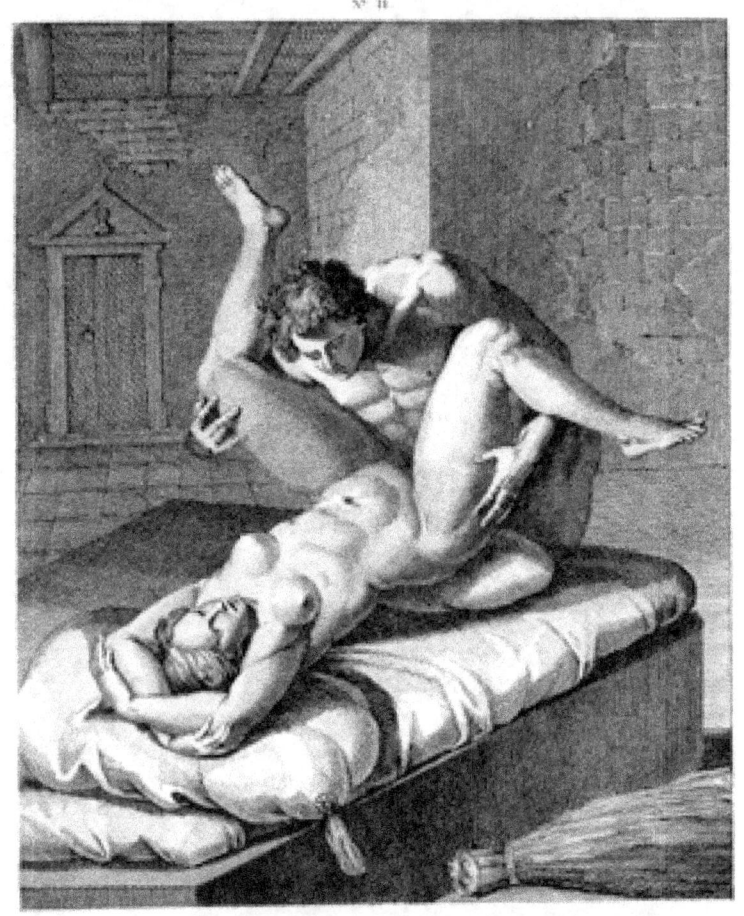

POLYENOS ET CHRISIS

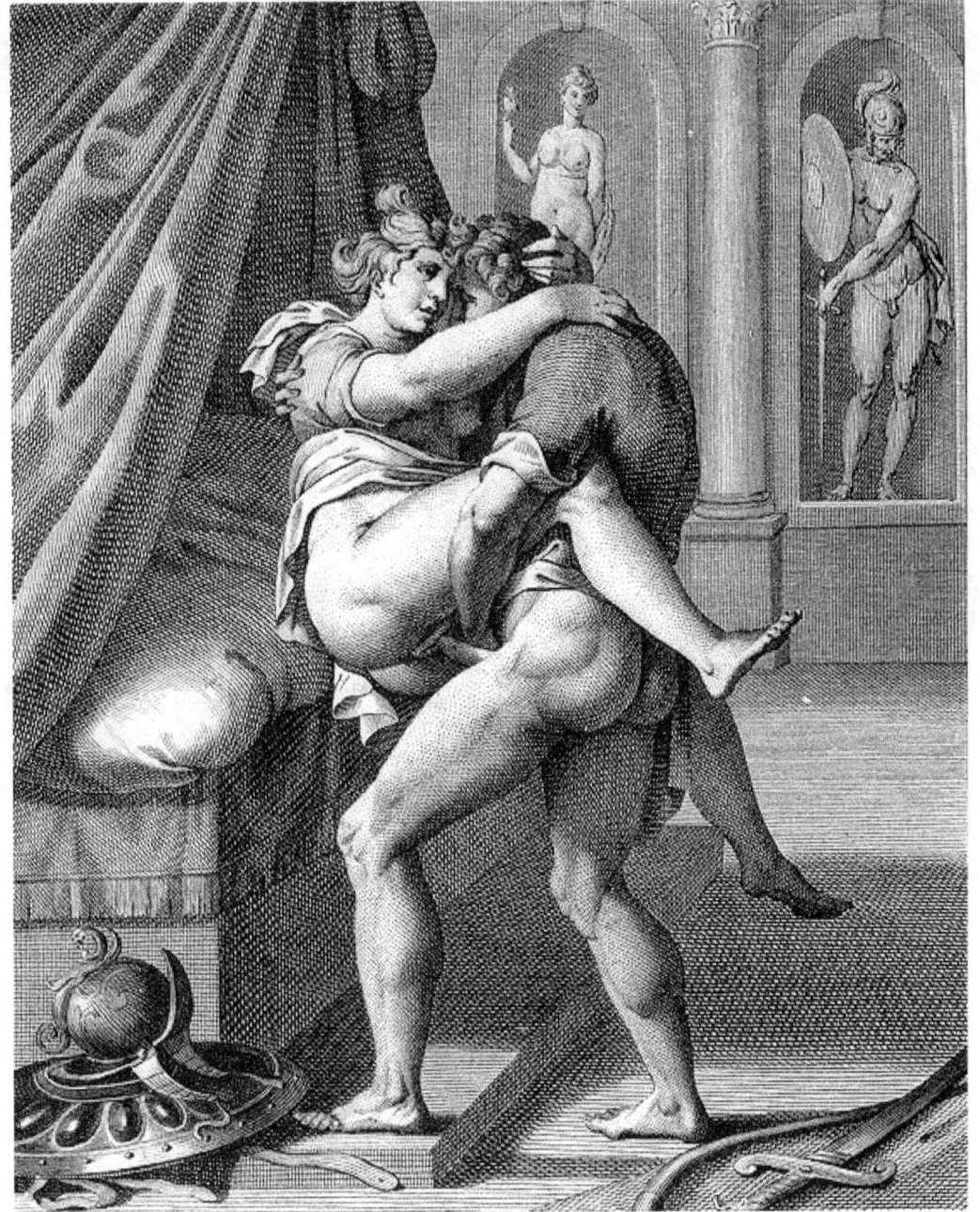

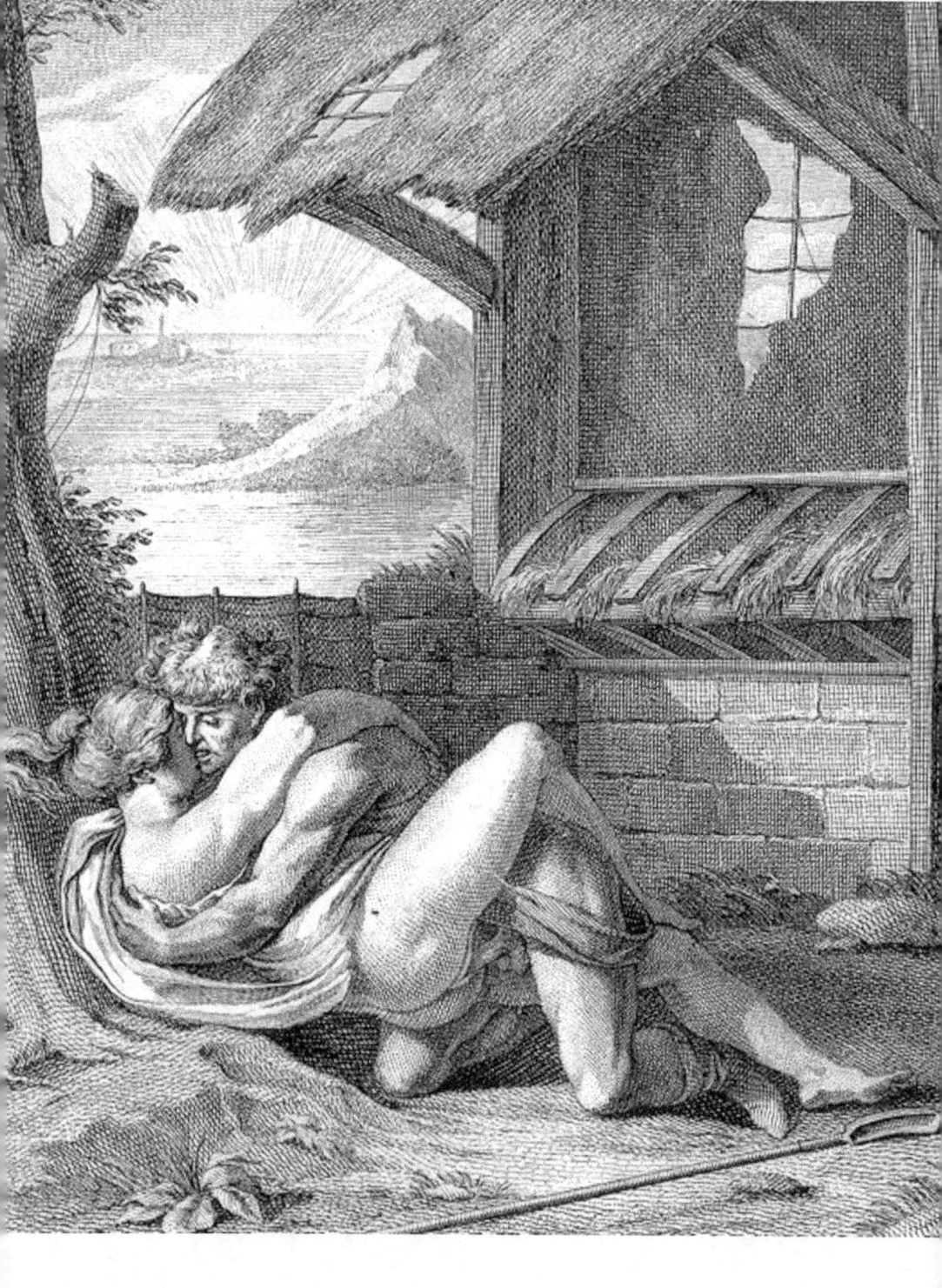

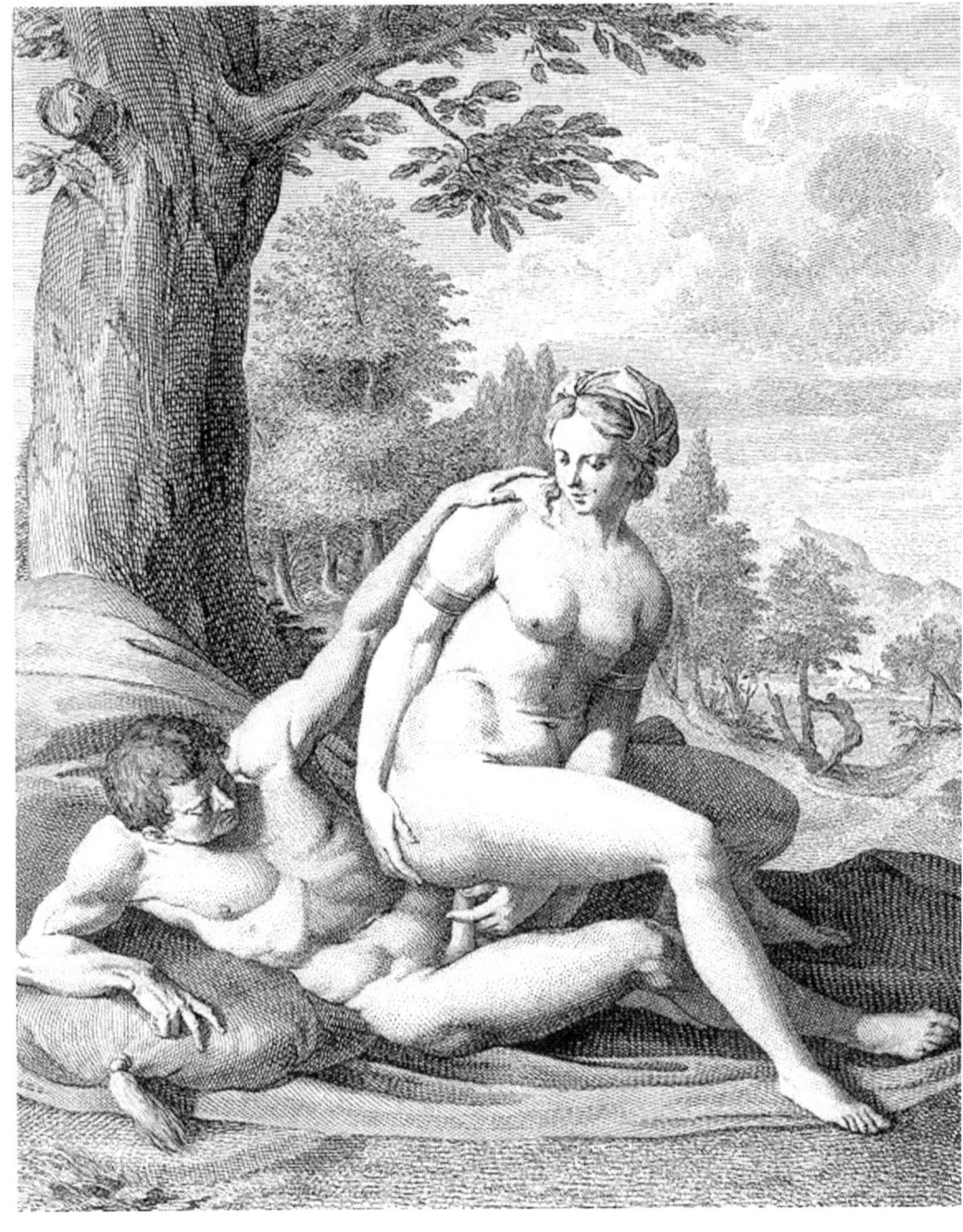

FRANCESCO PARMIGIANINO:
WITCHES' SABBATH

As I've noted above, many of the 'great' artists of Renaissance and post-Renaissance art have produced 'erotic art', 'erotic art' meant for selected clients, not for mass consumption, in addition to the eroticism in their 'great' works. Thus, the 'great' Rembrandt van Rijn drew a couple copulating on a bed, Henri Fuseli drew a woman sucking the nipples of a woman, her hand on her clitoris, Francois Boucher drew half-naked people groping each other, Francesco Parmigianino drew a hilarious *Witches' Sabbath*, featuring a witch astride a gigantic phallus, Francisco de Goya drew two people sucking each other's genitals, Nicholas Géricault painted two people writhing under Caravaggesque drapes, and William Turner sketched people lovemaking.[1]

1 Henry Fuseli: *Lesbian Couple*, c. 1815-20, Edward Croft-Murray, London; François Boucher: *Pastoral Scene*, c. 1750s, Cary von Karwath, Vienna;Francisco de Goya (?): *Sixty-Nine*, c. 1790s, G. Lo Duca, Paris; Rembrandt: *Ledakant*, c. 1646, British Museum; J. M. W. Turner: *Sheet of Sexual Drawings*, c. 1820s, British Museum; Théodore Géricault: *Lovers*, 1815-6, oil on canvas, 24 x 32.5cm, private collection, Geneva; Francesco Parmigianino: *Witches' Sabbath*, 1530s, British Museum

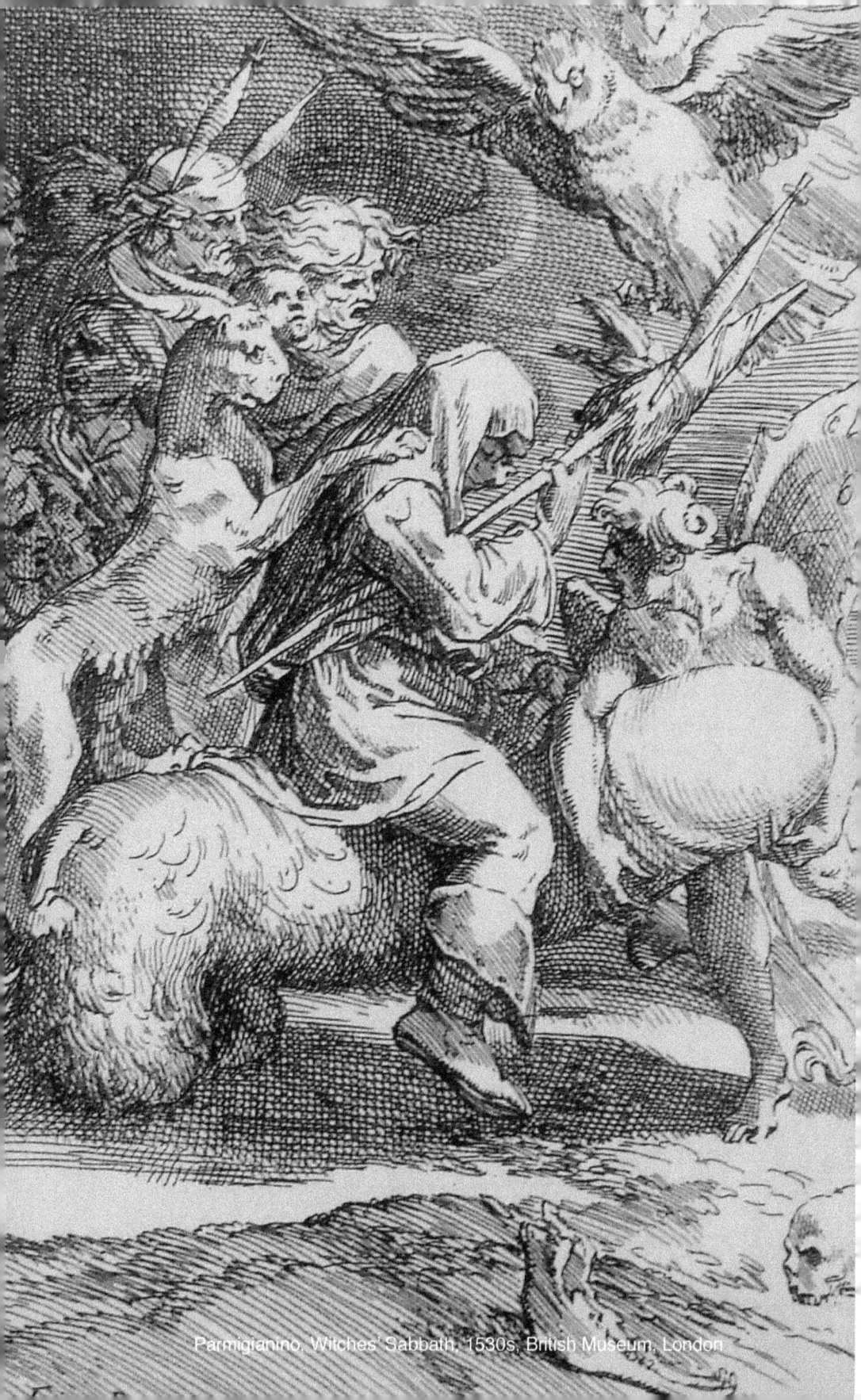

Parmigianino, Witches' Sabbath, 1530s, British Museum, London

PETER PAUL RUBENS

Painters such as Peter Paul Rubens do not hide their interest in the eroticism of art. Rubens' paintings are wild romps through fields of nakedness, through acres and acres of flesh.[1] When you see a large number of Rubens' paintings together, the effect is overwhelming: no other painter created such a shivering, trembling vision of shivering, trembling flesh. Among other post-Renaissance painters, there is a wealth of eroticism in Caravaggio, Ribera, Murillo, Tiepolo, Gentileschi, Zurbáran and Veronese.

---

1 see for instance his *Diana and Her Nymphs Surprised by Fauns*, oil, 50 x 124in, Prado, Madrid

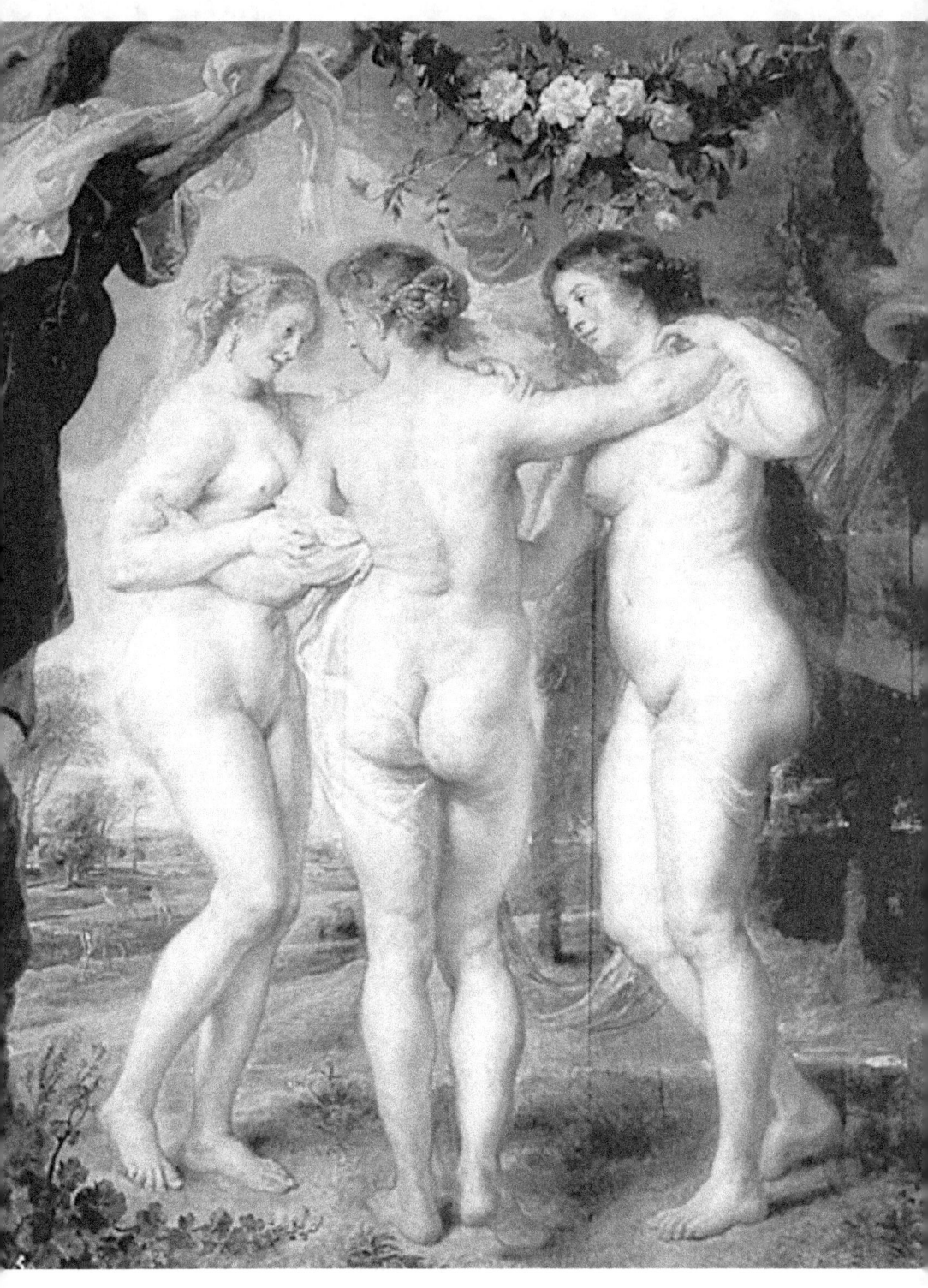

Peter Paul Rubens, The Three Graces, 1638-40, Prado, Madrid

JEAN FOUQET

An intriguing mix of the erotic and the spiritual, the sacred and the profane, occurs in Jean Fouquet's *The Melun Diptych*, where the Madonna bares her breast. This alone is not remarkable, although the breast is certainly more openly and erotically displayed, as spectacle, than in most Madonna art. The model for this voluptuous Mother of God, though, was Agnès Sorel, mistress of King Charles VII.[1]

1 See Marina Warner: *Alone of All Her Sex*, 203

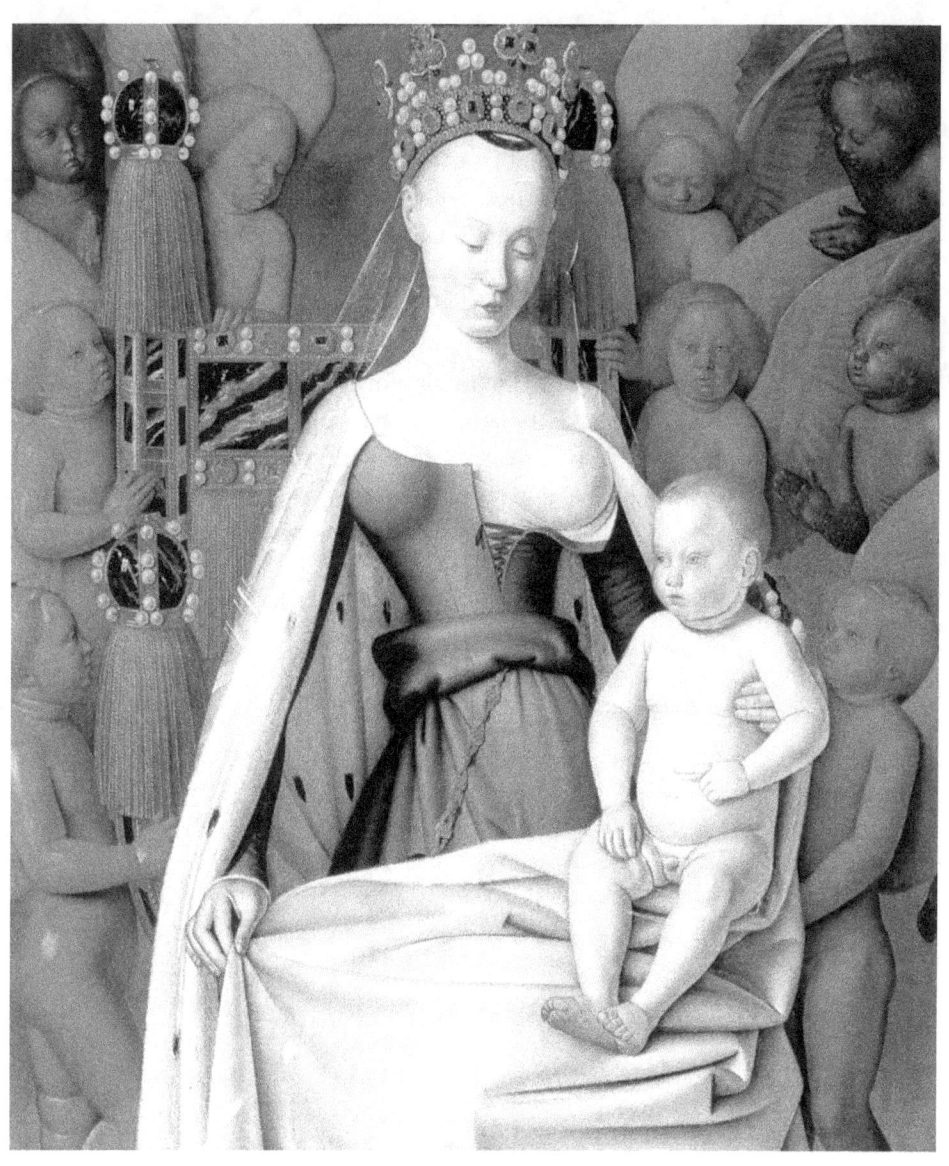

Jean Fouquet, The Melun Diptych, c. 1450

FRANCOIS BOUCHER

Erotic art may defined as simply 'æstheticized sexual representation' (L. Nead, 103), that is, erotic feelings processed through
the mechanisms of 'high culture'. For some feminists, there is no
doubt that the enjoyment of the female nude is pornographic, and
is largely inseparable from the lustful consumption of pornography. The boundaries between 'art' and 'pornography' are
being constantly blurred, constantly reset and rewritten. For
instance, Louise O'Murphy, the model for Boucher's famous nude
Mademoiselle O'Murphy, became King Louis XV's personal
prostitute (his 'mistress', as critics call them) after the King saw
Boucher's painting. The high art 'possession' or pleasure of the
female nude in Boucher's painting became the real 'possession' of
Louise O'Murphy's body. Clearly, kings can 'buy' what they
like: they can have the best art, and 'have' the best women.

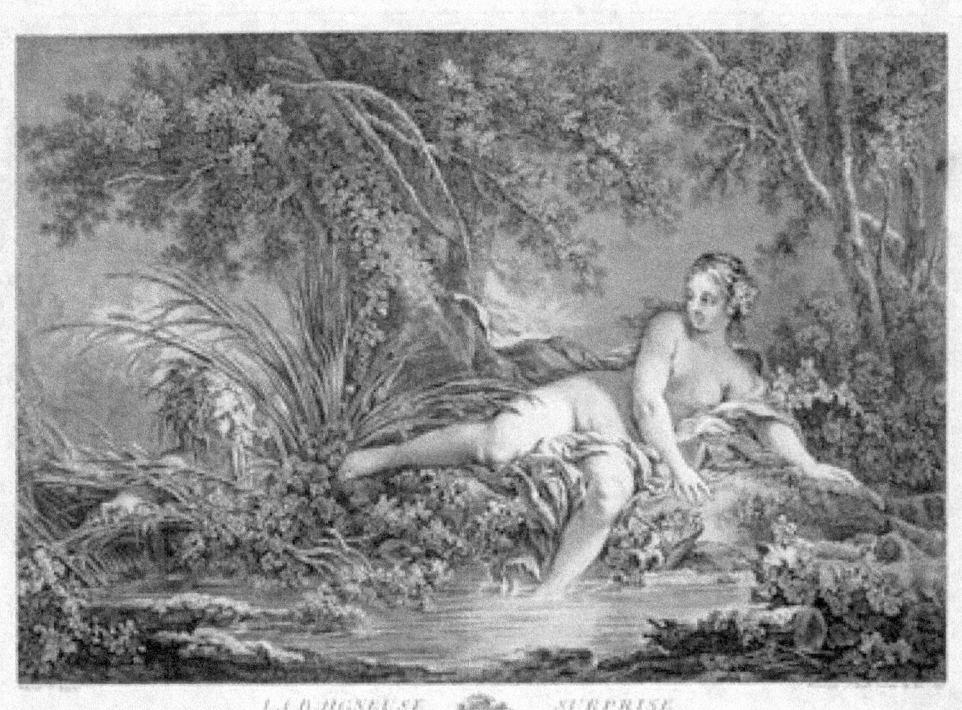

François Boucher, La Baigneuse Surprise

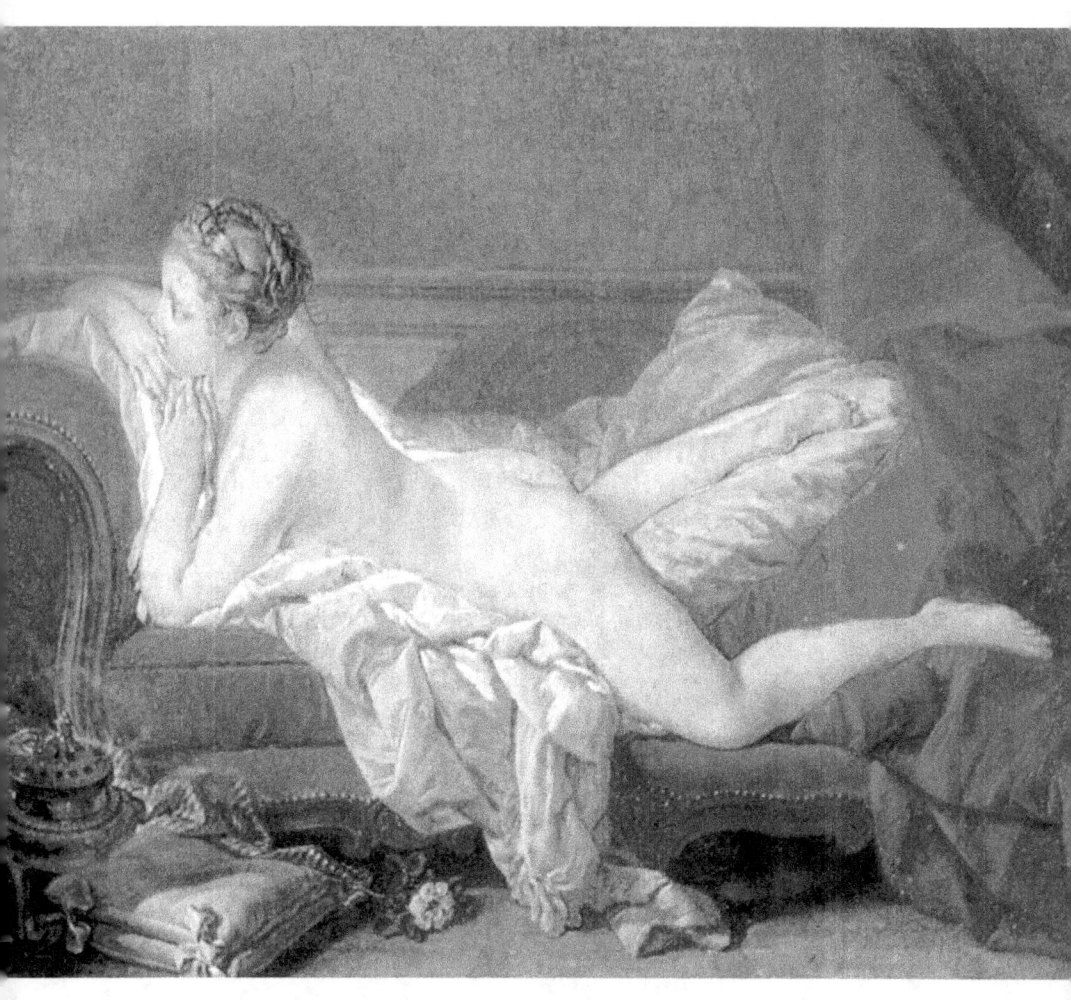

François Boucher, Madamoiselle O'Murphy, 1751

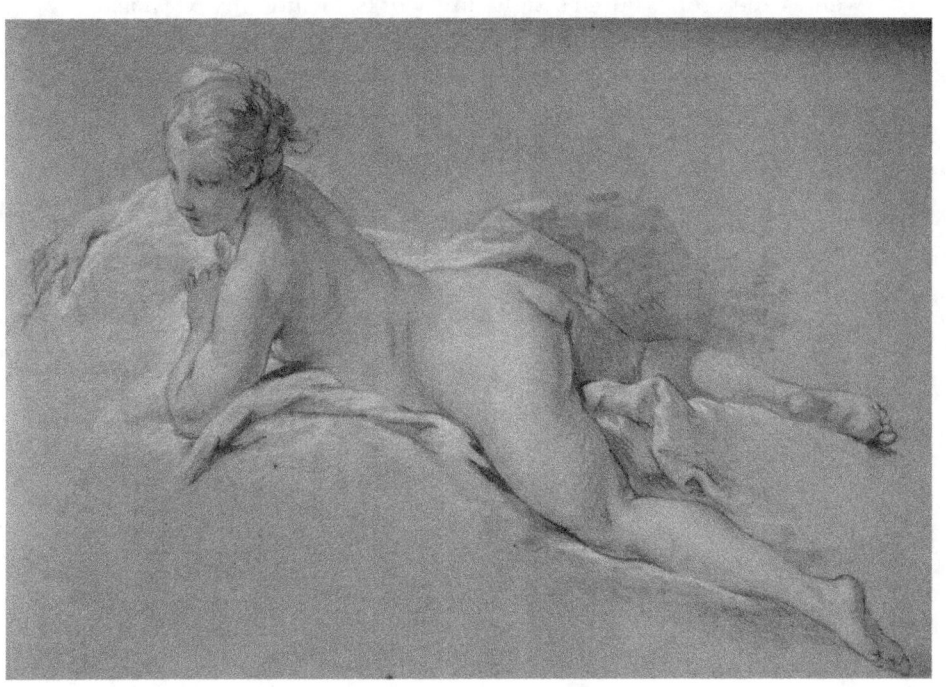

François Boucher, sketch

JOHN HENRY FUSELI

The Swiss artist John Henry Fuseli is a master of the macabre as well as the erotic. Fuseli's signature works include his *Nightmare* an influential slice of Romantic Gothic imagery. But *Sturm und Drang* art is only element in Fuseli's eccentric and individual work, which includes many erotic subjects, and nudes.

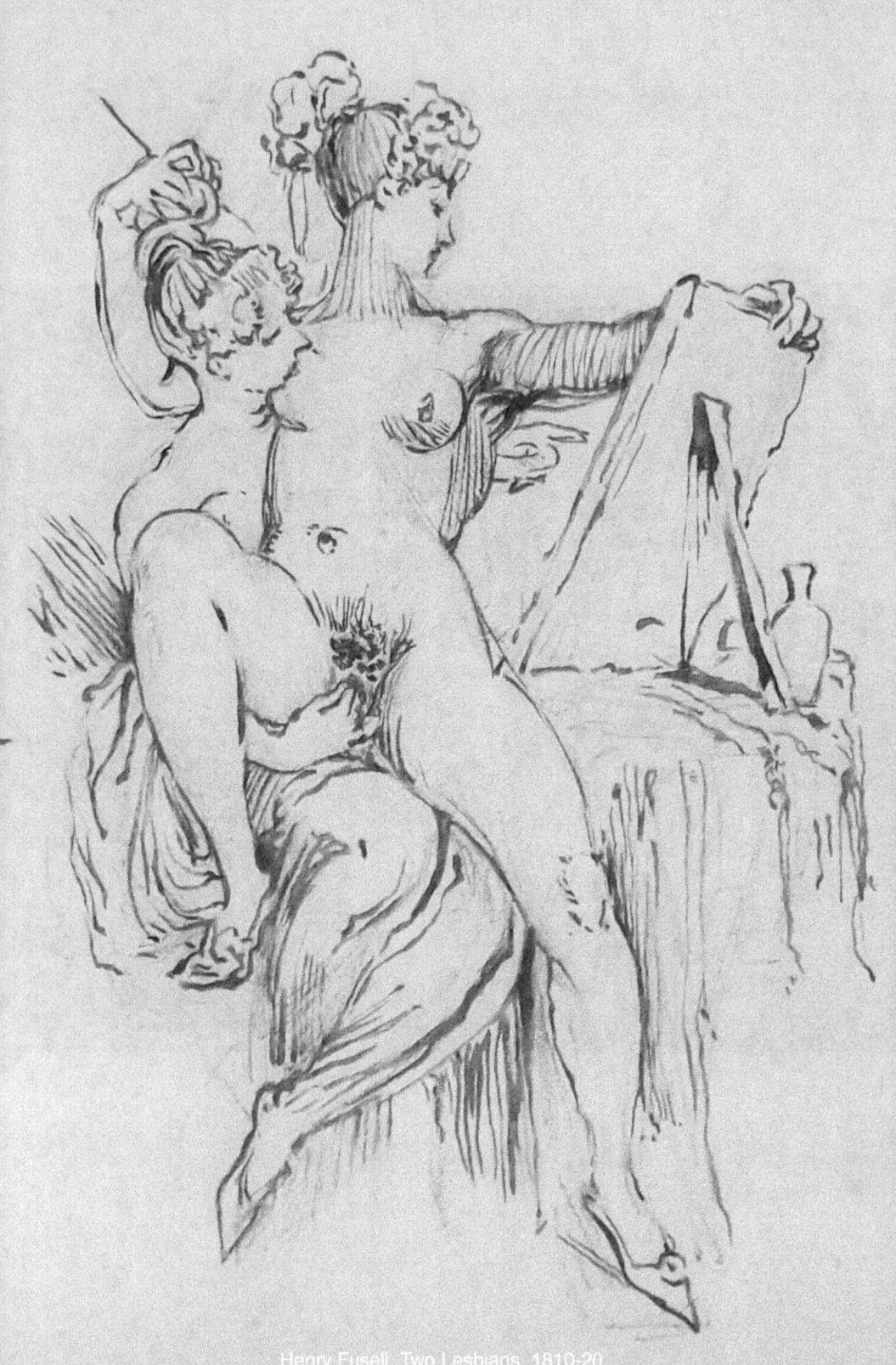

Henry Fuseli. Two Lesbians, 1810-20,
private collection

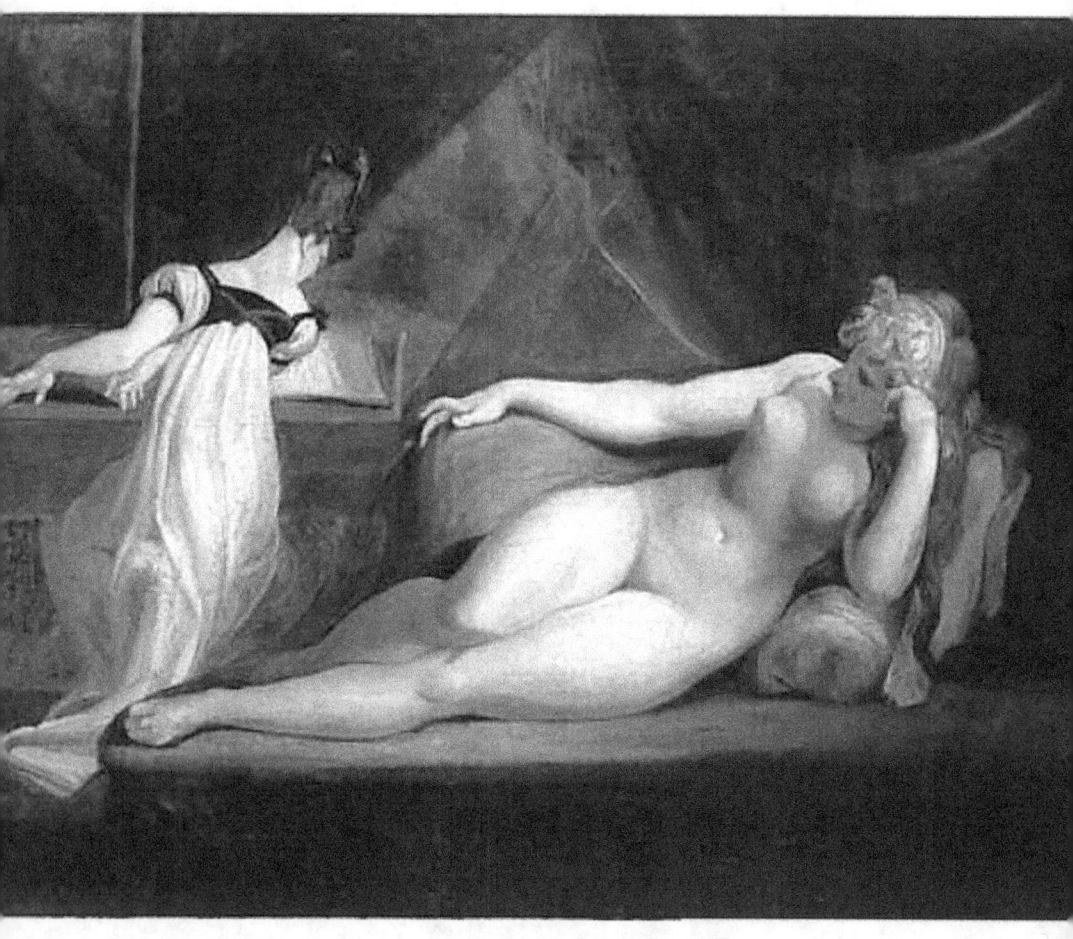

Henry Fuseli

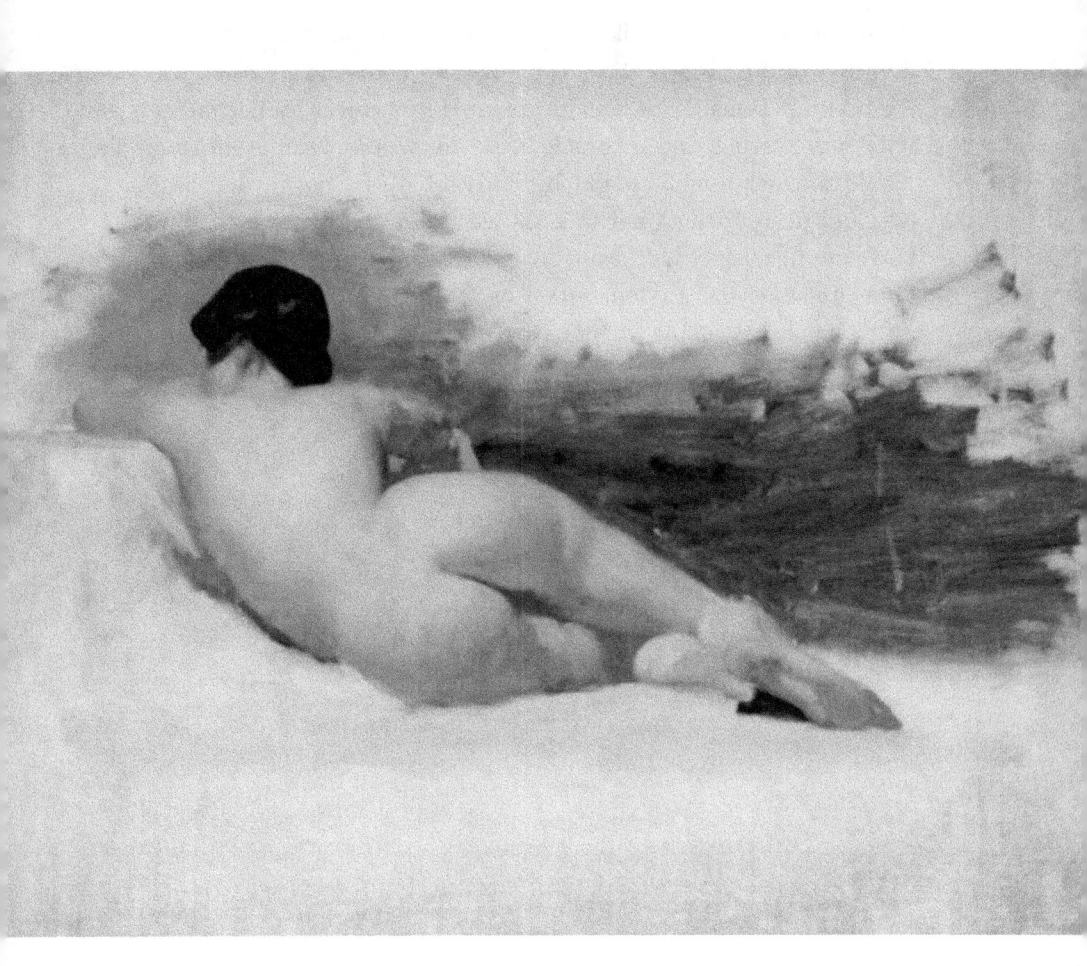

Henry Fuseli

REMBRANDT VAN RIJN

A mythic image that allowed for artists to paint a scene that depicted nudity and eroticism, magic and heterosexual love, was the myth of Danae. She was imprisoned in a tower by her father, who was warned by an oracle that she would bear a son that would murder him. The god Jupiter (Zeus) saw her, lusted after her, and descended to her in a shower of gold, which she caught between her legs; the result was Perseus. Painters depict the moment when the golden semen of the phallic deity falls on the nude Danae, as in the versions by Correggio, Titian, Rembrandt and Mabuse.[1]

---

1 Rembrandt van Rijn: *The Danae*, 1636, oil on canvas, 186 x 201cm, Hermitage St Petersburg; Titian: *Danae*, 1553-4, oil on canvas, 128 x 178cm, Prado, Madrid; Mabuse (Jan Gossaert: *Danaë*, 1527, Alte Pinacothek, Munich; Correggio: *Danaë*, 1531/2, canvas, 161 x 193cm, Borghese Gallery, Rome

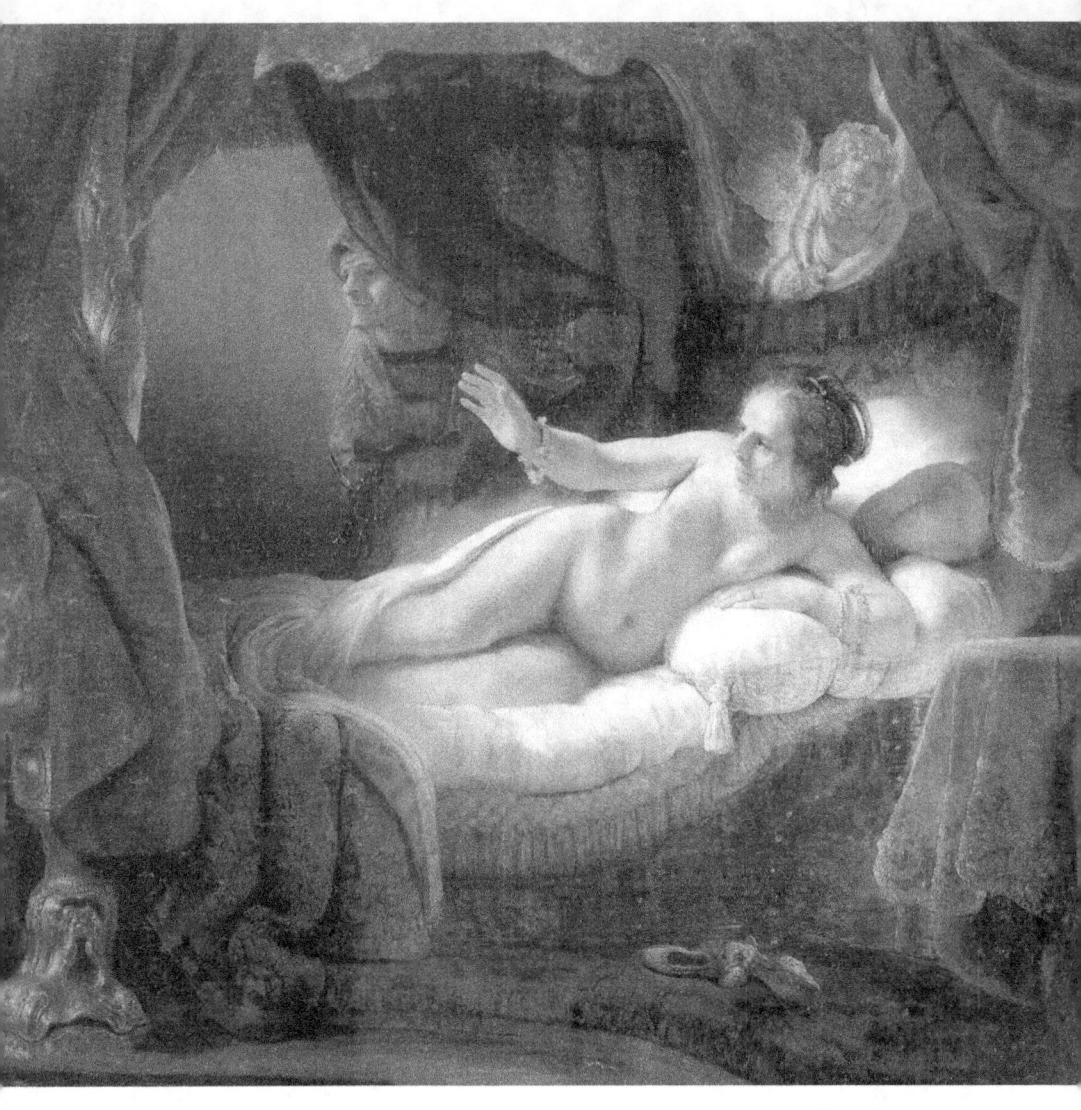

Rembrandt van Rijn, Danae, 1636, St Petersburg

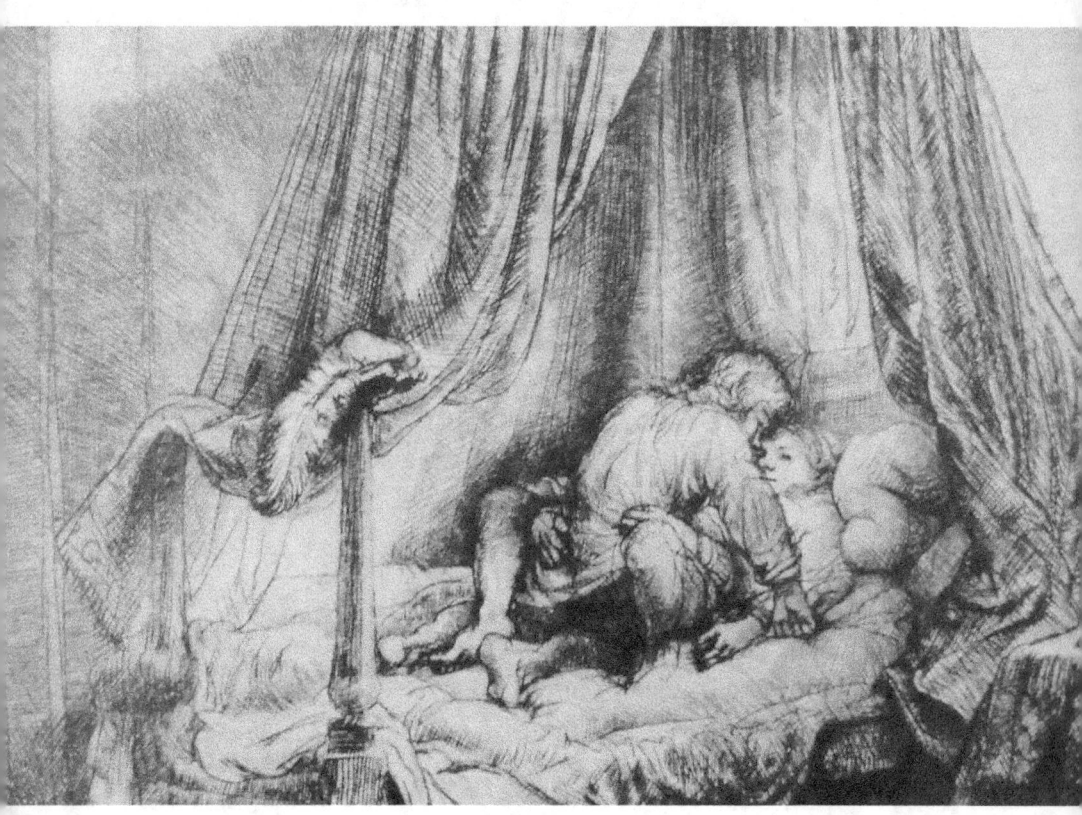

Rembrandt van Rijn, Ledakant, 1646

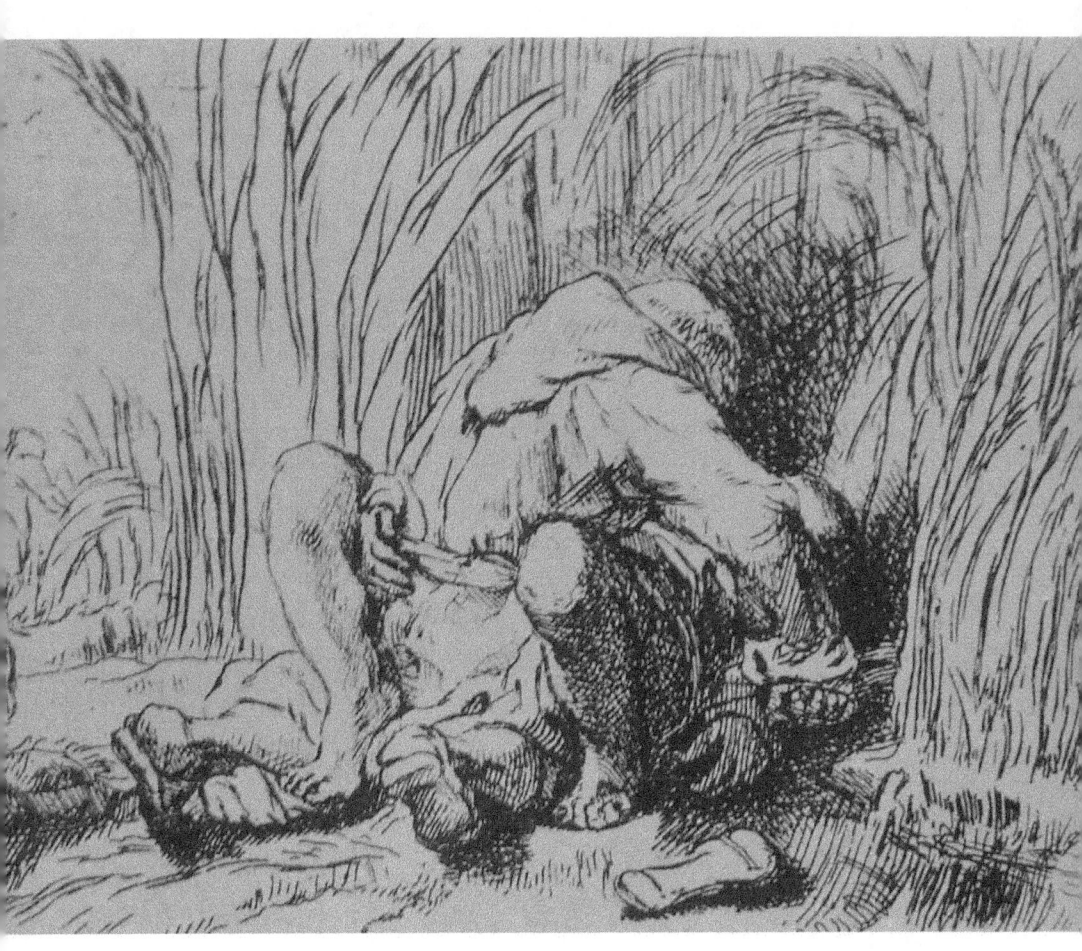

Rembrandt van Rijn, The Monk In the Cornfield

ANIMA

In the Jungian system, Beatrice, Laura, Cleopatra, Isolde, Eurydice, Ariadne and all those women of myth, poetry and legend, are incarnations of the *anima*, which is, as Carl Jung explains, something all males possess: '[e]very man carries with him the eternal image of woman, not the image of this or that particular woman, but a definitive feminine image.'[1] The *anima* is 'a personification of the unconscious in a man, which appears as a woman or a goddess in dreams, visions and creative fantasies', write Emma Jung and Marie-Louise von Franz, glossing Jung's *anima* concept.[2]

Male painters throughout history have depicted their version of the *anima*, it seems. Each (male) painter has a version of the 'inner feminine figure', as Carl Jung calls it.[3] For painters, this idealized *anima* figure seems to be another manifestation of that obscure object of desire, the eroticized woman, a mirror for male lust. The equation is: the more sublime and voluptuous the woman is painted, the more sublime and voluptuous is the artist's desire. The artist's model, then, can be seen as a Jungian *anima*, heavily eroticized, a Lacanian phallic mirror.

1 C. Jung: *The Development of Personality*, vol. 17, Routledge, 1954, 198; Marie-Louise von Franz: *The Psychological Meaning of Redemption Motifs in Fairy Tales*, Inner City Books, Toronto 1980, 39f
2 Emma Jung & Marie-Louise von Franz: *The Grail Legend, tr.* Andrea Dykes, Sigo Press, Boston, Mass., 1980, 64
3 C. Jung: *Memories, Dreams, Reflections*, Collins 1967, 210-1

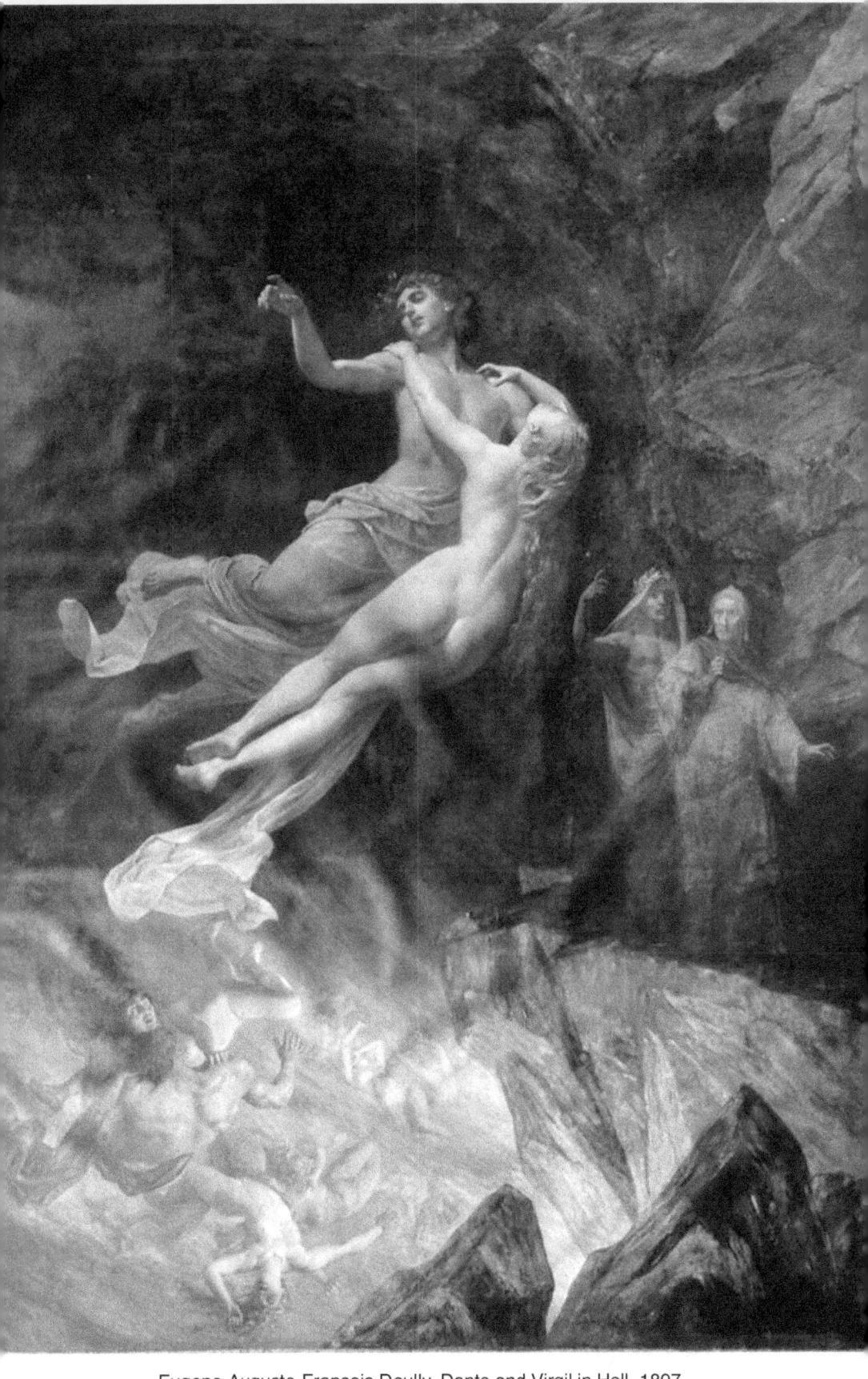

Eugene-Auguste-Francois Deully, Dante and Virgil in Hell, 1897

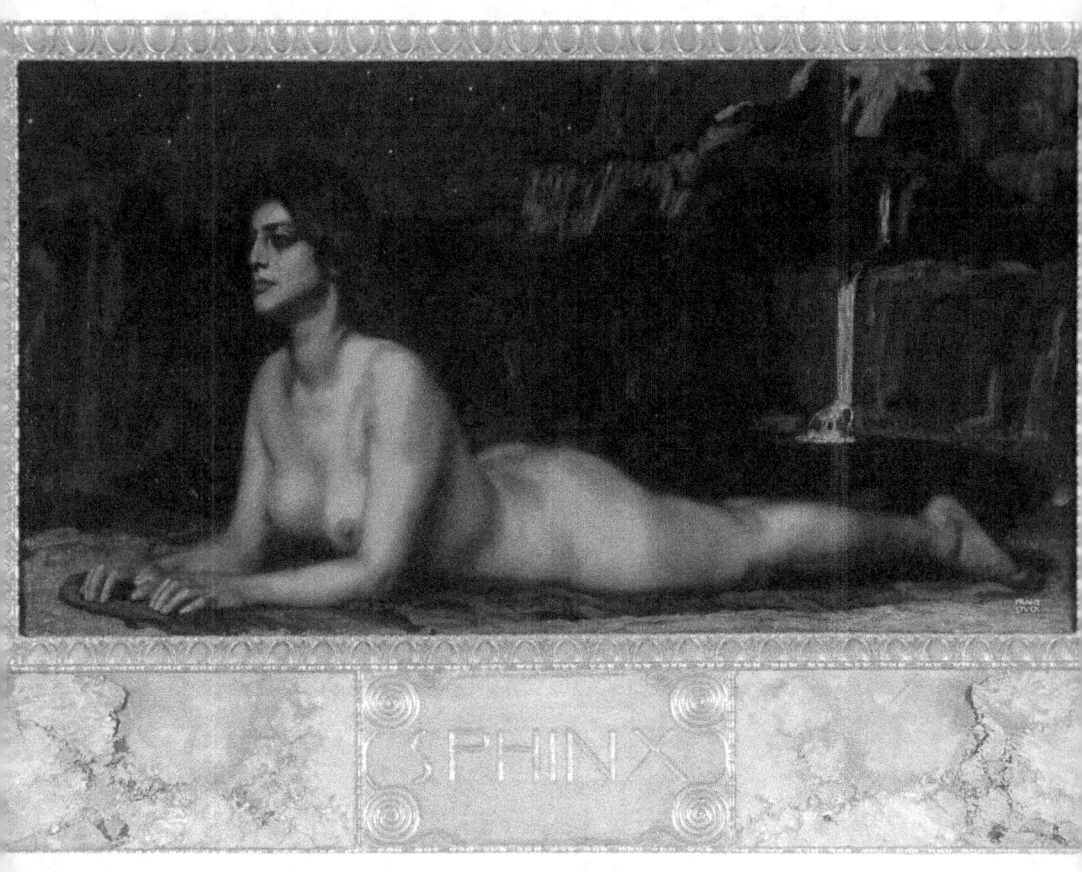

Franz von Stuck, Sphinx

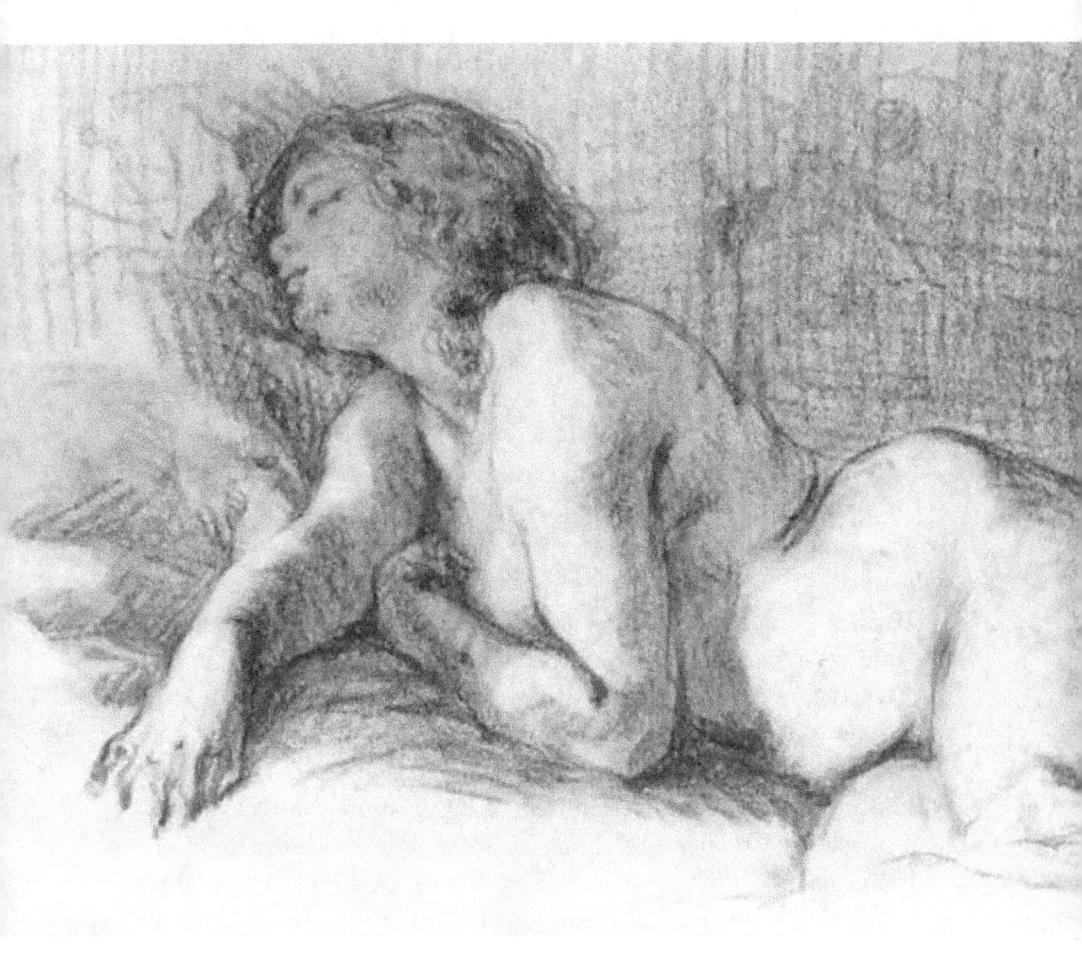

Jean-Françoise Millet

ARTISTS AND MODELS

Seen in Lacanian theory, the female model becomes the 'obscure object of desire' feared and desired, ever unreachable, the manifestation of eternal loss.[1] We can see elements of the Lacanian lack, desire, repression, mirror stage, Symbolic Order and œdipal anxiety in the modern artists who create specifically erotic images. In the output of artists such as Pierre Renoir, Henri Matisse, Jules Pascin, Aristide Maillol, Auguste Rodin, Gustav Klimt, Amedeo Modigliani and Pablo Picasso, one finds loss, desire, repression and anxiety quite clearly. The art they produced is fiercely heterosexual, glorifying women, even as, in some cases (Picasso) the paintings seem to denigrate women. Renoir, in paintings such as *Bather Arranging Her Hair*, Pascin in *The Prodigal Son*, and Lawrence Alma-Tadema in *In the Tepidarium*, produced works that exalt women as sexual objects. The soft flesh is available but also distinctly not available; there is acres of skin, especially in Pascin's painting, but it is not touchable either.[2] These nude paintings remain chimeras, never to be possessed, always to be yearned for. As Nicolas Poussin wrote of painting: '[p]ainting is nothing but an imitation of human actions, which alone are, properly speaking, inimitable'.[3] Poussin recognizes that painting is always an imitation, a mirror; the real thing can never be possessed in art. It is the same in erotic art – indeed, it is most dramatically expressed in erotic art – this paradoxical fear and desire, this simultaneous desire and loss, this ambiguous conflict between possession and dispossession.

1 Toril Moi: *Sexual Textual Politics*, 99f; Anika Lemaire: *Jacques Lacan*, Routledge & Kegan Paul 1977; Elizabeth Wright: *Psychoanalytic Criticism*, Methuen 1984
2 Pierre Renoir: *Bather Arranging Her Hair*, 1885, canvas, 92 x 73cm, Sterling and Francis Clark Institute, Williamstown, Mass.; Lawrence Alma-Tadema: *In the Tepidarium*, 1881, wood, 24 x 33cm, Lady Lever Art Gallery, Port Sunlight; Jules Pascin: *The Prodigal Son*, 1928, oil on board, 15 x 18in, private collection, Switzerland
3 In R. Goldwater, 154.

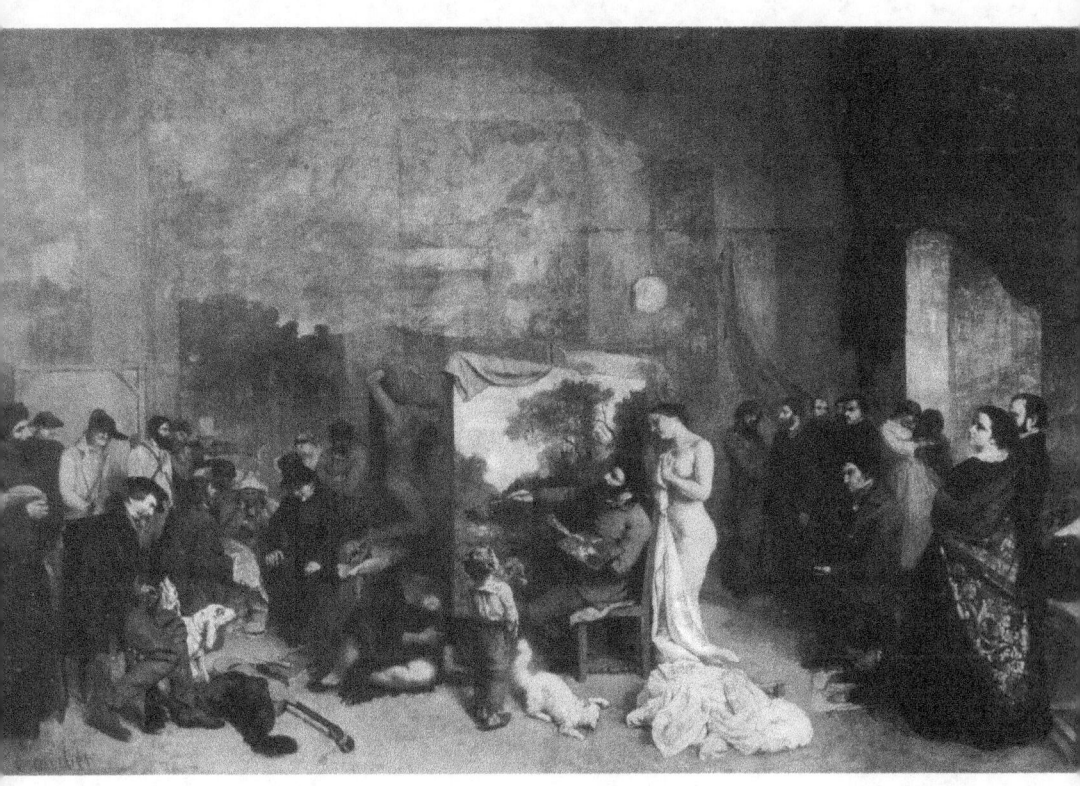

Gustave Courbet, The Studio, 1855, Musée d'Orsay, Paris

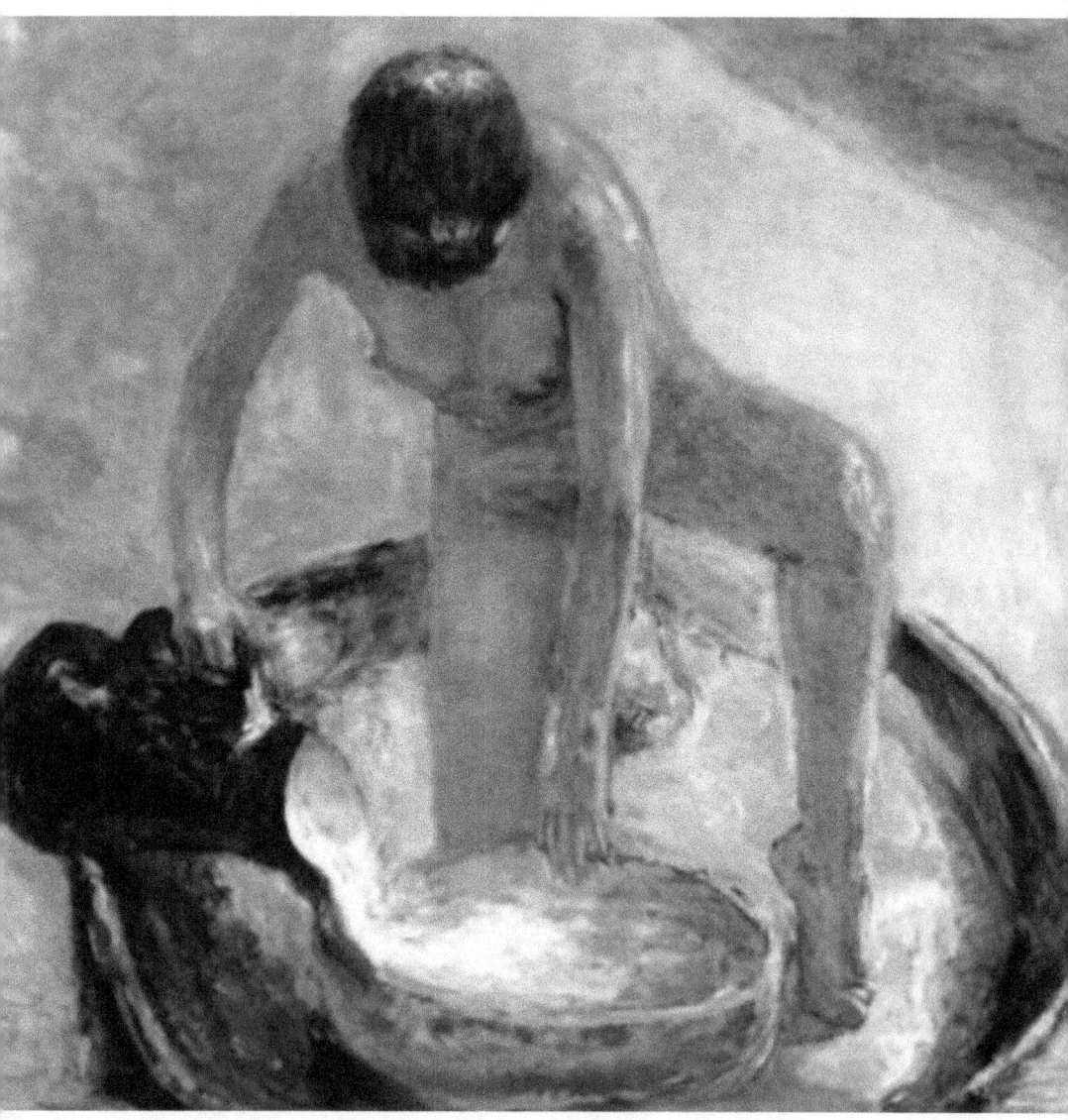

Pierre Bonnard, Nude Crouching In a Tub

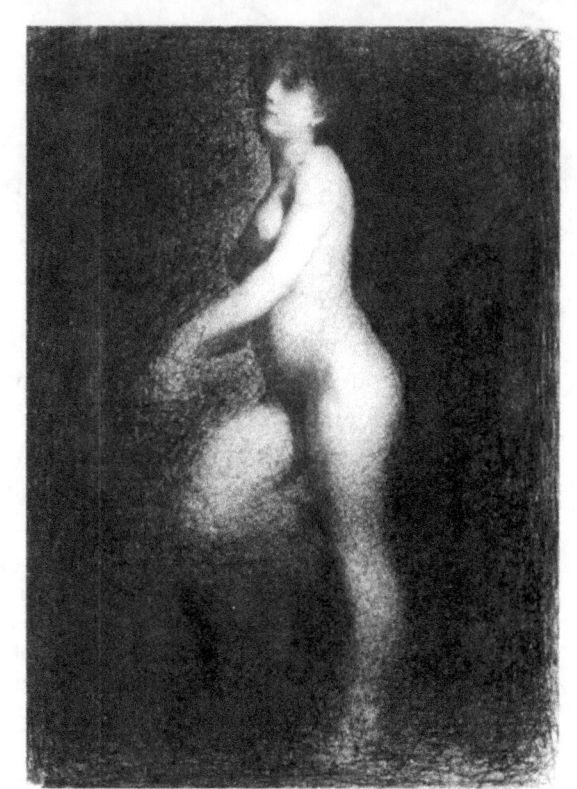

Georges Seurat

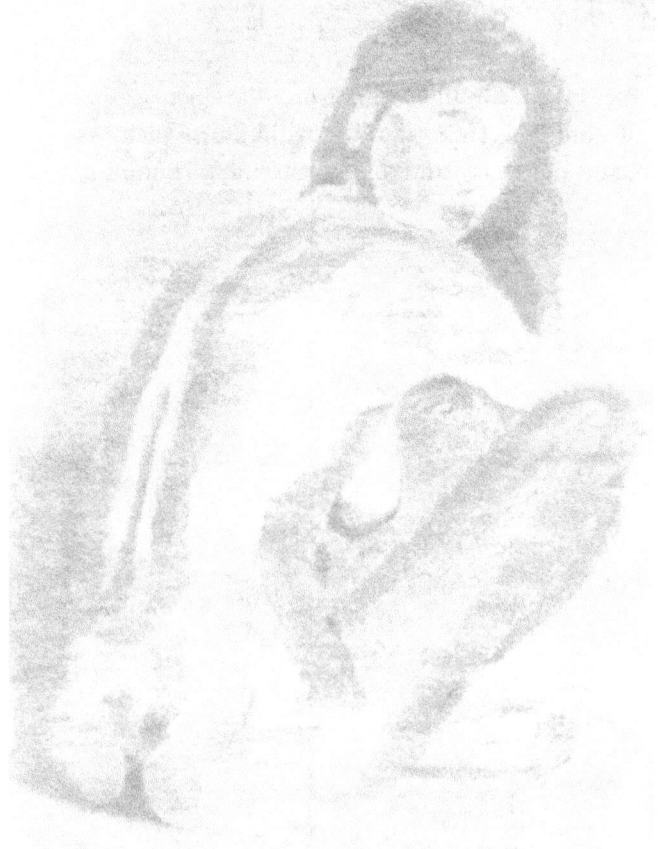

THE FEMALE NUDE – 19TH CENTURY

The female nude is the apotheosis of 'high art', yet it constantly wavers around the borderline between art and pornography. The female nude is erotic *and* obscene, in the male system, both desired and loathed, both representable and un-representable.

Lynda Nead writes in *The Female Nude* (71):

> The body is, therefore, central in the formation of individual identity and is the site of the subject's desires and fantasies, actions and behaviour. Once one rejects the perception of the body as a biologically determined and pre-cultural given and moves towards the conception of 'embodied' subjects, the way is opened for feminist interventions within the definition of the female body.

The 19th century saw an enormous increase in the number of nudes being produced in painting, particularly linked to the academies and art schools. This rise in nude painting reflected the social changes of the 19th century, such as the increase in population, the rise of mercantile capitalism, the increase in prostitution, the decline of authoritarian institutions such as organized religion, and the increasing dependence on technology,

William Bouguereau, Evening Mood, 1882

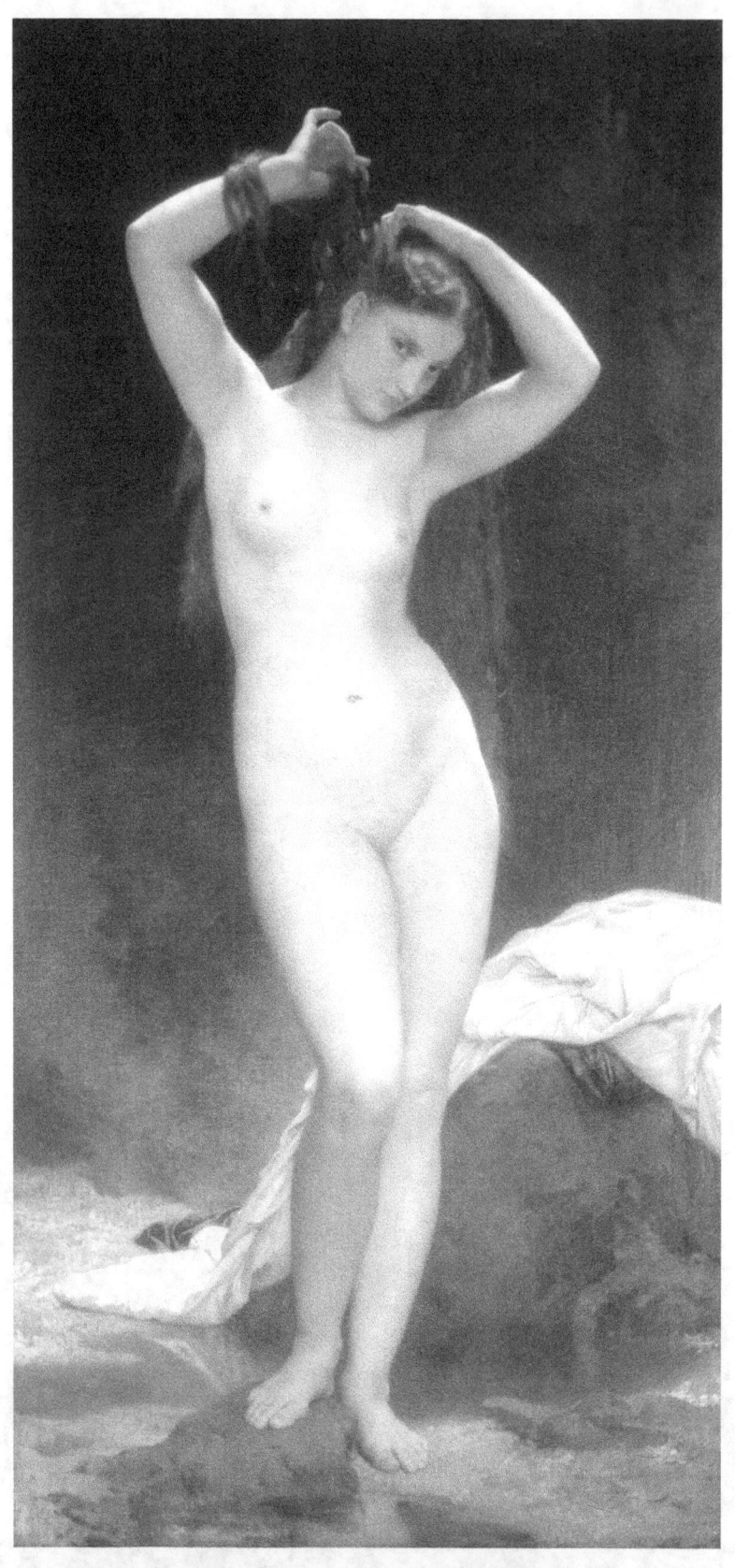

William Bouguereau, The Bather, 1870

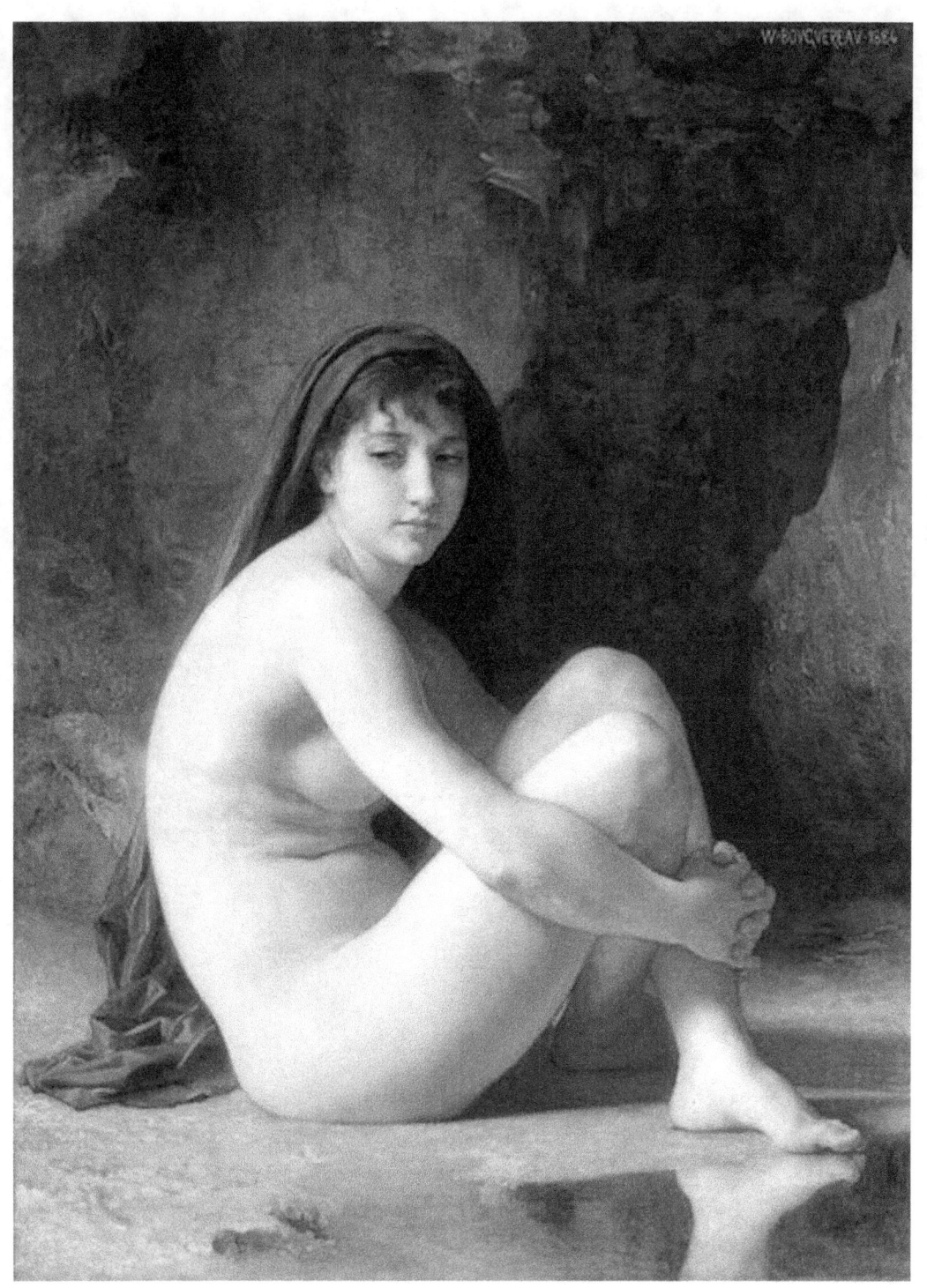

William Bouguereau, Seated Nude, 1884

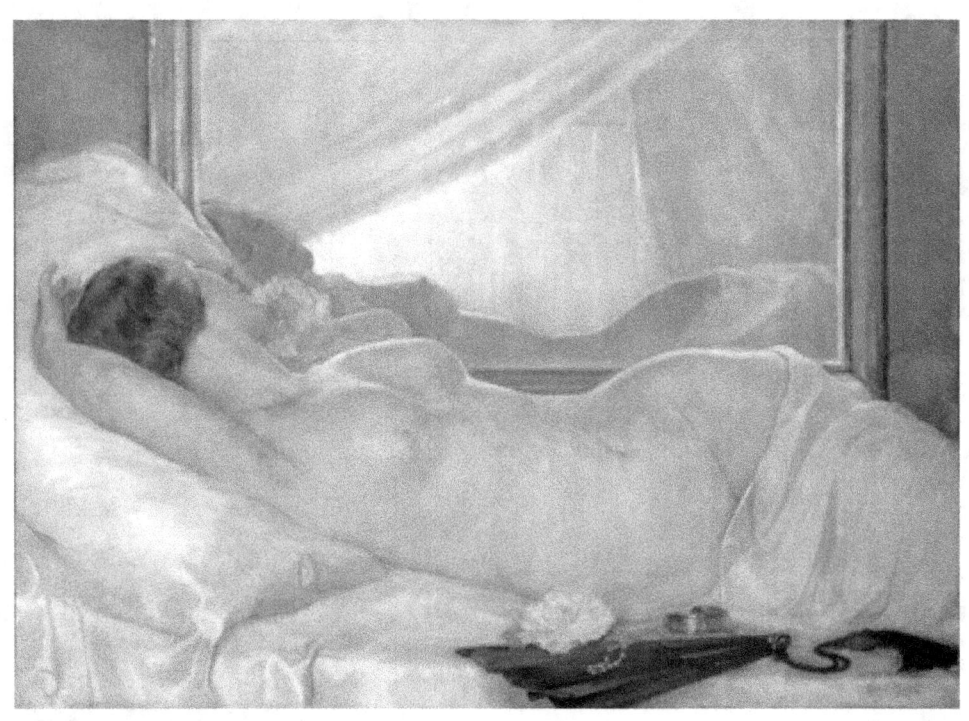

Eugène Huc

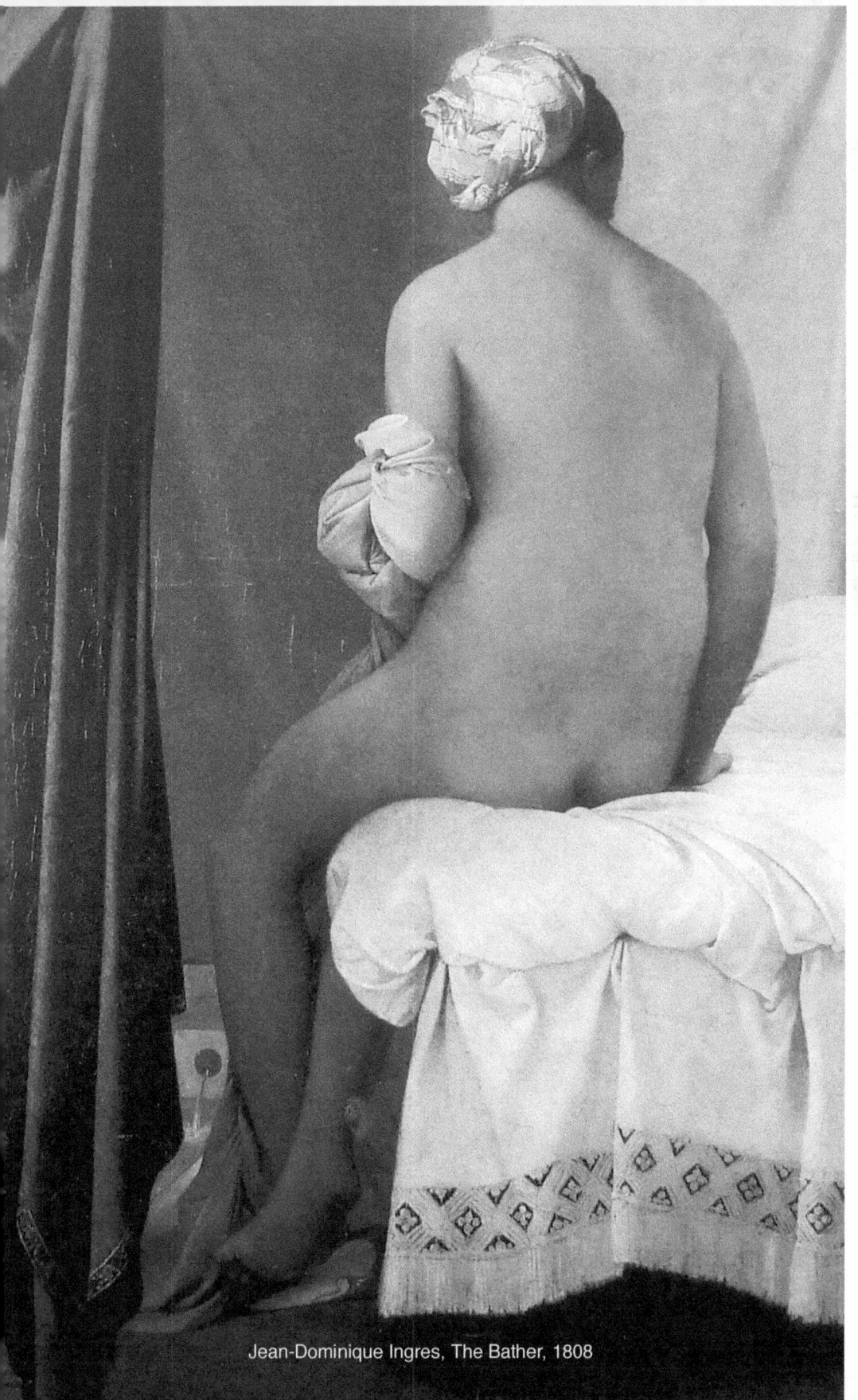

Jean-Dominique Ingres, The Bather, 1808

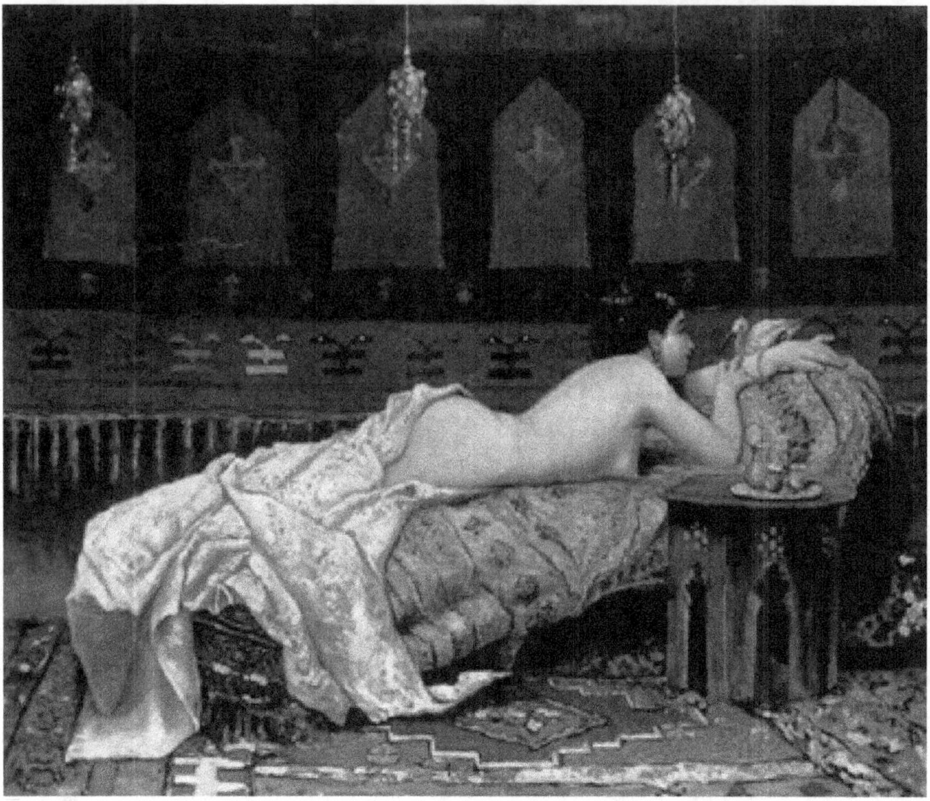

Francesco Paolo Michetti (above).
Paul Bouchard (below).

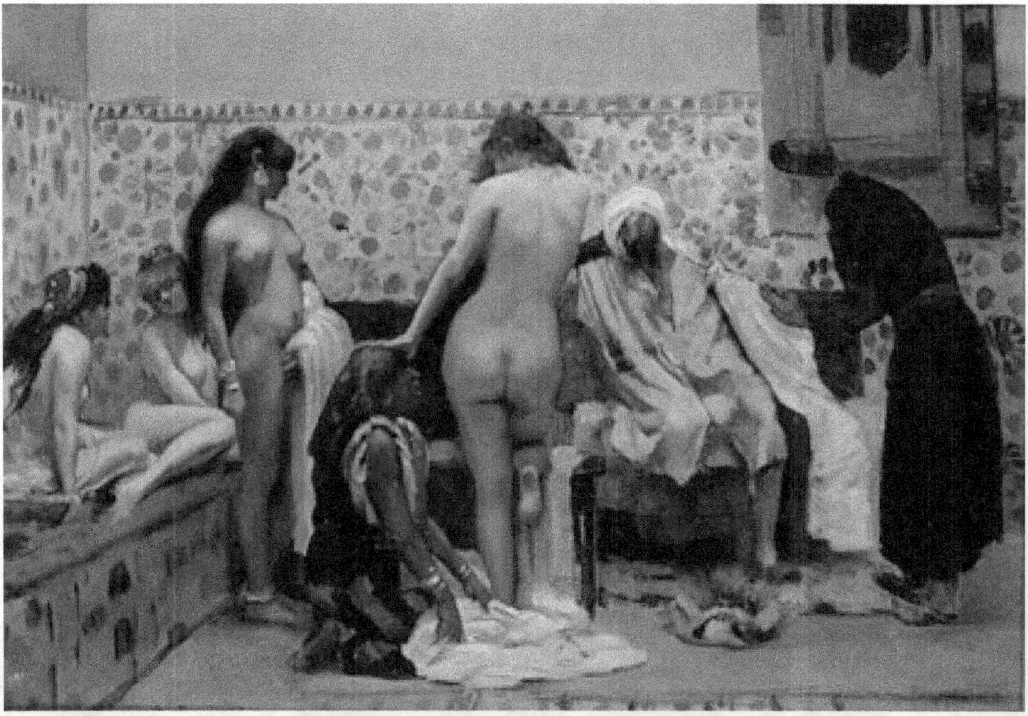

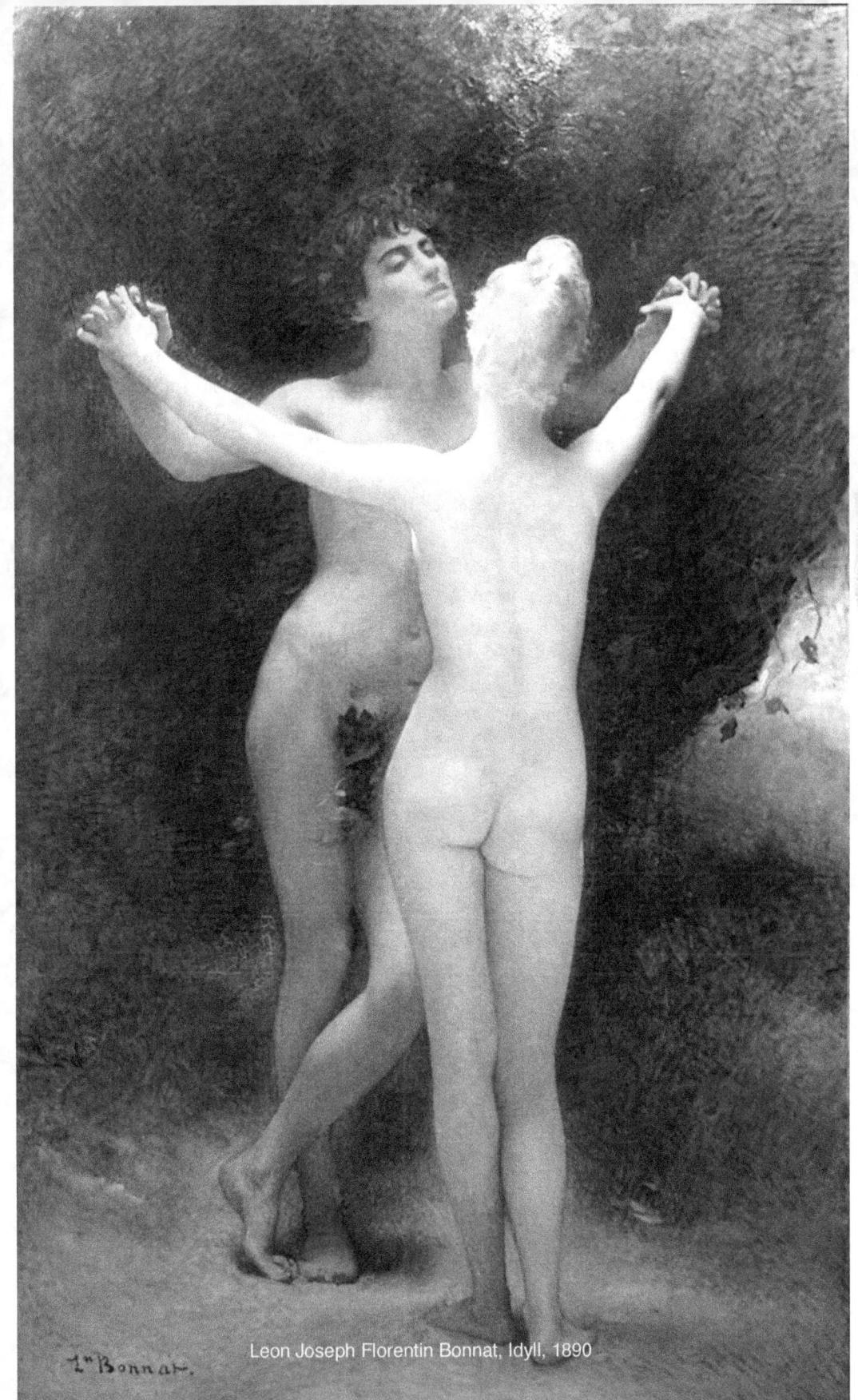

Leon Joseph Florentin Bonnat, Idyll, 1890

CHRISTIANITY AND PORNOGRAPHY

Pornography subverts the laws of Christianity, but it is based on the same laws. Porn comes out of the same world, the same politics, the same culture, as Christianity. Not only is there much of Christianity in pornography, there is much of pornography in Christianity. For instance, Christian history is a catalogue of sadomasochistic events and acts, some really horrific scenes of torture and oppression. More acts of terror have been carried out in the name of God than in the name of 'freedom' or 'truth' or 'honour'.

Painters throughout Western history have reflected the violent acts of Christianity, portraying them as heroic gestures: many painters portrayed St Sebastian full of arrows (Andrea Mantegna, Antonella da Messina, Pietro Perugino, Henrick Terbruggen, and, more recently, Eric Gill and Egon Schiele). In the 19th century, the obsession with portraying the suffering in Catholicism continued.

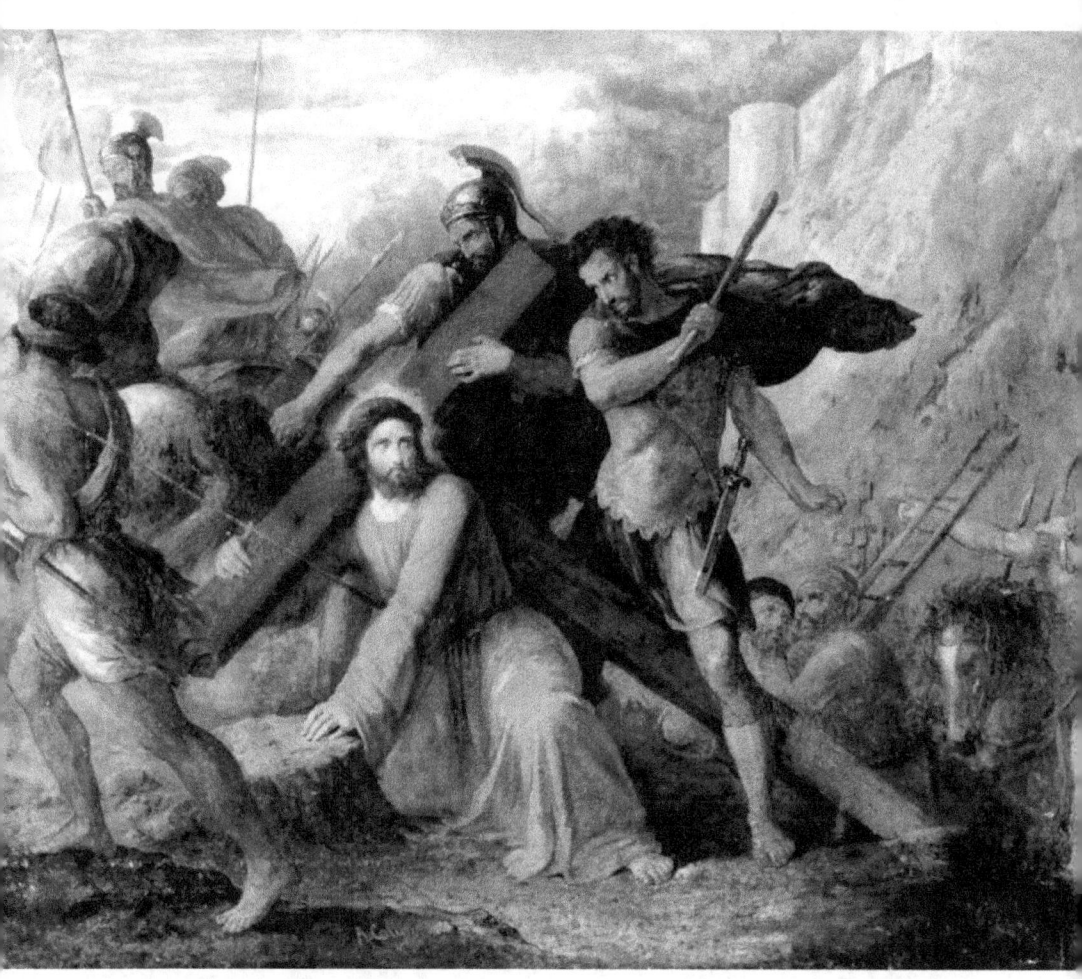

Alexandre-Marie Colin, Christ Falling On the Way To Calvary, 19th century

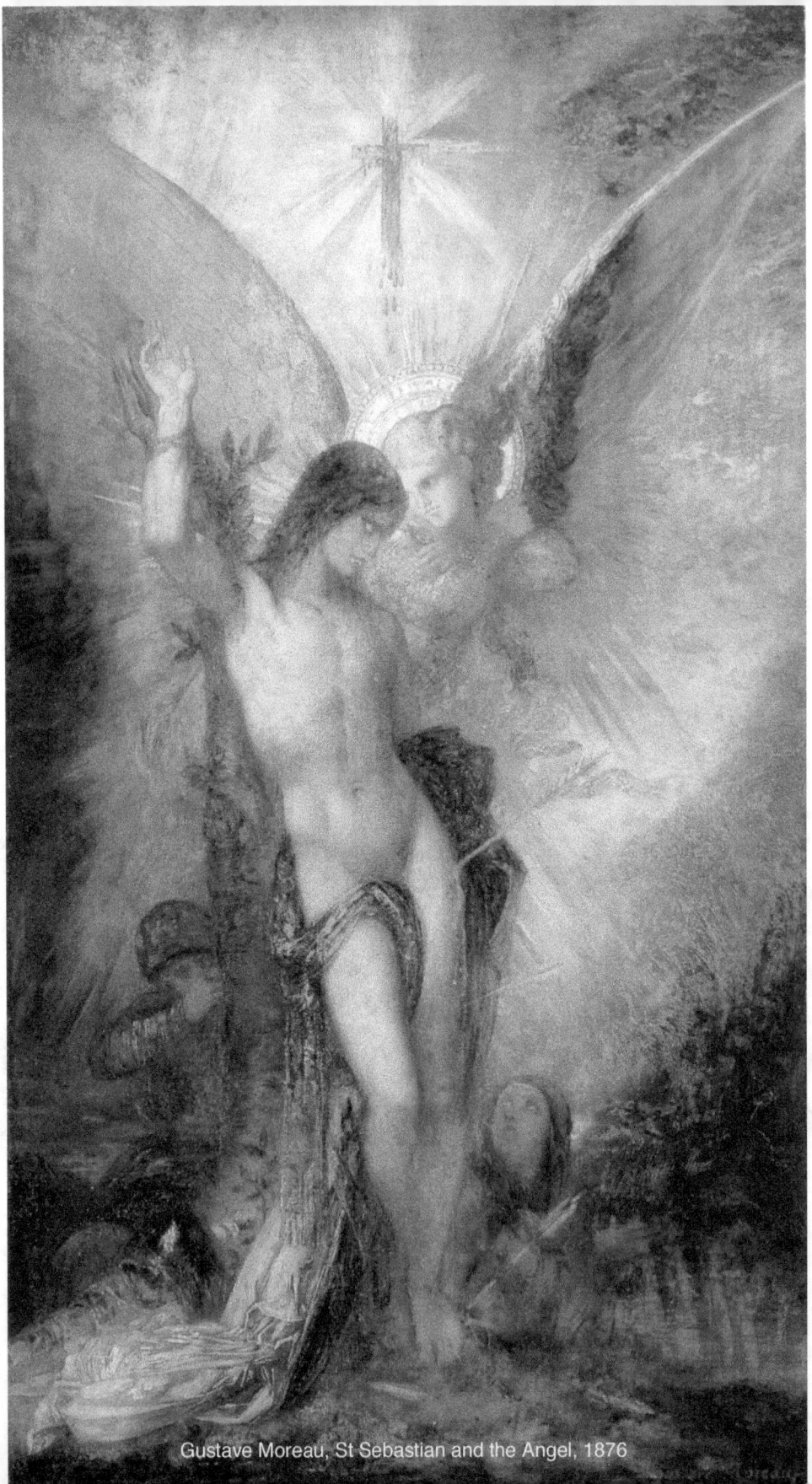

Gustave Moreau, St Sebastian and the Angel, 1876

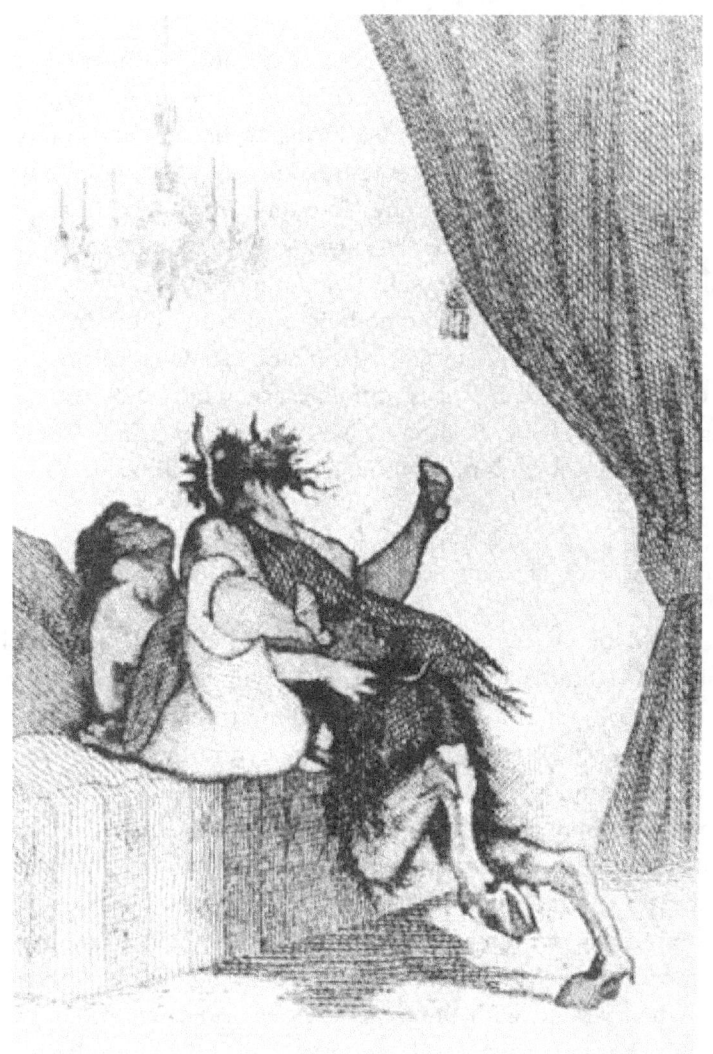

Félicien Rops, from Le Diable du
Corps, by André de Nerciat

CHRISTIANITY

In the patriarchal view, religion is sexy, and sex is religious. Artists in the 19th century often combined sexual and religious imagery (it was another way of exploring eroticism – and could be powerful precisely because the repression and exertion of power in the social realm was so strong). Western art, like pornography, draws on the Judæo-Christian insistence on sin, death, vice, fornication, dirt and suppression. The father of Christianity is not Jesus but St Paul. Jesus wrote nothing; St Paul wrote everything, setting down the views of Christianity in that fanatical prose in the *Corinthians* and *Galatians* and *Romans*, which gets so many things wrong about flesh and spirit and marriage. Michael Foucault writes of some of the strictures of Christianity:

> Christianity associated it ['the sexual act'] with evil, sin, the Fall, and death, whereas antiquity invested it with positive symbolic values.[1]

In Christianity, women are the 'gateway to Hell' as the early theologian Tertullian poetically put it; women are evil, sinful, lustful ('the Devil is a woman' is a common theme in mediæval philosophy as well as pop songs). From Eve in the *Old Testament* to the Virgin and Magdalene in the *New Testament*, women are definitely second class citizens in the eyes of Western religion. Women-hating is startling in its violent manifestations – not just in wife-beating, which occurs everywhere and, one supposes, at every moment of human history, but also in the mass movements, such as the fight against witchcraft in the Middle Ages and later, when, armed with the *Malleus Maleficarum*, the Witchfinder Generals hunted down and tortured and killed hundreds or thousands, some say millions, of women.

1 M. Foucault: *The Use of Pleasure*, 14

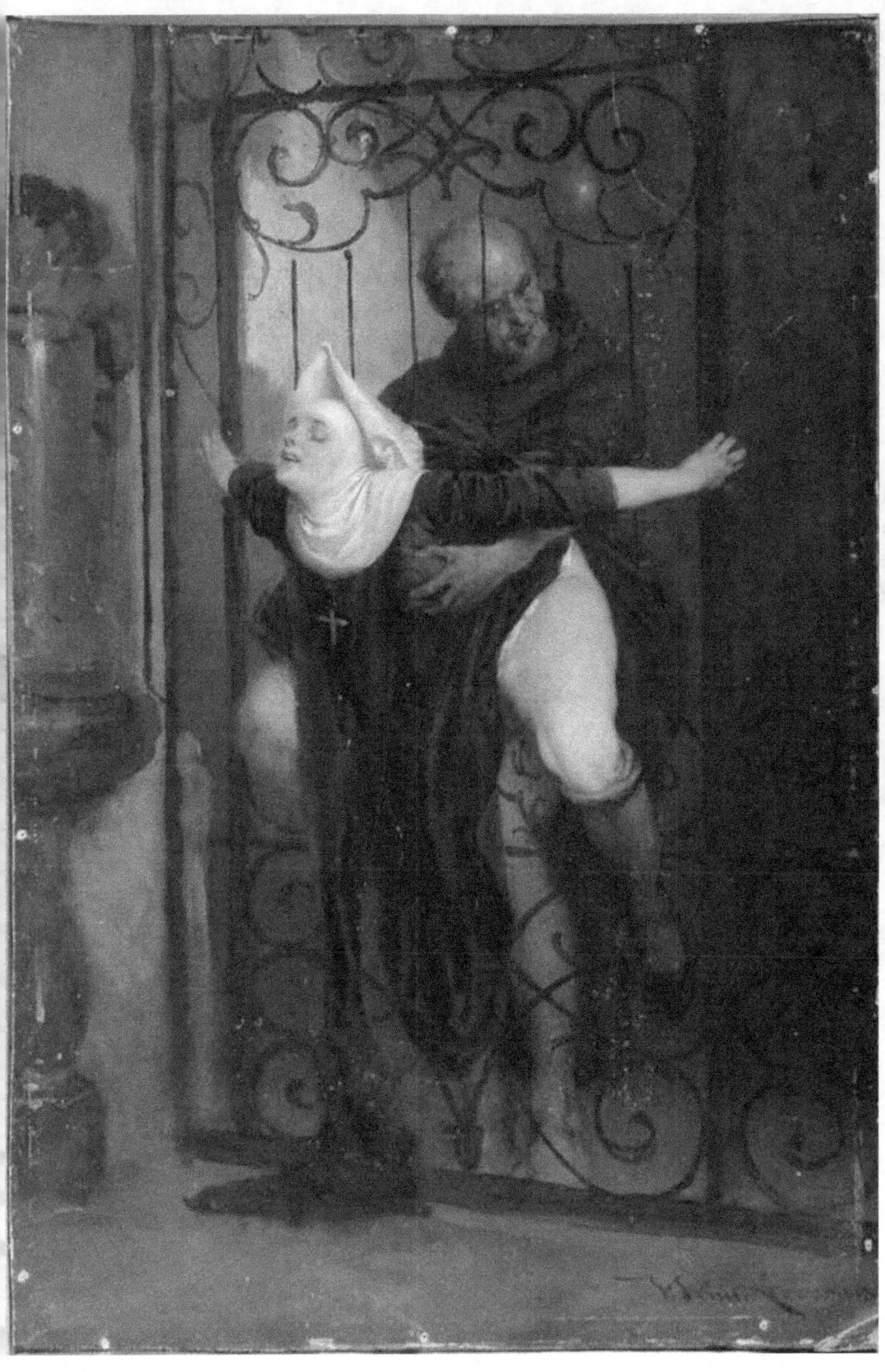

Heinrich Lossow, The Sin, 1880

FEMME FATALES

The *femme fatale* type neatly melds sex and death, desire and fear, contact and loss, for the (male) artist. She appears in Medusa, Salomé, Delilah, Jezebel, Judith, Lilith, Ninuë (the lover of Merlin), Venus, Helen of Troy, La Belle Dame Sans Merci, and Cleopatra. These female 'types' combined beauty with death, immense power and all manner of sadistic, masochistic and fetishistic fantasies. These are the women who will whip you to death, if you wish, as in Leopold Sacher-Masoch's *Venus in Furs*. Figures such as Cleopatra provided the longed for combination of socio-political, religious sovereignty, wild eroticism, intrigue, magnificent settings and gory love-deaths. As Max Lake informs us:

> The amatory skills of Cleopatra passed into legend while she lived. Apart from the rapid seduction of both Julius Caesar and Mark Antony, she is reported to have fellated one hundred noblemen in a single evening. Her Greek nickname was *meriochane*, 'she who parts wide for a thousand men.'[1]

---

1 Max Lake: *Scents and Sensuality: The Essence of Excitement*, John Murray 1989, 58

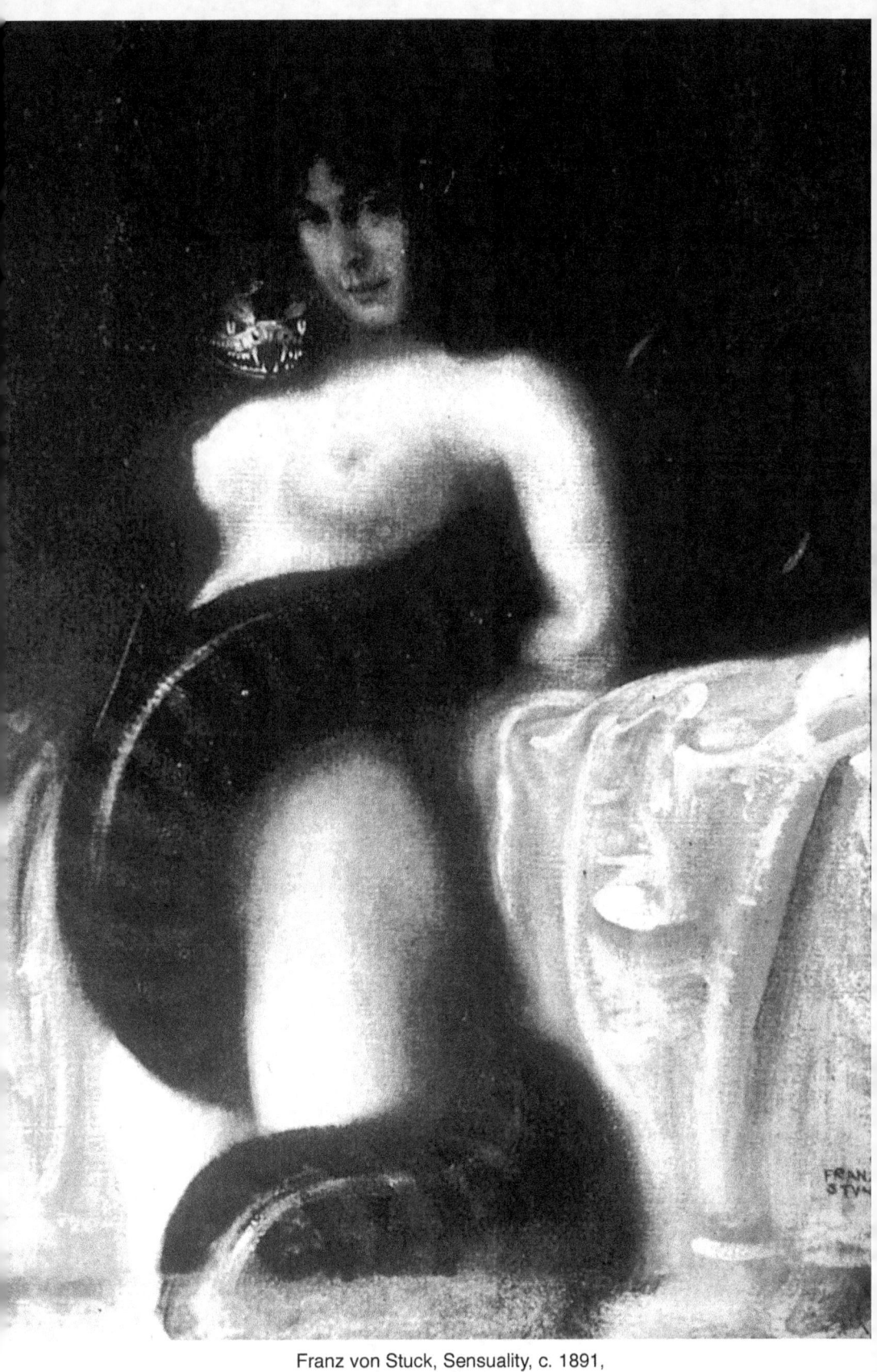

Franz von Stuck, Sensuality, c. 1891,
collection: Abraham Somer, Los Angeles

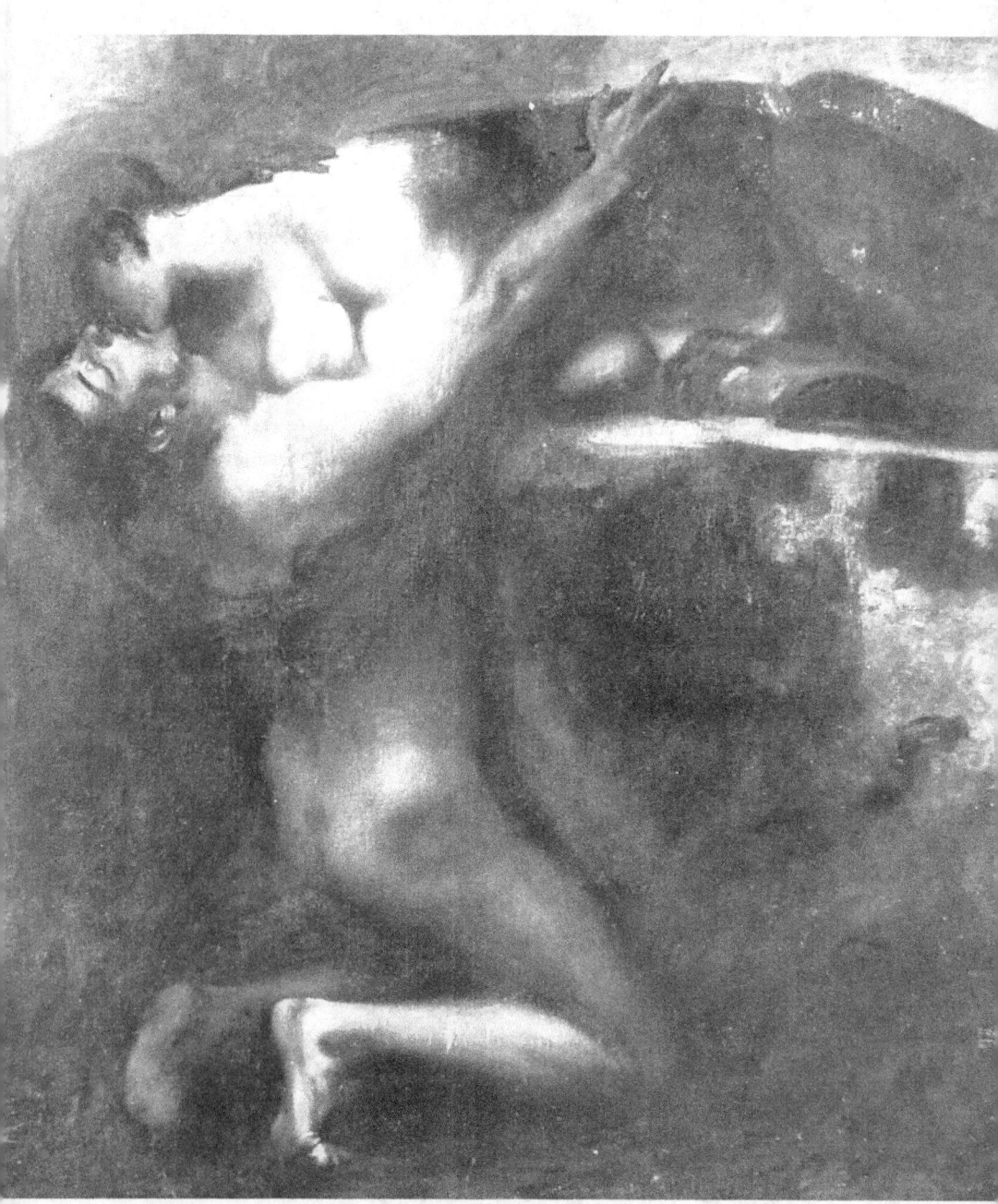

Franz von Stuck, Sphinx

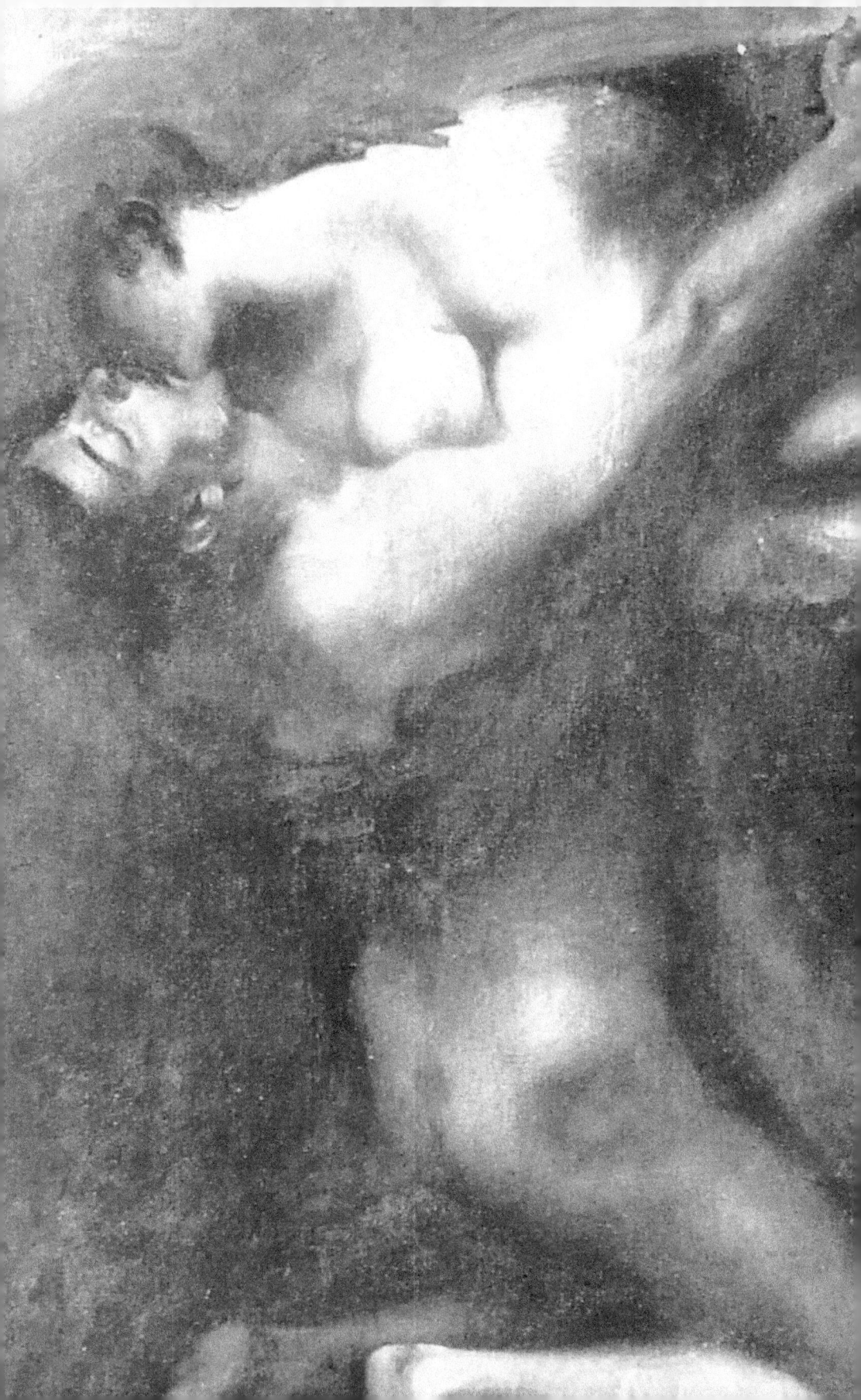

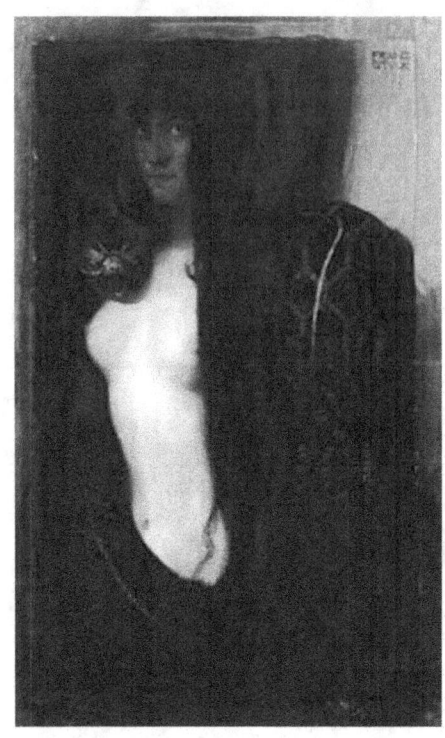

Franz von Stuck,
Wounded Amazon (below).

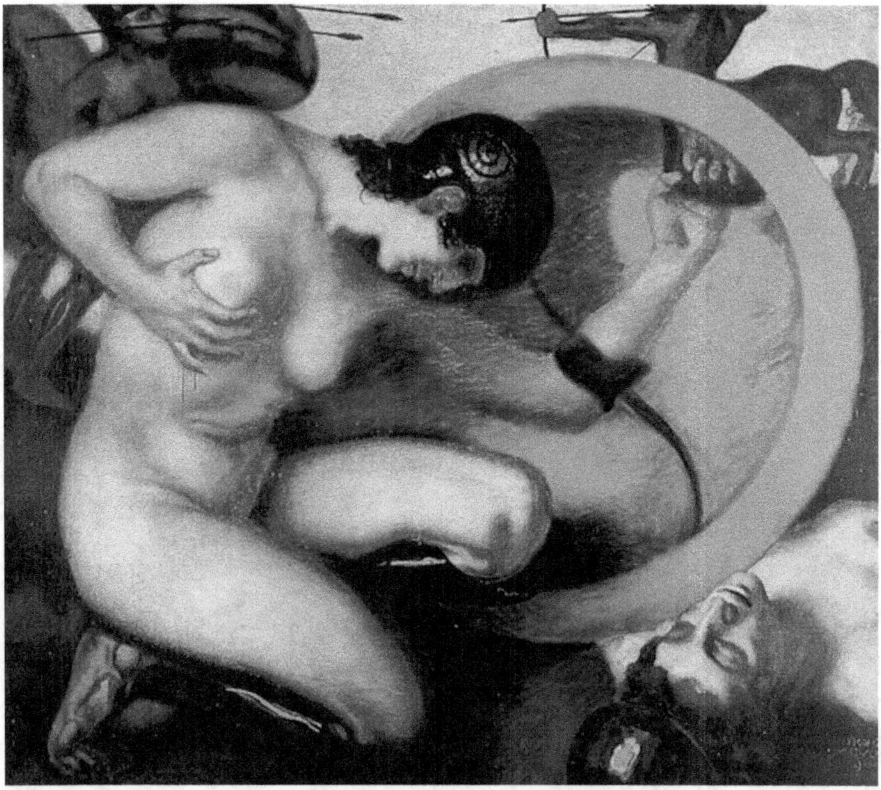

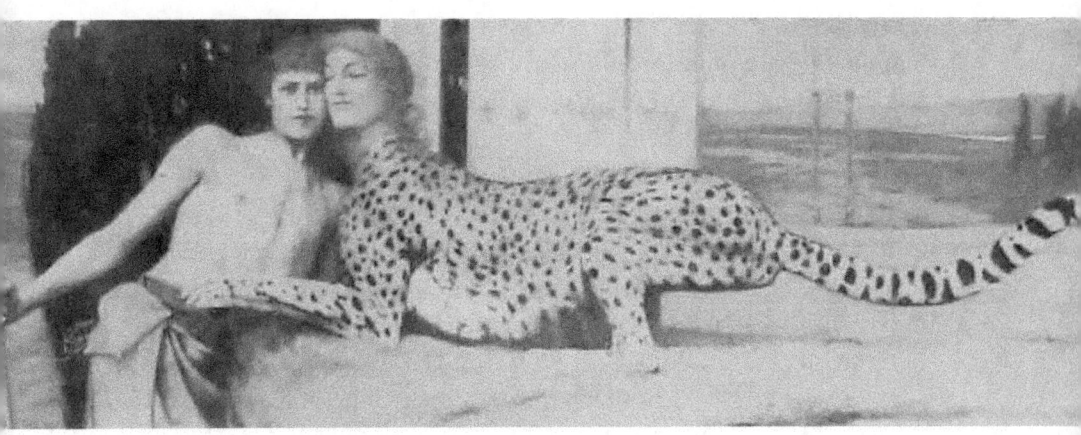

Fernand Knopff, The Caresses of the Sphinx, 1896, Brussels

SYMBOLIST AND DECADENT ART

Symbolist art, Decadent art, *fin-de-siècle* art, whatever you want to call it, is the most pornographic of 'high art'. Other art movements that followed Symbolism – Surrealism, for instance, or Pop Art – simply improvize on the excesses of Symbolist art. For in artists such as Gustave Moreau, Edvard Munch, Félicien Rops, Odilon Redon, Jean Deville and Franz von Stuck – one discovers figurative art at its most excessive. The high priest of the Symbolist era is undoubtedly Gustave Moreau. His images make the Pre-Raphaelites in Britain seem positively watered-down, and the Pre-Raphaelites themselves are as contrived, luxuriant, and mythical as any group of artists.

The Symbolist and Decadent age is marked by 'gory exoticism', as Mario Praz puts it (289), by mysticism and black magic, the macabre, the æstheticism of 'beauty', opulence and indulgence, where the key phrase is from Paul Verlaine: 'Je suis l'Empire à la fin de la décadence'.[1] The Symbolist age was summed up by works of literature such as Arthur Rimbaud's *Une Saison en Enfer*, Lautréamont's *Chansons de Maldoror*, Edgar Allan Poe's horror stories, and Charles Baudelaire's *Flowers of Evil*. Other works which characterize the epoch include: *Salambô*, J.-K. Huysmans' *A Rebours*, Péladan's *Le Vice suprême, Parsifal*. Some of the key artists of the Decadent and Symbolist age include Richard Wagner, Honoré de Balzac, J.-K. Huysmans, Walter Pater, Gustave Flaubert, Gustave Moreau, Oscar Wilde, Arnold Böcklin, and Stéphane Mallarmé. Rimbaud argued for a 'rational derangement of all the senses', and showed how marvellous poetry could be when it was unfettered and wild, in his *Les Illuminations*. Rimbaud's tenets, of the 'seer' poet, of madness, of magic, of rebellion, provide the basic ground for many art 'movements', from Symbolism through Surrealism to Pop Art (and rock music).

---

1 Verlaine: *Selected Poems*, tr Joanna Richardson, Penguin 1974, 180

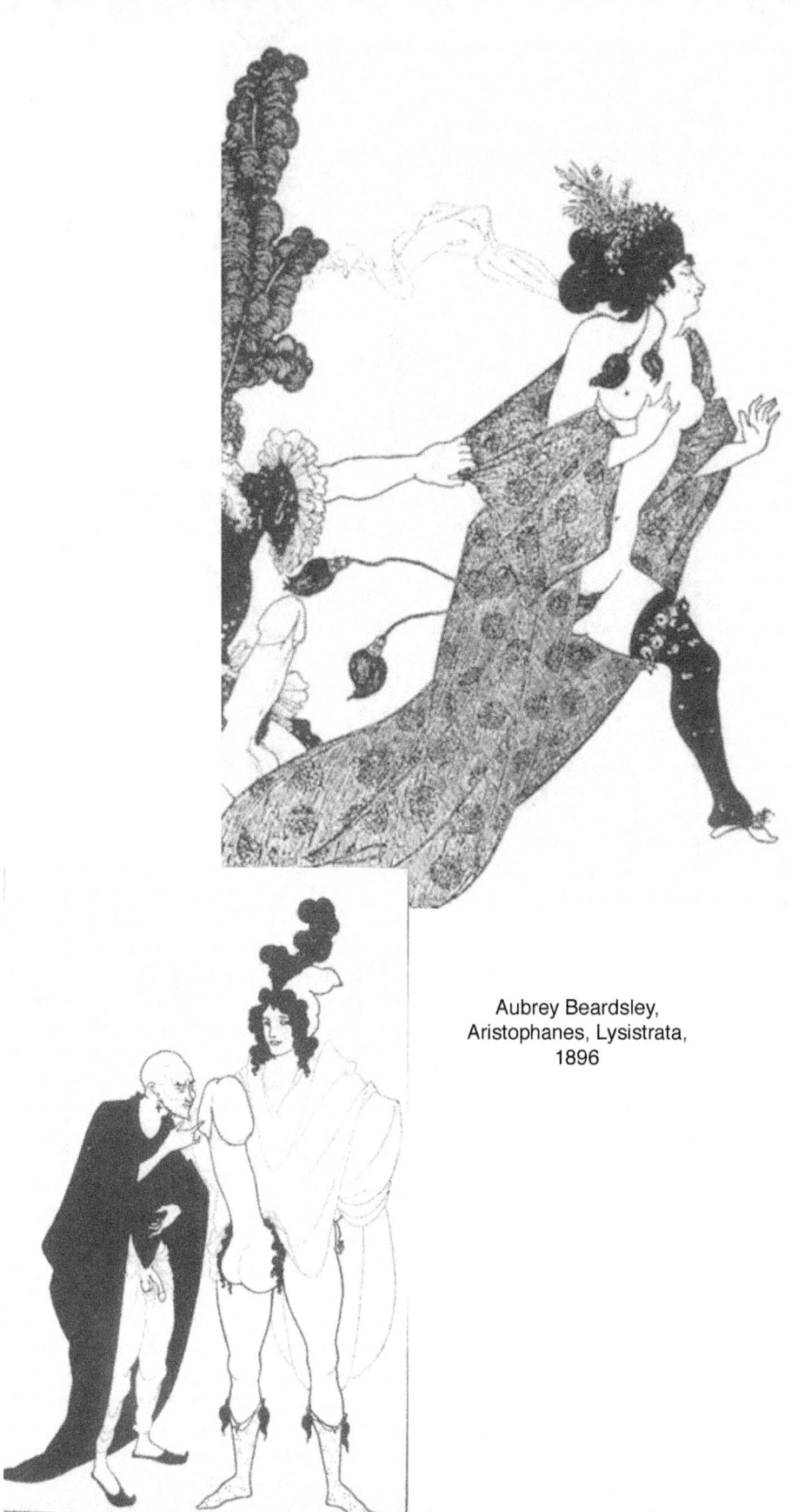

Aubrey Beardsley,
Aristophanes, Lysistrata,
1896

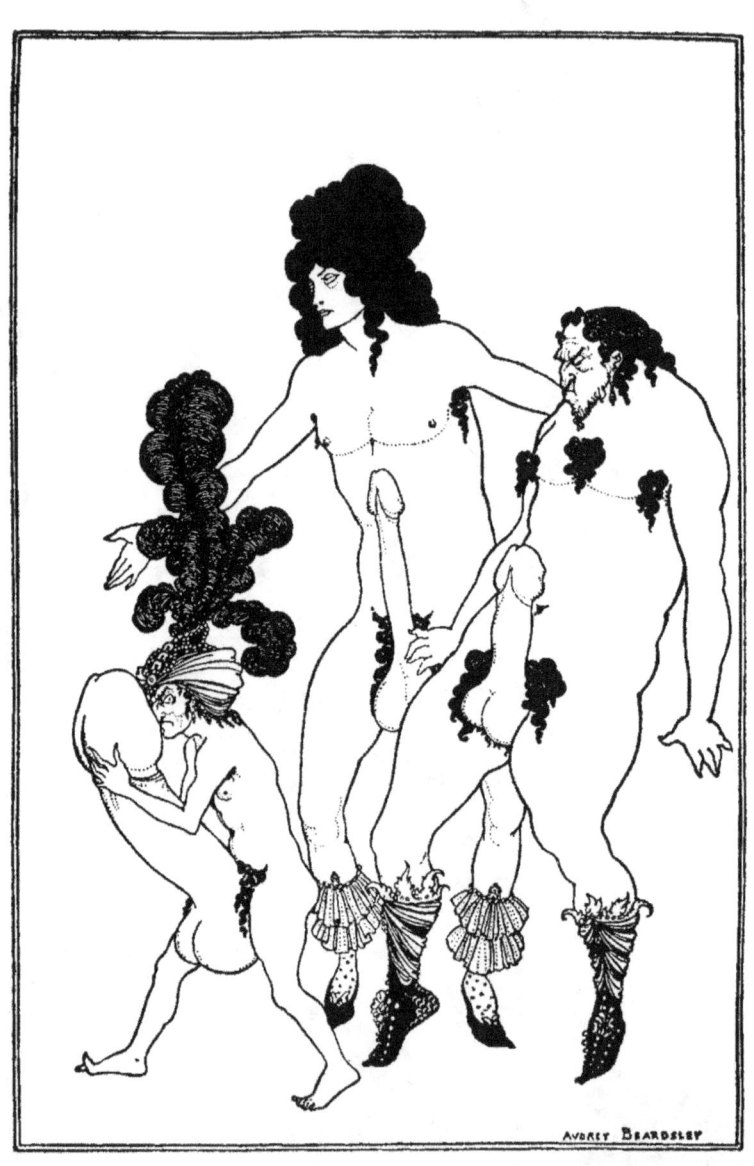

Aubrey Beardsley, Aristophanes, Lysistrata, 1896

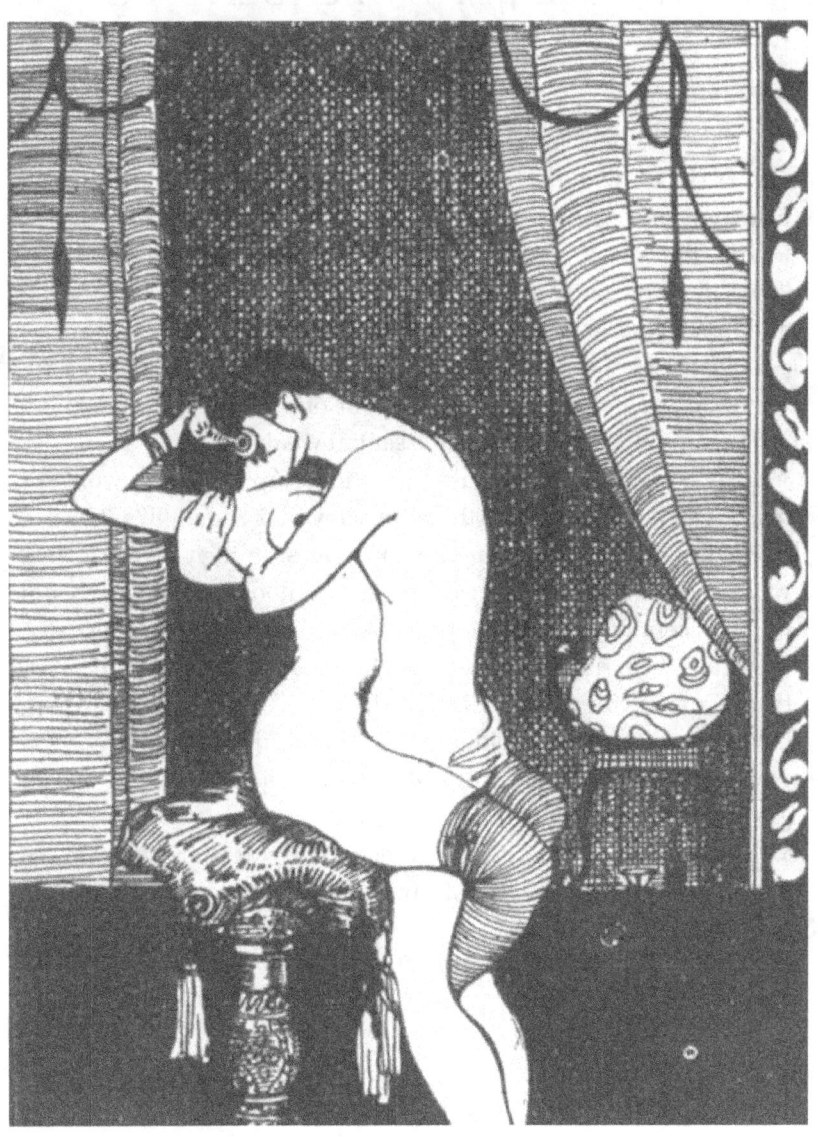

Anonymous, from Fanny Hill by John Cleland, 1889

SYMBOLIST AND DECADENT ART

The representation of women is central to Symbolist and Decadent art, as it is to 19th century art as a whole. The result is a misogynism which is often fierce and vicious. Edward Burne-Jones, the most celebrated of the Pre-Raphaelites, wrote: '[t]iresome the modern woman is. I like women when they're good and kind and pretty – agreeable objects in the landscape of existence – give life to it'.[1] This is a typical sexist comment of the Victorian age. John Burgan, a professor of divinity at Oxford, said: '[w]oman's strength lies in her essential weakness'.[2]

Some late 19th century paintings appropriate women's mysteries, such as childbirth, as in Giovanni Segantini's *The Evil Mothers*, which depicts women tied to trees by their own hair in a wilderness, punished for rejecting motherhood.[3] Many images of the 19th century do nothing more than objectify women sexually, depicting them as sex objects: many artists did not hide their lust; their women are openly displayed, legs akimbo, spines arched, heads thrown to one side, as in standard pornography. The women in many images of 19th century art pose in a porno-graphic fashion: in Henri Gervex's *Rolla*, in many works by Félix Vallotton, in Auguste Rodin's' frenetic sculptures of kisses, in the artworks of Félicien Rops, Gustave Moreau, Jean Delville, etc.[4]

1 Burne-Jones: "Conversations", in Kestner, 107
2 Burgan, 1884, in Joan Burstyn: *Victorian Education and the Ideal of Womanhood*, Croom Helm 1980, 33.
3 Segantini: *The Evil Mothers*, 1894, oil on canvas, 120 x 225cm, Kunsthistorisches Museum, Vienna
4 Gervex: *Rola*, 1878, oil on canvas, 175 x 220cm, Musée des Beaux-Arts, Bordeaux; Félix Vallotton: *The Spring*, 1897, oil on board, 48 x 60cm, Musée du petit Palais, Geneva

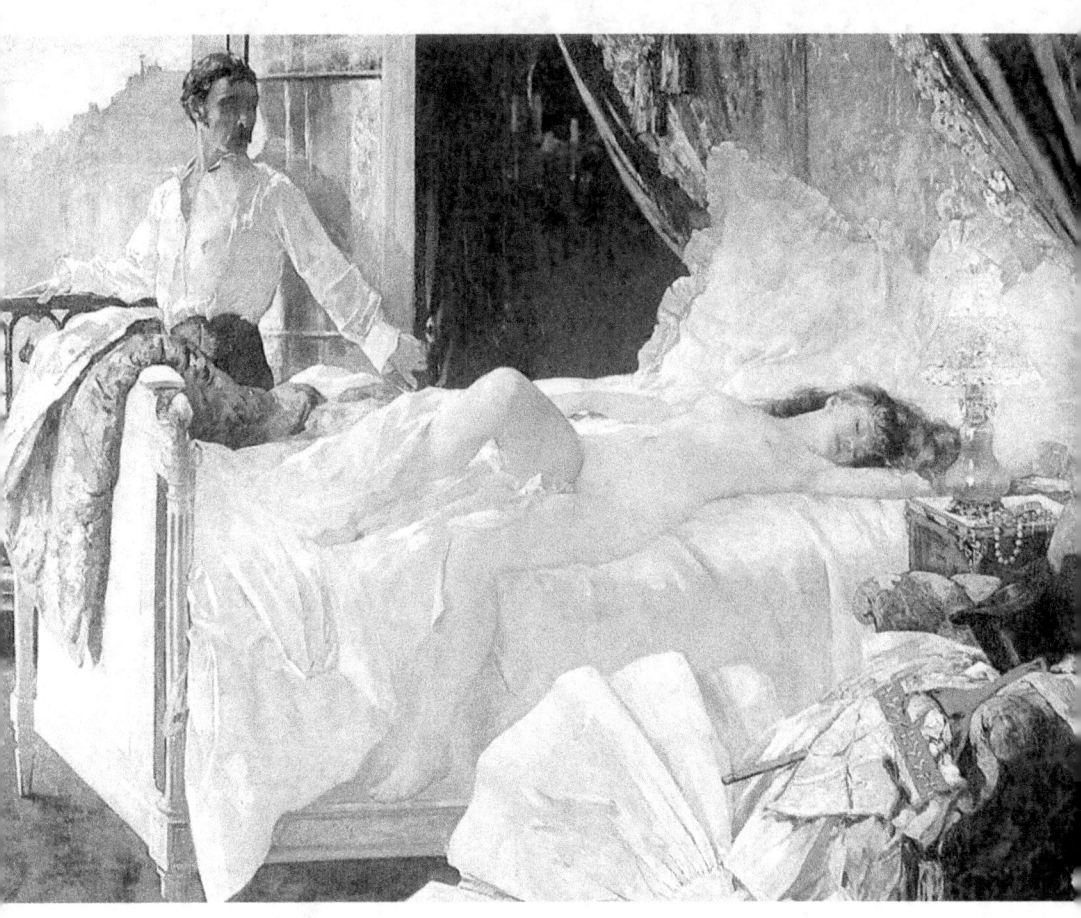

Henri Gervex Rolla, 1878

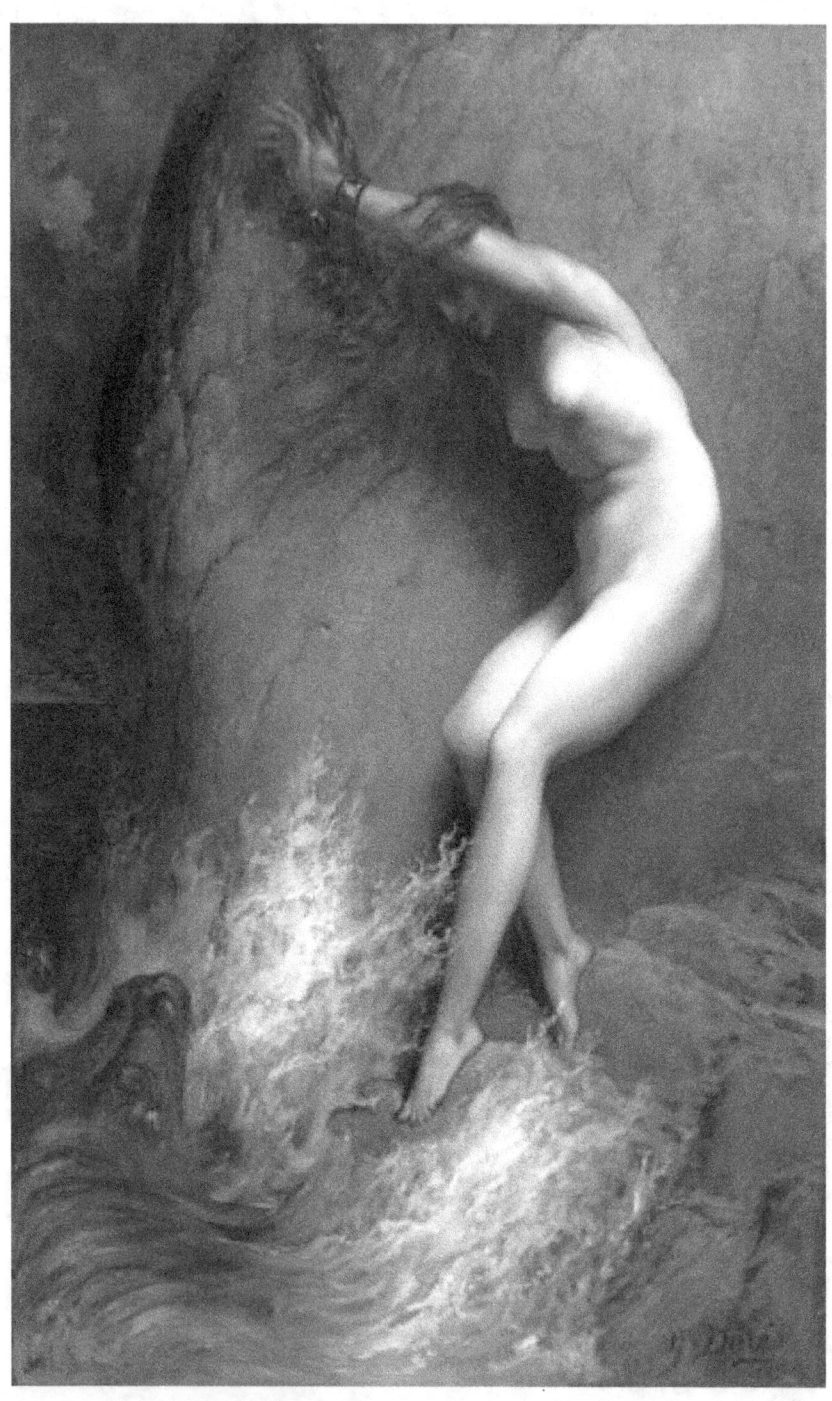

Gustave Doré

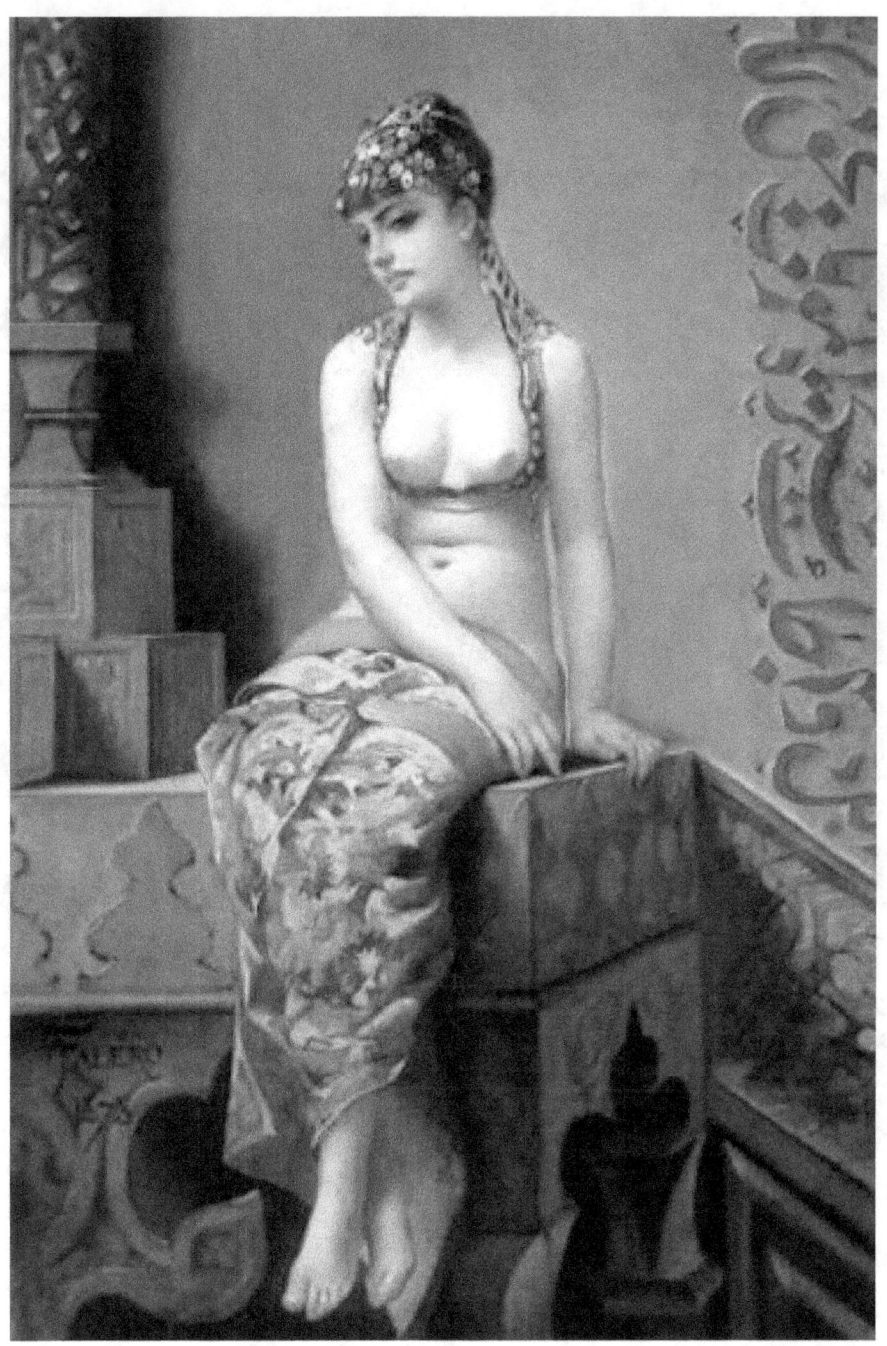

Luis Ricardo Falero

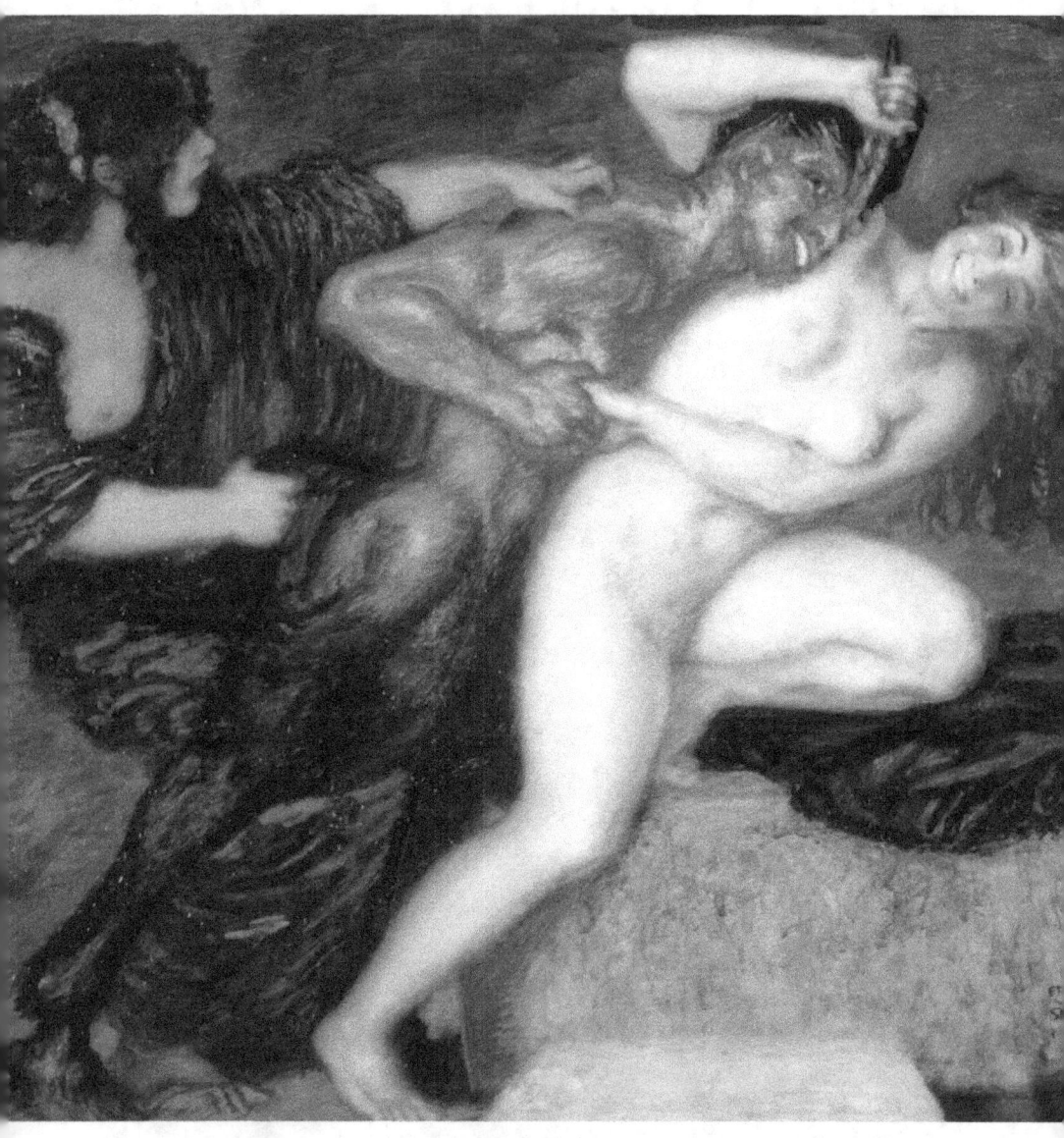

Franz von Stuck, Scherzo

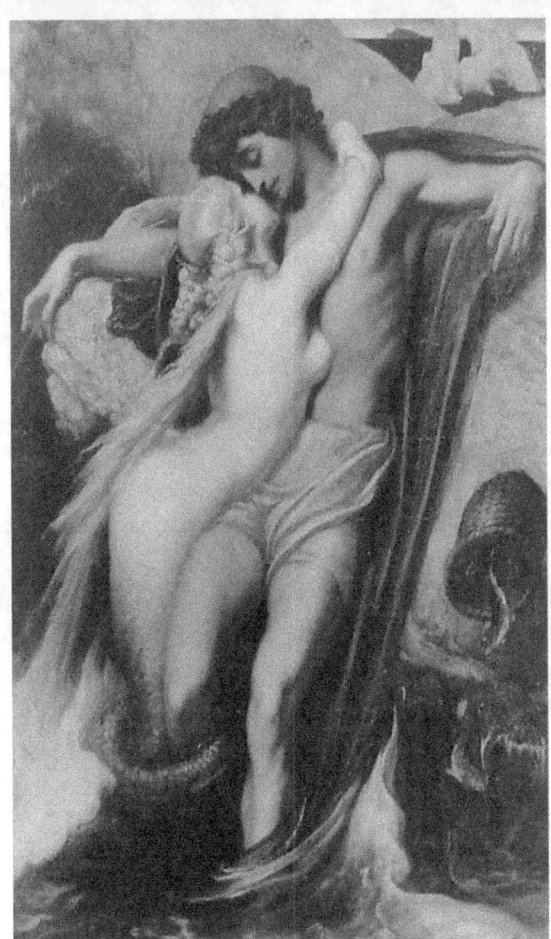

Classic Victorian nude imagery, by Lord Leighton: The Fisherman and the Siren,
1858, Bristol, above; and Actaea, the Nymph of the Shore, 1868, Ottawa, below.

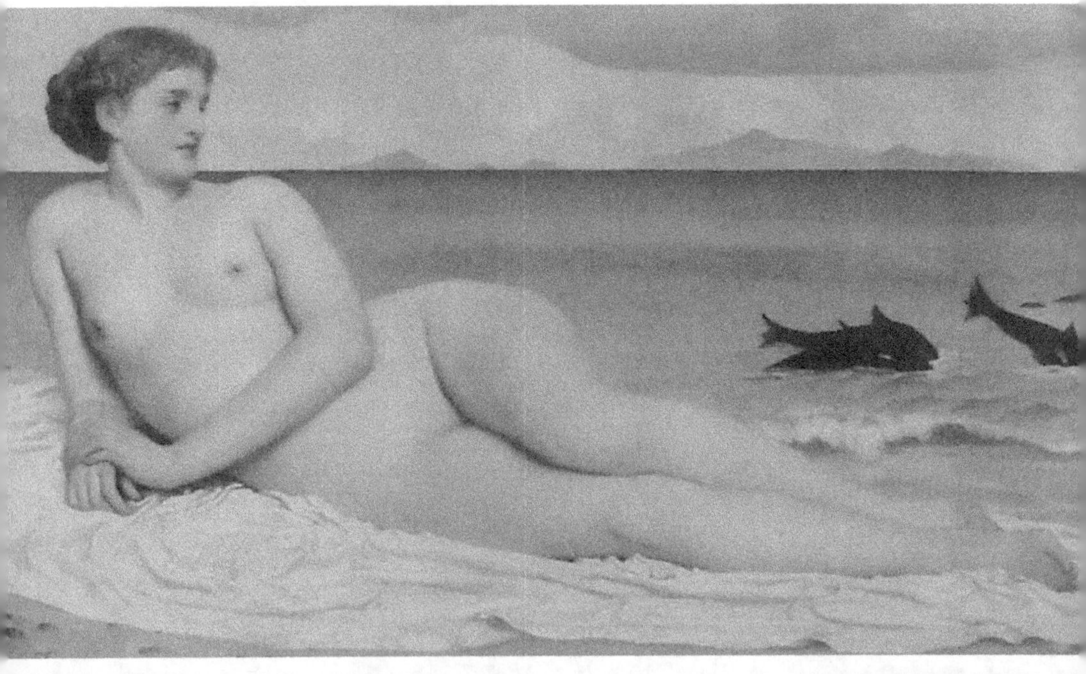

OTTO GRENIER: *THE DEVIL SHOWING WOMAN TO THE PEOPLE*

The depictions of women as mythical beings in Symbolist and Decadent are sometimes misogynistic, occasionally extremely so. If the 'holy whore', whether Aphrodite, Cleopatra or the Sphinx is the Queen or Goddess of Symbolist, Satan is undoubtedly the hero, which is only right for a culture founded on the Marquis de Sade and Charles Baudelaire. Women and death are merged throughout Western art. In many Symbolist pictures, for instance, the figure of death with the sickle is a woman,[1] while in Otto Greiner's *The Devil Showing Woman to the People*, Satan holds up a woman, naked of course, in stockings, of course, as a sex object.[2] Indeed, much of Symbolist art, and modern art, can be seen as 'the Devil showing woman to the people'. The Devil is the artist, showing women in various forms of sexual objectification, from 'high art' nudes to hardcore pornography.

---

1 in Odilon Redon's *Death: My Irony Surpasses All Others*, 1889, lithograph, 26 x 19cm (from Flaubert's *The Temptation of St. Anthony*, another key work of the Symbolist/Decadent era), Bibliothéque Nationale, Paris; Félicien Rops: *Mors Syphilitica*, Bibliothéque Nationale, Paris; Alfred Kubin: *The Best Medicine*, 1901-2, pen and India ink, 17 x 29cm, private collection; Gauguin: *Madame La Mort*, 1899, charcoal and India ink, 24 x 29cm, Musée d'Orsay
2 Otto Greiner: *The Devil Showing Woman to the People*, 1897, chalk on paper, 39 x 29cm, Art Gallery of Ontario, Toronto

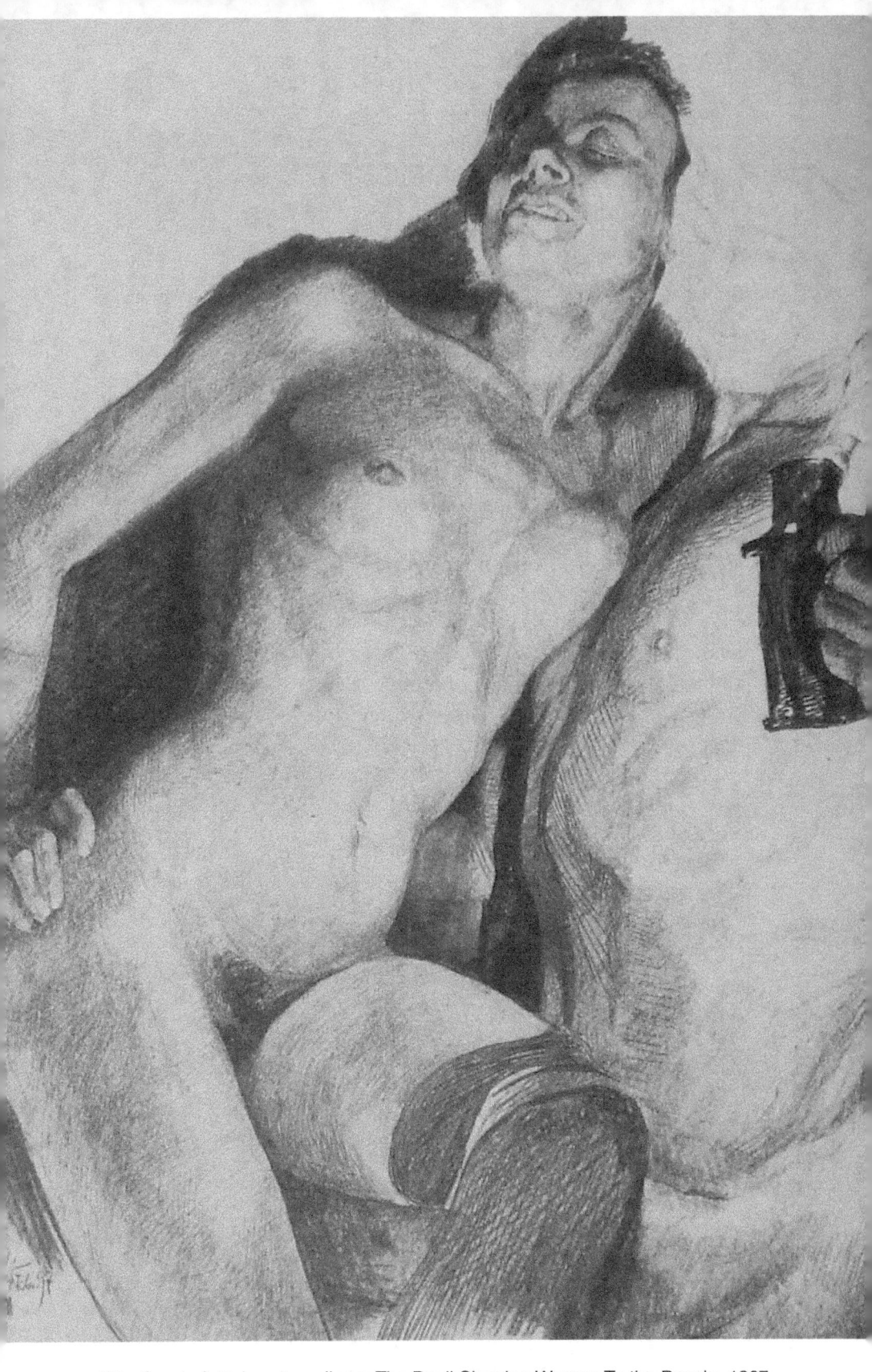

Otto Grenier's truly extraordinary The Devil Showing Woman To the People, 1897

GUSTAVE MOREAU

Gustave Moreau's world is supremely heterosexist. Women conform to stereotypes, to whores, witches, virgins, maidens, etc. Semele swoons over the radiance of the god Jupiter. Moreau's painting is the apotheosis of the religious cult of Symbolism and Decadence, which makes a religion of æsthetic depictions of sex and death and decadence. The word, *decadence*, from Paul Verlaine, connotes profuse amounts of eroticism, debauchery, declining state power, Imperialism and 'perversions'.

Gustave Moreau's is the poet's painter, the painter of 'poetic' visions, someone whom J.-K. Huysmans praised in the Bible of the Decadent era, *À Rebours* (*Against Nature*). Moreau is the painter of pure emotion: 'I only believe what I do not see and uniquely what I feel', he remarked.[1] Moreau's art brings together all the crucial elements of Symbolist art; the mysticism, eroticism, nostalgia (for Byzantium, Greece, Rome), Imperialism, romanticism, decadence, occultism and dreams.

---

1 G. Moreau, quoted in J. Paladilhe, 134

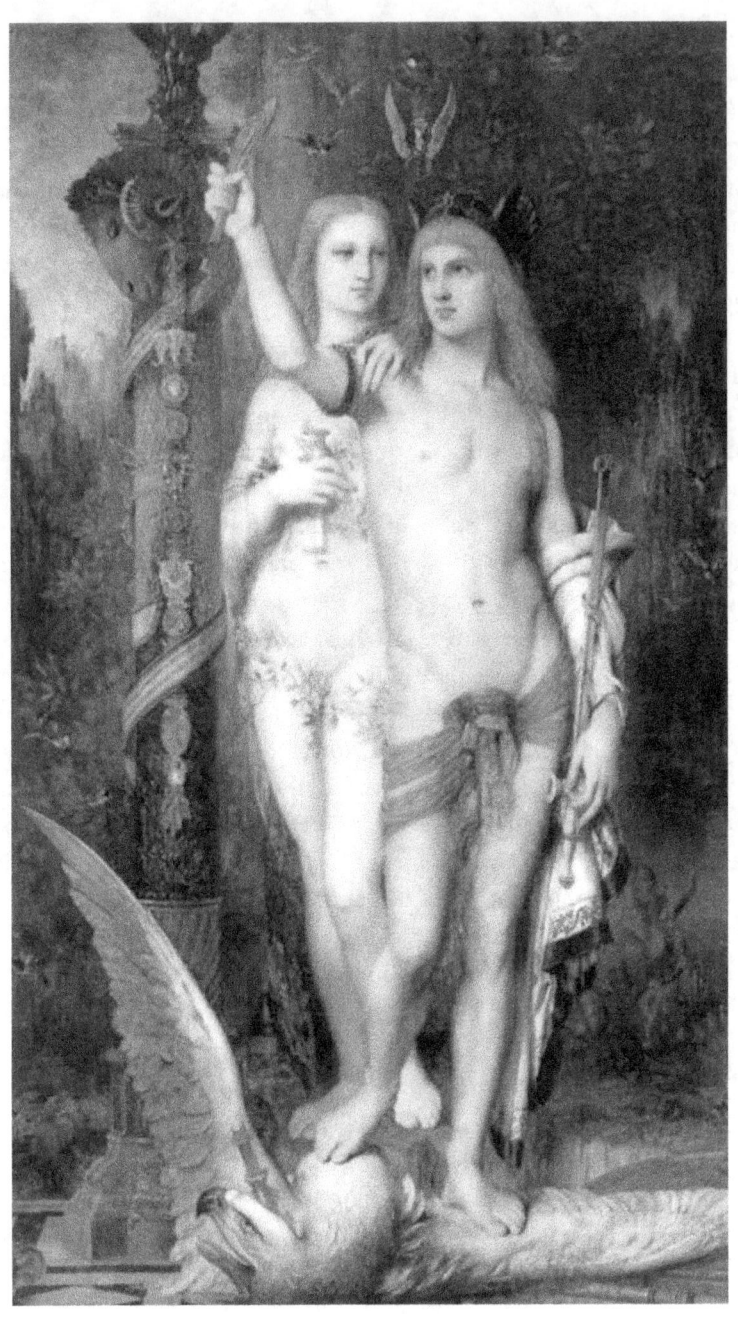

Gustave Moreau, Jason and Medea

GUSTAVE MOREAU

Gustave Moreau's paintings are soaked in dream imagery – not the hallucinatory sort that people think can only be obtained from by use of LSD – but by the visions of poets have in their dreams. Dreams of ancient and timeless worlds, where rituals or mysterious scenes, such as Salomé dancing, or Hercules amongst Thespius' daughters, occur endlessly and statically.[1] Moreau's world is of an eternal Orphic dreaming: he painted Orpheus' head on the lyre, as did Odilon Redon, who is even dreamier than Moreau, if that is possible.[2] Moreau's people seem to be asleep, when they are not wide awake with religious enlightenment. Salomé in many drawings and paintings dances with eyes closed.[3]

The half-asleep figures emphasize the passivity and interiority of Gustave Moreau's mythopoeic world. There is little confrontation, although there is anguish and pain aplenty. Salomé dominates his art. She is the ultimate castrating force. For Freudians, Salomé in Moreau's art is the return of the castrating mother. Moreau's famous *The Apparition* orchestrates in the most decorative and stylized manner, more mannered than Mannerist art, more baroque than Baroque art, more romantic than Romantic art, the anguish of fear and desire, the fear of rejection and loss, the craving for contact and sublimation.[4]

1 G. Moreau: *Salomé Dancing Before Herod (Tattooed Salomé)*, 1876, oil on canvas, 92 x 60cm, Gustave Moreau Museum, Paris; *Hercules Among the Daughters of Thespius*, begun 1852, oil on canvas, 258 x 255cm, Gustave Moreau, Paris
2 Odilon Redon: *Orpheus*, c. 1913-6, pastel, 70 x 57cm, Cleveland Museum of Art; Moreau: *Thracian Girl Carrying the Head of Orpheus*, 1866, oil on canvas, 154 x 99.5cm, Louvre, Paris
3 G. Moreau: *Salomé Carrying the Head of St John the Baptist*, pencil and ink, 30 x 19cm, Gustave Moreau Museum, Paris; *Salomé*, study, oil on wood, 23 x 33cm, Gustave Moreau Museum, Paris; *Salomé*, pencil, 60 x 36cm, Gustave Moreau Museum, Paris
4 G. Moreau: *The Apparition*, 1876, watercolour on paper, 106 x 72cm, Louvre, Paris

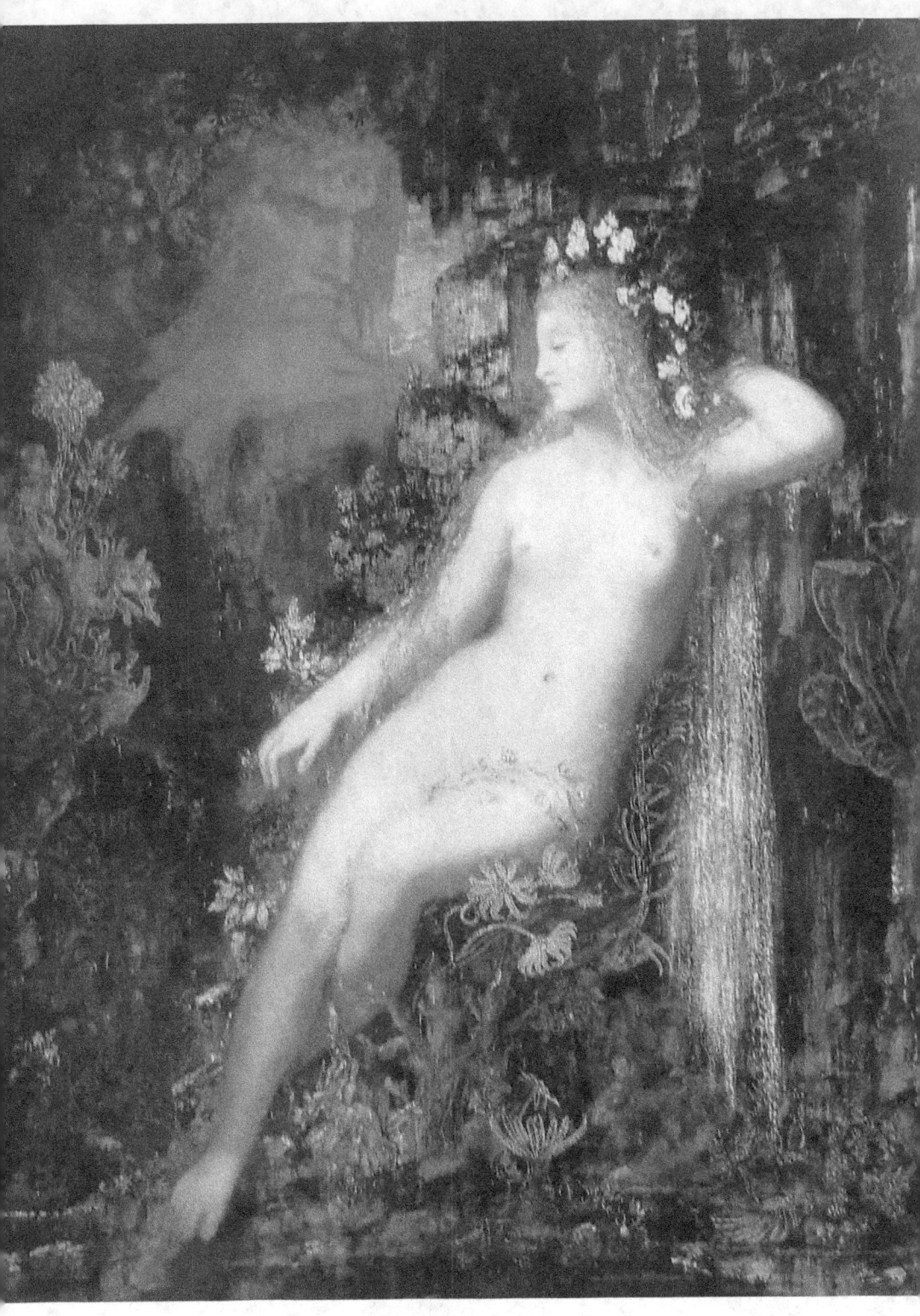

Gustave Moreau, Galatea, 1880

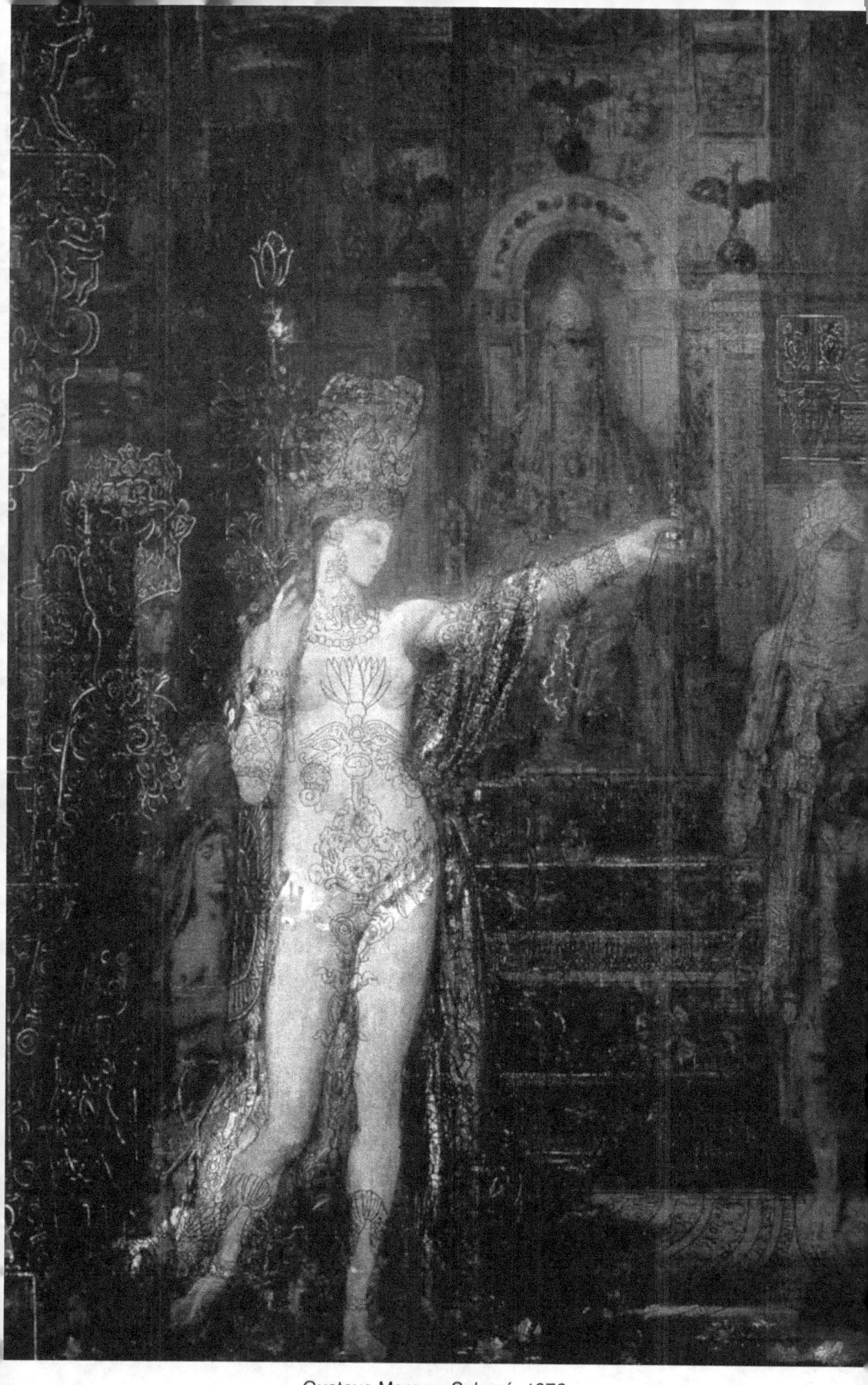

Gustave Moreau, Salomé, 1876

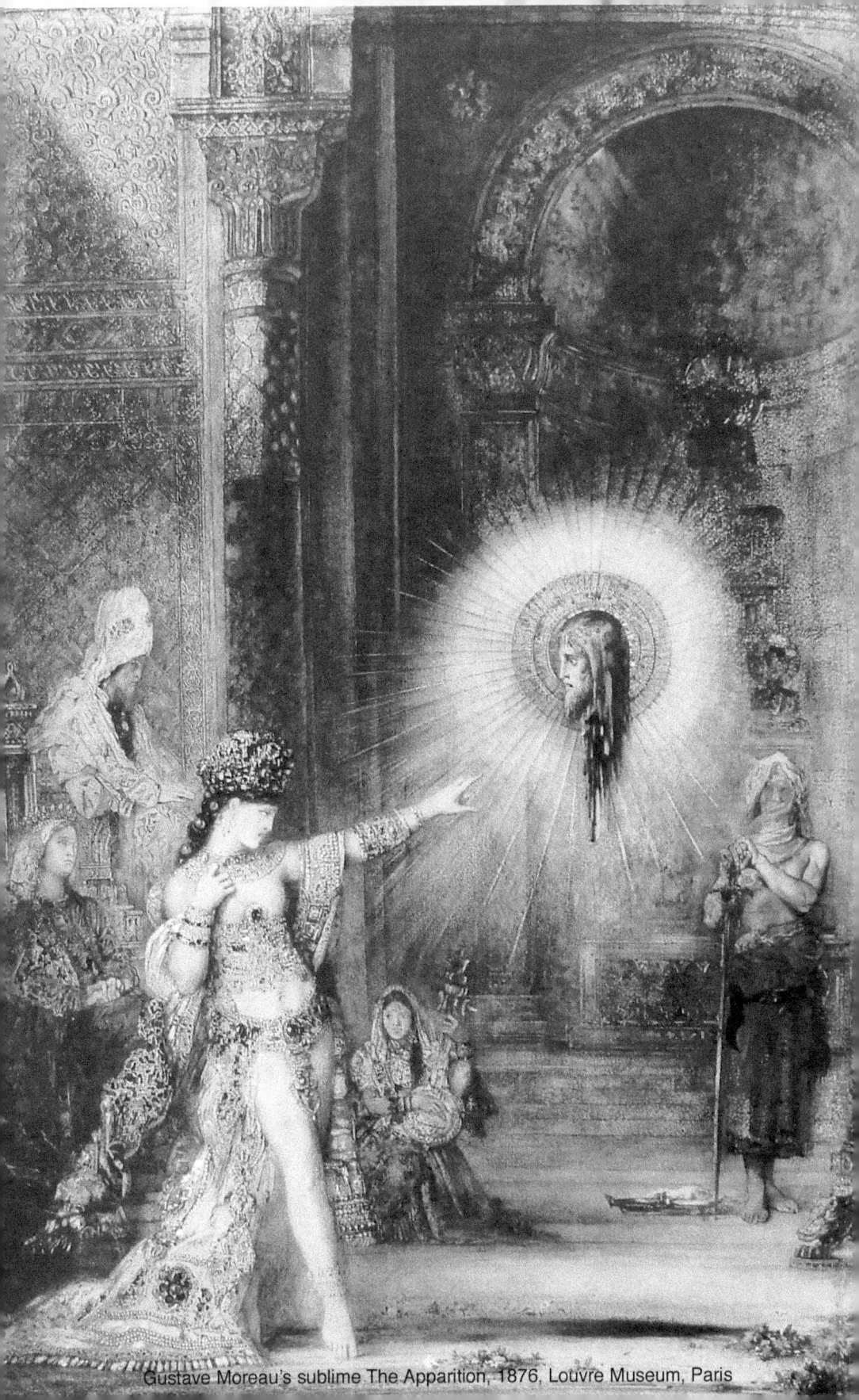

Gustave Moreau's sublime The Apparition, 1876, Louvre Museum, Paris

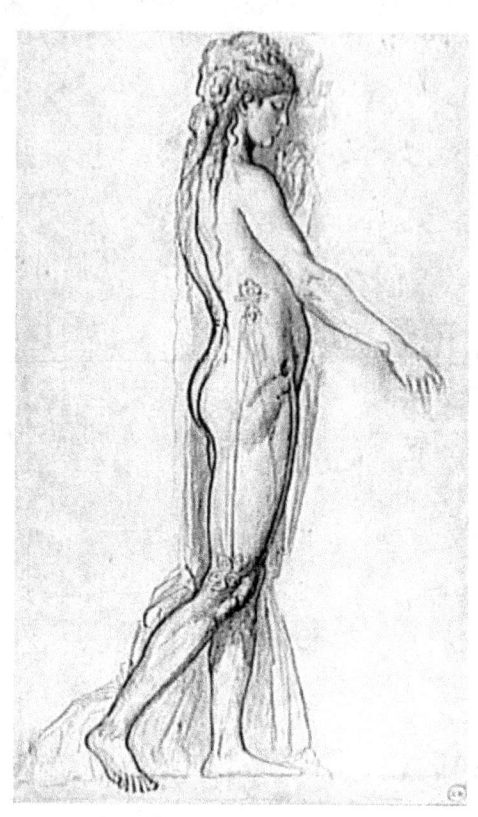

Gustave Moreau, Study for
Salomé (above)

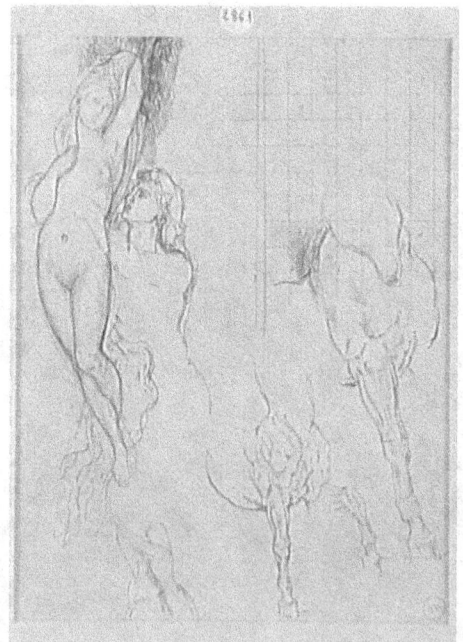

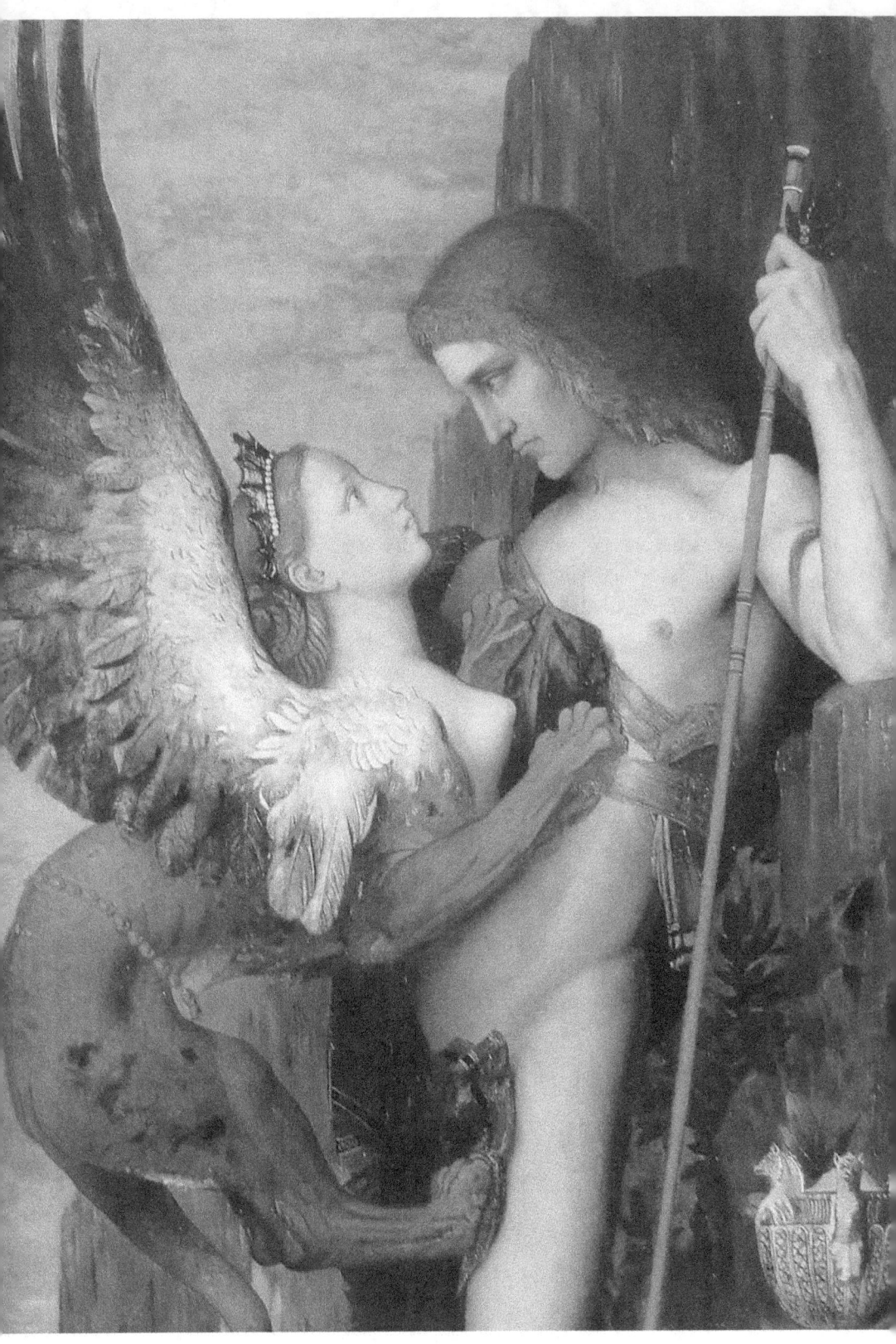

Gustave Moreau, The Sphinx

GUSTAVE MOREAU

However astonishing the fantastical but realist paintings of the Pre-Raphaelites or any 19th century artist may be, those of the French master Gustave Moreau outdo them all. He is the supreme champion of 'fantasy art', of any kind. His paintings are the richest imaginable, in terms both of content – in the exotic, Byzantine architecture, the incredibly ornate costumes, the flamboyant gestures – and of physicality and technique.

For Gustave Moreau's paintings, when he finished them, are extraordinarily densely painted. Layers of oil are laid upon each other, so that the surface of the amazing *Jupiter and Semele* is actually jewel-like.[1] *Jupiter and Semele* is an image of pure sex: it is manufactured deliberately to be an orgasmic and orgiastic feast for the eye, where the pleasure of looking causes multiple orgasms. Moreau's painting is as voluptuous as painting can get. It is a multiple voluptuousness, because the form and the content breed continuously, creating myriad pleasures. The painterly technique, the drawing, the colours and the forms combine with the images of Greek, Byzantine, Roman and Oriental architecture to create a marvellous vision of phallic power. For Jupiter (Zeus) is the supreme phallic god of antiquity – he lusts after and rapes just about every Goddess he can. Sitting on his throne, Jupiter in Moreau's last completed painting is a phallus, adored by the woman swooning in bliss beside him.

---

1 Gustave Moreau: *Jupiter and Semele*, 1896, oil on canvas, 213 x 118cm, Musée Gustave Moreau, Paris

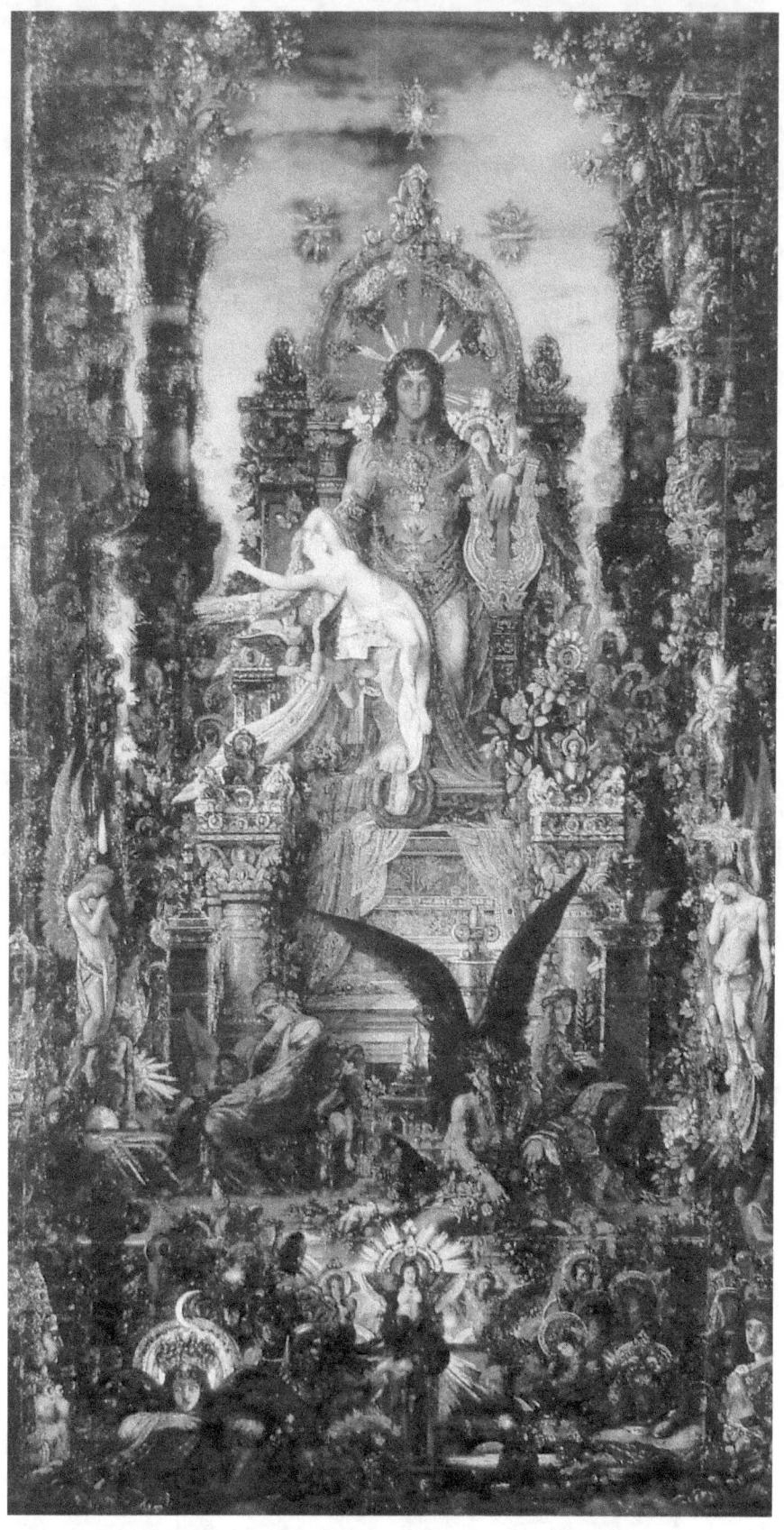

One of Gustave Moreau's masterpieces: Jupiter and Semele, 1896, Paris

JEAN DELVILLE

Only Jean Delville, with the exception of Félicien Rops, comes closest to Gustave Moreau's extravagant vision. Painters such as William Blake, Henry Fuseli and John Martin had depicted phantasma-gorical vistas, but Moreau's art is the apotheosis of visionary art. Delville, like Odilon Redon and Moreau, painted Orpheus' head, and emphasized the dreaming nature of art (floating heads were popular in Symbolist art).[1] It was Deville who created that archetypical image of *fin-de-siècle* occultism, the bizarre portrait of the wife of the Symbolist poet Stuart Merrill.[2] Like Fernand Khnopff's *I Lock the Door Upon Myself*, Delville's image is marked by haunted eyes, weirdly bright eyes which stare at the viewer.[3] These eyes are possessed, perhaps by spirits, born from some ectoplasmic Spiritualist evening session in Paris.

It is Deville who provides the wildest depiction of the King of late 19th century art, Satan, in *Trésor de Satan*, where the fiery archangel dances manically over a flow of nude bodies writhing in a Rubens-like manner at the bottom of the sea.[4] More writhing nude bodies occur in Delville's *L'Amour des Ames*, where the lovers are rising amidst swirls of fire and light above the sea. It is a cosmic image, with its stars and planets in the background, reminiscent of theosophical imagery, the pictures done under hypnosis, like those of A.E. Waite and the Golden Dawn artists.[5] But Delville's most powerful image is that of the extraordinary Goddess in the aptly titled *Idol of Perversity*, which is a phrase that could apply to much of Symbolist and Decadent art, which made idols out of perversity.[6]

1 Jean Deville: *Orpheus,* 1893, oil on canvas, 79 x 99cm, collection: Mme Gilléon-Growet, Brussels
2 J. Deville: *Portrait of Madame Stuart Merrill*, 1892, coloured chalk, collection: E. Jannss-Junior
3 F. Khnopff: *I Lock the Door Upon Myself*, 1891, oil on canvas, 72 x 140cm, Neue Pinakothek, Munich
4 J. Delville: *Trésor de Satan*, Musées Royaux des Beaux-Arts, Brussels
5 J. Delville: *L'Amour des Ames*, lithograph, Bibliothéque d'Art et d'Archélogie, Paris
6 J. Delville: *Idol of Perversity*, 1891, private collection

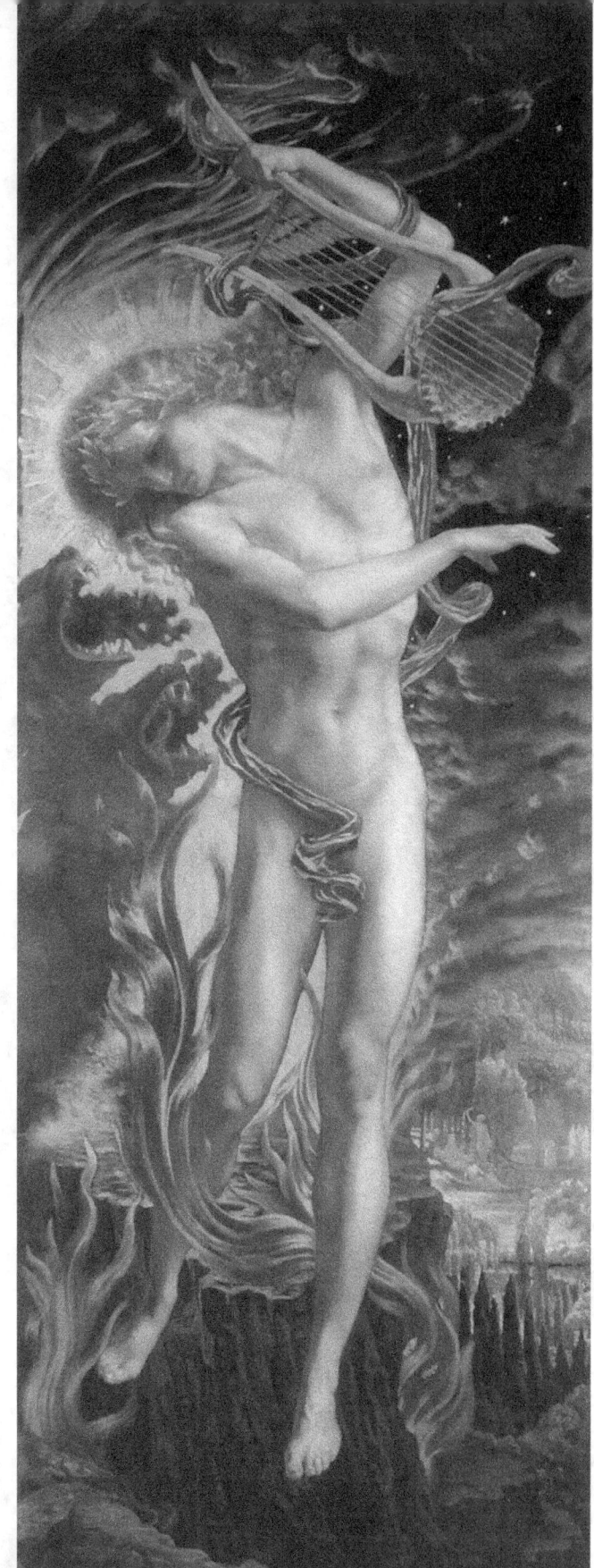

Jean Delville,
Orpheus,
late 19th century

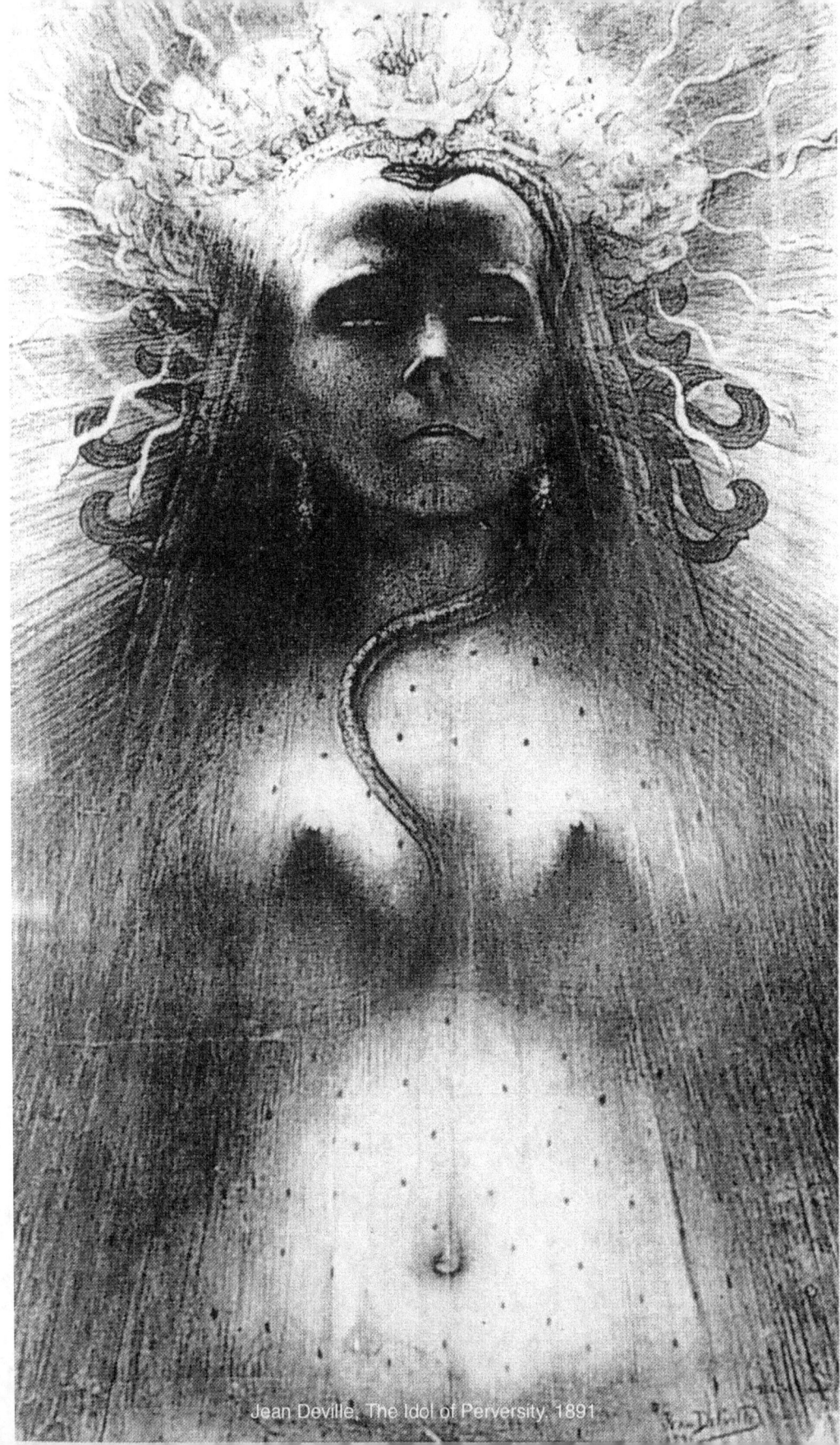
Jean Deville, The Idol of Perversity, 1891

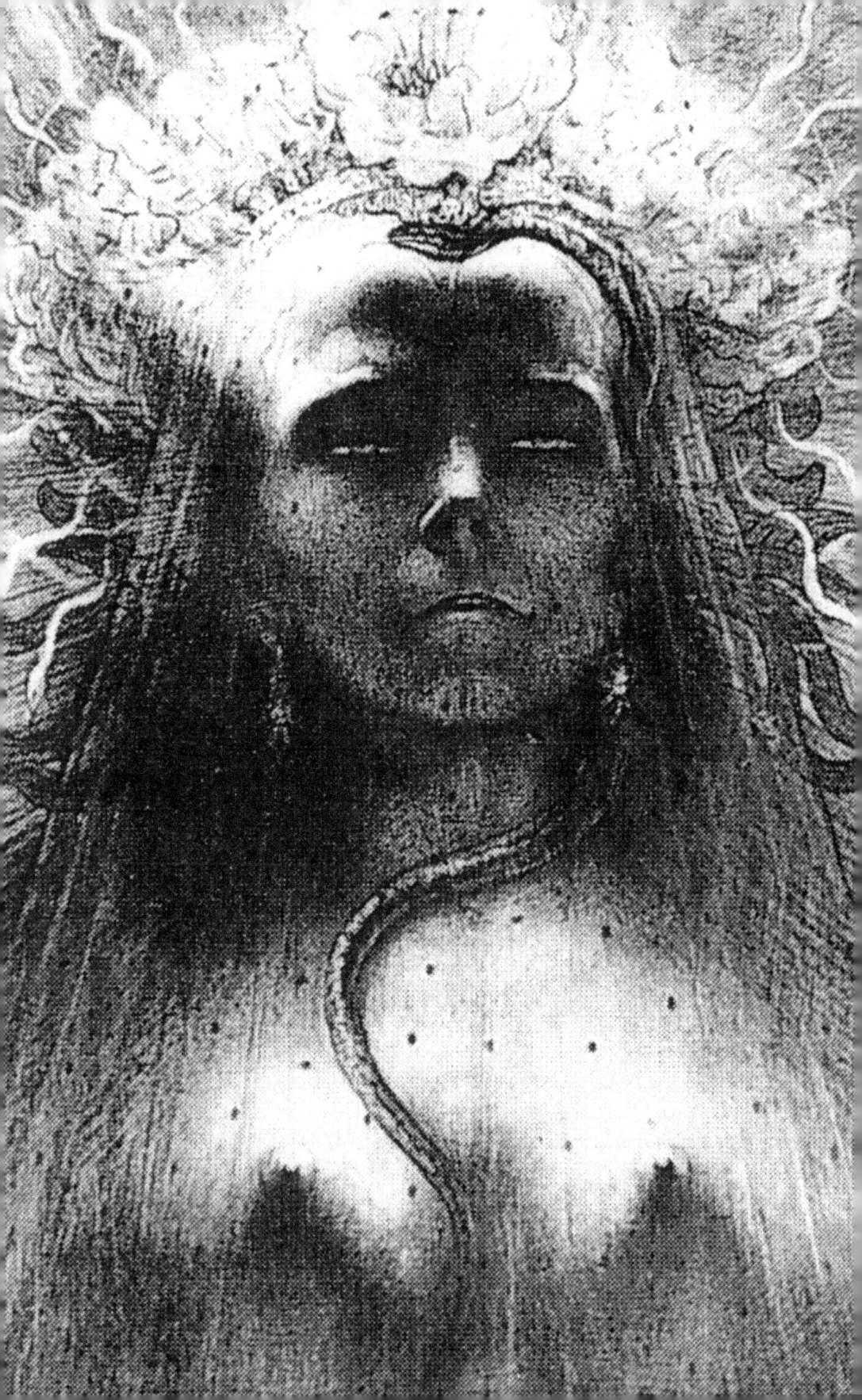

FÉLICIEN ROPS

In Félicien Rops' (1833-98) art, Satan appears as an ithyphallic wraith, like Pan gone Gothic, brandishing his erect penis as an image of terror. Erotic art centres on desire – psychologically and politically as well as physically. In *Les Sataniques*, a series of fantastical etchings, Rops fuses sex and death and religion: Satan is shown on the Cross, a blasphemous image in itself, for nowhere else in Western high art do we see Satan on Christ's Cross. Satan is strangling a woman (naked of course) with her own hair.

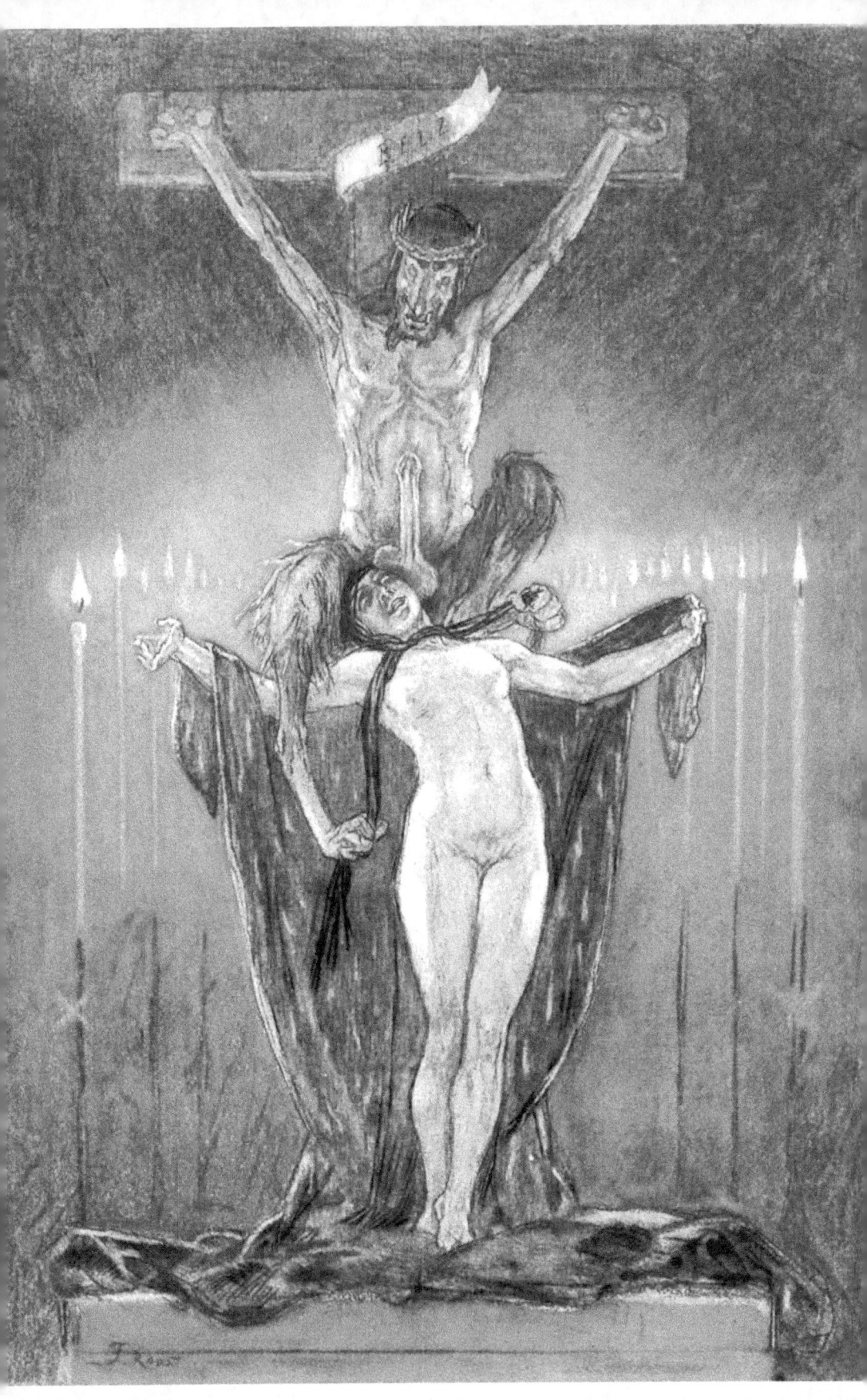

FÉLICIEN ROPS

Félicien Rops' images of torture and eroticism (erotic torture, or torturous eroticism) are also ridiculous. His image of Mary Magdalene masturbating in front of a little wooden cross upon which a phallus is crucified is hilarious.[1] She stares up at the crucified prick as she rubs herself between her legs. Great fun.

1 Rops: *Mary Magdalene*, c. 1885, collection: Simon Wilson, London

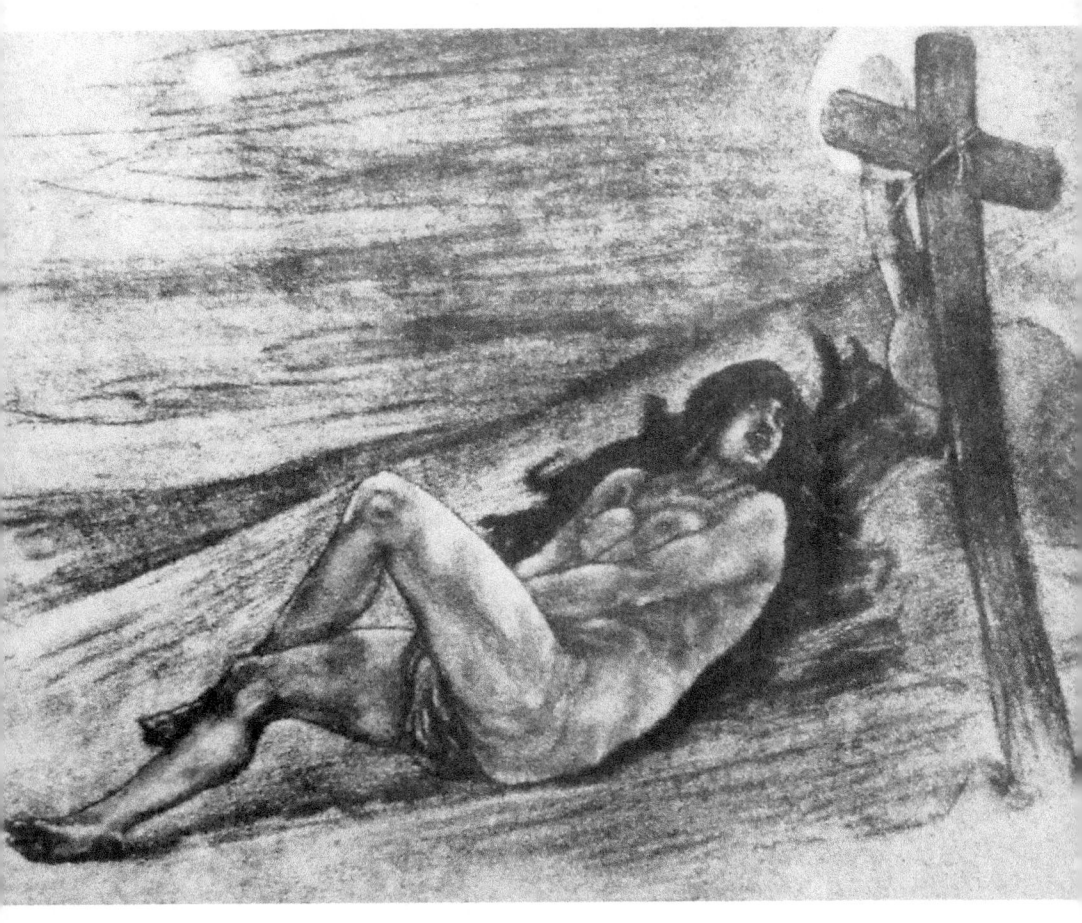

Felicien Rops, Mary Magdalene

FÉLICIEN ROPS

Félicien Rops' etchings are all cock, all phallic energy gone wild. A woman impales herself on the phallus of a statue of a crazily grinning Pan or Satan, flanked on each side by bizarre dwarf-like beasts, each holding up six foot erect penises. In another image, Satan appears as a ram's skull, a familiar motif (deriving again from Pan, perhaps). The phallus this time is a massive snake-like thing which curls downwards and enters a woman, who's naked of course.[1] The phallus becomes a ridiculous motif or image all too quickly. Many people have noted how silly it looks. Hence it is so heavily censored in the modern era, although we do see many phallic metaphors and equivalents – the thrusting red sports car, the articulated lorry, the tank, the missile, the jet plane, the atomic bomb, the gun, the knife, the skyscraper, the computer, all those 'tools' of modern life.

---

1 Rops: *Les Sataniques*, 1884, Piccadilly Gallery, London

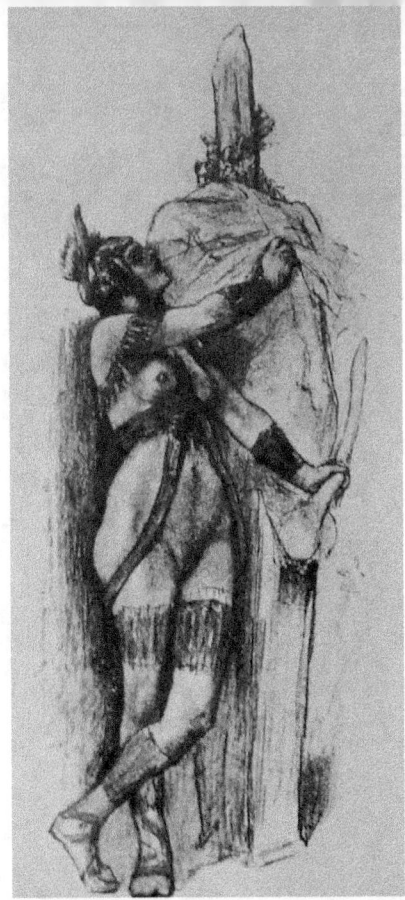

The inimitable Félicien Rops, French fin-de-siècle Decadence at its most extreme.

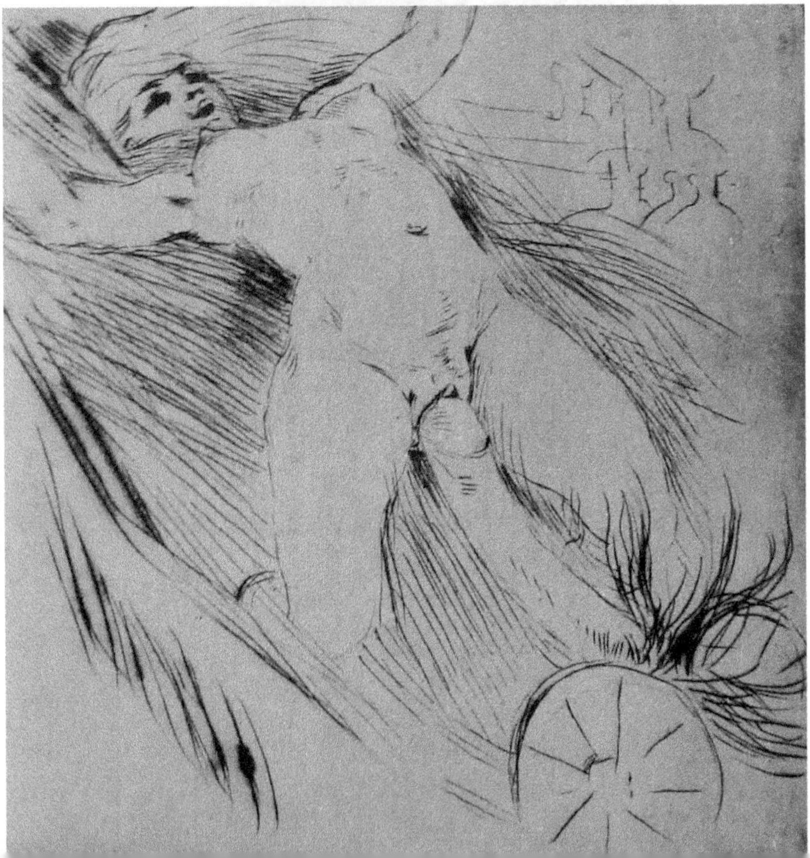

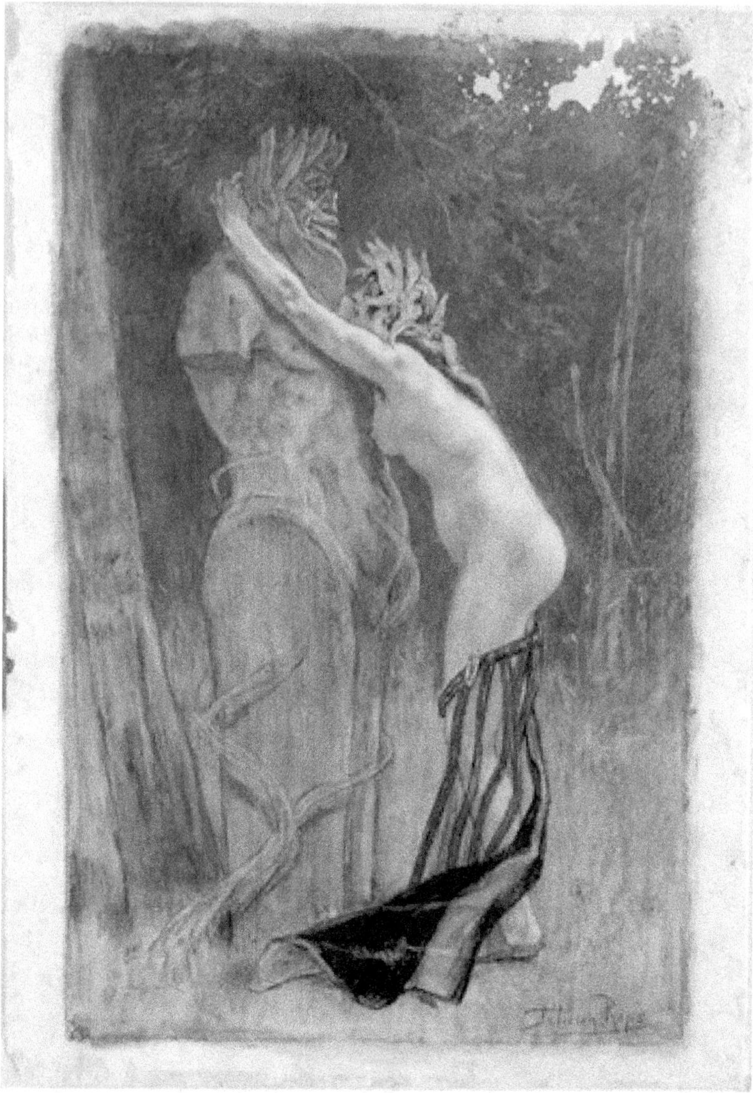

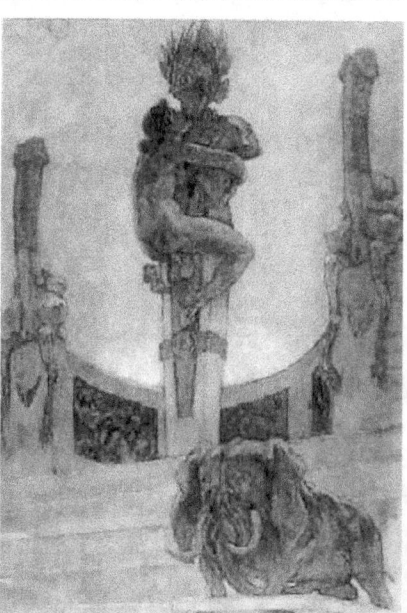

Félicien Rops, Hommage
To Pan (above)

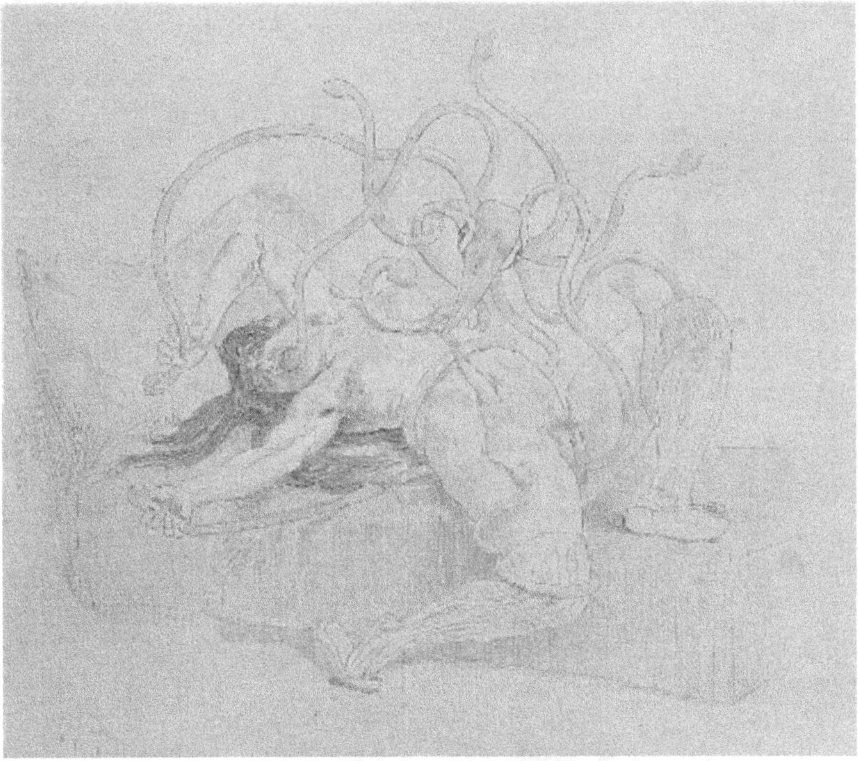

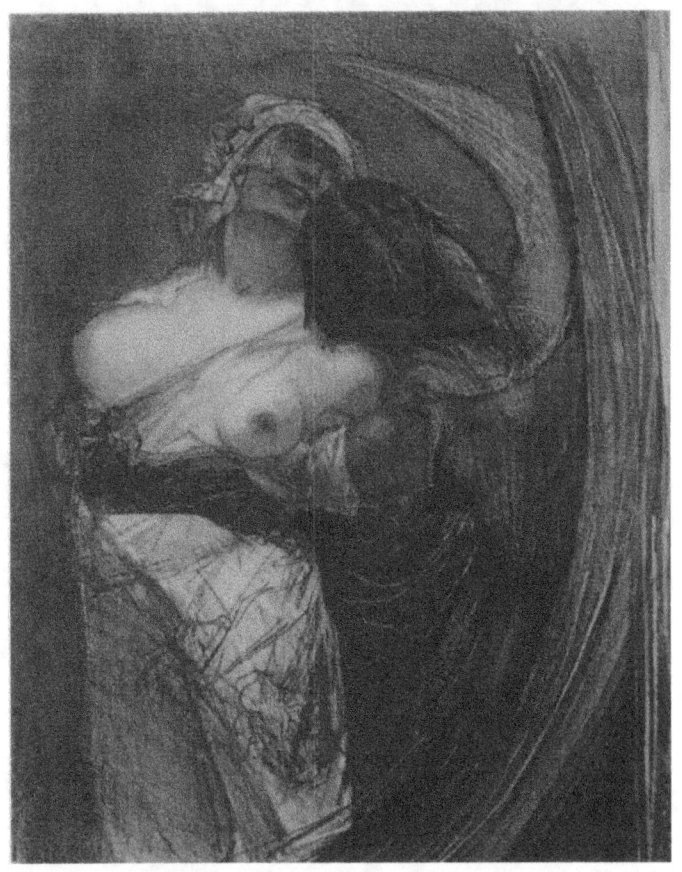

Félicien Rops, The Cold Devils, c 1860 (below).

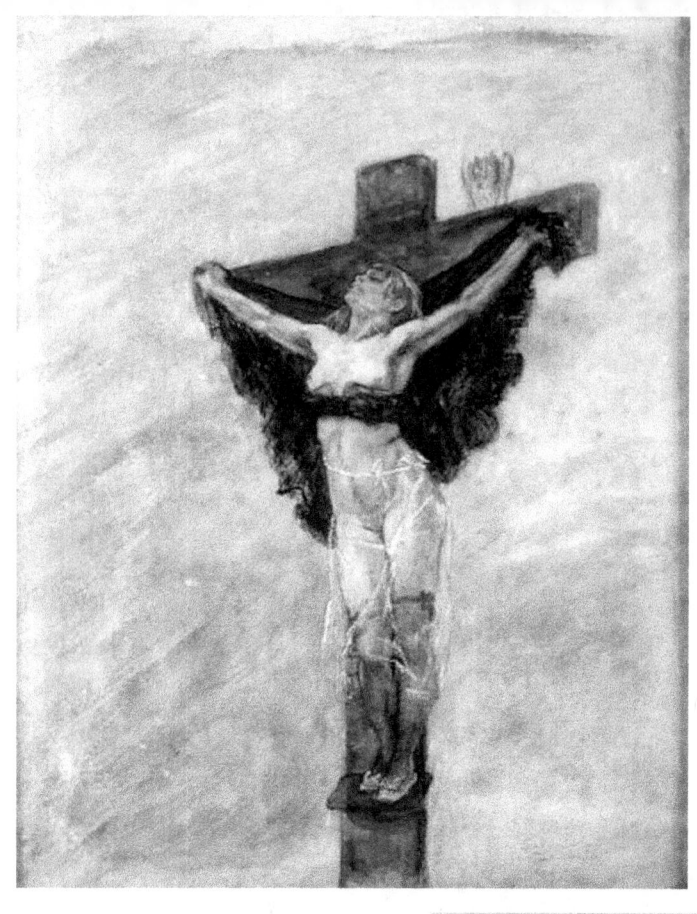

Félicien Rops

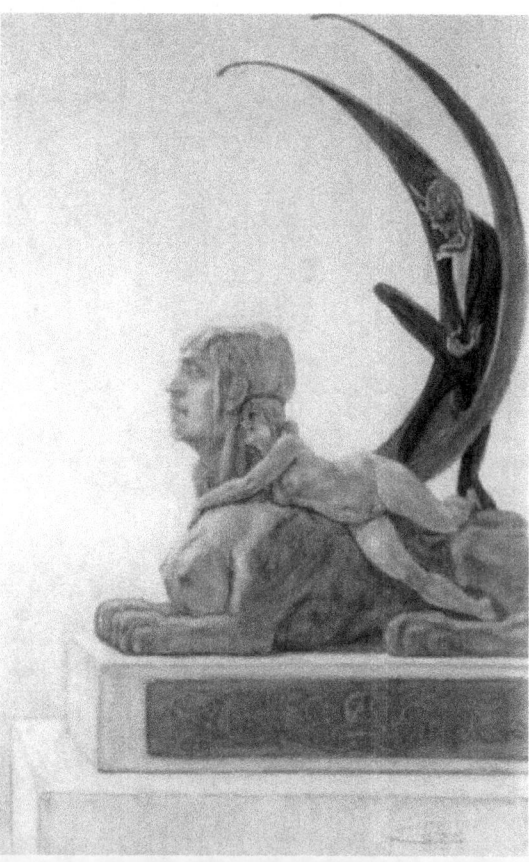

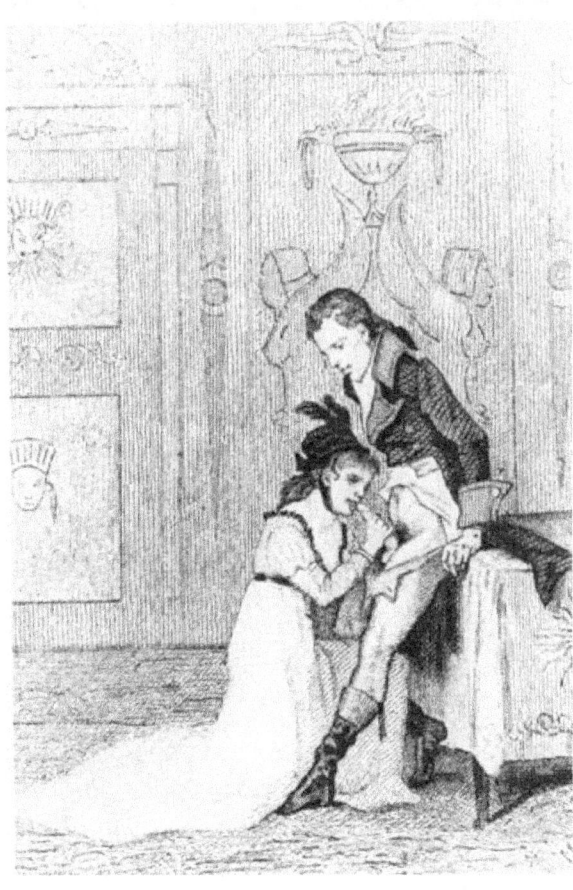

Félicien Rops, from Le Diable du Corps
by André-Robert Andréa de Nerciat
(1739-1800)

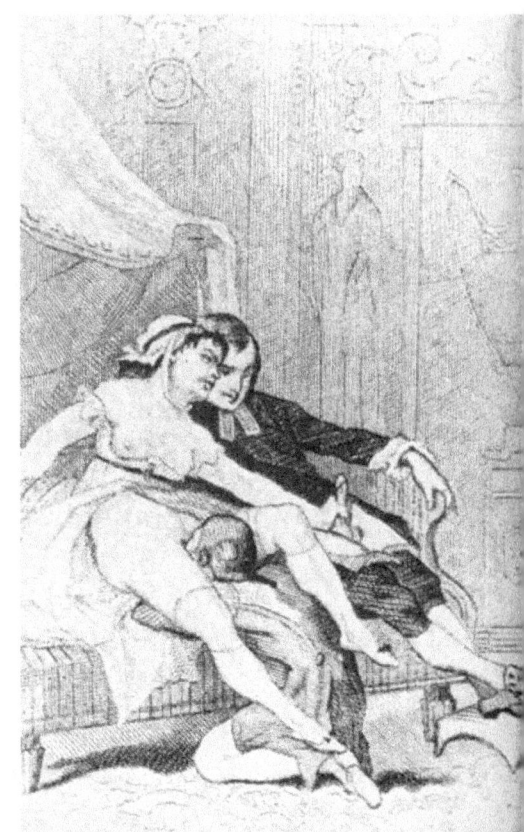

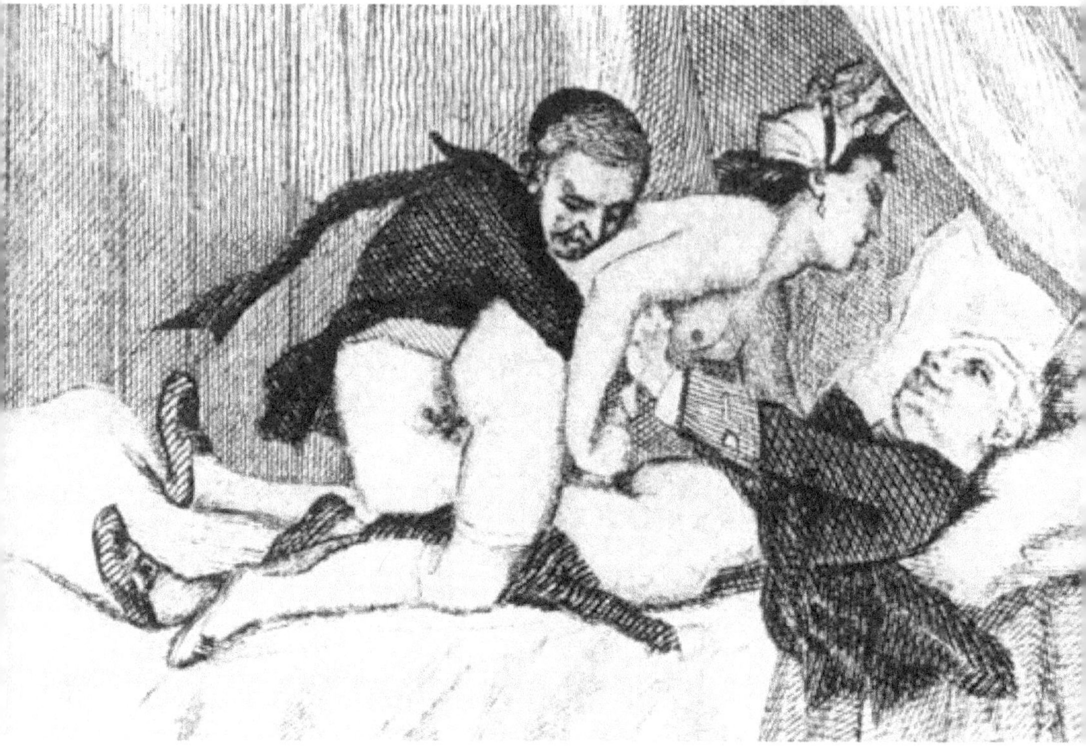

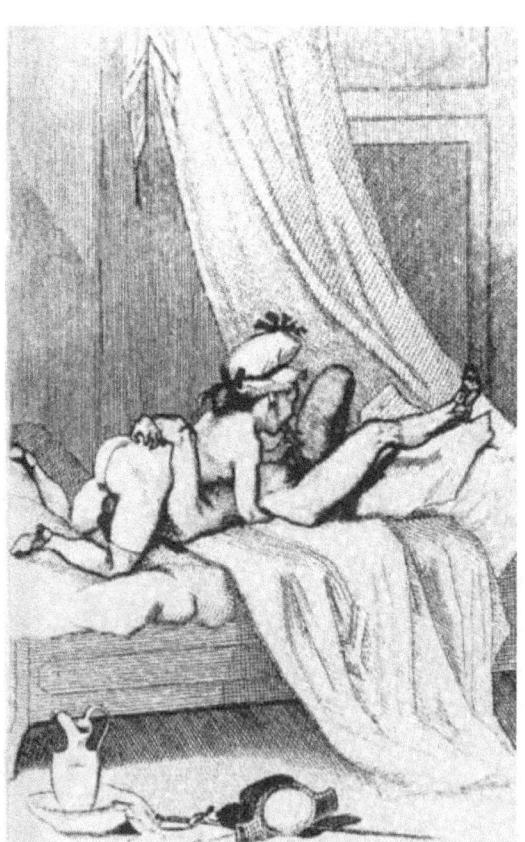

Félicien Rops,
Le Diable du Corps

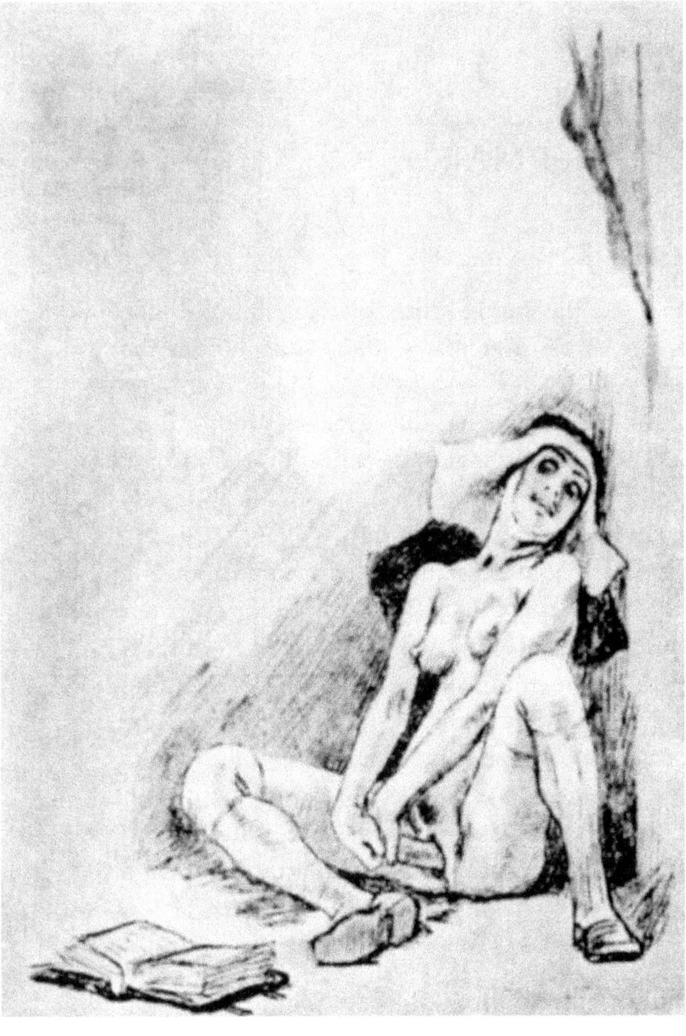

Félicien Rops, Sainte Thérèse
(left).

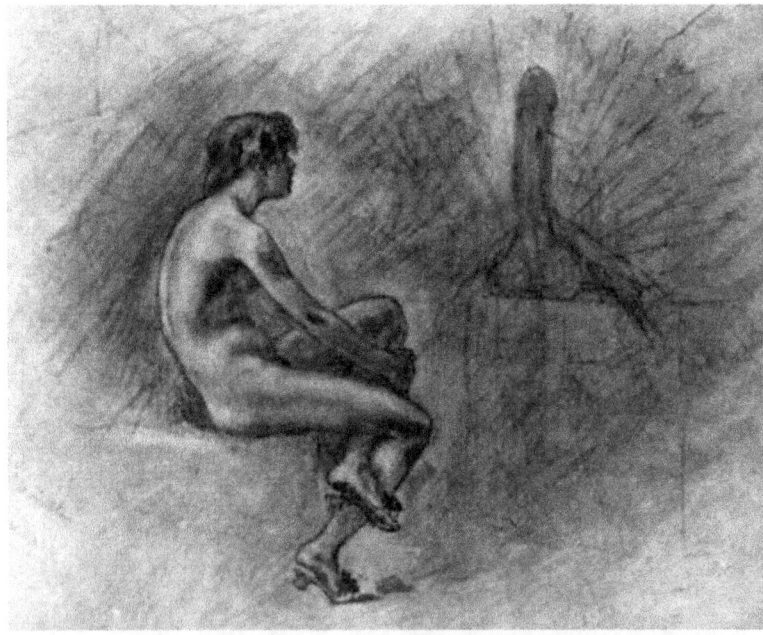

MERMAIDS

There is deep sexism in the Judæo-Christian Fall, for it is the woman who picks the apple and offers it to Adam. From the beginning, in the Judæo-Christian tradition, it is the woman who makes men 'fall'. In some depictions, the sexism is doubled, by having the serpent shown as a snake-woman – the torso of a woman, the legs, like those of a mermaid, as in Michelangelo Buonarroti's *Temptation and Expulsion* (1508-12).[1]

The symbol of the half-woman/ half-fish, still in use today,[2] is another manifestation of patriarchal people's projection of their sexual fears onto women, so that what lies 'below the waist' is feared and objectified as something slimy and fishlike, something dark, from the depths of the unconscious, which is the sea. The mermaid appears sculpted on mediæval churches, some of the mermaids expose their genitals, like the *sheila-na-gig* figure, which again fuses sacred and profane, spiritual and sexual, desire and fear.[3] The mermaid appears in much of Victorian art, as an image of men's ambivalent views of female sexuality – in E.M. Hale's *Mermaid's Rock* (1894), for instance, or John William Waterhouse's Pre-Raphaelite *A Mermaid* (1901).[4]

---

1 Michelangelo: *Temptation and Expulsion*, 1508-12, fresco, Sistine Chapel, Vatican, Rome
2 See the depiction of the Mary Magdalene in the wilderness sequence of Universal's film *The Last Temptation of Christ* (1988, USA)
3 See Anthony Weir & James Jerman: *Images of Lust: Sexual Carvings on Mediæval Churches*, B. T. Batsford, 1986, 48ff
4 John William Waterhouse: *A Mermaid*, 1901, 38.5 x 36.3in, Royal Academy of Arts, London; Edward Matthew Hale: *Mermaid's Rock*, 1894, 48 x 78in, City Art Gallery, Leeds

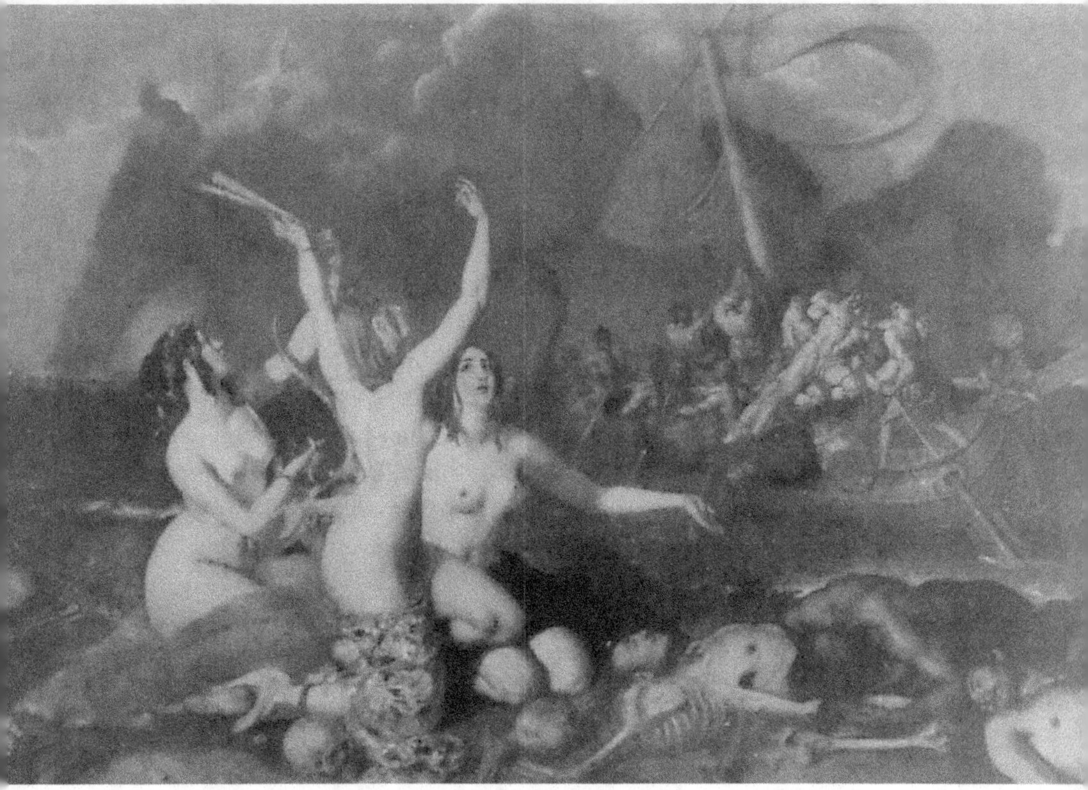

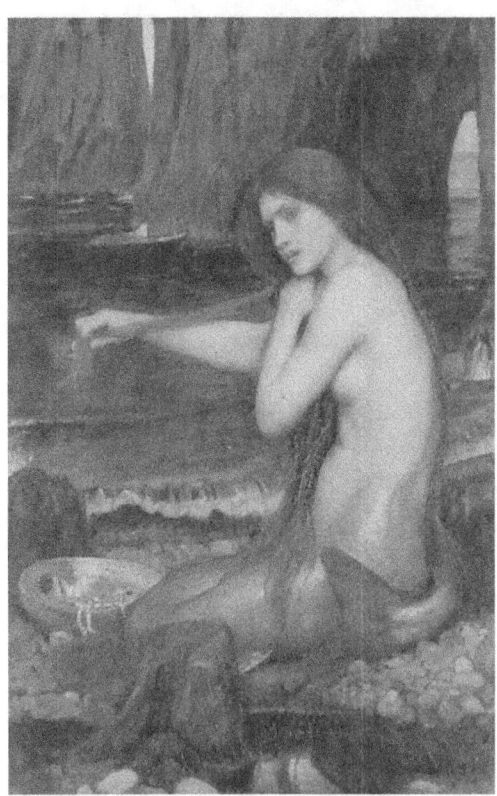

A favourite theme in 19th century painting: sex, death, nudity and the sea.
William Etty's The Sirens and Ulysses, 1837, Manchester. above.

J.W. Waterhouse,
A Mermaid, 1901, Royal Academy, London, below.

PRE-RAPHAELITES

Pre-Raphaelite art hides its gender bias under a surface of mediævalism, Gothic imagery, Arthurian motifs and a breathless romanticism. But the images of women are often stereotypical, reductive, eroticized: there is the purer-than-pure woman, with her unreal, pale skin, who bends wistfully like the Madonnas in Renaissance *Annunciations* (in Edward Burne-Jones' *The Baleful Head*)[1] or they are conniving, nefarious witches (as in the *Morgan Le Fay* painting of Frederick Sandys).[2]

British 19th century painters sometimes rival even Gustave Moreau, the most exotic of figurative visionaries, in the depiction of really bizarre and potentially sexist scenes. Frederic Leighton, for instance, painted a very voluptuous mermaid coiling her tail around a drowned sailor. It is a variation on the theme, depicted by Félicien Rops, Eric Gill and Auguste Rodin, among others, of a nude, long-haired woman, a Mary Magdalene figure, embracing a swooned, seemingly passive male.[3] Frederick Sandys' *Danaë* portrays a dreamy Goddess raising her arm to reveal her body. This painting is clearly pornography, right down to the thin dress she wears, revealing her breasts in a manner similar to women's wet Tee shirt contests.[4]

---

1 Edward Burne-Jones: *The Baleful Head*, 1885-7, oil on canvas, 155 x 130cm, Staatsgalerie, Stuttgart
2 Frederick Sandys: *Morgan Le Fay*, 1864, oil, Birmingham Art Gallery
3 Frederic Leighton: *The Fisherman and the Syren*, 1858, 26.5 x 18.5in, Bristol Art Gallery
4 Frederick Sandys: *Danaë in the Brazen Chamber*, 1867, chalk on paper, 26 x 17in, Bradford Art Gallery

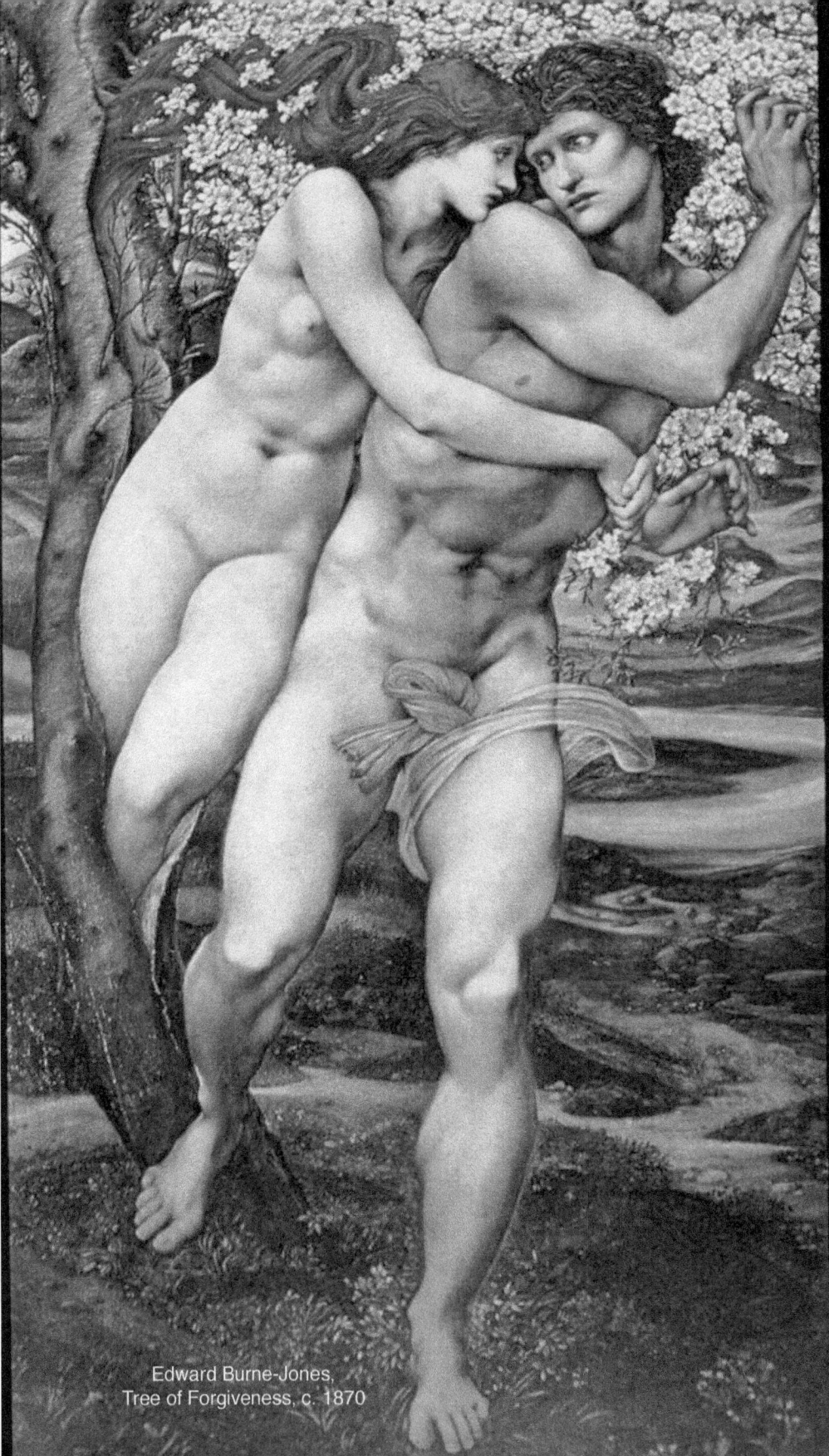

Edward Burne-Jones,
Tree of Forgiveness, c. 1870

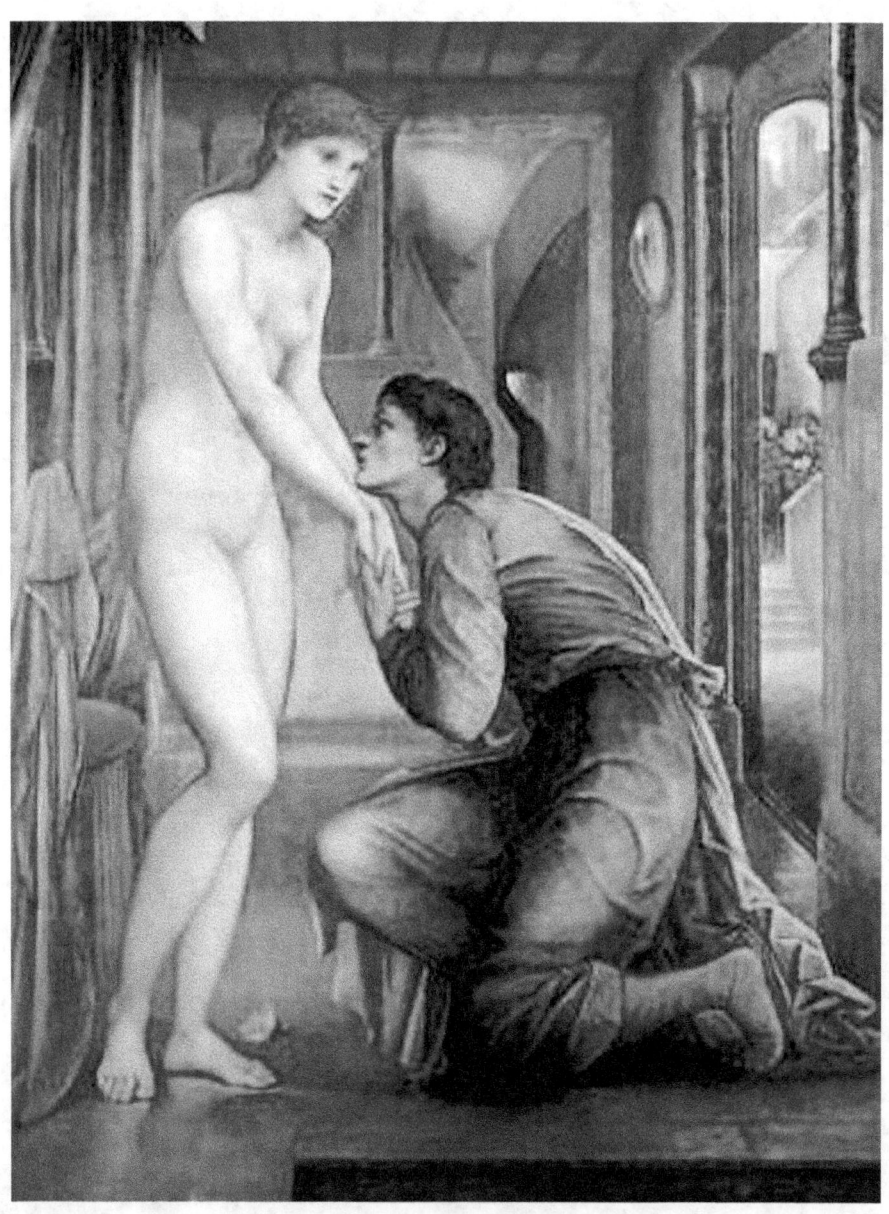

Edward Burne-Jones, Pygmalion, 1878, Birmingham, England

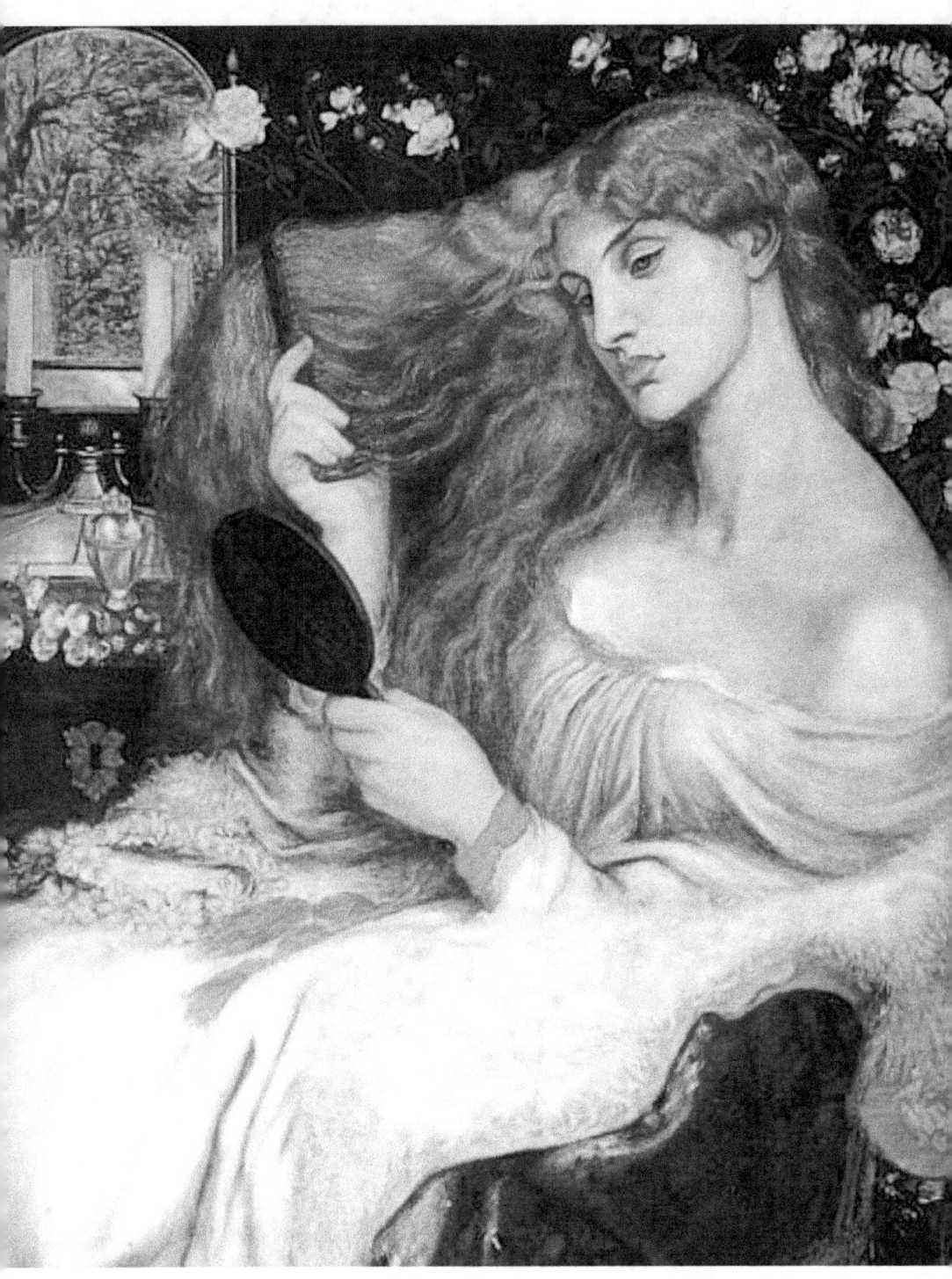

Dante Gabriel Rossetti, Lady Lilith, 1866-68, Delaware Art Museum

THOMAS ROWLANDSON

Thomas Rowlandson (1756-1827) is one of the great social commentators among British artists, capturing in a sprawling, vivacious and often humorous manner the variety of life in early modern Britain. His erotica is well-known, and a clear ancestor of saucy British postcard humour, of *Carry On* movies, of the nudge-nudge, wink-wink, *Monty Python* style of British comedy.

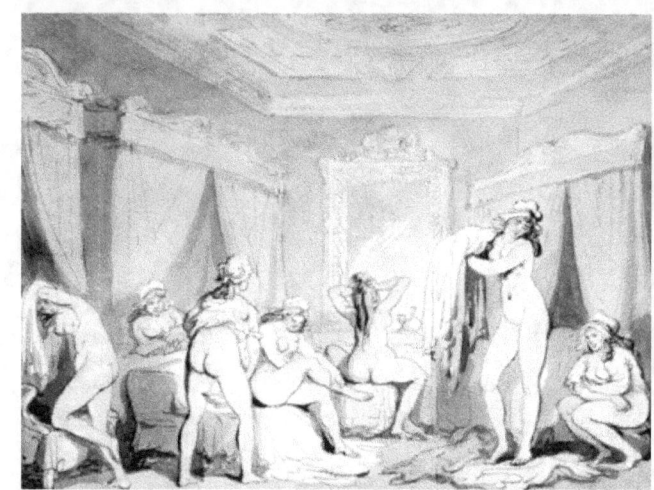

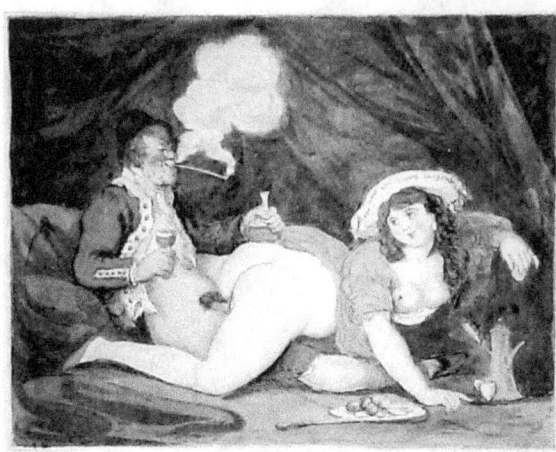

Thomas Rowlandson.
This page and following pages

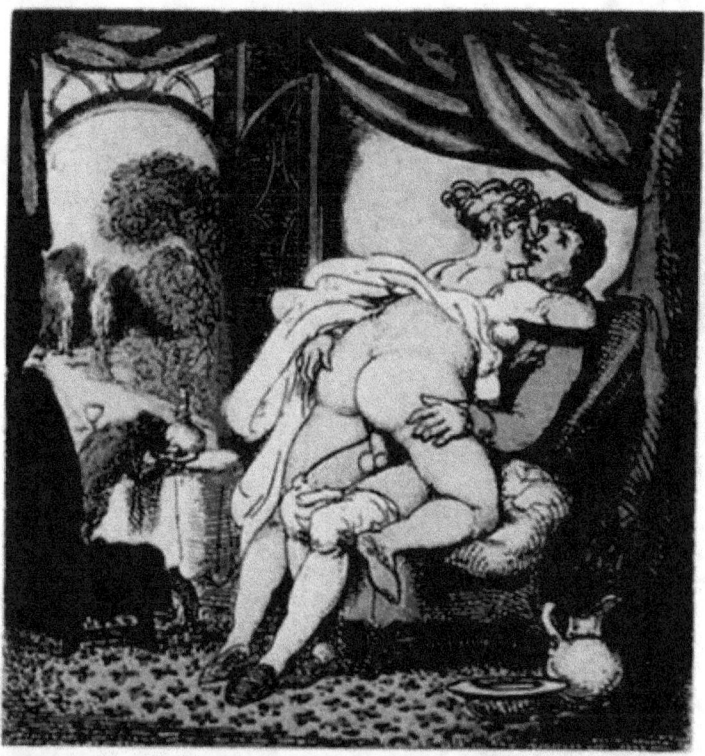

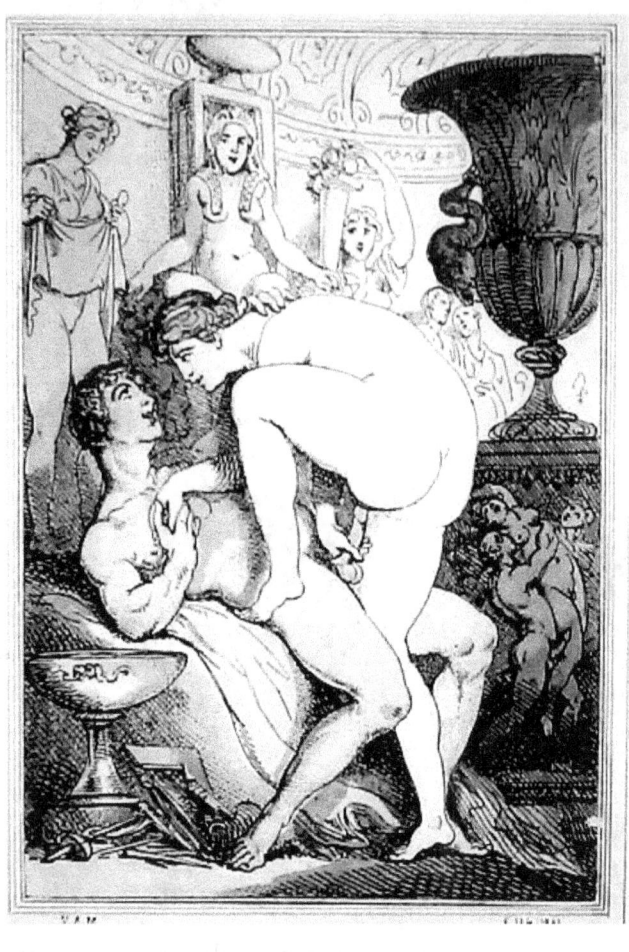

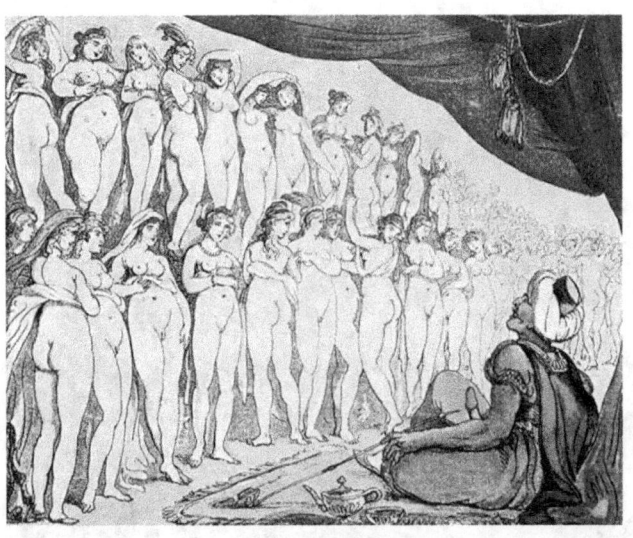

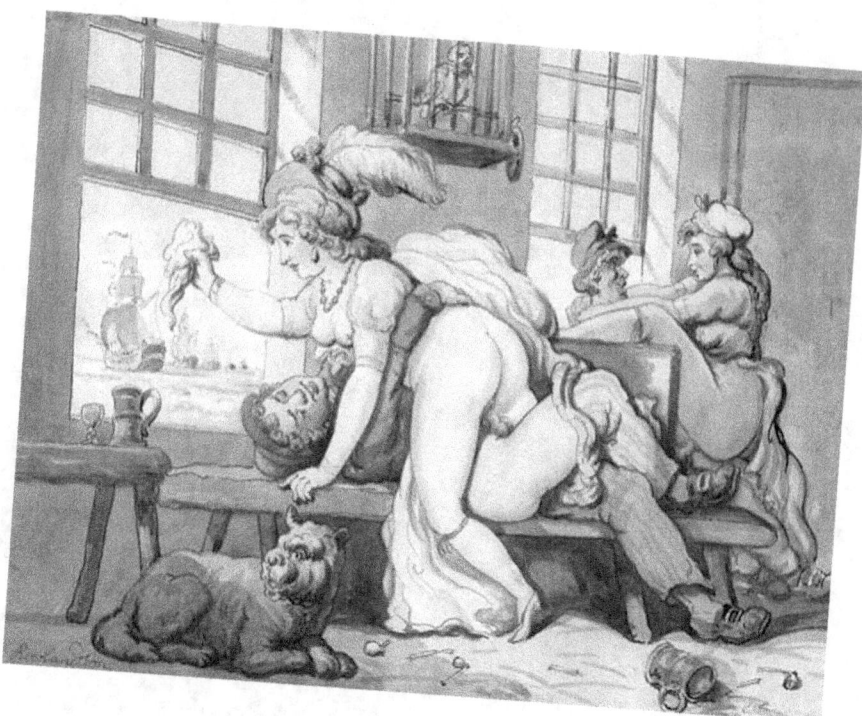

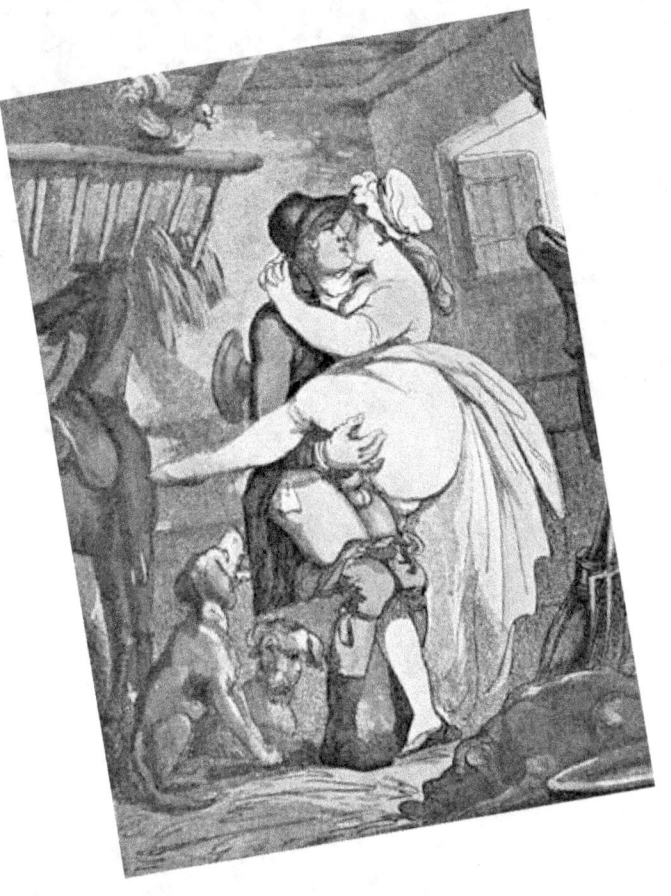

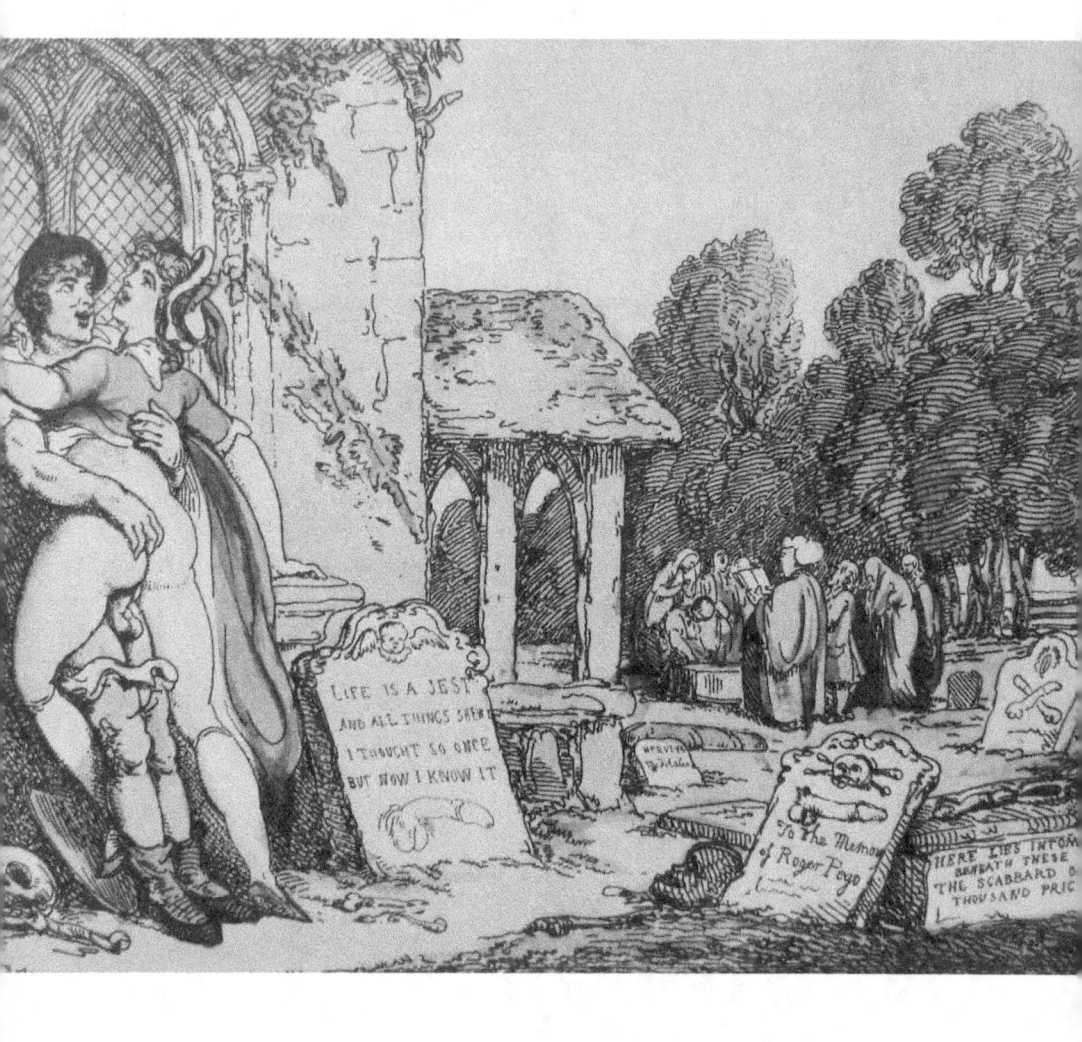

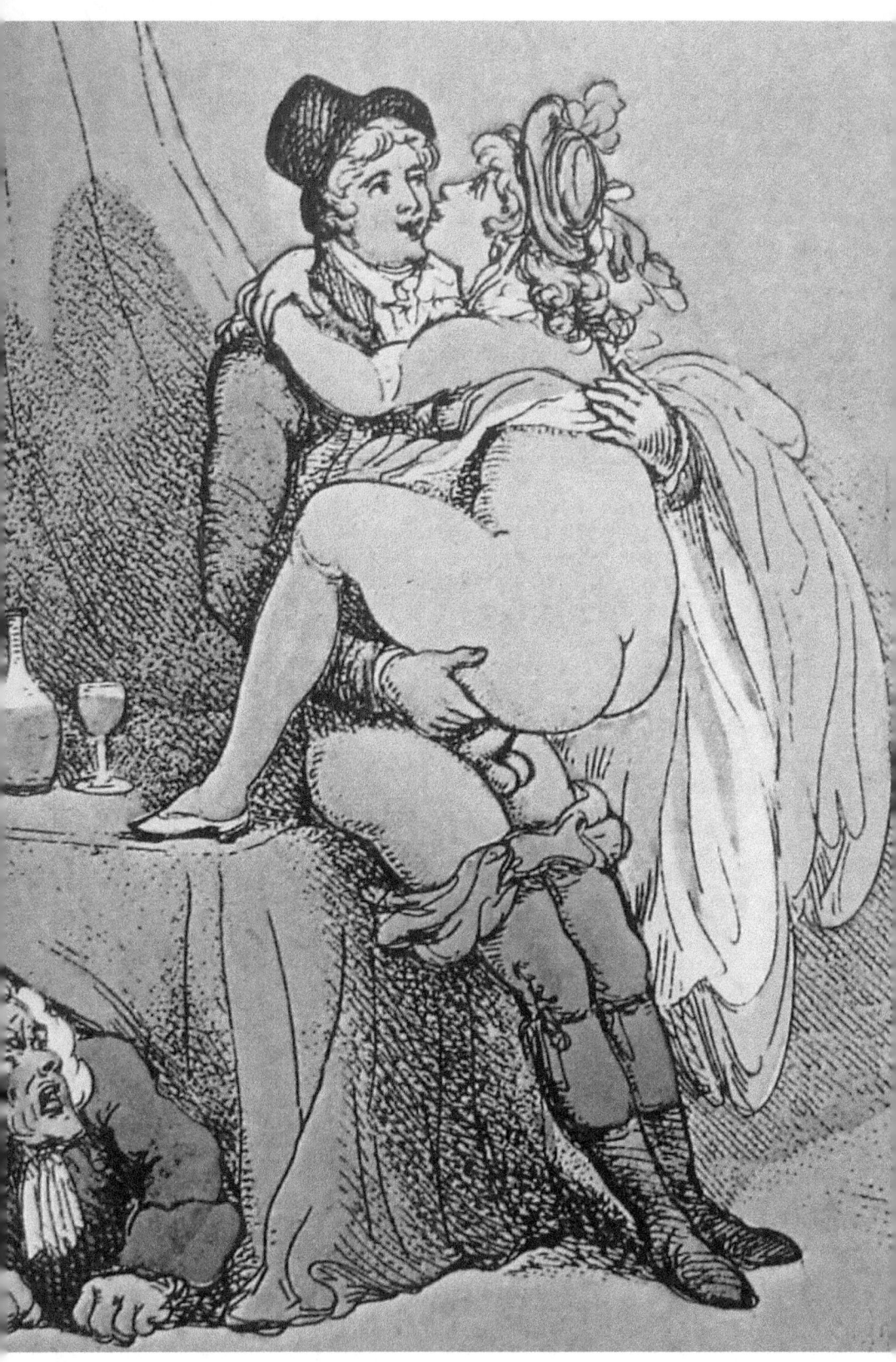

GUSTAVE COURBET:
ORIGIN OF THE WORLD

Gustave Courbet painted a woman's torso, seen from below. With her legs spread, the picture is really a close-up of a vagina, and is clearly pornographic. Maxime Du Camp described how Courbet's painting presented pornography as 'high art':

> In the dressing room of this foreign personage [the Turkish collector Khalil Bey] one sees a small picture hidden under a green veil. When one draws aside the veil one remains stupefied to perceive a woman, lifesize, seen from the front, moved and convulsed, remarkably executed, reproduced *con amore*, as the Italians say, providing the last word in realism. But, by some inconceivable forgetfulness, the artist, who copied his model from nature, had neglected to represent the feet, the legs, the thighs, the stomach, the hips, the chest, the hands, the arms, the shoulders, the neck, and the head.[1]

It has cosmic aspirations, for the title is *The Origin of the World*, again echoing the mythology of the Goddess, and woman as the site of all time and space.[2] For a long time the painting's whereabouts were apparently unknown: now it's on public view in the Musée d'Orsay in Paris.

1 Maxime Du Camp: *Les Convulsions de Paris*, Hachette, Paris 1889, II, 189-190
2 G. Courbet: *The Origin of the World*, 1867, Musée d'Orsay, Paris.

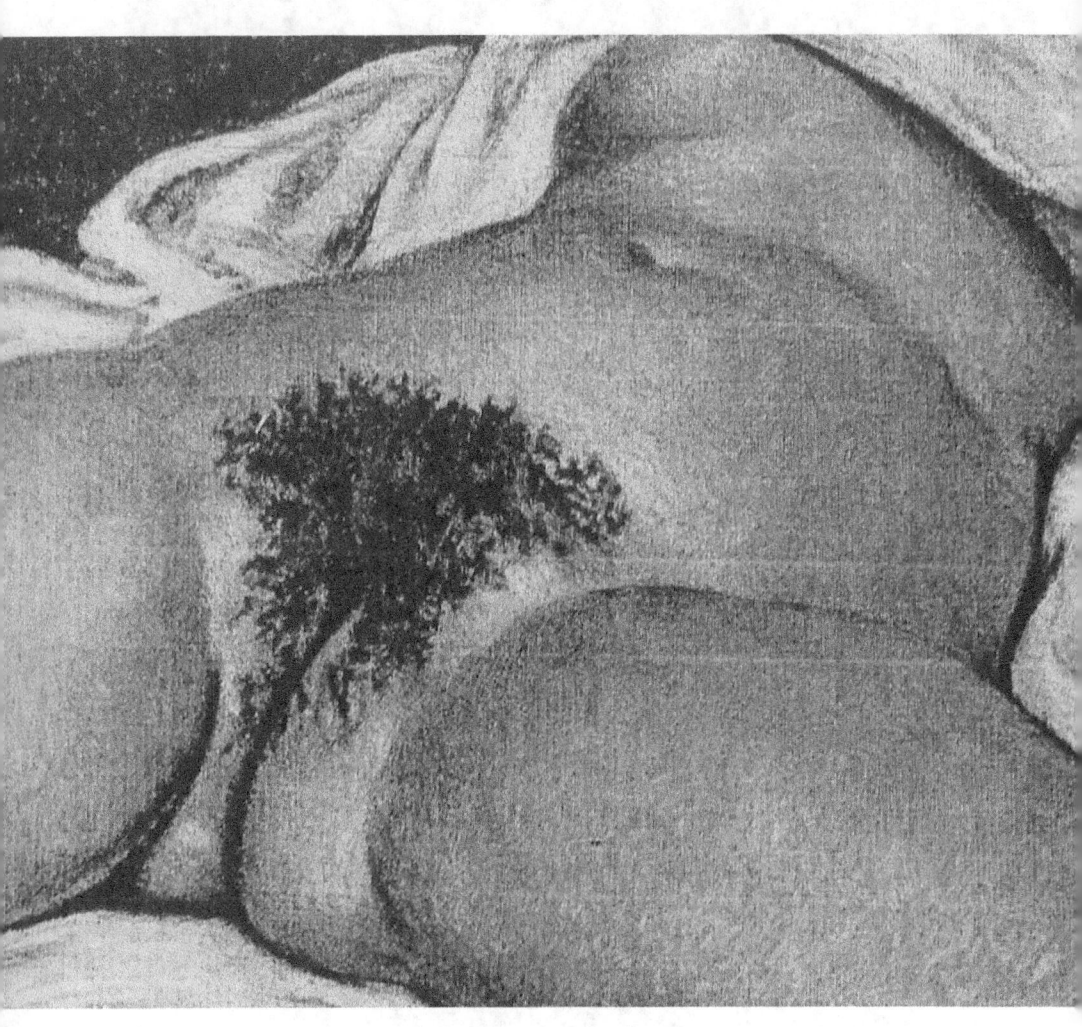

Gustave Courbet, The Creation of the World

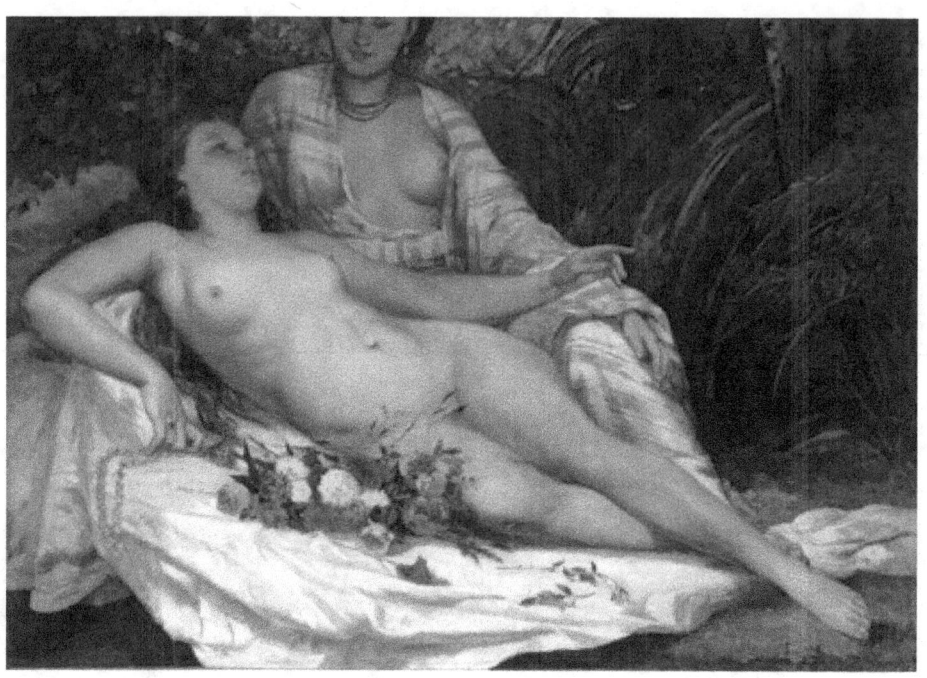

Gustave Courbet, Two Bathers (above).
Woman Lying Down, 1862.

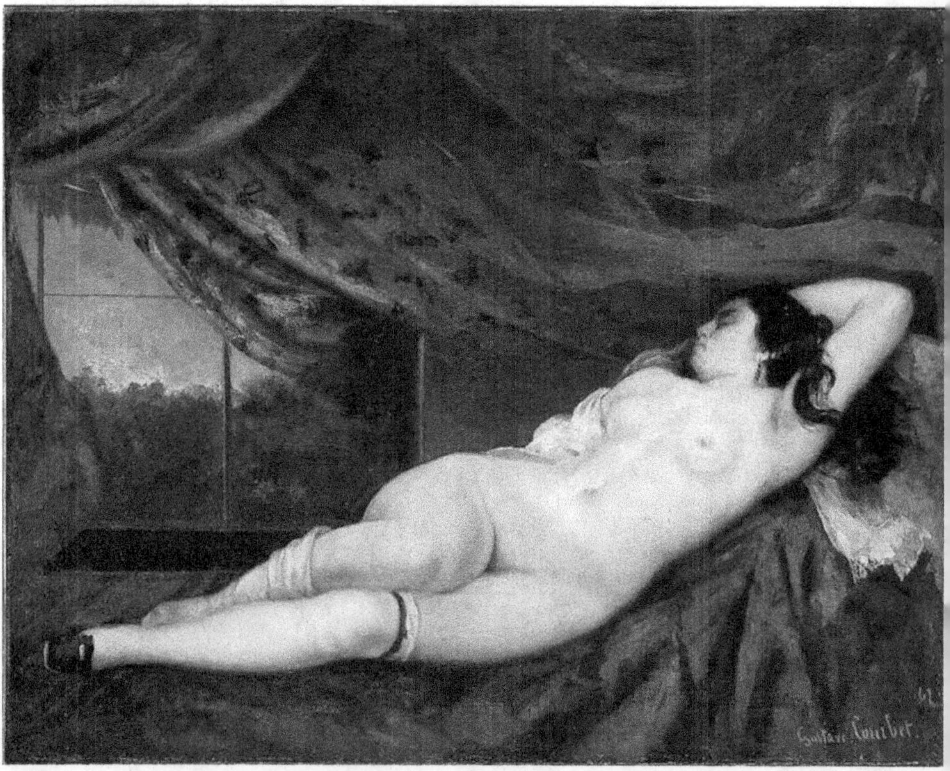

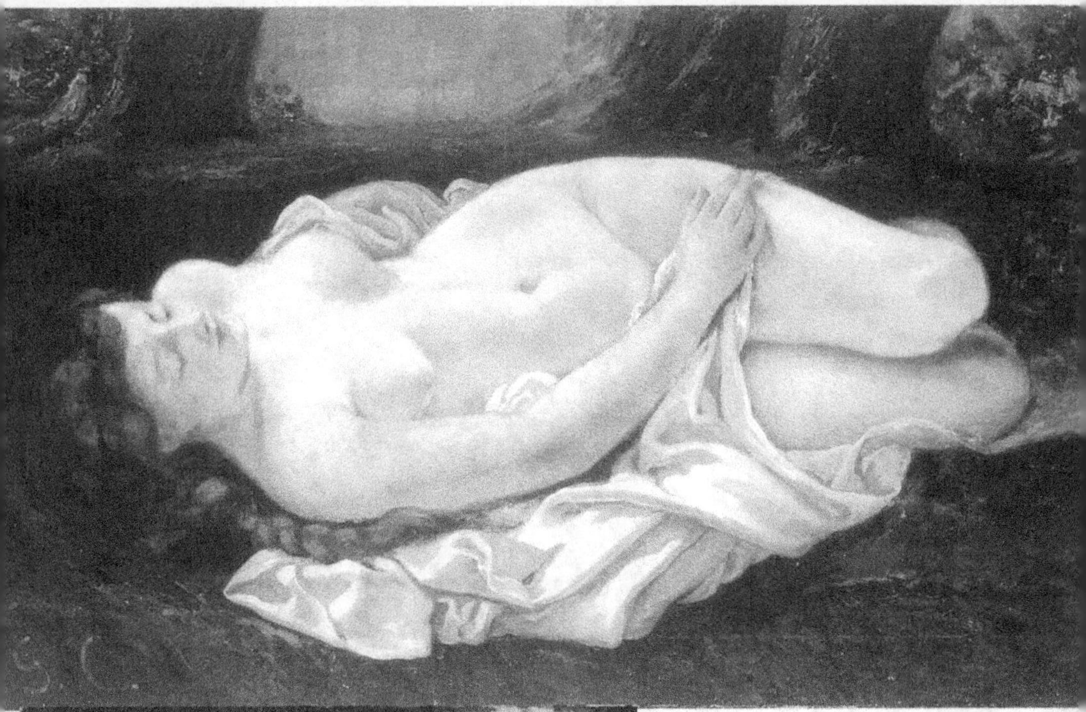

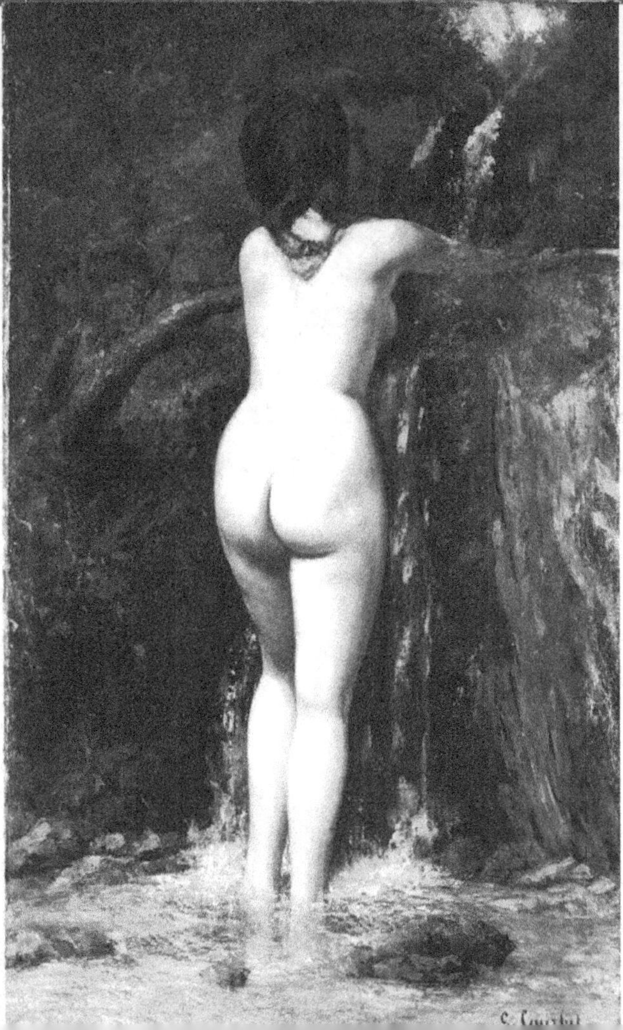

Gustave Courbet, Source, 1862
(left). Reclining Woman (above).

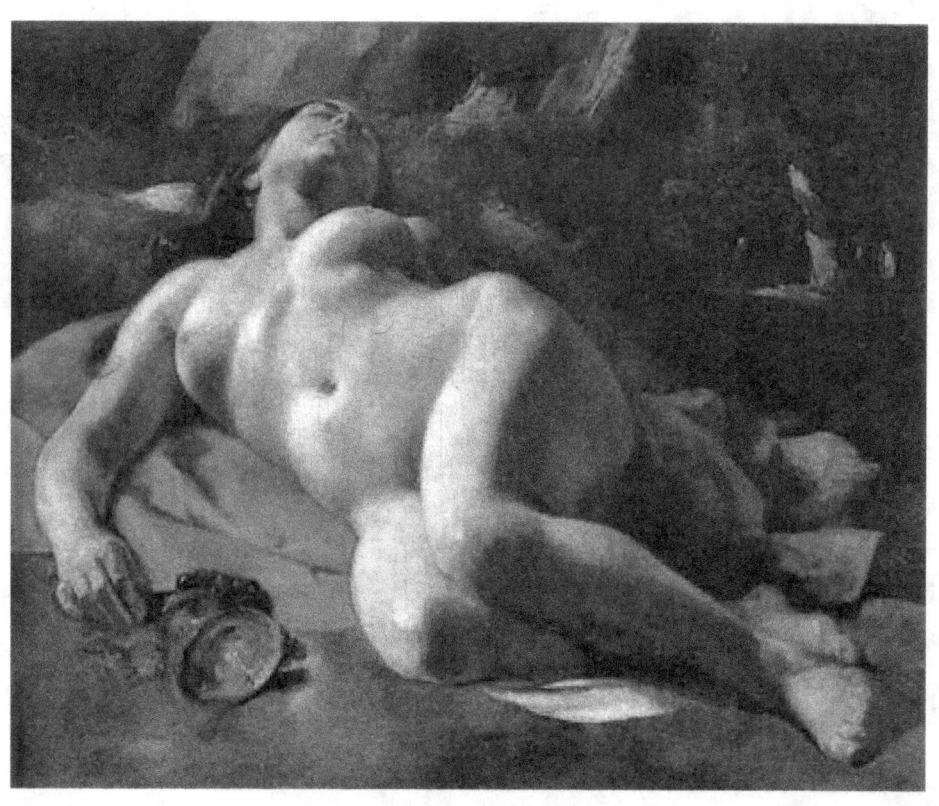

Gustave Courbet, La Bachante, 1844-47

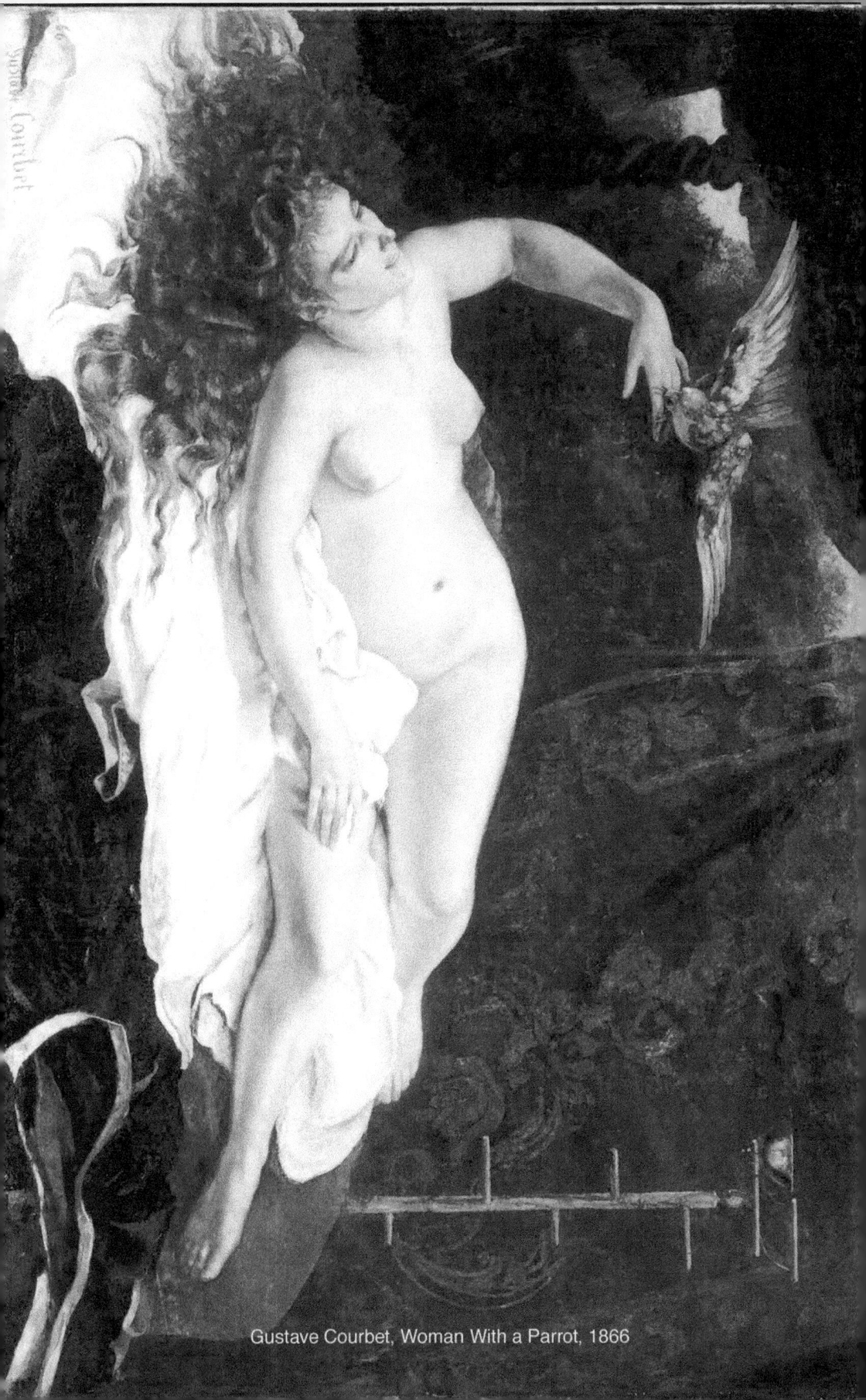

Gustave Courbet, Woman With a Parrot, 1866

J.M.W. TURNER

Many major artists have produced erotic art, from Titan to J.M.W. Turner. Titian drew in charcoal and chalk two people having sex, the woman (as ever) underneath, the man on top (as ever), while Turner made a (rare) sketch of people making love – the people are anonymous and faceless, while the genitals, as in all good erotica, are emphasized.[1]

1 J.M.W. Turner: *Sheet of erotic drawings*, c. 1820s, pencil & wash, 10.5 x 14.5in, British Museum, London; Titian: *A Couple in Embrace*, c. 1750, charcoal & white & black chalk on blue paper, 25.1 x 26cm, Fitzwilliam Museum, Cambridge

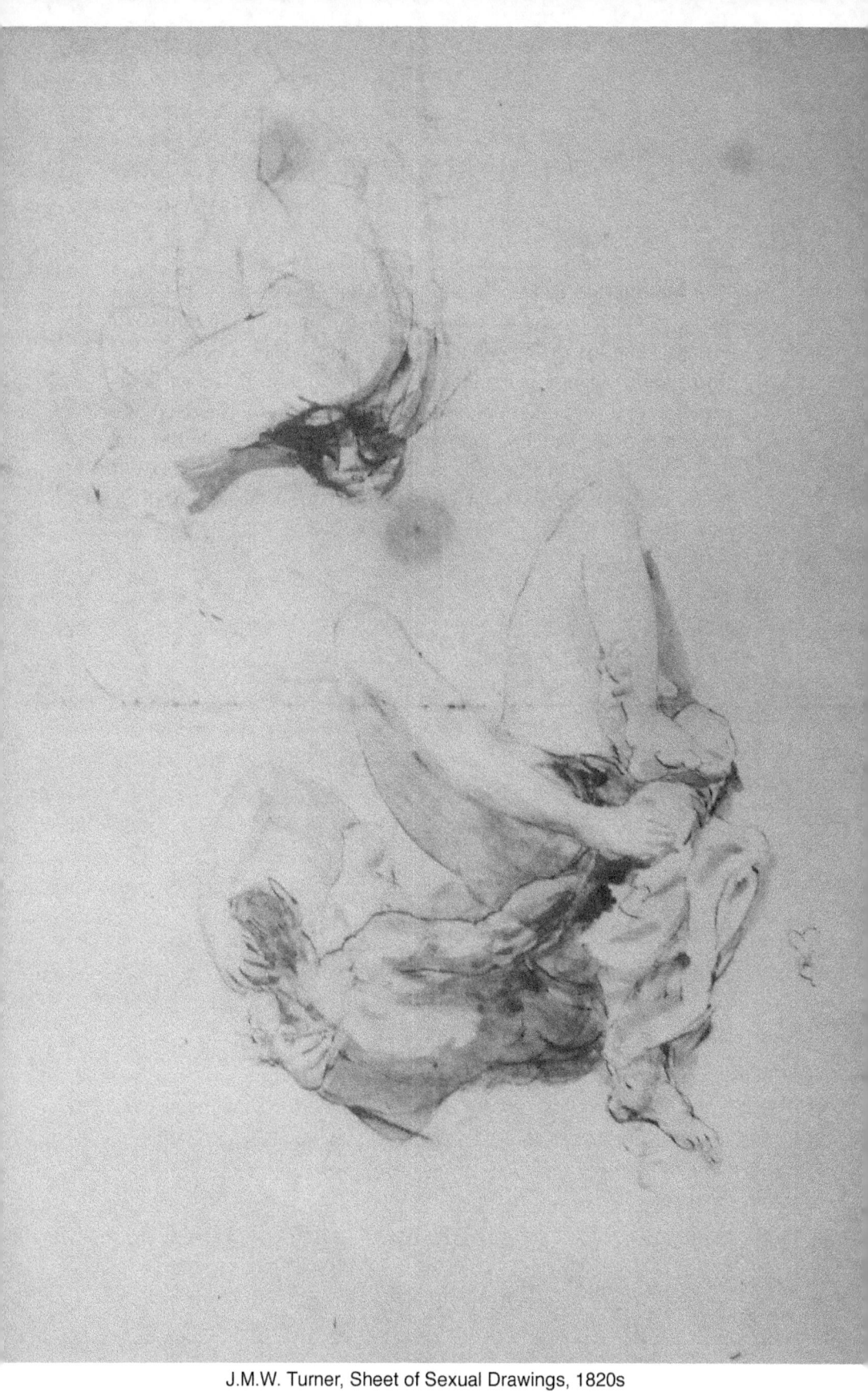

J.M.W. Turner, Sheet of Sexual Drawings, 1820s

THE MARQUIS DE SADE

The Marquis de Sade is quite astonishing. De Sade is the high priest of metaphysical eroticism, as championed by the European artistic élite, such as Charles Baudelaire, Jean Cocteau, the Surrealists, Algernon Swinburne, Lautréamont, Fyodor Dostoievsky and John Cowper Powys. Among visual artists, the inheritors of the Sadeian pornographic ethic include Pablo Picasso, Hans Bellmer, Jean Cocteau, Max Ernst, Allen Jones, and David Salle. Many artists have had a go at illustrating de Sade's work.

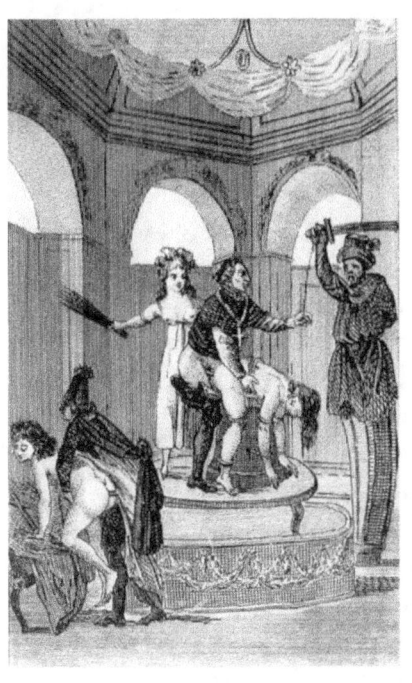

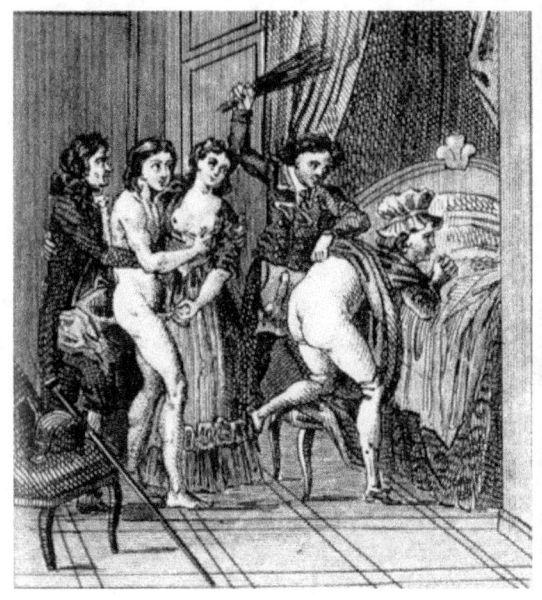

Illustrations from Justine,
late 18th century

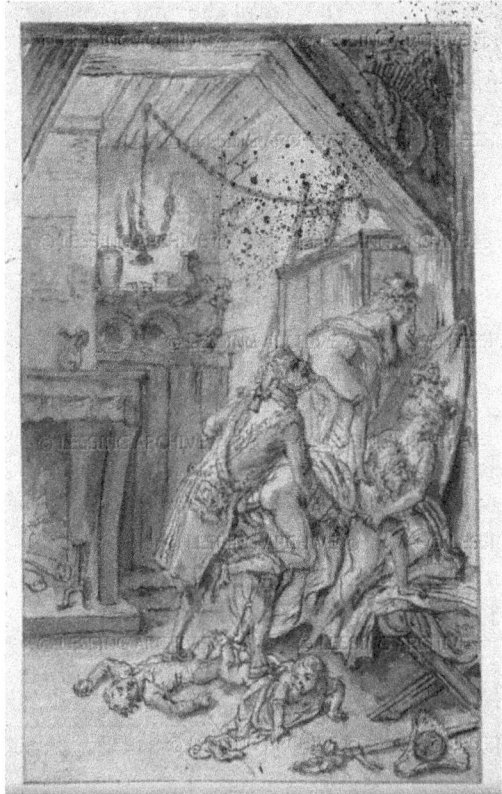

EDGAR DEGAS

Pierre Bonnard's paintings mythicize the intimate day-to-day activities of his beloved, as art has always done, so that drying the body after a bath becomes a religious ritual. The same thing happens in the art of Edgar Degas. In both Degas' and Bonnard's works, the voyeur is built into the image. One is always aware of looking. One is always aware that the image is constructed for the pleasure of the artist. The viewer is a voyeur in Degas' art, in so much of art. As Degas said: '[i]t is as if you looked through a keyhole.'[1] This is emphasized in Degas' art by the studied indifference to the viewer, when the women turn their backs to the viewer, and in Bonnard's art one often looks through doorways or mirrors or frames of some kind. Both artists, as in late Picasso, emphasize the act of looking, the pleasure of seeing.

Edgar Degas' nudes, with their gorgeous pastel colours, spatial flatness, ritualized poses and gestures are brilliant graphic orchestrations, and seem at first to be simply formal explorations, as the poet Paul Valéry maintained.[2] These are the images, of nude bathing women, that Degas is famous for.[3] In fact, Degas' nudes have much to do with voyeurism, with scopophilia, with framing the obscure object of desire, so that the woman retains her 'looked-at-ness', to use Laura Mulvey's term from her key essay on visual pleasure.[4]

1 Quoted in P.A. Lemoine: *Degas et son œuvre*, Paris, 1946-9, I, 107
2 'All his life, Degas sought in the Nude, observed from all sides, in an unbelievable quantity of poses... the unique system of lines that would formulate any given moment of the body with the utmost precision and the utmost generality", wrote Paul Valéry (*Degas Danse Dessin*, Gallimard, Paris 1938, 59).
3 Egdar Degas: *Woman Drying Herself*, c. 1890-5, pastel, National Gallery of Scotland, Edinburgh; *The Tub*, c. 1885, pastel and gouache, 71.1 x 71.1cm, Hillstead Museum, Farmington, Connecticut
4 Laura Mulvey: "Visual Pleasure and Narrative Cinema", *Screen*, 16, 3, 1975

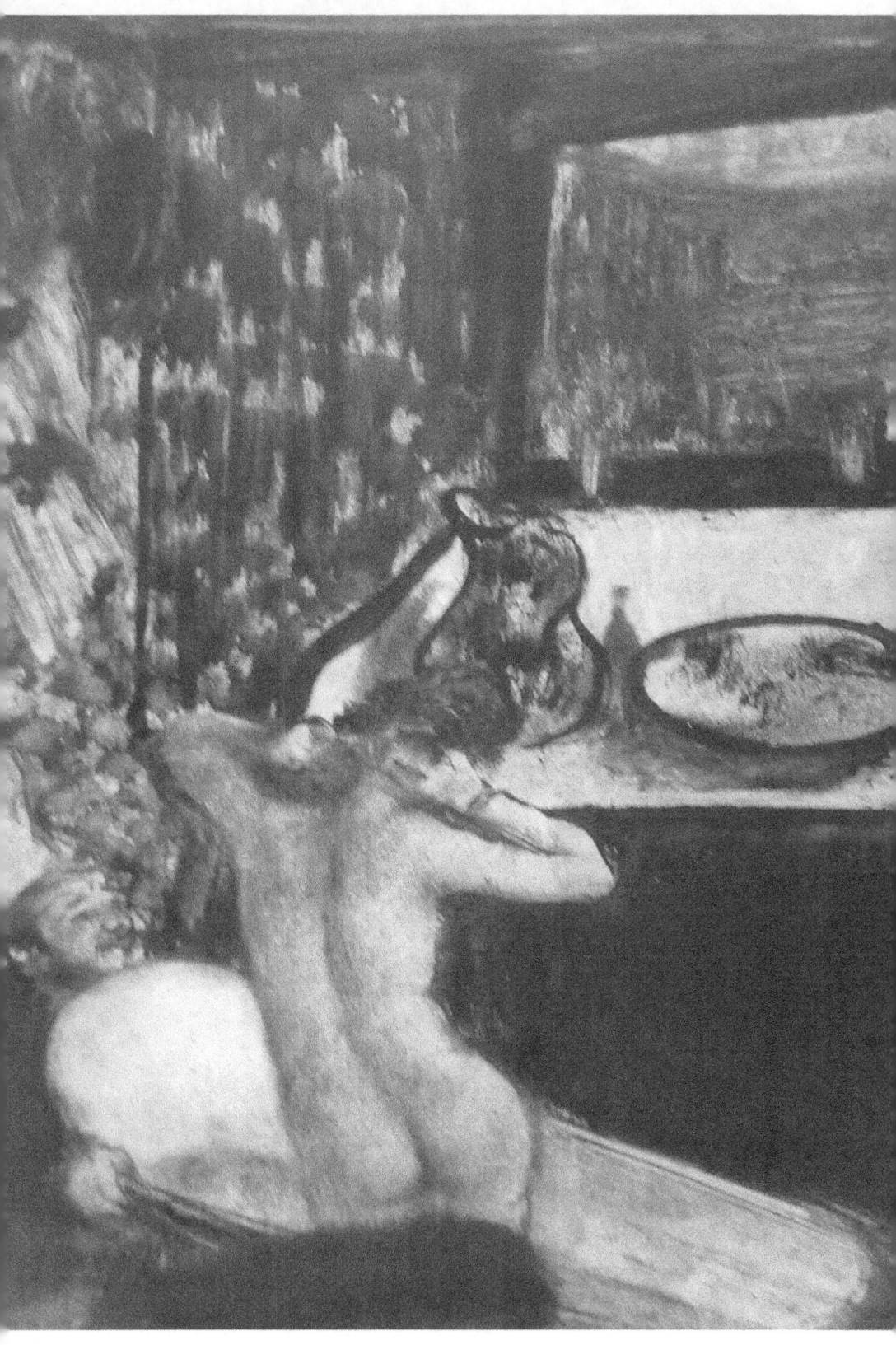

Edgar Degas, The Bath

EDGAR DEGAS

Edgar Degas' tender, sensual and tightly-controlled images try to erase the artist's viewpoint. Degas would like us to believe that he wasn't really there, drawing those women crouching on bathroom floors. They turn away from the artist, and Degas denies his interest in them, which is obviously erotic. But Degas cannot erase his erotic looking, his pleasure in brushing over with pastels every inch of skin of these anonymous women. For instance, Degas so often draws the hips, buttocks and back, and the women, bent over, are like the women of erotica, who always show off their bodies, and often their butts and hips.[1]

Although Edgar Degas' nudes can be seen as detached and aiming for a cool objectivity, Degas is drawing, time after time, nude women, who go about their tasks of cleaning and washing, and sit, like cats, self-absorbed. Degas heavily invests in his subjects, in these nude women. He is very interested in them, it seems, despite his professed detachment. His interest has an erotic component which if *he* can deny it, his art cannot deny it. Degas' nudes, then, can be seen as celebrations of the female nude, which turn out to be formulaic.

---

1 See Edgar Degas' *The Tub*, c. 1891, pastel on paper, Burrell Collection, Glasgow; *Aprés le Bain*, charcoal on paper, Victoria & Albert Museum

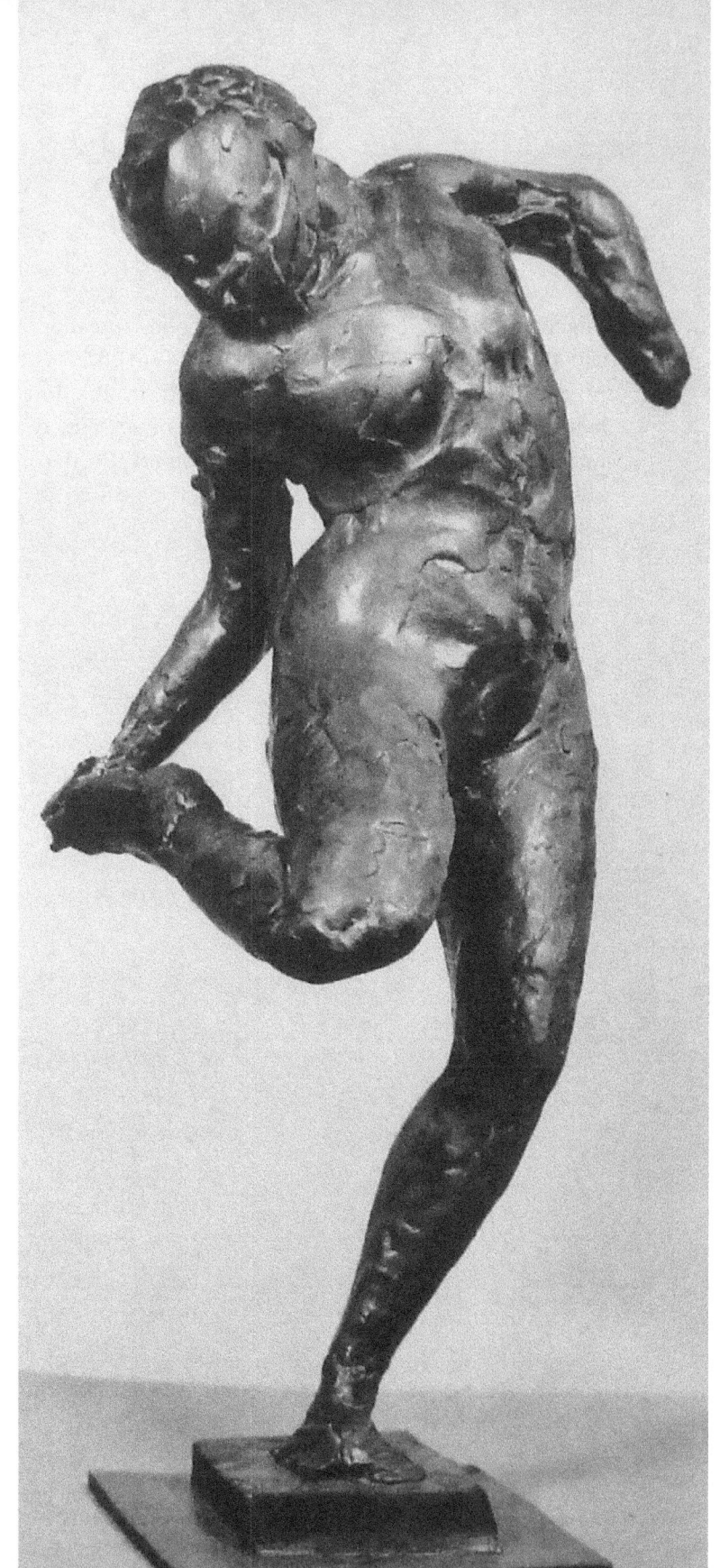

Edgar Degas,
Dancer Looking At
the Sole of Her
Right Foot, 1882-95,
New York

EUGÈNE DELACROIX

Eugène Delacroix is one of France's great Romantic artists. His signature work is *The Death of Sardanapalus* of 1827, with its image of a voluptuous slave being murdered in the foreground, a haunting image of the Romantic fusion of sex and death, which lingers on everywhere in Western erotic art. By the way, if you are ever in Paris, I highly recommend a visit to the Delacroix Museum.

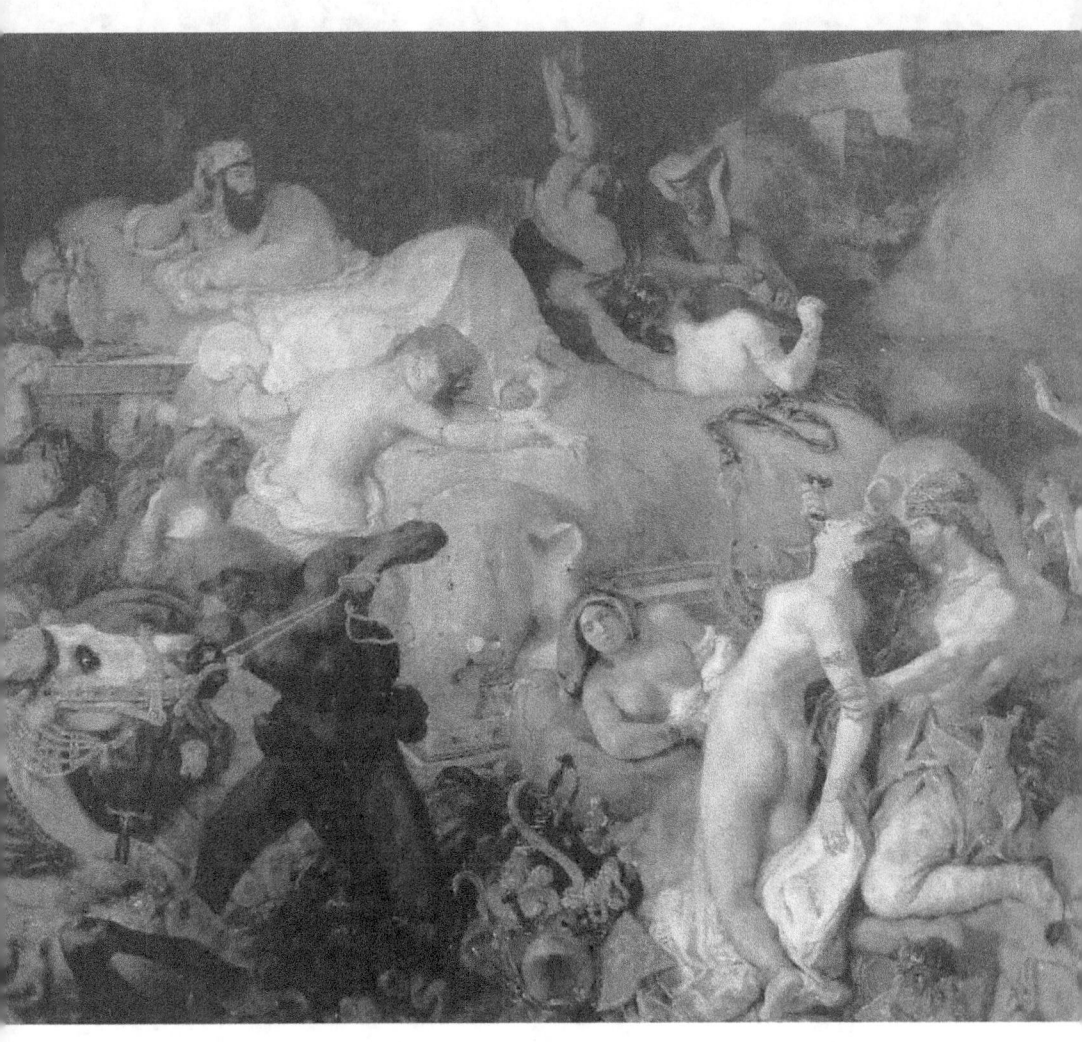

Eugene Delacroix, The Death of Sardanapalus, 1827

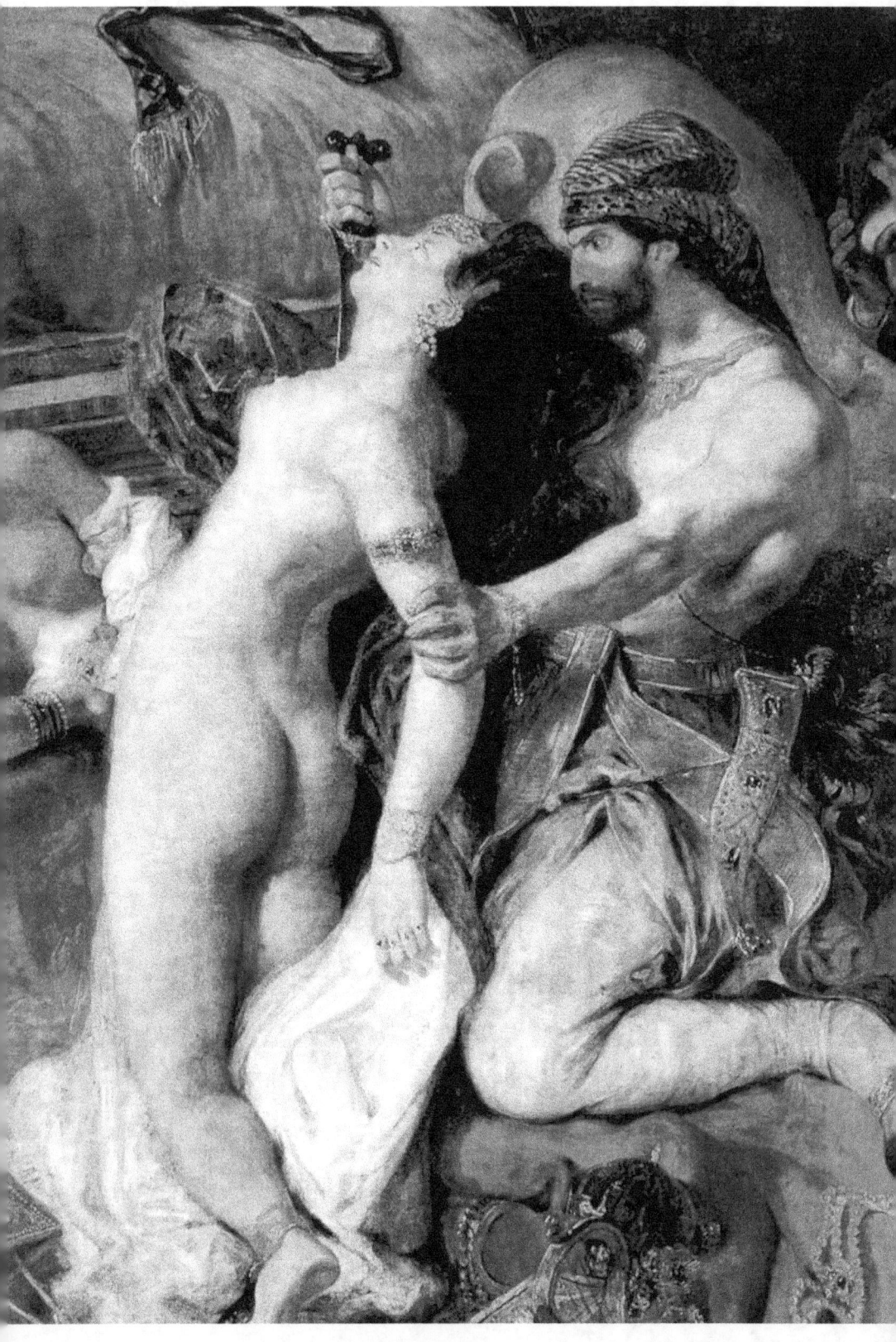

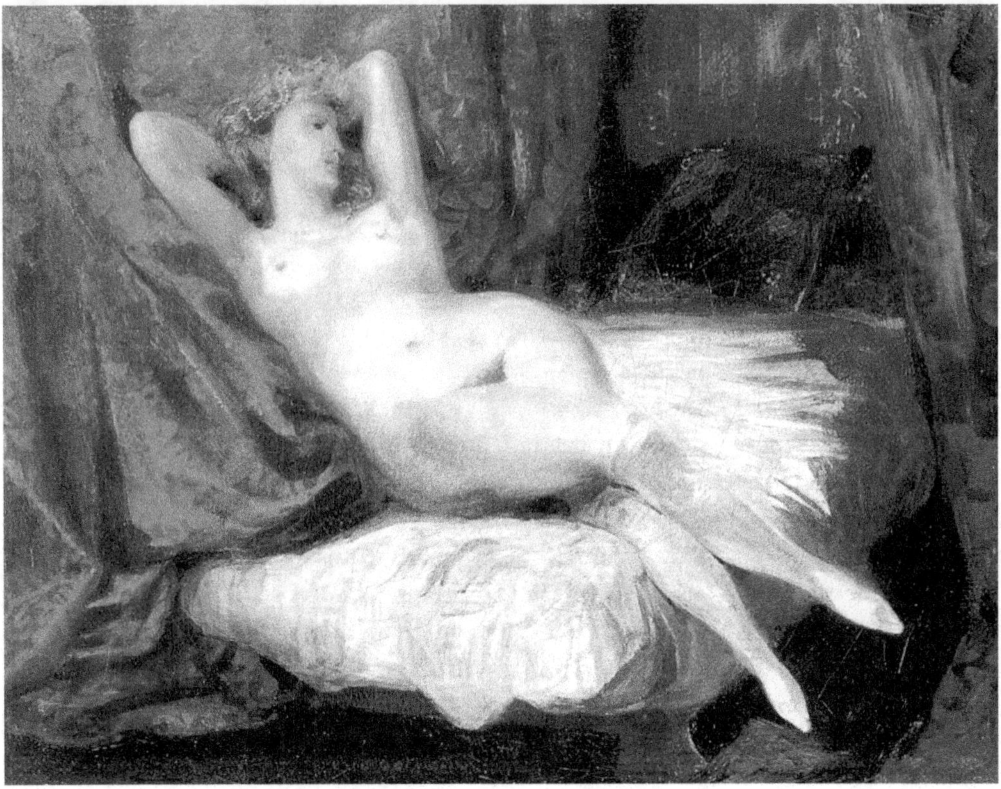

Eugène Delacroix

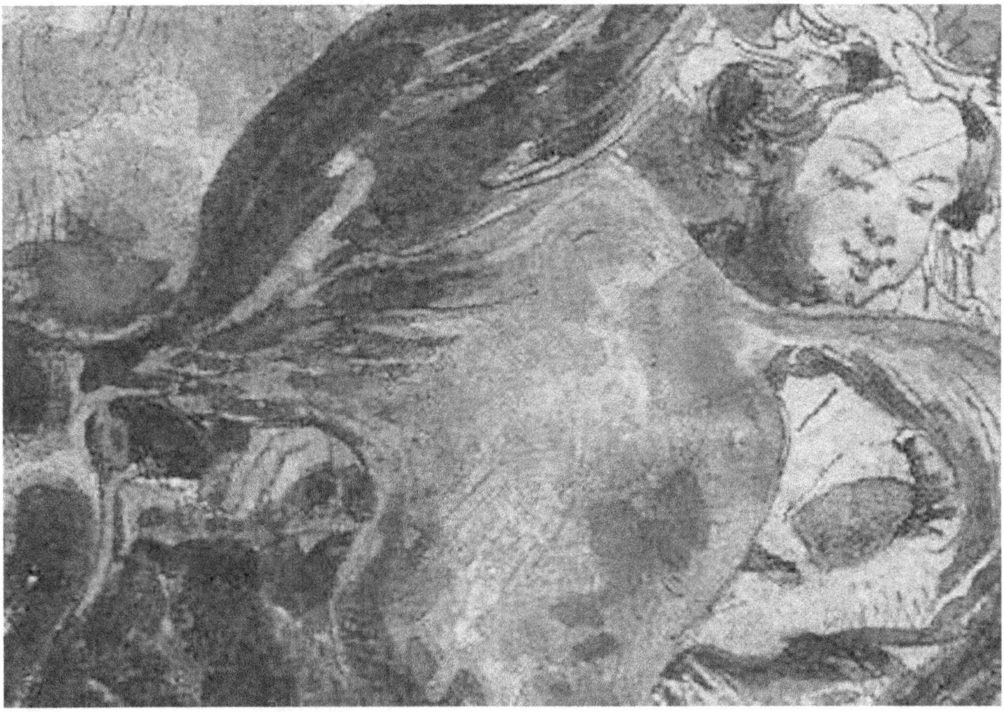

PIERRE RENOIR

Many artists love their subjects. Their paintings are acts of love. As Alfred Sisley says, speaking of landscape, but his notion also applies to the human figure: '[e]very picture shows a spot with which the artist himself has fallen in love'.[1] On canvas, they try to recreate their love of their subject. We see this especially in the nude, whether the male or female nude. Artists such as Pierre Renoir said they painted with their penis. The paintbrush becomes a phallus, gilding and caressing the (obscure) object of desire. The painter creates the Jungian *anima*, the beloved woman, the soul-mate on the canvas.

---

[1] In R. Goldwater, 309.

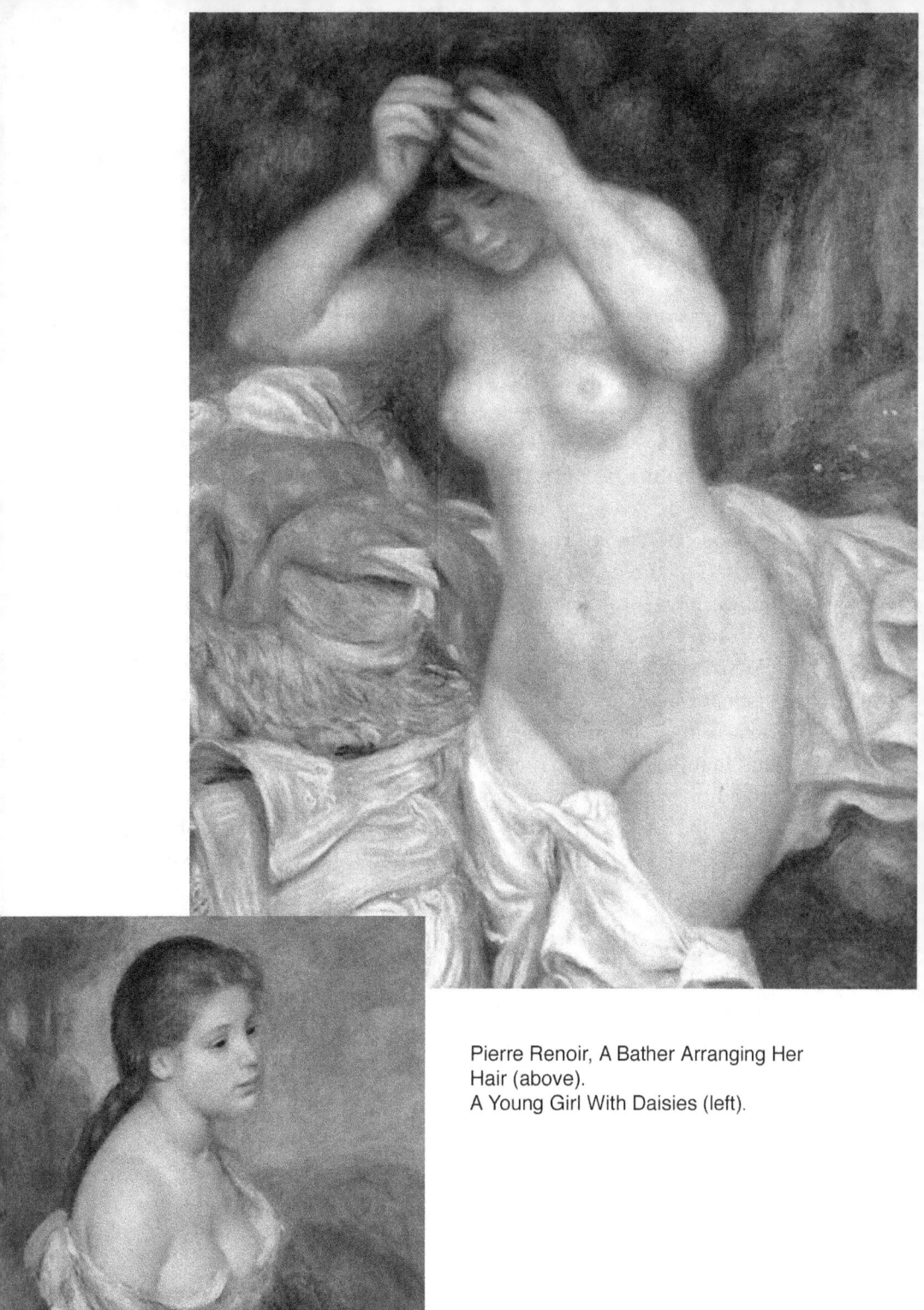

Pierre Renoir, A Bather Arranging Her
Hair (above).
A Young Girl With Daisies (left).

ÉDOUARD MANET

Personal, private erotic art became increasingly public. Thus, Édouard Manet's *Déjeuner sur l'Herbe* (1863) puts the nude into a contemporary setting.[1] The picture is not idealized, the woman is not on a pedestal, the intention is not to be timeless and ethereal, as in so many nudes. Manet's approach is to be direct, to move towards naturalism, as in his infamous *Olympia* (1863).[2]

Édouard Manet is often described as the founder of modern art, and one can see why, for in the art of Manet the seamlessness of the picture surface breaks down, and painting becomes increasingly a matter of marks on a canvas. The naturalism/ realism, the everyday subject matter, the indifference to the painting-viewer relation, make Manet 'modern'. A case could be made for many other painters – such as J.M.W. Turner, or Eugène Delacroix, or Jacques-Louis David, or Titian, or Giotto – as being the 'founder' of modern art. It doesn't really matter. But Manet's straightforward treatment of sexuality is powerful. Not necessarily 'new', but new in Western painting. Manet's *Olympia* broke and reworked the traditional relations between female sexuality, representation, 'high' art, and consumption.[3]

1 E. Manet: *Déjeuner sur l'Herbe*, 1863, Louvre, Paris
2 E. Manet: *Olympia*, 1863, Louvre, Paris
3 See T.J. Clark: "Preliminaries to a Possible Treatment of *Olympia* in 1865", *Screen*, 21:1, Spring 1980, 18-41, and T.J. Clark: *The Painting of Modern Life: Paris in the Art of Manet and His Followers*, Thames & Hudson 1985, 79-146

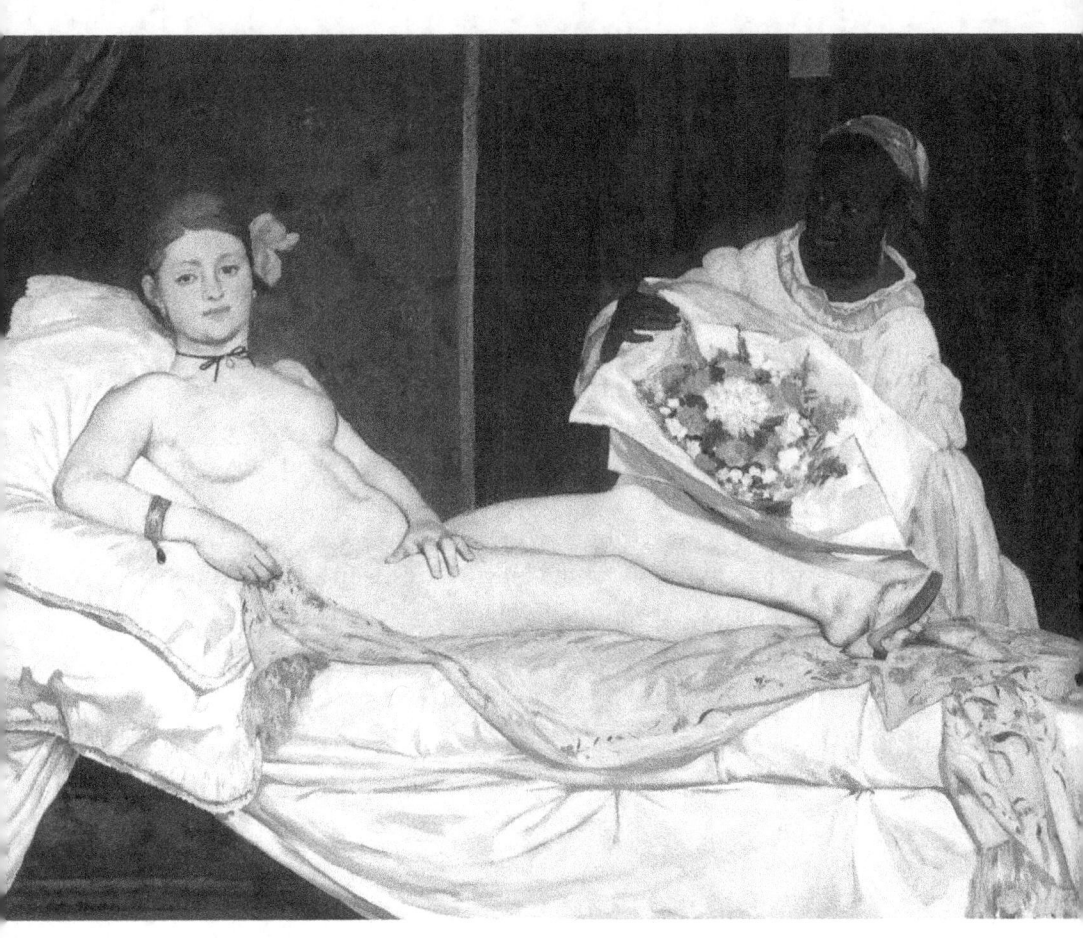

Edouard Manet, Olympia, Musée d'Orsay, Paris

VELÁSQUEZ AND GOYA

Two of the most famous female nudes in the whole history of art, Diego Velásquez' *Venus* and Francisco de Goya's *Naked Maja*, offer views of women as voluptuous sites of pleasure.[1] These are images of pure desire, pure wish-fulfilment, pure pleasure, which are also pornographic. There is no doubt that the painted 'high art' female nude, as an image, is very like the pornographic image, which offers women as sexualized objects of male lust. They are part of a continuum of representation. What different-iates 'high culture' nudes from the nudes in pornography is largely to do with context, with the sociopolitical environment in which the nudes are consumed. You can put Goya's *Naked Maja* into a soft core pornographic context and it would send only a few conflicting signals with the rest of the photography there. Fashions change – in costume, hair, make-up, pose and props – but it is startling how similar the female nude is in art. The funda-mental relation, of sexualized women being offered up to be looked at and lusted over by desirous males is remarkably similar the world over, and through history.

1 Diego Velásquez: *The Rokeby Venus*, 1649-50, oil on canvas, 122.5 x 177cm, National Gallery, London; Francisco de Goya: *Naked Maya*, 1800-5

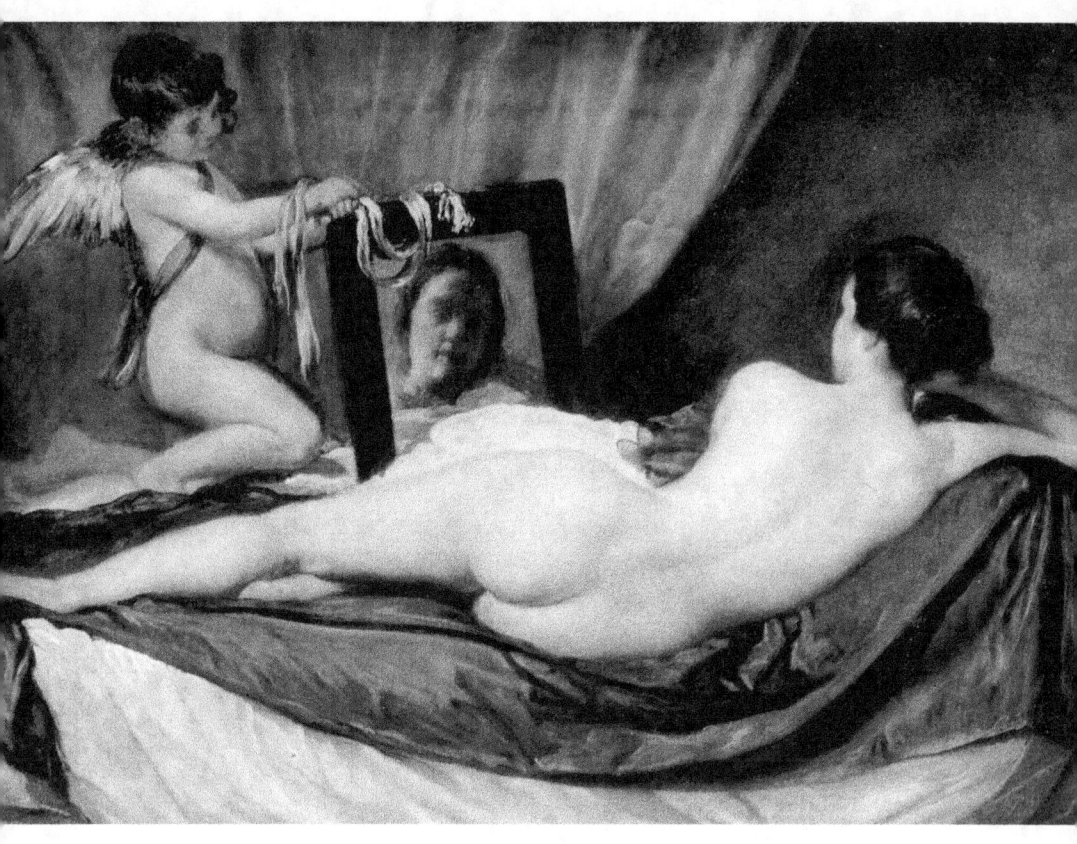

Diego Velásquez, Rockeby Venus, 1649-51,
National Gallery, London

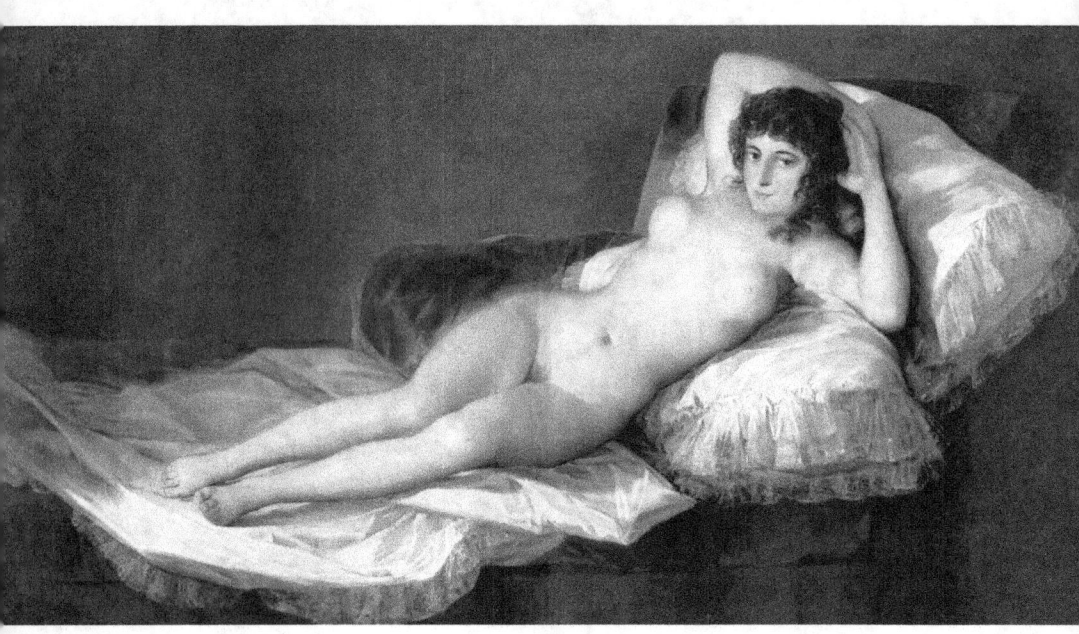

Francisco de Goya, Naked Maja, c. 1801, Prado, Madrid

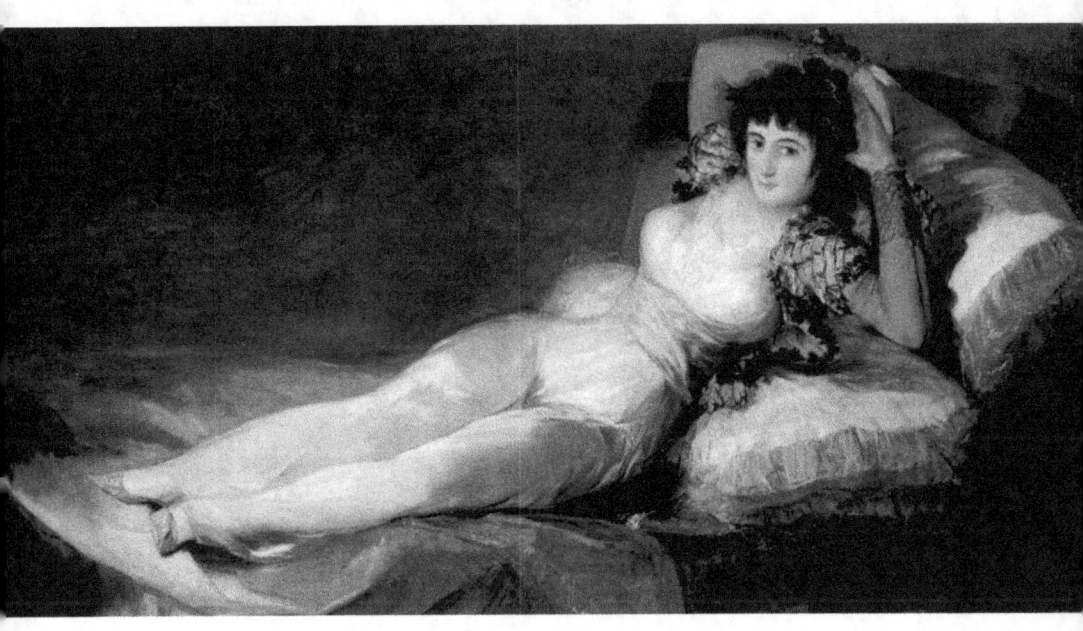

Francisco de Goya, Clothed Maya, 1801

J.A.D. INGRES

J.A.D. Ingres eulogized the female form in some of the art's most celebrated nudes (such as in his *A Sleeping Odalisque*). Ingres is the epitome of the cool, Neo-Classical, post-Baroque artist. Ingres follows in the footsteps of artists such as Giorgione in his *Concert Champêtre*, Jacopo Tintoretto in his *Susannah and the Elders*, Pierre Renoir in his *La Nymphe de la Source,* Leon Kroll in his *Nude*, or John Everett Millais in his *The Night Errant*.[1]

---

1 John Everett Millais: *The Night Errant*, oil on canvas, Tate Gallery, London; Jacopo Tintoretto: *Susannah and the Elders*, 1555-6, oil on canvas, Kunsthisorisches Museum, Vienna; Ingres: *A Sleeping Odalisque*, oil on canvas; Giorgione: *Concert Champêtre*, oil on canvas, Musées Nationaux, Paris; Leon Kroll: *Nude*, 1933-4, oil on canvas, 48 x 36in, Metropolitan Museum of Art, New York

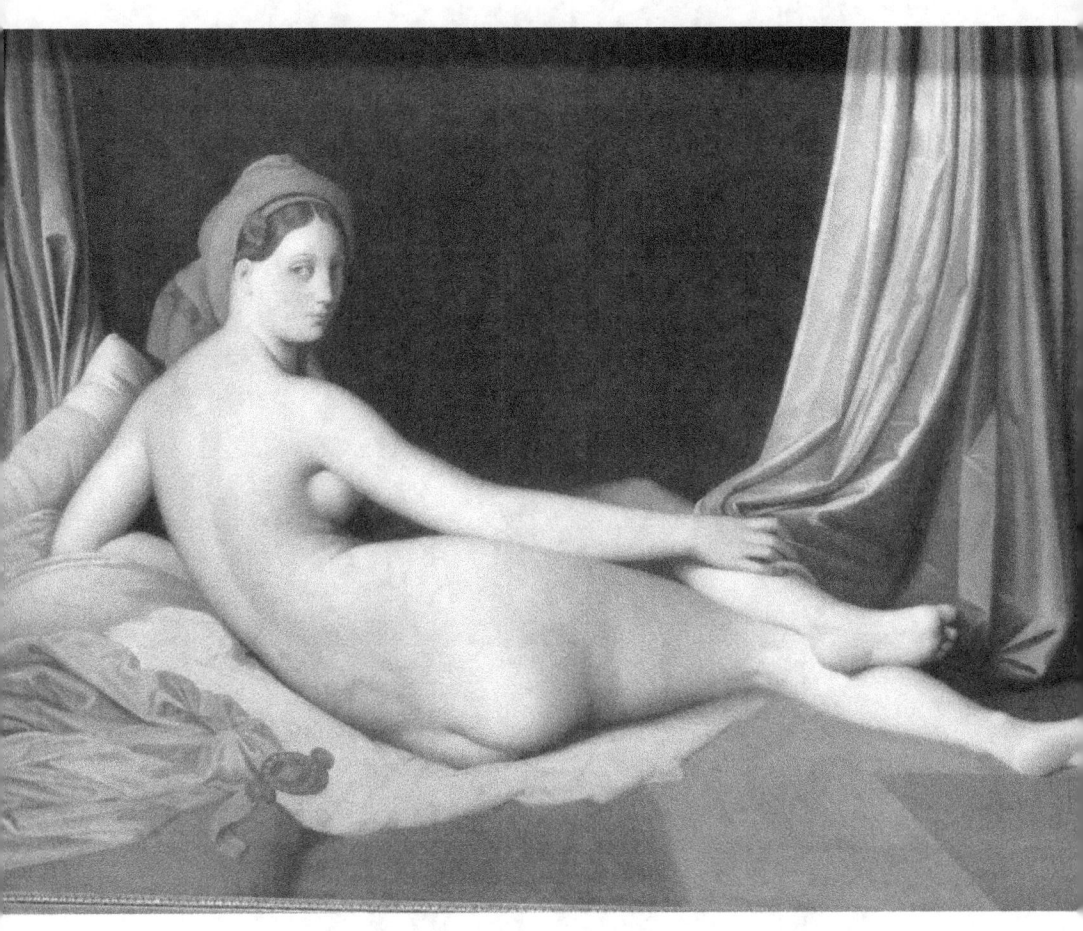

J.A.D. Ingres, Odalisque, Metropolitan Museum of Art

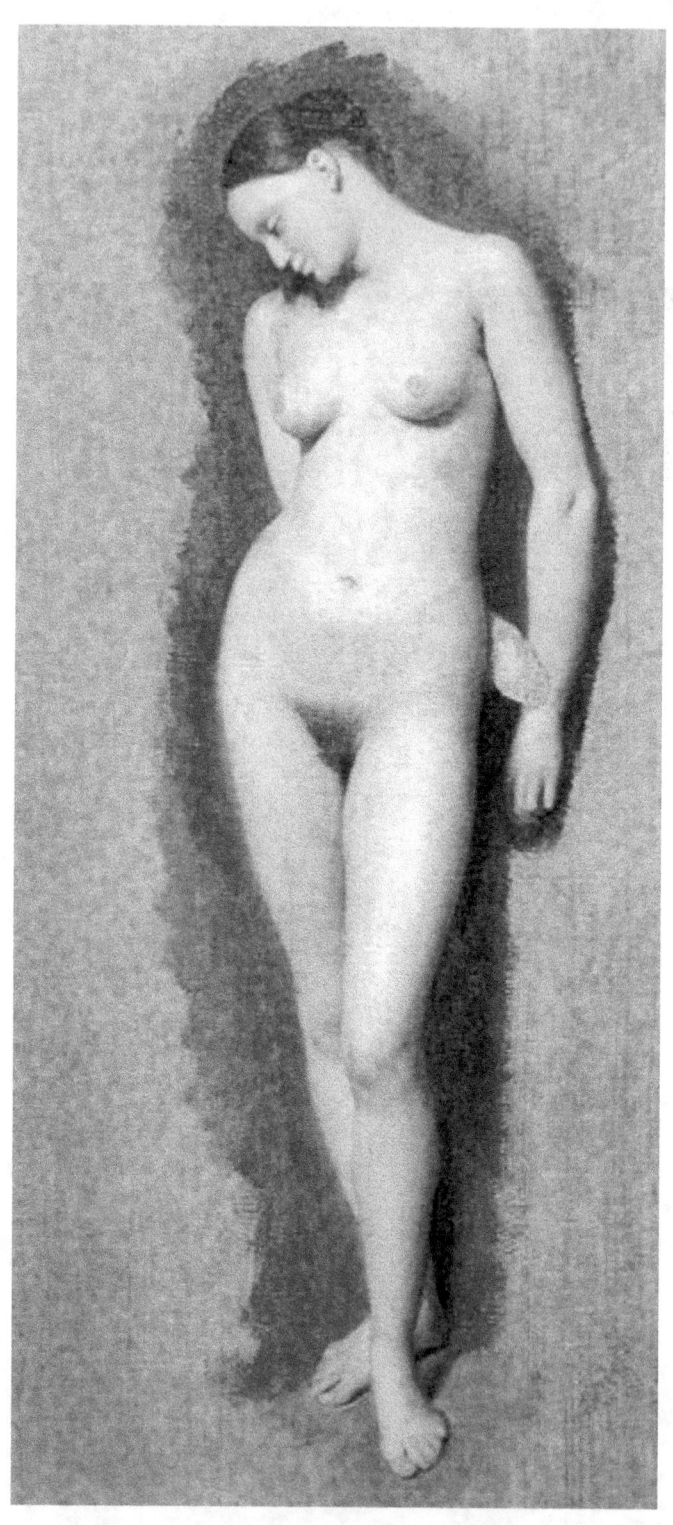

Jean-Dominique Ingres, Nude Study

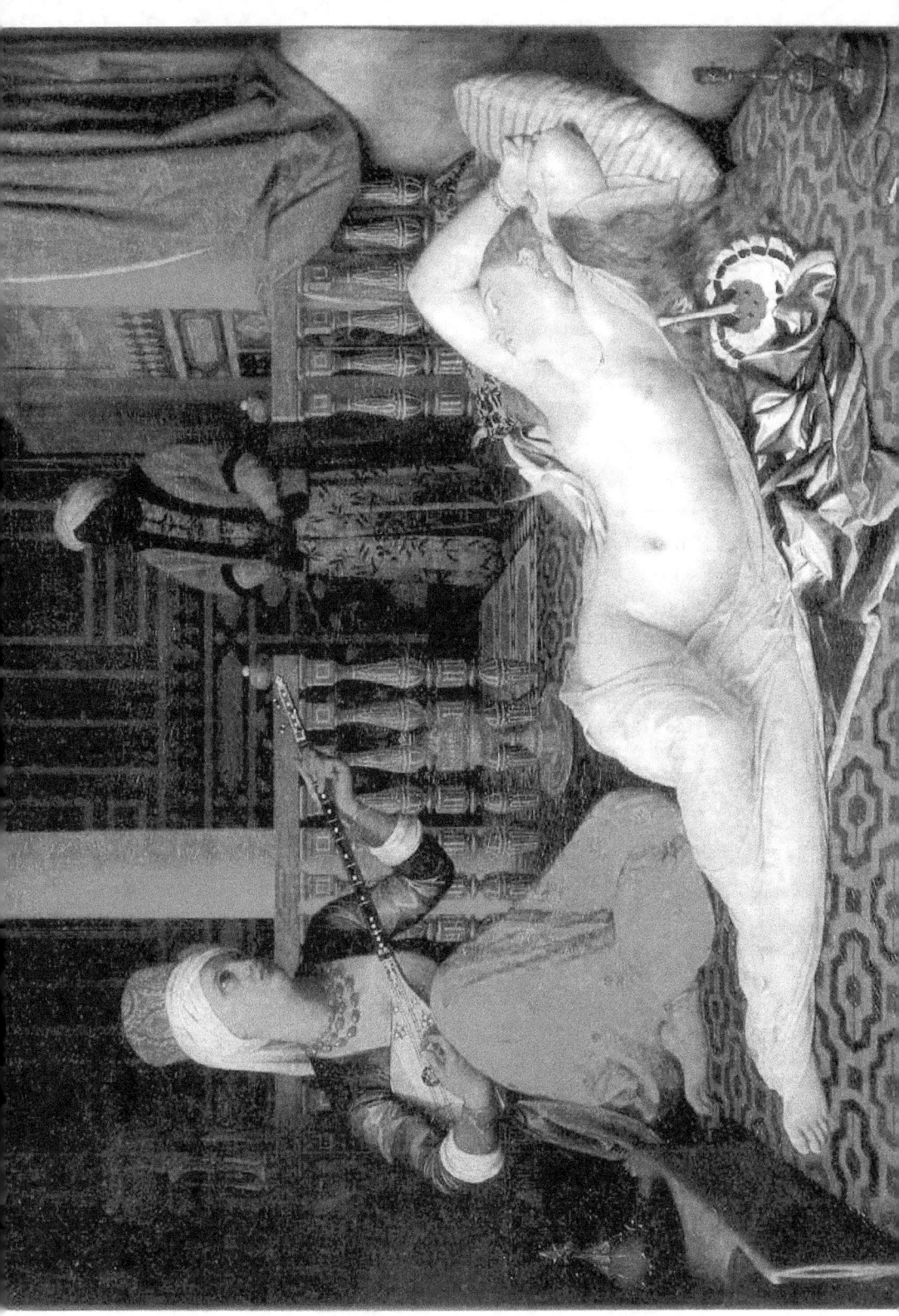

Jean-Dominique Ingres, Odalisque

EGON SCHIELE

Egon Schiele (1890-1918), Gustav Klimt's disciple, is the embodiment of *fin-de-siècle* Vienna, the decadent *zeitgeist* of the 'city of dreams' which was obsessed with itself, which psychoanalyzed itself endlessly, which simultaneously celebrated and suppressed eroticism.

Egon Schiele, like Pablo Picasso or Eric Gill, is one of the 'great' modern erotic artists.[1] He is daemonic compared to Gustav Klimt.[2] His view of sex is the usual masculinist, bourgeois one that sex = pain and pain = being truly alive. He said: 'I am a human being. I love death and I love life.'[3] Schiele wrote from prison in 1912: 'I believe that man must suffer from sexual torture as long as he is capable of sexual feelings.' Schiele's poetry is a mass of Expressionist meditations on the painful moments of life – sex, death, birth, violence:

> An eternal dreaming
> full of the sweetest overabundance of life –
> restless – with heavy pangs within, in the soul. –
> It blazes, burns, yearns for battle, –
> spasm in the heart
> Calculating – and madly alert with excited lust.
> (from 'Self-Portrait')[4]

1 See Alessandra Comini: *Egon Schiele*, Braziller, New York 1976; Jane Kallir: *Gustav Klimt, Egon Schiele*, Galerie St Etienne, Crown, New York 1980; Rudolf Leopold: *Egon Schiele*, Phaidon 1973; Peter Selz: "Egon Schiele", *Art International*, 4, no. 10, 1960, 39f
2 Otto Benesch: *Egon Schiele als Zeichner*, Vienna 1950, "Egon Schiele", *Art International*, II, 1958-9, no. S 9-10
3 Quoted in F. Whitford, 193
4 Quoted in E. Schiele: *I, Eternal Child*, 44

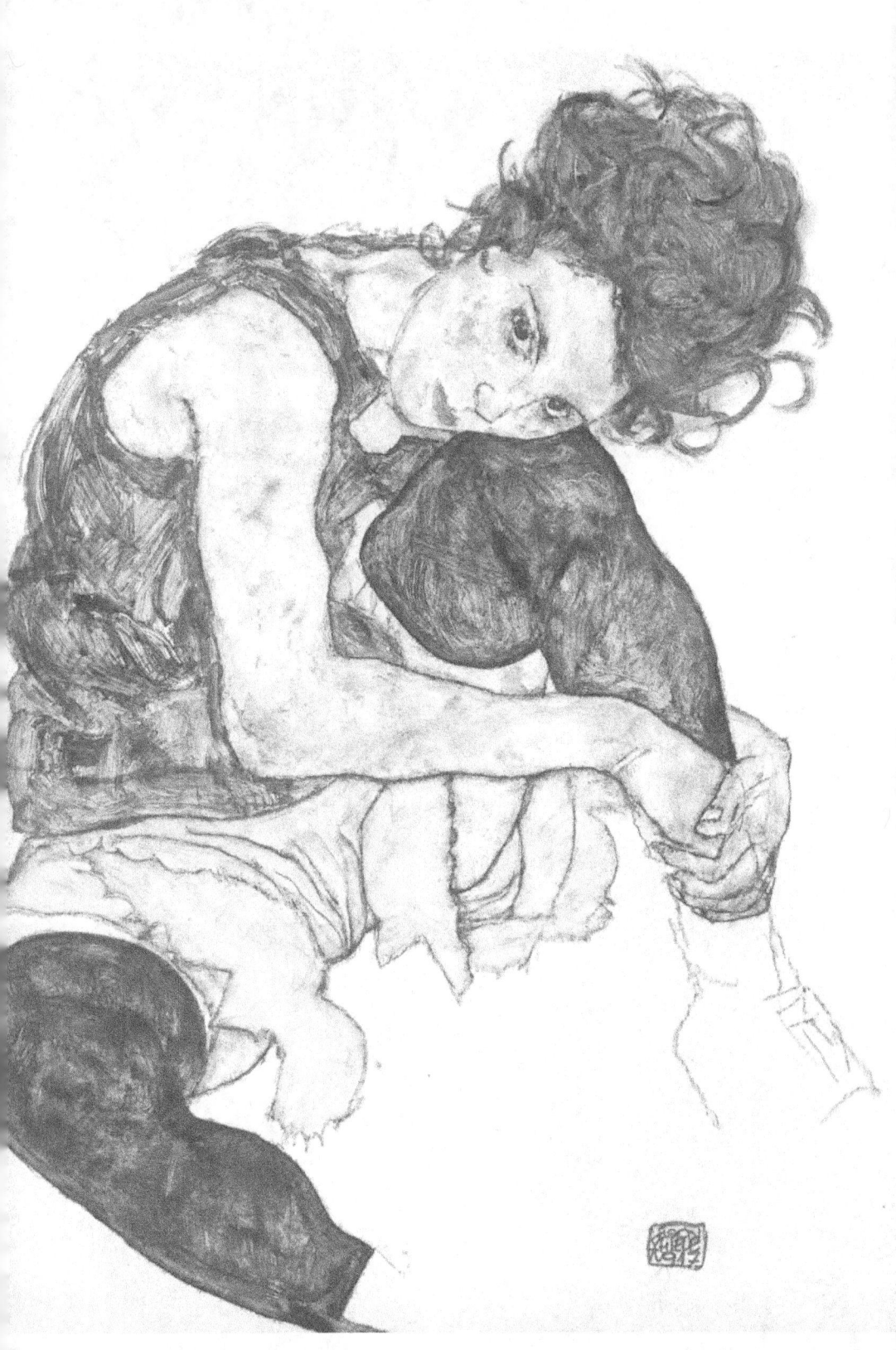

Egon Schiele, Edith, the Artist's Wife, 1917

Egon Schiele, Girl With
Black Hair, 1911 (right).

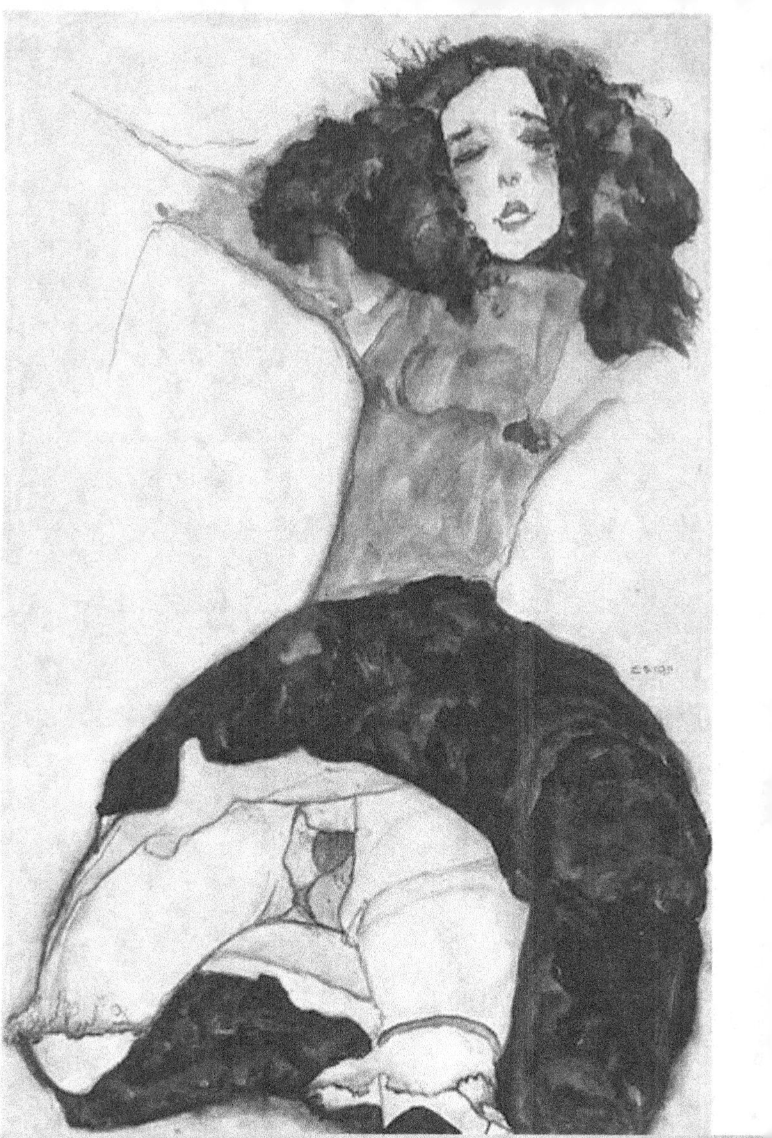

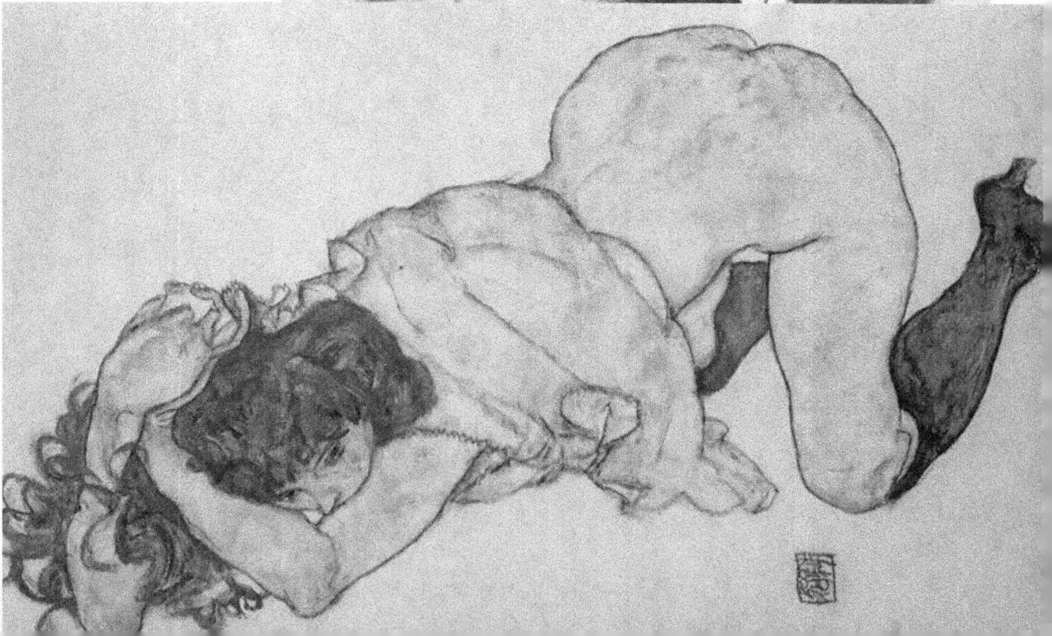

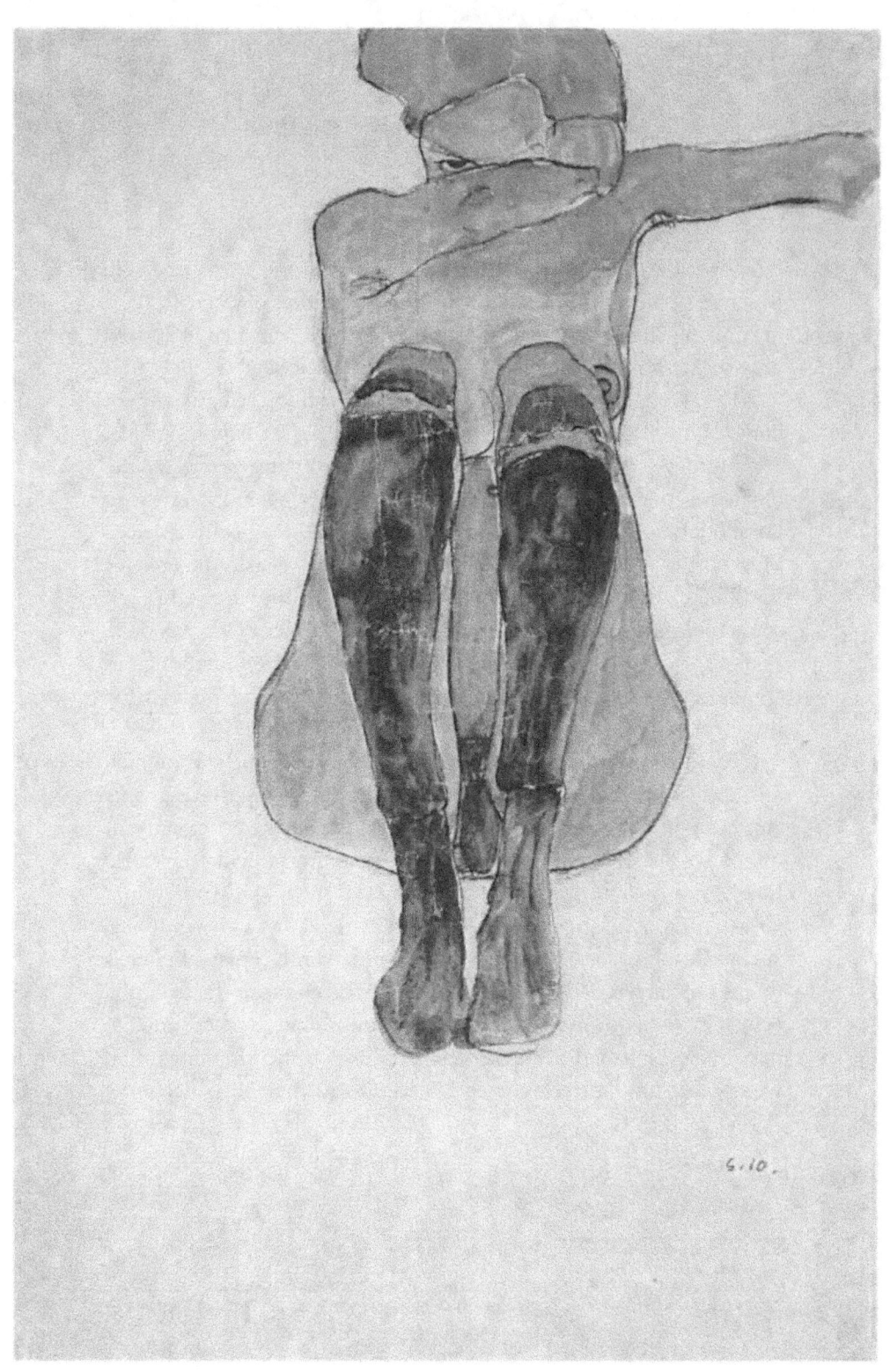

Egon Schiele, Nude, 1910

EGON SCHIELE

Egon Schiele's art is characterized by his nervy, stark line. He was not a painter in the richly sensuous tradition of Peter Rubens or Eugène Delacroix. Schiele's oil paintings are like coloured drawings. His drawings, though, are viciously realist and incisive. He does not miss a single blemish or irregularity of bone, skin, muscle or hair. Drawings such as *Recumbent Woman* are ruthless realistic: the sagging flesh of the woman, the blemishes on the skin, the hairy armpit and the indifference of the model are all recorded with a forensic, pathological intensity.[1] This sort of picture is a far cry from the chaste images of traditional, male, academic art. Schiele's' drawings do not romanticize or soften the subject, as Gustav Klimt or Georges de la Tour do. Schiele's thin, spindly figures have something in common with those of Alberto Giacometti (in the latter's *Diego*, for instance).[2]

There are a number of elements in Egon Schiele's art which are the hallmarks of erotic art. Firstly, there is the massive emphasis on sexuality. Always the observer's aware not only of the body, but of the erotic nature of the figure in Schiele's work. Like Gustav Klimt, he produced endless drawings of women in a variety of poses, most of them characterized by twisted limbs, spread legs, heads thrown to one side, hands splayed across thighs or torsos. While Klimt's recline in comfort, luxuriantly, Schiele's women are distinctly uncomfortable, restless, itchy, twitchy, dissatisfied. Schiele did produce erotic drawings that were seemingly direct copies of Klimt, such as the *Reclining Woman* of 1911.[3]

---

1 Egon Schiele: *Recumbent Woman*, 1914, pencil and gouache, 30.4 x 47cm, Graphische Sammlung Albertina, Vienna
2 A. Giacometti: *Diego*, 1953, oil, 100 x 81in, Guggenheim Museum, New York
3 Egon Schiele: *Reclining Woman*, 1911, pencil and gouache, 31.5 x 44cm, Fischer Fine Art, London

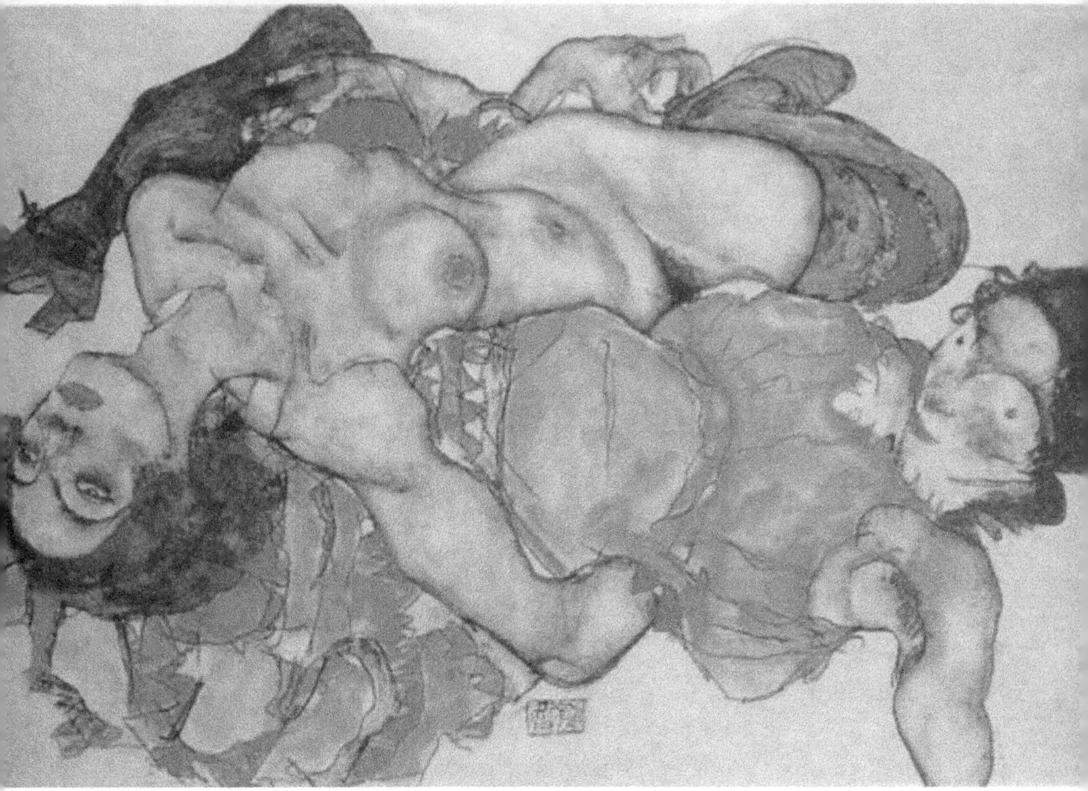

Egon Schiele, Two Women Lying Entwined, 1915, Vienna (above).

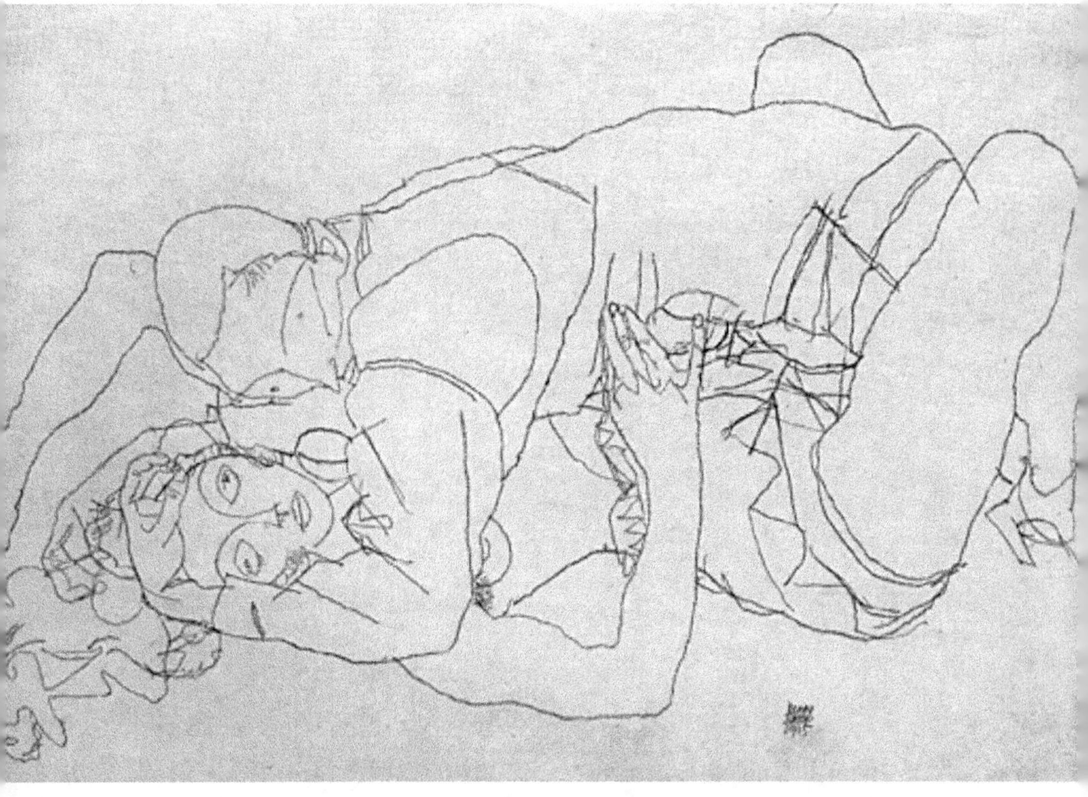

EGON SCHIELE

The *Reclining Girl*[1] of 1910 shows a young woman lying back with her finger on her clit, emulating Gustav Klimt's images of woman masturbating. Egon Schiele plays with expectations however, for his model is young, underage perhaps, something of a Lolita figure. Many of Schiele's women are like this: young, underdeveloped, thin, boyish, to use the terms of patriarchy. Schiele favours women that are 'boyish', yet he emphasizes vulvas and breasts. His models are androgynous, both feared and desired, both male and female. Schiele appropriates the androgyny theme in Symbolist art and infuses it with his own tortured form of eroticism. As Frank Whitford writes, expressing the paradoxical fear and desire theme of art and porn:

> Physically immature, thin, wide-eyed, full-mouthed, innocent and lascivious at the same time, these Lolitas from the proletarian districts of Vienna arouse the kind of thoughts best not admitted before a judge and jury. (82)

---

1 Egon Schiele: *Reclining Girl*, 1910, pencil, 55.7 x 37cm, Neue Galerie am Landesmuseum Joanneum, Graz

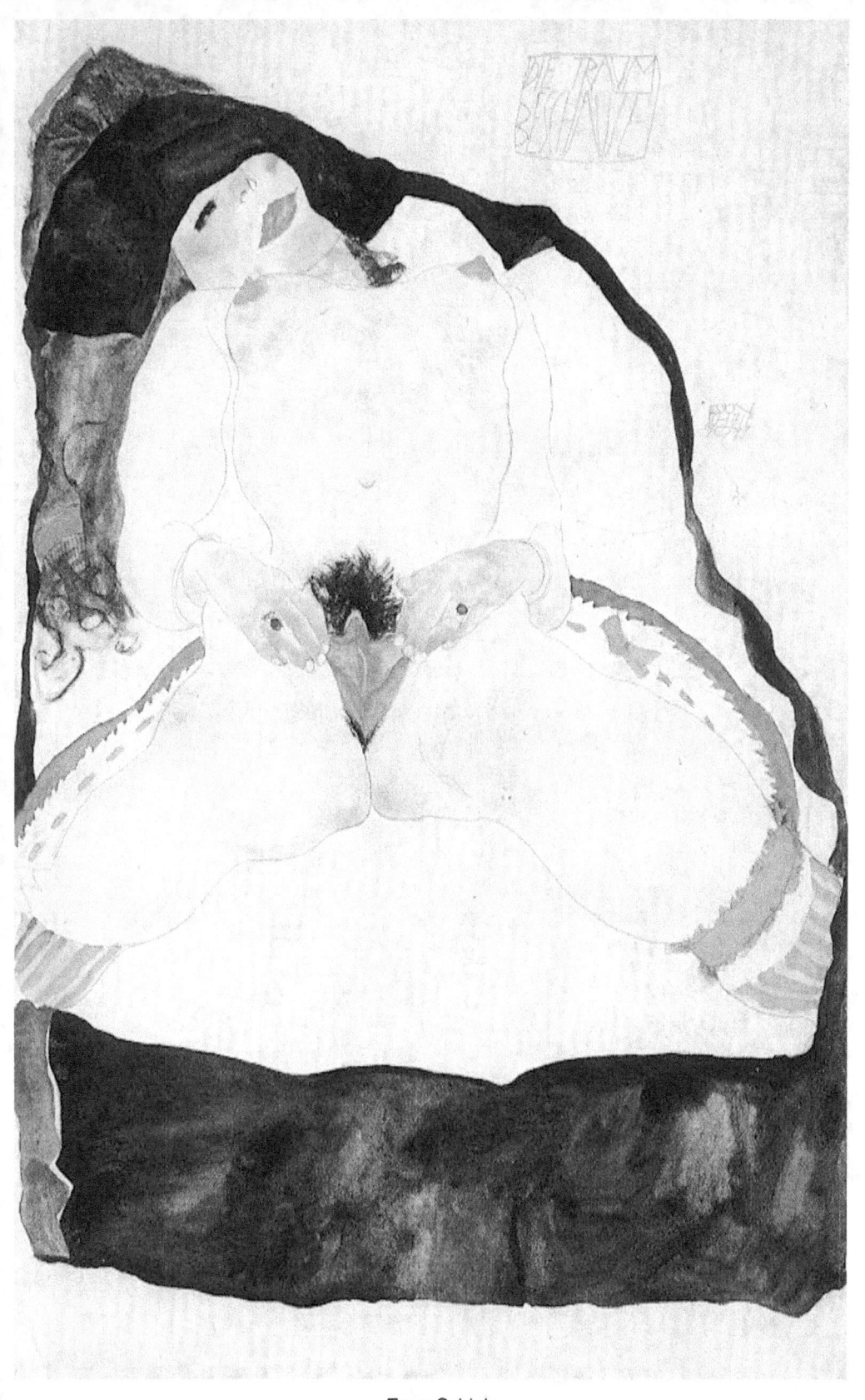

Egon Schiele

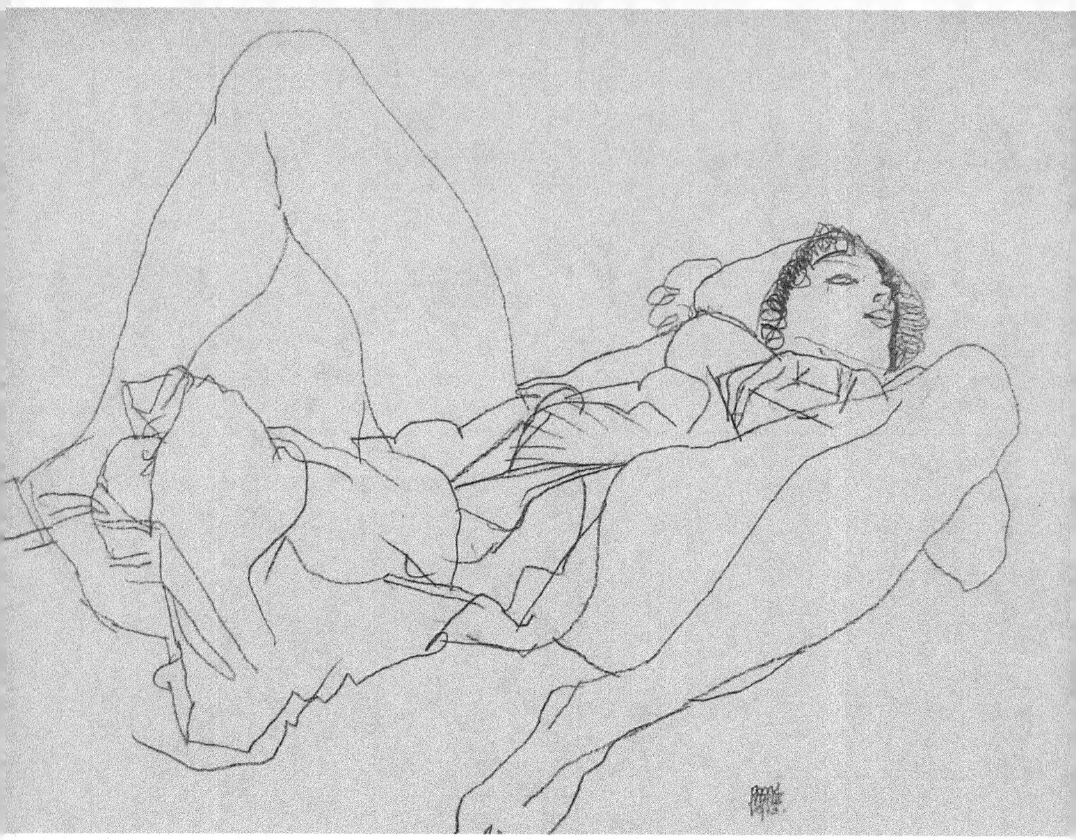

Egon Schiele, Reclining Nude With Spread Legs, 1913 (above).
Reclining Nude With Raised Chemise, 1914 (below).

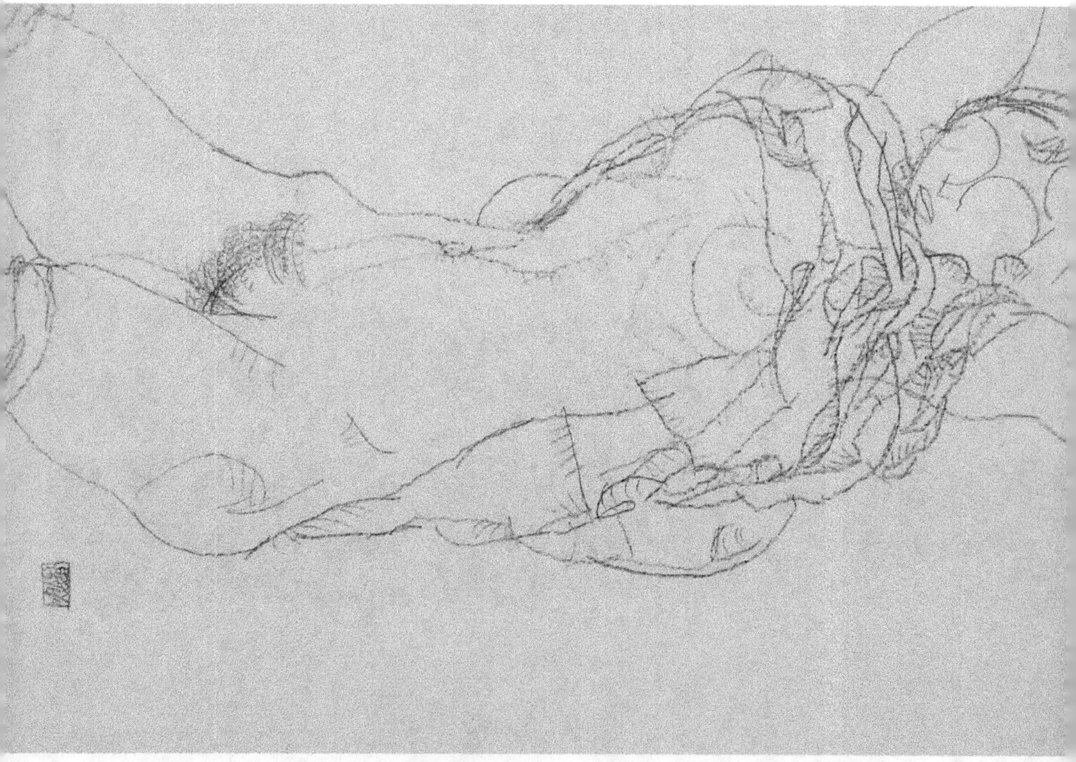

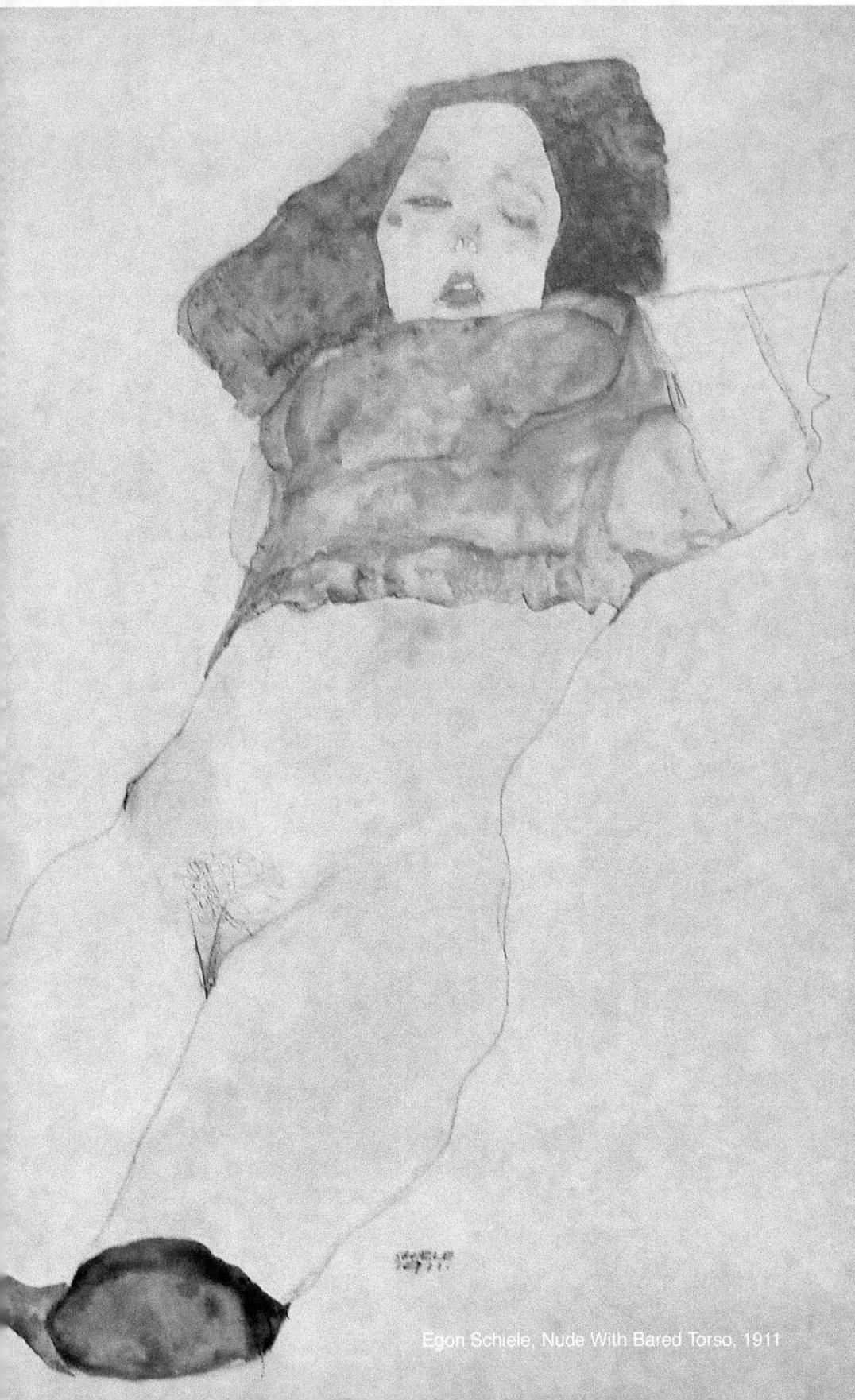

Egon Schiele, Nude With Bared Torso, 1911

EGON SCHIELE

Another aspect of Egon Schiele's art that is found in both erotica and art is fetishism. So many of Schiele's models wear stockings – striped stockings or purple stockings.[1] Schiele has one of the sharpest eyes for a startling graphic image. All of his art is very *stylish*, very fashionable. It always *looks good*, as fashion can. The dresses and stockings are part of the stylistic design, integrated as ornament, as in the work of Gustav Klimt, and are as crucial as the angular limbs or looks of complicity.

The 1911 drawing of a semi-nude woman lying on her front is typical of Egon Schiele's stylish erotica.[2] She lies with eyes closed, her legs are apart, to reveal her vulva, which Schiele has, as usual, coloured red with watercolour over his pencil drawing. This is usual enough in erotica and pornography, and in Schiele's art, this focusing on the woman's genitals. What is unusual, perhaps, is the fashionable items that Schiele clothes his model in: a stripey skirt, the stripes are very colourful: light blue, red, dark blue, orange, black, purple. She wears a check shirt, the colours here again are bright: green, red, orange, black and white squares. The overall effect is a combination of erotica and fashion. In Schiele's drawings, everything in the picture is fetishized, not just the model.

---

1 Egon Schiele: *Girl with Striped Stockings*, 1910, gouache, 31.5x 44cm, private collection; *Nude with Purple Stockings*, 1911, watercolour, 45 x 31.4cm, private collection
2 Egon Schiele: *Reclining Nude, Half Length*, 1911, pencil & watercolour, 18.8 x 12.4in, private collection, New York

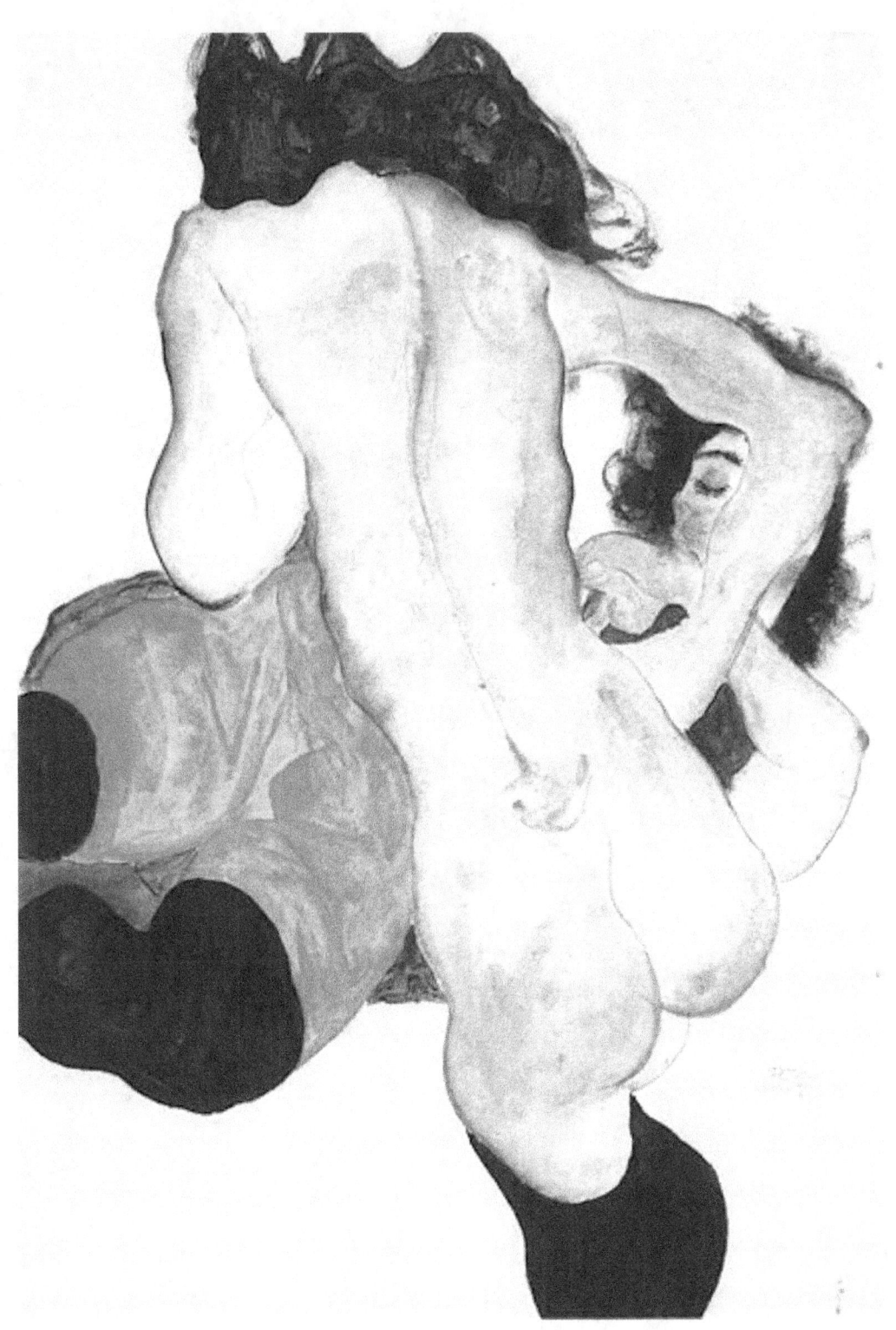

Egon Schiele, Two Lovers

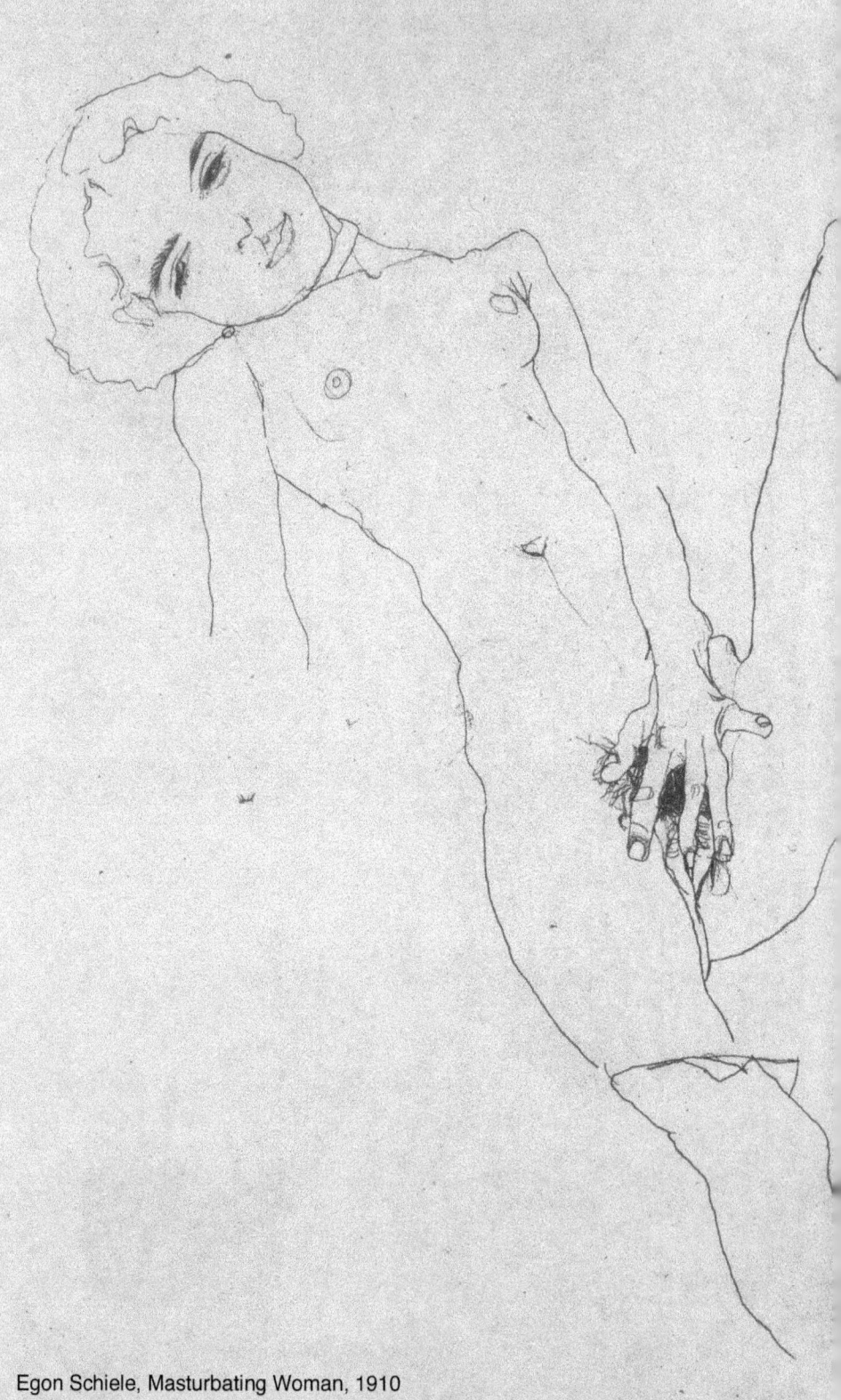

Egon Schiele, Masturbating Woman, 1910

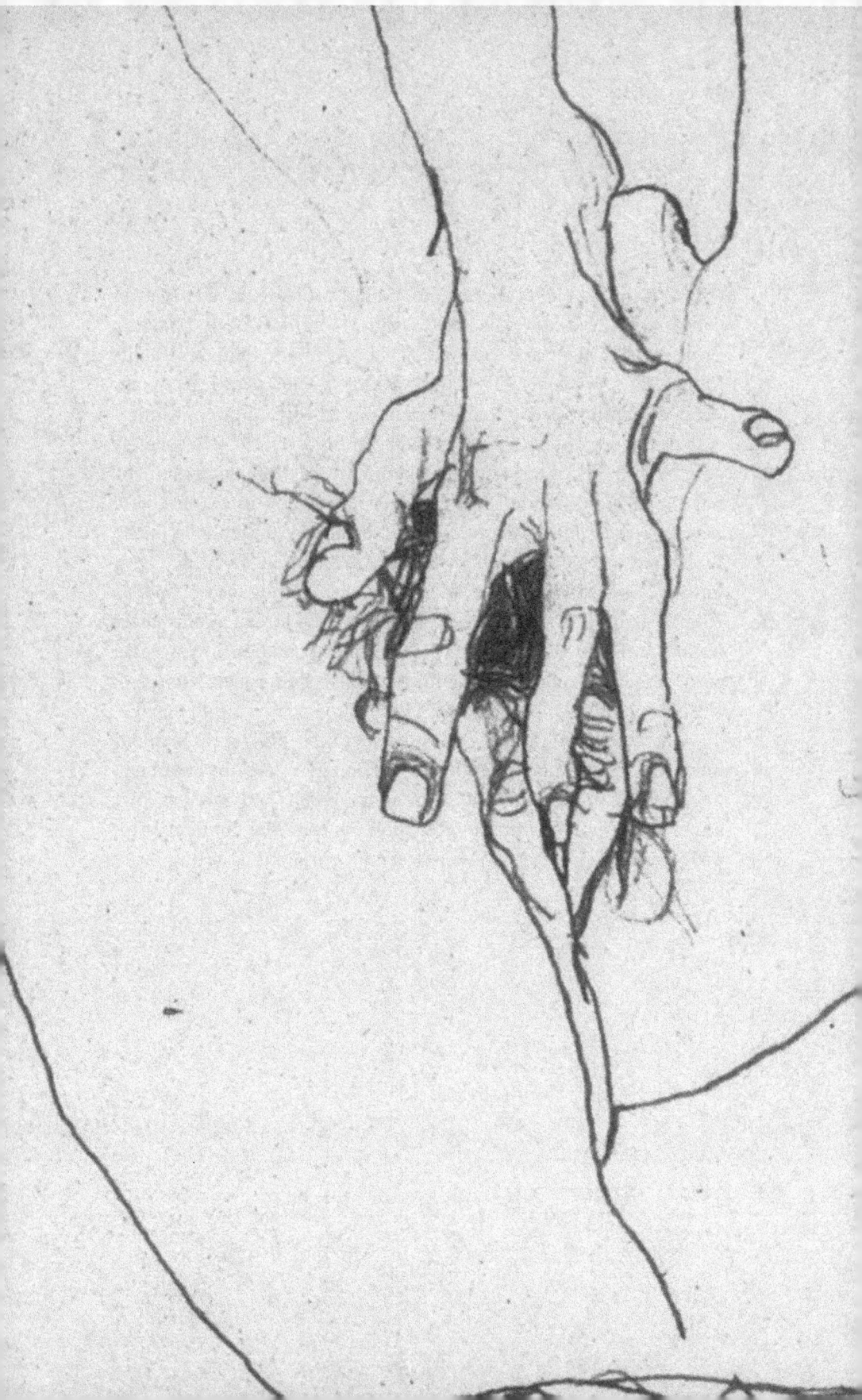

GUSTAV KLIMT

Gustav Klimt is one of those 'acceptable' erotic artists, whose art is consumed these days as mild erotica, regularly appearing in prints and posters and calendars, next to Henri Matisse, Claude Monet and Vincent van Gogh. Klimt never strays from the heterosexist norm of soft-core pornographic consumption. Klimt is ruthlessly, vigorously heterosexual in his art. He passionately adores women, and is a modern summary of all male artists who have loved and painted women. In paintings such as *Danae*, *The Kiss* and *Woman*, Klimt produced luxuriant, post-Symbolist, post-Byzantine icons of femininity in that Art Nouveau style of Vienna termed 'Secessionstil'.[1] Decadence or over-indulgence is one of Klimt's hallmarks. At times, only Gustave Moreau seems more luxuriant. Klimt depicts naked or half-naked bodies flowing over each other, entwined and writhing but also half-asleep, their eyes closed or half-open, as in stuck in some slow motion opium orgy.[2]

Gustav Klimt flattens every element of his representations onto one picture plane, and turns the image into pure ornamentation and decoration. He is supremely stylish, and rarely allows any evil serpent to slither in and spoil his basically tame nostalgic paradise. In his friezes, one sees the epic grandeur asserting itself.

---

1 G. Klimt: *Danae*, c. 1905, 77 x 80cm, Galerie Weltz, Salzburg; *The Kiss*, 1907-8, 180 x 180cm, Österreichische Galerie, Vienna; *Woman*, 1913, pencil 56 x 35cm, Vicktor Fogarassy Collection,
2 See, for instance, Gustav Klimt's *The Virgin*, 1912-3, Narodny Galerie, Prague

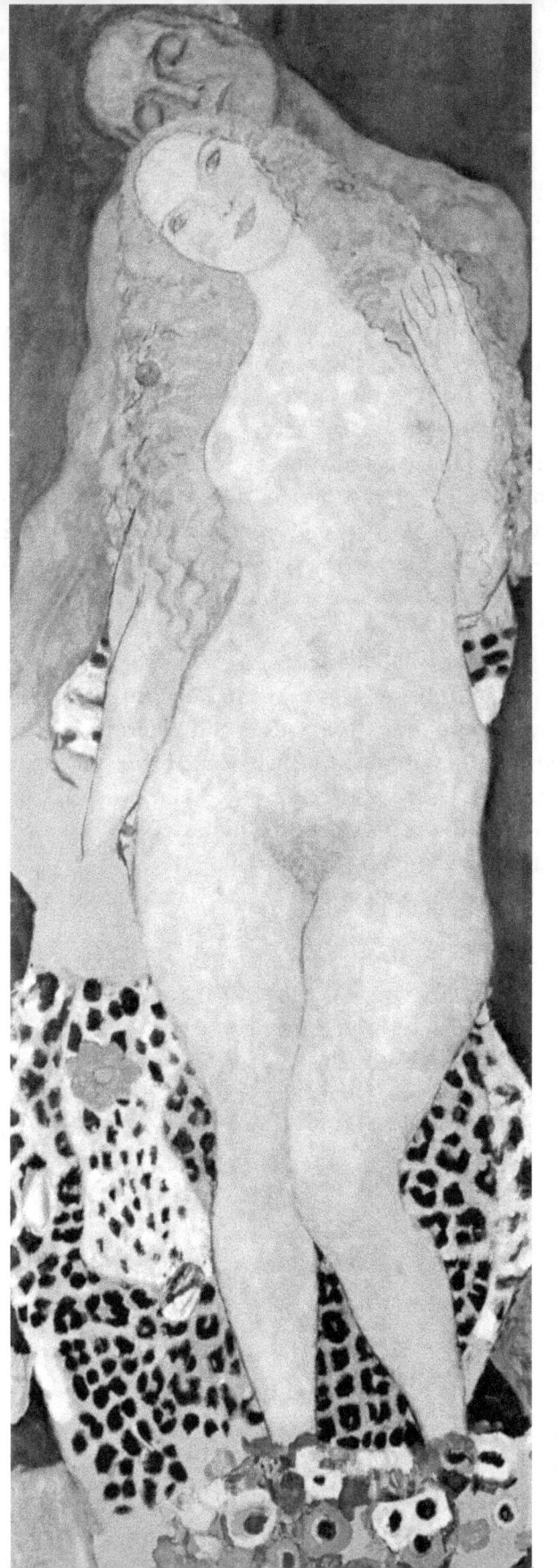

Gustav Klimt,
Adam and Eve

GUSTAV KLIMT

Gustav Klimt's art is relentlessly ornamental. He dispenses with three dimensionality, and goes for an abstract flatness, as in *The Fulfilment* – which features an erotic embrace like that depicted in *The Kiss* – where the background is a mosaic of swirls.[1] Klimt's art is utterly sensual, in its intent, and the signals it gives off: the lush colours, the profuse use of gold, the swirling shapes, the intricate patterns, flowing lines and the exaltations of the human form. In portraits such as that of Adele Bloch-Bauer, Klimt's paintings are as voluptuous as paintings get, with their profusions of gold, acres of gold, walls of gold.[2]

In the drawings the eroticism is more specific: Gustav Klimt drew women reclining, legs drawn up, masturbating, their hands moving dreamily over their vulvas and clitorises as they look at the viewer. They have titles such as *Reclining Woman*, or *Seated Woman, with Open Legs*.[3] Auguste Rodin was the immediate precursor of Klimt's masturbating nudes: Klimt had seen Rodin's erotic drawings,and they inspired him.[4]

As with the images of erotica and some porn, these are anonymous women, any women, with faces but no names, no characters.[5] These are orgasmic images, celebrating female orgasm. This form of eroticism is not confined to the 'private' drawings, drawings which can be seen as a private form of pornography: Gustav Klimt's famous *Judith* stares voluptuously at the viewer with her eyes half-closed, in a orgasmic state.[6] It is a pose cultivated by Hollywood stars, the seductive, luscious look to camera.

1 G. Klimt: *The Fulfilment*, c. 1905-9, Musée des Beaux Arts, Strasbourg
2 G. Klimt: *Adele Bloch-Bauer*, 1907, Österreichische Galerie, Vienna
3 G. Klimt: *Reclining Woman*, 1912-8, pencil, 37 x 56cm, Grapische Sammlung Albertina, Vienna
4 A. Rodin: *Reclining Female Nude*, c. 1900, pencil, 12.2 x 8in, Musée Rodin, Paris
5 G. Klimt: *Seated Woman, with Open Legs*, 1916/7, pencil, 57 x 38cm; *Recumbent Semi-Nude*, 1914/5, blue crayon, 37 x 56cm, Historical Museum, Vienna
6 G. Klimt: *Judith I*, 1901, Österreichische Galerie, Vienna

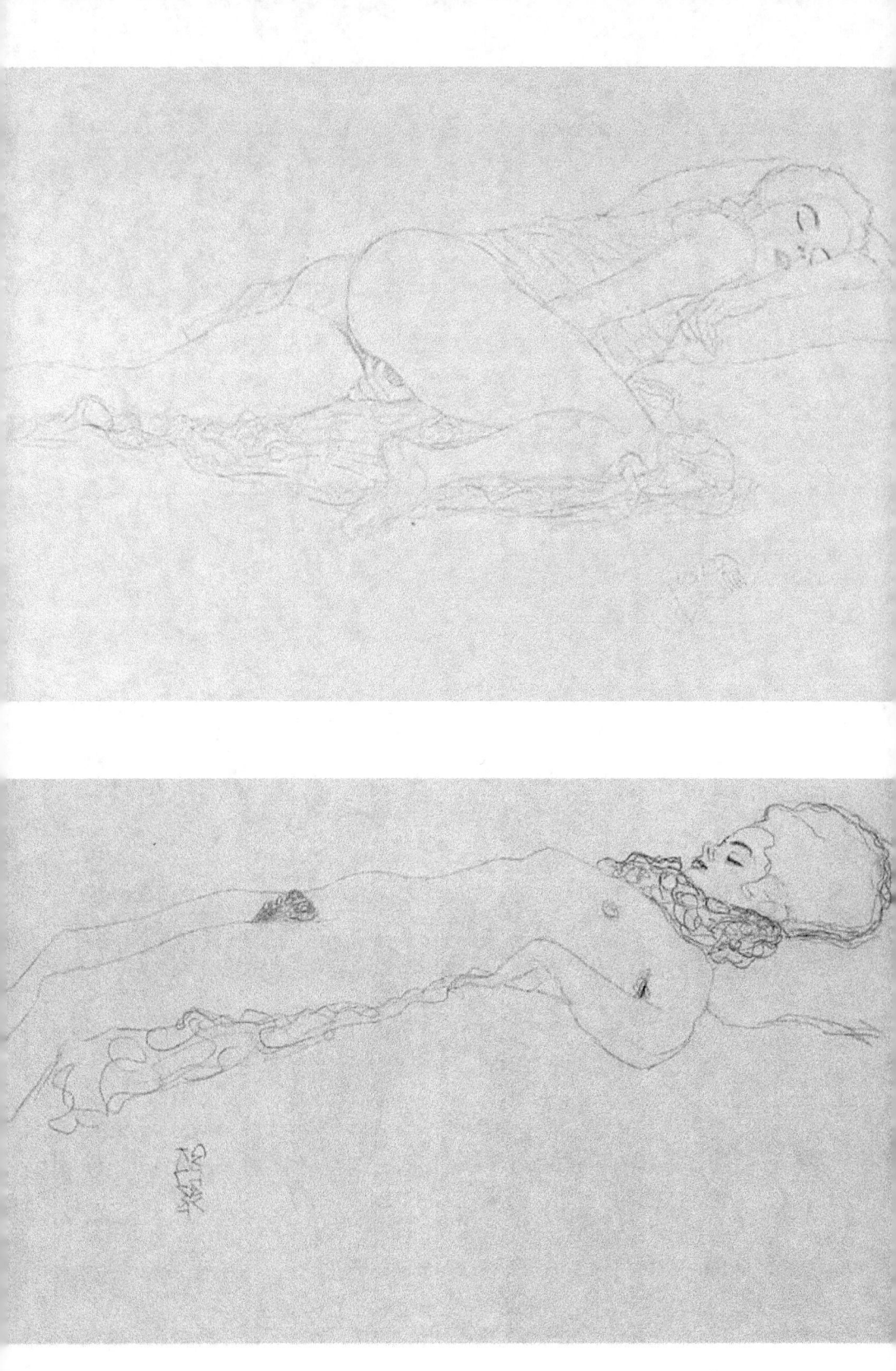

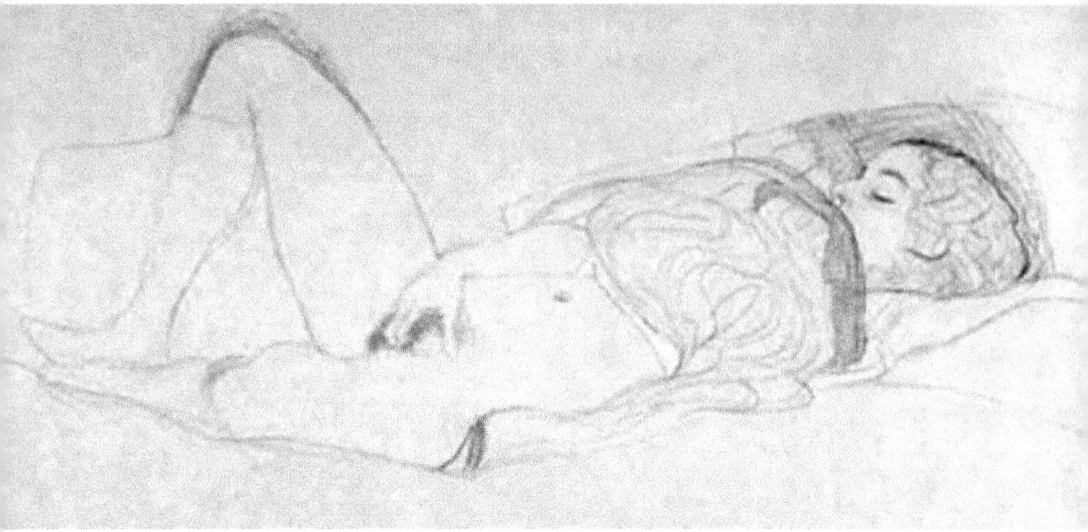

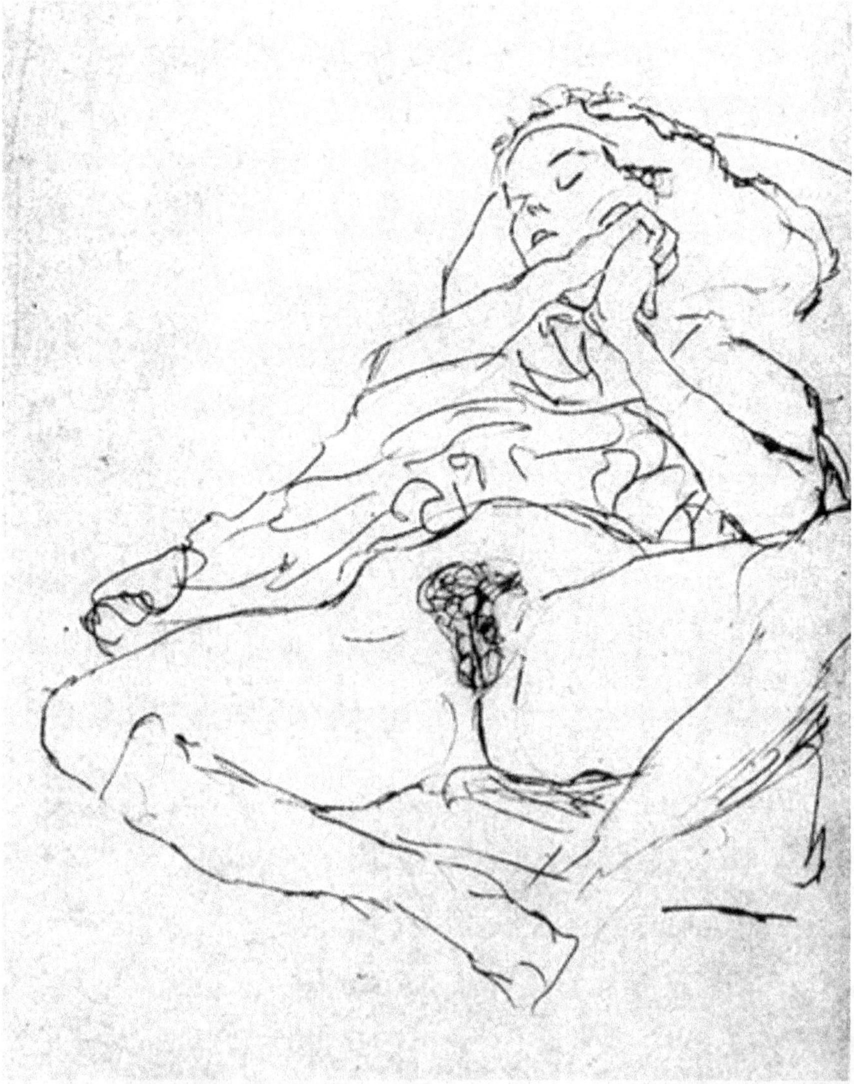

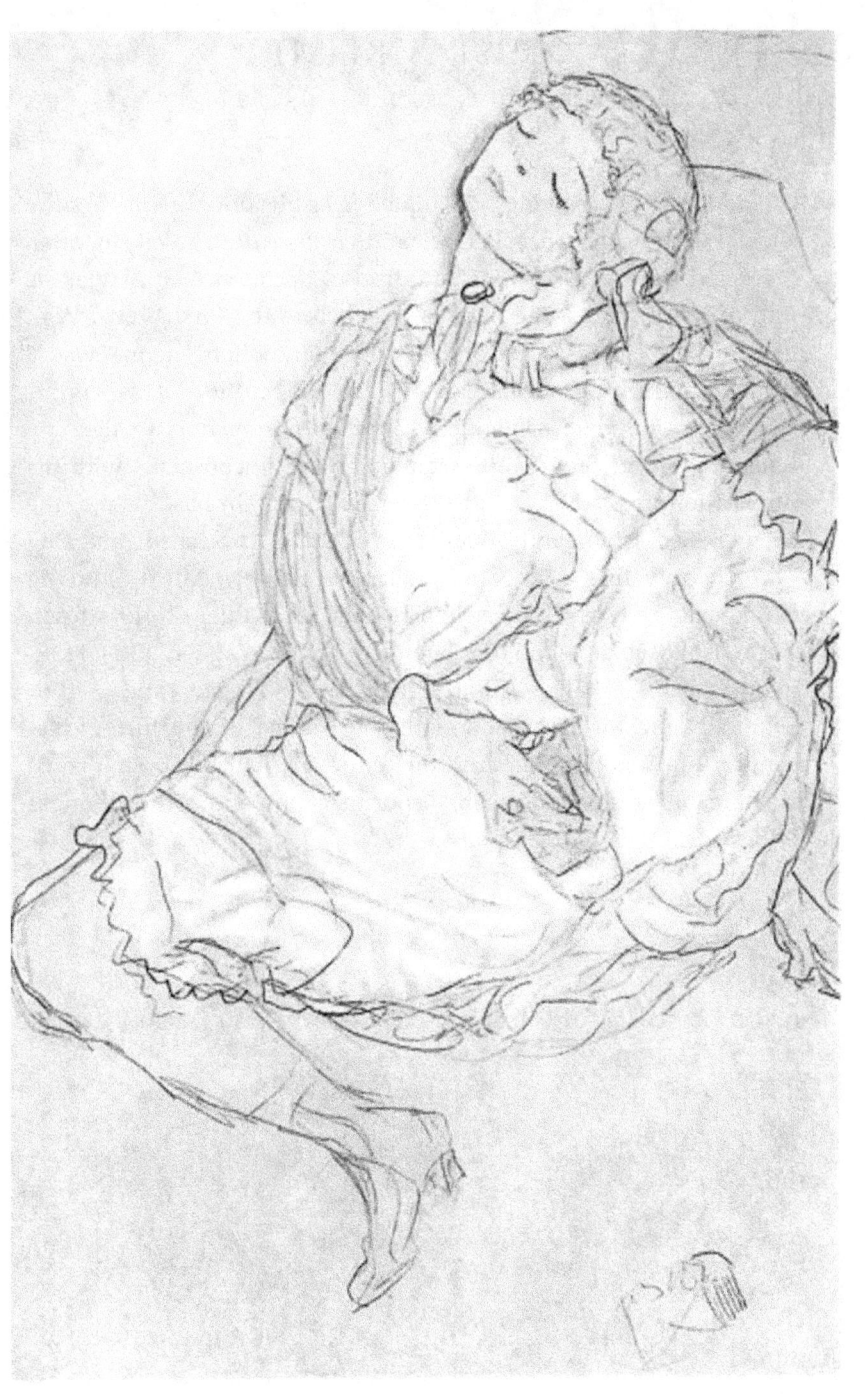

GUSTAV KLIMT

Gustav Klimt's drawings circulated as soft porn in *fin-de-siècle* Vienna among the art collectors and *cogniscenti*. The city is often marketed now as a seething cauldron of decadence and style, the End of the Empires, the heady years before the First World War, like Berlin before the Second World War, when Vienna was a fevered mass of eroticism, death, art and culture. This mythic Vienna is the over-romanticized *mittel European* city, the city where Sigmund Freud was opening up the unconscious with the publication in 1899 of *The Interpretation of Dreams*, where the Vienna Secession and Wiener Werkstäte produced amazing graphic and fine art. Names such as Robert Musil, Ludwig Wittgenstein, Karl Kraus, Freud, Gustav Mahler, Kolo Moser, Oscar Kokoschka, Arnold Schoenberg, Otto Wagner, Josef Hoffmann, JosePH Stalin, Adolf Hitler, Leon Trotsky and Arthur Schnitzler are all associated with the Vienna of the turn-of-the-century era, making it a cultural centre to rival the best. Vienna was the city of sex and death, of pornography and prostitution, as critics attest.[1]

---

1 See Frank Whitford: *Egon Schiele*, Thames & Hudson 1981, 92f

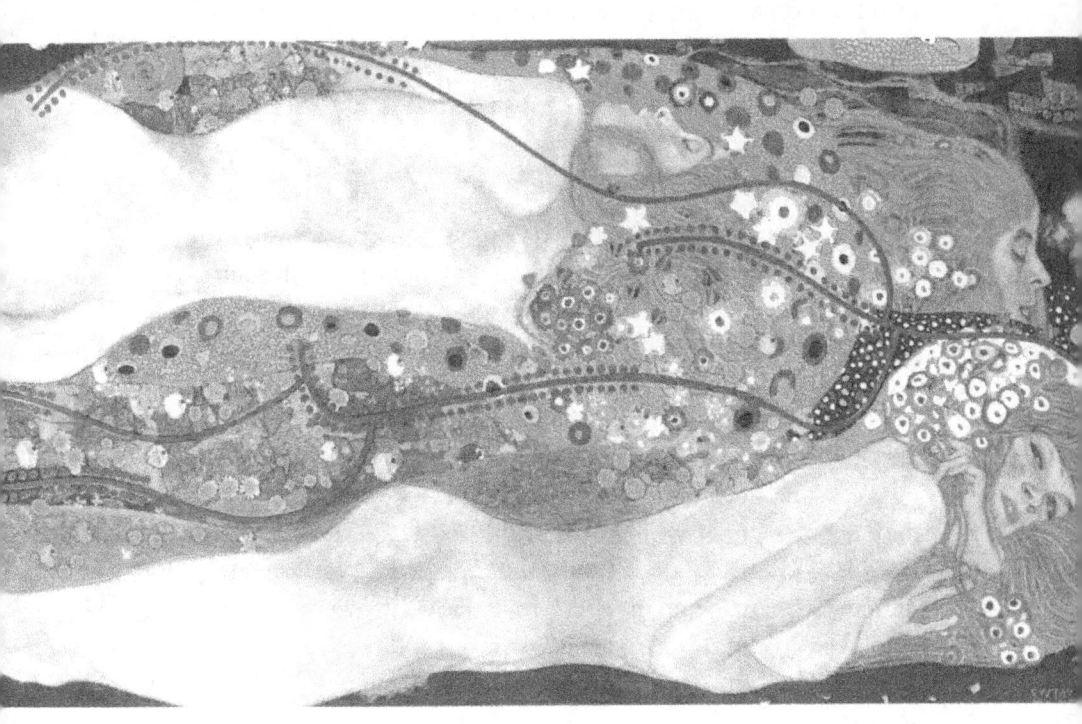

Gustav Klimt

GUSTAV KLIMT

The drawings of women lying back with their legs spread are pure pornography – the *Seated Nude*, for example.[1] *Goldfish* depicts in oil a woman, nude of course, squatting, buttocks prominent.[2] Women are seen as water, that symbolic 'feminine' element, in *Flowing Water*.[3] *Water Serpents I* is the usual Gustav Klimt offering,[4] a semi-nude woman sliding down the picture, eyes closed, dreamy, asleep perhaps, or in bliss, blissed-out, her hair, long of course, flowing around her. So many of Klimt's figures are elongated, slipping vertically down the painting, caught in a cascade of ornamentation. This is the standard Klimtesque scenario, this dreamy nude slipping past the viewer, as in his university pictures and large-scale paintings: *Philosophy, Medicine, Jurisprudence*.[5]

Gustav Klimt's depictions of women are archetypical, absolutely at the centre of mainstream Western art. His lesbian imagery, for instance, is, essentially, that of pornography. When he paints pregnant women, as in the great *Beethoven Frieze*, or in *Hope II*, he uses a much censored image in Western art.[6] The nude, pregnant woman still provokes controversy when it is displayed in the popular media or in art today. Klimt's pregnant women, though, are simply part of his overall exaltation of women.

1 G. Klimt: *Seated Nude with Closed Eyes*, 1913, pencil, 57 x 37cm; *Reclining Semi-Nude Woman*, 1913, pencil, 56 x 36cm, both Historical Museum, Vienna
2 G. Klimt: *Goldfish*, 1901/2, oil on canvas, 150 x 46cm, Dübi-Miller Foundation, Kunstmuseum, Solothurn
3 G. Klimt: *Flowing Water*, 1898, oil, 52 x 65cm, St Etienne Gallery, New York
4 G. Klimt: *Water Serpents I*, 1904-7, oil, gold leaf, mixed media on parchment, 19.6 x 7.8in, Österreichische Galerie, Vienna
5 G. Klimt: *Philosophy*, 1899-1907, oil on canvas, 430 x 300cm, destroyed; *Medicine*, 1900-7, oil on canvas, 430 x 300cm, destroyed; *Jurisprudence*, 1903-7, oil on canvas, 430 x 300cm, destroyed
6 G. Klimt: *Beethoven Frieze*, 1902, casein, gold leaf, semiprecious stones, mother-of-pearl, gypsum, charcoal, pastel and pencil on plaster, 216 x 636cm, Österreichische Galerie, Vienna; *Hope II*, 1907-8, oil and gold on canvas, 110.5 x 110.5cm, Museum of Modern Art, New York. See Marian Bisanz-Prakken: "The Beethoven Exhibition of the Vienna Secession", in Erika Nielsen, ed: *Focus on Vienna 1900*, Houston German Studies, no. 4, Fink, Munich 1982; Peter Vergo: "Gustav Klimt's Beethoven Frieze", *Burlington Magazine*, 115, no. 839, 1973, 109f

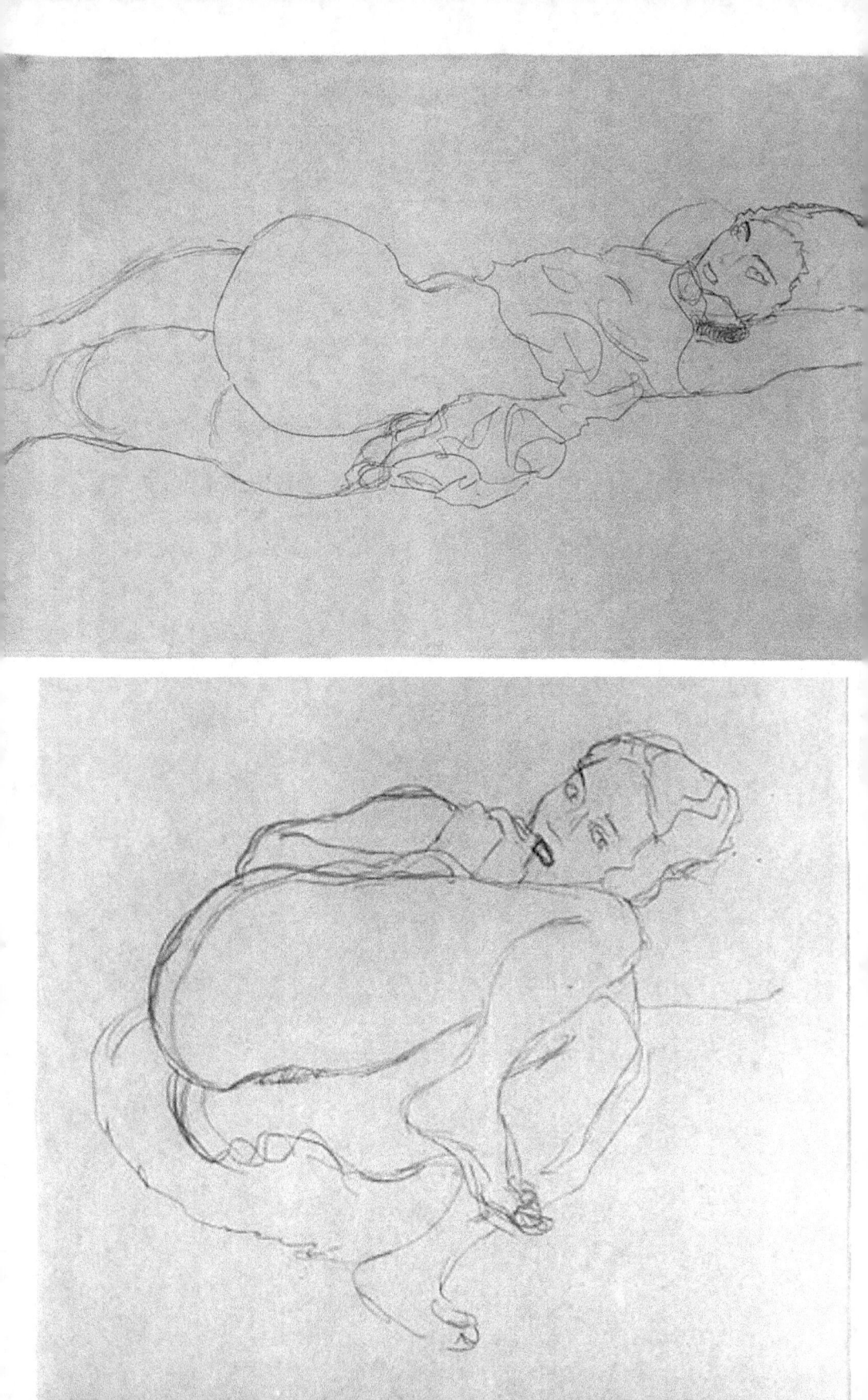

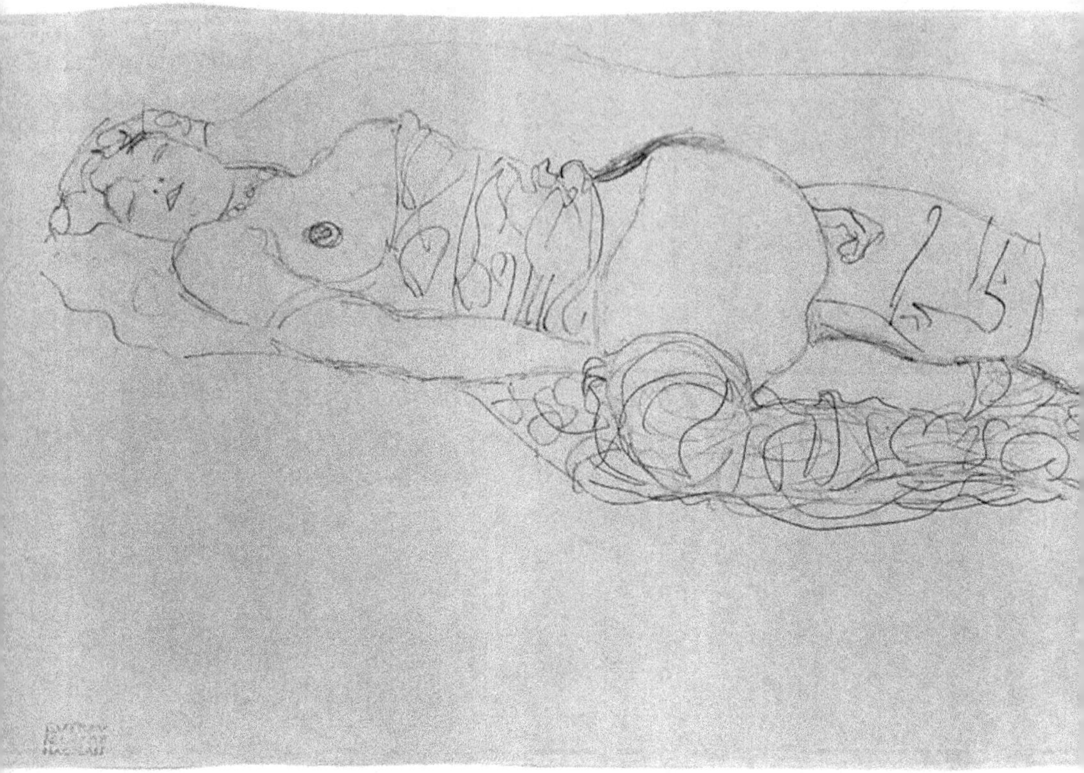

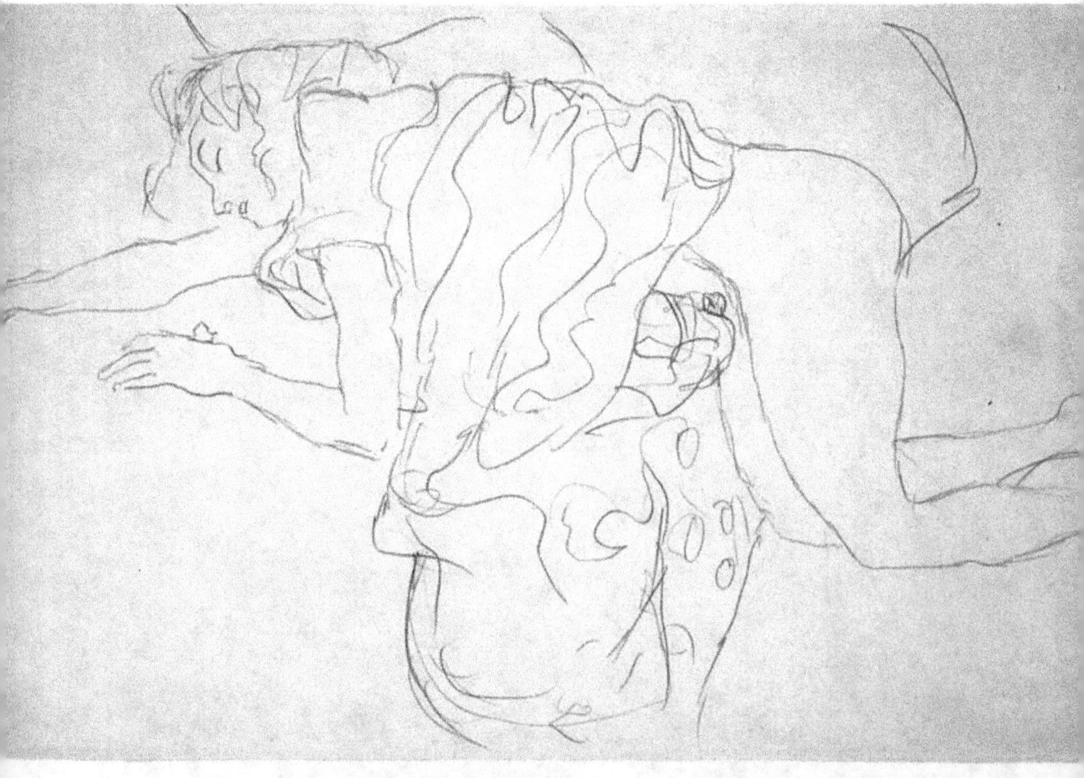

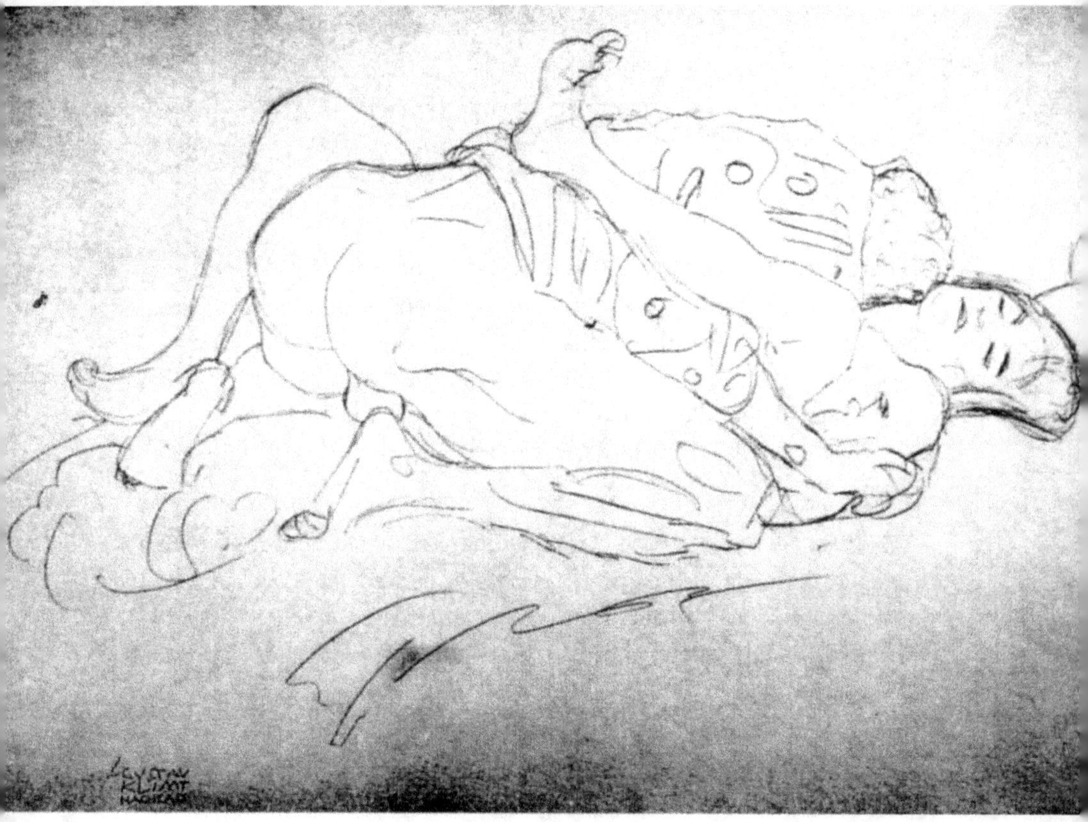
GUSTAV KLIMT NACHLASS

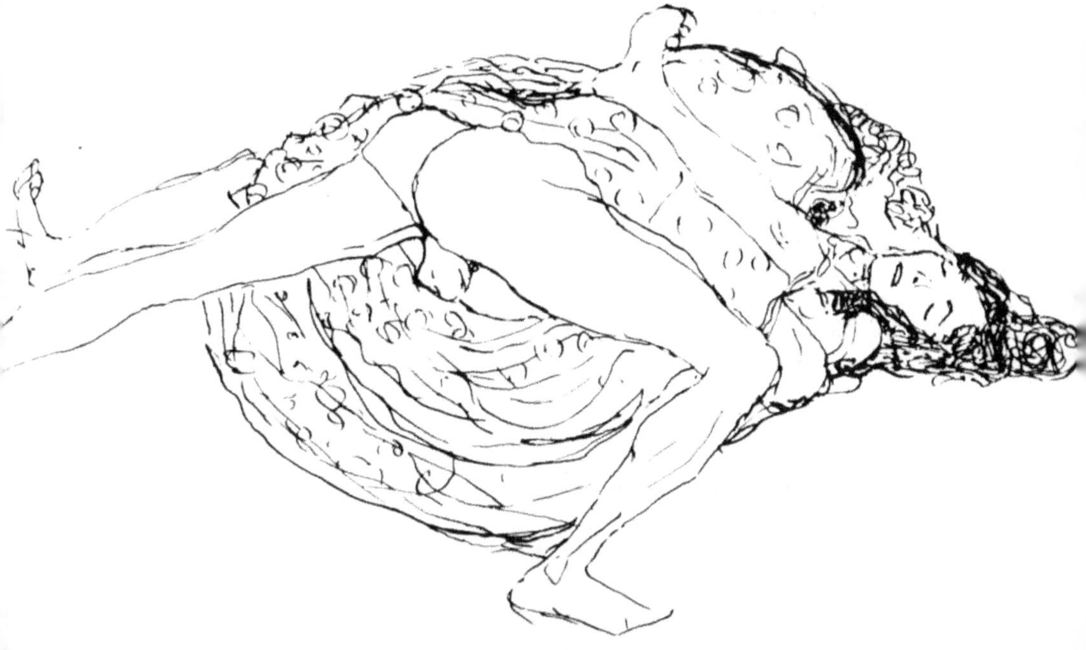

AUGUSTE RODIN

There are a number of renowned modern artists who are unrestrained in their exaltation of women. Auguste Rodin is a typical example. Of the *Venus de'Medici*, Auguste Rodin wrote:

> Notice all the voluptuous curvings of the hip... And now, here, the adorable dimples along the loins... It is truly flesh... You would think it moulded by caresses!

Auguste Rodin is the classic womanizer artist, who made love to his models physically as well as psychologically and æsthetically. His models became his mistresses (such as Camille Claudel). Like many artists, he produced erotica for private consumption.

But enthusiastic eroticism infuses everything Auguste Rodin created. Sculptures such as *The Metamorphoses of Ovid* is typical – it depicts two lovers embracing.[1] The sculpture *Christ and the Magdalene* is more controversial, for it depicts Mary Magdalene sexually embracing the crucified Christ.[2] The image is blasphemous, fusing sex and religion in that age-old fashion. This eroticization of Mary Magdalene occurs also in the art of Félicien Rops and Eric Gill.

---

1 A. Rodin: *The Metamorphoses of Ovid*, plaster, height 13in
2 A. Rodin: *Christ and the Magdalene*, 1894

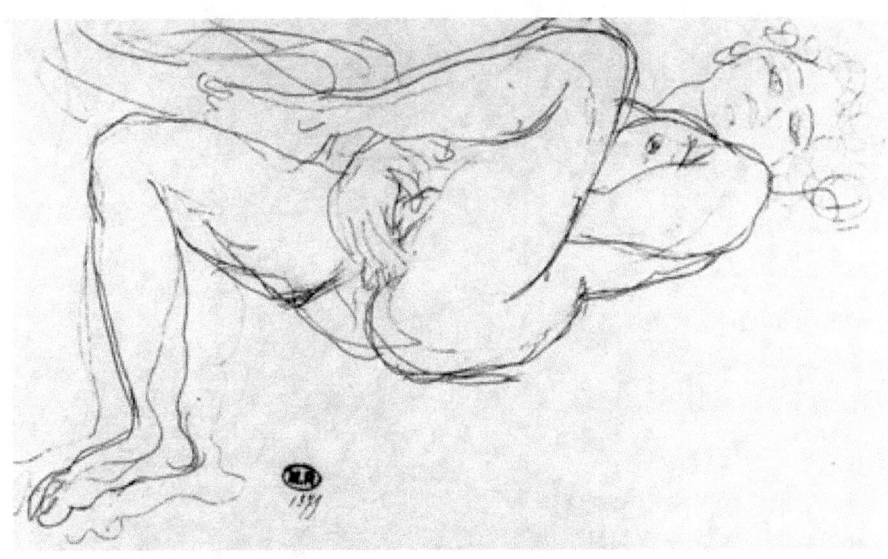

Auguste Rodin, drawings

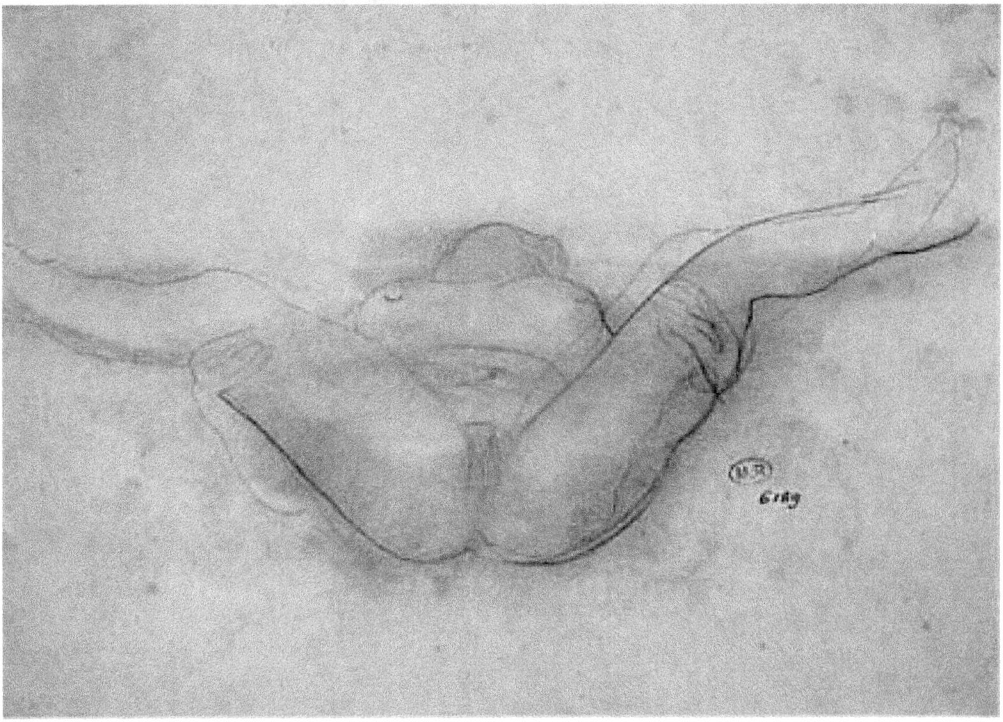

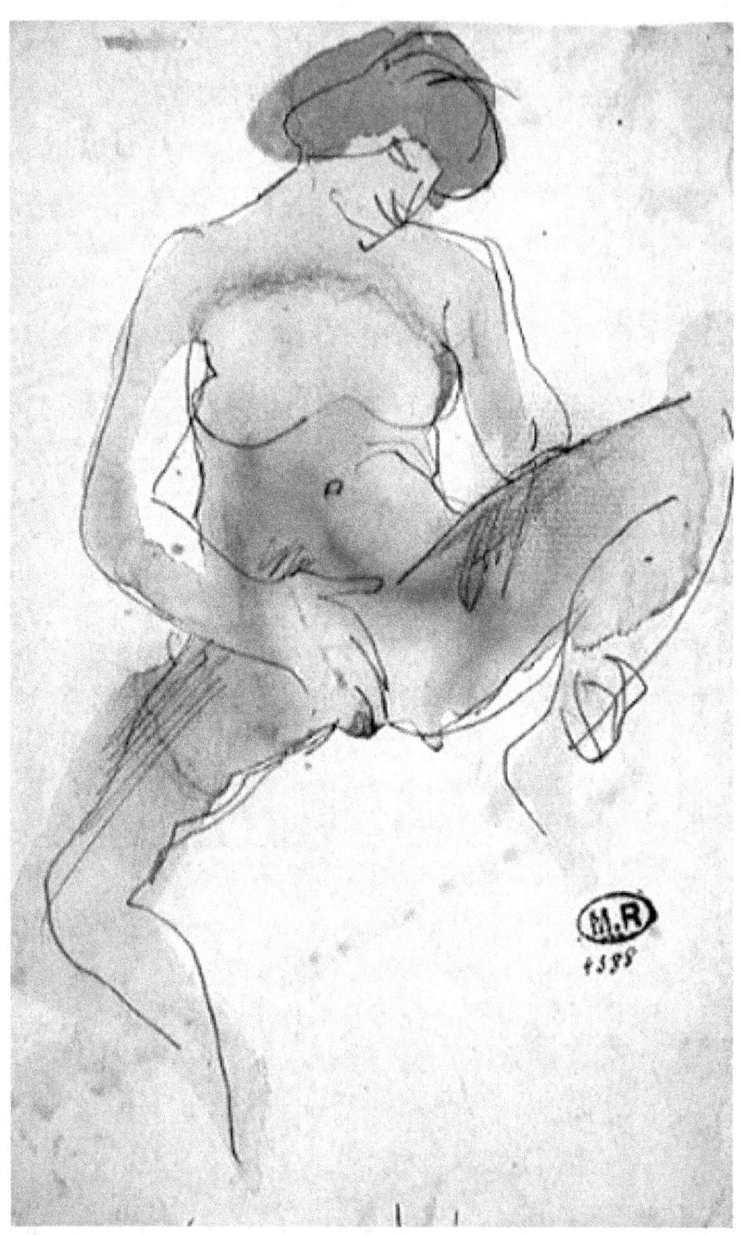

Auguste Rodin

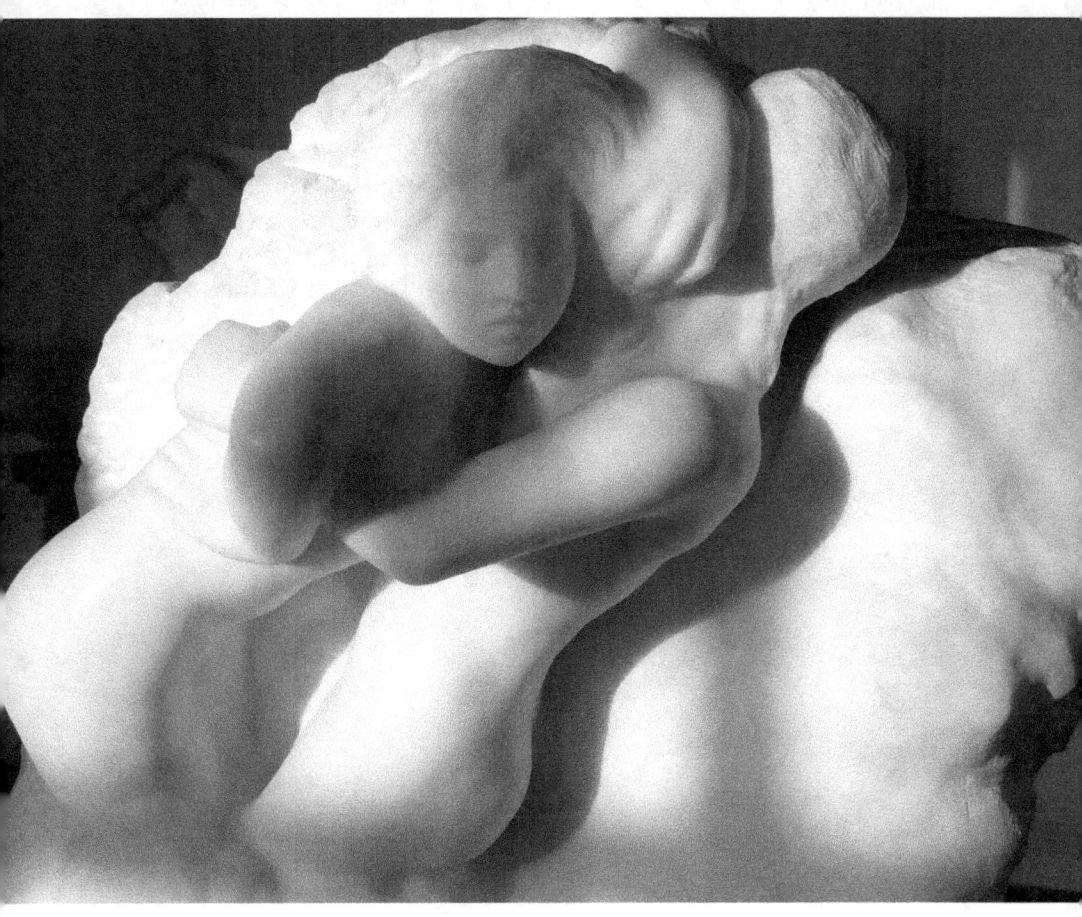

Auguste Rodin

EXPRESSIONISM

The Expressionists' worldview seems more authentic, closer to real life than, say, that of the Impressionists or the Neo-Classicists. In Expressionism we get a sharp sense of the harshness of existence. There are few smiles or laughs in Expressionist art – think of the art of Karl Schmidt-Rottluff, Max Pechstein or Alexander Kanoldt – yet their view of life seems closer to the real thing than that of many other artists. But in amongst the apparently sombre or dour images there are many wild colours and much exuberance – especially in the art of Ernest Kirchner, Alexei von Jawlensky, Kees van Dongen and Gabriele Münter.

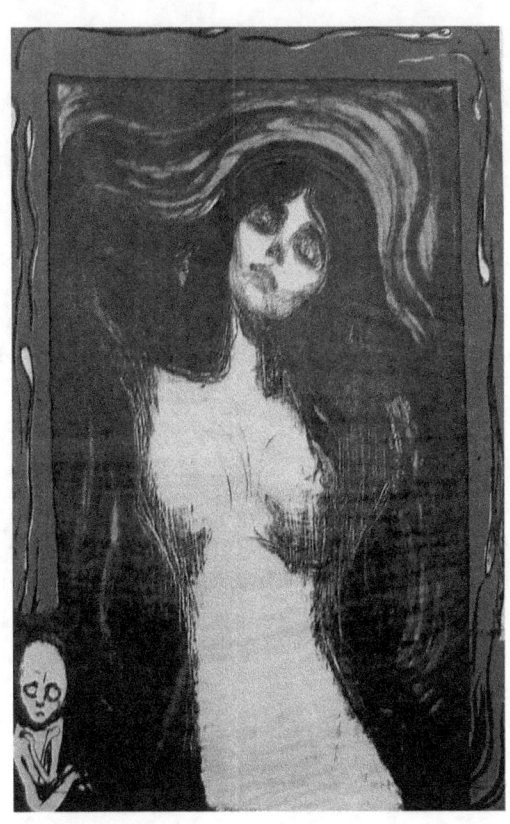

Sexuality in the tortured Scandinavian manner:
Edvard Munch's The Kiss and The Madonna

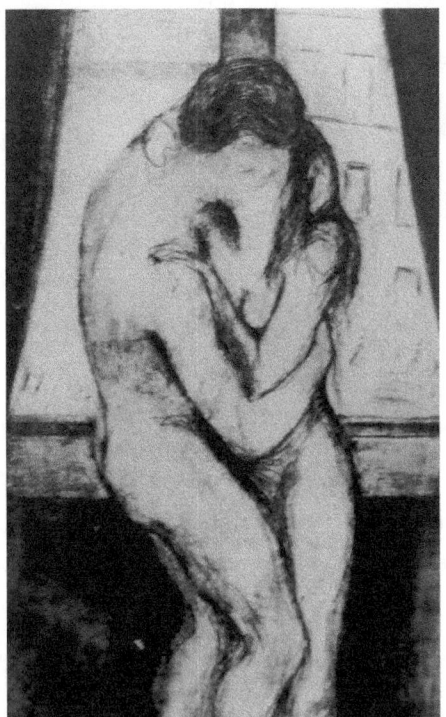

ERNEST LUDWIG KIRCHNER

Agony is one of the hallmark of Expressionist art, and this is true in the depictions of sexuality. Again, it is women who dominate the sexual discourse of the Expressionists. As with the Symbolists and the Viennese Secessionists and New Artists, the Expressionists use women as subjects and sexual objects, as sites of fears and desires about sexuality and life, as vehicles of lust and despair. The emotional and moral ambiguity is apparent in so much of Expressionist art. In Ernest Kirchner's art, for instance, we find simultaneous love and hate of his subjects, which he communicates with his vigorous descriptive lines and his offbeat use of colour, such as in *Five Women In the Street*.[1] Kirchner's portrait of a woman with her blouse pulled down to show her breasts is essentially no different from softcore pornographic images.[2] For art historians, Kirchner's eroticization of his subject is redeemed because of its 'artistic merit'. But no amount of art historical discussion of Kirchner's innovative colouration[3] obscures the fact that his painting objectifies women sexually.

1 Ernest Ludwig Kirchner: *Five Women in the Street*, 1913, 120 x 90cm, Wallraf-Richartz Museum, Cologne
2 E. Kirchner: *Semi-nude Woman With Hat*, 1911, 76 x 70cm, Wallraf-Richartz Museum, Cologne
3 See Wolf-Dieter Dube: *The Expressionists*, 42f

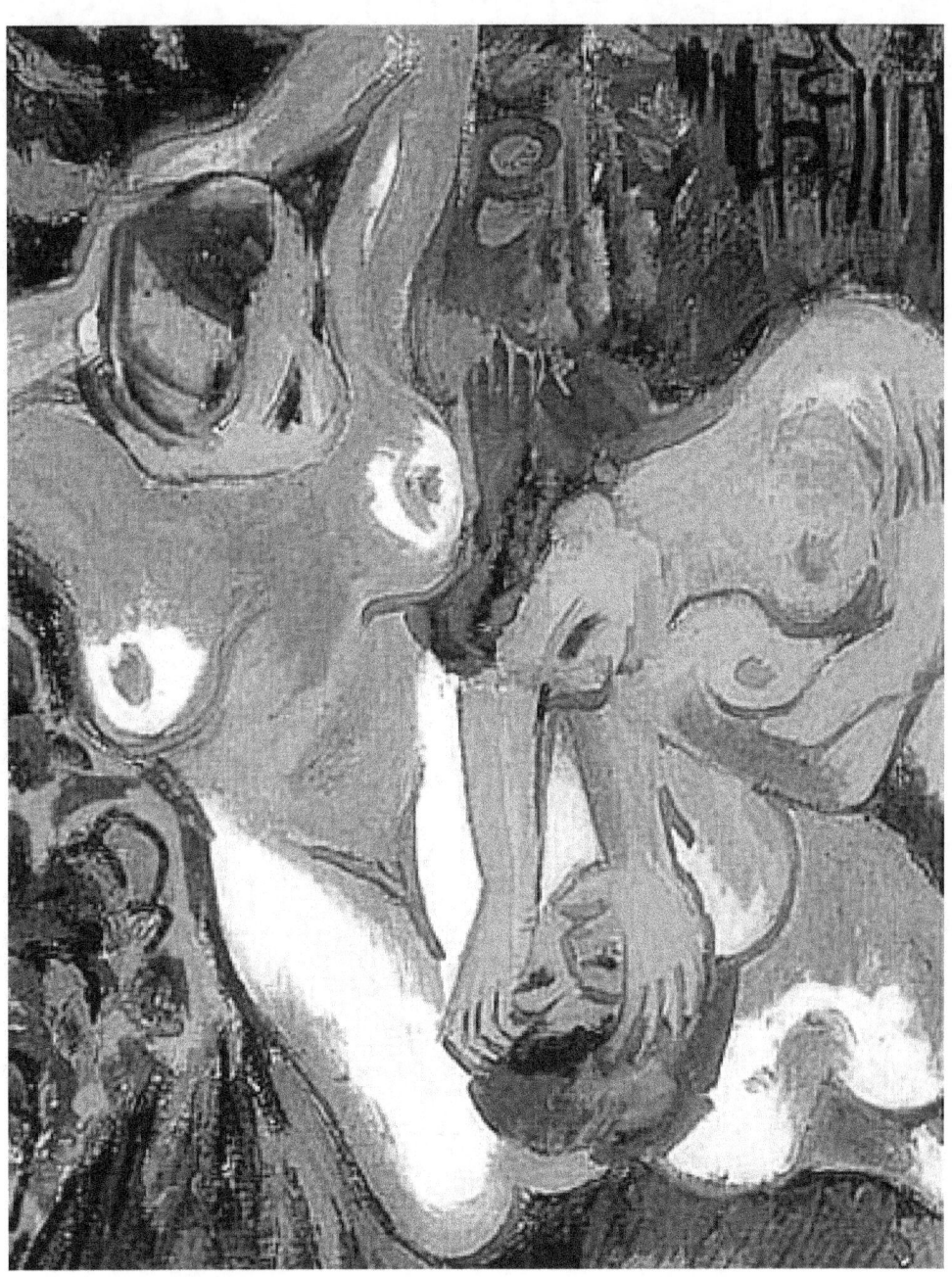

Ernest Ludwig Kirchner, Bathers On the Lawn, 1919

OTTO MUELLER

Otto Mueller's motif is a group of young women sitting in long grass. He painted variations on this theme many times.[1] The women are nude, have sallow eyes but no individual personality. They are 'types', with their pointed knees and elbows. They are made up of straight lines, and painted in a style that is deliberately 'primitive' or crude. Mueller's nude women are clearly erotic for him, though they are anonymous, abstracted, curiously bland, as if, once he had painted them, Mueller was scared by what he had created. So he takes all the individuality out of them, and turns them into a series of shapes. Pablo Picasso did this with his Avignon women, though they have more personality, more of a sense of self than Mueller's nude women.[2]

1 Otto Mueller: *Two Girls in the Grass*, 1905, tempera, 141 x 110cm, Staatsgalerie, Munich
2 Pablo Picasso: *Les Demoisels d'Avignon*, 1907, MOMA, New York

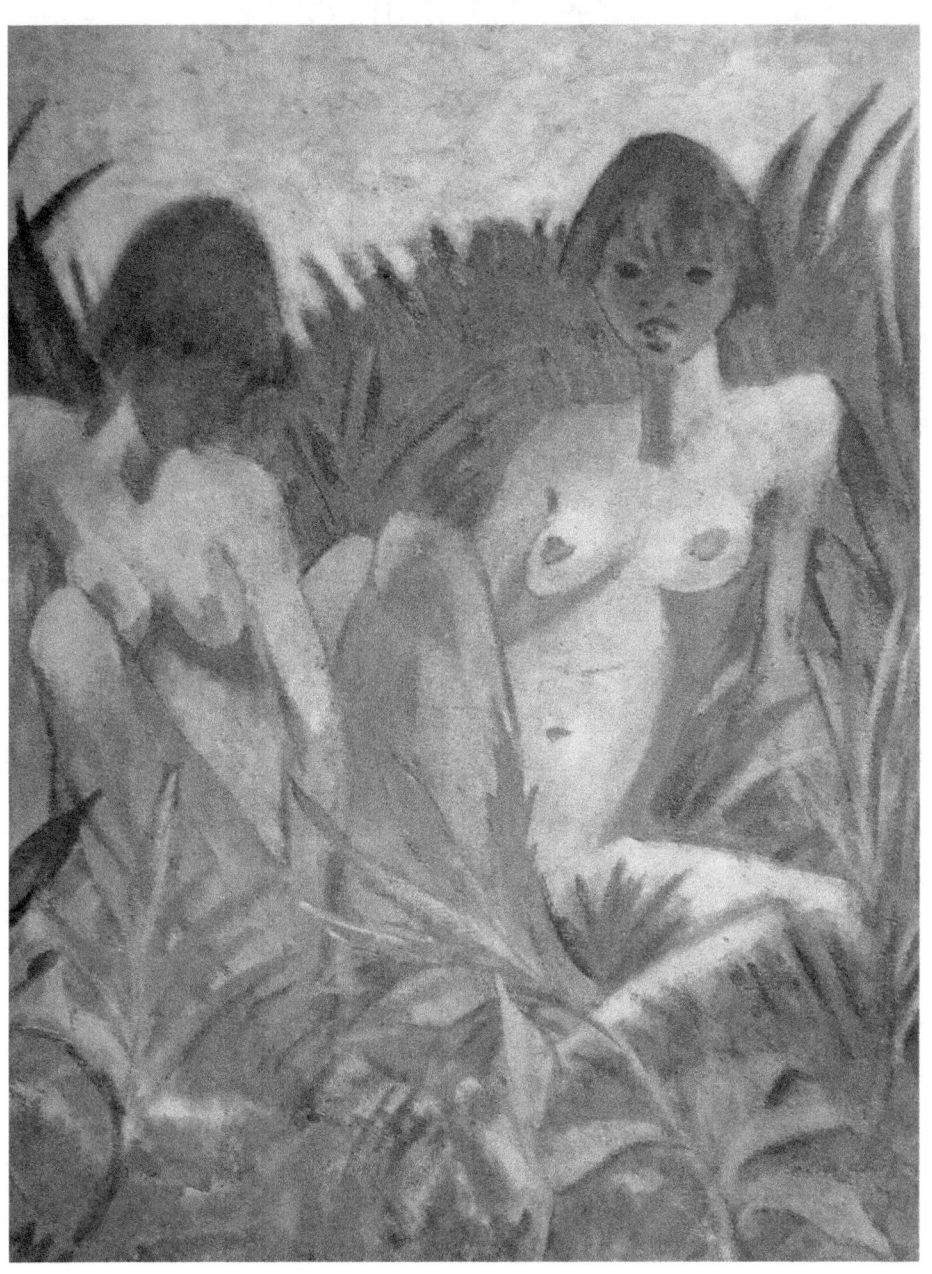

Otto Mueller, Two Girls In the Grass

ARISTIDE MAILLOL

Love infuses every gesture Aristide Maillol makes. There are no blemishes, no irregularities, no awkward poses in Maillol's city of women. Each figure is softly rounded, softly drawn or sculpted. It seems as if make artists have loved creating rounded forms in women since time immemorial – large-hipped women appear not only throughout Western art (in the art of Peter Rubens, Titian, Rembrandt van Rijn, and Henri Matisse), but also in prehistoric imagery, in those faceless, stone "Venuses". These 'large' women are less like potential lovers than mothers. They seem to conform to the Freudian and Lacanian emphasis on the mother as the male's first lover. The 'large' women in the works of Pablo Picasso, Henri Matisse, Auguste Rodin, Aristide Maillol and Paul Gauguin are motherly, so clearly the mother figure of psycho-analysis, and the Goddess of ancient mythology.

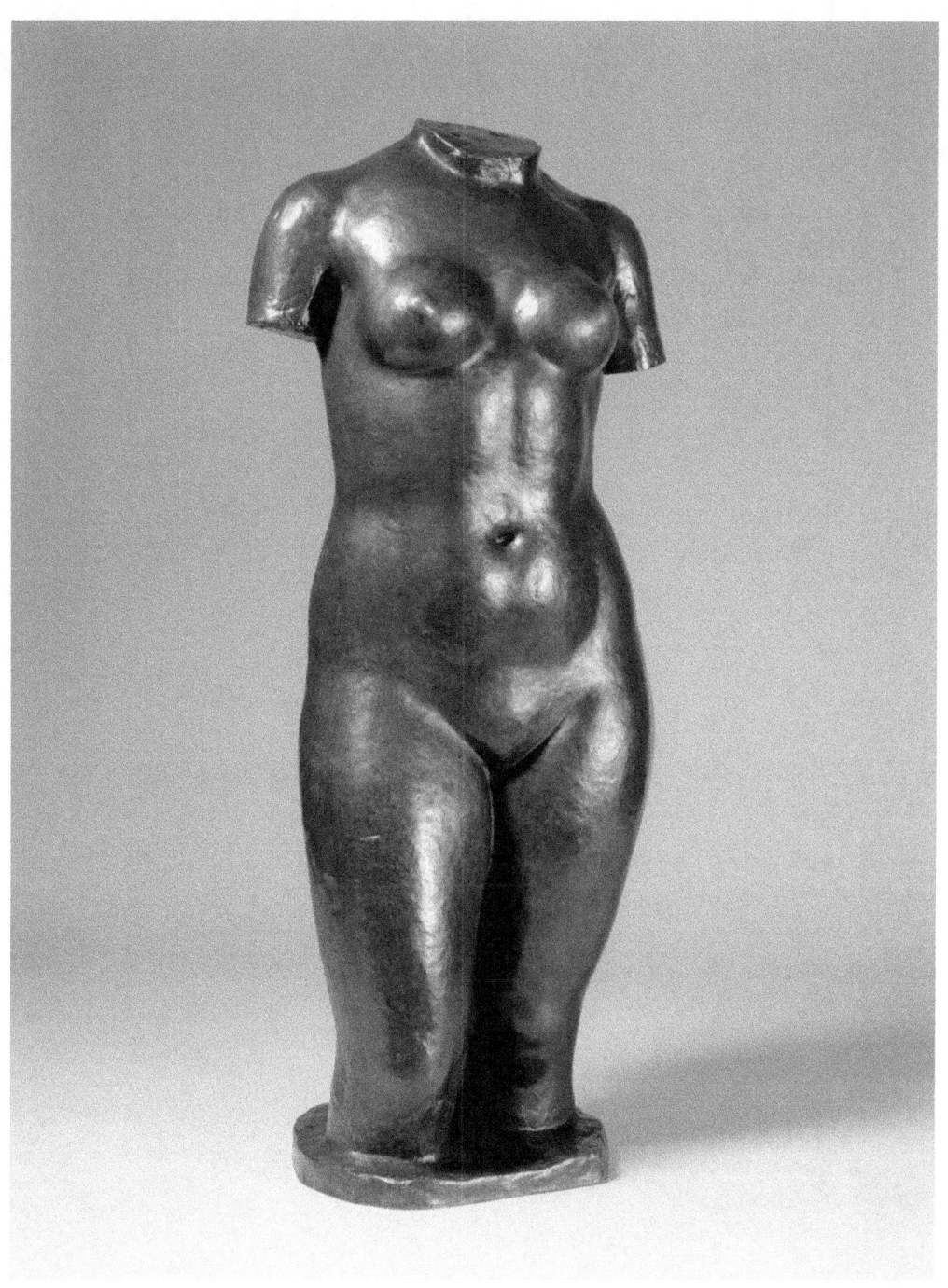

Aristide Maillol, Torso of a Young Woman, 1935,
Montreal Museum of Fine Arts

JULES PASCIN

Jules Pascin (1885-1930) is best remembered today as part of the circle of (post-) Expressionists (which included Chaim Soutine and Marc Chagall), in Paris in the 1920s. His nudes and erotica are less well-known, but noted for their sensuality.

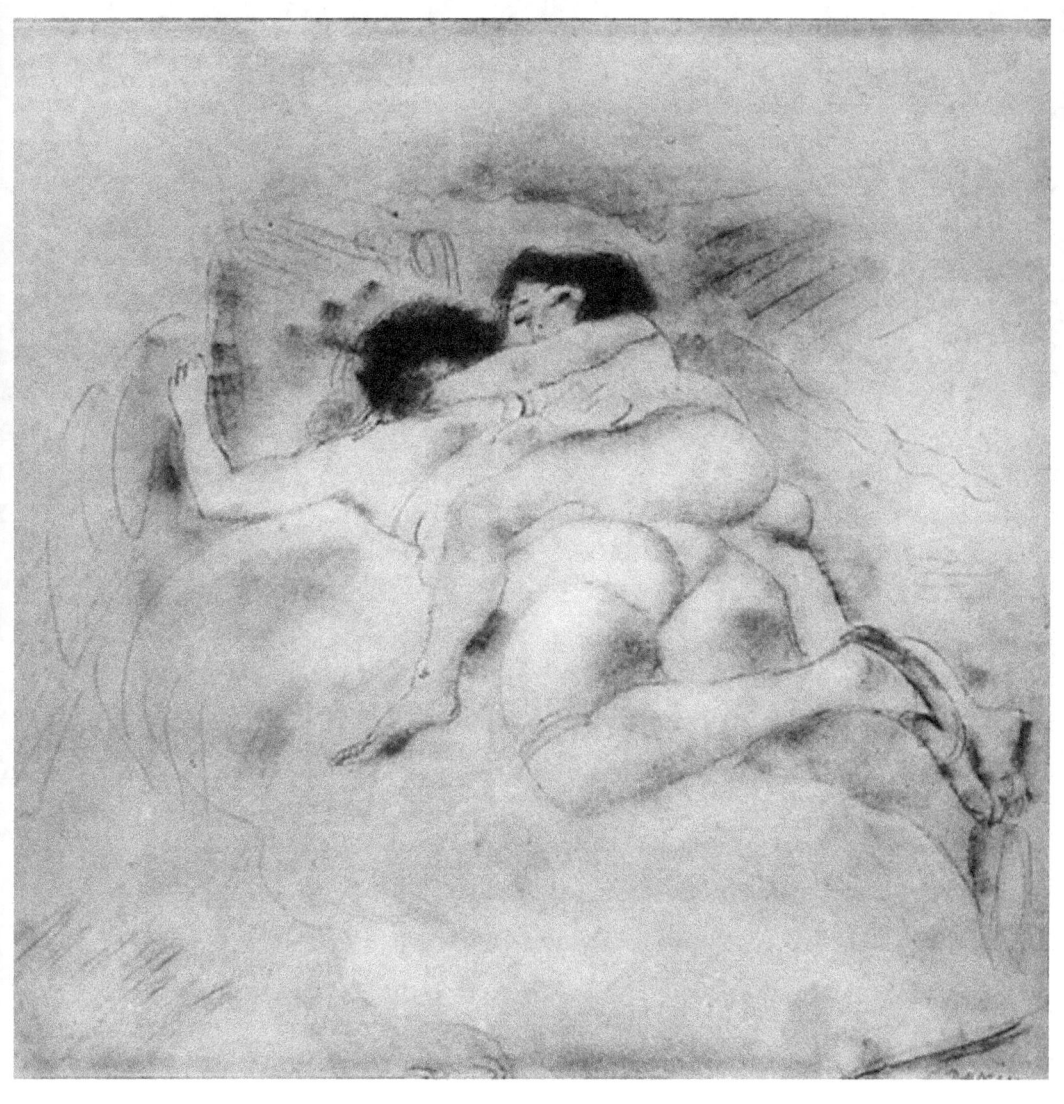

Jules Pascin

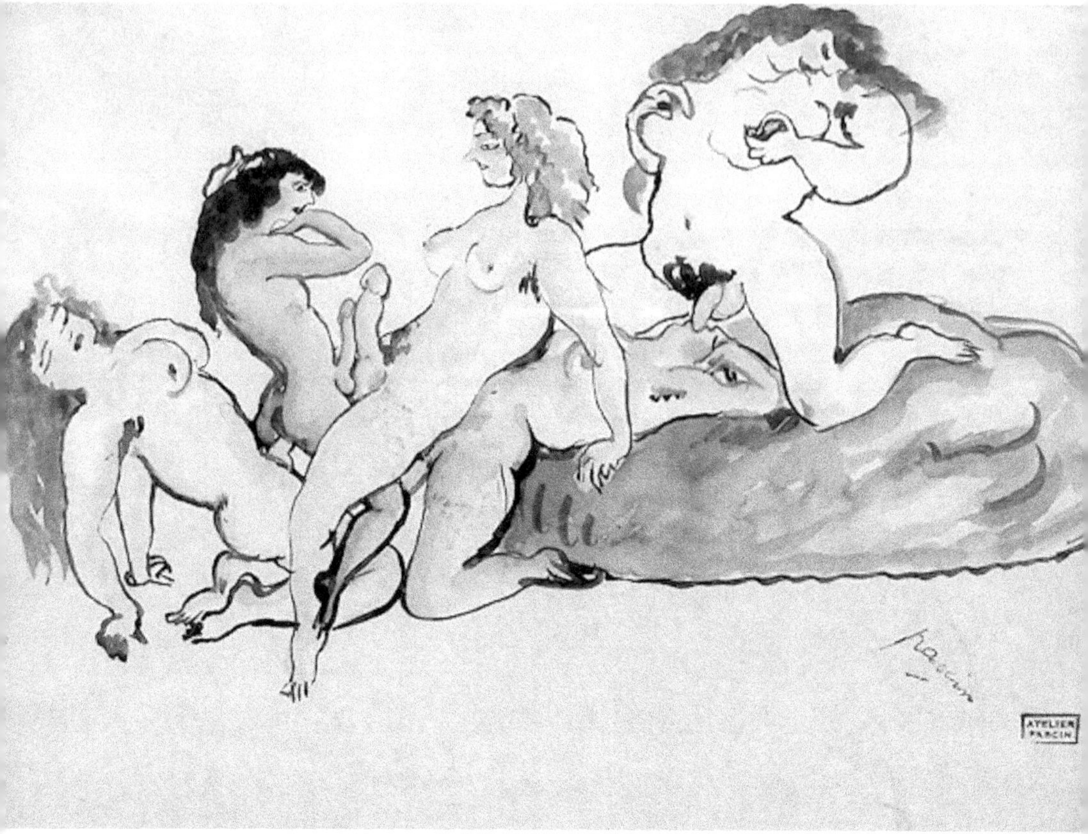

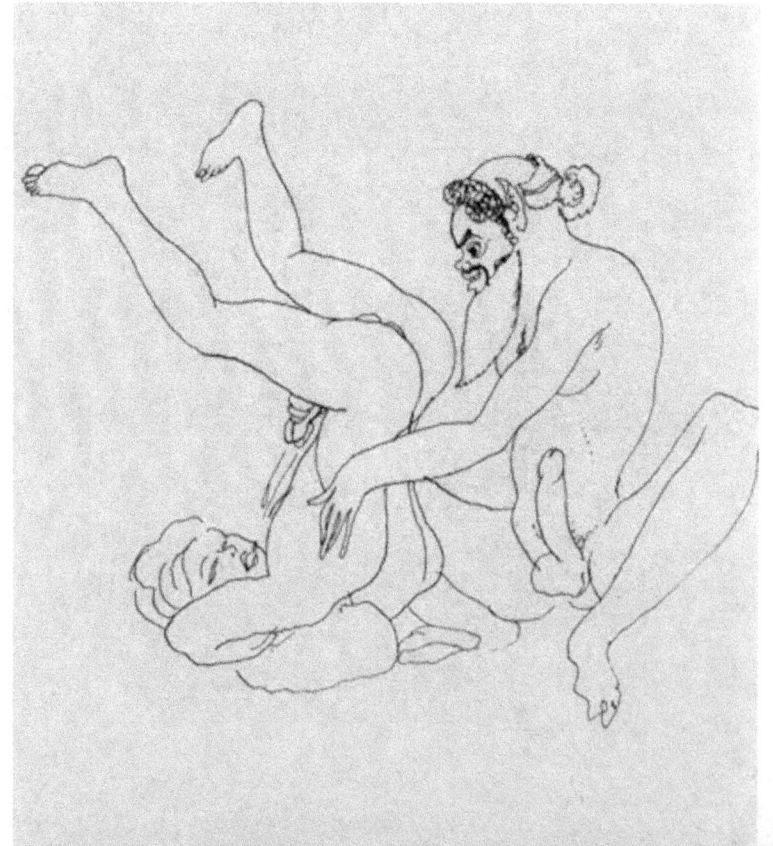

Jules Pascin

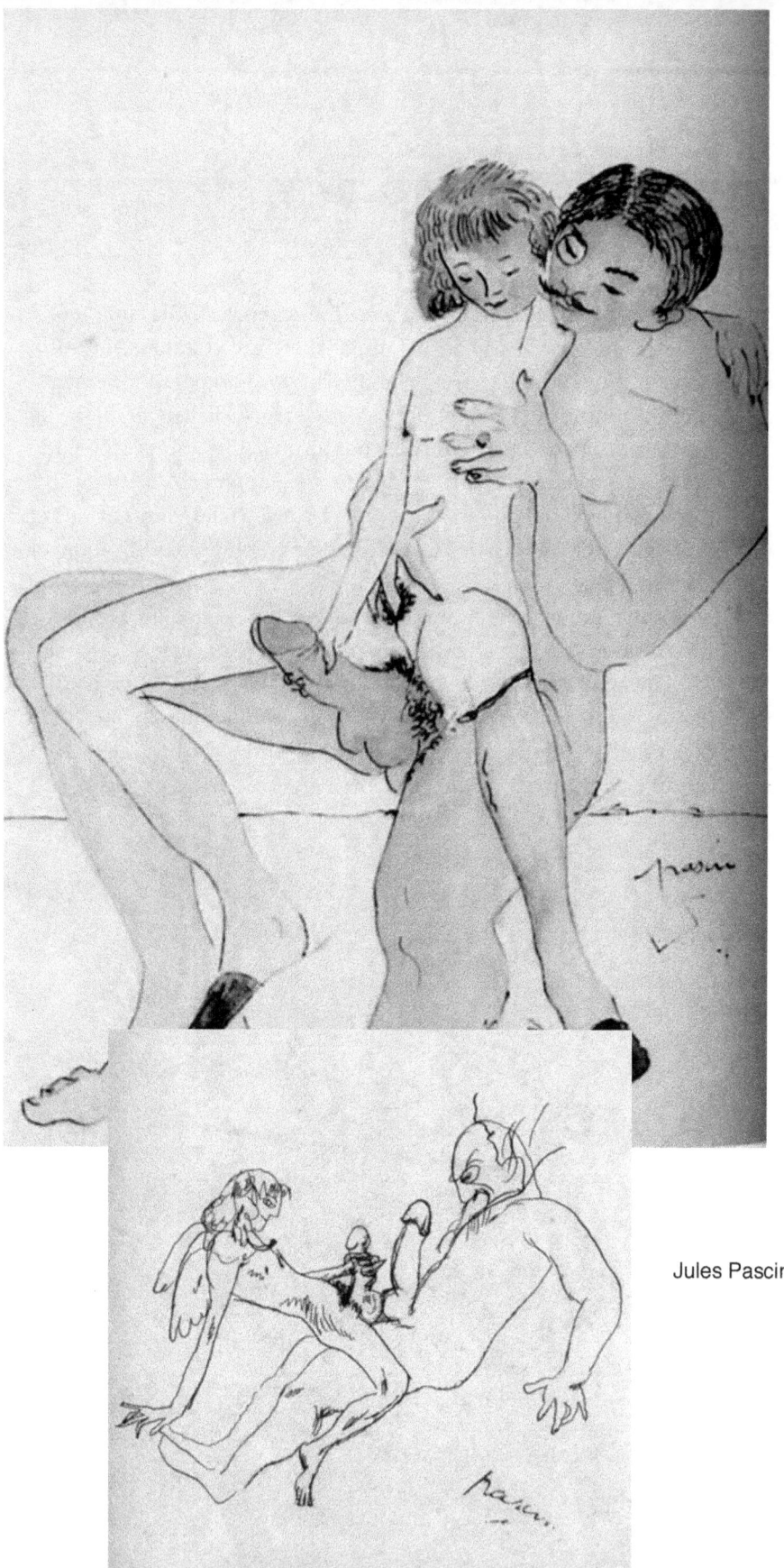

Jules Pascin

PHOTOGRAPHY

Eroticism in photography follows the same æsthetic and moral patterns as those found in painting. There are countless nudes in photography, ranging from 'high art' to pornography. Images such as those by US photographer Harry Callahan of his wife Eleanor seem to be distanced and formal, like the pastel nude drawings of Edgar Degas.[1] But the cool approach, of 'high art' photography, as in the art of Degas (who himself used photography), masks the age-old pornographic objectification of women.

Many erotic photographs have been marketed in the same way that erotica has always been marketed – as images of desire for consumption by devotees. One of the differences is that photographs can be reproduced in huge quantities – far more than the woodblock printing mechanisms of the early 19th century, for instance.

---

1 Callahan: *Eleanor, Port Huron*, 1954, 17 x 16.5cm, Museum of Modern Art, New York

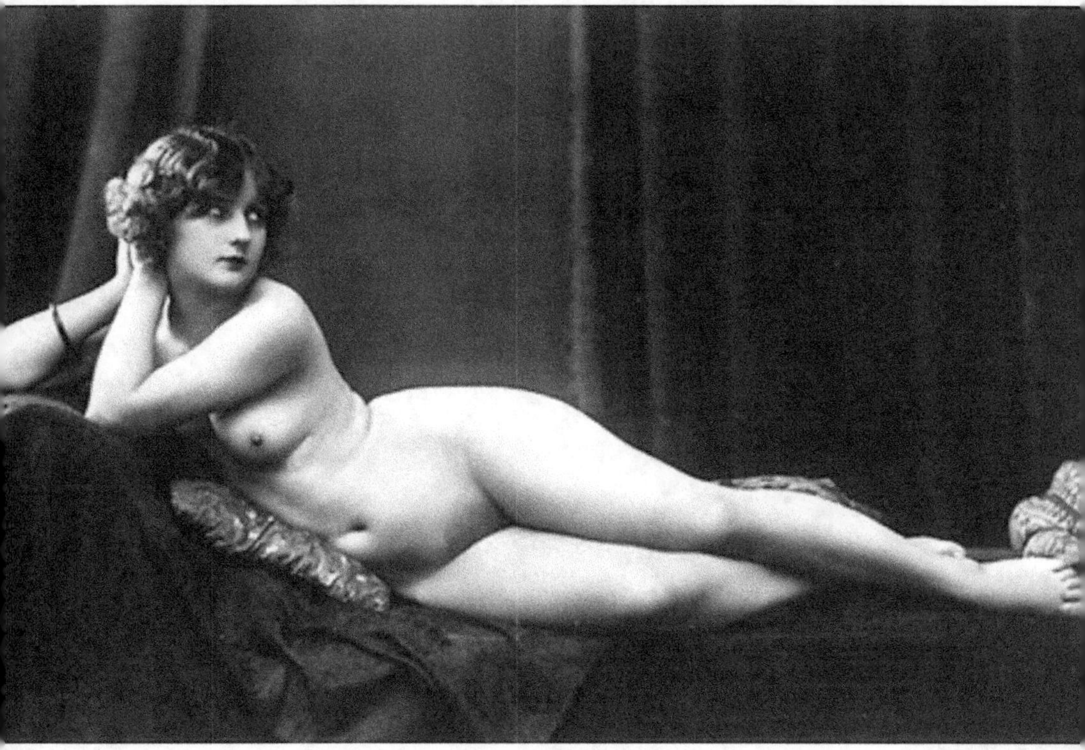

Julian Mandel
(This page and following pages)

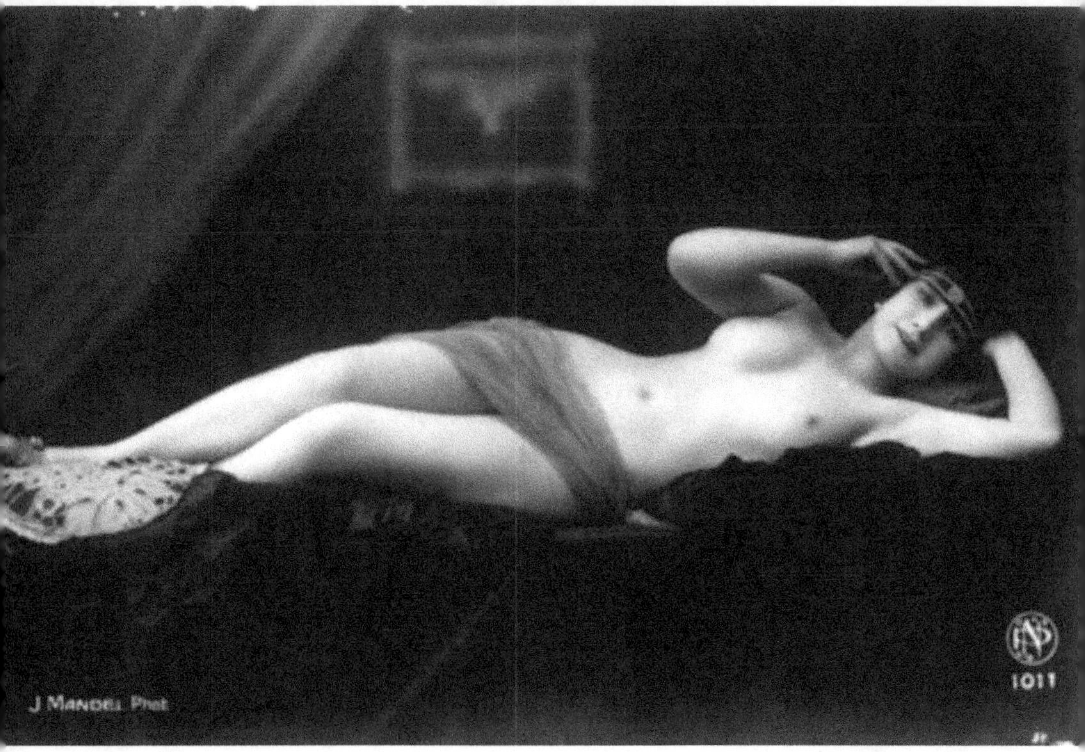

J MANDEL Phot

1011

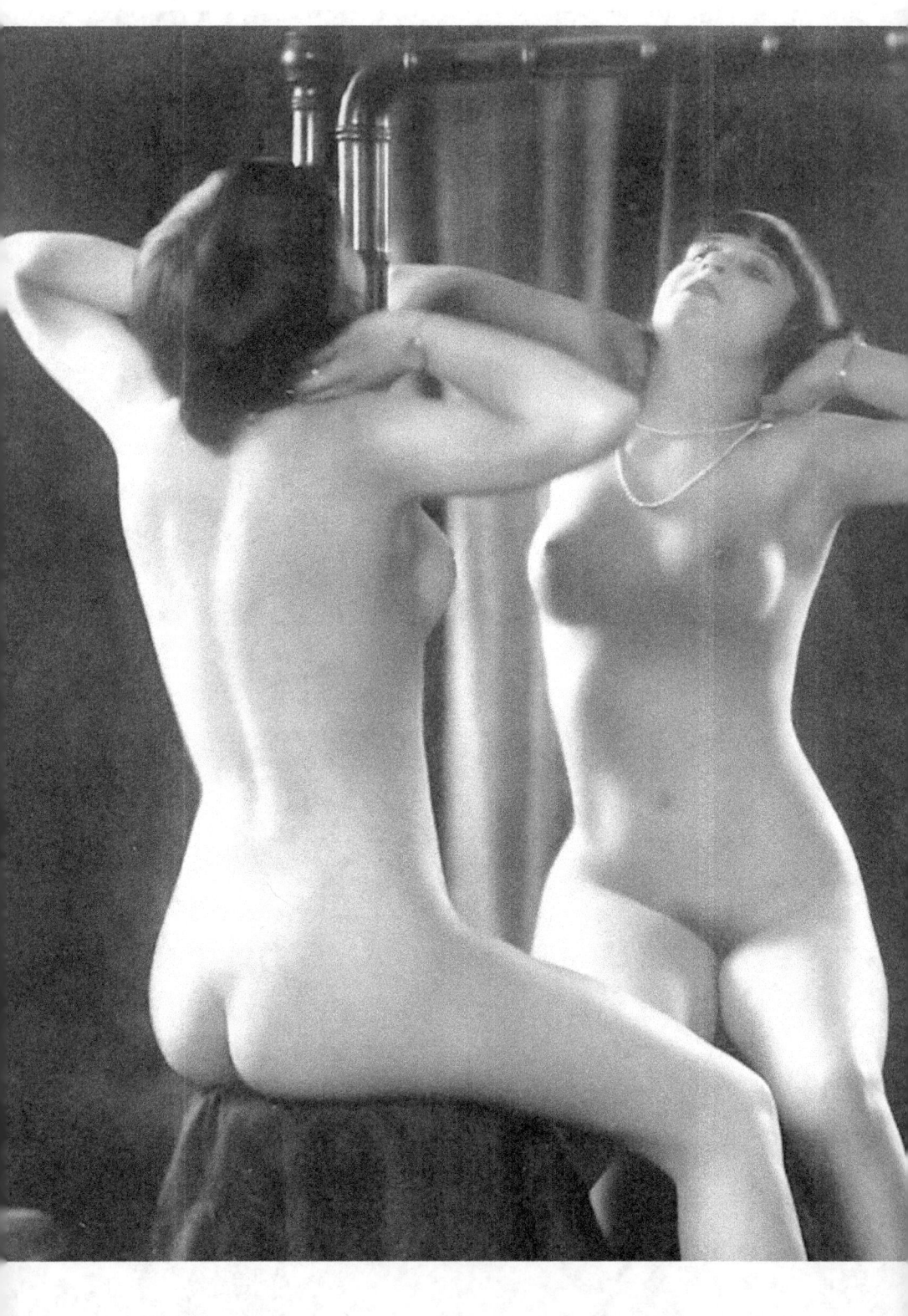

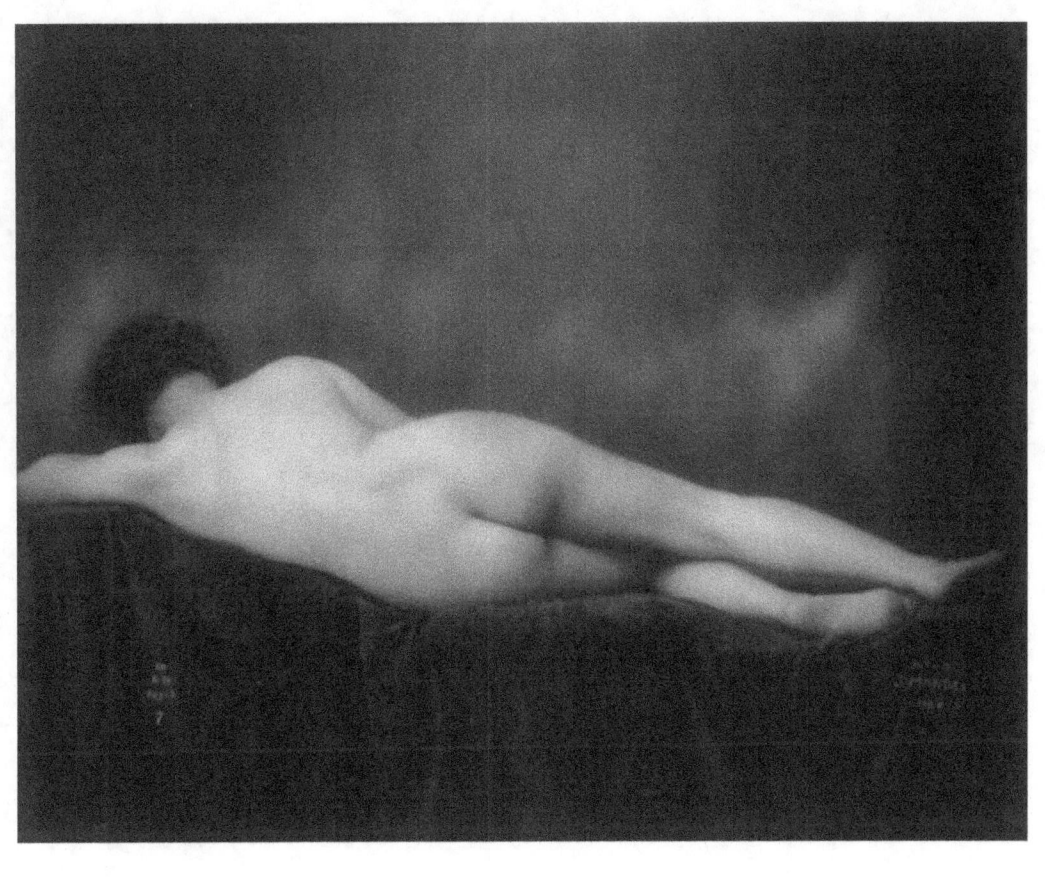

PHOTOGRAPHY

Many photographic nudes are fetishized or eroticized as in pornography. A lot of photography beloved of amateur photographers is essentially soft porn, where 'models' are depicted in swimsuits or topless, against coloured backgrounds and the 'models' have glamorous hairstyles and glossy make-up. These pictures are featured on the covers of amateur photography and digital art magazines. These magazines are full of copy on computer art, digital and photographic techniques, but the examples of the genres of photography they use to illustrate their technical articles – sport, nature, landscape, portrait – are used side-by-side with erotic images of women.

And in many of these photographs included here, many of which are anonymous, the same conflicting issues are at work: desire and pleasure on one side, and technology and the mass media on the other; self-expression and art on one side, and taste and censorship on the other.

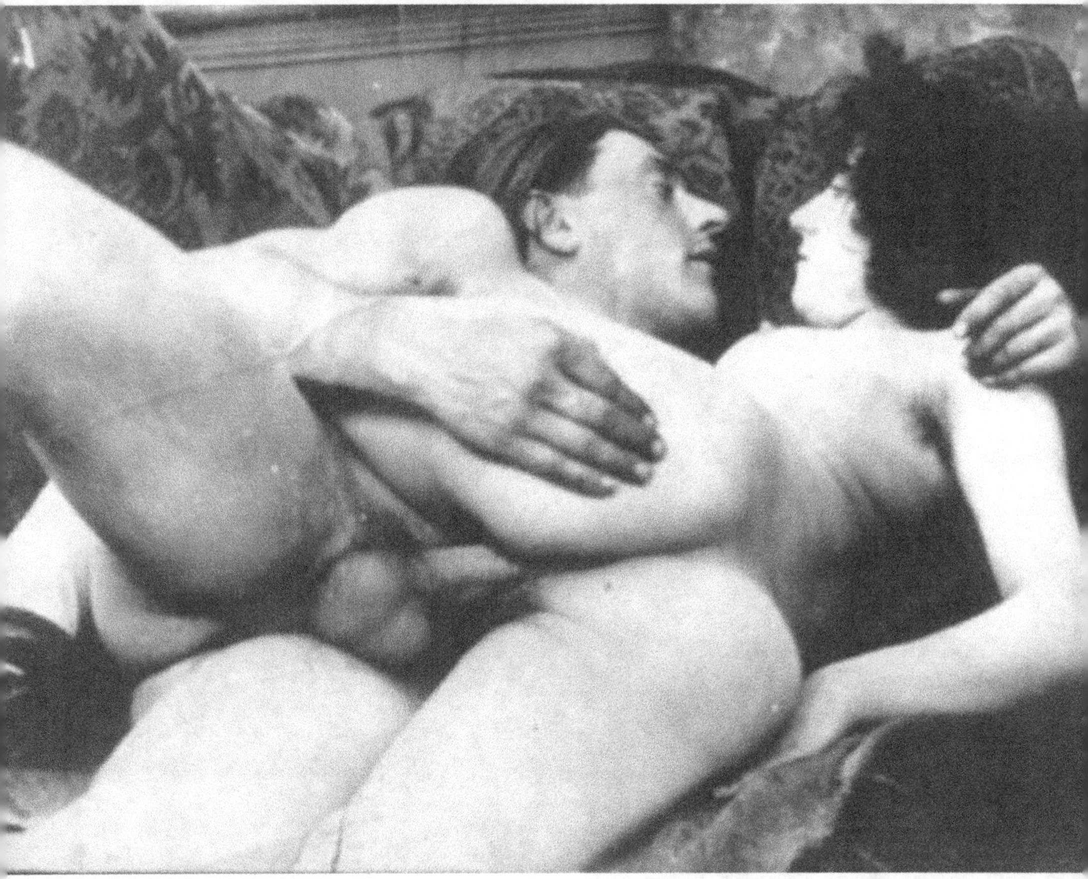

Anonymous, early 20th century

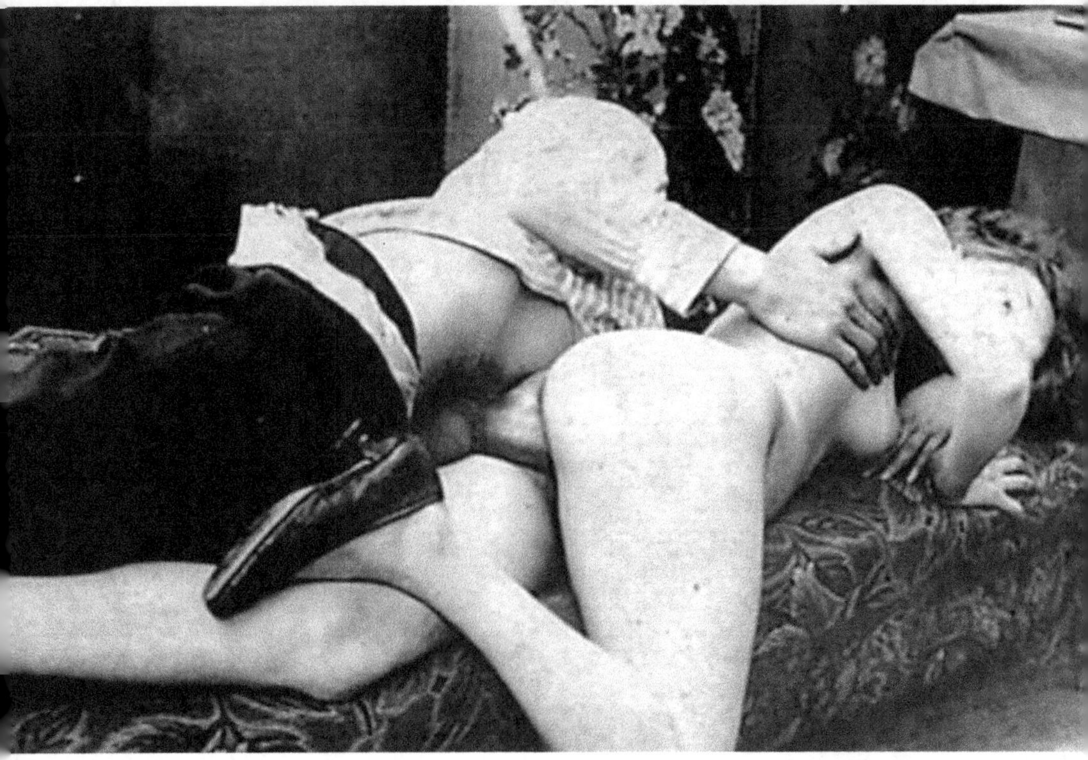

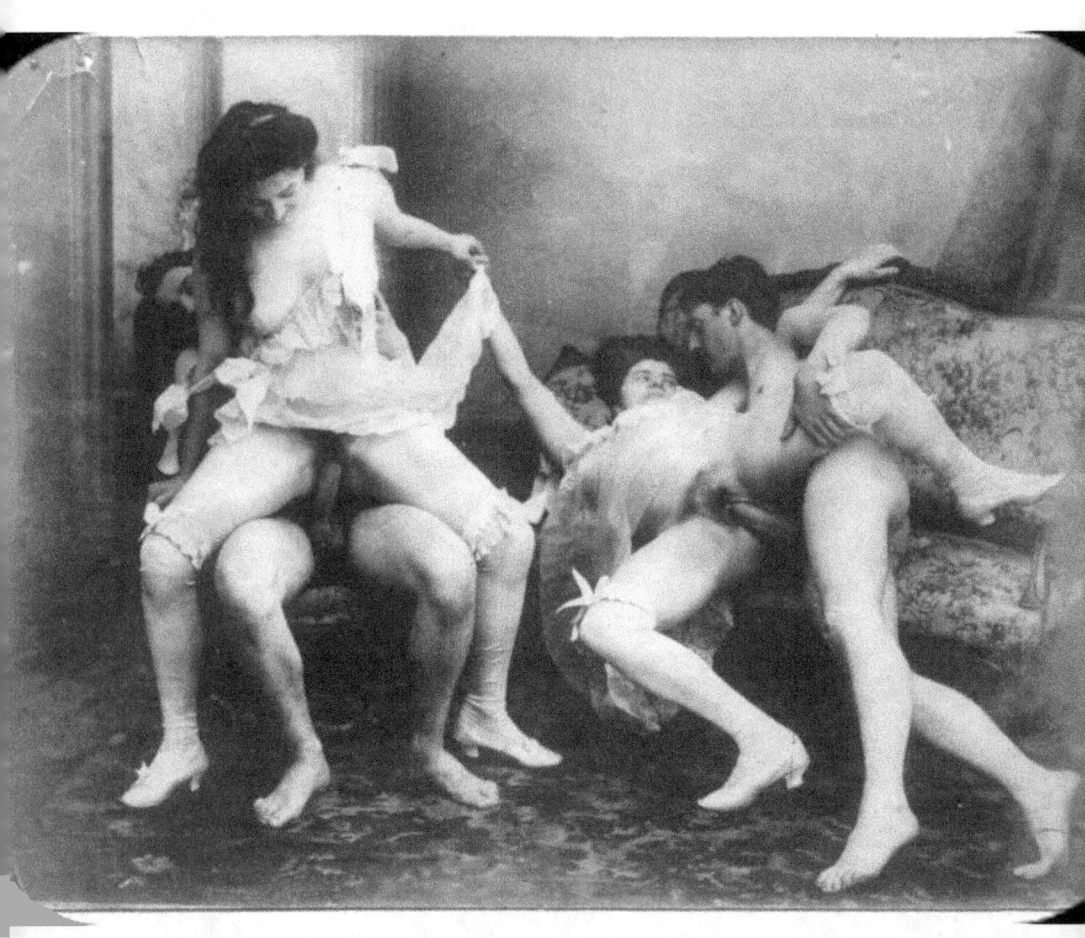

Anonymous, late 19th century

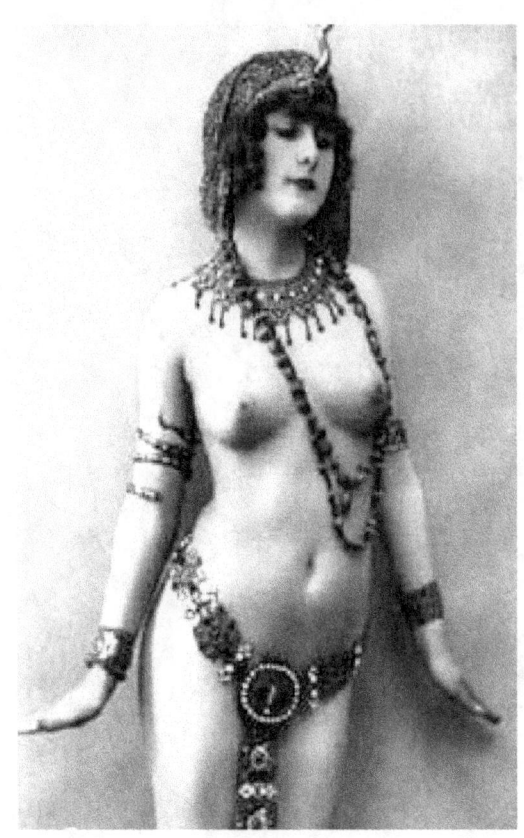

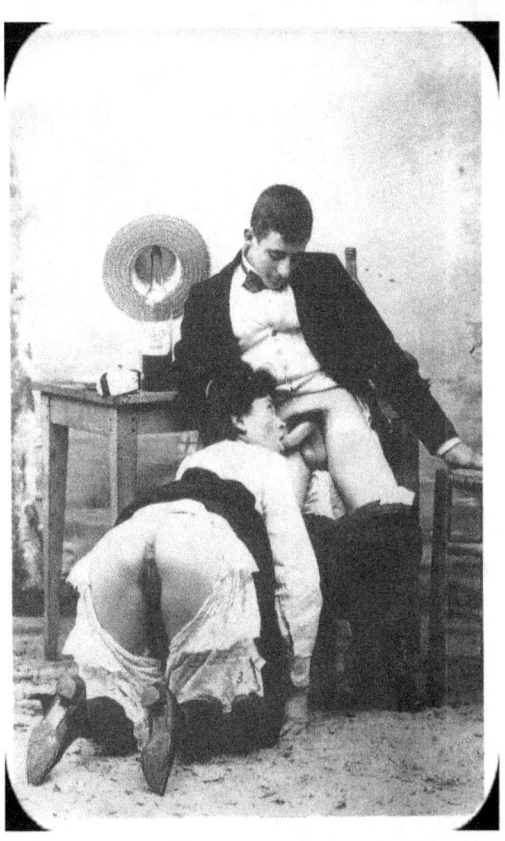

Late 19th century photographs, anonymous

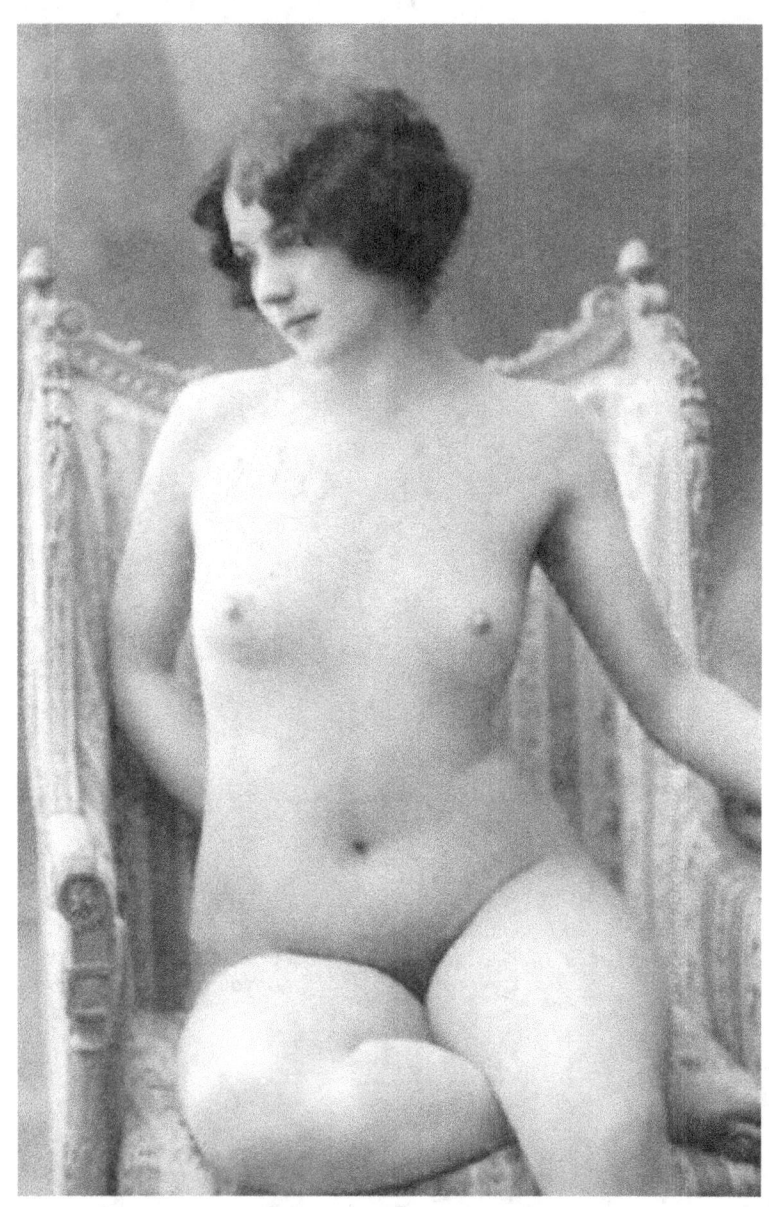

Jean Agélou, c. 1910s

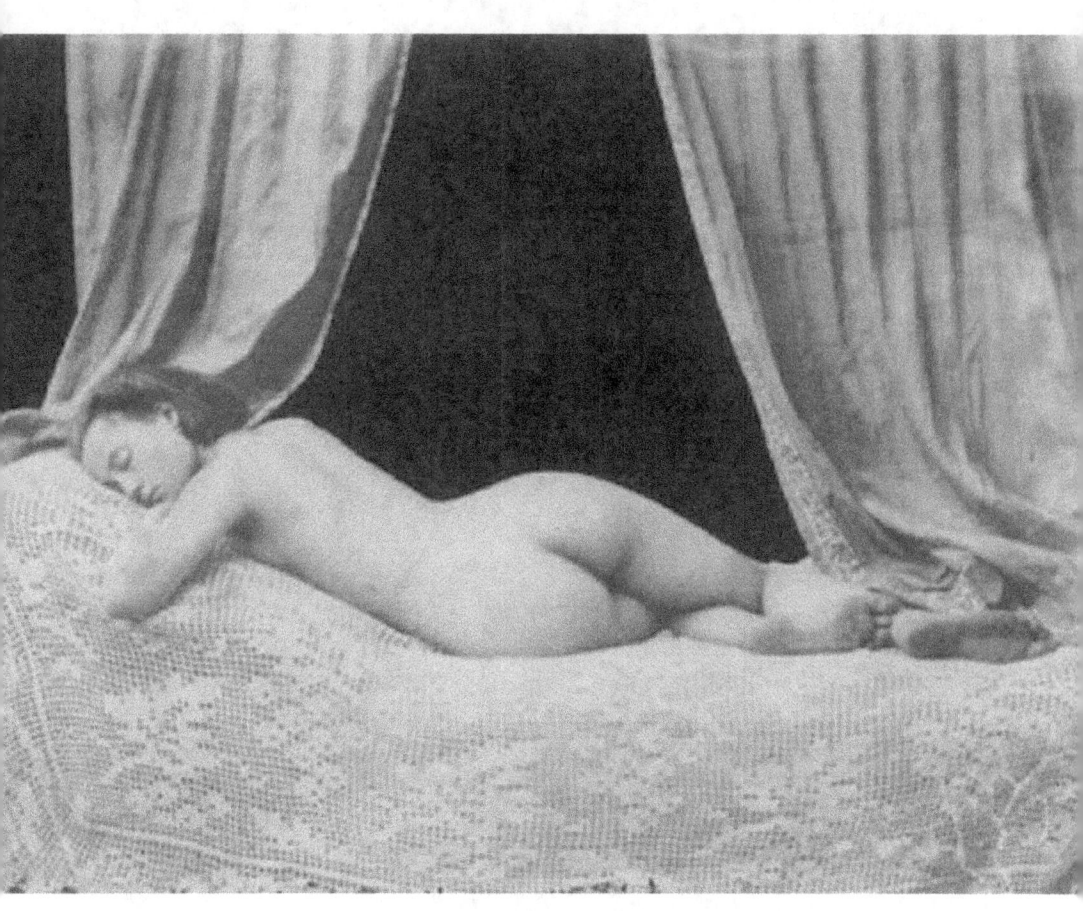

Anonymous, 19th century

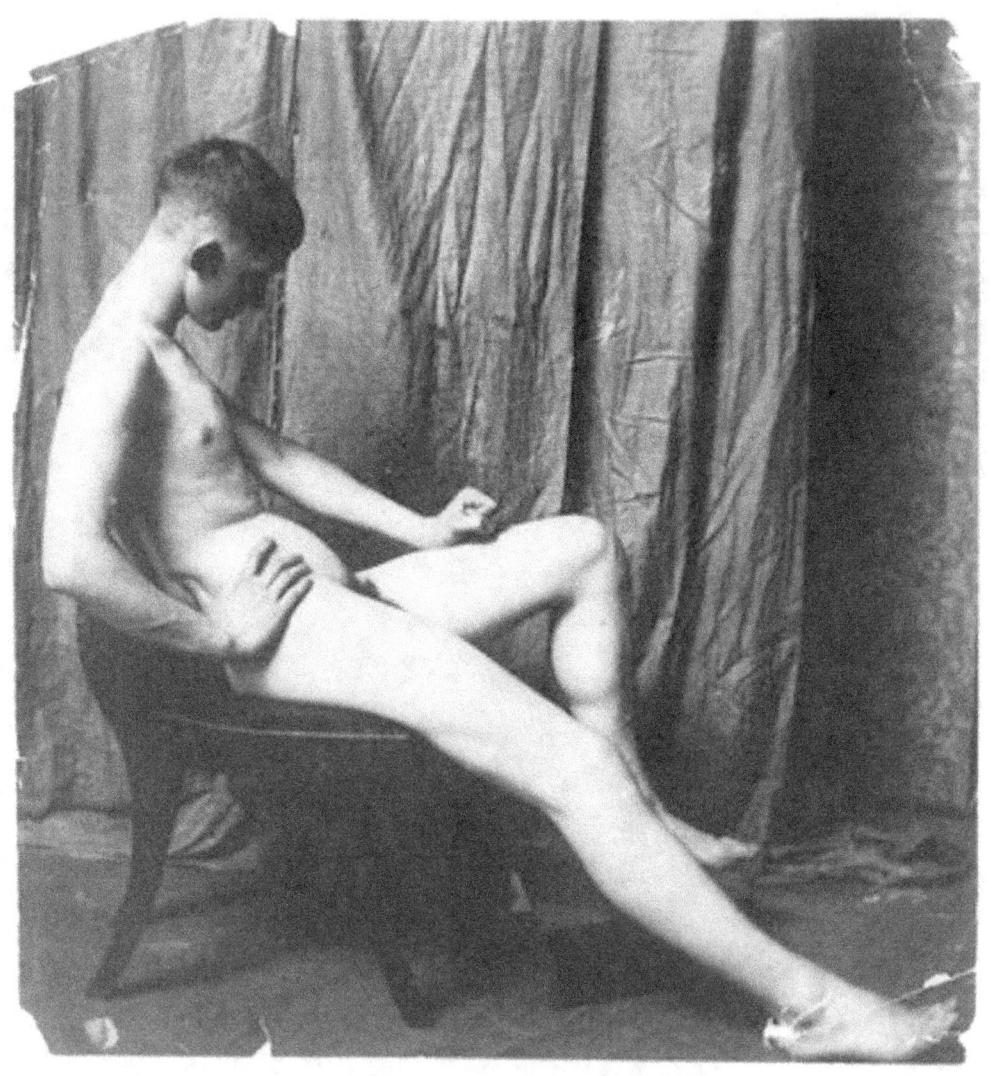

Male Nude (possibly Bill Duckett), 1880s,
Art Students' League of Philadelphia.

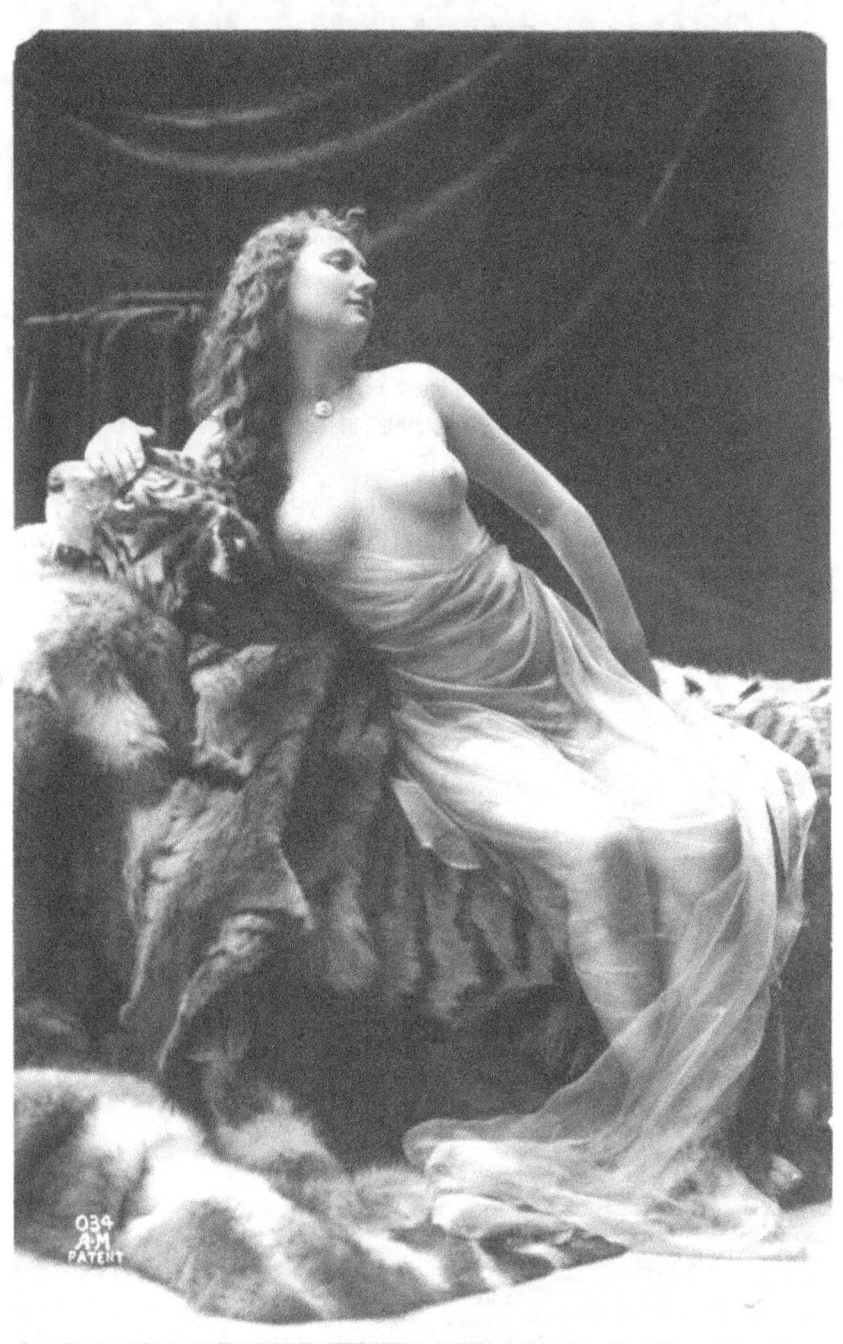

Anonymous, late 19th century

PIERRE LOUŸS

The works of Pierre Louÿs (1870-1925) include many photographs, including plenty of erotica (one of Louÿs' books was a study of women's asses, entitled *La cul de la femme*). Some classic, revered movies have been based on Louÿs' work: for instance, his book *La femme et le pantin* was adapted as the Josef von Sternberg-Marlene Dietrich movie *The Devil Is a Woman* (1935) and the last film of Luis Buñuel, *That Obscure Object of Desire* (1977). *La femme et le pantin* was also the basis of a 1992 TV movie, a 2007 TV movie, and movies in 1920, 1929 and 1946.[1]

Pierre Louÿs' erotic poetry included *Astarte* and *Songs of Bilitis*,[2] novels such as *Aphrodite* (1896) and *La femme et le pantin* (1898), and erotic works such as *Les Aventures du roi Pausole* (1901), *Pervigilium Mortis* (1916), and *Manuel de civilité pour les petites filles à l'usage des maisons d'éducation* (1917).

---

1 Other movies based on Pierre Louÿs' work include: *Bilitis* (1977), *A Woman Like Satan* (1959), *Aphrodite* (1982), *Les filles de leur mère* (1985), *The Adventures of King Pausole* (1933), *Take Me Naked* (1966) and *The Merry Monarch* (1933).
2 Claude Debussy set some of the *Chansons de Bilitis* to music in 1898.

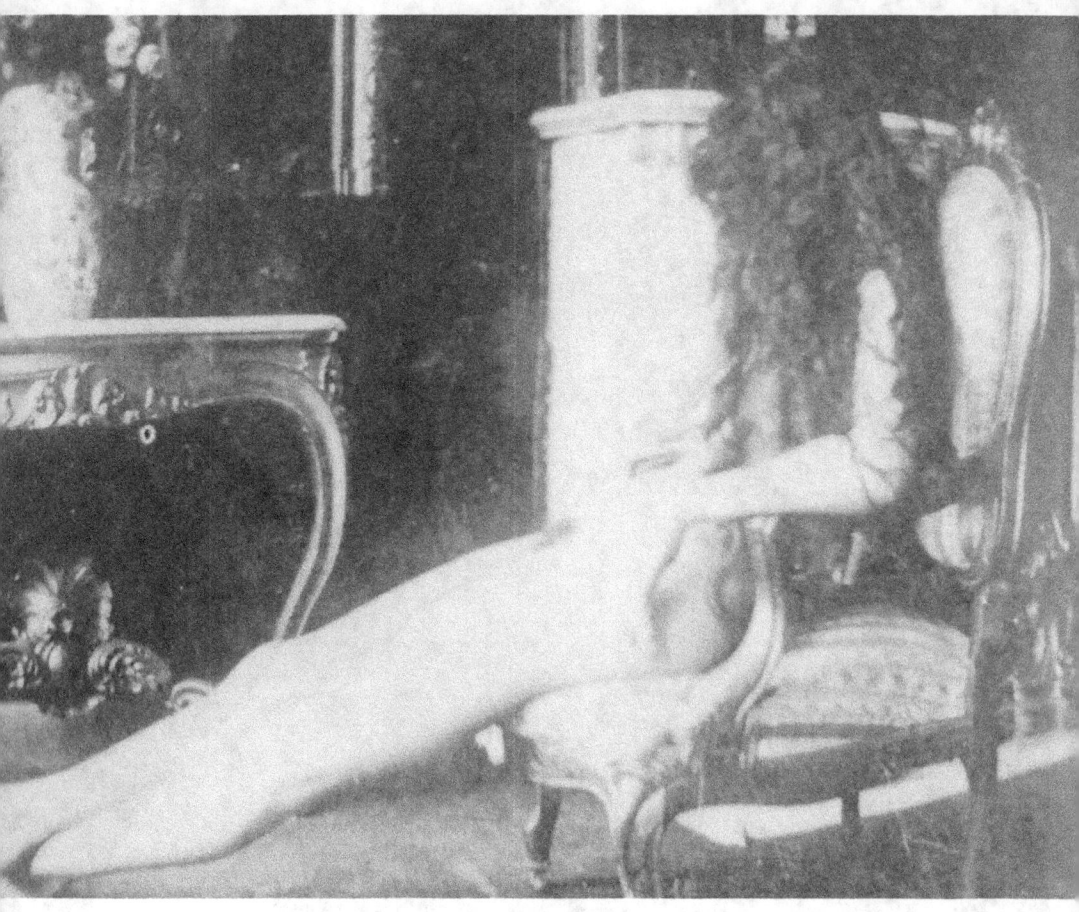

Pierre Loüys on this page and the following pages.
One of the great erotic artists of the modern era,
Louÿs wrote erotica and took many erotic photos.

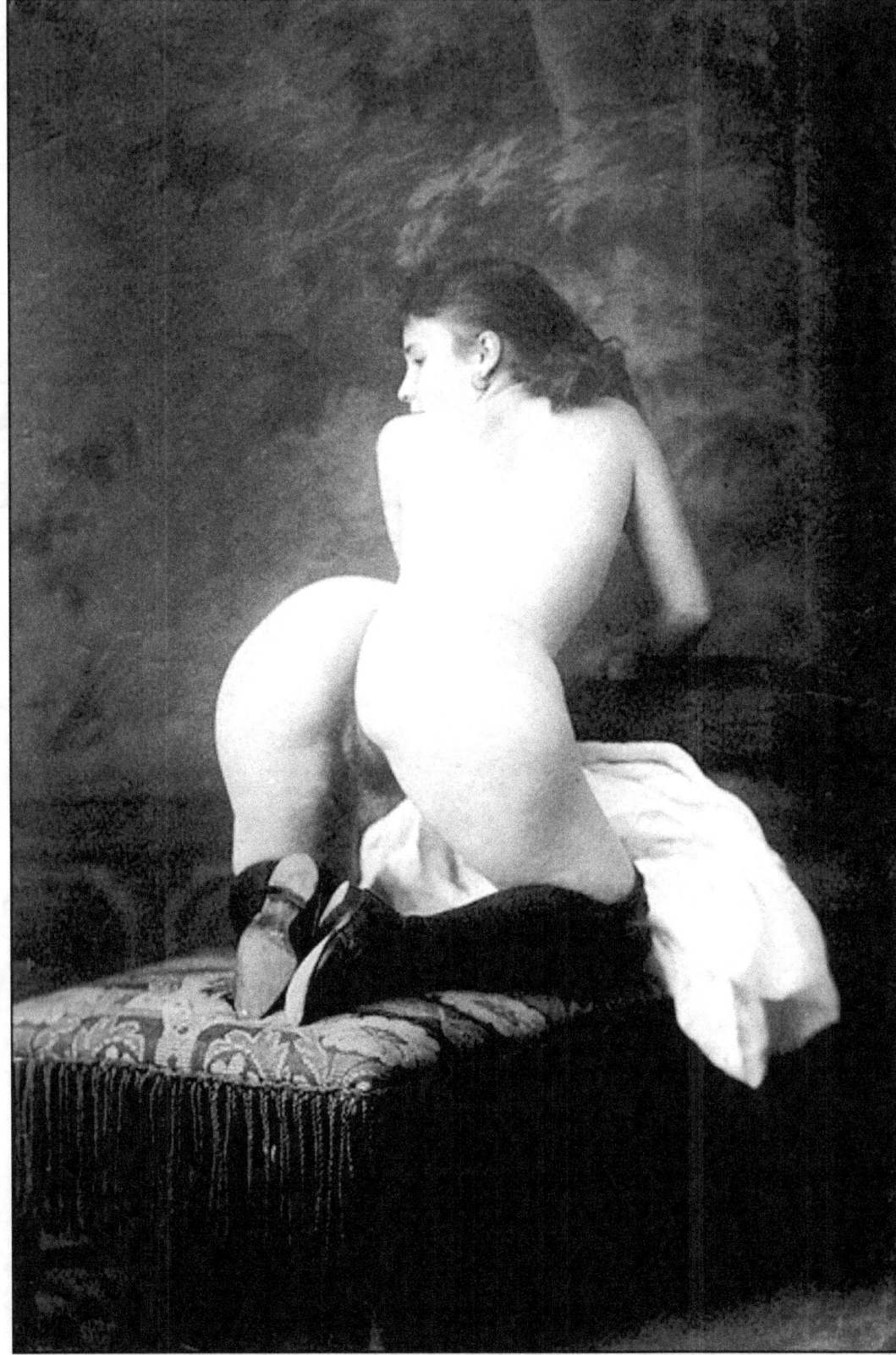

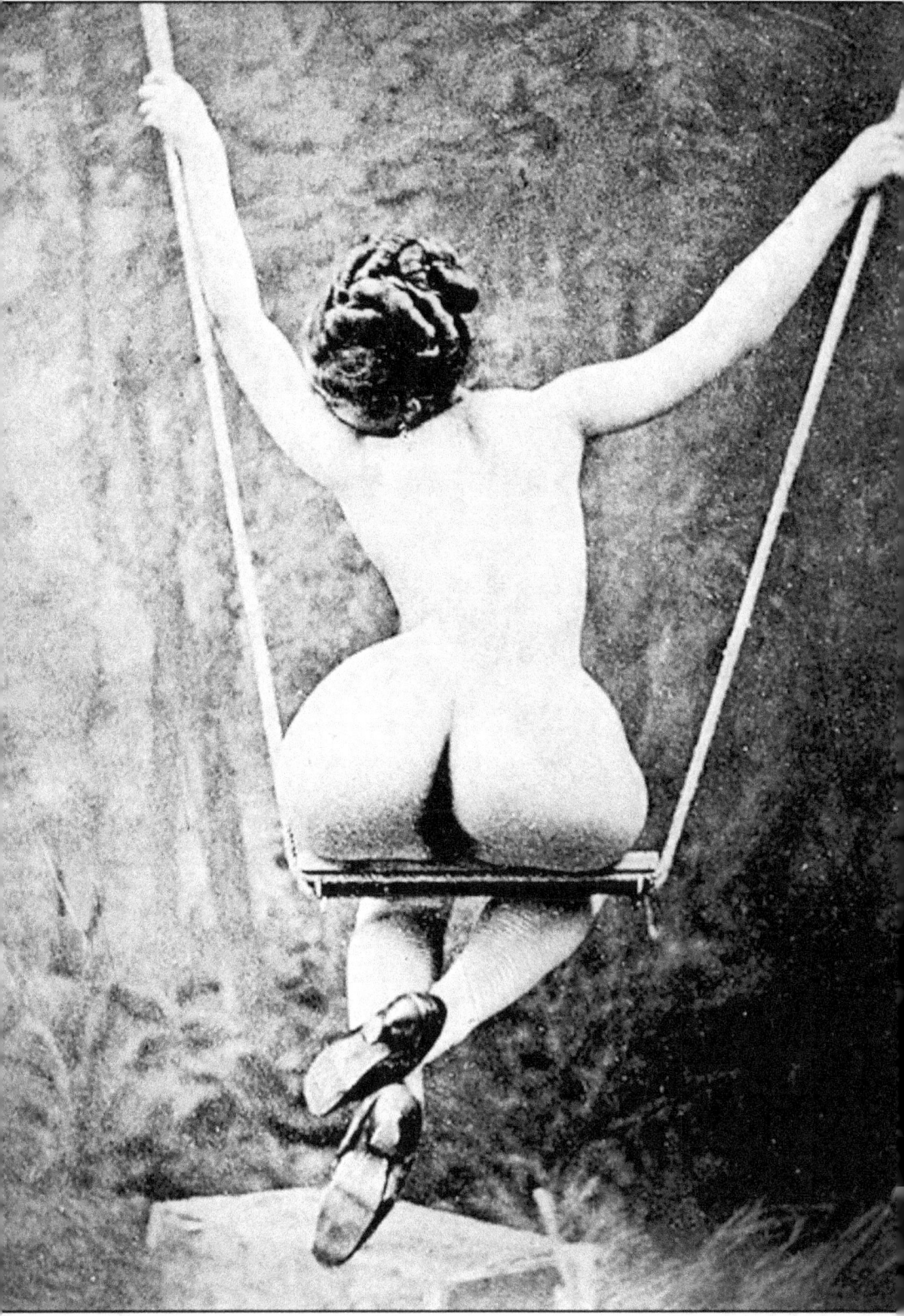

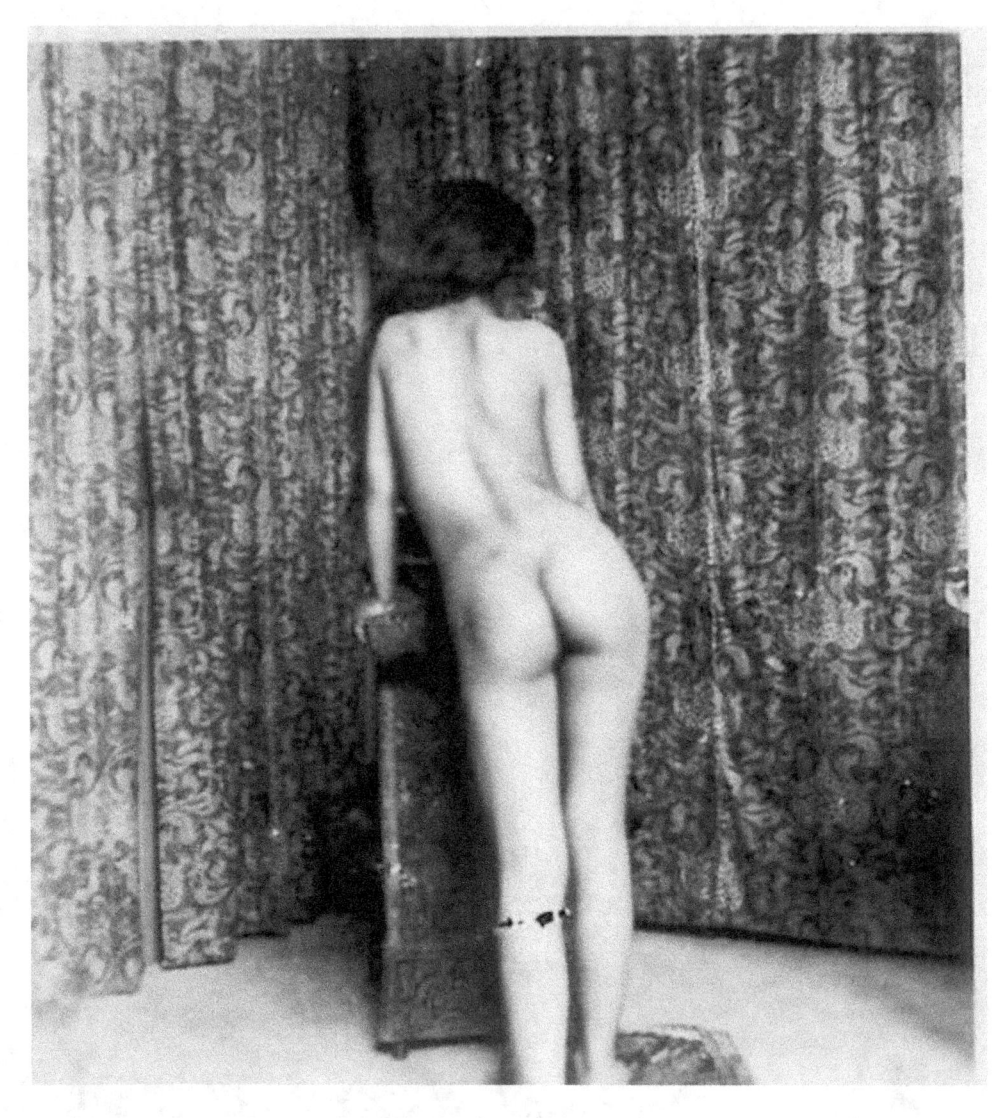

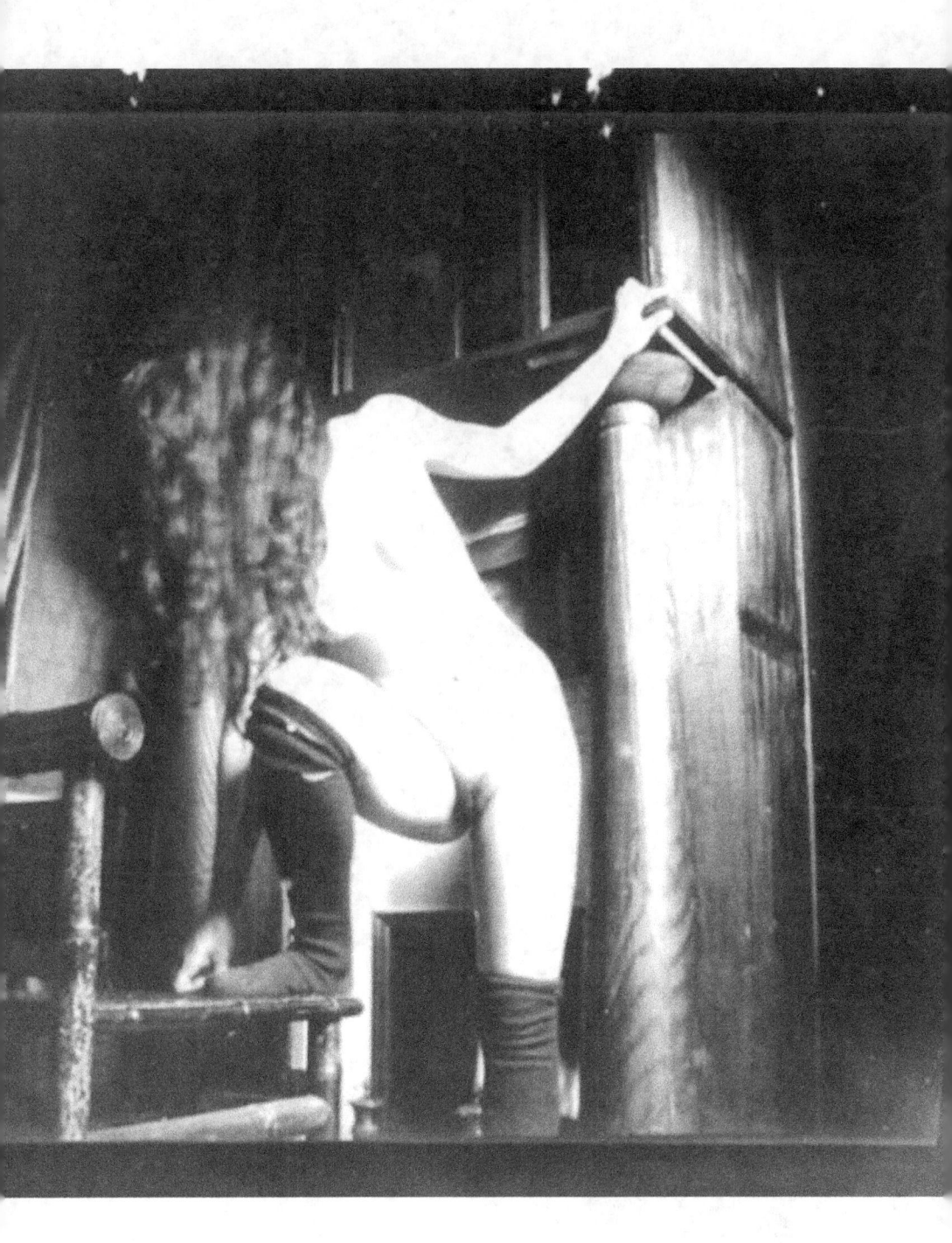

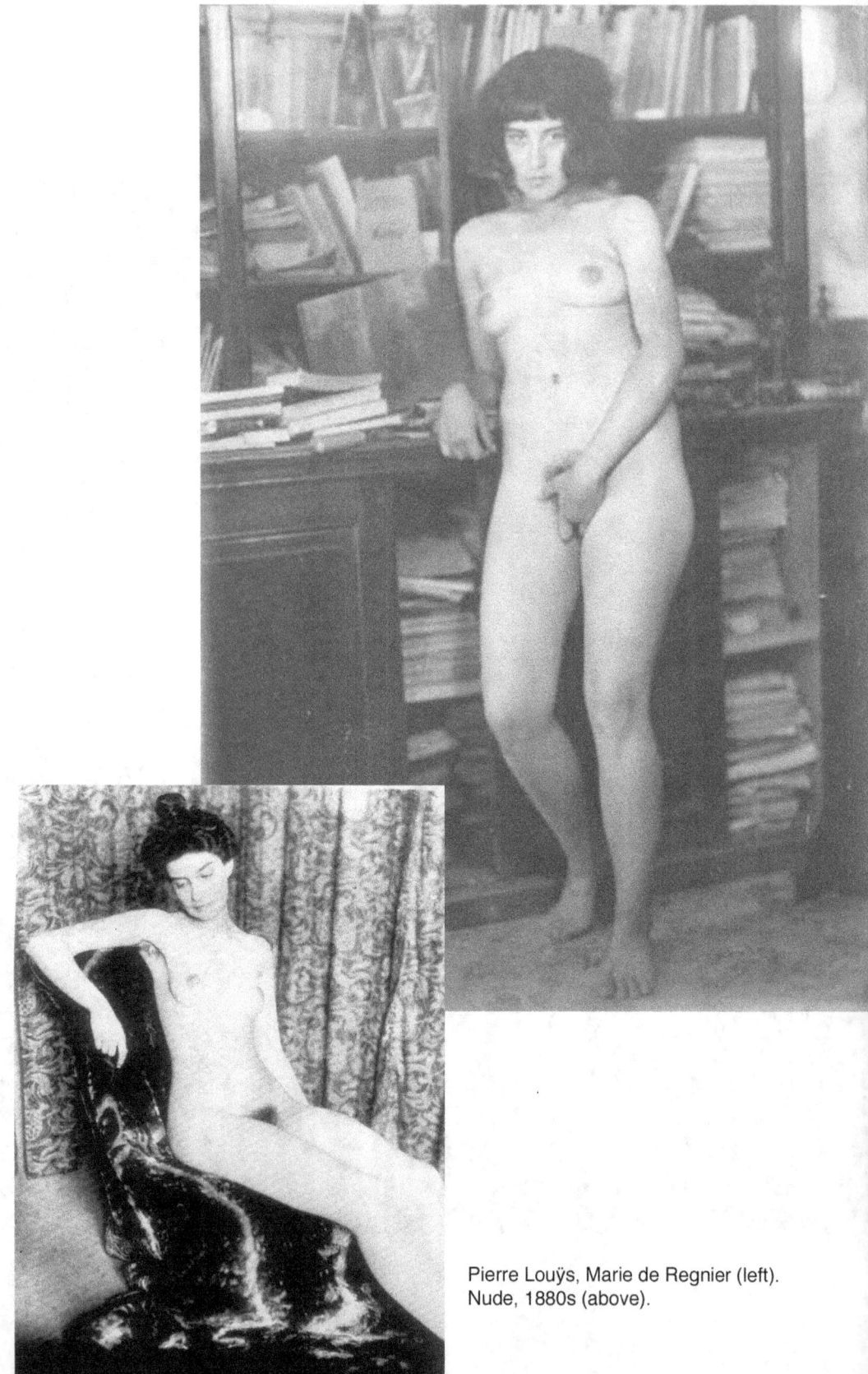

Pierre Louÿs, Marie de Regnier (left).
Nude, 1880s (above).

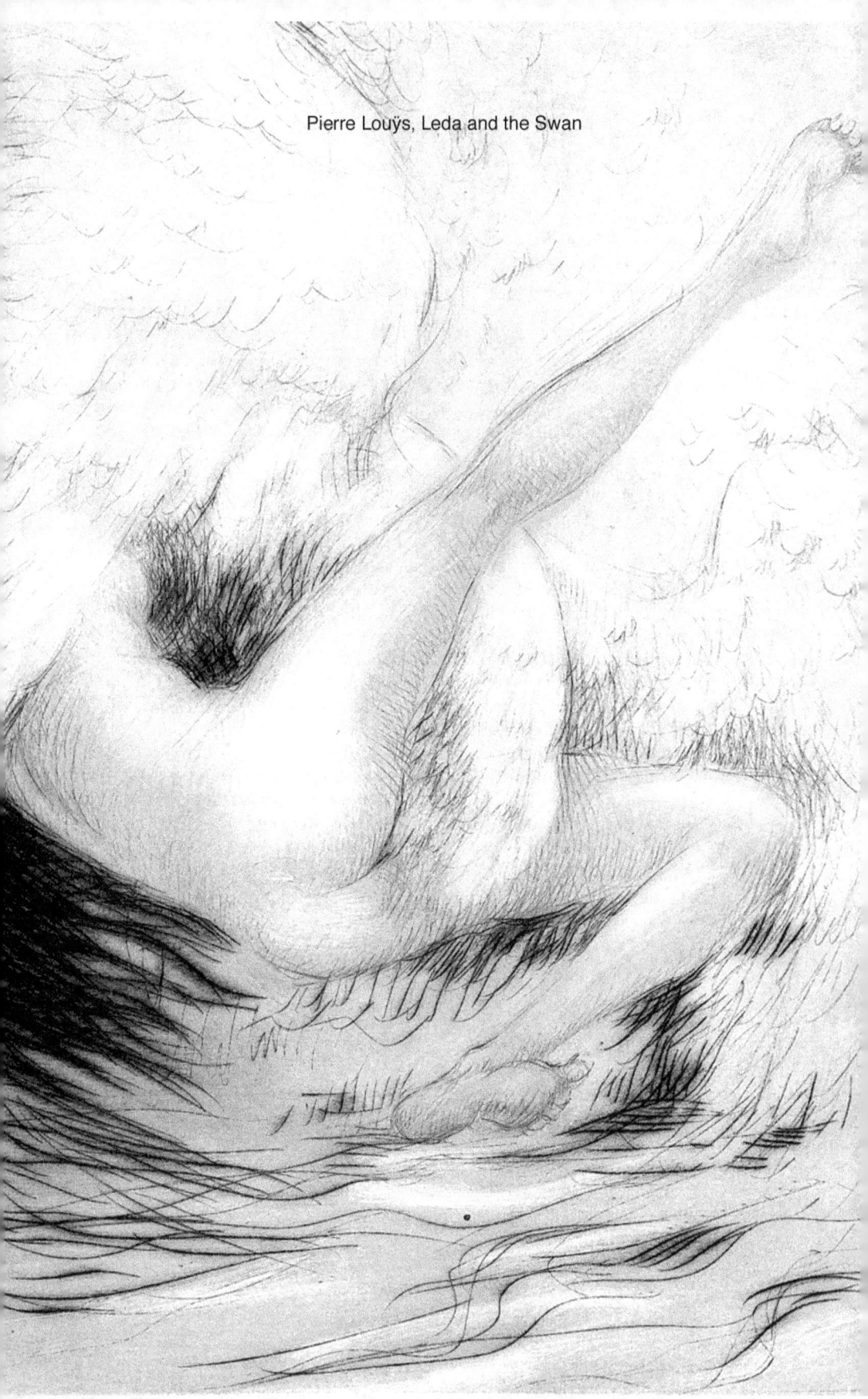

Pierre Louÿs, Leda and the Swan

PAUL AVRIL – *FANNY HILL*

Fanny Hill: Memoirs of a Woman of Pleasure (1748) by John Cleland (1709-89), is one of the classics texts in the history of erotica, along with *Moll Flanders, The Romance of Lust, The Perfumed Garden,* and of course *The Kama Sutra.* Paul Avril was one of the key modern erotic artists. This is an extract from *Fanny Hill:*

> He threw up my petticoat and shift, whilst my thighs were, by an instinct of nature, unfolded to their best; and my desires had so thoroughly destroyed all modesty in me, that even their being now naked and all laid open to him, was part of the prelude that pleasure deepened my blushes at, more than same. But when his hand, and touches, naturally attracted to their center, made me feel all their wantonness and warmth in, and round it, oh! how immensely different a sense of things, did I perceive there, than when under my own insipid handling! And now his waistcoat was unbuttoned, and the confinement of the breeches burst through, when out started to view the amazing, pleasing object of all my wishes, all my dreams, all my love, the king member indeed! I gazed at, I devoured it, at length and breadth, with my eyes intently directed to it, till his; getting upon me, and placing between my thighs, took from me the enjoyment of its sight, to give me a far more grateful one, in its touch, in that part where its touch is so exquisitely affecting.

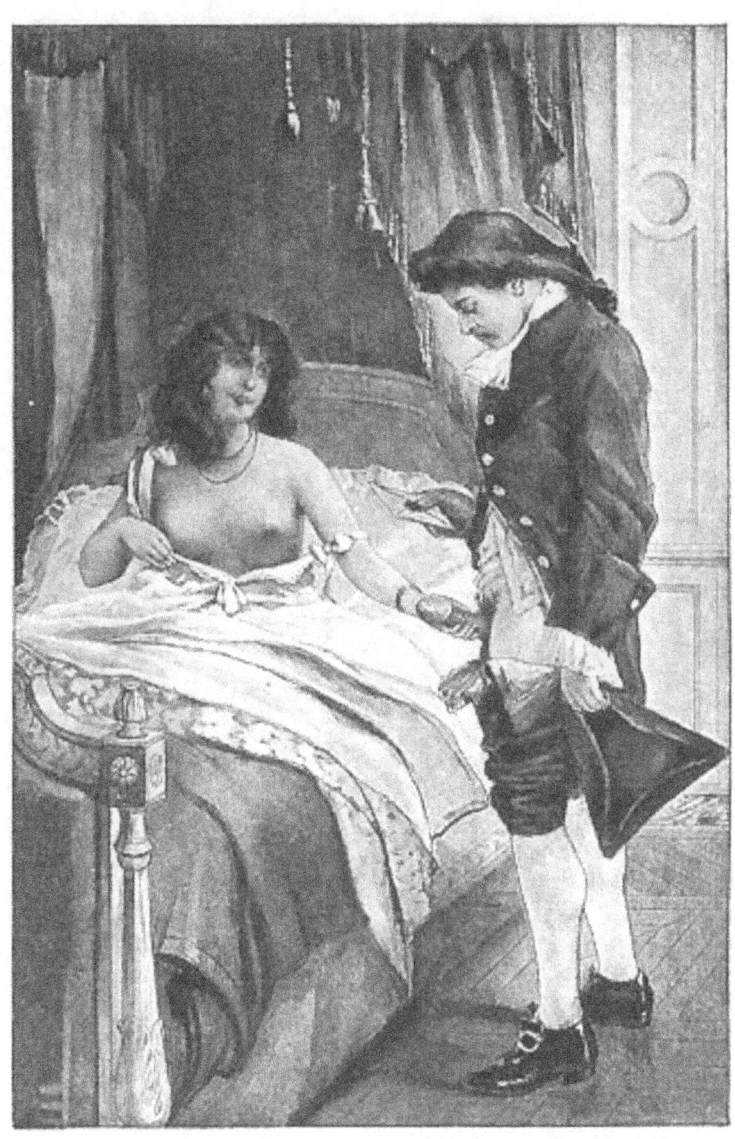

Paul Avril, from Fanny Hill (1908), this page and over,
followed by images from De Figuris Veneris (1906).

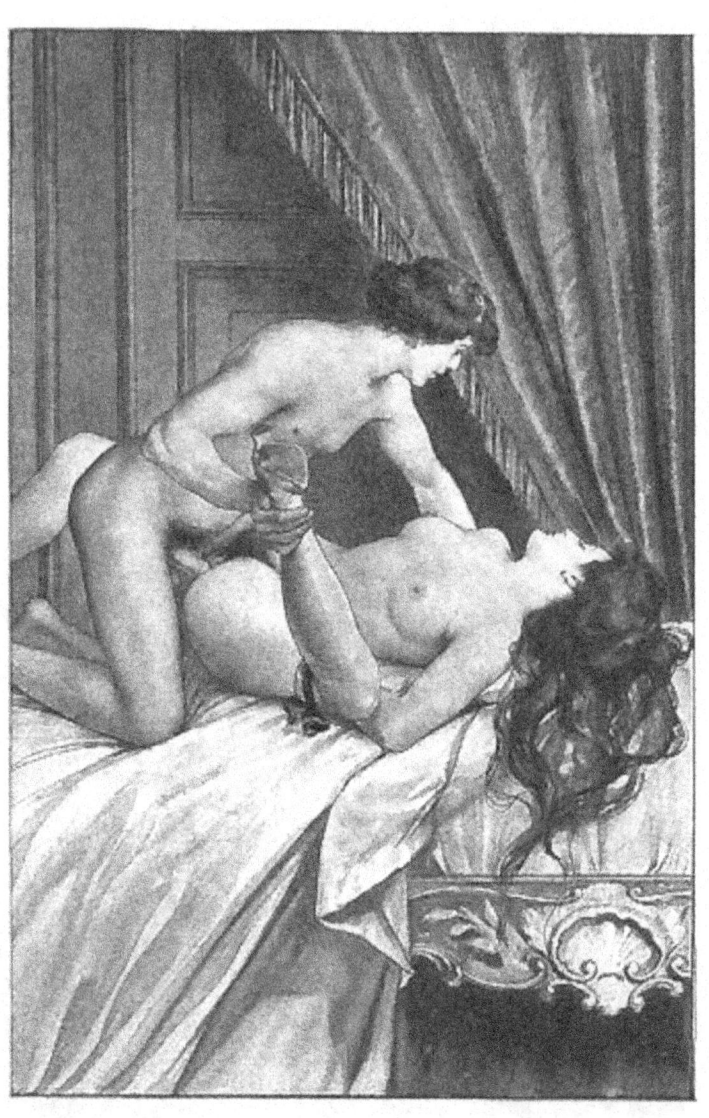

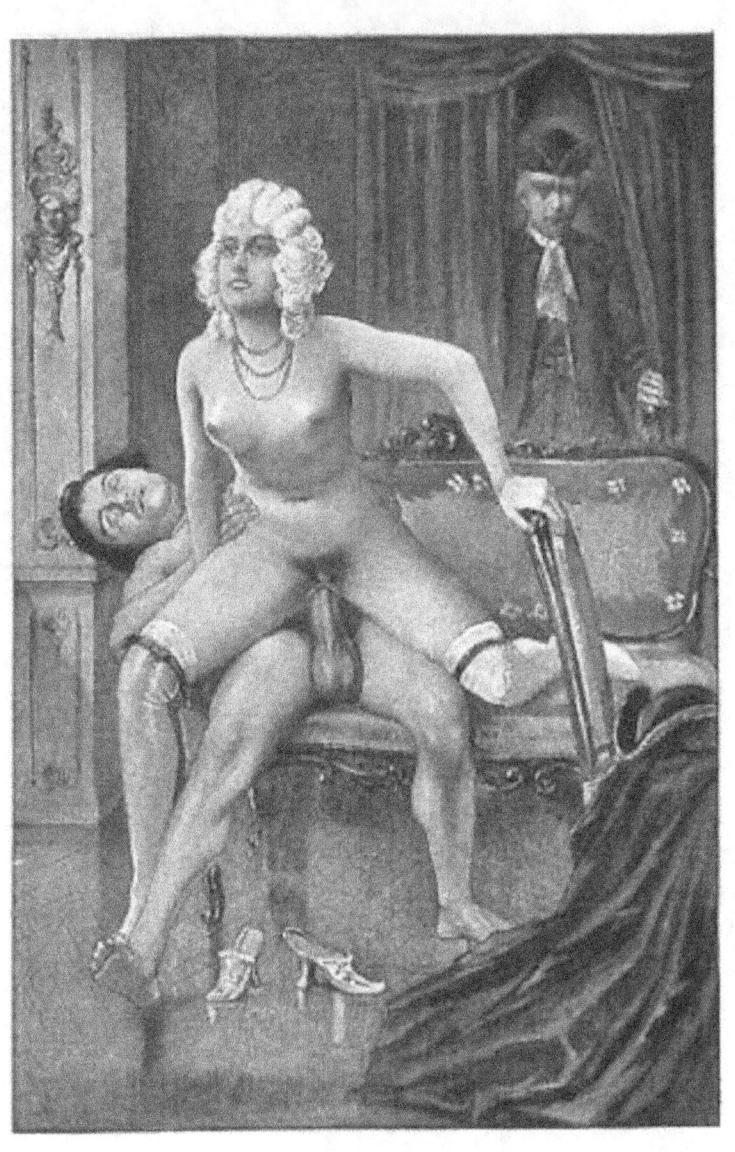

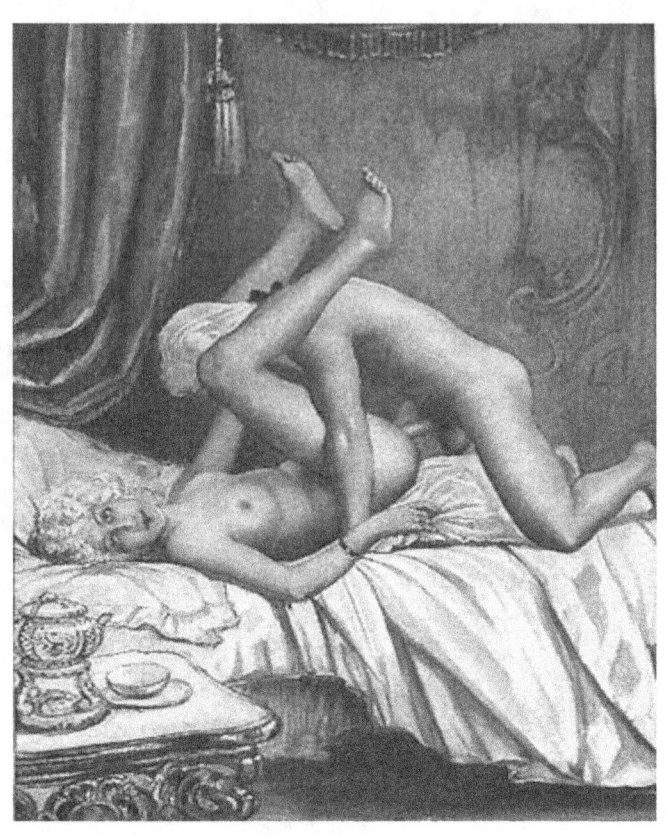

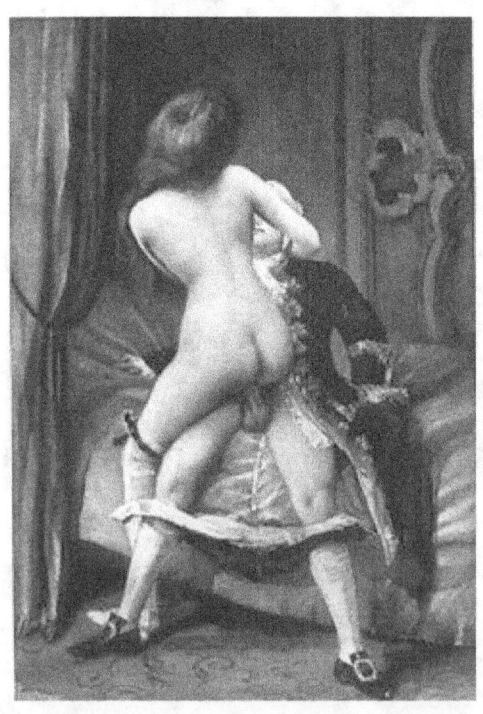

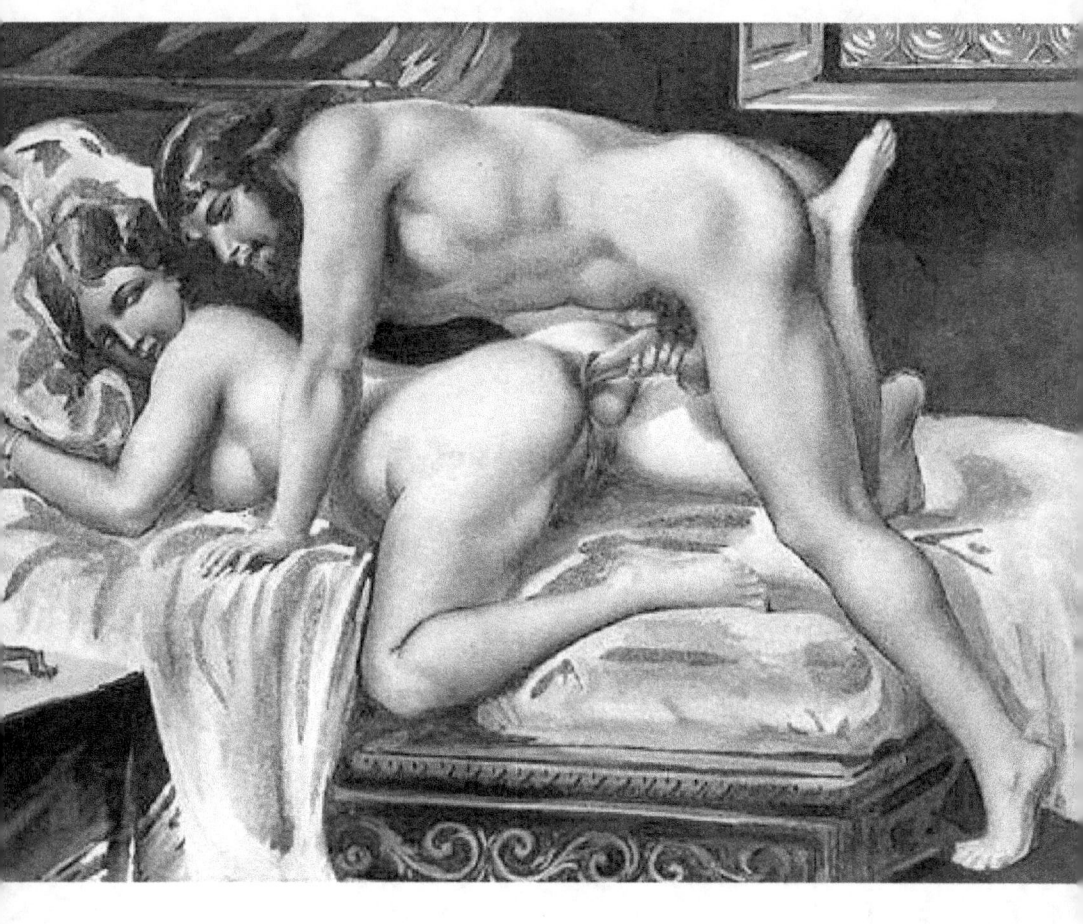

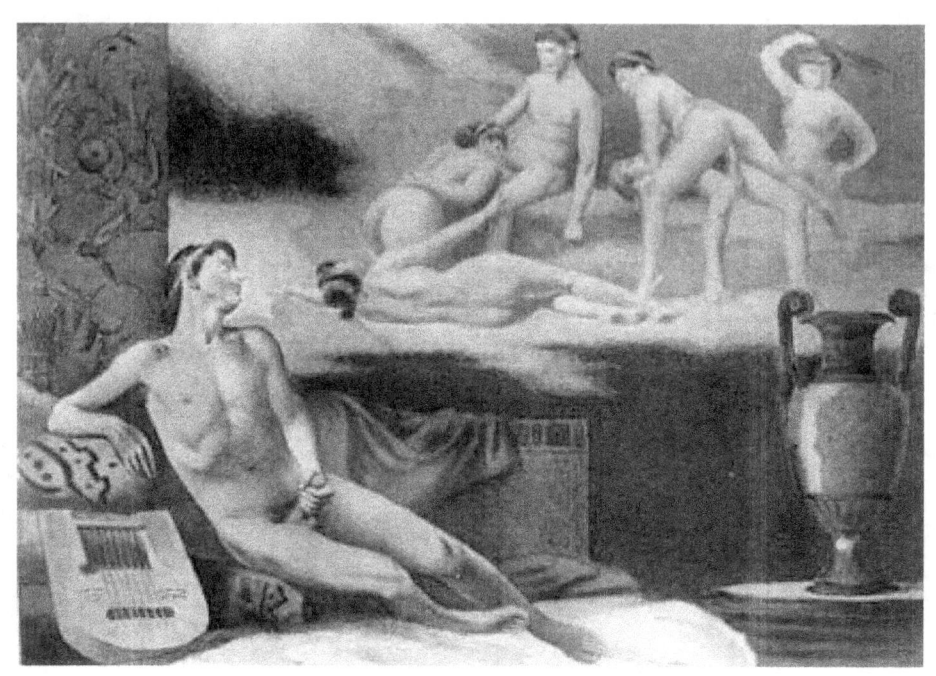

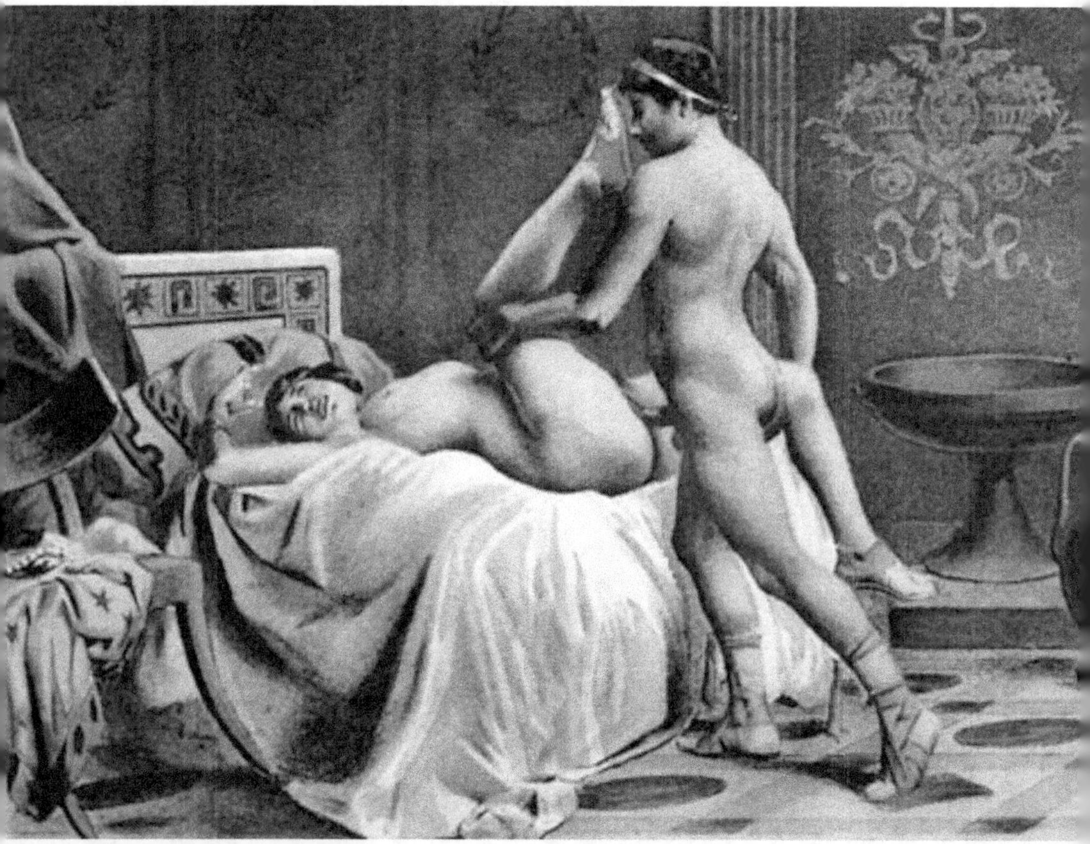

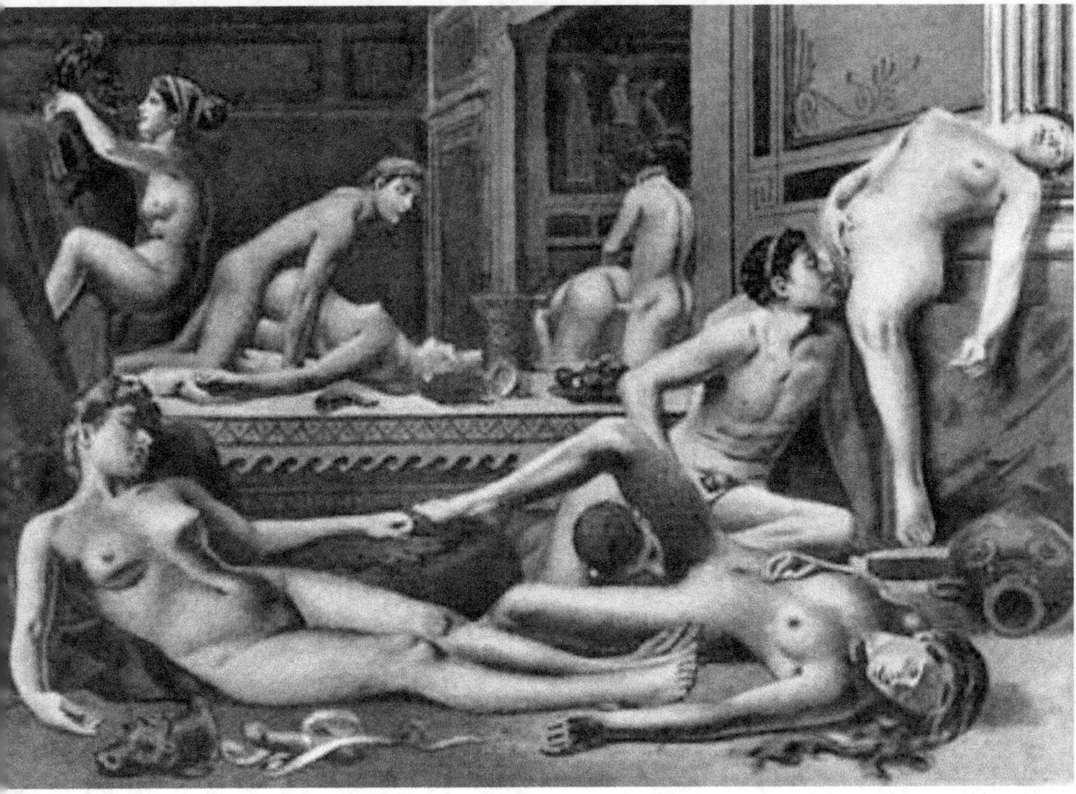

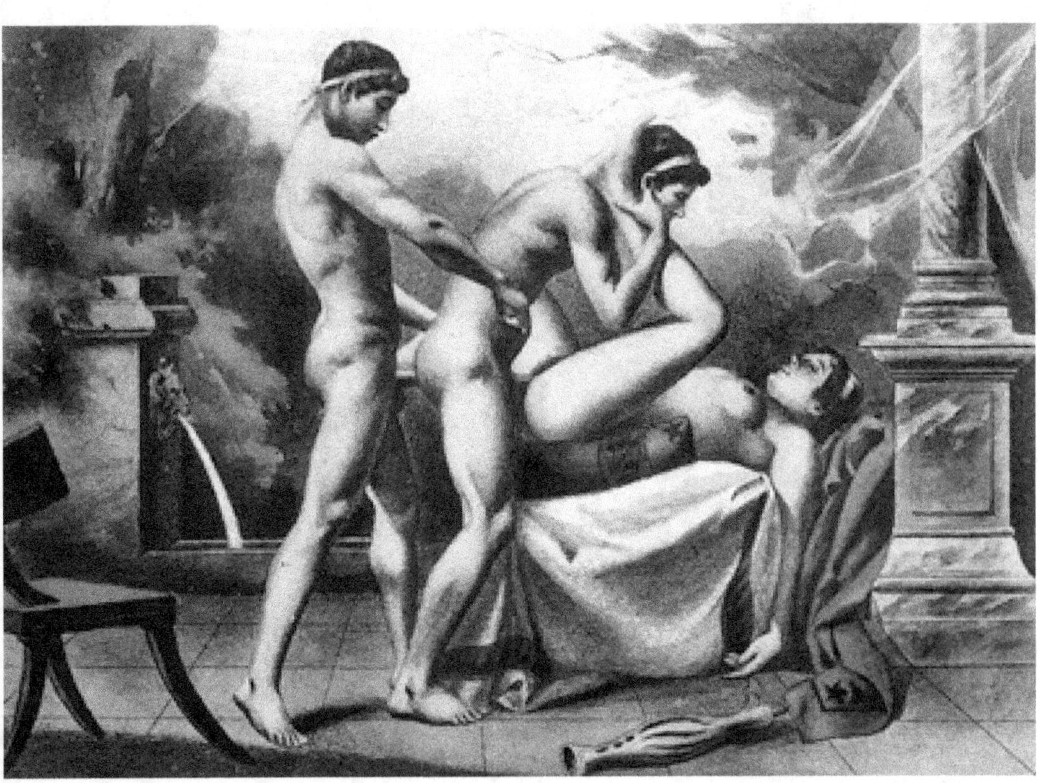

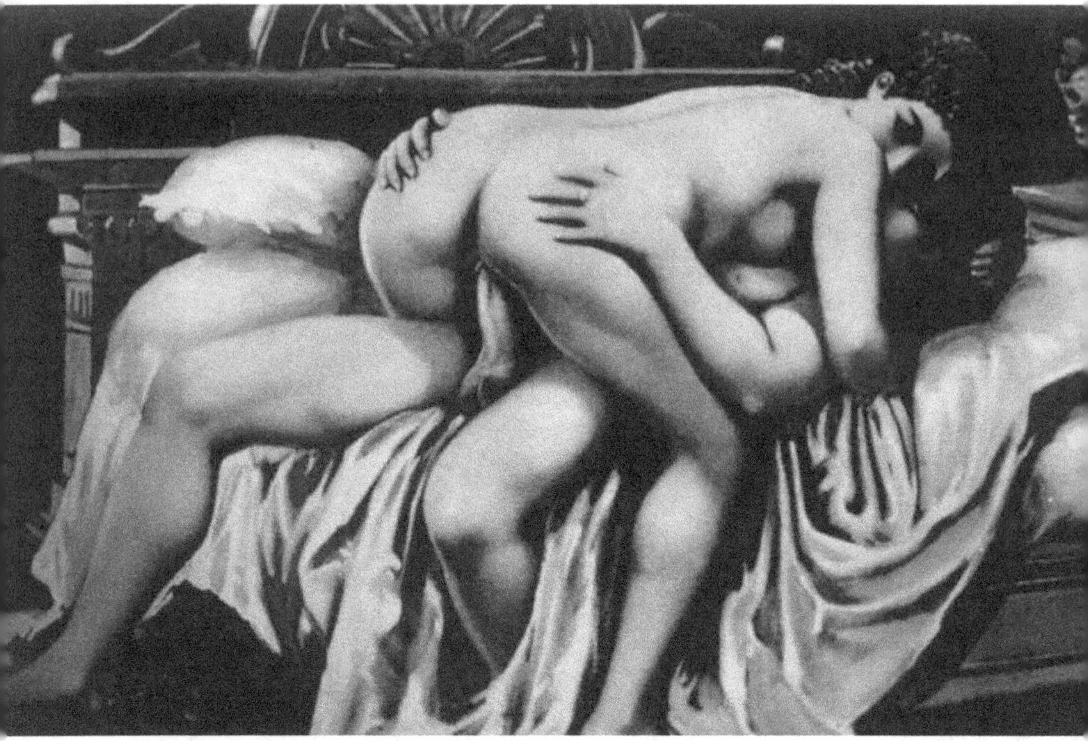

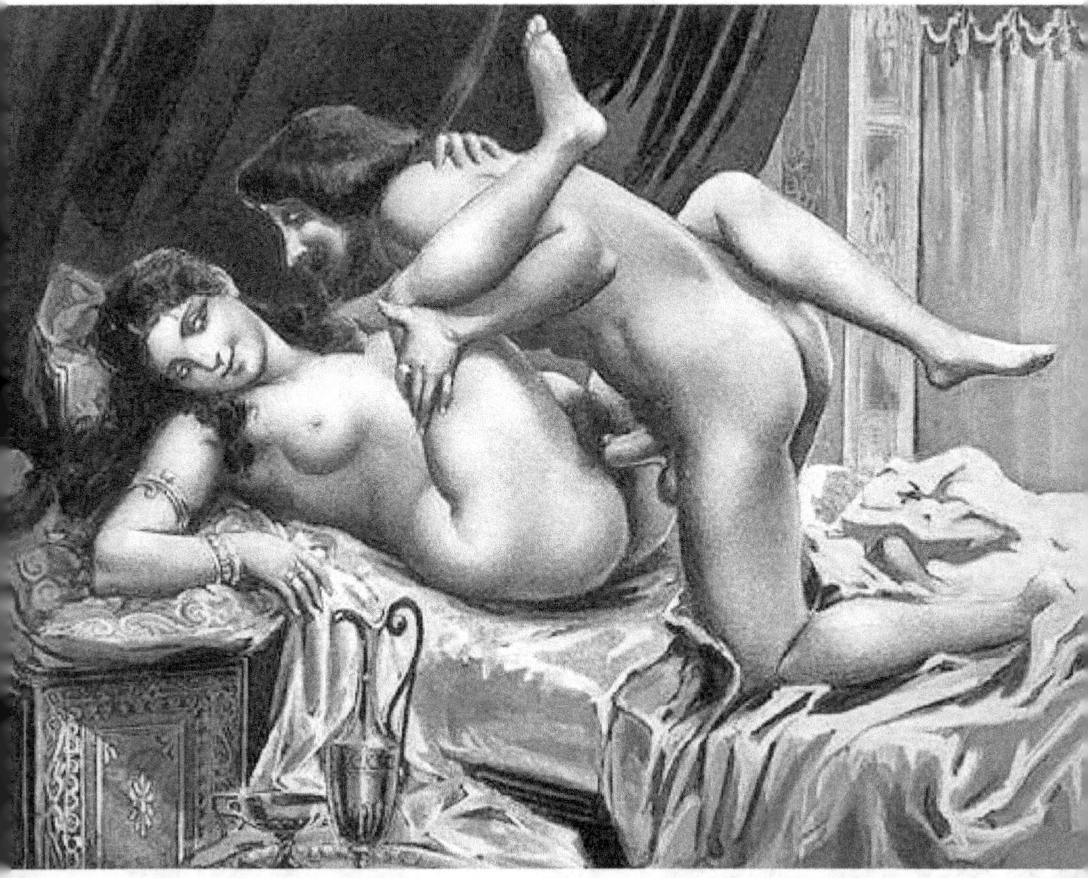

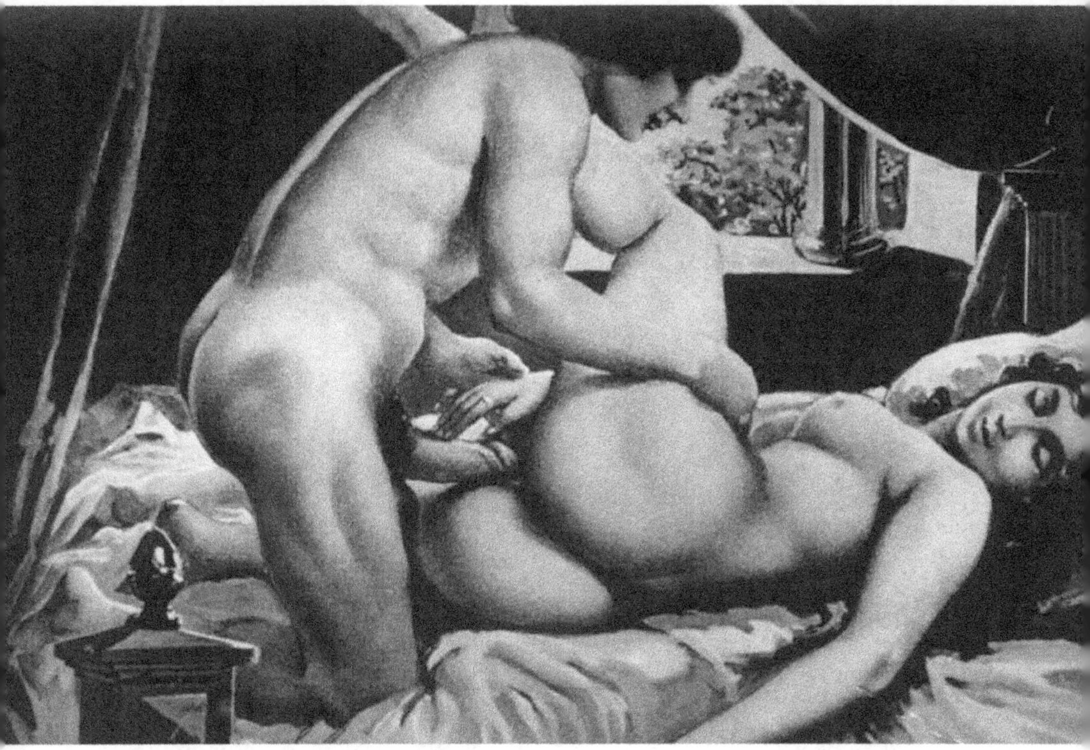

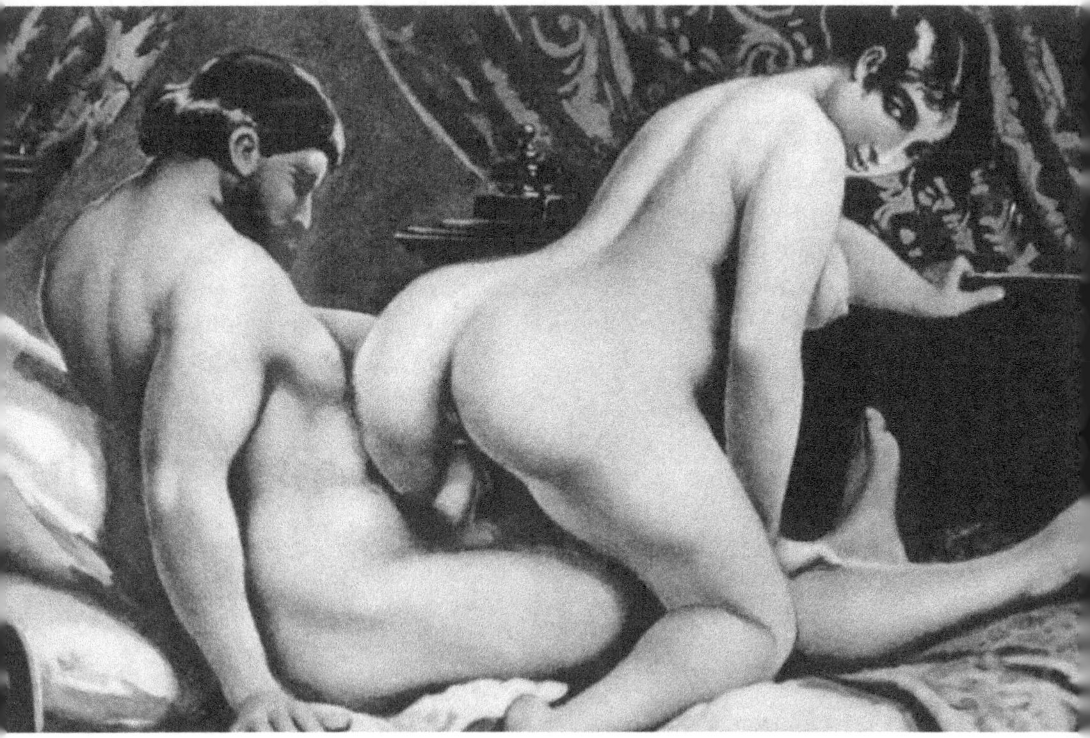

ERIC GILL

Eric Gill (1882-1940) is one of the major erotic artists of the 20th century. For him, eroticism was a vital part of life, and should be openly displayed in art. He moved from nudes to Madonnas easily and simply in his art: sex and religion were part of the same mystery for him. He built eroticism into most of his depictions of people. He continually drew attention to a figure's genitals. He was obsessed, for instance, by pubic hair. He was also fascinated by the penis, particularly his own.

Despite being open about sexuality, Eric Gill did keep some of his art secret. There are private drawings in the collections of the Victoria and Albert Museum and the British Museum in London, which depict, for instance, some seventy drawings of penises. The drawings are careful anatomical studies, complete with measurements. Some of the phallic drawings show Gill masturbating, or on a bed, or in a mirror. Sometimes the drawings of penises enter the critically acceptable arena, as in the prints entitled *The 'Most Precious Ornament'*.[1]

Eric Gill was meticulous in his recording of sexual activities. His private writings reveal a secret code for 'acts' such as anal intercourse. He also 'experimented' with dogs, incest and group sex.[2] So many male artists have drawn, painted or sculpted their penises: Jasper Johns, Egon Schiele, Pablo Picasso, Hans Bellmer, Robert Rauschenberg, Salvador Dali, and Tom of Finland. Men love their dicks. As did the ancients: from the Cerne Giant in Dorset, with its 30-foot long dick, to ithyphallic cave paintings of the palæolithic era.

1 Eric Gill: *The 'Most Precious Ornament'*, 1937, print, Victoria & Albert Museum
2 See Fiona MacCarthy: *Eric Gill*, Faber 1989

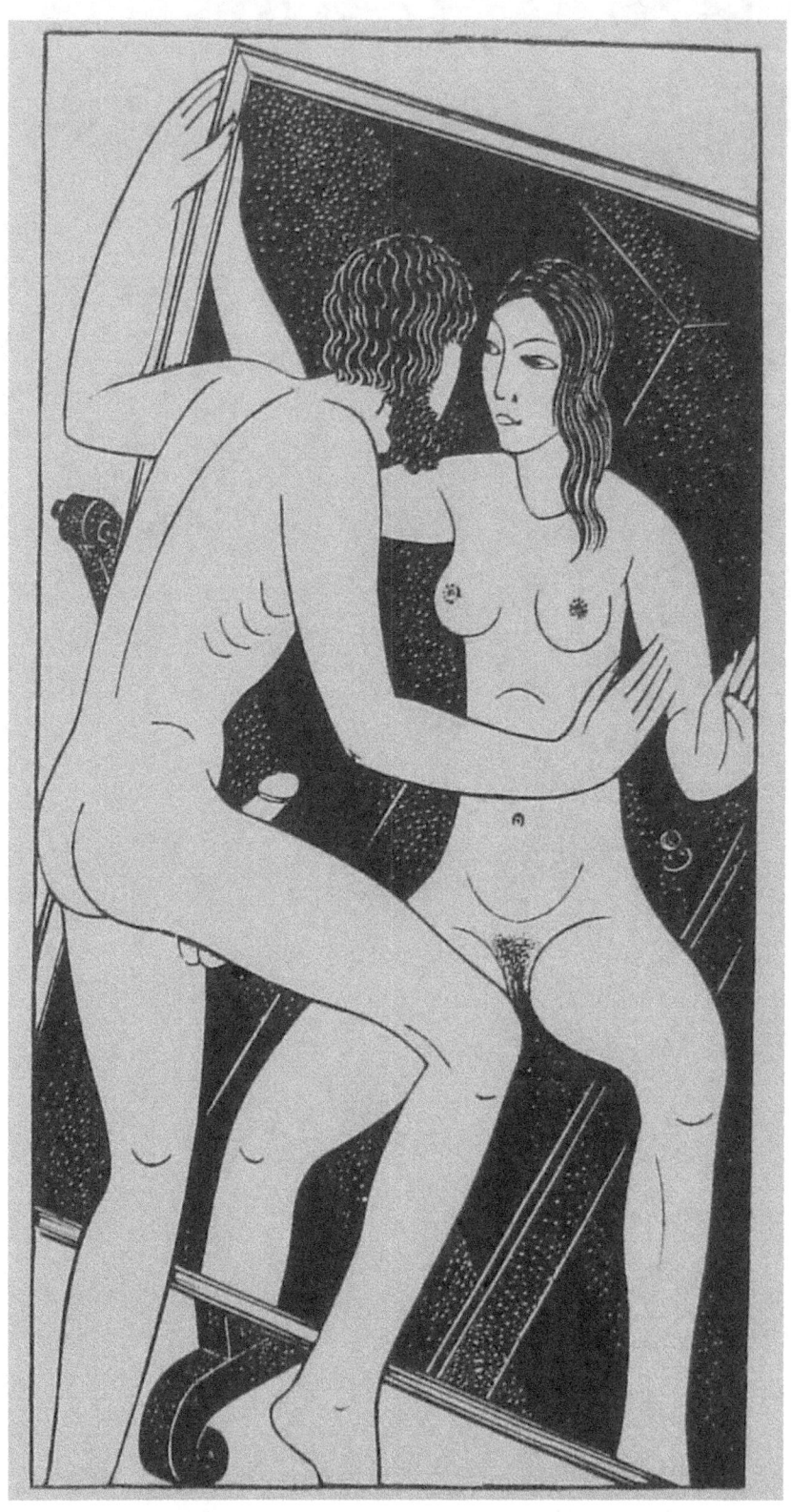

Eric Gill, Artist and Mirror, 1932

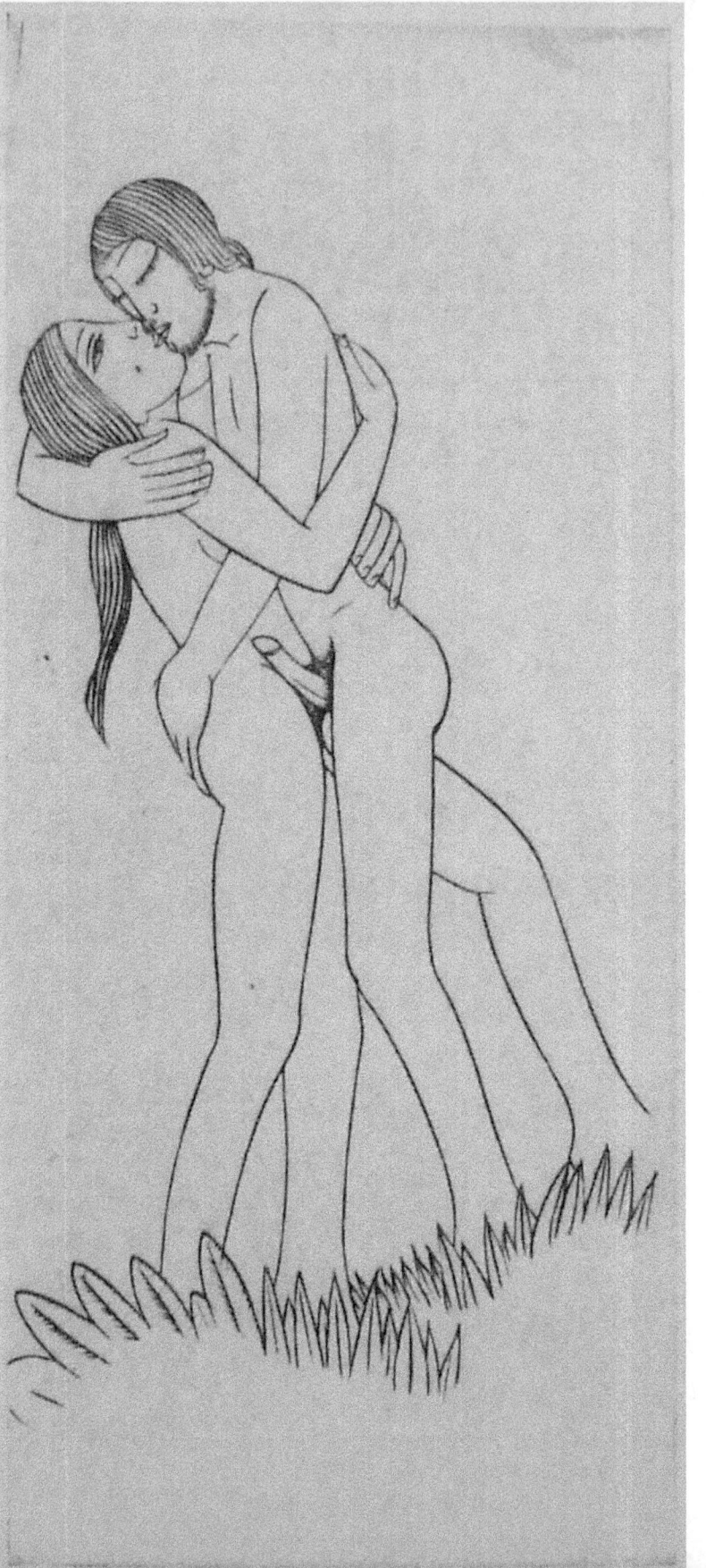

Eric Gill,
Earth Wrestlir
1926

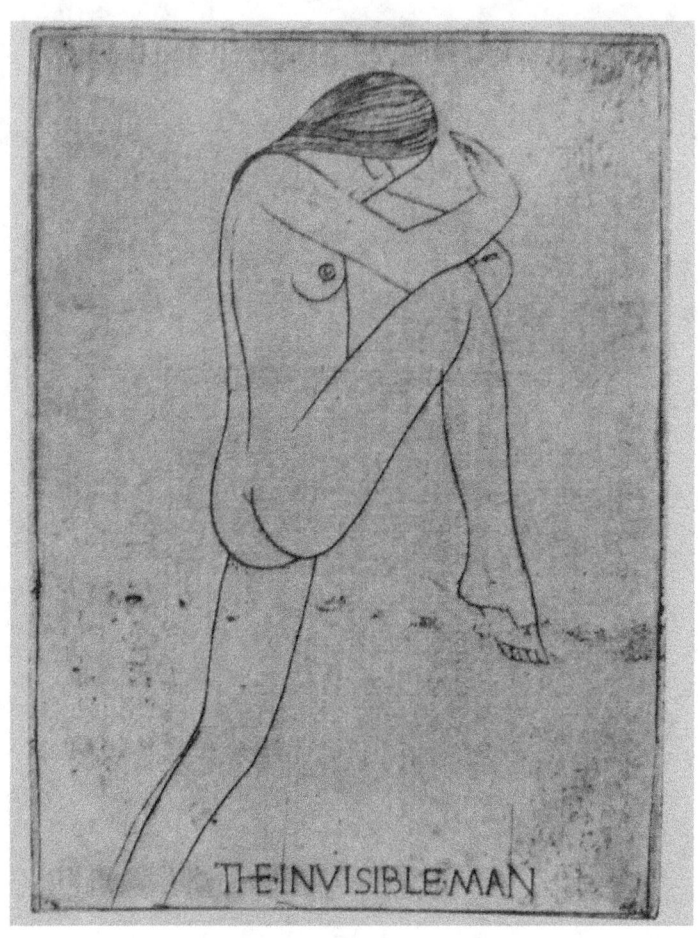

Eric Gill, The Invisible Man, 1924

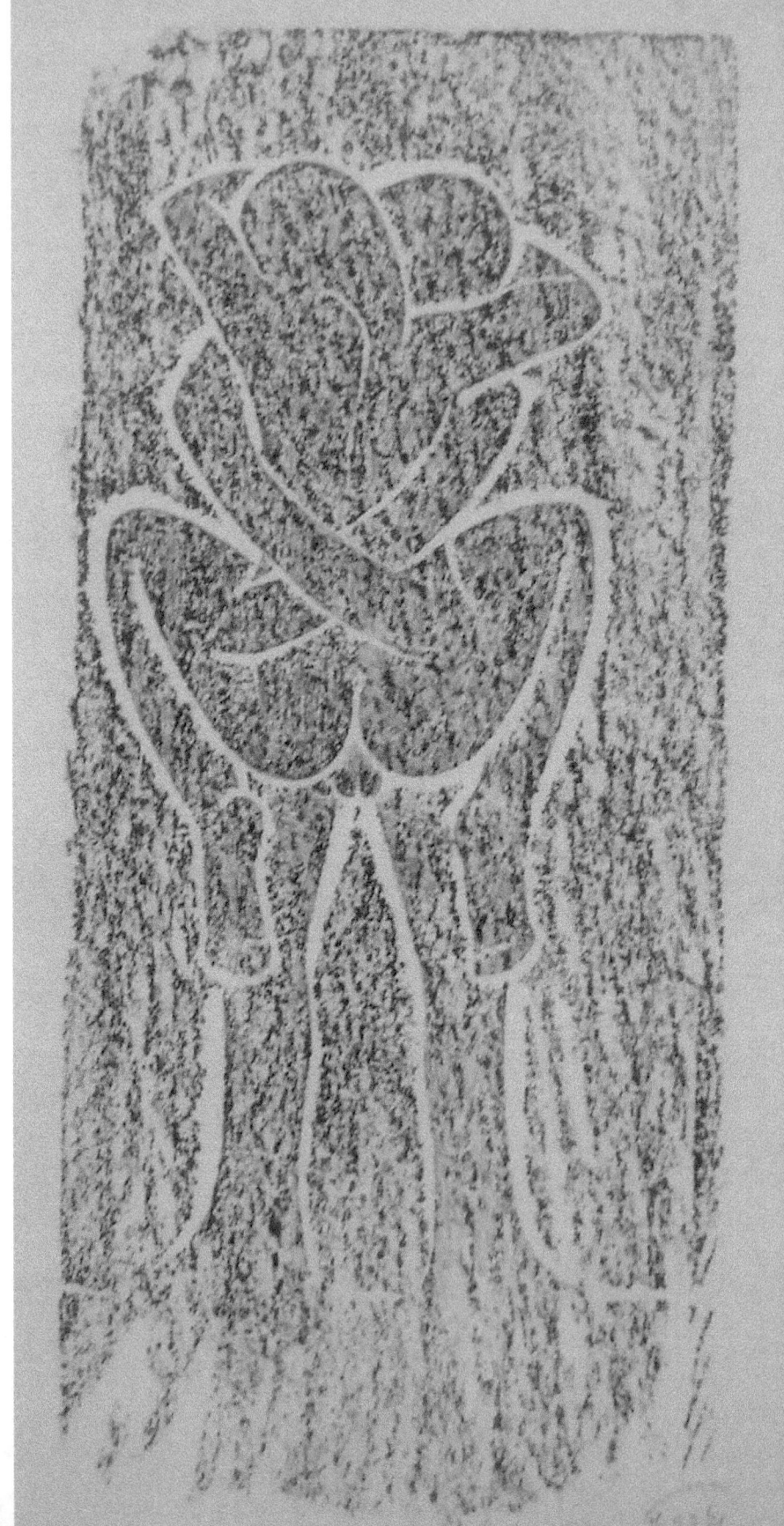

Eric Gill,
rubbing of
Lovers Relief,
1921
(whereabouts
unknown)

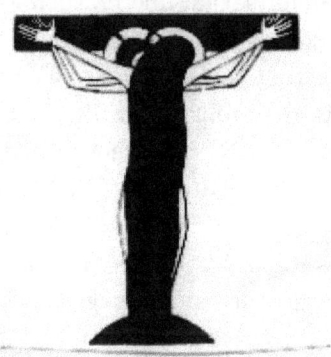

Eric Gill, Nuptials of God, 1922: the naked Mary Magdalene
making love to Chris on the Cross

ERIC GILL

In Eric Gill's art one finds all the usual tensions of Western art: the relation between women and fertility, agriculture, nature and nurture; the constant eroticization of people, the reduction to sexual identities; and the idea that sex can instigate a social and spiritual renewal or revolution.

Eric Gill's sense of sexuality is distinctly heterosexual, as with other campaigners for sexual liberty, such as D.H. Lawrence. Like Lawrence, Gill exalted women and the idea of 'woman'; like Lawrence, Gill secretly admired the male form: in both Gill and Lawrence there is an emphasis on the phallus, the symbolic erect phallus, which meant religious rebirth, as Lawrence showed in *The Escaped Cock*, a novella of the 'phallic' man, the new Adam. Lawrence's testament of erotic revolution, *Lady Chatterley's Lover*, was admired by Gill, and Gill illustrated it, depicting Mellors and Connie making love, kneeling on grass.[1] (There is also a bisexuality, or multi-sexuality, in Gill's art – or in his life, rather, than in his art. And he also experimented with sex with animals).

---

1 Eric Gill: *Lady C*, 1931, print, 2nd state, Victoria & Albert Museum

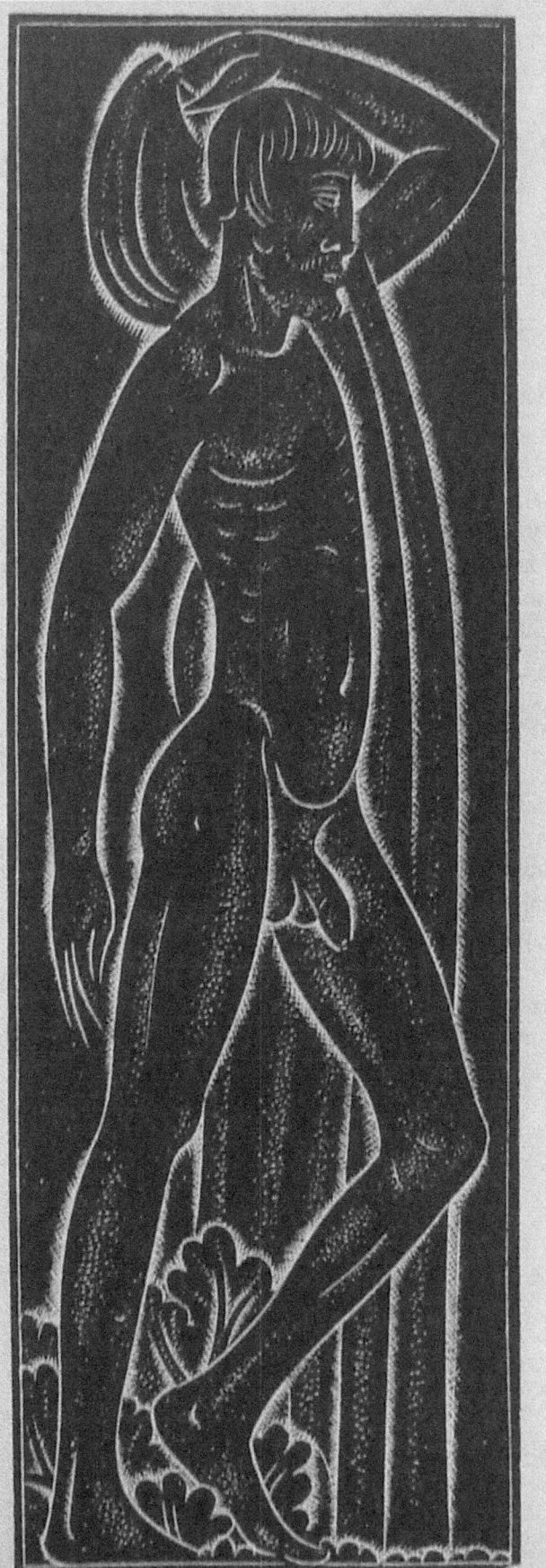

Eric Gill,
Mellors, 1930

ERIC GILL

Like D.H. Lawrence, Eric Gill believed in the holiness of sex and the holiness of art. Sex, art and religion were a continuum for Gill, as for Lawrence and others, such as Gustav Klimt, Michelangelo Buonarroti and Pablo Picasso. For Gill, as for so many artists, making art was a holy activity. Gill espoused the tenets of William Morris and the Arts and Crafts movement, maintaining that craftsmanship was sacred. 'The point is that human works should be holy, for holiness is properly their criterion', wrote Gill in a late essay. The Word of God was the first creative act, Gill said, and writers such as André Gide concur with this view. Gill wrote:

> What is a work of art? A word made flesh. That is the truth, in the clearest sense of the text. A word, that which emanates from the mind. Made flesh; a thing, a thing seen, a thing known, the immeasurable translated into terms of the measurable.[1]

In many images, Eric Gill depicted sex in sacred ways, either by giving his pictures of copulating couples a religious context – a title, perhaps, as in *Earth Wrestling*, or he puts the hand of God above the lovers, and rays of light emanate from the hand, blessing the sex act, as in *Earth Receiving*.[2] The image of the couple making love below the hand of God perfectly summarizes Gill's view of sex, of sex as a religious experience.

---

1 Eric Gill: "The Priesthood of Craftsmanship", *Blackfriars*, in Goldwater, 456-7
2 Eric Gill: *Earth Wrestling*, 1926, engraving on copper, Victoria & Albert Museum; *Earth Receiving*, 1926, engraving on copper, 12.4 x 8.8cm, University of Texas, Austin

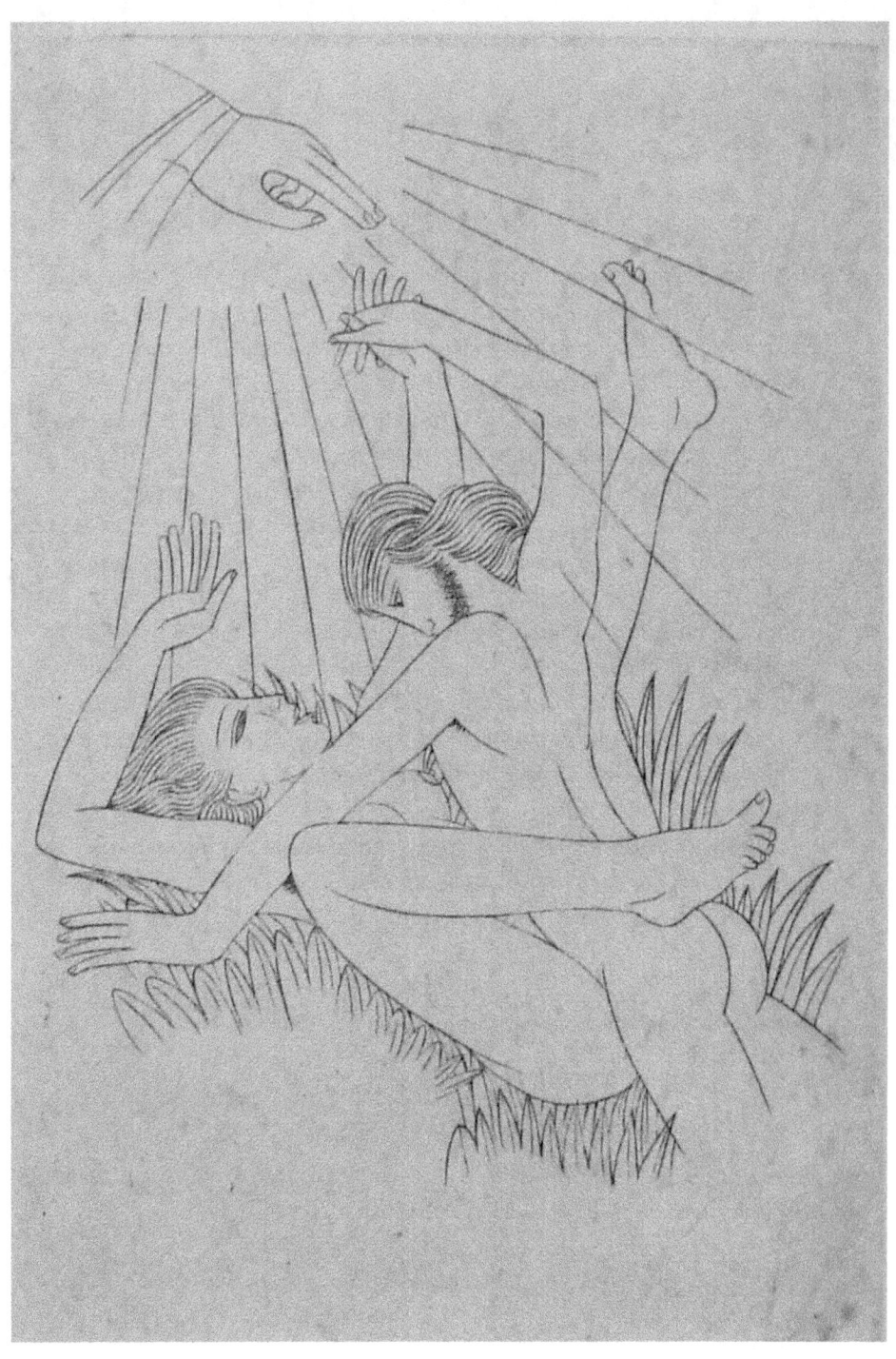

Eric Gill, Earth Receiving, 1926

ERIC GILL

In most of his religious-erotic images, Eric Gill is wildly phallic and heterosexual. The woman is definitely 'passive' and the male is 'active'. The woman, as Earth, 'receives', while the man does the fucking. The woman 'gives' herself, gives of herself, in Eric Gill's art, as in his series of erotic prints illustrating the most sensual poem in the *Bible*, the *Song of Songs*, where the woman offers her breasts to the man.[1] According to Marina Warner (*Alone*, 126), the *Song of Songs* is immensely erotic: '[t]here has never been a more intense communication of the experience of desire.' The *Cantia Canticarum* allows for depictions of unbridled sensuality. The nuptial imagery allows for artists to be as sensual as they dare in a religious setting. Gill's merging of eroticism with Catholicism operates within the mystical tradition of Catholicism, as espoused by St Bernard, Jan van Ruysbroeck, St Theresa and St John of the Cross. It is a wild and ecstatic mysticism which describes religious bliss in very sensual terms.

In the art of Eric Gill, eroticism veers from moments of tender affection, as in *Approaching Dawn*, from an illustration of Geoffrey Chaucer's *Troilus and Creseyde*, to undiluted erotica, such as in *The Chinese Maidservant*, which shows a woman bending over, revealing her buttocks. The aim of such images is to sexualize the female body, to make it available to the (male) gaze.

---

1 Eric Gill: *Ibi Dabo Tibi*, 1925, Victoria & Albert Museum

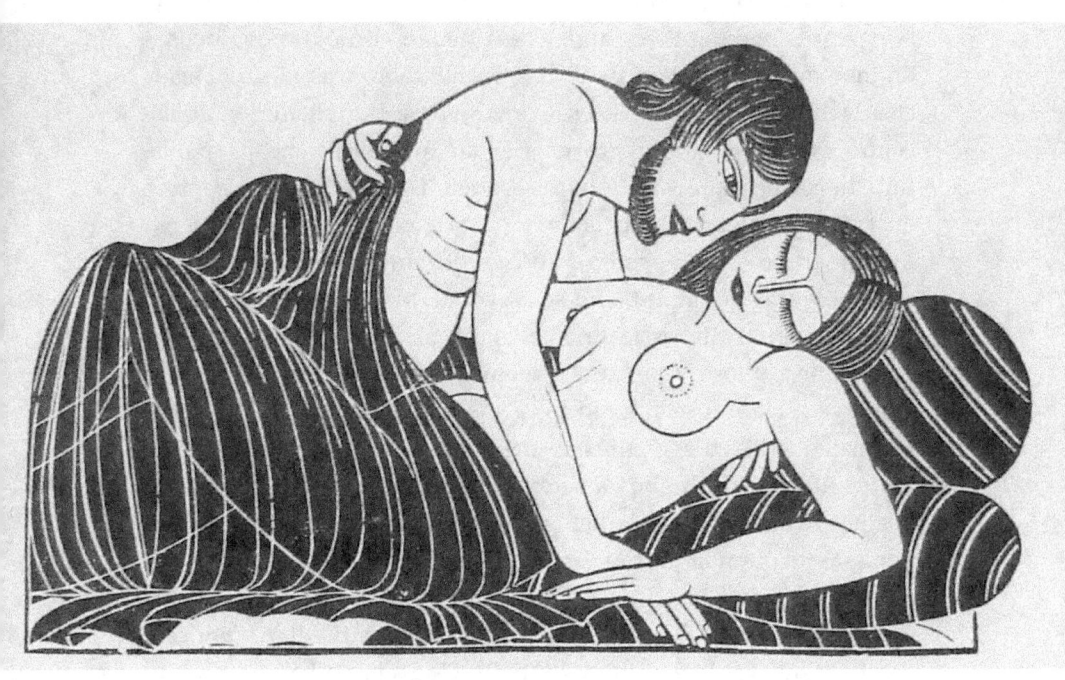

Eric Gill, The Juice of My Pomegranates, 1925

ERIC GILL

In other images, such as *Lot's Daughter*, Eric Gill depicts two people making love in a picture employing plain, unadorned marks,[1] as found in Taoist sex manuals,[2] or in the 'acrobatic' fucking of *Lovers in Tent* or *Lovers, the Raised Bottom*, which depicts two people making love,[3] and, as so often in pornography, focuses on the penis and vagina, as if that was all there was to sex. This is clearly the case in Eric Gill's works, where the phallus is at the centre of pleasure and power. Sex in his works means penile thrusting. The man is on top, the woman is underneath, accepting everything. Gill's art reveals the same power relations as depicted in high art, low art, pornography, advertizing, TV and the media: male power is dominant, and sex revolves around the phallus.

There is no clitoris in Eric Gill's art. Similarly, D.H. Lawrence condemned those 'cocksure' women who took control and employed 'clitoral sex', as in his *The Plumed Serpent*. It's only the vulva. For Gill, the phallus is the 'transcendent signifier', as in the print *Eve* which shows a female nude with a snake between her legs, curling towards her groin, clearly the snake here is the penis, as so often in patriarchal art.[4]

Often, Eric Gill's ithyphallic imagery is laughable, as in his *God Sending*, which shows Jesus flying towards the Earth with an erection, his head beaming with light, God's hand behind him, in Heaven, sending Christ on his way.[5] Here is that most blasphemous of images: not only an erotic Christ, but Christ with an erection!

1 Eric Gill: *Lot's Daughter*, 1926, pencil and watercolour, 13.5 x 1.6cm, University of Texas, Austin
2 *The Leaping White Tiger*, album leaf in ink and colours on silk, Chinese K'ang-hsi period 91622-1722), C. T. Loa collection, Texas
3 Eric Gill: *Approaching Dawn*, 1927, in *Troilus and Cresseyde*, Golden Cockerel Press; *Lovers, the Raised Bottom*, 1934, Victoria & Albert Museum
4 Eric Gill: *Eve*, 1926, print, Victoria & Albert Museum
5 Eric Gill: *God Sending*, 1926, engraving on copper, Victoria & Albert Museum

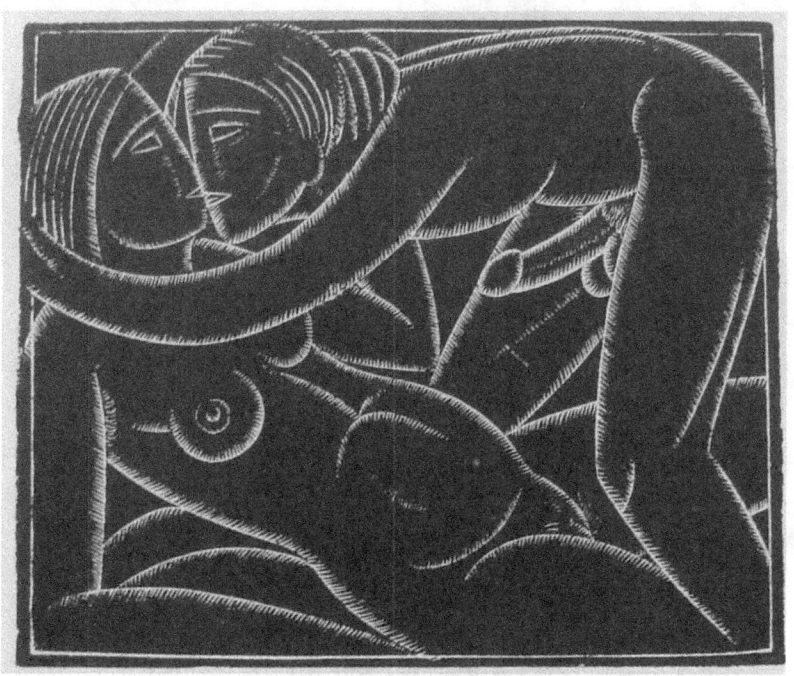

Eric Gill, Lovers, 1924

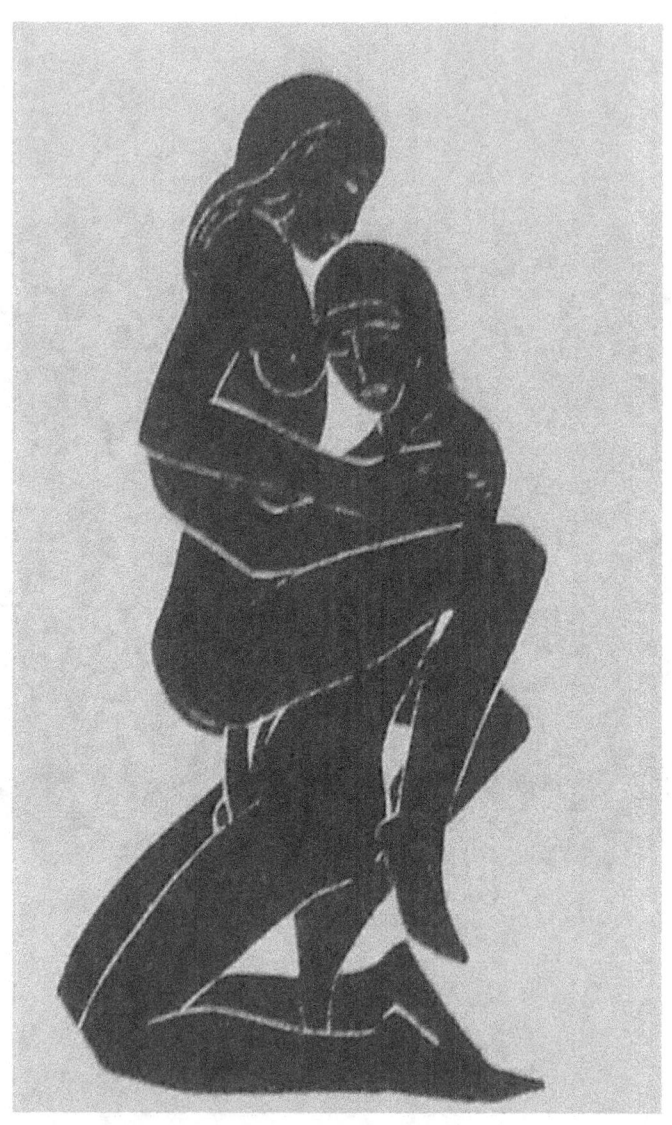

Eric Gill, Lovers, Kneeling, 1920

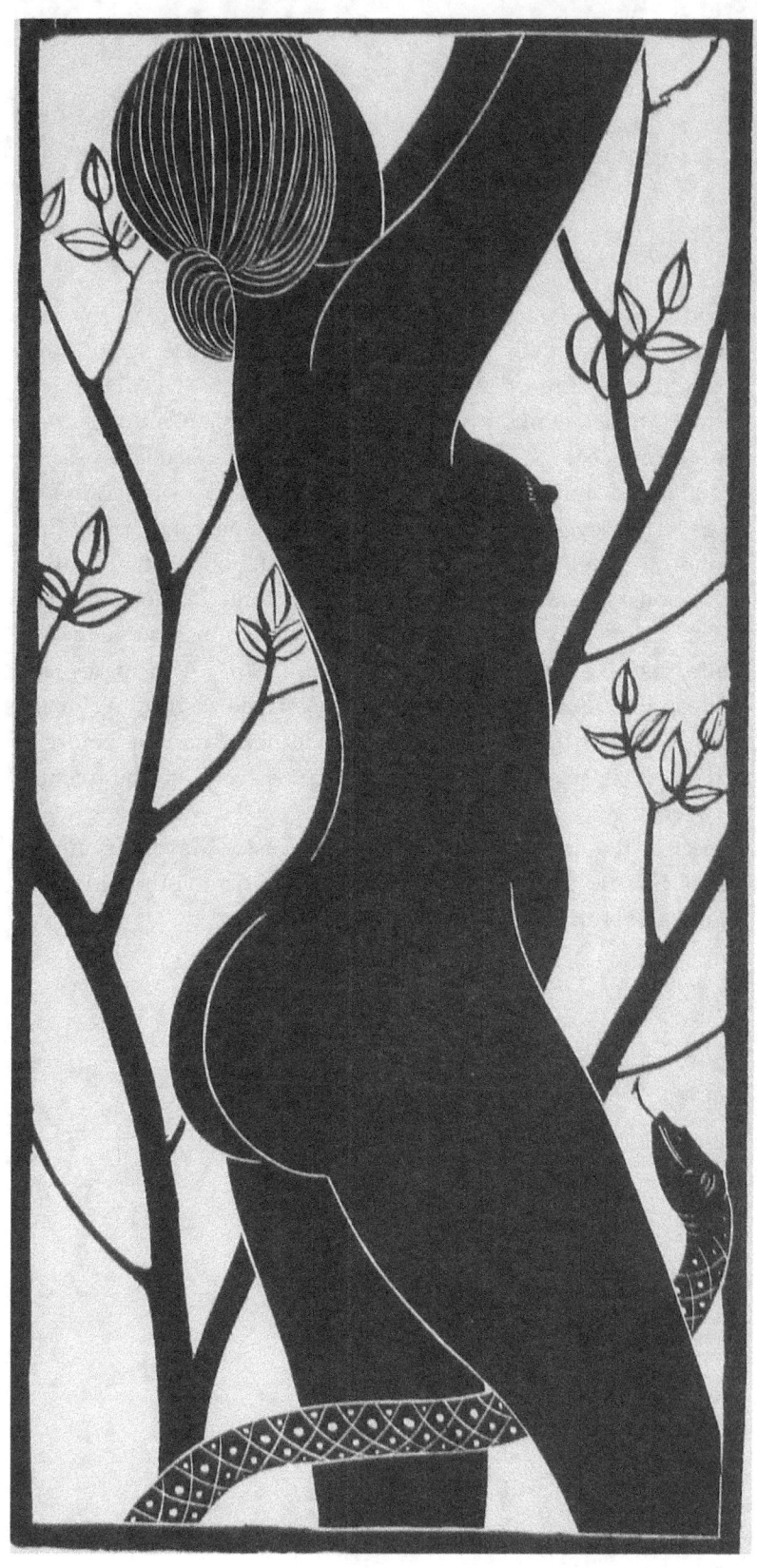

Eric Gill, Eve, 1926

AMEDEO MODIGLIANI

Amedeo Modigliani's nudes seem to be the archetypical 'modern master' nudes, with their sleek bodies at once 'pure', like Classical sculpture or the colder-than-cold lines of J.A.D. Ingres, yet also quite definitely sensual-sexual. Modigliani's nudes are – apart from being women (of course) – 'available', passive, relaxing back for the viewer's enjoyment, just like women in skin mags.[1] Their eyes are closed, their arms are open, they show their bodies to the viewer, not always sad, but often smiling mysteriously (with what eroticists call a 'come on' look on their faces). 'Come and get me', these nude women in Modigliani say, really, just like the women in the art of Titian, J.A.D. Ingres, and Jean-Honoré Fragonard ('come and get me, but don't really touch'). And if the models or figures do not state it as boldly as that, it is implied in their passive pose, and in the relation between viewer and subject. The *connection* between viewer and subject in the art of Modigliani, as in Picasso, Matisse, Bonnard, Degas, Schiele, Klimt, Titian, Ingres, Boucher, and other 'high art' painters, is erotic.

---

1 Amedeo Modigliani: *Recumbent Nude*, 1917-8, private collection; *Seated Nude*, c. 1917, Courtauld Institute of Art, London

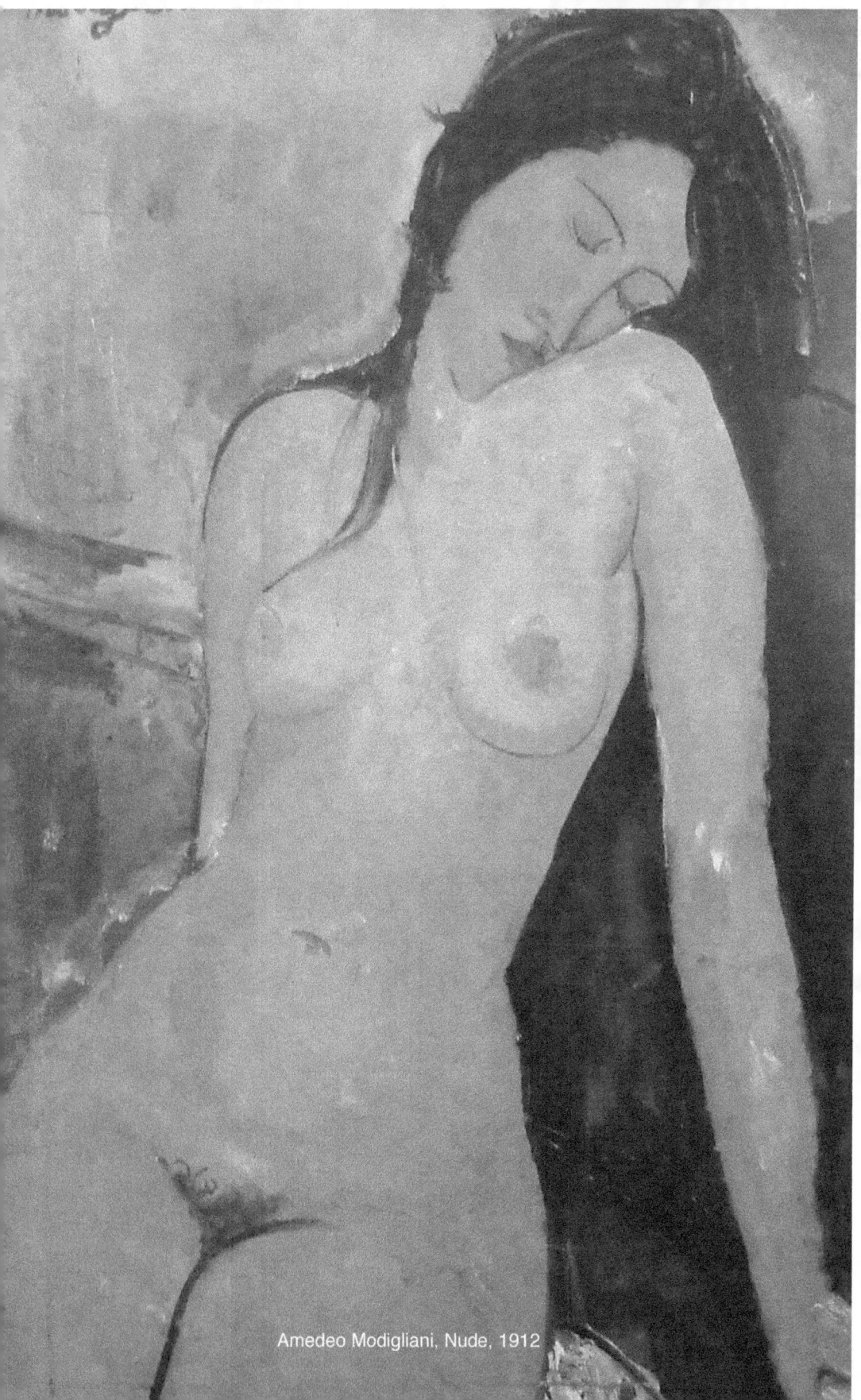

Amedeo Modigliani, Nude, 1912

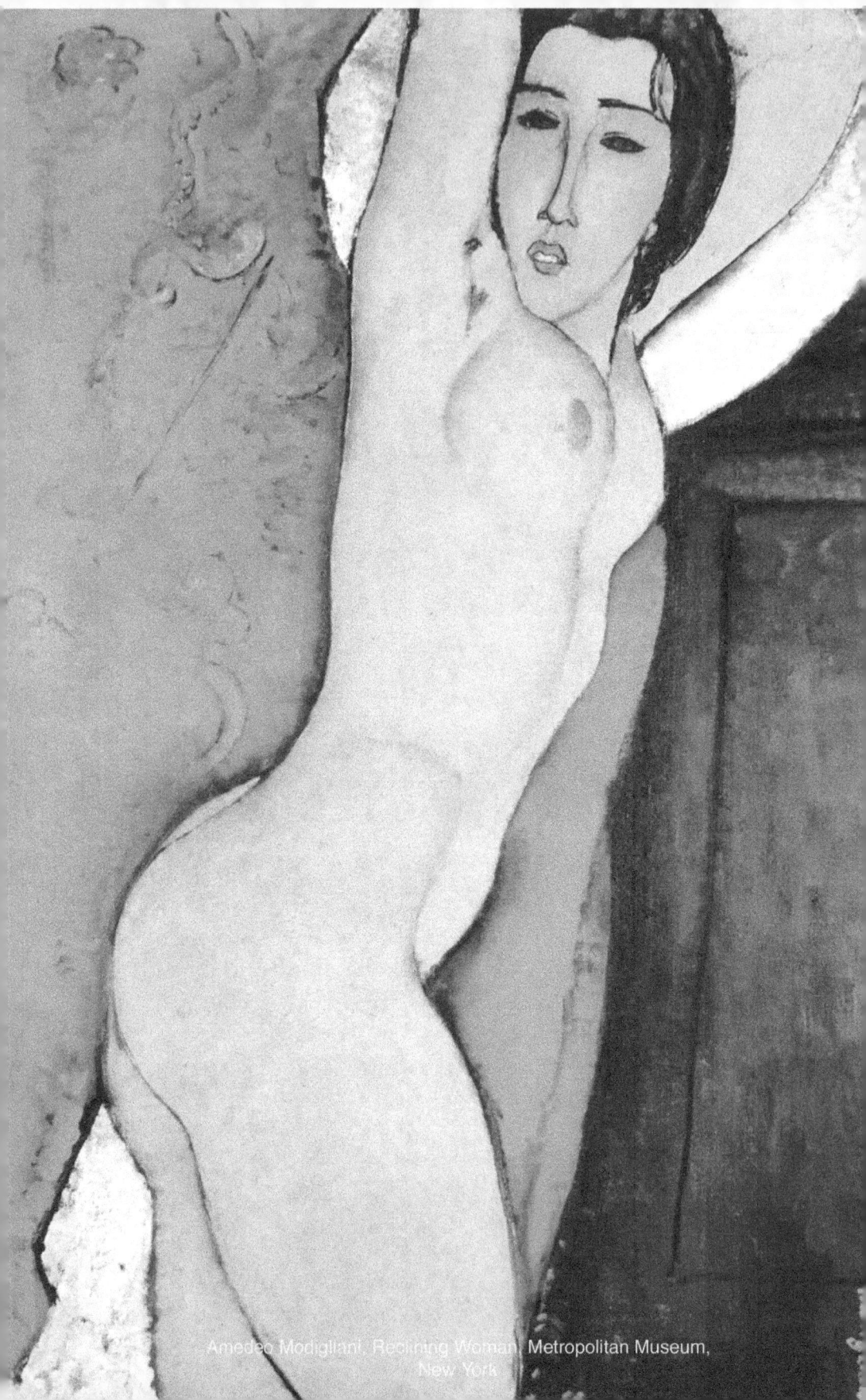

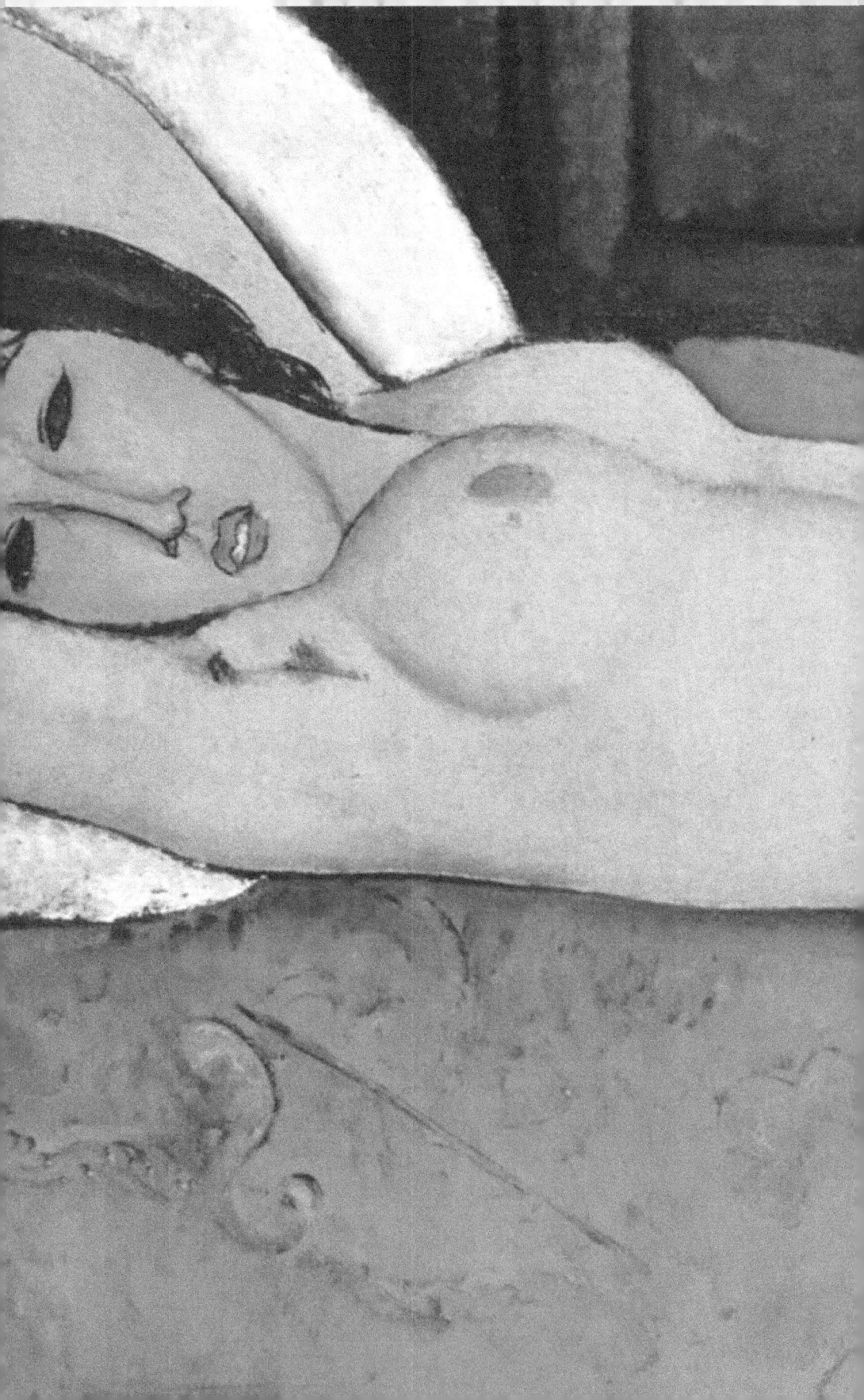

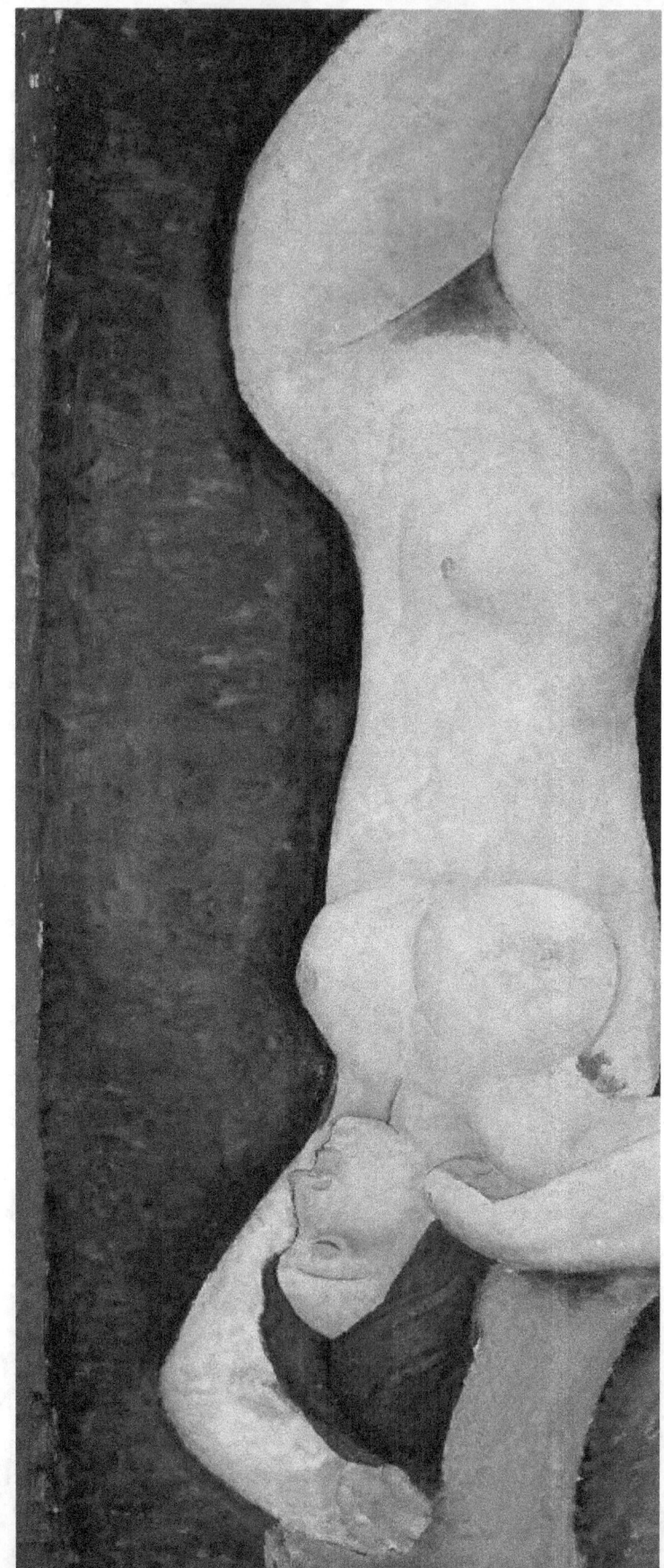

Amedeo
Modigliani,
Reclining
Nude, 1919

APPENDICES

Extra illustrations, including from the following artists:

Henry Fuseli (1741-1825), a Swiss artist.

•

Peter Fendi (1796-1842), from a collection of 40 erotic prints published in 1910.

•

André de Nerciat, from *Le Diable* (1803).

•

Antoine Borel (1743-1810).

•

Heinrich Lossow (1843-97), from the *Metamorphoses, The Triumph of Cupid*.

•

Johann Nepomuk Geiger (1805-80), a painter and lithographer from Vienna.

•

Otto Schoff (1888-1938), a German graphic artist, from *Loose Engravings* (1920).

•

Mihály Zichy (1827-1906), a Hungarian born artist, from *Liebe* (1911).

•

Martin van Maële (October 12, 1863-September 5, 1926), a French illustrator, including some images from *La Grande Danse Macabre des Vifs*.

•

Ernest Gerhard, a German artist, from *Die Laterne* (1925).

•

F. Christophe, from *Die Verfuhrung*, 1925.

- Achille Jacques-Jean-Marie Devéria (February 6, 1800-December 23, 1857), French painter and lithographer, from *Diabolico Foutro Manie* (1835).

- Almery Lobel Riche (1880-1950).

- William Bouguereau (1825-1905), a French painter known for his academic paintings of female figures.

- Gustav Klimt (1862-1918).

- Egon Schiele (1890-1918).

- Plus a selection of more images from the history of erotic art.

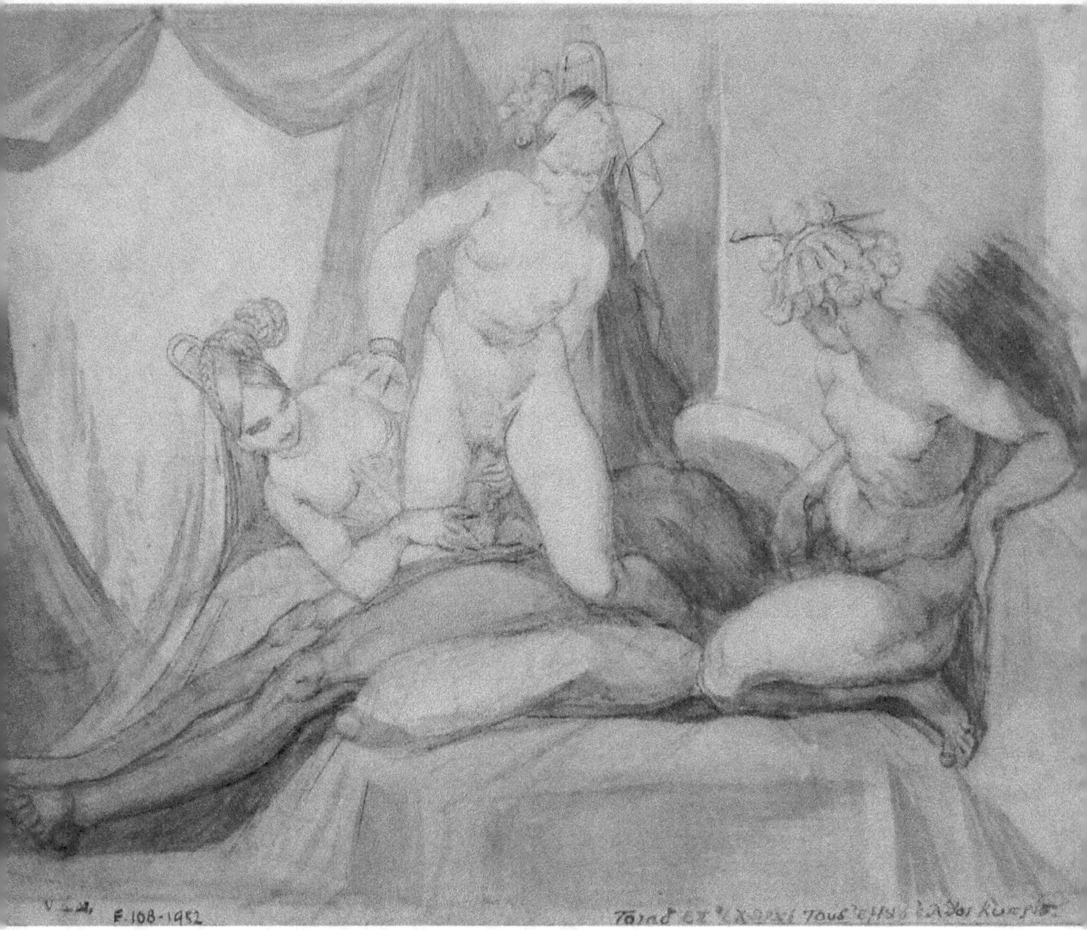

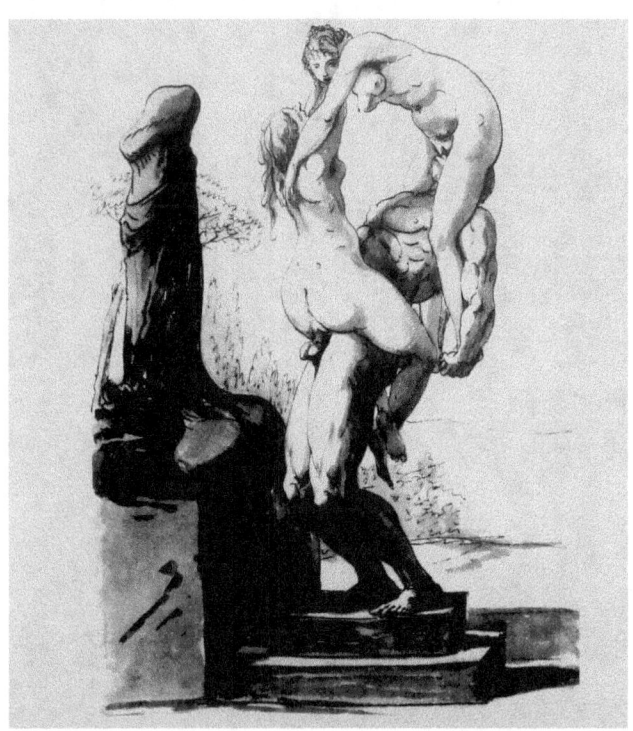

Henry Fuseli, Orgy Scene, 1809-10, Victoria & Albert Museum, London, above.

Jean-Baptiste Regnault, left.

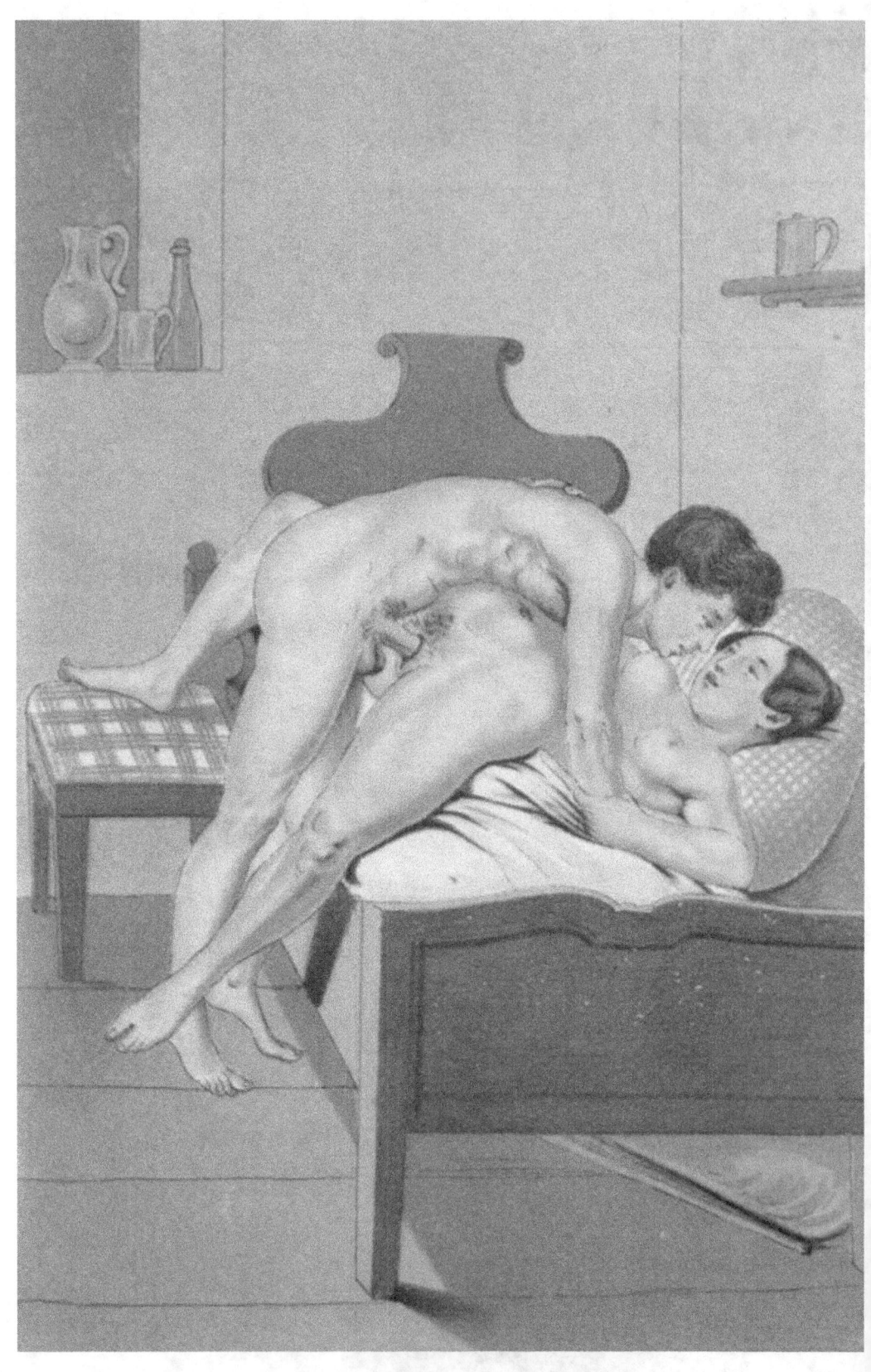

Peter Fendi, this page and following pages

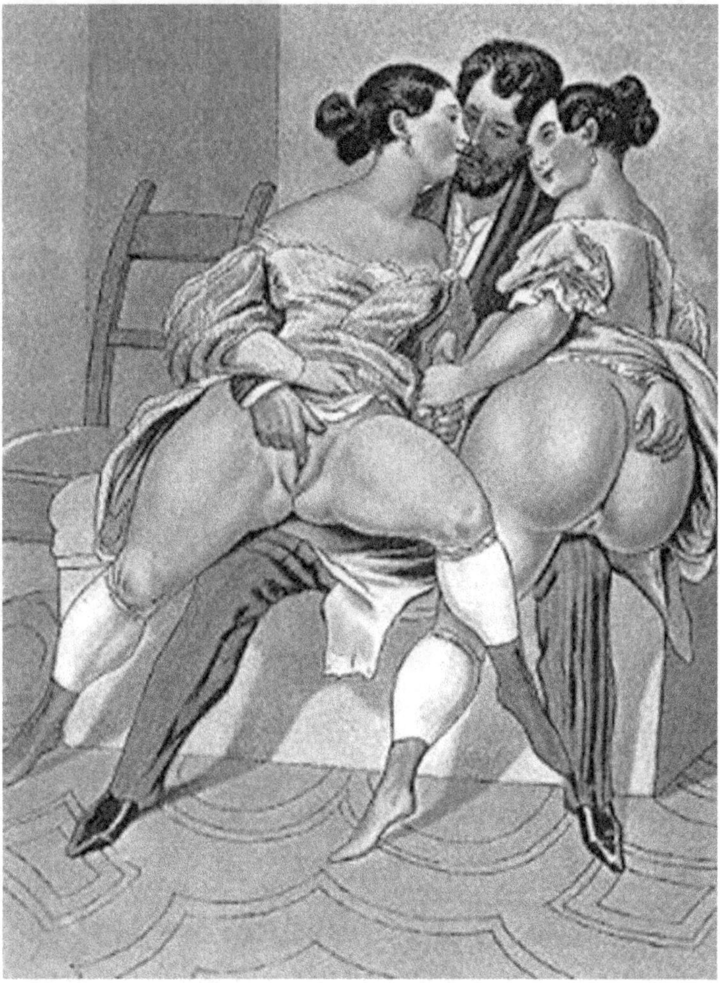

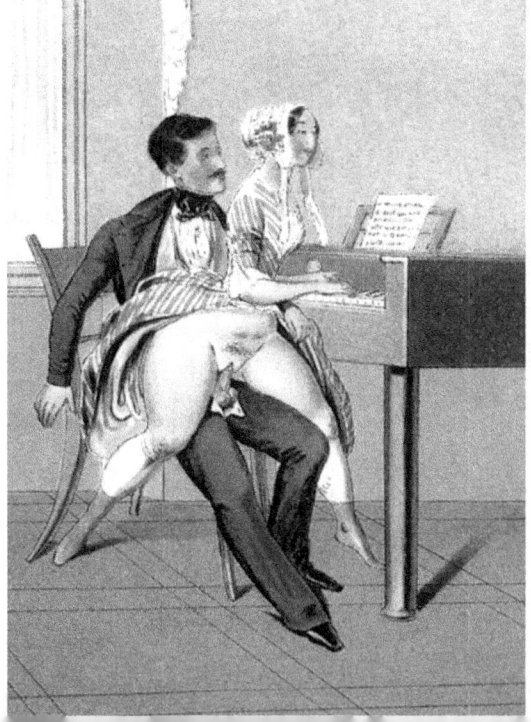

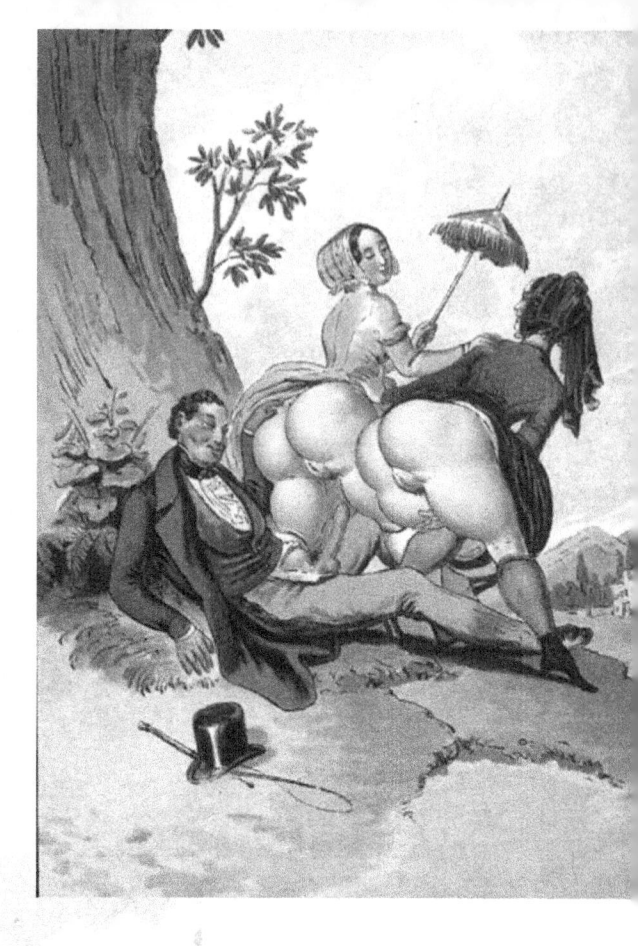

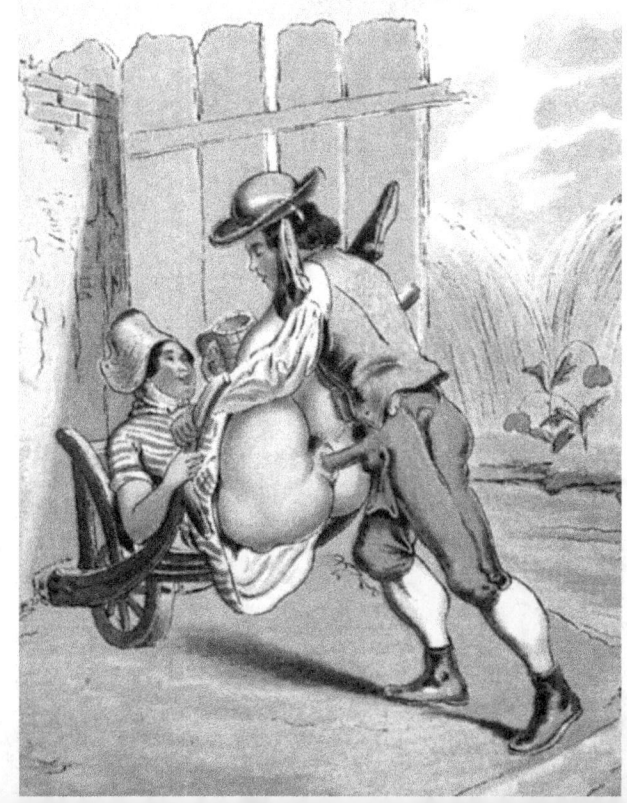

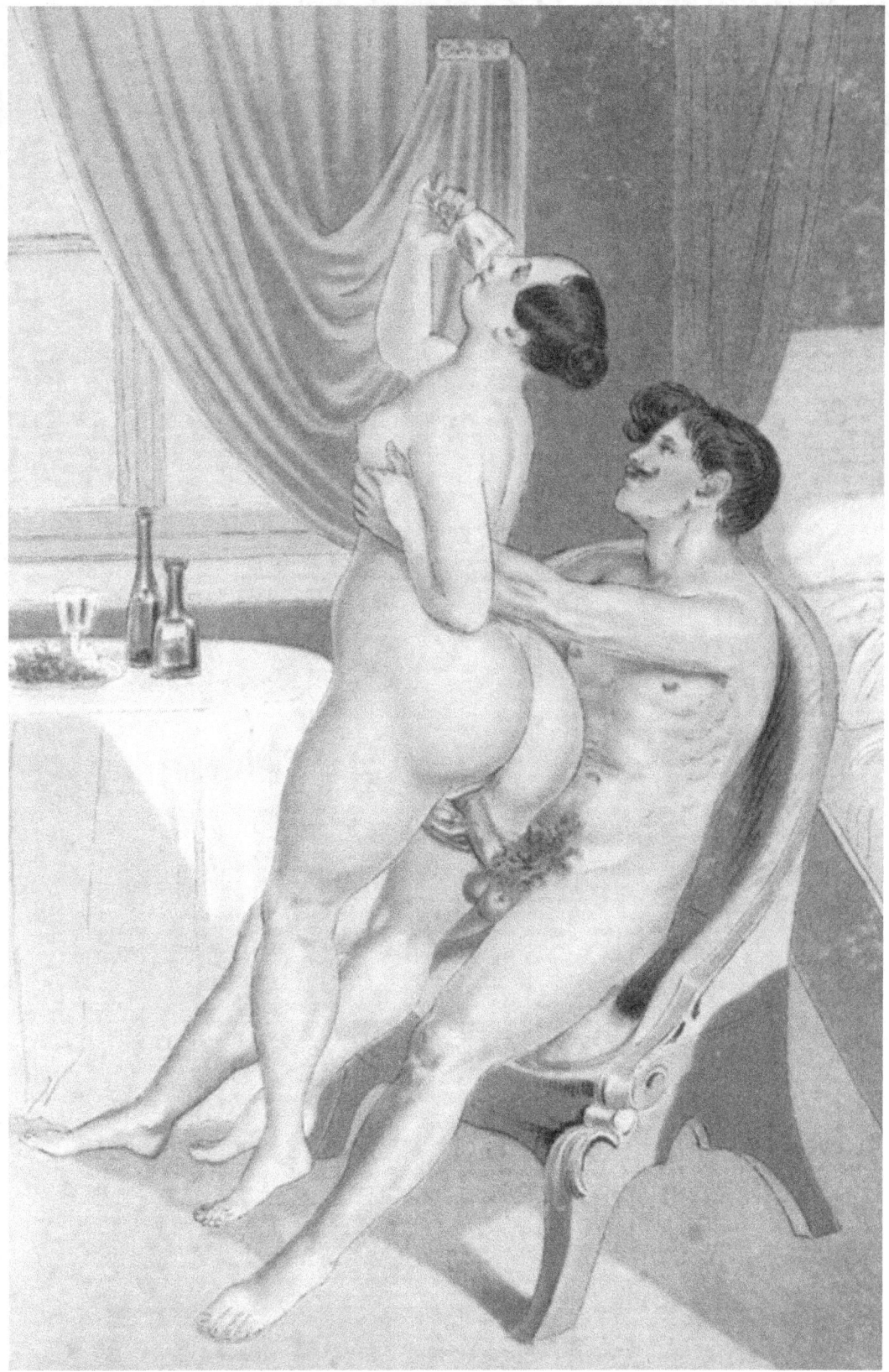

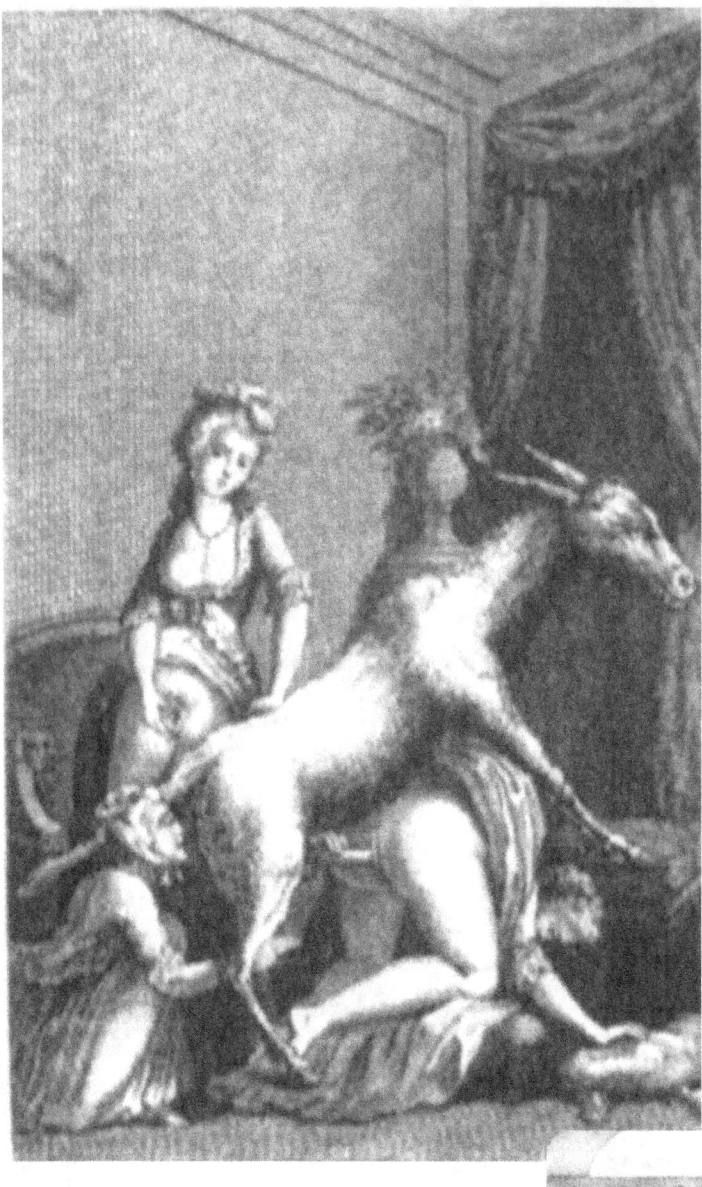

From Le Diable du corps,
by André-Robert Andréa de Nerciat, 1786
this page and following pages.

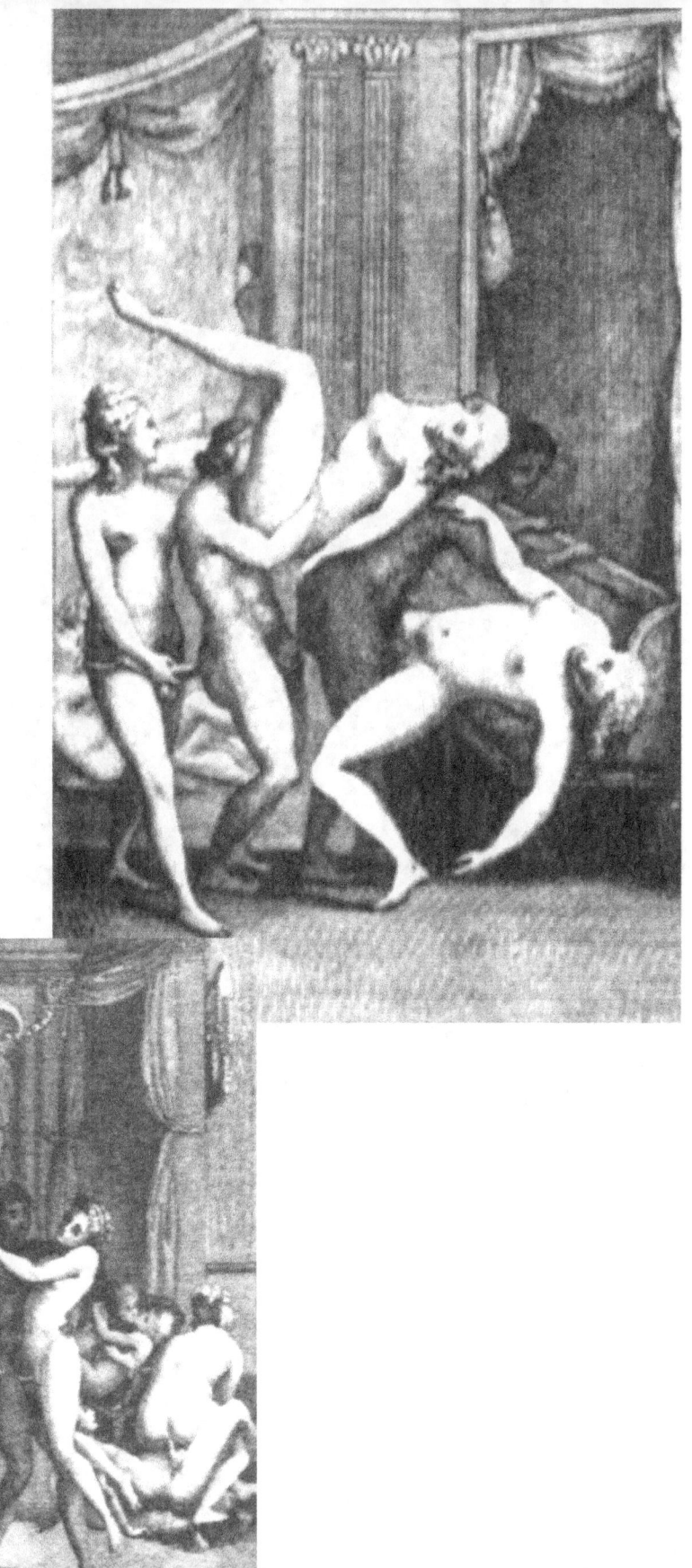

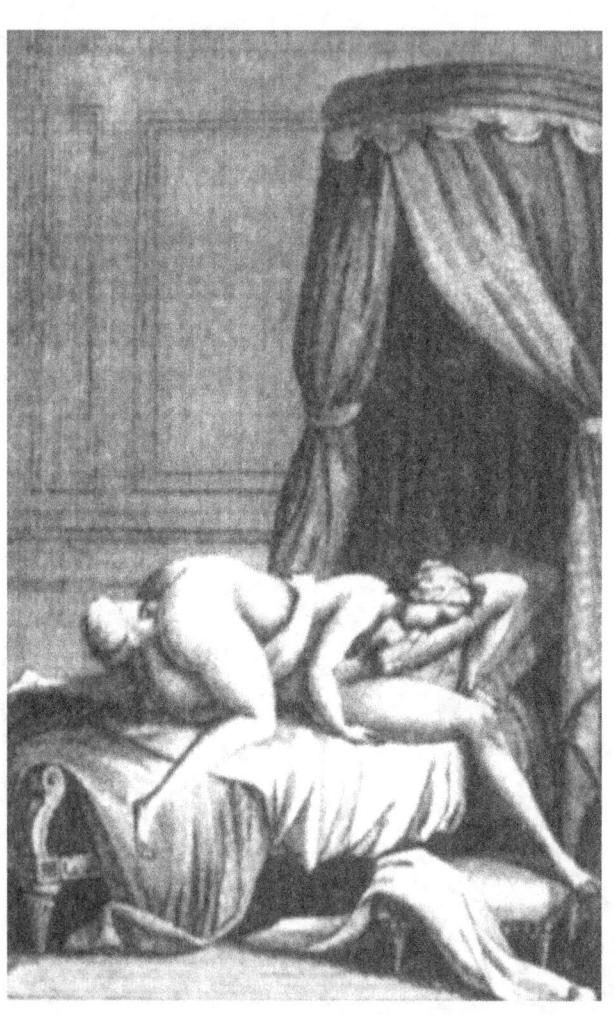

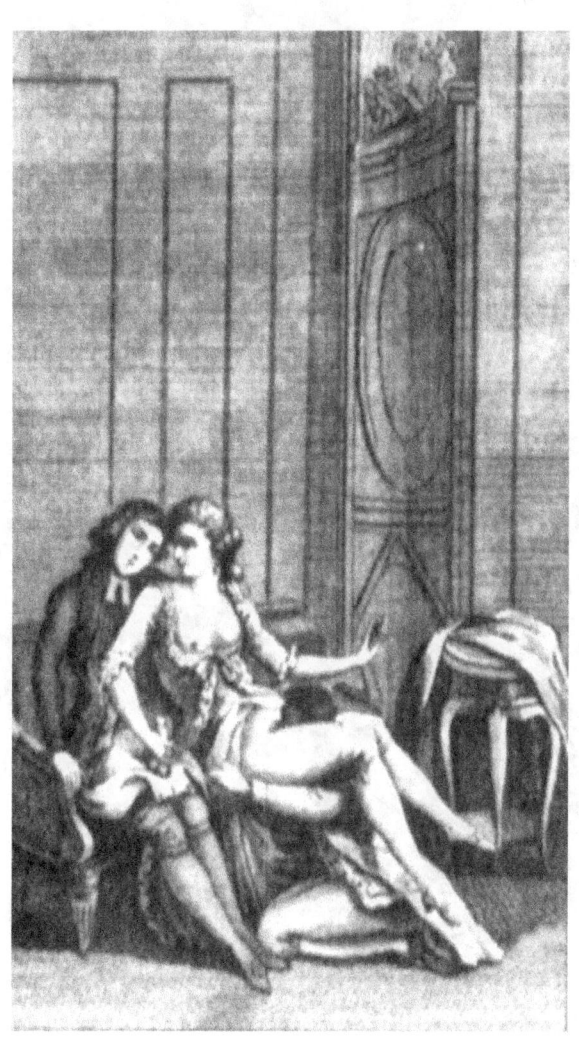

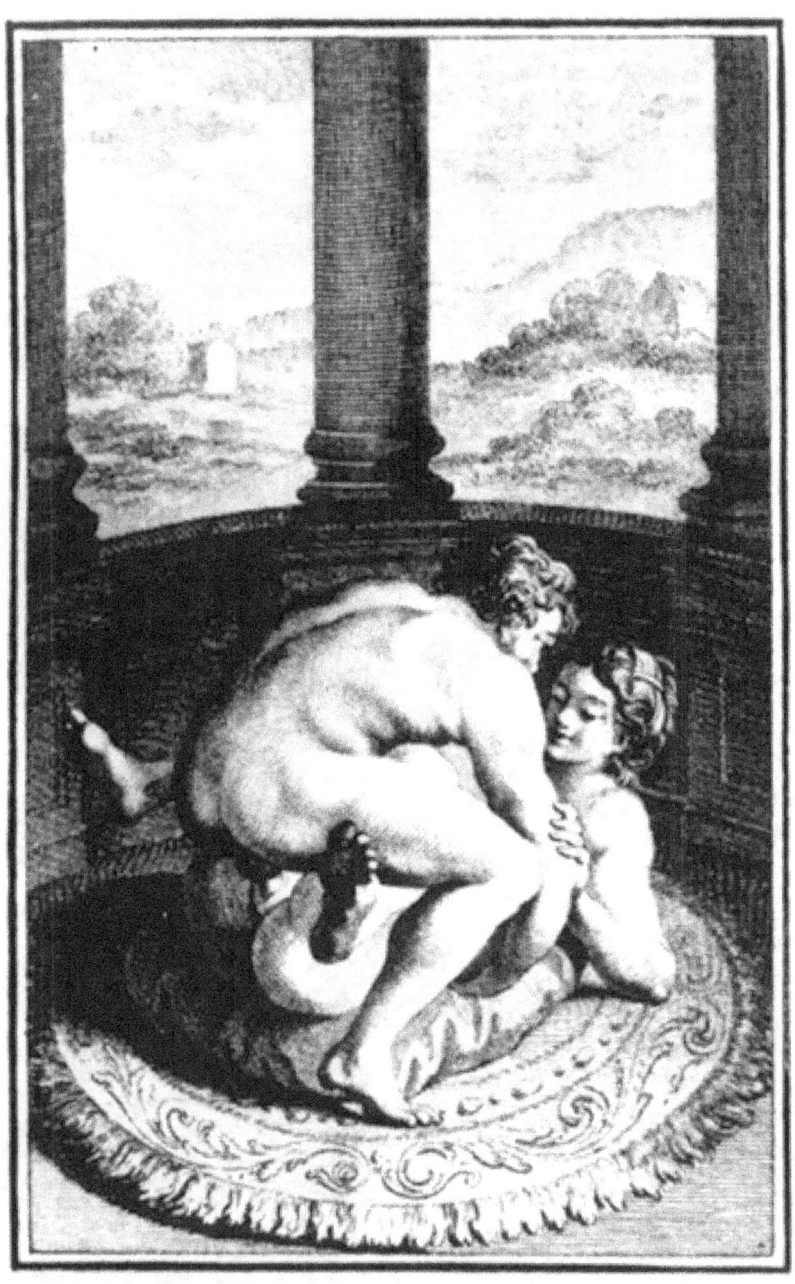

Antoine Borel, this page and following pages

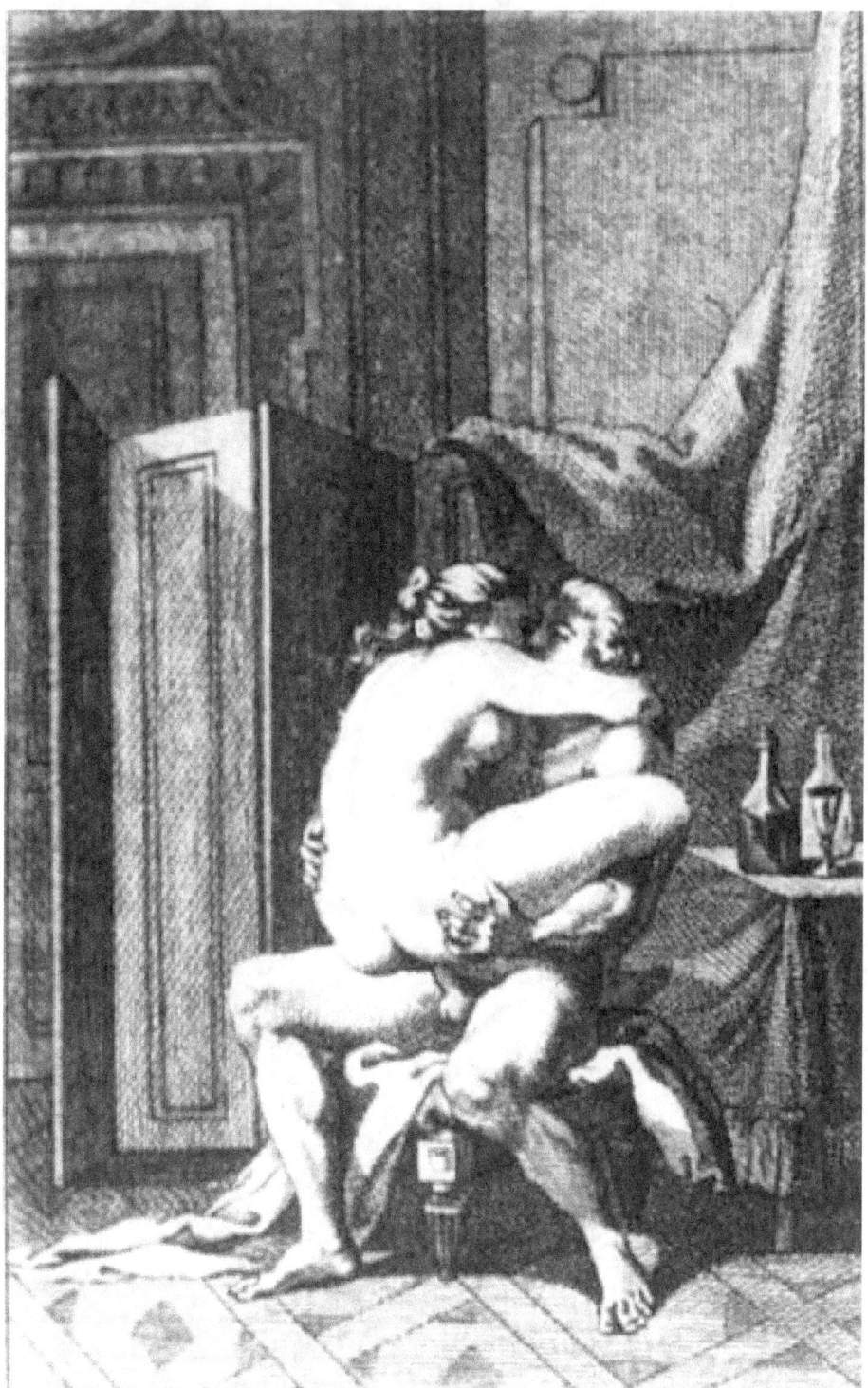

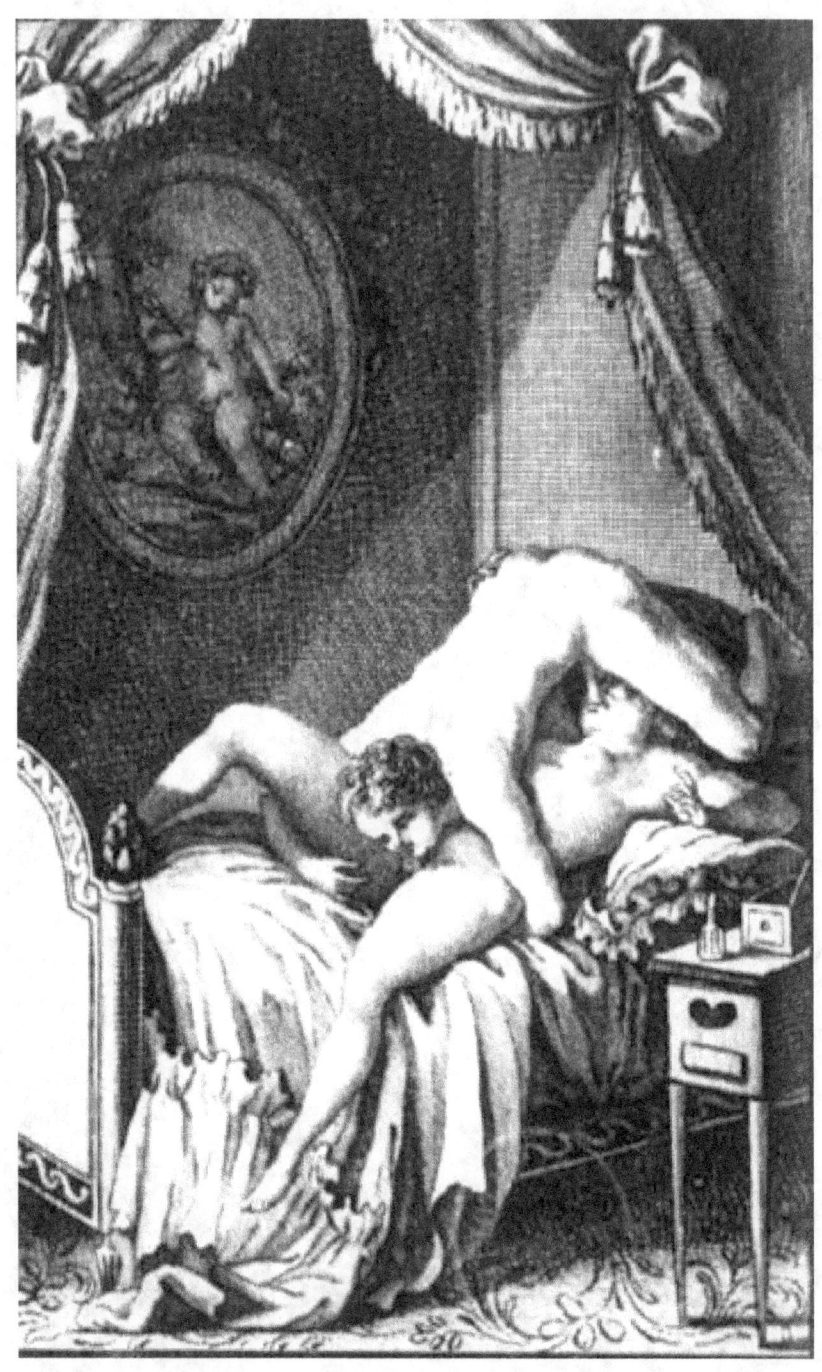

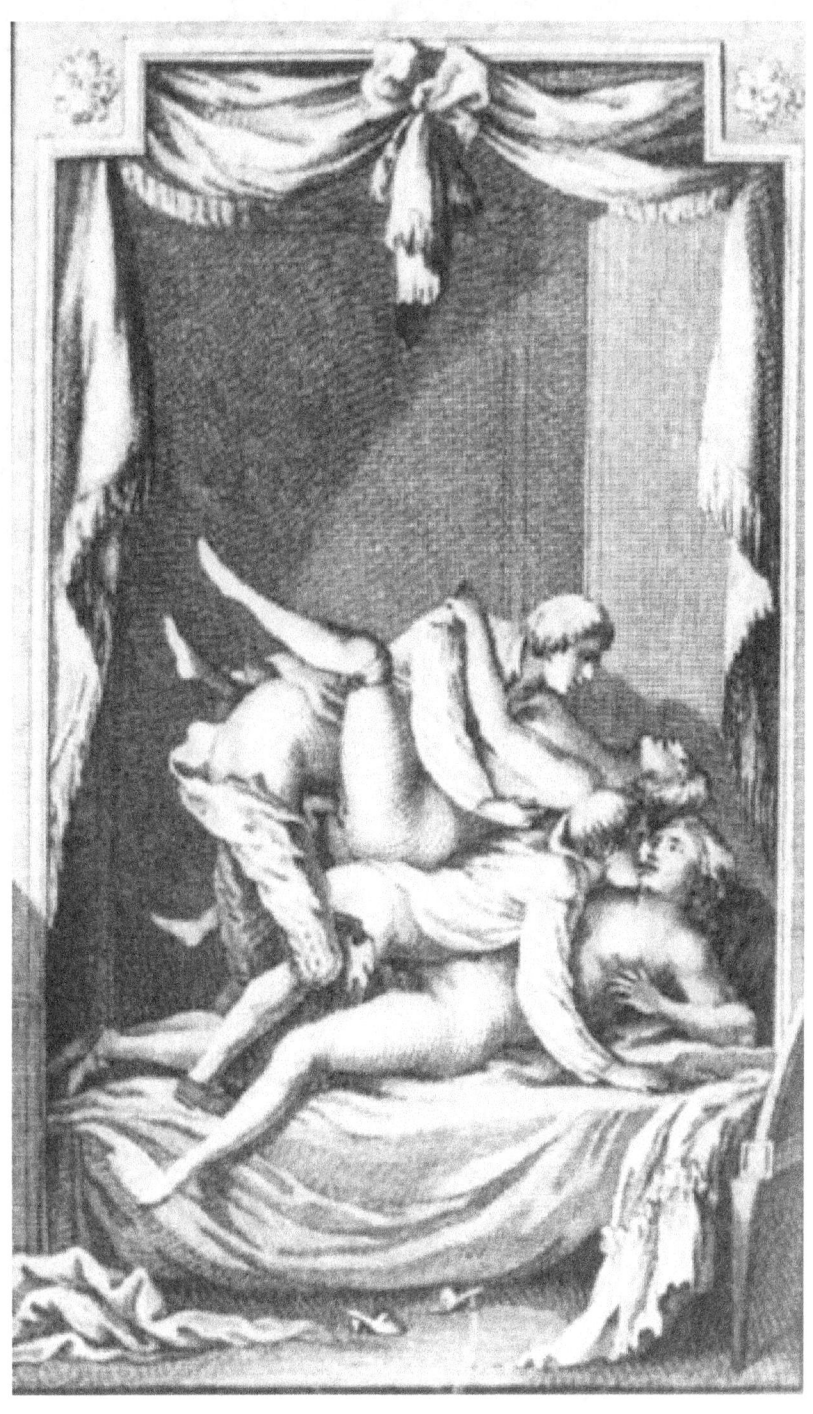

Antoine Borel, illustration for Mémoires de Saturnin,
by Jean-Charles Gervaise, 1787

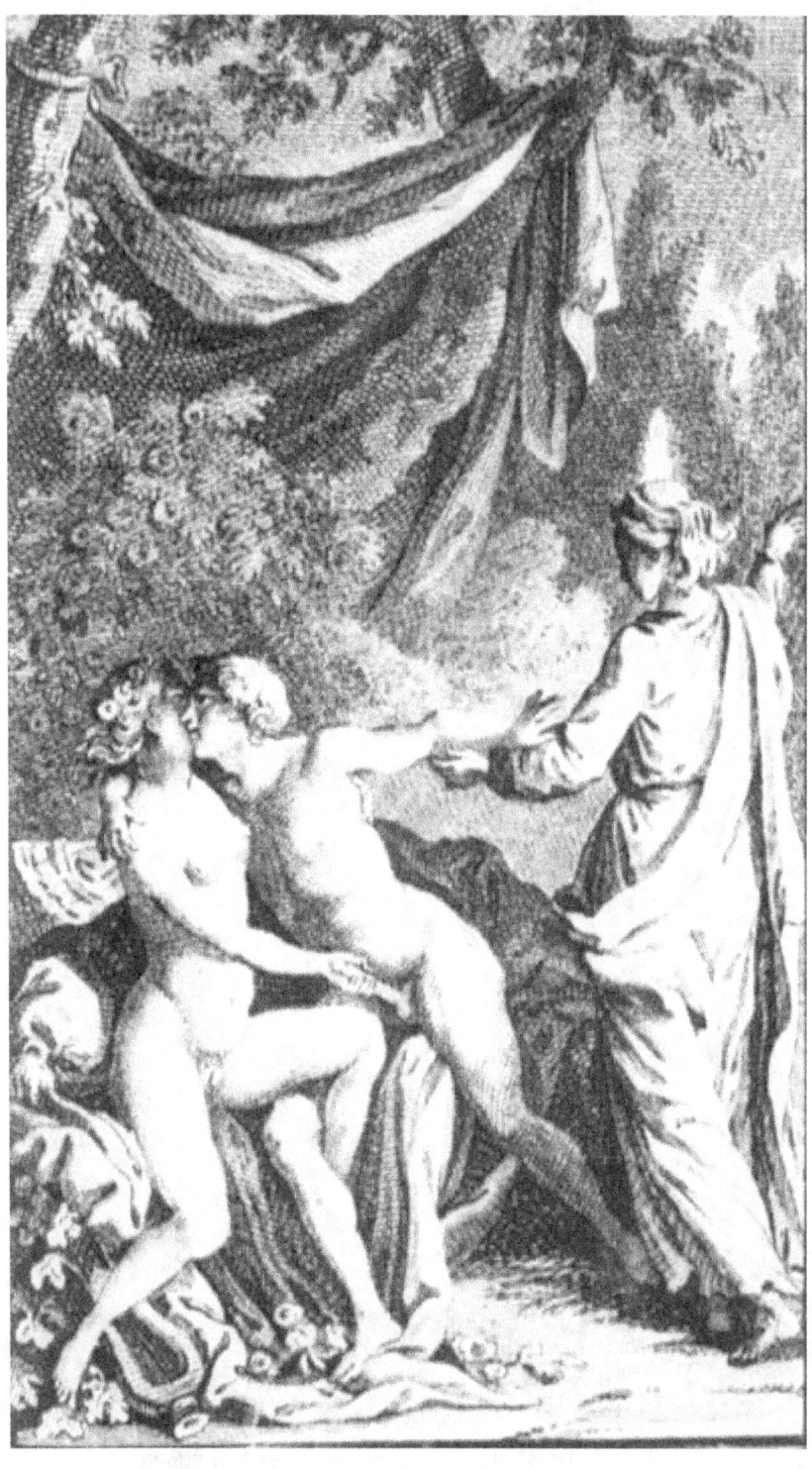

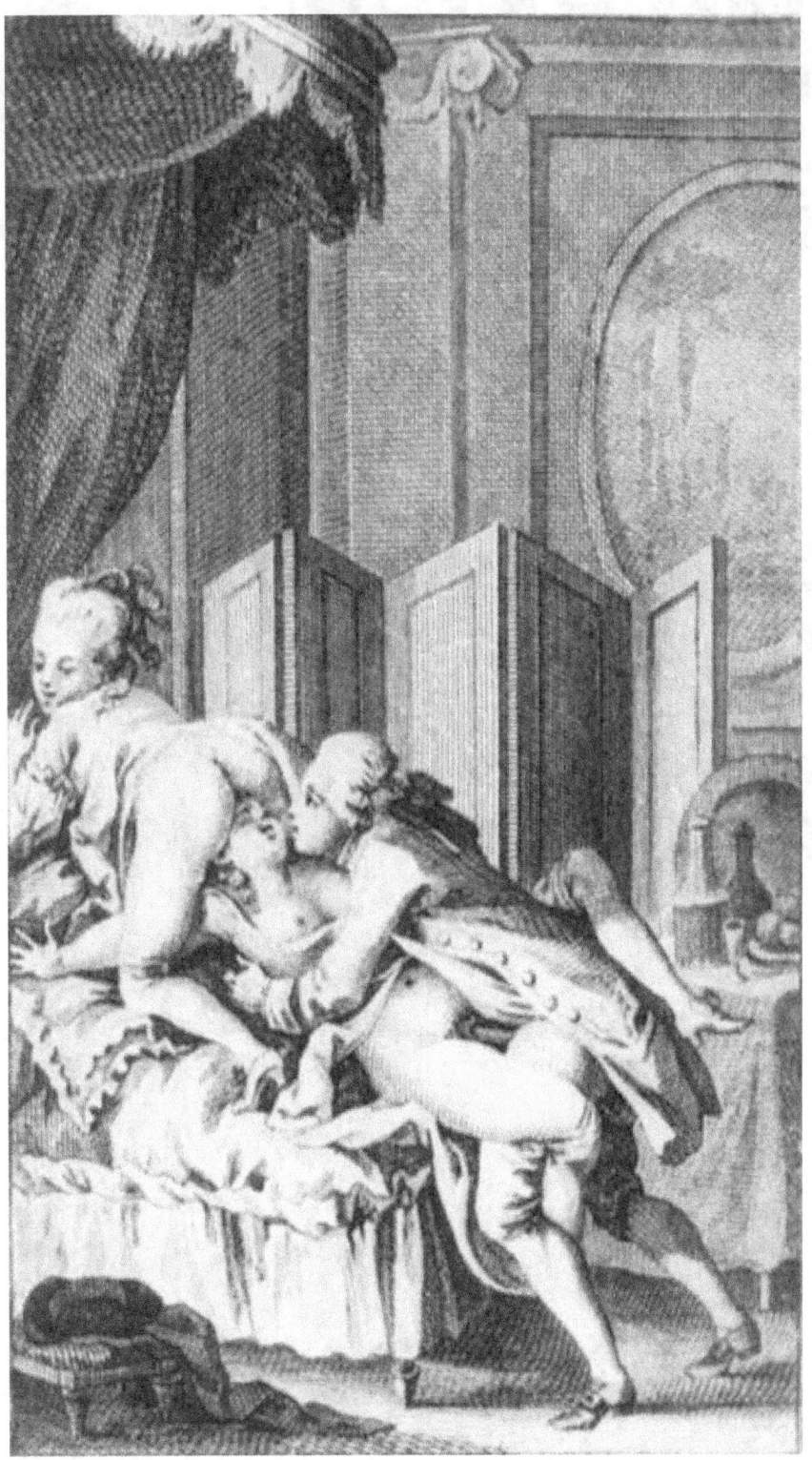

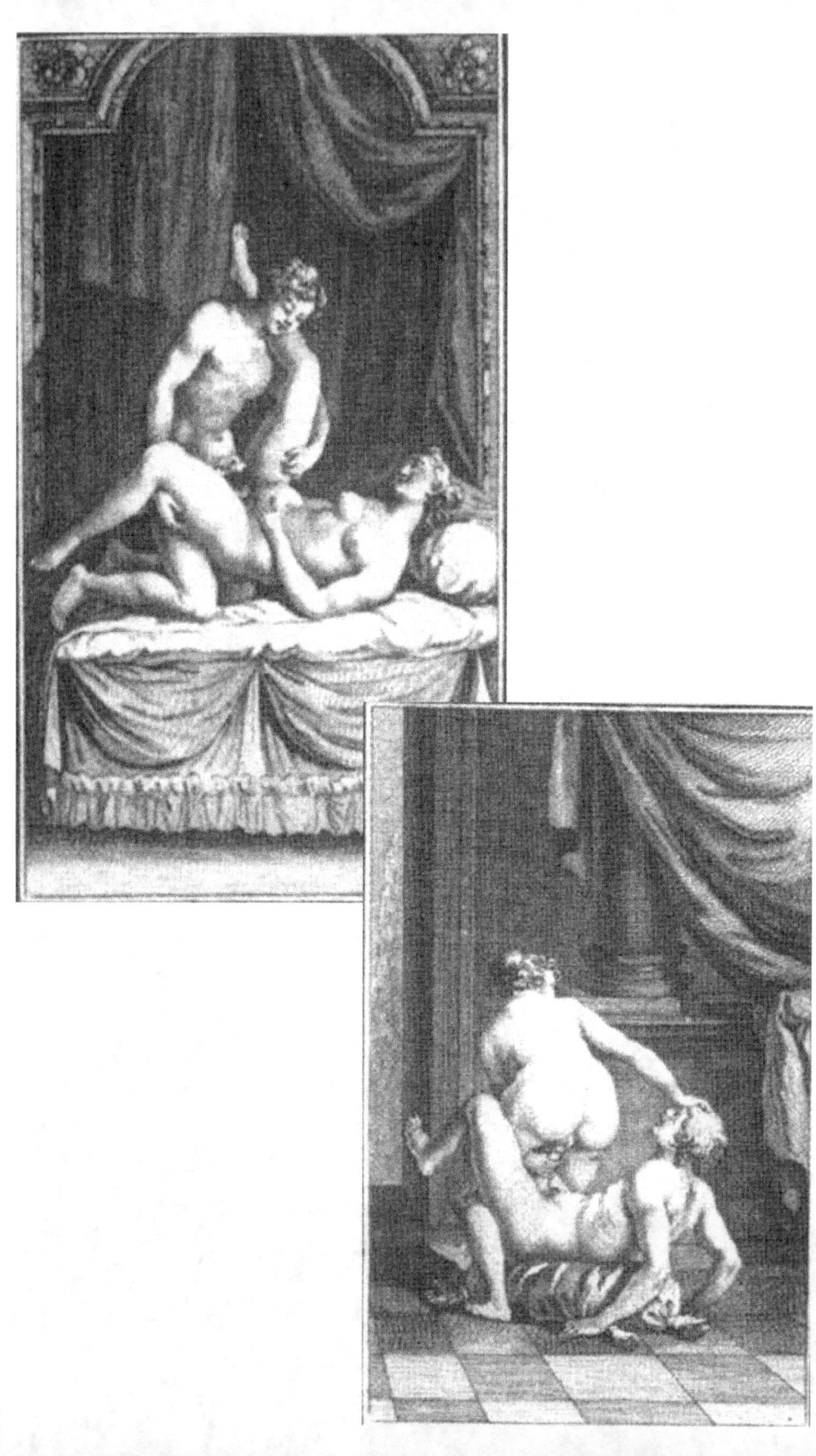

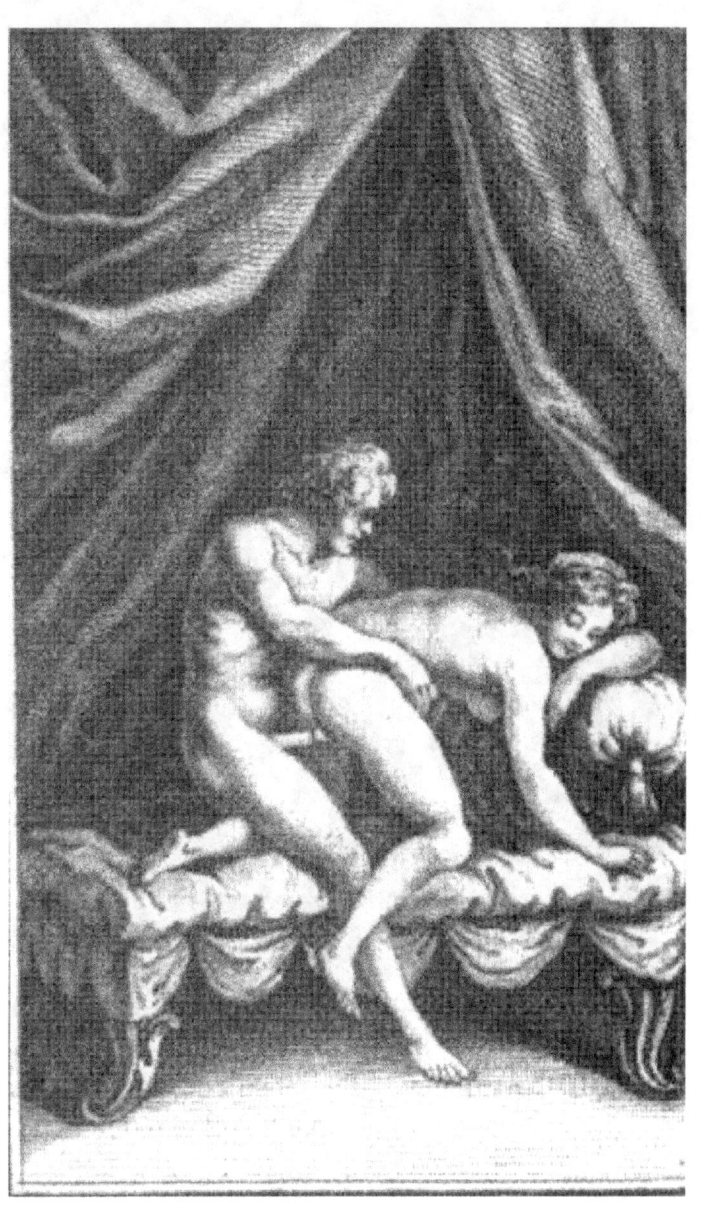

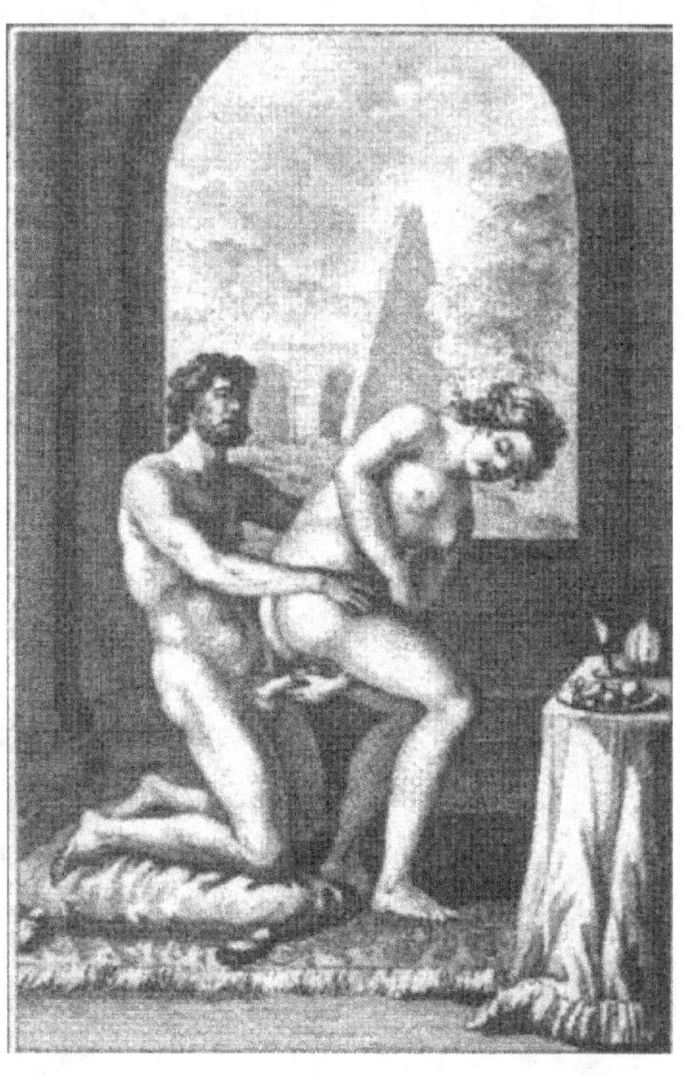

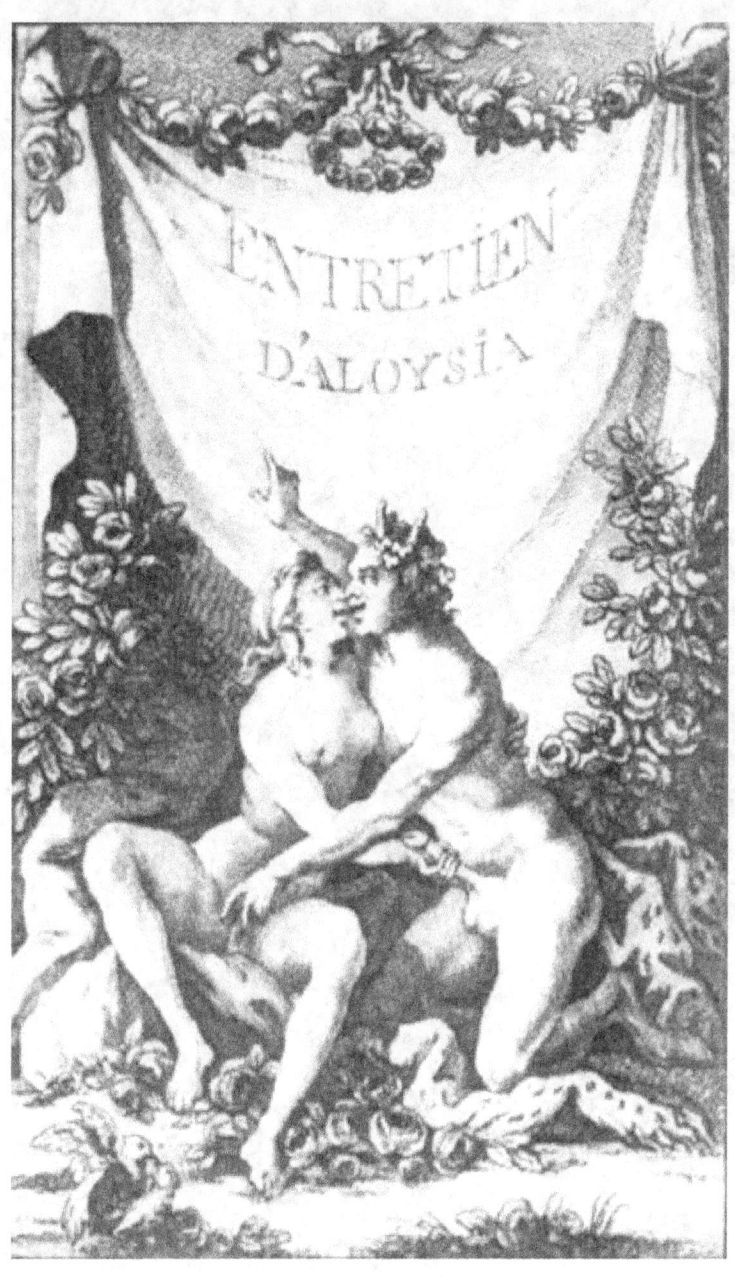

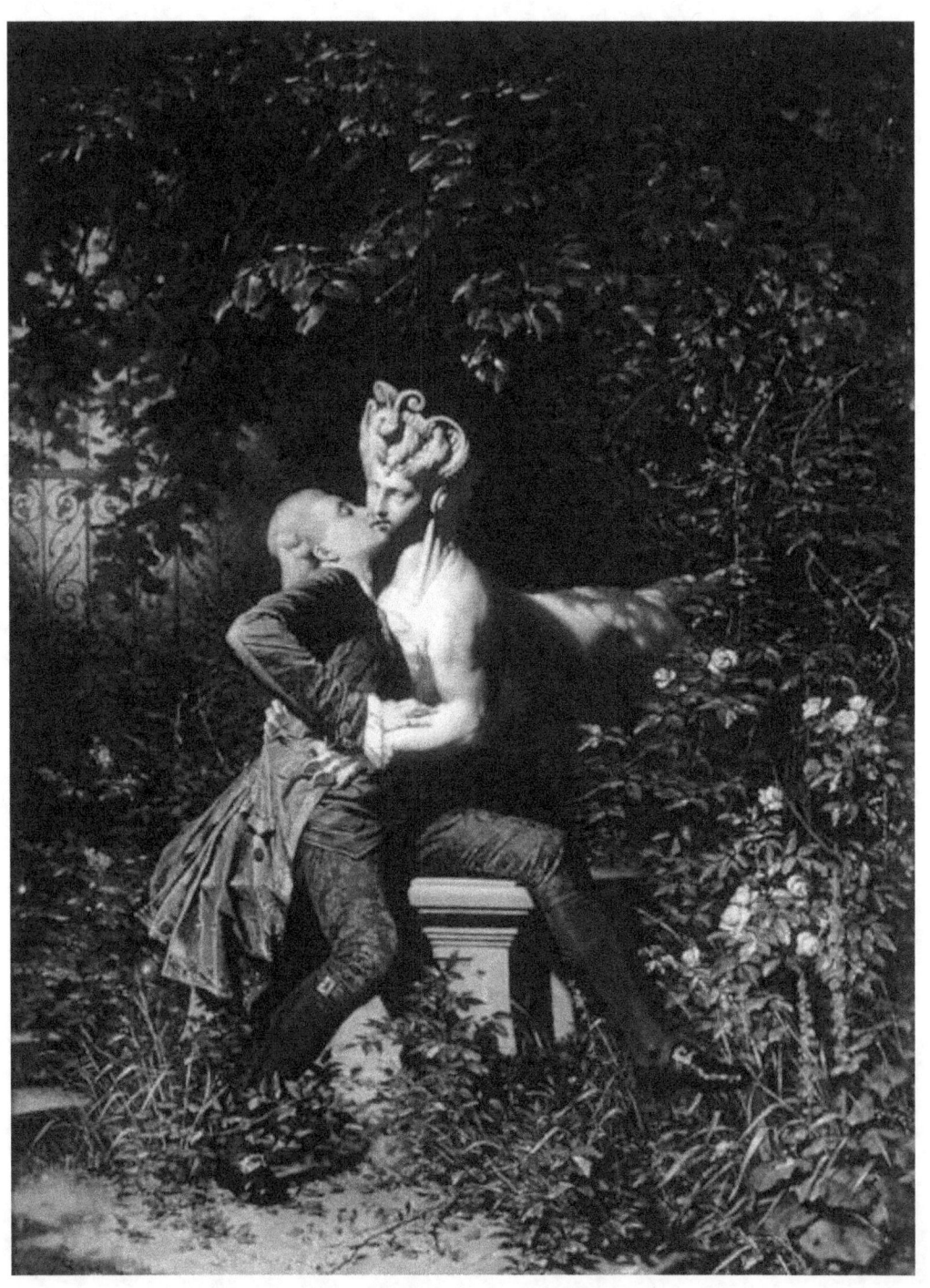

Heinrich Lossow, The Enchantress, 1868

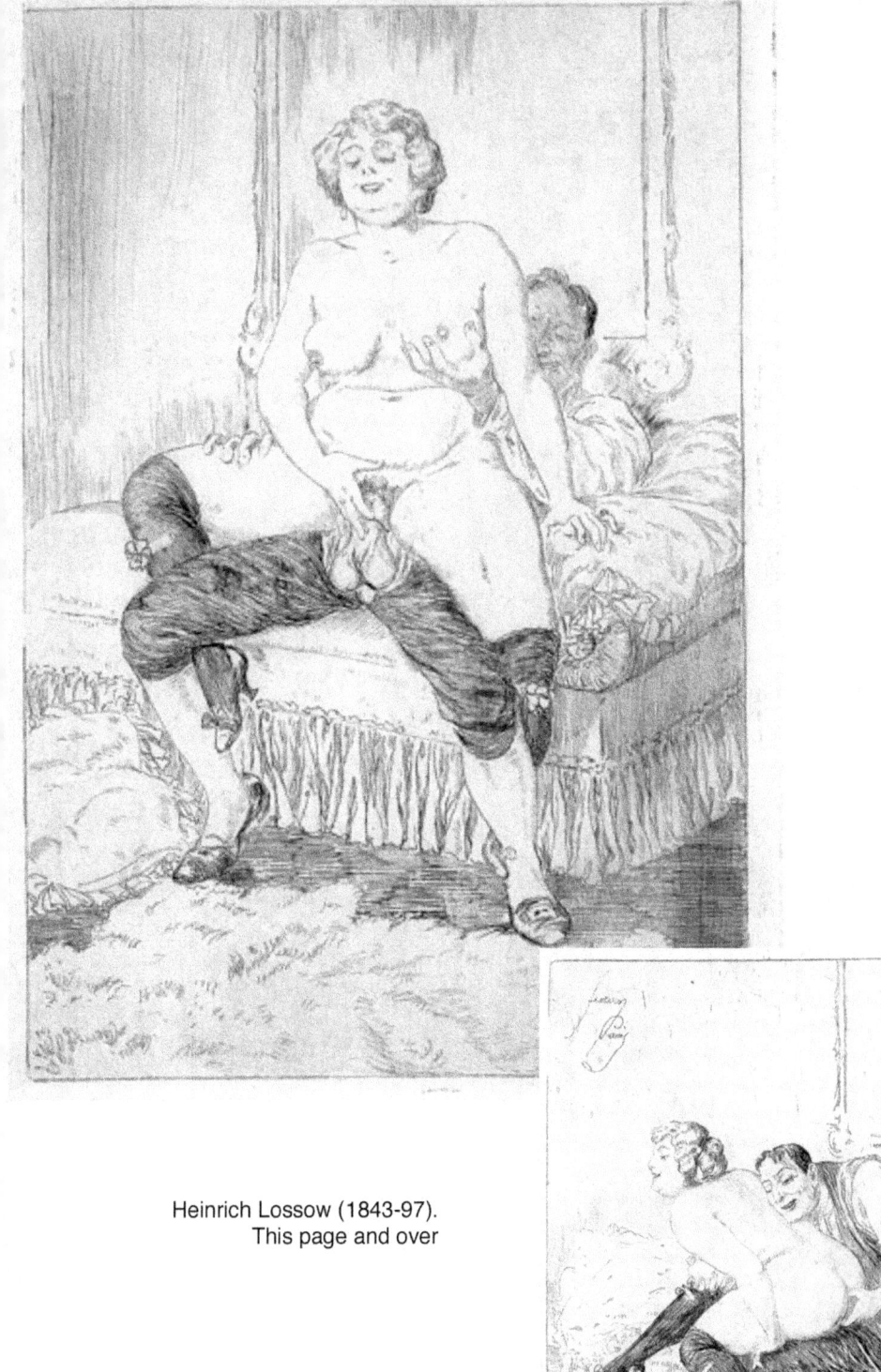

Heinrich Lossow (1843-97).
This page and over

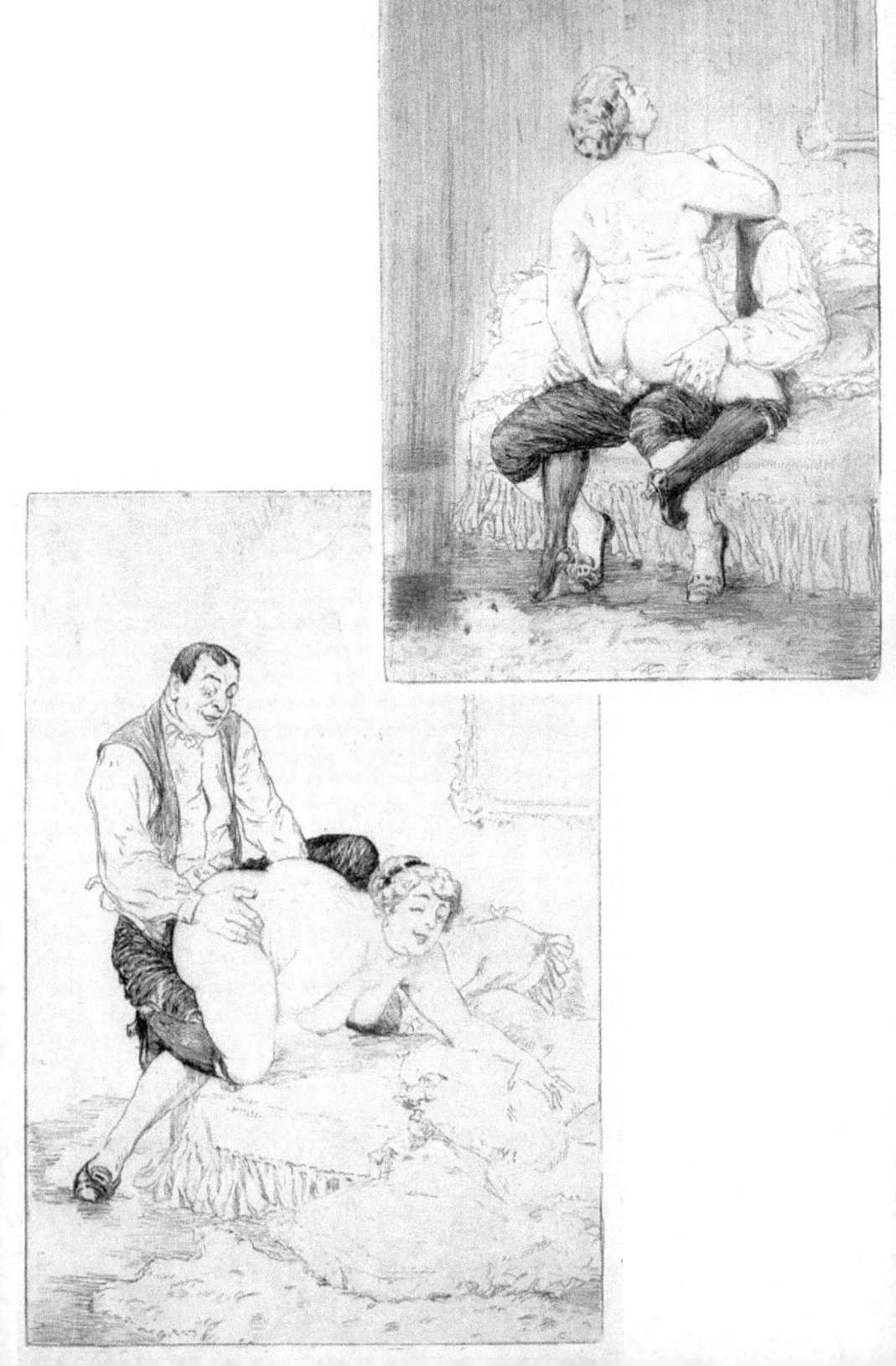

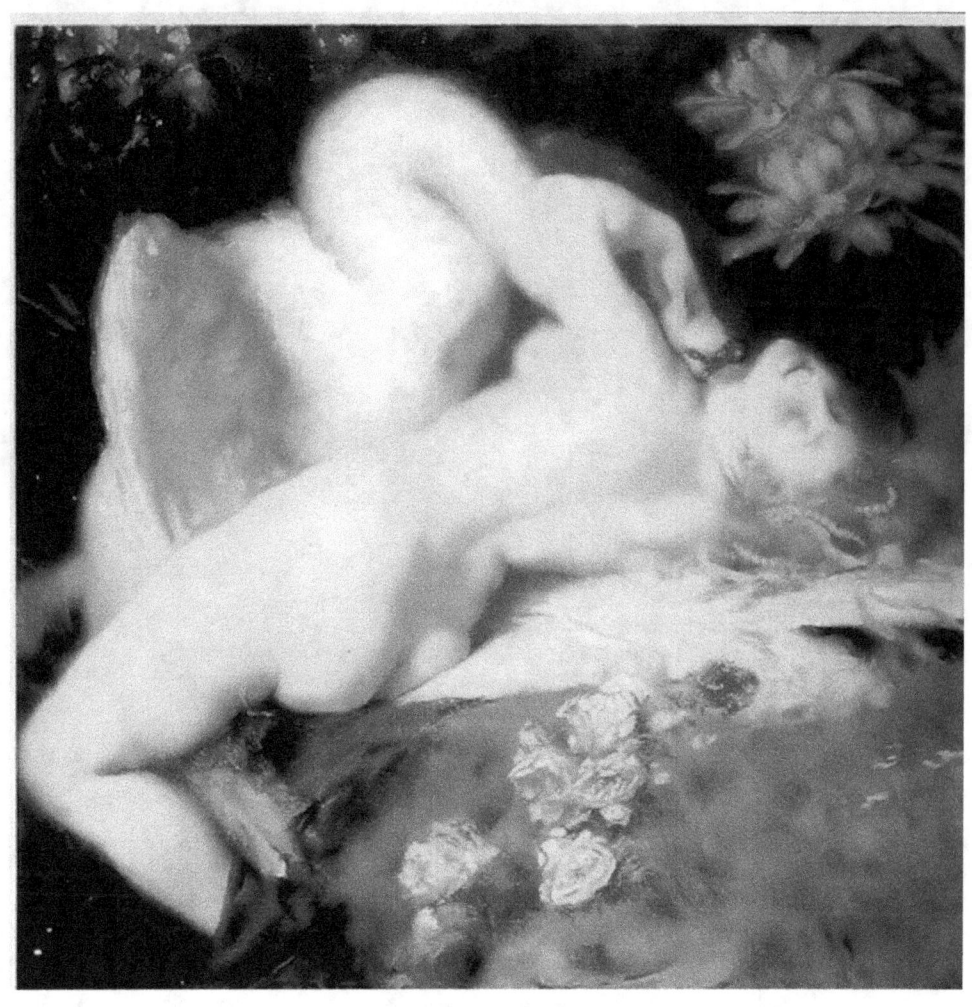

Heinrich Lossow, Leda and the Swan

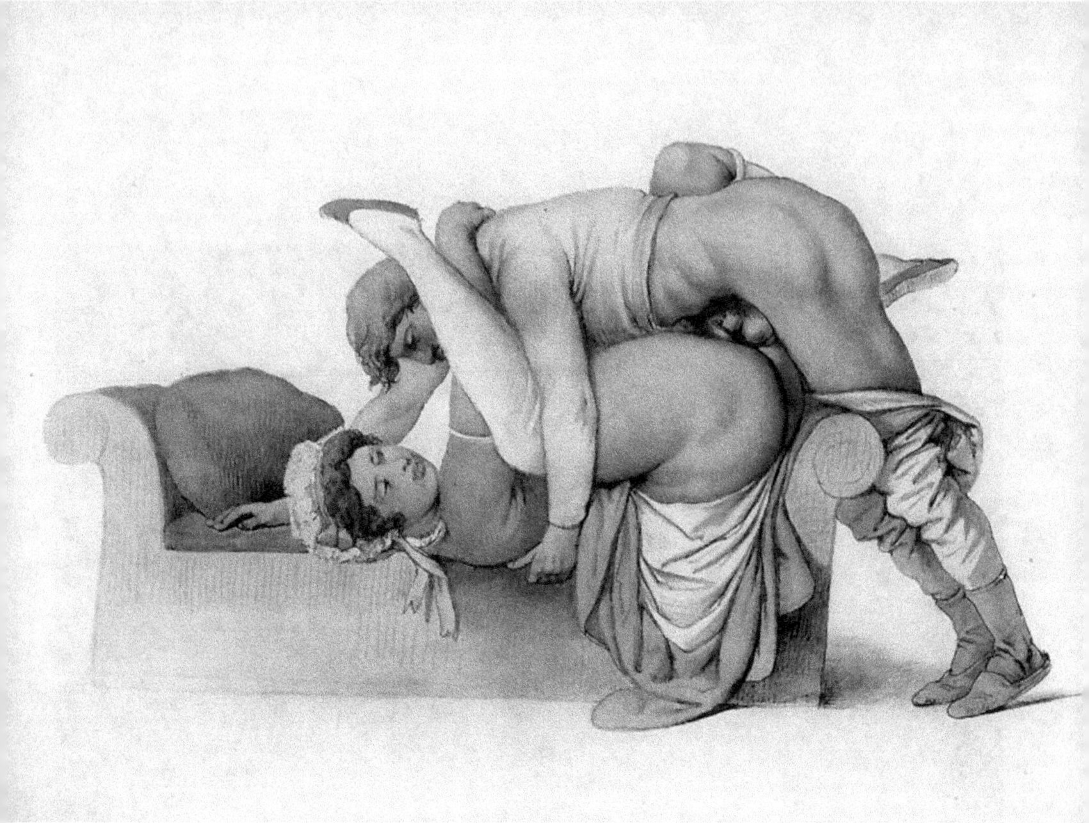

Johann Nepomuk Geiger, this page and the following pages.

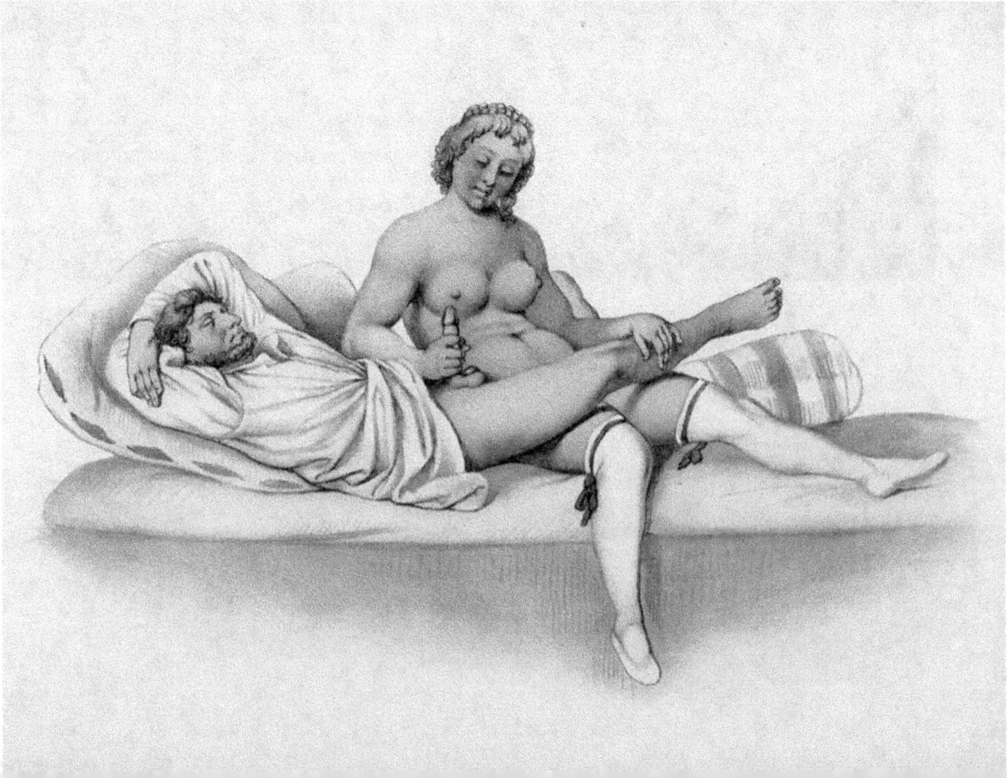

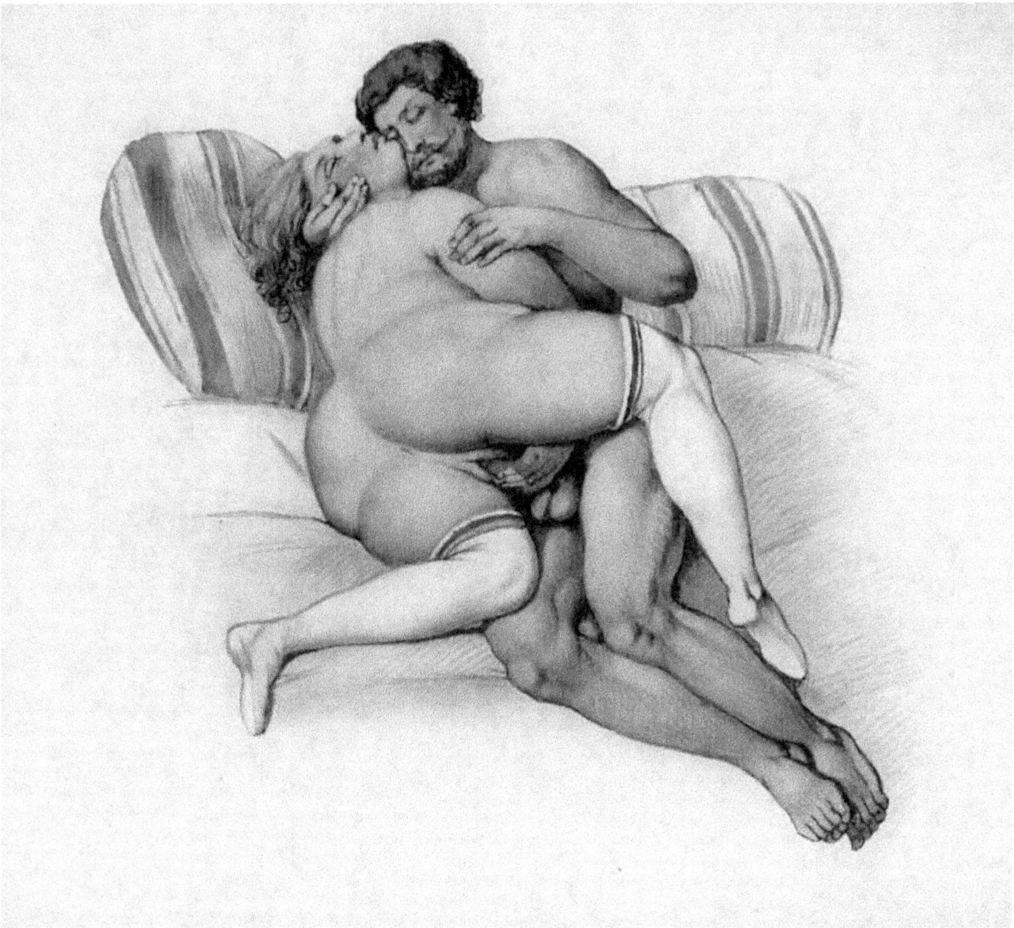

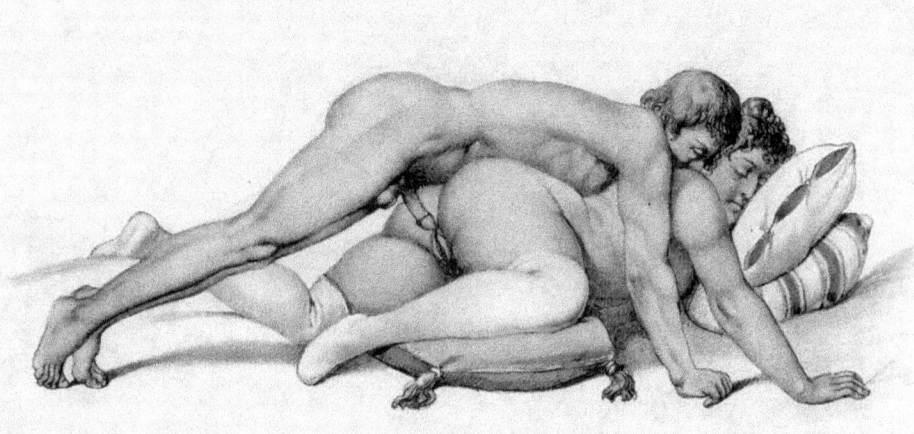

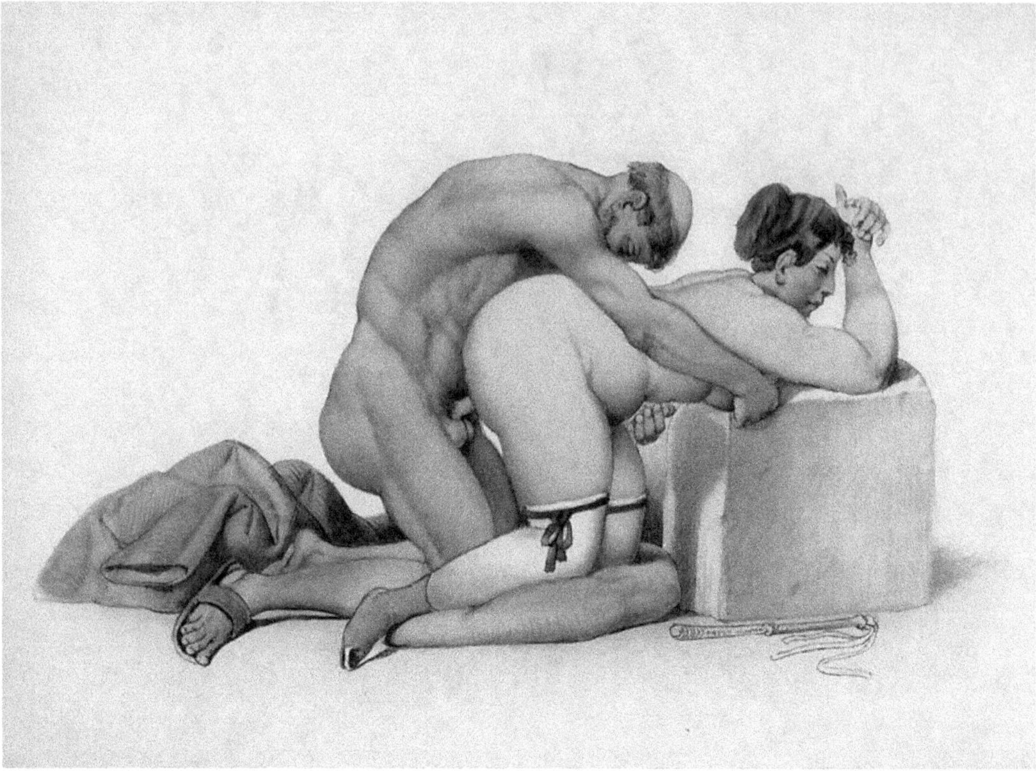

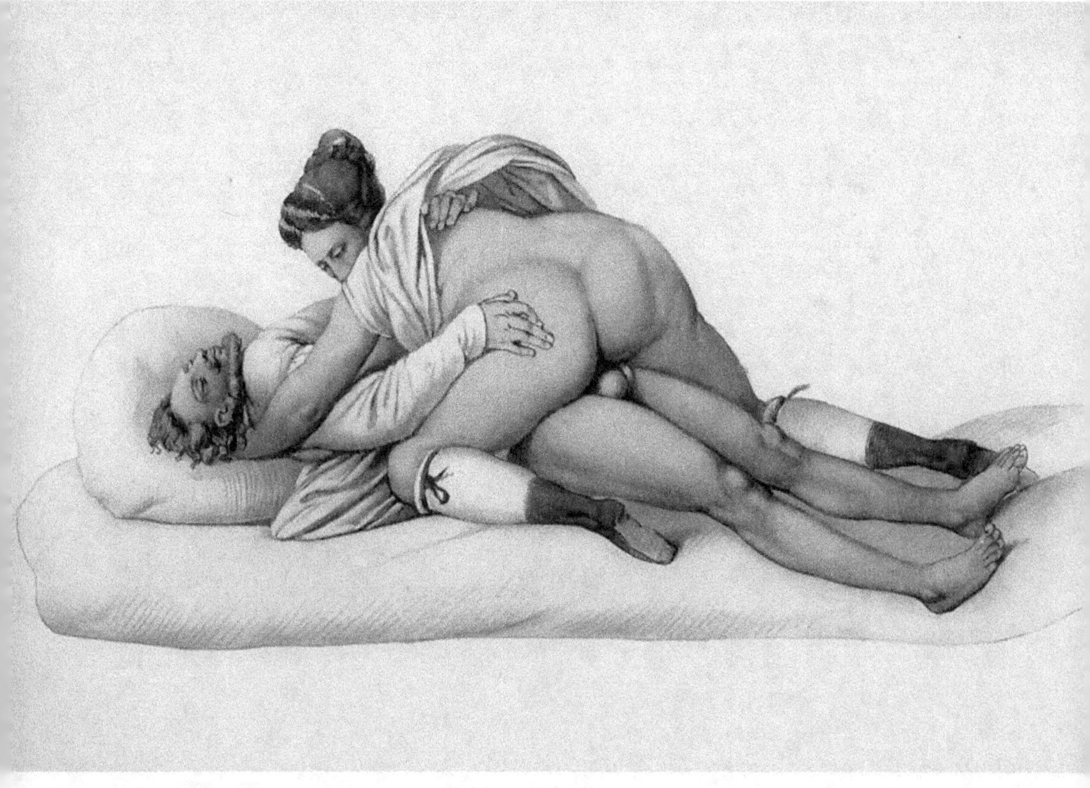

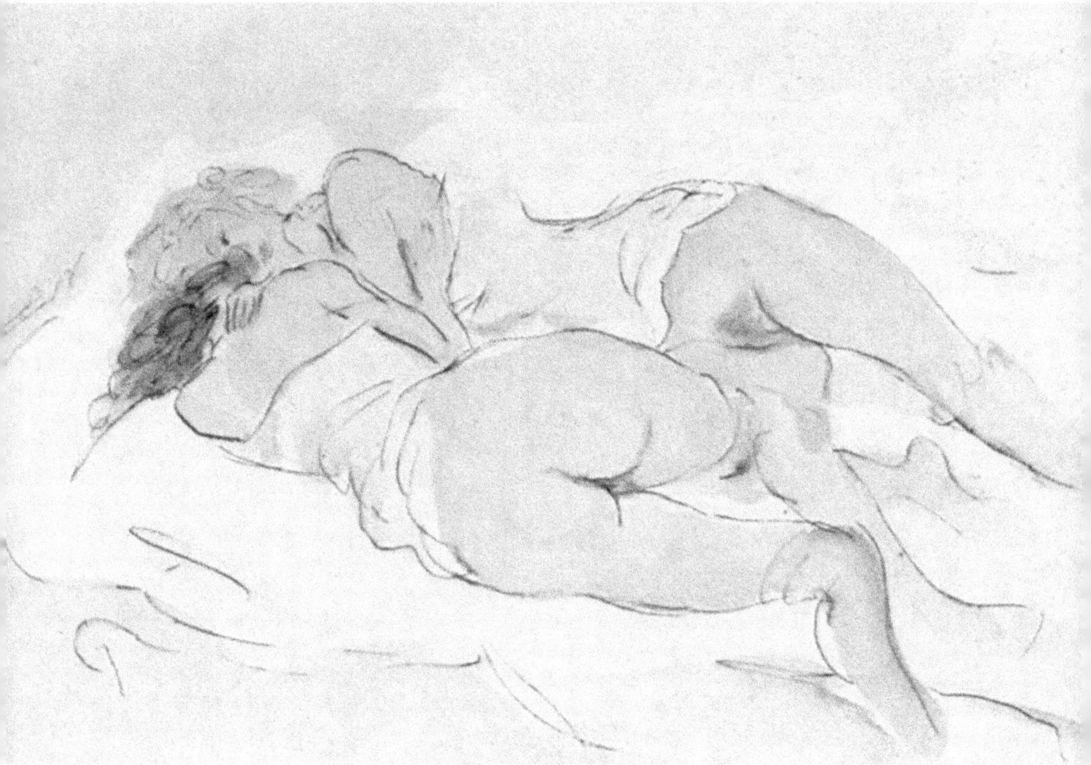

Otto Schoff, this page and following pages

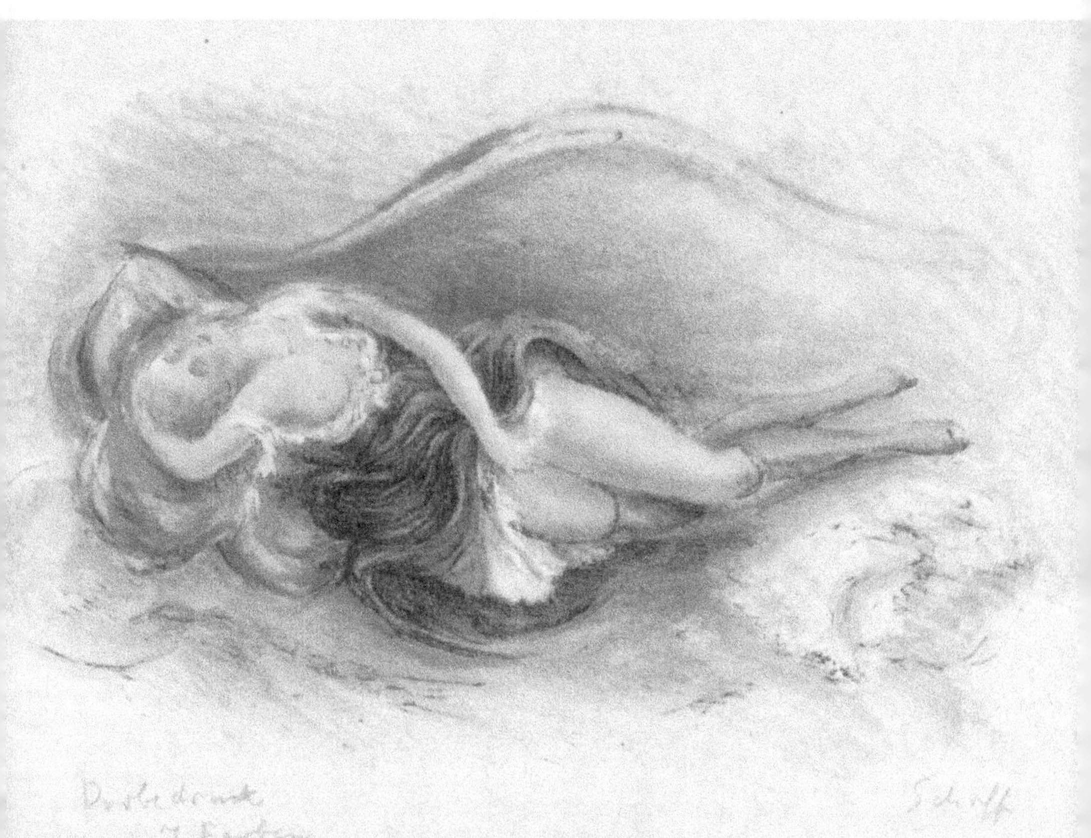

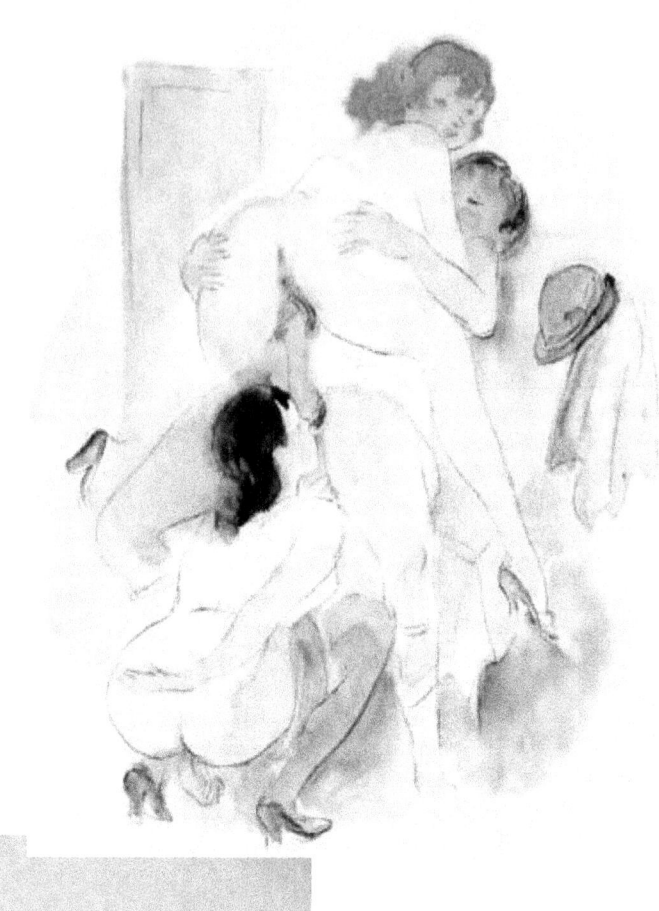

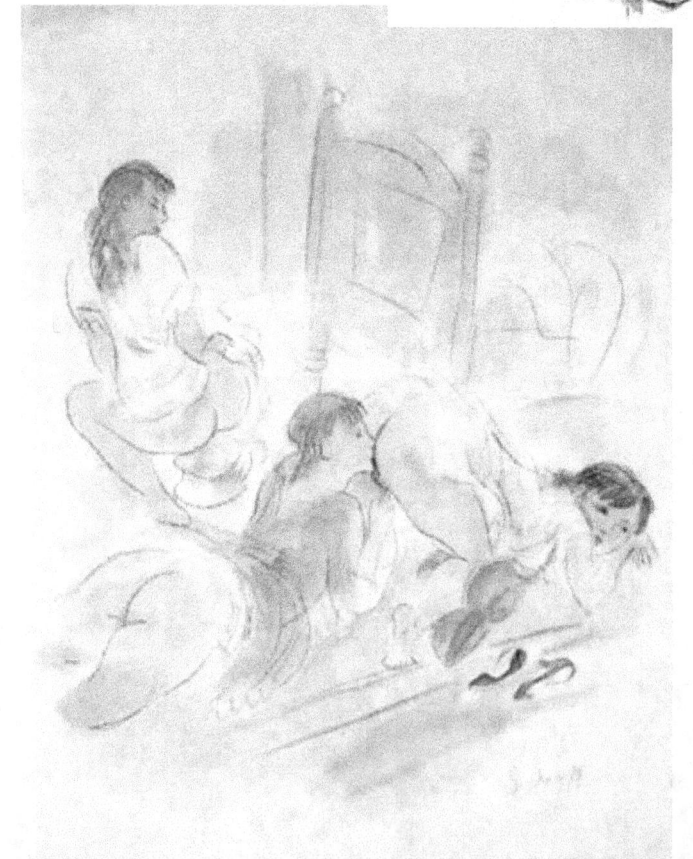

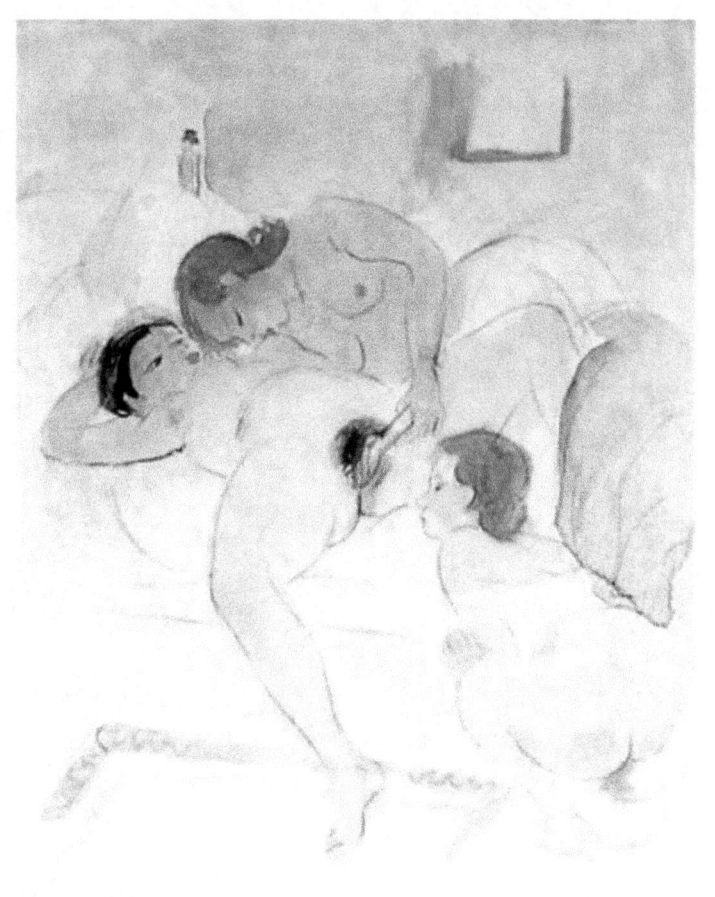
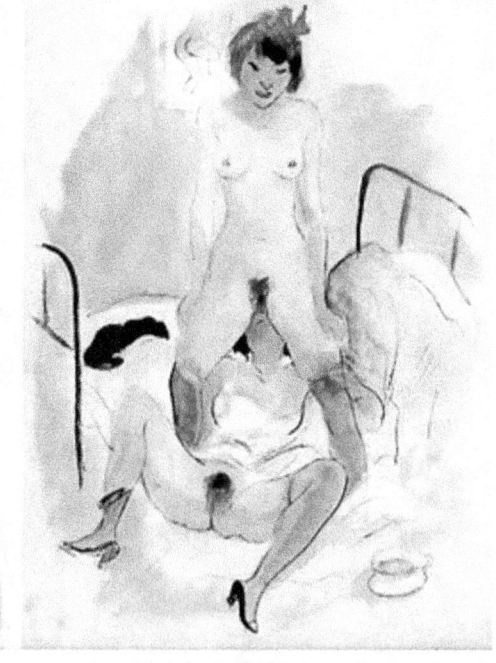

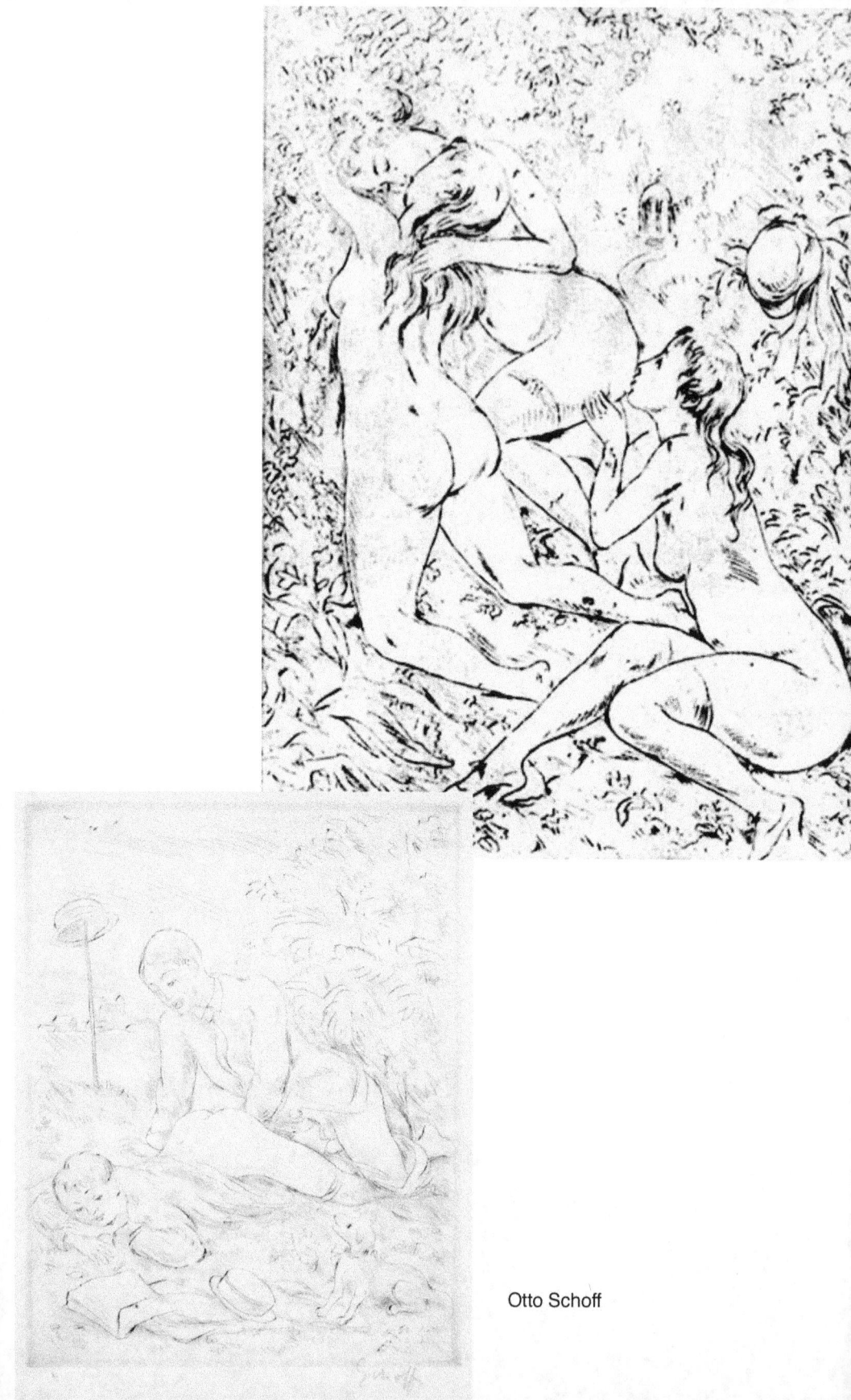

Otto Schoff

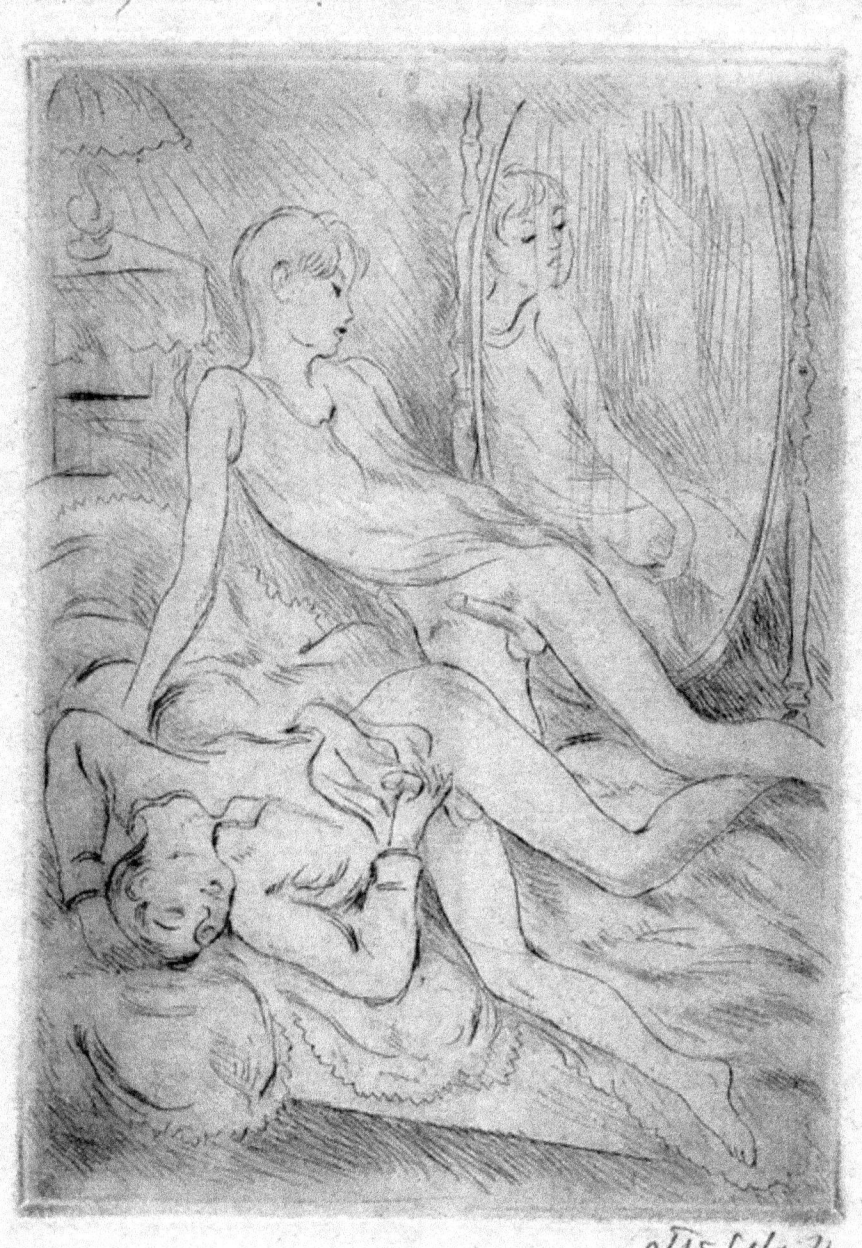

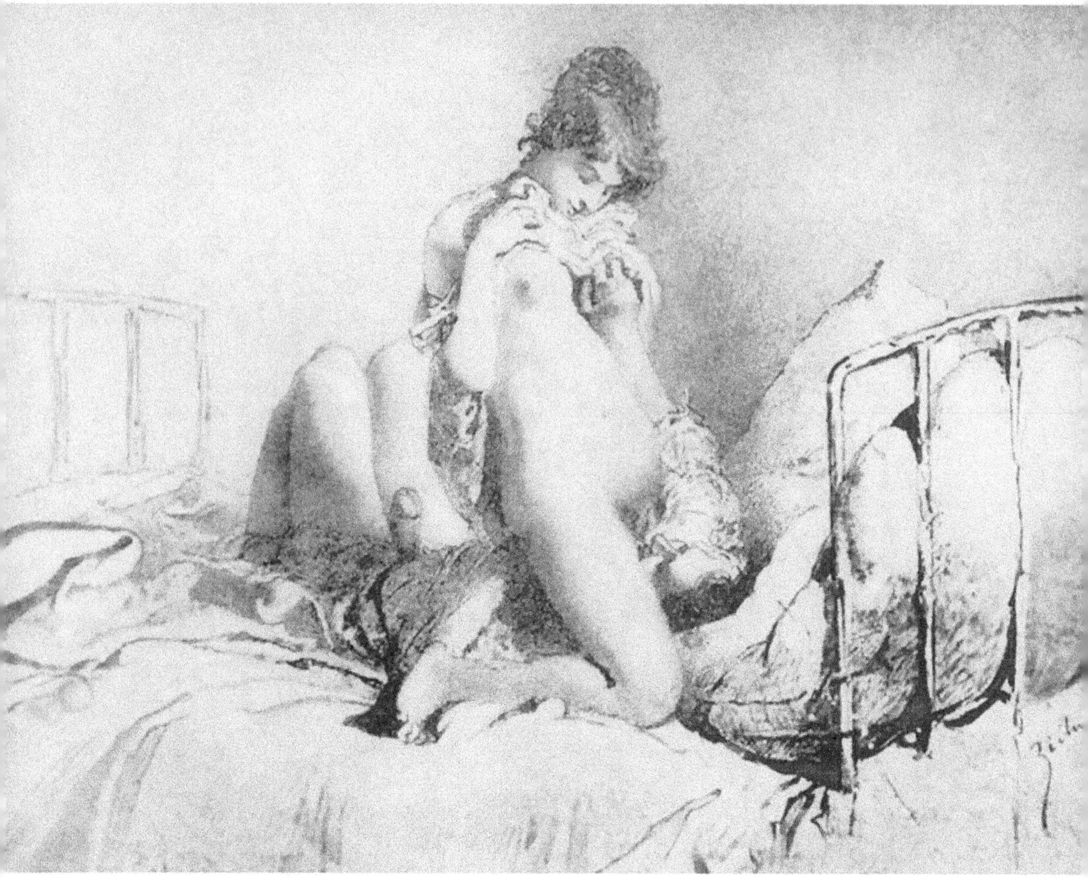

Mihály Zichy (1827-1906), from Liebe, 1911. This page and following pages

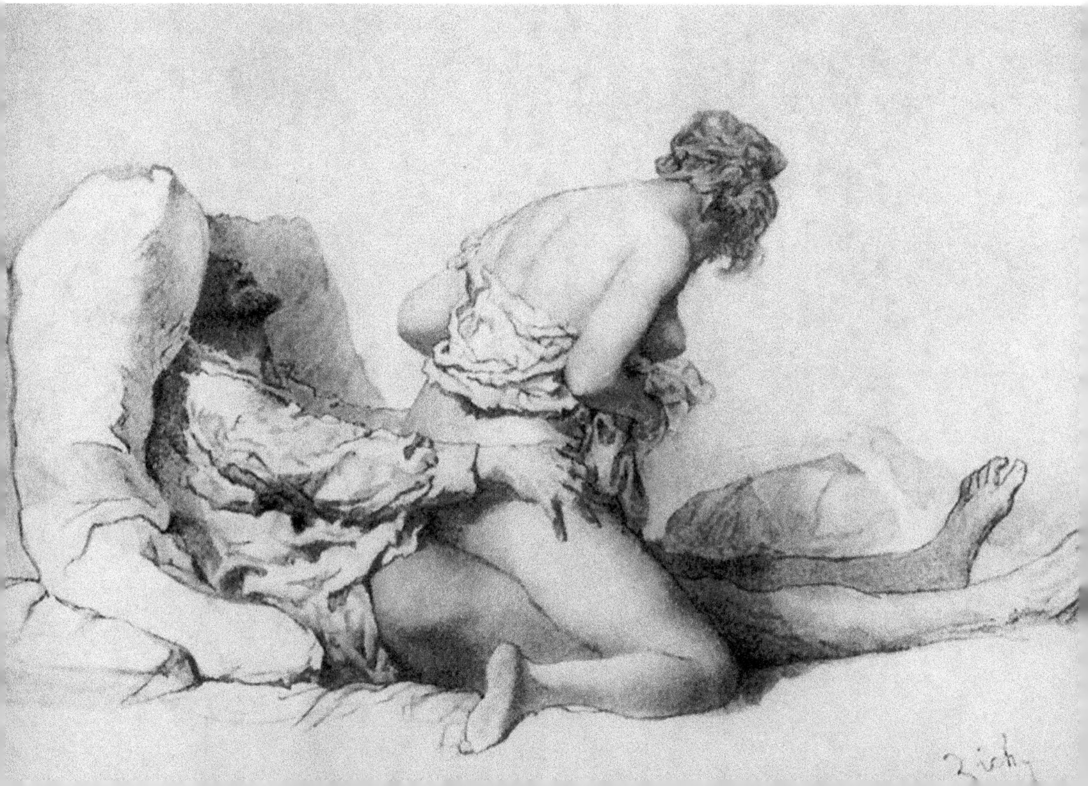

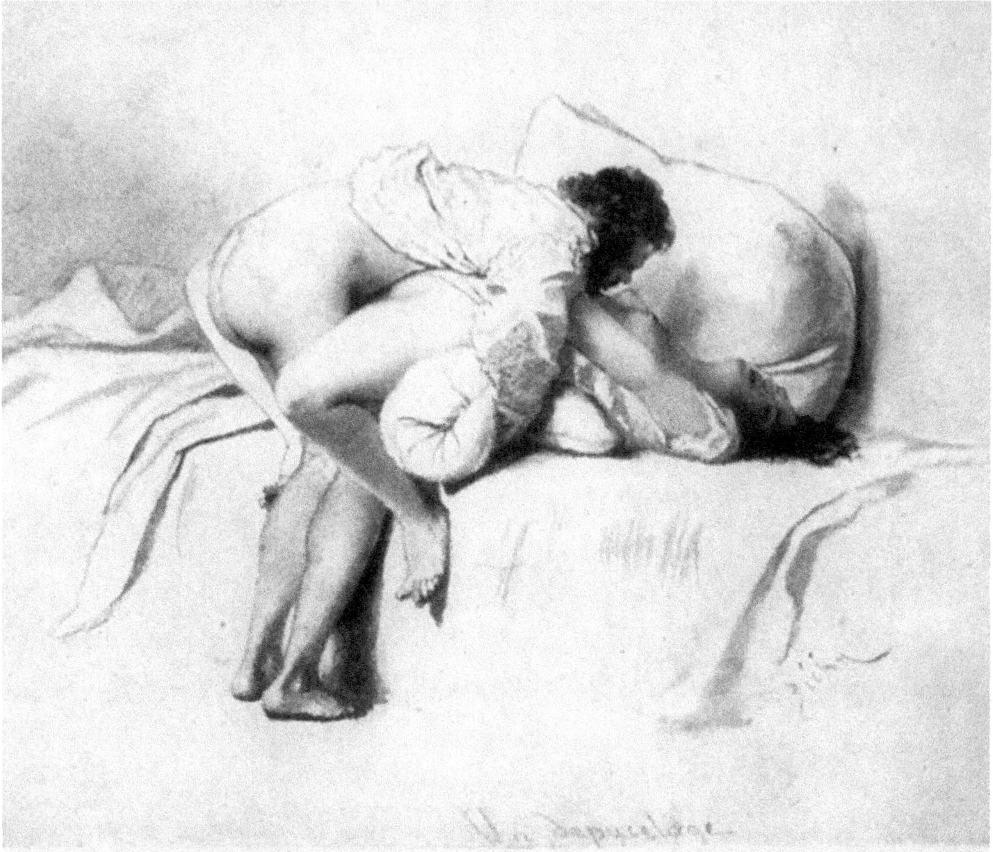

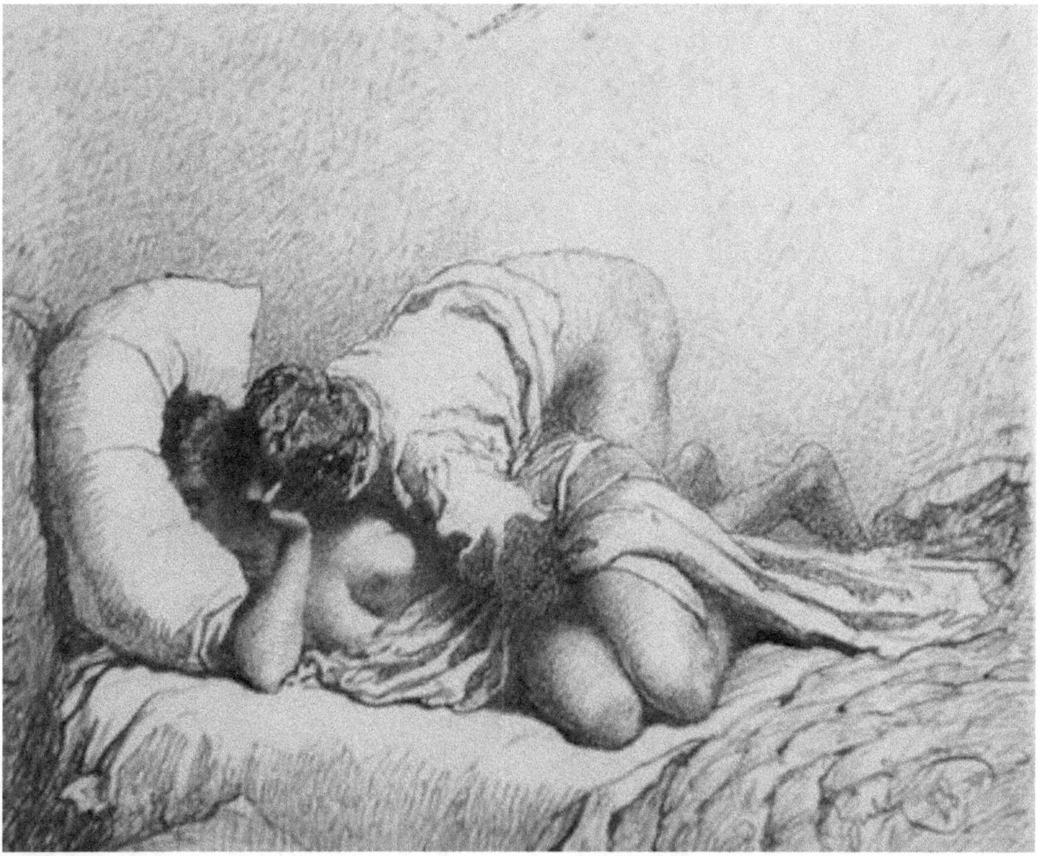

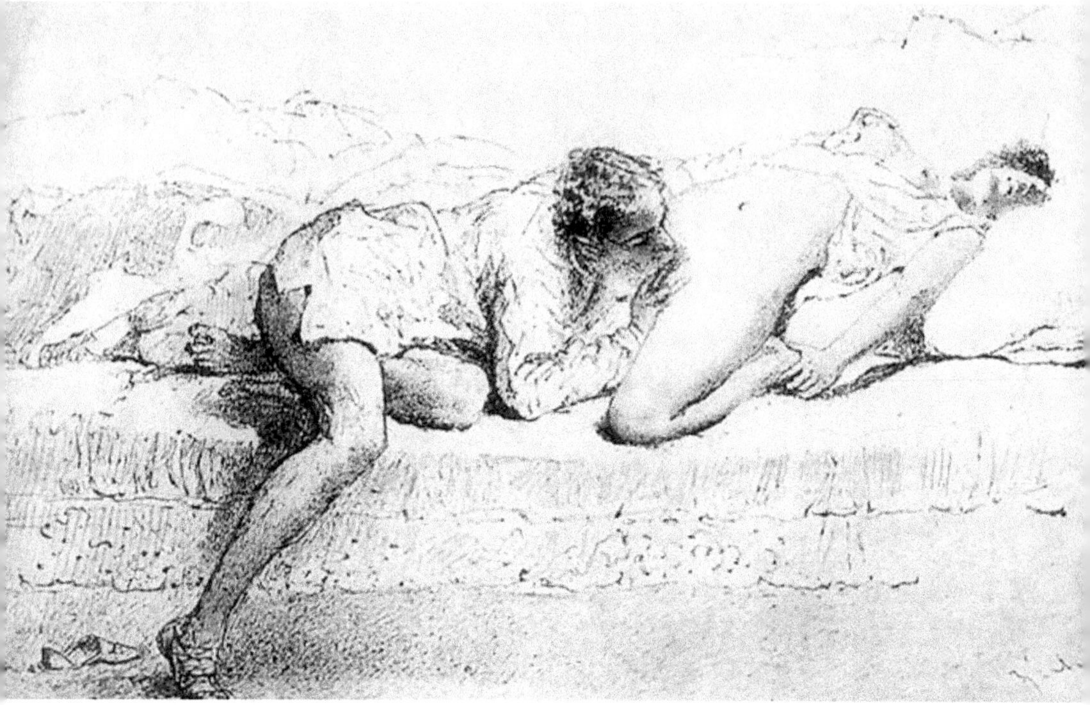

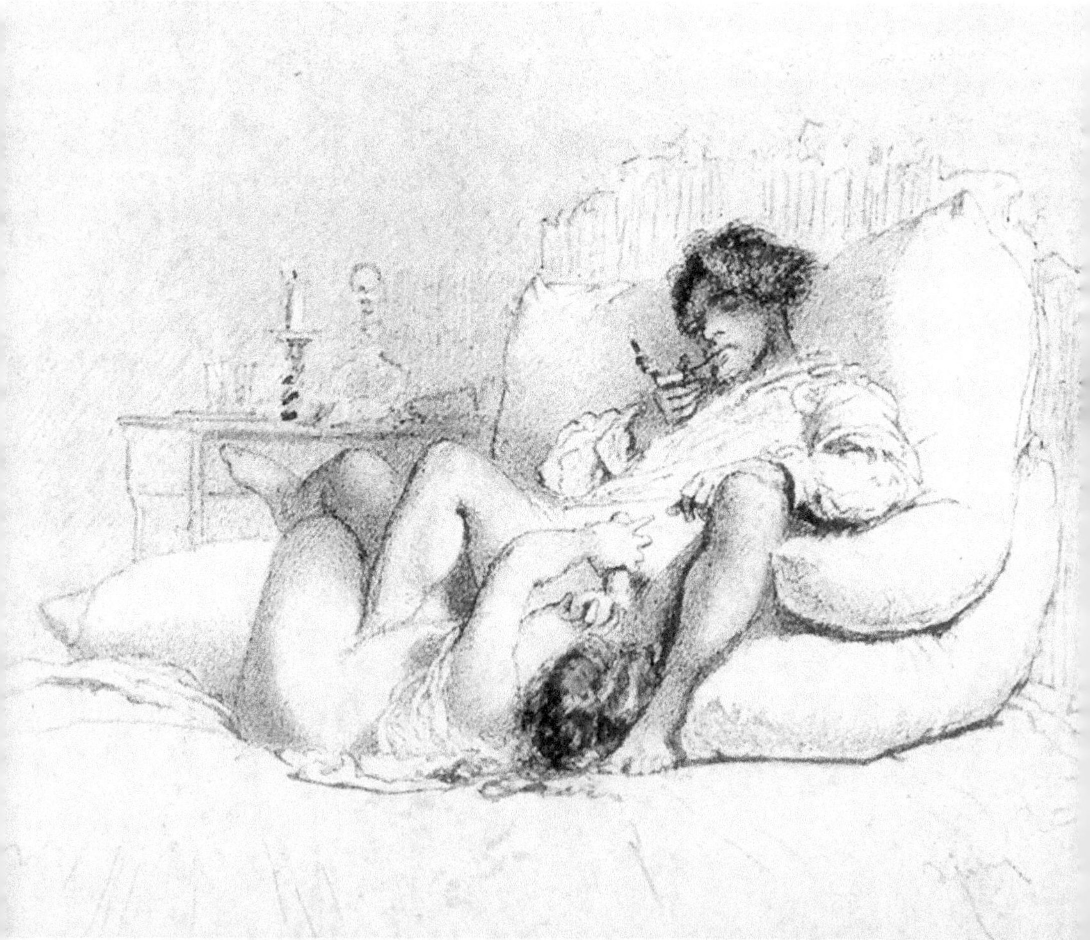

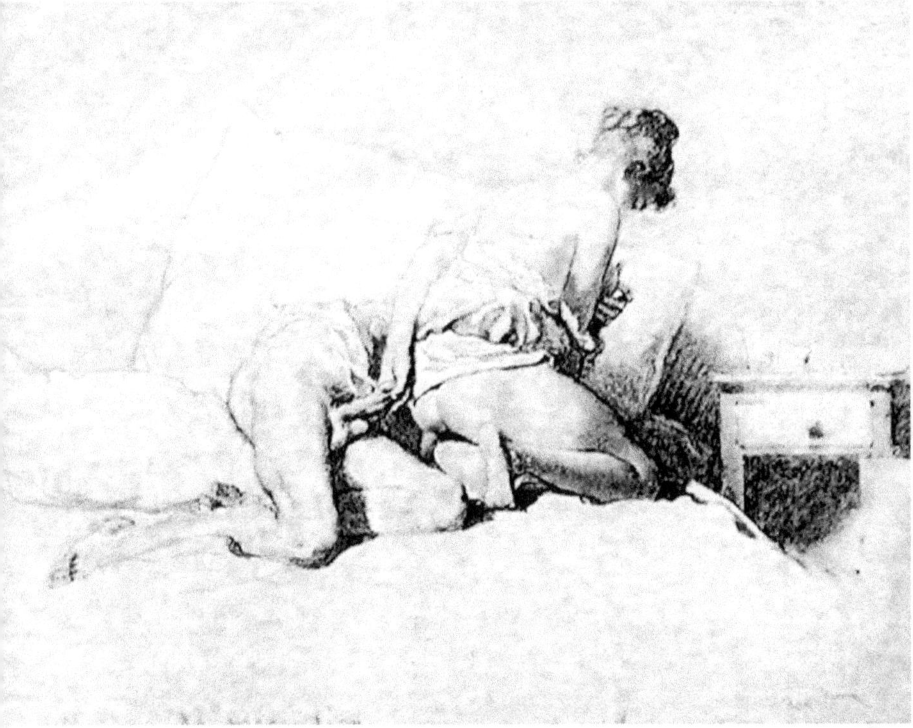

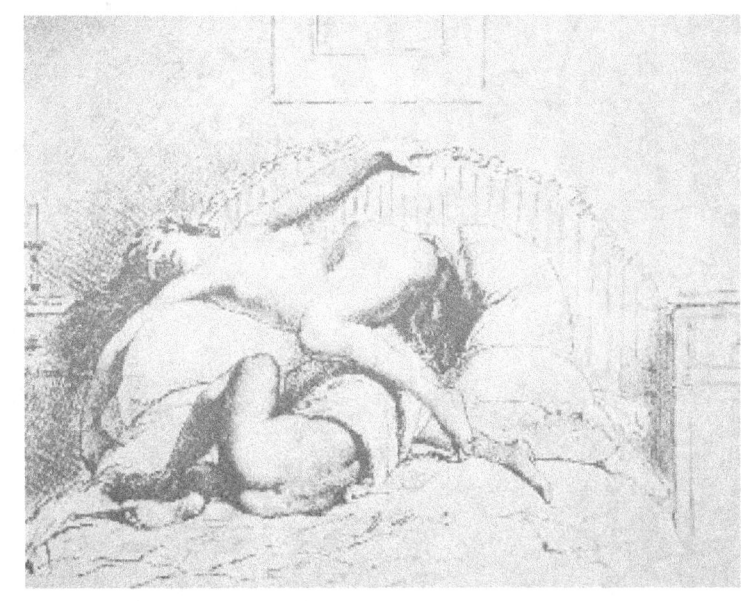

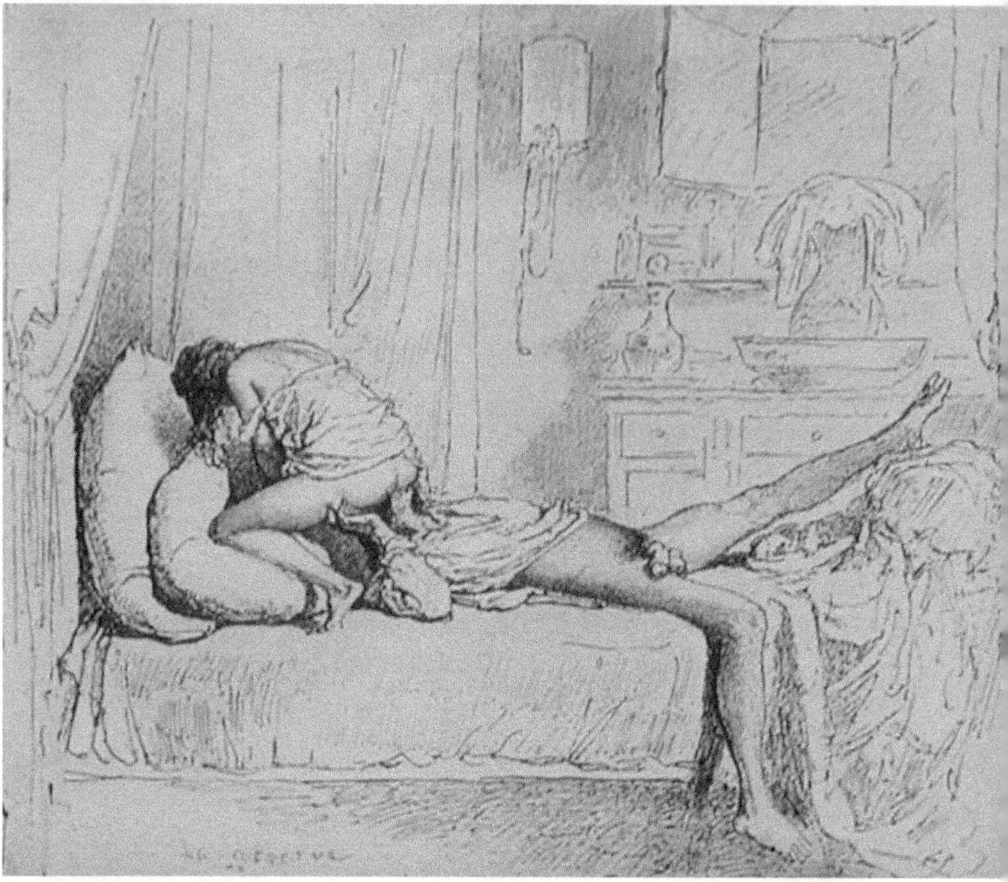

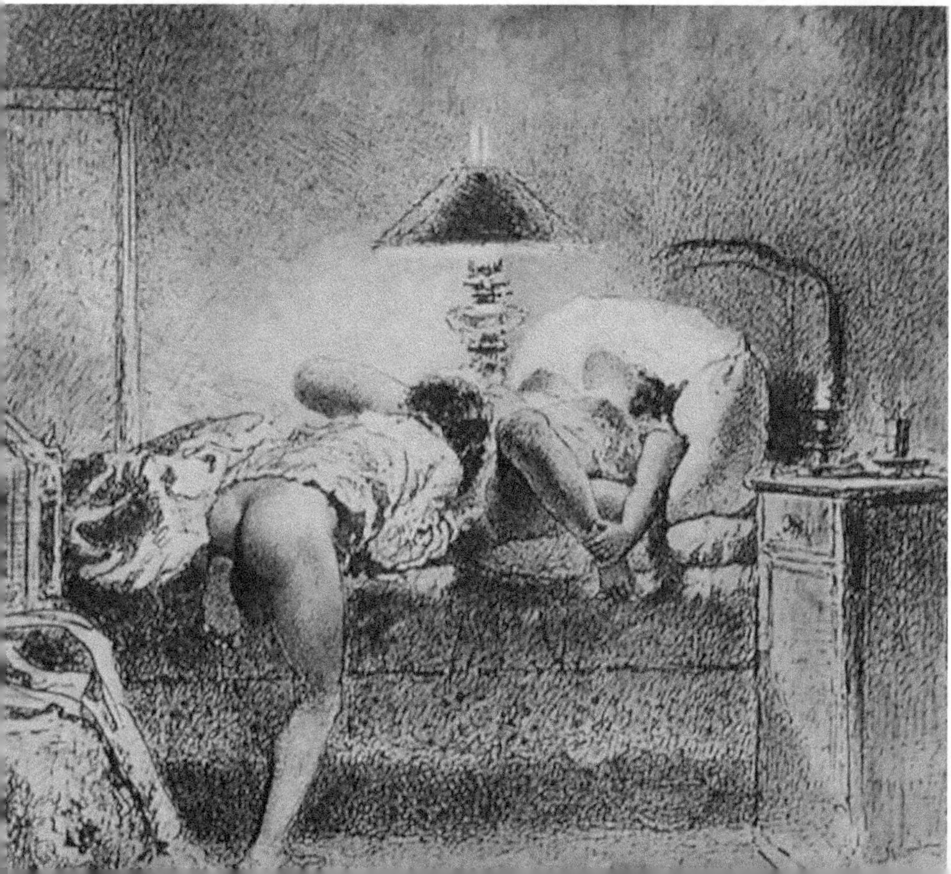

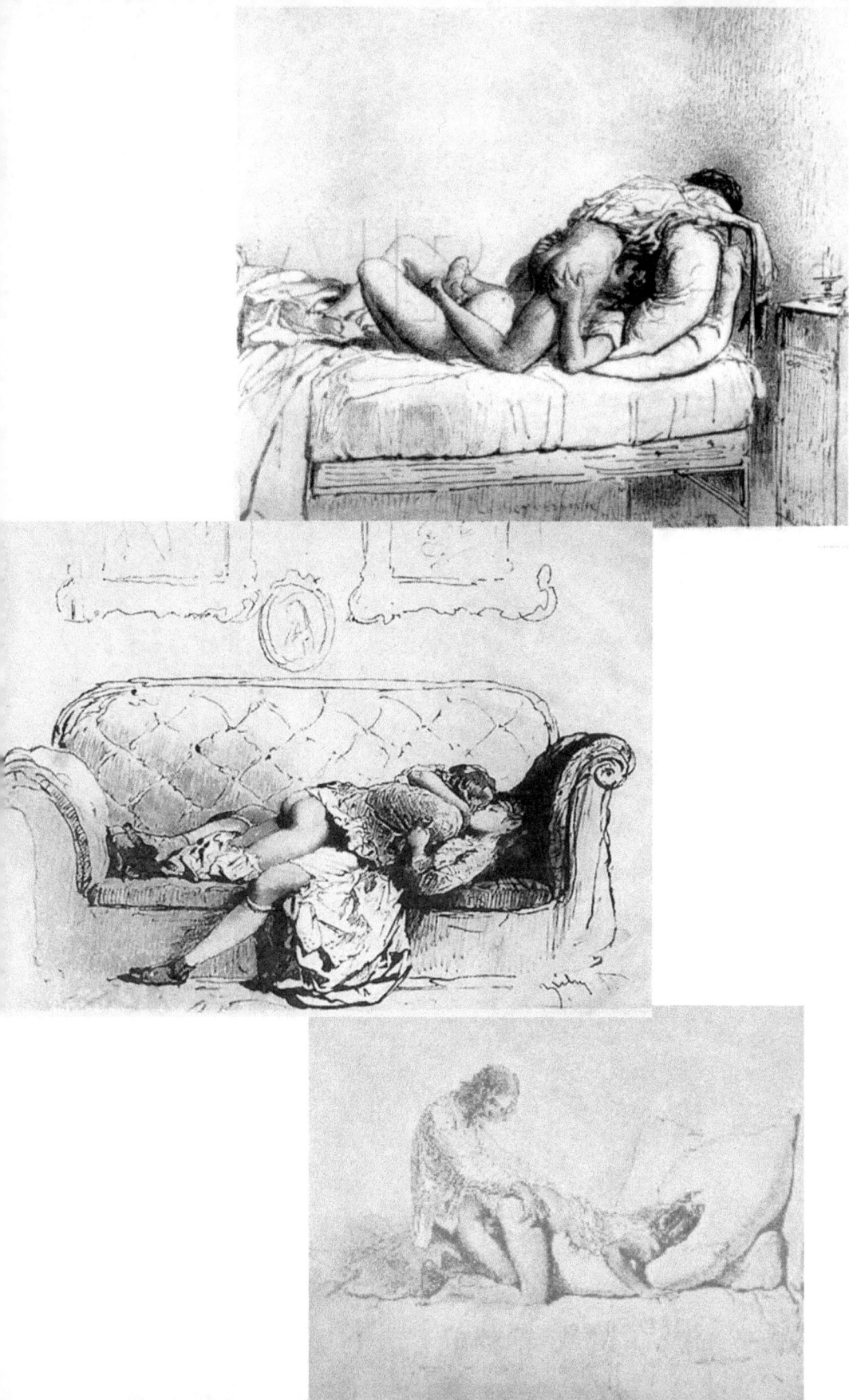

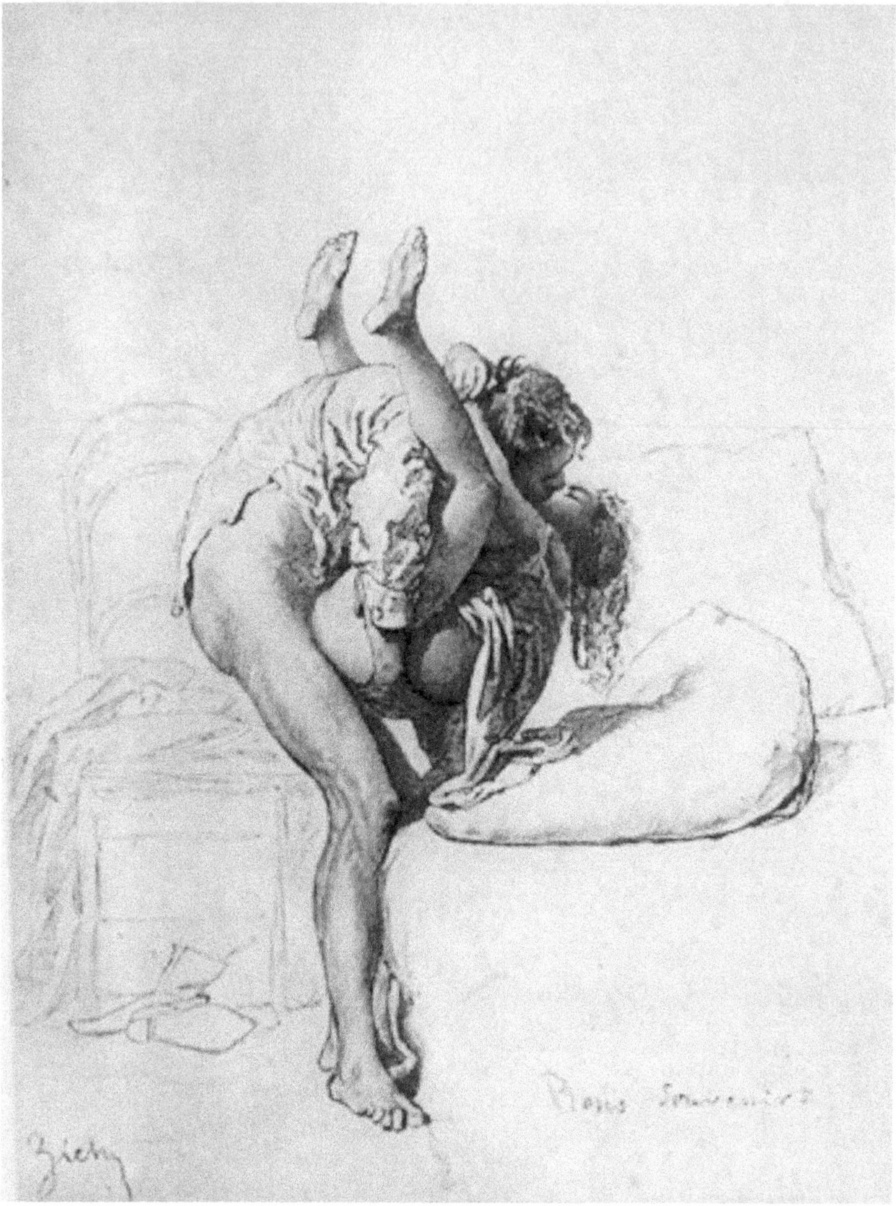

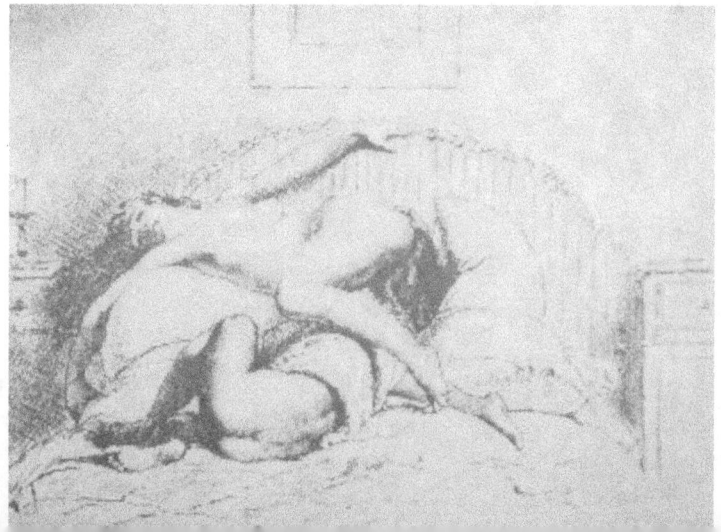

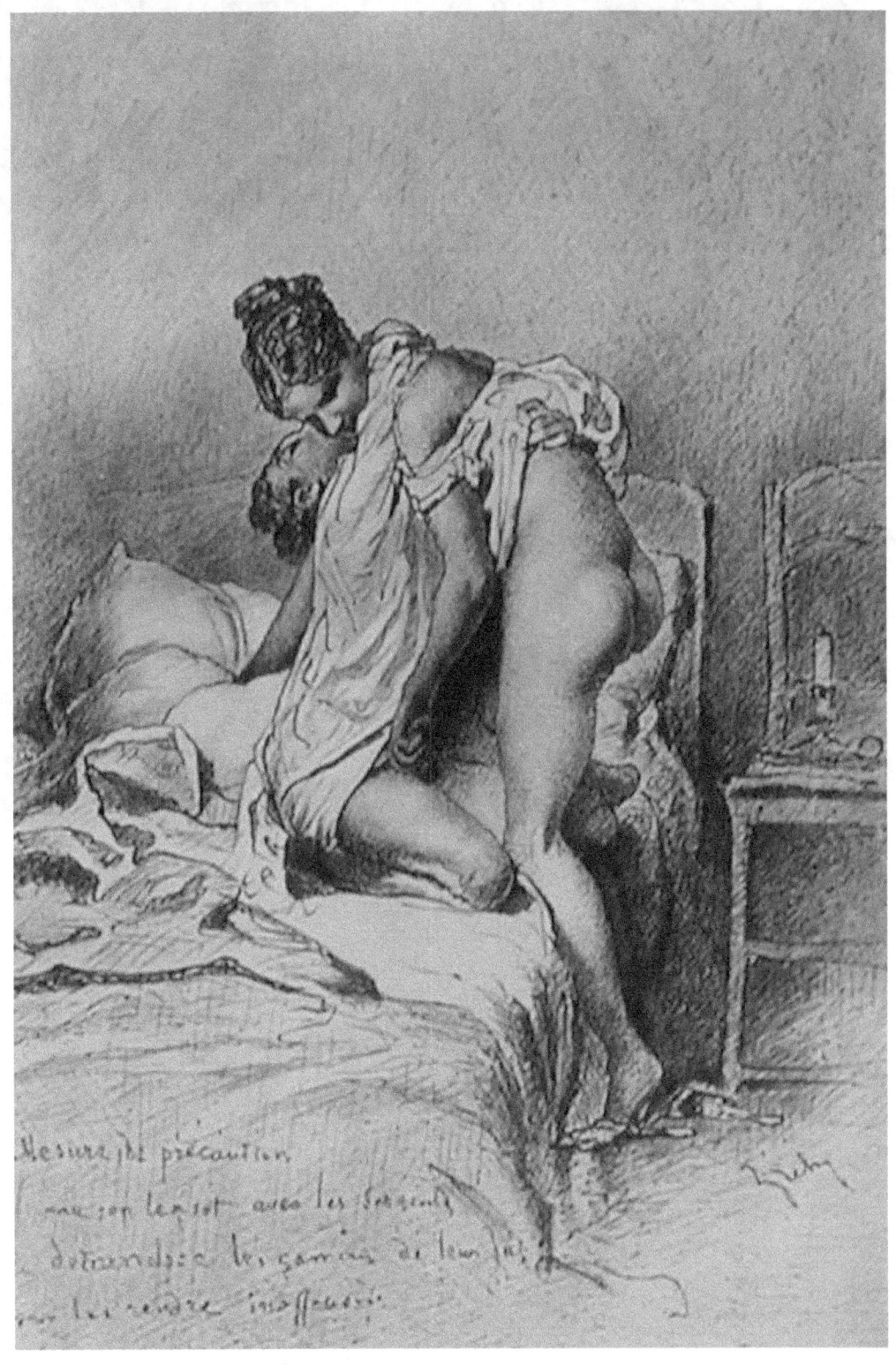

Mesure et précaution
que son temps avec les * serments*
détendre les *garnis* de leur lit
les rendre inoffensifs

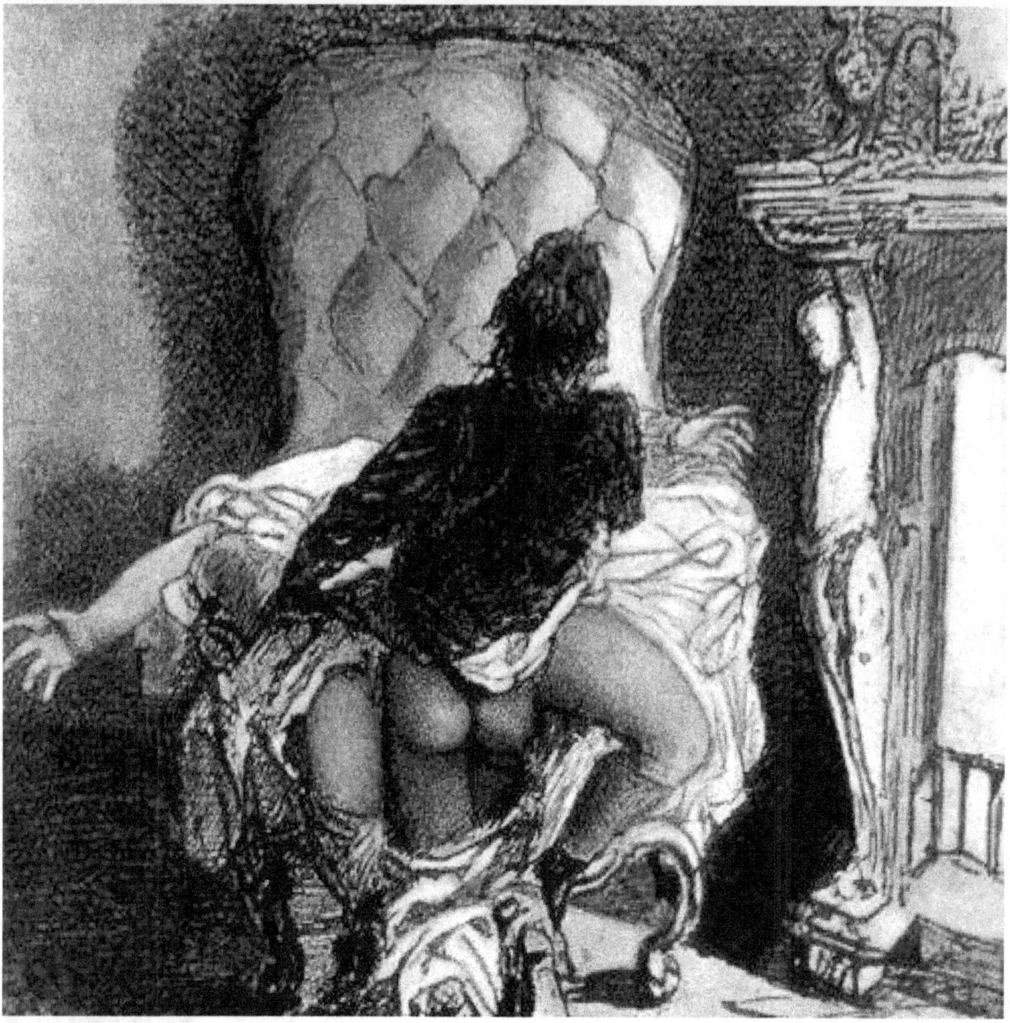

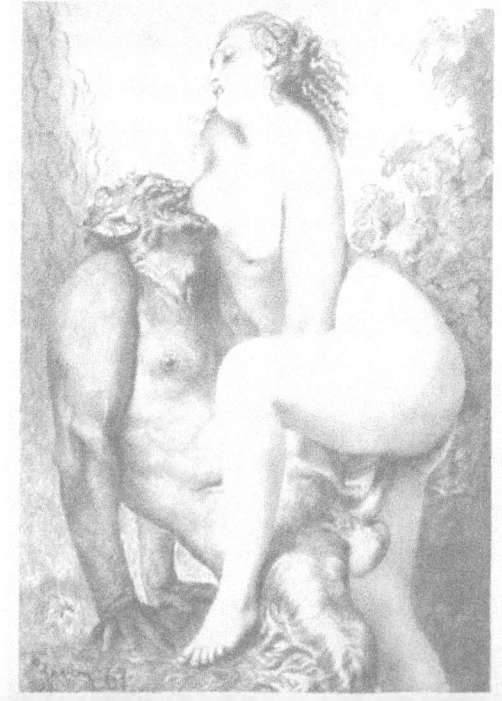

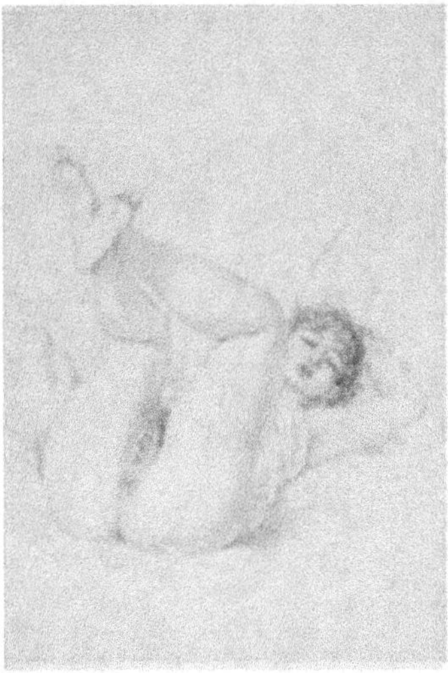

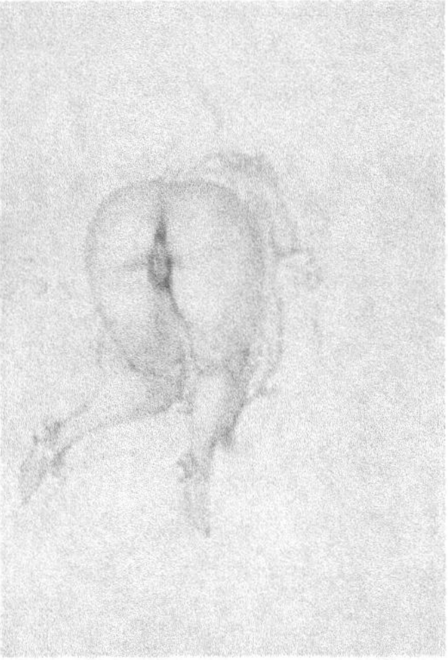

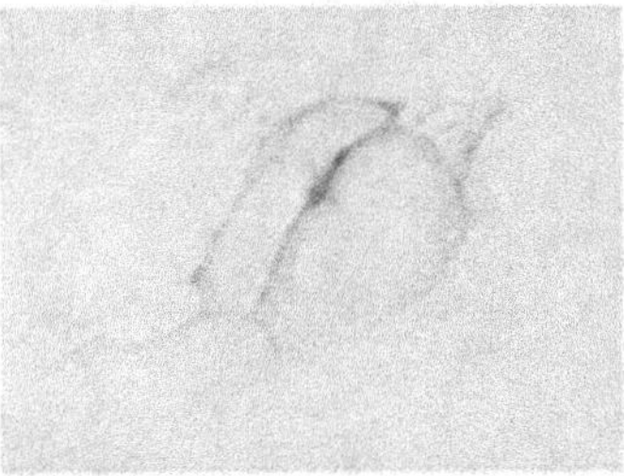

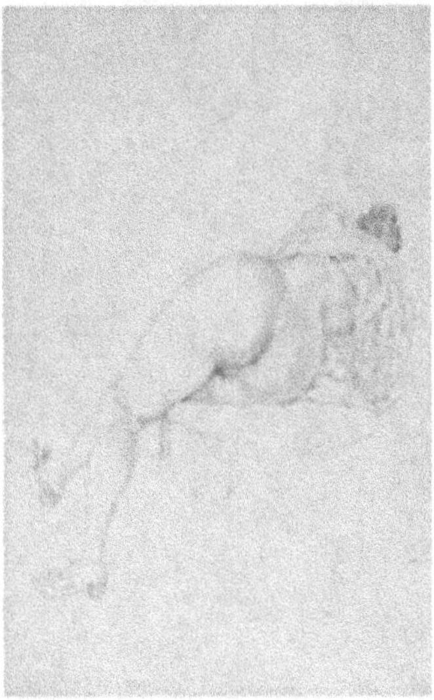

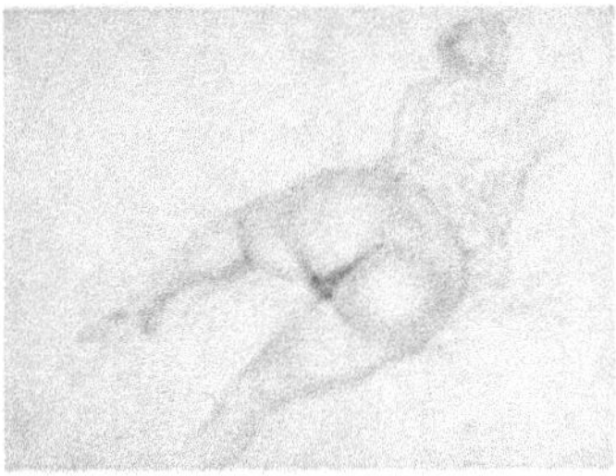

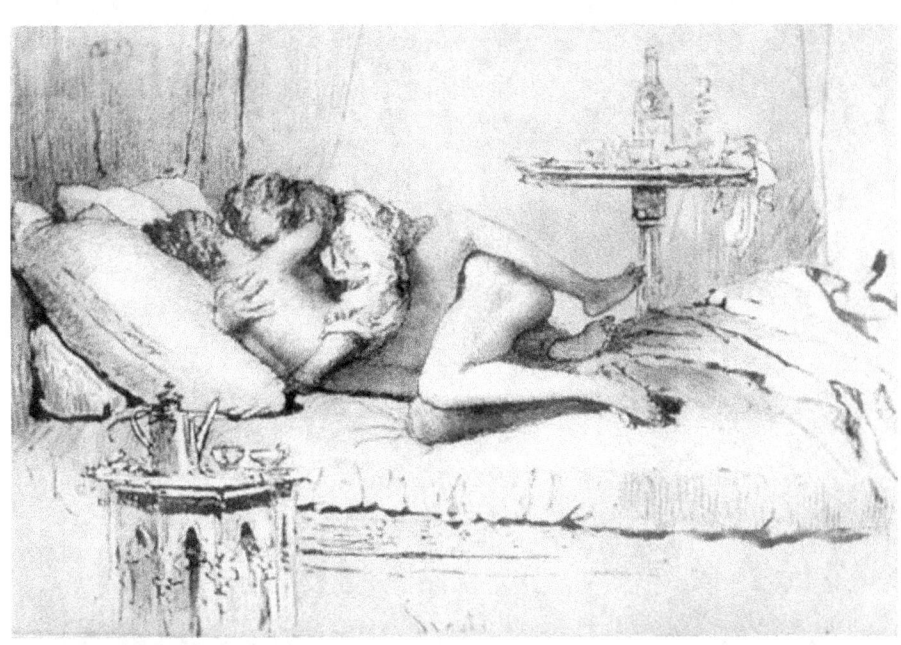

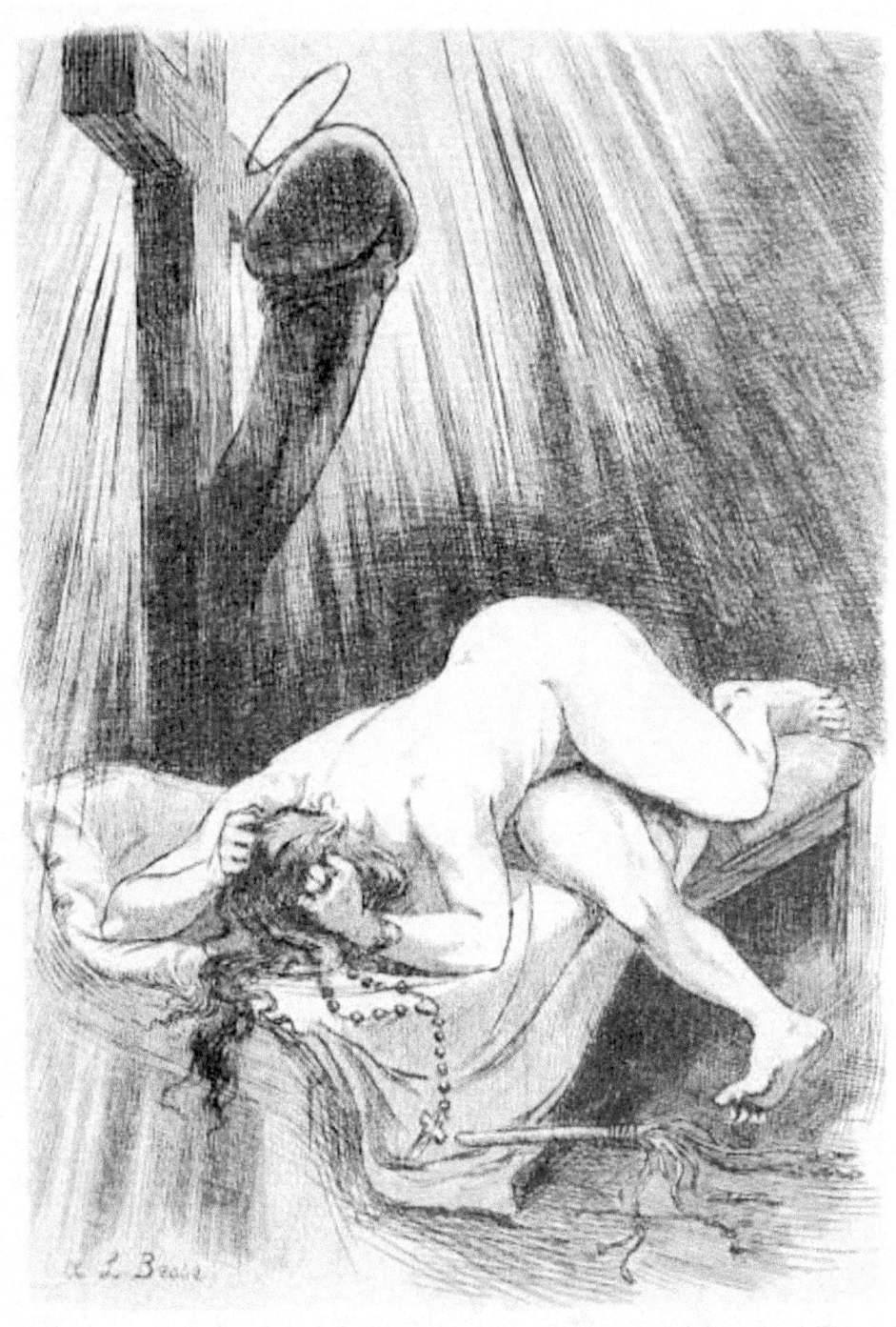

Martin Van Maele, this page and following pages

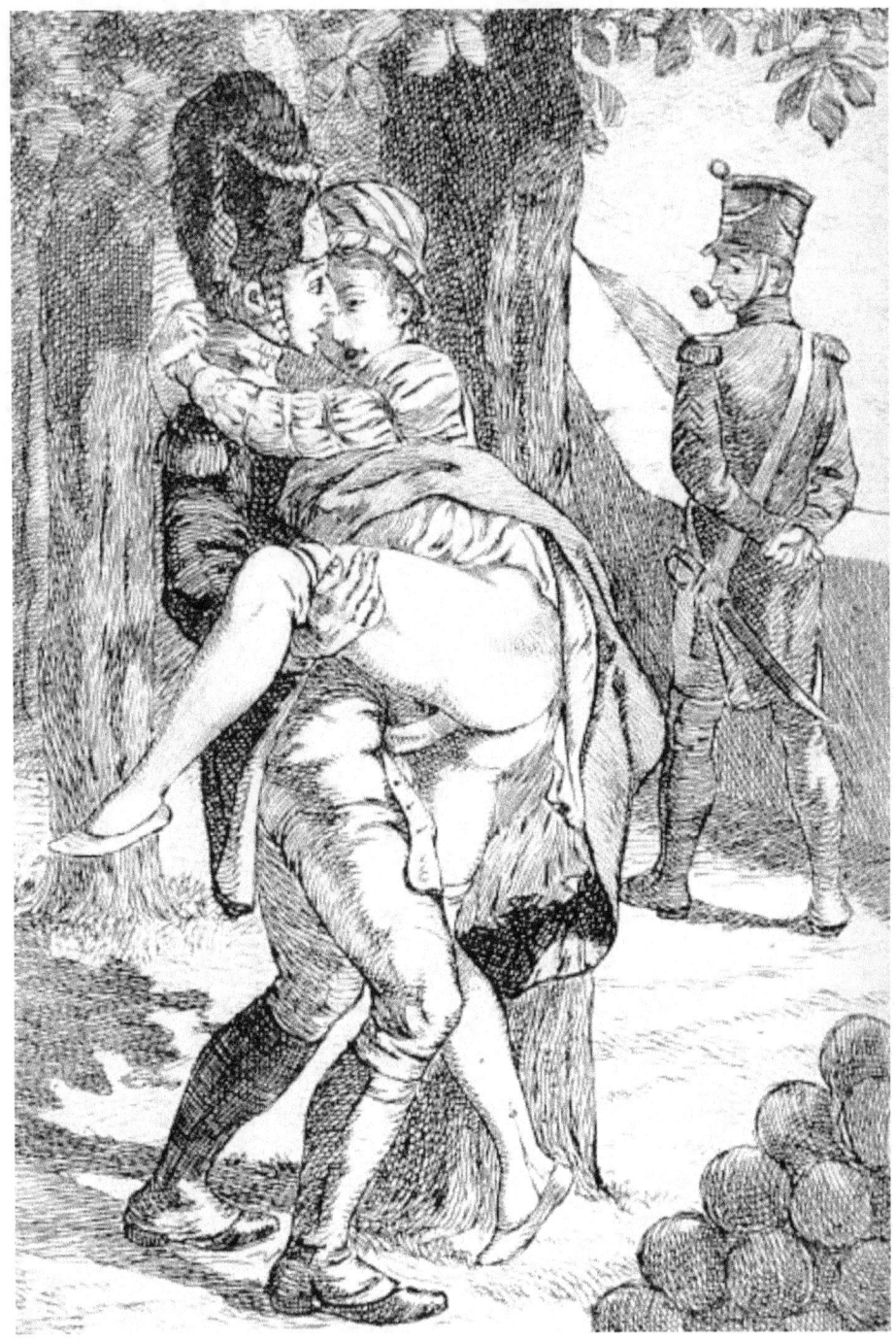

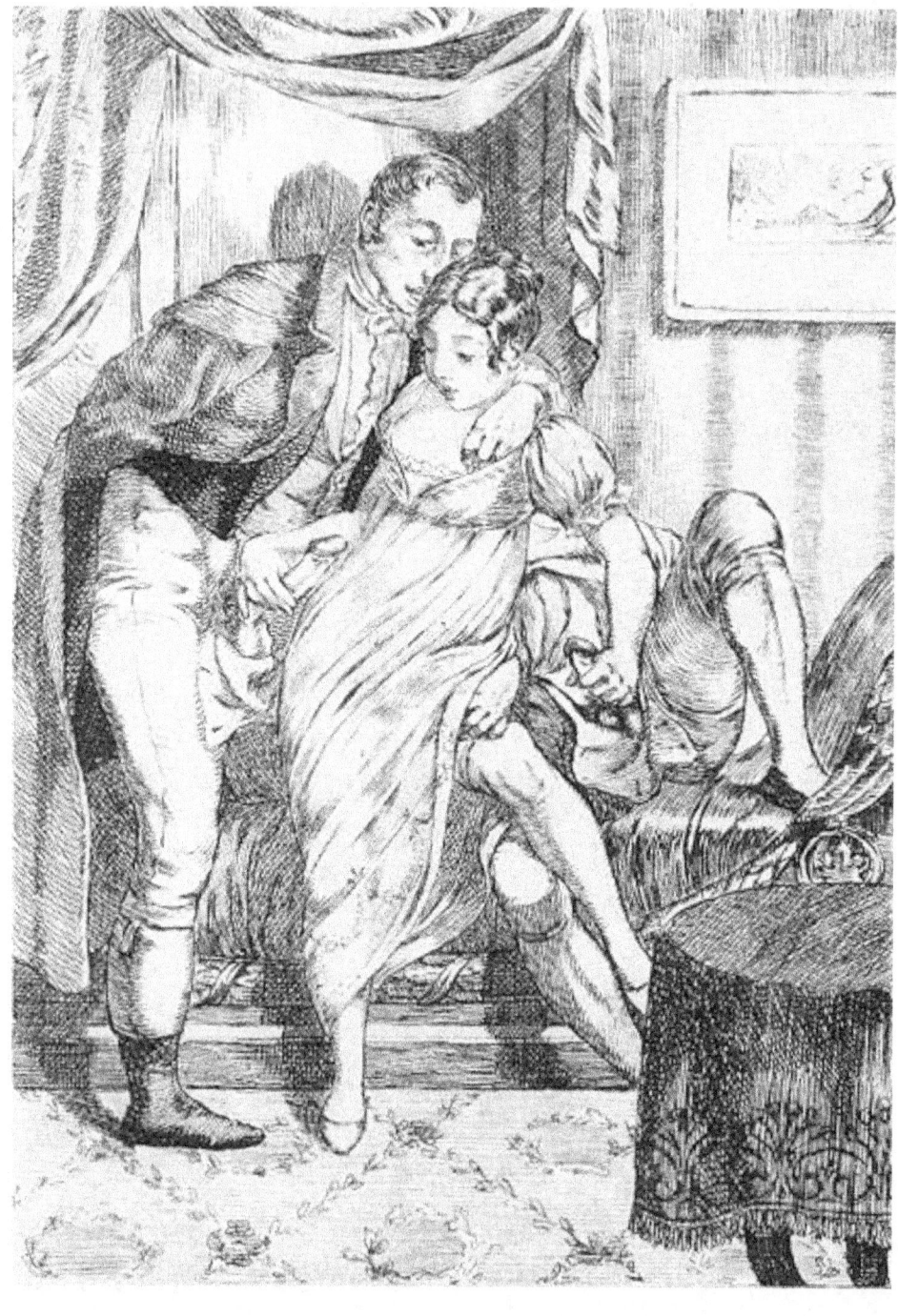

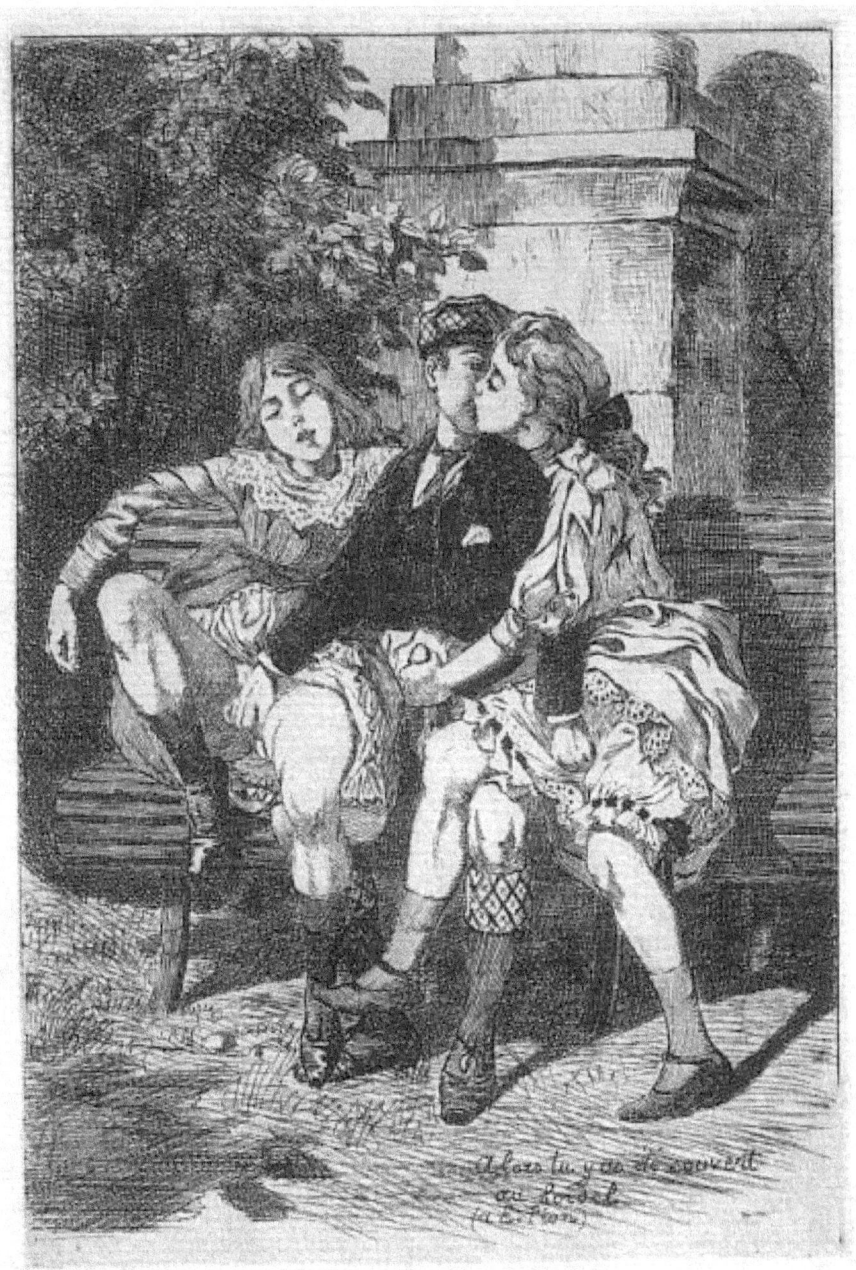

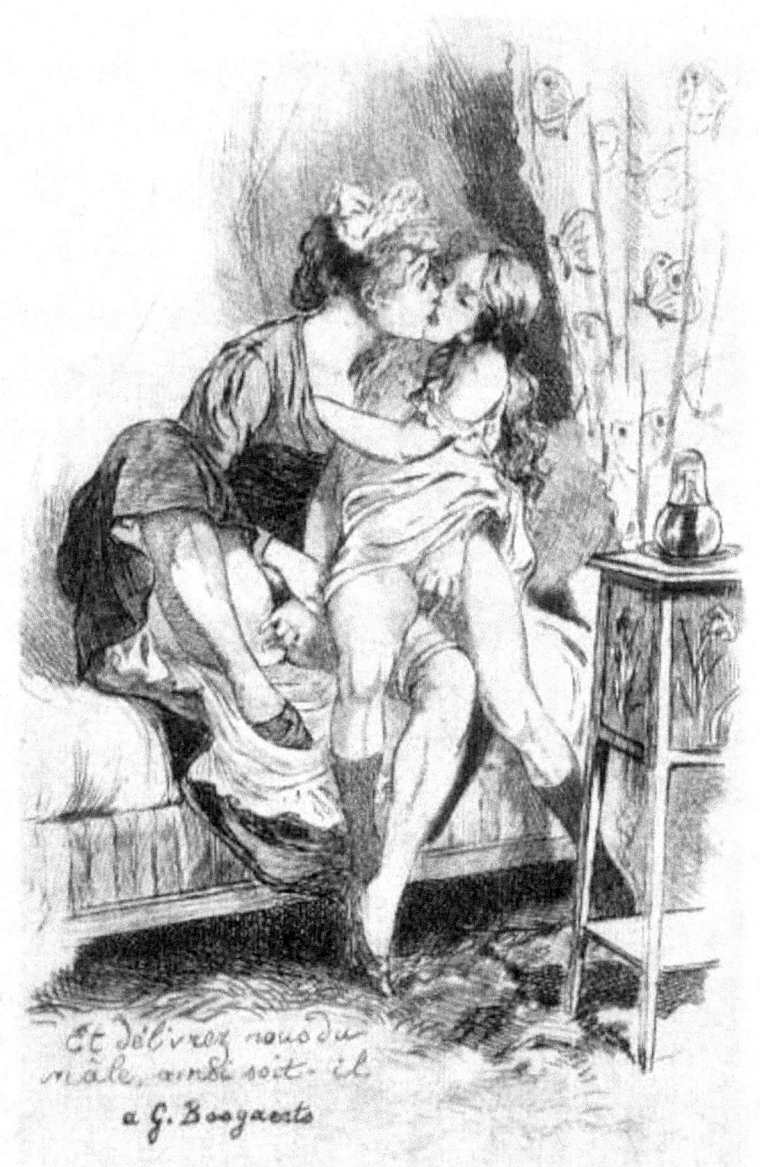

Et délivrez nous du
mâle, ainsi soit-il
a G. Boogaerts

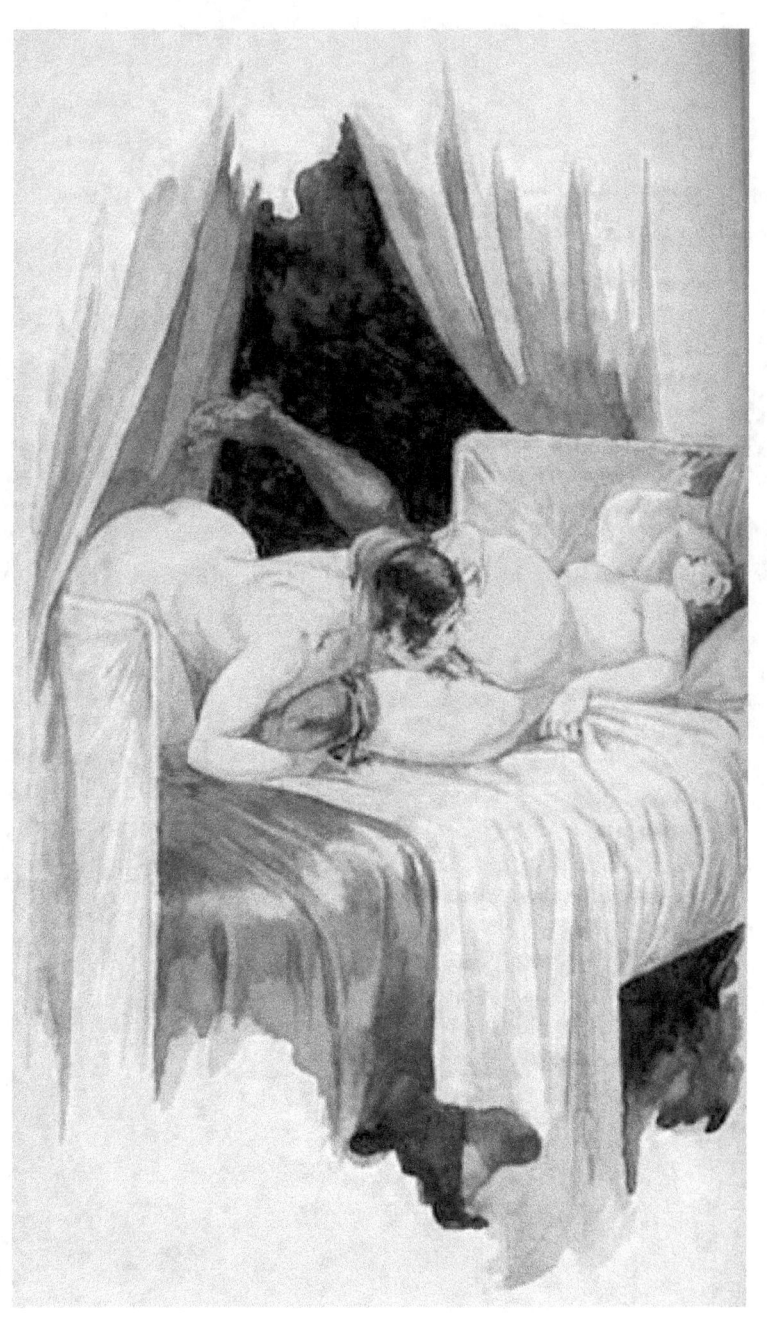

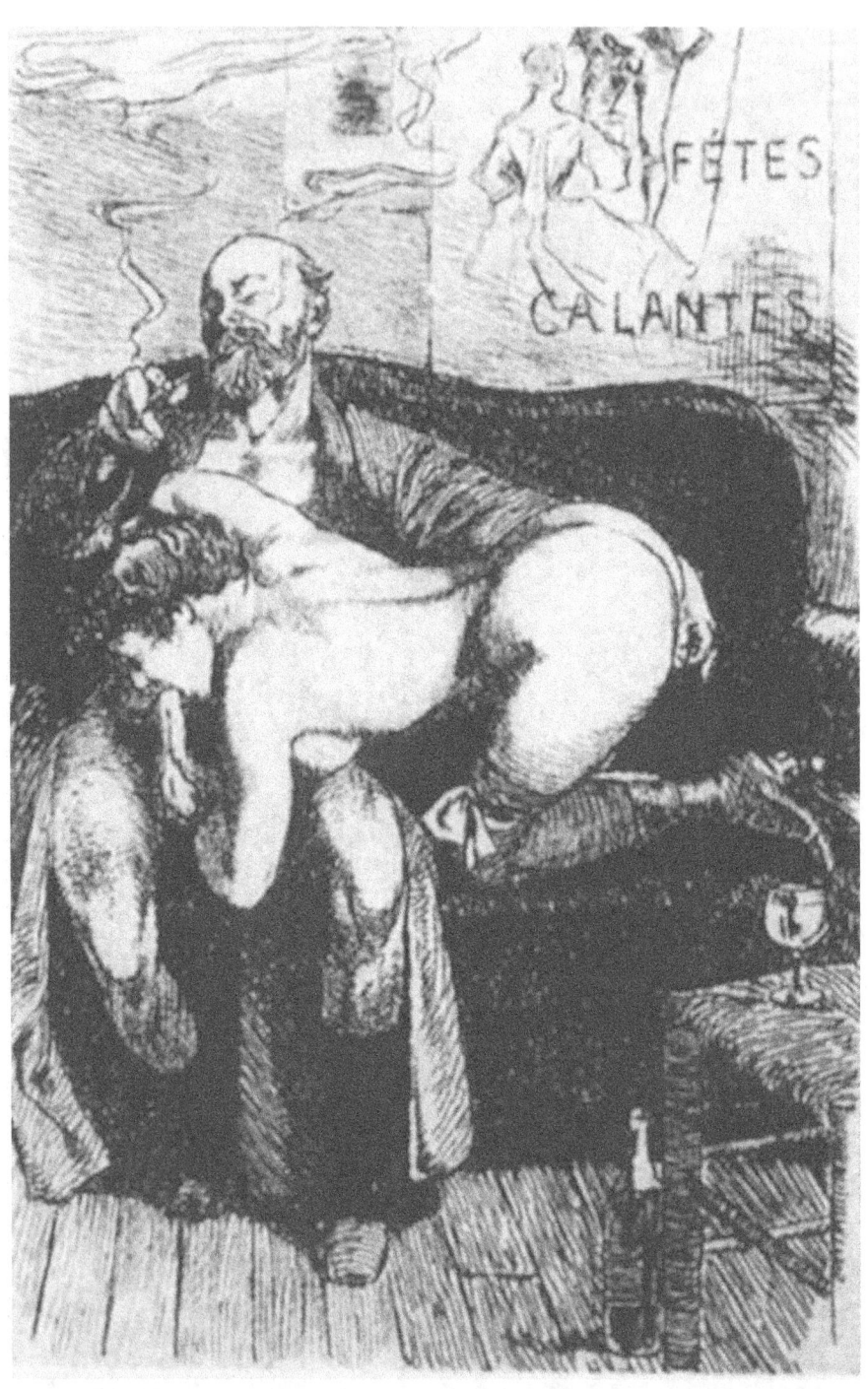

Martin van Maele, illustration for Paul Verlaine's Trilogie Érotique, 1907.
This page and following pages

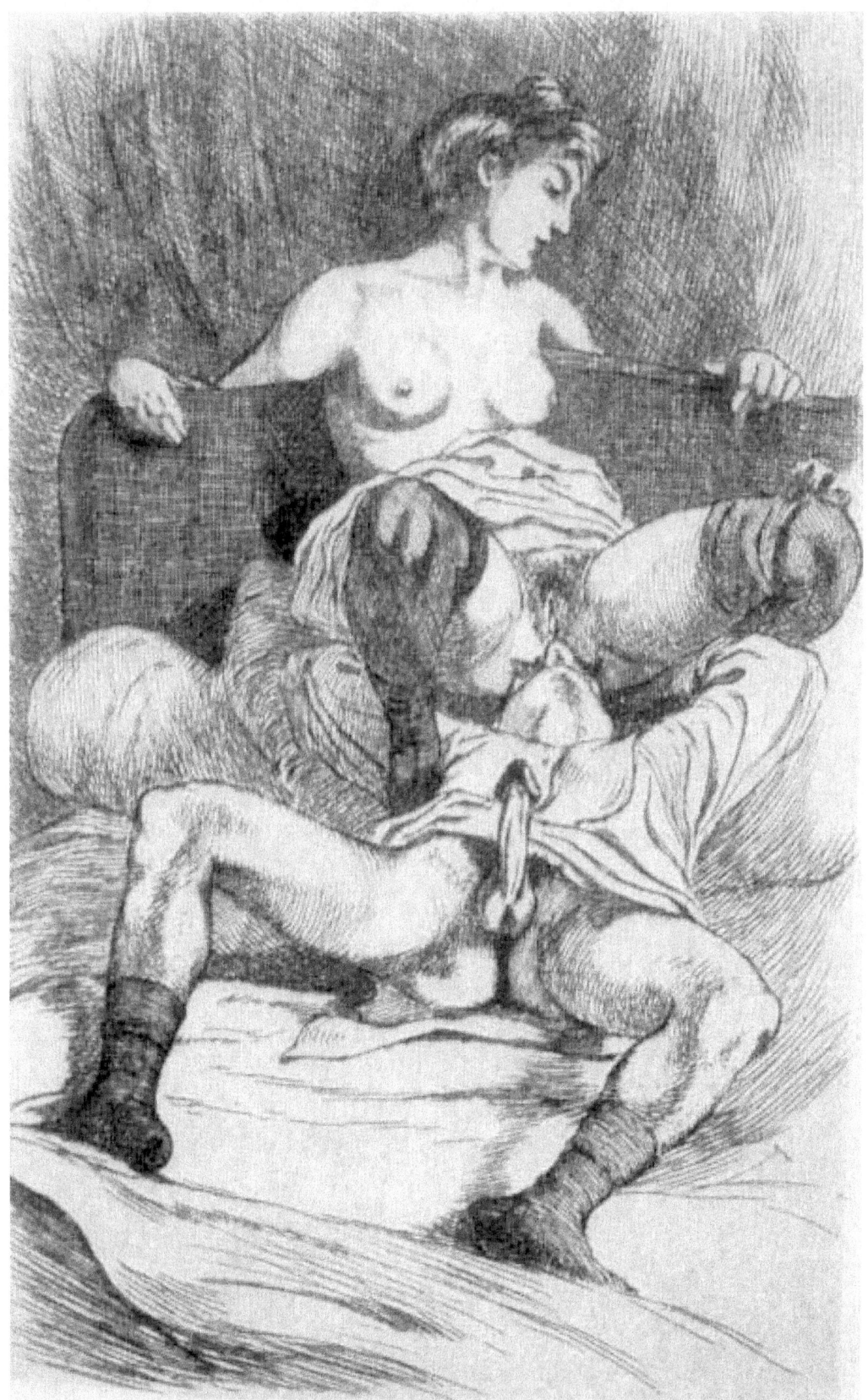

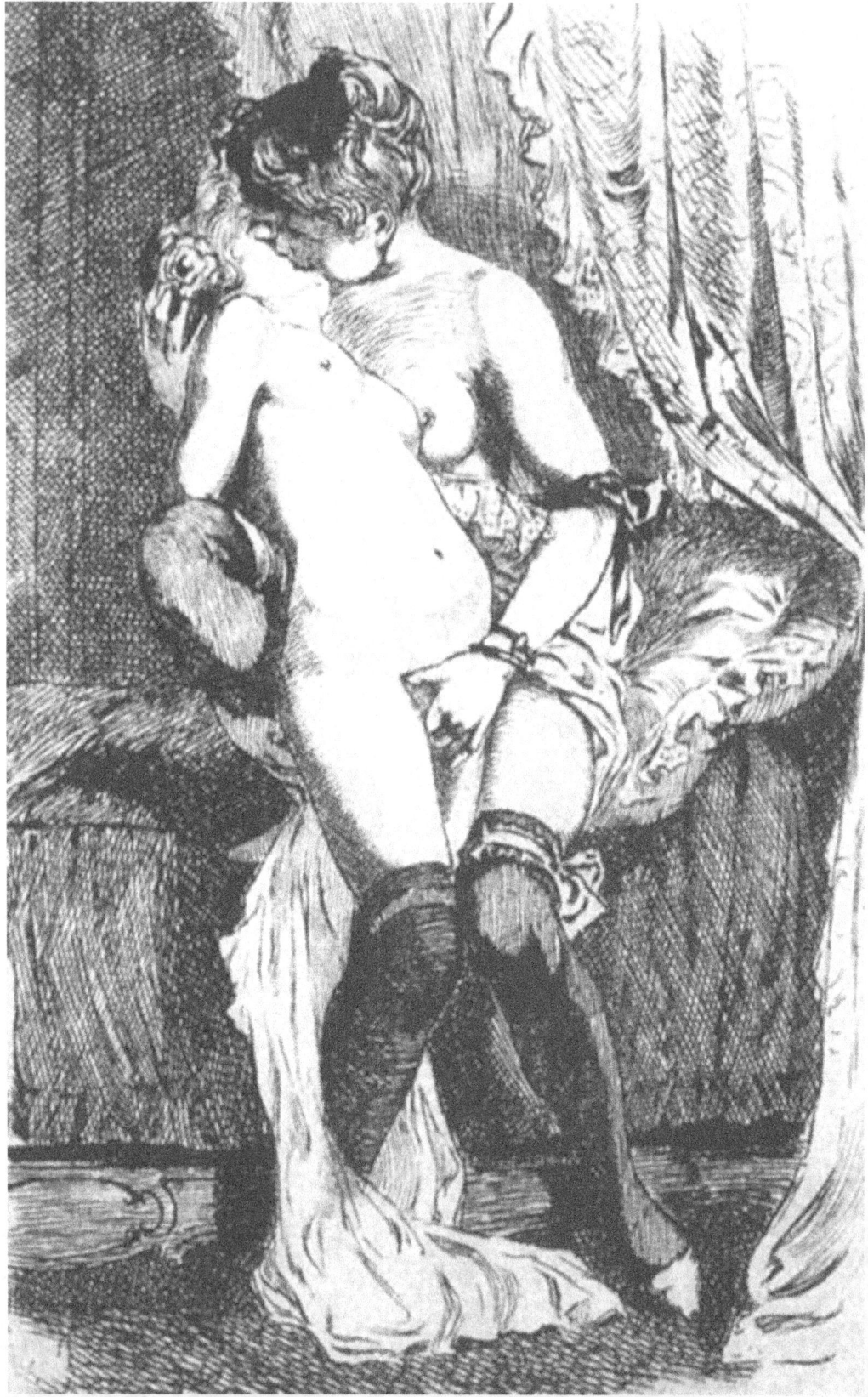

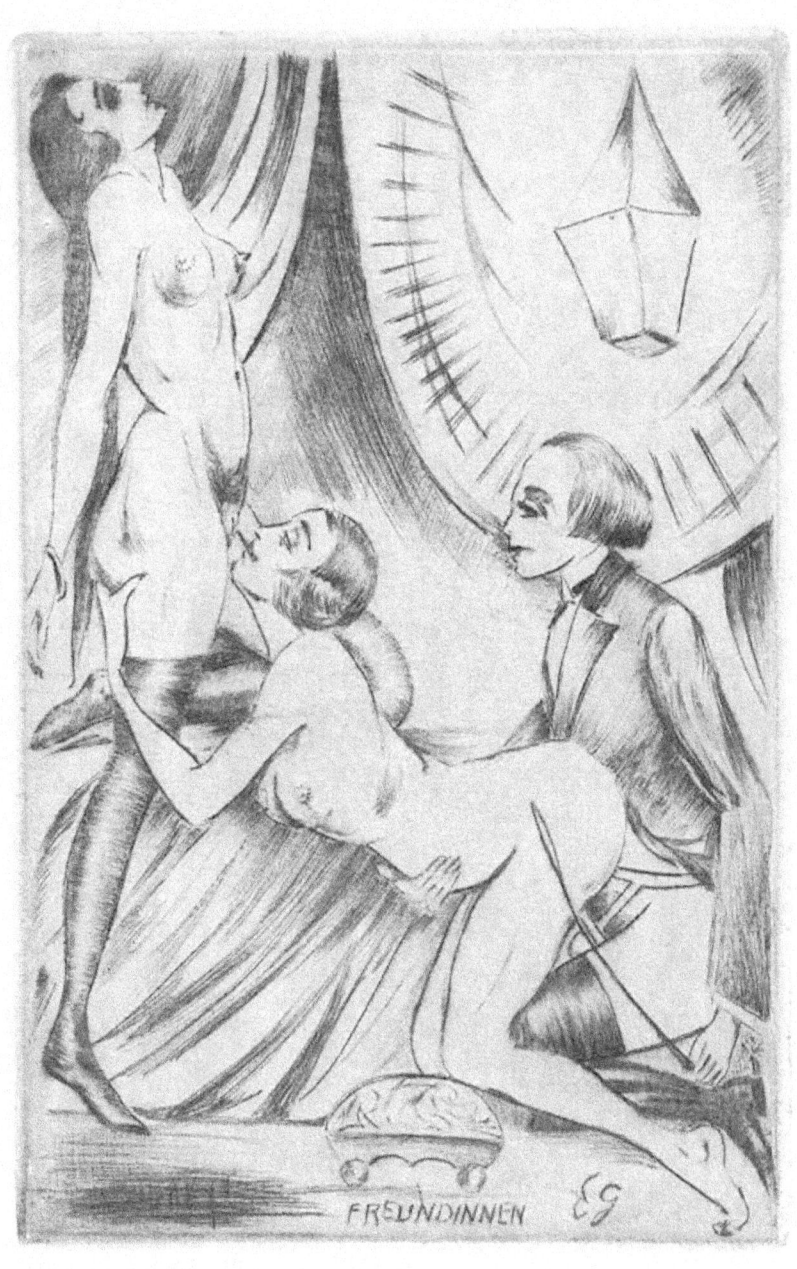

Ernest Gerhard, from Die Laterne (1925).

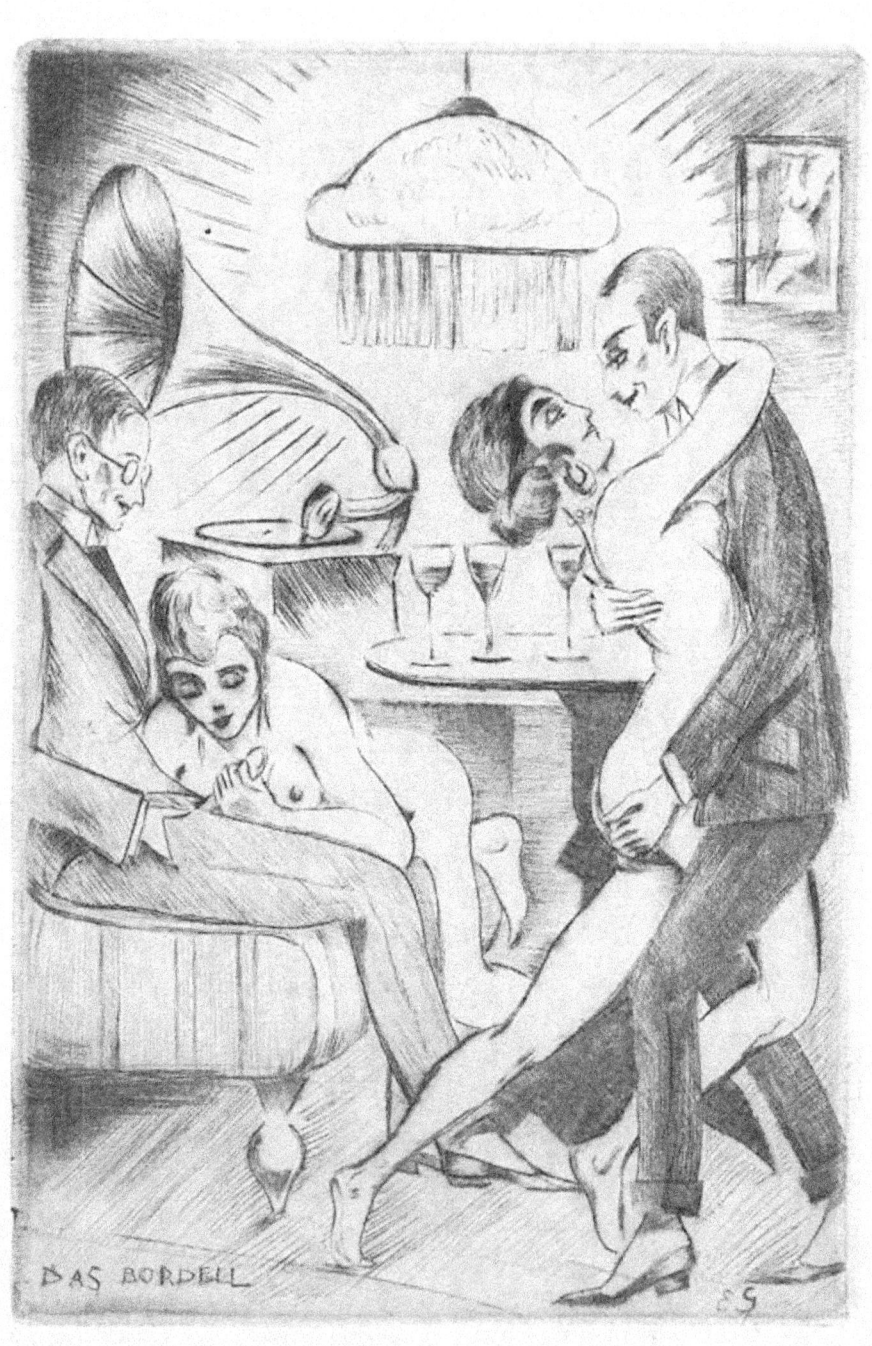

DAS BORDELL

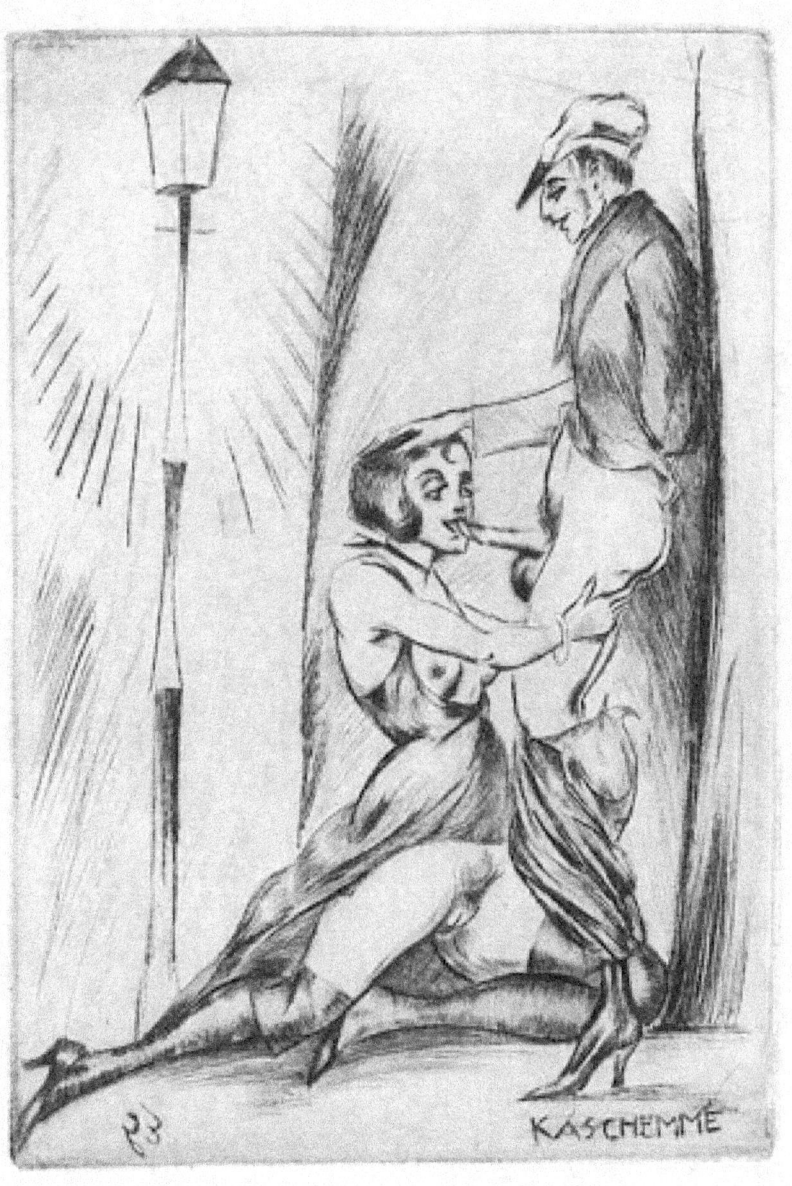

KASCHEMME

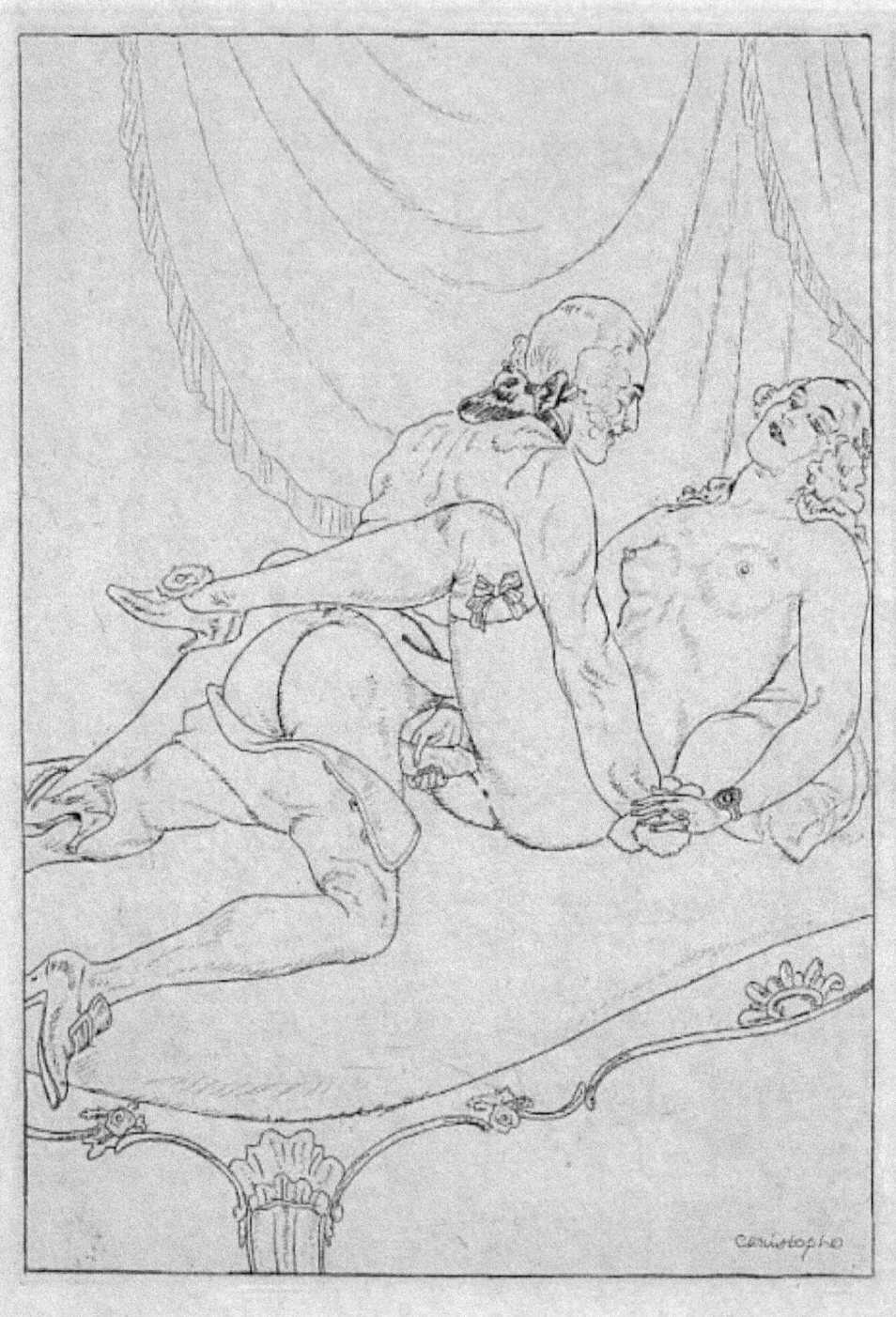

F. Christophe, from Die Verfuhrung,
this page and following pages

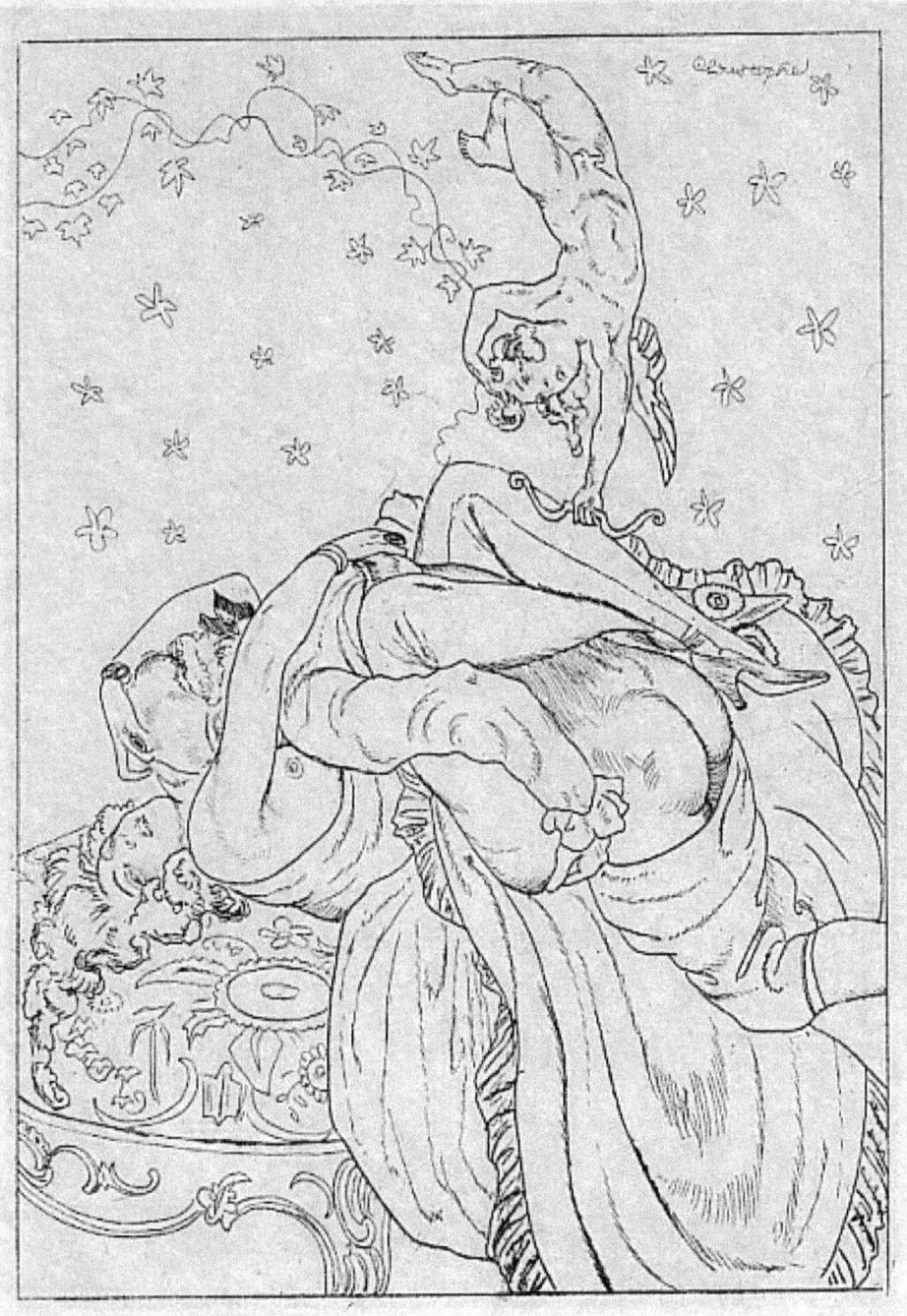

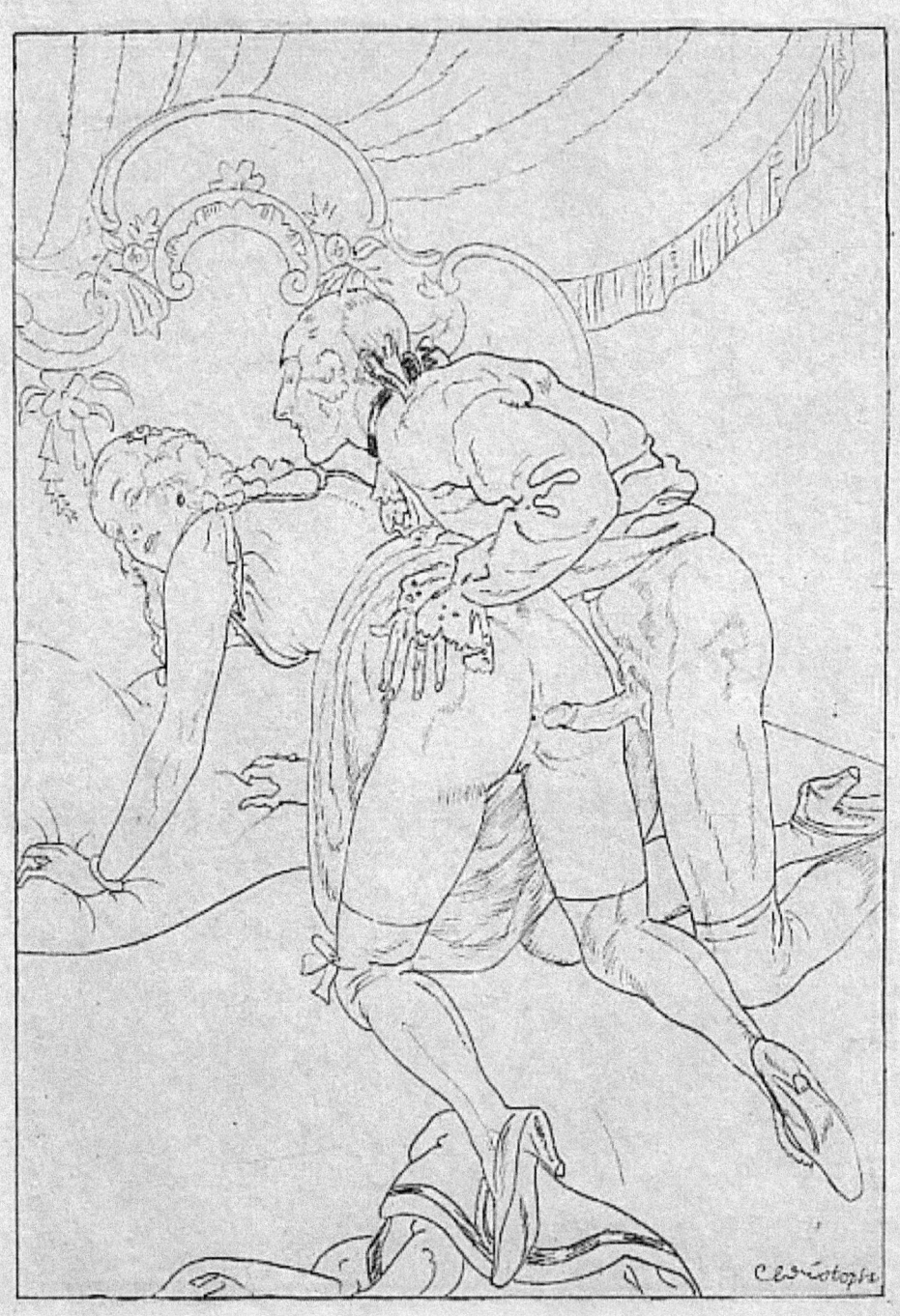

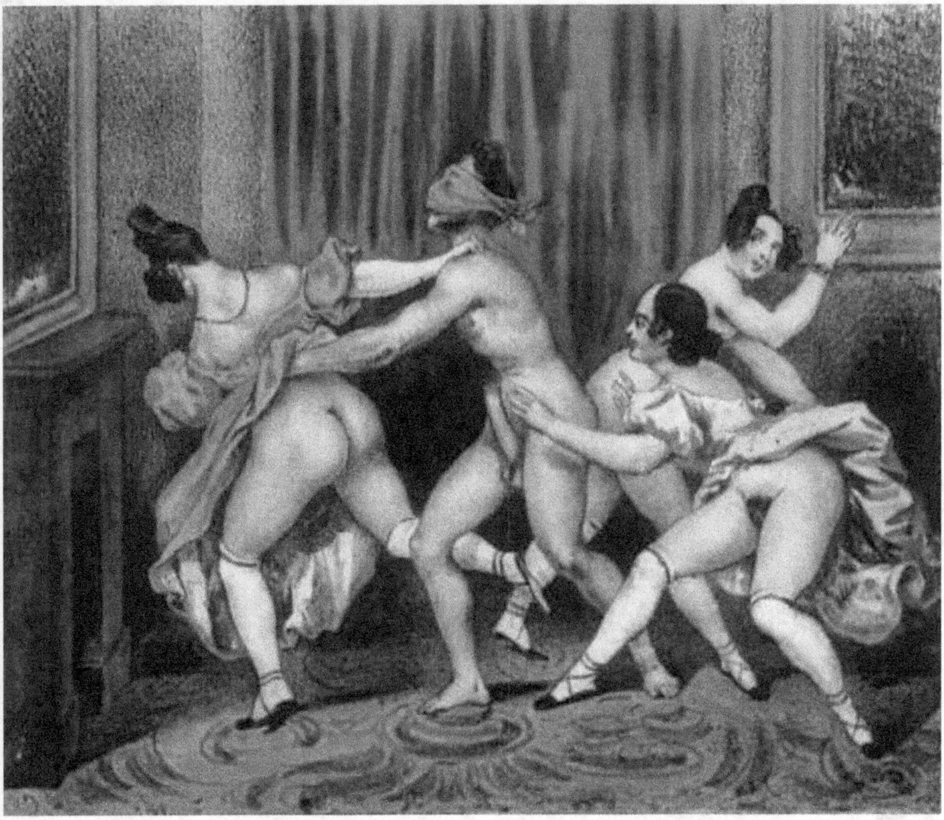

Achille Deveria (1800-1857), this page and following pages

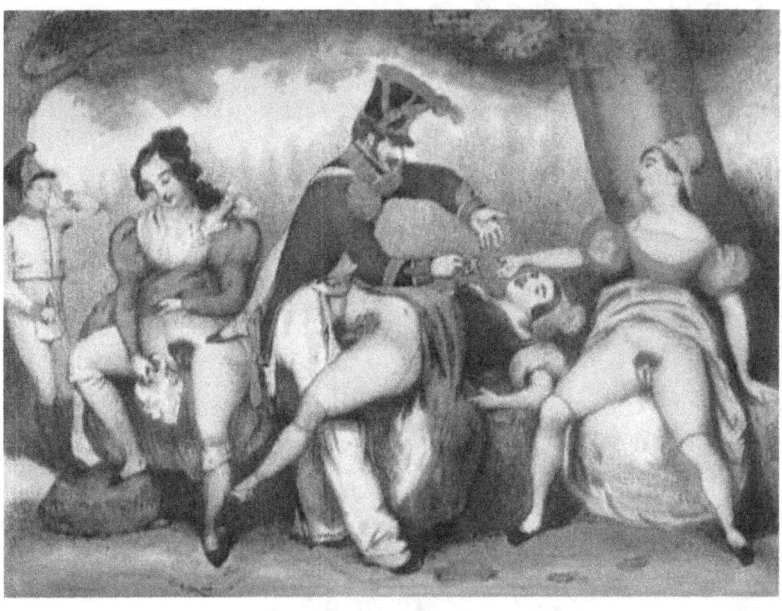

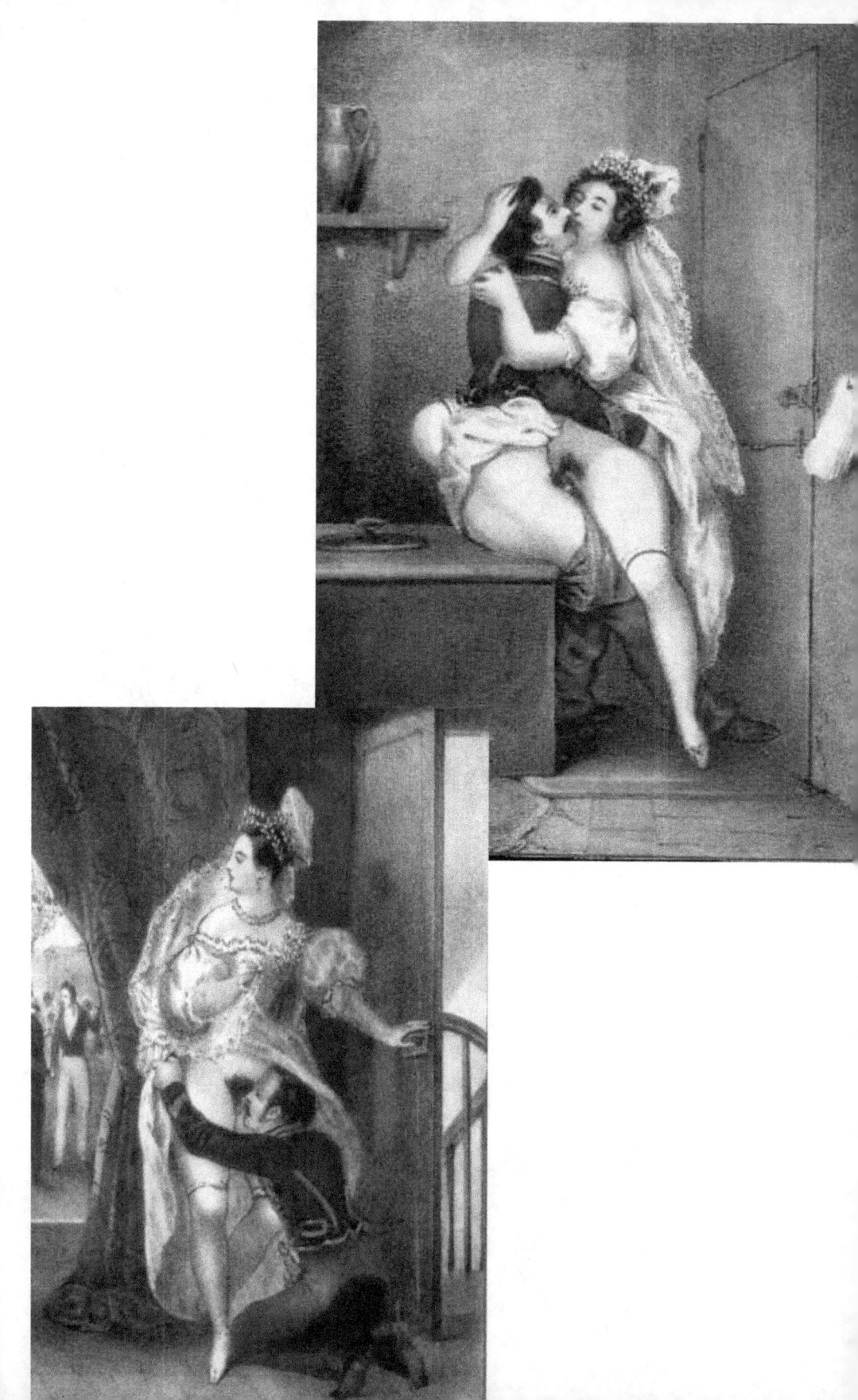

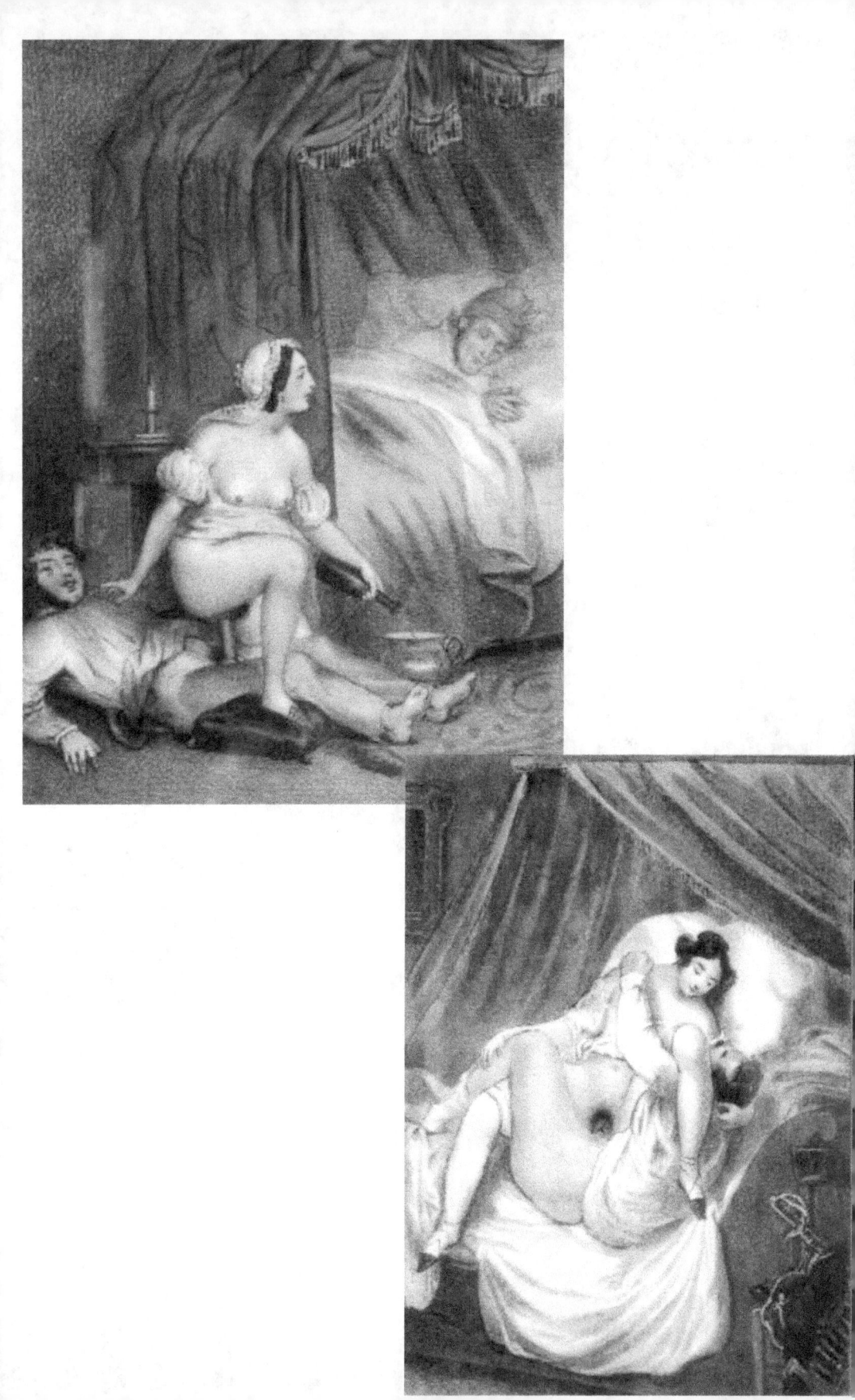

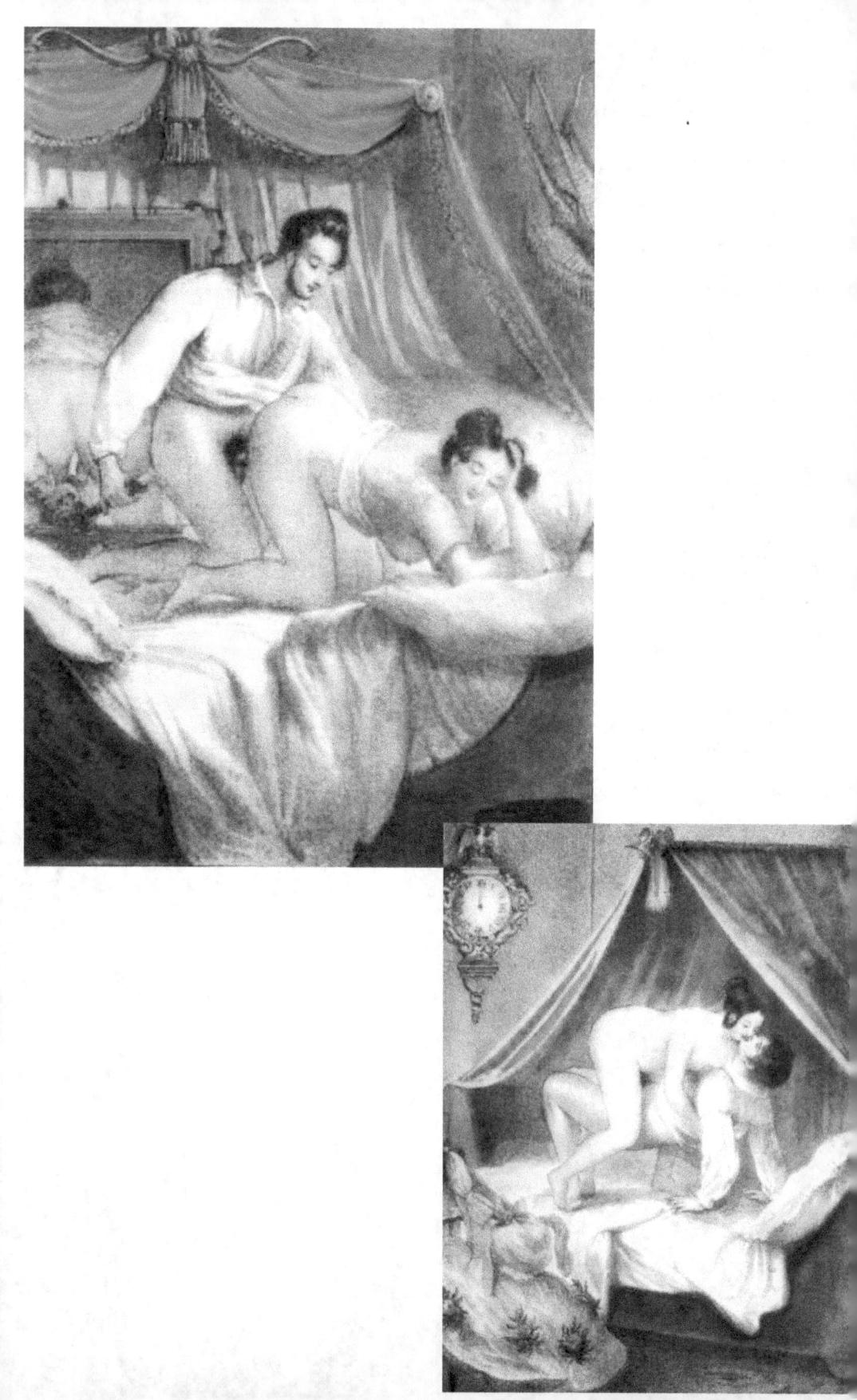

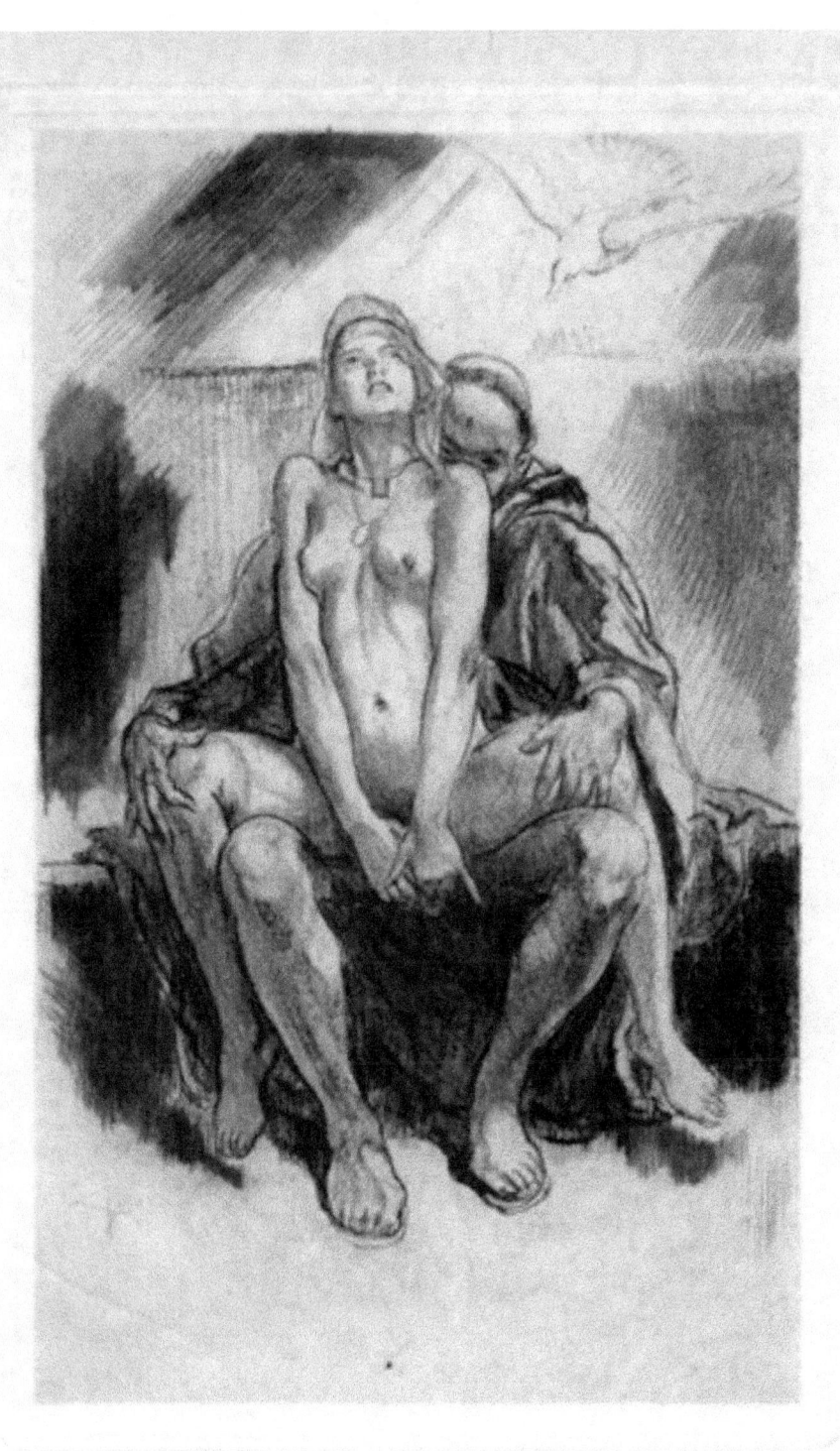

Almery Lobel Riche
(this page and following pages)

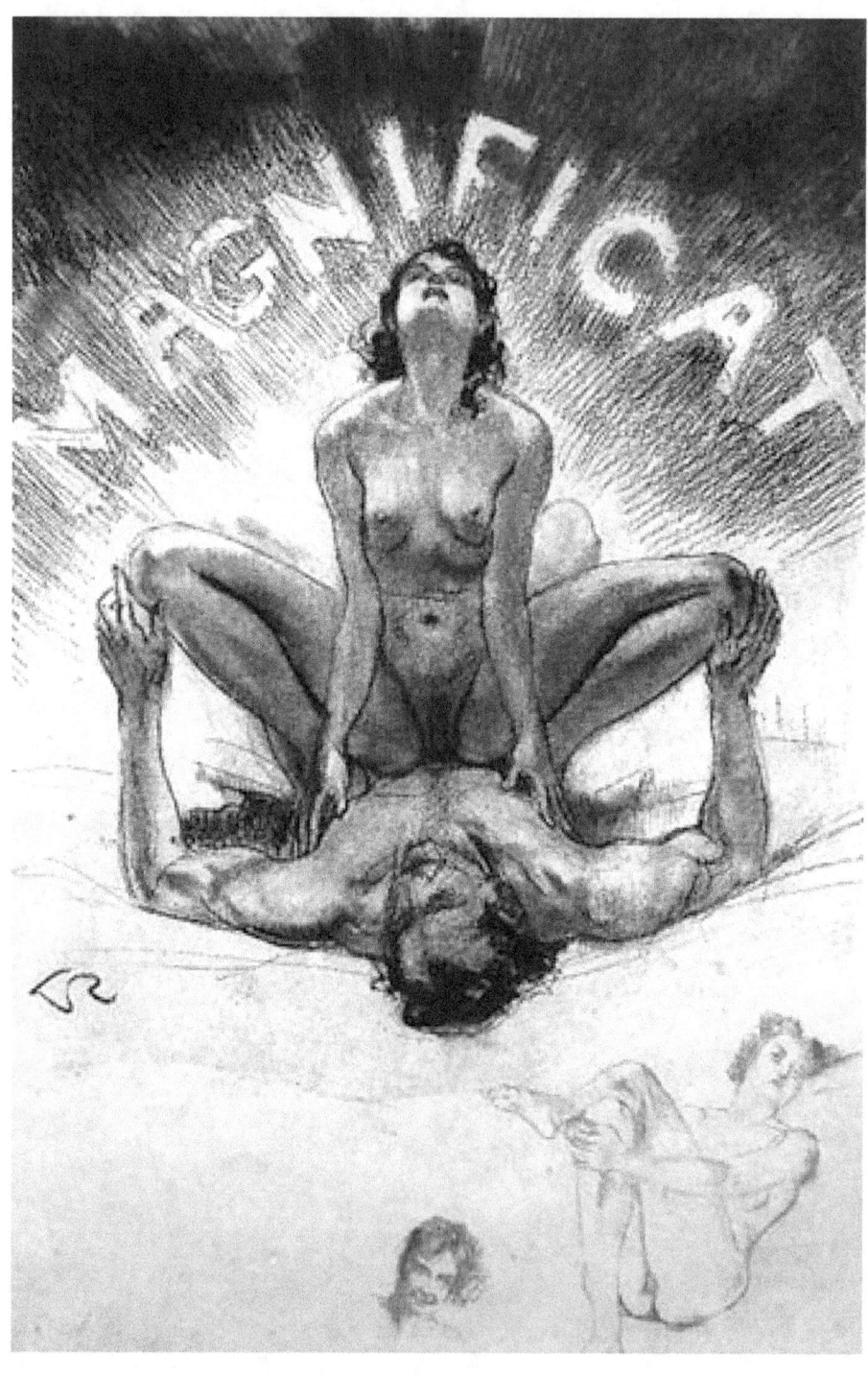

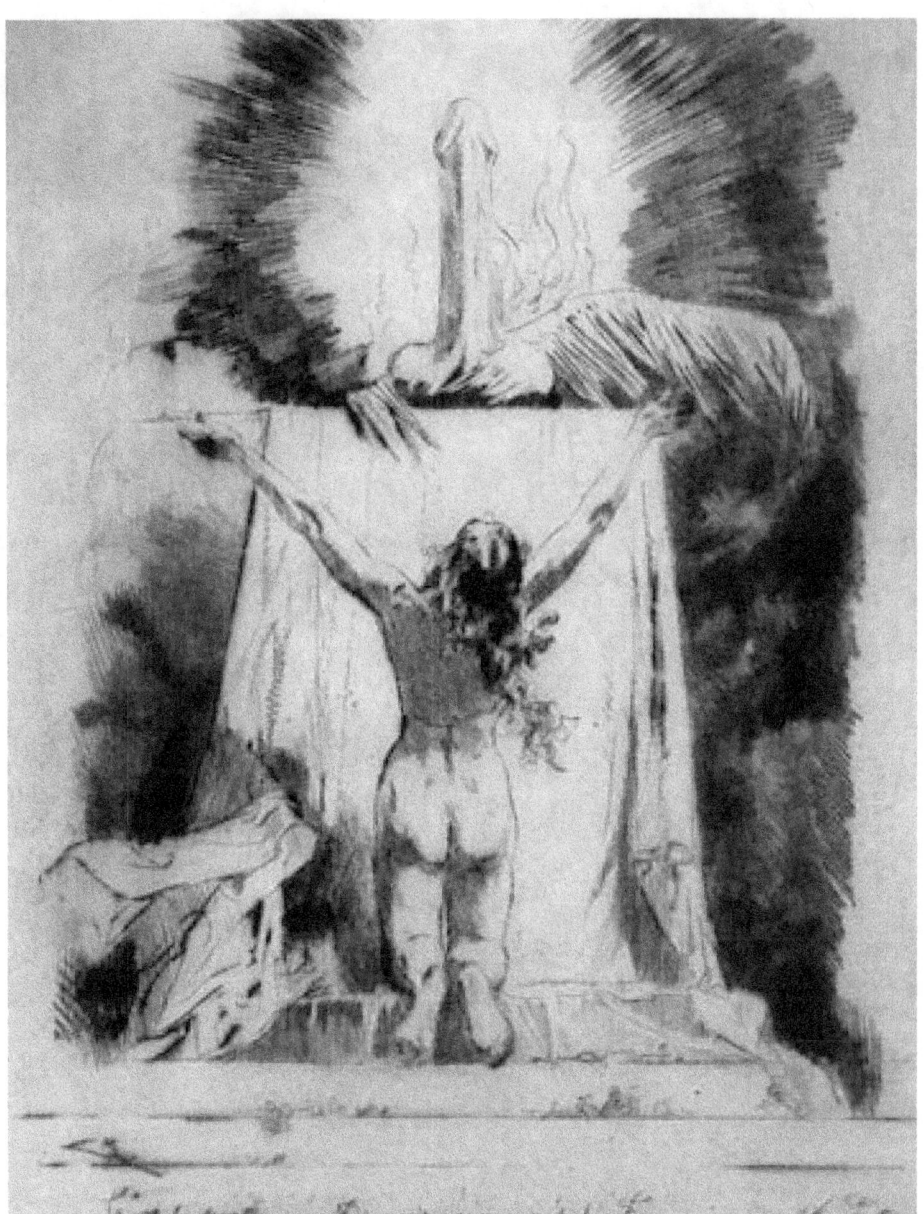

C'est le sceptre que Dieu met aux mains de la Femme
Et la verve qui jaillit dans son cerveau.

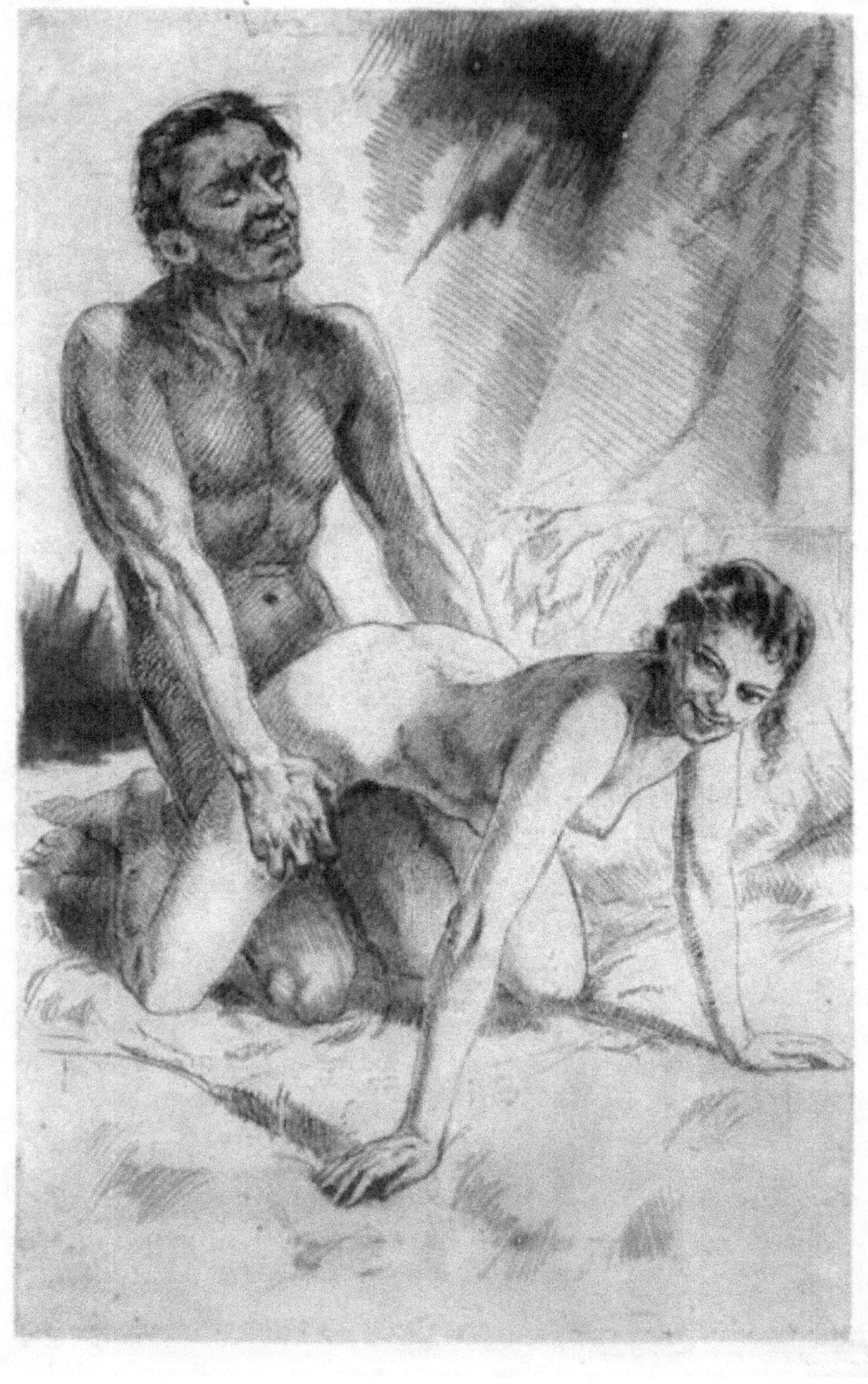

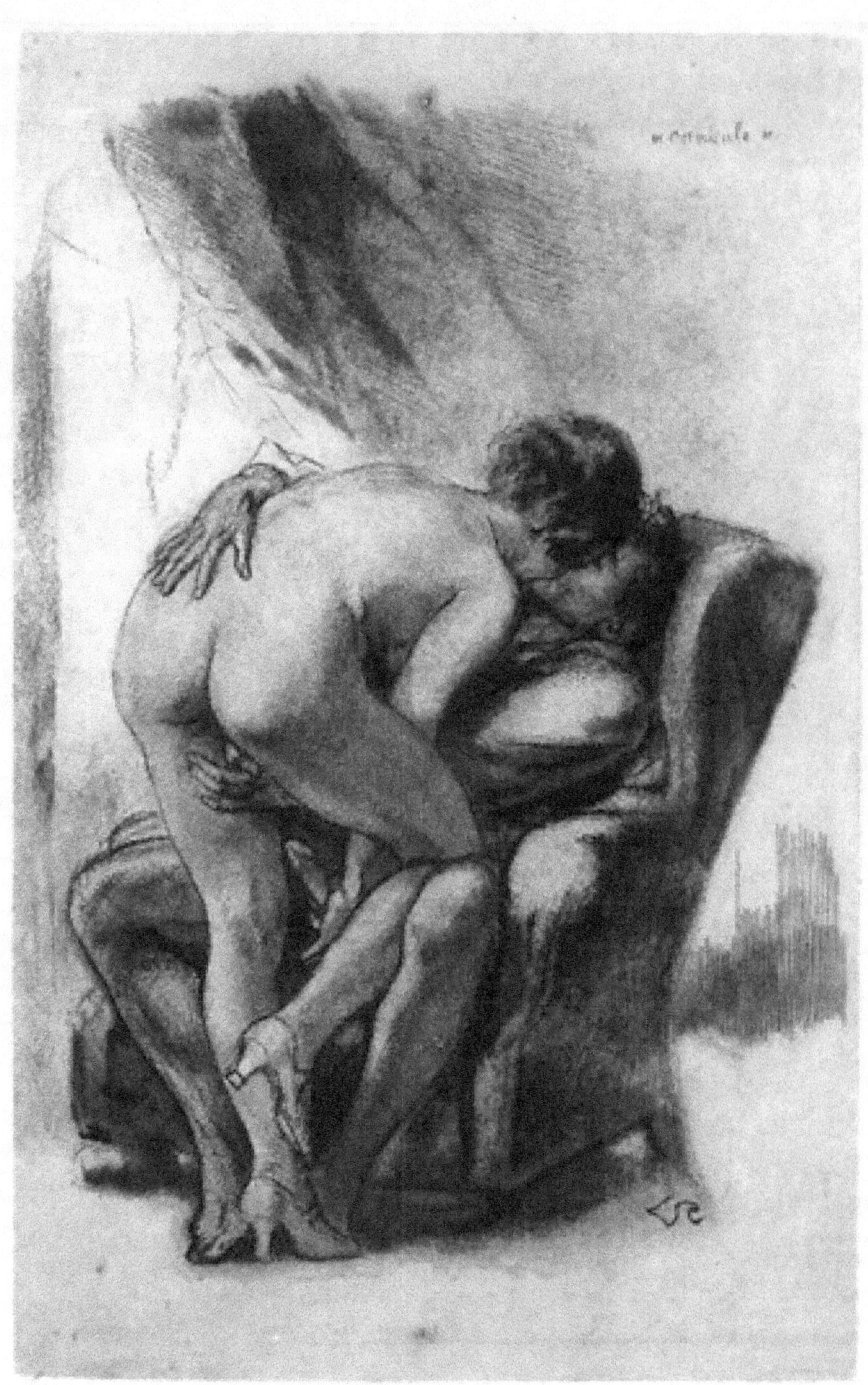

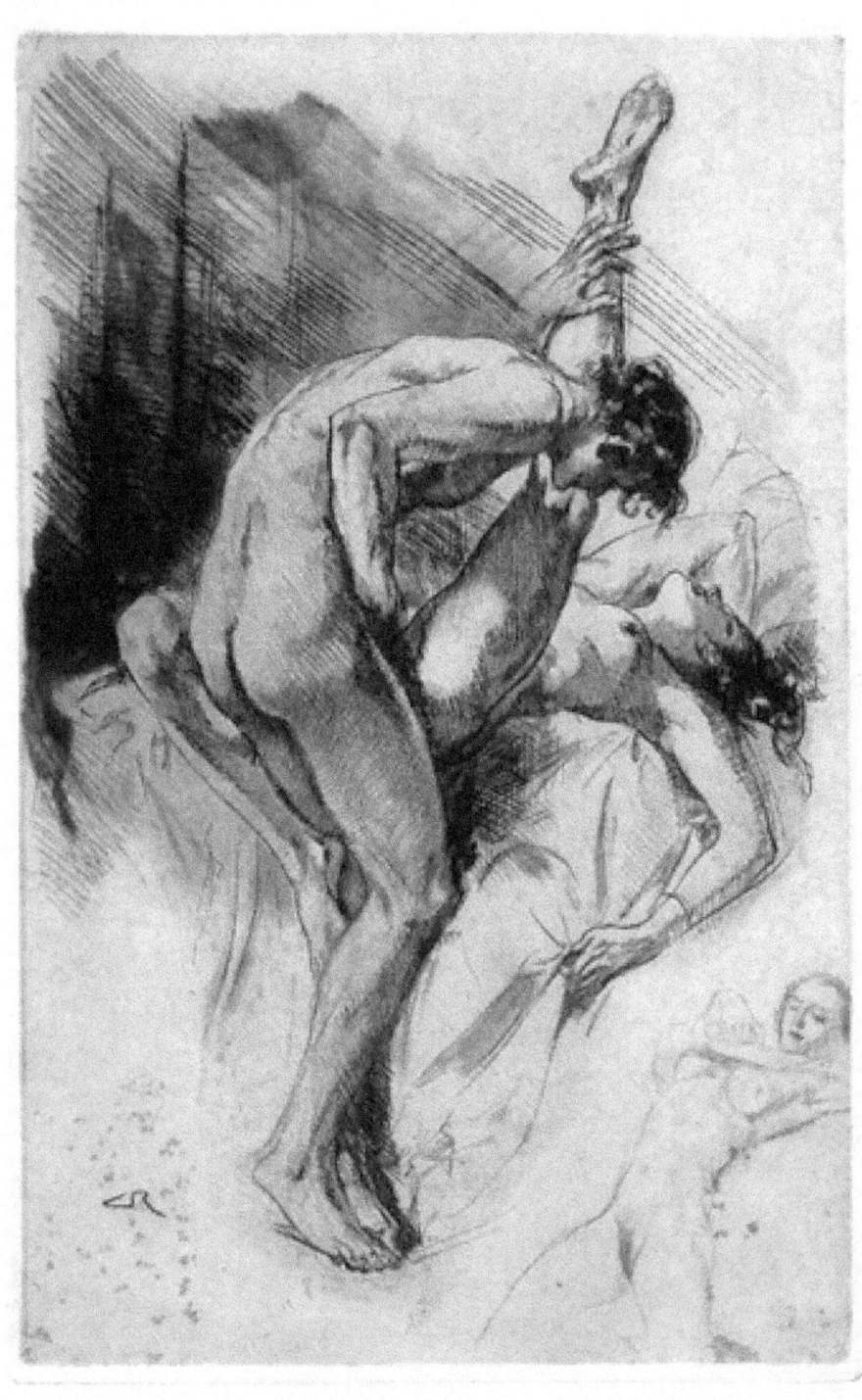

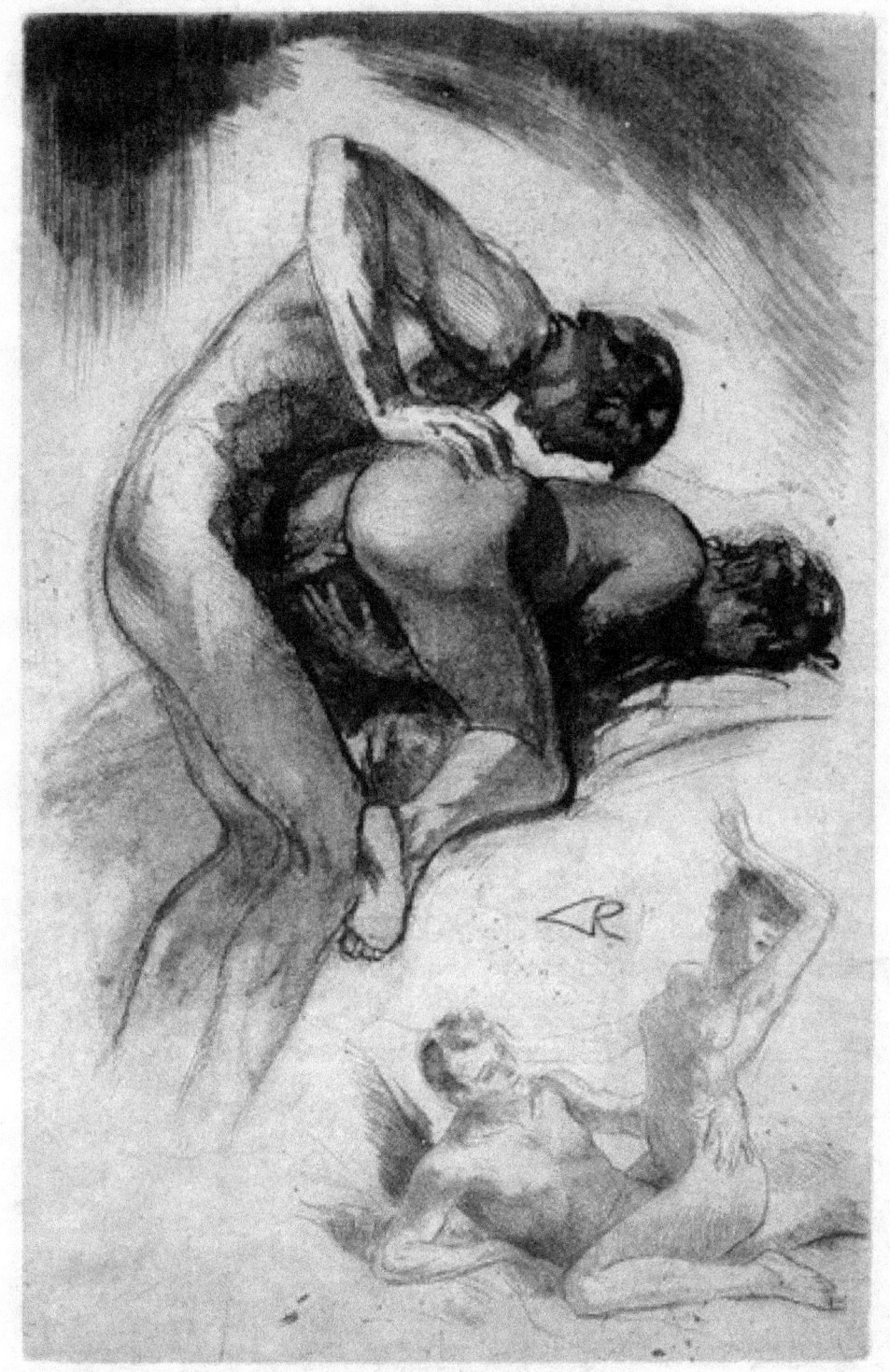

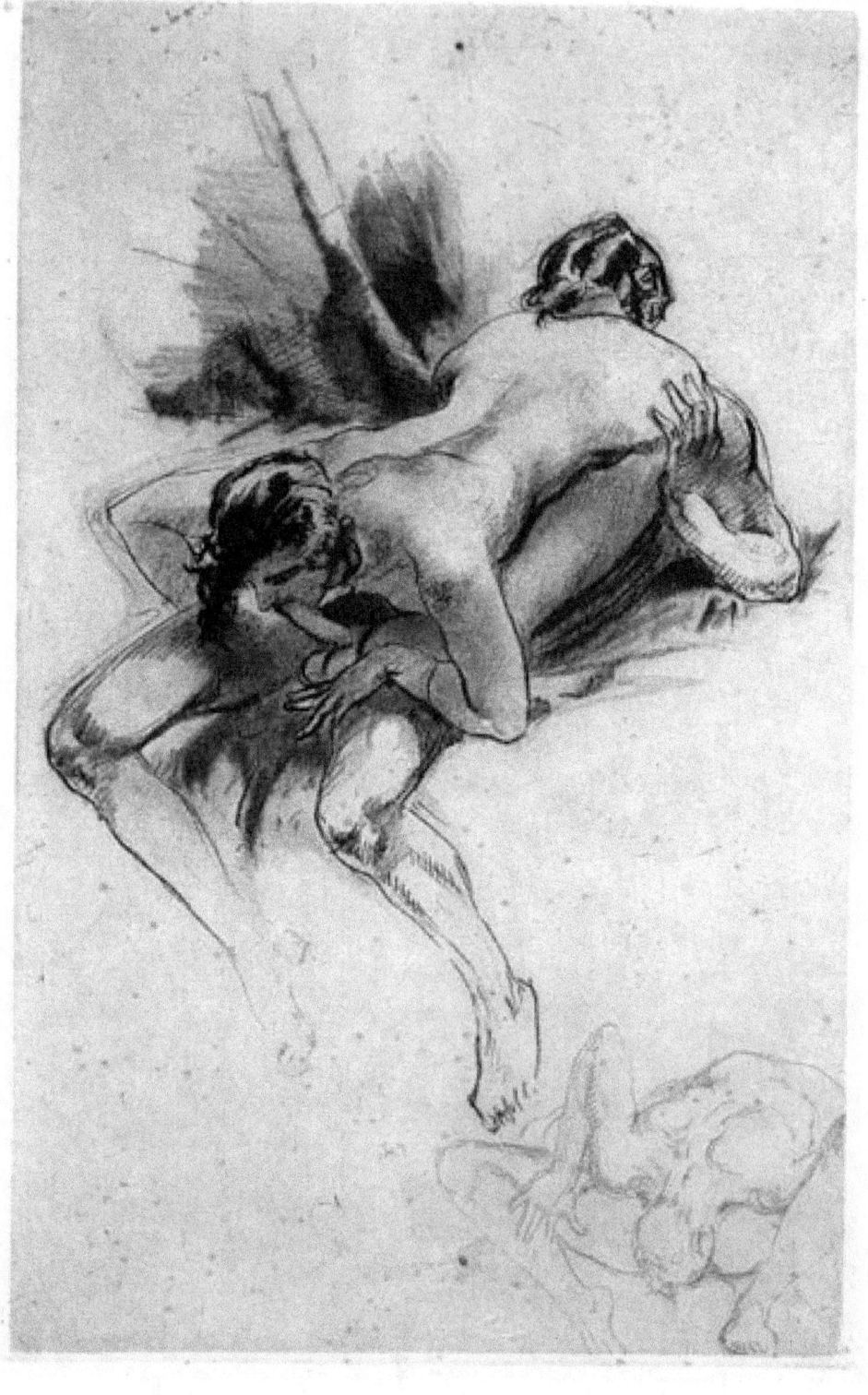

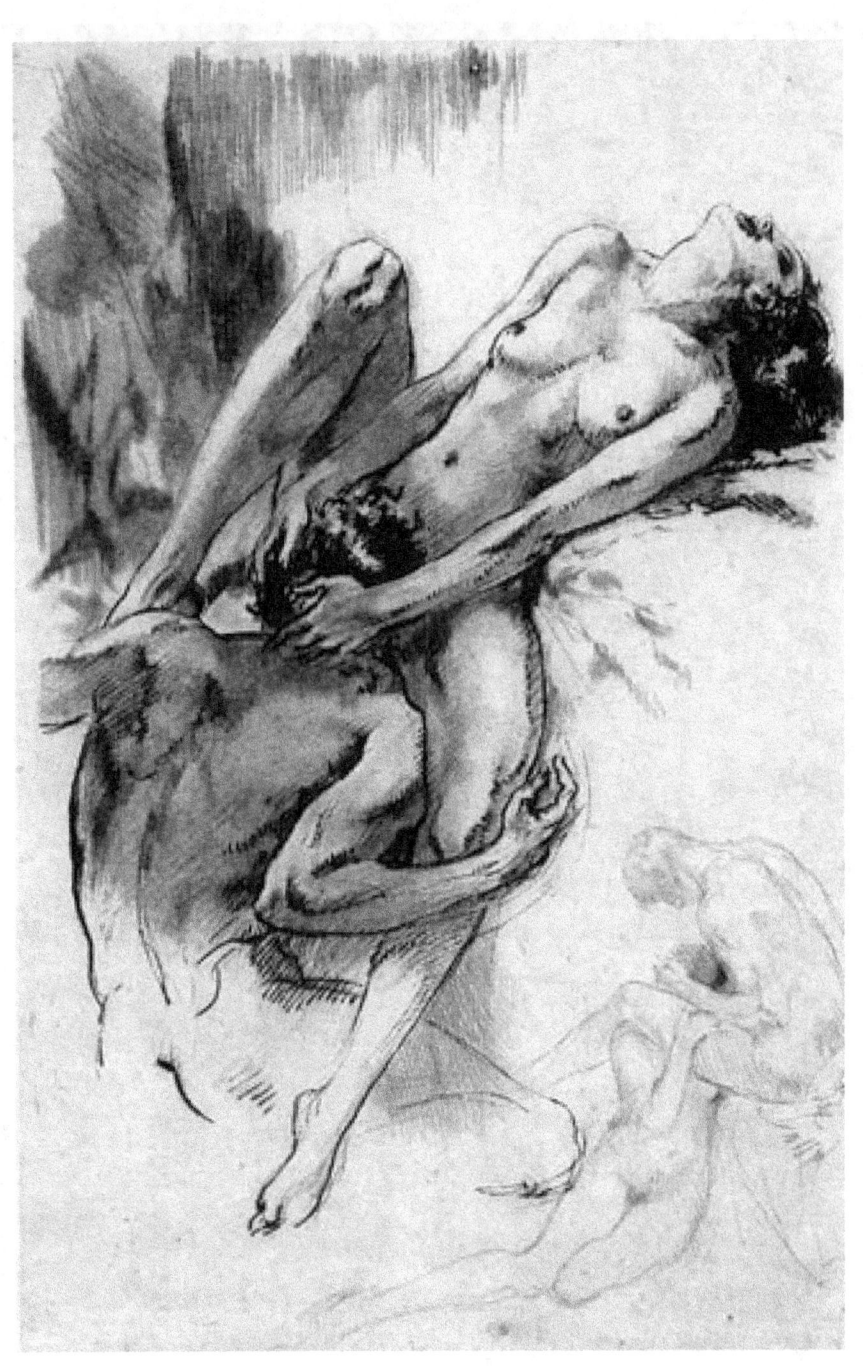

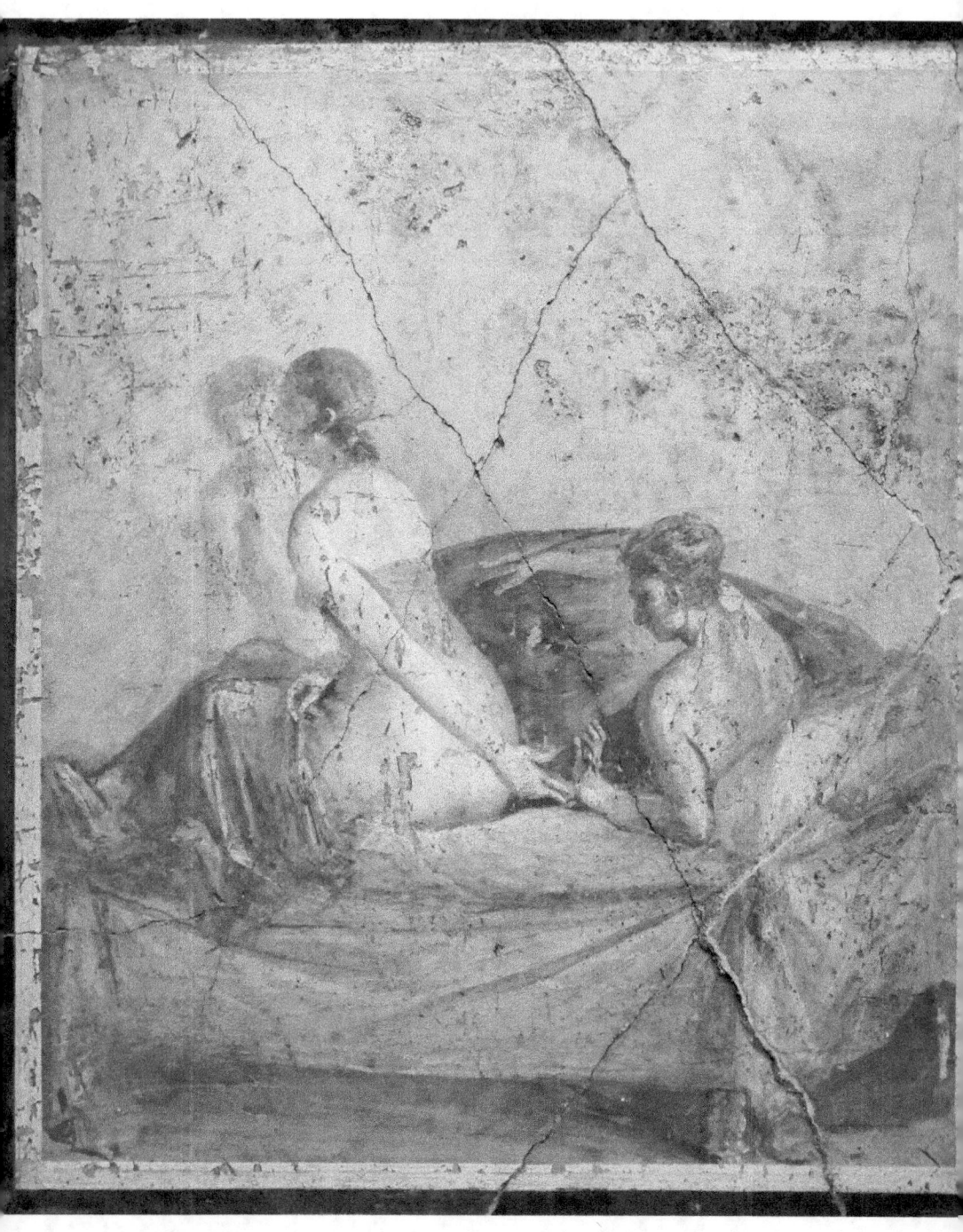

Pompeii

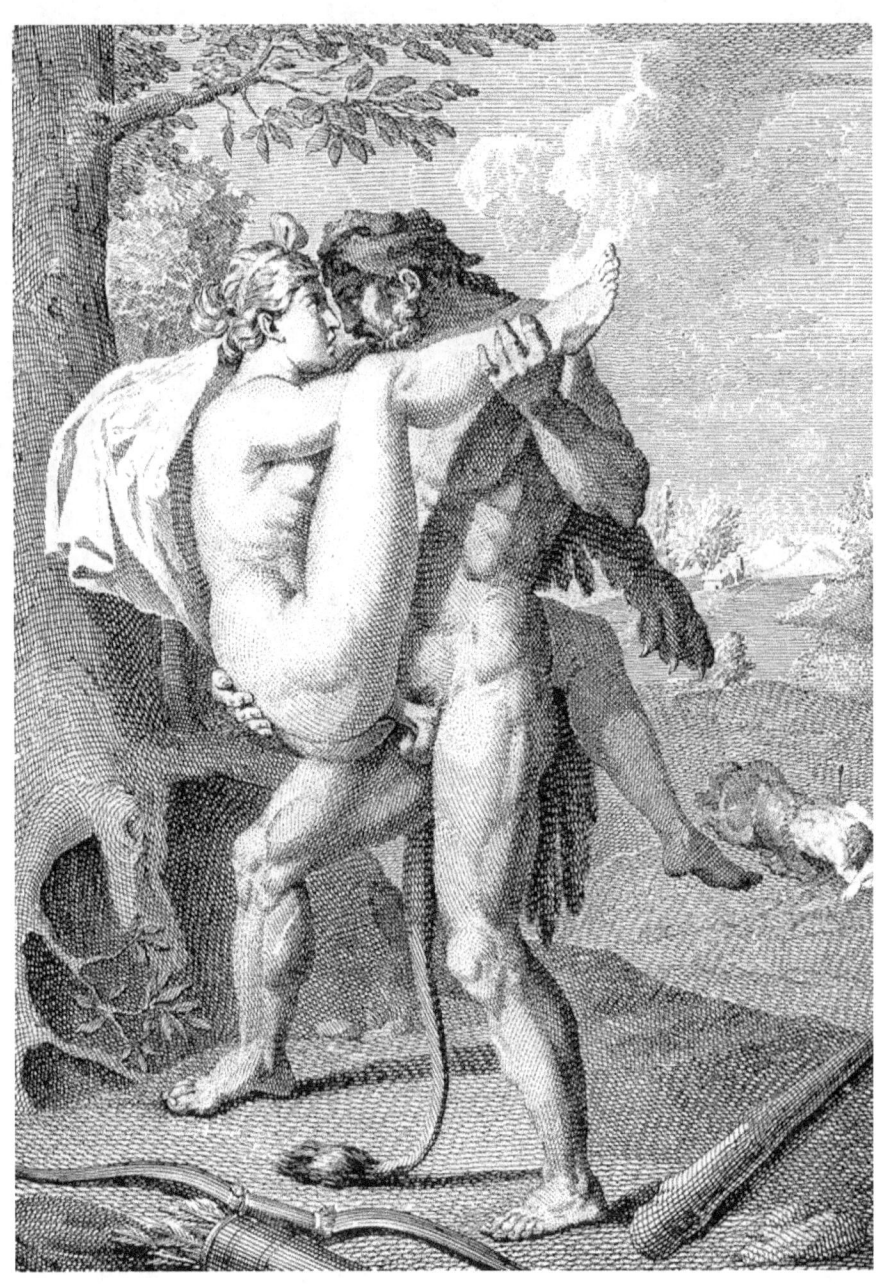

Agostino Caracci

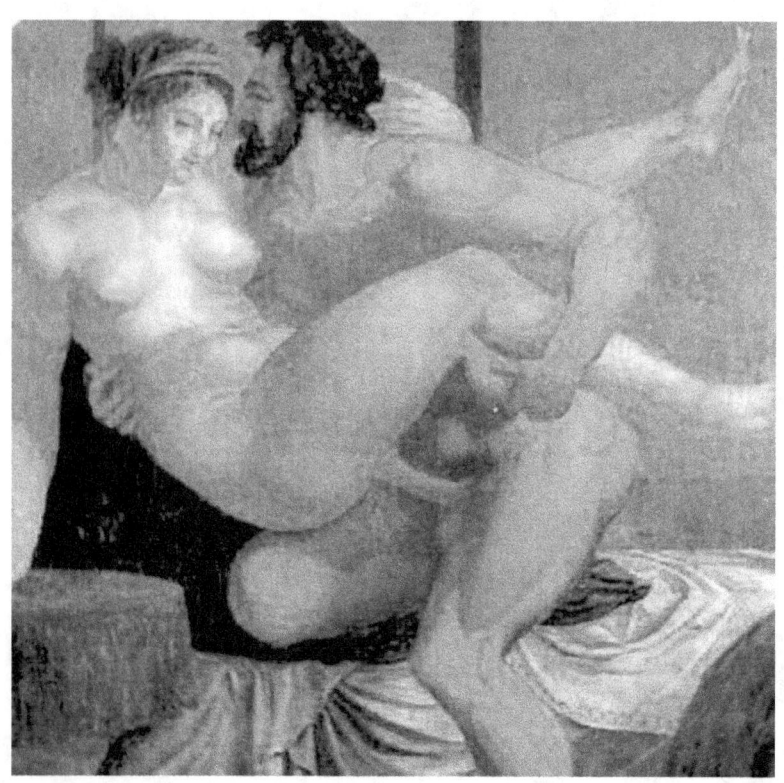

French school, late 18th century

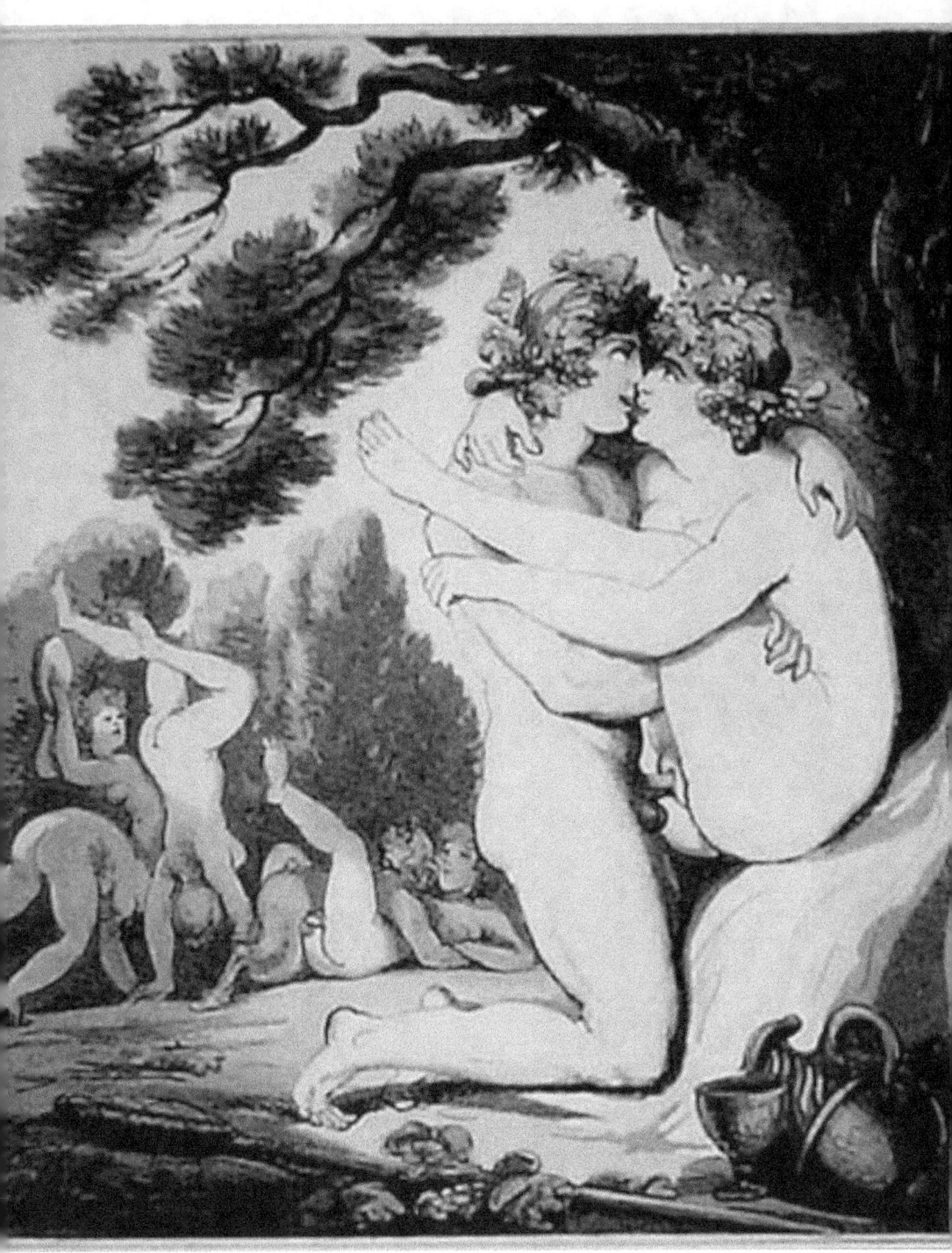

Thomas Rowlandson

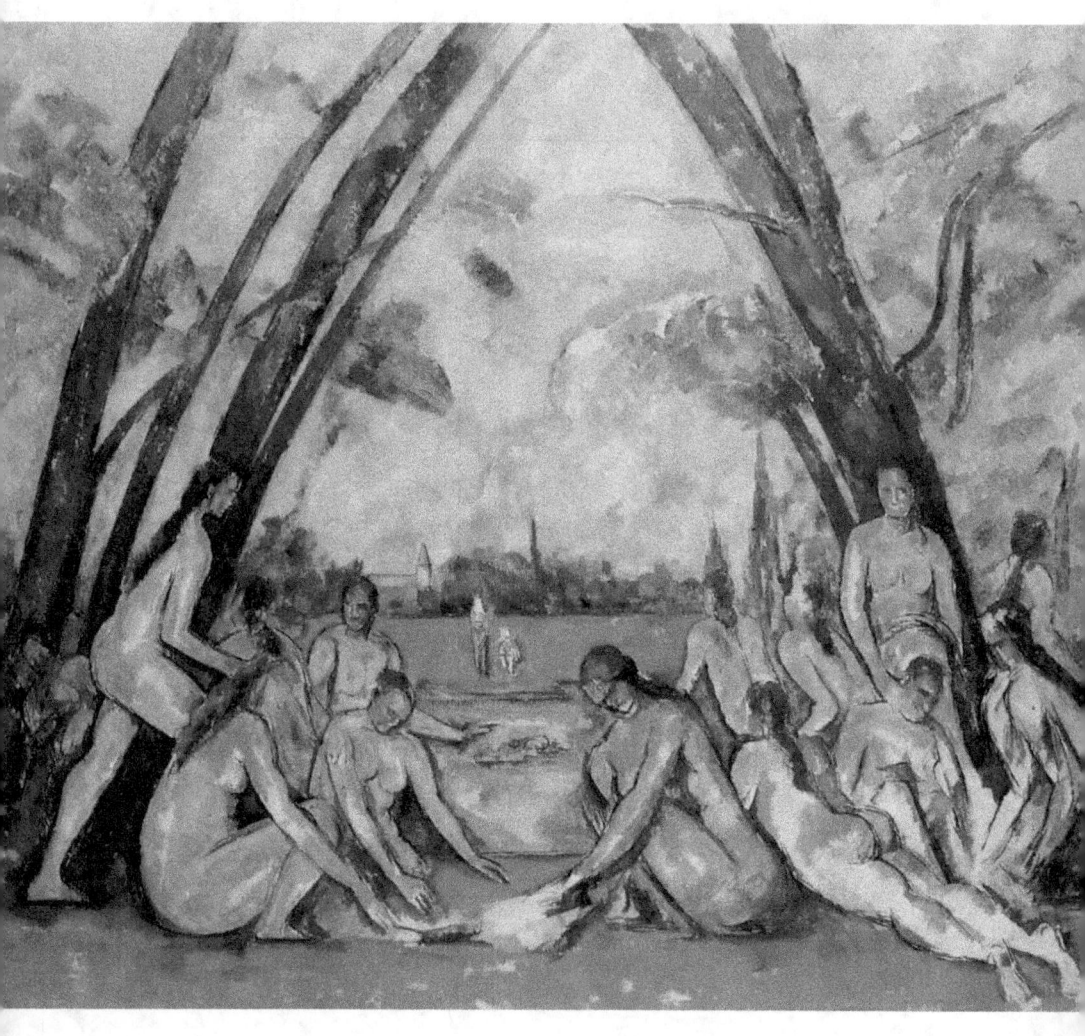

Paul Cézanne, Large Bathers, 1906,
Philadelphia Museum of Art

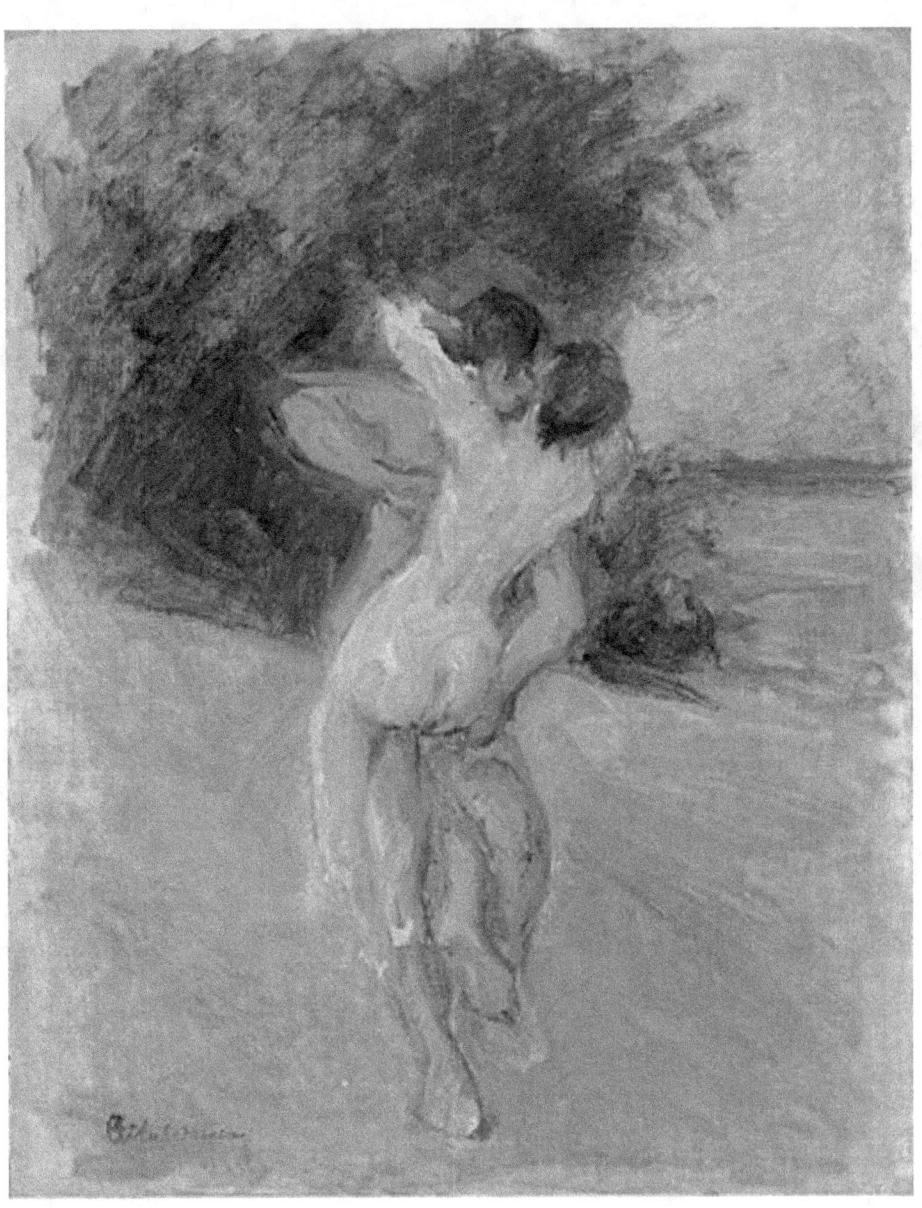

Max Lieberman

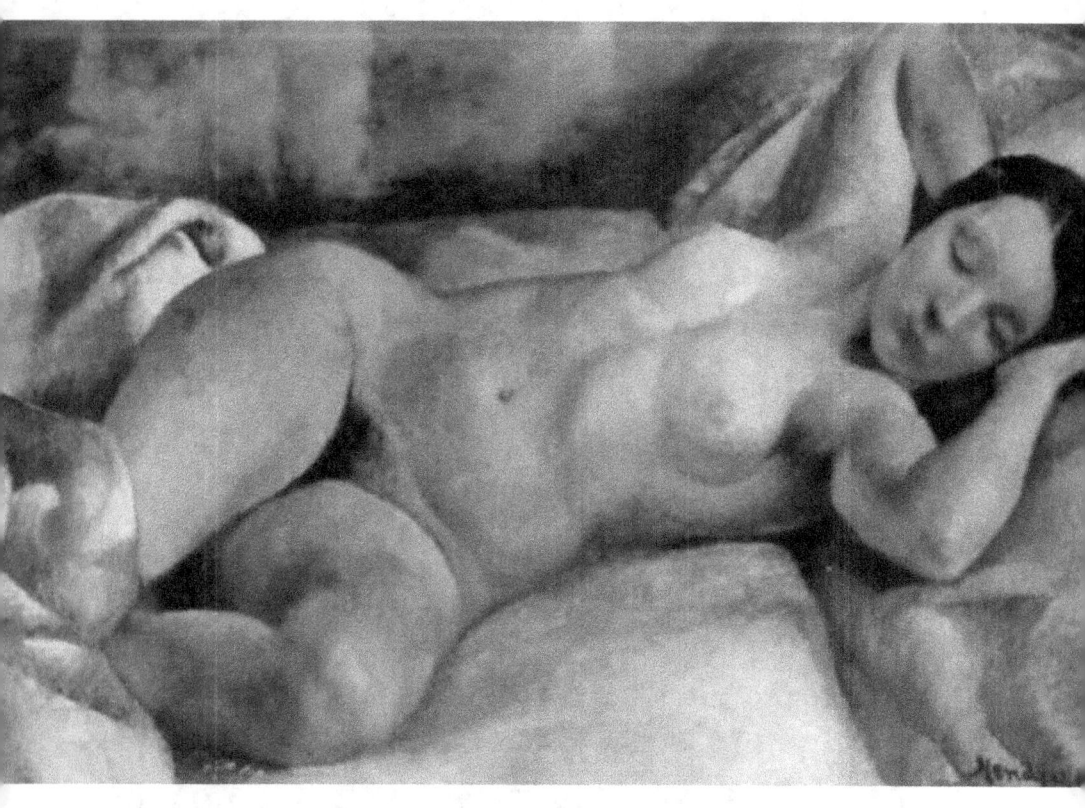

Maurice Medjinsky, Kiki, 1921

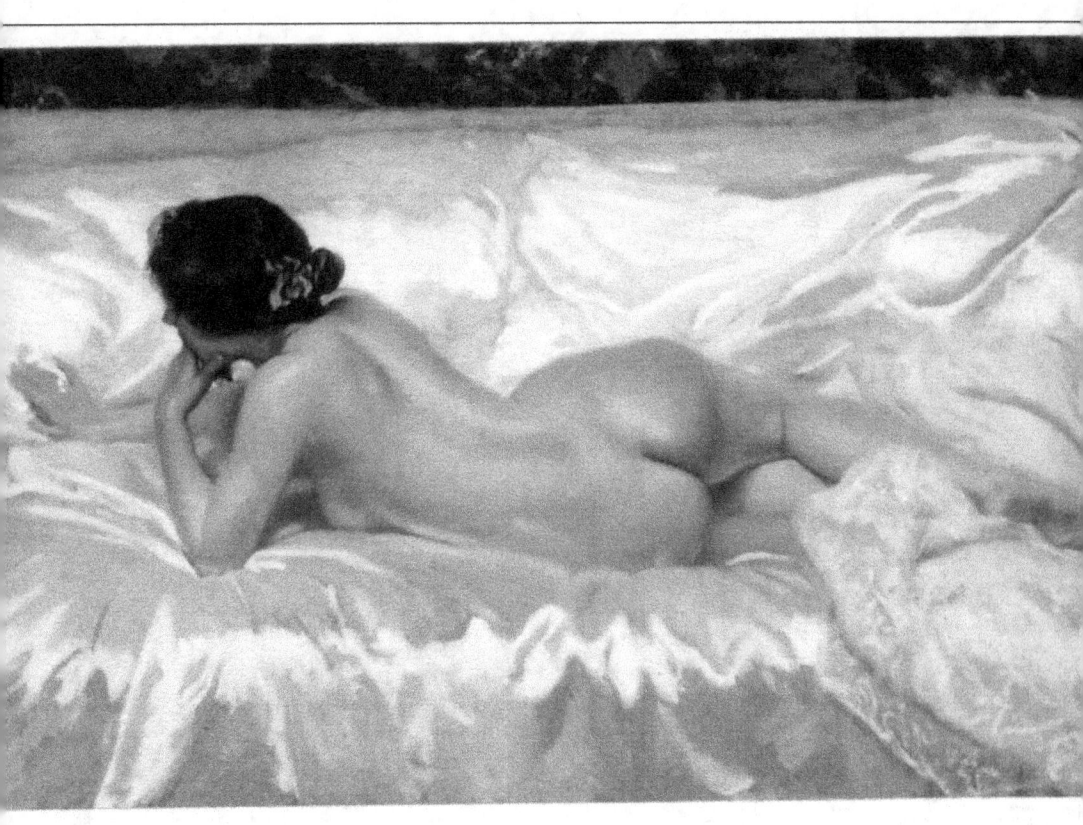

Joaquin Sorolla, Female Nude, 1902

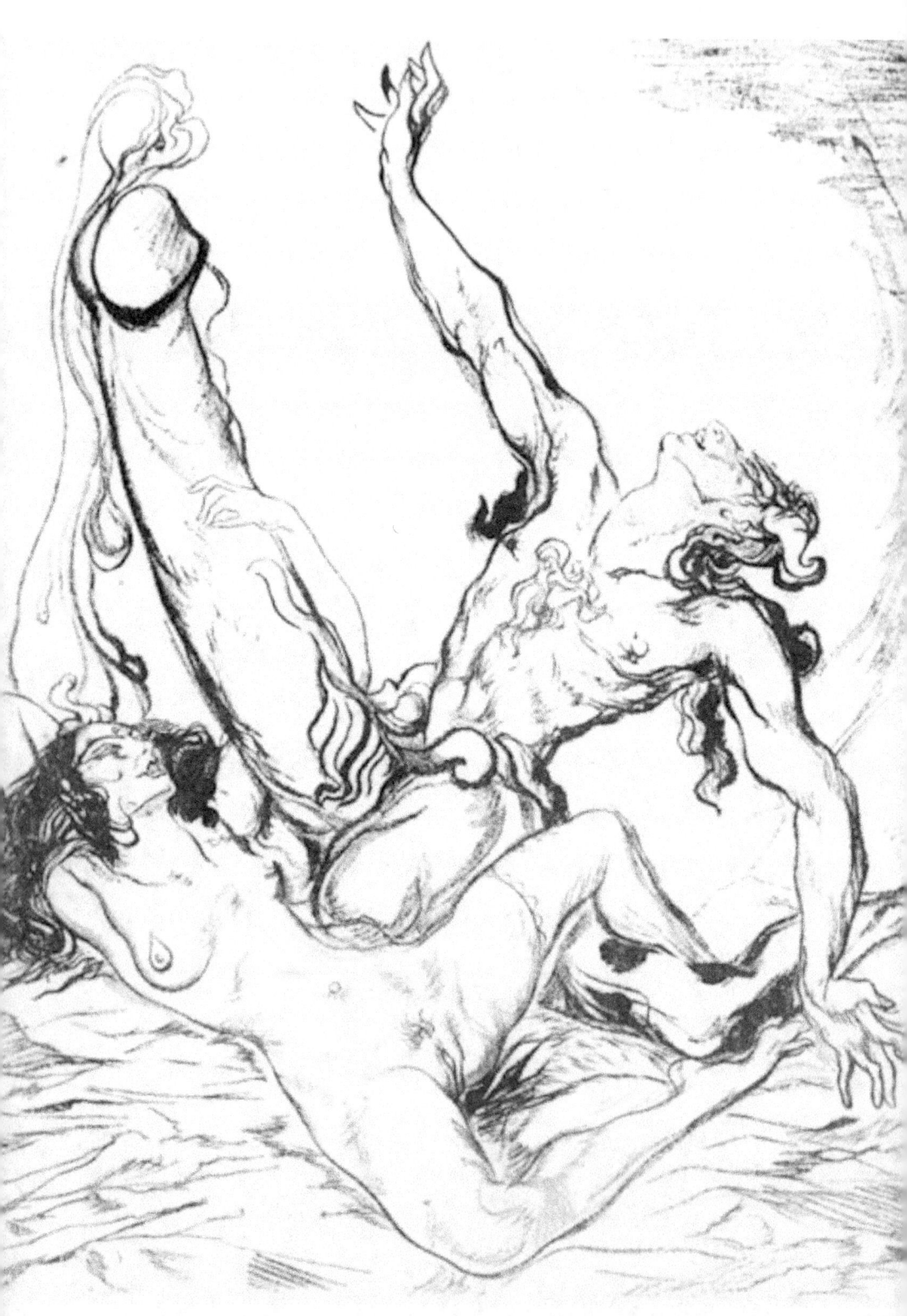

Nicolas Sternberg, from Les orfe vres a la Saint-Éloi (1430), Paris, 1930

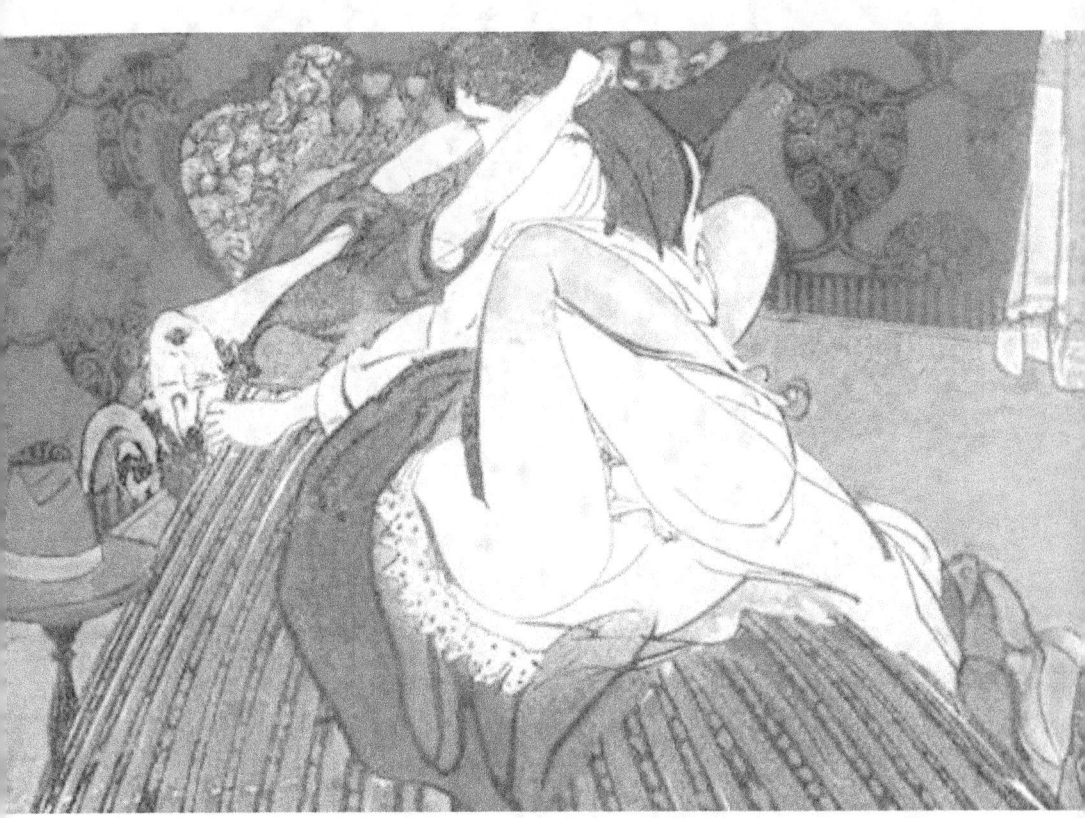

Albert Weisgerber (1878-1915), Passion

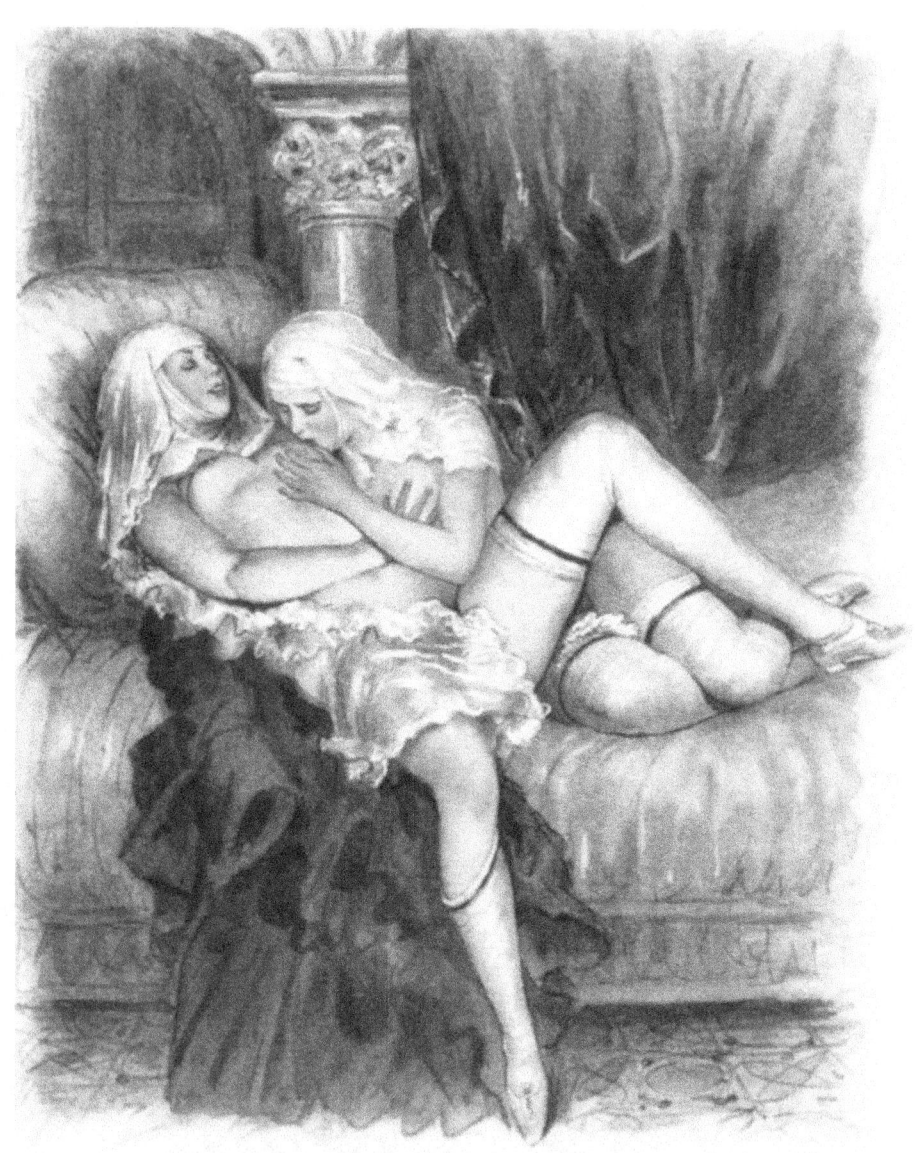

Paul-Émile Bécat, illustration for
Les Ragionamenti by Pietro Arentino (1534)

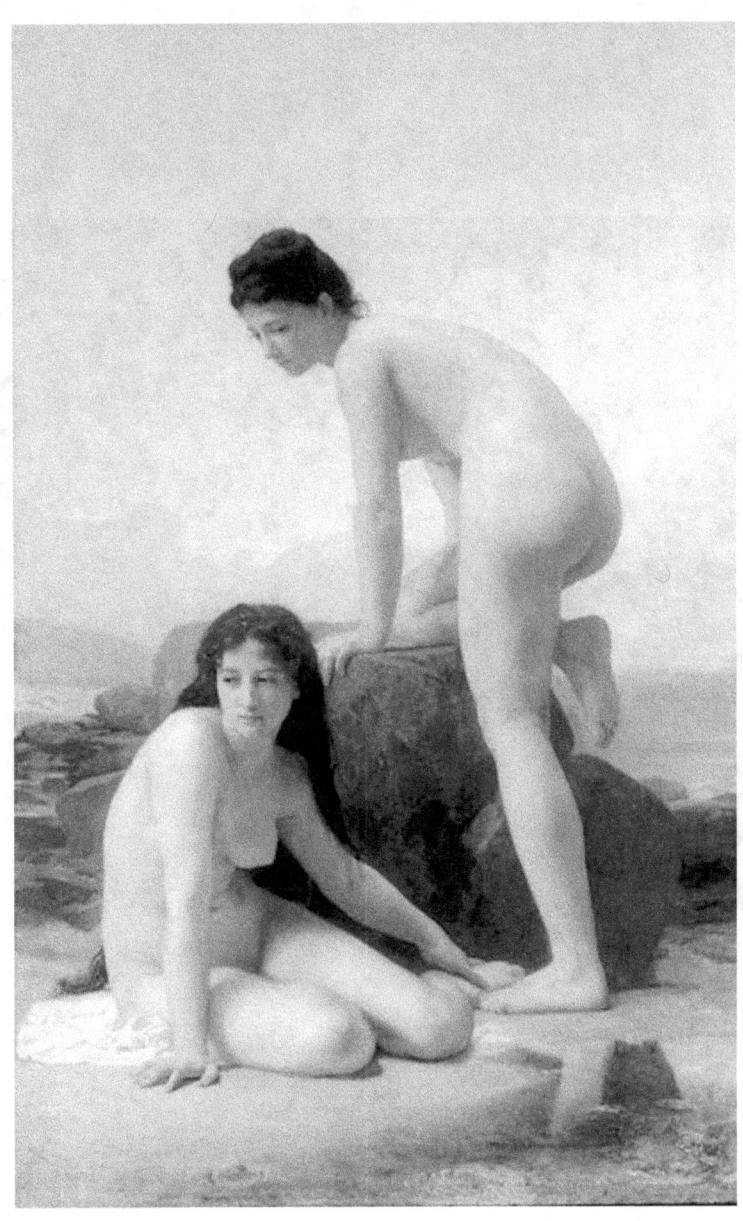

William Bouguereau, Les Deux Baigneuses, 1884

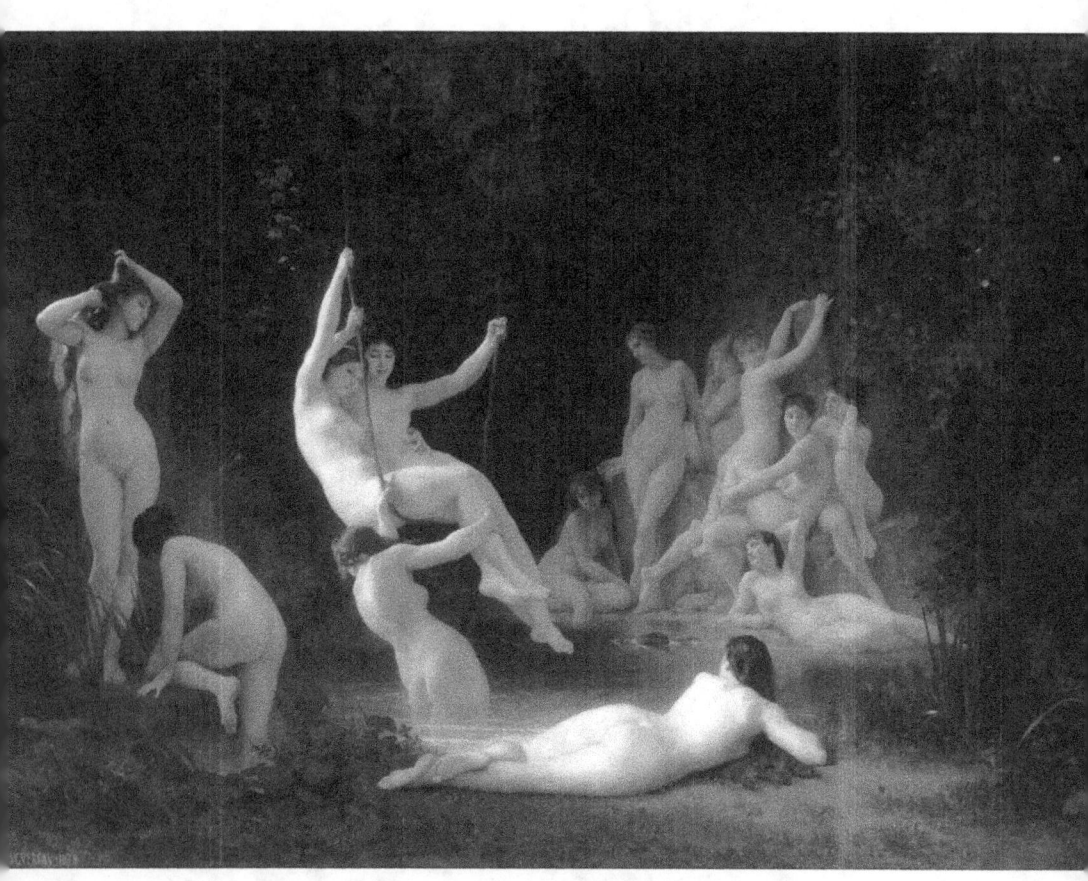

William Bouguereau, The Nymphaeum

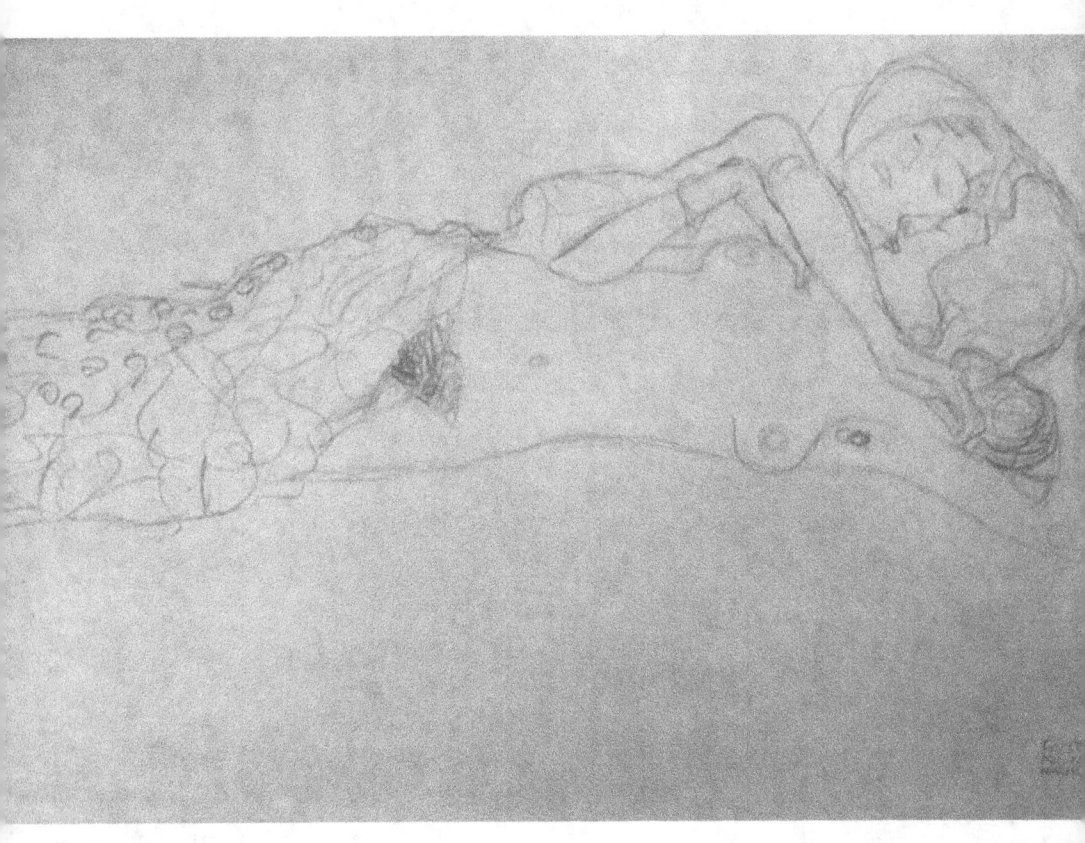

Gustav Klimt

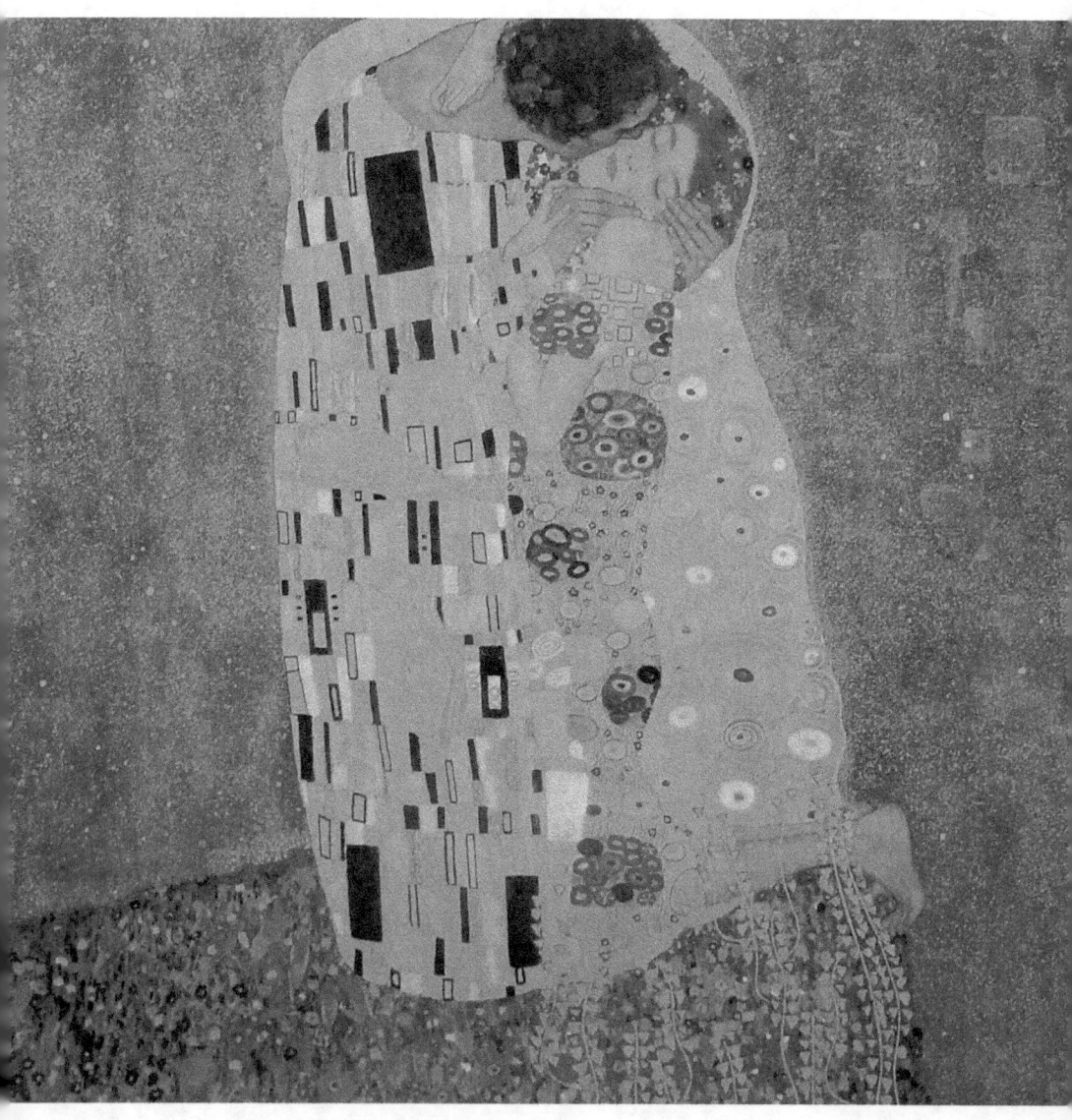

Gustav Klimt, The Kiss

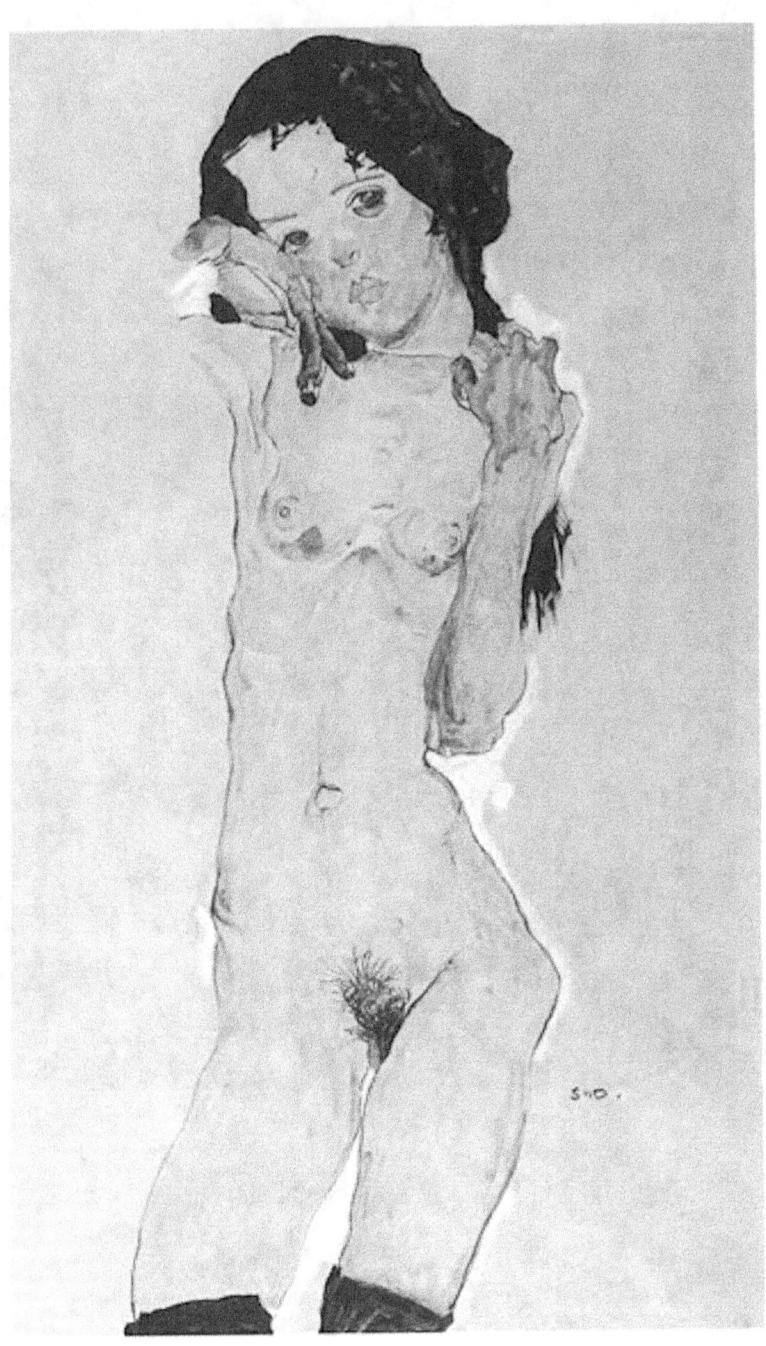

Egon Schiele, Black Haired Nude Woman, Standing, 1910, Vienna

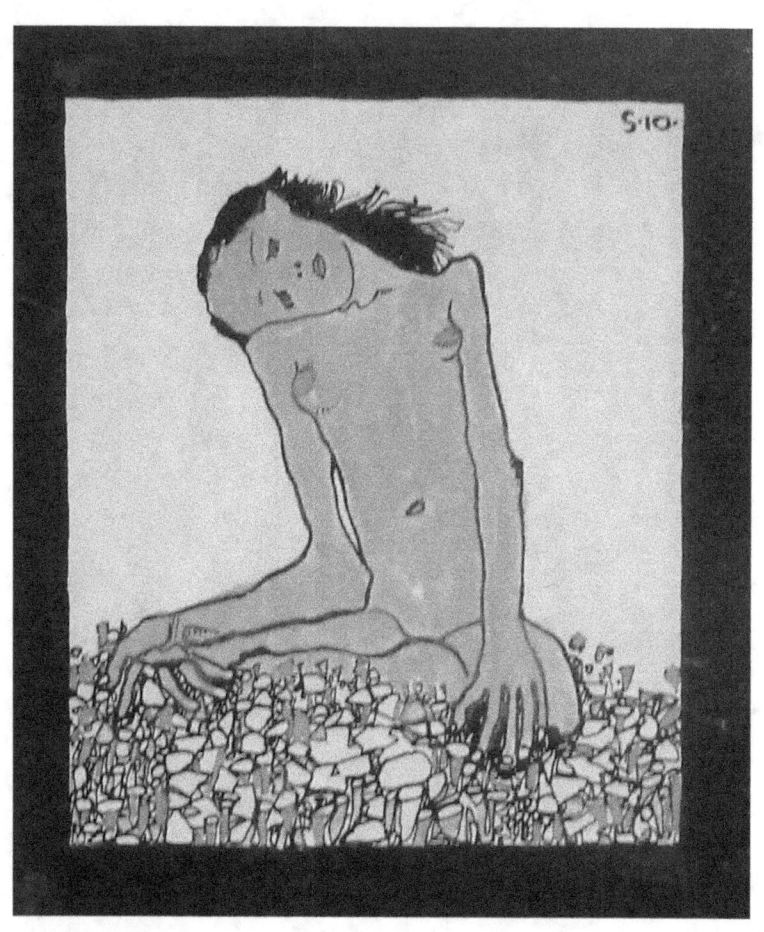

Egon Schiele, Girl Sitting In a Flowery Meadow, 1910

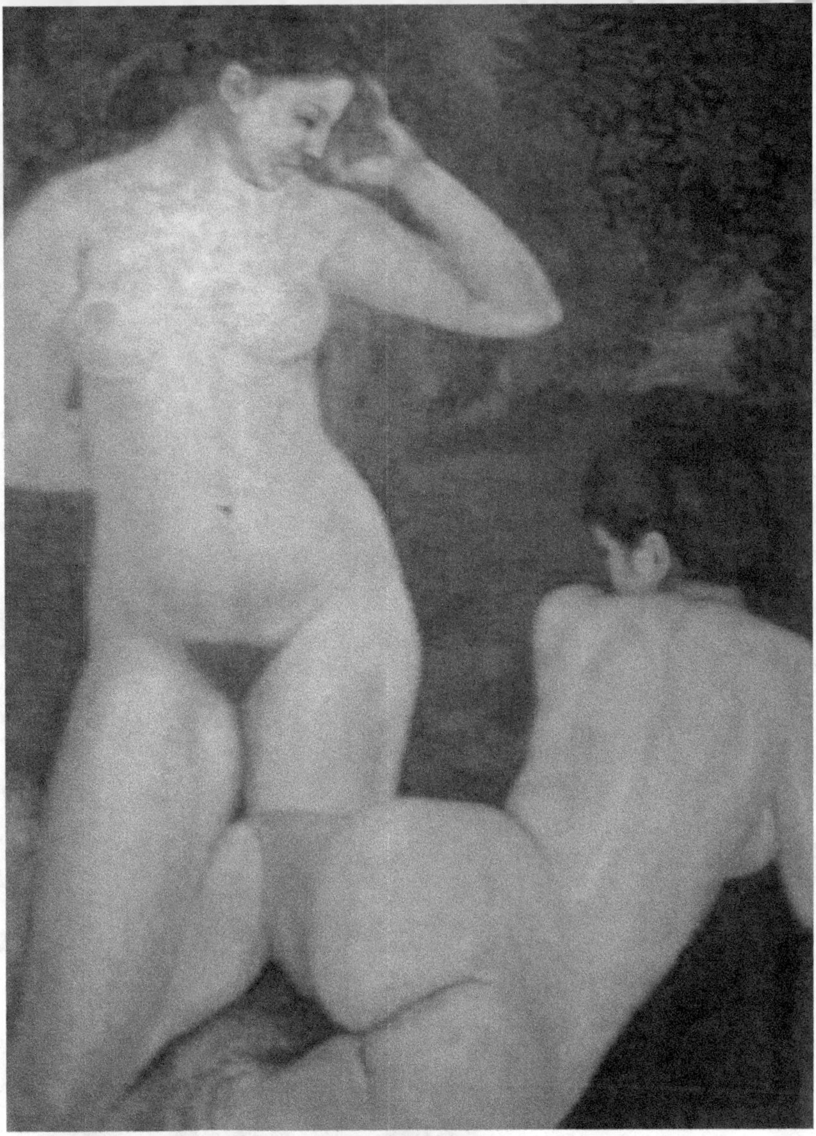

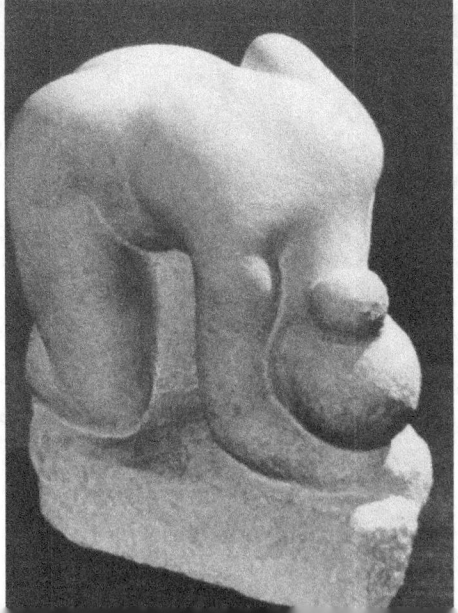

Aristide Maillol, Nudes (above).
Kneeling Bather (left).

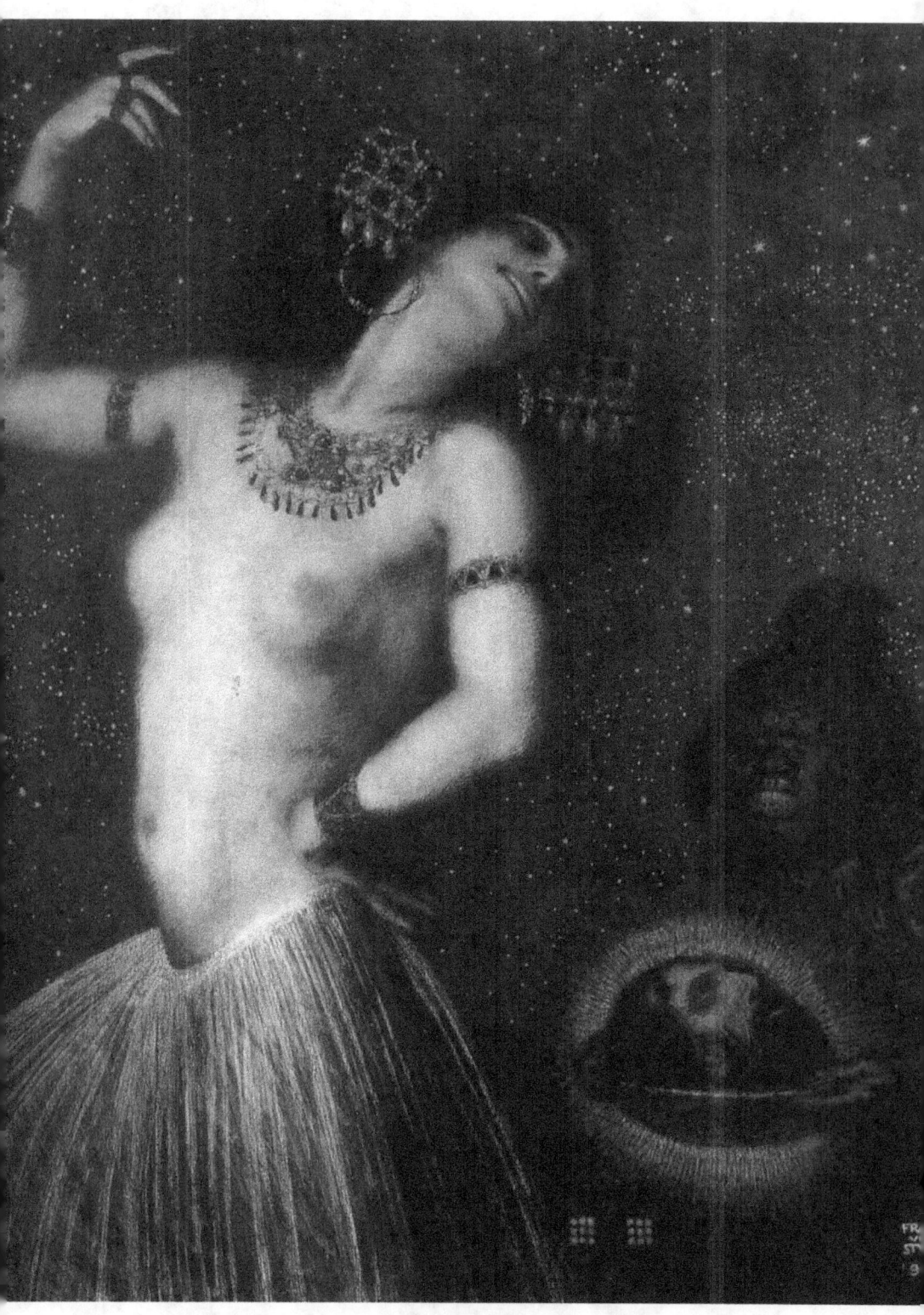

Franz von Stuck, Salomé, 1906

BIBLIOGRAPHY

E. de Antonio & M. Tuchman: *Painters Painting,* Abbeville Press, New York, NY, 1984

C.G. Argan: *The Renaissance*, Thames & Hudson, London, 1969

I. Armstrong, ed. *New Feminist Discourses: Critical Essays on Theories and Texts,* Routledge, London, 1992

J. Atkins: *Sex in Literature,* volume 2: *The Classical Experience of the Sexual Impulse,* Calder & Boyars, London, 1973

P. Bade: *Femme Fatale: Images of evil and fascinating women,* Ash & Grant 1979

M. Baxandall: *Painting and Experience in 15th Century Italy*, Oxford University Press 1988

—. *Patterns of Intention: On the Historical Explanation of Pictures*, Yale University Press 1985

G. Bazin: *A Concise History of World Sculpture*, David & Charles, Newton Abbot 1981

J. Beck: *Italian Renaissance Painting*, Harper & Row, New York, NY, 1981

B. Berenson: *The Italian Painters of the Renaissance*, Phaidon, London, 1952

—. *Looking at Pictures with Bernard Berenson*, selected by Hann Kiel, Abrahams, New York, NY, 1974

B. Bernard: *The Queen of Heaven: A Selection of Painting the Virgin from the Twelfth to the Eighteenth Centuries,* Macdonald/ Orbis, London, 1987

—. *The Bible and Its Painters*, Orbis, London, 1983

F. Bonner *et al*, eds. *Imagining Women Cultural Representations and Gender*, Polity Press, Cambridge 1992

S. Bramly: *Leonardo: The Artist and the Man*, Michael Joseph 1992

A. Brahama: *Italian Renaissance Painters of the Sixteenth Century*, National Gallery 1985

J. Burckhardt: *The Altarpiece in Renaissance Italy*, Phaidon, London, 1988

T. Burckhardt: *Sacred Art in East and West*, Perennial Book, Middlesex 1967

W. Chadwick: *Women, Art, and Society*, Thames & Hudson, London, 1990

—. *Women Artists and the Surrealist Movement*, Thames & Hudson, London, 1991

A. Chastel: *Art of the Italian Renaissance*, tr. P. & L. Murray, Alpine Fine Arts Collection, London, 1985

—. *The Studios and Styles of the Renaissance, Italy 1460-1500,* tr. Griffin, Thames & Hudson, London, 1966

G. Chester & J. Dickey, ed. *Feminism and Censorship: The Current Debate*, Prism Press, Bridport, Dorset 1988

H.B. Chipp, ed. *Theories of Modern Art*, University Press of California, Los Angeles, 1968

J.E. Cirlot: *A Dictionary of Symbols*, Routledge, London, 1981

Kenneth Clark. *The Nude*, Pantheon Books, 1957

B. Cole: *The Renaissance Artist at Work*, John Murray, London, 1983

J.C. Cooper: *An Illustrated Dictionary of Traditional Symbols*, Thames & Hudson, London, 1978

K. Davis *et al*, eds. *Coming to Power, Writings and Graphics on Lesbian S/M*, Alyson Publications, Boston 1983

L. Dresen-Coenders, ed. *Saints and She-Devils: Images of Women in the 15th and 16th Centuries*, Rubicon Press 1987

W. Dube: *The Expressionists*, Thames & Hudson, London, 1972

S.C. Dubin: *Arresting Images: Impolitic Art and Uncivil Actions*, Routledge, London, 1992

G. Duby & M. Perrot: *Power and Beauty: Images of Women in Art*, Tauris Parke Books,

A. Dworkin. *Intercourse*, Arrow, London, 1988

—. *Pornography: Men Possessing Women*, Women's Press, London, 1984

C. Eisler: *Early Netherlandish Painting: The Thyssen-Bornemisza Collection*, Sotheby's Publications, London, 1989

A. Elsen: *Modern European Sculpture 1918-45*, New York, NY, 1979

J. Evans, ed. *The Flowering of the Middle Ages*, Thames & Hudson, London, 1966

J. Evola: *The Metaphysics of Sex*, East-West Publications, London, 1985

M. Foucault: *The History of Sexuality*, Penguin, London, 1981

—. *The Use of Pleasure: The History of Sexuality*, vol. 2, Penguin, London, 1987

C. Franklin, ed. *Erotic Art by Living Artists*, Directors Guild Publishers, Renaissance, California 1988

S.J. Freedberg: *Painting of the High Renaissance in Rome and Florence*, Harper & Row, New York, NY, 1972

S. Freud: *Leonardo da Vinci*, tr. A. Tyson, Penguin, London, 1963

E. Gadon: *The Once and Future Goddess*, Aquarian Press 1990

Fred Gettings: *The Hidden Art: A Study of the Occult Symbolism in Art*, Studio Vista, London, 1978

P. Gibson & R. Gibson, ed. *Dirty Looks: Women, Pornography, Power*, British Film Institute, London, 1993

M. Gimbutas: *The Language of the Goddess*, Thames & Hudson, London, 1989

R. Goldwater & M. Treves, eds. *Artists on Art*, John Murray, London, 1975

E.H. Gombrich: *Norm and Form: Studies in the Renaissance I*, Phaidon, London, 1985

—. *Symbolic Images, Renaissance Studies II*, Phaidon, London, 1985

S. Griffin: *Pornography and Silence: Culture's Revenge Against Nature*, Women's Press, London, 1981

J. Hale: *Italian Renaissance Painting*, Phaidon, London, 1977

J. Hall: *A Dictionary of Subjects and Symbols in Art*, John Murray, London, 1984

M. Esther Harding: *Women's Mysteries*, Rider, London, 1989

F. Hartt: *History of Italian Renaissance Art: Painting, Sculpture, Architecture*, Thames &

Hudson, London, 1987

N.G. Heller: *Women Artists: An Illustrated History,* Virago, London, 1987

J. Hobhouse: *The Bride Stripped Bare: The Artist and the Nude in the Twentieth Century,* Cape, London, 1988

A. Hollander: *Seeing Through Clothes,* Viking Press, New York, NY, 1980

M. Humm: *Feminisms: A Reader,* Harvester Wheatsheaf, 1992

—. ed. *The Dictionary of Feminist Theory,* Harvester Wheatsheaf 1989

M. Jacobs: *A Guide to European Painting,* David & Charles 1980

—. *Mythological Painting,* Phaidon 1979

P. Julian: *Dreamers of Decadence: Symbolist Painters of the 1890s,* tr. R. Baldick, Pall Mall Press, London, 1971

S. Kappeler: *The Pornography of Representation,* Polity Press, Cambridge 1986

D. Kelder: *Pageant of the Renaissance,* Pall Mall Press, London, 1969

J.A. Kestner: *Mythology and Misogyny: The Social Discourse of Nineteenth-Century British Classical-Subject Painting,* University of Wisconsin Press, Madison 1989

C. Kramarae & P.A. Treichler, eds. *A Feminist Dictionary,* Pandora Press, London, 1987

J. Kristeva: *The Kristeva Reader,* ed. Toril Moi, Blackwell 1986

—. *Desire in Language: A Semiotic Approach to Literature and Art,* ed. L. Roudiez, tr. T. Gora *et al,* Blackwell 1982

J. Lacan and the *Ecole Freudienne: Feminine Sexuality,* eds. J. Mitchell and J. Rose, Macmillan, London, 1982

A. Le Normand-Romain *et al. Sculpture: The Adventure of Modern Sculpture in the Nineteenth and Twentieth Centuries,* Skira, Geneva, 1986

L. da Vinci: *The Drawings of Leonardo da Vinci,* introduction A.E. Popham, Cape, London, 1964

M. Levey: *High Renaissance,* Penguin, London, 1975

—. *Early Renaissance,* Penguin, London, 1967

F. Licht: *Sculpture, 19th and 20th Centuries,* Michael Joseph, London, 1967

L. Lippard: *From the Center: feminist essays on women's art,* Dutton, New York, NY, 1976

—. *Six Years: The Dematerialization of the Art Object from 1966 to 1972,* Praeger, New York, NY, 1973

E. Lucie-Smith: *Symbolist Art,* Thames & Hudson, London, 1972

—. *Sexuality in Western Art,* Thames & Hudson, London, 1991

F. MacCarthy: *Eric Gill,* Faber, London, 1989

E. Marks & I. de Courtivron, eds. *New French Feminisms: an Anthology,* Harvester Wheatsheaf 1981

J.C.J. Metford: *Dictionary of Christian Lore and Legend,* Thames & Hudson, London, 1983

Michelangelo: *The Complete Paintings,* Granada, London, 1980

E. Mitsch: *The Art of Egon Schiele,* Phaidon 1975

T. Moi: *Sexual/Textual Politics: Feminist Literary Theory,* Routledge, London, 1988

E. Mullins: *The Painted Witch: Female Body, Male Art,* Secker & Warburg, London,

1985

L. Mulvey: *Visual and Other Pleasures*, Macmillan, London, 1989

S. Munt, ed. *New Lesbian Criticism: Literary and Cultural Readings*, Harvester Wheatsheaf, London, 1992

P. & L. Murray: *The Penguin Dictionary of Art and Artists*, Penguin, London, 1976

L. Murray: *High Renaissance*, Thames & Hudson, London, 1977

L. Nead: *Female Nude: Art, Obscenity and Sexuality*, Routledge, London, 1992

E. Neumann: *The Great Mother*, Princeton University Press, NJ 1972

S. Nicholson, ed. *The Goddess Re-awakening: The Goddess Principle Today*, Theosophical Publishing House, New York, NY, 1989

J. Paladilhe. *Gustave Moreau*, Thames & Hudson, London,1972

E. Panofsky: *Studies in Iconology*, Harper & Row, New York, NY, 1972

—. *Early Netherlandish Painting*, Harvard University Press, Mass., 1953

R. Parker & G. Pollock. *Old Mistresses: Women, Art an Ideology*, Routledge & Kegan Paul, London, 1981

W. Pater: *The Renaissance*, Oxford University Press 1980

R. Payne: *Leonardo da Vinci*, Robert Hale, London, 1979

K. Petersen & J.J. Wilson: *Women Artists: Recognition and Reappraisal from the Early Middle Ages to the Twentieth Century* Women's Press, London, 1978

G. Pollock: *Vision and Difference: femininity, feminism and histories of art*, Routledge, London, 1988

M. Praz: *The Romantic Agony*, tr. Davidson, Oxford University Press 1933

P. Rawson: *The Art of Tantra*, Thames & Hudson, London, 1973

Peter Redgrove. *The Black Goddess and the Sixth Sense, Bloomsbury, London, 1987*

F. Roh: *German Art in the Twentieth Century: Painting, Sculpture, Architecture*, Thames & Hudson, London, 1968

M. Roskill: *What is Art History?*, Thames & Hudson, London, 1976

G. Saunders. *The Nude: a new perspective*, Herbert Press, London, 1989

E. Schiele: *I, Eternal Child: Paintings and Poems*, tr. A. Hollo, Grove Press, New York, NY, 1985

P. Selz. *German Expressionist Painting*, University of California Press, Berkely, CA, 1974

—. *Art in Our Times: A Pictorial History 1890-1980*, Thames & Hudson, London, 1982

E. Showalter, ed. *The New Feminist Criticism*, Virago, London, 1986

Penelope Shuttle & Peter Redgrove. *The Wise Wound*, Paladin/ Grafton, 1978/86

M. Sjöo & B. Mor: *The Great Cosmic Mother*, Harper & Row, San Francisco 1987

F. Stella. *Working Space*, Harvard University Press, Cambridge, MA, 1986

—. *Frank Stella*, Madrid, 1995

K. Stiles & P. Selz, eds. *Theories & Documents of Contemporary Art: A Sourcebook of Artists' Writings*, University of California Press, Berkeley, CA, 1996

V.I. Stoichita: *Leonardo da Vinci*, Abbey Library, London, 1978

S. Rubin Suleiman, ed. *The Female Body in Western Culture: Contemporary Perspectives*, Harvard University Press, Cambridge, Mass., 1986

William Thompson. *The Time Falling Bodies Take to Light: Mythology, Sexuality and the*

Origins of Culture, St Martin's Press, New York, NY, 1981

A. Tilly: *Erotic Drawings*, Phaidon 1986

P. Trevor-Roper: *The world blunted through sight: An inquiry into the influence of defective vision on art and character*, Thames & Hudson, London, 1970

W. Tucker. *The Language of Sculpture*, Thames & Hudson, London, 1974

L. Venturi: *Renaissance Painting, from Leonardo to Dürer,* Skira/ Macmillan 1979

—. *Italian Paintings*, Zwemmer, London, 1950

P. Vergo: *Art in Vienna: 1898-1918: Klimt, Kokoschka, Schiele and Their Contemporaries,* Phaidon 1975

G. de Vries, ed. *On Art: Artists' Writings on the Changed Notion of Art After, 1965*, Cologne, 1974

B. Walker: *Body Magic*, Paladin, London, 1979

—. *Tantrism: Its Secret Principles and Practices*, Aquarian Press, Wellingborough 1982

Marina Warner. *Alone Of All Her Sex: The Myth and Cult of the Virgin Mary*, Picador, London, 1985

—. *Monuments and Maidens*, Weidenfeld & Nicolson, London, 1985

Valerie Wayne, ed. *The Matter of Difference: Materialist Feminist Criticism of Shakespeare*, Harvester Wheatsheaf, Hemel Hempstead, 1991

P. Webb: *The Erotic Arts*, Secker & Warburg, London, 1983

D. Wheeler: *Art Since Mid-Century: 1945 to the Present*, Thames & Hudson, London, 1991

F. Whitford: *Egon Schiele*, Thames & Hudson, London, 1981

L. Williams: *Hard Core*: Power, *Pleasure, and the 'Frenzy of the Visible'*, Pandora, London, 1990

C. Wilson: *The Sexual Misfits: A Study of Sexual Outsiders*, Collins, London, 1989

H. Wolfflin: *Classic Art*, Phaidon 1952/80

G. Woods *et al*, eds. *Art Without Boundaries*, Thames & Hudson, London, 1972

M. Wudram: *Art of the Renaissance*, Weidenfeld & Nicolson, London, 1985

M. Yorke: *Eric Gill: Man of Flesh and Spirit*, Constable, London, 1981

WEBSITES

eroticbibliophile.com
eroti-cart.com
deltaofvenus.com
erotomane.org

CRESCENT MOON PUBLISHING

web: www.crmoon.com e-mail: cresmopub@yahoo.co.uk

ARTS, PAINTING, SCULPTURE

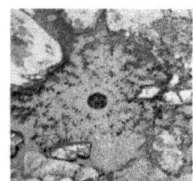

The Art of Andy Goldsworthy

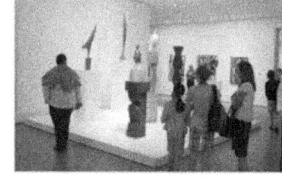

Andy Goldsworthy: Touching Nature
Andy Goldsworthy in Close-Up
Andy Goldsworthy: Pocket Guide
Andy Goldsworthy In America
Land Art: A Complete Guide
The Art of Richard Long

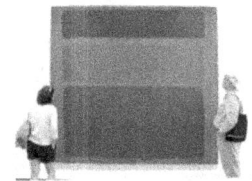

Richard Long: Pocket Guide
Land Art In the UK
Land Art in Close-Up
Land Art In the U.S.A.
Land Art: Pocket Guide
Installation Art in Close-Up
Minimal Art and Artists In the 1960s and After
Colourfield Painting
Land Art DVD, TV documentary
Andy Goldsworthy DVD, TV documentary
The Erotic Object: Sexuality in Sculpture From Prehistory to the Present Day
Sex in Art: Pornography and Pleasure in Painting and Sculpture
Postwar Art
Sacred Gardens: The Garden in Myth, Religion and Art
Glorification: Religious Abstraction in Renaissance and 20th Century Art
Early Netherlandish Painting
Leonardo da Vinci

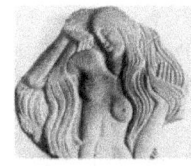

Piero della Francesca
Giovanni Bellini
Fra Angelico: Art and Religion in the Renaissance

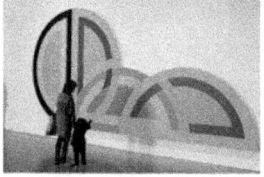

Mark Rothko: The Art of Transcendence
Frank Stella: American Abstract Artist
Jasper Johns
Brice Marden

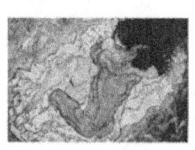

Alison Wilding: The Embrace of Sculpture
Vincent van Gogh: Visionary Landscapes
Eric Gill: Nuptials of God

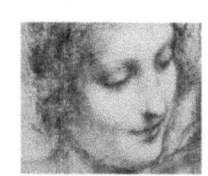

Constantin Brancusi: Sculpting the Essence of Things
Max Beckmann
Caravaggio
Gustave Moreau
Egon Schiele: Sex and Death In Purple Stockings
Delizioso Fotografico Fervore: Works In Process 1

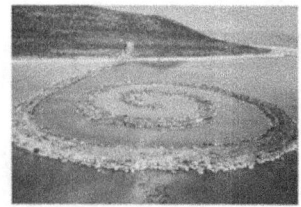

Sacro Cuore: Works In Process 2
The Light Eternal: J.M.W. Turner
The Madonna Glorified: Karen Arthurs

MEDIA, CINEMA, FEMINISM and CULTURAL STUDIES

J.R.R. Tolkien: The Books, The Films, The Whole Cultural Phenomenon
J.R.R. Tolkien: Pocket Guide
The *Lord of the Rings* Movies: Pocket Guide
The Cinema of Hayao Miyazaki
Hayao Miyazaki: *Princess Mononoke*: Pocket Movie Guide
Hayao Miyazaki: *Spirited Away*: Pocket Movie Guide
Tim Burton : Hallowe'en For Hollywood
Ken Russell
Ken Russell: *Tommy*: Pocket Movie Guide
The Ghost Dance: The Origins of Religion
The Peyote Cult
Cixous, Irigaray, Kristeva: The *Jouissance* of French Feminism
Julia Kristeva: Art, Love, Melancholy, Philosophy, Semiotics and Psychoanalysis
Luce Irigaray: Lips, Kissing, and the Politics of Sexual Difference
Hélene Cixous I Love You: The *Jouissance* of Writing
Andrea Dworkin
'Cosmo Woman': The World of Women's Magazines
Women in Pop Music
HomeGround: The Kate Bush Anthology
Discovering the Goddess (Geoffrey Ashe)
The Poetry of Cinema
The Sacred Cinema of Andrei Tarkovsky
Andrei Tarkovsky: Pocket Guide
Andrei Tarkovsky: *Mirror*: Pocket Movie Guide
Andrei Tarkovsky: *The Sacrifice*: Pocket Movie Guide
Walerian Borowczyk: Cinema of Erotic Dreams
Jean-Luc Godard: The Passion of Cinema
Jean-Luc Godard: *Hail Mary*: Pocket Movie Guide
Jean-Luc Godard: *Contempt*: Pocket Movie Guide
Jean-Luc Godard: *Pierrot le Fou*: Pocket Movie Guide
John Hughes and Eighties Cinema
Ferris Bueller's Day Off: Pocket Movie Guide
Jean-Luc Godard: Pocket Guide
The Cinema of Richard Linklater
Liv Tyler: Star In Ascendance
Blade Runner and the Films of Philip K. Dick
Paul Bowles and Bernardo Bertolucci
Media Hell: Radio, TV and the Press
An Open Letter to the BBC
Detonation Britain: Nuclear War in the UK
Feminism and Shakespeare
Wild Zones: Pornography, Art and Feminism
Sex in Art: Pornography and Pleasure in Painting and Sculpture
Sexing Hardy: Thomas Hardy and Feminism

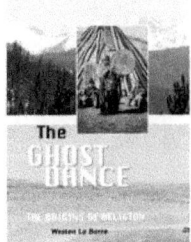
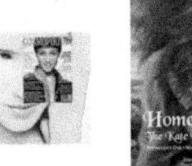
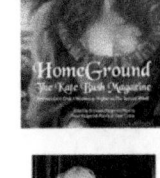
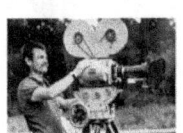
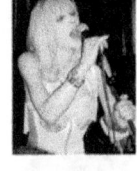
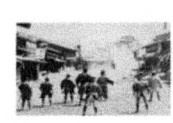
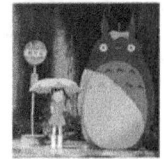
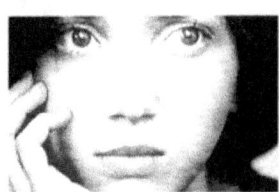

The Light Eternal is a model monograph, an exemplary job. The subject matter of the book is beautifully organised and dead on beam. (Lawrence Durrell)
It is amazing for me to see my work treated with such passion and respect. (Andrea Dworkin)

CRESCENT MOON PUBLISHING
P.O. Box 1312, Maidstone, Kent, ME14 5XU, Great Britain. www.crmoon.com

cresmopub@yahoo.co.uk   www.crescentmoon.org.uk

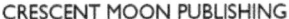